DATE DUE

			PRINTED IN U.S.A.

DRAMA
CRITICISM

Guide to Gale Literary Criticism Series

For criticism on	Consult these Gale series
Authors now living or who died after December 31, 1959	*CONTEMPORARY LITERARY CRITICISM (CLC)*
Authors who died between 1900 and 1959	*TWENTIETH-CENTURY LITERARY CRITICISM (TCLC)*
Authors who died between 1800 and 1899	*NINETEENTH-CENTURY LITERATURE CRITICISM (NCLC)*
Authors who died between 1400 and 1799	*LITERATURE CRITICISM FROM 1400 TO 1800 (LC)* *SHAKESPEAREAN CRITICISM (SC)*
Authors who died before 1400	*CLASSICAL AND MEDIEVAL LITERATURE CRITICISM (CMLC)*
Authors of books for children and young adults	*CHILDREN'S LITERATURE REVIEW (CLR)*
Dramatists	*DRAMA CRITICISM (DC)*
Poets	*POETRY CRITICISM (PC)*
Short story writers	*SHORT STORY CRITICISM (SSC)*
Black writers of the past two hundred years	*BLACK LITERATURE CRITICISM (BLC)*
Hispanic writers of the late nineteenth and twentieth centuries	*HISPANIC LITERATURE CRITICISM (HLC)*
Native North American writers and orators of the eighteenth, nineteenth, and twentieth centuries	*NATIVE NORTH AMERICAN LITERATURE (NNAL)*
Major authors from the Renaissance to the present	*WORLD LITERATURE CRITICISM, 1500 TO THE PRESENT (WLC)*

ISSN 1056-4349

R

DRAMA
CRITICISM

Criticism of the Most Significant and Widely Studied
Dramatic Works from All the World's Literatures

VOLUME 9

Lawrence J. Trudeau, Editor

GALE

DETROIT · LONDON

STAFF

Lawrence J. Trudeau, *Editor*

Susan Trosky, *Permissions Manager*

Kimberly F. Smilay, *Permissions Specialist*
Stephen Cusack, Kelly Quin, *Permissions Associates*
Sandy Gore, *Permissions Assistant*

Victoria B. Cariappa, *Research Manager*

Michele P. LaMeau, *Research Specialist*
Julie C. Daniel, Tamara C. Nott, Tracie A. Richardson,
Norma Sawaya, Cheryl L. Warnock,
Research Associates

Mary Beth Trimper, *Production Director*
Deborah Milliken, *Production Assistant*

C. J. Jonik, *Desktop Publisher*
Randy Bassett, *Image Database Supervisor*
Michael Ansari, Robert Duncan, *Scanner Operator*
Pamela Reed, *Photography Coordinator*

Library of Congress Catalog Card Number 92-648805
ISBN 0-7876-2016-5
ISSN 1056-4349

Printed in the United States of America
Published simultaneously in the United Kingdom
by Gale Research International Limited
(An affiliated company of Gale Research Inc.)

10 9 8 7 6 5 4 3 2 1

Contents

Preface   vii

Acknowledgments   xi

List of Authors   xv

Special Volume Devoted to

Anton Pavlovich Chekhov
1860-1904

Preface

*D*rama Criticism (*DC*) is principally intended for beginning students of literature and theater as well as the average playgoer. The series is therefore designed to introduce readers to the most frequently studied playwrights of all time periods and nationalities and to present discerning commentary on dramatic works of enduring interest. Furthermore, *DC* seeks to acquaint the reader with the uses and functions of criticism itself. Selected from a diverse body of commentary, the essays in *DC* offer insights into the authors and their works but do not require that the reader possess a wide background in literary studies. Where appropriate, reviews of important productions of the plays discussed are also included to give students a heightened awareness of drama as a dynamic art form, one that many claim is fully realized only in performance.

DC was created in response to suggestions by the staffs of high school, college, and public libraries. These librarians observed a need for a series that assembles critical commentary on the world's most renowned dramatists in the same manner as Gale's *Short Story Criticism* (*SSC*) and *Poetry Criticism* (*PC*), which present material on writers of short fiction and poetry. Although playwrights are covered in such Gale literary criticism series as *Contemporary Literary Criticism* (*CLC*), *Twentieth-Century Literary Criticism* (*TCLC*), *Nineteenth-Century Literature Criticism* (*NCLC*), *Literature Criticism from 1400 to 1800* (*LC*), and *Classical and Medieval Literature Criticism* (*CMLC*), *Drama Criticism* directs more concentrated attention on individual dramatists than is possible in the broader, survey-oriented entries in these Gale series. Commentary on the works of William Shakespeare may be found in *Shakespearean Criticism* (*SC*).

Scope of the Series

By collecting and organizing commentary on dramatists, *DC* assists students in their efforts to gain insight into literature, achieve better understanding of the texts, and formulate ideas for papers and assignments. A variety of interpretations and assessments is offered, allowing students to pursue their own interests and promoting awareness that literature is dynamic and responsive to many different opinions.

Each volume of *DC* presents:

- 8-10 entries

- authors and works representing a wide range of nationalities and time periods

- a diversity of viewpoints and critical opinions.

Organization of an Author Entry

Each author entry consists of some or all of the following elements, depending on the scope and complexity of the criticism:

- The **author heading** consists of the playwright's most commonly used name, followed by birth and death dates. If an author consistently wrote under a pseudonym, the pseudonym is listed in the author heading and the real name given in parentheses on the first line of the introduction. Also located at the beginning of the introduction are any name variations under which the dramatist wrote, including transliterated forms of the names of authors whose languages use nonroman alphabets.

- A **portrait** of the author is included when available. Most entries also feature illustrations of people, places, and events pertinent to a study of the playwright and his or her works. When appropriate, photographs of the plays in performance are also presented.

- The **biographical and critical introduction** contains background information that familiarizes the reader with the author and the critical debates surrounding his or her works.

- The list of **principal works** is divided into two sections, each of which is organized chronologically by date of first performance. If this has not been conclusively determined, the composition or publication date is used. The first section of the principal works list contains the author's dramatic pieces. The second section provides information on the author's major works in other genres.

- Whenever available, **author commentary** is provided. This section consists of essays or interviews in which the dramatist discusses his or her own work or the art of playwriting in general.

- Essays offering **overviews and general studies of the dramatist's entire literary career** give the student broad perspectives on the writer's artistic development, themes and concerns that recur in several of his or her works, the author's place in literary history, and other wide-ranging topics.

- **Criticism of individual plays** offers the reader in-depth discussions of a select number of the author's most important works. In some cases, the criticism is divided into two sections, each arranged chronologically. When a significant performance of a play can be identified (typically, the premier of a twentieth-century work), the first section of criticism will feature **production reviews** of this staging. Most entries include sections devoted to **critical commentary** that assesses the literary merit of the selected plays. When necessary, essays are carefully excerpted to focus on the work under consideration; often, however, essays and reviews are reprinted in their entirety.

- As an additional aid to students, the critical essays and excerpts are often prefaced by **explanatory annotations**. These notes provide several types of useful information, including the critic's reputation and approach to literary studies as well as the scope and significance of the criticism that follows.

- A complete **bibliographic citation**, designed to help the interested reader locate the original essay or book, precedes each piece of criticism.

- The **further reading list** at the end of each entry comprises additional studies of the dramatist. It is divided into sections that help students quickly locate the specific information they need.

Other Features

- A **cumulative author index** lists all the authors who have appeared in *DC* and Gale's other Literature Criticism Series, as well as cross-references to related titles published by Gale, including *Contemporary Authors* and *Dictionary of Literary Biography*. A complete listing of the series included appears at the beginning of the index.

- A **cumulative nationality index** lists each author featured in *DC* by nationality, followed by the number of the *DC* volume in which the author appears.

- A **cumulative title index** lists in alphabetical order the individual plays discussed in the criticism contained in *DC*. Each title is followed by the author's name and the corresponding volume and page number(s) where commentary on the work may be located. Translations and variant titles are cross-referenced to the title of the play in its original language so that all references to the work are combined in one listing.

A Note to the Reader

When writing papers, students who quote directly from any volume in *Drama Criticism* may use the following general formats to footnote reprinted criticism. The first example pertains to material drawn from periodicals, the second to materials reprinted from books.

¹Susan Sontag, "Going to the Theater, Etc.," *Partisan Review* XXXI, No. 3 (Summer 1964), 389-94; excerpted and reprinted in *Drama Criticism,* Vol. 1, ed. Lawrence J. Trudeau (Detroit: Gale Research, 1991), pp. 17-20.

²Eugene M. Waith, *The Herculean Hero in Marlowe, Chapman, Shakespeare and Dryden* (Chatto & Windus, 1962); excerpted and reprinted in *Drama Criticism,* Vol. 1, ed. Lawrence J. Trudeau (Detroit: Gale Research, 1991), pp. 237-47.

Suggestions are Welcome

Readers who wish to suggest authors to appear in future volumes of *DC,* or who have other suggestions, are cordially invited to contact the editor.

Acknowledgments

The editors wish to thank the copyright holders of the excerpted criticism included in this volume and the permissions managers of many book and magazine publishing companies for assisting us in securing reproduction rights. We are also grateful to the staffs of the Detroit Public Library, the Library of Congress, the University of Detroit Mercy Library, Wayne State University Purdy/Kresge Library Complex, and the University of Michigan Libraries for making their resources available to us. Following is a list of the copyright holders who have granted us permission to reproduce material in this volume of *DC*. Every effort has been made to trace copyright, but if omissions have been made, please let us know.

COPYRIGHTED EXCERPTS IN *DC*, VOLUME 9, WERE REPRODUCED FROM THE FOLLOWING PERIODICALS:

Canadian American Slavic Studies, v. 22, Spring-Summer-Fall-Winter, 1988.—*Comparative Drama,* v. 15, Winter, 1981-82. © copyright 1981, by the Editors of *Comparative Drama.* Reproduced by permission.—*The Critical Review,* Melbourne, n. 16, 1973. Reproduced by permission.—*The Hudson Review,* v. XXX, Winter, 1977-78 for "Three Sisters" by Howard Moss. Copyright © 1977 by The Hudson Review, Inc. Reproduced by permission of the Literary Estate of Howard Moss.—*Modern Drama,* v. XXVI, September, 1983; v. XXXIV, September, 1991. © 1983, 1991. University of Toronto, Graduate Centre for Study of Drama. Both reproduced by permission.—*Poetics Today,* v. 8, 1987. © The Porter Institute for Poetics and Semiotics. Reproduced by permission of Duke University Press.—*The Saturday Review,* v. L. July 8, 1967. © 1967 Saturday Review Magazine, © 1979 General Media Communications, Inc. Reproduced by permission of Saturday Review Publications, Ltd.—*Slavic and East European Journal,* v. 22, Winter, 1978. © 1978 by AATSEEL of the U.S., Inc. Reproduced by permission.—*Slavic Review,* v. 44, Fall, 1985. Copyright © 1985 by the American Association for the Advancement of Slavic Studies, Inc. Reproduced by permission.—*The Slavonic and East European Review,* v. 65, January, 1987. Reproduced by permission.—*The South Carolina Review,* v. 14, Spring, 1982. Copyright © 1982 by Clemson University. Reproduced by permission.—*Soviet Literature,* n. 1, 1985 for "Chekhov's Realism" by Pyotr Palievsky. Reproduced by permission of the author.

COPYRIGHTED EXCERPTS IN *DC*, VOLUME 9, WERE REPRODUCED FROM THE FOLLOWING BOOKS:

Bentley, Eric. From "Apologia" in *The Brute and Other Farces.* By Anton Chekhov. Edited by Eric Bentley. Translated by Eric Bentley and Theodore Hoffman. Applause Theatre Book Publishers. Copyright (c), 1958 by Eric Bentley. All rights reserved. Reproduced by permission.—Bentley, Eric. From *In Search of Theater.* Applause Theatre Books, 1992. Copyright 1953, renewed 1981 by Eric Bentley. All rights reserved. Reproduced by permission.—Chances, Ellen. From "Chekhov's 'Seagull': Ethereal Creature or Stuffed Bird?" in *Chekhov's Art of Writing: A Collection of Critical Essays.* Edited by Paul Debreczeny and Thomas Eekman. Slavica Publishers, 1997. Copyright © 1977 by Slavica Publishers, Inc. All rights reserved. Reproduced by permission of the author.—Egri, Péter. From *Chekhov and O'Neill: The Uses of the Short Story in Chekhov's and O'Neill's Plays.* Akadémiai Kiadó, 1986. © Akadémiai Kiadó, 1986. Reproduced by permission of the publisher and the author.—Ehre, Milton. From *Chekhov for the Stage.* Northwestern University Press, 1992. Copyright © 1992 by Northwestern University Press. All rights reserved. Reproduced by permission.—Esslin, Martin. From "Chekhov and the Modern Drama" in *A Chekhov Companion.* Greenwood Press, 1985. Copyright © 1985 by Toby W. Clyman. All rights reserved. Reproduced by permission of Greenwood Publishing Group, Inc., Westport, CT.—Fergusson, Francis. From *The Idea of a Theater: A Study of Ten Plays: The Art of Drama in Changing Perspective.* Princeton University Press, 1949. Copyright, 1949, by Princeton University Press. Renewed 1976 by Francis Fergusson. Renewed 1977 by Princeton University Press. Reproduced by permission.—Frayn, Michael. From the introduction to *The Seagull: A Comedy in Four Acts.* By Anton Chekhov. Translated by Michael Frayn. Methuen, 1986. Translation copyright © 1986 by Michael Frayn. Reproduced by permission.—Frayn, Michael. From the introduction to *Uncle Vanya: Scenes from Country Life in Four Acts.* By Anton Chekhov. Translated by Michael Frayn. Methuen, 1987. © 1987 by Michael Frayn. All rights reserved. Reproduced by permission.—Gaskell, Ronald. From *Drama and Reality: The European Theatre Since Ibsen.* Routledge & Kegan Paul, 1972. © Ronald Gaskell 1972. Reproduced by permission.—Gilman, Richard. From *Chekhov's Plays: An Opening into Eternity.* Yale University Press, 1995. Copyright © 1995 by Richard Gilman. All rights reserved. Reproduced by permission.—Gottlieb, Vera. From *Chekhov and the Vaudeville: A Study of Chekhov's One-Act Plays.* Cambridge University Press, 1982. © Cambridge University Press 1982. Reproduced by permission.—Guthrie, Tyrone. From "A Director's Introduction" in *Uncle Vanya: Scenes from Country Life in Four Acts.*

PHOTOGRAPHS AND ILLUSTRATIONS APPEARING IN *DC,* VOLUME 9, WERE RECEIVED FROM THE FOLLOWING SOURCES:

Moscow Art Theater production of *The Seagull* by Anton Chekhov, 1905, photograph. From ***Konstantin Stanislavsky: Selected Works.*** Compiled by Oksana Korneva. Raduga Publishers, Moscow, 1984. —Act I from the 1898 Moscow Art Theater production of *The Seagull* by Anton Chekhov, photograph. —Act III of a Moscow Art Theater production of *The Seagull* by Anton Chekhov, 1905, photograph. From ***Konstantin Stanislavsky: Selected Works***. Compiled by Oksana Korneva. Raduga Publishers, Moscow, 1984. —Act III of a Moscow Art Theater production of *The Cherry Orchard* by Anton Chekhov, 1904, photograph. From ***Konstantin Stanislavsky: Selected Works.*** Compiled by Oksana Korneva. Raduga Publishers, Moscow, 1984. —Act IV of the Moscow Art Theater production of *The Three Sisters* by Anton Chekhov, photograph. From ***Konstantin Stanislavsky: Selected Works.*** Compiled by Oksana Korneva. Raduga Publishers, Moscow, 1984. —Andrews, Harry, Simone Signoret, Vanessa Redgrave, and Alfred Lynch in Sidney Lumet's 1968 film adaptation of Chekhov's *The Seagull,* photograph. The Kobal Collection. Reproduced by permission. —Anton Chekhov's dacha, wing built in 1894, 1895, Melichowo, Russian Empire, photograph. Austrian Archives/Corbis. Reproduced by permission. —Aschcroft, Peggy, Gwen Frangcon-Davies, and Carol Goodner, in John Gielgud's 1938 production of Chekhov's *Three Sisters* at the Queen's Theatre, London, photograph. Hulton-Deutsch Collection/Corbis. Reproduced by permission. —Barber, Frances, Derek Jacobi, and Imogen Stubbs, in the 1995 Chichester Theatre production of Chekhov's *Uncle Vanya,* photograph. Robbie Jack/Corbis. Reproduced by permission. —Bondarchuck, Sergei (left), Irina Kupchenko (facing), with others, in a scene from a Russian film adaptation of Chekhov's *Uncle Vanya,* 1970, photograph. The Kobal Collection. Reproduced by permission. —Chekhov, Anton, photograph. Corbis-Bettmann. Reproduced by permission. —Chekhov, Anton, with family and friends, 1890, Moscow, photograph. Austrian Archives/Corbis. Reproduced by permission. —Chekhov, Anton, 1888, photograph. Austrian Archives/Corbis. Reproduced by permission. —Chekhov, Anton, 1901, photograph. From ***Konstantin Stanislavsky: Selected Works.*** Compiled by Oksana Korneva. Raduga Publishers, Moscow, 1984. —Chekhov, Anton, with his brother Nikolai, 1880, photograph. Austrian Archives/Corbis. Reproduced by permission. —Chekhov, Anton, c. 1900, photograph. Hulton-Deutsch Collection/Corbis. Reproduced by permission. —Chekhov, Anton, photograph. The Library of Congress. —Chekhov, Anton, with the Moscow Art theatre troupe, reading his play *The Seagull,* 1899, Moscow, photograph. Austrian Archives/Corbis. Reproduced by permission. —Cover of the first edition of Chekhov's *Three Sisters,* illustration. —Dench, Judi, and Alan Cox, in a 1994 National Theatre production of Chekhov's *The Seagull,* London, photograph. Robbie Jack/Corbis. Reproduced by permission. —Funeral cortege of Anton Chekhov reaching the Kusnetska Bridge, 1904, Moscow, photograph. Austrian Archives/Corbis. Reproduced by permission. — Heard, Daphne, and Laurence Olivier, in his 1970 film adaptation of Anton Chekhov's *Three Sisters,* photograph by Norman Gryspeerdt. The Kobal Collection. Reproduced by permission. —Jacobi, Derek, and Jane Wymark in an Old Vic production of Anton Chekhov's *Ivanov,* 1978, London, photograph. Hulton-Deutsch Collection/Corbis. Reproduced by permission. —Interior of the Moscow Art Theater, photograph. From ***Stanislavsky: My Life in the Theatre.*** Academia, 1936, Soviet Union. —Knipper, Olga, as Ranyevskaya in Anton Chekhov's *The Cherry Orchard,* photograph. —Knipper, Olga, and Anton Chekhov, 1902, photograph. —Lawrence, Josie, John Dougall, and Mark Lockyer, in the 1995 Royal Shakespeare Company production of Anton Chekhov's *The Cherry Orchard,* photograph. Robbie Jack/Corbis. Reproduced by permission. —Mason, James, and Elsa Lanchester, in the 1933 Old Vic production of Anton Chekhov's *The Cherry Orchard,* London, photograph by Sasha. Hulton-Deutsch Collection/Corbis. Reproduced by permission. —Moscow Art Theater cast from *Three Sisters* by Anton Chekhov, 1901, photograph. From ***Konstantin Stanislavsky: Selected Works.*** Compiled by Oksana Korneva, photograph. Raduga Publishers, Moscow, 1984. — The Moscow Art Theater troupe, 1900, photograph. From ***Konstantin Stanislavsky: Selected Works.*** Compiled by Oksana Korneva, photograph. Raduga Publishers, Moscow, 1984. —Nemirov-Danchenko, Vladimir, photograph. From ***Konstantin Stanislavsky: Selected Works.*** Compiled by Oksana Korneva. Raduga Publishers, Moscow, 1984. —Olga Knipper as Masha, in Act I of *Three Sisters* by Anton Chekhov, photograph. —Purnell, Louise, and Ronald Pickup, in Laurence Olivier's 1970 film adaptation of Chekhov's *Three Sisters,* photograph by Norman Gryspeerdt. The Kobal Collection. Reproduced by permission. —Purnell, Louise, Jeanne Watts, and Joan Plowright, in Laurence Olivier's 1970 film adaptation of *Three Sisters* by Anton Chekhov, photograph by Norman Gryspeerdt. The Kobal Collection. Reproduced by permission. —Scene from the 1971 Russian film adaptation of *The Seagull* by Anton Chekhov, photograph. The Kobal Collection. Reproduced by permission. —Scene from the Moscow Art Theater production of *The Seagull* by Anton Chekhov, 1898, photograph. ***From Stanislavsky: My Life in the Theatre.*** Academia, 1936, Soviet Union. —Smoktunovsky, Innokenty, and Irina Kupchenko, in a Russian film adaptation of *Uncle Vanya* by Anton Chekhov, 1970, photograph. The Kobal Collection. Reproduced by permission. —Stanislavsky, K. and Maria Petrovna Lilina, in a Moscow Art Theater production of *The Cherry Orchard* by Anton Chekhov, 1908, photograph. From ***Stanislavsky: My Life in the Theatre.*** Academia, 1936, Soviet Union. —Stanislavsky, K. and Olga Knipper, in a Moscow Art Theater production of *Three Sisters* by Anton Chekhov, 1901, photograph. From ***Stanislavsky: My Life in the Theatre. Academia.*** 1936, Soviet Union. —Stanislavsky, K. and Olga Knipper, in a Moscow Art Theater production of *Uncle Vanya* by Anton Chekhov, 1904, photograph. From ***Stanislavsky: My Life in the Theatre.*** Academia, 1936, Soviet Union. —Stanislavsky, K., in the Moscow Art Theater production of *Three Sisters* by Anton Chekhov, 1901, photograph. From ***Konstantin Stanislavsky: Selected Works.*** Compiled by Oksana Korneva. Raduga Publishers, Moscow, 1984. —Stanislavsky, Konstantin, as Astrov in a Moscow Art Theater production of Chekhov's *Uncle Vanya,* 1899, photograph. From ***Konstantin Stanislavsky: Selected Works.*** Compiled by Oksana Korneva, photograph. Raduga Publishers, Moscow, 1984. —Warner, David, in the 1968 film adaptation of Chekhov's *The Seagull,* directed by Sidney Lumet, photograph. The Kobal Collection. Reproduced by permission.

List of Playwrights Covered in *DC*

Volume 1
James Baldwin
William Wells Brown
Karel Capek
Mary Chase
Alexandre Dumas (*fils*)
Charles Fuller
Nikolai Gogol
Lillian Hellman
Christopher Marlowe
Arthur Miller
Yukio Mishima
Richard Brinsley Sheridan
Sophocles
Thornton Wilder

Volume 2
Aristophanes
Albert Camus
William Congreve
Everyman
Federico García Lorca
Lorraine Hansberry
Henrik Ibsen
Wole Soyinka
John Millingon Synge
John Webster
August Wilson

Volume 3
Bertolt Brecht
Pedro Calderón de la Barca
John Dryden
Athol Fugard
Langston Hughes
Thomas Kyd
Menander
Joe Orton
Jean-Paul Sartre
Ntozake Shange

Volume 4
Pierre-Augustin Caron de
    Beaumarchais
Aphra Behn
Alice Childress
Euripides
Hugo von Hofmannsthal
David Henry Hwang
Ben Jonson
David Mamet
Wendy Wasserstein
Tennessee Williams

Volume 5
Caryl Churchill
John Pepper Clark
Adrienne Kennedy
Thomas Middleton
Luigi Pirandello
Eugène Scribe
Lucius Annaeus Seneca
Sam Shepard
Paul Zindel

Volume 6
Amiri Baraka
Francis Beaumont and
    John Fletcher
Ed Bullins
Václav Havel
Clifford Odets
Plautus
Tom Stoppard

Volume 7
Frank Chin
Spalding Gray
John Lyly
Emily Mann
Pierre Carlet de Chamblain de
    Marivaux
Peter Shaffer
Terence
Ivan Turgenev
Derek Walcott
Zeami

Volume 8
Aeschylus
Jean Anouilh
Lonne Elder III
John Ford
Brian Friel
Oliver Goldsmith
Charles Gordone
Larry Kramer
Marsha Norman

Volume 9
Anton Pavlovich Chekhov

Anton Pavlovich Chekhov
1860-1904

INTRODUCTION

Chekhov is one of the most important playwrights in all of Western drama. His name has been linked with those of Molière, Schiller, and Shakespeare for the impact his work has had on the history of theater. With a small handful of plays he overthrew the long-standing tradition of works that emphasize action and plot, in favor of dramas that treat situation, mood, and internal psychological states. The content and dramatic technique of Chekhov's four masterpieces, *The Seagull, Uncle Vanya, Three Sisters,* and *The Cherry Orchard* inaugurated fundamental changes not only in the way plays are composed but in the way they are acted, a revolution that persists to this day in works written for film and television, as well as those composed for the stage.

BIOGRAPHICAL INFORMATION

Chekhov's grandfather was a serf who bought his freedom, and his father was the owner of a small grocery business in Taganrog, the village where Chekhov was born. When the family business went bankrupt in 1876, the Chekhovs, without Anton, moved to Moscow to escape creditors; Anton remained in Taganrog until 1879 in order to complete his education and earn a scholarship to Moscow University. There, he studied medicine and, after graduating in 1884, went into practice. By this time he was publishing sketches, mostly humorous, in popular magazines. Chekhov did this to support his family, and, although he wrote literally hundreds of these pieces, he did not take them very seriously. In 1885, however, he moved to St. Petersburg and became friends with A. S. Suvorin, editor of the journal *Novoe vremja,* who encouraged the young writer to develop his obvious gifts.

At this time, and for several years afterward, Chekhov's writings were profoundly influenced by Leo Tolstoy's ideas on ascetic morality and nonresistance to evil. But after Chekhov visited the penal settlement on the island of Sakhalin, which he would make the subject of a humanitarian study, he rejected Tolstoy's moral code as an insufficient answer to human suffering. In the late 1880s Chekhov began to produce what are regarded as his mature works in the short story form. At the same time he began experimenting with the writing of plays. In the 1880s he composed a number of comic one-act plays, or "vaudevilles," often adapted from his short stories. *Ivanov,* his first full-length work (aside from the early untitled and never-performed drama commonly referred to as *Platonov*), was staged in 1887, and *The Wood Demon* appeared two years later. Both *Ivanov* and *The Wood Demon* were unsuccessful when they were produced. His first major work as a dramatist, *The Seagull,* was also a failure when

it was staged in a disastrous 1896 production at the Alexandrinsky Theater in St. Petersburg. A discouraged Chekhov vowed never to write for the stage again. However, two years later, in their debut season, the Moscow Art Theater mounted an acclaimed revival of *The Seagull* which established both Chekhov as an accomplished playwright and the Moscow Art Theater company as an important new acting troupe.

Around this time Chekhov rewrote *The Wood Demon,* transforming it into *Uncle Vanya.* The new play was performed several times in the Russian provinces before it received its first professional staging by the Moscow Art Theater in 1899. The same company also presented the first performances of *Three Sisters* (1901) and *The Cherry Orchard* (1904). In 1901 Chekhov married Olga Knipper, an actress with the Moscow Art Theater. Because of his worsening tuberculosis, from which he had suffered since 1884, Chekhov was forced to spend most of his time in the Crimea, where, it was believed, the warm southern climate was better for his condition, and in European health resorts; consequently, he was often separated from his wife, who typically performed in Moscow. He died in a Black Forest spa in 1904.

MAJOR WORKS

Chekhov's interest and participation in the theater had its origins in his schooldays at Taganrog, when he acted and wrote for the local playhouse. His first serious effort in drama was written in 1881, during his residence in Moscow. This work, *Platonov,* initiated the first of two major periods of the author's dramatic writings. The works of this first period are conventional melodramas characterized by the standard theatrical techniques and subjects of the times. *Platonov,* a long and somewhat declamatory social drama, features a leading character whose reformist ideals are negated by the indifference of others and by his own ineffectuality. Chekhov's next drama, *Ivanov,* is less bulky and more realistic than its predecessor, though critics still view it as a theatrically exaggerated and traditional piece. Written during the Tolstoyan phase of Chekhov's works, *The Wood Demon* was his first attempt at the artistic realism fully achieved only in his later dramas. This didactic morality play on the theme of vice and virtue is criticized for the same dramatic faults as the other works of this period.

The dramas of Chekhov's second period constitute his major work in the theater. These plays are primarily noted for their technique of "indirect action," a method whereby violent or intensely dramatic events are not shown on stage but occur (if at all) during the intervals of the action as seen by the audience. Chekhov's major plays, then, contain little of what is traditionally regarded as "plot," and consist primarily of quotidian activities performed by the characters and conversations in which allusions to the unseen events are intermingled with discussions of daily affairs and seemingly random observations. Though not portrayed on stage, momentous events are thus shown by the characters' words and actions to be pervasive in their effects. By focusing more closely on the characters' reactions to events than on the events themselves, Chekhov's plays are able to study and convey more precisely the effects of crucial events on characters' lives. Although Chekhov utilized elements of this method in *Ivanov* and *The Wood Demon,* these works remain in essence traditional melodramas. The first drama in which the technique of indirect action is extensively employed is *The Seagull.* In this play, the highly charged, traditionally "dramatic" events—the affair between Trigorin and Nina, Treplev's suicide attempts—occur off stage. No "crises" in the usual sense are shown. What are presented are the precipitating events and consequent effects on the characters—Treplev's and Nina's idealism and the subsequent despair of the one and the resignation of the other. Even though Treplev's suicide attempts and Trigorin's seduction of Nina are resolutely kept off stage, their presence points to the fact that Chekhov was thus far unable to completely eradicate melodramatic elements from his work. Likewise, Vanya's attempt to shoot Serebriakov in *Uncle Vanya* and Tuzenbach's death in a duel in *Three Sisters* are remnants of the older tradition which Chekhov was unable to do without. Only *The Cherry Orchard* appears free of such theatrical "high points." In this play no-one dies. No shots are even fired—either on or off stage.

The static quality of Chekhov's plays, in which nothing much seems to happen, is evoked by their content as well as their apparent "plotlessness." A common theme throughout Chekhov's four major plays is dissatisfaction with present conditions accompanied by a perceived inability to change oneself or one's situation. Treplev tries and fails to revolutionize the nature of drama. Uncle Vanya feels he has wasted his life supporting the fraud Serebriakov and believes he has no alternative but to continue on as he has. The three sisters feel smothered in the stultifying atmosphere of a provincial town and appear incapable of taking action to realize their dream of returning to Moscow. Ranevskaya and Gaev are faced with the loss of their beloved childhood home but cannot act decisively to prevent its sale. Chekhov escapes pessimism in these works by including characters who express optimism—or at least some degree of hopefulness—regarding the future. Sonya in *Uncle Vanya,* Vershinin in *Three Sisters,* and Trofimov in *The Cherry Orchard* all anticipate some future state in which all present ills and discontents will be remedied.

The past, too, as well as the future, exerts significant influence on the behavior of Chekhov's characters. To Treplev in *The Seagull,* Arkadina and Trigorin represent the artistic past that he is attempting to overthrow. Vanya feels the burden of the past in the form of the years wasted supporting Serebriakov. Masha, Irina, and Olga long for the Moscow of their childhood. Ranevskaya in *The Cherry Orchard* is tormented by the memory of her drowned son and her subsequent flight to Paris. But it is the present that concerns Chekhov most in these plays. Affected by the past, leading to some unseen future, the present with all its complexities and uncertainties is the stuff of which Chekhov's plays are made. Life as it is really lived, rather than highly melodramatic and theatrical incidents, Chekhov insisted, is the proper subject for plays. "After all, in real life," he observed, "people don't spend every minute shooting at each other, hanging themselves, and making confessions of love. They don't spend all the time saying clever things. They're more occupied with eating, drinking, flirting, and talking stupidities—and these are the things which ought to be shown on the stage. A play should be written in which people arrive, go away, have dinner, talk about the weather, and play cards. Life must be exactly as it is, and people as they are. . . . Let everything on the stage be just as complicated, and at the same time just as simple as it is in life. People eat their dinner, just eat their dinner, and all the time their happiness is being established or their lives are being broken up."

CRITICAL RECEPTION

Although the Moscow Art Theater production of *The Seagull* was a great success for both the company and the playwright, Chekhov was infuriated by the staging, contending that director Konstantin Stanislavsky had ruined the play. The sets, the lighting, the sound effects—which, famously, included the croaking of frogs and the chirruping of crickets—and the acting all emphasized elements of tragedy in a play that its author vehemently insisted was a comedy. A similarly heated disagreement arose between author and director over *The Cherry Orchard,* which Chekhov subtitled "A Comedy," but which, in the Moscow Art Theater staging, was presented as a nostalgic parable on the passing of an older order in Russian history. Stanislavsky and his actors stressed, to Chekhov's dismay, the pathos of the characters' situation.

Chekhov never applied the term "tragedy" to his works: aside from labelling *The Seagull* and *The Cherry Orchard* "comedies," he called *Uncle Vanya* "Scenes from Country Life" and *Three Sisters* simply "A Drama." Nevertheless, the plays have routinely been interpreted as tragedies in countless performances and critical studies. Until recently, actors, directors, and scholars alike perceived a mood of sadness and despair blanketing all of Chekhov's major plays. Among such interpreters, Chekhov has earned a reputation as a portrayer of futile existences and as a forerunner of the modernist tradition of the absurd. The view of Chekhov as a pessimist, however, has always met with opposition, especially from Russian critics, who have seen him as a chronicler of the degenerating landowner classes during an era of imminent revolution.

A common response of early reviewers of performances of Chekhov's works throughout Europe and North America was to dismiss the plays as meaningless assemblages of random events. Early critics censured their seeming plotlessness and lack of "significant" action. However, much critical attention has subsequently been paid to the organizational and structural principles of Chekhovian drama. Scholars have shown that by the meticulous arrangement of sets, sound effects (including verbal effects: witness, for example, the "Tram-tam-tam" exchange between Masha and Vershinin in Act III of *Three Sisters*), and action, as well as the characters' speeches, Chekhov creates scenes and situations which appear static and uneventful on the surface but which are charged with significance and meaning. (It was the care with which he had arranged the various elements of his plays that led to Chekhov's exasperation with Stanislavsky: the director's myriad stage effects obscured or obliterated the delicate balance of parts that the writer sought.)

The subtlety and indirection of Chekhov's method of presentation required a new style of acting, free of the big gestures and declamation characteristic of traditional acting. A restrained, allusive style was essential, and here Chekhov was well served by the Moscow Art Theater, with its new emphasis on internalizing character and conveying elusive psychological states. Scholars and theater historians have repeatedly stressed that Chekhov, together with Stanislavksy and the Moscow Art Theater, forever transformed the ways in which plays are conceived, written, and performed.

The reception, then, of *The Seagull, Uncle Vanya, Three Sisters,* and *The Cherry Orchard* extends far beyond theater reviews and critical studies, and the influence of these plays continues to be felt by writers, actors, directors throughout the world.

PRINCIPAL WORKS

PLAYS

Platonov 1881
Ivanov 1887
Leshy [*The Wood Demon*] 1889
Chaika [*The Seagull*] 1896
†*Dyadya Vanya* [*Uncle Vanya*] 1896?
Tri sestry [*Three Sisters*] 1901
Vishnevy sad [*The Cherry Orchard*] 1904

SHORT FICTION

Pëstrye rasskazy 1886
Nevinnye rechi 1887
V sumerkakh 1887
Rasskazy 1889
The Black Monk, and Other Stories 1903
The Kiss, and Other Stories 1908
The Darling, and Other Stories 1916
The Duel, and Other Stories 1916
The Lady with the Dog, and Other Stories 1917
The Party, and Other Stories 1917
The Wife, and Other Stories 1918
The Witch, and Other Stories 1918
The Bishop, and Other Stories 1919
The Chorus Girl, and Other Stories 1920
The Horse-Stealers, and Other Stories 1921
The Schoolmaster, and Other Stories 1921
The Schoolmistress, and Other Stories 1921
The Cook's Wedding, and Other Stories 1922
Love, and Other Stories 1922

COLLECTED WORKS

Chekhov: Polnoe sobranie sochinenii 1900-1904
Polnoe sobranie sochinenii i pisem A. P. Chekhova 1944-51
The Oxford Chekhov 1964-1980

---

*The date of this early, untitled play of Chekhov's is conjectural. Commonly referred to as *Platonov,* after its central character, it has also been called *That Worthless Fellow Platonov* and *Play without a Title.*

†The date of *Uncle Vanya* is uncertain. A reworking of the earlier *Wood Demon,* the play was probably composed by Chekhov in 1896; a letter of Chekhov's dated in December of that year seems to refer to *Uncle Vanya* as a completed work. Provincial productions of the play were mounted soon afterward, but it did not receive its first professional staging—in a Moscow Art Theater production—until 1899.

Overviews and General Studies

A. Skaftymov (essay date 1948)

SOURCE: "Principles of Structure in Chekhov's Plays," in *Chekhov: A Collection of Critical Essays,* edited by Robert Louis Jackson, Prentice-Hall, 1967, pp. 69-87.

[*The following is an abridged version of an essay that was first published in Russian in 1948. Skaftymov addresses the "question of the unity of form and content" in Chekhov's plays.*]

There is a rather large and in many respects substantial body of secondary literature on Chekhov's dramaturgy.

Contemporaries noted a peculiarity in Chekhov's plays at the time of the first productions. At first they interpreted this peculiarity as Chekhov's inability to manage the problems of continuous living dramatic movement. Reviewers spoke of "prolixity," of the lack of "stagecraft," of "insufficient action" and weakness of plot. In reproaching Chekhov, contemporaries wrote that "he himself does not know what he wants," that "he does not know the laws of drama," that he does not fulfill the "most elementary demands of the stage," that he writes some sort of "reports," that he gives little pictures with all the chance accidentality of photography, without any thought, and without expressing his own attitude.

K. S. Stanislavsky and V. I. Nemirovich-Danchenko noted the so-called "undercurrent,"[1] the most essential principle in the dramatic movement of Chekhov's plays. They revealed the presence of a continuous, internal, intimate, lyric current behind the external, prosaic episodes and details; and in their endeavors at creative staging, they correctly directed all their efforts toward rendering this emotional current more perceptible to the spectator. The new, infectious force of Chekhov's plays became evident.

During this time critics ceased to speak of Chekhov's ineptitude in the field of drama. They reconciled themselves to the "absence of action" in his plays just as they did to the plays' evident strangeness; they defined Chekhov's plays as a special "drama of mood," and thereby seemed to answer all the questions for a time. Only a few critics continued to look back to traditional "dramatic laws," and as a mild reproof to Chekhov continued to speak of a "looseness" and of the "diffuseness of a Chekhovian scenario."[2] This reproof, however, no longer testified to dissatisfaction or ill will. They "forgave" Chekhov for his peculiarity. All the articles on Chekhov's plays now enumerated everything that contributed to the "mood": elements of lyric coloring in the characters' speeches, sound accompaniment, pauses, and so forth.

Chekhov and Olga Knipper in 1902.

Later on these same devices and peculiarities were described in special studies (Yuriev, Grigoriev, and Balukhaty). S. D. Balukhaty's contributions to the study of Chekhov's dramaturgy were especially considerable. In two books and several separate studies, he traced the history of the writing and first productions of each play and gathered a great deal of material characterizing Chekhov's own attitude toward his activities as a dramatist and the attitude toward his plays on the part of the critics and public. He carefully described the structure of each play and thoroughly mapped out the process of gradual formation of those special features and devices which constitute the specific character of Chekhov's plays. All this aids considerably in the study of Chekhov's drama.

Regrettably, even Balukhaty presents all the peculiarities of dramatic structure merely in a descriptive manner. The question of the unity of form and content in Chekhov's plays remains altogether untouched.

Much remains unclear. Specifically, what was the nature of the new attitude toward reality which required new forms for its expression? What ideological kind of creative force drew Chekhov to put together this particular complex of dramatic peculiarities? What motivated Chekhov to devise new methods of dramatic movement? Why does everyday reality occupy such a large and free place in his plays? Why does he abolish tightness of plot and substitute for it episodic, disconnected scenes, and why does he change all forms of interaction of dialogue? And mainly: how is it that all these peculiarities harmonize with each other; what is the nature of their interdependence; what underlying defining principle do they have in common?

The statement that Chekhovian drama is not drama in the usual sense, that it is "lyric drama" or a "drama of moods," and more precisely of "melancholy moods," has only descriptive value. Furthermore, it has little concrete meaning. It is true that in such a description, functional explanations are found for such elements as sound accompaniment, pauses, etc. But why, for the purposes of lyricism, was it necessary to resort to indirect rather than direct expression of feeling, moods, and so forth? If it is a matter of "lyricism" or "moods" in general, with the added note that this lyricism has a sad, melancholy character, then are the scattered quality of the everyday details, the absence of plot, and other purely Chekhovian features absolutely necessary for its expression?

Obviously, calling attention to the lyricism and melancholy mood of Chekhov's plays is inadequate as an answer to these questions. One must consider the qualitative substance of those "moods," that is, see what thoughts and ideas are connected with them. Only then will the essence of Chekhovian forms be revealed as the specific nature of content—a content which could only, and exclusively, be expressed through the given forms.

Balukhaty's suggestion that Chekhov, with his new type of drama, was seeking to supersede the old canon of the drama of everyday life explains little. It is true that Chekhov was dissatisfied with the "tried and true poetics" of the drama of everyday life, that he was "seeking to overcome the schematic character of the drama of everyday life" just by using new "elements and colors from everyday life," to "create in the theater the illusion of life," and "to construct new, fresh dramatic forms in place of the former, conventional typification of scenes and characters."[3] But one can hardly agree that Chekhov includes "facts, actions, intonations, and themes," in a drama merely because they were "new," "strikingly impressive," and because they had not yet been "utilized" on the stage; that merely for the sake of such "novelty," Chekhov "avoids vivid, dynamic elements," simplifies the plot fabric, and substitutes "an apparently unsystematic combination of facts and actions" for "the dramatically conceived, strictly motivated movement of themes one finds in the drama of everyday life."[4] Supposedly, Chekhov did all this in order to "tone down the customary 'theatricality' of plays and to revivify dramatic writing by *naturalistic* and *psychological devices* within the complex structure and relations of routine, ordinary life."[5]

The suggestion of a striving for novelty does not define the real nature of that novelty. If the term "naturalistic" is understood to mean Chekhov's striving not only toward novelty, but also toward the utmost truthfulness, that is, toward the closest approximation of the forms of life itself, then, of course, it would be generally correct to say that Chekhov discovered certain new aspects of reality, and in his creative work as an artist-realist sought to reproduce them. But a striving for truthfulness is insufficient as an explanation. . . . The crucial question is why Chekhov stubbornly and persistently sought to combine so many diverse elements of reality, the unity of which makes up the specific substance of his plays. He must obviously have perceived some sort of connection between all these elements of reflected life. . . . This article is an attempt to reveal the structural peculiarities of Chekhov's plays as an expression of a special dramatic quality of life discovered and interpreted by Chekhov as an attribute of his epoch.

As we know, theater critics reproved Chekhov most of all for introducing into his plays superfluous details from everyday life, and thus violating the laws of stage action. The presence of such details was put down to his ineptitude, to the habits of the writer of tales and short stories, and to his inability or unwillingness to master the requirements of the dramatic genre. These views were expressed not only by newspaper and theater reviewers who were distant from Chekhov and did not know him, but even by those who clearly wished him well (for example, A. Lensky and Nemirovich-Danchenko).

Chekhov himself, at the time he was writing the plays, apparently experienced the greatest difficulty and confusion on this point. While working on *The Wood Demon,* he saw that instead of a drama (in the usual sense) he was arriving at something like a story. "*The Wood Demon* is suitable for a novel," he wrote A. S. Suvorin October 24, 1888.

> I am perfectly well aware of this myself. But I haven't the strength for a novel. I might be able to write a short story. If I wrote a comedy *The Wood Demon,* then not actors and a stage would be in the forefront, but literary quality. If the play had literary significance, it would be due to that.

After *The Wood Demon,* Chekhov turned away from the theater for some time. Seven years passed. He was now at work on *The Seagull.* His purpose was not to get rid of details from everyday life, but to overcome the seeming incompatibility between such details and the demands of dramatic genre and to effect a synthesis of these details. "Details" in the new play were, he knew, prevalent to a degree inadmissible in the usual play, but obviously, he could not forsake them. While working on the play, he wrote: "I am afraid to make a mess of it and to pile up details which will impair the clarity." And further: "I am writing the play not without satisfaction, although I sin terribly against the conventions of the stage. It is a comedy, three female parts, six male, four acts, a landscape (view of a lake); much conversation about literature, little action, tons of love." And then again: "I began it *forte* and finished *pianissimo*—despite all the rules of dramatic art. A story has emerged. I am more dissatisfied than satisfied, and reading my new play, I am again convinced that I am not at all a playwright." (Letters to Suvorin, October 21 and November 21, 1895.)

All of this indicates that for Chekhov in his excursions into drama, some sort of reproduction of the sphere of everyday life was an indispensable condition; he was unwilling to forsake it. . . . "They demand," he said,

> that the hero and heroine be theatrically effective. But really, in life people are not every minute shooting each other, hanging themselves, and making declarations of love. And they are not saying clever things every minute. For the most part, they eat, drink, hang about, and talk nonsense; and this must be seen on the stage. A play must be written in which people can come, go, dine, talk about the weather, and play cards, not because that's the way the author wants it, but because that's the way it happens in real life.[6]

> Let everything on the stage be just as complex and at the same time just as simple as in life. People dine, merely dine, but at that moment their happiness is being made or their life is being smashed.[7]

At first glance, such statements seem incomprehensible. Was there not everyday life in the earlier drama of everyday life which had developed over the course of the entire nineteenth century? Take A. N. Ostrovsky (1823-1886)—whom, of course, Chekhov could not fail to know—don't people eat, drink, hang about, and talk nonsense in his plays? Can it be that his characters come, go, dine, talk, and so forth only because "that's the way it happens in real life"? Is not the entire structure of an Ostrovsky play directed toward the attainment of the greatest likeness in life? Are not all devices of plot, development, and denouement in Ostrovsky created in order to approximate the truth of everyday life? There were, of course, conscious deviations from this criterion. But these were unavoidable, an obligatory convention. And even in these instances the author's efforts were nevertheless directed toward achieving the closest resemblance to those situations which were regarded as possible in everyday life.

But let us not stop here. Are not the dramatic collisions which make up the heart and meaning of a play, drawn as belonging to everyday life? All images of people, types, and characters always have been represented as figures from everyday life, that is, as something established, of long standing, and characteristic of the general way of life in a given environment. At any rate, authors were always striving in this direction. . . .

The principal justification for the nineteenth century play of everyday life was always one and the same: its closeness to reality and to the most universal and enduring qualities of life and people. Out of this demand arose the notion of "typicality," binding for all alike and accepted as the basis for all literary and dramatic judgments. It gave a common direction to everyone's efforts—one which met with varying success, to be sure, and brought about the creation of a peculiar but widely shared style of everyday life realism. In spite of all the variety of thematic and ideological problems, all the subtleties in ways of selecting and arranging material, everyone more or less had to present everyday life not only as a framework, but as a theme facilitating the most exact verisimilitude. One can scarcely point to any play of this kind where elements of the common flow of life are not represented, where, specifically, tea is not drunk, where there is no eating and drinking, and where quite "ordinary" conversations do not take place.

Chekhov, of course, knew this. It is clear that, when he spoke of the necessity for everyday ordinariness in a dramatic reproduction of life, he had in mind some other reality which he had observed, something unlike anything he had seen in his predecessors.

Wherein lay the difference?

One of the salient features of pre-Chekhovian drama is that everyday life is absorbed into, and overshadowed by, events. The humdrum—that which is most permanent, normal, customary, and habitual—is almost absent from these plays. Moments of the even flow of life appear at the beginning of the play, as an exposition and a starting point, but subsequently, the entire play, the entire fabric of dialogue is taken up with events; the daily flow of life recedes into the background and is merely mentioned and implied in places.

In plays of this type . . . where the stage situation serves merely as an occasion for the characteristic descriptive utterances of the *dramatis personae,* there are no entangling events. But these plays are not finished works of art; even for the authors they were no more than preliminary studies, episodic genre sketches. In most of the other plays . . . the elements of commonplace tranquility always, in essence, foreshadow an event and are directed toward it. They foretell an event, giving information about the conditions under which it will occur; or they comment on its meaning by revealing in dialogue certain traits in the characters without which the event would not occur. . . .

Furthermore, in the earlier drama, everyday life is nothing but the customary manners and morals of people. In each play the intent is to expose, display, and comment on some social vice or imperfection. Depending on the depth and breadth of the author's understanding and ability, the central event of the play absorbs into itself both the roots and manifestations of the evil at issue, as well as its consequences. Basically, the characters appear either as bearers of the vice depicted or as its victims. Some characters are introduced for subsidiary aims: to forward the intrigue, to reveal the qualities of the main characters, or to explain the author's point of view (the *raisonneur*). Within these limits there are countless variations. But despite all the variety of world views, talents, and objects depicted, and despite marked differences in the writers' mastery of drama, all the previous drama of everyday life is similar in its one objective: to mark and isolate some everyday traits in people, and for this purpose to show an event in which the characters act in accord with these selected traits.

The everyday elements of each play, then, are chosen only as they illustrate the social or ethical meaning of some feature of typical life like ignorance, despotism, acquisitiveness, flippancy, official swindling, social indifference, obscurantism, and so forth. . . . The result is a concentration of the ordinary dialogue on some morally significant trait or other which is embodied in the principal event. All other details of everyday life are merely extraneous, have no direct bearing on the problem, and could easily be omitted. The even humdrum of life is almost absent from these plays.

In Chekhov it is entirely different. Chekhov does not seek out events; on the contrary, he concentrates on reproducing the most ordinary features of day-to-day existence. Chekhov saw the drama of life being performed in that ordinary flow when things are left to themselves and nothing happens. The peaceful flow of life as it is lived was, to Chekhov, not simply a "setting" and not simply an exposition serving as a transition to the events, but the central area of life's dramas, that is, the direct and fundamental object of his creative act of representation. So, contrary to all traditions, Chekhov moves events to the periphery as if they were details; and all that is ordinary, constant, recurring, and habitual constitutes the main mass, the basic ground of the play. Events that do occur in Chekhov's plays do not fracture the general atmosphere of everyday conditions. Events spread themselves evenly throughout the interweaving of divergent interests, everyday habits and happenings; they are not knots where everything centers, but rather, they merge into the general multicolored fabric; each event serves as a thread, a detail in the pattern.

Chekhov's method of revealing everywhere—not only in the plot—the substance of the play is not yet apparent in *Ivanov.* Ivanov's inner drama, which organizes the play's principal movement, is brought out in the event which integrates the plot—the story of Ivanov and Sasha Lebedev. Much of the substance here, too, however, lies outside the strict plot field: for example, scene v in Act I (Shabelsky and Anna Petrovna), most of Act II (the guests at Sasha's estate), scenes i, ii, iii, iv in Act III, with the conversations of Lebedev, Shabelsky, and Borkin on political events in Germany and France, the conversations about tasty foods and snacks, and the subsequent intrusion of Kosykh with his passion for cards. None of this bears directly on the story of Ivanov and Sasha. Everywhere in the play one is reminded of the permanent and diverse aspects of life.

In *The Wood Demon,* this sense of an external, humdrum, protracted, and ordinary atmosphere, conveyed

through neutral, everyday, trivial details, emerges quite distinctly. The play's event (the flight of Elena Andreevna) has the status of a local episode. The most important and larger part of the play's canvas is crowded with ordinary affairs, when there is no special intention to attract interest to the central event.

In *The Seagull,* the most notable events are centered on Treplev. But the play is not entirely concentrated around this most obvious pivot. Its driving impulse is felt autonomously and independently in Nina Zarechnaya, Trigorin's life, Arkadina's life, the lovesick Masha Shamraeva, the ill-starred life of Medvedenko, Dorn's weariness, and Sorin's peculiar kind of suffering. Common life flows on and everywhere preserves its common forms. Each of the participants has his own inner world and sorrow, and each plays his own little part in the general ensemble.

In *Uncle Vanya* and *The Three Sisters,* there are even fewer events. In *Uncle Vanya,* the most prominently placed are Voynitsky's relations to Elena Andreevna and Serebryakov; in *The Three Sisters,* the relations of Masha and Vershinin and of Irina and Tusenbach. But these moments, so prominent, nevertheless do not provide a backbone of plot for the play as a whole. In the general flow of the play these moments remain episodes; they are seen as individual consequences of a way of life that was formed long ago and is common to all, a way of life that is sensed equally throughout the play and among all the characters in situations that have long been chronic.

At the center of *The Cherry Orchard* stands the sale of the estate and Ranevskaya's emotional upheavals and sufferings connected with it. But throughout the play the drama of Ranevskaya is absorbed into the flowing processes of common everyday life. From the first scenes, even Varya is shown to have her special anxieties and secret sorrows. Lopakhin is worried by the immediate business of the next day. Even Epikhodov, Firs, Simeonov-Pishchik, and Dunyasha have their minor, but still special inner worlds. And later, throughout the whole length of the play, everybody's common, everyday concerns continue to go on around Ranevskaya.[8]

In none of the plays do one or two persons bear the inner conflict all by themselves. Everyone suffers (except for a very few, cruel people).

. . . The bitter taste of life for these people consists not in a particular sad event, but precisely in the drawn-out, habitual, drab, monotonous dullness of every day. Workaday life with its outwardly tranquil forms is introduced into Chekhov's plays as the main sphere of the hidden—and most widespread—states of dramatic conflict.

What interests Chekhov in the humdrum of everyday existence is the general feeling of life, that state of pervasive inner tonicity in which man lives from day to day.

The dramatic characterization of everyday life, based on the depiction of customs, morals, and manners, proved unsuited to Chekhov's purposes. His choice of prosaic details was determined not by their ethical and thematic meaning, but by their significance in the general emotional content of life. But because this principle was not understood at first, it seemed that they had been deposited haphazardly, following no internal law.

At the end of Act I of Ostrovsky's *Let's Settle It Among Ourselves,* Bolshov, having a conversation with Rizhpolozhensky and Podkhalyuzin, picks up a newspaper, as if by accident, and reads there a declaration concerning "bankrupts." Now everyone can understand the reason for this episode because it is connected with the basic theme of the play. No one doubts the internal propriety of this seemingly "accidental" detail, because it so clearly corresponds to all that is happening and will happen to Bolshov.

But consider: in Act II of *The Three Sisters,* Chebutykin reads from a newspaper: "Tsitsikar. Smallpox is raging here." Neither Tsitsikar nor smallpox bears any relation whatsoever to Chebutykin, or to any other person, or to anything that is happening or will happen on the stage. A newspaper report happens to catch his eye. He reads it through and it has no direct bearing on anything that is being said around him. Subsequently, it is left without any echo. Why is it there?

In Act I of *Uncle Vanya,* again without any connection to what is happening, Marina walks around the house and clucks: "Cheep, cheep, cheep." And again, one asks: what is its purpose?

In Act II of *The Seagull,* Masha stands up in the middle of a conversation, walks in a "lazy, limping gait," and announces: "My foot is asleep." Why is this necessary?

There are many such "accidental" remarks in Chekhov. The dialogue is continuously bursting, breaking, and becoming confused by some apparently unnecessary and altogether extraneous triviality. The result was bewilderment. People were astonished by the seeming incongruities, by the insignificance of the thematic content, and by the accidentality of much of the dialogue and many of the characters' individual remarks.

One can remain bewildered, however, only so long as one does not grasp the new dramatic principle whereby all these seemingly meaningless particularities are drawn in and unified. They take on life and meaning not by what they connote, but by the complex sense of life they convey.

When Chebutykin, immersed in his newspaper, reads: "Tsitsikar. Smallpox is raging here," this sentence is addressed to no one, and is not intended to provide information. It is simply one expression of boring tranquility, the idleness, sluggishness, and insubstantial character in the play's general atmosphere. Again, when Solyony and Chebutykin argue as to whether the word *chekhartma* or *cheremsha* means a meat or a plant of the onion family, this passing episode has meaning not for its thematic content, but simply because of the triviality and the stage of half-exasperation it expresses. . . .

The internal state of an individual is superimposed on the common variegated fabric and from it derives its particular meaning, background, and emphasis. Remarks are charged not only with particular meaning for the character who is speaking, but, when spoken neutrally, take on vast meaning that illumines the condition of the other characters present.

When Marina, during one pause, imitates a chicken's "cheep, cheep, cheep," it not only says something about Marina, but also gives expression to the tedium that weighs upon the other characters present: here the upset Voynitsky and the bored Elena Andreevna. When at the end of the play, Marina says: "I, sinner that I am, have not eaten noodle soup in a long time," her words are not especially meaningful and might even seem superfluous. But in the context of the play, they say less about Marina's homely desire for food than about the succession of pleasant and tranquil, but dull days which have now begun again for Uncle Vanya and Sonya.

Chekhov's methods of rendering the tedium of life were not created all at once, but rather they developed and grew complex according to the peculiar problems of each play.

In *Ivanov,* Chekhov points to the spiritual destitution and emptiness surrounding Ivanov and Sasha when he stuffs the dialogue with frankly boring conversations by Lebedev's guests (Act II), and Ivanov's guests (at the beginning of Act III). More of these conversations, their emptiness all the more obvious, filled the first versions of the play. Chekhov was thus faced with the danger that his depiction of tedium might itself become tedious to the audience. This danger compelled him to forgo some motifs and to shorten these episodes.[9]

Subsequently, Chekhov communicated the impression of emptiness and tedium in the everyday flow of life without emphasizing the tedious and uninteresting elements; he would merely touch on them, hinting at people's boredom through a gesture or intonation which revealed the direct, but also the hidden, emotional meaning of a seemingly insignificant sentence.

During a general conversation, Masha, in *The Seagull,* gets up and says: "It must be time for lunch. (Walks in a lazy, limping gait.) My foot is asleep. (Exits.)" The audience grasps not only Masha's boredom but the whole feeling of a scene on a typical endless day.

At the end of Act II of *Uncle Vanya,* when Elena Andreevna, upset by a conversation with Sonya about love, happiness, and her own fate, waits to hear whether or not she may play the piano, the watchman taps in the garden. Then he leaves, at Elena Andreevna's request, and his voice echoes in the silence: "Hey you! Zhuchka! Boy! Zhuchka!" This juxtaposition of a neutral, peaceful, ordinary detail with the pathos of a joy that is denied, opens a perspective on the calm, eternal indifference of the everyday flow of life: life—you have to recognize it—passes and goes its way.

By means of such juxtapositions as these, the homely detail in Chekhov acquires an enormous capacity for conveying emotion, and you feel behind each detail the synthesizing force of a feeling for life as a whole.[10]

What is the source of the conflict? Who and what causes suffering? Until we arrive at the substance or the peculiar essence of Chekhovian conflict, we shall formulate it merely as the contradiction between what is given and what is desired, that is, the discrepancy between what a man has and what he strives for. Who or what brings about this breach between man's desired and real existence?

In other drama, the source of conflict, generally speaking, lies in the contradiction and conflict of human interests and passions. The conflict is based on a violation of moral norms, as when one will encroaches upon the resisting interests and wills of others. Therefore, the notion of some kind of guilt is always connected with the dramatic suffering. The source of the conflict, consequently, is the faulty, criminal, evil, or misdirected will of a person or persons; a battle of wills breaks out—the battle with obstacles, and all sorts of peripeteia.

Some defect in social relations always lies at the base of the dramatic conflict, and conflict consists of a collision between healthy and honorable human desires and a dark, evil force. Basically, one of two kinds of villains is involved: either the "domestic" oppressor, who, by his own despotic conduct, corrupts and disfigures life for those around him; or the newcomer, the bearer of evil. The latter is an adventurer or a swindler, and by deception he forces his own way into the confidence of his victims in order to achieve his mercenary and dishonest aims.

The poor who are dependent on the rich experience most of the dramatic suffering; or it falls on younger members of the oppressor's family, who are deprived of their rights: the daughter, the governess, or less often, the son or wife. The victims of the deception are honest, trusting people, primarily women, who for one reason or another attract the deceiver's interest, then, betrayed by blinded feelings, find themselves in his snare. . . . Social relations changed, customs changed, new vices arose, other problems were posed. . . . The drama of everyday life, however, remained the same, because it retained in every respect its basic aims: to depict customs and morals, to edify, to expose and indict vice.

Chekhov is different and has an entirely different point of departure for his critique of reality. Chekhov's first mature play, *Ivanov,* does solve a problem having to do with social types, but at the same time it is polemically directed against preconceived and hasty judgment of people.

Ivanov perpetrates a number of acts which by their own outward appearance naturally arouse moral indignation. Everyone condemns him. Yet the play, by its dual illumination of Ivanov, outer and inner, cautions as it goes along against customary moral judgments and calls for a more complex understanding of those reasons, motives, and incentives which govern a man's behavior. . . . In *Ivanov,* instead of moralizing directly, Chekhov elucidates the emotional state of his hero and suggests the notion of involuntary guilt, as when one man causes another's misfortune without any desire whatsoever to do so. . . . [11]

In his second play, **The Wood Demon,** Chekhov was concerned with the same idea. The play again wars on the lack of attention people give to each other. It attacks preconceived labels and stereotypes which prompt one to judge people without any real basis for doing so. All the mutual suspicions and accusations which, ultimately, led to the misfortune turn out to be false. Everyone regrets his mistake (except Serebryakov, the most obtuse and self-satisfied of all the characters; and in the first draft of the play, even he is remorseful).

Dramatic conflicts in Chekhov consist not in the opposition of strong wills, but in contradictions inherent in the objective conditions of life, contradictions before which the individual will is powerless.

In **The Seagull,** in **Uncle Vanya,** in **The Three Sisters,** and in **The Cherry Orchard,** "no one is to blame," no one individually and consciously prevents another's happiness. Who is to blame that in **The Seagull,** Medvedenko loves Masha, and Masha loves Treplev, and Treplev loves Nina Zarechnaya, and Nina loves Trigorin, and so forth? Who is to blame that the professions of writing and acting do not in themselves bring happiness to Treplev and Zarechnaya? Who is to blame that Voynitsky regards Serebryakov as an idol worthy of the sacrifice of an entire life, and that when Serebryakov proves to be a hollow man Voynitsky's life goes by in vain? Who is to blame when Astrov cannot summon the feelings for Sonya that would make her happiness? Who is to blame for the lonely and inane life that tortures Astrov, disfigures him spiritually, and wears away his feelings to no purpose? Who is to blame in **The Three Sisters,** where, instead of leaving for Moscow, the Prozorov sisters begin to sink even further into the drabness and fog of provincial life? Who is to blame when their knowledge and sensibilities find no application and wither to no purpose? Who is to blame when Ranevskaya and Gaev, by virtue of their own moral and psychic condition, are unable to make use of Lopakhin's well-meaning advice? Who is to blame for the general state of life in **The Cherry Orchard,** where the characters wheel about in lonely suffering, where people do not and cannot understand each other. Who is to blame when people's sincere feelings and mutual good will do not give warming joy, but life remains drab, dirty, unhappy, and sad?

No one is to blame. Then, since no one is to blame, there are no real adversaries; and since there are no real adversaries, there are not and cannot be struggles. The fault lies with the complex of circumstances which seems to lie beyond the influence of the people in the play. The unfortunate situation is shaped without their willing it, and suffering arrives on its own.

It is not that Chekhov's people are not judged at all. It is not that there is no distinction between human virtues and defects, or that human conduct is not shown to be a source of evil. All that is there. But evil in Chekhov operates outside the sphere of direct, willful activity as if it were merely some involuntary fruit of life (though it is evil all the same). Even in the most negative of Chekhov's characters, it is not their wills that are presented first and foremost, but the quality of their feelings. Their wills do not create the action of the play. Wicked people in the plays only make worse a situation that is already bad in itself. The better people turn out to be powerless. A mass of petty, ordinary details entangles man; he flounders in them and is unable to extricate himself. Life passes irrevocably and in vain, continuously, inconspicuously giving out what people do not need. Who is to blame? This question resounds continuously throughout each play. And each play answers: individuals are not to blame, but the entire makeup of their lives. People are to blame only in that they are weak.

What is the substance of the conflict? It was defined generally above as the contradiction between what is given and what is desired. But such a definition still leaves out the specific Chekhovian quality. The contradiction between what is given and what is desired is to be found everywhere, and every play is structured on this conflict; but Chekhov established his own, specific sphere of the desired.

In the earlier, pre-Chekhovian drama of everyday life, the desired is projected as liberation from the vice that hinders life. In each of the given plays, the setting to rights of life is conceived to be limited to the areas encompassed by the evil operating in the play. The fate of people is considered with reference to that aspect immediately subject to the interference and influence of the given vice. The characters' individual desires, as a whole, are contained within these limits. Remove the action of the vice, and a state of happiness is obtained. The destructive influence may prove to be so profound, however, that the restoration of the "norm" proves impossible; then catastrophe results. But whichever way the characters' fate is structured, even in these cases, it remains within restricted thematic limits. That is what happens in all of Ostrovsky's plays. . . .

The particular conflict in which a Chekhovian character finds himself also proceeds from some perfectly concrete desire that has not been or cannot be fulfilled. In *The Seagull,* it is anguish over unrequited love or longing for the joy of a writer's or an artist's fame. In *Uncle Vanya,* suffering, caused by the consciousness of the irrevocable and joyless passing of life, moves into the main focus beside the motif of desired, but unattainable love (Voynitsky, Sonya, Astrov, and Elena Andreevna). In *The Three Sisters,* the concrete desire is a yearning to escape from the provinces to Moscow. In *The Cherry Orchard,* it is connected with the change awaited in the fate of the estate.

Yet it is not difficult to see that these concretely designated yearnings do not, in themselves, take in the entire scope of that longing for the better which is felt in the play. Each private desire is accompanied by expectation of a change in the entire substance of life. The dream of fulfillment of a given desire lives in the soul of each personage with a longing for the satisfaction of more poetic interests that embrace all of life. Each person's suffering consists in the fact that these higher spiritual elements do not find application and conceal themselves in intimate thoughts and daydreams. Thus the particular, private desires always have an extended meaning. They appear as vehicles for the inner longing for another, bright existence in which vague, lofty, poetically beautiful, secret dreams can be realized.

The melancholy of Masha Shamraeva and Sonya, the belated outbursts of Voynitsky and Astrov, the Prozorov sisters' continuously voiced yearning to move to Moscow, contain a suffering brought about by the general drabness and emptiness of the life they lead. They all want a complete transformation, they want to reject the present and set off for some new and bright horizon.

When Nina Zarechnaya aspires to be an actress she has a notion of some higher spiritual happiness which is not granted to mere mortals, about which one dreams only from a distance. For the Prozorovs, that many-featured daydream calling from afar is Moscow. What they will obtain in Moscow or what and how it will fill their lives—of this not a word. At the focal point of the play, one finds only a spiritual unrest, a feeling of life's incompleteness, a surging impulse, and an expectation of something better. The concrete forms in which this desire takes shape and becomes concentrated vary with each character. Each in his own way wants and expects something better. And in each case the inner unrest and dissatisfaction is expressed in a personal form: in Tusenbach it is different from what it is in Vershinin; in Solyony it is even more different; in Andrei Prozorov it is different again; and so forth. But in everyone, private desires are united with the common longing to begin some kind of different life. You feel an individual's distress only to feel the drabness and incoherence of life as a whole.

In *The Cherry Orchard,* personal and private outbursts are brought even more clearly into the realm of life's general disorder. The fate of the estate interests everyone in his own way, but behind each private interest, everyone thinks and feels desires of a more general character, as is obvious in the role of Petya Trofimov. Ranevskaya suffers not only because of the loss of the estate, but also because of the entire wasteland of her life. And even Lopakhin, in his dreams of summer cottages, in the end anticipates a general, fundamental change. "Oh, if it all would pass more quickly, if somehow our awkward, unhappy life would quickly change!" "Lord, thou gavest us immense forests, unbounded fields, and the widest horizons; and living here we should, by all that is true, be giants." This plea for eventual universal happiness finds passionate and overt expression in the lyric endings of the plays, in the words of Sonya, Olga, and Anya. . . .

Chekhov's dacha, where he wrote The Seagull *and a number of other works.*

The spectator is drawn into this lofty atmosphere of longing by various means, like things and sounds; and also by dialogue on subjects very different on the surface, but really in their emotional tone closely related and similar in meaning: love, happiness, nature, art, the past, and so forth. There are even theoretical discussions, usually inconclusive. They are cut short and abruptly left hanging in midair. Their significance lies not so much in their theoretical content as in the sense of helplessness and weariness which gives rise to them. They are symptoms of a dissatisfaction and inner upheaval which perhaps are not realized fully and equally by everyone all the time.

These lofty desires find strong resistance in the flow of life. . . .

The next question is that of the movement of the tragic element, of its development in the play. What are the progressive changes of situation that make up what we call "development of action"?

It is very characteristic of Chekhov that his selection of things to take place onstage and not offstage leans toward life's most constant and most time-consuming features. . . . The play opens with the characters already in a state of habitual, wearying discontent. The roots and causes of the present burdensome situation lie somewhere in the distant past. The chronic spiritual malaise is dragged out now day after day. This kind of suffering does not cease to be suffering, but has a peculiar character and its own discreet forms of expression. Hidden, it erupts and becomes noticeable only momentarily.

At the beginning of Act I of **The Seagull,** everyone but Nina Zarechnaya and, in part, Treplev (and Arkadina, who is always satisfied) has been only half-alive for a long time, can hardly endure life, and only frets and mourns after the happiness that has been denied to him. In **Uncle Vanya,** Voynitsky's situation was established long ago, and now, as his feeling for Elena Andreevna awakens again, it is only exacerbated. Astrov has long been sadly accustomed to the tedious, cold, and exhaust-

ing routine of his workaday existence and knows perfectly well that his situation is hopeless. Sonya, too, has
languished for a long time. The Prozorov sisters have for
years been yearning for Moscow. Life itself long ago
conditioned the "unhappy" existence of the characters in
The Cherry Orchard.

The development of the plays consists in the recurrence
of hopes for happiness, followed by their being exposed
as illusions and then shattered. Nascent hopes for happiness or at least for some improvement in the situation
summon various persons to actions which have the character of events; but these events are never developed in
the play. Chekhov quickly returns his hero to a new
version of the everyday condition to be endured once
again. The event provoked by the hero's enthusiasm for
his new purpose occurs only behind the scenes. On the
stage it makes itself felt only in the protracted and total
tedium which has again set in.

In *The Seagull,* Nina Zarechnaya's fate changes. Illusions of happiness engulf her, an attempt to realize these
hopes occurs (she draws nearer to Trigorin, she becomes
an actress), and then the hopes are exposed as false.
Happiness, she discovers, was not to be obtained even
there. The moment of joy, however brief and illusory
(her love affair with Trigorin), is not shown on the stage.
Only the result is shown: the return to days of prosaic
suffering. The false, happy excitement is already a thing
of the past, life has become once more days to endure,
and with this sad new humdrum state of things, Nina
comes back on the stage. Masha Shamraeva, from act to
act, hopes to overcome her melancholy by some new,
decisive act (she gets married, again offstage). But there
is no improvement. . . . *Uncle Vanya* contains almost no
events. Voynitsky's feeling for Elena Andreevna is only
an element in the final clarification and realization of his
sealed fate. He struggles with no one and nothing. The
shot at Serebryakov was only an indirect expression of
his vexation at the mistake of his life which he had
already realized. His joyless life is bound to remain the
same as before. The play quickly restores him to his
earlier, outwardly smooth, but bitter, humdrum existence.
The same is true also of Sonya. Astrov, from the very
beginning, knows that his situation is irremediable, and
his drama is marked by bitter self-irony. "The entire
meaning and drama of man are internal," Chekhov said
apropos of *Uncle Vanya.* "Sonya's life had drama in it
up to this moment; it will have drama in it after this
moment, but the moment itself is simply an incident, a
continuation of the shot. And the shot, after all, is not
drama, but an incident."[12] . . .

[In *The Three Sisters*] Irina hopes for a renewal in life
when she starts to work. She becomes a telegraph operator, then serves on the town council. The days are past
when all this was new to her. . . . Chekhov takes up the
situation when the new post has already become tedious,
drab, and burdensome, when it is already clear that the
changes which occurred have added no joy whatsoever.
Andrei marries Natasha. But again, the event is not
onstage when it is still something new; only its joyless

result receives stage embodiment; we see the marriage
only when illusions have already disappeared and the
monotonous protraction of life's useless passing has already set in. . . . Chekhov presents the bitter thought, the
bitter feeling, human suffering, not when they are fresh,
but when they have passed within, have become part of
an established state of mind, and are hidden from others
by outwardly usual behavior. As a result, the movement
of action acquires exceptional complexity. . . .

The resolution of the conflict corresponds to the specific
nature of its content. The final chord has a double ring:
it is both sad and bright.

If the dramatic tension has to do with the whole tenor of
life, if no one individual is to blame, then one can expect
that the way to something better lies only in a radical
unheaval of life in its entirety. The arrival of something
better depends not on the removal of local obstacles, but
on the transformation of all forms of existence. And until
there is such a transformation, each person in the separateness of his being is powerless before the common
fate. Therefore, in the end, Chekhov's heroes do not find
their lot improved. Life remains dismal and drab. Nevertheless, all the plays end with an expression of a passionate dream and a belief in the future. Each play emphasizes the confidence that in time life will become different, clear, joyful, and rich with radiant feeling. Life,
however, remains joyless—but only temporarily and only
for those who are still weak. . . .

The double emotional chord at the end (sadness about
the present, and the bright promises of the future) is the
synthesis of that judgment on reality which is realized in
the movement of the entire play: it is impossible to reconcile oneself to the view that people must live without
joy, that everything vital and poetic in man must remain
fallow, that it must die impotent inside; life must change,
must become "beautiful"; one must build such a life,
work. "Such a life is necessary to man, and if it does not
exist at this time, then he must anticipate it, wait, dream,
prepare for it."

NOTES

[1] V. I. Nemirovich-Danchenko, Predislovie "Ot redaktora" in N. Efros'
'Tri sestry' v postanovke Moskovskogo khudozhestvennogo teatra
(Petrograd, 1919), p. 10.
[2] Ju. Sobolev, *Chekhov* (Moscow, 1934), p. 241.
[3] S. D. Balukhatyj, *Chekhov-dramaturg* (Leningrad, 1936), p. 113.
[4] *Ibid.*
[5] *Ibid.,* p. 18. [My italics—A. S.]
[6] "Vospominanija D. Gorodetskogo," *Birzhevye vedomosti* (1904), No.
364.
[7] "Vospominanija Ars. G. (I. Ja. Gurljand)," *Teatr i iskusstvo* (1904), No.
28.
[8] For further discussion on this point, see my essay "O edinstve formy i
soderzhanija v 'Vishnevom sade' Chekhova" ["On the Unity of Form and
Content in Chekhov's *The Cherry Orchard*"] in my collection of essays,
Stat'i o russkoj literature (Saratov, 1958), pp. 356-390.
[9] See my essay "P'esa Chekhova *Ivanov* v rannikh redaktsijakh" ["The
Early Versions of Chekhov's *Ivanov*"] in *Stat'i o russkoj literature,* pp.
339-355.
[10] In his representation of everyday life, Chekhov is sometimes thought to
resemble Turgenev, especially as represented in *A Month in the Country.*
It is true that one might see some analogy, notably in Act I in the insig-

nificance of the conversation, in the remarks that cross and interrupt each other, in the general, peacefully bland mood as the characters play cards, wait for dinner, and so forth. But the substance of all these peculiar features in Turgenev bears no resemblance to Chekhov. In Turgenev the details are without relation to the essence of the characters' experience. The dramatic interest passes outside and around the details. Thus, the nature of the dramatic conflict in Turgenev is entirely different from that in Chekhov.
[11] We find this same thought in "Verochka" (1887), written at the time he was working on *Ivanov*: "For the first time in his life he [the hero] knew by experience how little man depends on his own free will, found himself in the position of a decent and sincere man who, against his own will, brings cruel and undeserved suffering to his fellow man."
[12] L. Sulerzhitskij, "Iz vospominanij o Chekhove," *Shipovnik,* No. 23, p. 164.

Hingley, Ronald (essay date 1950)

SOURCE: "Chekhov's Last Years: His Approach to Drama," in *Chekhov: A Biographical and Critical Study,* George Allen & Unwin, 1966, pp. 219-44.

[*In the following excerpt from a work that was first published in 1950, Hingley examines the essential characteristics of Chekhovian drama.*]

A 'REVOLUTIONARY' DRAMATIST

Chekhov was admirably fitted to become the leading dramatist of the Moscow Art Theatre because he thoroughly agreed with Nemirovich-Danchenko and Stanislavsky in wanting to get away from the conventions and atmosphere of the existing Russian stage. His four major plays—*The Seagull, Uncle Vanya, Three Sisters* and *The Cherry Orchard*—mark a break with tradition so startling that many critics call him a 'revolutionary' dramatist. In defining the revolution which he accomplished it is impossible to avoid paradoxical language—he is frequently said to have 'purged the theatre of theatricality', to have written 'undramatic drama' and 'tragedies, the essence of which consists in the absence of tragedy'.

Like the directors of the Art Theatre he objected to an over-concentration on a small number of characters, and seems to have been feeling his way towards this position as early as 1887 when he wrote *Ivanov,* in which he claimed that there was not a single hero or villain. Though *Ivanov* certainly lacked heroes and villains in the ordinary stage sense, it did contain, in the title role, a big part calculated to overshadow all the others, and suitable for performance by one of the old-style star actors. No such character appears in any of the four major plays. Naturally some of the parts are bulkier than others, but there is a much more even distribution of emphasis than had been customary in earlier drama.

Together with this tendency went a relative lack of action. The average pre-Chekhov play seemed to move from one emotional crest to another, treating the audience to an exciting succession of fights, quarrels, confessions of love, adulteries, suicides, murders and the like. There are many passages in Chekhov's letters showing that he deliberately rejected this conception of the drama:

'After all, in real life,' he observed, 'people don't spend every minute shooting at each other, hanging themselves and making confessions of love. They don't spend all the time saying clever things. They're more occupied with eating, drinking, flirting and talking stupidities—and these are the things which ought to be shown on the stage. A play should be written in which people arrive, go away, have dinner, talk about the weather and play cards. Life must be exactly as it is, and people as they are—not on stilts. . . . Let everything on the stage be just as complicated, and at the same time just as simple as it is in life. People eat their dinner, just eat their dinner, and all the time their happiness is being established or their lives are being broken up.'

This passage, similar to various statements by Chekhov on his approach to the short story, forms an excellent introduction to his method in the four major plays, although even in them he did not entirely dispense with such examples of stage action as shootings and confessions of love. His earlier dramatic work shows that an avoidance of such action had not always been part of his policy. This is particularly true of his earliest surviving play, which is sometimes referred to as *Platonov,* and which has considerably more than its share of startling effects. It includes, among many other examples of dramatic action, two unsuccessful attempts at murder, averted at the last minute, the murder of the hero, the attempt of one heroine to throw herself under a train, and a whole succession of hysterical love scenes. *Ivanov,* the next long play, also had a fair allotment of lurid incident such as is not usually encountered in ordinary life. Chekhov said of this play that he conducted it quietly and peacefully on the whole, but that at the end of each act he gave the audience a 'sock in the jaw'. It will be remembered that the most violent of these dramatic punches had been packed in the last act, which concludes with Ivanov's suicide on his wedding morning. It was a long way from this to the methods of the later plays. In *The Wood Demon,* which succeeded *Ivanov,* and was later transformed into *Uncle Vanya,* Chekhov was feeling his way towards his new approach. Unfortunately the harsh reception of *The Wood Demon* deterred him for a time from further experiment. The quieter manner adopted in this play led to its condemnation by critics on the ground that the treatment was more appropriate to a story or novel than to the stage. It is generally agreed to be unsuccessful, and even such a sympathetic member of the audience as Nemirovich-Danchenko pronounced it unfit for production.

Returning to the assault on the new drama, Chekhov produced in *The Seagull* the first representative specimen of his mature manner. In this play, as in its successors, he tends to avoid any concentration on exciting dramatic incidents. The characters are for the most part apparently absorbed in trivialities; they usually allow the audience to learn only in passing of important changes in their relationships and lives, such as might have been made the subject of vivid scenes by earlier dramatists. For example, the eventful career of Nina Zarechnaya (including her relations with Trigorin and his desertion of her) is hardly presented on the stage. The same applies to Treplev's two attempts at suicide, though on the second occasion the audience is allowed to hear the revolver shot. Revolver shots were for a long time Chekhov's last link with the more violent methods of the traditional theatre, and he said that he was very pleased when he managed to dispense with them for the first time in **The Cherry Orchard.**

The Cherry Orchard provides an especially interesting illustration of Chekhov's use of incident in his later plays. Though he talked about writing a play in which people do nothing more than 'arrive, go away, talk about the weather and play cards', he never managed to carry out this policy with complete ruthlessness. Something had to happen, even in a Chehkov play, and the main incident of **The Cherry Orchard** is one which seems to be very important to all the characters—the loss of the house and estate belonging to Gaev and his sister. There was a lot of fuss and worry about this, but it is typical that after the sale had taken place the whole affair should somehow seem very much less momentous. In fact Gaev himself gaily proclaims that 'now everything is all right. Before the sale of the cherry orchard we all suffered and got excited, but afterwards, when the question was finally and irrevocably decided, we all grew calm and even cheered up.'

Another way in which Chekhov wished to break with the old theatre was by avoiding stock theatrical types. He shows what some of these were in another passage from his correspondence:

> Retired captains with red noses, bibulous reporters, starving writers, consumptive hard-working wives, honourable young men without a single blemish, exalted maidens, kind-hearted nurses—all these have been described already and must be avoided like the pit.

Though he kept his plays free from these old favourites Chekhov feared that some of the characters might be misinterpreted along traditional stage lines, and it will be remembered that he did not even trust the Art Theatre to give the right interpretation in certain instances. Lopakhin in **The Cherry Orchard** must on no account be turned into a conventional stage merchant, nor Uncle Vanya into a stage landowner; the officers in **Three Sisters** must not strut about like stage soldiers—on all these points Chekhov gave explicit instructions. The characters were ordinary, simple people who must be played plainly and sincerely so as to create exactly the effect they would make in ordinary life. It was natural that Chekhov should also seek to avoid stock situations. 'Remember,' he wrote, 'that confessions of love, the deception of wives and husbands, tears, whether widows', orphans', or anyone else's, have long ago been described.' He goes on to say that 'the subject must be new and you can do without a plot.'

Plot occupies just as small a place in the plays as it does in the stories. To Chekhov the exchange of small-talk was often a sufficient vehicle for the presentation of complex and subtle emotions. Again and again his characters speak of trivialities at a time when their thoughts are quite clearly engaged on something quite different. A conversation illustrating this takes place at the end of **The Cherry Orchard** between Lopakhin and Varya, both of whom know that this is a likely moment for Lopakhin to propose, and that if he misses the opportunity his marriage with Varya is never likely to take place. All that comes out in the dialogue, however, is a few banalities about the weather, the fact that the thermometer is broken, and that Varya has lost something while packing. Though the dialogue turns on such neutral themes the real situation makes a greater impact on the audience than might have been possible if Chekhov had handled it directly.

Chekhov's indirect method often enabled him to obtain extremely subtle effects, but he was always ready to be simple and straightforward when the occasion demanded it. This is often noticeable in the way he introduces information to the audience. He has not always been to any particular pains to dovetail his exposition into natural dialogue in the way usually considered necessary by playwrights. His characters often give information which must clearly be known already to the people with whom they are conversing, and which is really intended for the audience. Olga's first speeches in **Three Sisters** are a case in point, for they include many items which would not be news to her sister Irina with whom she is speaking.

> Father died exactly a year ago, this very day, May 5th—your nameday, Irina. . . . He was a General in command of a brigade. . . . Father received his brigade and left Moscow with us eleven years ago.

A similar straightforwardness of approach is to be found in numerous passages where various personages give character-sketches of themselves, again for the benefit of the audience.

Whether he was being direct or indirect, Chekhov's words were equally packed with meaning. Stanislavsky had a very keen appreciation of this, for as actor and producer he naturally made an especially thorough study of Chekhov's text. His general conclusion was that behind each of Chekhov's words 'there stretched a whole range of many-sided moods and thoughts, of which he said nothing, but which arose of their own accord in one's mind'. Stanislavsky found that a play like **Three Sisters** was so saturated with meaning that, although he acted in it hundreds of times, every single performance revealed something new to him about it.

ATMOSPHERE IN CHEKHOV'S PLAYS

The quality of Chekhov's plays, so charged with emotional significance in spite of their surface innocence, has stimulated Russian critics to look for a suitable name to describe his technique. His drama has been called 'lyrical'; it has been called 'internal', as opposed to the earlier, 'external' variety, and it has also been called the 'drama of the under-water current', since the operative dramatic stresses are so often submerged. The most common description is 'the drama of *nastroenie',* a concept already discussed in relation to the stories, where it was shown that 'mood' or 'atmosphere' are the best English equivalents.

An examination of the plays shows that Chekhov's methods of presenting *nastroenie* are similar to those employed in the stories. The same use is made of memories of the past, hopes for the future, and the state of mind associated with unsuccessful love. Chekhov often chose to present situations particularly calculated to throw such sensations into relief. Leave-takings were very suitable for the purpose—for example, those involved in the departure of the regiment at the end of *Three Sisters.* It had been stationed for some years in the provincial town where the action takes place, so that, when it came to leave, intimate associations had to be broken off, with little prospect of them ever being renewed. The emotions attendant on such an occasion blended harmoniously into the Chekhov mood. Similar emotionally-charged partings are to be found in *Uncle Vanya* and *The Cherry Orchard.* Madame Ranevskaya's arrival at the beginning of the latter play shows that the reverse process is equally capable of evoking atmosphere. She arrives back in her home early one morning after an absence of several years and cannot restrain her tears at the sight of the old nursery where she slept as a little girl. She ranges from laughter to tears as she revives her memories of such varied things as her brother's habit of interspersing his conversation with imaginary billiard strokes, and the wonderful sight of the orchard in bloom.

In the plays, as in the stories, Chekhov also makes use of the beauties of nature in building up atmosphere. For example, the audience is not long allowed to forget the lake which figures so prominently in *The Seagull* that it has even been suggested that Chekhov regarded it as one of the *dramatis personae.* The cherry orchard plays an even more important part in conditioning the mood of the play to which it gives its name. 'White, white all over,' Madame Ranevskaya addresses her orchard on her return. 'Oh, my orchard! After a dark, foul autumn and a cold winter you are young again and full of happiness; the angels of heaven have not forsaken you.' Again and again the characters refer to the orchard. In the minds of Ranevskaya and her brother it is bound up with countless childhood memories. The old servant Firs remembers how forty or fifty years ago they used to send cherries by the wagon-load to Moscow and Kharkov, after subjecting them to a special preserving process—now nobody can remember the recipe. To Trofimov the orchard typifies an obsolete social structure, but serves as a reminder of the beautiful life which he believes is possible on earth. He develops this theme to Anya, the young daughter of the house.

> All Russia is our orchard. The earth is large and beautiful and there are many wonderful places in it. Think, Anya, your grandfather, your great-grandfather and all your ancestors were serf-owners, possessors

of living souls. Do you not feel that human creatures are looking at you from every cherry in the orchard, from every leaf and trunk? Don't you hear their voices?

Whereas all these characters relate the orchard to the past in their various ways, the businessman Lopakhin is more concerned with its future. Nobody listens to him when he points out that the cherry trees must be cut down so that summer bungalows can be built. Finally the orchard has to be sold, and it makes its last contribution to the atmosphere of the play at the very end when the curtain goes down to the sound of axes as the work of felling begins.

As anyone who has seen the play will remember, this is a particularly brilliant use of sound in the theatre. The same play provides many other examples, including the dance music which serves as a background to the third act—an eloquent commentary on the household crisis with which it coincides. An examination of the stage directions in the plays provides innumerable more illustrations of Chekhov's feeling for sound. Stanislavsky says that Chekhov himself sometimes used to confer with the sound-effects man to make sure that the noises produced were in exact accord with what he had in mind. At the beginning of the third act of *Three Sisters* an alarm is sounded in warning of a fire, and, according to Stanislavsky, Chekhov went to a lot of trouble experimenting with various apparatus in the hope of reproducing the typical and unmistakable 'soul-searing' note of a church bell in a Russian provincial town. One remarkable sound effect has caused some embarrassment to producers, and illustrates the production of *nastroenie* on a more surrealist level. This is the 'distant, dying and mournful sound of a breaking string', which is heard twice in *The Cherry Orchard.* The play does not make it entirely clear how this noise is supposed to have originated, but Chekhov certainly regarded it as important in evoking the right sort of mood in his audience. Stanislavsky was a more than eager co-operator in producing sound effects, and often seems to have overdone it in Chekhov's opinion. His introduction of bird calls and croaking frogs were not always appropriate to the season in which the scene was supposed to be taking place, and his fondness for choruses of chirping crickets was a standing joke. There was plenty of scope for his ingenuity in correctly reproducing the sounds which actually appeared in the stage directions. It should not be thought, however, that the plays were swamped with sound effects, for Chekhov retained his usual sense of balance in this matter. The point is not so much that he used such effects—they appear to a greater or lesser extent in any play—but that he used them with unusual subtlety. They were a particularly useful method of creating atmosphere, and one which is interesting because it was not available to Chekhov in the short stories.

CHEKHOV'S PLAYS AND THE 'CHEKHOV LEGEND'

Chekhov's plays raise once again the complicated question of his pessimism and of the 'Chekhov legend' in which it is embodied. This legend could not have arisen without some basis in fact, and the most superficial examination of the four last plays does something to show how it originated. The first of them, *The Seagull,* begins with this exchange of remarks:

MEDVEDENKO: Why do you always wear black?

MASHA: I am in mourning for my life. I am unhappy.

Andrew's soliloquy in *Three Sisters* is in the same style:

Oh, where is my past, where has it disappeared to— the time when I was young, happy, intelligent, when my thoughts were fine, when my present and future were lit up with hopes? Why is it that, almost before we have begun to live, we become boring, grey, uninteresting, lazy, indifferent, useless, unhappy?

Only a small minority of Chekhov's personages are satisfied with their fate, and even these are usually people whose futility is patent to almost everybody else but themselves—the smug charlatan Serebryakov in *Uncle Vanya,* the absurd schoolmaster Kulygin in *Three Sisters* and the conceited man-servant Yasha in *The Cherry Orchard.* These figures are clearly antipathetic to Chekhov. Decidedly exceptional is Doctor Dorn in *The Seagull,* who can look back with satisfaction to a reasonably happy and contented life, and who yet enjoys the respect of his fellows and the apparent approval of Chekhov. Another exception is the hard-working Doctor Astrov in *Uncle Vanya,* with his interest in forestry schemes. However, even Astrov describes himself as a man lost in the dark without a light to guide him, and this is pre-eminently true of the rest of Chekhov's heroes, who mostly drift along without knowing where they are going. They are not usually men of action, and such action as they take is generally ineffectual. Even when they fire revolvers, a form of violence which, as has been seen, Chekhov occasionally permits them, they are more likely than not to miss.

The characters lose few opportunities for airing their frustrations. The younger people usually want something in the future, and nearly always it is something which they do not look like getting. His three sisters have attached their mental fantasies to life in Moscow, where, they imagine, all their worries and cares would disappear at once. They never go there, of course, and even if they had gone it seems unlikely that it would have made much difference. With the older characters frustration often takes the form of laments over a wasted life and lost opportunities. Sorin in *The Seagull* suggests himself as a subject for a story on the theme *L'homme qui a voulu.*

In my youth I wanted to become a writer—and didn't become one; I wanted to speak eloquently—and spoke revoltingly. . . . I wanted to get married—and I didn't; I wanted to live in the town, and here I am ending my days in the country.

When it is pointed out to Sorin that he has at any rate attained the distinction of becoming a senior civil servant, he replies that that was one of the things he hadn't wanted. Uncle Vanya regrets almost every feature of his past life, including the fact that he had not proposed to Elena before she became the wife of Serebryakov.

Ten years ago I met her at my sister's house. She was seventeen at the time and I was thirty-seven. Why didn't I fall in love with her then and make a proposal? Why, it would have been so easily possible! And now she would be my wife. . . . Yes . . . Now we should both have been woken up by the storms; she would have been afraid of the thunder, and I would have held her in my arms and whispered, 'Don't be afraid.'

Among the sources of frustration in Chekhov's plays love occupies pride of place. Broadly speaking no one is allowed to be in love with anyone who is in love with them, and on the rare occasions when this rule is broken some external circumstances can be relied upon to create an effective obstacle. In *The Seagull* the love-pattern presents a remarkably complicated picture, as follows:

Medvedenko loves Masha
Masha loves Treplev
Treplev loves Nina
Nina and Arkadina love Trigorin

This chain-formation was not repeated in any of the later plays, but in them love is frustrated with equal consistency.

It is obvious that anyone prepared to identify Chekhov with his own characters could find abundant evidence in the plays to support the 'Chekhov legend'. During his lifetime the idea sometimes did arise in Russia that Chekhov himself was a sort of Uncle Vanya, but this impression dissolved as his work and biography became better known. It was seen that Chekhov, far from identifying himself with his gloomier heroes, was often laughing at them, and it even began to be thought that he conceived his plays as scathing satires directed against the futility and morbid self-pity of intellectuals belonging to his generation. This view was almost equally mistaken. Perhaps Chekhov's attitude was puzzling because it was so simple. He was merely following his usual policy of putting on the stage ordinary people in an everyday environment. He might ridicule them or sympathize with them (very often he seems to have been doing both simultaneously) but his general attitude was not one of wholesale condemnation or approval.

It is inevitable that the 'ordinary' people in Chekhov's plays should produce an effect in some ways the reverse of ordinary in England, since the characters and life described are so peculiar by our standards. However, this very properly lends them an extra element of interest on the English stage, provided that they are acted (as they very often are) simply and sincerely, in the way Chekhov intended. Chekhov's world must seem equally

The Moscow Art Theater company, 1900. Chekhov is standing in the back row, seventh from the right; Olga Knipper is seated in front of him; and Maxim Gorky is fifth from the right in the back row.

unfamiliar to all except the oldest generation of present-day Russians. It is worth remembering, however, that the plays were regarded by his contemporaries as true and representative pictures of their society. The fact that three of them are set in country houses belonging to the land-owning upper class does much to explain the accent on frustration. Members of this class could look back to a period earlier in the century when they had played a much more important part in Russian life. At the time when Chekhov was writing they had long forfeited their position of cultural leadership, and were fast losing their wealth. Any mention of a Russian landowner in literature of the second half of the nineteenth century is almost certain to be followed by the information that his estates are mortgaged and that he is heavily in debt. The more sensitive members of the class realized that their way of life was dying out, but they were so conditioned by education and environment as to be unable to do anything about it, and submitted to the social trend which brought about their complete extinction thirteen years after Chekhov's death. It was natural, therefore, that the country houses in which Chekhov sets his plays should distil an atmosphere of regret and aimlessness.

If Chekhov managed to present this situation without undue melancholy, it was due principally to the sympathetic humour with which he regarded it. This emerges in many ways, including the extraordinary manner in which he handles his dialogue—frequently used to emphasize the isolation of the characters one from another. Disconnected remarks are placed in juxtaposition to show how the various personages, absorbed in their own interests, ignore, or do not hear, what other people have to say. As an example of many-sided disjointed dialogue, Nemirovich-Danchenko singled out the second act of *Three Sisters.* This contains in a very short space of time a succession of remarks, often entirely disconnected, on a bewildering variety of themes, including the fact that Tusenbach has a triple-barrelled name, that Irina was rude to a woman in the post-office, that her new hair-style makes her look a boy, that Andrew has lost two hundred roubles at cards, that the doctor hasn't paid his rent for eight months, that life will be wonderful in two or three hundred years, and that Balzac was married at Berdichev. Among exchanges which emphasize the estrangement of the characters one from another, is included:

NATASHA: Babies understand very well. I said, 'Hallo, Bobik. Hallo, darling,' and he gave me a special sort of look. You think it's just a mother's partiality, but it isn't, I assure you. He's a remarkable child.

SOLYONY: If that child was mine I'd cook him in a frying-pan and eat him.

Mutual misunderstanding does not always operate on such a crude level, and a rather gentler example of this form of humour is to be found in a passage from *The Cherry Orchard*:

DUNYASHA: The clerk Epikhodov made me a proposal after Easter.

ANYA: You're always on about the same thing . . . I've lost all my hair-pins.

DUNYASHA: I just don't know what to think. He loves me. He loves me so much.

ANYA: (*tenderly, looking at the door of her room*) My room, my windows! Just as if I'd never gone away. I'm home! Tomorrow morning I'll get up and run into the orchard.

The element of humour became more noticeable with each play that Chekhov wrote, and it is most prominent in *The Cherry Orchard*. It will be remembered that Chekhov in his letters widely advertised the fact that he regarded this play as a farce, and it is quite true that many of the characters might have stepped straight out of one of his own vaudevilles—for example, Simeonov-Pishchik, whose name alone is ridiculous enough. This gentleman, with his inveterate borrowing, and claim to be descended from the horse which Caligula made a member of his Senate, is very much a figure of fun. When a servant offers his hostess a bottle of pills, he intervenes:

You shouldn't take medicine, dear lady. . . . It does you neither good nor harm. . . . Give them to me, most respected lady. (*Takes the pills, pours them on his palm, blows on them, puts them in his mouth and drinks them down with kvas.*)

This is not the only excursion into farce in the play. People fall downstairs, break billiard-cues and lose their goloshes. At least half of the characters are presented in comic terms. These include, apart from Simeonov-Pishchik, the absurd governess Charlotta Ivanovna, most of the servants, and Gaev with his general ineptitude, mock billiards strokes and eloquent speeches which are liable to be addressed to the furniture. Similar comic touches appear in the other plays, though they figure most prominently in *The Cherry Orchard*.

Chekhov himself was seriously convinced that *The Cherry Orchard* and—what is more surprising—*The Three Sisters* were 'gay comedies, almost vaudevilles'. Stanislavsky has recorded his insistence on this point in the face

of much opposition. 'Right up to his death Chekhov could not reconcile himself with the idea that *The Three Sisters* and *The Cherry Orchard* were sorrowful tragedies of Russian life.' Neither Chekhov himself nor the 'sorrowful tragedy' school of thought seem to have expressed the true position on the subject. The plays are not comedies or tragedies in the accepted sense of either word, nor are they exclusively gay or sorrowful. They contain rather an extremely subtle blend of both elements. That the evocative atmosphere peculiar to Chekhov should combine harmoniously with broad farce is perhaps a surprising fact, but *The Cherry Orchard* is there to prove the possibility of such a combination.

David Magarshack   (essay date 1960)

SOURCE: "Introductory," in *Chekhov the Dramatist,* Hill and Wang, 1960, pp. 13-49.

[*In this essay, Magarshack explores Chekhov's views on art and the Russian theater of his day, as expressed in his letters and occasional writings.*]

CHAPTER I

The plays of Chekhov, like those of any other great dramatist, follow a certain pattern of development which can be traced through all its various stages. His last four plays, moreover, conform to certain general principles which are characteristic of the type of indirect-action drama to which they belong. Chekhov himself was fully aware of that. Already on November 3rd, 1888, in a letter to Alexey Suvorin, he clearly stated that all works of art must conform to certain laws. "It is possible to collect in a heap the best that has been created by the artists in all ages," he wrote, "and, making use of the scientific method, discover the general principles which are characteristic of them all and which lie at the very basis of their value as works of art. These general principles will constitute their law. Works of art which are immortal possess a great deal in common; if one were to extract that which is common to them all from any of them, it would lose its value and its charm. This means that what is common to them all is necessary and is a *conditio sine qua non* of every work which lays claim to immortality."

Chekhov did not claim immortality for his plays. He was too modest for that. What he did claim for them, however, was something that any immortal work of art is generally supposed to possess, namely, the power so to influence people as to induce them to create a new and better life for themselves. "You tell me," Chekhov said to the writer Alexander Tikhonov in 1902, "that people cry at my plays. I've heard others say the same. But that was not why I wrote them. It is Alexeyev (Stanislavsky) who made my characters into cry-babies. All I wanted was to say honestly to people: 'Have a look at yourselves and see how bad and dreary your lives are!' The important thing is that people should realise that, for when they do, they will most certainly create another and better life for themselves. I will not live to see it, but I know that it will be quite different, quite unlike our present life. And so long as this different life does not exist, I shall go on saying to people again and again: 'Please, understand that your life is bad and dreary!'

"What is there in this to cry about?"

The misinterpretation of Chekhov's plays by the Moscow Art Theatre led to constant conflicts between their author and its two directors. These conflicts became particularly violent during the production of *The Cherry Orchard.* "The production of *The Cherry Orchard,*" Olga Knipper, Chekhov's wife and one of the leading actresses of the Moscow Art Theatre, wrote, "was difficult, almost agonising, I might say. The producers and the author could not understand each other and could not come to an agreement." Chekhov himself wrote to Olga Knipper: "Nemirovich-Danchenko and Alexeyev positively see in my play something I have not written, and I am ready to bet anything you like that neither of them has ever read my play through carefully." And to a well-known Russian producer Chekhov said: "Take my *Cherry Orchard.* Is it my *Cherry Orchard*? With the exception of two or three parts nothing in it is mine. I am describing life, ordinary life, and not blank despondency. They either make me into a cry-baby or into a bore. They invent something about me out of their own heads, anything they like, something I never thought of or dreamed about. This is beginning to make me angry." And what is true of Chekhov's Russian producers is even truer of his English and American producers, though in their case the idea that the characters in Chekhov's plays represent curiously unaccountable "Russians" adequately conceals their own confusion and helplessness.

This general bewilderment would have been fatal to the popularity of Chekhov's plays were it not that, being a playwright of genius, Chekhov paints his characters with so exquisite a brush that no caricature can strip them of their essential humanity. If neither the spectators nor those responsible for the production and performance of the plays can see the wood for the trees in them, the trees themselves are so brilliantly delineated that they are quite sufficient to ensure the comparative success of any of Chekhov's famous plays. It must not be forgotten, however, that their success is only "comparative", for so far Chekhov has failed to become a really "popular" playwright either in England or America, and it is doubtful whether one in a thousand of the regular playgoers in these countries has ever seen a play of his or, indeed, knows anything about it.

Nor has Chekhov been particularly fortunate in his critics. Disregarding the host of critics in and outside Russia whose aesthetic appreciation of Chekhov derives entirely from their own sensibilities and who seem to delight in losing themselves in a welter of half-tones and feelings too exquisite for anyone but themselves to detect, two critical appreciations of Chekhov as a playwright sum up an attitude that is still prevalent among the more thought-ful admirers of Chekhov's genius. One of them comes from Tolstoy. Peter Gnyeditch, a Russian novelist and playwright who was for some years in charge of the repertoire of the Imperial Alexandrinsky Theatre in Petersburg, recounts the following observation made by Tolstoy to Chekhov in his presence: "You know I can't stand Shakespeare, but your plays are even worse. Shakespeare after all does seize his reader by the collar and lead him to a certain goal without letting him get lost on the way. But where is one to get to with your heroes? From the sofa to the . . . and back?" And to Gnyeditch himself Tolstoy remarked that Chekhov had not "the real nerve" of a dramatist. "I am very fond of Chekhov and I value his writings highly," Gnyeditch reports Tolstoy as saying, "but I could not force myself to read his *Three Sisters* to the end—where does it all lead us to? Generally speaking, our modern writers seem to have lost the idea of what drama is. Instead of giving us a man's whole life, drama must put him in such a situation, must tie him in such a knot as to enable us to see what he is like while he is trying to untie it. Now, as you know, I have been so bold as to deny the importance of Shakespeare as a playwright. But in Shakespeare every man does something, and it is always clear why he acts thus and not otherwise. On his stage he had signposts with inscriptions: moonlight, a house. And a good thing too! For the entire attention of the spectator remains concentrated on the essential point of the drama; but now everything is the other way round."

And in an interview published in the Russian journal *Slovo* on July 28th, 1904, about a fortnight after Chekhov's death, Tolstoy summarised his objections to Chekhov's plays in these words: "To evoke a mood you want a lyrical poem. Dramatic forms serve, and ought to serve, quite different aims. In a dramatic work the author ought to deal with some problem that has yet to be solved and every character in the play ought to solve it according to the idiosyncrasies of his own character. It is like a laboratory experiment. But you won't find anything of the kind in Chekhov. He never holds the attention of the spectators sufficiently long for them to put themselves entirely in his power. For instance, he keeps the spectator's attention fixed on the fate of the unhappy Uncle Vanya and his friend Dr. Astrov, but he is sorry for them only because they are unhappy, without attempting to prove whether or not they deserve pity. He makes them say that once upon a time they were the best people in the district, but he does not show us in what way they were good. I can't help feeling that they have always been worthless creatures and that their suffering cannot therefore be worthy of our attention."

The Seagull, it is interesting to note, Tolstoy roundly dismissed as "nonsense." Alexey Suvorin, the well-known Russian newspaper publisher and a life-long friend of Chekhov's, records in his diary on February 11th, 1897, that Tolstoy told him that the play was "utterly worthless" and that it was written "just as Ibsen writes his plays."

"The play is chock full of all sorts of things," Tolstoy declared, "but no one really knows what they are for.

And Europe shouts, 'Wonderful!' Chekhov," Tolstoy went on, "is one of our most gifted writers, but *The Seagull* is a very bad play."

"Chekhov," Suvorin remarked, "would die if he were told what you thought about his play. Please, don't say anything to him about it."

"I shall tell him what I think of it," Tolstoy said, "but I shall put it gently. I'm surprised that you think he would take it so much to heart. After all, every writer slips up sometimes."

Tolstoy, according to Suvorin, thought that Chekhov should never have introduced a writer in *The Seagull.* "There aren't many of us," he said, "and no one is really interested in us." Trigorin's monologue in Act II he considered the best thing in the play and he thought that it was most certainly autobiographical, but in his opinion Chekhov should have published it separately or in a letter. "In a play it is out of place," he declared. In his short story 'My Life,' Tolstoy concluded with what, if he only knew, would have appeared to Chekhov the most devastating criticism of his play, "Chekhov makes his hero read Ostrovsky and say, 'All this can happen in life,' but had he read *The Seagull,* he would never have said that."

Apart from his purely moral objections to Chekhov's characters Tolstoy's main criticisms of Chekhov's plays concern their structure and their apparent lack of purpose. Accustomed to the drama of direct action, Tolstoy expected the unravelling of the knot which the playwright ties round his hero to supply the key to his character, to reveal the man as a whole. He also expected a play to solve the problems society has so far failed to solve and in this way supply the answer to the question: where does it all lead to?

Curiously enough, English criticism, too, seems to regard the same apparent lack of purpose as characteristic of Chekhov's drama, though, unlike Tolstoy, most of the critics consider that as something praiseworthy. Discussing *The Seagull,* Mr. (as he then was) Desmond MacCarthy[1] asks: "What is it all about?" and his answer is: "It is a question more than usually difficult to answer in the case of *The Seagull.* I am obliged to turn it aside," he goes on, "and say that it is a beautiful study in human nature, penetrating, detached, and compassionate. . . . It has no theme." Still, the critic admits that he often said to himself that "a work of art to have any value must somewhere carry within it the suggestion of a desirable life," which he does not apparently find in Chekhov's plays, and he therefore suggests that it is to be found "in the mind of Chekhov himself, in the infection we catch from the spirit of the whole play; in the delicate, humorous, compassionate mind which observed, understood and forgave." The same critic, in another notice of *The Seagull* eleven years later,[2] answers the same question: "What is *The Seagull* about?" as follows: "It is a study of a group of people, penetrating, detached and compassionate." As for the purpose of the play, "the point that *The Seagull* drives home," he writes, "is that the person

who possesses what another thinks would make all the difference to him or her is just as dissatisfied as the one who lacks it. By means of these contrasts Chekhov shows that what each pines for makes no difference in the end."

As for *Uncle Vanya,*[3] Mr. MacCarthy finds that Chekhov's "favourite theme is disillusionment and as far as the kind of beauty he creates, beneath it might be written 'desolation is a delicate thing'." Generally, Chekhov's play, according to the same distinguished critic, reveals "an atmosphere of sighs and yawns and self-reproaches, vodka, endless tea, and endless discussion." And thirteen years later, the same critic, writing of *Uncle Vanya* again,[4] declared that "though Chekhov was far from ineffectual himself, the ineffectiveness of his generation was his inspiration. And his final conclusion about the play is: "Besides inventing the play without plot and theatrical effects, Chekhov was also the poet and apologist of ineffectualness."[5]

Discussing *The Cherry Orchard,*[6] Mr. MacCarthy states as a matter of fact ("we all know") that "the essence of Chekhov's drama" is "the rainbow effect, laughter shining through tears." And in a notice of *The Three Sisters*[7] he finds Chekhov's heroines to be "forlorn, ineffectual young women" and comes to the conclusion that "Chekhov's supreme gift was to bring the observation of character to a most delicate sense of justice," and that his method was "to develop character and situation by means of a dialogue which follows the broken rhythms of life, and by making every remark, every gesture of his characters reflect the influence of group relations of the moment."

While disagreeing entirely with Tolstoy about the value of Chekhov's plays as works of art, Mr. Desmond MacCarthy, who in this respect represents English criticism as a whole, agrees with him about the absence of a well-defined aim in them as well as about the general ineffectualness of their characters. The only trouble about this now widely held view is that Chekhov himself dissented violently from it. Before, then, deciding whether Chekhov or his critics and producers are right, it is necessary to find out what Chekhov thought the final aim and form of a dramatic work ought to be, and what his attitude to contemporary drama was. For Chekhov had very definite ideas about both, and these most certainly influenced his work for the stage.

CHAPTER II

Chekhov was not, as is generally supposed, a great short-story writer who took up drama seriously only during the last seven or eight years of his all too short life. He was a born dramatist whose first works of importance were three full-length plays, two written in his late teens and the third in his early twenties. He took up short-story writing for two reasons: first, because he had to support a large family which was entirely dependent on him, and the writing of short stories was the quickest way of doing it; secondly, because the state of the Russian stage in the eighties and the nineties of the last century was such that no serious playwright could hope to have his plays performed, let alone earn a decent living in the theatre. Even Alexander Ostrovsky, whose reputation as a playwright had long been established, was not able to do so. It was indeed this hopeless position of the serious playwright in Russia towards the end of the nineteenth century that made Chekhov look on fiction as his "legal wife" and the stage as "a noisy, impudent and tiresome mistress." But the remarkable fact about a Chekhov short story is that it possesses the three indispensable elements of drama: compactness of structure (Chekhov's term for it was "architecture"), movement, that is dramatic development of plot, and action. "The reader," Chekhov wrote to the writer Ivan Leontyev on January 28th, 1888, "must never be allowed to rest; he must be kept in a state of suspense." The dialogue in Chekhov's short stories is essentially dramatic dialogue and that is what chiefly distinguishes them from the short stories of other fiction writers. Many of these short stories, particularly the early ones, have been adapted for the Russian stage, but the "adaptation" consisted mainly in lifting Chekhov's dialogue and using the descriptive passages as stage directions. Chekhov himself "adapted" five of his short stories for the stage on the same principle, that is, he merely lifted the dialogue, adding his own stage directions, and, if his story was too short, expanding it to the necessary length of a one-act play. Commenting on a play by the Norwegian playwright Bjoernstjerne Bjoernson in a letter to Suvorin on June 20th, 1896 (that is, *after* he had written *The Seagull*), Chekhov remarked that it was of no use so far as the stage was concerned because "it has no action, no living characters and no dramatic interest." This is surely the best comment ever made on the distortion the plays of Chekhov have suffered on the stage, and especially on the English and American stage, by being denied just the quality Chekhov himself valued most both as playwright and as short-story writer, namely, action.

Chekhov, then, was a born playwright and his knowledge of the stage, too, was first-hand. As a boy in his native town of Taganrog he had often appeared on the amateur and professional stage and earned general recognition as a talented actor. Replying on March 4th, 1893, to an invitation to take part in a literary evening, Chekhov pointed out that he was a bad reader and, what was even worse, suffered from stage-fright. "This is silly and ridiculous, but I can't do anything about it," he wrote. "I have never read in public in my life and never shall. A long time ago I used to act on the stage, but there I concealed myself behind my costume and make-up and that gave me courage." And writing to Suvorin on April 18th, 1895, about an amateur performance of Tolstoy's *The Fruits of Enlightenment,* planned by a number of Moscow writers in aid of some charity, in which he had agreed to take the part of the peasant, Chekhov declared: "I used to act quite well in the past, though now I fear my voice will let me down."

His purely professional attitude towards drama (as opposed to the now so common "literary" one) can further be gauged from the fact that he did not consider a play of his completed before it had been thoroughly revised by him at rehearsals. Thus he wrote on November 27th, 1889, to the poet Pleshheyev who had asked his permission to publish *The Wood Demon,* "I never consider a play ready for publication until it has been revised during rehearsals. Wait, please. It is not too late yet. When the play has been revised at the rehearsals, I shall take advantage of your kind offer without waiting for an invitation."

Chekhov's only reason for writing a play was the likelihood of its being performed on the stage. Moreover, when writing a play he usually bore in mind the actors who were most likely to appear in its leading parts and, as in the case of *Ivanov,* he never hesitated to alter a play radically if a different actor or actress took a part he had originally intended for someone else.

"I sent you two versions of my *Ivanov,*" he wrote to Suvorin on January 7th, 1889. "If Ivanov had been played by a resourceful and dynamic actor, I should have altered and added a lot. I felt in the mood for it. But, alas, Ivanov is played by Davydov. That meant that I had to write shorter and duller dialogue, keeping in mind that all the subtleties and 'nuances' will be overlooked, become ordinary and tedious. Can Davydov be gentle one moment and furious another? When he plays serious parts there seems to be a kind of handmill turning round and round in his throat, dull and monotonous, which is speaking instead of him. I am sorry for poor Savina who has to play the part of my uninspiring Sasha. I would gladly have altered it for Savina, but if Ivanov mouths his part, I can't do anything for Sasha, however much I alter her part. I am simply ashamed that Savina will have to play goodness knows what in my play. Had I known earlier that she would play Sasha and Davydov Ivanov, I should have called my play *Sasha* and made everything revolve round this part and just attached Ivanov to it. But who could have foreseen that?"

Such an attitude may appear curious to a modern playwright, but that is only because the modern playwright has become detached from the stage. To Shakespeare or (in Russia) to Alexander Ostrovsky, to playwrights, that is, whom Chekhov called "specialists of the stage," such an attitude would not have appeared at all strange, and indeed both of them wrote their plays for and around well-known members of their companies.

What was Chekhov's attitude to the theatre? What did he think of the actors of the Imperial and private stage in Moscow and Petersburg? What were his views on the problems of acting and did he think a play ought to have a well-defined aim of its own, an aim that should be intelligible to the spectator? What, finally, were his ideas on the form and structure of a play and what did he consider to be the playwright's place in the theatre?

These questions occupied Chekhov's mind continually and were of decisive importance to his whole career as a dramatist.

Chekhov left a scathing description of the state of the theatre in Moscow in an article he contributed to the Petersburg weekly *Fragments* in 1885. What Chekhov found so appalling about the Moscow Imperial stage was the reign of mediocrity on it. "At the Bolshoy Theatre," he wrote in his article, "we have opera and ballet. Nothing new. The actors are all the old ones and their manner of singing is the old one: not according to the notes, but according to official circulars. In the ballet the ballerinas have been recently joined by Noah's aunt and Methuselah's sister-in-law." The state of affairs at the Moscow Imperial dramatic theatre, the Maly Theatre, was no better. "Again nothing new," Chekhov declared. "The same mediocre acting and the same traditional ensemble, inherited from our ancestors." As for the Moscow private theatre owned by Korsh where *Ivanov* was soon to be given its first try-out, it bore, Chekhov wrote, "a striking resemblance to a mixed salad: there is everything there except the most important thing of all—meat." There were two more private theatres in Moscow at the time, one near the Pushkin memorial, known as the Pushkin Theatre, where plays were performed for only half the season, and the theatre owned by the famous impresario Lentovsky. "Whether Lentovsky's theatre," Chekhov wrote, "will be given up to operettas, pantomimes or tragedies, or whether the celebrated clown Durov will be showing his learned pig there, is so far unknown to Lentovsky himself, who is at present preoccupied with designing vignettes for some grand, stupendous, nebulous enterprise." There were, besides, "fifty thousand amateur theatres," but Chekhov had no use for them, and even the foundation three years later of the Society of Art and Literature by Stanislavsky and the actor and playwright Fedotov was looked upon by Chekhov with unconcealed derision, the pretentiousness of the name of the society being sufficient to make Chekhov sceptical about its founders.

In a letter to Suvorin on February 14th, 1889, Chekhov roundly dismissed the Russian theatre as it existed at that time as "nothing but a sport. I don't believe in the theatre as a school without which it is impossible to exist," he declared. In **"A Boring Story"** which he wrote between March and September, 1889, Chekhov discussed the vexed problem of the theatre as a place of entertainment at greater length and came to the conclusion that such a theatre was a mere waste of time. "A sentimental and credulous crowd," he writes, "can be persuaded that the theatre in its present state is a 'school'. But anyone who knows what a school is really like will not be deceived by such a facile statement. I don't know what the theatre will be like in fifty or a hundred years, but under present conditions it can serve only as entertainment, and as entertainment it is too expensive to be worth while. It deprives the State of thousands of gifted young men and women who, if they did not dedicate themselves to the theatre, could have become good doctors, farmers, teachers, army officers; it deprives the public of its evening hours—the best time for intellectual work and fireside chats. Not to mention the sheer waste of money and the moral injury suffered by the public from seeing a wrongly presented case of murder, adultery or libel on the stage."

This criticism of the theatre as entertainment Chekhov puts into the mouth of the hero of his story, an old professor of medicine, and Chekhov was always very careful to make his heroes speak and think "in character". But there can be no doubt that, though Chekhov himself would not have expressed these ideas in so extreme a form, they were substantially his own ideas on the theatre of his day. It was certainly Chekhov the playwright who was speaking through the mouth of his hero when he condemned the music played in the intervals between the acts of a play as "quite unnecessary" and "as adding something utterly new and irrelevant to the impression created by the play." It was only with the foundation of the Moscow Art Theatre that this "unnecessary and irrelevant" custom was abolished.

CHAPTER III

Three notices which Chekhov contributed to Moscow journals in 1881, that is to say, at the very beginning of his literary career, reveal him as a thoughtful student of the stage and a merciless critic of bad acting. Two of these deal with Sarah Bernhardt who was on tour in Russia and appeared on the Moscow stage in December of 1881. Chekhov was not an admirer of the divine Sarah. While dramatically effective, he found her too artificial. "Every sigh of Sarah Bernhardt's," he wrote, "her tears, her convulsions in the death scenes, her entire acting is nothing but a cleverly learnt lesson. Being a highly intelligent woman who knows what is and what is not dramatically effective, and who, besides, possesses most excellent taste and a knowledge of the human heart, she knows how to perform all those conjuring tricks which at one time or another take place in the human heart at the behest of fate." Chekhov's strongest objection to Sarah Bernhardt's acting was based on the fact that the great French actress always acted herself. "She transforms everyone of her heroines," Chekhov wrote, "into the same kind of unusual woman she is herself." Furthermore, Chekhov found that Sarah Bernhardt was not anxious to be natural on the stage (an interesting and highly significant criticism this). "All she cares about," he declared, "is being unusual. Her aim is to startle, astonish and stun. There is not a glimmer of talent in all her acting, but just an enormous amount of hard work." It was Sarah Bernhardt's hard work that, Chekhov thought, provided the clue to her great success on the stage. "There is not one trivial detail in her big or small parts," he wrote, "that has not passed through the purgatory of hard work." And after expressing his "most respectful admiration" for Sarah Bernhardt's "industry", Chekhov advised the Russian actors to take a lesson from her. "That the majority of our actors do very little," he wrote, "can be gathered from the fact that they all seem to stand still: not a step forward—anywhere! If only they worked as hard as Sarah Bernhardt, if only they knew as much as Sarah Bernhardt, they would go far. But, unfortunately, where the knowledge of the art of the stage is concerned, our big and small servants of the Muses lag far behind and, if an old truth is to be believed, knowledge can only be achieved by hard work.

"We watched Sarah Bernhardt," Chekhov sums up his impressions of the French actress, "and we were thrown into raptures by her great industry. There were moments in her acting which almost moved us to tears. If our tears did not flow it was only because the whole charm of her acting was spoilt by its artificiality. But for that confounded artificiality, those deliberate conjuring tricks and over-emphasis, we should most certainly have burst into tears, and indeed the whole theatre would have shaken with thunderous applause. Oh, genius! Cuvier said that genius was always at loggerheads with mere agility, and Sarah Bernhardt is certainly very agile."

There was one important quality of acting, however, that Chekhov did appreciate in Sarah Bernhardt: it was her ability to *listen*. That ability, though, was shared by the rest of her French company. They were all excellent listeners, and that was why, Chekhov thought, they never felt out of place on the stage. It was different with the Russian actors. "This is how we do it:" Chekhov wrote, "when Mr. Mashkeyev is saying his lines on the stage, Mr. Wilde, who is listening to him, has his eyes fixed on some far-away point and keeps coughing impatiently, and as you watch him, you cannot help feeling that what he is thinking of at the moment is: 'That has nothing to do with me, old man'!"

What Chekhov admired, therefore, and what he demanded from his actors, was natural acting, the sort of acting for which the great Russian actor Shchepkin became famous and which Stanislavsky later on made into the cornerstone of his own system of acting. He realised, as Stanislavsky did many years later, that such acting required a great deal of hard work as well as observation of life. "Our actors," Chekhov complained in a letter to Suvorin on November 25th, 1889, "never observe ordinary people. They know nothing of landowners, business men, priests, or Civil Servants. On the other hand, they are quite capable of representing billiard markers, rich men's mistresses, drunken card-sharpers, and generally those individuals whom they happen to observe incidentally during their pub-crawls and drinking-bouts. The real trouble is that they are so frightfully ignorant."

Chekhov's dissatisfaction with the state of the Russian stage of his time is expressed even more forcibly in a notice on a performance of *Hamlet* at the Pushkin Theatre which he wrote on January 11th, 1882. It is the only dramatic criticism of a Shakespearean performance Chekhov ever wrote, and for that reason alone it deserves to be quoted at length. Chekhov begins his notice with a parable of a sage who could not be dragged away from his books but whom one of his disciples discovered one night in "a far from respectable place" with a pretty French girl on his knees, sipping champagne.

"What are you doing, Herr Professor?" his disciple exclaimed in dismay, turning pale with surprise.

"A foolish thing, my son," the sage replied, pouring out a glass of wine for his disciple. "I am doing a very foolish thing."

"But why?" the disciple asked.

"To let in a little fresh air, my son," the sage replied, lifting his glass. "To wine and women!"

The disciple drank, turning even paler with surprise.

"My son," went on the sage, stroking the hair of the pretty French girl, "clouds have gathered in my head, the atmosphere has grown heavy, and lots and lots of things have accumulated. All that has to be aired and purified and put in its proper place. It is to do that that I am committing this piece of folly. Folly is a regrettable thing, but very often it does freshen things up. Yesterday I felt like rotting grass, but tomorrow morning, *O bone discipule,* I shall be as fresh as a daisy. Three cheers for an act of folly committed once a year! *Viva stultitia!*"

"If folly," Chekhov continues, "sometimes acts in so refreshing a manner, how much more must it be true of its opposite extreme." And he goes on to explain that nothing needed refreshing so much as the Russian stage. "Its atmosphere," he writes, "is leaden and oppressive. It is covered inches-thick in dust and enveloped in fog and tedium. You go to the theatre simply because you have nowhere else to go. You look at the stage, yawn, and swear under your breath."

But, Chekhov contends, it is impossible to put new life into the stage by an act of folly because the footboards are all too used to acts of folly, as it is. It must be brought to life by the opposite extreme, and, he adds, "this extreme is Shakespeare. I have often heard people ask whether or not it is worth while performing *Hamlet* at the Pushkin Theatre," Chekhov writes. "It is an idle question. Shakespeare must be played everywhere for the sake of letting in fresh air, if not for the sake of instruction or some other more or less lofty purpose."

Hamlet, Chekhov was glad to report, was accorded a delighted welcome by the audience of the Pushkin Theatre which seemed to enjoy itself hugely. Chekhov goes on to criticise the performance, and again in these criticisms a clue can be discovered to his own ideas of acting.

"Mr. Ivanov-Kozelsky,"[8] he writes, "is not strong enough to play Hamlet. He understands Hamlet in his own way. Now, for an actor to understand a character in his own way is not a fault, provided the actor does not let his author down. Mr. Ivanov-Kozelsky whined through the whole of the first act. Hamlet never whined. No man's tears are cheap, and certainly not Hamlet's. On the stage," Chekhov declares, "as though in anticipation of the fate that would befall his own characters, "tears must not be shed without reason. Mr. Ivanov-Kozelsky," he goes on, "was frightened of the ghost, so greatly frightened indeed was he that I felt sorry for him. He made a hash of Hamlet's speech to his father. Hamlet was an irresolute man, but he was no coward, all the more so since he had already been prepared for the meeting with the ghost. The scene in which Hamlet invites his friends to swear

on the hilt of his sword was not successful: Ivanov-Kozelsky did not speak but hissed like a gander chased by
boys. His conversation with Rosencrantz and Guilden-
stern lacked dignity. He gave himself airs in their presence. It is not enough," Chekhov goes on, again as though
in anticipation of the way in which his own characters
would be mangled and distorted on the stage, "it is not
enough to feel and to be able to convey one's feelings
correctly on the stage; it is not enough to be an artist; an
actor must also possess a great fund of knowledge. An
actor who undertakes to play Hamlet must be an educated man. The scene between Hamlet and his mother was
excellently played. So was the scene in the churchyard.
There was a great deal of charm in Ivanov-Kozelsky's
acting, but all this charm was due to his ability to feel,
and to that alone. He underlined every word, watched his
every movement, counted his steps. This is the fault of
every beginner. Hamlet's death in horrible convulsions
and a fearful voice should have been replaced by a natural one."

As for the other actors, Chekhov found that "Claudius
was not bad," and, he added significantly, "he knew how
to kneel." On the other hand, "the queen, the ghost,
Horatio and the rest were bad. Still, the First Player was
good enough and though I am told that Ophelia had a
better voice than Miss Baranova, she did not play so
badly."

After criticising the small stage, the bad scenery and
costumes, and the unnecessary cuts, Chekhov concludes
his notice by praising "the genius of the man who first
suggested a performance of *Hamlet* on the stage of the
Pushkin Theatre. Far better," he declares, "a badly acted
Shakespeare than some dreary trash."

This being Chekhov's opinion of the Russian stage and
the Russian actors, what did he think of the Russian
audiences? There were moments when the Russian audiences made him lose heart. "Why and for whom do I
write?" he exclaims in a letter to Suvorin on December
23rd, 1888. "For the public? But I do not see it and I
believe in it less than in house demons: it is uneducated,
badly brought up, and its better elements are unfair and
ill-disposed to us. I can't make up my mind whether this
public does or does not need me." But he drew the line
at blaming the Russian audiences for the bad state of the
theatres. "The public," he wrote to Suvorin in November
of the same year, "is everywhere the same: intelligent
and foolish, generous and ruthless, all depending on its
mood. It always was a herd in need of good shepherds
and dogs and it always went where the shepherds and
dogs made it. You profess to be outraged that it should
laugh at silly jokes and applaud high-sounding phrases;
but it is the same audience that packs the theatre to see
Othello and that weeps when listening to Tatyana reading her love letter in *Eugene Onegin*. However foolish it
may be, it is in general more intelligent, more sincere
and more good natured than Korsh or any actors and
playwrights, while Korsh and the actors imagine that
they are the more intelligent ones. A mutual misunderstanding."

*Stanislavsky as Shabielsky, in a 1904 Moscow Art Theater
production of* Ivanov.

CHAPTER IV

A scathing description of the type of playwright who was
all too common in his day, was given by Chekhov in
1886 in a small sketch under the title of **"Dramatist."**
The playwright, "a dim personality with lustreless eyes
and a catarrhal physiognomy," is shown paying a visit to
his doctor. His complaints include breathlessness, belch-
ing, heartburn, depression and a bad taste in the mouth.

"What do you do for a living?" asked the doctor.

"I am a playwright," the individual replied not without
pride.

The doctor, filled with respect for his patient, smiled def-
erentially. Since such an occupation implied great nervous
strain, he asked his patient to describe his mode of life.
The playwright told him that he usually got up at twelve,
and at once smoked a cigarette and drank two or three
glasses of vodka. After breakfast he again had some beer
or wine, the choice depending "on his finances". Then he
usually went to a pub and after the pub he had a game of

billiards. At six o'clock he went to a restaurant to have his dinner, but his appetite was so bad that to stimulate it he was forced to have six or seven glasses of vodka. Then at the theatre he felt so nervous that he again had to consume large quantities of drink. From the theatre he went to some night-club where he usually stayed till the morning.

"And when do you write your plays?" asked the doctor.

"My plays?" the playwright shrugged. "Well, that depends . . ."

Asked by the doctor to describe "the process of his work," the playwright gave this illuminating, though not by any means exaggerated, account of the way "popular plays" were usually written in those days: "First of all, I get hold of some French or German piece either by accident or through some friends (I haven't got the time to keep an eye on all the new foreign plays that are published myself). If the play is any good I take it to my sister or hire a student for five roubles. They translate it for me and I, you see, adapt it for the Russian stage: I substitute Russian names for the names of the characters and so on. That's all. But don't run away with the idea that this is easy. It isn't at all easy!" the "dim individual" declared, rolling up his eyes and heaving a sigh.

The Russian stage in the eighties and nineties of the last century was indeed flooded with such "adaptations" of, mostly, French plays, and one of Chekhov's own brilliant one-act comedies actually owed its origin to one such adaptation of a French play.

Two years later Chekhov gave the following description of an original Russian play by E. P. Karpov, who was later to become the producer of the Petersburg Alexandrinsky Theatre and who was chiefly responsible for the failure of *The Seagull*:

"The other day I saw *Crocodile Tears,* a rubbishy five-act play by a certain Karpov, author of *On the Meadow, The Agricultural Board, The Free Bird,* etc." he wrote to Suvorin on November 11th, 1888. "The whole play, even if one overlooks its wooden naïvety, is an utter lie and travesty of life. A dishonest headman of a village gets a young landowner, a permanent member of the local agricultural board, into his power and wants him to marry his daughter, who is in love with a clerk who writes poetry. Before the marriage a young, honest land-surveyor opens the eyes of the landowner, who exposes his would-be father-in-law's crimes, the crocodile, i.e., the headman of the village, weeps, and one of the heroines exclaims: "And so virtue is triumphant and vice is punished!" which brings the play to an end.

"Horrible! After the play Karpov stopped me and said: 'In this play I have shown up the liberal milksops and that is why it was not liked and was abused. But I don't care a damn!'

"If ever I say or write anything of the kind, I hope that you will hate me and have nothing to do with me any more."

And in a letter to Leontyev on the same day Chekhov wrote:

"You want to have an argument with me about the theatre. By all means, but you will never convince me that I am wrong about my dislike of these scaffolds where they execute playwrights. Our contemporary theatre is a world of confusion, stupidity and idle talk. The other day Karpov boasted to me that he had shown up 'the silly liberals' in his third-rate *Crocodile Tears* and that that was why his play was disliked and abused. After that my hatred of the theatre grew more violent and I grew even more fond of those fanatics who are trying to make something decent and wholesome out of it."

It was in another letter to Leontyev that Chekhov summed up his attitude to his contemporary playwrights in these words: "Our gifted writers have a great deal of phosphorus, but no iron. We are, I am afraid, no eagles, but just pretty birds who know how to sing sweetly."

It is an amazing fact that the accusation of lacking "iron", which Chekhov brought against the writers of his own day, should even in his lifetime have been brought against him by those who were so influenced by this general absence of a clearly perceived aim in their own writings that they naturally assumed that Chekhov, too, was like them. And yet there was no more outspoken a critic of this contemporary trend in literature than Chekhov. Writing to Suvorin on October 27th, 1888, Chekhov declared: "I dislike everything that is being written today. It makes me feel bored. Everything in my own head, however, interests, moves and excites me—and from this I conclude that nobody is doing what ought to be done, and that I alone know the secret of how to do it." Chekhov was quick enough to modify this seemingly arrogant statement from a young man of twenty-eight by adding that he supposed every writer thought the same, but in his case it happened to be true. Among his contemporaries, that is to say, among the young popular writers of the eighties and nineties, he was the only one to demand from the creative artist "a conscious attitude towards his work", though at first he insisted that it was not the business of a writer to provide a solution of social problems. "In *Anna Karenina* and *Eugene Onegin,*" he wrote to Suvorin in the same letter, "not a single problem is solved, but they satisfy you completely because the problems in them are formulated correctly. It is the duty of the judge to put the questions to the jury correctly, and it is for the members of the jury to make up their minds, each according to his own taste." In another letter to Suvorin earlier in the same year Chekhov is even more specific. "The creative artist," he writes, "must not set himself up as a judge of his characters or of their opinions, but must be an impartial witness. If I happen to hear a rather confused discussion about pessimism which does not solve anything, I have to report this conversation in the form in which I heard it, and it is for the members of the jury, i.e. for my readers, to express an opinion about it. My business consists in being talented, that is, in being able to distinguish the important depositions from the unimportant ones and in being able to throw light on my characters and to speak their language. . . . It is time that writers, and particularly those of them who are artists, should admit that it is impossible to make anything out in this world, as indeed Socrates and Voltaire so admitted. The mob thinks that it knows and understands everything, and the more stupid and ignorant it is, the wider does the scope of its knowledge and understanding seem to stretch. But if an artist in whom the mob believes is bold enough to declare that he does not understand anything of what he sees around him, then that alone will be a big step forward."

The vexed problem of the ultimate aim of art is of particular importance so far as Chekhov the playwright is concerned. Chekhov's insistence on the absolute objectivity of the writer led him at first to assume a standpoint which is barely distinguishable from that of the art-for-art's sake school. Indeed, it led him to write the only purely naturalistic play he ever wrote—**"On the Highway,"** a play that was forbidden by the censor on the ground that it was "sordid". The failure to differentiate between Chekhov's plays of direct-action and his later plays of indirect-action is to a certain extent due to the failure to realise that Chekhov's attitude towards the ultimate aim of art underwent a complete change during the seven years that separate his last play of the direct-action type from his first play of the indirect-action type. It is not only the purely structural form of the plays that underwent a change but also their inner content. If during his first period as a playwright Chekhov seemed to assume that artistic objectivity was incompatible with the presence of a "message" in a work of art, it was due mainly to his own struggles to achieve personal freedom and eradicate all traces of slavishness which his upbringing by a bigoted and despotic father had left on his mind. "My holy of holies," he wrote to the poet Pleshcheyev on October 4th, 1888, "is the human body and brain, talent, inspiration, love and personal freedom—freedom from force and lies, whatever form the last two may take. That is the programme I should like to have followed if I were a great artist. . . . I am not a liberal, or a conservative, or an evolutionist, or a monk or an indifferentist," he declares in the same letter. "I should like to be a free artist and—that is all. . . . I hate lies and violence of any kind. Phariseeism, stupidity and licence are to be found not only in middle-class homes and police stations; I see them in science, in literature, and among our young people. I consider a label or a trade-mark of any kind to be a prejudice." In a letter to Suvorin on January 2nd, 1889, he replied to the assertion of the Russian novelist Dmitry Grigorovich who wrote to him that "talent and freshness will overcome everything". It was much truer to say, Chekhov declared, that "talent and freshness may spoil a great deal. For in addition to the profusion of material and talent, something no less important is required. First of all, a mature mind and, secondly, *a feeling of personal freedom,* which I did not possess before."

But even during the period when Chekhov drove his conception of the creative artist's objectivity to the extreme of denying that a work of art must possess what is commonly known as "a message", he deeply resented any accusation of being merely a naturalistic writer. In reply to the criticism of his short story **"Slime"** (an early story published in September, 1886) by Maria Kisselev, an old friend of his, who accused him of being too much preoccupied with "dunghills" and urged him to concentrate on finding "the pearl in the dunghill", Chekhov made a detailed statement on his attitude to literature and the aims that should animate a serious writer in clothing contemporary life in an artistic form, a statement that is of the greatest possible significance to his early work for the theatre.

"I do not know who is right," Chekhov wrote on January 14th, 1887, "Homer, Shakespeare, Lope de Vega or, in general, the ancients who were not afraid of rummaging in 'dunghills' but were much more steadfast than we are so far as morals are concerned, or our contemporary writers who are prudes on paper but cold cynics in spirit and in life. I do not know whose taste is worse: the taste of the ancient Greeks who were not ashamed of glorifying love as it really is, or the taste of the readers of Emile Gaboriau, Eugenia Marlitt or Peter Boborykin?" At the age of twenty-seven Chekhov did not feel himself competent to give an answer to this question, just as he felt incompetent to give the right answer to the question of nonresistance to evil or the freedom of conscience. His correspondent's references to Turgenev and Tolstoy, who, she claimed, avoided the "dunghill" Chekhov brushed aside as irrelevant. "Their fastidiousness," he wrote, "proves nothing; after all, the generation of writers before them considered even descriptions of peasants and low-grade civil servants as beneath their dignity. And, besides," he goes on, "one period of literature, however rich in content, does not give us the right to draw any conclusions in favour of one literary movement or another. References to the corrupting influence of a certain literary movement do not solve the problem, either. Everything in the world is relative and approximate. There are people whom even children's books will corrupt and who seem to derive delight from reading the piquant passages in the Psalms and Solomon's Proverbs. But there are also people who remain unaffected by 'dirt'; indeed, the more familiar they become with it, the cleaner they are. Publicists, lawyers, and doctors, who are familiar with all the secrets of life are, as a rule, much more moral than bishops. And, finally," Chekhov maintained, "no literature can possibly outdo life by its cynicism: you can't make a man drunk on a glass of liquor if he has already drunk a whole barrel."

As for his correspondent's claim that it was the duty of literature to dig for "the pearl" in "the dunghill", that, Chekhov contended, meant disowning literature itself, for literature, he wrote, "is a creative art just because it shows us life as it is. Its purpose," he went on, "is absolute and honest truth, and to narrow down its functions to such a specialised field as the extraction of 'pearls' is as fatal as, for instance, compelling Levitan to paint a tree without showing its dirty bark and yellow leaves." Chekhov was ready to admit that the "pearl" was an excellent thing in itself, "but a writer," he insisted, "is not a confectioner, a cosmetician or an entertainer. He is a man who has to fulfil certain duties; he is a man who has entered into a contract with his conscience and his sense of duty, and however much he may hate it, he must overcome his fastidiousness and soil his imagination with the dirt of life . . . To a chemist," Chekhov went on, "the notion of dirt does not exist. A writer must be as objective as a chemist. He must renounce every subjective attitude to life and realise that dung-hills play a very honourable part in a landscape and that vicious passions are as much a part of life as virtuous ones." On the other hand, Chekhov admitted that writers must observe the rules of decency, but, he added, "it is only that that we are entitled to demand from the realists."

Chekhov concluded his letter by deploring any outside interference with literature. "The fate of literature would be lamentable indeed," he declared, "if it were left to the mercy of personal prejudice. That is first of all. Secondly, no police exists that could possibly consider itself competent in literary matters. I admit that self-restraint is necessary, for charlatans, too, find their way into literature, but, however much you tried, you could never invent a better police for literature than the critic and the author's own conscience. People have been inventing all sorts of things since the creation of the world, but they have not invented anything better than that."

This letter was written shortly before Chekhov wrote *Ivanov,* his last direct-action play, and the views expressed in it are therefore important in assessing the literary merits of his plays of that period. He had acknowledged himself to be a realist pure and simple and had taken for his watchword the phrase "life as it is". But it would be a grave mistake to think that Chekhov never budged from this position. Indeed, the seven years that separate *The Wood Demon* (1889), the play in which he had unsuccessfully attempted to find a different approach to drama, from *The Seagull* (1896), the first play in which he was supremely successful in his new medium of indirect action plays, were years of great heart-searchings for Chekhov, years in which his formula "life as it is" underwent a profound change. His endless recasting of *Ivanov* and his final dissatisfaction with the play, to which he began to refer in his letters as *Bolvanov* (*bolvan* meaning "blockhead" in Russian), shows that even at that early date Chekhov was beginning to be conscious of the dilemma inherent in the strict adherence to the principle of complete objectivity. In his letter to Suvorin of October 27th, 1888, he summed up the problem in these words: "If one were to deny the problem and the intention in creative art, then one would have to admit that the artist worked without premeditation under the influence of some mental aberration, and if, therefore, some writer were to boast to me that he had written a story without any previously thought out design but just by inspiration, I should call him a madman." But he still insisted that while it was right to demand from an artist a conscious attitude towards his work, it was only "the correct formulation of the problem" and not its solution that was compulsory for him. Two years later, however, in reply to Suvorin's

criticism of his short story **"Thieves,"** he admitted that "no doubt it would be pleasant to combine a sermon with art," but, he pointed out, he found such a combination personally impossible for technical reasons. "For to depict horse-thieves in seven hundred lines," he wrote on April 1st to Suvorin, "I have to think and talk all the time in their tone and feel as they do, otherwise, if I were to add subjectivity, my characters would become blurred and the story would not be as compact as all short stories ought to be. When writing I rely entirely on the reader to add the missing subjective elements in the story."

But Chekhov soon discovered that it was impossible to rely on the reader to draw the right moral from his stories. Indeed, one of the "fat", i.e. "highbrow", monthlies in Moscow, *Russian Thought,* to which he was to become a regular contributor later on, had so misunderstood the whole purpose of his writings that it bluntly accused him of being "an unprincipled writer". That was the last straw. On April 10th, 1890, Chekhov wrote a furious letter to Vukol Lavrov, the editor of the monthly, in which he repudiated the accusation of lack of principle as a libel which made any future business relations between them and the usual civilities of acquaintanceship impossible. This letter is important in that it reveals the inner conflict that was going on in Chekhov's mind at that particular time. Indeed, his defence against Lavrov's criticism is rather lame, and the fury of his letter must be chiefly ascribed to his own realisation of its lameness. "I have never been an unprincipled writer," he declared, "or, which is the same thing, a scoundrel. It is true that my whole literary career is an uninterrupted sequence of mistakes, sometimes gross mistakes, but that is explained by the limitation of my gifts and not at all by my being a good or a bad man. I have never blackmailed anyone, I have never written anything of a libellous nature, I have never informed on anyone, flattered anyone, or lied to anyone, or insulted anyone—in short, I have never written a single line of which I need be ashamed. If I were to assume that by 'unprincipled' you have in mind the melancholy fact that I, an educated man, who have often appeared in print, have done nothing for those I love, and that my activity has vanished without a trace, without, for instance, being of the slightest use to our agricultural boards, our new courts of justice, the freedom of the press, and so on, then *Russian Thought* ought in justice to consider me as its colleague and not accuse me, for it never did more than I—and that not because of any fault of mine."

Chekhov went on to defend himself against an accusation which obviously hurt him to the quick by claiming that even if he were to be judged as a writer pure and simple, he did not deserve to be publicly stigmatised as unprincipled, and he advanced the curious plea that he was really a doctor and not a writer at all, and that even as a writer he had so far got on excellently with all his literary friends. Finally, he pointed out that in the conditions of the strict censorship that prevailed at the time, it showed a peculiar lack of tact on Lavrov's part to bring such an accusation against writers.

CHAPTER V

Chekhov's reference to the stringent censorship was the only valid argument he used to rebut Lavrov's criticism. In his great plays he had to resort to all sorts of evasions in order to circumvent that particularly obnoxious obstacle. But his letter undoubtedly reveals a great uneasiness of mind and is indeed an indirect admission that there was some justice in Lavrov's accusation. His fury with *Russian Thought* was short-lived. He was, above all, honest with himself. On November 25th, 1892, in a letter to Suvorin he re-defined his position as a writer by finally relinquishing his standpoint of strict objectivity and placing the "aim" of a work of art, i.e. its moral purpose, at the head of all its other distinguishing marks.

Chekhov began his letter by casting a critical eye over the successful writers and artists of his time. His main objection to them was that they lacked "alcohol" to make their readers "drunk and enthralled". Had any of these writers ever given the world "one drop of alcohol?" Were not "Korolenko, Nadson and all our modern writers just lemonade? Have the paintings of Repin and Shishkin," he asked Suvorin, "ever turned your head?" And he went on to characterise these writers in the phrase he later put into Trigorin's mouth: "Charming, talented. You are delighted," he wrote, "but at the same time you can't forget that you want to smoke." Comparing the achievements made in his day by science and technology, Chekhov could not help concluding that the writers of his time found life "flabby, sour and dull" and that they themselves, too, were "sour and dull. All this," he concluded, "is not caused by our stupidity or lack of talent or, as Victor Burenin[9] thinks, by our self-conceit, but by an illness which is for an artist worse than syphilis or sexual impotence." These writers lacked "something", something very essential, something that made all the difference between mere entertainment and real art. What was that "something"? Chekhov went back to the classics in search of it. "Remember," he wrote, "that the writers whom we consider immortal or even just good, the writers who have the power of keeping us enthralled, all possess one highly important characteristic in common: they get somewhere and they call upon us to go with them, and we feel not only with our reason but with the whole of our being that they have some aim, like the ghost of Hamlet's father, who did not come back for nothing and did not trouble Hamlet's imagination for nothing. Some of them, according to how great they are, have aims that concern their own times more closely, such as the abolition of serfdom, the liberation of their country, politics, beauty, or simply vodka, others have more remote aims, such as God, life beyond the grave, human happiness, and so on. The best of them are realists and depict life as it is, but because every line they write is permeated, as with a juice, by a consciousness of an aim, you feel in addition to life as it is, also life as it should be, and it is that that delights you. But what about us? We depict life as it is, but we refuse to go a step further. We have neither near nor remote aims and our souls are as flat and bare as a billiard table. We have no politics, we do not believe in revolution, we deny the

existence of God, we are not afraid of ghosts, and so far as I am concerned, I am not afraid of death or blindness, either. But he who wants nothing, hopes for nothing and fears nothing cannot be an artist." In another letter belonging to the same period, he wrote that the writers of his time were "like maniacs who are writing books and plays for their own pleasure. One's own pleasure is of course an excellent thing while one is writing," he declared, "but afterwards?"

So the great realisation had come at last, and though for the time being Chekhov pretended that he, too, was suffering from the same illness, it was merely his modesty speaking. Already in his short story **"Ward No. 6,"** which he wrote shortly before his letter to Suvorin, he had shown "a consciousness of an aim" that entitled him to a place among the foremost creative artists in fiction, but that consciousness was already discernible in many of his earlier stories in spite of his adherence to the principle of strict objectivity. For objectivity is as much the hallmark of a great artist as the consciousness of a high moral purpose, and, as Chekhov points out, it is the combination of the two that is characteristic of all great art, or, in other words, of realism as opposed to mere naturalism.

Having reached that conclusion, Chekhov later not only refused to include **"On the Highway"** in the collected edition of his works, but entirely suppressed it. And the main reason for his bitter conflict with the directors of the Moscow Art Theatre was their failure to see the high moral purpose of his plays, a failure that is still characteristic of most of his producers in England and America. What differentiates Chekhov's early from his four last plays is not only a difference of technique. It is the much more important question of the final aim of the plays, the moral purpose that is absent from his early plays and forms so essential a part of his later ones. For it is these later plays that, in Chekhov's own words, "are permeated by a consciousness of an aim", and are meant to make the spectator see not only "life as it is", but also "life as it should be".

The greatest mistake English and American producers of Chekhov's plays have been making is to accept the view that Chekhov's drama is essentially a drama of frustration. This is only true of his two plays of direct action; of his last four plays the opposite is true: it is a drama of courage and hope. It was Stanislavsky who was mainly responsible for treating Chekhov's plays as plays of frustration and it was he who imposed this view on the rest of the world. But the bitter conflict between Chekhov and Stanislavsky is well known, and the most obvious mistake some producers make is in either overlooking this conflict altogether or drawing the wrong conclusion from it. They all ignore the final aim of the four great plays. Indeed, they usually go so far as to deny that such an aim exists and purposely play down or entirely ignore those parts of the plays which deal with this aim. Hence the spurious "Chekhovian" atmosphere which is laid on so thickly in every production of a Chekhov play. Ironically enough, it is they who, instead of expressing Chekhov's ideas, express the ideas of the Russian woman critic Sazonova, which appalled Chekhov when he read her strictures of his letter to Suvorin of November 25th, 1892. Suvorin himself was so astonished to read Chekhov's views on the ultimate aims of a work of art, which were so much at variance with Chekhov's former views, that he sent his letter to Sazonova for her comment and then sent those comments on to Chekhov, whose reply to Suvorin is both illuminating and decisive.

"That the last generation of writers and artists had no aim in their work," Chekhov wrote to Suvorin on December 3rd, 1892, "is quite a legitimate, consistent and interesting phenomenon, and the fact that Sazonova was aghast at my letter does not mean that I was insincere or acted against my conscience. It is you yourself who have read insincerity into it, for otherwise you would not have sent her my letter. In my letters to you I am often unjust and naïve, but I never write anything I do not believe in. But if you want insincerity, there are tons of it in Sazonova's letter. 'The greatest miracle is man himself, and we shall never grow tired of studying him.' Or 'The aim of life is life itself'. Or 'I believe in life, in its bright moments, for the sake of which one not only *can* but also *must* live; I believe in man, in the good sides of his nature,' and so on. Do you really think this is sincere, or does it indeed mean anything? This is not an outlook on life, but sheer nonsense. She underlines 'can' and 'must' because she is afraid of speaking about what is and what must be taken into account. Let her first of all tell us what is, and then I shall be glad to listen to what can and must be done. She believes in 'life', which means that she does not believe in anything if she is intelligent or that she simply believes in the peasant's God and crosses herself in the dark as if she were a silly old woman.

"Under the influence of her letter," Chekhov goes on, "you write to me about 'life for life's sake'. Thank you very much. Why, her letter which is supposed to be so full of the joy of life is more like a graveyard than mine. I wrote that we had no aims and you rightly drew the conclusion that I considered them necessary and that I would gladly go in search of them, while Sazonova writes that it is wrong to tempt man with all sorts of benefits which he will never get—'you must be thankful for your present mercies', and in her opinion our misfortune consists solely in our looking for some more remote and higher aims. If this is not just female logic, then it is the philosophy of despair. He who is sincerely convinced that higher aims are as unnecessary to man as they are to a cow and that 'our whole misfortune' lies in having those aims, has nothing left but to eat, drink and sleep, and when he gets sick of all that, to take a good run and smash his head on the sharp edge of a trunk. I am not abusing Sazonova. All I mean is that she does not appear to be a very cheerful person."

CHAPTER VI

Mention has already been made of Chekhov's views on the paramount importance of action in a play. What are the other general conditions that Chekhov regarded as necessary to an aspiring playwright? First of all comes a thorough, first-hand knowledge of the stage. "Beginning with the next season," Chekhov wrote to a fellow-dramatist in March 1889, "I shall start visiting the theatre regularly and educating myself scenically." To his eldest brother Alexander, who had sent him a general outline of a play he was proposing to write, Chekhov wrote: "Don't forget to visit the theatre a few times and make a thorough study of the stage. You'll then be able to compare and that is important." Another rule that Chekhov was never tired of enjoining on his fellow-dramatists was the need for originality. "Try to be original in your play," he advised his brother, "and, as far as possible, intelligent, but do not be afraid to appear silly. Complete freedom of expression is necessary, but remember that only he is free to express his views who is not afraid to write stupid things. Incidentally, love declarations, infidelities by husbands and wives, and tears shed by widows, orphans and other people have been described long ago." In a further letter to his brother he gives another list of characters that a playwright should avoid: "Retired captains with red noses, drunken press reporters, starving writers, consumptive and hard working wives, honest young men without a blot on their characters, lofty-minded young ladies, and dear old nannies." Eleven years later, in a letter to Suvorin, he adds this illuminating note on the need for originality in a playwright's characters: "An educated nobleman who wants to become a priest—this is rather old-fashioned and does not arouse curiosity. You should have taken a young scientist, or a secret Jesuit who dreams of the union of the churches, or anyone else who would have cut a much more imposing figure than a nobleman who is about to take holy orders." Discussing another character in Suvorin's play, Chekhov remarks: "The father seems to have no weakness of any sort. He does not drink, he does not smoke, he does not play cards, and he is not ill. You ought to attach some kind of quality to him and give the actor something to hang on to." And he adds this rather significant note on the importance of sex in plays: "Whether the father does or does not know about his daughter's false step is not very important. Sex, no doubt, plays a great role in the world, but not everything depends on it, not by any means; and it is not everywhere that it is of decisive importance."

A play, in Chekhov's view, must above all be compact. "The more compact and the tighter a play is," he writes to a fellow dramatist, "the brighter and more expressive it is." He warns the same dramatist against becoming a professional playwright, that is to say, a playwright to whom the mere tricks of the stage are more important than the subject matter of his plays. A playwright, he insists, must above all be a poet and an artist. He must conquer the stage and not let the stage conquer him. All the same, so keen was Chekhov's perception of the requirements of the stage that in a letter to another fellow dramatist he coined the aphorism: "You must never put a loaded rifle on the stage if no one is going to fire it."

In addition to compactness and expressiveness, Chekhov laid great stress on "plasticity of phrase". He warned his brother against preciosity of language. He objected to the dialogue of one of Suvorin's plays because the language of its characters was "like a white silk dress which is all the time reflecting the sun and on which it hurts you to look. The words 'vulgarity' and 'vulgar'," he adds, "are old-fashioned now." Writing to Gorky in January 1899, Chekhov warned him against lack of gracefulness and restraint in his first play, defining "gracefulness" in these words: "When a man spends the least possible number of movements on some definite action, then that is gracefulness."

Another principle of writing plays Chekhov stuck to all through his career as a playwright concerned the elimination of what he called "the personal element". Writing to his eldest brother in May, 1889, he declared: "Your play will be no good at all if all the characters are like you. Who cares about your life or mine or about your ideas or mine?" A further principle, which is very characteristic of Chekhov's later plays especially, is that "an author must always be humane to the tips of his fingers". But admirable as this last principle is, it has undoubtedly been responsible for a great deal of "sensitive" criticisms of Chekhov's plays which tend to obscure their more important points.

There is another piece of advice Chekhov gives to his brother which is characteristic of the external form of a Chekhov play and which might as well be noted here. Every full-length play of Chekhov's has four acts and the importance of each act in its relation to the play as a whole was defined by Chekhov as early as May 8th, 1889, in a letter to Alexander: "The first act," he wrote, "can go on as long as an hour, but the others must not last longer than thirty minutes. The climax of the play must occur in the third act, but it must not be too big a climax to kill the fourth act."

It was Chekhov's custom first to produce a rough draft of a play and then go on improving it. With *Ivanov* and *The Wood Demon* (*Uncle Vanya*) this procedure was much more drastic, the two plays in their final form undergoing vital alterations. This process of re-shaping a play Chekhov considered required much greater ability from the playwright than the initial process of writing the play. In a letter to the poet Pleshcheyev on January 15th, 1889, written soon after the completion of the final draft of *Ivanov,* he referred to this particular aspect of the playwright's craft in connexion with the "tragic laugh" that was one of the characteristics of his friend and fellow dramatist Ivan Leontyev (Shcheglov). "No," he writes, "I do not envy Jean Shcheglov. I understand now why he laughs so tragically. To write a good play for the theatre one must possess a special kind of talent (one can be an excellent novelist and at the same time write bunglingly incompetent plays); but to write a bad play and then attempt to make a good one out of it, to resort to all sorts of tricks, to delete, re-write, insert soliloquies, resurrect the dead, bury the living—to do all that one must possess a much greater talent. That is as difficult as making a silk purse out of a sow's ear. Here you will not only laugh tragically, but neigh like a horse."

One more important aspect of Chekhov's attitude to the stage still remains to be elucidated, namely his views on the playwright's place in the theatre. It was undoubtedly Chekhov's great good fortune that among the greatest admirers of his genius was Nemirovich-Danchenko, one of the founders of the Moscow Art Theatre, who prevailed on Stanislavsky almost by main force to put on *The Seagull* during the Moscow Art Theatre's first season, thus being responsible for Chekhov's close association with one of the most progressive theatres in Russia. But this association with Stanislavsky and Nemirovich-Danchenko was also one of Chekhov's greatest misfortunes inasmuch as both producers were, at the outset of their stage careers at any rate, what is commonly known as producer-autocrats who brooked no interference either from their actors or from their authors and who quite honestly held the view (all too common among producers) that they had a right to interpret a play any way they liked. Ordinarily this would have brought about an early break between Chekhov and the Moscow Art Theatre, for Chekhov would never have agreed to his elimination from the production of his plays and the complete disregard of his own interpretation of them. As early as 1887, he insisted on the playwright's right to have a deciding voice in anything that concerned the production of his plays. Writing to Nicolai Leykin, editor of the humorous weekly *Fragments* to which he had been contributing regularly during the early years of his authorship, Chekhov made it quite plain that he would never resign his position in the theatre to the producer. Leykin had written to him: "An author who habitually interferes with the production is a nuisance to the actors, his instructions being mostly silly." To which Chekhov replied: "The author is the owner of the play and not the actors. Everywhere the casting is left to the author, provided he is not absent. Besides, till now *all* my instructions were helpful and the actors did as I told them. If the author is to be completely eliminated from the production of his plays," he concluded, prophetically as it turned out, "then goodness knows what will happen. Remember how Gogol used to fly into a temper when his play was being produced! Wasn't he right?"

Holding such views, how did it happen that Chekhov let Stanislavsky and Nemirovich-Danchenko ride roughshod over his own conception of his plays? The answer to this question is simple: at the time his plays were being performed at the Moscow Art Theatre Chekhov was already a stricken man who could take no direct part in their production. He was condemned to live in the Crimea and the few rehearsals he managed to attend in Moscow were insufficient for him to correct the cardinal misunderstanding of his ideas by the two producers. (He did, however, take an active part in the rehearsals of *The Three Sisters* before the revival of the play in the autumn of 1901.) That was the reason for his frequent outbursts of anger during the rehearsals and his refusal to advise the actors how to play their parts. His stock reply to the actors, "You'll find it all in the text," was just an evasion forced on him by his complete helplessness to make his producers see the positive ideas he had taken so much pains to present in an artistic form. In face of such utter blindness on the part of his producers and their inability to raise themselves above the prevailing ideas of their time, Chekhov was powerless: he was too ill to do anything. The irony of it was that this cardinal misinterpretation of his plays seems to have agreed with the mood of that particular period in Russian history so that in spite of it the plays were (after a time) successful. There is, of course, the further fact that with so great a playwright as Chekhov the failure to grasp the ruling ideas of his plays, the inability to understand their structure, and even the plain distortion of their characters, leaves so much that is original and artistically true that the spectator has plenty left he can thoroughly enjoy. That, however, does not justify the view that Chekhov's outbursts of angry protests against the misinterpretation of his plays were merely the unaccountable tantrums of genius. Chekhov, as is plainly evident from his letters, does not belong to the type of writer who is devoid of critical ability. He was, in fact, a very profound literary critic as well as a man who possessed the invaluable capacity for self-criticism. It took him about seven years to work out his new formula of the play of indirect action, and there can be no doubt that he arrived at his new form of dramatic expression only after a careful and painstaking analysis of the technique of playwriting, including a thorough study of Greek drama,[10] a fact of some consequence to the understanding of the structure of his last four plays.

NOTES

[1] *The New Statesman,* November 14th, 1925.
[2] Ibid., May 30th, 1936.
[3] Ibid., May 16th, 1914.
[4] Ibid., February 13th, 1937.
[5] Ibid., January 27th, 1945.
[6] Ibid., October and, 1926.
[7] Ibid., February 5th, 1938.
[8] A famous Russian actor.
[9] A member of the staff of Suvorin's paper, *Novoye Vremya.*
[10] Among the large number of well-thumbed books Chekhov sent to the public library of his native town of Taganrog were the best available translations of the complete plays of the Greek dramatists.

Charles B. Timmer (essay date 1960)

SOURCE: "The Bizarre Element in Čechov's Art," in *Anton Čechov, 1860-1960: Some Essays,* edited by T. Eekman, E. J. Brill, 1960, pp. 277-92.

[*In this essay, Timmer traces Chekhov's use of the "bizarre," defined as "a statement, or a situation, which has no logical place in the context or in the sequence of events, the resulting effect being one of sudden bewilderment."*]

I

A study in literature, whether on Gogol', Dostoevskij or Čechov is bound to involve a study in anti-reason: it cannot limit itself to a study of aesthetic laws only, unless we are prepared to assume that the grotesque, the bizarre, the absurd elements in the works of these authors are unexplainable phenomena.

The grotesque, the bizarre, the absurd,—by using these words I realize that I am bringing to the foreground certain aspects of Čechov's art, which to my knowledge did not thus far have the attention they undoubtedly deserve. It is certainly not my ambition to exhaust the subject in these notes; my purpose is merely to outline it and to make an attempt to trace the difference between the technique of the bizarre in Čechov's last works and his use of the bizarre element in his early stories; for example, between a little scene like this in **The Cherry Orchard** (1903-04):

VARJA: The estate will be up for sale in August.

ANJA: Oh dear!

LOPACHIN: (*puts his head through the door and bleats*) M-e-e-e . . . (*Disappears*)[1]

and 'bizarre' stories like **"On Christmas Eve"** (1883), **"At Sea"** (1883), **"Oysters"** (1884), **"The Mistress"** (1882), **"In the Home for Incurables and the Aged"** (1884) and many others from Čechov's early period, stories that are bizarre either in style or theme, or both. When we consider Čechov's literary output as a whole, we cannot fail to notice one remarkable fact, namely, that the bizarre element is abundantly represented in the early, the 'Čechonte' stories, that it gradually disappears in his later and riper work, but reappears, more profusely than ever, in his plays.

But what really is the meaning of the bizarre in art and what is its function? When do we call a certain phenomenon, a situation, a statement *bizarre*?

The word defies precise definition. However, it is possible to mention one inherent quality:—its irrelevancy, and one typical effect:—its capability of producing bewilderment. In this it differs from the grotesque, which really is nothing but comical exaggeration, showing us the ludicrous side of 'extreme situations'; it likewise differs from the absurd, which lies already wholly in the realm of the irrational. The *bizarre* is not necessarily absurd: it is, as it were, a statement, or a situation, which has no logical place in the context or in the sequence of events, the resulting effect being one of sudden bewilderment; the bizarre brings about a kind of mental 'airpocket': one gasps for breath, until the tension is relieved by laughter. The *absurd* is contrary to reason and does not necessarily contain this element of playful, whimsical strangeness, which is so characteristic for Čechov in the youthful wantonness of his art, a strangeness, which comes so strikingly to light again in many characters and situations in his plays. It is difficult, if not impossible to draw a distinct line between such conceptions as 'the absurd', 'the bizarre', 'the grotesque'; they often overlap and flow together. And besides, in all these matters the factor of personal appreciation by the reader or spectator and therefore of subjective interpretation influences the definition. A few examples by way of illustration, taken from Čechov's Notebooks—this rich fund of grotesque, bizarre and absurd fancies and observations, may throw some

Act III of a 1905 Moscow Art Theater production of The Seagull. *Stanislavsky as Trigorin, Maria Petrovna Lilina as Masha, and Marya Liudomirovna Roksanova as Nina.*

more light on the matter. Thus the following situation might be called simply 'grotesque': "A shy young man came on a visit for the night; suddenly a deaf old woman of eighty came into his room, carrying a clyster-pipe and administered a clyster to him; he thought that this must be the usual thing and so did not protest; in the morning it turned out that the old woman had made a mistake."[2] Here my contention that the characteristic quality of the grotesque lies in the exaggeration, in the hyperbolism of a *possible* situation, is clearly demonstrated by the English translation of this passage,[3] in which, possibly for reasons of modesty, the clyster-pipe is replaced by a cupping glass and the victim is bled. Suppose another translator would go one step further and change the syringe for a cup of tea—then the grotesque element would have disappeared altogether. The bizarre element can be found in a statement like this: "When I become rich, I shall have a harem in which I shall keep fat naked women, with their buttocks painted green." This is a good example of that particular kind of 'mental leap', so typical of the bizarre, with the clear-cut caesura in the logical sequence after the third section of this statement. Finally, the absurd is demonstrated in a note of the following kind: "N., a singer; speaks to nobody, his throat muffed up—he takes care of his voice, but no one has ever heard him sing." Which, in my opinion, is a good exampe of irrational behaviour.

In the beginning of his career as a writer the bizarre element in Čechov's work comes very close to the grotesque; wherever it appears in his later prose-writings and in his plays, it has more in common with the absurd. This is important and fully in harmony with the well-known fact that the laughter in Čechov's stories gradually dies down. In his early period it seems hardly likely that Čechov used the bizarre deliberately as a consciously worked out technique: it rather appears that bizarre thoughts, statements, situations found their way in his work quite naturally, as the fruit of unbridled inspiration; they arose understandably from a youthful *brio,* playfulness and boldness in the author himself; they are, if I may quote Dylan Thomas, "A portrait of the artist as a young dog". More often than not the stories, in which the bizarre element is very evident, can be found in that group of narratives, which Čechov himself did not include in his collected works and which form a part of his literary inheritance. The genuinely grotesque-bizarre stories are published under the penname 'Čechonte', a pseudonym rather bizarre in itself, at least for Russian ears.

Quite frequently the stories, containing bizarre elements, are written in the first person singular or plural, e.g. **"The Crooked Mirror", "At Sea", "The Confession", "The Only Remedy", "At a Spiritualist Seance", "The**

Ninny", "A Charitable Publican", "The Guardian", "From the Reminiscences of an Idealist", "The Dream", etc. They are often provided with a sub-title in the way of "A Christmas Story", or "A Psychological Etude", or "Lament of a Ruined Man". In all these cases the bizarre character of the story is evoked by a peculiar blend of mystification, exaggeration and the deadly serious tone of the story-teller. A story like **"At Sea"** for instance, bearing the sub-title "A Sailor's Story", deals with anything but life at sea; this tale gives a perfect demonstration of the method of disguise and it leaves a peculiar impression of bewilderment and oppression with the reader, who at the same time feels inclined to laugh the whole thing off. The bizarre in stories of this kind, as also in **"On Christmas Eve"**, an early story, written in a pseudo-romantic vein, and in quite a few others is realized by way of a subtle mockery of the 'terrible'; the element of horror is played with, rather flippantly sometimes, with the effect that horror becomes funny. Most of these stories have a definite point, with a surprising denouement, which does not however solve a problem or a mystery, but intensifies the comical effect of the narrative. Upon finishing his play *Ivanov,* Čechov wrote in a letter to his brother Aleksandr: "This is the first play I wrote, ergo—I was bound to make mistakes. The subject is complicated and not stupid. Every act I end just like my stories: throughout the whole act everything goes on peacefully and smoothly, but towards the end I give the spectator a punch on the nose."[4] It is in this "punch on the nose", in this sudden uncovering of "green-painted buttocks", that the typical bizarre element in Čechov's early work is revealed and it is not without reason that his second collection of stories, which Čechov published in 1886, bore the title *Motley Stories.* Nor is it fortuitous that Čechov did not include in this collection any work of his hand that had appeared under his own name in the literary magazine *New Times,* work that he wanted to save for 'a more important publication'. Seen against the background of Čechov's later, much more complicated and serious output, we can understand that the author at the height of his creative powers felt rather reluctant to include certain of his bizarre 'trifles' (as he calls them) in his collected works, although Čechov's harsh judgment seems to us unwarranted: in their class these stories are priceless.

As I pointed out, the bizarre gradually disappears in Čechov's later work, or rather, it loses its grotesque aspect and approaches more and more that particular attitude towards things, which we call the absurd. Here it must be stated at once, however, that the absurd as such in Čechov's art is always treated merely incidentally, never programmatically, dogmatically or from the platform of a certain philosophy. For Čechov life as such (existence) is neither absurd nor intelligible. The absurd elements in his stories should therefore not be confused with the absurd as idea. The absurd is the confrontation with the irrational; it is, what in relation to human judgment is considered as unreasonable. If we think of a scientist, whose knowledge in a certain field of science is unique and of immeasurable value to mankind, who suddenly dies in a car-accident, we may speak of an absurd occurrence, the absurd in this case consisting in the fact that such a tremendous wealth of knowledge and experience can be destroyed within a fraction of a second. Death in its finality is bizarre in so far as it causes bewilderment, it is absurd in so far as we consider it unreasonable. Čechov had a wonderful feeling for the whole scale of subtle shades between the bizarre and the absurd in life and death. The long standing controversy, whether Čechov was an optimist or a pessimist, with ardent partisans on both sides, loses its meaning, when we realize that Čechov, like every sensitive artist, was torn between two contrary insights: that the world, or life as such, is unreasonable and at the same time, that man cannot leave off trying to find a reasonable explanation for this world, or, in the words of Albert Camus, this philosopher of the absurd (whose own death can stand as an example of absurdity): "Ce monde en lui-même n'est pas raisonnable . . . Mais ce qui est absurde, c'est la confrontation de cet irrationnel et de ce désir éperdu de clarté dont l'appel résonne au plus profond de l'homme."[5] Čechov's dithyrambic dreams of a better life in the future, expressed in his last plays and in some of his stories, are no proof of his "optimism", but only of his desperate desire to find a solution to the problem of the antagonism, existing between absurd reality and rational ideality, his desire to bring about a peace between life as it is lived:—an apparently bizarre and senseless undertaking,—and life as it could be projected in the mind:—beauty, justice and harmony. On the other hand, if Čechov were convinced that such a peace would a priori be impossible, that the search for a reasonable explanation of the world is an enterprise, foredoomed to failure, then we might be justified in calling him a pessimist; but he never made such a statement, on the contrary: somewhere, at some time in the future the solution will be found, he says. This is not optimism, but the firm conviction that life itself generates hope. Converted to secular values, we may compare Čechov's faith with the 'Credo quia absurdum' of Tertullian, philosophically speaking the most optimistic statement ever made, if we put the stress on the 'credo', but at the same time the most pessimistic one, if we realize that we can never overcome the absurd, that we, as long as there is life, shall never be able to say: we believe in it, because it is reasonable. In other words: that faith can never be replaced by knowledge, Čechov's dream of happiness 'after two hundred years' is nothing else than this *désir éperdu de clarté,* of which Camus speaks. In fact, hope and expectation are blended so masterfully in Čechov's art with hopelessness and despair, the technique of evoking bizarre effects by letting hope clash on despondency is handled so skilfully, that we can say without hesitation that here we find the clue to that unique fascination, which emanates from his work and the spell it exercises on the reader. A perfect demonstration of this we find in stories like **"Dreams"** (1886), or **"Happiness"** (1887), in **"Peasants"** (1897), **"In the Ravine"** (1900) and many others. In the story **"Happiness"** an old shepherd is telling about the treasures, hidden, according to legend, somewhere in the vast Russian steppe. A young shepherd listens attentively to the old man's stories. "But, if you find the treasure, what are you going to do with it?", he asks in the end. The old man does not know; all through his long life he has dreamed of finding one of these legendary treasures, but the thought, what to do with it, has never occurred to him: that was not important. The young man also starts to wonder at the curious fact that only old men and women were so interested in these treasures, only the old kept constantly talking about them. At last the young shepherd falls silent and thinks about all the things he has heard in the course of the summer night. "He was not interested so much in happiness in itself, which he did not need, and which he could not comprehend, as in the fantastic, the fairytale side of human happiness . . .", concludes Čechov.

One of Čechov's notions of the bizarre,—and probably one of the most important ones,—is that in an apparently hopeless life there is still hope, that, as I said before, life itself generates hope. That, if there is seemingly no way out,—there *is* nevertheless a way out: by being interested, fully, humanly interested in "the fantastic, fairytale side" of every situation. To the question of what life *means,* Čechov had no other answer than: it is what it is, as in *Three Sisters,* when Maša asks: "Isn't there some meaning?" and Tuzenbach answers: "Meaning? . . Look out there, it's snowing. What's the meaning of that?"[6] In the same play the final conclusion of Andrej, when Čebutykin asks him: "What about your wife?" is: "My wife is my wife".[7] But even if every life is condemned to end in failure, even if it has many terrible aspects, it still is hopeful, because it is life, because it can be seen and felt and tasted and experienced, because it can be told. In the story **"Peasants"** this hope, this life, this Čechovian conception of indestructible continuation is impersonated in the little girl Saša, who as an innocent witness of poverty and misery wanders through the whole story with eyes to see and to bear witness. The little girl is not a judge, she just observes and sees. The fact that in life there are eyes to see the injustice, the absurdity, is enough: this is all the hope there is. Well, and this is precisely the case with Čechov himself: *he just sees.* And to see, really to see, with inquisitive, child-like eyes, means to discover the hidden relationships in life, to reveal its fairytale side. In many of Čechov's stories it is the child, or the grown-up with the childlike mind that sees in this manner: it is the child and the artist, who possess this talent for discovering. And again, it is children and artists who have the genuine taste for the bizarre, the feeling for the absurd; it is they also, who can recreate it, because playfulness is an intrinsic part of their being, they represent the *homo ludens* with his taste for freedom. In Čechov's first long story **"The Steppe"** (1888) it is through the eyes of the little boy Egoruška that the steppe and life in it are recreated. In the story **"In Exile"** (1892) it is the poor, illiterate Tartar with the mind of a child, who understands and grasps the 'hidden relationships' and stammers the truth in his broken Russian: "The gentleman is a good soul, very good, and you are a beast, you are bad! The gentleman is alive and you are dead . . . God made man that he should be alive, that he should have happiness, sorrow, grief, and you want nothing, so you are not alive, but a stone! A stone wants nothing and so do you . . .".[8]

When comparing the bizarre in Čechov's work with the bizarre in Dostoevskij, we find some striking differences in their approach, both in technique and its application. In the great novels of Dostoevskij the bizarre element is mainly demonstrated in some of the secondary characters and they are always slices of enlarged humanity. Mentally, intellectually, the reader believes in a captain Lebjadkin (*Evil Spirits*), in a Lebedev (*The Idiot*) and queer characters like these, although they possess a reality, built up out of isolated psychological components and the bizarre in them lies in their psychological hyperbolism. Lebedev in *The Idiot* is a vulgar scoundrel and a drunk, but at the same time a man, who prays at night for the salvation of the unfortunate comtesse Du Barry; he is a specialist in the exegesis of the Apocalypse, and in some casual, enigmatic remarks he gives a clue to the main theme of the whole novel. In the hundreds of characters in Čechov's stories not one is in this sense 'enlarged' and hyperbolic; they always stay human in every respect; the bizarre with them,—even with the queerest characters we meet in his plays,—does not appear so much in what they are, as well in what they do. Looking for the bizarre in Čechov's work, we do not find it in the characters, but in their situation, in their mutual relationships. The reason for this may be found in the fact that Čechov's characters nearly all are 'whole', while Dostoevskij's characters are practically all 'split personalities', or combined doubles; they are dramas, tragedies *in themselves,* while Čechov's people through their interrelationship create tragedies and dramas *amongst themselves.* Čechov's characters long for things they do not possess (Moscow, talent, love, gooseberries), or for what they are not and cannot be (famous, active, energetic) and the author knows how to uncover the bizarre element in such hopeless longing: in this respect the epithet of "a cruel talent" could be given to Čechov also! But Dostoevskij's heroes are both mean and noble, both evil and good, both vulgar and highminded; alternatively the one or the other quality breaks out and suppresses the opposite impulse. Therefore the bizarre with Dostoevskij is one of inner conflict and of being; with Čechov of outer conflict and of situation. In 1886 Čechov wrote in a letter to his brother Aleksandr: "Heaven forbid that we indulge in the use of commonplaces! The best would be to avoid in your stories the description of the mental state of your heroes altogether. You must try to develop this state out of the actions of your heroes."[9] This is exactly the opposite of Dostoevskij's method, where the action is rather a result, the outcome of the mental state of the hero, of what I call his 'inner conflict'. Nikolaj Čikildeev in the story **"Peasants"** had to give up his job as a waiter in a Moscow hotel because of ill health and returned with wife and child to his native village, where he slowly withers away. In the famous description of a night at the peasant-cottage Čechov relates, how "Nikolaj, who had not slept all night, got down from the stove. He took his dress-coat out of a green chest, put it on, and going to the window, stroked the sleeves, fingered the coat-tails—and smiled. Then he carefully removed the coat, put it away in the chest, and lay down again."[10] There is no question in Nikolaj's bizarre behaviour in the middle of the night of a description of inner conflict: Nikolaj is quite an ordinary man, but he is placed in an extraordinary situation, a man beyond hope and help, who attires himself at night with the only remaining attributes of his former happiness and dignity. In the given situation the bizarre lies in the fact that the ex-waiter, placed in the position of a parasite on the village-life, caresses as a symbol of liberty and human dignity an object, a waiter's dress-coat, which in fact should stand as a symbol for human servitude and humiliation.[11] It will be clear, from an example like this, that the technique of the bizarre, as used by Čechov in this passage, is quite a far cry from the overt and wanton caprices in his 'Čechonte'-period; now the bizarre comes to us as a technique, subtly handled by a masterhand and only recognizable as bizarre through the intellectual cooperation of the reader.

II

In the confrontation with the bizarre man is conscious of his existence as an enigma. Although Čechov, being through education a man of science himself, believed in the civilizing and beneficent powers of knowledge and enlightenment, his faith was not a blind faith in nineteenth century positivism and progress. Nobody saw clearer than Čechov the danger of the so-called 'intellectualism', nobody realized better the limits of pure rationalist thinking. Stories like e.g. **"A Dreary Story"** (1889), **"Ward No. 6"** (1892), or **"The Black Monk"** (1894) provide ample substance for this contention. Čechov himself was a highly intelligent man, a keen observer, capable of putting two and two together in all the phenomena of life. But here he added one element to his intelligence—and in this we recognize his genius,—namely, his readiness to accept, to admit and to tolerate the statement that two and two can be five, at least to grant the possibility of such a statement, were it only as a form of protest. Protest against what? My answer would be: a protest against the *law*.

Amongst the few types of wholly negative characters in the work of Čechov, a prominent place is given to the "man in a shell", of whom it is said that "the only things that were clear to him were Government regulations and newspaper notices in which something was forbidden."[12] This man-in-a-shell type of the intelligentsia, this Belikov, has a close relative in a slightly different hero, one somewhat more sociable and congenial, but likewise inclined to terrorize his neighbourhood: the type of the Von Koren in the story **"The Duel"** (1891), or his pendant L'vov in the play *Ivanov* (1887-89). They are the personifications of what we may call the 'guardians of duty', 'the pillars of law and order',—men, who are honest, correct, intelligent, but absolutely devoid of imagination, men with no feeling, no taste and no understanding at all for the *bizarre*. Both the story **"The Duel"** and the play *Ivanov* are built up around three heroes: in **"The Duel"** this trio is formed by Laevskij, Von Koren, and Samojlenko. In the play *Ivanov* we meet the same trio in the persons of Ivanov, L'vov and Lebedev. The positions of these three types are clear: Laevskij/Ivanov is the man fighting with, and eventually becoming the victim of the

bizarre; Von Koren/L'vov is the man who does not admit the existence of the bizarre, while Šamojlenko/Lebedev accepts the bizarre as an intrinsic part of life. In the last act of *Ivanov,* when Ivanov, a prey to despair and harassed by self-accusations, informs his bride Saša that he cannot marry her, when L'vov walks around as a Nemesis, firmly decided to unmask Ivanov once and for all, then the 'fool' Lebedev, this apparent good-for-nothing, utters some words of plain common sense. In a conversation with his future son-in-law and friend Ivanov it is he, who exclaims: "Look at things simply, as everybody else does! In this world everything is simple. The ceiling is white, the boots are black, sugar is sweet. You love Saša, she loves you. If you love her—stay with her, if you don't love her—go, we won't bear you any malice. It's really as simple as that!"[13]

With Čechov, just as with Shakespeare, we must above all things be attentive to what the 'fool' has to say. The Lebedev-element, this third aspect of human intelligence, is innocence, presented—as is so often the case—in the disguise of foolishness. It is the voice of life itself as it is lived, when we are told: "In this world everything is simple!", an observation which must sound as the height of absurdity in the ears of pathetic Ivanovs, caught in a mess of guilt-complexes, or of the stern L'vovs who want to reduce life to a complicated system of regulations. But what we hear in Lebedev and Samojlenko, apart from a certain amount of *naïveté,* is the voice of confidence, this utter and stable confidence that cannot be shaken by all the horrors in the world. It is Čechov's confidence in the regenerating powers of life. It is the voice of unassailable innocence in human intellect, of its inviolable virginity. It is the voice that will be heard "two hundred years from now . . ." The Lebedevs and Samojlenko's together with the little girl in **"Peasants"**, with Lipa in **"In the Ravine"**, with Gusev in the story of that name, with father Anastasij in **"The Letter"**, with the Tartar in **"In Exile"**,—these are the ones, of whom I said that they are the children and artists, who see and accept the bizarre, who are free and possess the talent for discovering the hidden relationships.

However, it is not Čechov's philosophy or outlook on life, that I am concerned with here. The problem of the grotesque-bizarre-absurd in his art is not a philosophical problem, but one of style and technique. I already pointed out that in the 'Čechonte'-stories the bizarre element appears to be used as a series of outbursts of youthful spontaneity rather than a consciously applied literary technique. It was found that this element gradually disappears in his stories of a later date; whenever we find traces of it, it is used with much restraint and *consordino,* the technique is usually applied in the form of a quick, unexpected shifting of various moods. We only need to compare a story like **"At Christmas Time"** (1900) with one of the 'Čechonte'-stories to see the difference in function of the bizarre. At first glance this element seems to be present in this story as well with the same nonchalant brio as for instance in **"For Stealing Apples"** (1880), but soon it becomes clear that it is used in quite a different technique; while in the early story the bizarre was nothing but ornament, here it is the canvas, on which the story is embroidered.

But it is especially in the plays, and most of all in *Uncle Vanja, Three Sisters* and *The Cherry Orchard,* that we find the technique of the bizarre applied consciously and deliberately with an eye on the effect it will produce. The functions of the bizarre as consciously applied technique are manifold. In the first place there is the function of *retardation* of the action. A good example can be found in the last act of *Uncle Vanja.* In the stage-directions at the beginning of this act it says: *On the wall a map of Africa, obviously serving no useful purpose here.*[14] The 'purpose' of this map, indeed a rather bizarre object in the study of an estate somewhere in the Russian province, becomes clear when Astrov takes his final leave. Astrov is firmly resolved to take his departure and to stay away for a long time to come, but he does not want to go at all. There really is nothing more to be said, but everybody feels the necessity of some remark being made, never mind what, only so that the final moment may be put off. It is then that Astrov walks up to the map of Africa and says: "I suppose down there in Africa the heat must be terrific now!" On this bizarre and quite irrelevant remark of the doctor in the prevailing situation Vanja reacts laconically with the words: "Yes, very likely."[15]

Apart from retardation the above example reveals another function of the bizarre and a very important one too, namely, to give a suggestion of indifference. It is well known, what importance Čechov attached to 'coldness', 'non-attachment' in the creative process. The impact of emotions, of distress, delight, of grief and joy is felt much stronger, when they are suggested and not described. If, in the given situation, Astrov would have said: "How awful to have to leave your people; I don't want to go, but have to, you know!" or something of the kind, the impression on the spectator would be nil, because that would be exactly the thing he had expected. Instead, Astrov says: "I suppose down there in Africa the heat must be terrific now!" and this element of restraint, applied in a scene that is charged with emotions, greatly intensifies the impression on the spectator. The element of the bizarre as a technique to retard the action and restrain the emotions is used frequently by Čechov in his plays.

A third function of the bizarre is the communication of a hidden meaning. This end is often attained by way of an understatement. It may happen that one of the characters makes an apparently nonsensical remark, which stupefies the reader or spectator. In *Three Sisters* the old and doting doctor Čebutykin has the habit of reading aloud from some old newspaper he always carries around with him. In act II, in the midst of a lively conversation on the meaning of happiness, he suddenly, reading from his newspaper, remarks: "Balzac was married at Berdičev".[16] This in the given context seemingly quite senseless remark is repeated twice, showing that the author did not regard it as just a casual interjection by a drunk, but that these words were meant to communicate some hidden message, an allusion to something, which, however, is nowhere explained in the further development of the conversation. But what possible meaning could be concealed in the bizarre observation of an old, dilapidated country-physician, in a play, the action of which takes place around 1900, while the words "Balzac was married at Berdičev", read from a newspaper, point to an event that surely happened before Balzac's death in 1850? The theme of the play is the expectation of happiness: Veršinin projects the 'coming happy life' in the future; the sisters believe that they will find happiness and fulfilment as soon as they will be in Moscow. When we remember that Berdičev is an ugly little bordertown in Western Russia, the remark of Čebutykin becomes meaningful, without losing its bizarre character: it means to say that, if Balzac could find his happiness in such a doghole as Berdičev, it is quite unnecessary to go to Moscow to look for happiness, because it can be found anywhere, and further: why project your dreams of happiness in the future, when we only need to open some old newspaper in order to find ample proof of happiness and fulfilment in the past? The function of the bizarre in this instance is first to stupefy and to shock, to disrupt the logical sequence of thoughts by some eccentric observation, secondly to provide this observation with an undercurrent of deeper meaning. Another example of this technique we find in the long story **"The Duel"** (the scene, when doctor Samojlenko and Von Koren carry on an animated conversation about the 'superfluous man' Laevskij). In the course of the conversation both get more and more excited. There is a third person in the room, a young deacon, a rather silly man who chuckles and giggles all the time, a man in whom we recognize once more one of these typical Čechovian fools, who are not directly involved in the conflict, but who at unexpected moments come forward with their comments and who, in this respect, have a rather similar function to that of the 'chorus' in the Greek tragedy. When the conversation between Samojlenko and Von Koren reaches its climax and both are about ready to cut each other's throat, this little, insignificant deacon suddenly makes the casual observation: "Our Eminence does not travel by coach through his diocese, he always goes on horseback . . ." and then he compares the bishop in his humility and simplicity with a Biblical character. The interruption had nothing whatsoever to do with the conversation, there was no talk at all about bishops, coaches or horses and to all appearance the deacon's words are out of place and sheer nonsense. Yet it brings the conversation to a sudden stop, the heat of the quarrel has abated and the observation carried a hidden meaning as well: the hint to both hotheaded antagonists to follow the bishop's example and to be more humble.

In **"Gooseberries"** (1898) Čechov makes the following observation: "What is terrible in life goes on somewhere behind the scenes . . .".[17] The bizarre is indeed quite frequently an eruption of the terrible on the smooth surface of common everyday life. Such an eruption takes place in the story **"The Murder"** (1895), in which the bizarre is an intrinsic part of the whole intrigue and a man is murdered, because during Lent he wanted to help himself at dinner to some oil; the instrument he is killed with is the oil-bottle.

Sometimes Čechov does not leave the bizarre unexplained, but reveals the meaning of it in an exposé, for instance, in **"The Lady with the Pet Dog"** (1899), in the following fragment: "One evening, coming out of the physicians' club with an official with whom he (the hero) had been playing cards, he could not resist saying: 'If you only knew what a fascinating woman I became acquainted with at Jalta.'" The official has no better reply to this beginning of a lover's confidential confession than the sordid and bizarre words: "Dmitrij Dmitri! . . . You were right this evening: the sturgeon was a bit high!"[18] Whereupon Čechov enters into a long explanation of why the hero was so infuriated by the vulgarity of the official's words.

A further function of the bizarre,—and this mainly in the plays again,—is to emphasize the salient features of certain characters, in other words, to show them in their absurdity. One of the most bizarre characters in Čechov's plays is Solenyj in **Three Sisters,** a sinister man, belonging to the family of the 'men-in-a-shell', in so far as meanness and limitations are not only the result of social maladjustment, but also caused by his private inhibitions. He has a very important function in the drama and is, as his name indicates, the salt in the play. His condition of being a potential murderer Solenyj can only cover up by spraying his hands frequently with perfume. Everything he says or does is absurd.

In order to give a note of the bizarre to his characters Čechov often makes use of the attribute of gluttony. Quite a few of his early comical stories are based on this human weakness. But this element also appears in his later stories and in the plays. The official in **"The Lady with the Pet Dog"** could only think of sturgeon when his partner wanted to talk about his beloved; Piščik, another bizarre character in **The Cherry Orchard** pours all the pills from a pill-box, brought by the valet to madame Ranevskaja, into his hand and eats them . . . We also hear that during Easter week he had consumed a gallon and a half of cucumbers.[19] Solenyj, in **Three Sisters,** referring to Bobik, Nataša's baby, remarks: "If that child were mine, I'd fry him in a frying pan and eat him,"[20] in which words he certainly betrays his radicalism. A little later it appears that he has eaten all the chocolates from a box of sweets on the table. Gaev, in **The Cherry Orchard,** frequently takes a box of caramels out of his pocket and sucks one.

Bizarre attributes are often used in drawing a character. Thus one notices Gaev's passion for billiards in **The Cherry Orchard** and his use of technical terms of the game, mostly in situations when he is confused and bewildered. Bizarre attributes, used in drawing Maša's character in **The Sea-gull,** are the black dress she wears and her opening-line in the play: "I am in mourning for my life";[21] in the case of Sorin, in the same play, it is his habit to use stock-expressions like: "and all that", "and all the rest of it", "and so on, and so forth",[22] which are all that is left of *l'homme qui a voulu,* the man, who in his youth had dreamt of becoming a literary man—and didn't . . . The pathos of an utterly lonely woman, the

governess Šarlotta Ivanovna in **The Cherry Orchard,** is accentuated by her bizarre talent to amuse the company with card tricks; equally bizarre is the way she makes her appearance in the first act with a little dog on a line and introduces herself with the words: "My dog eats nuts too".[23]

All this shows that in Čechov's plays the element of the bizarre both helps to build up a character and aids in preparing the surprise moment in the development of the action. Once they are firmly established as "queer characters", their quasi irrelevant observations cause a break in the dialogue. And here we touch upon one of the principal aspects of the bizarre, lying in the fact that, while all these observations and odd demeanours should normally bring about a certain bewilderment or at least some response in the others, this is not the case: more often than not there is no reaction at all, as if the others did not exist, as if the words were spoken in a void, as if all those persons were living in a vacuum, in other words: the bizarre is accepted, or rather tolerated, but not reacted upon. When in **The Cherry Orchard** the servantgirl Dunjaša, anxious to pour out her heart to her young mistress, says to Anja: "Epichodov, the clerk, made me a proposal just after Easter",[24] the answer is: "I've lost all my hairpins." When in the second act of this play Šarlotta Ivanovna all of a sudden starts to complain about her fate and says: "Always alone, alone, nobody belonging to me . . . and who I am, and why I'm on earth, I don't know",[25] there is no response from the others. When in the third act of **Three Sisters** Čebutykin has broken the clock and Irina says: "That was mother's clock", the old doctor declares in drunkenness: "Perhaps . . . Well, if it was hers, it was . . ."—and then continues: "What are you staring at? Nataša has got a little affair on with Protopopov, and you don't see it . . . You sit here and see nothing, while Nataša has a little affair on with Protopopov . . ."[26] The only reaction to this grave accusation comes from Veršinin, who says: "Yes" and then immediately resumes his conversation about his own affairs. Time and again we hear in Čechov's stories and plays the desperate complaint: "To whom shall I tell my grief?", which is used as motto in the story **"Misery"** (1886),—but there is no response and by this frequently used technique Čechov succeeds in producing that oppressive atmosphere of human loneliness which is so typical for his art; the inability of people to understand each other, their complete lack of interest and attention is the core of all tragedy. Human coldness, indifference and careless cruelty—these form the main subject and the leading theme of many of Čechov's stories and plays.

Finally, in some of the plays, especially in **Three Sisters,** echov succeeds in attaining a bizarre effect by frequently putting quotations from other writers in the mouth of his characters. In many cases these quotations have a definite function in the play, both to reveal a character and to create a certain "mood", to evoke an atmosphere. Two of the best known of these functional quotations in **Three Sisters** are: "A green oak grows by a curving shore, and round that oak hangs a golden chain . . .",[27] which are the opening-lines of Puškin's poem "Ruslan and Ljudmila", and: "He had no time to say 'Oh, oh!', before that bear had struck him low . . .",[28] two lines from Krylov's fable "The Peasant and the Farmhand", the first quotation being used by Maša, the second one by Solenyj, and not just once, but several times on appropriate occasions, thus becoming something like motives, played by solo-instruments in a symphonic work. Apart from literary quotations Čechov uses quotations, taken from actual life. An example of a quotation from life can be found in a letter by Ol'ga Knipper to Anton Pavlovič, written in 1900, in reply to a complaint of the author that he was becoming bald. In this letter Ol'ga Knipper writes: "I shall give you a fine recipe for falling hair. Take half a bottle of methylated spirit and dissolve in it two ounces of naphtaline, then rub the skin with this lotion . . .". Ol'ga Knipper took her recipe so seriously that she hastened to write to Čechov a few days later that she had made a mistake in it: it should not be two ounces of naphtaline, but only half an ounce. But Čechov had already used the original passage in *Three Sisters,* first act, where he lets the *'fool'* Čebutykin read the recipe from his newspaper.[29] The motive for the well-known Tra-ta-ta conversation,—possibly the most mysterious and original 'love-talk' in literature,—between Maša and Veršinin at the end of the third act of *Three Sisters* is likewise taken from real life and based on an actual experience Čechov had in a restaurant. These examples,—and the notes in Čechov's notebooks could easily provide further ample material,—show, how keen an eye Čechov had for the bizarre, how much value he attached to such phenomena and how anxious he was to apply this material in his art. I wonder, whether it is only a matter of coincidence that Čechov's biographers managed to dig up such a remarkable variety of bizarre incidents in the life of the author. If we may believe one of his biographers, N. Telešov, the bizarre did not even leave Čechov on his deathbed: in the evening of July 15th 1904 in Badenweiler the doctor had ordered the sick man to drink a glass of champagne. Anton Pavlovič took the glass, remarked to his wife: "I have not tasted champagne in a long time", drank the glass to the bottom, lay down on his left side and died. "The oppressive silence of the night,—Telešov tells us,—was only disturbed by a large night-moth that had flown in through the open window . . . After the doctor had gone, in the complete silence and stuffiness of the summer night, suddenly, with a terrific blow, the cork shot out of the half finished champagne bottle . . .".[30]

Notes

[1] Anton Chehov, *Three Plays,* transl. by Elisaveta Fen, London 1953, p. 30.
[2] *The Personal Papers of Anton Chekhov,* New York 1948, p. 104. The translation of the Notebook is by S. S. Koteliansky and Leonard Woolf and quoted here with some corrections.
[3] The passage referred to reads in the English translation: "Suddenly a deaf old woman came into the room, carrying a cupping-glass, and bled him". Cf. A. P. Čechov, *PSSP* XII 284: "Vdrug vošla starucha let 80, gluchaja, s klistirnoj kružkoj i postavila emu klistir."
[4] *PSSP* XIII 372.
[5] Albert Camus, *Le mythe de Sisyphe,* Paris 1942, p. 37.
[6] Anton Chehov, *Three Plays,* transl. by Elisaveta Fen, London 1953, p. 126.
[7] Id. p. 162.

[8] *The Stories of Anton Tchekov,* ed. by Robert N. Linscott, N.Y. 1932, p. 180.
[9] *PSS* XIII 215.
[10] *The Portable Chekhov,* ed. by Avrahm Yarmolinsky, N.Y. 1947, p. 339.
[11] Cf. A. Derman, *O masterstve Čechova,* Moskva 1959, p. 42.
[12] *The Portable Chekhov,* ed. by Avrahm Yarmolinsky, N.Y. 1947, p. 356.
[13] Anton Chehov, *Three Plays,* transl. by Elisaveta Fen, London 1953, p. 251.
[14] Anton Chehov, *The Seagull and Other Plays,* transl. by Elisaveta Fen, London 1954, p. 140.
[15] Id., p. 150.
[16] *The Plays of Anton Tchekov,* transl. by Constance Garnett, N.Y. n.d. p. 146.
[17] *The Portable Chekhov,* ed. by Avrahm Yarmolinsky, N.Y. 1947, p. 381.
[18] Id., p. 424.
[19] *The Plays of Anton Tchekov,* transl. by Constance Garnett, N.Y. n.d. p. 72.
[20] Id., p. 147.
[21] Id., p. 3.
[22] Id., p. 46.
[23] Id., p. 64.
[24] Ibidem.
[25] Id., p. 80.
[26] Id., p. 161.
[27] Anton Chehov, *Three Plays,* transl. by Elisaveta Fen, London 1953, p. 98.
[28] Id., p. 99.
[29] Id., p. 96. Cf. *Teatr, ežemesjačnyj žurnal dramaturgii i teatra,* Moskva 1960, I: A. Vladimirskaja, *Zametki na poljach.*
[30] N. Telešov, *Zapiski pisatelja,* Moskva 1950, pp. 86-87.

Maurice Valency   (essay date 1966)

SOURCE: "The Sound of the Breaking String," in *The Breaking String: The Plays of Anton Chekhov,* Schocken Books, 1983, pp. 289-301.

[*In the following excerpt from a work that was first published in 1966, Valency places Chekhov in the context of the social and cultural upheavals of his time.*]

Chekhov's drama, like Ibsen's, represents a world in transition. In Ibsen's Norway, wherever that might be, the impact of modern thought in the latter half of the nineteenth century brought about a relatively peaceful revolution. In Russia the idea of the state was formulated along particularly rigid lines, and the transition from the old to the new was accompanied by impressive rites of passage. In his *Autobiography,* Gorky speaks with something like awe of an old policeman's description of the invisible thread that issued from the heart of the Tsar and wound through his ministers down to the least of his soldiers in a web that encompassed the nation.[1] To many, life under these conditions seemed intolerable; but the thought of breaking the tie caused much uneasiness.

One of the constant complaints of the time centered on the breakdown of communication between fathers and sons, and the abyss that divided the older generation from the younger. This is, no doubt, a universal complaint in all periods, but the social and economic situation of Russia in the latter half of the nineteenth century made the break particularly sharp and deep. The golden

The interior of the Moscow Art Theater.

string that connected man with his father on earth and his father in heaven, the age-old bond that tied the present to the past, was not to be broken lightly. When at last it snapped, the result, we have discovered, was both world-shaking and soul-shaking.

It was on the threshold of this cataclysm that Chekhov set his stage. He was primarily an ironist, and his plays were, on the whole, comedically conceived. But Chekhov was taking the pulse of a dying world. It died well, with courage and gayety; nevertheless, the description of its agony could not be altogether funny. His plays are full of laughter, but in each we hear the sound of the breaking string; and from the contrast between what seems, from one viewpoint, comic, but tragic from another, Chekhov developed a form of drama, a dramatic polyphony, which is unparalleled in the history of the theatre.

The technique of suggestion and implication through which this result was achieved had been fully worked out in his stories before Chekhov attempted to employ it on the stage. The short story called **"The Wife,"** for example, concerns the relations of a husband and his estranged wife with regard to the relief of a neighboring village in time of famine. In the behavior of these two people is implied the whole story of their past, what amounts virtually to a novel. None of this is actually related. But by the end of the story, what has not been said has become completely clear, and one realizes that two stories have been told simultaneously, the one related directly, and the other altogether implied. Similarly, **"About Love"** is the story of an adulterous relationship that does not take place. It results in an intimate characterization of the narrator, Alekhin, who is understood mainly by reference to what he does not do and does not say. It would be an error to conclude from such examples that Chekhov was primarily concerned with novel forms of narration. He was, on the contrary, much inclined to a very simple and unaffected style, and disliked anything that smacked of trickery. But the things that most interested him as a writer were often too intangible for direct communication. In consequence, he developed a curiously tangential method of approach.

The difficulty of representing on the stage anything that cannot be directly stated is enormous. Unlike the novelist, the playwright relinquishes control of his material the moment it is played, and the audience is at liberty to do with it what it pleases. The theatre therefore inclines one to an uncompromising frontality of approach, and its conditions are generally unsuitable for any but the simplest and most unambiguous effects. This is particularly true of characterization. In the theatre it is usually assumed that the audience will be briefed quite precisely as to the nature of the characters by the end of the first act—such was the Scribean practice. Anything that changes this impression is then in the nature of a major effect, a surprise, or a recognition.

None of Chekhov's plays follows this prescription. His characters do not announce themselves, nor do they lend themselves readily to definition. Like real people, they are the subject of surmise and inference, and the author furnishes only the barest clues as to his intention. When the Moscow Art Theatre presented **The Sea Gull,** its directors went to great lengths to explore the personality of the principal characters in the interests of a truly realistic production. Chekhov's approach to these problems was characteristically oblique. Stanislavsky had been playing Trigorin in the elegant costume of a successful writer. When he managed in time to elicit from Chekhov a judgment of his interpretation, Chekhov's only comment was: "Excellent. Only he wears checked trousers, and his shoes have holes." He was somewhat more expansive with Kachalov, who also undertook this role for a time: "His fishing-rods are homemade, you know, all crooked and bent; he makes them himself with a penknife. His cigar is a good one, perhaps even a very good one; but he never removes the cigar band." And after a moment's earnest thought, he added: "But the main thing is his fishing rods." Similarly, during the rehearsals of **Uncle Vanya,** he wrote to Stanislavsky to explain Astrov's last scene: "He whistles, you know. Whistles. Uncle Vanya cries, but Astrov whistles."

These were, in fact, very useful clues to the characterization in each case, though willfully—one might even say mischievously—enigmatic. Even in the interests of his own production, Chekhov did not trouble to spell out for his cast the process of reasoning through which the character of Trigorin might be deduced from the holes in his shoes or the crudeness of his fishpoles. Here, as elsewhere, he contented himself with pointing to the external fact, the superficial manifestation of the inner situation.

That this epigrammatic mode of representation was learned rather than innate can hardly be doubted. Experience had taught him the futility of long explanations. In 1888, he had written copious notes analyzing the characters of **Ivanov,** and he had coached Davydov for hours in connection with the Petersburg production, all to no avail. Even toward the end of his life, in his letters to Olga Knipper he furnished from time to time detailed analyses of character and action, which nobody in the acting company understood or heeded. But he had his special magic, and used it to good effect. He knew that

a moonlit landscape could be evoked by the highlight on the neck of a bottle; and in a man who whistled while others wept one could divine the depths of the soul's despair.

Until the last years of the nineteenth century, only the greatest dramatists had attempted anything on the stage beyond the depiction of the obvious. Traditionally, a play was an acted story, an observable pattern of events, but it was considered necessary in the course of a dramatic action for the author to reveal something of the secret life of his characters. This was accomplished in the simplest manner. Even in the nineteenth century, we find the characters of drama eager to explain themselves to us verbally in soliloquies or, more subtly, in the relation between what they do and what they say. Until the advent of symbolism, drama was an art that made things clear. Only the greatest plays preserved their mystery.

Impressionism was the great innovation of the later nineteenth century. The impressionists declined to look below the surface and, in the novel as on the stage, impressionist art was primarily concerned with the definition of external experience. For the impressionists, and their semi-scientific brethren, the naturalists, a character was what he seemed to be, and nothing more. The reaction was inevitable. Long before 1891, the year Huret published the results of his *Enquête* on the future of literature, it had become evident that a literary art which declined to look beyond appearance could have no great future.

The immediate result of the reaction to the school of Médan was a renewal of interest in symbolism and psychology, both of which attempted to probe the surface in order to discover what lay beneath the external tissue of experience. Chekhov had no taste for the metaphysical; but the workings of the human psyche interested him very much. His attitude from first to last remained staunchly impressionistic. He was concerned primarily to describe the face of nature; but its physiognomy fascinated him and, like all the major writers of his day, he came readily under the influence of symbolism.

Maeterlinck's essay *Le Tragique quotidien* was not published until 1896, the year of **The Sea Gull**; but Chekhov had been reading him for some time in French, and in the summer of 1897 he wrote Suvorin of the great impression Maeterlinck's plays had made upon him. Maeterlinck had written of the need for a quiet drama, the drama of every day, which would convey the true sound of life:

> Here, we no longer live with barbarians, nor is man now fretting in the midst of elementary passions, as though these were the only things worthy of note; he is at rest, and we have time to observe him. It is no longer a violent, exceptional movement of life that passes before our eyes—it is life itself.[2]

It must have occurred almost as readily to Chekhov as it had to Maeterlinck that in "life itself" there is something other than the obvious component, and that, consequently, naturalism, even at best, is a needlessly shallow evaluation of experience. People are primarily visible to the sensual eye, but only in their solidity, their opacity; the eye sees them and understands nothing. If they are to be understood, they must be perceived with the eye of the mind, armed with all the perceptive powers of which the mind is capable. Chekhov was unwilling to speculate, and refused to predicate anything of a general nature with regard to the substrate. Nevertheless, he was very much aware of the invisible life. He noted the outward detail of his world with the vigilant eye of the impressionist, but the result was valuable to him chiefly insofar as the outer world furnished a basis for the exploration of the world within, and it was in the relation of the two worlds that he found the true substance of his art.

In **"The Lady with the Little Dog"** the contrapuntal nature of the double life is demonstrated in a very elementary form. Gurov, the hero of the story,

> had two lives, one open, seen and known by all who cared to know it, full of conventional truth and conventional falsehood, exactly like the lives of his friends and acquaintances, and another life that ran its course in secret. And through some strange, perhaps accidental combination of circumstances, everything that was of interest and importance, and essential to him, everything about which he felt sincerely and did not deceive himself, whatever constituted the core of his being, was hidden from other people; while all that was false in him, the shell in which he hid in order to conceal the truth . . . all that life went on in the open. And, judging others by himself, he believed nothing that he saw, and always considered that every man led his real, and most interesting life under the cover of secrecy, as under the cover of night . . . [3]

It was Chekhov's special gift as an artist that he was able to penetrate to the core around which the outer life is shaped; but it was characteristic of his native reticence that beyond a certain point he did not betray his characters. With Chekhov, the revelation of truth was a matter involving the greatest circumspection. He never pretended to understand what he did not understand, and he scrupled to make a display of what he knew. In **"The Black Monk,"** Kovrin lives his true life in the company of the mysterious apparition he has called forth from within himself. His well-meaning wife and her father, by means of diet and bromides, succeed in driving away the phantom which absorbs his attention, and are surprised when the excitement and the joy of his life vanish also. Once he is cured of his hallucination, the man is ruined, and his resentment knows no bounds. When the phantom monk returns at last, Kovrin is happy once again, and it is now that he suffers the hemorrhage that puts an end to him.

This is all Chekhov tells. But the intimation is clear. Kovrin's secret life, his essential life, is inseparable from the disease he hides in his breast, his tuberculosis, which works silently and secretly within him, and at last appears before his eyes as his dearest friend and greatest

solace, his sincere admirer, the black monk. Such is the compensation he has invented for his mediocrity; and the fantasy is more than merely compensatory. It is a work of art precisely suited to his psychic needs, realized step by step until it destroys him. This growing death which he nourishes is, in short, his life, the illusion of greatness which at once sustains and consumes him. In the same way, in **The Sea Gull,** Treplev cannot endure the thought of his mediocrity. For him also the idea that he is a genius is his link with the vital principle; when this link snaps, his life comes to an end.

The art of Chekhov is, seemingly, limpid, a more or less humorous representation of the life of his time. In fact it is the art of the incomprehensible, the half-surmised, the enigmatic. It elicits, not a feeling of satisfaction but a revery, a mood that is very often disturbing. Chekhov speaks not to the mind, as perhaps he intended, but to the soul, reaching inward through a train of associations over which he exercises only a partial control. There is certainly something in this method that suggests the poet, or better still the composer; and Chekhov's work has, in consequence, often been called poetry, and compared with music. But if this art is musical, it is, on the whole, a discordant music that it makes. Chekhov was often compassionate, but more often brutally ironic. His was not a gentle art.

It is perhaps for this reason that Chekhov seems to us in our day so astonishingly modern. He was no ordinary realist. Had he been, his work would very likely have withered with his age, as he feared it might. In his own day, and in his country, he was admired for things that no longer seem important; and even now there is surely a tendency among Russian critics to exaggerate his role as a precursor of the Revolution. Tolstory admired him greatly as an artist; but he thought his plays were pointless. Of all his stories, Tolstoy liked **"Dushechka"** best—**"The Darling"**—which he considered a beautiful portrayal of womanhood, completely overlooking the irony of the characterization.[4]

The truth of "life as it is," which Chekhov thought it the function of the artist to reveal, was not, indeed, a truth perceptible to the realist. The life with which he was concerned was not the life which people exhibit. His was another order of realism. For those who are mainly aware of the external life, it is Chekhov's comic tales which are primarily valuable, and the works of his later period seem to them the product of a mind which ceased at a certain point to be amusing.[5] But after half a century of earnest psychologizing, we tend to look beyond the jester in Chekhov, beyond the ironist, and for the first time, perhaps, we become aware of his terrifying insight into the guarded depths of the personality, the dark continent of the mind which only the artist can enter without intrusion.

Chekhov's characters are never wholly detached from the matrix. They stand out in various degrees of relief, never wholly in the round, physically and psychically a part of their environment, something to be contemplated along with the other things of nature, rivers and trees, the sky, the flight of geese, the lightning. For Chekhov all such manifestations of life were equally animate and equally mysterious, a source of wonder in themselves and in their mutual relations. Chekhov never ceased to be the boy traveling across the steppe toward the distant city, and he transmitted best of all the sense of surprise, the feeling of awe that life can arouse in a fresh and receptive mind. Perhaps because death was so near to him, he had no strong terminal sense. Man ends; but his story is endless. Chekhov's plays are not finished. When the curtain has fallen, the play goes on; there is still the sense of flux. We say farewell, and the brigade moves on toward other horizons. With Chekhov the story is soon told; but behind the story there is an eternity of stories, there is the eternal story:

> Yalta was hardly visible through the morning mist; white clouds stood motionless on the mountain tops. The leaves did not stir on the trees, cicadas chirruped, and the monotonous, hollow sound of the sea, rising from below, spoke of peace and the eternal sleep that awaits us. So it must have sounded when there was no Yalta, and no Oreanda; so it sounds now, and so it will sound, indifferent and hollow, when we are no more. And in this permanence, in this complete indifference to the life and death of each one of us, there is hidden perhaps a pledge of our eternal salvation, of the unceasing movement of life on the earth, of the unceasing movement toward perfection.[6]

It is in such passages that we sense the nature of the Chekhovian "Beyond," the strangely unreal atmosphere in which the realities of his later plays are suspended. It is an atmosphere less mysterious and less explicit than the Maeterlinckian *au-delà,* and certainly more intelligible. Like many of Chekhov's stories, his plays, *The Sea Gull, The Three Sisters,* and *The Cherry Orchard,* are presented with utmost realism, but they are presented *sub specie aeternitatis,* so that everything in them seems provisional and ephemeral in its nature, and the action seems curiously insignificant, a trifle in comparison with the vast process of which it forms a part.

Men live and suffer and die and are forgotten; the wave piles high on the beach, recedes, returns, endlessly repeating its monotonous cycle. It is perhaps quite aimless and meaningless; yet we are permitted to see in it the symbol of our salvation. The doubt, the question, is at the bottom of all. It is the true source of the unity of these plays, and the ultimate principle of their form. In consequence of the doubt which shaped them, they have a dream-like quality which is emphasized by somnambulistic characters for whom the borders of reality seem blurred. And, indeed, beyond the action of these plays we are made aware through dubious signs of another and more questionable reality to which these symbols barely reach; and which is perhaps not there.

Late in his life, it is said, Chekhov came to the conclusion that his works were essentially of exemplary and didactic character. Tikhonov recalls that in the course of a discussion in Moscow Chekhov remarked: "You say that you have wept over my plays. Yes, and not you alone. But I did not write them for that; it is Alexeyev who has made such cry-babies of my characters. I wanted something else. I wanted to tell people honestly: 'Look at yourselves. See how badly you live and how tiresome you are!' The main thing is that people should understand this. When they do, they will surely create a new and better life for themselves. I will not see it, but I know it will be entirely different, not like what we have now. And so long as it does not exist, I will continue to tell people: 'See how badly you live, and how tiresome you are!' Is that what makes them weep?"[7]

Evidently, at this stage of his career, the work of preparing the future of humanity, of which Vershinin speaks so vaguely, was taking a more definite form in Chekhov's mind, and he was willing to present his work primarily as social criticism. Unquestionably Chekhov said things of this sort from time to time, and especially when he found it necessary to defend himself against the charge, often repeated, that his writings made no point and carried no message. But while such statements are understandable in the circumstances, and even perhaps to his credit, the truth is that, as a dramatist, he was a very minor social critic, but a very great artist. It is doubtful that anyone will wish to read *Uncle Vanya, The Three Sisters,* or *The Cherry Orchard* for purposes of edification, and it seems quaint that Chekhov should have suggested the possibility; but they have the universal validity of the highest art.

It seems altogether unlikely that Chekhov ever wrote with a particular point in mind. His work is never argumentative, seldom demonstrative. It is descriptive, representational. When he found a subject to his liking, he proceeded, apparently, to set it down as a painter might, filling in his canvas with broad, and often seemingly unrelated, touches which in the end are seen to make a *Gestalt.* Chekhov was certainly concerned with meaning, but not often with message. His works leave one with a sense of a deeply felt and complex experience, in part emotional, and in part intellectual, but never with the feeling of having digested a sermon or an *exemplum.* Apart from his often-expressed faith in the future of humanity, it is quite impossible to say what Chekhov believed. He affirmed life. He gave to the transitory a permanent form, an intimation of eternity; and he fixed the cultural elements of his time in patterns that are beautiful in themselves, and universally intelligible. It is the traditional role of the artist. His work comes as close to life as the work of Gogol and, since like him he was inclined to caricature, he strove for a likeness. But from the intellectual standpoint he was never precise: he displayed mainly his ambivalence. His plays are never definite in function or in aim and, as works of art, they seem as irrelevant to such concerns as the paintings of Brueghel or Vermeer.

It was evidently Chekhov's idea that the elemental forces of the universe express themselves most clearly in the individual, and that it is by observing the behavior of individuals that we become aware of the great tides that sweep the world. All of Chekhov's plays are small in subject matter, plays of the drawing-room and the garden. Yet no one has painted a broader canvas, or unfolded a deeper perspective. It was his aim to write simply and accurately. No modern dramatist is more complex; and few have elicited more diverse interpretations. In the belief that a representation of life involves everything that can be truly said about it, he noted in detail the symptoms of the world's malaise. So far as he could see, his world was a tissue of absurdities. It made no sense, and was probably no longer viable. He had only general therapeutic measures to suggest. Perhaps it could be nursed back to health. If not, it would die; and a new world would rise from its ashes. The question of how precisely this was to happen seemed, at the moment, unanswerable. But in two or three hundred years at the most, he was certain, the answer would be clear, and perhaps even the question. In the meantime, there was nothing for it but patience. Life was painful, but it was amusing; on the whole, an interesting and exasperating experience that one would not willingly forego. There was no more to be said on the subject. "You ask, what is life?" he wrote Olga some months before his death. "That is just the same as asking what is a carrot. A carrot is a carrot, and nothing more is known about it."[8]

Chekhov expressed no great faith in his chances of survival on the literary scene. In 1901 he remarked to Ivan Bunin that he did not expect his works to live over seven years. "But even though they read me only seven years more," he added, "I have less than that to live. Six."

He exaggerated. He had only three years more to live, barely that; but he would surely be read for centuries. He was not like other writers of his age, who spoke well, but only for their time, and were certain to pass away with it. Better than any among his contemporaries he expressed the transition between the old world and the new; his viewpoint was universal, his insights were at the same time Olympian and intensely human, he saw the jest where others saw only the injustice, and sensed the pain where others were moved chiefly to laughter. It is much to his credit that he saw life in the round, and also that he was not much concerned to formulate it philosophically. After all, he was soon to die, and for him the word *nichevo*, which his characters speak so often, had a special connotation.

In a noisy age, Chekhov greatly cultivated the gift of understatement. Therefore his words come to us softly and clearly through the hubbub of his time, and in this manner he is emphatic beyond any of his contemporaries, more convincing than Tolstoy, more effective than Gorky. Occasionally in his world there arises a scream of anguish or a shriek of laughter; but not often. His world, in general, is quiet, so quiet that when a string breaks in the sky, we hear it.

NOTES

[1] M. Gorky, *Autobiography,* New York, 1949, pp. 468.
[2] Maeterlinck, *Le Tragique quotidien.* In *Le Trésor des humbles,* Paris, 1949, pp. 127 ff.; translated in part in B. Clark, *European Theories of the Drama,* p. 412.

[3] "The Lady with the Little Dog." In *Selected Works,* III, 186 f.; translated in Yarmolinsky, *Chekhov,* pp. 430 f.; Garnett, *Tales,* Vol. III: *The Lady with the Little Dog and Other Stories,* New York, 1917, pp. 24 f.
[4] See the fine study by Sophie Laffitte, *Chekhov et Tolstoy,* in Eekman, *Anton Čechov,* pp. 131 ff.
[5] E.g. Prince Mirsky, *Contemporary Russian Literature,* New York, 1926, pp. 84 ff.
[6] "The Lady with the Little Dog." In *Selected Works,* III, 178 f.; Garnett, *Tales,* Vol. III, p. 18; Yarmolinsky, *Chekhov,* 419.
[7] "Chekhov v neizdannykh dnevnikakh sovremennikov" in *Literaturnoe nasledstvo,* LXVIII, Moscow, 1960, pp. 479 ff.
[8] Letter to Olga Knipper, 20 April 1904. In Garnett, *Letters,* p. 386. For a good discussion of the various viewpoints, from the time of Skabichevsky and Shestov to that of Chukovsky, with regard to Chekhov's temperament, see Hingley, *Chekhov, A Biographical and Critical Study,* pp. 103 ff.

Kenneth Rexroth   (essay date 1967)

SOURCE: "Chekhov's Plays," in *Saturday Review,* Vol. L, No. 27, 8 July 1967, p. 18.

[*In this essay, Rexroth comments on the profound change in the nature of drama brought about by Chekhov.*]

It comes as a bit of a shock to sit yourself down and deliberately think, "In the first half of the twentieth century, the position once occupied in ancient Greece by Aeschylus, Sophocles, and Euripides was held, in the estimation of those who sought serious satisfaction in the modern theater, by Ibsen, Strindberg, and Chekhov." What had happened in two thousand years? Had it happened to the audiences, or to the playwrights, or to the self-evolving art of drama? Or was the change more profound than this, more profound even than a change in the meaning of civilization—was it a change in the very nature of man? We still say we enjoy *Antigone*; but if we go directly from a performance of that play to Chekhov's *Three Sisters,* it is difficult not to believe that the men of Classic times were different from us, a different kind of men.

In certain plays, both Ibsen and Strindberg set out deliberately to compete with the great past, with Shakespeare or Schiller or Sophocles or Aeschylus. The results are hardly competition. *Peer Gynt* or *Damascus* bears little resemblance to the past, though certain Strindberg plays do contain distorted reflections of Euripides. But Chekhov—what would the Greeks have made of *The Sea Gull*? They would have classed it with Menander, with the New Comedy of domestic conflict and absurd situation. So did Chekhov. We seldom pay attention to half-titles in "Collected Plays," but there it says, right on the page—*"The Sea Gull, A Comedy in Four Acts." Ivanov* is called "a drama"; *Uncle Vanya,* "scenes of country life"; *Three Sisters,* a "drama"; *The Cherry Orchard,* certainly the saddest of all, "A comedy."

So simply Chekhov states his aesthetic, and with it a philosophy of life. If we take these heartbreaking plays as tragedies in the sense in which *Oedipus the King* is a tragedy, we are self-convicted of sentimentality. No one has ever had a more delicate sentiment, a more careful sensibility, when it comes to portraying, and so judging, the lives of more-than-ordinary men and women—but no one was ever less a sentimentalist—than Chekhov. This is why he outraged a swashbuckling sentimentalist like D. H. Lawrence, who hated him and who couldn't understand why he didn't come down hard on the right side and plump for the Good Guys and The Life Force.

Chekhov always insisted that the five plays of his maturity that his audiences insisted were tragedies were simply developments, precisely in maturity, of the hilarious short farces of his youth. But if Uncle Vanya's impotent pistol shots and Irina's "Moscow, Moscow, we'll never see Moscow now!" are not tragic, then Chekhov is mocking us, and his characters—and, not least, his actors—too. No. Chekhov is the master of an art of such highly refined modesty that he can present his people in their simplicity on a stage and let life itself do the mocking.

He wanted a new theater, a theater that would tell it the way it really was. There has been plenty of realist and naturalist theater in Russia in his day and since, but there is only one Chekhov. The naturalist theater uses a whole armamentarium of devices to create an illusion of "real life" and then drive home its points, all derived from the storehouse of literary and dramatic morality.

There have been many more lifelike plays than Chekhov's. His is not a circumstantial naturalism of décor and talk and event—it is a moral naturalism. These lost people, off in the vast provinces of Russia, frustrated, aimless, hopeless, or full of utopian unrealizable hopes, all alike coming to trivial ends, actually make up a highly stylized theater of their own, as formal or classic as the Commedia dell' Arte or Plautus and Terence.

What is realistic, or naturalistic? What is "life as it really is"? This is the silent moral commentary that underlines every speech, like an unheard organ pedal. Is it a judgment? In the sense in which "Judge not lest ye be judged" is a judgment.

There is something intrinsically ridiculous about all the people in all the plays. Chekhov's is truly a theater of the absurd. Yet we never think of them as very funny—and we don't think of them as very sad, either. The play as a whole may sadden us, as life saddens us with all the massive pathos of mortality, but Chekhov's people we simply accept.

We do not judge Uncle Vanya to be a fool or Irina to be a silly girl or Trigorin to be an ass and a cad, although they certainly say foolish and silly and asinine things. And when that recurrent character who always says, "Some day life will be splendid, and people in those far-off days will look back on us and pity us in our filth and misery and thank us for having endured our agonies for them, so that they might be" speaks his recurrent part, we neither laugh nor sigh nor believe, but at the most think, "Perhaps. Not likely. It won't matter."

Chekhov would have been horrified if anyone had cold-bloodedly accused him of teaching a moral—but so he does. We accept these tragic comedies, these sorrowful farces of Chekhov's the way we would accept life itself if we were gifted with sudden wisdom. Chekhov places us in a situation, confronting the behavior of a number of human beings in what seems to them, at least, an important crisis. We are so placed, so situated and informed, that we can afford to be wise. We can regard the affairs of men as they should be regarded, in the aspect of timelessness. But this is what Sophocles does.

Once we accept both the idiom of Chekhov and the idiom of Sophocles we can compare them, and we can see very clearly the great precision and economy with which Chekhov works. His plays are pre-eminently, in modern times, playwright's plays, a joy for a fellow craftsman to see or read. How right everything is! How little time or speech is wasted! How much every line is saturated with action! Sophocles, Molière, Racine—very few other playwrights have been as accurate and as economical.

It is this genius for stating only the simplest truth as simply as can be that makes Chekhov inexhaustible—like life. We can see him for the hundredth time when we are sick of everything else in the theater, just as we can read his stories when everything else, even detectives and science fiction, bores us. We are not bored because we do not feel we are being manipulated. We are, of course, but manipulated to respond, "That's the way it is." Since the professional manipulators of the mind never have this response in view, we are quite unconscious of Chekhov's craftiness—that he is always interfering on the side of suspended judgment.

Quite unlike those of Ibsen and Strindberg, who were tireless preachers and manipulators, Chekhov's people are not alienated. They have trouble, as men have always had, communicating, but the cast of each play forms a community nonetheless. They would all like to live in a society of mutual aid if only they could define the means and ends of aid itself. One feels that Ibsen and Strindberg didn't like any of their casts very much and made them up of people who wouldn't listen to Ibsen and Strindberg. Chekhov doesn't want to be listened to. He isn't there. He is out of sight, in the last row of the balcony, listening. "I imagine people so they can tell me things about themselves." This is an unusual, but certainly an unusually effective, credo for a playwright.

It is easy to accept Orestes or Hamlet as an archetype. Hundreds of books are written analyzing the new pantheon of heroes who make up the inner dramas of our unconscious. They are very spectacular personages, these. It is hard at first to believe a playwright who comes to us and says, "The schoolteacher and the two stenographers next door to where you live in Fort Dodge—these are the real archetypes." But until we have learned this—and most of us will never learn it, however many Chekhov plays we see; not really, not deep in the bowels of compassion, but only as we learn things in books—we will never learn to approach life with the beginnings of wisdom: with that wisdom so characteristic of Sophocles.

J. B. Priestley (essay date 1970)

SOURCE: "Chapter 7," in *Anton Chekhov,* A. S. Barnes & Co., 1970, pp. 70-82.

[*In the essay below, Priestley admires the psychological depth of Chekhov's characters, arguing: "It is this depth, where consciousness dissolves into the fathomless unconscious, where new half-realized meanings gleam and then vanish like fish in some deep lake, that constantly renews for us the fascination of [Chekhov's] drama."*]

The first Chekhov play I ever saw was *The Cherry Orchard.* This was in 1925 when it had its first London run. (There had been a single Stage Society performance as far back as 1911.) I took a girl with me, an intelligent girl who was a newly qualified doctor, and I remember that she left the theatre feeling bewildered and rather resentful. But the play, even in this faulty production, had enchanted me. The magic of it lingered for days. Since then I have seen many different productions of *The Cherry Orchard.* The best I ever saw was when I was in Russia in 1945, in a performance beginning at the curious hour of noon on Sunday, and it was of course being given by the Moscow Art Theatre, largely by players who had been trained and directed by Stanislavsky. Compared with that, the performance given by the Moscow Art Theatre during its visit to London in 1958 was disappointing. Incidentally, almost all the earlier British and American productions of Chekhov were too slow, heavy, lugubrious, missing the shot-silk 'laughter-through-tears' effect. Chekhov himself would have detested them.

After so many years I do not remember what my girl-doctor companion said after we left the theatre that evening in 1925. But it is a fairly safe guess to suppose she told me that 'nothing happened'. It was a common complaint for some time against Chekhov and his four last plays. In point of fact a great deal happens in these plays, and indeed in *The Seagull, Uncle Vanya* and *The Three Sisters* there are moments that might have come from melodrama. It is not the dramatic substance of these plays that used to leave audiences feeling bewildered and dissatisfied: it is Chekhov's peculiar method. What he does in effect is to turn the conventional 'well-made' play upside down and inside out. It is almost as if he had read some textbooks on the art of playwriting and had then done the opposite of everything they recommended. It is common form in conventional drama to endow the leading characters, if only for the sake of the inevitable 'conflict', with more power of will and sense of purpose than most of us can pretend to have. Chekhov reverses this. Instead of heightening and hardening the will in his characters, he depresses and softens it: most of them are even more uncertain and weaker than we are. Again, in the 'well-made' play, the characters are so intent upon shaping neat scenes, are so anxious to reach the climax of the conflict, they cannot find time to tell us they dislike tomato soup or have an old uncle who still plays the 'cello. But if they are Chekhov characters, then they have time to tell us anything that comes into their heads.

There is a fascinating thing here that has escaped general notice. Chekhov himself, following some secret train of thought, was always surprising other people by making inconsequential remarks, just like so many characters in his plays. The others might be arguing about Marxism and he would say, 'Have you ever been to a stud farm?' Or the subject might be literature, and he would announce out of the blue, 'One ought to go to Australia.' Stanislavsky describes how Chekhov, a devoted angler, when he was out fishing with some theatrical friends, suddenly burst out laughing, and when they asked him what was the matter, he replied, 'Listen! Artem can never play Ibsen.' But what was a little idiosyncrasy in his own talk was broadened and deepened to become a highly original method in his drama. It enables us to come closer to his characters. It reminds us how difficult true communication can be. (Act Two of *The Cherry Orchard* originally ended with a scene between Charlotta, the eccentric governess, and Firs, the very old valet, who tried—entirely in vain—to explain their lives to each other. But it was decided during rehearsal to shorten the act and this scene had to go—most unfortunately, in my opinion.) This method also reminds us how essentially lonely we are, most of our time. Finally, it gives Chekhov's drama, on the surface so lackadaisical and inconsequential, rhythm and development in depth.

It is this depth, where consciousness dissolves into the fathomless unconscious, where new half-realized meanings gleam and then vanish like fish in some deep lake, that constantly renews for us the fascination of his drama. He can be disliked—anybody and anything can be disliked—but if we like him at all, then we can take his plays over and over again. I have seen dreadful productions of Chekhov, who makes demands that too many companies cannot meet, but even during the worst of them something of the magic has remained. He has, so to speak, an extra dimension. Many of his friends, while they loved him for his unfailing kindness, generosity and charm, found something teasingly elusive in his personality. He can be equally elusive in his plays. What is farcical turns into pathos, comedy dissolves into tragedy, while this in turn reveals a glint of irony. Let us take, as an obvious example, all those speeches about life being wonderful sometime in the future. As we hear or read those speeches we can almost see an enigmatic smile hovering above them. Whatever else Chekhov may be doing, he is not seizing an opportunity to declare his faith in progress. (But I am not saying he had no such faith, only that he was not writing plays to prove it.) Any attempt to saddle him, as a dramatist, with a political-economic-social purpose seems to me quite wrong. He goes to work on a deeper level.

Like many of his tales, his plays make us movingly aware of waste and loss. With the exception of his lovable old innocents, his characters, though they may suffer from self-deception and weakness of will, make us feel that Time has cheated them. It is as if Anton Chekhov, as distinct from the practical sensible Dr A. P. Chekhov, felt strongly when in a creative mood that there is some secret, which might reveal a very different scheme of

Chekhov's funeral, 1904.

things, that we have lost. There is a curious speech by Vershinin in *The Three Sisters,* beginning: 'I often say to myself: suppose one could start one's life over again, but this time with full knowledge? Suppose one could live one's life as one writes a school composition, once in rough draft, and then live it again in a fair copy?' It is worth noticing that although there is a great deal about love in these four plays, not one of them offers us an example of a happy lasting sexual relationship. And there is a significant entry in one of his notebooks: 'Love is either the residue of something that is degenerating and that was once tremendous or else a part of something that will become tremendous in the future. But in the present it cannot satisfy, it offers much less than is expected of it.' He may have had in mind the the heady false romanticism common enough in the Russia he knew. But his conclusion—'it offers much less than is expected of it'—is oddly prophetic to us now, when among so much uncertainty, fear, hidden despair, sex is being asked to carry too heavy a load.

However, it is time to take a seat in the theatre and look at the plays themselves. From here on it must be understood that my criticism is very personal, an expression of my own likes and dislikes; it could not be anything else

and remain honest; but at least I can add that I have seen many productions of these plays, including some in Moscow itself, and that my own theatrical experience has been very considerable. In any order of all-round merit, I would say that the last of these plays, *The Cherry Orchard,* comes first; then, a little below it, *The Three Sisters* (often called simply *Three Sisters,* but this sounds a bit brutal in English); and then, some way below and both on the same level, *Uncle Vanya* and *The Seagull.*

We have seen already how immensely popular *The Seagull* became as soon as it was produced by the Moscow Art Theatre. It is far closer to conventional drama than Chekhov's later plays. It is nothing like so subtle and elusive. Its characters create definite 'scenes'. And it offers us actresses and authors—incidentally, the last we shall see in Chekhov. Nor is it surprising that the first act should have been so rapturously received at its opening performance. It is a wonderful first act, strikingly original, and broad, rich and deep. I could enjoy seeing it again and then leaving the theatre. Not that the rest of the play is bad—far from it—but it has weaknesses more obvious as the play develops. One of them is that it has too large a circle of unrequited lovers: the A loves B, B loves C, C loves D pattern soon becomes irritating. Then

Trigorin and Treplev are hard to accept. What Chekhov did here was to divide his own personality into three: Trigorin being the popular storyteller self he was getting tired of, Treplev being the self struggling with new forms of expression, and Dr Dorn being his doctor-self, significantly sympathetic to Treplev's efforts. None of them quite succeeds as a separate creation, an independent character. Trigorin, a part notoriously difficult for actors, is presented as a weak, shallow, fashionable author, yet he shows an all-consuming devotion to his art that is neither weak nor shallow and would set him apart from fashionable hacks. (He says some very good things of course, but are they in character—and which character?) Again, unless I have been deceived about Treplev as a highly original young writer, then I cannot accept his suicide. Finally, though this is a minor criticism, Dr Dorn seems to carry weight that he never really uses. The women, especially Nina, are good acting parts but hardly memorable characters. The play itself is fine theatre, which explains its popularity, but even so I am now ready to leave after that wonderful first act.

I am happy to announce that the production of **Uncle Vanya** I most enjoyed was an English one, that by the Old Vic in 1945, with Richardson as Uncle Vanya, Olivier as Astrov, Joyce Redman as Sonya, Margaret Leighton as Yelena. Even though it has the advantage of a very moving last act, **Uncle Vanya** is not an easy play for an English-speaking audience to accept. Its main theme—that old Professor Serebryakov and his beautiful young wife, Yelena, are not worth the sacrifices that Uncle Vanya and Sonya have been making for them—is straightforward enough. But the Professor's social importance is not obvious to us, and we could do with a little more of him. The over-excitable Uncle Vanya, very much a Slav type, is always in danger of appearing quite farcical, and the scene in which he fires at—and misses—the Professor has always seemed to me, as people say, 'a bit much'. As we know, this play is based on a much earlier one, **The Wood Demon.** It was completed, probably rather hastily, in 1896, but there is some evidence that Chekhov may have worked on it as early as 1890. Certainly if he had been still revising it by the time he was writing **The Three Sisters** and was now at ease with his own method, the rather awkward soliloquies in **Uncle Vanya** would have been taken out, and, for example, Dr Astrov would have been less obviously explicit about his forests and the waste of the countryside. The old underlying theme of waste and loss is here again, but this play may be taken as a symbolic presentation of the Russia of the 1890s, when so many glittering empty types like the Professor and his wife were being maintained by the long hard work and the drastic economies of the Uncle Vanyas and the Sonyas—who must 'live through a long, long chain of days and weary evenings' and know no rest this side of the grave, only in Heaven.

There are some great plays that offer more to the imaginative reader than they do to the playgoer. (After seeing many productions of *King Lear* and *Antony and Cleopatra,* I think they are best enjoyed at home.) Chekhov's **The Three Sisters** is not one of these plays. So long as

the production is worthy of it—and it is a difficult play to stage—it must be seen to be fully appreciated. I have described already how Chekhov took endless trouble over this play, constantly sending on textual revisions and advice to actors after he had been compelled to go abroad. The best production of it I ever saw was at the Moscow Art Theatre in 1945, with Tarasova, a magnificent actress, playing Olga Knipper's original part, Masha. (My only reservation about this production, superb in every detail, is that because it tried to keep together as many as possible of the players trained by Stanislavsky, the cast as a whole tended to be much older than the characters they were playing.) The first act, in which we have to be introduced to so many people, is rather awkward, and the opening scene, between the three sisters, offers us too much obvious exposition. On the other hand, the play gains in force and depth as it goes along, and the last act—properly produced and using a big stage—is overwhelming. There is no better example of Chekhov's unique 'laughter-through-tears' effect than the scene in which the little teacher, Kuligin, puts on the false beard in a pathetic attempt to amuse his wife and her two sisters. There is much irony in the play as well as great pathos, as one illusion after another fails the test of reality; but it is not intended as a complicated proof of human futility. While Anton Chekhov tenderly removes each illusion, Dr A. P. Chekhov is suggesting we should not waste the life we have by allowing idle dreams to rob it of colour, flavour and zest.

We have seen already how Chekhov found **The Cherry Orchard** hard to compose—and it *was* composed rather than written, almost like another *Das Lied von der Erde.* And not simply because he was then a very sick man, working under a sentence of death. But I think this influenced him to a degree beyond his conscious appreciation, so that while he protested over and over again that he was writing—or had written—a comedy, he was not aware how much sadness was seeping through. (Stanislavsky must have felt this, so that he was not really at cross-purposes with Chekhov, though he may have wanted to make too much of the dying aristocracy theme.) But Chekhov must have found his 'comedy' hard to compose because it carried his unique dramatic method as far as it would go, while at the same time he had to handle a large and varied group of characters. Furthermore, he gave each act its own particular atmosphere: first, the waiting up in the dark hours and then the arrival at dawn; secondly, the revealing talk in the immense calm early evening; thirdly, the semi-hysterical atmosphere of the late party; and finally the hurried tearful departure from the desolate house. All four are wonderful in their own way, but to my mind the masterpiece is Act One, which has long seemed to me the finest single act in the whole of modern drama. Technically it is a marvel, but over and above what can be analysed it has a peculiar magic that is renewed year after year.

Too much can be made of the cherry orchard itself. It gave Chekhov a beautiful image for his title, and the sale of it helps to shape the drama. But it is the house and not the orchard that is the centre and heart of the play. All the characters—even Lopahin, who begins by telling us so—are intimately connected with the house. But this is not a play about closing a house or selling an orchard. What then is it 'about'? It is about time and change and folly and regret and vanished happiness and hope for the future. A little girl I once knew, quiet for once and sitting in a corner, was asked what was the matter, and replied: 'Life in this world'. *The Cherry Orchard* is about life in this world. Coldly considered, its characters are far from being admirable: Madame Ranevsky is a foolish woman only too anxious to return to a worthless young lover; Gaev is an amiable ass who talks too much; Anya is a goose and her Trofimov a solemn windbag; Lopahin, the practical self-made man, is confused and unhappy; Epihodov a clumsy idiot; Dunyasha a foolish girl; Yasha an insufferable jumped-up lad; and Firs far gone in senility. But Chekhov, who knows all this better than we do, is not coldly considering these people. Even more, I suspect, than we are consciously aware of, he is revealing them to us in a strange light, infinitely tender and compassionate, that might illuminate a man's mind when he is in effect saying farewell to this life. Chekhov talked vaguely about another play he was planning to write, but I think he never meant this seriously. He had already said goodbye in *The Cherry Orchard,* his masterpiece.

A final point about Chekhov as dramatist. He came to have an enormous influence upon younger writers. Now a man may be a magnificent dramatist himself and yet be a bad influence. This, in my opinion, is true of Shaw, who, out of his unusual temperament, experience, witty ebullience, was able to create unique comedies of debate. He is an easy man to enjoy and a very difficult man to follow, with the result that we have had far too many mediocre comedies, loud with argument, written under his influence. The opposite is true of Chekhov. Since his time we have had many Chekhovian plays. None of them rivals *The Cherry Orchard* or *The Three Sisters,* but they are not worse plays because of his influence, they are all better than they might have been. While appearing at first so indifferent to the immediate demands of the Theatre, in the end Chekhov liberated and enriched it.

David Magarshack (essay date 1972)

SOURCE: "Introduction," in *The Real Chekhov: An Introduction to Chekhov's Last Plays,* George Allen & Unwin, 1972, pp. 9-18.

[In the following, Magarshack examines misinterpretations of Chekhov's plays by theater directors, translators, and others.]

> *The stage is a scaffold on which the playwright is executed.*
>
>   Chekhov (Letters)

Chekhov's chief executioners both in Russia and England (not to mention the United States) have been the directors, who quite consistently disregard Chekhov's

intention in writing his plays, inevitably producing a crude distortion of their characters and a travesty of their themes. 'It is highly necessary', Mr Basil Ashton declared in a letter to the *New Statesman* (II September 1970)

> for anyone who really cares about the classics to insist on the theatre providing a few directors who respect their author, rather than seeking, solely, to air their egos. . . . It is only by the *writings* of dramatists that the theatre survives, and directors should consider this fact as strongly as modern conductors seem able to consider the importance of the composer. As I happen to be a director myself, I cannot be accused of self-interest when I repeat that a director is only of any use when he serves the dramatist and allows the public to see and understand what the dramatist intended.

Chekhov himself had no delusions about the 'egos' of the directors. 'Chuck the theatre,' he advised a fellow-writer. 'With a few exceptions it is nothing but an asylum for megalomaniacs.' It is not a director's 'ego', however, that is the chief culprit in the 'execution' of Chekhov on the stage and screen. What makes him so consistently ignore Chekhov's intention is his complete ignorance of the background of Chekhov's plays as well as of his personal life, of his views of the literary and political problems of his day, and of the circumstances relating to the genesis of his plays. It is the total incomprehension of the central themes of Chekhov's plays that explains why directors are so prone to indulge in wild fantasies. Their ignorance of Chekhov's personal life all too often results in grotesque inventions, which have led some well-known actors to make up to look like Chekhov in the part of Trigorin in *The Seagull.*

It was ignorance of Chekhov's attitude to the literary and political problems of his day that led Stanislavsky to describe Chekhov's comedies as 'great tragedies of Russian life'. This cardinal misconception gave rise to the sadness-cum-despair syndrome which became such a characteristic feature of most Chekhov productions.

This was already manifest in Stanislavsky's production of *The Seagull* at the close of the first season of the Moscow Art Theatre in December 1898. It was the last play of the season. The theatre had scored a moderate success with its first play, a mediocre historical drama by Count Alexey Tolstoy, but the other five plays in its repertoire had been dismal failures. The whole future of the Moscow Art Theatre depended on the success or failure of *The Seagull.* It was a resounding success and the theatre was saved. At the time this success was attributed to the 'mood' of the play and the *mises en scène.* Stanislavsky was responsible for both. The 'mood', which was to become so generally accepted as the most characteristic feature of Chekhov's plays, may have corresponded with the despondent mood of the Russian educated classes before the revolutions of 1905 and 1917, but it had nothing whatever to do with Chekhov's play. As for the *mises en scène,* they were made up entirely of the inventions and gimmicks Stanislavsky had used so successfully in his amateur productions: the nocturnal countryside noises of croaking frogs, the crake of the landrail, the chirrings of the crickets, the ominous reddish light hovering over the darkness, and the slow tolling of a distant church bell which, Stanislavsky explains in his 'score' of *The Seagull,* 'help the audience to get the feel of the sad monotonous life of the characters'. Here we have the birth of the sadness-cum-despair syndrome, which threw Chekhov into a fit of blind fury when the play was performed for him later. Indeed, Chekhov was so furious with Stanislavsky's misinterpretation of his comedy that, unable to demand Stanislavsky's dismissal from his own theatre, he kept insisting on the instant dismissal of the young actress who played Nina and whose 'sad and monotonous' mood and bursts of loud sobbing (neither she nor Stanislavsky had the faintest idea of the real meaning of the last scene of the play), Chekhov declared had ruined his play. He was to say the same thing about Stanislavsky's production of *The Cherry Orchard.*

The two never got on. Chekhov treated Stanislavsky with half-amused contempt. Stanislavsky, as he was to admit many years later in his reminiscences, thought Chekhov to be 'supercilious and insincere'. But the reason for their disagreement lay much deeper than mere personal antipathy, and it also explains why Stanislavsky so persistently misunderstood and misinterpreted Chekhov's plays. To Chekhov, the son of an impoverished former serf, the sale of the Gayev estate and its unproductive cherry orchard was, as he makes Trofimov explain to Anya at the end of Act II, merely the inevitable consequence of the life of people who for centuries had lived at the expense of those whom they did not admit 'further than their entrance hall'. They were not tragic figures at all, but characters in a comedy. To Stanislavsky, the son and heir of a rich factory owner, they were, on the contrary, characters of 'a great tragedy', as indeed he would have regarded the failure of his father's lucrative business as 'a great tragedy'.

The most extraordinary thing in the whole history of European drama is the contemptuous dismissal by directors of Chekhov's own description of *The Seagull* and *The Cherry Orchard* as comedies. They are quick enough to acknowledge Chekhov as one of the greatest dramatists of his age, but they do not seem to take him seriously when he claims his two plays to be comedies. Do they really believe that Chekhov did not know the difference between a comedy and a tragedy? The main reason for this almost unanimous disregard of Chekhov's intention in writing the two plays is, of course, that both plays seem to end unhappily for some of their chief characters. In *The Seagull,* Konstantin's suicide is generally interpreted as being due to an unhappy love affair. B. N. Livanov, director of the Moscow Art Theatre's first revival of *The Seagull* after over sixty years, did not hesitate to distort Chekhov's intention by the insertion of new dialogue and to mutilate the play by completely ignoring Chekhov's stage directions. According to Livanov, Konstantin commits suicide because he is 'disillusioned by Nina's rejection of him'. This is what Stanislavsky and countless other directors took to be the reason for Konstantin's suicide. When, towards the end of

the last act, Konstantin asks Nina where she is going, and she replies simply enough that she is going back to the town, Stanislavsky interpolates the melodramatic note: 'This is where he really dies'. But, surely, if disappointed love made him commit suicide, he should have 'died' earlier at the time when Nina had told him that she was still in love with Trigorin.

Konstantin's suicide does not make *The Seagull* into a tragedy, in the dramatic meaning of the word, any more than does Uncle Vanya's suicide at the end of the third act of *The Wood Demon*—the first Tolstoyan version of *Uncle Vanya*—which Chekhov also described as a comedy and provided with a happy ending strictly in accordance with the Tolstoyan notion (made abundantly plain in Tolstoy's famous story 'The Devil') that a man who lusts after a married woman ought to put a bullet through his head. Konstantin's suicide has a much deeper significance. It concerns Konstantin's realisation that his uncritical acceptance of the ideas of the *avant-garde* symbolist movement had resulted in his failure as a writer, a theme which has wider implications and is as pertinent today as it was in Chekhov's day.

Chekhov strongly objected to being labelled a 'realist'. To him labels like 'realism' or 'naturalism' were just, as he expressed it through the mouth of Uncle Vanya, 'nothing but a lot of nonsense'. Indeed, what makes *The Seagull* and *The Cherry Orchard* comedies in the strict meaning of the word is that both plays are based on the principle that characterises both low and high comedy, namely, the incongruity between reality and delusion. The clash between things as they are and things as they are believed to be by the characters of a comedy is also one of the most characteristic aspects of a Chekhov play. When Mrs Ranevsky is told that her estate and the unproductive, though aesthetically beautiful, cherry orchard are quite certain to be sold at a public auction, she refuses to believe it, while her brother Gayev, a confirmed escapist, takes refuge in his obsession with billiards (a situation that would have appeared more credible to English and American audiences if his obsession had been with golf). When the slow-witted country schoolmaster Medvedenko declares at the very beginning of the first act of *The Seagull* that Nina and Konstantin are in love and that in Konstantin's play 'their souls will unite in an endeavour to give expression to one and the same artistic ideas', the preciosity of such an utterance should immediately arouse the suspicions of a perceptive audience and prepare it for the following scene between Nina and Konstantin, which far from being a love scene, as it is usually played, shows the first serious rift in the boy-and-girl romance of the two chief characters of the comedy.

The Moscow Art Theatre's last production of *The Seagull* shows all too clearly how easy it is for a director to destroy and mutilate a great play by totally ignoring the playwright's intention. Stanislavsky at least was very careful not to interfere with Chekhov's text, which cannot be said of Livanov who had no compunction at all in amending, cutting, rewriting and, generally, mangling Chekhov's text to satisfy his own philistine ideas of how the play should have been written. English and American directors have it much easier. It is the translator who does most of the mangling for them.

Chekhov burst upon the English stage at a time when Stanislavsky and his Moscow Art Theatre were at the height of their fame in the West. It was natural, therefore, that Stanislavsky's idea of Chekhov's plays as 'tragedies of Russian life' should have been accepted without question. It was also at the same time—that is, in the early twenties—that the only widely recognised translator from the Russian was Constance Garnett, whose admirable zeal and indefatigable perseverance was only equalled by her inadequate knowledge of Russian which never rose above the dictionary level. It was Constance Garnett who for a long time monopolised the presentation of Chekhov plays on the English stage, leaving a ghastly legacy of misconceptions and misrepresentations that made them synonymous in the mind of the English spectator with sadness, gloom and despair.

The frequent mistranslations of Russian colloquial expressions and idioms necessarily introduce an element of quaintness which is totally absent from the original text. This element of quaintness is intensified by the attempt, so beloved by directors who have no idea of their author's intention, to convey the 'Russian' atmosphere, either by the introduction of Russian words into the dialogue or by insisting that the actors should use Russian names and patronymics which are usually mispronounced so horribly that no Russian would be able to recognise them. Why insist on patronymics when they not only confuse the audience but also interfere with the rhythm of English speech, and when the slightest Russian variation of them, such as Potapych instead of Potapovich in the *Three Sisters,* is quite meaningless to an English or American ear? The same is true of the Russian diminutives which are also invariably mispronounced and whose infinite variations convey different meanings beyond the comprehension of an English-speaking audience. Why insist on making the actors pronounce Petya or Alexandr when all it means is 'darling Peter' and 'Alexander'? What actually happens, therefore, is that what the director takes to be the 'Russian atmosphere' is not Russian at all. It is nothing but a fraud perpetrated upon an audience to cover up a director's ignorance.

This failure to see the hidden meaning of a word or a name is also true of American translators of Chekhov's plays. Korney Chukovsky, the well-known Russian critic, translator and poet, has this to say about Miss Marian Fell's translations of Chekhov plays in his recently-published book on *Translation as a High Art Form*:

> Marian Fell excelled herself in her translations of Chekhov plays. She has made up a hundredfold for all the howlers and mistakes ever made by her Russian colleagues. The Russian scholar and art critic Batyushkov, mentioned in *Uncle Vanya,* becomes a Greek Orthodox priest, for she seems to have confused the surname Batyushkov for *batyushka,* the Russian word for a priest. In another play she has transformed the

radical critic Dobrolyubov into St Francis of Assisi by translating his name literally as 'a lover of goodness' and jumping to the conclusion that Chekhov must have meant St Francis. In *Ivanov* Count Shabelsky says that he has spent twenty thousand roubles on all sorts of cures. She translates it: 'In the course of my life I have nursed several thousand sick people.' Indeed, the whole character of Count Shabelsky has been smashed to smithereens by her translation of a short sentence. Chekhov wrote: *'Tebya, brat, zayela sreda',* which means, 'You, my dear fellow, are the victim of your environment.' Miss Fell, mistaking *sreda* for the Russian word for Wednesday, translates it: 'You have got out of your bed on the wrong side.' She describes Gogol as a Russian fabulist. Every page of Miss Fell's translation of Chekhov's plays is teeming with blunders which completely distort Chekhov's text. But let us suppose for a moment that, overcome with shame, Miss Fell eliminated all her howlers and mistakes, that *batyushka* became, as in Chekhov, Batyushkov, that St Francis became Dobrolyubov, that, in short, her translations became a faithful translinear rendering of the Russian text, even then it would have been of no use at all, for it would have lacked the most important quality of the original, its style, without which Chekhov is not Chekhov.

But, style apart, it is the ignorance of the background of the plays that more often results in the total misconception of their author's intention. A good example of this is Constance Garnett's substitution of Chekhov's Hamlet quotation in the first act of *The Seagull* by another quotation from the same play. When Chekhov first submitted his play to the censor prior to its performance at the Alexandrinsky Theatre in Petersburg, the censor objected to several passages at the beginning of the first act in which Konstantin referred in scathing terms to his mother's relationship with Trigorin. For a son to speak so disrespectfully of his mother was considered to be quite inadmissible in a public performance of a play. Chekhov was told that unless he deleted those passages he would obtain no permission for the performance of his play on the stage of what at the time was not a private but a state theatre. He, therefore, decided to make Konstantin recite Hamlet's lines to Gertrude, 'Nay, but to live in the rank sweat of an enseamed bed', etc., so as to reveal Konstantin's disapproval of Arkadina's relations with Trigorin and, at the same time, make it quite impossible for the censor to object to it. To introduce the lines and to heighten their dramatic effect, he had to give Arkadina Gertrude's preceding lines, as a cue for her son's violent outburst. Constance Garnett totally failed to grasp the relevance of the Hamlet quotation. She therefore substituted two lines Hamlet uses for the introduction of his own play: 'And let me wring your heart, for so I shall / If it be made of penetrable stuff', an utterly inappropriate quotation, for it was not Konstantin's intention to wring anybody's heart, but merely to give a dramatic form to the cosmic conflict between the two primary super-human figures of the World Soul and Satan as conceived by the poet and mystic Vladimir Solovyov, one of the leading figures of the Russian Symbolist Movement, of which Konstantin was an ardent adherent. Needless to say, Constance Garnett completely misses

Elsa Lanchester and James Mason in a 1933 Old Vic production of
The Cherry Orchard

the meaning of the seagull theme (as, indeed, do most of the directors and actors of the play) by the mistranslation of a single word in Nina's speech in the last act by making Nina say, 'What matters is not fame . . . but knowing how to be patient', instead of 'knowing how to endure'.

The mistranslation of a single word may sometimes be enough to ruin a Chekhov play by reducing one of its chief characters to a state of utter idiocy. There was the case of a well-known director who used a 'new' translation of *The Cherry Orchard* (directors are very keen on using 'new' translations without bothering to find out whether the translator has the qualifications for it) in which Trofimov's advice to Lopakhin not to throw his arms about is translated: 'Don't flap your hands'. Lopakhin in this production kept flapping his hands all through the play. He would do so even in the middle of a speech, pausing to flap his hands whenever he wished to emphasise a point. It was no use explaining to the director in question the utter senselessness of Lopakhin's hand-flapping. He seemed quite convinced that the flapping had some deep meaning, some mystic revelation of the 'Russian soul', some Dostoevskian streak of submissiveness and suffering in the far from submissive or suffering Lopakhin.

Quite often a translator will deliberately mistranslate a single word to justify a generally accepted perversion of a Chekhov character. Elisaveta Fen, the translator of the Penguin edition of Chekhov's plays, does just that in translating the second line of Chebutykin's version of 'Tarara-boom-di-ay' as 'I'm sitting on a toomb-di-ay', as a final confirmation of the Chekhovian sadness-cum-despair syndrome. Miss Fen, of course, knows very well that the Russian word *toomba* does not mean a tomb but a round stone post at the corner of a street in a Russian town. The intention of the second line is simply to put the finishing touch to the man who describes himself as 'not a human being at all', whose creed is that 'nothing matters', and who does nothing to save his favourite Irene's husband-to-be from being shot dead in a duel at which he as doctor is present. Miss Fen has become the victim of the general lunacy which is so characteristic a feature of the Chekhov cult.

Another feature of this cult is boredom. 'In *Uncle Vanya*', an English critic wrote in a recent issue of a well-known Sunday paper, 'the whole theme is the boredom of comfortable provincial life'! [*Sunday Times*, 15 November 1970]. The view of a lunatic? Not at all. It simply is one more proof of the well-known phenomenon, namely that once somebody or something becomes the object of a cult then even the craziest idea can be accepted without questioning. That is the explanation of why an English director does not hesitate to sit down with several translations of a Chekhov play and proceed to write his own 'version', for he is convinced that he *knows* what Chekhov *ought to have written,* and he manipulates his or somebody else's version of the play accordingly: gloom, despondency, a dialogue that makes no sense, a few Russian words scattered here and there, a general atmosphere of gloom and despair, and scenery that is the work of some celebrated stage designer and that by itself is sufficient to kill the play stone dead. There is, furthermore, the strong itch felt by some ignorant, fashionable directors to introduce a 'new slant' into a Chekhov play. In one production of *The Cherry Orchard* Mrs Ranevsky, it is made apparent, was about to have, or is having, an affair with Yasha of all people, for does not Gayev declare that his sister is an immoral woman? It is true that such idiocies are rare, though not so rare as an attempt to raise a laugh in the audience by making Arkadina destroy the whole meaning of the first scene of the second act of *The Seagull* by sagging and holding her side after trying to convince everybody how young she still is.

Stanislavsky was fully aware of the uncontrollable impulses of actors and directors to contrive something 'new', to give full scope to some new trend, some passing whim, some gimmick that might provide publicity and help to furbish their reputations. His remedy can be summed up in one word: *subtext*—undertext, which does not mean reading between the lines of the text, but an attempt to reconstruct the life of the characters from the sometimes insufficient data of the text. Unfortunately, the *subtext* does not prevent a director who is ignorant of the background or the genesis of the play or of the dramatist's intention in writing it, from superimposing his own ideas on it and in this way distorting both its meaning and the motives of its characters. Chekhov himself was loath to discuss his plays with the actors. But he did say something to them that sounds so simple that very few people have paid any attention to it. 'Why don't you *read* my play? It is all there!' In fact, *it is all there*. The trouble is that in reading a Chekhov play, directors and actors seem to be bereft of all commonsense by the nonsense that has been written and accepted by critics, academics and directors for the past seventy years. When urged that new movements in drama justified a new approach to his plays, Chekhov's reply was that no conditions justified a lie.

Siegfried Melchinger   (essay date 1972)

SOURCE: "Chekhov and the Craft of Theater," in *Anton Chekhov,* translated by Edith Tarcov, Frederick Ungar Publishing Co., 1972, pp. 62-84.

[*In the essay below, Melchinger investigates the ways Chekhov overthrew the theatrical conventions of his day.*]

In 1902, Chekhov wrote to Alexander Tikhonov:

> You say you wept over my plays. You are not the only one. But I did not write them for this. It was Stanislavsky who made them so tearful. I intended something quite different.

Chekhov's judgment of Stanislavsky's productions of the Chekhov plays—as numerous passages from letters and witnesses' observations testify—can be summarized in a sentence he wrote about the production of *The Cherry Orchard* a few weeks before his death: "Stanislavsky has ruined my play."

It is said that dramatists cannot judge the productions of their plays. That may be true of those who do not understand the theater, but not of Chekhov, who knew and understood the stage. When he was still an adolescent in Taganrog his favorite pastime was attending the theater. When he went to Moscow as a nineteen-year-old, to study medicine and to rescue his family from their poverty-stricken life, the theater attracted him more than anything else. He wrote his stories to earn a living. Now that a heavily edited draft of *Play without a Title (Platonov)*—on which he must have worked for a long time and with much passion—has been found among his posthumous papers, we know what really was in his thoughts.

When Chekhov was writing this play, he had a plan, a program for the theater. Later, for a while, he abandoned this plan and made concessions to the conventional stage. But in his major works he returned to his Platonov plan. His contemporaries found the newness and innovation of this plan so strange and shocking that they hooted two Chekhov plays off the stage on opening nights. Not one of his plays was a success in its first production. His works needed time to succeed. The reason was not, as their later success has proved, a lack of dramatic effec-

tiveness, but rather their unusualness. There were times when Chekhov went daily to the theater, to study the conditions of the stage and the conduct and attitudes of the actors. One of these periods occurred while *The Sea Gull* was in rehearsal. His understanding of actors was extremely astute. After all, he eventually was to be married to an actress. One of his contemporaries who worked in the theater reported: "Every false note, every cliché, every fatuous or vulgar nuance made Chekhov wince. . . . Often he would interrupt the actors and plead, 'Please, no theatricality! Let it be simple, just simple!'"

So far, Chekhov's judgment of Stanislavsky's Chekhov theater has not been taken seriously. The Chekhov tradition as originally conceived by the Moscow Art Theater became dated not because there was a quest for the kind of theater Chekhov really had in mind, but rather because of the great changes in theater in general throughout the world. Surprisingly, some of the Chekhov productions in recent years are closer to the concepts of the true Chekhov theater than is the conventional style for producing Chekhov, whose alleged authenticity originated with Stanislavsky. I have in mind: the Milan production of *Platonov,* directed by Giorgio Strehler; the Stockholm production of *The Sea Gull,* directed by Ingmar Bergman; *The Three Sisters,* produced in Stuttgart under the direction of Rudolf Noelte and, also produced in Stuttgart, *The Cherry Orchard,* directed by Peter Zadek; and the Prague production of *The Three Sisters,* under the direction of Otomar Krejča. . . .

While Chekhov was still alive, the true plan and character of Chekhov's work was recognized by some of the younger people. Among those who early appreciated the true Chekhov was Vera Kommissarzhevskaya. She was Chekhov's favorite among the actresses who worked in his plays. (She was the first Sea Gull in the unfortunate Saint Petersburg production that was booed off the stage.) She was among the young rebels who broke early with Stanislavsky. Chekhov wanted to write a play for her after she had left Stanislavsky's ensemble. In her own theater, which she and her brother directed, she provided Meyerhold with a chance for his revolutionary experiments. Meyerhold, another of the young rebels, also had been an actor of the Art Theater and a student of Stanislavsky. He had portrayed Treplev in the famous *Sea Gull* production of 1898. Meyerhold discovered in Chekhov's dramaturgy "new paths that are closed to the methods of psychological realism." He sharply criticized Stanislavsky's overuse of the scenic details that he loved so (an "ocean of objects"), and the sentimental atmosphere, which had made Stanislavsky's production of *The Cherry Orchard* so intolerable to Chekhov. For the third act, in which a ball is taking place while the news about the sale of the cherry orchard is expected, Meyerhold demanded a cold and hard delivery, the projection of a "nightmare," a "horror"; he wrote to Chekhov, "Your play is abstract like a symphony." When Meyerhold in the style of that period spoke of "symbolism" or even "mysticism," he meant to characterize the antirealistic element in Chekhov's plays, the "rhythmic movement" of the work as a whole.

Especially revealing are the observations of Gorky, whom Chekhov loved as a human being, whose talent he recognized at once, and whom he reprimanded for his carelessness as an artist (he has no sense of architecture, doesn't know how to build). "Do you know what you are doing?" Gorky wrote to Chekhov in 1900. "You are flogging realism to death! And it will soon be dead for a long time." Gorky sensed the fundamental tension between the musicality and the coldness in these plays and recognized, above all, their great art of simplicity: "You are a man who can create a character with a mere word, and with a sentence tell a story." This brings to mind Chekhov's words: "The most important thing is to construct a sentence." Gorky said of *Uncle Vanya* that he saw more meaning in this play than others did, something "powerful," which he too called "symbolism." Chekhov, in turn, wrote that Gorky deserved great merit for being the first writer in Russia and in the whole world to express contempt and revulsion for the *meshchanstvo* (usually translated as "petty bourgeoisie," or as "that conservative stratum of society that stagnates in personal egotism," or as "the establishment") and so stimulated the protest of others. Chekhov shared in this protest, but he wanted to do more—he wanted to provoke this protest in the audience. After writing the lines to Tikhonov, quoted at the beginning of this chapter, Chekhov continued:

> I wanted to say simply and honestly, "Look at yourselves, look how badly and boringly you lead your lives!" The most important thing is that people come to recognize this. As soon as they understand it, they will have to live differently and better. I will not live to see it, but I am convinced that life will be quite different then, not to be compared with that of today. But in the meantime I will not stop from repeatedly saying to people: "Just look how boringly and badly you are living!" Yet what is there to weep about?

Chekhov's is "a theater that shows, that exposes," to quote from Ilya Ehrenburg's essay, in which he pleaded that the modern and contemporary quality in Chekhov be recognized.

Gorky expressed it thus:

> Chekhov understood, with a high measure of art, how to recognize and describe the trivial in life. . . . The trivial always found in him a severe critic. . . . This great, wise man, who observed everything, who encountered this boring, gray mass of weak people, looked at the lazy inhabitants of his homeland and said to them, with a sad smile and in a tone of mild but profound reproach, with an expression of hopeless sorrow,—"Ladies and gentlemen, you are living badly!"

Vakhtangov, another revolutionary of the Russian theater, who directed Gerhart Hauptmann's *Friedensfest* ("the Feast of Reconciliation") in the Studio, was reprimanded by Stanislavsky's partner Nemirovich-Danchenko because he brought out the "shrill tones" too sharply. Gorky stood by the young director. Gorky severely opposed the "mania to muffle and mute everything," which had angered him previously in Stanislavsky's production of *The Lower Depths*. He demanded instead, in the sense of Chekhov, "genuine art"—the art of protest.

But we must beware of being unjust. Stanislavsky's historical merit cannot be ignored. It will not be diminished by the observation that he led the Russian theater in a direction different from the one Chekhov had in mind. Perhaps even, considering the course of history, his was the only direction possible. Chekhov's goals were perhaps too much in advance of the times to be comprehensible to his contemporaries. His aggressive opposition to the theater as he found it was as clear as that of Stanislavsky. It was the aggressive opposition of their generation—that of the youth of that epoch in Europe. In 1881, when Chekhov was in the process of finishing his work on *Platonov,* Zola wrote, urging that naturalism be utilized for the stage. He expressed what moved them all: anger toward the pompousness, the dishonesty, the corruption of the theater, a theater that was dominated by the pathos with which the tragedies were presented and the overacting of the stars. The new password was: reality and truth. But years were to pass before reality and truth would reach the Russian stage: in 1887 it would reach the Théâtre Libre in Paris (Antoine); in 1889, the Freie Bühne in Berlin (Otto Brahm, Hauptmann); in 1892, the Independent Theatre in London (Grein, Shaw); in 1896, the Moscow Art Theater. Reading Stanislavsky's memoirs, one gains some insight into the many difficulties and obstacles he had to overcome, from the day he founded the Moscow Society for Art and Literature (in 1888), whose niveau Chekhov hardly took seriously, until he could finally back up his opposition to the present state of the theater with a viable program for the future. Perhaps he would not have been able to achieve this had he not met Nemirovich-Danchenko, his intellectual and literary collaborator. Taking all this into account, one has to admire even more the genius of Chekhov. The *Platonov* play of the twenty-one-year-old Chekhov was written before the publication of Zola's pamphlet, and at a time when Stanislavsky was still dreaming of nothing but operettas and vaudevilles.

The Russian theater, of course, had an advantage over that of the rest of Europe. Since Gogol and Stchepkin, and the first production of Gogol's *Government Inspector* in 1836, it had a tradition of realism. This satirical comedy was even part of the repertoire of the Imperial Theater. It is indeed astonishing that its performance was tolerated in this land where despotism ruthlessly suppressed the slightest expression of an independent impulse. But the Czar was amused when he saw civil servants satirized. The aristocracy, more and more hard-pressed by the rising bourgeoisie, encouraged derision of the new capitalist class. And so Ostrovsky could become the program director of the Imperial Theater. It was in the year of Ostrovsky's death that Tolstoy wrote the naturalistic peasant drama *The Power of Darkness*. However, it was not to be performed until 1889, and then in Paris, by Antoine, not in Russia.

The form of satire seduced the Russian dramatists and actors into caricature. But in Chekhov's plan there was no place for caricature. "Even if it were in the interest of the theater to caricature human beings, it would be a lie. It is simply unnecessary. A caricature, of course, will sharpen an image and so be more easily understood. But it is better to work out the drawing of a sketch with care than to smear it up with showy and shoddy strokes."

Caricaturing actors have a tendency to hamming. In their indignation at the low niveau of the Russian theater Stanislavsky and Chekhov were in agreement. The actors were despised by society and often led slovenly, debauched lives. Many of them became alcoholics. Only those who were able to rise to a position in the Imperial Theaters were guaranteed a measure of respectability. But even there conditions were in an unbelievable state of muddle and slovenliness. Chekhov believed, . . . that the major cause of the scandalous uproar and failure of the 1887 premiere of *Ivanov* was that the actors did not know their lines and that they were drunk by the last act. He reported that what had been recited on the stage was unbelievable. In 1882 this was his judgment: "The Russian actor has everything—except education, culture, and manners, in the good sense of the word." Besides the slovenly bungling, he found the stars' method of upstaging the rest of the cast, the acting up front before the footlights, especially distasteful. And exactly this, despite all his admiration, he had already criticized in 1881 in the acting style of Sarah Bernhardt, who was the rage of the Moscow audience when she played there on tour: "She wants to be striking, to amaze." It was the style of the *coup de théâtre,* the objective of which was to exhibit the virtuosity of the stars. The *coup de théâtre* was the style of *La Tosca* and *La Dame aux Camélias* and other plays by Sardou and Dumas fils. These writers had given up romantic melodrama and were devoting themselves to what was considered realistic theater at the time. But what they deemed "dramatic" was identical with effect. The material was taken "from life," not because it was life that was to be shown, but because this material yielded effects with which a Bernhardt could bring an audience to their knees. The same exaggeration that blurred and hammed up what was truly comic also blurred and hammed up the tragic. With the one it became caricature; with the other it resulted in *coup de théâtre.*

One can imagine what a great impression the Meininger troupe, during their 1885 tour, made on the young Russians, who had read Zola and wished to see resurrected on the Russian stage what once Pushkin, Gogol, and Turgenev had realized—and what Tolstoy and Dostoyevsky now were achieving in the novel (1877, *Anna Karenina;* 1880, *The Brothers Karamazov;* 1886, *The Death of Ivan Ilyich*). In the troupe's performances seriousness, accuracy, and discipline worked in ensemble: it was a "holiday of art," as Stanislavsky wrote. Their productions, with their spirit of solidity and seriousness, made a lasting impression on the young Russians interested in drama. Yet people, even Stanislavsky, also took exception to the exaggeratedly emotional acting of the Germans.

These two principles—solidity and seriousness—were to form the cornerstone of the Moscow Art Theater. And Chekhov understood well what an advance these new standards would bring about in the Russian theater. To have them succeed was a historical feat and accomplishment, and Chekhov did not withhold recognition of this achievement. He never did like Stanislavsky, though he later respected him, but he felt warm sympathy for Nemirovich-Danchenko. He felt even more warmth for the actors, whose esprit de corps and sense of ensemble-playing he praised. He would have felt much warmth toward them even if he had not found his future wife, Olga Knipper, among them. What these actors did on the stage for the sake of art and truth moved him deeply. "One must wrest the stage out of the hands of the merchants," he said, "and give it over into the hands of literary people; otherwise it will perish." Yet it was clear to him, from the time of the production of *The Sea Gull* in 1898 to that of *The Cherry Orchard* in 1904, that the director and the actors of the Art Theater took the path to his plays "without me." They believed they knew better than he did. And their success seemed to prove them right. Stanislavsky—who always thought of himself as "a slow one"—deserves respect for describing the late insight he gained while writing his memoirs in 1925—an insight that, as he wrote, gave him "new horizons":

> The works of all geniuses who, like Chekhov, represent a cornerstone, outlive generations; generations do not outlive them. . . . It is possible that some of what is Chekhov, in this or that work, may appear dated and for the postrevolutionary era no longer valid—yet Chekhov, in *how* he has presented his material, has not even begun to come to full flower in our theater. The chapter about Chekhov in the history of our theater is far from finished; we have not yet studied him thoroughly enough, have not yet penetrated to his inner essence. We have closed the book prematurely. We must open it anew, to study it thoroughly and read to the end.

Stanislavsky had not understood the *how* in Chekhov. He had distorted the *how* because of his fixation on elements that, though contained in Chekhov's work, he had interpreted wrongly. He directed theater of atmosphere—mood theater—and the mood, which dominated this theater, was that of ennui. In Chekhov, mood is an element among others, though one he knew how to use as few have before him. And ennui was for him the opposite of what Stanislavsky made of it. That is, it was not to Chekhov tearful, melancholic, elegiac, sentimental. It was something hateful, as it would be for a man who suffered bitterly from ennui after he was forced (by his physicians) to endure it—a man who, according to Gorky, conceived of work as the basis of all culture and civilization. What Chekhov brought to the stage as boredom or "ennui" is best translated as "emptiness." This ennui, this boredom of his epoch, is only superficially different from that of today: we, of course, have the added element of noise.

The consciousness of emptiness, then as today, is numbing. And it is as hateful today as it was then because those who suffer it have no desire and no courage to face the truth, as it is, and to draw from that the necessary conclusions. It is this which Kierkegaard calls "indifference"—and nothing enraged Chekhov more, as we know, than to be accused of "indifference": "I hate lies and violence in any form. . . . Don't I protest, from the beginning to the end, against the lie?" This hateful thing has to be protested, as Gorky had demanded and Vakhtangov had done. The worst one can do with it is to transform it into mood. To lull the audience into a sniveling, tearful sentimentality relieves it of the task which Chekhov meant to confront it with. As he so often said,

> They [the audience] shall be the jury: they have to reach the verdict. The artist's task is to observe, to choose, to unmask, to sum up. And these tasks presuppose a question. If there is no question asked to begin with, there is nothing to unmask, to expose, to select. . . . Those are right who demand that the artist must have a conscious relationship to his work. But they often confuse two concepts: the solution of the question, and the right way of asking it. The commitment of the artist is only to the second task. . . . It is the duty of the court to formulate the problem correctly, but it is up to the members of the jury to solve it, each according to his own insight.

Chekhov once observed that it would seem very agreeable to combine art and sermon, and then to put the whole burden on "the gospel" that is being preached, without first bringing the reader or the audience to the point where they can believe in that gospel. For him, he said, this would be simply "technically impossible." He said, "When I present a horse thief, they want me to say, it is bad to steal a horse. But everyone knows that well enough, without my saying so."

Chekhov's basic principle is scientific: it is objectivity. Its application demands extreme coolness. "Only he who is cool is just." True justice determines the organization of the material, which has to be presented both objectively and convincingly, if "the jurors" are to discover the truth. In this, above all, the controversy with Stanislavsky came to a head. For Stanislavsky believed that it was the task of the director to reinforce the mood, to make it as inescapable as possible, through details and stage effects.

Meyerhold reported that in the scene in *The Sea Gull* in which Arkadina says farewell to the servants, Chekhov had specified that there be three of them. Stanislavsky, however, had a whole mass of people come onto the stage, among whom was a woman with a crying baby in her arms. "Why this?" Chekhov asked him. The answer was, that this was "just like in real life" and "realistic." Chekhov laughed, "So, this is realistic!" After a brief silence he continued: "But this is the stage—and the stage is art! If you take a good portrait painting, cut out the nose, and put into the hole a real nose, that is realistic—but the painting is ruined."

As for the crying baby Chekhov said, "This is superfluous. It is as if you play pianissimo on the piano and the lid falls, crashing down on the keys." Again, the answer was that it was often like this in real life, and that often a forte, suddenly, breaks into a pianissimo.

"Undoubtedly," Chekhov replied. "But the stage has its own conditions. Don't you know that you don't have a fourth wall? The theater is art; it expresses the quintessence of life. It is unnecessary to fill it up with superfluous details."

The quintessence is contained in the text. What is not in the text must not be brought onto the stage. He was cross when the actors begged him to explain their parts to them. "It is all written down in the text. I am just a doctor." It was indeed all written down in the text.

This is how Chekhov described one part of his *Platonov* plan:

> In real life people don't spend every minute shooting each other, hanging themselves, or making declarations of love. They don't dedicate their time to saying intelligent things. They spend much more of it eating, drinking, flirting, and saying foolish things—and that is what should happen on the stage. Someone should write a play in which people come and go, eat, talk about the weather, and play cards. Life should be exactly as it is, and people should be exactly as complicated and at the same time exactly as simple as they are in life. People eat a meal, and at the same time their happiness is made or their lives are being ruined.

That has sounds of Zola. But what is decisive is not the goal, not the imitation of reality, but the method. It is the opposite of the "well-made play," the *pièce-bien-faite,* as, from Eugène Scribe (1791-1861) to Henrik Ibsen (1828-1906), it has been "dramatically" developed.

Chekhov was not fond of Ibsen: "He doesn't understand anything about life." Ibsen himself admitted that he had learned his dramatic technique from that of the well-made play. According to its pattern, he had constructed his plot, which, by means of its dramatic climax, proved its effectiveness as theater. Chekhov believed that plot is unimportant for the stage. He rejected "the dramatic" when it was the result of calculated effect. His friends in the theater rebuked him because, allegedly, he did not understand "dramatic" as they understood it. Six years after writing *Platonov* he was ready to make a compromise—in *Ivanov.* It failed—because the gap between the truth he sought to show and the stage effects he was utilizing could not be bridged.

The method Chekhov discovered as he designed the *Platonov* plan (more correctly, he *re*discovered it, for the Greeks and Shakespeare had known this plan before him) was that of the dual planes of the stage—one of which is indirect. When people talk to one another, the truth usually is not contained in what they say but rather in what they do not say. They talk in order to talk. They talk, often without answering each other. They talk past each other, each preoccupied with himself. They talk, in order to deceive themselves. There is always a pause, because they either don't understand one another or they don't really hear one another. But in these pauses life goes on; decisive things can happen in these intervals of silence. And so Chekhov discovered (*re*discovered) the dramatic meaning of silence.

This was both understood and misunderstood in the Moscow Art Theater. Indeed, Nemirovich-Danchenko and Stanislavsky recognized the uniqueness in Chekhov's indirect method. Chekhov's method was to bring about a revolution in the art of the theater and was even to shed new light on the presentation of the works of a Sophocles or a Shakespeare. A contemporary of Chekhov's described the technique that evolved from this indirect method:

> The inner dialogue, and the charm of that which is only half-expressed—this was what the performers of the Art Theater projected. Chekhov had abolished the old concept of plot and action, and now the theater discovered that the word is far from being the most important element in the art of the theater. The word is only an indication of inner emotions, one that is neither complete nor perfect but only a guide that can lead to the soul of the character. But often and at the most dramatic moments the word becomes mute and yields to silence. This silence is full of meaning, full of the whole energy of the spoken words that have gone before, and of the latent presence of the thousands of words that are to follow or that perhaps will never be said. This silence is stronger than the most violent scream, and it contains more meaning than a hundred words that are determined by a defined meaning. Thus the goal of the drama becomes his silence. And it must be acted out and projected so that it resounds and breaks out into a thousand colors.

The Moscow Art Theater staged Chekhov's silence in exaggerated ways. First, they padded it with innumerable details of silent acting, with such effects as the crying baby in the farewell scene in *The Cherry Orchard,* in their effort to achieve the "purest" reality. Second, they strove with all their resources to express emotions through silent acting, so that the audience simply could not overlook what went on in the "inner dialogue." Chekhov felt that this was not his but another kind of theater, and exactly the theater he wanted to avoid. Here is an example.

In the last scene of *Uncle Vanya* there occurs, again, a leave-taking. Astrov, the doctor, a central character, steps up to a map of Africa that hangs on the wall and says, "The heat must be awful in Africa now—just awful!" Olga Knipper wrote to her future husband how marvelously Stanislavsky played this scene: "How much bitterness, how much experience of life he expressed in that line! And how he pronounced the words, with a kind of bravura that was most exciting!" And she reported that he had also played the preceding love scene in this way. Chekhov was horrified. He answered:

> You write that, in this scene, Astrov turns to Yelena like a passionate lover—"He holds on to his emotion

like a drowning man to a straw." But that is wrong, all wrong! Astrov likes Yelena, he is attracted by her beauty. But in the last act he knows very well that nothing will come of it, that Yelena will disappear from his life, and he speaks in this scene in the same tone he uses when talking of the heat in Africa. He kisses her merely to while away the time.

Later, Chekhov wrote directly to Stanislavsky: "Astrov whistles, you see. He whistles. Uncle Vanya weeps, but Astrov whistles." After this Stanislavsky (and it indeed speaks well for him) changed his interpretation of the role. Yet this example demonstrates how right Chekhov was when he said that Stanislavsky was still seeking to present "old theater." The acting-out of silence was for Stanislavsky what once had been the old *coup de théâtre.*

Chekhov hated overexplanations; he admonished the young Meyerhold not to exaggerate in presenting the nervousness of a lonely man. "Let it be in the tone of your voice and in your eyes, but don't project it with your hands and feet. Do it with grace, with sparse, expressive gestures." On the same subject he wrote to Olga, "Most people are nervous, most of them suffer, and only a few feel acute pain. But where—on the street or in the house—do you see people nervously running back and forth and constantly clutching their heads?"

The word "grace" is curious and noteworthy. This is how Chekhov defined what he meant by the word "grace": "When a person performing a particular action uses a minimum of movement—that is grace."

The silence Chekhov prescribes is exactly the opposite of "the acting out of silence." It is nothing other than silence, motionlessness, concentration. The Japanese actors of the *No* theater have developed this art of "doing nothing" to its highest level. Chekhov surely never saw them. But for many years he had studied actors on the stage, and he knew how much they were able to say when they were silent. He had seen Eleonora Duse; and perhaps Yermolova, too, had done similar acting. He knew how ambiguous spoken words could be. He fashioned his dialogue with this in mind. His dialogue consists of what is said and what is not said (perhaps what cannot be said).

People have counted how often the word "pause" appears in Chekhov's stage directions. Yet such a count can only be superficial; the number of pauses in Chekhov is far greater than the overt instructions indicate. The pauses occur when the actor is walking or making gestures or emptily chattering away. Chekhov's "pauses" demand of the actor the highest degree of concentration, absolute motionlessness, a distillation of thoughts and emotions in which the character is to be immersed.

Stanislavsky's use of sound effects in the stagings of Chekhov's plays has become famous. In a play that was set on a summer afternoon in the country, the theatergoer himself was to experience the illusion that he himself was spending a summer afternoon in the country. And this is how Stanislavsky justified the innumerable details with which he elaborated Chekhov's stage directions.

Certainly, Chekhov's plays require more sound effects than were ever used before on the stage. However, the sound effects Chekhov prescribes are not illusion-creating but dramaturgic. They are not there to provide mood and atmosphere—they are there to "speak." By means of the Chopin waltz Treplev plays backstage in the last act of *The Sea Gull,* he is present on the stage—giving his commentary on the dialogue. The strange sound that is twice called for in *The Cherry Orchard* tears at one's nerves. It is, as Meyerhold has said, "symbolic," so far as the assonance to the "tearing of a string" [of a violin] is to be taken literally. It is part of the elements of a theater whose effects, exactly calculated, are chosen from all the possibilities available to the stage. This sound effect does not occur "by chance"; it is not an imitation of reality. It is part of a thought-out plan in a work of art, in which chance only exists when it is intended, in which everything superfluous has been eliminated.

As there must be no misunderstanding of Chekhov's concept and use of "mood" and "atmosphere," so there must be no misunderstanding of his concept and use of "simplicity," which is so prominent and important in his observations. He criticized the verbal "extravagance" of Gorky. "Strike out all adjectives . . . ," he said to him. "Write 'The man sat down in the grass.' Basta." Chekhov's simplicity is not the language of the "simple man"; it is, like his silence, a distillation.

Chekhov once wrote to the critic Menshikov apropos one of his articles: "There is something missing in your article. You have given too little space to the character of language. It is important for your readers to know why a primitive man or a madman will use only one or two hundred words, while a Shakespeare can make use of tens of thousands."

Gorky wrote to Chekhov, observing that his language had a "magical quality, both terse and powerful." Gorky also said that Pushkin, Turgenev, and Chekhov created the Russian language.

The art of Chekhov's language lies in its terseness and brevity—"The art of writing consists less in good writing than in cutting out what is bad writing." As he so often said, everything superfluous has to be cut out. When Olga wrote to him that she was coming to grips with a monologue in *The Three Sisters,* he cabled her, "Omit everything except one sentence: 'A woman is a woman.'" When the superfluous was cut away, what emerged was not naturalism but art.

His contemporaries, Stanislavsky among them, began early to perceive the musical quality of his dialogue. As Chekhov wrote to a woman writer, everything depends on the construction of the sentence. "One must take care," he added, "that it be musical." This musicalness is neither romantic nor sentimental. He hated prose that sounded like "poetry." And the always low-keyed tone in which

the actors of the Moscow Art Theater spoke their lines got on his nerves. Like music, there is contrast in speech: there is forte, piano, diminuendo and crescendo, accelerando, ritardando and rubato. Whole scenes are as tightened and unified as one single bow and have to be played as such, while others are divided into exactly delineated, carefully composed parts. Pauses are parts of the composition—they are its fermatas and caesuras. Chekhov's plays have to be performed like musical compositions. (This was a goal that Stanislavsky, according to the report of his students, also set himself in his later years.)

Chekhov's structures are so terse and severe that any tampering will shake their frame. Just as Stanislavsky failed because he padded out these concentrated forms, so modern directors have failed because of their rearrangements and deletions. When Chekhov said, "It is all written down in the text," he meant not only that nothing should be staged that was not written down, but also that nothing should be left out that was written down. How could he have reproached Gorky for understanding nothing of the architecture of writing, if he had not known so exactly what meaning good architecture has for a play?

The only material of which Chekhov's plays are built are life and truth. "In art, only in art," he used to say, "one cannot lie." The plan he set himself when he wrote *Platonov,* which developed in opposition to both the idealistic and the conventional theatrical styles, culminated in bringing onto the stage an "encyclopedia of life"—as he said at the time, of Russian life. Even in his later years he did not think it possible that his plays could be performed outside Russia. It is absurd to maintain that he wished to present a naturalistic picture of his epoch (Ehrenburg commented on this refreshingly and clarifyingly), but it is equally absurd to assume that he wanted to bring the whole of Russia onto the stage. His was quite a different kind of material—and material that he knew exactly. When he criticized Tolstoy for being "ignorant," his argument was that Tolstoy wrote about syphilis while not knowing anything about how and what syphilis was. Behind the Russian foreground Chekhov presented the quintessence of all human life. Thomas Mann spoke of his uncanny gift for identifying himself with other human beings, for putting himself into their situations and condition. The writer Alexander Kuprin, who knew him well, said, "He saw and heard while looking into a person's face, hearing his voice, watching his walk, that which was hidden." Out of all this grew an "amalgam of personal observations and feelings, and of his experiences, his conjectures, and his power of imagination" (Ehrenburg).

Chekhov took over nothing exactly as he found it in life. He detested both subjectivism and naturalism. The art of composition for him boiled down to what he called his "encyclopedia," which he brought onto the stage in sparse and concentrated form. His models were Shakespeare, Cervantes, and Pushkin. *Platonov* got out of hand because the young Chekhov lacked the experience and mastery of so concentrating his material. In the next plays he was to write—*Ivanov* and *The Wood Demon* (out of which *Uncle Vanya* was to emerge)—he made up for this youthful lack of experience with concessions to the contemporary conventional theater's "dramatic" demands for "melodramatic" effect-filled scenes.

Finally, in *The Sea Gull* he succeeded in wringing out of his "encyclopedic" intention the conciseness that his vision demanded. He knew that the images that now emerged were truly art. Through distillation he shaped the rambling and accidental in true life into a form that enabled him to project the quintessence of life's truth. He let it show through the nonexisting fourth wall of the stage, so that the audience could see and recognize it. So the quintessence was brought before the audience, the jury that had to reach its verdict. Chekhov's theater, then, is one of showing, exposing.

Nothing is to be omitted if the encyclopedia is to be complete. Not illness, not chance, not dirt ("To the chemist nothing is dirty; the writer must be just as objective as the chemist"). The method of Chekhov's art was like that of a science, whose goal is the exact, precise, and subtle presentation of truth. He stayed cool as he wrote, though he loved the material with which he worked: human beings and life.

Whatever is said about Chekhov must be said in contradictions. He was a physician, yet he was also a patient and seriously ill. He "laughed through tears," as Gorky said. He wrote comedies, and they were played like tragedies. He looked through the manner and pretensions of his time and knew, and hoped, that everything was going to be different in the future, everything except that which no one can change: nature, the nature of mankind, and the nature of life.

In 1933 Gorky wrote of him:

> He had such tired hands; when they touched things, they often seemed half reluctant, half unsure. This was also the quality of his walk. He moved like a doctor in a hospital in which there are many patients but no medicines—a doctor who is not really convinced that the patients should be cured.

Janko Lavrin   (essay date 1973)

SOURCE: "Anton Chekhov," in *A Panorama of Russian Literature,* Barnes & Noble, 1973, pp. 175-86.

[*In the following excerpt, Lavrin investigates Chekhov's "method of showing the tragic nature of everyday existence in its ordinary everyday conditions."*]

The impact of Chekhov on world literature seems in some respects stronger than that of any other modern Russian author after Dostoevsky. This applies to his plays even more than to his stories,[1] since he happens to be one of the reformers of the modern theatre and drama. Chekhov himself proclaimed (in one of his letters) the theatre of

his time a 'skin disease, a world of muddle, of stupidity and high-falutin' which should be swept away with a broom.' He did not mind being such a broom even in the late 1880s when the only conspicuous reformer in this respect was Henrik Ibsen. Chekhov's inauguration of drama devoid of traditional plot and big theatrical gestures, not to mention the old declamatory pathos, was a courageous feat in those days, although he may have faltered now and then under the weight of his own experiments. His *Ivánov,* for example, was given a brilliant first performance in the Alexandrinsky theatre at St Petersburg on 31 January, 1889. Its reception was favourable, which, however, could not be said of his next play, *The Seagull (Cháika),* produced in October 1896. Chekhov felt so depressed by its failure that he thought of giving up the theatre altogether. But on 17 December 1898, a very successful production of *The Seagull* took place in the Moscow Art Theatre. Less than a year later another triumph was scored in the same theatre by Chekhov's *Uncle Vanya (Dyáyda Ványa)*—a modification of his less pessimistic play *The Wood Demon (Léshiy).*[2]

Chekhov thus became closely connected with the Moscow Art Theatre, run by Stanislavsky and Nemirovich-Danchenko. In 1900 he wrote for it *The Three Sisters (Tri sestrý)* and in 1903—roughly one year before his death—he completed *The Cherry Orchard (Vishnyóvy sad).* In addition, he was responsible for several one-act plays some of which are dramatised short stories. They abound in farcical situations, quite in the tradition of the old vaudevilles which were always great favourites with the Russian audiences. Such of his one-act plays as *The Proposal (Predlozhénie)* and *The Bear (Medvéd')* are of international repute.

Chekhov's plays, like so many of his stories, depict the blind-alley of the rootless and decaying intelligentsia either against the background of their country estates, as in *Ivanov, The Seagull, Uncle Vanya,* and *The Cherry Orchard,* or against the provincial town atmosphere as in *The Three Sisters.* His characters are 'superfluous' individuals in a more acute sense even than those of Turgenev. They do not know what to do with themselves, and their minds are further complicated by the strange inner barrier separating them even from those whom they had once regarded as their nearest and dearest. Such is Ivanov, the principal character of the play under the same title. Treplev in *The Seagull,* Voinitsky, Dr Astrov, and Sonya in *Uncle Vanya* belong to the same category, not to mention, Masha, Olga and Irina in *The Three Sisters* (first performed on 31 January, 1901).

According to Chekhov a sensitive person, confronted by the rough and ready style of life he has to face or contend with, is almost doomed to failure, and a failure of this kind, morally speaking, may not be to his credit, since success is only too often a prerogative of pushful vulgar types. This is why Chekhov looks with sympathy upon those *hommes manqués* who have been crushed because they expected from life more than it could give. Some of them still cherish hopes for a better future by trying to believe that the price they have to pay is not entirely in vain. Maybe they are paying the bill for the happiness of future generations whose lives will be less muddled and stupid—a thought which by no means alleviates their own ordeals, but may at least prevent them from slamming the door on the last glimmer of hope. Still, Chekhov's characters have to foot the bill. Quite a few of them accept the bill in this spirit simply in order to avoid the danger of utter nihilism and despair.

> Those who will live a hundred or two hundred years after us, and who will despise us for having lived our lives so stupidly and tastelessly—they will, perhaps, find a means of being happy, but we. . . . There is only one hope for you and me. The hope that when we are asleep in our graves we may, perhaps, be visited by pleasant visions.[3]

Such is Dr Astrov's comment in *Uncle Vanya.* But the same emergency faith is voiced by Vershínin in *The Three Sisters* and by Trofimov in *The Cherry Orchard.* Amidst all his despondence Chekhov himself arrived at a solace of this kind, as one can judge from his letter to Diaghilev (December, 1902), in which he says:

> Modern culture is but the beginning of a work for a great future, a work which will go on, perhaps, for ten thousand years, in order that mankind may, even in the remote future, come to know the truth of a real God—that is, not by guessing, not by seeking in Dostoevsky, but by perceiving clearly, as one perceives that twice two is four.

Flashes of such faith did not redeem, however, that quagmire of Russian reality which Chekhov had to endure and which he used as the raw material for his stories and plays. The surprising thing is that he was able to transmute it into perfect art, the devices of which are also worth studying in connection with his dramatic technique.

Chekhov did his best to 'de-theatralise' the theatre by depriving it of everything 'heroic', noisy and artificial. But in doing this he increased the effect of his plays in a strangely suggestive manner. In his early play, *Ivánov,*[4] he still depended on tradition, albeit he purposely abstained from a worked-out plot and made use of what he called the 'belletristic', as distinct from the dramatic, method in the old style. 'Each act I finish as I do my stories,' Chekhov says in a letter; 'I develop it quietly and calmly, but at the end I give a slap to the spectator. All my energy is centred on a few really strong passages, but the bridges connecting these passages are insignificant, weak and old-fashioned.' The main hero, Ivanov, is an unheroic 'superfluous' intellectual—a victim of those Russian circumstances he is unable to overcome. He has lost his hold upon life and feels, at the age of thirty-five, an old man.

> Exhausted, overstrained, broken, with my head heavy and my soul indolent, without faith, without love, without an objective in life, I linger like a shadow among men and don't know what I am, what I am

Peggy Ashcroft as Irena, Gwen Ffrangcon-Davies as Olga, and Carol Goodner as Masha in John Gielgud's 1938 staging of Three Sisters *at the Queen's Theatre.*

living for, what I want. . . . My brains do not obey me, nor my hands, nor my feet. My property is going to ruin, the forest is falling under the axe. My land looks at me like a deserted child. I expect nothing, I regret nothing; my soul shudders with the fear of the morrow. . . . What is the matter with me? To what depths am I making myself sink? What has brought this weakness on me?

But there is no answer. Surrounded by fools and nonentities, Ivanov—an essentially decent fellow—sinks deeper and deeper into the morass of his own despondence. In his bewilderment he does not mind offending even his consumptive wife who adores him and whom he used to adore. After her death he is free to marry Sasha, who had been secretly in love with him all that time; but for no apparent reason he shoots himself, when on the point of taking her to the altar. His is the tragedy of a sensitive man doomed to failure, although he himself does not know why. There is no plot in the play and even the normal logical causation (the 'bridges' connecting the passages) seems to be absent; yet as a picture of life transformed into art the play is convincing and impressive.

In *The Seagull,* written some eight years later, Chekhov's peculiar technique is more pronounced than in *Ivanov.* This time, too, the plot is replaced by a string of seemingly casual happenings, cemented by that lyrical 'atmosphere' which became—both in his plays and narratives—the principal if not the only unifying factor. Here the tragedy of frustration in Treplev and Nina is the more poignant because of all the trivialities leading up to it. While Nina, after her disappointments, finds shelter in the profession of an actress, Treplev cannot fill the void of his life even with his initial success in literature. These are his parting words to Nina, after she had vainly deserted him for the writer Trigorin who cared for her as little as for a shot seagull:[5] 'You have found your path, you know which way you are going, but I am still floating in a chaos of dreams and images, not knowing of what use it is to anyone. I have no faith and I don't know what my vocation is.' Chekhov once again made use of the 'belletristic' method, but was not quite sure whether to approve of it or not, and he said so in a letter to Suvorin (November 1895): 'I began it *forte* and finished it *pianissimo* against all rules of dramatic art. It came out like a story. I am more dissatisfied than satisfied with it, and, reading over my newborn piece, I became once more convinced that I am not a playwright at all.' He certainly was not a playwright in the traditional sense, some further proof of which he gave in *Uncle Vanya, The Three Sisters,* and *The Cherry Orchard.*

In *Uncle Vanya* we meet the same type of intellectual gentleman victimised by a trivial existence, as in *Ivanov* and *The Seagull.* The plot as such is replaced by a series of 'scenes of country life in four acts'. The 'atmosphere' is all important, while the subject-matter is as simple as it can be. A famous but now retired university professor, suffering from conceit and gout, comes with his beautiful second wife Elena to settle down on his estate, where his brother-in-law, Voinitsky (Uncle Vanya), and his daughter from a first marriage, Sonya, have been toiling for years in order to add to his income. Much admiring the professor's fame and learning, Voinitsky has spent the whole of his adult life in serving him—only to discover at the age of forty-seven that the supposedly great man was nothing but a puffed-up ignoramus. Voinitsky, now a weary middle-aged man, realises his mistake, but the lost years cannot now be retrieved. To make things worse, he is in love with Elena, who is too indolent to respond even to the advances of the younger and more interesting wooer, Doctor Astrov—a man still in the process of going to seed. As though lost in his own void, Voinitsky is frightened of the present and the future. 'I am forty-seven. If I live to be sixty, I have another thirteen years. It's a long time. How am I to get through those thirteen years? What shall I do? How am I going to fill them up? . . .' In his rancour he fires two shots at the pitiably frightened celebrity and, having missed, thinks of suicide. But it all ends *pianissimo,* that is peacefully. The learned professor and his frigid wife depart. Life returns to its old routine. Both Sonya (whose love for Astrov is now frustrated for good) and Voinitsky find a questionable escape in accountancy and petty drudgery about the estate in order to increase, once again, the professor's income.

The Three Sisters is written in a similar vein, but with a greater amount of lyrical touches. Again there is no plot. We are introduced to three sisters—members of the intelligentsia. After the death of their father (a cultured high-ranking officer) the sisters and their brother have remained stuck in a provincial garrison town which they loathe. Their determination to return to Moscow, where they were born, only expresses their desire for a fuller life. But the provincial mire is stronger. Neither they nor their brother, who is preparing for a university career, succeed in extricating themselves. Instead of living, they are compelled to vegetate. 'I am nearly twenty-four,' complains Irina. 'I have been working for years, my brains are drying up, I am getting thin and old and ugly and there is nothing, nothing, not the slightest satisfaction, and time is passing, and one feels that one is moving away and being drawn into the depths. I am in despair and I don't know how it is I am alive and have not killed myself yet.' It is no fault of theirs that all their efforts are futile and that things go from bad to worse. Their brother, moreover, marries a mean and vulgar *petite bourgeoise* who openly deceives him with another man. And as in *Uncle Vanya,* Chekhov ends this play *pianissimo,* with apparent resignation camouflaged by hard work.

The tone is somewhat gayer in *The Cherry Orchard*—a cleverly dramatised string of comic and semi-tragic incidents. The bankruptcy of the irresponsibly carefree, or rather careless, Ranevskaya and her brother Gayev is here symbolic of the inner as well as the outer inefficiency of that landed-gentry class which, not so long ago, had dominated Russian life. Ranevskaya's country-house, together with its magnificent cherry orchard, is bought by the self-made businessman Lopakhin—the son of a former serf. And the first thing the new owner does is to fell the orchard in order to make room for a suburban housing-estate, planned out on a most profitable basis. Lopakhin thus emerges as the new social force—a capitalist on a large scale. But the 'eternal student' and revolutionary Trofimov has little respect for him. 'I can get on without you. I can bypass you.' He and the girl he loves are still young enough to flatter themselves with the illusion that they, and not the money-grabbing Lopakhin, are in the front rank of humanity; nevertheless Lopakhin is the only one who triumphs at the end of the play.

The Cherry Orchard was written especially for Stanislavsky. But Chekhov himself did not approve of the interpretation the Moscow Art Theatre gave it. He actually complained in a letter to his wife that its two directors, Nemirovich-Danchenko and Stanislavsky, had never read his plays properly, and least of all *The Cherry Orchard.*

Chekhov's technique stands outside that tradition of the Russian dramatic art which goes from Fonvizin—via Griboyedov—to Gogol's *Government Inspector,* although his small farcical pieces may be reminiscent of Gogol. On the other hand, his 'belletristic' method had an interesting Russian precedent in Turgenev's *A Month in the Country* which, like *Uncle Vanya,* could be called 'scenes from country life' rather than a play in the traditional style. Finally, the playwright Alexander Ostrovsky contributed certain elements to the Chekhovian drama, however different Ostrovsky's aims and reasons may have been from those of Chekhov's. As an innovator Chekhov also had some features in common with Ibsen, but with reservations.

Like Ibsen in his later plays, he reduced the external action to a minimum. He replaced it not so much with Ibsen's psychological inner tension as with an accumulation of those lyrical-impressionistic touches which keep the seemingly disjointed incidents together. But the similarity between the symbolic use of the seagull in Chekhov's play of the same title and that of the wild duck in the well-known drama by Ibsen is hardly accidental. Analogies could also be found elsewhere, especially in Chekhov's frequent use of the double dialogue, the spoken words of which serve only as a mask for what one wants, or rather does not want, to say. However, there are essential differences between these two pioneers of modern drama. As a rule Ibsen relegated the tragic guilt of his main characters to the past (i.e. to the time before the play began) and gave all his attention to the psychological *dénouement* as seen through the workings of the hero's conscience, tossed between two contradictory sets of values. Even in his realistic middle-class dramas he was still rooted in the romantic tradition. His characters show a strong will opposing or fighting the surrounding conditions to the end. Thus Stockmann in *An Enemy of the People* is the bourgeois equivalent of such a heroic-romantic figure as Brand. The ex-Pastor Rosmer in *Rosmersholm* is also a romantic idealist. Even Nora in *A Doll's House* rises to the stature of a rebel determined not to put up with her position of a doll petted by a smug philistine husband. And as for the master-builder Solness, Borkmann, and the sculptor Rubek, they all perish in an attempt to assert their own will and freedom against fate; but their very defeat, however catastrophic, can be regarded as a romantic self-affirmation. In each case we watch how the inner change of the hero is due to a sudden perception of a truth which gives a new direction to his will even if he may no longer be destined to live up to it.

Chekhov proceeds differently. Having discarded the old plot, he does not replace it by a conflict of values in the manner of Ibsen for the simple reason that his very point of departure is the bankruptcy of all values. Nor do we find in him that logical and psychological consistency of characters in which Ibsen excelled. Chekhov depicted a disintegrating life in that seemingly casual way to which Tolstoy once referred (with disapproval) as a 'scattered composition'. Tolstoy himself greatly admired Chekhov's stories, but was somewhat critical of his plays. 'As you know,' he once told him, 'I do not like Shakespeare; but your plays are even worse'. . . . Yet there was a system in Chekhov's method of cementing the 'scattered' bits and slices of life together and he did so with a skill in which he proved to be master of his art.

By his method of showing the tragic nature of everyday existence in its ordinary everyday conditions Chekhov also made a contribution to the new style of acting. The

success of Chekhov's plays depended and depends largely on all sorts of nuances, of psychological imponderables, not to mention the importance of pauses, of tempo, as well as of the deeper 'symbolic' side of words, gestures and inflections. After all, it was not for nothing that Chekhov was proclaimed by Andrey Bely a precursor of Russian symbolism.

Chekhov's symbolism is more vague and elusive than, say, that of Ibsen. Also his characters are too fatalistic or else too pathetic in their passivity to be tragic in Ibsen's sense. They have neither enough faith nor enough stamina to fight for, let alone shape, their own destinies. The originality of Chekhov is in fact due more to the way in which he showed that the very drabness of life can be turned into significant art. And he did this not only in a new light, but also with that peculiar understatement which, together with his short-hand realism, could not help influencing a number of other literary and dramatic creations of our era.

Notes

[1] In England it was Katherine Mansfield in particular who wrote her stories under Chekhov's stimulus.
[2] This play which, incidentally, has a happy ending, was subsequently excluded by Chekhov from the collected edition of his works.
[3] All quotations from Chekhov's plays are taken from Constance Garnett's translation of Chekhov's works (Chatto and Windus).
[4] Chekhov's first long and not very successful play *Platonov* (1881) remained in manuscript, but some of its characters and themes served for his other plays, especially for *Ivanov*.
[5] The tragedy of Nina with Trigorin was partly based upon an actual love affair of the singer Lika Mizinova (one of Chekhov's friends) and the writer Potapenko.

Peter Mudford (essay date 1979)

SOURCE: "Anton Chekhov," in *The Art of Celebration,* Faber and Faber, 1979, pp. 110-22.

[In this excerpt, Mudford explores how Chekhov's characters struggle between present despair and hope for the future.]

> What beautiful trees—and how beautiful, when you think of it, life ought to be with trees like these!
> ***Three Sisters,*** Act Four

Tolstoy once complained to Chekov in conversation: 'You know I cannot abide Shakespeare, but your plays are even worse.'[1] Chekov's plays lacked, in his opinion, a point of view. Chekov, who felt an unequalled love and affection for Tolstoy, admitted the truth in what he was saying; but could not do anything about it.

> I have often been blamed, even by Tolstoy, for writing about trifles, for not having any positive heroes . . . but where am I to get them! Our life is provincial, the cities unpaved, the villages poor, the masses abused. In our youth we all chirp rapturously like sparrows on a dung-heap, but when we are forty, we are already old and begin to think of death. Fine heroes we are![2]

In Chekov's view, the life of the individual was all too often unfulfilled and impoverished, spiritually as well as materially. If he had probed more deeply, he might have reached a view of character not unlike Ibsen's in his later works. But Chekov depicted that frustration as the result of forces at work in life and time, without involving himself in its particular emotional or psychological causes. Again, he placed more emphasis on the Russian temperament as an explanation of the tendency to philosophise and delay action, than, for example, upon the influence exerted by heredity which preoccupied Ibsen throughout his life. Chekov's characters too can perceive their defects; and knowing they will not change, they look to future generations to avoid their errors. 'Humanity is perpetually advancing, always seeking to perfect its own powers,'[3] says Trofimov in **The Cherry Orchard.** 'One day all the things that are beyond our grasp at present are going to fall within our reach, only to achieve this we've got to work. . . .'[4] Hope for the future only partly conceals the 'lacrymae rerum'. Although the individual may not be rewarded, he must continue to work, search and hope. Chekov's recognition—not without irony—that this was how many people lived aroused his love and admiration for human beings in their hard and often thankless pilgrimage; this in turn gave to his works a more compassionate tone than was present in Ibsen's.

Unlike Tolstoy, Chekov had none of the advantages of social position to protect him in his youth from coming to know how hard life was for the majority of men. In the small town of Taganrog, on the sea of Azov, where his father kept a general store, Chekov was schooled by the daily struggle for existence. His father worked him long hours in the shop, and bullied the family at home. His incompetence in business, and his religious zeal, inspired mainly by his love of church music, brought neither material comfort nor spiritual joy to his family's life. Compulsory attendance at church made Sundays and holy days dreadful occasions for his children. Anton Chekov was later to say: 'I was brought up in religion, and received a religious education . . . And what is the result? I remember my childhood as a pretty gloomy affair, and I'm not a bit religious now.'[5] In his art, as in his life, Chekov derived no consolation from traditional belief; what he asserted as positive good had to be won against the hard and dull facts of life, as he knew it. The slave, he said, had to be squeezed out of him drop by drop. The characters he created reflected his experience of how much depended on the inner resources of the individual.

After the death of his father, when he was nineteen, Chekov assumed responsibility for his family's finances. While training to become a doctor, he started to write the stories that were later to make him famous. Throughout his life, he continued to believe in the benefits which people would derive from scientific progress and education. Although he came to see himself first as a writer, he continued to practise medicine in times of epidemic, or in cases of want. He was active in setting up local libraries and creating improved facilities in schools. By travelling to the convict settlement on Shakhalin, off the

coast of Japan, he sought to bring about an improvement in the conditions he found there. All these activities extended what he wanted to achieve in his writing:

> I only wished to tell people honestly, 'Look at yourselves, see how badly and boringly you live!' The principal thing is that people should understand this, and where they do, they will surely create for themselves another and better life.[6]

Nothing that Chekov experienced—not even the filth, disease and drunkenness of the peasants—tempted him to feel that things could not be improved, but only to question how the same waste might be avoided in the future. The answer which he reflected in his art was a personal one, and depended upon individual endeavour: the will to endure so that in the future life might be better. . . .

Chekov's view of the individual admits the recurrence of failure and waste. But being the least doctrinaire of writers, he does not conceive this as the result of cold and impersonal forces, which stand in the way of human endeavour, so much as the operation of life upon the individual, fashioning him in a particular way, and often rendering him impotent in relation to what he most desires. Chekov was also able to bring to most of his characters an affectionate warmth, because his observation of their failings did not destroy his sense of humour. Since he recognised so much to be immutable within the brief course of an individual life, he could only regard the discrepancy between what people wanted, and what they achieved, as finally comic. His knowledge of provincial life also sharpened his eye for the unsophisticated and ludicrous attempts which human beings make to put things to rights; and this matched a style which never became over-complex, or, in the bad sense, urbane. However brief his stories, they focus upon incidents which reveal the quality of life, and its limited possibilities at a particular moment of time. . . .

Chekov's characters appear to a greater degree than Ibsen's the product of their choices; their decisions, often lightly taken, lead to more serious consequences than they could have foreseen. Chekov's irony is directed against the resulting waste; but it is tempered by his awareness of how swiftly life's opportunities disappear, and by the irrevocable consequences which flow from trivial acts. Sometimes, as in **"The House with a Mezzanine,"** the opposition of the stars, as much as missed opportunity, causes the lack of fulfilment, but again time only offers very fleetingly a change of potential happiness. A young landscape painter, staying in perpetual idleness on a friend's estate, meets the Volchaninovs, who live nearby. The family consists of a mother and two daughters. The painter recognises the limitations and inadequacies of his existence. He feels pain, sadness, loneliness, and uncertainty of direction. For one night, his love for the younger sister, Zheyna, transforms his pain:

> . . . I dreamed of her as my little queen, who together with me would possess those trees, those fields, this

mist, this sunset, this exquisite, wonderful countryside, in the midst of which I had felt till now so hopelessly lonely and unwanted. . . .[18]

But the following day, Zhenya has vanished for ever.

What people feel themselves to have missed forms at the centre of their lives a depressing hollow, making them appear to themselves and to others ineffectual and incomplete. The transience of opportunity also in varying degrees absolves them. Like the house itself, with its attic storey and green-shaded light, love is briefly seen, and never forgotten. While Chekov extends the interest of the story by the argument between the painter, and Lydia, the elder sister, as to the relative importance in an impoverished country of medicine and art, their debate remains a battle of words, less important than the stifled relationship. In the late plays he adds another dimension to the gentleness and discrimination with which his characters had always been portrayed, by emphasising their desire for the future to be brighter for all men than the fleeting and incomplete present, and by highlighting the courage with which they confront their contribution to that end.

In these plays, Chekov developed a style of dramatic writing that enables us to see, without being told, how distraught people are; and how hard, in spite of their ineffectualness, they try to find a way of resolving their grief. Some, like the unloved and unsuccessful Trepliev in **The Seagull,** cannot bear their inability to do so. Others, like Nina who cannot reciprocate Trepliev's love, learn through suffering 'how to endure things . . . how to bear one's cross and have faith.'[19] In the last three plays, **Uncle Vania, Three Sisters** and **The Cherry Orchard,** the most subtle and painful feelings within the characters are made clear to the audience by Chekov's artistry; and they see, sometimes with almost unbearable clarity, why things cannot be changed, however much people desire them to be. Nothing can turn Trepliev into a successful writer, or make Trigorin faithful to Nina. Chekov's art is wrought from present feeling, and is unconcerned with experiences long since passed. Lacking a historical perspective, he can concentrate on the immediate experience, and perceive its value in relation to the quality of a continuing life. The moments as they pass in Chekov's drama form a pattern of growing awareness of what each character is, and must endure—apparent to themselves, as to his audience.

The Seagull is somewhat less refined in technique than the last three plays; and because of that the theme of self-fulfilment stands out the more starkly. Inability to reciprocate love, and a lack of equivalence in people's desires, convey incompleteness. Masha is touched by Medviedenko's love, but cannot return it. Trepliev adores Nina, who does not care for him; and Masha loves Trepliev, who scarcely notices her. But the seagull symbolises another kind of frustration, and of fulfilment: that of the creative life itself. Trepliev, when he enters with the dead seagull, prophesies that he will soon kill himself; and at the play's end he does so. Thwarted in his love for Nina, he also fails to find himself as a writer; floating

Derek Jacobi and Jane Wymark in a production of Ivanov *at the Old Vic Theatre, 1978.*

about in a world of dreams and images, he lacks any sense of direction, or the power to impose the new artwork of which he dreams on his audience. Poor as Trigorin's writing may be, when compared, as he compares it, with that of Dostoevsky, he is supported by fame, wealth and popularity; and short-lived as his own affections may be, he is nonetheless adored by Nina. Trepliev does not enjoy his good fortune in love or work. He tries to fly but cannot. Nina suffers no less when Trigorin deserts her after the death of their child; but she turns her suffering to creative advantage; and while achieving scarcely more success as an actress than Trepliev does as a writer, she 'grows stronger in spirit every day'. She becomes the seagull that flies, as opposed to Trepliev's seagull that destroys itself.

Chekov portrays them both with more sympathy than Trigorin or Arkadina who, in spite of their public success, display an unchanging self-regard and lack of concern for others. All that has happened to them in the two-year interval between Acts Three and Four has left them the same. Chekov often used fixity in character for comic effect—as he does here in the case of the retired lieutenant, Shamrayev—but also to convey a humanity restricted by lack of any deep feeling. The importance of matching one's dreams to one's possibilities, and accepting the consequences, is suggested in the contrast between Nina's and Trepliev's end; but Chekov still attaches more importance to the individual who endures and searches than to the person whose experience of living does not run deep. In *The Seagull,* as in the later plays, he also uses Nature in its permanence and stillness to create a contrast with the distress of human life, and implicitly to suggest through it a beauty which human life ought to contain.

Like several of Ibsen's plays, *Uncle Vania* derives its dramatic tension from the effects of disruption upon an established way of life. The retired Professor Serebriakov and his young wife, Yeliena, return to the estate which the Professor owns; the estate is run by Vania, the brother of the Professor's first wife, and Sonia, his daughter. Vania is upset by the Professor's disturbance of their routine, by the youth and beauty of his wife, and by the fact that in spite of his eminence he is obviously a nincompoop. Vania is forty-seven, and knows that life is slipping him by, that he has achieved nothing. 'It would even be pleasant to hang oneself on a day like this,' he says. The old nurse comments, indirectly, as she feeds the chickens: 'Chook, chook, chook!'[20] All this 'pother o'er our heads' is insignificant. Vania is in love with the Professor's young wife, Yeliena (or thinks he is); Sonia loves Dr. Astrov, a regular visitor to the estate—but the doctor, through the endless monotony and fatigue of his work, has grown dead to feeling (though he too is attracted by Yeliena). All except Serebriakov sense the emptiness and incompleteness of their lives; and he has a pain in his left leg. As Vania says to Yeliena (not without bathetic humour): 'My life, my love—look at them—where do they belong? What am I to do with them? My feeling for you is just wasted like a ray of sunlight falling into a well—and I am wasted too.'[21] To Yeliena this talk of love is just stupid. Astrov's confession to Sonia is painful in a different way:

ASTROV: I don't love human beings . . . I haven't cared for anyone for years.

SONIA: Not for anyone?

ASTROV: No one. I feel a sort of fondness for your old nurse—for the sake of old times. . . .[22]

He goes on talking, but his loquacity conceals as much as Sonia's silence. The real dialogue between them, which we can read in their tone, expression and gesture, remains unspoken.

In Act Three, Serebriakov clumsily announces his intention of selling the estate which Vania has looked after for so long. Vania attempts to shoot him, and repeatedly misses. At the opposite extreme to Sonia's stillness, Vania's frenzied excitement suggests how deeply these lives are shaken by their desires, and the misfortunes of existence. When finally the storm has passed, and the sound of the Professor's carriage recedes once more from the house whose tranquillity it shattered, it carries away Vania's love, just as Astrov's decision not to come to the house till summer buries Sonia's. It is an ironic and painful irrelevance that at the moment of departure Astrov should stare at the map of Africa and remark: 'I suppose down there in Africa the heat must be terrific now.'[23] There can be nothing more personal for them to say to each other. But Sonia and Vania, in spite of all they suffer, and must endure in the future, do not quite despair:

SONIA: Well, what can we do? We must go on living! We shall go on living, Uncle Vania. We shall live through a long, long succession of days and tedious evenings . . . we shall work for others, now and in our old age, and we shall have no rest . . . Over there, beyond the grave . . . we shall rejoice and look back at these troubles of ours with tender feelings, with a smile—and we shall have rest.[24]

In these moments when Sonia has finally lost hope in the fulfilment of her love for Astrov, she has to construct something upon which to rejoice. However much truth we may or may not feel in Sonia's general view of things, we cannot, after what she has suffered, doubt either her courage or her sincerity. Sonia's sorrow belongs to a heart that remains glad; in her hope and steadfastness she symbolises a sustained goodness at the centre of harsh and suffering existence. This is not lack of viewpoint, but a confident assertion of those values which are stronger than the arbitrariness and unhappiness of the world.

Chekov's tone has become more sombre in *Three Sisters,* the least comic and most tautly structured of his plays. In *Uncle Vania,* people are often blind to the effect of their actions, but not deliberately malicious. In *Three Sisters,* Solyony cannot accept that Irene does not love him, and even less that the Baron is his rival. In the first act he threatens to put a bullet in the Baron's head out of ill temper (a threat which is sometimes in production meaninglessly directed at Chebutykin); and in the fourth act he does so out of jealousy. Solyony, humourless and destructively mean, is only worse in degree than Natasha, the wife (after Act One) of Andrey, brother to the three sisters. Incapable of seeing how cruel she is to her husband, whom everyone knows she deceives, and to the old servant Anfisa, whom she wants turned out of the house, relentlessly and apparently unknowingly she takes over her husband's home and life, destroying him with her vulgarity, and shallowness of spirit. As Andrey is forced to admit by the end of the play, something about her 'pulls her down to the level of an animal—a sort of mean, blind, thick-skinned animal—anyway not a human being. . . .'[25] Chebutykin, one-time doctor, and now alchoholic, destroys in another way. Not having done a stroke of work since he left the university he feels that nothing is worth the effort, and that, anyway, nothing matters.[26] He makes no attempt to stop the duel between Solyony and the Baron; and when the Baron is killed, consoles himself with the newspaper: 'Let them cry for a bit. . . .'[27]

These three characters in different ways represent the negative and destructive self, incapable of looking beyond themselves for a justification of their present suffering. Work, tedious and spiritless though it may be, is seen both as a palliative for that pain, and as a hope. Vershinin exclaims: 'We've just got to work and work . . . All the happiness is reserved for our descendants, for our remote descendants.'[28] But that scarcely balances the hardship it causes in the present. Andrey finds no satisfaction in his work for the Council Office, and regrets increasingly his missed academic career. Irene, who begins with a longing for work, cannot bear what she has to do in the post office: 'It's the sort of work you do without inspiration, without even thinking. . . .'[29] Olga is worn out by her work at the school: 'Tomorrow I'm free,' she says. 'Heaven, what a joy!'[30] Masha, married to a master at the High School, is 'so bored, it's simply disgusting'.[31] In love too they are equally unhappy and unfulfilled. Masha's affair with Vershinin (himself married to a woman he finds despicable) is doomed to end when his regiment is posted away; Irene agrees to marry the Baron, admitting she does not love him, but promising to be loyal and obedient—only to have him killed in a duel by Solyony; and Andrey's love for Natasha is ended by their marriage. In such a world what people say to each other often sounds irrelevant and absurd, and their hopes for the future, whether in Moscow or lives still unborn, sound like a means of cheering themselves up. But they are not only that. In Chekov's high art the distinction between good and bad is that between those who have the faith to go on working, searching and hoping, and those who do not care, or do not think it worth the effort. His vision of reality is nourished by a belief in people who suffer and do not give up, while conscious that any rewards will not be for them to enjoy.

The Cherry Orchard (1904), Chekov's last play, expresses in its most poignant and subtle form his attitude to time. He regarded the play as a comedy, and so in the divine sense it is. What seems so important and permanent to individuals at the time, like this family's love of the cherry orchard, must inevitably undergo change. Madame Liuba cannot grasp this. Almost penniless, and compelled to sell her estate, she insists upon giving a gold coin to a passing tramp, and behaving as though the orchard is not going to be sold. Even when both silly and misguided, characters in Chekov's plays have the ability, as Liuba does, to convince one of their basic goodness. And it comes across the more strikingly for the irrelevance which threatens to overrun everything.

Act Two, in particular, impresses this upon us. The action takes place at an old wayside shrine in the country which suggests a state of limbo—the place where these people happen to be. At the opening, Charlotta, the governess, takes a shotgun off her shoulder and says thoughtfully: 'I don't know how old I am. I haven't got a proper identity-card, you see.'[32] Later Lopakhin, destined to buy the estate, reminds Liuba and Gayev: 'We must decide once and for all: time won't wait. . . .'[33] But in limbo time doesn't exist: 'Who's been smoking such abominable cigars here?'[34] Liuba asks in reply to Lopakhin, and goes on to admit how senselessly, recklessly she is spending her money. Lopakhin complains that they don't seem

to understand the estate is up for sale, Liuba asks, 'What are we to do? Tell us, what?'[35] They way of life they have always known will never be changed, and disappear; and Trofimov, the eternal student, will always be present to comfort as well as chide them: 'The whole of Russia is our orchard. The earth is great and beautiful, and there are many, many wonderful places on it.'[36] In a world so entrenched in a sense of its permance, the remote sound of a string, snapping—perhaps a cable in one of the mines—causes the most disturbance. Like the Serebriakovs, though far less obtrusively, it suggests the raid of time upon stillness. In that stillness the voices of the unfulfilled—Sonia, Anya, Liuba, Gayev—desirous, if not capable, of faring forward, are heard. Like the cherry orchard itself, time overtakes them; but not before their uniqueness and the 'ground of their beseeching' has been portrayed with all the fineness and subtlety of Chekov's art. The cherry orchard is an image of great beauty: doomed to be cut down, but remaining memorable as something which Time cannot change or touch. The curtain of the theatre itself discovers it every time that it rises: 'It is May, but in the orchard there is morning frost. . . .'[37]

Chekov is like Hardy in that his mastery comes from a quality perceived within people. Without Hardy's elaborate stage-setting, his characters appear to us more directly as 'only undefeated because they have gone on trying'. Both through his work as a doctor and through his imagination, Chekov knew how much poverty, boredom and indifference worsened the quality of people's lives. His art, in its content and formal beauty, speaks quietly and resiliently against such things; and the brighter future for which his characters work and hope expresses the nature of their particular quests. Time and circumstance operate against their chance of fulfilment. While recognising the amount of waste in all existence, Chekov celebrated its goodness, not only in what people are, but in what they intend.

NOTES

[1] Quoted by Ernest Simmons in *Chekov, A Biography*, London, 1963, p. 495.
[2] *Ibid.*, p. 581.
[3] Chekov, *Plays*, translated by Elisaveta Fen, Penguin Classics, Harmondsworth, 1959, *The Cherry Orchard*, Act II, p. 363.
[4] *Ibid.*, pp. 363-4.
[5] Simmons, *op. cit.*, p. 17.
[6] *Ibid.*, p. 581.
[7] *Lady with Lapdog, and other stories*, translated by David Magarshack, Penguin Classics, Harmondsworth, 1964, *Ward Number Six*, p. 143.
[8] *Ibid.*, p. 143.
[9] *Ibid.*, p. 175.
[10] The Oxford Chekov, Vol. 6, *Stories 1892-93*, translated by Ronald Hingley, London, 1971, *Neighbours*, p. 104.
[11] *Ibid.*, p. 115.
[12] *Ibid.*, p. 117.
[13] *The Darling*, translated by David Magarshack, *op. cit.* (note 7), p. 255.
[14] *Ibid.*, p. 260.
[15] *Ibid.*, p. 263.
[16] *Ionych, op. cit.* (note 7), p. 243.
[17] *Ibid.*, p. 250.
[18] *The House with an Attic, op. cit.* (note 7), p. 228.
[19] *Plays, op. cit., The Seagull*, Act IV, p. 181.
[20] *Plays, Uncle Vania*, Act I, p. 195.
[21] *Ibid.*, Act II, p. 205.

[22] *Ibid.,* Act II, p. 211.
[23] *Ibid.,* Act IV, p. 244.
[24] *Ibid.,* Act IV, p. 245.
[25] *Plays, Three Sisters,* Act IV, p. 318.
[26] *Ibid.,* Act I, p. 266.
[27] *Ibid.,* Act IV, p. 329.
[28] *Ibid.,* Act II, p. 281.
[29] *Ibid.,* p. 278.
[30] *Ibid.,* p. 293.
[31] *Ibid.,* Act III, p. 304.
[32] *Plays, The Cherry Orchard,* Act II, p. 354.
[33] *Ibid.,* p. 357.
[34] *Ibid.,* p. 357.
[35] *Ibid.,* p. 359.
[36] *Ibid.,* pp. 367-8.
[37] *Ibid.,* Act I, p. 333.

Irina Kirk (essay date 1981)

SOURCE: "Chekhov's Plays," in *Anton Chekhov,* Twayne Publishers, 1981, pp. 126-56.

[Kirk provides a detailed examination of each of Chekhov's full-length plays.]

Chekhov wrote his first plays at the age of eighteen, but all that survived of those efforts are the titles: a drama *Without Fathers,* a comedy *Laugh It Off If You Can,* and a one-act comedy **"Diamond Cuts Diamond."** (These titles are mentioned by Chekhov's eldest brother, Aleksandr, in a letter of October 14, 1878.) The manuscript of the earliest preserved play by Chekhov was discovered after his death and published in 1923. Because of the missing title page it was published as *A Play without a Title,*[1] but later it was named *Platonov* after the play's main character. Although the manuscript is undated there is evidence that the play was written in 1881, since Chekhov's brother Mikhail refers to it in his introduction to the second volume of Chekhov's letters. Apparently Chekhov took this play to the then-famous actress Mariya Yermolova with hopes that it would be performed at the Maly Theatre, and its rejection caused him great disappointment.

The play lacks artistic merit. It is too long, melodramatic, and as Mikhail wrote, "unwieldly," but it does offer interesting material for a study tracing some of Chekhov's themes and characters to their original sources. It is also significant as Chekhov's first effort to portray those sociological problems and conflicts that resulted from the emancipation of the serfs in the last two decades of the nineteenth century.

As in any period of transition there was uncertainty and confusion among the land-owning class, and many felt a helpless frustration at their inability to cope with change. Platonov, formerly a rich landowner and now a village teacher, is, in the words of one of the characters, "an admirable representative of our modern uncertainty."

To escape his frustration, Platonov involves himself with different women. Married to Sasha, a pious and innocent woman, he is having an affair with Anna, a general's widow. On discovering this, Sasha throws herself under a train, but is saved by the horse thief Osip. In the third act, she finds out that her worthless husband has also been trying to revive his old love for Sonya, who viewed him in her student days as a second Byron.

Sonya decides to "save" Platonov, and she offers him a new, meaningful life with her: "I'll make a worker out of you. We'll be decent people, Mikhail. We shall eat our own bread. We shall live by the sweat of our brows. We shall have calloused hands. I shall work, Mikhail" (p. 116). Platonov agrees to this scheme without much conviction or enthusiasm, but just as he prepares to leave, he is summoned to court "in the case of an assault committed upon the person of Mariya Grekhova daughter of Councellor of State." The summons does not deter Platonov, but at this point he finds it convenient to spend two weeks with Anna, prior to leaving with Sonya forever.

The last act is filled with every theatrical cliché and melodramatic device possible. Sasha poisons herself with matches, Sonya throws herself on her knees in the presence of Anna and begs Platonov to leave with her, and Mariya Grekhova comes in to announce that she is withdrawing her summons and that she too loves Platonov.

Exasperated, Platonov vows to revenge himself on all these loving women: "They all love me. When I get well I'll corrupt you. Before I used to say nice things to them, but now I'm corrupting them all" (p. 162). Sonya relieves him from the necessity of fulfilling such an ambitious vow by shooting Platonov with a pistol and wounding him fatally. The play ends with a lament of Colonel Triletsky, Sasha's father: "The Lord has forsaken us. For our sins. For my sins. Why did you sin, you old jester? Killed God's own creatures, drank, swore, condemned people . . . The Lord couldn't put up with it any more and struck you down" (p. 165).

Such lamentations were not part of Chekhov's later art, but the spiritual bankruptcy, the destructive forces of ennui, and the idea that work is man's salvation were to become some of his recurring themes. The figure of a bored, impoverished landowner unable to revive his youthful ideals and resentful of any efforts to save him appears again in Chekhov's next play, *Ivanov.*

I IVANOV

It is apparent that Chekhov himself rejected *Platonov* so completely that he considered *Ivanov* his first play. In a letter to his brother Aleksandr in October of 1887 Chekhov said, "It is the first time I have written a play, ergo, mistakes are unavoidable. The plot is complicated and not stupid. I end each act like a short story. All the acts run on peacefully and quietly, but at the end I give the spectator a punch in the face. My entire energy is concentrated on a few really powerful and striking scenes; but the bridges joining them are insignificant, dull, and trite. Nevertheless, I am pleased, for however bad the play may be, I have I think, created a type of literary significance."[2]

The type Chekhov created was not new in Russian literature. Aside from the fact that Ivanov was a reworked version of Platonov, he was similar to many so-called superfluous men who dominated Russian novels since the early nineteenth century. Behind his melancholy, boredom, and cosmic fatigue stood his idealistic past, where his powers were directed toward passionate speeches about progress, human rights, and agricultural improvements. It is the discrepancy between what he had dreamed he would become and what he actually did become that lies at the source of his illness. As a part of his rebelliousness and youthful dreams, Ivanov married a Jewish girl, Sarah, who gave up her inheritance and her faith to become his wife. As the play opens, Sarah is suffering from tuberculosis, Ivanov's lands are mortgaged to Lebedev, and he himself is about to become involved with Sasha, a young and idealistic daughter of Lebedev who is bent on saving Ivanov. Chekhov said of Sasha (letter of Dec. 30, 1888 to Suvorin), "She is the type of female whom the males do not conquer by the brightness of their feathers, their fawning or their bravery, but by their complaints, their whining, their failures. She is a woman who loves a man at the moment of his downfall. The moment Ivanov loses heart, the girl is at his side. That was what she was waiting for . . . She is not in love with Ivanov but with that task of hers."[3]

Ivanov's relationship to his wife is seen and evaluated by different people: by common gossipers (act 2), by Dr. Lvov, by Sarah, and by Ivanov himself. The issue becomes a catalyst that reveals the degree of honesty each character has toward himself and others.

According to gossip, Ivanov is a murderer, a blood sucker, and a thief: an opinion that is a crude distortion of the truth. Dr. Lvov pronounces a similar judgment on Ivanov. Unlike the gossips, Lvov is motivated by sincere honesty and by a genuine concern for Sarah's health. Dr. Lvov correctly sees that Ivanov's lack of reaction to the fact that his wife is dying and his behavior with Sasha are largely responsible for Anna's death. Still, he fails to take into account Ivanov's idealistic past and his present ennui. Chekhov writes of the doctor: "He belongs to the type of honest, straightforward, excitable, but also narrow-minded and plain-spoken man."[4] As the count says of Lvov, he is "like a parrot who thinks of himself as a second Dobrolyubov." His role is thus a caricature of the liberal *narodnichestvo* (populism) dramas popular at the time.

Ivanov's reaction to Dr. Lvov is indicative of his attitude toward himself. Ivanov is not intentionally evil, but he feels himself powerless to resolve all the contradictions and complexities of his weak nature. Thus he admonishes Dr. Lvov for his harsh judgment, which is lacking in depth and perception:

> No, doctor. We all have too many wheels and gears for us to be judged by first impressions or by a few

external traits. I don't know you, you don't know me, and we don't know ourselves. Isn't it possible to be a good doctor—and at the same time not understand people? You'll have to admit that, unless you're blind.

(p. 43)[5]

Although Ivanov does not fully accept Lvov's definition of him, he realizes that he alone is responsible for his life. Still he cannot reconcile himself to his present ennui:

> I can stand all these things! Anxiety, depression, bankruptcy, the loss of my wife, premature old age, loneliness, but I just can't bear the contempt I have for myself. The shame that I, a strong, healthy man, have somehow become a kind of Hamlet, a Manfred, just about kills me! Oh, I know there are fools who are flattered when you call them a Hamlet, but to me it's an insult! It wounds my pride, I'm oppressed with shame, and I suffer . . .

(p. 29)

Ivanov agrees with the doctor that his passivity is the indirect cause of both his wife's death and of his financial problem.

The dramatic action of this play is developed in accordance with the painful self-revelation which in the end drives Ivanov to suicide. Ivanov's psyche is revealed through his own remarks about himself, his gestures, his reactions, and the pauses in his speech.

Each act places an emphasis on Ivanov's estrangement from his surroundings. This is frequently comic, as in the contrast between Ivanov and Borkin, but it is just as often tragic. The comic episodes balance the tragic ones and serve as parodies, reflecting as if in a distorted mirror the plight of the main character. Both Count Shabelsky, Ivanov's uncle, and Lebedev, chairman of the County Council, speak of their idealistic past with humor, yet Ivanov cannot feel indifferent to what he has become, and hence he suffers. Ivanov's relationship with Sasha is parodied by Shabelsky's vacillating intention to marry the rich young widow Babakina. Just like Ivanov, the count reasserts his honesty at the end of the play, telling Babakina he hates her. However, Ivanov must pay a tragic price to extricate himself from his marriage to Sasha. Lvov's aggressive honesty is a parody of what Berdnikov calls Ivanov's "subjective honesty." Although the doctor acts honorably, Ivanov's passive honesty enables him to judge himself and others with more insight than Lvov.

Chekhov wrote to Suvorin about *Ivanov* on January 7, 1889: "In the conception of Ivanov I hit approximately on the dot, but the performance is not worth a damn. I should have waited."[6] Chekhov's conception was to portray the "superfluous man" of the 1880s in all of his psychological complexity, but he had not yet mastered the dramatic subtleties of characterization. The excess of monologues and self-explanatory speeches in *Ivanov* kept it well within the bounds of the traditional theater, while Chekhov was striving to achieve something new. In a letter of October 10-12 to his brother Aleksandr he says of *Ivanov,* "Korsh hasn't found a single mistake or fault in it so far as stage technique is concerned which proves how good and sensible my critics are."[7] Korsh hadn't found a mistake because *Ivanov* conformed to the requirements of the conventional play.

Ivanov is certainly a vast improvement over *Platonov.* It is much more concise, and Chekhov realized the importance of ending each act definitely. At the end of the first act Sarah leaves her house to follow Ivanov, and at the end of the second act she appears at the very moment of Sasha's and Ivanov's kiss. The third act ends with Ivanov's rebuke to Sarah that she will soon die, and the fourth act with his suicide.

Chekhov failed to make an original creation out of a character that had become stock in Russian literature. As Suvorin said, "Ivanov was a ready-made man." Chekhov denied the charge and replied (February 8, 1889) that Ivanov was not static because he was "ready-made" but because the author's hands were unskillful. Chekhov obviously tried to portray the inner emotional life of his hero, but didn't know how to do it except with worn-out devices.

II THE WOOD DEMON

While Chekhov was writing *The Wood Demon* he was at the same time at work on "A Boring Story." However, whereas "A Boring Story" displays all the control of an admirable craftsman, *The Wood Demon* confirms Chekhov's own suspicion that he was not yet a playwright. When the play was passed by the censor in October, 1889, it was rejected by the Literary-Theatrical Committee of St. Petersburg, among whose members was Grigorovich. Lensky, an actor of the Moscow Maly Theatre for whose benefit night the play was submitted, wrote Chekhov two weeks later, "Write stories. You are too scornful of the stage and the dramatic form. You respect these things too little to write plays."[8] Nemirovich-Danchenko was more charitable and more perceptive. He wrote, "You ignore too many of the requirements of the stage, but I have not observed that you scorn them; simply, rather, that you don't know what they are."[9]

In December, Chekhov finally sold the play to the private Abramov Theatre in Moscow, and it was presented on the Moscow stage on December 27th. The criticism of the play was singularly severe. The kindest review came from a magazine *The Actor,* No. 6, 1890 which said, "Chekhov's talent, without a doubt, is above the play he wrote, and the play's strange qualities are explained, probably, by the speed of the work and a sad delusion regarding inescapable qualities of every dramatic work." Chekhov added his personal criticism of *The Wood Demon,* which had also failed his own artistic expectations. In a letter to Urusov, literary critic and chairman of a drama society, he stated, "I cannot publish [*The Wood Demon*]. I . . . am trying to forget it."[10] (The play was in fact later revised and staged as *Uncle Vanya.*)

Chekhov did succeed in removing the conventional plot from *The Wood Demon,* but he had not yet mastered the technique of portraying inner psychological action. The play is too mechanical, undisciplined, and verbose. The inner psychological moments which in later plays would be depicted by a suggestive line of speech or a mere gesture, are expressed in loud monologues or bathetic dialogues. The play is also undermined by unconvincing coincidences and melodramatic situations. Letters and diaries serve to communicate information in a contrived manner, characters appear on stage at the proper moments as if by chance, and in Act Four a fire is created to get Khrushchev off stage. The play ends with the clown Dyadin's remark which ironically defines not only his own absurdity but also the play's: "That is delightful—Just delightful" (p. 124).

The theme and characterization are developed in accordance with the love relationships in the play. Serebryakov, an old and insufferable professor, is married to a very young and beautiful woman, Elena. The stupid boor Orlovsky and the Byronic rake Fedor both crudely attempt to seduce Elena, but receive only moral lectures for their pains.

Chekhov was obviously under the influence of Tolstoi's teachings at this time. The passive but virtuous Elena delivers speeches on the sanctity of marriage, purity, loyalty, and self-sacrifice. Although Elena is unjustly maligned throughout the play she is inwardly sustained by her false belief that she is the paragon of Russian womanhood:

> Oh, to be free as a bird, to fly away from all your drowsy faces and your monotonous mumblings and forget that you've even existed at all! Oh, to forget oneself and what one is . . . But I am a coward; I am afraid, and tortured by my conscience. I know that if I were to be unfaithful, every other wife would do the same thing and leave her husband, too. But then God would punish me. If it weren't for my conscience, I'd show you how free my life could be.

> (p. 96)

There is another love triangle between the professor's spoiled daughter Sonya, the idealistic "wood demon" Dr. Khrushchev, and the scoundrel Zheltukhin. Khrushchev eventually proposes to Sonya, who accepts his offer, at which point she too starts mouthing Tolstoian precepts: "There is no evil without some good in it. Our sorrow has taught me that we must forget our own happiness and think only of the happiness of others. Our lives should be a continual act of self-sacrifice" . . . (p. 113).

All the characters are united by the thematic leitmotif of their wasted lives, and by their attempt to delude themselves with rationalizing philosophy. The "wood demon" Khrushchev sums up the lives of everyone in the play as follows:

> We say that we are serving humanity, but at the same time we inhumanly destroy one another. For instance,

did you or I do anything to save George? Where's your wife, whom we all insulted? Where's your peace of mind, where's your daughter's peace of mind? Everything's been destroyed, ruined. You call me a Wood Demon, but there's a demon in all of you. You're all wandering lost in a dark forest, you're all groping to find a way in life. We know just enough and feel just enough to ruin our own lives and the lives of others.

(p. 117)

Voinitsky has sacrificed his entire identity to Serebryak-ov, whom he has worshipped as a great genius for years, only to discover his mistake when it is too late. Serebry-akov, whose entire youth was devoted to work, tries desperately to achieve happiness as an old man by exercising the power of his position, but he only succeeds in destroying those around him. Elena is proud of her "virtue," but she is a failure in her inability to love anyone and quite rightly defines herself as a "worthless, empty and quite pathetic woman" (p. 93). Fedor and Zheltukhin are leading senseless lives, and justifying themselves with cynicisms modeled after Lermontov's Byronic hero Pechorin.

Though *The Wood Demon* was a failure in terms of its artistry, its conception of form revealed the trend toward dramas of "inner action" which was to become fully actualized in Chekhov's later plays. *Uncle Vanya,* which was modeled after *The Wood Demon,* will give the most concrete example for studying the development of Chek-hov's technique from banal melodrama to masterful dramatic art.

III THE SEAGULL

Perhaps it is fitting that after the failure of *The Wood Demon,* Chekhov would want to write a play about art and the nature of artists. *The Seagull* marks Chekhov's maturity as a playwright, and it is also the most innovative of his plays. Chekhov wrote *The Seagull* in 1895, and in a letter to Suvorin (October 21, 1895) he said that he was working on it with pleasure, "though I sin terribly against the conventions of the stage. It is a comedy with three female parts, six male, a landscape, a view of a lake, much talk about literature, little action, and five tons of love."[11]

It was the "sinning against convention" that was most probably responsible for the scandalous failure of *The Seagull* at its first performance on October 17, 1895. The play's initial engagement lasted only five days, and it was greeted with satirical invective from the St. Petersburg audience, as well as from the art critics who reviewed it. Very few people were astute enough to appreciate *The Seagull*'s innovative use of mood, subtext, and symbolism as a new dramatic form.

The theme of *The Seagull* deals with the complex relationship between art, love, and life. Konstantin's play in the first act serves to polarize the characters' feelings around this subject, and to reveal the role of each individual in both a thematic and a dramatic sense.

At the beginning of *The Seagull* Masha, Medvedenko, and Polina are united by their total unconcern with the content of Treplev's play. They are all totally immersed in love conflicts and art has no relevance to their lives. On the other hand, for Sorin, who has failed in his ambitions to be a writer as well as in love; for Nina, who aspires to be a great actress; for Treplev's mother Arkadina, who is a famous actress; for the idealistic Dr. Dorn; and for the popular author Trigorin, there is an intimate relationship between art and personal identity.

Arkadina views her son Konstantin's attempt to create "new forms" in the theater as both a personal and a professional threat. Treplev is aware of his mother's animosity toward this assertion of his rebellious individuality, and he mockingly recites Queen Gertrude's lines to Arkadina before his play is performed. The oedipal power struggle between Konstantin and his mother is thus transferred onto the more abstract level of art, where it can be interpreted as the battle waged by every new generation to replace worn-out art forms.

Arkadina's lover, Trigorin, also feels no affinity for Konstantin's play. He confesses to understanding neither its abstract symbolism nor its emotional intensity. For Trigorin creative writing is not a dynamic process of discovery, but rather it is a rational process with a given methodology: "I take every word, every sentence I speak, and every word you say, too, and quickly lock them up in my literary warehouse—in case they might come in handy sometime" (p. 148). Like Arkadina, Trigorin desires to dominate the young, creative energy which he himself cannot generate. His destructive love relationship with Nina parallels Arkadina's power over her son.

Dorn is the only member of the "older generation" who truly understands, and sympathizes with Treplev's efforts. It is interesting that Dorn, who is an experienced man, shares the same abstract notion of art as the naive and alienated Konstantin. Dorn's remarks to Konstantin are supportive, but at the same time they offer valuable critical advice:

There must be a clear and definite idea in a work of art—you must know why you're writing—if not, if you walk along this enchanted highway without any definite aim, you will lose your way and your talent will ruin you.

(p. 139)

Treplev asserts that "one must portray life not as it is, not as it should be, but as it appears to be in dreams" (p. 131). Nina replies that, on the contrary, art must express life's strongest emotion, love. Nina not only has a strongly idealistic vision of the role of love in art, she also sees it as paramount in the life of the artist himself. And, although Treplev and Nina disagree on the focus of art in human relationships, they are both united by their naive dreams and by the shock of reality they must suffer.

Judi Dench as Arkadina and Alan Cox as Treplev, in a 1994 National Theatre production of The Seagull.

Nina's and Treplev's parallel struggle to overcome the frustrations of reality and to establish a real artistic identity is symbolized by the central image of the seagull Treplev has wantonly killed. The impetus for this symbol was an incident that occurred when Chekhov's friend Levitan and he were walking in the wood and Levitan shot a woodcock. Chekhov picked up the wounded bird and Levitan asked him to crush its head with a gun stock. Chekhov replied he could not do it, but Levitan continued to plead with him to end the bird's suffering. Chekhov wrote to Suvorin on April 8, 1892: "I had to obey Levitan and kill it. One more beautiful, enamored creature gone, while two fools went home and sat down to supper."[12]

Nina's identification with a seagull is mentioned when she first arrives at the Treplevs' in Act One. Although her family has forbidden her to visit there, she longs "for this lake, as if I were a seagull" (p. 130). Later, at the end of act 2, the writer Trigorin interprets the dead seagull as a premonition of Nina's own fate in love: "A young

girl like you has lived in a house on the shore of a lake since she was a little girl; she loves the lake like a seagull. Then a man comes along, sees her, and having nothing better to do, destroys her like this seagull here" (pp. 150-151). When Nina's unhappy romance with Trigorin, as described in act 4, becomes an actualization of this "fiction," Nina associates her identity entirely with a wounded seagull and even signs her letters to Treplev "the seagull."

But Nina's dedication to art ultimately reverses her fate. In her last speech she declares her triumph to Konstantin with the following words:

> I've become a real actress. I enjoy acting! I revel in it! The stage intoxicates me, and on it I feel very beautiful. While I've been here, I've spent a lot of time walking and thinking . . . thinking . . . and I feel that my spirit's growing stronger every day. I know now, Kostya, that what matters most for us, whether we're writers or actors, isn't fame or glamor, or any of the things I used to dream of. What matters most is knowing how to endure, knowing how to bear your cross and still have faith. I have faith now and I can stand my suffering when I think of my calling, I'm not afraid of life.
>
> (p. 174)

Thus, although Trigorin's interpretation of the seagull correctly foretold Nina's tragedy in love, it failed to take into account her success as an artist.

On the other hand, the seagull assumes an entirely different symbolic meaning in terms of Trigorin's fate. In the second act Konstantin shoots the seagull as a demonstration of his failure in love, and as a symbolic act to Nina that he might be his own next victim. Thus, Konstantin's ultimate failure is ironically not in his unrequited love for Nina. Rather, it is the result of his inability to find a direction in art. In the last act Konstantin says to Nina of himself:

> TREPLEV, *sadly.* You've found your road, you know where you're going—but I'm still floating about in a maze of dreams and images, without knowing what it is I am to do . . . I have no faith, and I have no calling.
>
> (p. 174)

Konstantin has become his own victim because he is caught between the power of his imagination to visualize and his impotence to actualize that vision into art. His final self-destructive frustration is resolved in the act of suicide, where his identification with the seagull becomes complete.

There are other symbols in the play that evoke different responses from the characters and are related to the thematic development. The lake on Arkadina's estate represents a promise of fulfillment: to Treplev it is associated with his play and with his love for Nina, to Trigorin it offers the solace of fishing (p. 168), and to Nina it is the lure that she will become a great actress. At the end of act 1 Dorn speaks to Masha of "sorcerer's lake," remarking on its power to evoke dreams. In the last act the lake's glassy surface is ruffled by chaotic, stormy winds, just as the dreams of each of the characters have been thrashed about by the forces of reality.

Flowers are also used as a symbol of the beauty and tender fragility of dreams. Polina jealously destroys the flowers that Nina presents to Dorn (p. 145), which parallels Arkadina's attitude toward Treplev and Trigorin's attitude toward Nina. Trigorin speaks of his wasted dreams as being like "flowers, torn from their roots" (p. 148), and at the end of the play Nina reminds Treplev of their youth, when feelings were "like tender, exquisite flowers" (p. 175). In *The Seagull* it seems that flowers, like youthful dreams, are destined to be trampled on or destroyed by time and indifference.

There are no real dramatic climaxes in *The Seagull* until Treplev's suicide at the end of the play. The plot develops with the introduction of the major characters in act 1, focuses on the love triangles between Trigorin-Nina-Treplev, Nina-Trigorin-Arkadina, and Medvedenko-Masha-Treplev in acts 2 and 3, and shows the resolutions of these conflicts in act 4. At the end of the play Treplev has abandoned Nina to return to Arkadina, Masha has married Medvedenko although she still loves Treplev, and both Nina and Trigorin have been jilted. Chekhov did not even portray Nina's affair with Trigorin on the stage, but used the messenger technique to report it to Dr. Dorn, and thus to the audience, in act 4.

Both David Magarshack in his book *Chekhov the Dramatist* and Maurice Valency in *The Breaking String* emphasize that *The Seagull* is the first of Chekhov's plays to use the dramatic technique of indirect action. Unlike *Ivanov* and *The Wood Demon,* where thoughts and ideas were revealed through standard plot developments, *The Seagull* highlights the more subtle psychological reactions of its characters through dialogue and symbolism.

Another innovation in *The Seagull* is Chekhov's wedding of comic and tragic elements. Although Arkadina's egoism, Treplev's fanatical attachment to his mother, and Trigorin's passion for fishing evoke a comic response, the reader understands each character too well to laugh without sympathy. The humor in *The Seagull,* which has its source in the frequent absurdity of human behavior, is never without a sadness that dreams very rarely come true. This thematic focus will be repeated in Chekhov's three later plays *Uncle Vanya, Three Sisters,* and *The Cherry Orchard.*

IV UNCLE VANYA

Having failed in the first two plays, Chekhov worked on *Uncle Vanya* without sharing his conception of it with anyone. Thus there are no indications anywhere as to when the play was written. Chekhov mentions its existence for the first time in a letter to Suvorin dated December 2, 1886: "Two long plays have to be set up still; *The Seagull* which is known to you, and *Uncle Vanya,* which is not known to anyone in the world."

The play first appeared in the anthology of plays and then in a provincial theater, where it was an immediate success. Chekhov was surprised at the favorable reception of the play and wrote to his brother Mikhail on October 26, 1898:

> My *Uncle Vanya* is being performed throughout the provinces and is a success everywhere. So you see, one never knows where he'll make it and where he won't. I never counted on this play at all.[13]

It appeared first at the *Khudozhestvenny* (Art) Theatre in Moscow on October 26, 1899. The critics of the capital were impressed. It was said that in the play, "the terrible prose of life has been elevated into a chef d'oeuvre of poetry." Perceptive critics like Ignatev noticed the absence of action, and wrote that "*Uncle Vanya* is significant in that the heroes have no will, no goal, do not know whether the circumstances are profitable for them or not, nor what kind of behavior will be theirs in the next moment. They are passive . . . Here the unity of action is substituted by the unity of mood."[14]

In fact, all but a few critics approved of the play. Tolstoi summed up the play in the following way to the actor A. A. Sanin, "Where is the drama? In what does it consist?"[15]

The action of *Uncle Vanya* consists of the movement from an established routine to the brief disturbance of that pattern, which contains a moment of illumination for the characters and a return to routine. The impetus for the shift in consciousness is the presence of Professor Serebryakov and his young wife Elena, whose extraordinary beauty arouses a longing for life in the others. Only they prove unequal to the challenge, and must deal with the failure of their dreams. The moment of illumination shows the characters that their inability to truly live has already determined not only their present, but their future, and this knowledge becomes an irrevocable part of their being. The question is no longer how to live, but as Voinitsky expresses it, "with what to fill the passing years?" (p. 216).

The themes of self-destruction and the violation of beauty are introduced at the beginning of act 1. In the opening scene, Dr. Astrov (the rewritten Dr. Khrushchev from *The Wood Demon*) asks the old nurse, Marina, whether he has changed in the eleven years she has known him. Her answer is the first expression of the theme which will be restated throughout the play on different levels: "Oh yes. You were young, handsome then, and now you seem like an old man. And you drink too" (p. 178). The nurse uses the Russian word *krasota,* "beauty," for "handsome," and it becomes a thematic leitmotif which is very prominent in the first two acts, subsides in the third act, and is totally absent from the last act, except in Sonya's final speech.

The two central images embodying physical beauty are the Russian forests and Elena. The idealistic Dr. Astrov plants new trees every year because, as Sonya says:

> He claims that forests beautify the earth, and so teach man to understand the beautiful, and instill in him a feeling of respect and awe. Forests temper the severity of the climate. In countries where the climate is warmer, less energy is wasted on the struggle with nature and that is why man there is more gentle and loving; the people there are beautiful, supple, and sensitive, their speech is refined and their movements graceful.
>
> (p. 185)

Astrov believes that man's creative and rational powers should be devoted to the preservation of that which is aesthetic in the environment, so that in a thousand years' time the earth might still retain its loveliness.

On the other hand, Vanya has a cynical attitude toward the preservation of forests. He is much more interested in the utility of the trees on his estate than in their beauty, and feels no compunction in burning logs in his fireplace or using wood for his barns. This attitude is not surprising in view of his physical appearance, which is described as "disheveled" (p. 179).

Both Astrov and Voinitsky are united in their love for the beautiful Elena. When Astrov realizes that he is infatuated with Elena he abandons his forest and medical practice to "seek her out greedily" (p. 207). Yet Astrov's tragedy is that while his attraction to Elena reveals his lack of a personal life, it does not involve his emotions. At the beginning of the play he says, "I don't love anyone" (p. 178), and this becomes the leitmotif which is confirmed in the last scene. His parting kiss to Elena is one neither of love nor of passion, but simply a gesture toward a momentarily aroused feeling that at one time in his life could have been real. Astrov's nature, as indicated by his desire to heal and to preserve the beauty of forests, is creative, yet he fails in the design of his own life.

Apparently Stanislavsky did not understand that point, for in his letter to Olga Knipper Chekhov writes in regard to the last scene:

> In accordance with your orders I hasten to reply to your letter where you ask about the last scene of Astrov and Elena. You write that Astrov in that scene behaves with Elena as with someone madly in love, that he clutches at his feeling as a drowning man for straw. But this is incorrect, completely incorrect. Astrov likes Elena, she overwhelms him with her beauty, but in the last act he already knows that nothing will come of it, that Elena will disappear from him forever— and he talks with her in this last scene in the same tone of voice as the heat of Africa, and kisses her, just simply out of nothing to do. If Astrov plays this scene violently, then the entire mood of the fourth act will be destroyed.
>
> (September 30, 1899)[16]

In opposition to Astrov's character, Uncle Vanya could perhaps be called destructive. Astrov accuses him of harboring this quality in respect to the forests, and Elena remarks on it in regard to other people:

> As Astrov said just now, see how thoughtlessly you destroy the forests, so that soon there will be nothing left on earth. In just the same way you recklessly destroy human beings, and soon, thanks to you, loyalty and purity and self-sacrifice will have vanished along with the woods. Why can't you look with calm indifference at a woman unless she belongs to you? Because . . . the doctor is right. You are all possessed by a devil of destructiveness; you have no feeling, no, not even pity, for either the woods or the birds or women, or for one another.
>
> (p. 187)

Yet just as Astrov fails to create, Uncle Vanya does not succeed in culminating his destructive impulses. He has already sacrificed the greater part of his life in a false dedication to the professor, who is a fraud. When Vanya becomes aware of the implications of his wasted life he attempts to shoot the professor and then himself. Both times he fails, and as a further insult to his masochistic pride, no one attempts to arrest him. Uncle Vanya is denied even the comfort of being thought of as a madman or a potential murderer; he is just a jester, devoid of any distinguishing personal trait. In his failure to destroy lies his inability ultimately to act out anything at all.

Uncle Vanya does not arouse anyone's sympathy. There is something comic in his love for Elena and in his homely dreams of a mediocre life with her. It is also obvious that while Elena responds to Astrov as a man, she does not to Uncle Vanya. Elena succeeds in resisting the temptation to consummate her attraction to Astrov, but in the best Freudian fashion takes his pencil as a souvenir of the possibility of an affair.

Astrov is said to be Chekhov's favorite character. Indeed, he is close to Chekhov in the lack of sentimentality with which he treats his profession as a doctor, in his lack of illusions, in his interest in alleviating the ills of Russia, in his desire to preserve the beauty in the world, and in his uncommitted personal life. (Chekhov wrote **Uncle Vanya** before he married Olga Knipper.)

The secondary characters seem superfluous at first glance, and apparently add nothing to the action of the play. As in other Chekhov plays, they serve as distorting reflections of the main characters, parodying their essential traits. Marina's main function in life is to feed others: she is perfectly satisfied with the routine and is disturbed only when something interferes with it. After Sonya has been rejected by Astrov, she settles down in the same routine and her function in life becomes the feeding of others. Telegin gave his property for the sake of strangers (his wife's children); and Uncle Vanya, like Telegin, can say at the end of his life, "I did not forsake my duty." The irony in both cases lies in the fact that neither Uncle Vanya nor Telegin had any duty toward the people for whom they gave up their own lives and that thus they

Frances Barber, Derek Jacobi, and Imogen Stubbs, in a 1996 Chichester Theatre staging of Uncle Vanya.

failed in their duty to themselves. Mariya Vasilevna, with her perennial reading and note taking in the margins of books, is a parody of Professor Serebryakov, who writes books that have as much value to others as reading does to Mariya herself. Marina, Telegin, and Mariya Vasilevna represent the unaware, who apparently settled into a pattern very early in life and who would never question its merits or the possibility of anything else. Juxtaposed to the indifference of these people are the longings of Uncle Vanya, Astrov, Elena, and Sonya. They too finally accept the routine of their lives. The difference is that they are conscious of their fate, whereas the other three remain ignorant.

Structurally **Uncle Vanya** is a very carefully wrought play. The particularly Chekhovian innovation is in the author's ability to combine all the elegiac elements and at some point to turn them into a comic situation. The tragic elements that constantly verge on the comic, and the ridiculous scenes that often inspire melancholy are probably what is meant by a special Chekhovian mood. It remains to examine how this particular mood is created. The details, though realistic in nature, make an appeal to the imagination. They illuminate the characters beyond their words and actions, and at times reveal their destiny. In addition, Chekhov uses landscape or simple objects for the same purpose of indirect dramatization.

Seemingly, nothing important is said in the opening lines of the play. On closer examination, it becomes obvious that those few lines already contain not only an introduction of the characters, but also the direction of the action and a hint of the outcome. The opening scene takes place in a garden. Cosy routine is indicated by the table set for tea; and the guitar, an accompaniment to the play, is there. It is cloudy. Marina offers tea to Astrov, and on his refusal, some vodka. To her offer he replies that he does not drink vodka every day. He adds that it is stifling. All these small details will receive amplification later: the cloudy weather will turn into a storm symbolic of the psychological storm gathering among the characters; it will be shown how the life on the estate is the kind that stifles human beings; and the vodka will become a means by which the self-destruction of Astrov will be accomplished.

Significantly, the insensitive characters do not notice the weather, so that the effect is one of two contrapuntal voices expressing the awareness and unawareness of the spiritual stifling. Upon entering, Serebryakov exclaims, "Superb, superb, what glorious views!" (p. 180); Voinitsky says, "It's hot and humid" (p. 180); and Telegin, the unconscious voice, says (although not in answer) "The weather is enchanting, the birds are singing, we all live in peace and harmony . . . what else do we want?" (p.

180). These remarks about the weather are a method of characterization, and they reveal as much about the characters as any of their speeches on profound subjects. Elena, who reconciles herself to life rather than actively reacting to it, says at the moment of tension between Voinitsky and his mother, "What a fine day. Not too hot." Uncle Vanya reples, "Yes, a fine day to hang oneself" (p. 184).

In act 2, the wind rattles the window and the sounds of the approaching storm alternate with the tapping of the night watchman, a sound that signifies the security of the household routine. Lightning strikes once, as the revelation of their destinies will later strike the participants. They begin to express their frustrations and their longings in various ways.

Serebryakov complains of being old and sick; Uncle Vanya laments his wasted life; Astrov (awakened by the storm) expresses his bohemianism by ordering Telegin to play his guitar when everyone is asleep and by asking for cognac. He also talks about beauty, and promises Sonya that he will never drink again. Sonya confesses her love for Astrov to Elena and Elena expresses her gathering frustration by wanting to play the piano: "I shall sit and play and cry, cry like a small child" (p. 200). But before she hears the answer of her husband, "It is forbidden," the pause is filled with another sound, that of the watchman, signaling the predominance of domestic routine over poetic longings. Elena tells him to stop his knock, but she herself is forbidden to express her own longings in the sounds of music. As Astrov says, "the storm passes us by, it only touched us by its tail." And so it does, except that the air is not cleared; it is heavy with unexpressed sounds.

In act 3, the storm moves inside. From act 1, which takes place in the afternoon, we move to the second act that takes place at night. In act 3, which will contain the central illumination, we are back in the daytime. At the beginning, Voinitsky announces the impending meeting at which the professor will make some kind of announcement. Yet before this announcement, which later elicits a violent reaction from Uncle Vanya, there is a scene that further motivates that response: Voinitsky sees Elena in Astrov's arms. A vision of his own happiness with Elena that had once been possible, together with the professor's ensuing speech concerning the sale of the estate, ignites Vanya's pathetic anger, although it resolves nothing.

As the Soviet critic, Ermilov noted, there is "a correlation of the final act with that earlier life on the estate, which existed here 'beyond the limits of the play,' even before Act One and the Serebryakovs' 'intrusion.'"[17] Every character says in his own way what Uncle Vanya said to the Professor: "All will be as before." Act 1 is set in the garden, an enclosed space. Act 4 takes place in Uncle Vanya's room, which is significantly both his bedroom and the office of the estate. All avenues of escape are obstructed; at the window stands a big table with account books, papers, and other objects that signify the estate. Both doors lead not outside but into some other enclosed

spaces. The unexplored life is symbolized by a map of Africa hanging on the wall, which as Chekhov says is "apparently not needed by anyone here." It is an autumn evening and all is quiet. Thus the scene is set for the future arrival of winter, of death; it is recomposed "beyond the limits of the play."

The offer of a glass of tea which Astrov refused in the opening of the play is here again declined, but the glass of vodka refused earlier in the play is accepted. Astrov thus breaks his pledge to Sonya, but that was made in act 2 before the storm and the revelation that self-destruction was inevitable.

Right after Astrov accepts the vodka he begins talking as in the opening scene, but his subject matter is not his passing youth, nor generalizations about the trivial life. Rather, there follows a mundane conversation about his horse's lameness and the blacksmith. It is at this point that the famous remark about heat in Africa is made by Astrov. The existence of the faraway, sunny, unexplored continent is dismissed by a banal and meaningless remark: "I suppose it is terribly hot in Africa now." (p. 221). Probably it is in this same manner that the unexplored regions of their lives have also been dismissed. Those unknown regions with all their potentialities are not needed here, as the map itself is not needed. When Maksim Gorky saw *Uncle Vanya* he wrote to Chekhov:

> In the last act of *Vanya* when after a long pause, the doctor speaks of the heat of Africa, I trembled with admiration of your talent and with fear for people and for our colorless wretched life. How magnificently you struck at the heart of things here, and how much to the point![18]

The routine has returned, and the predominant voices in this act are those concerned with routine: noodles, accounts, twenty pounds of oil, and Sonya's last speech that contains words like "bearing the trials that fate sends us," "humbly," "the long, long chain of days." Earthly dreams have finally been substituted by those that have nothing to do with life or people, those of skies alight with jewels and angels. There is a need to have faith. Against the familiar sounds of the night watchman, Telegin's guitar, and Mariya Vasilevna's scribbling in the margins of the book, Sonya's closing words, "We shall rest," (p. 223) sound like a death sentence.

V THREE SISTERS

The success of *Uncle Vanya,* together with pressure from the Moscow Art Theatre for another play, prompted Chekhov to start serious work on *Three Sisters.* Chekhov labored over the manuscript from August to November of 1900, during which time he was very skeptical in his appraisal of its artistic merit. He was afraid that there were "a great many characters" and that it would "come out indistinct or pale." Tolstoi agreed with this appraisal of the play, complaining that "nothing happened" in it. After Chekhov visited Tolstoi in the Crimea during the winter of 1901-1902, he described the great artist's criticism of his plays as follows:

> He was still confined to bed but talked a great deal about everything and about me, among other things. When eventually I get to my feet and make my farewells, he pulls me back by the arm, saying: "Kiss me!" and after giving me a kiss he suddenly bends over swiftly to my ear and says in that energetic quickfire old man's voice of his: "But I still can't stand your plays. Shakespeare's are terrible, but yours are even worse!"[19]

"Indistinct" and "pale" can hardly be applied to the final manuscript of *Three Sisters.* To begin with, Chekhov's innovative conception of dramatic structure differs radically from that of the traditional play with three or five acts that places the climax in the middle act. In contrast to this, Chekhov portrays the effects of passing time with an evenly balanced dramatic structure, in which the first two acts form a contrasting mirror to that which will follow.

The play begins in a spring that is full of hope for the three sisters, who have faith that they will return to Moscow before the fall. When the curtain goes up, Olga, Masha, and Irina are framed on stage alone together, but gradually the other major characters join them to celebrate the youngest sister Irina's name day. The tone is optimistic and it is clear that the sisters feel they will soon move to Moscow with their brother who they hope will become a university professor. The arrival of Vershinin, an old acquaintance from Moscow, further raises their spirits, acting as a link to them between the past and future. But at the beginning of act 2 these lighthearted feelings and hopes have been dispelled because of Andrei's unfortunate marriage to the vulgar, materialistic Natasha.

Significantly, the season is now winter, a time of sterility and barrenness, which is indeed the effect of Natasha's dominion over the household. In act 3 the season is not mentioned but there is a fire raging that is a symbolic representation of the destructive havoc being wreaked in the lives of the Prozorov sisters. The last act is set in autumn, which ironically recalls Irina's original prediction four years earlier that they would be settled in Moscow by the fall. The wide range of possibilities that life in Moscow represented has been permenently placed out of reach, and the sisters must adjust to the confines of a provincial existence.

Natasha, who in act 1 was a guest in the house, has now succeeded in evicting the sisters from the premises altogether. Natasha's final smug assertion of power over the sisters avenges her for her earlier position of servility to them. Natasha criticizes Irina's belt, which directly echoes Olga's admonition to her in the first act concerning the bright green belt she was wearing. However, although Natasha has attained material power, she has instilled neither respect nor even fear in the sisters. In the end they remain spiritually unified as in the beginning by a

faith in life and in the possibilities of human nature. In the last scene Olga, Masha, and Irina are framed together on the stage, mirroring the first representation of them in the play and underlining the fact that their spiritual unity can not be destroyed by personal hardships.

The play is also united by imagery that runs throughout its four acts. In the beginning of the play Irina says she feels as if she were "sailing along, with a great blue sky above me and huge white birds soaring about." Tuzenbakh responds by calling Irina his "little white bird," and the association of a bird's freedom of migration with Irina's desire to fly away to Moscow is thus implied. Tuzenbakh uses the image of a bird again in act 2, although this time the context of his speech forms an ironic comment on Irina's feelings of identity with a bird. In an argument with Vershinin, who argues for faith in the future, Tuzenbakh responds with a metaphor that people are like migrating birds: to the unknowledgeable observer a bird's flight might seem free, yet even these creatures are constantly obeying laws of nature that bind them to pre-established patterns:

> And life won't be any different, no, not only a couple of hundred years from now, but a million. Life doesn't change, it always goes on the same; it follows its own laws, which don't concern us and which we can't discover anyway. Think of the birds flying South in the autumn, the cranes, for instance: they just fly on and on. It doesn't matter what they're thinking, whether their heads are filled with great ideas or small ones, they just keep flying, not knowing where or why. And they'll go on flying no matter how many philosophers they happen to have flying with them. Let them philosophize as much as they like, as long as they go on flying.
>
> (p. 250)

Irina will never reach Moscow because her life is governed by certain arbitrary laws of fate, and hence any identification of her with a bird is tragically closer to this interpretation than the optimistic one she originally conceived. In act 4 Chebutykin again compares Irina to a bird, stressing that she is free of him because she can fly faster than he:

> CHEBUTYKIN, *moved.* My precious little girl, my dear child! You're gone on so far ahead of me, I'll never catch up with you now. I've been left behind like a bird that's too old and can't keep up with the rest of the flock. Fly away, my dear, fly away, and God bless you!
>
> (p. 276)

Clothing imagery also unites this play. In the beginning Olga, the eldest, is wearing a blue school uniform, Masha a black dress, and Irina a white frock. These costumes are not only indicative of each woman's character, but also of their future fate. In act 4, after a lapse of four years, Olga is involved with teaching to the exclusion of everything else, Masha is mourning Vershinin's departure, and Irina is planning to be married. Nothing has changed.

The narrative technique employed by Chekhov is disjointed conversation between characters, which sometimes points to their isolation from one another, but which can also be used to develop a series of associations that are united subtextually. A good example of this device is given in the following lines:

> MASHA But man has to have some faith, or at least he's got to seek it, otherwise his life will be empty . . . How can you live and not know why the cranes fly, why children are born, why the stars shine in the sky! . . . You must either know why you live, or else . . . nothing matters . . . everything's just nonsense and waste . . . *A pause.*
>
> VERSHININ Yes, it's sad when one's youth has gone.
>
> MASHA "It's a bore to be alive in this world, friends," that's what Gogol says.
>
> TUSENBACH And I say: it's impossible to argue with you, friends! Let's drop the subject.
>
> CHEBUTYKIN *reads out of the paper.* Balzac was married in Berditchev.
>
> (pp. 250-251)

Vershinin responds to Masha's generalizations about waste in a personal sense, commenting implicitly that, for them at least, only the timing of their meeting has blocked fulfillment. Masha responds with another generalization, that the course life takes is often boring, and at that moment Chebutykin comments that Balzac was married in Berdichev, which although seemingly unrelated to Masha's statement, serves as evidence of its veracity. This technique will later be used even more effectively in *The Cherry Orchard.*

Olga, Masha, and Irina are united by a longing for the excitement and love that is lacking in their lives, and to them Moscow is a sort of "earthly paradise." As the other characters are introduced, it is revealed that they too are searching for fulfillment in life: whether it be of the most base, materialistic sort, as in the case of Natasha, or the most abstract form of a "dream for mankind," in the case of Vershinin. Masha and Vershinin are the most idealistic characters in *Three Sisters.* The lyrical mood associated with Masha is first developed with her recitation of the first two lines from Pushkin's *Ruslan and Ludmila:* "A green oak grows by a curving shore, / And round that hangs a golden chain." Masha's melancholy longing for beauty and for a more poetic life finds its echo in Vershinin's abstract vision of the future:

> Why in two or three hundred years life on this earth will be wonderfully beautiful. Man longs for a life like that, and if he doesn't have it right now he must imagine it, wait for it, dream about it, prepare for it: he must know more and see more than his father or his grandfather did.
>
> (Act 1, p. 237)

A love affair develops between the two of them despite the fact that they are both married and that their ephemeral, lyrical happiness will have the same doomed fate as all their dreams. Masha and Vershinin's love has a fairy-tale quality, and they often communicative with snatches from a melody which expresses the poetic quality of their feelings for one another.

The youngest sister, Irina, also longs for a different sort of life, which will be enobled by meaningful work and beautified by a passionate love. She feels sure that fulfillment awaits her in Moscow, if only she could break away from the dreary provincial town which binds her to a boring, mechanical job and to relationships with men to whom she is indifferent.

Three men are in love with Irina: the elderly Dr. Chebutykin, the young profligate Soleny, and the dependable but unexciting Count Tuzenbakh. Dr. Chebutykin was once the unsuccessful suitor of Irina's mother, and he has transferred his unrequited affections to her. The inappropriate and slightly unpleasant quality of the doctor's attachment to Irina are underlined by two symbols that draw attention to his ignorance and to his old age. The samovar that Chebutykin presents to Irina on her twentieth birthday is the traditional gift for a silver wedding anniversary, and it causes consternation among the sisters rather than pleasure. Later, the doctor breaks the clock that belonged to Irina's mother, symbolizing his desire to erase time and also his carelessness toward other people's deepest feelings. Chebutykin's constant reading of the newspaper and quoting of trifles from it draws attention to the poverty of his mind, and again to his old age.

Irina's other unsuccessful suitor, Soleny, is much more dangerous and evil than the doctor. Whereas the doctor is indifferent to those around him, Soleny views himself as a second Lermontov, who has the right to harm others. When Irina refuses to return his love, he tells her that she shall have no successful suitors, and determines to kill Tuzenbakh. Soleny is identified with the animal violences of a bear from the beginning of the play. He attempts to defend himself against Masha's just criticism of him in the first act with lines from Krylov's fable: "He had hardly time to catch his breath, Before the bear was hugging him to death." However, it is clear in the last act that Soleny himself is the bear, and Tuzenbakh his victim. Before accompanying Soleny to the duel, Chebutykin recites these same lines back to Soleny, making the identification absolutely clear. Another symbol that delineates Soleny's character is the bottle of scent which he constantly sprinkles over his hands and chest, an act which indicates his desire to expiate himself from guilt.

Like the three sisters, their brother Andrei is a refined idealist who dreams of becoming one day a professor at Moscow University. He is constantly associated with his violin and with the books he reads even after all hope for an academic career has vanished. Andrei is the victim of his own inaction, as well as of his coarse wife Natasha and her lover Protopopov. Natasha is a woman with neither refinement nor kindness, who is interested only in advancing her material position in life. After her marriage to Andrei, she exercises despotic control over the household, makes a cuckold of her husband, and finally evicts the three sisters from their own house althogether. A lighted candle, symbolizing destructive fire, becomes Natasha's leitmotif as she gradually gains more power. Although her lover Protopopov never appears on the stage, it is clear that this influence is likewise evil. Masha's initial mistrust of Protopopov and her association of him with the bear of Russian folklore prove to be well founded.

Three Sisters further develops the theme of the meaning of human life which was broached by Sonya at the end of *Uncle Vanya.* The only two characters in the play who are not philosophically inclined, Natasha and Protopopov, are those who are shortsighted enough to triumph in temporal power relationships. All the other characters are in some way caught in a web of dreams that makes them more ineffectual in life than they might otherwise be.

In the end, all these characters must adjust to the frustrations of life in some way: for the doctor it is with indifference, for Andrei it is with resignation, and for Soleny it is with violence. Irina, Olga, and Masha must abandon their dreams of going to Moscow and must also deal with life as it is. At the end of the play Irina again speaks of work, and Masha and Olga advocate devoting themselves to improving life for future generations. There is a dignity in the three sisters' struggle to create meaning in life after it has been stripped of their most beautiful illusions, which makes this Chekhov's most serious play. It is a drama with comic elements rather than vice versa.

VI THE CHERRY ORCHARD

After the success of *Three Sisters* in Yalta, Chekhov wanted to write another play that he said would be a joyful comedy. He wrote to his wife on March 7, 1901: "The next play I am going to write will be funny, very funny, at least in conception."[20]

Chekhov took two years to write *The Cherry Orchard.* Perhaps his illness slowed his pace, or maybe he sensed that this would be his last major work, and he wanted to make it a masterpiece. At any rate, while Chekhov was writing *The Cherry Orchard* he surrounded it with an aura of mystery that indicates his own very personal attitude toward the play. By the summer of 1902, Chekhov still had not told anyone the title of his forthcoming play, and it was only to comfort his ill wife that he told her and she was the first to know. "Do you want me to tell you the name of my new play?"[21] he asked her. Olga later recalled that even though they were alone in the room, Chekhov would not say the title out loud, but whispered it to her.

Apparently the prototypes that would later be developed into the characters of *The Cherry Orchard* were in Chekhov's mind for some time. When he was in Europe in 1901, Chekhov wrote his wife about the Russian women living a dissipated life there, and singled out Monte Carlo as a representative city. Originally, Ranevskaya was designated in Chekhov's notebooks as just such an elderly Russian woman. Chekhov also told Stanislavsky about a Russian landowner who stayed in bed all day if he was not dressed by his servant: an obvious exaggeration of Gaev's passive personality. Several people whom Chekhov knew had Epikhodov's qualities, although each of his friends thought they recognized someone else in this figure. Sharlotta was modeled on an English governess who was Chekhov's neighbor; although to that woman's cheerful, goodhumored, and eccentric nature, Chekhov added a dimension of loneliness and alienation.

Chekhov considered Varya as "a fool, but a kind fool." He thought of Lopakhin as perhaps being the main character, and designated this role for Stanislavsky right from the beginning. Chekhov did not conceive of Lopakhin as simply a vulgar representative of capitalism and the new bourgeois class. He made the point in one of his letters that a serious, pious girl like Vavara couldn't have fallen in love with Lopakhin as she did if he were just an insensitive merchant.

When *The Cherry Orchard* was first produced on January 17, 1904, it was not greeted as a success. Some complained that "nothing happened," others remarked that the theme of the decaying landowning class was already exhausted by playwright Alexander Ostrovsky. These criticisms totally overlooked Chekhov's intention to address the audience on the subtextual level of unconscious sensibility, rather than on that of surface dramatic action.

Francis Fergussen sees the four acts of *The Cherry Orchard* in classical terms.[22] He identifies the first act as the prologue (the stating of necessary facts: in this case the cherry orchard's imminent scale); the second act as the agon (the conflict of characters in a drama: here between the values the characters attach to the cherry orchard and their efforts to save it); the third act as the peripety (when the cherry orchard is sold and the fact is announced at the party); and the fourth act as the epiphany, or completion of action, which occurs when the characters must accept the loss of the cherry orchard.

The plot structure is not nearly as meaningful as the impact of events on the inner sensibilities of the characters. The loss of the cherry orchard serves as a catalyst that elicits revealing responses from each of the characters.

Mrs. Ranevskaya and her brother Gaev are totally without practical ability, yet both pride themselves on their refinement and appreciation of beauty. Neither of them is capable of acting like a merchant, and thus even as their world crumbles beneath them they continue to uphold the same values. Lyubov squanders her remaining money on luxuries, and Gaev insulates himself from the world by playing an imaginary game of billiards. Likewise, the old servant Firs makes the cherry orchard an inviolable aesthetic symbol of the traditional order. He fondly remembers days of prosperity when the sale of the sweet dark cherries yielded enough income to support the entire estate in splendor. However, these memories will die with Firs' generation, and offer no philosophy to the young people in the play.

Trofimov and Anya have adopted a more impersonal and optimistic view of the cherry orchard's loss. The student Trofimov argues at the end of act 2 that "The whole of Russia is our orchard. The earth is great and beautiful and there are many wonderful places in it" (p. 316). Trofimov and Anya thus view the loss of the orchard as the inevitable and positive redistribution of resources from a privileged class to the whole Russian people. However, the irony will be that the profiteering merchant Lopakhin rather than "the people" will benefit from the sale of the property and that, furthermore, his plans for "development" will destroy its beauty.

Character portraits are further developed by the parodies that exist between the gentry and their servants. Sharlotta's lack of identity and her ludicrous behavior are a satirical reflection of Ranevskaya. Dunyasha is a parody of the whole idea of the delicate young noblewoman. Epikhodov with his twenty-two miseries is a parody of Gaev, as too is the "spoiled" Yasha, who insists "How uncivilized this country is."

Yasha's coarse words to Firs, *"Nadoel ty ded, xot' by ty skoree podox"* ("How you bore me, old man. Why don't you just go away and die. It's about time.") (p. 325), are a parody of the irresponsible attitude which Ranevskaya, Varya, Gaev, Anya, and Trofimov later show toward the old servant. Although they wouldn't be capable of consciously sharing Yasha's cruel attitude, at the end of the play, not one member of the family is concerned enough to ascertain that Firs has actually been sent to the hospital, and he is left alone to die.

The characters are also depicted through Chekhov's astute description of their speech peculiarities. Ranevskaya's dialogue is composed of emotional, sentimental, and at times melodramatic expressions which convey her helplessness. Such lines as: "I dream," "I'll die," "Have pity on me, my darling table"; and the repetition of the phrases "Perhaps it would be good to," "I don't know what to think," and "I'm expecting something" underline her feeling of insecurity. On the other hand, Ranevskaya's warmhearted nature is expressed in her speech by the constant use of endearing terms. She often addresses people as "my darling, my friend, my dear," and repeats these words tenderly.

Gaev's speech is at times prosaic, repetitive, and empty of meaning. His diversion of imaginary billiards is a defense against reality which preoccupies and soothes his mind, and it is highly fitting that he always seems to be sucking a gumdrop as he describes fictive games. However, Gaev is sentimental, and he periodically pronounces lyrical apostrophes to the past, to nature, and even to an old bookcase he is fond of. Although these oratorical speeches are scorned by the younger generation, there is

much truth in them, especially in his declamation to nature:

> Oh nature, glorious nature, shining with eternal light, so beautiful and indifferent . . . you whom we call Mother, you unite within yourself both life and death, you create and you destroy. . . .
>
> (pp. 314-315)

Lopakhin's speech is predominantly practical, although folk words such as *nebos'*, *prorva*, and *ob tu poru* intrude into his conversation. He often refers to numbers, and his vulgarity is reflected in his use of such words as "pig," "idiot," *baba*, and *bolvan*. On the one occasion that Lopakhin quotes from *Hamlet* his lack of education is further evident in the error, "Okhmeliya, get thee to a monastery!" (p. 316).

The student Trofimov's speech is educated and refined, and it is filled with imagery and metaphors. Like Vershinin, Trofimov has faith in the future, and his words to Anya are reminiscent of those spoken to Masha in *Three Sisters*:

> To free ourselves of all that is petty and ephemeral, all that prevents us from being free and happy, that's the whole aim and meaing of our life. Forward! We march forward irresistibly toward that bright star that shines there in the distance. Forward! Don't fall behind, friends!
>
> (p. 316)

Trofimov's effeminate appearance and his rationalization of celibacy with the line, "We are higher than love" (p. 322) render him comic. In act 3 he chides Ranevskaya for not being able to accept the truth about her lover, yet he himself can't face the implications of the fact that he has never had a mistress.

These very peculiarities which are so important to Chekhov's characterization do not serve the plot but rather play a vital role in the development of the play's comedy. Each character's idiosyncrasies are amusing in themselves, and everybody is preoccupied with his own subjective view to the point that communication becomes comic. Conversations have the quality of a mosaic, and the juxtaposition of phrases is artistically arranged to underline the absurd tragedy of human isolation. The following passages serve to illustrate this point:

LYUBOV: The nursery!

VARYA: How cold it is! My hands are numb! [*To Lyubov*] Your rooms are the same as always . . .

LYUBOV: The nursery, my dear, beautiful room! . . . .

GAEV: The train was two hours late. Just think of it! Such efficiency!

SHARLOTTA: And my dog eats nuts, too.

(p. 292)

Josie Lawrence, John Dougall, and Mark Lockyer, in a 1995 Royal Shakespeare Company presentation of The Cherry Orchard.

FIRS: I've lived for a long time. They were planning to marry me before your father was born . . . I remember everyone was happy at that time . . .

LOPAKHIN: That was the good life all right! All the peasants were flogged.

FIRS: [*not having heard him*] That's right! The peasants belonged to their masters, and the masters belonged to the peasants; but now everything's all confused.

GAEV: Be quiet, Firs. Tomorrow I've got to go to town . . .

(p. 312)

The use of symbolism is as important in this play as in *Three Sisters.* The significance of the cherry orchard itself has already been discussed. The color white is used to draw attention to the purity and beauty of Gaev's and Lyubov's past. In act 1 Varya mentions that one of Lyubov's favorite rooms is white (p. 292), and later when they look out at the orchard Gaev and Lyubov remark upon its whiteness, imagining their mother among the trees (p. 301). Firs, who lives according to the old traditions, is often dressed in a white waistcoat, and on one occasion he is wearing white gloves. Varya

is constantly carrying a ring of keys, which draws attention to her position of practical authority in the house. At the end of the third act, when Lopakhin announces that he has bought the orchard, she flings these keys at him.

The most important symbol in **The Cherry Orchard** is the breaking string that is sounded first near the end of act 2, and then again at the end of the play. In his book *The Breaking String,* Maurice Valency says of it:

> The symbol is broad; it would be folly to try to assign to it a more precise meaning than the author chose to give it. But its quality is not equivocal. Whatever of sadness remains unexpressed in **The Cherry Orchard,** this sound expresses.[23]

Valency adds that the breaking string is associated with the melancholy of a passing generation. He notes that in act 2 it is heard after Gaev's apostrophe to nature has been rejected by the young people listening to him, and again at the end of the play, after Firs has been abandoned.

The melancholy fatalism that is a constant undercurrent in **The Cherry Orchard** enlarges the scope of its comedy.

It is not a funny play in the traditional sense of the word, but rather in the framework of a more conscious, modern concept of humor of Henri Bergson's conception. The isolation that every human being lives in, the passing of time, and the imminence of death are cosmic tragedies. Only a great artist such as Chekhov could succeed in portraying the comic aspects of metaphysical questions which have been plaguing man for centuries.

VII EPILOGUE

In the recollections of those who were professionally involved with Chekhov's creations, actors and directors, the playwright emerges in the same light as the author of short stories who is able to zero in on a small part to reveal the whole.

"When we asked him," writes Olga Knipper, describing the actors' interaction with Chekhov, "he replied suddenly, as though not to the point, as though he was speaking in general and we did not know whether to interpret his remark seriously or in jest. But it seemed so only in the first minute, and then instantly we sensed that this remark, seemingly uttered in passing, began to penetrate the brain, the soul, and from a barely perceptible human character trait all the essence of Man began to emerge."[29]

K. Stanislavsky recalls that when he first played Trigorin in *The Seagull,* Chekhov praised his acting ability highly yet added that "but it isn't my character. I didn't write that."

To Stanislavsky's question in what did he err, Chekhov replied, "He has checkered pants and his shoes have holes in them." And he refused to elaborate.

"And he always made his remarks in this manner, briefly and imagistically. They surprised one and remained in one's memory. It was as though A. P. gave us charades from which it was impossible to rid oneself until one could fathom them."[25]

"I deciphered this charade only six years later," writes Stanislavsky, "when we performed *Seagull* again."

Stanislavsky says that even when he directed one of Chekhov's plays for the hundredth time he never failed to discover something new in the well-known text and in the well-known feelings evoked by the play.[26]

It is this immeasurable depth of a writer that affords his readers the joy of perpetual discovery and that makes Chekhov alive today, the only immortality to which he would aspire.

NOTES

[1] A. P. Chekhov, *Polnoe sobranie sochinenii i pisem,* vol. 12 (Moskva, 1949). In this edition the play appears as *P'esa bez nazvanija* (A Play without a title). All references are to this edition, pp. 7 - 165.
[2] *Pis'ma,* vol. 12, p. 58.
[3] Ibid., p. 117.
[4] Ibid., p. 116.
[5] *Six Plays of Chekhov.* New England versions and introduction by Robert W. Corrigan (New York, 1962). All of the following page references to Chekhov's plays refer to this edition.
[6] *Pis'ma,* vol. 12, p. 120.
[7] Ibid., p. 58.
[8] Gitovich N. I., *Letopis' Zhizni i tvorehestva A. P. Chekhova* (Moscow, 1955) p. 245.
[9] Ibid., p. 246.
[10] Avrahm Yarmolinsky, *Letters of Anton Chekhov* (New York, 1973) p. 353.
[11] *Pis'ma,* vol. 12, p. 248.
[12] Yarmolinsky, *Letters,* p. 209.
[13] Ibid., p. 319.
[14] *Russkie vedomosti,* 1899, No. 298.
[15] Quoted in *Chekhov* by Ernest J. Simmons (Boston, 1962), p. 495.
[16] *Pis'ma,* vol. 12, p. 311.
[17] Ermilov, "*Uncle Vanya:* The Play's Movement," in *Chekhov: A Collection of Critical Essays,* ed. R. L. Jackson (Englewood Cliffs, N.J., 1967), p. 119.
[18] M. g. A. Ch., *Perepiska, stat'i, vyskazyvaniia,* (M-L, 1937), p. 11.
[19] Recalled by Bunin, Chekhov "Vospominanlay I. A. Bunina" in *Chekhov Literature Nashedstuo,* vol. 68 (Moscow, 1960) p. 660.
[20] A. I. Reviakin, *Vishnevyi Sad A. P. Chekhova* (Moskva, 1960), p. 43.
[21] Ibid., pp. 45 - 46.
[22] Francis Fergussen, *The Idea of a Theater* (Princeton, N.J., 1949), p. 163.
[23] Valency, *The Breaking String* (New York, 1966), p. 287.
[24] Olga Knipper, *A. P. Chekhov v vospominaniiah sovremennikov* (Moskva, 1960), p. 686.
[25] Ibid., pp. 379 - 380.
[26] Ibid., p. 397.

J. L. Styan (essay date 1981)

SOURCE: "Chekhov's Contribution to Realism," in *Modern Drama in Theory and Practice, Volume 1: Realism and Naturalism,* Cambridge University Press, 1981, pp. 81-91.

[*In the excerpt below, Styan views the inducement of ironic detachment in the audience as Chekhov's most important contribution to realist theater. Styan states: "It is this effect of distancing, together with the troubling relevance of his human and social themes and the elusive lyricism of his stage, which has made Chekhov an immeasurably pervasive influence on the form and style of realistic drama in the twentieth century."*]

The Moscow Art Theatre went on to produce the last plays of Anton Chekhov (1860-1904), each with a structure more fragile than that of *The Seagull* with its comparatively conventional plotting. These were Chekhov's masterpieces, *Uncle Vanya* (1899), *Three Sisters* (1901) and *The Cherry Orchard* (1904). Whereas Stanislavsky largely developed his thinking about the art of the theatre after Chekhov's death, it was during the production of these plays that Chekhov increased his understanding of stage realism. He learned by experience and largely taught himself.

Three Sisters was the first play he wrote knowing who might play the parts. This factor might be thought to make it easier to write 'to the life', but in practice the availability of a company who could be counted on to indulge his experiments presented him with the greater challenge. After seeing this play in rehearsal and performance, he continued to worry at its text to get it right. *The Cherry Orchard* gave him even more trouble. He cast and recast the parts in his mind, and the play was three years in the writing. However, he was a dying man by the time it was produced, and he was spared the work of rewriting it. As a result of his agonizing, his achievement was of such a stature as called for a redefinition of naturalism, and made Ibsen's look old-fashioned. Stark Young spoke for the post-Ibsen generation when he found that only Chekhov's plays as performed by the MAT gave him 'the thrill that comes from a sense of truth', for only they carried realism 'to an honest and spiritual depth and candour'.

Chekhov's comment on the actors of the St Petersburg *Seagull* had been, 'They act too much', for, like his contemporaries in the west, he was in full revolt against the popular drama and its style of acting. He was particularly incensed at the derivative nature of the traditional fare on the Russian stage: a French or German piece would be merely translated into Russian and have its characters' names changed accordingly. He also deplored the kind of false, external acting which went with this kind of shallow dramatic enterprise: after Bernhardt's visit to Moscow in 1881, he took even the divine Sarah to task, saying, 'Every sigh of Sarah Bernhardt—her tears, her death agonies, all her acting—is only a cleverly learned lesson . . . There's not a glimmer of talent in her acting, only a lot of hard work.'

At this time, the physical conditions of performance prevented any fundamental improvement. In a letter to his brother Alexandre of 20 November 1887, Chekhov described the opening night of an earlier play, *Ivanov,* in Moscow:

> Curtain rises. Enter the person for whom the benefit is being given. Diffidence, ignorance of the parts, presentation of the bouquet, combine to make me unable, from the first phrase, to recognize my play. Kiselevsky, on whom I placed great hopes, did not pronounce a single phrase correctly. Literally: *not one.* In spite of this, and the prompter's mistakes, act I was a great success. Many curtain calls.

> (Translated Avrahm Yarmolinsky.)

There was little hope of an actor's catching the subtleties of the new dialogue when he expected to take a bow upon entrance before stepping into the action, and even then to stop to receive applause for his points throughout the scene. Nor was there much chance of conveying an ensemble quality in the portrayal of family life when each speaker drifted downstage centre to hear the voice of the prompter. Chekhov and his drama badly needed the reformed stage of the MAT.

In his last years Chekhov knew a little of Ibsen from Moscow productions, but he made it clear that he did not approve of Ibsen's kind of realism. Doubtless Chekhov recognized the forms and trappings of the well-made play still presented in the Norwegian: the big conflicts, the *scènes à faire* and the preconceived roles and attitudes, all lacking the quiet irony with which Chekhov himself saw human behaviour. He saw *Hedda Gabler* in 1900 and thought Hedda's suicide too sensational—'Look here', he said to Stanislavsky, 'Ibsen is not really a dramatist.' At that time, Chekhov had already learned to write an objective, underplayed curtain scene. Even the most Chekhovian of Ibsen's plays, *The Wild Duck,* which Chekhov saw in 1901, he found 'uninteresting'. He saw *Ghosts* just before his death in 1904, and again the curt verdict: 'A rotten play'. It was Ibsen's lack of humour and his posture as a moralist which disturbed the Russian, whose aim was to keep his characters flexible and his mind open.

Chekhov himself pursued a unique objectivity in his naturalism. 'Freedom from force and falsehood, no matter how they manifest themselves', he wrote to his editor Pleshcheyev on 4 October 1888. He refused to moralize, and part of the discomfort of watching Chekhov on the stage comes of having no moral position to espouse. 'I have not introduced a single villain nor an angel, although I could not refuse myself buffoons; I accused nobody, justified nobody' (this in a letter of 24 October 1887). So it is that we can be angry with Mme Ranevsky for letting the orchard slip through her fingers, like the money we twice see her give away so recklessly, but we can also understand her inability to manage a situation wholly foreign to her nature and upbringing. The well-known assertion by Chekhov that 'a writer should be as objective as a chemist' (14 January 1887) could sum up the reasons why he goes beyond Ibsen and Strindberg in his realism. Chekhov had been trained as a physician, but his pursuit of a scientific ideal of truth, one in which the writer was required to be as impersonal as a doctor examining a patient, really came of his extraordinarily sharp eye for spotting incongruity in human behaviour. This kind of objectivity forced upon the audience a role equivalent to that of a jury presented with a mass of circumstantial and contradictory evidence—it must stand back and coolly sort it out.

By the time Chekhov wrote *The Cherry Orchard,* the last vestiges of romantic sensationalism had disappeared from his playwriting. There is no shot fired on or off the stage, no death of one of the characters to upset the balance of interest. Epihodov's pistol is all for laughter, and Charlotta's hunting gun amusingly illuminates her character. Every love scene in the play, Anya with Trofimov, Yasha with Dunyasha, Varya with Lopakhin, is designed for an incisive moment of comic irony. The triumph of Lopakhin, who becomes the new owner of the very estate where his family had formerly worked as serfs, is undercut by his drunken good humour, and any grand and knowing statement in his public announcement of the purchase in act III is not to be found. There is no villain, no hero, no moral, just a calm and amused treatment of a potentially enormous and explosive situation, that of the breaking up of the old order and the disintegration of a whole class of society. In form and style, *The Cherry Orchard* was a final rejection of the ways of the nineteenth-century stage and drama.

Chekhov had unwittingly prepared himself to become Russia's greatest playwright by writing hundreds of short stories to order: it was the kind of particularity and economy that could serve the stage well. The stringent requirement of no more than 1,000 words for each of his early stories taught him to work by a highly selective and impressionistic method, pruning ruthlessly at every opportunity. 'Brevity is the sister of talent', he wrote in a letter of 11 April 1889, and his stories are little jewels of compressed character and suggested situation. His regular advice to the new authors who regularly flooded him with their manuscripts was to avoid generalizations, acquire a glancing style of writing, and deal in fine details: observation and the study of actual life, he reiterated, were the essential pre-requisites of a good writer. So in *The Cherry Orchard* Chekhov discovered that a caramel popped into Gaev's mouth could illuminate the man's character in a flash, as well as neatly undermine what he had just said; or the brash handling of a Parisian cigar could indicate vividly that Yasha had ideas above his station, but knew how to flatter the servant girl sitting beside him even by puffing smoke into her face.

A richer, submerged life in the text is characteristic of a more profound drama of realism, one which depends less on the externals of presentation. In Chekhov's last two plays, the hints and suggestions are more minute and prolific, so that the spectator's attention to the surface clues becomes more intense: 'It is necessary that on the stage everything should be as complex and as simple as in life. People are having dinner, and while they're having it, their future happiness may be decided or their lives may be about to be shattered.' By applying this formula to *Three Sisters,* for example, we recognize the reason for Olga's horror at Natasha's ill-treatment of the old servant Anfisa from our sense of Olga's background; or we reach our own sceptical conclusions, from the youthful enthusiasms she displayed before, about Irina's ardent intention to earn an honest living; or we understand Masha's reluctance to pick up life again with her husband Kuligin from the abject pride he takes in his school and his headmaster.

Chekhov went much farther than Ibsen in providing suggestive settings for his plays, but without having any symbolic image intrude upon the realistic content. The progression of the scenes in *Uncle Vanya* takes us from outside the house deeper and deeper into the heart of the household, and finally into Vanya's own room—by which time his soul is bared. The sets in *Three Sisters* trace the dispossession of the family from the comfort of their drawing room to the confined action of act III in a bedroom, and finally in act IV to the garden outside the house, which is now occupied by the dispossessors Natasha and her lover Protopopov. In *The Cherry Orchard* we pass from the nursery, the one growing point for the life of the whole family, out to the orchard and a little beyond, almost to the fringes of a new industrial town, and then back again, as if to depict in the stage settings the cycle of the characters' existence, and perhaps the cycle of nature itself.

So, too, the weather and the seasons change significantly from scene to scene. The heat of a hot, humid summer afternoon in act I of *Uncle Vanya* reinforces the soul-destroying routine of life on the estate, until the storm breaks by act III and feelings spill out. In *The Cherry Orchard,* the chill of spring gives way to the warmth of summer, and then to the returning chill of incipient winter, suggesting a steady passage of time to match the cycle of the cherry trees from their blossoming to their destruction, as well as the change from hope to despair in the family. Meyerhold recognized afterwards that Chekhov's strength did not lie in such surface effects as the chirping of crickets and the barking of dogs; rather, the unique rhythms of his drama created a 'mystic lyricism' designed to feed the imagination of his audience.

Yet 'lyricism' is inadequate as a word with which to identify the Chekhovian drama. Just as the direction of Chekhov's art as a writer of stories was towards creative reporting, so his craft as a playwright was towards 'documentary'. His naturalistic ideal was to let actuality speak for itself without apparent manipulation or distortion for didactic purposes. In giving *Uncle Vanya,* the first of his wholly naturalistic plays, the subtitle *Scenes from Country Life,* he seemed to be declaring his new role as a descriptive recorder. This play, like the two that follow it, essentially lacks a central figure, and by the dry and untheatrical way it opens and then has the title character slump on a seat dishevelled and yawning as if he had just rolled out of bed, Chekhov was challenging, if not insulting, the Moscow audience and its expectations. Judged at a superficial level, the play seems to take for a theme the problem of absentee landlordism, the poverty of rural Russia, and the indifference of the Russian intellectual, so that its author could be a kind of social historian. At quite another level, he tries to probe the nature of day-to-day living in all its triviality and futility.

Chekhov brought the same objective approach to the petty life of provincial Russia in *Three Sisters,* and to the world of *The Cherry Orchard* a sense of the pressure of social change. In a hundred tangential details Chekhov is the sly social critic gently pricking the conscience of his audience. There is no better example of this facility than when he obliquely touches the Jewish question in *The Cherry Orchard.* We hear the pathetic Jewish orchestra scraping together a living on two occasions in the play: once in the distance across the fields, and once after Mme Ranevsky has hired them to play at her unfortunate party. She betrays her feelings of guilt towards the Jews in so doing, and even though she cannot pay them ('Offer the musicians some tea', she says in a sorry voice) and we do not see them, the incident is a reminder of the persecution of the Jews under the Tsars.

In rejecting the traditional structure of interest and excitement in his plays Chekhov took an extraordinary risk. He set himself the task of presenting mediocrity, futility and boredom to his audience without boring it, and of making a broad, general statement without losing the particularity needed to make a sharp and realistic impact. Chekhov's documentary method supplied a strong

Chekhov on *Ivanov*:

To Alex. Chekhov

Moscow. Oct., 1887.

Ask Fedorov or Byezhetsky to insert the following notice in the theatrical news:

"Comedy, *Ivanov,* by A. P. Chekhov, in four acts. Read before one of the Moscow literary circles (or something of that kind), it produced a very strong impression; the subject is new, the characters are outstanding, noble, etc.," . . . It is not necessary to praise the play in this notice. Limit yourself to commonplaces.

I wrote the play unexpectedly, after a certain conversation with Korsh. Went to bed, thought up a theme, and wrote it down. I spent less than two weeks on it. I cannot judge of the merits of the play. It is to come out in a surprisingly short time. Everybody likes it. Korsh did not find a single error or sin against the stage, which is a sad indication of how good and attentive my judges are. I write a play for the first time, ergo, mistakes should be therein. The plot is complicated and not silly. I finish up each act as if it were a story: the action goes on quietly and peacefully, and at the end I give the audience a sockdologer. All my energy was spent on a few really brisk, forceful climaxes; but the bridges joining these are insignificant, loose, and not startling. Still, I am glad; no matter how bad the play is, I created a type that has literary value; I have produced a rôle which only as great a talent as Davidov will undertake to play, a rôle in which an actor can reveal himself, and display true ability. . . .

My play has fourteen characters, five of them women. I feel that my ladies, with the exception of one, are not thoroughly well developed.

Modern playwrights begin their plays with angels, scoundrels, and clowns exclusively. Well, go seek these elements in all Russia! Yes, you may find them, but not in such extreme types as the playwrights need. Unwillingly, you begin forging them out of the mind and the imagination, you perspire, and give the matter up. I wanted to be original: I did not portray a single villain, not a single angel (though I could not refrain when it came to the clown), did not accuse anyone, or exculpate. Whether all this is well done, I do not know.

Letters of Anton Chekhov, in *Letters on the Short Story, Drama and Other Literary Topics,* by Anton Chekhov, edited by Louis S. Friedland, Minton, Balch, 1924, pp. 115-63.

sational, larger-than-life eccentricity, but by his unusual gift for observing people. His aim was to bring about an audience's understanding and conviction. In lieu of a strong plot and striking events, Chekhov placed weight on a character's motives: from the start, the sisters' dream of Moscow is as hopeless as the redemption of the cherry orchard, and so the audience is persuaded to examine the behaviour of these people under commonplace and recognizable stresses.

Audiences accustomed to the traditional control of an unfolding narrative and provocative action on the stage—the imperatives of 'What will happen next?'—were naturally troubled. Without a central character upon whom to focus attention and whose moral guidance to follow, they had little to hold on to. One sister would have been a convenience, but three were a distraction. These qualities, together with Chekhov's oblique way of presenting the human comedy without explicit social commentary, were unprecedented in modern drama. Even Tolstoy was deceived into thinking that Chekhov lacked a governing theme or idea. For some playgoers, therefore, Chekhovian comedy has been relegated to the category of an acquired taste, for which an audience has to make a special effort of perception.

As for the actor, he is delighted to learn quickly that in the mature Chekhov play, every character has a complete life story embedded in his lines. Chekhov creates a rich and rounded character by supplying a hundred fragmentary impressions. And just as an audience has to decipher the code in the lines if it is to disclose the feelings and memories latent in them, so had the actor to decipher Stanislavsky's 'subtext'. The Chekhovian way with character was especially rewarding for actors who had acquired the skills of the Stanislavsky System: Chekhov never lets an actor down, and, like Shakespeare's characters, the larger parts are inexhaustible in their spectrum of possibilities. Even lesser semi-choric or background parts like Telegin, the guitar-playing parasite in *Uncle Vanya,* or the old nurse Anfisa in *Three Sisters,* invite the actor to contribute something of himself. No actor need feel like a supernumerary in a Chekhov play.

A singular problem for an audience watching a play by Chekhov, however, is to take in so large a group of highly individualized characters, for Chekhov habitually deals in whole families. Watching a play of his becomes an exercise in observing interactions and speculating upon interrelationships, constantly having to explain from the context of character and situation why something is said and done. In *Three Sisters,* Masha suddenly takes off her hat, silently indicating that she has decided not to leave: so we are compelled to seek the reason why she has changed her mind in what Vershinin has said or done. In *The Cherry Orchard,* Varya unexpectedly throws a pair of goloshes at Trofimov and, while it is true he is looking for them, she has no real reason to be so angry with him: we find the answer in her apparently unrelated disappointment in a character who is not even on the stage—Lopakhin, who has let her down again by failing to propose marriage to her.

compensatory element, however, by showing him a technique of full and engrossing character-drawing. He created memorable characters, not by working on some sen-

The lack of focus on a single character after *The Seagull* is also compensated for by the proliferating patterns into which Chekhov contrived to have his characters fall. If his three sisters are each carefully contrasted in age and position, their attitudes nevertheless intersect at the mention of their old home, and they share a common nostalgia for Moscow. In *Uncle Vanya,* the characters fall easily into opposing parties of tormentors and victims, masters and slaves, and were it not for the ironic chorus of the Nurse, the old mother and Telegin, the melodramatic conflict of opposites would have been less muffled. By the time of writing *The Cherry Orchard,* Chekhov has subtly made each character at war with itself, so that a small cast represents a large variety of other discords—of youth and age, of financial solvency and insolvency, of contrasting social classes of complacency and ambition, of marital needs. A few people become a microcosm of society, and introduce an unending complexity of interwoven thematic threads into the play. The patterns of accord and contradiction into which Chekhov's creatures fall increasingly affect the structure of rhythm and mood on his stage from moment to moment, and produce a new kind of 'poetic' drama.

Because of Chekhov's submerged character relationships, few other dramatists have demanded ensemble playing of such a high order. Epithets like 'orchestrated' and 'symphonic' began to creep into Stanislavsky's critical vocabulary, while discussion and rehearsal prior to a production took longer and longer. Today only a truly repertory company can blend the ingredients needed for a successful Chekhov production, for it takes time, not only to individualize character, but also to relate two or more such individuals: group acting can be convincing only if every character has drawn completely upon his history, and has developed an affective relationship with every other. And only if the group forms a unified whole can an audience assimilate the human values in the play feelingly. The implications of the Professor's announcement that he is going to sell the estate in *Uncle Vanya* touches every person in the family differently, and only the audience, perceiving the whole, can see how the proposal joins and divides each one, and how they support and fail each other in their moment of need.

Chekhov's method of juxtaposing individual attitudes in order to reveal an incongruous situation in its entirety is also one reason for his keen impact as a comic artist. Only by writing comedy did he maintain his objectivity in the face of the great social changes of his age, but his idea of the comedy suitable for a realistic play was by no means based upon the traditional exaggeration of character and the incongruity of situation. Chekhov's characteristic way of securing a balanced view was not to exaggerate but to undercut. *The Seagull* achieved this balance less well because it was constrained by the powerful ingredients of an earlier melodramatic form—in a realistic context, seduction and suicide are impossible to undercut. The relationships in the play are emotionally too intense, especially coupled as they are with the distracting suggestion of a conflict of innocence and evil among the principals. When Chekhov came to write *Uncle*

Vanya, the feelings of Vanya, a man who has given twenty-five years of his life to a false idol, Professor Serebriakov, are certainly as intense as those of Konstantin Treplev, but the detachment of the audience is wonderfully secured when Vanya fires at the Professor and misses: the anticlimax of this incident in the third act, with the great man cowering in fear and the middle-aged rebel throwing a tantrum and casting aside his weapon in disgust, is irreducible by any comic evaluation.

Chekhov wrote comedy, yet comedy with a bitter aftertaste, again typical of his method. For we also *like* Vanya, and his cause is worthy. In a world where justice triumphs some of the time, Vanya *should* have shot the Professor. The juxtaposing of pathetic and ridiculous incidents, the thrusting of farcical elements into a tense emotional situation, suppress any moralizing tendency and repeatedly induce the ironic detachment of the audience. It is this effect of distancing, together with the troubling relevance of his human and social themes and the elusive lyricism of his stage, which has made Chekhov an immeasurably pervasive influence on the form and syle of realistic drama in the twentieth century.

This is not to say that many modern plays or productions have been able to keep the infinitely delicate balance without which Chekhov's kind of realism amounts to very little as good theatre. The bulk of twentieth-century realistic comedy swings crazily between the grim and the giddy.

Richard Peace (essay date 1983)

SOURCE: "Introduction," in *Chekhov: A Study of the Four Major Plays,* Yale University Press, 1983, pp. 1-15.

[*In the following essay, Peace focuses on the "emotional atmosphere" or "mood" Chekhov evokes in his plays.*]

Chekhov, as a playwright, is the inheritor of a Russian tradition which, deeply indebted to Western models, nevertheless has its own recognisable idiom; in the words of one critic it exhibits 'a magnificent picture gallery, but no great narrative ingenuity'.[1] Although this characterisation specifically refers to the 'comedic tradition that leads from Griboyedov to Chekhov, the observation is broadly true for Russian literature as a whole, with its emphasis on character (i.e. psychology) at the expense of the neatly tailored plot.

Chekhov is also the inheritor of another Russian tradition, according to which seminal plays were written by authors excelling in other genres (Pushkin, Gogol, Lermontov, Turgenev, Tolstoy). Chekhov only achieved success in the theatre towards the end of his life, when he already enjoyed an established reputation as a writer of short stories. This fact undoubtedly conditioned his approach to dramatic art; his stage settings at times contain evidence of a striving for total authorial control more appropriate to description in the short story than to the business-like deployment of properties and scenery for a producer and actors. Thus in Act IV of **Uncle Vanya** the stage directions describe the map of Africa as: [*obviously useless to anyone here*]; the setting for the first act of **The Three Sisters** has the direction: [*outside it is sunny, gay*]; and Chekhov's prescriptions for the set of Act II of **The Cherry Orchard** (with its town *'which can be seen only in very good, clear weather'*) push the technology of scenic illusion to its limits.² Such directions are at once specific and yet intangible. They recall the descriptive devices of Chekhov's short stories; for they are in essence indicators of mood.

'Mood' may seem a term over-used in Chekhovian criticism, but it is an indispensable concept. The very essence of mood is its lack of precision: it is a complex, emotional, only just subrational reaction to meaning and significance not clearly apprehended: a response to elusive suggestion rather than precise statement. Unfortunately its very vagueness has often led to its being used in criticism as a woolly dampener to further analysis and discussion.

Chekhov's preoccupation with the elusive, less dynamic emotions of 'mood' appears to cut across the traditional concept of drama as action. Thus Harvey Pitcher comments on the development implied in the reworking of the earlier **Wood Demon** into **Uncle Vanya**: 'What Chekhov has done is to replace a play of action by a play of emotional content.'³ The observation is good as far as it goes, but Pitcher (who wishes 'to bury alike both Chekhov the social partisan, and Chekhov the ironist') reduces everything to 'emotion' and is against 'vast coded documents which can only be deciphered with the utmost patience'.⁴ The truth lies somewhere in between: literature is not an abstract art—it cannot abrogate meaning. Chekhov's world is poised between emotion and reason, and his drama combines mood with action, much as his comedy mixes laughter with pathos.

The emotional atmosphere (mood) of a Chekhov play is achieved through numerous devices. His titles may call obvious attention to symbol (**The Seagull, The Cherry Orchard**) but for the creation of mood such symbolism must retain a degree of ambiguity throughout. The sets, in their evocation of significant place, are also redolent of symbolism (the nursery in **The Cherry Orchard**; the study-cum-estate office in **Uncle Vanya**; the garden and the trees in the final act of **The Three Sisters**). A natural setting may be conducive to a lyrical mood, and atmosphere can be evoked through sounds—some musical: piano, guitar, concertina, snatches of song; some ominous: a distant shot, a breaking string, the thud of axes. Omen itself has a distinct role to play in the building up of vague feelings of presentiment. Akin to this is the extensive use of literary quotation, which surrounds each play with a penumbra of partially stated meaning. This shadowy periphery is also the abode of nonappearing characters, whose influence upon those on stage may often be considerable, and from this realm beyond the wings there stray from time to time odd episodic characters, vatic vagrants whose presence is inexplicably disturbing.

Conversations, which seem disconnected and are interrupted by random remarks, contrive, nevertheless, to suggest some interrelated significance.⁵ The device is most obvious at the beginning of **The Three Sisters,** where two apparently unrelated conversations form a dramatically meaningful whole. Nonsense words (*tram, tam, tam* or *ta-ra-ra bumbiya*) can also be imbued with significance, and gestures and small actions communicate meaning symbolically and visually (Gayev's imaginary billiard game, and the constant looking at watches). Above all there is the adroit use of pauses, where silence takes on an eloquence denied to mere words.⁶

All these devices have a common factor: they are referential and allusive—they suggest rather than state. As such they invite interpretation, and must have seemed to Nemirovich-Danchenko and Stanislavsky ready-made material for the new director-dominated productions of the Moscow Arts Theatre. The interpretation of mood was one of the chief sources of disagreement between author and producer, but although Chekhov on occasion seemed to be in despair at the way his plays were being staged, the only advice he seemed capable of giving was to hint in the enigmatic, elusive spirit of the plays themselves. To Stanislavsky's appeals for elucidation Chekhov replied: 'But I have written it all. I am not a producer. I am a doctor.' Such observations as he did vouchsafe were felt by Stanislavsky to be 'puzzles' (rebuses).⁷ In this respect Chekhov's attitude to his later plays appears to differ markedly from his earlier urge to analyse and interpret **Ivanov.**⁸

Chekhov did not invent 'mood' in the theatre, but he brought its techniques to perfection. A. N. Ostrovsky's play *The Thunderstorm* (1859) has many of the lyrical, poetic qualities often associated with Chekhovian theatre. The symbolism of the title and the motif of birds are developed in the play itself. Ostrovsky's outdoor sets breathe an almost Chekhovian magic, and atmosphere is created through omens (the mural depicting Gehenna) as well as by episodic vatic characters (the mad noblewoman). Particularly Chekhovian are the sounds of the guitar, the snatches of song and the literary quotations: Ostrovsky's autodidact Kuligin seems to find at least a nominal echo in Chekhov's representative of provincial intelligentsia in **The Three Sisters**—Kulygin. Moreover, like Chekhov, Ostrovsky is interested in the psychology of his characters (particularly his heroine) rather than in dramatic action as such.

Turgenev's play *A Month in the Country* has also been seen as a forerunner of Chekhovian theatre. Here too action is subordinated to psychological portraiture. Valency, in comparing Chekhov's methods with those of Turgenev, has made a strong case for the innovatory nature of Turgenev's characterisation, which he claims is the technique of impressionism: the characters 'discover themselves little by little, and are constantly surprised at the things they feel and do'.⁹ Nevertheless for the purposes of his plot Turgenev relies on the well-worn device of eavesdropping—a stock situation also found in his novels. It is significant that Chekhov uses this theatrical cliché in his early plays *Platonov* and *Ivanov*, but in his later plays it is used only once (*Uncle Vanya*) and there its psychological role transcends any suggestion of a mere hackneyed mechanism of plot.[10] Indeed the recurrent situation of the true Chekhovian play is not overhearing but 'underhearing'—the inability, even refusal, of one character to listen to another. Such psychological 'deafness' had already been developed as a social theme in Griboyedov's *Woe from Wit* (1825), indeed Chekhov's comic characters Ferapont (*The Three Sisters*) and Firs (*The Cherry Orchard*) may owe something to Griboyedov's Tugoukhovsky, but, more importantly in *The Cherry Orchard,* as in *Woe from Wit,* the younger generation is the bearer of truths which an older generation does not wish to know; Lyubov Andreyevna, like Famusov before her, covers up her ears in a symbolic act of non-hearing.[11]

Nevertheless, *A Month in the Country* is obviously far closer than *Woe from Wit* to the later plays of Chekhov. It is closer in its naturalism as well as in its poetic symbolism. Turgenev, as he does elsewhere, uses trees symbolically. Thus Rakitin, whose very name is derived from a tree (*rakita* = 'willow') attempts to evoke a romantic mood in his wayward mistress by poetic words on nature, but his contrast of the strong oak to the radiant birch is obviously to be taken as a symbolic statement about himself and Islayeva. Like Gayev in *The Cherry Orchard* he is rebuked for such elevated thoughts on nature. The motif of trees recurs frequently in Chekhov's plays, but his symbolic use of the theme is at once more subtle and more generalised. This scene between Rakitin and Islayeva strikes yet another Chekhovian note in the 'silences' which Turgenev calls for in his stage directions.[12]

The allusive quality of Turgenev's writing is important. In Act IV of *A Month in the Country* Shpigel'sky seeks to explain himself through a song, but more significant is the use of literary quotation. Rakitin is the friend of Islayeva's husband, and when in Act I Islayeva tells Rakitin: 'You see, I, like Tatyana, can also say: "What's the point of dissembling?"' her fragment of quotation alludes to far more than it actually states: it indicates her love for Rakitin, whilst at the same time asserting her faithfulness to her husband. Every Russian audience would catch the reference to Chapter Eight, stanza XLVIII of Pushkin's *Eugene Onegin,* would know what precedes these brief words and what comes after:

> I love you (what's the point of dissembling)
> But I have been given to another.
> I shall be eternally faithful to him.[13]

The impact of any play depends as much on its audience as it does upon its performers, and the special susceptibilities of a Russian audience are often overlooked by Western critics. Education in Russia has traditionally been based on oral skills to a greater extent than in most English-speaking countries. Every educated Russian has a rich fund of poetry which he knows by heart, and public recitations of poetry, both classical and contemporary, are a prominent feature of Russian cultural life. Anyone who has attended such a recital, given perhaps

by a well-known actor, will know that the performer has only to falter a moment for there to be innumerable voices from the audience prompting him with the correct lines, so that the impression may be gained that the audience knows the poem better than the reciter himself.

Far more, perhaps, than in any other culture, a writer in Russia can play upon the literary memory of his audience or of his readers. It is important to bear in mind this ability of a Russian audience to participate in the creative act through its literary memory, when we come to look at the use Chekhov makes of literary quotation in his own plays (such as the repeated quotation in *The Three Sisters* of lines from Pushkin's *Ruslan and Lyudmila*).

The tradition of censorship in Russia has been such that readers and audiences alike have long been attuned to the finer points of oblique statement and innuendo. Theatre in Russia can be particularly vibrant; producers and actors have a way of bringing pointed meaning to words which look innocuous on the printed page. Thus classics of the nineteenth-century repertoire, such as *Woe from Wit,* or the stage adaptation of Dostoyevsky's story *The Village of Stepanchikovo and its Inhabitants* can be played in such a way that without any deviation from the text a Soviet audience is aware of its relevance for contemporary life.[14]

Having said this, it must also be conceded that Chekhov could not always count on his audiences. The dispiriting failure of the opening night of *The Seagull* was as much due to the audience's expectations, as was its spectacular success when it was later produced by the Moscow Arts Theatre. Chekhov's plays were unfamiliarly new; but for all that, they built on the work of previous dramatists. When Styan lists among Chekhov's new techniques: 'experiments with the empty stage, his use of sounds to enlarge the area of our perception or to illuminate the condition of a character', we must not forget that, almost seventy years before, Gogol had shown him the way.[15] At the end of Act IV of *The Government Inspector* the stage is left empty for the departure of Khlestakov, which is impressionistically conveyed through off-stage conversations, cries and the sound of troyka bells. Chekhov, like Gogol, shuns the subplot, but suggests intrigue beyond the confines of the stage through his use of non-appearing characters—a device which goes back, in fact, to Griboyedov.[16]

Elements of the Chekhovian play may even be seen in eighteenth-century comedy. Thus in *Uncle Vanya* Marina's 'comic' prop of the knitted sock, has its precursor in D. I Fonvizin's *Brigadier* (1769) which opens, like the Chekhov play, with one of its characters (the brigadier's wife) knitting a sock on stage.[17] V. V. Kapnist had also experimented with the ironical effects of the interdependence of apparently unrelated conversations in his comedy *Malicious Litigation* (*Yabeda*) of 1798. In Act I scene viii of Kapnist's play an attorney conducts one conversation with the chairman of a civil court about his employer's litigation, whilst at the same time he carries on another with the chairman's wife concerning goods which he has brought with him as bribes.[18]

Scene from a 1971 Russian film adaptation of The Seagull.

One can sense Chekhov himself experimenting with his techniques in the earlier playlets. Thus *Swan Song* (1887) which is the dramatic reworking of the short story **"Kalkhas,"** can be seen as an exercise in the extended use of literary quotations, and *Tatiana Repina* (1889), which is Chekhov's theatrical reply to Suvorin the dramatist, has been seen by at least one scholar as: 'the first glimmerings of the drama of mood'.[19] The playlet is remarkable in that it is constructed entirely of parallel and apparently unrelated areas of speech, through which Chekhov suggests ironical commentary (scandalous gossip conducted against the background of the wedding service). A second Chekhovian feature is the centring of *Tatiana Repina* not on dramatic action but on a ritualised event, capable of charging the playlet with its own 'ready made' atmosphere and drama.

Success in the theatre for Chekhov was by no means immediate, yet he wished to write plays almost from the start of his literary career. His first attempt dates from 1878—a play without an authenticated title, which is usually referred to as *Platonov* in English (after its chief protagonist) but should perhaps be called *Fatherlessness* (*Bezotsovshchina*). It has a long rambling plot, but it is full of glimpses of the mature Chekhov, and Donald

Rayfield is probably right to see it as the source of all his later plays.[20] *Ivanov,* Chekhov's next full-length play, certainly appears to be a reworking of *Platonov*. It exists in two versions (1887 and 1889) both of which, unlike the earlier play, were staged. In its revised version *Ivanov* enjoyed a measure of success, nevertheless it cannot be regarded as a truly Chekhovian play. Its hero, Ivanov, is married to a young Jewish heiress, who has not brought him a dowry because she has been disowned by her staunchly religious parents. Heavily in debt, Ivanov becomes involved in a liaison with another heiress, Sasha, the daughter of a friend and neighbour. Ivanov's behaviour drives his consumptive wife to an early death, but when he is free to marry Sasha he is denounced by his wife's doctor, and because of this, and the malicious gossip which surrounds him, he commits suicide (in the first version he succumbs to the pressure and dies a rather improbable natural death). Ivanov is hardly an edifying character, yet it is obvious that Chekhov is presenting him as a candidate for his audience's sympathy.

John Tulloch has persuasively argued that Chekhov based his portrait of Ivanov on the scientific theories of the time, and that the play has to be seen more as a sociomedical case study of neurasthenia. He stresses that

Chekhov had the professional outlook of a doctor, which in the Russian tradition implied medicine with a sociological bias.[21] Yet one might also quote the words of Ivanov himself: 'It is possible to be an excellent physician and at the same time not know anything about people.'[22] If *Ivanov* shows evidence of Chekhov's professional outlook as a Russian doctor, it also bears the trademarks of his other, and more important, profession—the calling of a Russian writer. His hero fits into that tradition of Russian writing (Griboyedov, Lermontov, Turgenev, Goncharov, Dostoyevsky among others) which sought to create typical 'heroes' of their time. Chekhov's very insistence on the name Ivanov seems designed to assert the typicality of his 'Russianness'.[23]

The decade of the 1880s, after the assassination of Tsar Alexander II in 1881, was a period of political repression and stagnation in Russian intellectual life. It was a time when heroism seemed impossible; a period of so-called 'little deeds' (*malyye dela*). It is in these terms that Sasha angrily taunts local society, in her defence of Ivanov:

> Or if you could all *do* something, something quite small, hardly noticeable, but something a bit original and daring, so that we young ladies could look at you and say 'Oh', admiringly, for once in our lives![24]

Ivanov, himself, is a typical intellectual figure of his period, but as such he is aware of literary echoes from a previous age:

> I'm dying of shame at the thought that I, a healthy, strong man, have somehow got transformed into a sort of Hamlet, or Manfred, or one of those 'superfluous' people, the devil knows which! There are some pitiable people who are flattered when you call them Hamlets or 'superfluous', but to me it's a disgrace! It stirs up my pride, a feeling of shame oppresses me, and I suffer.[25]

The term 'Hamlet' was almost synonymous with 'superfluous man' (cf. Turgenev's story *The Hamlet of the Shchigrovskiy Region*). References to Hamlet are particularly pronounced in *Platonov* (as well, of course, as in the later play *The Seagull*). Nevertheless the true era of the so-called 'superfluous man' had been the three decades between 1825 and 1855 which corresponded to the reign of Tsar Nicholas I. Like the period of the 1880s this was a time of repression, which had also been occasioned by a political event—the suppression of the Decembrist uprising in 1825. Ivanov exhibits the characteristics of key figures in the literature of this earlier period. Like Griboyedov's Chatsky he is at odds with local society.[26] Like Turgenev's Rudin he is a man full of great potential, which he seems incapable of realising; and again like Rudin, he demurs when his 'heroine' suggests that they should abscond. Nevertheless the terms of his reply suggest yet another of these 'superfluous' heroes: 'I feel too lazy to walk to that door, and you talk of America . . .'[27]

The laziest man in Russian literature is the hero of I. A. Goncharov's novel *Oblomov* (1859). Like the other fig-

ures discussed above, Oblomov is incapable of forming a serious relationship with a strong heroine, yet she, Olga Ilinskaya, wishes to 'resurrect' him. In a similar way Sasha is accused by Ivanov of having set herself the goal of resurrecting the human being in him and he characterises their love affair as a literary stereotype:[28]

> And this love affair of ours is all just something commonplace and trite: 'He lost heart and lost his grip on things. She appeared, cheerful and strong in spirit, and held out a helping hand.' It's beautiful, but it's only like what happens in novels. In real life you don't . . .[29]

In Goncharov's novel the psychological motivation of Olga Ilinskaya is equally as fascinating as that of Oblomov himself. Sasha provides us with an insight which could be just as valid for Olga:

> There are a lot of things men don't understand. Every girl is more attracted by a man who's a failure than by one who's a success, because what she wants is active love. . . . Do you understand that? Active love. Men are taken up with their work and so love has to take a back seat with them. To have a talk with his wife, to take a stroll with her in the garden, to pass time pleasantly with her, to weep a little on her grave—that's all. But for us—love is life.[30]

In a variant of this scene Sasha actually calls Ivanov 'Oblomov', but Chekhov discarded such open identification.[31] In reinterpreting Goncharov he undoubtedly wished to avoid the ready-made stereotype, and a polemical point is the disowning of positive features which certain critics had attributed to Oblomovism itself:

> IVANOV. I can't enjoy spiritual idleness and see it as something noble and lofty. Idleness is idleness, weakness is weakness—I don't know any other names for them.[32]

Central to the play is the assertion that man is psychologically far more complex than the gossip-mongers of local society and the self-appointed moralist, Dr Lvov, can ever imagine. In an important speech in Act III, scene vi, Ivanov not only rebukes Lvov for his simplistic view of human motivation, but at the same time appears to take up Lebedev's observation in the preceding scene, that man is a mere samovar.[33] This polemical point about the complexity of human psychology will be illustrated more impressively in the later plays: in *Ivanov* itself it has more the role of a programmatic statement.

Nevertheless it is national psychology and sociological interpretation which are uppermost in the detailed explanation of his play communicated to Suvorin in a letter of 30 December 1888. It appears from this that *Ivanov* is about the Russian temperament itself, which Chekhov sees as conditioned by periods of excitability followed by troughs of depression. He even draws a graph to illustrate his argument showing that with each successive phase the troughs of depression get lower:

Disillusionment, apathy, nervous instability, being easily tired are the invariable results of excessive excitability and such excitability is characteristic of our young people in the highest degree. Take literature. Take the present . . .[34]

Although Chekhov here seems to be offering a national and social account of the medical condition known as manic depression, his view of the polarisation of the Russian temperament between excitability and depression, bouts of activity and periods of lethargy, is not new. The critic N. A. Dobrolyubov, pointing to a similar pattern in Russian history, had likened the intelligentsia of his day to the legendary folk hero Ilya Muromets who slept for thirty years then awoke to perform doughty deeds.[35]

Chekhov's argument in his letter to Suvorin, as we have seen, is partly based on literature, and here he may have had *Oblomov* in mind; for there had also been 'highpoints' of activity in Oblomov's life (initially, as a young man, under the influence of Shtolts and later in response to Olga). Indeed, in giving his hero both the name and the patronymic of Ilya (Ilya Ilyich) Goncharov may have been seeking to link him with the symbolic figure of Ilya Muromets.

In *Ivanov,* the aristocratic Shabelsky says of Ivanov's self-appointed critic Dr Lvov, that he thinks of himself as a second Dobrolyubov, and regards him (Shabelsky) as a rogue and a serf-owner, because he wears a velvet jacket and is dressed by a manservant.[36] There are clear references in this to Dobrolyubov as the critic of 'Oblomovism'. In 1859 Dobrolyubov had written an extremely influential article on Goncharov's novel (*What is Oblomovism?*) in which he had argued that Oblomov was the summation of all the gentleman heroes in literature up to that point: that he was the quintessential 'superfluous man'. A similar objective seems to have been in Chekhov's mind when writing *Ivanov*:

> I cherished the daring dream of summing up all that has been written up to now about whining and melancholy people, and to put an end to these writings with my *Ivanov.* It seemed to me that all Russian men of letters and playwrights had felt the need to depict the depressed man, and that they had all written instinctively without having definite images and a view on the matter. In conception I more or less got it right, but the execution is worthless, I should have waited.[37]

It is interesting that this same letter contains the often quoted statement about himself as a writer of lowly origin who had to squeeze the slave out of himself drop by drop and who one day woke up to find real human blood in his veins. His injunction to write a story about such a figure was never fulfilled. The nearest he came to depicting such a social parvenu in positive terms was in his play *The Cherry Orchard.* Lopakhin has certain autobiographical features and is a more credible version of Goncharov's Shtolts—the practical man of affairs of mixed social origin.

In 1886 Chekhov published a 'Literary Table of Ranks' in the humorous publication *Splinters (Oskolki)* (No. 19, 10 May).[38] This parody of the hierarchy of ranks in the civil service left the top grade as yet unoccupied, but placed Tolstoy and Goncharov together in the second grade. Nevertheless in 1889, after the production of the second version of *Ivanov,* Chekhov reread *Oblomov* and, in a letter to Suvorin at the beginning of May, wrote of his disillusionment with the novel and its author: he had completely revised his views of its artistic merits. In his next letter to Suvorin (4 May 1889) Chekhov defends himself against the charge of laziness, but fears that he is like Goncharov: 'whom I do not like and who is ten times head and shoulders above me in talent'.[39]

In *The Wood Demon* (1889) Hélène is seen as the embodiment of laziness, and she is characterised by Voynitsky as an 'Oblomov'.[40] This reference was removed when the play was rewritten as *Uncle Vanya,* and Chekhov strongly objected to critics who attempted to interpret the play in terms of Goncharov's novel:

> I have read reviews of *Uncle Vanya* only in the *Courier* and *News of the Day.* I saw an article about 'Oblomov' in the *Russian Record,* but I didn't read it. I can't stand this making something out of nothing, this forced linking with *Oblomov,* with *Fathers and Sons* etc. You can forcibly compare any play with what you want, and if Sanin and Ignatov had taken Nozdrev and King Lear instead of Oblomov, it would have turned out equally profound and readable. I do not read such articles, so as not to foul up my temper.[41]

Given such a categorical authorial pronouncement, it might seem that any critic would be foolish to draw further parallels between Oblomov and Chekhov's heroes, yet the echoes are there in the later plays; indeed in the recurrent theme of ineffectuality confronted by the exhortation to work we have something of the dilemma which lies at the heart of Goncharov's novel.

Chekhov felt the parallel with Oblomov even in his own life. We have already seen that in reply to Suvorin's charge of laziness, he conceded that he felt like Goncharov, and he made a similar excuse to Stanislavsky towards the end of his life as he was working on *The Cherry Orchard*:

> I was ill, but am recovered now, my health has improved, and if I do not work as I ought, it is because of the cold (it is only eleven degrees in my study), lack of company and, probably, laziness, which was born in 1859, that is one year before me.[42]

The reference to the publication date of *Oblomov* is unmistakable, yet Chekhov was anything but a lazy man; he did, however, suffer from a debilitating disease, and did not wish to face up to it. A jocular condemnation of the 'Oblomov' within himself was one way of minimising his symptoms and coping with a problem he knew to be incurable. The charge of 'Oblomovism' from others was another matter—it touched on a sensitive area of his own life, even though the term was applied solely to his heroes. It is undeniable, nevertheless, that the protagonists of his plays lack drive: 'The usual Chekhovian character is a halfhearted participant in an action that barely excites his interest.'[43] Through such heroes Chekhov was not merely purging an element which he most dreaded in himself, he was also portraying a state of mind endemic in Russian society at the end of the nineteenth century. In the political reaction which followed the assassination of Tsar Alexander II even the most energetic leaders of the intelligentsia suddenly felt themselves superfluous. M. Ye. Saltykov-Shchedrin (of whose great output Chekhov felt envious)[44] expressed this mood most strikingly in his Gogolian 'Fairy Tale' *The Adventures of Kramolnikov* (1886)—Kramolnikov wakes up one morning and suddenly realises that he doesn't exist.[45] Such new 'non-people' could obviously be related to the former 'superfluous men', of whom Oblomov had been seen as the epitome. But *Oblomov* is also a novel about social change (it purports to have been written in answer to the question: 'where do beggars come from?').[46] The reforms of the 1860s, anticipated in Goncharov's novel, had resulted by the turn of the century in a rapidly changing society. The old landowning gentry were a waning social force, losing ground to the new and energetic entrepreneur, whom Goncharov had not so much depicted, as prophesied, in the figure of Shtolts. The social theme is important for all Chekhov's plays and it is significant that its dominant motif is dispossession.

It has often been observed that Chekhov's theatrical technique combines a subtle blend of naturalism and symbolism.[47] He wrote at a time when the Russian theatre had found, in Stanislavsky, its great exponent of showing life as it is. The Moscow Arts Theatre productions stressed the naturalism of the plays to the point where, Chekhov felt, it became absurd. The naturalism of sets, acting and effects was boldly emphasised, and Stanislavsky was particularly fond of multiplying incidental, off-stage sounds far in excess of those called for by the author. Stanislavsky tells the following story against himself:

> 'Listen!' Chekhov told someone, but so that I could hear, 'I shall write a new play and it will begin like this: 'How marvellous, how silent! No birds can be heard, no dogs, no cuckoos, no owls, no nightingales, no clocks, no bells and not a single cricket.' Of course he was getting at me.[48]

Stanislavsky's philosophy of production, his famous 'method', was constantly developing. Later he would take a different view of his earlier Chekhov productions.[49]

Nevertheless, naturalism as such was not the order of the day. Throughout Europe the 1890s marked an almost universal flight from the humdrum and everyday; symbolism, decadence, impressionism dominated the *fin de siècle* mood. Chekhov was aware of these currents, and in his new theatre of the 1890s he contrived, whilst retaining the naturalistic surface, to incorporate an element of intangibility and mystery proclaimed in the new art forms—a dimension characterised by Valency as the 'Chekhovian "Beyond"': 'The strangely unreal atmosphere in which the realities of his later plays are suspended. It is an atmosphere less mysterious and less explicit than the Maeterlinckian *au-delà,* and certainly more intelligible.'[50]

Chekhov's earlier heroes, Platonov, Ivanov and Voynitsky (in the **Wood Demon**) are romantic figures alienated from the prosaic world in which they live. Not only do they convey a sense of looking back to an earlier period of Russian literature, but such self-indulgent, self-destructive romanticism is artistically at odds with the naturalistic vehicle of the plays themselves. It is significant that **The Seagull,** the play which gave Chekhov his first major success, and marked the onset of the theatre of mood, should project the romantic, alienated hero at odds not merely with the society around him, but more importantly with that society's concept of theatre. Treplev, in calling for new forms, is Chekhov struggling to find a way out of his own artistic impasse. The rivalry between Trigorin and Treplev reflects a debate within the author himself. The first 'Chekhovian' play is a play of re-evaluation and self-examination.[51]

NOTES

[1] M. Valency, *The Breaking String: The Plays of Anton Chekhov,* New York, 1966, p. 17 (cf. also *ibid.* p. 222).
[2] Cf. Francis Fergusson, '*The Cherry Orchard*: A Theatre-Poem of the Suffering of Change', in *Chekhov, A Collection of Critical Essays,* ed. R. L. Jackson, Englewood Cliffs, New Jersey, 1967, p. 152.
[3] Harvey Pitcher, *The Chekhov Play,* London, 1973, p. 78.
[4] *Ibid.* pp. 4, 214.
[5] Nils Ake Nilsson denies any significance other than compositonal to such remarks. See his 'Intonation and Rhythm in Chekhov's Plays' in Jackson, pp. 172-3. Valency, however, considers that 'it is seldom that the associative links are entirely lacking', but adds: 'It is entirely probable that the seemingly disjunctive nature of Chekhov's dialogue reflects his own habit of mind.' See Valency, p. 237. Pitcher considers such speech habits a trait common to Russians. See Pitcher, p. 28.
[6] 'During the pauses it is as though inaudible words are carried across the stage on light wings', Yu. Aykhenval'd (quoted in *PSS*, XIII, p. 510).
[7] K. S. Stanislavsky, *Moya zhizn' v iskusstve,* Moscow, 1962, p. 328.
[8] Cf. Chekhov's long letter to Suvorin on *Ivanov* (30 Dec. 1888) *PSS* (Letters), III, pp. 108-16.
[9] Valency, p. 45.
[10] Styan, however, sees Voynitsky's surprising of the 'amorous' scene between Astrov and Yelena as 'a grotesque stage trick'. See J. L. Styan, *Chekhov in Performance. A Commentary on the Major Plays,* Cambridge, London, New York, Melbourne, 1971, p. 126.
[11] Harvey Pitcher denies 'lack of communication' as a theme in Chekhov's plays. See Pitcher, p. 25.
[12] Cf. I. S. Turgenev, *Polnoye sobraniye sochineniy i pisem v dvadtsati vos'mi tomakh (Sochineniya)* III, Moscow, 1962, pp. 75-6.
[13] *Ya vas lyublyu (k chemu lukavit'?)*
No ya drugomu otdana,
Ya budu vek yemu verna.
Cf. Turgenev, *Poln. sob. soch. (Soch.),* III, p. 58. Pushkin's 'Novel in Verse' is itself full of literary allusions. For Russians literary echoes not only permeate literature, they also permeate life. See Peace, *Russian Literature and the Fictionalisation of Life,* Hull, 1976.
[14] In Ostrovsky's play *The Forest* an actor manages to pass an outspoken judgement on local society by reciting a speech from Schiller's *Die Räuber,* and cannot be brought to account because, as he says, it has been passed by the censor. See A. N. Ostrovsky, *Polnoye sobraniye sochineniy v dvenadtsati tomakh,* Moscow, 1974, III, p. 337.
[15] Styan, p. 339.
[16] For the influence of Gogol on Chekhov see Peace, *The Enigma of Gogol, An Examination of the Writings of N. V. Gogol and their Place in the Russian Literary Tradition,* Cambridge, 1981, pp. 52, 89, 150, 191, 204, 247, 299, 321 n. 31, 330 n. 38, 337 n. 16.

[17] See *Russkaya literatura* XVII *veka,* compiled by G. P. Makogonenko, Leningrad, 1970, p. 290. Rayfield compares *Platonov* with *The Brigadier.* See D. Rayfield, *Chekhov: The Evolution of his Art,* London, 1975, p. 98 (but cf. Platonov's own rejection of the 'raisonneur' figures of Fonvizin, *PSS,* XI, p. 38).

[18] Makogonenko, pp. 495-6. The following part of this exchange seems particularly pointed semantically:

> KRIVOSUDOV. But I fobbed him off. He would have gone on with a whole lot of improbable things about the case, but I shut him up.

> NAUMYCH [*to* FEKLA]. A pound of mustard.

> KRIVOSUDOV. I got him off my hands.

> NAUMYCH. How much, sir, my master to you is indebted [*to* FEKLA] a skirt length of silk.

[19] A. S. Dolinin (quoted in *PSS,* XII, p. 368; cf. also *ibid.* p. 316).
[20] Rayfield, p. 94.
[21] J. Tulloch, *Chekhov: A Structuralist Study,* London and Basingstoke, 1980, pp. 7, 90.
[22] *PSS,* XII, p. 56.
[23] Cf. Rayfield, p. 101. Chekhov spoke to V. G. Korolenko of writing a drama to be called *Ivan Ivanovich Ivanov*—'you understand. There are thousands of Ivanovs, an ordinary man, absolutely not a hero . . .', *PSS,* XII, p. 412. Chekhov also commented: 'The word Russian often crops up when I describe Ivanov.' See *The Oxford Chekhov,* trans. and edit. Ronald Hingley, London, New York, Toronto, 1967, II, p. 295.
[24] *PSS,* XII, pp. 29-30.
[25] *Ibid.* p. 37.
[26] His uncle Shabel'sky says that he himself played at being Chatsky as a young man, *PSS,* XII, p. 33. Rayfield notes the influence of *Woe from Wit* on both *Platonov* and *Ivanov.* See Rayfield, p. 98.
[27] *PSS,* XII, p. 38.
[28] *Ibid.* p. 72.
[29] *Ibid.* p. 57.
[30] *Ibid.* p. 59.
[31] *Ibid.* p. 250 (cf. Hingley on Chekhov's 'endearing distrust of clichés and literary stereotypes', *The Oxford Chekhov,* II, p. 6).
[32] *PSS,* XII, p. 71.
[33] Cf. *ibid.* pp. 50, 54-6.
[34] *PSS* (Letters), III, p. 111 (a somewhat similar view on the Russian as a sieve was expressed to Gorky. See Jackson, p. 202).
[35] N. A. Dobrolyubov, *Sobraniye sochineniy,* Moscow 1935, I, pp. 183-4 (cf. also the use of Dobrolyubov's term 'A Realm of Darkness'—*temnoye tsarstvo*—in *Ivanov, PSS,* XII, p. 34).
[36] *PSS,* XII, p. 33.
[37] *PSS* (Letters), III, p. 132.
[38] *Ibid.* p. 421.
[39] *Ibid.* pp. 201-2, 203.
[40] *PSS,* XII, p. 165.
[41] *PSS* (Letters), VIII, pp. 319, 596 and *PSS,* XIII, pp. 419, 459.
[42] *PSS* (Letters), XI, p. 142.
[43] Valency, p. 246.
[44] *PSS* (Letters), II, pp. 332, 512.
[45] Ye. M. Saltykov-Shchedrin, *Sobraniye sochineniy v dvadtsati tomakh,* Moscow, 1976, XVI(1), p. 197.
[46] I. A. Goncharov, *Sobraniye sochineniy v shesti tomakh.* Moscow, 1972, IV, p. 510.
[47] Cf. Stanislavsky, *Moya Zhizn',* p. 275 and Vs. Meyerhold, 'Naturalistic Theater and Theater of Mood', Jackson, pp. 62-8.
[48] Stanislavsky, *Moya Zhizn',* p. 329.
[49] Vl. Prokof'ev, *V sporakh o Stanislavskom,* Moscow, 1976, p. 86.
[50] Valency, p. 298.
[51] 'Written after a vow not to work for the theatre again, it is an act of vengeance', Rayfield, p. 202.

Leslie Kane   (essay date 1984)

SOURCE: "Chekhov," in *The Language of Silence: On the Unspoken and the Unspeakable in Modern Drama,* Fairleigh Dickinson University Press, 1984, pp. 50-76.

[*In the following essay, Kane investigates Chekhov's use of language and silence in his plays, arguing: "Aware that speech, like time, is an anthropocentric effort to limit, control, and elucidate the chaos of experience, Chekhov relies on the unspoken to expose and examine the elusive and the enigmatic both within and beyond man."*]

Anton Chekhov, respected for the concision, objectivity, sensitivity, and humanity of his short stories, began writing for the theatre in the 1880s. He was, in the opinion of Robert Corrigan, "the first playwright who sought to create in his plays a situation which would reveal the private drama that each man has inside himself and which is enacted everyday in the random, apparently meaningless and undramatic events of our common routine."[1] *The Sea Gull, Uncle Vanya, The Three Sisters,* and *The Cherry Orchard,* written at the end of the nineteenth century and the beginning of the twentieth, represent perfection of the Chekhovian dramatic form: the subtle, complex interplay of expression and suggestion.

Chekhov achieves the coalescence of phenomenal and psychological experience by fusing thought and technique.[2] His experimentation with dramatic form, content, and linguistic methodology results from his intention to present the complexity, universality, and essential mutability of life. Therefore, examination of Chekhov's symbolist and naturalist techniques, his use of the quotidian, and his apparently static structure can lay the foundation for an estimation of this playwright's distinctive use of the unspoken.

In *The Breaking String* Maurice Valency suggests that the dominant literary trend of the fin de siècle was symbolism and that Chekhov, responsive to literary experimentation, came very much under its influence.[3] Affinity to symbolism is apparent in Chekhov's lyrical interpretation of experience, concern for the transitory nature of beauty, evocation of mood, literary reference, and use of nuance, intimation, and suggestion, as well as his exploitation of symbols and emphasis on imprecision. Indeed, it is the dramatist's reliance on introspection and the synthesis of concrete reality with interior mood that most clearly align Chekhov to symbolist techniques.

A skeptic living in an age characterized by doubt and unrest, Chekhov did not share the symbolist's mysticism but nevertheless maintained that there is discrepancy between what man has and what he strives for. Central to his mature work is a spiritual unrest, rooted in awareness of life's mysteries and incompleteness coupled with the expectation of something better.

It would be a mistake, however, to label Chekhov a symbolist, just as it would be erroneous to label him a naturalist or social critic.[4] Chekhov wears all these hats and is defined by none. "Life as it is"—the barren facts of substantial reality and private, half-conscious perceptions, illusions, suspicions, and reveries of insubstantial experience—provide the content for this artist's drama; he provides the artistic form to realize and imaginatively distill its essence. Emphasizing the importance of artistic objectivity, Chekhov writes:

> In life people do not shoot themselves or hang themselves, or fall in love or deliver themselves of clever sayings every minute. They spend most of their time eating, drinking, running after women or men, talking nonsense. It is therefore necessary that this be shown on the stage. A play ought to be written in which people should come and go, dine, talk of the weather or play cards not because the author wants it that way but because that is what happens in real life.[5]

Taking his cue from the authenticity of Chekhov's portrait of reality and the dramatist's insistence on objectivity, John Lahr stresses the impact of Zola's naturalism on the naturalistic character of Chekhov's dramas.[6] And Robert Brustein concurs that the seemingly "arbitrary landscape, character details, aimless dialogue, silences, shifting rhythms and poetic mood" which typify Chekhovian drama constitute the most convincing attempt at dramatic verisimilitude of the modern theater.[7] However, we are admonished, by Chekhov's own correspondence, to distinguish between scientific accuracy and creative artifice. "I may note incidently," he writes to Grigori Rossolimo, "that artistic considerations do not always allow me to write in complete harmony with scientific data; on stage you cannot show death by poisoning as it actually occurs."[8]

Clearly, Chekhov is neither a symbolist nor a naturalist, but an astute artist who employs techniques peculiar to both schools of thought to create an "artifice of reality," to use Bernard Beckerman's term, which subtly balances subjectivity and objectivity, interiority and exteriority, vague intimations and clearly delimited detail, psychological time and anthropocentric chronicity in order to achieve emotional realism.[9] The seemingly formless Chekhovian form is a meticulously constructed dramatic composition stripped bare of the lines of construction to convey naturally the desired effect of fluidity and fixity. Lacking in intrigue, complication, climax, and denouement, the mature plays are a sequence of scenes wherein spatial arrangement supplants linear arrangement and unity of mood supplants unity of action.[10]

Both Valency and F. L. Lucas have noted the importance of Maeterlinckien static drama to the development of Chekhov's methodology.[11] Chekhov's plays employ the substitution of the effects of an event for the event itself, the use of nuance and suggestion to evoke mood, the use of quotidian dialogue, family gatherings in restricted areas, and an apparently quiescent structure that belies cyclical and chronological fluctuation.[12] But Chekhov's is the more gentle, subdued, and deeply analytic art. Maeterlinck's static drama evokes an atmosphere of spiralling anxiety, but Chekhov's drama elicits sustained *nastroenie;* Maeterlinck's gatherings are excruciating and funereal, Chekhov's characteristically ceremonious, social occasions such as name day celebrations, summer reunions, and farewell gatherings. The focus of Maeterlinck's static plays is the silent progression, intrusion,

oppression, and finality of death, but death is displaced in Chekhovian drama by the agonizing, progressively debilitating process of dying. Ossifying in their rural surroundings, Chekhov's characters eventually wither and waste away, witness to and participant in the destruction of themselves, their environment, their social order.[13] Characteristically, in addition, Chekhov eschews the archetypes of young and old, preferring to reflect emotional, material, spiritual, and temporal dispossession through varying states of decrepitude. In *Uncle Vanya,* for example, Vanya and Sonya are threatened with the loss of their estate; in *The Three Sisters* and *The Cherry Orchard* eviction and dispossession are an accomplished fact. Spiritual deterioration is illustrated in these plays by Andrey's loss of hope, Nina's loss of innocence, Mme. Ranevsky's loss of beauty, Masha's loss of Vershinin. For all, the loss of time is the most shocking and the most difficult to accept. Vanya's reaction is typical:

> VANYA: Day and night the thought that my life has been hopelessly wasted weighs on me like a nightmare. I have no past, it has been stupidly wasted on trifles, and the present is awful in its senselessness.
>
> (205)

Significantly, epiphanic awareness comes to Chekhov's characters when it is too late to reverse their ossification and deterioration. They are, and remain, helpless and passive in the face of social and cosmic forces which determine their lives.

Like Maeterlinck's pilgrims, Chekhov's characters wait, but for the anxious wait for Sisters of Mercy, priests, news of death, and escape from entrapment the Russian static dramas substitute the less terrifying, but no less anxious, tiresome, and debilitating wait for trains, for carnival people, for auctions, for lovers, for duels, for the release from boredom, for the realization of dreams—and, always, for tea.

Unlike nineteenth-century playwrights for whom the quotidian either depicted customary manners and morals or was overshadowed by events, Chekhov moved events to the periphery, as if they were details, and brought the ordinary, constant and recurring to center stage. Like Maeterlinck, he exploited the daily flow of the customary and habitual, not as setting but as subject of his art. To support his artistic representation of "life as it is" and to dramatize continuity and perpetuity, Chekhov employed the four-act structure, preferring the elongated form to the Maeterlinckien one-act structure and the naturalistic *quart d'heure.*[14] Emphasizing progression in time, rather than in action, Chekhov provides us with great specificity of detail: intricate arrival/departure patterns, pertinent "acts of God," the exact season, date, and age of the characters.[15] Nature figures importantly in the Chekhovian tapestry, providing a beautiful background for the drab foreground and graphically showing the cyclical and degenerative pattern of life. For example, in the first acts of *The Three Sisters* and *The Cherry Orchard* the reunion coincides with the springtime; the mood is expectant and exultant. In Act 4, on the other hand, the mournful farewell is set against the autumn sky and the imminent destruction of the trees; the mood is one of distress and disillusionment. Similarly, in Act 1 of **The Sea Gull** the heat of the summer season mirrors the burning passion of the lovers Treplev and Nina who are united in the birth of their artistic creation; but by Act 4 we learn that Nina has carried, delivered, and buried Trigorin's baby. His career aborted and his love for Nina unrequited, a despondent Treplev takes his own life on a night when the wind howls through the chimney and windows are shuttered against the draft.

Simultaneous with chronological progression, Chekhov focuses attention on the changing state of consciousness of each character. By particularizing temporal details, the playwright fashions a fragment of time in which everything, or more accurately, nothing, takes place. And by subordinating plot to characterization and event to stasis, he diverts attention from process to motive, from phenomenal reality to psychological.[16] The pervading effect, as William Gerhardi observes, is "at once static and transitory," indeed "static in its absolute transitoriness."[17]

However, the seemingly quiescent surface belies fluidity. The conclusion of each play (superficially similar to the beginning, but strikingly different in its lack of hope) confirms the swift passage of time which has gone unnoticed. Loss displaces promise; weariness displaces vitality; waste displaces beauty; resignation displaces hope.

Chekhov, cognizant of the iconoclastic nature of his structure and content, wrote to Alexei Suvorin in 1895, "I sin frightfully against the conventions of the stage . . . lots of talk on literature, little action and tons of love."[18] Significantly, the playwright fails to note that love in his dramas is either painfully or perpetually unsatisfied and unsatisfying or, if satisfied, painfully transitory. Beckerman suggests that the number of transitory and unfulfilled love affairs, with the central position they occupy in Chekhov's plays, is notable when seen against the background of the decay of aristocratic society.[19] But the number is crucial, less for its social relevance than for the multivalent human responses associated with it. Chekhov chose as central a universal emotion, ambivalent and evanescent in nature, which defies the limitation of time, place, and verbal expression. Unlike Maeterlinck's silent plays which primarily evoke the condition of fear, his drama elicits the vacillating, prismatic, confounding emotion of love tempered by joy, expectation, hope, disillusionment, and the searing pain of loss and rejection. Put differently, Chekhov's treatment of love is a function of his treatment of time: at once static and transitory, at once empirically verifiable and psychologically imprecise, at once measured and illimitable.

Because Chekhov's drama is a forum of emotion, not idea, the universal, evanescent, insubstantial, and undefinable emotions of loneliness and loss take their place with love in the broad spectrum of life experience that the dramatist impressionistically presents. Typically, Chekhov draws his content from life as it is; but the well

he taps is deep and dark, and the emotions he evokes are inextricably linked to his use of the unspoken.

Chekhovian dialogue performs a great number of essential dramatic functions: revealing character, furthering the action (more particularly, inaction), uncovering theme, and arousing in the spectator a mood similar to that of the character.[20] However, this playwright fulfills these dramatic necessities in an innovative way: by simulating aimless, fluid speech and thought. So convincing is the Chekhovian linguistic artifice that it may appear to be an irrational choice and accidental arrangement of words. But Chekhov is a consummate craftsman; what appears alternately fluid and fixed is in fact achieved by the intricate counterpointing of speech and silent response. Crucial to a study of Chekhov's use of the unspoken is the relationship of symbolist and naturalist techniques, deceptive stasis, cyclical flux, and the quotidian to this dramatist's linguistic innovations. The distinctive elements of his methodology may be considered under these topics:

1. disjunctive, indirect speech
2. colloquial dialogue
3. negation
4. repetition and echoing
5. pauses
6. counterpointing through overstatement and understatement
7. silent scenes
8. mute characters
9. silence as a metaphor for isolation
10. silence as a metaphor for evanescence
11. silence of the playwright

Oblique disjunctive speech elicits imperceptible fluctuation both within the mind of the speaker and between speakers. Repetitions, recurring motifs, and pauses reinforce the apparent stasis suggested by the eventless drama, and the continued use of negations (which have the effect of nullifying the statement just made) effectively slow or reverse the progression of time. Overstatement and understatement, moreover, report, by their exaggeration, both the emotional condition of the speaker and the quotient of attention and reception his comments receive from the listener. Kahn observes that through antiphonal counterpointing the dramatist achieves the impact of ironic statement that has the "special effect of not actually being stated."[21]

Unlike his predecessor in the symbolist theatre, the Russian playwright did not wish to accentuate the distance between speech and silence, the quotidian and the profound, the human and the mystical. Demonstrating grace and artistry of concision, Chekhov softens the harsh lines of Maeterlinck's polarized portrait through resonance, achieving in language the indistinctness and imprecision which typify all of his art.[22] The resonances produced by choral speaking, negative statement, understatement and overstatement, and the repetitive use of pauses narrow the gap between speech and silence while simultaneously revealing the distance between thought and meaning, between illusion and reality, between a person's conception of himself and the conceptions of his companions, and between speaker and listener. Indeed, Chekhov manifests his modernity by his awareness of man's essential fragmentation and isolation. Chekhovian characters escape to the relative security of memory or the relative promise of philosophy in order to forge a link in time and meaning. But as Corrigan observes, Chekhov, more than any other dramatist of the late nineteenth and early twentieth century, was very conscious of the existential loneliness of the human condition. In order for him to portray life as it is, Chekhov had to define his characters by their "solitude and estrangement from life" and not by their participation in it.[23] Chekhov employs restricted settings to underscore the fact that his characters are always in close physical contact, but rarely, if ever, in emotional contact. Efforts to break out of the imprisonment of isolation are foiled or gently mocked: confidences are ignored, confessions fall on deaf ears.

Aware that speech, like time, is an anthropocentric effort to limit, control, and elucidate the chaos of experience, Chekhov relies on the unspoken to expose and examine the elusive and the enigmatic both within and beyond man. Disjunctive, indirect speech is particularly well suited to the dramatization of exterior and interior experience. Citations from the mature plays clearly illustrate the discontinuity in conversation when one voice drifts off and another picks up the dropped line, in situations of physical or emotional stress or exhaustion, in the reversal or corrected direction of a thought. In the arrival scene of *The Cherry Orchard,* for example, the thoughts of Mme. Ranevsky, Gaev, Charlotta, Pishtchik, Dunyasha, and Varya overlap and cut across one another. What the dialogue lacks in continuity, it gains in authenticity. Mme. Ranevsky, exhausted from the long trip and the trauma of returning from Paris nearly destitute, is nevertheless exhilarated by the sight of her beloved nursery. Memories of her childhood flood her mind and fill the moment. Time and speech momentarily stop for her, and then through tears she remembers the presence of her own daughter, Varya. "Varya's just the same as ever," she notes, but for Gaev, who has been impatiently waiting two hours for her delayed train, time did not stand still. Grumbling about the delay and the ineptitude of the rail system, Gaev demands, "What do you think of that," but he might as well be talking to himself. At the same moment, Charlotta informs Pishtchik that her dog "eats nuts, too." In all the confusion, both literal and linguistic, Pishtchik replies, "Fancy that," but one hardly knows whether this remark is to answer Mme. Ranevsky, Gaev, or Charlotta—or in fact all three (64).

Through the use of quotidian expressions and situations, this dramatist reveals disjunction not only between participants in a conversation, but also between the thoughts of one speaker. In the last act of *The Cherry Orchard* Pishtchik arrives in time to say farewell to the departing family; but in his effort to cover all the subjects on his mind he jumps from one to another without apparent logic or continuity:

PISHTCHIK: What! *(in agitation)* Why to the town? Oh, I see the furniture . . . the boxes. No matter . . . *(through his tears)* . . . no matter . . . men of enormous intellect . . . these Englishmen. . . . Never mind be happy. God will succour you . . . no matter . . . everything in this world must have an end *(kisses Lyubov Andreyevna's hand).* If the rumour reaches you that my end has come, think of this old horse, and say: "There was once such a man in the world . . . Semyonov-Pishtchik . . . the Kingdom of Heaven be his!" . . . most extraordinary weather . . . yes. *(Goes out in violent agitation, but at once returns and says in the doorway)* Dashenka wishes to be remembered to you *(goes out).*

(110)

The passage shows that disjunctive speech is often broken by negative statements which have the effect of linguistically erasing not only what has been said, but also the progression in thought and time that speech implies. Thus Chekhov dramatizes the flux between statement and counterstatement and the stasis achieved by nonprogressional verbal action.

Although indicative of stress and discarded thought, negation also implies an imposition of silence on a subject that the speaker refuses to participate in and continue. An excellent illustration of this technique can be found in the beginning of act 4 of *The Three Sisters* when Tchebutykin is approached by Irina, Kuligin, Andrey, and Masha for information about the impending duel between Tusenbach and Solyony. To each who wants to continue the topic the doctor offers a variation of this negative statement: "What happened? Nothing. Nothing much *(reads the paper).* It doesn't matter!" (172-75). The newspaper provides escape for the doctor, but it is negation that short-circuits conversation.

In addition to the use of negatives to evoke the impression of stasis, Chekhov expands and sophisticates the technique of repetition, which had been used extensively, and obviously, by Maeterlinck to intensify mood and to reinforce fixity. Chekhovian repetitions, while admittedly tedious, do not intensify mood; rather, they elicit and continually perpetuate a condition such as entrapment, monotony, frustration, loneliness, despair. In these plays of "come and go" (structured around intricate arrival/departure paradigms), motifs, phrases, and pauses repetitively come and go. Significantly, repetition, like other aspects of Chekhovian drama, works simultaneously on the realistic and psychological levels and, more importantly, is cumulatively effective. The speaker who reiterates a particular emotion or illusion reveals a compulsive pattern of behavior from which he is unwilling or unable to extricate himself. Thus Kuligin is "content, content, content," or at least he will steadfastly hold to that illusion, while Masha is "bored, bored, bored" with Kuligin. Olga and Irina are typified by their chant "to Moscow," its continued repetition gaining the impact of prayer. With each repetition, however, the disparity between the first expression and those which succeed it, as well as the emotional, spiritual, and linguistic deterioration of the speaker, is progressively laid bare.

Vladimir Ivanovich Nemirovich-Danchenko, co-founder of the Moscow Art Theater.

The words repeated, moreover, are of less importance than the mental baggage which the reiteration conveys. This is illustrated by the central role that memory plays in the dramas. In memory images are neither recorded nor recalled in strict chronological or spatial order, but rather according to emotional impact and stimulus. Chekhov dramatizes the ability of broken shards of reverie to break through consciousness and find verbal form. A characteristic citation from *The Three Sisters* illustrates the cumulative effect of fragments intermittently reiterated: Masha, who continually recalls phrases from Pushkin's *Ruslan and Lyudmila,* tries to calm herself after Vershinin's departure by reciting the lines. The confusion of her words, however, reflects emotional chaos, signifying to her that she is not in control of her life. "What does 'strand' mean? Why do these words haunt me?" she mourns, seemingly aware for the first time of her entrapment (183). That the words lack meaning does not mean she will be freed from the grip they have on her mind.

Repetitions, however, need not be compulsive. "Echoing," a nuanced, associational variation of the technique of repetition, is particularly effective in these plays of come and go in which reunion and separation of the family are experienced differently by each member. In echoing, the same words are subject to multiple interpretations comparable to the refraction of light by a prism or to a symphonic theme and variation. In the farewell scene of *Uncle Vanya,* for example, Sonya, Marya, Marina, Astrov, and Vanya take note of the departure of Yelena and Serebryakov. The phrase "They've gone" is repeated in turn by each, but the unspoken emotions of loss, relief, and anticipated loneliness inform their mood more accurately than the words they all share. Similarly, the technique is masterfully employed in *The Cherry Orchard,* where, in the opinion of Francis Fergusson, each of the characters, in his own way, gains insight into his or her situation and that of the doomed estate.[24] Essentially, Fergusson maintains by offering a multiplicity of nonverbal responses simultaneously with common expression, Chekhov evokes a condition or an emotion which precedes the emotionally charged attitude of the characters. Undoubtedly, the associational effect of this technique derives in good part from undefined, infinite silence.

The principal recurring motif in Chekhovian theatre is the pause. Static and nonprogressional, and comparable to the rest in musical composition, the pause is an essential and integral element of structure which effectively stalls the advancement of thought, action, and time. Moreover, nonverbal hesitation is cumulatively effective and responsible in great part for the oppressive sense of timelessness in Chekhov's world. This dramatist's treatment of the unspoken includes the silence of impasse, anticipation, reflection, reverie, doubt, revelation and cover-up, helplessness, isolation, and complicity. Although interesting studies have been written on the quantitative nature of the Chekhovian pause, a simple count of pauses as they appear in stage directions constitutes a superficial examination of this dramatist's extensive use of the unspoken.[25] Also to be considered are his use of silent scenes, such as those of Irina left alone at the end of act 2 of *The Three Sisters* and of Gaev and Mme. Ranevsky at the end of *The Cherry Orchard,* his use of mute characters, his use of silence as a metaphor for entrapment, evanescence, and isolation, and his own silence. These uses will subsequently be examined more fully; now, however, it is necessary to reiterate that nonverbal responses are inextricably linked to verbal techniques in Chekhovian drama, just as expression/suggestion informs all the elements of this dramatist's art. In these eventless plays attention must be focused both on all the events that are not explicitly dramatized and on many responses that are not explicitly communicated.

Crucial to an understanding of Chekhov's reliance on silent response is the centrality of the motifs of love, loneliness, and loss—all emotions, essentially untranslatable, which would be immeasurably reduced in significance, complexity, and verisimilitude if verbally defined and delimited. The following characteristic passage from *Uncle Vanya* illustrates both the coalescence of verbal and nonverbal discursiveness and the gamut of silent responses from revelation to impasse, doubt, anticipation, and reflection. Yelena, who has approached Astrov on Sonya's behalf, finds herself embroiled in a suggestive tête-à-tête with the attractive doctor:

YELENA (*perplexed*): Bird of prey! I don't understand.

ASTROV: A beautiful, fluffy weasel. . . . You must have a victim! Here I have been doing nothing for a whole month. I have dropped everything. I seek you greedily—and you are awfully pleased at it, awfully. . . . Well, I am conquered; you knew that before your examination *(folding his arms and bowing his head)*. I submit. Come and devour me!

YELENA: You are mad!

ASTROV (*laughs through his teeth*): You—diffident . . .

YELENA: Oh, I am not so bad and so mean as you think! I swear I'm not *(tries to go out)*.

ASTROV (*barring the way*): I am going away to-day. I won't come here again, but . . . *(takes her hand and looks round)* where shall we see each other? Tell me quickly, where? Someone may come in; tell me quickly . . . *(Passionately)* How wonderful, how magnificent you are! One kiss. . . . If I could only kiss your fragrant hair . . .

YELENA: I assure you . . .

ASTROV (*preventing her from speaking*): Why assure me? There's no need. No need of unnecessary words. . . .

(221-22)

Notably, Yelena leaves unspoken her attraction to him, as she leaves unspoken her assurances that, happy in her marriage, she has no interest in pursuing their blossoming relationship. Moreover, the pause which breaks the doctor's speech elicits the chaos of emotions breaking in his heart and mind: the relief of revealing his passion, the exhilaration of seduction, the sexual excitement of Yelena's presence, the frustration of her reluctance to agree upon a meeting place.

Yelena's laconism illustrates one of the most important applications of silence in Chekhovian theatre. It is through their muteness that some of Chekhov's characters, like Masha, Andrey, and Varya, maintain the privacy of their thoughts. It must be remembered that speech shares with time the characteristic of irreversibility; thus, we postulate that characters who prefer the silence of isolation do so to separate themselves not only from the judgment and recrimination of others, but also from a confrontation with the truth within themselves. We note, moreover, that when these withdrawn and normally taciturn characters participate in dialogue, the psychic distance between them and their external reality is emphatically underscored, not necessarily by what they say, but rather by the fact that they speak at all. Corrigan maintains that the use of muteness reveals Chekhov's modernity: his

most profound insight is knowing each man is alone and that he seeks to maintain his solitude, though he also knows that for each man solitude is unbearable.[26] Chekhov's characters alternatingly break out of entrapment in self to attempt to relate to others, only to comprehend once more the limitations of their ability to verbalize elusive emotions and the limitations of those who would hear, if they cared to. Thus, typically, Andrey holds his peace while Natasha torments him, questions him, emasculates him, bores him, and lectures him. His response, "I have nothing to say," is counterpointed by the conversation with Ferapont which immediately follows his passive conflict with Natasha (138-39). Significantly, duologue disintegrates into monologue, further emphasizing the solitariness of the individual and the willful or indifferent silent response of the other. Andrey's confession to Ferapont is met with the old man's reply, "I don't hear well" (140). In Chekhovian drama the silence of the mute, broken intermittently, is most often met with the silence of exclusion or incomprehension.

Inarticulateness informs Chekhov's characters and similarly informs the playwright himself. In a frequently quoted letter, Chekhov responds to Suvorin's criticism of his taciturnity, which the latter had equated with indifference and moral irresponsibility:

You scold me for objectivity, calling it indifference to good and evil, lack of ideals and ideas. . . . Of course it would be nice to combine art with sermonizing, but that kind of thing I find extraordinarily difficult and well-nigh impossible because of technical considerations.[27]

Admittedly, Chekhov valued restraint and concision in art, and in fact he often chided fellow artists for their excessive verbalism.[28] Neither lack of space nor other "technical considerations," however, prevented Chekhov's subjective intrusion into his material. It is not the form which precedes the artist, but the artist who devises and controls the medium. Chekhov's style of compression, which eschews subjectivity, can be explained by his perception of the artist's role: distillation, not amplification of the complexity of life. He trusted the reader of his short stories to supply subjective observation; similarly, we can assume that he expected the audience attending the dramas to do likewise. But Suvorin failed to realize that the absence of verbalized commentary did not preclude nonverbal commentary. Unlike his stage characters who talk too much or too little, Chekhov maintains his silence. Employing imprecision delicately and evocatively to convey empirical and psychic experience, this playwright refuses to limit his world by defining himself or his art, because he believes that "the artist . . . must pass judgment *only on what he understands*."[29] Siegfried Melchinger observes that Chekhov lived in a loquacious epoch, and his laconism was thus interpreted as harshness, but it might just as easily have been accurately interpreted as skepticism.[30] The doubt which plagued Chekhov personally and clouded the historical period, shrouds his gray people and gray world. Compassion replaces indifference.

Chekhov's attitudes about the role of the artist and the interrelationship of speech, silence, and temporality can be traced directly to the professional and personal life of the artist, the socio-political milieu of fin de siècle Russia, the author's experimentation and expertise in the short-story form, and the literary heritage of Russian theatre which he inherited.

Chekhov's debt to his training and career in medicine is immense; it provided him with analytical methodology, subject matter, and firsthand exposure to inexplicable and irremediable suffering.[31] Tuberculosis, which debilitated the playwright and finally claimed his life in 1904, increased daily his awareness of and sensitivity to man's vulnerability and ultimate mortality: in his mature plays the alternatingly static and transitory condition dramatized is one of suffering. Typically, Drs. Dorn, Astrov, and Tchebutykin lament their helplessness; Dorn cannot relieve Masha's pain, Astrov has no medication for Vanya, and Tchebutykin, drinking to kill his own pain, can neither help the wounded injured in the fire nor save the life of the Baron. Although Chekhov does not explicitly exploit the shifting political scene and the social depression in his Russia, the reality of the menacing and tedious situation provides the macrocosmic contrast for the unrelieved mental and physical suffering of his characters.

Valency maintains that Chekhov's drama profited most from his short-story writing (his most prolific period immediately antedates *Uncle Vanya*), in which he perfected the techniques of concision, portraiture, and imprecision, from the tradition of Ostrovsky, Tolstoy, and Turgenev and from the theatrical reform in 1882 which Ostrovsky initiated. Ostrovsky's emphasis on the quotidian and Turgenev's on life as a process of self-realization figured importantly in Chekhov's use of epiphanic structure and his portrayal of life as it is.[32]

Chekhov's success in the Russian theatre, however, cannot be directly attributed to his dramatic or linguistic versatility and innovativeness, but rather to the uneasy marriage of the avant-garde playwright with the fledgling Moscow Art Theatre in 1898. Nemirovitch-Dantchenko, noting in Chekhov's plays a release from antiquated stage clichés and a depth of psychological perception, encouraged the merger between Chekhov and Stanislavsky, who was less than enthusiastic about the playwright.[33] Everything we know of this union, from Chekhov's correspondence, the reminiscences of Nemirovitch-Dantchenko, and the prompt-book of Stanislavsky, suggests a difficult but rewarding symbiotic relationship between Chekhov and the M.A.T. In Chekhov the ensemble acting company found a native playwright to whom they could readily respond, and Chekhov found a group of accomplished actors who could sensitively bring to life the nuance, resonance, and complexity of his eventless, quiescent dramas. However, Stanislavsky's definition and dramatization of Chekhov's modern realism differed so sharply from that of the playwright that Chekhov complained that Stanislavsky was ruining his plays. The most obvious and most crucial excess for which Chekhov faulted Stanislavsky was the latter's insistence

upon natural noises to fill the absence of sound created by the pauses. What the artist had intentionally left evocatively undefined, imprecise, and unexpressed, he would too often find filled not with silence, but with sound.[34]

It is *The Three Sisters,* produced by the M.A.T. on 31 January 1901, which we will subject to exegesis to illuminate Chekhov's idiosyncratic use of the unspoken as it evolves and develops within the text. Although this play contains the greatest number of specifically indicated pauses, it is not for this reason that we look at its text but because, as has been argued, Chekhov's subtle and sophisticated treatment of silence entails in it a coalescence of explicit expression and implicit suggestion, an integral interplay of indicated silences and vague intimations. In this four-act drama duologues are linked by the recurring motifs of love and loss, by references to past and future time, and by the central symbol, Moscow. In order to appreciate the intricate texture of what is only superficially formless, we will need to establish the significance of, and the content and fluctuation both within and between, conversational units.

The initial conversation in *The Three Sisters* typifies the contrasting and associational nature of Chekhovian dialogue. Olga's monologue immediately focuses upon the dissimilarity between Irina's name day and their father's funeral one year ago, and in the pause necessitated by the clock's chiming twelve times, Olga moves deeper into the sadness and loneliness of that time. But the thought of loss and the beauty of springtime elicit still another memory of loss: Moscow displaces both father's death and the gloomy mood. With all that the city implies in terms of culture, vitality, and education, Moscow evokes an enthusiastic expression of longing in Olga, but characteristically Chekhov undercuts her words by the technique of choral speaking. Tusenbach, chatting in another room, answers Tchebutykin's comment with "Of course it's nonsense"; and although this statement is not intended to reply to Olga's, it has the effect of rendering ironic comment on it. Reiterating the longing to escape from provincial morass, Olga's words drift off into reverie, and Irina, echoing the dream of return to Moscow, finishes the statement left incomplete by her sister's silence. Similarly her voice drifts off into silent reverie.

Unlike her younger sister, Olga's longings are not limited to the return to Moscow. This twenty-eight-year-old spinster schoolteacher muses, "If I were married and sitting at home all day, it would be better." Pausing to reflect on the contentment, serenity, and inner peace that married life would offer her, Olga adds, "I should be fond of my husband." Once again Tusenbach's response, directed now to Solyony, cuts across Olga's statement and mocks her wistful ruminations (120-21). Intimated but left unspoken is Olga's awareness that at her age and in their financial situation, her opportunities for marriage are indeed meagre.

This initial dialogue has introduced several important, recurring motifs: loss/promise, death/birth, longing/disillusionment, purpose/uselessness, interiority/exteriority, light/darkness, coming/going, escape/entrapment, and joy/ sadness. The unspoken may be presented by silent response, overstatement undercut by negation, understatement, choral speaking, and silent protagonist. Significantly, Masha's refusal to join in the conversation of her two sisters or to respond to Olga's comments signals the lack of unanimity of the three sisters. The dream of Moscow is counterpointed by Masha's disillusionment, their joy by her sadness, their talk of escape by her entrapment in a marriage that yields none of the contentment about which Olga dreams, their faith in promise by her loss of innocence, their emphasis on memory by her forgetfulness. Masha's silent presence implicitly conveys that her sisters' expectations are illusory.

Typically, Chekhov juxtaposes the optimism of Olga and Irina with the cynicism of Tchebutykin, and the next conversational unit employs both fluctuation between one philosophical posture and another and within the mind of a single speaker. Tacitly, the motifs of promise, longing, escape, and purpose are juxtaposed to Tchebutykin's sense of loss, disillusionment, entrapment, and uselessness. One observes, moreover, that his disjunctive speech is continually punctuated by negative statements that have the effect of terminating discussion, rendering ironic comment, and providing figurative, if not literal, escape for the old doctor. The lethargy which typifies this character, however, is displaced by Irina's vitality. Overcome with her beauty and the depth of his love for the girl that might have been his daughter, Tchebutykin addresses Irina, "My white bird . . ." (p. 121). His voice drifts off, the emotions too diffuse to define. Their conversation is broken off by the doctor's departure to retrieve her name day present, and it is only after his exit that we understand that the old man has been impatiently and silently awaiting the arrival of the present. The silence of expectation and the paradigm of coming and going figure importantly in this act, as they inform the structural and linguistic methodology of the play. We await the arrival of Kuligin, Vershinin, and Natasha and the return of Tchebutykin, but while we wait, Masha, a nonparticipant in the conversation and the party mood, decides to go. Feeling the need to offer explanation to her sister Irina, she tries to explain that she is melancholy today, but in her disjunctive speech punctuated by pauses we understand that mourning, unexpressed and uncommunicated to the others, both for her father and for herself, prohibits her participation. Irina discontentedly remarks, "Oh, how tiresome you are . . . ," and Olga tearfully adds, "I understand you, Masha"; but what is clearly implied by the playwright is that neither sister conveys the disappointment she feels nor understands emotions that for Masha are elusive and enigmatic (124).

Masha repeatedly says, "I'll go," but she postpones her departure to make two observations; in stark contrast to her prior laconism, Masha fires a caustic retort to Solyony and renders negative judgment on Protopopov. Chekhov leaves unspoken any further comment on Protopopov, the intruder in this static drama who will menace both the family and the Prozorov homestead though he neither appears nor is heard in the play. This character,

comparable to death in *L'Intruse,* makes his presence and power known through tangible and intangible effects on the other characters. Here, the casual and connotative mention of Protopopov in the conversational unit is particularly effective because it is delivered by Masha, who has so insistently kept her counsel, and because it is prophetic.

Attention returns to Tchebutykin, whose present, a samovar, is a most inappropriate gift for Irina. Each sister echoes reprimand and Tusenbach chimes in, "I warned you," but the doctor does not respond to their criticism. Rather he explains, "I am an old man, alone in the world, a useless old man. . . . There is nothing good in me except for my love for you, and if it were not for you, I should have been dead a long time ago . . ." (124-25). His voice drifts off, the thought left unfinished; confused, he has revealed his deep love for their dead mother, who obviously comes to his mind in an emotional moment eliciting birth and death, love and loss.

The awkwardness of the moment is displaced by the arrival of Vershinin, the new battery commander, known to General Prozorov and a regular visitor to the Prozorov home. He tries to place the women, whom he knew as three little girls, and simultaneously they try to place him in their memory. Once again memory links present and past, and once again the mention of Moscow subtly reiterates the motifs of joy and sadness, coming and going. Significantly, it is Olga and Irina who chat with him while Masha, silent and reflective, searches her mind. "Now I remember," she interrupts, but the picture her memory produces is one of a younger, more attractive man. Chekhov reintroduces the theme of love and loss as we learn that the "love-sick" major has not made a very happy match. The most essential and most elusive loss, that of time, to which Vershinin alludes, becomes the topic of a typical philosophical peroration. Tusenbach engages in conversation with Vershinin; but the conviviality of the moment is disrupted, as is their speech, by the intrusion of Solyony, whose "chook, chook, chook" is rude not only to Tusenbach, but also to Vershinin (128). No further comment is made by Tusenbach or the others gathered, but the silence of the group excludes Solyony, who, like Protopopov, will continue to intrude upon the lives of this family to weave, repetitively and inexorably, a web of disaster.

The only member of the Prozorov family who has not made an appearance is Andrey; his music precedes him. In his absence, his sisters take the opportunity to praise his many talents. Indeed, there is a most awkward silent moment when Irina shows Vershinin the present her brother has made for her birthday; in stark contrast to his usual loquacity, the battery commander is speechless. "Yes . . . it is a thing . . ." is all he can reply (129), his dumb silence conveying how little he thinks of Andrey's handiwork. Rather than speak of craft, the two men speak of education in an exchange that reiterates the theme of promise and foreshadowed loss. The playwright offers no comment on Andrey, but his pessimism with regard to the value of education renders ironic comment on his professed career goals. Andrey's pessimistic attitude elicits Vershinin's famous "future" speech, but what is most pertinent about their conversation is not the political positions each takes, but rather the emotional posture each reveals. Masha, who has been vacillating in her decision to stay or go, simply says, "I'll stay to lunch." Her understatement is startling and suggestive. It is for Irina, young, impressionable, romantic, to sigh and say, "All that really ought to be written down . . ." (130). Her older sister, however, conveys in her silence of communion, if not awe, a deep attraction to Vershinin.

Vershinin continues to speak about possibilities and promise, punctuating with a pause his desire to live again in a house like the Prozorovs' and to live as a bachelor. When at this moment Masha's husband, Kuligin, enters the room and joins in the conversation, for Masha it is an intrusion. The conversation immediately turns to "going," but it is not a departure which Masha welcomes. Whereas earlier in the afternoon she searched for excuses to leave, now with Tusenbach and Tchebutykin she distractedly searches for an excuse to prevent her departure. Anguished, Masha breaks down, "Oh yes, don't go! . . . It's a damnable life, insufferable . . . ," but her incomplete sentence emphasizes the fact that her verbalized despair is only the tip of the iceberg (133).

Masha's outburst is covered by the noise of the crowd entering the dining room for lunch. In the silence, made more apparent by the noise which precedes it, Tusenbach pauses to brace himself for his declaration of love to Irina. Repeatedly he asks, "What are you thinking of?" but her silent response conveys that she does not share his love. She tries to change the direction of his thoughts from love to work, and as her voice drifts off, Natasha, muttering to herself, arrives to intrude upon their privacy. Significantly, the last conversational unit of the act is a reversed replay of this romantic exchange between Irina and Tusenbach. Natasha, who has run from the dining room, embarassed by the teasing of the others, has Andrey in hot pursuit, assuring her of his ardent love and the playful affection of his family. His disjointed speech conveys the excitement and passion that he feels, and unlike Tusenbach Andrey is rewarded by a kiss. Intrusion marks this passionate moment, as the unseeing lovers are observed by Roddey and Fedotik, two officers arriving late for the luncheon. Their silence of amazement passes ironic comment on the passionate lovers, for intimations have been made throughout the act that Natasha would marry Protopopov and that Andrey's affection for the provincial girl is only a ruse to tease his sisters.

The silent, passionate scene which concludes act 1 is strikingly counterpointed by the initial conversational unit of act 2. Chekhov subtly and evocatively links the two acts through a common setting markedly different in mood. Springtime is replaced by a blizzard and sunshine by darkness. The noisy conviviality of the party and the silent affection of the lovers is juxtaposed with the uneasy silence of anticipation and tension which permeates the room, Natasha's calculated and purposeful intrusion

upon Andrey's privacy, and Andrey's insistent laconism. Approaching Andrey's room, Natasha appears distracted. "Reading?" she inquires of her husband. "Never mind, I only just asked . . ."; but obviously she has something more on her mind than the late arrival of her sisters-in-law. Continuing to babble about their son Bobik, the carnival people, and his obesity, Natasha suddenly realizes that Andrey has maintained his silence throughout her speech. Affectionately she asks, "Andryushantchik, why don't you speak?" Tacitly Chekhov conveys, by innuendo and mincing tones, vicious quips, and emasculating comments that explain in good part Andrey's reticent response to his wife, that time passing has affected their relationship. We note that her shy affection has metamorphosed into assertive verbiage; and though he says he has nothing to say, his silence of complicity implies that he has no say. Indeed, carefully picking her moment and feigning absentmindedness, Natasha wonders, "Yes . . . what was it I meant to tell you? . . . Oh, yes; Ferapont has come from the Rural Board, and is asking for you" (138-39). Obviously, Natasha has already said what she "meant" to tell him, that she intends to dispossess his sister Irina and put baby Bobik in her room, but her disjunctive speech not only exposes emotional realism but also reinforces the impression of distance and lack of verbal communication between Andrey and herself.[35]

It is only in the duologue between Andrey and Ferapont that we learn that Ferapont has been kept waiting for hours, because no one told Andrey that he was there. Once again the motif of waiting reappears and informs the characters and their responses. Whereas Natasha had been agitated and anxious, the long wait seems to have little effect on the old servant and for Andrey tediousness characterizes life. "It's dull at home . . . *(a pause),*" he notes, but his few words addressed to the old man are emphasized by his inability to continue speaking. Getting a grip on his emotions, he tells Ferapont that for amusement he reread his university lecture notes. "I laughed. . . . Good heavens!" What he does not say is that he laughed until he cried, that boring reality is blessedly relieved by his nightly dreams. Pathetically, Ferapont replies, "I can't say . . . I don't hear well . . . ," but we surmise that he could not say if he could hear well. Andrey, understanding that he has sought protection from ridicule and condemnation by confessing to a deaf man, is agonizingly aware that, although he is among family and friends, he is "a stranger—a stranger . . . A stranger, and lonely. . . ." Ferapont's "Eh?" is underscored by a pause. Andrey has hesitated to verbalize his thoughts, then hesitated to find the proper word to describe his anguish, then repeated and conveyed his obsession with alienation, and Ferapont's monosyllabic response implies a silence of bafflement. The brief conversational unit advances the motifs of promise and disillusionment, coming and going, light and shadow, memory and forgetfulness. Andrey's parting words, "Goodbye *(reading).* Come to-morrow morning and take some papers here. . . . Go . . . *(a pause),*" significantly fall on deaf ears. Ferapont has already gone, leaving the distracted, disappointed young man alone with his pain (139-41).

After Andrey has again sequestered himself in his room, the audience hears a conversation between Masha and Vershinin obviously begun before their entry into the dining room. The formerly taciturn Masha is now loquacious. Relating her former respect for Kuligin, she continues, "And now it is not the same unfortunately. . . ." In the pause that follows, the absence of speech underscores the depth of her sadness at having to admit to Vershinin, and to herself, that "unfortunately" things are not what they once were. Compassionately and intuitively he replies, "Yes . . . I see . . . ," his voice drifting off to the picture she has wordlessly drawn of her marriage and wordlessly evoked of his (141). The motif of disappointment in love sounded by Masha is echoed by Vershinin, who speaks of his own marital relationship. Styan maintains that although Vershinin claims never to speak of it, he incessantly does and wins Masha by his confession: "Don't be angry with me. . . . Except for you I have no one—no one . . . (a pause)," maintaining, moreover, that this is a ploy to seduce Masha.[36] But there is a pitiful aspect to this character which Styan fails to accept. If it is only to Masha that Vershinin confesses, then his is indeed the reverse of Andrey's confession to Ferapont, for Masha thrives on Vershinin's anguish and loneliness and reaps the benefits of his protestations of love. Laughing softly, Masha pleads, "Please don't do it again . . . (In an undertone) You may say it though; I don't mind . . . (covers her face with her hands), I don't mind. . . ." The pauses reveal that Masha's heart responds while her mind rejects; her contradictions reinforce her vacillation between reason and passion.

This private emotional scene is counterpointed by one with another couple, but they are unrequited lovers. The pause in Irina's speech reflects neither embarrassment nor infatuation, but rather exhaustion. Tusenbach's talk of joy is countered by her sadness and disillusionment with work. She attempts to explain that "It is work without poetry, without meaning . . . ," but weary in mind and spirit her voice drifts off. In the silence she hears the doctor's signal and entreats Tusenbach, "Do knock, dear . . . I can't . . . I am tired" (143). She is too tired to complete the sentence, too tired even to send a signal.

Tchebutykin joins them and quietly sits reading his paper while Masha and Irina lovingly tease him, but a silence settles over the group. In fact, it is so quiet that Irina inquires of normally talkative Vershinin, "Why are you so quiet?" He explains that he is longing for a cup of tea; what he leaves unspoken is that he is longing to be alone with Masha. Surrounded by family, Vershinin seeks to cover his emotions with silence, but this tactic becomes unbearable. Finally he suggests that Tusenbach and he discuss something, anything, while they wait for tea. Agreeably, Tusenbach concurs. "What shall we speak about?" he asks, but Vershinin answers his question with a question: "What?" "Let us dream . . . ," he suggests; and in the pause following the suggestion we are aware that this is what Vershinin has silently been doing while the others spoke. While the men philosophize about happiness, Masha counterpoints the seriousness of the topic with a joyful, private laugh. But her laugh turns to the silence of contemplation and metaphysical yearning when she intrudes upon the conversation to passionately assert, "One must know what one is living for or else it is all nonsense and waste." The pause which punctuates her protestation reveals the depth of her emotion and the need to believe what the words say rather than the truth she knows the silence suggests (143-47).

Fedotik, Natasha, and Anfisa join the group and the long-awaited tea arrives. Anfisa calls Masha to the table and to Vershinin she says, "Come, your honor . . . excuse me sir. I have forgotten your name." Anfisa hesitates, embarrassed by a lapse in memory that is realistically acceptable, but Chekhov pokes fun at Vershinin, who obviously has been a frequent visitor to the Prozoroz house for at least a year and a half. The mood has changed with the intrusion of the others, and Masha, reluctant to share Vershinin with the others, and unwilling to sit at the table with Natasha and Solyony, leaves her emotions unexpressed. Rather, she asks Anfisa to serve Vershinin and her separately; but alas, no sooner than Vershinin has said, "We have no happiness, and never do have, we only long for it," a letter arrives informing him that once again his wife has attempted suicide. Sadness silently intrudes upon joy, entrapment in marriage supplants escape in love affairs. Noting Vershinin's absence, Anfisa expresses her annoyance that she has just served him tea, but Masha is unwilling to verbalize the cause of her anguish. Instead, she viciously snipes at Anfisa and all around her, leaving herself open to their criticism. Typically, Masha's emotions remain undefined, her distress and disappointment at Vershinin's abandonment unexpressed to her family and friends. Once again we note the motifs of coming and going, purpose and usefulness, longing and disillusionment, superficial conviviality and essential loneliness (148-49).

The motif of expectation is revived at the conclusion of this act as we remember that the carnival people have been expected. But Natasha, whispering to Tchebutykin, leaves it to him to convey to the others that they are not welcome. Masha, who does not accept Bobik's poor health as a credible excuse for Natasha's rudeness, searches for words to describe her sister-in-law. The motifs of escape and entrapment, promise and loss, light and darkness inform the conclusion of the act as they did the initial scene. Andrey sneaks away with Tchebutykin to lose himself gambling, while Solyony sneaks in to surprise Irina. When he inquires "Are you alone?" she responds "Yes," but quickly seeks to cut off conversation by an abrupt "Good-bye" (153). He professes his love as if he had not heard her response and speaks as if unaware of Natasha's intrusion into the room. The motif of coming and going characterizes the conclusion of this act, as the arrival of the carnival people, the arrival of Vershinin, Kuligin, Solyony, Roddey and Fedotik is counterbalanced by the departure of these, in addition to the departure of Andrey and Tchebutykin and the departure of Natasha for a sleigh ride with Protopopov. Primarily through counterpoint, disjunctive speech, and echoing Chekhov reinforces linguistically the physical oscillation and emotional fluctuation of his characters. Irina, left alone at the end of act 2, moans repetitively, "Oh, to go to Moscow, to Moscow!" Entombed in the desolate room now deserted by the others, she is walled in by loneliness.

Juxtaposed with the silent, empty scene which concludes Act 2 is the cluttered, crowded bedroom which Irina and Olga share that, in a state of disarray, is the initial scene of act 3.[37] In shifting the physical setting from the dining room to a more personal sanctum deeper within the house, Chekhov registers linguistically the literal and metaphoric disorder and disjunction. We observe that the act is composed of an intricate network of conversational units which overlap and cut across one another and essentially share the motif of confession and lack of comprehension. The initial conversational unit involves Anfisa, who has kept her deteriorating relationship with Natasha a secret. Succumbing to the mental and physical strain of the fire, she begs Olga to intercede on her behalf. Olga's disjunctive speech punctuated by pauses exposes the depth of her anguish at the physical deterioration of her beloved nurse and the linguistic barrage which Natasha fires at her. The motif of purpose and usefulness is reiterated as Natasha orders the "useless" Anfisa, whom Olga has had resting, out of the room. There is pause in which Natasha gathers her strength and arrogance: "Why do you keep that old woman, I can't understand!" Anfisa has just admitted to Olga that she is an old woman, Masha discourteously has called the nurse an old woman, and admittedly her visage reveals that she is an old woman; nonetheless, Natasha's use of the term shocks Olga. "Excuse me," Olga retorts, taking a moment to understand the full meaning of Natasha's intent, "I don't understand either. . . ." Understanding is epiphanic awareness; Olga sees as if for the first time Natasha's baseness and coldness, but her revulsion remains unspoken. Natasha characteristically pauses to change the subject and explain that as mistress of the house she must have order. She fails to explain the correlation between old age and disorder, except to imply that old can be defined as obsolete. Natasha maintains the flow of conversation while Olga, her mind spinning with the catastrophic events of the evening and the implication that she will be head mistress, finds herself unable to continue speaking with Natasha. Catching her breath with a drink of water, her words sticking in her throat, Olga responds to Natasha, "You were so rude to nurse now . . . Excuse me, I can't endure it . . . It makes me faint." She cannot endure callousness, she cannot endure Natasha, but her disgust will remain unspoken and her outburst unfinished. Natasha makes a feeble attempt at apology, and it is Masha's unverbalized disgust expressed through silent observation and then physical withdrawal that counterpoints Olga's complicitous silence. The duologue is concluded with the same note of lack of mutual comprehension on which it began. Olga observes, "This night has made me ten years older," but Natasha responds unhearing, "We must come to an understanding . . . that old witch shall clear out of the house tomorrow!" Obviously the old servant was the initial, superficial subject for this tête-à-tête between Olga and Natasha, but more was conveyed in the evocative, threatening, aggressive, and alternatingly placid moments which

surround and inform the disjunctive speech (pp. 157-59). Natasha's dispossession of Anfisa anticipates and draws fire from the dispossession of Olga from her room, just as the dispossession of Irina in act 2 was prepared and adequately anticipated. Although she hesitates before changing her tone, Natasha intends to press on for full power of the upstairs management.

Natasha's departure and Kuligin's entrance reverse the tone and prepare for the drunken profundity of Tchebutykin. Significantly, the doctor's emotional confession is dismissed as drunken prattle, just as Gaev's perorations are dismissed as the gabble of a senile old man. Kuligin observes that Tchebutykin is a "bit fuddled," and this superficiality is typical of the comprehension of those gathered. The focus is empirical rather than psychological; Tusenbach is presently organizing a musical benefit for the fire victims. Similarly, Vershinin's comment that the brigade is being transferred goes almost unnoticed: what is intimated is characteristic of Chekhov's artistry. Vershinin's comment is not followed by any exclamation, but rather an evocative generalization. Tusenbach remarks wistfully, "The town will be a wilderness." A wilderness indeed. It is only in act 4 that we begin to perceive the consequences of this statement (159-61).

At this moment, as if to underscore the loss, disappointment, and despair all experience at the news of departure, but characteristically do not verbalize, Tchebutykin smashes the china clock. Returning to the same motif that he sounded earlier, the doctor affirms that negation is affirmation, but the others have been listening without hearing. Seeking to strike out at their deafness, he chants, "Natasha has got a little affair on with Protopopov, and you don't see it" (161). Offering Vershinin a date, Tchebutykin departs, having expressed for the first time a truth known by the others for some time though the silence of evasion afforded them comfortable escape from reality.

Reflecting on all that has transpired during the catastrophic blaze, Vershinin reiterates the motifs of promise and loss, joy and sadness, light and darkness, longing and disillusionment. Anxious and distraught over the proposed departure of the brigade, he speaks in order to control and to conceal his emotions. Masha, silent throughout the act, picks up her pillow and joins Vershinin, her silent response to his comments on the future implying support and compassion. Inspired, Vershinin continues, but knowing that his philosophizing is often annoying in its verbosity he apologizes: "I have such a desire to talk about the future. I am in the mood." The pause which follows underscores the depth of his despair, a despair he hopes to talk his way out of. Concluding his reverie, Vershinin notes, "I am in such a strange state of mind to-day. I have a fiendish longing for life . . . (sings)." No one, not even Tusenbach, answers Vershinin's proselytizing. All that remains unspoken in his speech is his fiendish love for Masha (162-63).

Although the others are present, this conversation appears to be understood only by Masha, for whom it is intended.

Masha responds, "Tram-tam-tam!" to which Vershinin echoes, "Tam-tam!" In their special Morse love code, their unanimity is implicitly and nonverbally conveyed.

Solyony enters the room and the mood changes. He upsets Irina and awakens Tusenbach, who sleepily confesses to Irina all that Vershinin left unsaid when conversing with Masha. Unfortunately, his confession of love falls on deaf ears. It is Masha now who has something on her mind, and she encourages not only Tusenbach, but also her own husband, Kuligin, to go. Finally alone with her sisters, she blurts out her frustration at the injustice and waste of her brother's reckless gambling. She is obviously revolted by more than the loss of the family estate; her sense of injustice is related to the loss of her lover and her ultimate entrapment in the provinces with Kuligin. Masha's resentment is counter-pointed by Irina's confused, disjunctive speech reflecting a literal and emotional world in disorder. Even her illusion of Moscow seems to slip away as she sobs, "Life is slipping away and will never come back, we shall never, never go to Moscow . . . I see that we shan't go. . . ." Irina had dreamed of meeting her Prince Charming in Moscow; now her repetitions of the word *nonsense* and her incomplete phrases suggest that she wishes that it were not "nonsense." But the repetitive use of negations reinforces the circularity of the thinking as well as the nonprogression of time. Natasha crosses through the room during this emotional scene, and Masha, silent during her sister's confession, interrupts to note that Natasha "walks about as though it were she had set fire to the town" (165-66). Natasha's culpability for the destruction of the Prozorov home, however, goes unverbalized; it is only Natasha's adultery which pricks Masha's mind at this moment and inspires her to confess her sin of adultery to her sisters.

Masha encounters isolating and censuring silence, just as Tchebutykin, Andrey, and Irina have learned that one is essentially alone. A shocked Olga hides behind a screen refusing to hear, while Irina, who just confessed her despair and disillusionment, meets Masha's confession with the silent response of tacit approval. Her long-suppressed confession spent, Masha vows "silence . . . silence . . ." (166-67).

But if the night of raging fire is nearly over, the torrent of confessions is not. Andrey, who clearly had had and wasted potential, promise, and purposefulness, breaks his self-imposed silence about his wanton gambling and its concomitant threat to his sisters, his abdication of responsibility as the head of the family, and his cuckoldry. Initially, Andrey employs language defensively, but then his linguistic control is broken disjunctively by pauses. The sisters, exhausted by the long evening of calamities and confessions, refuse to listen to him. Powerless to respond in anger or to offer compassion, the sisters convey by their silence their annoyance with, and censorious exclusion of, their brother. Indeed, Andrey admits more to himself than to them that in marrying Natasha he had thought they would be happy, and we recall Andrey's passionate confession of love to Natasha which concluded act 1 and stands in direct contrast with this broken, disjunctive speech. Gone is the promise of love, the joy of marriage, the longing for future. Andrey negates all the positive qualities of Natasha which he has previously enumerated, and the negations serve to establish an erasure of words in time, as he tries to erase their memory in his mind. Weeping, Andrey begs for the understanding and the forgiveness of his sisters, "Dear sisters, darling sisters, you must not believe what I say, you mustn't believe it . . . *(goes out)*." Because Chekhov has chosen a tumultuous night in which the family is thrown together in need and in trial to help themselves and others, their confessions, otherwise awkward and melodramatic, do not seem unnatural. However, repetitive confessions have a cumulative effect, so that the final prayer which Irina utters, "There's nothing in the world better than Moscow! Let us go, Olya! Let us go!" seems no more credible than Andrey's confession or Masha's assertion that she will maintain silence. Chekhov's characters can maintain neither silence nor speech; they inform by an integral interplay of both (168-69).

Act 3, characterized by its disorder, dispossessions, and dispersion, by its staccato confessions, its clanging fire bells and hysterical outbursts, by its claustrophobic entrapment in Olga's bedroom, is juxtaposed in Act 4 to the quiescent stillness of the autumnal garden, evoking an atmosphere of departure and death. Act 1, marked by the arrival of the soldiers, is complemented in act 4 by dispersion; the intricate paradigm of arrival/departure is reflected once again through echoing and choral speaking. Chekhov, a master of farewells, conveys unsuccessful attempts to communicate loss and forgetfulness and the sadness of departure by filtering the departure through several lenses. Just as in the conclusion of *Uncle Vanya* when Marya, Astrov, Vanya, Sonia, and Marina acknowledged the departure of Serebryakov and Yelena, similarly, Irina and Tchebutykin take note of the departure of Fedotik and Roddey. The mood is restive. Andrey quietly wheels the baby carriage while Irina confesses her uneasiness about Tusenbach to Tchebutykin. Moreover, Masha, anxious about the arrival and imminent departure of Vershinin, also seeks out the companionship of the old doctor. Whereas her baby sister, loquacious as always, chats with Tchebutykin about her anxiety, Masha, as in act 1, is taciturn, maintaining her withdrawal from conversation and obviously distracted by her thoughts. Sitting close to the doctor she hesitates and then decides against revealing her pain. Could words possibly define or delimit it? Instead of speaking of her agony, Masha changes the direction of her thoughts and asks the old doctor a question which has probably been in the recesses of her mind for years that is dredged to the surface by present events. "Did you love my mother?" she inquires. The response is immediate: "Very much." But to her next question: "And did she love you?" Tchebutykin's silent response communicates his unwillingness or inability to reveal that confidence. His refusal to give an immediate, affirmative reply suggests that the love was unrequited, but essentially Tchebutykin maintains the enigma by leaving the past love undefined. Trying to conceal her personal loss through language, Masha attempts to speak about Andrey, but her voice breaks off.

Louise Purnell as Irina, Jeanne Watts as Olga, and Joan Plowright as Masha, in Laurence Olivier's 1970 film adaptation of Three Sisters.

She can neither be quiet nor concentrate on one subject. The wait is agonizing. Reiterating the motif of departure, Masha takes note of the birds escaping. Distraught about the duel, Masha links her personal loss to that of the Baron and by implication, although unstated, to her sister Irina, so happily expecting to depart tomorrow to marry Tusenbach and begin a new life. Characteristically, Tchebutykin responds, "It doesn't matter," but he pauses, as if to imply that Masha is not to believe him. Postponing his departure for the duel, Tchebutykin appears to contribute to the eventless atmosphere in act 4 which is building into an intolerably static and emotionally suffocating one.

After much intimation, Tusenbach arrives to speak to Irina, but they succeed in talking about nothing. His parting speech to her is poignant and emotional, broken by pauses in which he seeks to cover up the truth of the duel and reveal the truth of his love. On the subject of the duel he is silent; on the subject of her love for him she is silent. Both silences, however, stunningly underscore the lack of confirmation. Styan views the Baron's silence as a "gesture of helplessness," but I would add that his chosen silence is not one of dumb apathy.[38] It is

a fertile silence of awareness and acceptance. Indeed, so sensitive and perceptive does Tusenbach appear that Irina wants to accompany him, but in alarm he goes off, only to turn around and call "Irina" for the last time. She asks, "What is it?" but, covering up the fact that he has no one thing to say, he asks, in a magnificent Chekhovian touch, to have coffee made for him. Irina's silent response to his request and departure is crucial; Chekhov's directions are explicit: "Irina stands lost in thought," then silently sits in a swing, presumably to await his return (177-79).

Time has been of constant concern throughout this play: the specific time for departures, the time of the duel, the undefined passing of time indicated by Olga's new position as head mistress, and Natasha's new offspring, Sophie. Set against the coming and going in the garden, Andrey, normally taciturn with the others, converses with Ferapont, who has in the last four years lost even more of his hearing faculties than was obvious in his last tête-à-tête with Andrey. The motifs of longing and escape, purpose and uselessness are reiterated, but Ferapont is unable to respond to Andrey. Finally the long-awaited Vershinin has arrived, but from the moment of his arrival we are made aware that time has been spent elsewhere. There are only a few brief moments for farewell. Using the stock phrase, "Forgive me if anything was amiss," Vershinin gives this commonplace a deeper resonance of implicit acknowledgment of self-deception by the pause which follows it.[39] Olga, despite her refusal to face the fact of her sister's love affair with Vershinin, is deeply saddened and speechless at his departure. We note in her silence the agony of separation that she feels personally and feels vicariously for Masha. Awkwardly waiting now for Masha's arrival from the recesses of the garden where she has been secluded anticipating her lover's arrival, Vershinin asks, "What am I to theorize about? . . . *(Laughs)*." Without his philosophy, Vershinin is lost; it is his defense against vulnerability, despair, and the creeping ravages of time. Continually consulting his watch, he is anxious about time passing: the time which seemed to drag so long in anticipation is now contracted, compressed, and fleeting in departure. Masha sobs violently and Vershinin's characteristic articulateness disintegrates into disjunctive phrases broken by silences: "I . . . must go . . . I am late. . . ." The wrenching of separation is conveyed by their emotional, primarily nonverbal responses (181-82).

Vershinin's departure dovetails with the arrival of Kuligin; obviously Masha's husband had discreetly waited for the departure of her lover. Intending to console her and claim her as his wife, Kuligin is nonetheless embarrassed by Masha's breakdown, which anticipates and foreshadows that of Irina. In the excitement of Vershinin's departure, Irina, awaiting the arrival of her lover, is forgotten by the others who try to calm the distracted Masha muttering disjointed words from the refrain which has haunted her for years. Fluctuating between hysteria and emotional control, Masha struggles to resume or restore her former life. Irina comes to console Masha and to silently share a farewell embrace; ironically, within moments it will fall to Masha, the more experienced in love and loss, to embrace and console her bereaved sister. Similarly, it falls to Tchebutykin, the doctor, oldest friend, and pseudo-father, to convey the truth of Tusenbach's death. Reiterating his characteristic "it doesn't matter," the exhausted Tchebutykin sings, "Tarara-boom-dee-ay," while the three sisters huddle together. Essentially separate individuals, their words and silences echo the different way in which each perceives loss in love and in life, as well as the devices, linguistic and other, by which they attempt to shield themselves from the agony of separation and the absurdity of existence.

Gone is the promise of vitality and love and contentment, gone the dream of Moscow, gone the possibility of escape. Characteristically, Chekhov neither defines nor delimits their words and their silences. Maintaining the ambivalence of mood by which he has realistically and emotionally shown the psychic lives of these characters, Chekhov underscores the contrast between the words of the three sisters and their stillness, their earnestness, with Tchebutykin's careless singing. Styan accurately suggests that "to define our final sensations by the final words of the three sisters, simply because they speak, is

to treat fictions as truths, characters as mouthpieces, and to disregard the contribution of the whole series of impressions."[40]

Chekhov symphonically concludes his masterpiece of mutability and perpetuity by linguistically reinforcing flux and fixity. Olga bravely and confidently declares, "We shall know what we are living for, why we are suffering," but her pause more honestly conveys the prevailing doubt and hesitation. The fervently hopeful words of the three sisters, like their embrace, are undercut by the silent response of resignation, anticipated loneliness, and retreat into illusion. Indeed, once again escape into the future obliterates present pain. The conclusion of this static drama is only apparently quiescent, belying cyclical, psychological, and social flux. By the masterful use of the specific and obvious in concert with the imprecise and tacit we learn that Natasha and Protopopov are securely entrenched within the Prozorov home and the three sisters will disperse, just like the brigade which has so recently departed. Thus this drama of coming and going ends by reflecting on the transitory nature of beauty, of life, and of love, ending as it began, by reflecting on the quotidian and the enigmatic.

The concluding scene of *The Three Sisters* beautifully illustrates the typifying characteristics of Chekhov's mature drama: resonance of impression, synthesis of expression and suggestion, silence of the playwright. Focusing on the motifs of love, loneliness, and loss, all emotions essentially untranslated, Chekhov delicately and implicitly conveys ontological solitude through suggestion and evocative pauses.

In dramatizing immediacy and unintelligibility through a language of silence, Chekhov has not only achieved verisimilitude in his own drama, but also prepared the way for subsequent linguistic innovation in modern theatre. Our attention first turns to the Theatre of Silence which emerged on the dramatic horizon after World War I, descendent of Maeterlinck and Chekhov and child of global hostility.

NOTES

[1] Robert W. Corrigan, "The Plays of Chekhov," in *The Theatre in Search of a Fix* (New York: Dell, 1973), 131.
[2] A. Skaftymov, "Principles of Structure in Chekhov's Plays," trans. George McCracken Young, in *Chekhov: A Collection of Critical Essays,* ed. Robert Louis Jackson, Twentieth Century Views (Englewood Cliffs, N.J.: Prentice-Hall, 1967), 69-87. This valuable essay poses and attempts to answer the question of unity of form and content in Chekhov's plays.
[3] See Maurice Valency, *The Breaking String* (New York: Oxford University Press, 1966), for an excellent study of Chekhov's predecessors in the Russian theatre, influences on his oeuvre, the role of the short story, and his career as a playwright.
[4] On the issue of Chekhov's social criticism, see Maxim Gorky, "Fragmentary Reminiscences," in *Anton Tchekhov: Literary and Theatrical Reminiscences,* trans. and ed. S. S. Koteliansky (1927; reprint, London: Benjamin Blom, 1965), 98-101. Gorky maintains that no one before Chekhov depicted bourgeois existence with such merciless truth. See also Robert Brustein, *The Theatre of Revolt: An Approach to Modern Drama* (Boston: Little, Brown, 1962), chap. 4, "Anton Chekhov," 135-79, for a discussion of Chekhov's rebellion against the quality of Russian life.
[5] Quoted in David Magarshack, *Chekhov the Dramatist* (New York: Hill and Wang, 1960), 84.

[6] John Lahr, "Pinter and Chekhov: The Bond of Naturalism," *Drama Review* 13, no. 2 (Winter 1968): 137-45; rpt. in *Pinter: A Collection of Critical Essays,* ed. Arthur Ganz, 60-71, Twentieth Century Views (Englewood Cliffs, N.J.: Prentice-Hall, 1968), hereafter cited as *PCCE.*
[7] Brustein, *Theatre of Revolt,* 137.
[8] Chekhov to Grigori Rossolimo, *The Selected Letters of Anton Chekhov,* ed. Lillian Hellman, trans. Sidonie Lederer (New York: Farrar, Straus, 1955), 252-53.
[9] Bernard Beckerman, "Artifice of 'Reality' in Chekhov and Pinter," *Modern Drama* 21, no. 2 (June 1978): 153-61.
[10] See Magarshack, *Chekhov the Dramatist,* for a distinction between plays of a "direct" and "indirect" action; see also Francis Fergusson, *The Idea of a Theatre* (Princeton, N.J.: Princeton University Press, 1949), 163-72, for a study of the scene as a dramatic form.
[11] Regarding Maeterlinck's contribution to Chekhov's evocative, eventless drama, see Valency, *The Breaking String;* F. L. Lucas, *The Drama of Chekhov, Synge, Yeats and Pirandello* (London: Cassell, 1963).
[12] Chekhov's muted images, gray landscape, tonal resonance, and the evocative mood of memory and melancholy are reminiscent of Verlaine's symbolist poetry.
[13] See Brustein, *Theatre of Revolt,* for an interesting discussion of those forces of darkness (such as mediocrity, vulgarity, and illiteracy) which "intrude" into the Chekhovian world and displace accomplishment, humanity and education (148-50).
[14] Beverly Kahn, *Chekhov: A Study of the Major Stories and Plays,* Major European Authors (Cambridge: Cambridge University Press, 1977), 312.
[15] Corrigan, *Theatre in Search of a Fix,* 131-33.
[16] Brustein, *Theatre of Revolt,* 153.
[17] William Alexander Gerhardi, *Anton Chekov: A Critical Study,* rev. ed. (1923; reprint, London: MacDonald, 1974), 28.
[18] Chekhov to Alexei Suvorin, *Selected Letters,* 189.
[19] Beckerman, "Artifice of 'Reality,'" 155.
[20] Brustein, *Theatre of Revolt,* 155.
[21] Kahn, *Chekhov,* 10.
[22] In a letter to Maxim Gorky, 3 January 1899, Chekhov defines grace: "when a person expends the least possible quantity of movement on a certain art" (*Selected Letters,* 239).
[23] Corrigan, *Theatre in Search of a Fix,* 133.
[24] Fergusson, *Idea of a Theatre,* 172-73.
[25] For further consideration of the quantitative nature of the pause, see James Kolb, "Language, Sounds and Silence" (Ph.D. diss., New York University, 1974), especially chap. 2. Regarding the multivalent use of the unspoken in Chekhovian drama, consult Siegfried Melchinger, *Anton Chekhov,* trans. Edith Tarcov, World Dramatic Series (New York: Frederick Ungar, 1972). For perceptive commentary on the interplay of structure, setting, symbol, and language, see J. L. Styan, *Chekhov in Performance: A Commentary on the Major Plays* (Cambridge: Cambridge University Press, 1971).
[26] Corrigan, *Theatre in Search of a Fix,* 133-34.
[27] Chekhov to Suvorin, 1 April 1890 (*Selected Letters,* 98).
[28] Chekhov to Gorky, 3 January 1899 (ibid., 230). Regarding Chekhov's insistence on laconism, see Ivan A. Bunin, "A. P. Tchekhov," in *Anton Tchekhov: Literary and Theatrical Reminiscences,* trans. and ed. S. S. Koteliansky, wherein the poet quotes Chekhov, "It is very difficult to describe the sea. Do you know the description a schoolboy gave in an exercise? 'The sea is vast.' Only that. Wonderful, I think" (87).
[29] Chekhov to Suvorin, 1888 (quoted in Brustein, *Theatre of Revolt,* 147).
[30] Melchinger, *Anton Chekhov,* 4.
[31] Ronald Hingley, *Chekhov: A Biographical and Critical Study,* rev. ed. (1950, London: George Allen and Unwin, 1966), 49.
[32] See Valency, *The Breaking String,* 32-47.
[33] Vladimir Nemirovitch-Dantchenko, "Tchekhov and the Moscow Art Theatre," in *Anton Tchekhov: Literary and Theatrical Reminiscences,* trans. and ed. S. S. Koteliansky (1927; reprint, London: Benjamin Blom, 1965), 135-38.
[34] Vladimir Nemirovitch-Dantchenko, *My Life in the Russian Theatre,* trans. John Cournos (Boston: Little, Brown, 1936), 162-63. See also Brustein, *Theatre of Revolt,* 154, for an interesting footnote in which the critic observes, "It is a pity that so many modern realists have followed Stanislavsky's approach to reality and not Chekhov's."
[35] Regarding the brilliance of revelation by innuendo, see Styan, *Chekhov in Performance,* 182-83.
[36] Ibid., 186.
[37] See Kahn, *Chekhov,* 303-4, for an interesting discussion of the interrelationship of compressed space and the interminable night. See also Brustein, *Theatre of Revolt,* 158-59, for a discussion of this scene as a prelude to dispossession.
[38] Styan, *Chekhov in Performance,* 214-15.
[39] Ibid., 225.
[40] Ibid., 236.

Pyotr Palievsky (essay date 1985)

SOURCE: "Chekhov's Realism," in *Soviet Literature,* No. 1 (442), 1985, pp. 154-60.

[*In the following essay Palievsky discusses Chekhov's positive depiction of the common people, maintaining that the writer "formed an invisible link between a high ideal and the perceptions, requirements, tastes and foibles of the ordinary man."*]

Chekhov, viewed in historical perspective, gives the ideal of Russian literature a new impetus or, perhaps, considering the distinctive features of his work, one should say that he gives it new substance. In him, literature regains its primary solidity, restores and develops its sovereign mode of thought and image of life, and its objectivity is strengthened. Life (in all its fullness and through artistic imagery) comes into its own, asserting its primacy over dreams, negations, fantasies, impulses of the moment and projects no matter how wonderful they may be. Much more wonderful than all this is Chekhov's infinite truth of reality.

However, Chekhov, like other Russian classics, is inconceivable and puzzling outside the common ideal of Russian literature. Not to be aware of this in Chekhov is like failing to see the light that snatches Nikolai Gogol's exaggerated, grotesque characters out of unfathomable darkness or the underlying positive thrust of all the ideas that crowd Fyodor Dostoevsky's works.

And yet Chekhov's realist writing uncannily predisposes us for just that kind of self-deception. It is the price he has to pay for his objectivity at the first encounter with the reader. The reader's sense of being completely understood by the author creates an illusion that the writer is entirely on his, the reader's, side and sees the harsh world through his eyes. The author's sympathy is there all right, but it is only gradually that the reader becomes aware of a stern eye which is comparing man as he should and certainly could be with what he is.

Dostoevsky used to say that beauty would save the world, and he agonised in his search for beauty, not stopping at melodrama or stylised "lives of saints" in pursuit of the elusive beauty. These great outbursts of fantasy prompted by a distant ideal were accompanied by frustrations and failures. Chekhov, not retreating from life, discovered beauty in the most humdrum reality. He offered it for everyone to see, beauty that is unaware of itself but is perfectly real. All of a sudden, we become aware of beauty growing out of every chink and curbstone, no matter how crippled its form.

Tolstoy's perception of Chekhov's **"Darling"** as a "positive" character is highly revealing. To be sure, she was never "positive" in the sense of being a model to emulate; but there was indeed something irresistibly sympathetic about her, something profoundly genuine that had been superficially distorted by circumstances, lack of self-awareness, thoughtlessness, carelessness, etc. Tolstoy divined specific gift of Chekhov with amazing sharpness. Chekhov invests hundreds of similar characters, almost all the characters that come within his purview, with some "positive" and "beautiful" quality. This is true not only of his favourite type of an average member of the intelligentsia—doctor, officer, student, teacher, etc.—but also, in a rather odd way, in the most contrived and quaintest of his characters.

It is another question that these people prove to be unworthy of themselves, so to say. They often failed life's tests, compromised, succumbed to circumstance, squandered their fortunes. But there was an element of beauty in every *ordinary* person (a crucial word for Chekhov), or rather, Chekhov revealed it for us. He made the ideal and the beautiful shine within them, and around them in ordinary life.

Chekhov advanced farther than other Russian classics in his formulation of "a fine man". He managed to discern the latent potential in the infinite variety of ordinary "souls", and he found a remarkable form for persuading us of this ideal, combining in a mysterious way the sternest of attitudes with great sympathy. The inspiring example of his own personality that shines through his every line and the unassuming but salutary beauty contained in each of his characters prove the reality of "the fine man" given a person's conscious will to become such.

The late J. B. Priestley wrote: "Other writers may have been as acutely observant as he was, others may have known his wealth of social experience, others again may have shared his broad compassion, his tenderness with all genuine suffering; but where else is all this combined with so exquisite a sense, amounting to genius, of what must be said and what can be left out, of a setting, an atmosphere, a situation, a character, all presented in the fewest possible strokes? We have then at one end of this man's personality the approach and methods of science and at the other end the most delicate antennae in Russian literature. He is lancing (for nothing) peasants' boils in the morning, planning a garden, a school, a library, in the afternoon, and writing a little masterpiece at night. And all done without dogmatism and theorising and bitterly-held ideology; all done with delicacy and gentle humour and compassion. So I say again that here was the model for a new kind of man, but the mould was broken before our blind mad century was five years old. There has only been one Anton Chekhov."

One can agree with everything said above except one thing: that the mould was broken. What we are dealing with is a historical task and not a fashion for Chekhov pince-nez, like, say, a fashion for the Hemingway sweater and pipe. And it is a task that takes time to carry out. No one can say exactly how much time has been allotted. Gogol thought it would take two hundred years. But

perhaps his romantic enthusiasm made him shorten the time? Chekhov's characters kept saying—almost a century after Gogol—that "life will be unimaginably beautiful in two hundred or three hundred years". The important thing is that the Chekhov phenomenon and his artistic world marked a dramatic step forward, towards the implementing of that task and convinced people that it was indeed possible. Moreover, Chekhov demonstrated that the accomplishment of the task and the time in which it can be coped with, depend on our awareness of its realistic nature, on our active and responsible attitude, in short, on ourselves: there can be no such thing as a definite, say, "two-hundred-year-long" period set beforehand.

Chekhov's recipe for the ideal man was self-perfection. He came to grips with that task earlier on in life than Tolstoy (as a schoolboy, some attest) and he proved by his life that a) such an attitude was absolutely necessary in a changing society, b) that it was a hard and often daunting task, and c) that notwithstanding all this, it was a feasible task.

The programme was all-embracing, and, most important of all, he fulfilled it. Bit by bit, Chekhov purged literature of lies: highfaluting, exalted, ingratiating, stilted, didactic, rhetorical, romantic, decadent, liberal, conservative, etc. (their name is legion). And he purified and cleaned the image to full transparency which some people in his time, and even today confuse with blandness and colourlessness ("he has no ideas"). Meanwhile he had all the ideas but they were blended together just as all colours are contained in invisible "white": the fullness and integrity of truth and the historical road of that truth. In this sense he was perhaps the only artist of his time who achieved a perfect balance, even in comparison with Tolstoy.

Echoes of other major writers found in Chekhov are often interpreted as influences that he gradually overcame. This is true, but it is only part of the truth. Chekhov learned from Turgenev, Leskov and Gogol (see for example, his story **"The Steppe"**) and, most revealingly, from Tolstoy ("The Wager"). Far more important, though, was the fact that these were not just influences but intellectual encounters in which Chekhov probed the main ideas of Russian literature, testing their universality, like Pushkin, and offering new answers of his own. In doing so, he transferred them from "the realm of rarefied conjectures" into ordinary reality and, without rejecting them, corrected them in keeping with this infinite reality; through this process of interaction he pursued one big objective truth, the main goal of his searches. He undoubtedly put to the test "the superfluous man" by shifting him from the realm of "intellectual self-development" to ordinary life (the play, *Ivanov*), Shchedrin's "trifles of life"; some of the visions of Dostoevsky from whom he is traditionally considered to be very remote, as for example the type of Nikolai Stavrogin (in *Ivanov* and also in Dymov, a character in **"The Steppe"**) and Smerdyakov (in Yasha, a character in *The Cherry Orchard*).

Chekhov determined the "historical age" (the literary critic Dmitri Urnov's expression) of the traditional recurring characters of Russian literature, traced their social consequences and in a way brought them to their logical conclusion. This is not to say that he robbed them of their universal human relevance; on the contrary, it became more transparent and evident; but the concrete human substance of these characters was manifested in such a historical form that the inner problems of almost every such type reached a tragic pitch and, as it were, demanded a change in the very mode of existence of the type, even if nothing dramatic seemed to happen on the surface and the "type" himself was unaware of all this.

Chekhov never imposed his views, and he avoided "conclusions", leaving every character with new possibilities to which they were drawn by circumstances and the general drift of the author's thought. But this yardstick was constantly present in the general historical direction of his characters' evolution. We could trace, for example, the evolution of Pushkin's Savelych (*The Captain's Daughter*) into Firs (**The Cherry Orchard**); the idea of loyalty as embodied in the latter character was deprived of all social meaning and foundation, and suddenly all the roles were switched.

Chekhov used the same yardstick to test ideas which were still on their way, the roads of the future.

And here the most interesting instance was Chekhov's attempt to travel the Gorky road—a whole decade before Gorky appeared on the literary scene.

Chekhov is the most consistent artist among the Russian classics. He argues only through his images. Obviously, he considers these to be the most convincing and at the same time non-obligatory arguments, leaving the reader the necessary freedom, which Chekhov himself is known to have valued above all. Such an approach was intended to evoke a response from the reader thereby educating him culturally.

Chekhov's modesty as an integral part of his personality had above all an aesthetic significance. Modesty of nature—an old Shakespearian ideal—found in him the most consistent exponent among the world classics. His originality lay in the strictest adherence to this ideal. And even as he followed that road he revealed and formulated new principles of art.

"People are having dinner, just having dinner, and in the meantime their hapiness is being born or their lives are being broken." Or: "One must write simply: how Pyotr Semyonovich married Maria Ivanovna. That is all." These ideas of Chekhov's mean deliberate dissolving of "conceptual" thought in an image and the most rigid and disciplined control of thought by the reality of the image. The energy of the artist's thought, according to Chekhov, had to be fused, included in a network of relations, important and trivial, characteristic of given circumstances; the possibility of tracing the idea through all the trivia was a measure of its validity. In the world art of

the 20th century, which was beginning in his lifetime, Chekhov went largely against the current, and this was probably a conscious decision in view of the experience of new writers like Ibsen whom he knew well.

It has often been noted that instead of writing a novel which, by all the canons of modern literature, a serious writer should have written (and which he seemed to have meant to write) Chekhov eventually chose drama as the vehicle for the important message he wanted to convey. The subsequent development of world art has shown that this too was a conscious decision of Chekhov's.

Without any doubt, he was aware of the demands of the new reality with its dramatically increased volume of knowledge that necessitated brevity of form, and together with Tolstoy, he set out to meet that challenge. It may be said that he met these new demands earlier than others by compressing his novel into a *povest* (long short story). **"The Steppe,"** for example, is quite clearly a *Bildungsroman,* a novel concerned with a person's formative years, which shows a great variety of roads stretching before Egorushka—something the critics at the time did not notice or did not want to notice. In prose, dramatic breakthroughs in this direction were being made by other people who wrote some unsurpassed masterpieces, for example, Tolstoy in his *"Hadzhi Murad,"* which encompassed a whole epic within a story. But this was not so in stage drama where a new impetus was badly needed.

In drama, there was the biggest untapped potential for the "subtext" method pioneered by Chekhov in which what is left unsaid is often more important than what is said. The form of drama which did not allow the author to make any comment, the very conventionality of that form suited him best in order to introduce his innovations. Here again, as in everything, he did not follow the "synthetic" approach of poaching on other arts, but preferred to tap the inner potential of the genre. Chekhov extended all the elements of dramatic form, including action, in order to accommodate the underlying message. The message was often conveyed through an apparent discrepancy between elements (e.g. between words and actions or actions and content). On the other hand, this discrepancy indicated that all these elements are just external boundaries, outlines of the whole. And the whole, if it was to be expressed, needed something else, something that moved between these boundaries, something contained in the actor, his face, and inflections of his voice, in the translucent *mise-en-scène* reproducing life, the atmosphere.

In other words, his plays could not be acted poorly. Oddly enough, this was another specific trait of Chekhov's plays. He forced the stage director and the actor to be creative, but (and this is very important) not independently of the author, as in the *avant garde* theatre, not through "variant interpretations", but only in collaboration with the author in revealing the whole given in outline.

"You cannot judge a play without seeing it on the stage," said Chekhov.

He was particularly thorough and careful in getting rid of superfluous words, editing the monologues, as in the celebrated case involving **Three Sisters** when he cabled to an actor to replace an explanatory monologue with the words "A wife is a wife."

Whenever monologues appeared they expressed the opinion of the character and not the central idea of the play, although their vividness often led people to believe that it was the author's idea. For example, if a person proclaimed that "in two hundred or three hundred years, life on earth will be unimaginably beautiful" that, according to Chekhov, did not mean that this would really be so in three hundred years, but that the person did not wish to notice the life around him and, under various rhetorical pretexts, turned away from life or disdained it.

The main message was to be conveyed not through the words, but through a dramatic image augmented by various words.

Chekhov's principle, which he doggedly implemented, was that words are nothing but an empty husk without the people who utter them and who invest them with important meanings. Of course, he needed a new theatre to prove that idea, a theatre that could be called an "art" theatre in the true meaning of the word. And such a theatre was created.

Chekhov, for the first time since Pushkin, formed an invisible link between a high ideal and the perceptions, requirements, tastes and foibles of the ordinary man. Chekhov's words, "we all are the people" was no trite remark, but an expression of a well-thought-out historical programme which he pursued in his art and his life, never straying from his chosen path.

Martin Esslin (essay date 1985)

SOURCE: "Chekhov and the Modern Drama," in *A Chekhov Companion,* edited by Toby W. Clyman, Greenwood Press, 1985, pp. 135-45.

[*In the essay below, Esslin assesses the impact of Chekhov's revolutionary dramatic technique on the history of Western theater.*]

Anton Chekhov was one of the major influences in the emergence of a wholly new approach to the subject matter, structure, and technique of dramatic writing at the end of the nineteenth century. It can be argued that he, in fact, occupies a key position at the point of transition between a millennial convention of "traditional" and the emergence of "modern" drama.

What was it that the "modern" drama replaced? What was it that the multifarious types of traditional dramatic fiction, however different they might appear, had fundamentally in common—from Greek tragedy and comedy to the well-made play of the nineteenth century; what

were the characteristics that all these shared that were so decisively displaced by the new elements of the "modern"?

It was not what had so long been regarded as the hallmarks of the truly correct and classical form of drama: the Aristotelian unities of time, place, and action. After all, medieval drama, the Elizabethans, and the Romantics had superseded those by constructing rambling, epic plot-lines. But Greek drama and the French classical tradition, the medieval mystery plays and the Spanish theatre of the "siglo d'oro," Shakespeare and commedia dell'arte, Restoration comedy and the well-made play, do have a number of characteristics in common. Foremost among them is the assumption that the audience must be explicitly and clearly told what the principal characters' state of mind is at any given moment in the play, whether through the monologues of Shakespeare and the Elizabethans that are directly addressed to the audience, or the use of confidants in French classical drama, or, indeed through "asides" uttered in the presence of other characters who, by convention, were assumed to remain unaware of them.

Even more important perhaps was another basic assumption that underlay all language used in drama: that what a character said was not only what he or she meant to say, but that he or she was expressing it as clearly and eloquently as possible. Dramatic speech was deeply influenced by, and obeyed the rules of, the classical tradition of rhetoric as practised and formulated by Demosthenes, Cicero, and Quintilian, and as it was taught in the schools from the time of Socrates to the nineteenth century and beyond (in the United States, in public speaking courses in some colleges and universities to this day).

Similar ideas of a clear, transparent structure (derived from the rhetorical rules of statement of theme, development, and conclusion) also governed the construction of the plot from exposition through complication and reversal to a definite and conclusive ending.

That the theatre should attempt to present a picture of the world as it really is never occurred to the theoreticians or practitioners of pre-modern drama. The theatre was an art—and art was artifice, quite apart from the practical impossibility of creating a true facsimile of human life under the technological conditions of a stage in the open air, or lit by candles, with painted scenery, or no scenery at all. The theatre could only present the essential aspects of the human condition, compressed and idealised, according to a firmly established set of conventions (just as, for example, painting eliminated pubic hair in nudes and showed crowds of people in neatly stylised groupings).

It was the great change in the technology of theatre (with gas and later electrical lighting, hydraulic stage machinery, and so on) which, combined with the rise of the scientific world view, led to the idea that the stage could not only reproduce an accurate image of "real life," but should also become like an instrument of scientific inquiry into human behaviour, a laboratory in which the laws governing the interaction of human beings and social classes could be studied.

Yet Zola who first formulated the theoretical concept of the theatre of Naturalism and Ibsen who was the first to gain gradual acceptance for it—through scandal and the violent partisanship of radicals—found it very difficult to liberate themselves from some of the old conventions. Although Ibsen did away with the soliloquy and the "aside," although he tried to create, in his socially oriented drama, stage environments of the greatest possible realism—rooms with the fourth wall removed—structurally, he tended to adhere to the convention of the well-made play. Ibsen's analytical plots developed toward a climax with the relentless logic and compressed time-scale of French classical drama. Even so, his failure to let his characters explain themselves to the audience mystified even intelligent playgoers. As Clement Scott, in reviewing a performance of *Rosmersholm* in 1891, put it:

> The old theory of playwriting was to make your story or your study as simple as possible. The hitherto accepted plan of a writer for the stage was to leave no possible shadow of doubt concerning his characterisation. But Ibsen loves to mystify. He is as enigmatic as the Sphinx. Those who earnestly desire to do him justice and to understand him keep on saying to themselves, "Granted all these people are egotists, or atheists, or agnostics, or emancipated, or what not, still I can't understand why he does this or she does that."[1]

It was Chekhov who took the decisive step beyond Ibsen. He not only renounced the convention of characters who constantly explain themselves to the audience, but he also discarded the last remnants of the plot structure of the well-made play. As a natural scientist and physician, Chekhov rebelled against the artificiality of the conventional dramatic structure. As early as 1881, when he was embarking on his first full-length play, which he discarded (the untitled manuscript, usually referred to as *Platonov*) after it had been rejected by Ermolova, he formulated his ideas as follows:

> In real life people do not spend every minute in shooting each other, hanging themselves or declaring their love for each other. They don't devote all their time to trying to say witty things. Rather they are engaged in eating, drinking, flirting and talking about trivialities—and that is what should be happening on stage. One ought to write a play in which people come and go, eat, talk about the weather and play cards. Life should be exactly as it is, and people exactly as they are. On stage everything should be just as complicated and just as simple as in life. People eat their meals, and in the meantime their fortune is made or their life ruined.[2]

It took Chekhov some fifteen years before he himself succeeded in bringing this theoretical program to full practical realisation and fruition with *The Seagull.* For it was not easy to work out all the implications of the

endeavour to present real "slices of life" on the stage. It meant, for one, that the action on stage would have to get as near as possible to "real elapsed time," that is, that an hour on stage would have to correspond to an hour of "real life." How could one tell a story with a scope larger than that of one-acts (such as Chekhov's own *The Proposal* and *The Bear*) by adhering to this principle? The solution that emerged was to present a number of significant episodes showing the characters and their situation in detail and in as near to "real time" as possible in widely separated segments extracted from the flow of time (usually four acts)—so that the events of months and years became visible by implication through the way in which the situation in each vignette differed from the previous one. Thus, the relentless forward pressure of the traditional dramatic form was replaced by a method of narration in which it was the *discontinuity* of the images that told the story, by implying what had happened in the gaps between episodes.

Even more decisive, however, was the demand that the characters should not be shown in unnaturally "dramatic" and climactic situations but pursuing the trivial occupations of real life—eating, drinking, making small talk, or just sitting around reading the newspaper. The state of mind of the characters, the emotional tensions between them, the subterranean streams of attraction and repulsion, love and hate, now frequently had to be indicated indirectly, so that the audience would be able to apprehend them by inference. In other words, the playwright had to supply the signs from which the spectators, having been turned into equivalents of Sherlock Holmes, would deduce the meaning of seemingly trivial exchanges, and, indeed, the meaning of silences, words that remained unspoken. This, after all, is what happens in real life: we meet people and from the cut of their clothes, the accents of their speech, the tone of voice with which they address remarks to us about the weather, we have to deduce their character or their intentions toward us. In our small ways each of us has to be a semiotician decoding the signs supplied to us by our fellow human beings and the environment.

Another consequence of this program for a new drama was the abandonment of the central figure—the hero—of the drama. There are no subsidiary characters in real life, no Rosencrantzes and Guildensterns whose presence in the play is merely dictated by the requirements of the plot and who therefore remain uncharacterised. In the traditional drama such characters were emotionally expendable. It was the hero or heroine alone with whom the spectator was meant to identify, from whose point of view he or she was supposed to experience the action, living through, vicariously, the emotions felt by such central characters. The new drama required a far more detached, clinical attitude that would allow the audience to look at all the characters with the same cool objectivity.

Characters viewed objectively, from the outside rather than through identification, tend to appear comic. If we identified ourselves with the man who slips on a banana peel we would feel his pain; if we viewed him from the outside we could laugh at his misfortune. The characters in Chekhov's mature plays, in which he succeeded in putting his program into practice, are thus essentially comic characters, even if what happens to them (frustration in love, loss of an estate, inability to move to Moscow) is sad or even tragic. Thus, Chekhov's program for a new approach to drama implied the emergence of tragicomedy as the dominant genre.

Chekhov's conflict with Stanislavskii about the production of his plays centered around this demand for a cool, sharp objectivity that would preserve the essentially comedic form of the tragic events, while Stanislavskii wanted to milk the tragic elements to produce an elegiac and as Chekhov felt "larmoyant" effect.

The demand for absolute truth, full conformity with the randomness and triviality of "real life," from which Chekhov started out, was clearly inspired by the same positivist, scientific ideas that had led Zola to proclaim the program of Naturalism. But, paradoxically, the resolve to reproduce the casualness and triviality of ordinary life led to a higher rather than a lesser degree of "artificiality." For, if meaning was to emerge from the depiction of people pursuing commonplace activities, if the spectator was to be enabled to deduce significance from the multitude of signifiers offered by decoding what they revealed, every move, every word, every object had to be carefully planned and designed as a bearer of such meaning. In other words, as real randomness would be totally meaningless, it was merely the *appearance* of randomness and triviality that had to be evoked by creating a structure of which every element contributed to the production of meaning. This type of drama thus required a far greater degree of skill in weaving an intricate texture of great complexity which could, nevertheless, add up to the intended effect and meaning.

This also was the reason why Chekhov so strenuously objected to Stanislavskii's overloading his productions with a clutter of details not indicated in the text. The proliferation of off-stage sound effects and other naturalistic detail brought in for the sake of mere "reality" smothered the structure of the signifiers Chekhov had carefully written into his scripts.

The dense texture of signifying detail within each segment of seemingly "real time" and the building of a sense of larger time-spans through a discontinuous four-act structure require a very high degree of control over the expressive means at the disposal of the playwright, a sense of rhythm and orchestration that would unify the seemingly casual and disconnected elements and transform the text into a texture as complex as that of the counterpoint of an orchestral score. Thus, the program that started from a rejection of "the poetic" on stage paradoxically led to a new kind of more complex poetry. Chekhov himself, in his acrimonious discussions with Stanislavskii, repeatedly insisted that the theatre was an art, striving to produce the appearance of reality, but it was never to be confused with reality.

On the other hand, the cold, objective nature of this art makes it impossible for the playwright to take sides or to offer solutions to the problems posed in his or her work:

> You are right to demand that an author take a conscious stock of what he is doing, but you are confusing two concepts: answering the questions and formulating them correctly. Only the latter is required of an author. It is the duty of the court to formulate the questions correctly, but it is up to each member of the jury to answer them according to his own preference.[3]

Chekhov's drama thus rejects all moralising, just as it eschews the neat solutions that were required by the playwrights of traditional drama. With him "open form" entered the theatre.

It took a long time for Chekhov's revolutionary innovations to be recognised, let alone generally accepted outside Russia, where the successful production of his plays by Stanislavskii's and Nemirovich-Danchenko's Moscow Art Theatre (however much Chekhov himself disagreed with them) had established him as a major playwright.

In Russia Gorkii was deeply influenced by Chekhov's technique, although his plays were far more partisan and explicitly political than Chekhov's. But it was only after the discomfiture of the revolutionary avant-garde and the introduction of socialist realism as the leading aesthetic doctrine in the Soviet Union in the 1930s that the Moscow Art Theatre was elevated into the model for Soviet drama, and Chekhov became the official model, at least as far as the superficial and external aspects of his "realistic" technique were concerned. In spirit the stereotype of the contemporary Russian "realistic" play, with its openly propagandistic message, is far removed from Chekhov.

Western Europeans found it difficult at first to understand Chekhov's intentions. Early performances of *Uncle Vania* in Berlin (1904) and Munich (1913), *The Seagull* in Berlin (1907), Glasgow (1909), and Munich (1911) and *The Cherry Orchard* in London (1911) remained without lasting echo. There was one major exception: Bernard Shaw was so deeply impressed that he modeled his own *Heartbreak House* (1919) on *The Cherry Orchard.* He clearly saw the parallel between the death of the Russian upper classes and the inevitable decline of English society.

After World War I, tours by the Moscow Art Theatre to Germany, France, and the United States spread the Russian playwright's fame. In France the Pitoeff family, exiled from Russia, consolidated his reputation, but there too they only gained general acceptance for him after World War II.

It was in England that Chekhov first achieved recognition as a classic and one of the great innovators of drama. A production of *The Cherry Orchard* by J. B. Fagan (with the young John Gielgud as Trofimov) at the Oxford Playhouse in January 1925 was so successful that the play was transferred to London and ran there for several months. Yet the real breakthrough for Chekhov came with a series of productions of his late plays by the Russian emigré director Theodore Komisarjevsky at the small Barnes Theatre in London in 1926. By the end of the 1930s Chekhov had become a recognised classic in the English theatre. Since then Shakespeare, Ibsen, and Chekhov have been regarded as the standard classics of the English repertoire. No British actor or actress can lay claim to major status without having successfully portrayed the principal parts created by these playwrights.

The reasons for Chekhov's spectacular rise to the status of a classic in Britain are complex. The fact that pre-revolutionary Russia and England were both societies in which the upper classes spent a great deal of their time in country houses populated by a large cast of family members and guests may well have something to do with it. In these plays theatre audiences in England recognised their own way of life. Similarly, Chekhov's use of "subtext" has its affinities with the English penchant for "understatement." English audiences may thus have been more skilled than those of other countries in the art of decoding subtle nuances of utterance. The fact remains that actors like Gielgud, Laurence Olivier, Peggy Ashcroft, Ralph Richardson, Michael Redgrave, and Alec Guinness made Chekhov their own and that he has remained one of the most performed standard authors over a period of 50 years.

That an author so favoured by major actors would have an influence on the writing of plays in Britain was inevitable. Among the many direct, if shallow, imitators of the Chekhovian style are playwrights like N. C. Hunter (1908-1971) whose *Waters of the Moon* (1951) scored a big success by providing fat parts for "Chekhovian" actors; Enid Bagnold (1889-1981); or Terence Rattigan (1911-1977) who used Chekhovian techniques in plays like *The Browning Version* (1948) and *Separate Tables* (1954).

In the United States Chekhov's influence spread indirectly through the success of Stanislavskii's approach to the technique of acting, not least through the efforts of Chekhov's nephew Michael Alexandrovich Chekhov (1891-1955) who had emigrated to England in 1927 and moved to America in 1939. Undoubtedly playwrights like Tennessee Williams, Arthur Miller, William Inge, or Clifford Odets absorbed at least some of Chekhov's ideas about the "subtext" and the emotional overtones of seemingly trivial conversation.

Yet to look for the direct influence of Chekhov on individual playwrights is perhaps futile. His real influence, though mainly indirect, goes far deeper and is far more pervasive. For he was one of the major innovators who changed the basic assumptions upon which the drama of our time (and "drama" nowadays includes the dramatic material of the cinema, television and radio) is founded.

Many influences, often of a seemingly contradictory nature, have shaped present approaches to drama. George Buechner (1813-1837), also a physician and natural sci-

entist, but almost certainly unknown to Chekhov as he was only being rediscovered at the turn of the century, in many ways anticipated the technique of discontinuous plot development and the use of a type of dialogue that was both documentary and poetically orchestrated. The Naturalists—Ibsen, Strindberg, Gerhart Hauptmann, Arthur Schnitzler—eliminated the conventions of the soliloquy and aside; Frank Wedekind was a pioneer of dialogue in which people talked past each other, neither listening nor answering their interlocutor's points; the German Expressionists, following the lead of Strindberg in the last phase of his career, shifted the plane of the action from the external world to the inner life of the leading character so that the stage became a projection of his or her fantasies and hallucinations; Bertolt Brecht rebelled against the theatre as a house of illusions, the tight construction of continuous plot-lines and developed his own, discontinuous "epic" technique of storytelling; Antonin Artaud tried to devalue the word as an element of drama; and the "Absurdist" playwrights of the 1950s and 1960s (Samuel Beckett, Jean Genet, Arthur Adamov, Eugene Ionesco) created a non-illusionistic theatre of concrete stage metaphors.

Many of these tendencies seem to be in direct contradiction to Chekhov's program of a theatre that would faithfully reproduce the appearance of real life, its casualness and its seeming triviality. Yet, paradoxically, his example and his practise contributed a great deal to developments that, at first sight, may seem very far removed from his ideas and intentions.

Above all, Chekhov, more than any other innovator of drama, established the concept of an "open" form. By putting the onus of decoding the events on the stage on the spectators, by requiring them to draw their own conclusions as to the meaning as well as the ultimate message of the play, and by avoiding to send them home with a neatly packaged series of events in their minds, Chekhov anticipated Brecht's "Verfremdungseffekt" (which he may well himself have inherited from the Russian formalists' concept of "defamiliarisation," in turn directly related to Chekhov's practise). And at the other end of the spectrum a play like Beckett's *Waiting for Godot* carries Chekhov's technique of characters in apparently idle and trivial chatter to its extreme, creating a dramatic structure without action and completely open-ended. Here the trappings of Realism have fallen away, but the Chekhovian principle remains triumphant.

Chekhov's renunciation of high-flown poetic language and rhetorical explicitness (which went much further than Ibsen's attempts at realistic dialogue) produced another paradoxical consequence: the need to orchestrate the seemingly casual conversations, and the silences and hesitations in the characters' speech produced a new kind of poetry, a lyricism in which the rhythms and pauses coalesced into a new harmony. This created an emphasis on mood, on atmosphere, that was very different from the conscious lyricism of Symbolists like Maurice Maeterlinck or Neo-Romantics like the young Hugo von Hofmannsthal, a texture of often bitter ironies and coun-

Daphne Heard as Anfissa and Laurence Olivier as Chebutikin, in Olivier's 1970 film adaptation of Three Sisters.

terpoints between the overt meaning and the subtext. Chekhov's practise opened the way for a new concept of the "poetic" in the theatre, what Jean Cocteau has called the "poetry of the stage" as against mere "poetry on the stage": the formally prosaic statement that acquires its poetry from the context in which it is pronounced, its position within the rhythmic and semantic structure of a *situation.*

The new type of "lyricism" has become the main source of "the poetic" in contemporary drama, not only in stage plays but also in the cinema, where a host of great directors, from Jean Renoir and Marcel Carné to Antonioni and Robert Altmann have extracted poetry from the trivial dialogue and objects of real life situations.

By reducing the importance of overt action and "plot" Chekhov created a new focus of attention: the situation itself, the conjunction of characters, the subtle use of seemingly incongruous detail (like the map of Africa on the wall of Uncle Vania's study), the sparing use of sound

(like the strumming of a guitar) put the emphasis on the complex audiovisual *image* of the stage and made the stage itself into a poetic metaphor. Chekhov was one of the pioneers in moving the theatre away from putting its main emphasis on action in the simple, literal sense. A great deal is still happening in the seemingly static stage images of Chekhov, behind the apparently trivial dialogue. But it is complex and covert rather than on the surface and direct. Much of contemporary drama derives from this use of ambivalence and irony. Sonia's last words in *Uncle Vania* in a seemingly idyllic situation, with Maria Vassilevna working on her pamphlet, Marina knitting, Telegin softly playing his guitar, and Sonia herself kneeling before Vania, "We shall rest!" seem hopeful and the situation idyllic. Yet, at the same time, Sonia may not really believe what she is saying, and the idyllic situation enshrines, in reality, the horror of endless boredom and futility. Compare this with the last line of *Waiting for Godot*: "Let's go," followed by the stage direction "(They do not move)" to see a much reduced, almost minimalist, version of the same technique.

Chekhov's refusal to depart from the mere objective delineation of people and events in their inherent inner contradictions and ambivalences made him the pioneer of another main characteristic of contemporary drama: the emergence of the *tragicomic* as its prevailing mode. That the "death of tragedy" derives from the loss of moral certainties and metaphysically grounded principles is clear enough. Chekhov was one of the first to see this and to embody its consequences in devising a new genre of drama. As Friedrich Duerrenmatt has argued, modern people are far too deeply enmeshed in society's organisational framework ever to exercise the heroic privilege of assuming full and proud responsibility for their acts, to allow their misfortunes ever to be more than mere mishaps, accidents. Chekhov was the first to cast his drama in this mode of tragicomic ambivalence; the three sisters' inability to get to Moscow, the ruination of their brother's talents, the death of Tuzenbakh—all are prime examples of just such socially determined inevitabilities, such mishaps and accidents. Vania's failure to hit the professor is comic, although the situation is tragic. But even if Vania did shoot the professor it would still not be tragedy, merely a regrettable incident. If Harold Pinter speaks of his plays as being meant to be funny up to that point where they cease to be funny, he was formulating a perception of the tragicomic that directly derives from Chekhov.

There is only a small step from Chekhov's images of a society deprived of purpose and direction to the far more emphatic presentation of a world deprived of its "metaphysical dimension" in the plays of Beckett, Genet, Adamov, or Ionesco. Admittedly, the dramatists of the Absurd have left the solid ground of reality behind and have taken off into dreamlike imagery and hallucinatory metaphor. Yet it can be argued that Chekhov himself, by his very realism, blazed even that trail. In creating so convincing a picture of the randomness and ambivalence of reality, he, more than any other dramatist before him, opened up the question about the nature of reality itself. If every member of the audience has to find his or her own meaning of what he or she sees by decoding a large number of signifiers, each spectator's image of the play will be slightly different from that which his or her neighbour sees, and will thus become one's own private image, not too far removed from being one's own private dream or fantasy. The Theatre of the Absurd merely builds on that foundation by posing, less subtly, more insistently than Chekhov, the question: "What is it that I am seeing happening before my eyes?"

The Brechtian theatre, insisting as it does on the solid material basis of the world, also requires the audience to decode the signifiers of its parables by themselves. It also derives its poetic force from the ironic juxtaposition of ambivalent and contradictory signs to produce an ultimately tragicomic world view. While it is almost certain that Brecht was not consciously or directly influenced by Chekhov, his ideas pervaded the atmosphere of theatrical and literary modernism and, indeed, more complex lines of interconnectedness can be traced. Brecht's "Verfremdungseffekt," as has already been mentioned, owed a great deal to the Russian formalists' concept of *ostranenie*

(defamiliarisation). Moreover, Brecht was a great admirer of Vsevolod Meierkhold, who, before he broke away from Stanislavskii and the Moscow Art Theatre had been the first Treplev in Stanislavskii's **Seagull** and the first Tuzenbakh in the **Three Sisters** (it is said that Chekhov had written the part for him). Meierkhold's modernism thus derives indirectly from, and is an extrapolation into more daring innovation of, the demand for ruthless objectivity and open forms in the theatre. Meierkhold once sent Chekhov a photograph of himself, inscribed: "From the pale-faced Meierkhold to his God."

The greatest and most directly discernible impact of Chekhov's innovation on the modern theatre, however, is undoubtedly to be found in the field of dialogue. The concept of the "subtext" has become so deeply embedded in the fabric of basic assumptions of contemporary playwriting and acting that, literally, there can be hardly a playwright or actor today who does not unquestioningly subscribe to it in his or her practise.

Chekhov's ideas have not only been assimilated, but they have also been further developed by dramatists like Harold Pinter, whose use of pauses, silences, and subterranean currents of meaning clearly derives from Chekhov but goes far beyond him in the exploration of the implied significance of a whole gamut of speech-acts, from the use of trade jargon to that of tautology, repetition, solecisms, and delayed repartee.

Pinter's linguistic experiments, so clearly derived from Chekhov, have engendered a host of followers in Europe and the United States (where perhaps David Mamet is the foremost practitioner of this type of linguistic exploration).

The concept of the "subtext" has also led to attempts to bring onto the stage characters whose linguistic ability is so low that they are unable to express themselves clearly. Here the playwright, through the rudiments of a vocabulary they may still possess, has to show what goes on in their minds and emotions. The English playwright Edward Bond, in a play like *Saved* (1965), made extremely successful use of a technique clearly derived from Chekhov, by making fragments of illiterate speech and silences reveal the characters' thoughts and feelings.

In the German-speaking world the Bavarian playwrights Franz Xaver Kroetz and Martin Sperr, the Austrians Wolfgang Bauer and Peter Turrini, have also become masters of this type of highly laconic dialogue in which silences and half-sentences are used to uncover the mental processes of tongue-tied individuals.

It is only since the end of World War II that Chekhov has been received, by general consensus, into the canon of the world's greatest dramatists that extends from the Greek tragedians to Shakespeare, Lope de Vega, Calderon, Racine, Corneille, Moliere, to the great moderns—Ibsen and Strindberg. Today Chekhov may well be regarded as being even more important and influential than Ibsen and Strindberg.

His output of only four major, mature plays may be much smaller than theirs, but, in the long run, its originality and innovative influence may well prove much greater.

Chekhov's determination to look at the world not merely with the cool objectivity of the scientist but also with the courage to confront the world in all its absurdity and infinite suffering (without flinching or self-pity and with a deep compassion for humanity in its ignorance and helplessness) led him to anticipate, far ahead of all his contemporaries, the mood and climate of our own time. That is the secret of his profound and all-pervading influence on the literature, and, above all, the drama of the century that opened so soon after his early death.

NOTES

[1] *Daily Telegraph,* February 24, 1891, quoted in Michael Egan, ed., *Ibsen: The Critical Heritage* (London and Boston: Routledge and Kegan Paul, 1972), p. 168.
[2] Quoted in Siegfried Melchinger, *Tschechow* (Velber bei Hannover: Friedrich Verlag), p. 68.
[3] Chekhov's letter to Suvorin, October 27, 1888, in *Letters to Anton Chekhov,* trans. Michael H. Heim and Simon Karlinsky (New York: Harper & Row, 1973).

J. L. Styan   (essay date 1985)

SOURCE: "Chekhov's Dramatic Technique," in *A Chekhov Companion,* edited by Toby W. Clyman, Greenwood Press, 1985, pp. 107-22.

[*In the following essay, Styan looks at the characters, settings, plots, and moods of Chekhov's plays.*]

As the years pass and as Chekhov's plays are given different treatments and exposed to new and larger audiences, it grows increasingly clear that Chekhov was the complete playwright. In his awareness of the needs of the stage and its actors it might be said that he was also a complete man of the theatre. He held to a minimum of rules for writing a play, and he ruthlessly abandoned others that had been sanctified by centuries of tradition, but he could only do this because he enjoyed a full sense of the theatre. A sense of the theatre embraces not so much its *mechanics* of acting and staging, plotting, and character-drawing as the way a playwright may exactly manipulate an *audience* for its strongest, yet its subtlest and most rewarding, response. This account of the method by which Chekhov put his major plays together, therefore, will emphasize how he made them work in performance. Only once before in the story of the theatre, in the plays of Shakespeare, do we find such a bold sequence of experiments to secure an audience's maximum participation in the workings of the stage. On these grounds alone it is arguable that not only is Chekhov Russia's greatest dramatist and the consummate realist of the modern theatre, but also that he must rank with the two or three best the theatre has known.

We cannot know the limits of Chekhov's skills of the stage, nor exhaust his secrets. As with Shakespeare, the unknown remains constantly to be discovered: each play is worth seeing again, and new insights are possible each time it is played. One reason for this phenomenon may be that Chekhov always works with a multitude of the most delicate details of human behavior, the finely perceived elements of speech and action, and compounds them in so infinite a variety of ways that the dramatic imagination of the spectator is unpredictably expanded. Thus, like the actor and the director, the student of Chekhov's plays must begin to approach them through those details and elements.

His first major play, **The Seagull,** is by no means his most subtle, and it is introduced by two lesser characters, Medvedenko the schoolmaster and Masha the girl he wishes to marry. Yet this play captures its audience immediately on the rise of the curtain with two challenging lines:

MEDVEDENKO Why do you always wear black?

MASHA I'm in mourning for my life.[1]

The lines catch the audience by surprise, and in performance they echo in the mind through the scene. When, later in the first act, we see Arkadina in light summer clothes, we will be reminded of Masha's dress and Medvedenko's question. Meanwhile, the first decision for the actors must be how to speak the lines. Is Masha tearful and sad, or angry and sarcastic?—two quite opposed notions, and either of them possible. It is especially necessary to see the characters in their setting, in the garden, having returned from a walk on a hot evening. It is a quite romantic setting: this part of Sorin's park near a lake in the moonlight will seem enchanting and beautiful. Does this pair of lovers therefore enter with their arms about one another, and when they sit on the bench do they sit side by side? The ambiguity in the opening lines hardly permits such romantic behavior. In the production of the play at the Moscow Art Theatre in 1898, Konstantin Stanislavskii had Medvedenko and Masha stroll about the stage, the man smoking and cracking nuts. But this too could be wrong, since, although he has been wooing Masha for some time, he surely must not seem to be indifferent to her. How far is their entrance a comic one? Is it intended that they enter with Masha walking a little ahead of Medvedenko, as if she were trying to escape his attentions? He certainly is a bore who complains constantly about his life as an underpaid schoolteacher. In any case we soon learn that Masha has her eye on another man, Konstantin Treplev. Thus, if she is in fact running from him, her remark about being in mourning for her life may be spoken as an irritated rebuff or with a teasing laugh, depending on the degree of comedy perceived in the scene. The truth is that we cannot be sure, in their uneasy relationship with each other and their enigmatic relationship with the spectator, that any of these treatments is intended. Yet none can be ruled out.

Something of each approach is implied, and the audience is intended to be left in tantalizing uncertainty. The element of doubt is characteristic of the basic ingredient with which Chekhov works as a playwright in matters large and small. He sustains an ambiguity in tone and mood, character and incident, for as long as he dares—chiefly to engage his audience in the effort of participation, which will ensure that we have reexperienced as closely as possible the life of his stage, but also to strike a note of indeterminacy that we cannot easily identify as tragic or comic, but that certainly captures the ironic feeling of real life. In the first act of *The Cherry Orchard,* Lopakhin pops his head round the door and moos like a cow at Varia. With no more than this brief signal, Chekhov indicates the miserable situation that spinster finds herself in, aware that the family is in debt and unable to get Lopakhin to make the proposal of marriage that would solve her problems. At the same time, the trick undercuts with our laughter the solemn news that the orchard will be sold that very August. In the next act Ania and Trofimov separate for their "love scene" in the moonlight, but while the romantically inclined Ania waits in anticipation of a kiss, the inept "eternal student" can only make an irrelevant speech to an imaginary crowd of fellow Trofimovs, "Forward! Do not lag behind, friends!", a speech that quite passes over the girl's head; "How well you speak!" (Act II) is all she can say. Again the audience laughs, for she can think only of pleasing him; yet it also recognizes that another hope of saving the family's fortunes has been dashed. "God defend you from generalizations," wrote Chekhov in a letter to his brother Alexander (May 10, 1886).[2] His effort to avoid stereotypes of character or situation, to achieve a fresh observation of true human relationships, repeatedly required him to work for a particular effect that did not admit simple classification. He did this by a hundred and one touches in which the very process of our interpretation called for a new effort of understanding of a character in its situation. The pretty girl Natasha, who makes a late entrance into Irina's party in Act I of *Three Sisters,* is wonderfully young and shy—embarrassed at being late, checking in a mirror that her hair is in place after hurrying, uncertain of the right color to go with her dress, ready to burst into tears. We forgive her everything, even her lack of taste, although we may remember that Masha thought her cheeks were rosy because she had resorted to the Victorian practice of pinching them to make them red. Perhaps we forgive her this too, until we see her evolve into the ruthless little *hausfrau* of Act II. Even then we may excuse some of her treatment of the sisters, who in their pretensions must have been difficult to live with.

By such minutiae of ordinary life Chekhov controls the response of his audience. He eschewed the traditional methods of critical and satirical comedy, like the exaggeration of character and the eccentricity of behavior, even though he had mastered this kind of stagecraft in the five short "vaudevilles" he had written between 1888 and 1891, *The Bear, The Proposal, A Tragic Role, The Wedding,* and *The Anniversary.* In the mature plays there is no Gregory Smirnov to fly into a rage when thwarted by a pretty widow with dimples (*The Bear*) and no Ivan Lomov to clutch at his heart and fall into a faint when

insulted (*The Proposal*), unless we except the obsequious Waffles and his pathetic history in *Uncle Vania* or the lovelorn Epikhodov with his bookishness and his squeaky boots in *The Cherry Orchard.* Yet even these caricatures enjoy a three-dimensional quality that would satisfy many realists. Chekhov makes a point of creating every character, major or minor, with a complete life history. No two are alike, so that every line of dialogue contributes to the imagined whole, although the final character is unpredictable until we have pieced it together at the end of the play. Thus, the maidservant Duniasha in *The Cherry Orchard* has just sprung from young girlhood, so much so that Mme. Ranevskaia only just recognizes her after a five-year absence. At the beginning of that momentous summer in which the family is broken up, she cannot resist excitedly telling everyone of the proposal of marriage she has received from Epikhodov. When Iasha's pseudo-Parisian sophistication magnetizes the girl, she promptly forgets Epikhodov and tries to impress Iasha by aping the ladies with a powder-puff and a pretense to refined ways, "I'm going to go faint. I'm fainting!" (Act I). She is overwhelmed when the post office clerk calls her a "flower," and she offers herself to Iasha as someone "grown sensitive and delicate" (Act III). Thus, before the summer is over, we have the strongest suspicion that Iasha has seduced her and is leaving her pregnant. Duniasha's little drama is slight indeed, but it is complete and woven subtly through the stronger warp and woof of the play, one more illustration of the breaking up of the social structure represented there.

Character, however deceptively realistic, is in this way part of a guiding pattern. It is first a pattern of checks and balances achieved by carefully setting one character off against another. In *Three Sisters,* the reticent, doomed Baron Tuzenbakh is placed in contrast with his voluble Colonel Vershinin, who will survive his troublesome marriage and his tour of duty in the provinces. Natasha the intruder slowly gains ascendancy over the family as Olga's authority and security slip. In *The Cherry Orchard,* Mme. Ranevskaia's fecklessness is brilliantly in parallel with the landowner Pishchik's empty optimism, and while she loses everything he at the last moment has a stroke of sheer good luck when the Englishmen "come along" and find on his land "some sort of white clay"; or the vapid idealism of Trofimov, the son of a chemist, is in nice counterpoint with the practical, but equally inappropriate, thinking of Lopakhin, the son of a peasant. In *Uncle Vania,* the plain Sonia's unselfish altruism sits in pathetic contrast with the self-serving of the beautiful Helena who apparently can whistle up any man she chooses; and Telyegin supplies a bleak image of miserable dependency for Vania, who himself is shortly to recognize his powerless slavery to the professor. This device of implicit character comparison and contrast both undermines and controls the sentiment and emotionalism in each play, and encourages a subtle ambivalence in the action played out before the audience.

A powerful dramatic strategy came of Chekhov's decision never to allow us a simple or comforting moral response to a character's actions. He accepts unreservedly that the human personality is complicated, and he demonstrates his point again and again. At the time of writing the early *Ivanov* (1889), he wrote to Alexander,

> Present-day playwrights begin their plays solely with angels, villains, and buffoons. Now, search for these characters in the whole of Russia. Yes, you can find them, but not such extremes as are necessary for a playwright. . . . I wanted to be original; I have not introduced a single villain nor an angel, although I could not refuse myself buffoons; I accused nobody, justified nobody.

(October 24, 1887)

He is particularly careful to prompt contradictory, impersonal feelings about those who might otherwise have served him powerfully as villains. In *The Seagull,* the famous author Trigorin is the man who is responsible for the seduction of the aspiring young actress Nina, but we are never to see him as the elderly *roué,* or as the matinee idol of modern melodrama. From the start he is shown wearing old shoes and checked trousers, dissatisfied with his own success, trying to flee his responsibility to Arkadina by, of all things, going fishing, finding in Nina at best some copy for his next story. When Nina so romantically offers her life to him by drawing his attention to a line in one of his own books, he is arguably more the seduced than the seducer. In *The Cherry Orchard,* the merchant Lopakhin is the son of a peasant who has the opportunity to buy the very estate on which his ancestors were serfs, "where they weren't even admitted into the kitchen." What a sensational avenger this character could have been, and what a strongly satirical point Chekhov could have made! But Lopakhin is no stereotype. If he has made his money by hard work, it is a sensitive man who regrets the loss of the fields of poppies he must harvest for their oil. If it is his destiny to be the one to dispossess the family, he has always loved Ranevskaia like a mother, from the time when she comforted him as a little boy with a bloody nose. He buys the orchard almost reluctantly, as if unintentionally, even protectively, from under the nose of Deriganov—the unseen villain.

We think of Chekhov's characters before his plots, not because their dialogue is easy to read, but because they so readily come alive and are so rewarding to actors in the many submerged hints and suggestions of psychological depth with which their author has endowed them. As a result, each character, like Shakespeare's, is wholly individualized, never interchangeable, and in a good performance quite unforgettable. Nevertheless, Chekhov probably did not construct a play by elaborating his characters first. With the objectivity of a true comedian, he envisioned them as a group in a realistic situation, not so much a plot as a set of circumstances. It is a commonplace that Chekhov's plays present us with families, in which even the servants are part of the group. From the start he works for the conflicts and contradictions of a group reaction, one that embodies the same principles of balance and control in order to command his audience's unemotional, but not unfeeling, understanding and judgment.

In all this he was working determinedly against the theatricalism of the nineteenth-century stage—hence his frequent clashes with his director Konstantin Stanislavskii, who was essentially a product of his period, albeit an outstanding and intelligent actor and manager. But Chekhov was demanding and far ahead of his time. Along with the star system and the flamboyant style of speaking and acting, the "well-made" ordering of events, and the overdramatic scene, which Stanislavskii and his partner Nemirovich-Danchenko had themselves rejected when they agreed on their plans for the Moscow Art Theatre, Chekhov also found himself disapproving of the stage practice of Henrik Ibsen. The Norwegian playwright's major contribution to stage realism was to require a more natural prose dialogue and to choose subjects that illuminated more honest human problems, those unencrusted with melodramatic characters and incident; but he was largely unable to avoid building his plays as a series of duelling duologues, and dealing in big conflicts and obligatory scenes of crisis. Chekhov does not have much to say about his famous counterpart in the naturalistic movement, but when he saw *The Wild Duck,* probably Ibsen's most Chekhovian drama, he declared he found it "uninteresting"; *Ghosts* was a "rotten" play; and the suicide in *Hedda Gabler* was for him too sensational.[3] Chekhov's increasing impulse was to outlaw the obligatory scene and contrive to undercut what was potentially sensational, always moving closer to an ideal of balanced realistic theatre.

It is true that we can find certain Ibsenesque moments in the earlier Chekhov. The quarrel between Arkadina and Treplev, mother and son, in Act III of *The Seagull,* with explosive lines like "You are nothing but a Kiev shopman! . . . You miser! . . . You ragged beggar!" may be considered to have been written in the older tradition, as may the quarrel between Arkadina and her lover Trigorin later in the same act ("You won't abandon me? . . . I have no will of my own. . . . Now he is mine!"). But when a comparable scene between Mme. Ranevskaia and Trofimov surfaces in the third act of his last play, *The Cherry Orchard,* when the student accuses the older woman of having led an immoral life, the incident is neatly turned for comedy, so cooling the emotionalism and distancing the audience. As Trofimov storms out of the room, crying, "All is over between us!" Chekhov adds the reductive stage direction, "There is a sound of somebody running quickly downstairs and suddenly falling with a crash. Ania and Varia scream, but there is a sound of laughter at once":

LIUBOV What has happened? (Ania runs in.)

ANIA (*laughing*) Petia's fallen downstairs! (Runs out.)

LIUBOV What a queer fellow that Petia is!

As a result of this ambiguous encounter, Liubov and Trofimov are seen to be no less fond of one another, since she dances with him immediately after, while the incident has served to illuminate the weakness of both characters in a purely comic way and to keep the moral issue of Liubov and her French lover in critical perspective. The exchange follows the perfect pattern of anticlimax: the building of dramatic tension is swiftly undercut for laughter, but without wholly destroying the basic purpose of the heated confrontation when the excitement is defused. A residue of deeper feeling and a fuller understanding of the difference between the two generations are subtly carried over into the next segment of the play.

It would not be too much to say that the characteristic device in Chekhov's mature plays is indeed that of anticlimax, implying his deliberate refusal to allow the pathos beneath his scenes to dictate the response of his audience for very long. He was not always successful. At the end of *The Seagull,* he aimed to undercut the sensationalism of Treplev's suicide by arranging that it should take place offstage, but in so doing Chekhov found himself inadvertently building up a sensationalism by default. The very absence of direct comment on the sound of the offstage shot, and the careful underplaying of Dr. Dorn's information to those who heard it on the stage ("It must be something in my medicine-chest that has gone off"), followed by his aside to Trigorin ("The fact is, Konstantin Gavrilitch has shot himself"), called for the audience itself to supply the missing emotional response. The rule that "a writer has to be just as objective as a chemist," as proposed in Chekhov's letter to M. V. Kiseleva (January 14, 1887), would not serve in all cases in the theatre. The effect of the next shot fired in a Chekhov play, that of Vania's attempt on the life of Professor Serebriakov at the end of the third act of *Uncle Vania,* is more precisely regulated. The gun is now visible; but not only does the bullet miss its target, but also the ridiculous behavior of the principals to the affair is fully written in, so that little of the intended effect is left to chance. Serebriakov has run in "staggering with terror" and Vania has run in looking for him: "Where is he? Oh, here he is! (Fires at him) Bang! (a pause) Missed! Missed again! (Furiously) Damnation—damnation take it. (Flings revolver on the floor and sinks on to a chair, exhausted)" With the professor running in panic and ducking the shot, possibly behind a chair, in an uncharacteristically undignified fashion, and with Vania childishly crying "Bang!" before he flings his gun down in a tantrum of frustration, Chekhov guaranteed that a scene which carried a potentially tragic explosion of feeling must create a decisively comic image of Vania's ineffectuality.

As a naturalistic dramatist concerned to reveal the forces of the environment and the circumstances of ordinary people working on their lives, Chekhov's greatest achievement was this controlled objectivity. Nowhere does it prove its worth more than at the crisis of *The Cherry Orchard* in Act III. During the ill-timed party flung by Mme. Ranevskaia at the time of the sale of the orchard, both the audience in the theatre and that on the stage are awaiting confirmation of what is a long foregone conclusion, that the orchard has been lost. To look again at Lopakhin's "triumph": insofar as this representative of the peasant class will buy the estate, he could have been used to make a powerful political point, one that a lesser playwright might have exploited. Not so Chekhov. Here

was to be no triumph for the forces of "justice," only an occasion, long anticipated, that would bring sorrow to everyone concerned, and Chekhov used it to mark the uneasy end of an era. The ironic moment of Lopakhin's entrance into the party foreshadows the whole anticlimactic treatment of the end of the play. Varia, who as housekeeper holds the keys to the family and who still cherishes the hope of marrying him, offers a blow with Firs's stick at Epikhodov, but almost hits Lopakhin on the head. The incident is turned for a joke at which everyone laughs, but it ensures that the new owner is to make no grand entrance. Instead, it touches the edge of symbolism. While the gesture with the stick reminds Lopakhin and us of his peasant boyhood and shows him more as an intruder than as a tyrant, it releases for comedy all the tension of the auction. The moment is laughable and fleeting; it is lightly done, yet it is full of meaning.

From total anticlimax to the persistent undercutting of fine detail, Chekhov's method as a comedian was consistently deflationary. *The Seagull* was composed of many aborted affairs between the sexes (I try to avoid the term "love-affairs"), those between Treplev and Nina, Nina and Trigorin, Trigorin and Arkadina, Masha and Treplev, Masha and Medvedenko, Polina and Dorn: so many, indeed, that they would seem to identify the play as a farce as they proliferate and cancel one another out. "How hysterical they are," says Dorn at one point, "and what a lot of love" (Act I). Yet the general tenor of these affairs, felt through the realistic interaction between each pair of lovers, teases us with tragedy. In *The Cherry Orchard,* eight years later, Chekhov again compounds his love-affairs, between Ania and Trofimov, Charlotta and Pishchick, Epikhodov and Duniasha, Duniasha and Iasha, Varia and Lopakhin, but of these not one allows a true pathos. Even in the case of Varia and Lopakhin, Chekhov was careful to avoid building sufficient sympathetic feeling to color with any sense of disaster that delicious moment when Lopakhin bolts from Varia's presence rather than propose to her. If Nina of *The Seagull* can be admitted as a pathetic figure, the cry-baby Varia can never be.

Communication from stage to audience by a host of fleeting but suggestive details was a method that Chekhov learned in the hard school of short story writing, and it served him well in the theatre where an economy of means is *de rigueur*. For the writer of fiction, Chekhov's well-known *mot* occurs in a letter to Alexander on May 10, 1886: "You will get the full effect of a moonlight night if you write that on the mill-dam a pin-point of light flashed from the neck of a broken bottle." This statement in part explains the brevity and immediacy of his glancing, impressionistic style of prose. On the stage, the smallest and simplest element of voice, or pause, or gesture, can in its context have a momentous impact, and the slightest hint on the surface of the dialogue can plumb a profound subtext. *Three Sisters* is particularly rich in little lines that guide the listener toward the hidden life of the family. The following unforgettable touches are presented here without comment:

NATASHA I was saying to your sister this morning, "Take care of yourself, Irina darling," said I. *But she won't listen.*

(Act II)

and

OLGA Whoever proposed to me I would marry him, if only he were a good man. . . . *I would even marry an old man. . . .*

(Act III)

and in Act IV

MASHA Did you love my mother?

TCHEBUTYKIN Very much.

MASHA And did she love you?

TCHEBUTYKIN (*after a pause*) That I don't remember.[4]

On the stage the technique also appears in Chekhov's choice and use of props and costume. In Act I of *The Seagull,* Masha's defiant little habit of taking a pinch of snuff (evidently used to keep Medvedenko at bay) subtly descends to become her new drinking habit in Act III; by then she has married him, and her slight tipsiness neatly understates her resignation to her new condition. In the same play, the decline in old Sorin's health is marked out by his progress from a limp and a shuffle with a stick in Act I, to his appearance followed by Medvedenko pushing a wheelchair in his wake in Act II, to his attack of dizziness in Act III, until in Act IV we finally see him confined to his chair. Thus have the two years passed for him. In *Uncle Vania,* we note the hypochondriacal professor's inability or unwillingness to make the adjustment when he leaves the city for the heat of a rural summer: Vania reports, "It's hot, stifling; but our great man of learning is in his greatcoat and galoshes, with an umbrella and gloves too" (Act I). Through those summer months the old nurse Marina's endless knitting of woollen stockings against the arrival of the Russian winter warns us, as they grow in length from scene to scene, of the relentless cycle of the seasons which govern the lives of Vania and Sonia. In *Three Sisters,* it is the silence and soft whistling of Masha, together with her attention to her hat, which tells us how her mind is working in Act I: at one point she puts it on to indicate her boredom with the company and her intention of leaving in the middle of Irina's party, then, long after the appearance of the new Colonel Vershinin with the information that he has come from Moscow ("TUZEN-BAKH: Aleksandr Ignatevitch has come from Moscow. IRINA: From Moscow? You have come from Moscow?"), Masha suddenly takes off her hat again as she makes a quiet decision that no one seems to hear, "I'll stay to lunch." By such oblique indications does Chekhov tell his story.

The technique brings the feel of actual life to the stage, almost a "documentary" touch, in which the actuality of speech and behavior seems to dictate what happens, and the pursuit of its authenticity becomes for the dramatist almost an imperative in itself. Indeed, with *Uncle Vania,* which Chekhov subtitled **"Scenes from Country Life"** after Aleksandr Ostrovskii, he seems to aim at an ideal of realistic objectivity in which he promotes his balance of compassion and detachment by letting actuality speak for itself. This play above all his others presents a group of trivial people in order to show the dullness of life in provincial Russia. The challenge for the playwright is to prove that even if they are dull, an audience need not find them uninteresting. *Uncle Vania* takes the first important step toward a "documentary" representation of life, and this, in the memorable words of the Scottish documentary film pioneer, John Grierson, implies "the creative treatment of actuality."[5]

A critical crux in *Uncle Vania* may well be resolved by reference to the latent principles of documentary in the play. At the end, when Vania and Sonia must patch together their former lives after the visitors of the summer have departed, the girl tries to comfort her uncle with a moving speech which nevertheless remains wickedly ambiguous, and any director of the play must decide whether or not his actress will play for a rousing and optimistic ending. Such lines as "We shall rest, we shall rest!" must be tested by performance: is Sonia expressing the hope of all downtrodden people in need of courage to face the future, or are her words to be heard as painfully ironic, mere pieties that offer hope only in the next world? As usual, Chekhov is careful to leave the matter in doubt. Yet the student of the stage should not overlook the fact that Sonia and Vania are not alone. Chekhov once said that it is the day-to-day living that wears you down, and at the end of *Uncle Vania* he arranges that four others besides Sonia and Vania will contribute to the uncertain spirit of his curtain scene. The Watchman resumes his tapping offstage, Maria takes up her pen again and begins to scratch her notes, Marina continues to click her knitting needles, and Telegin quietly tunes and strums his guitar. These four are all making the faint sounds that are to form a dry, melancholy background to Sonia's speech, pacing and commenting on the scene as a whole— like Andrei who aimlessly pushes his baby-carriage across the back of the stage at the end of *Three Sisters,* or like the noise of the axe that falls with monotonous regularity on the trees at the end of *The Cherry Orchard.* The "silent" characters at the end of *Uncle Vania* represent the day-to-day living and provide a chilling perspective on Sonia's innocence.

Uncle Vania is "about" the socio-economic conditions in rural Russia at the end of the nineteenth century, but the toll paid by the human mind and spirit is conveyed as a sensory experience constructed out of noises heard in counterpoint with words, and neither words nor noises can be escaped by their audience. Chekhov's social criticism thus remains tangential and elusive, and properly so, and thus documentary becomes drama. *Three Sisters* exactly documents the nature of provincial life in a small town many miles from the great metropolis of Moscow. Its fragile cultural life depends on the presence of the officers from the regiment of artillery stationed nearby. It is easy to recognize that the chorus of voices crying for a return home to Moscow is ineffectual, and it is even easier to pass some sort of judgment that the three women should apply themselves and take a more positive attitude to life. It is Chekhov's purpose to show how the weight of trivial living bears down on the three of them remorselessly. While Irina clings hopelessly to her romantic notions of love, Masha settles for a shabby affair with the colonel of the regiment and Olga sacrifices herself to play the double role of breadwinner and mother to the family. As the audience comes to acknowledge the sisters' limitations as human beings and theatrically reexperiences, as it were, the increasing pressure of their circumstances, its criticism will be muted.

The general framework of Chekhov's balanced comedy admits a remarkable variety of muffled, but subversive, social criticism, and at unexpected moments he will disrupt the apparent calm of his scene. In that balmy summer afternoon of Act II in *The Cherry Orchard,* for example, Firs expresses his disapproval of the Emancipation in his longing for the past, and Lopakhin catches us with a throwaway line, "Those were fine old times. There was flogging anyway." Or Chekhov contrives to insert an oblique reminder of the Jewish persecution under Nicholas II when the pathetic Jewish orchestra is heard faintly and is then later hired for the ball in the next act by Mme. Ranevskaia, suggesting her sense of guilt and obligation. Or he introduces the disagreeable image of the drunken beggar who comes upon the family group sitting in the dusk, frightening Varia and affording them and us an ugly glimpse of what could happen to them all. In the same letter to Kiseleva mentioned above, Chekhov had insisted that "To chemists there is nothing unclean on earth," and with no jot of sensationalism his comedy admitted both the ugly and the painful. When near the end of the play Gaev volunteers that he has taken a job as a bank clerk, "I am a bank clerk now—I am a financier—cannon off the red" (Act IV), Chekhov's intention is more than to provoke a facile laugh. Gaev's line fits into the pattern of the play's constant reference to money and points to a devastating change in the social order: "How am I going to feed the servants?" demands Varia.

The fabric of Chekhov's drama is thus slyly interwoven with an acute commentary on the times. In his foreword to *Miss Julie* in 1888, Strindberg outlined an appropriate method for writing the dialogue of naturalism when he described how in his own play "the dialogue wanders, gathering in the opening scenes material which is later picked up, worked over, repeated, expounded, and developed like the theme in a musical composition."[6] If this sounds altogether too deliberate to describe Chekhov's way of working, it nevertheless implied that writing realistic dialogue was a matter of great discipline. The commonplace that Chekhov offered his audience "a slice of life" was always inadequate, since what appears to be an image of desultory and humdrum existence in fact carried a purposeful and meticulously designed "subtext" that moved relentlessly to a point. In another of Chekhov's famous assertions, "In life people don't shoot them-

selves or fall in love every minute. . . . They spend more time eating, drinking and talking nonsense, and while they're doing it, their lives may be shattered."[7] The method deceived Tolstoi, who thought of him as an impressionist painter for whom "it is all only mosaic without a governing idea," but it should not deceive the spectator in the theatre.[8] If there is no obvious "hero" on whose fortunes it might have been possible to focus attention, if there is no discernible issue of right or wrong in the representation of events on the stage, and if there is no "plot" in the Aristotelian sense, Chekhov achieves the dramatic unity these classical concepts all imply. If there is little plotting, there is much planning.

The unity of a Chekhov play arises when all its parts come together to form an experience greater than their sum. We look for this unity, therefore, in those elements that determine the rhythm of the experience and control the processes of the play in performance. They are the elements that can be seen to regulate both the actors on the stage and the responses of the audience. They can be found in every stroke of character and incident, but let us conclude this essay by indicating what may be most easily missed in reading the text of the plays.

Chekhov was well aware that the *setting* on his stage could speak powerfully to the spectator, who could not avoid seeing it, and he perfected a way that drew a partly realistic, but equally symbolic, visual pattern from act to act. In *The Seagull,* the scene changes from the romantic to the almost sordid: from Sorin's glorious park with its setting sun and rising moon reflecting the youthful idealism of Treplev and Nina in Act I, to the pretty croquet lawn bathed in sunlight outside the house, the domain of Mme. Arkadina and her little social circle in Act II; Act III takes us inside the house for the first time, and we see it disordered by the preparations for leaving; and Act IV moves still further into the heart of things, into the world of books and careless furniture that Treplev miserably inhabits. *Uncle Vania* follows a comparable pattern, beginning outside the house, but this time set on the edge of a plantation that lacks all romance; thereafter, Acts II and III move each time deeper into the house, until Act IV finds out Vania's own room, his bed and his personal jumble of account-books, scales, and papers, together with a starling in a cage and a map of Africa on the wall, all lightly suggesting the clutter of his mind and his ineffectual longing for escape.

The setting for *Three Sisters* is different by beginning inside the house and embracing us with its main public room for the first two acts. Columns suggest a former grandeur, and the partly seen dining room hints at the scale of the house. However, in Act II the evidence of Natasha and her baby is everywhere, and many subtle changes in the scene tell us of the passage of time. Act III continues the process of dispossession by confining us to Olga's bedroom, now shared with a displaced Irina, so that the confusion of beds and screens looks and feels uncomfortable. With Act IV, the sisters are finally found outside the house, with Natasha and her lover Protopopov inside, so that the visual symbolism of exclusion is complete. *The Cherry Orchard* dares a circular pattern of scenes in order to symbolize the cycle of life. It begins in the nursery, the one room where every member of the household has a rooted memory. It then passes to a spot beyond the orchard which manages to include in one composition a little of the rural estate and a glimpse of urban and industrial growth, with the family caught between the past and the future as it lolls about in a disused graveyard: the set seems required to bear too heavy a weight of meaning. Act III returns us nostalgically to the ballroom of the house as a background for the incongruity of the party, and Act IV comes full circle to the nursery of the first act, although it is now a scene of desolation: bare trees, furniture covered over, heaps of luggage—a setting that holds out no hope.

In parallel with each visual setting, mood and atmosphere are precisely adjusted, and Chekhov makes use of the seasons, the weather, and the time of day to regulate our changing image of the action. *The Seagull* begins in the twilight of a hot summer's day—"How stifling it is!", says Masha—and the heat seems to provide an excuse for the ruffled feelings which next afternoon explode in ill-temper and direct confrontation. In the last act, the final pathos of Treplev and Nina is set against a dark, wild night of wind and rain. *Uncle Vania* also begins sluggishly in the sultry heat of summer and proceeds through a restless night until the storm breaks, all to prepare the audience for the shock of the professor's announcement that he is planning to sell the estate which precipitates Vania's brainstorm. The last act dips down anticlimactically to the painful time when autumn is changing to winter in a characteristically Chekhovian going-away scene of bitter reflection and regret.

Three Sisters makes some use of the seasons, beginning in spring sunshine with the optimism of an impending party in the air; but in Act II the mood is utterly different as reality begins its advance with the gloom of a winter evening. In Act III, we feel the tensions and hostility arising from the sleeplessness and exhaustion of the fire in the night. For Act IV, Chekhov tries a new device: he ends his play in midday sunshine, although there is a touch of autumn in the air (Stanislavskii had leaves falling throughout the act), the better to capture the sisters' regret at the departure of the regiment, ironically colorful in dress uniforms and marching to the spirited music of a military band. In *The Cherry Orchard,* Chekhov falls back on the cycle of the seasons, which extend from the last frost of May to the first of the winter, matching the cycle of the orchard itself all in white blossom, in the brilliant light of the early morning sun as it rises in Act I, to the time when the trees are glimpsed standing starkly through the bare windows of Act IV. So the summer months of the calendar are quietly marked off as the sale of the estate approaches in Acts II and III, until the cold returns in Act IV—"three degrees of frost," remarks the practical Lopakhin. The story of the family's fortunes seems to be told by the changes in the cherry trees themselves, as if they were sentient creatures.

By such devices of setting and atmosphere Chekhov unifies his play and focuses on a central theme. The dramatic surface of *non sequiturs* and brilliant pauses, of centrifugal incidents and tangential comments, is misleading, like much else of his dramatic method. He suddenly fills his stage with people and as quickly empties it in the first acts of *Uncle Vania* and *The Cherry Orchard*—against all the "laws" of drama. Indeed, he works with an empty stage as effectively as with a full one. He appears to give as much time and attention to "minor" characters as to "major" ones. He scatters his scenes with distracting cues for music and song, some twenty or so in each of his last two plays. He loads his lines with two or three times as many unseen characters as are in the cast itself, and until one counts them it is hard to believe that there are 50 or so "offstage" characters in each of *Three Sisters* and *The Cherry Orchard.* So Chekhov's picture of humanity is infinitely extended by offstage mothers and fathers, sisters and brothers, grandfathers and aunts, friends and acquaintances, servants and workmen, porters and peasants, musicians and nurses, and cooks and gardeners. Who can ever forget Telegin's courageous wife, who ran away from him the day after their wedding "on the ground of my unprepossessing appearance" (Act I). Or Natasha's persistent lover Protopopov, or Kulygin's intimidating headmaster, or Pishchik's long-suffering daughter Dashenka?

This rich abundance in Chekhov's world of people is part of his illusion of reality, providing family backgrounds, giving depth to the lives of the few we see. Yet his most deceptive technique may be that of arranging for his characters to fall into patterns that indicate order in what otherwise seems to be at random—a kind of dramatic *Gestalten* awaiting the perception of an audience watching a performance. In *Uncle Vania,* each of the eight principals falls into a category of what might be thought of as a master-and-slave relationship. There are those who exercise a power over others without thought: Professor Serebriakov through his position in society and his ownership of land, and Ielena through her sex and her beauty. There are those who are as yet unreconciled to their servitude and see some possibilities of change: Vania, Sonia, and Astrov. And there are those who have succumbed to the dead hand of routine and the pressures they have no control over: Maria, Marina, and Telegin. In *Three Sisters,* the fortunes of the family change as the self-centered ones, Natasha, Solenyi, and perhaps Vershinin, prevail over the weaknesses of others, particularly the sisters and their brother Andrei.

It is with *The Cherry Orchard* that Chekhov perfects his magical technique of character patterning, and, had he lived, he would no doubt have explored further. In this play twelve characters appear to make ten times that number as each serves as a representative of more than one aspect of society. Thus, each is a richly individualized composite of many elements, while being at the same time one of a group identified by social or economic class, or sex, or age, and more, as each group is affected differently by the sale of the orchard. As members of the landowning class, Gaev and Mme. Ranevskaia lose their place in society, and pull down with them their immediate dependents, Ania and Varia. Meanwhile, the former peasants, Lopakhin and Iasha, acquire new economic and social responsibility, so that the financial distress of some is seen to be to the advantage of others; two generations after the Emancipation, the results of the upheaval on the changing structure of society are still being felt. If the cast is divided by sex, the loss of the orchard places a marital urgency on the spinsters, Varia, Duniasha, and introduces a human need that Lopakhin, Iasha, and Pishchik cannot understand and to which they cannot respond; Ania and Trofimov still move in an unreal, romantic fog where they are as yet content to remain "above love"; and Liubov, now a rather desperate lady, is thrown back on the resource of her Paris lover. If the cast is divided by age, those of the older generation whose lives are locked in the past view change as the loss of a whole way of life too precious to be contemplated; for those of the youngest generation, Ania, Trofimov, Iasha, and Duniasha, the sale of the orchard is a necessary break with the past and an opportunity for a new life; and those of middle years, Lopakhin, Varia, and Charlotta, are the realists who must face the demands of the moment, take stock of their financial position, find work. Such differences between the generations bring time alive on the stage. Only Firs, aged 87, is beyond class, sex, and time: he is the near-absurd chorus who is able to survey all the others, unaffected by events, and even as those he has loved forget him at the last, so the play ends on a crashing irony.

By Chekhov's dramatic techniques the audience is placed in the classic comic role of objective observer. It is finally academic to ask whether these plays are tragedies or comedies when their fugitive methods in performance call at one moment for the audience's compassionate understanding of the human condition and at the next for its unemotional judgment. Faced with the mass of detailed evidence, we the jury must temporarily withdraw and calmly try to reach a verdict. Our ambivalent, tragicomic response to the multitude of Chekhov's signals from the stage, apparently all at odds like the contradictions of life, reflects a process at the heart of his dramatic method and amazingly corresponds to the actual experience of living. In his *Preface to Shakespeare,* Samuel Johnson recognized that "the real state of sublunary nature . . . partakes of good and evil, joy and sorrow, mingled with endless variety of proportion and innumerable modes of combination,"[9] and thus justified the dramatic mixture in Shakespeare. In the world of his plays, Chekhov, like Shakespeare, generously embraces human life and does so with a little of the same impulse toward creative variety.

NOTES

[1] Anton Chekhov, *The Cherry Orchard, and Other Plays,* trans. Constance Garnett, Phoenix Library Edition (London: Chatto and Windus, 1935). Further quotations from *The Seagull, The Cherry Orchard,* and *Uncle Vania* are from this edition.
[2] S. S. Koteliansky and Philip Tomlinson, eds., *The Life and Letters of Anton Tchekhov* (London: Benjamin Blom, 1965). All subsequent citations from Chekhov's letters are from this edition.

[3] See Ernest J. Simmons, *Chekhov: A Biography* (New York: Little, Brown, 1962), p. 542; S. S. Koteliansky, ed. and trans., *Anton Tchekhov: Literary and Theatrical Reminiscences* (London: Routledge, 1927), pp. 156, 161; Anton Tchekhov, *The Letters to Olga Leonardovna Knipper,* trans. C. Garnett (New York: Benjamin Blom, 1966), p. 368.
[4] Anton Chekhov, *Three Sisters and Others Plays,* trans. Constance Garnett, Phoenix Library Edition (London: Chatto and Windus, 1935), pp. 30, 68, 80, emphasis added. Further quotes from *Three Sisters* are from this edition.
[5] *Grierson on Documentary,* ed. Forsyth Hardy (London: Collins, 1946), p. 11.
[6] August Strindberg, *Six Plays,* trans. Elizabeth Sprigge (Garden City, N.Y.: Doubleday, 1955), p. 69.
[7] Quoted in David Magarshack, *Chekhov the Dramatist* (London: John Lehmann, 1952), p. 118.
[8] Quoted in Dmitri Chizhevsky in *Anton Čechov: 1860-1960: Some Essays,* ed. T. Eekman (Leiden: E. J. Brill, 1960), and reprinted in *Chekhov: A Collection of Critical Essays,* ed. R. L. Jackson (Englewood Cliffs, N.J.: Prentice-Hall, 1967), p. 53.
[9] Samuel Johnson, *Johnson on Shakespeare,* ed. Walter Raleigh (London: Oxford University Press, 1908), p. 15.

Péter Egri (essay date 1986)

SOURCE: "The Mosaic Design," in *Chekhov and O'Neill: The Uses of the Short Story in Chekhov's and O'Neill's Plays,* Akadémiai Kiadó, 1986, pp. 68-117.

[*In the following excerpt, Egri demonstrates how themes and motifs from Chekhov's short stories are incorporated into "mosaic patterns" in* Three Sisters *and* The Cherry Orchard.]

The most intricate and refined strategy of composing a dramatic whole out of short-story-like units is the application of the mosaic design. It represents a total integration of short-story-oriented elements, minor motifs, even fragmentary motives, into a dramatic pattern. How conscious Chekhov was of the nature and merits of the procedure is witnessed by his letter of May 8, 1889, to his brother, Alexander Pavlovich: "The large number of revisions need not trouble you, for the more of a mosaic a work is, the better. The characters stand to gain by this. The play will be worthless if all the characters resemble you. . . . Give people people, and not yourself."[1] It is worth bearing in mind that for Chekhov the plasticity, objectivity and variety of the characters in a play can be obtained by the dramatic adoption of the mosaic technique, and conversely, the mosaic principle is applied to reach these very effects. Describing *The Wood Demon* (then a play in progress) in a letter of May 14, 1889, to A. S. Suvorin, Chekhov calls it "something of a mosaic", but this quality of the drama does not prevent him from stating: "it leaves upon me an impression of accomplishment."[2]

Unity created of seemingly accidental fragments is a familiar and recurring trait of Chekhov's epic works (**"The Steppe," "The Duel," "Three Years" "A Nervous Breakdown," "My Life," "Gooseberries," "On Official Duty"**);[3] the technique also crops up in his early long plays,[4] and it reaches the stage of perfection in the last two dramas, *Three Sisters* (1900) and *The Cherry Orchard* (1903).

The mosaic composition of *Three Sisters* can partly be explained by its strong and multiple reliance on a number of narrative works by Chekhov. In **"My Life"** (1896), a short novel consisting of short chapters not infrequently following a short story design, the thematic nucleus of *Three Sisters* may be discerned. Describing general conditions in the small town he lives in, Poloznev complains of the wide-spread bribery and corruption from which only very young girls surrounded by the atmosphere of moral purity and characterized by a noble spirit and high aspirations are exempt. They, however, do not know much about real life, and are threatened by the morass of petty bourgeois banality. The predicament of the three sisters in general and the plight of Masha married to the provincial schoolmaster Kuligin in particular can clearly be recognized.

"My Life" also anticipates the play by its heavy emphasis on the redeeming necessity of (physical) work. Poloznev, the son of an untalented architect, hates mechanical office work, becomes, like Irina, weary of being a telegraph clerk, and finds satisfaction in becoming a housepainter. Baron Tusenbach, who resigns his commission as a lieutenant and decides to start a new life in a brickyard, strikes the reader as a dramatic variant of Poloznev. Dolzhikova, the daughter of a well-to-do railway engineer, condemns the idleness, boredom and spiritual emptiness—in part Masha's condition—that attend wealth (the alienation of the rich), runs a farm, patronizes the building of a school, and when she feels overwhelmed by the dead-weight of almost insurmountable difficulties, becomes a singer and moves to the United States. Even Poloznev's sister, Cleopatra makes up her mind to work, to lead an independent life and earn her living as a teacher—like Olga and Irina—, or as a nurse, or to take on washing and scrubbing. In the end, however, her dreams and plans are thwarted; she—not unlike Masha—becomes the mistress of a married man, Dr. Blagovo, bears him a child, is deserted by him, and dies of tuberculosis.

The discussions between Poloznev and doctor Blagovo about the aims of mankind and the prospects of progress towards the indistinct happiness of a distant future anticipate the ethical conversations between Lieutenant Tusenbach and Lieutenant-Colonel Vershinin. So do the occasional changes of stances which are also responsible for a short-story-tinted oscillation. When (in Chapter 7) Poloznev is talking with Blagovo, he points out that although serfdom has been done away with, and capitalism is spreading, the majority feeds, dresses and defends the minority in the name of liberty and remains as hungry, underdressed and defenceless as it has been since the time of Batu Khan. The idea of progress seems to involve the development of the art of slavery. When, however, (in Chapter 8) he is having a conversation with Dolzhikova, Poloznev gives voice to the view that comfort and good life should be considered an inevitable concomitant of capital and culture. Similarly, in Act II of *Three Sisters* "Tusenbach professes to have no faith in the future, and it is Vershinin who is the apostle of work. But in the first act, we find Tusenbach on the windward

track, and it is his words which have the proper prophetic ring."[5] Such oscillations, modifications, adjustments and readjustments of attitudes do not simply express the indecision of characters; they also transmit the contradictory character of the social process itself, whose objective pattern consists of mosaic pieces of this kind.

In **"Gooseberries"** (1898), a short story both eloquent and ironic, Ivan Ivanich, an enlightened veterinary surgeon, attacks the narrow provincialism of his younger brother, Nikolay, a one-time financial clerk, who has resigned from the hurly-burly of everyday life, has moved out of town to seek refuge on a farm, to starve his wife to death, and to find his life's satisfaction in growing and relishing gooseberries, and professing "aristocratic" views: the time is not yet ripe for the people to be cultured, and occasional corporal punishment may be useful. The difference between life in the city and in the country prefigures the three sisters' longing for Moscow, just as the picture of petty provincialism appears to be a preparatory sketch for the portraits of Natasha, Kuligin and Chebutykin.

The distance between the city and the country are represented in Chekhov's short story, **"On Official Duty"** (1899), in terms of the contrast between Moscow (or St. Petersburg) and Sirnya, the small village where Lesnitsky, an impoverished nobleman, dissatisfied with life as an insurance clerk, commits suicide in one of the rooms of the local zemstvo. Lyzhin, the young magistrate, sent out to investigate the matter on the spot, yearns for Moscow with no less intensity than Olga, Masha and Irina in *Three Sisters*; for him Moscow and St. Petersburg represent the fatherland, the real Russia, whereas Sirnya is only the provinces, the colonies. When Lyzhin spends a night in the warm and comfortable house of the local squire, Von Taunitz, and meets his cultured and attractive daughters (who are not unlike the sisters in the play), as he waits for the blizzard to be over, he is overpowered by disconcerting ideas. He feels there is no life in the place, only bits of life, accidental fragments without meaning. He feels sorry for the girls, who are compelled to live cut off from the centre of culture, where nothing happens by chance, where even a suicide fits into the general scheme of things. The theme of *Three Sisters* is audibly sounded in the short story.

As if to underline the fortuitousness of life in the country, Lyzhin sees in a restless dream Lesnitsky, the dead clerk, and Loshadin, the miserable old peasant constable, struggling together through the snow. The sight of Loshadin (who foreshadows Ferapont, the old porter from the Rural Board in *Three Sisters*), and of Lesnitsky, whom he has so far seen only as the repellent object of an unpleasant investigation in an impossible place, arouses the young magistrate's social conscience. He feels responsible for their fates. Like Vershinin and Tusenbach in the play, Lyzhin experiences an insight into something more significant, broad and meaningful than his immediate interests; and like Chekhov, the short story writer, and Chekhov, the dramatist, composing a meaningful whole out of apparently mosaic-like fragments,

Louise Purnell as Irina and Ronald Pickup as Tuzenbach, in Laurence Olivier's 1970 film adapation of Three Sisters.

the magistrate realizes that the unhappy clerk and the old constable appeared accidental and unrelated only to one who saw his life as a fragment, but would be seen as parts of a single organism, marvellous and rational, by one who had the insight to see his life as part of the universal whole. Perceiving, through the operation of social conscience, the significance even of rural existence, observing the general in the particular, the necessary in the accidental, the whole in the fragments, the pattern in the mosaic pieces is the major artistic achievement of the author of **"On Official Duty"** and ***Three Sisters.***[6]

Chekhov's preliminary studies for the play were completed by a long short story divided into short-story-shaped chapters, **"In the Ravine"** (1899). The narrative is concerned with the way in which Aksinya, the serpent-eyed daughter-in-law of the merchant, Tsibukin, gradually and ruthlessly gains sway over the household. She deliberately scalds Nikifor, Tsibukin's infant grandson, when she learns that the old man has bequeathed him one of his

estates (on which she happens to have a brickyard); she ousts Nikifor's mother, Lipa, from the house (as Natasha does Anfisa, the old nurse in the play); and practically starves Tsibukin. With her uninhibited drive and unscrupulous energy, she is the prototype of Natasha in ***Three Sisters.***

Short story motifs and fragments of this kind combine into a mosaic composition in ***Three Sisters.*** The nature and function of the mosaic pattern emerges at the very opening of the play. No sooner has Olga remarked that the sunshine warming their home in this provincial town reminds her of the sun bathing the streets of Moscow than Chebutykin, the boorish doctor, gives his answer "The devil it is!", and Baron Tusenbach adds "Of course, it's nonsense."[7] They are not addressing their words to Olga; in fact, they are retorting to Solyony; yet the onlooker, who has not been given a chance to listen to Solyony's story, has the half-conscious impression that these words also refer to Olga's attitude, and thus constitute a comical check on the upsurge of desire. A direct reply would, at this point, have been farcical and crude. The absence of all rejoinder might have given a sentimental emphasis to Olga's day-dreaming. The juxtaposition of longing and laughter, of desire and derision, establishes an intricate relationship between the two poles: Olga's ideals are qualified as elegiac illusions by the soldier's sobriety; but these illusions are, to a certain extent, also justified and enhanced by Chebutykin's vulgarity. The doctor's attitude also appears in a double light: it is both "real" in the sense of being free of all illusions, and crude in the way it cynically relinquishes all ideals. The situation is further complicated by the fact that Tusenbach, who with his casually condescending, scornful remark seems at the beginning to belong, along with Chebutykin, to the pole of unadorned truth, later proves to be an idealist dreamer himself, and takes a position very different from Chebutykin's. It is, of course, only in the total design of the dramatic mosaic that the viewer becomes fully conscious of the wider implications of such tiny steps from mosaic piece to mosaic piece; a carefully, if seemingly casually, built design, in which subjective intentions and objective conditions are realistically related, and the elegiac and the coarse, the high and the low, the tragic and the comic mutually counterpoint, delimit but also highlight and intensify one another. The apparently loosely laid out darker and lighter pieces form a unified pattern in the concept of the author and the vision of the viewer in such a manner as to focus the human essence of the characters and their situations. This outlook and view, therefore, with its admitted naturalistic informality and impressionistic scintillation, define and follow the formal principles of a realistically arranged modern composition.

With the basic note thus struck, the dramatic composition reinforces the pattern. What could be more commonplace than a casual remark about some member of the family staying to lunch? When, however, it is Masha who makes the remark in the opening conversation in the play,[8] it assumes a special dramatic significance. This is because of the mosaic principle: the seemingly trivial statement, in fact, marks the point at which an attitude is reversed, a hidden psychological process breaks through, an emotional relationship is established.

Not long before her remark, Masha said she was going home and was not staying for Irina's name day party. She was glum and depressed, remembering the old days in Moscow, when her father, General Prozorov, was still alive, and at least thirty or forty officers came to a name-day party. When, however, the new battery commander, Lieutenant-Colonel Vershinin, newly come from Moscow, arrives and says he recalls Prozorov's home and his three daughters, and starts talking about the importance of the contribution intelligent and educated people living in a dull and dismal town make to rendering life unimaginably beautiful and marvellous in two or three hundred years, the sisters are animated—and Masha stays to lunch. A man has turned up with a presentiment of the future, with a sense of morality, and with an encouragement giving justification for suffering. Masha is on her way to falling in love with someone worthy of her

love. This is an exceptional moment presented without rhetoric; a piece of mosaic preceded and prepared by Masha's initial sadness and ennui; by her remark that she does not remember Vershinin; by her statement that she can recall him after all as the young lieutenant she used to tease as the love-sick major; by her observation to the effect that to know three languages in a provincial town is an unnecessary encumbrance like a sixth finger; and finally by his reassuring vision of how future happiness may justify present suffering. He has a notion of the meaning of life; he may become the meaning of her life. There is no way she can miss that lunch.

Tusenbach develops Vershinin's idea of the beauty of the future, and starts speaking about his own chief moral concern, the necessity of work to achieve it. Vershinin agrees with an absent-minded and curt "yes", and praises the lovely flowers and delightful rooms the sisters have. The abrupt change of subject, another mosaic piece, leads the conversation back to normal, prevents day-dreaming from becoming pathetic, and reestablishes the balance between what, by this very act, is proved exceptional and the sphere of everyday utterances. When Tusenbach tries to resume his favourite topic, he already feels he has to defend himself against the possible charge of being a sentimental German and assures everybody present that he is Russian, cannot even speak German, and had a father who belonged to the Orthodox Church . . .

The contradiction between Andrey's imaginary and real prospects is also brought home to the onlooker or reader by a mosaic motif. His sisters hope, and sometimes he himself trusts, that he will continue his studies and will become a professor. In fact, he is only the secretary of the Rural Board, and his sole prospect is to become a member of the Board. He grumbles to Ferapont about how life thwarts one's desires. The old, half-deaf porter from the Board admits he does not hear Andrey well. Andrey is pleased: "If you did hear well, perhaps I should not talk to you",[9] he sums up paradoxically his position characterized by loneliness, timidity, inability to establish human contact with anyone, absent-minded weakness and non-committal passivity—with which he encourages, without knowing it or wishing to do so, the predatory inclinations of his ruthless and vulgar wife, Natasha . . .[10]

In Andrey's and Ferapont's conversation, running on parallel lines interrelated but not intersecting, Moscow is evoked several times. The psychological reality and the physical unreality of its magic attraction are rendered in a fine movement and counter-movement: the nearer the image of Moscow floats in their desires, the farther it recedes in its tangible reality. For Andrey, it is a most desirable city, where one can sit in a huge restaurant not knowing anyone and still not feel like a stranger; for Ferapont, it is an anecdotal town where some merchants allegedly ate forty or fifty pancakes at a sitting, and ultimately it appears as a legendary, fabulous, mythical habitation where, as some contractor says, a rope is stretched right across the place . . .

That Moscow is, in fact, the recurring symbolic leitmotif of the reality of desires and the unreality of their fulfilment is made explicit in yet another microscopic mosaic scene: Irina, playing patience, exclaims happily that it is coming out right, and so they will go to Moscow, but Vershinin, newly come from there, replies: "you won't notice Moscow when you live in it. We have no happiness, . . . we only long for it."[11]

Act III of *Three Sisters* provides a tragicomic cluster and a whirling cavalcade of mosaic events. The longer the mosaic sequence is, the stronger the tragicomic effect turns out to be. The reason is illuminated by the devastating fire raging in the town. The spectator sympathizes with Vershinin, who rescues his two frightened little daughters, brings them to the sisters' house, and muses about the repulsiveness of the present and the beauty of the future; he sympathizes with Masha, who confesses her love for Vershinin to Olga and Irina, and yearns for Moscow; he feels sorry for Kuligin, who is cuckolded; he understands Tusenbach, who awakes from a dream and praises Irina's beauty glimmering white in the dark room, and wishes to work on her side; and to a certain extent, the spectator can even accept Andrey, who would withdraw from the insults of the outer world to the sheltered intimacy of his room and to the music of his violin; or Chebutykin, who has forgotten all he ever knew of medicine and, reduced to a semblance of life, considers life a mere appearance and drinks himself into oblivion.

But into the turmoil of smouldering desires, sufferings and grievances an inextinguishably comic ingredient is mingled by the circumstance that none of these persons, so desirous of a meaningful life and a valuable form of activity, bother to make an attempt to put out the fire. Vershinin even praises the soldiers out fighting the flames as splendid fellows, he gets dirty all over, but he only takes his daughters from his house (already out of danger) and runs away with them to the sisters—to find his hysterical wife there, screaming and angry. He desperately longs for real life, and sings out his "tam-tam!" in answer to Masha's "tram-tam-tam!", but this is about all he actually does. Somewhat incongruously, Kuligin finds it reassuring that, in spite of the wind, "only one part of the town has been burnt."[12] Baron Tusenbach is enchanted by Irina's melancholy paleness, declares he is going to the brickyard directly to start a new life devoted to physical work, and invites Irina to work with him—but in spite of their apparent agreement, neither stirs a limb to quench the fire or help its victims. Tusenbach's rival for Irina's love, or at least attention, Captain Solyony, when asked by Vershinin about the fire, casually answers that it is said to be dying down; what he does fume over is why he may not stay in the house if the Baron may, sprinkling himself with a bottle of scent the while. When asked for the eleventh time by Ferapont to give permission to the firemen to go through his garden on their way to the river, Andrey first bawls at the porter not to call him Andrey Sergeyevich but to address him as "your honour", then gives his leave, absent-mindedly adding that he is sick of the firefighters; he asks for Olga's key

to the cupboard, declares Natasha is a splendid woman, claims that his sisters are against her only because "Old maids never like and have never liked their sisters-in-law";[13] states peremptorily that he considers his membership at the Rural Board just as sacred and elevated as if he were a university professor; confesses he has mortgaged the house because he has lost thirty-five thousand roubles gambling; repeats that Natasha is an excellent, conscientious, honourable woman—and starts crying: "Dear sisters, darling sisters, you must not believe what I say, you mustn't believe it . . .".[14] Chebutykin cannot cure anyone any more: a woman he treated died a few days before, and she has come back to his mind; he finds everything nasty and disturbed in his soul and so gets drunk. That is why he cannot help the victims of the fire, and Olga—the only member of the company helping the helpless—cannot put them into his room because of his drinking bout.

Chekhov is far from exaggerating the contrast between the personal suffering of those safely ensconced and those afflicted by the fire; nor does he overdo the contradiction between what his characters should do, do not do, and do do. The fire is only a backdrop to the desires and hopes entertained, to failures and sufferings in the foreground. But since the characters consider the fire only a backdrop to their personal affairs, these affairs—despite the sincerity with which they are experienced and pursued—take on a tragicomic quality. To dream of the good life to come and to do nothing about it in an emergency is tragicomically incongruous. The seemingly disintegrated informal casualness and the cumulative effect of the mosaic scenes serve this purpose with a brilliant formal clarity.

It is in Act IV that the elegiac-tragic and the trivial-comic threads of the action are woven into an extremely evocative and unified pattern. The mediating agent is again the mosaic design. With the artillery brigade being transferred to another post, the sisters are heart-broken. Irina still has her chance for happiness: Tusenbach has resigned his commission; they are planning to marry the following day; then Tusenbach hopes to start working at a brickyard, and Irina wishes to take up teaching at a school. But the jealous and irritable Solyony is threatening to kill Tusenbach in a duel. When Masha suggests that Chebutykin ought to prevent the duel, his answer is negligently cynical and nihilistic: "The baron is a very good fellow, but one baron more or less in the world, what does it matter?"[15] The interaction of pathos and bathos mutually limit, but also strengthen, one another.

To drive his point home effectively, yet unobtrusively, Chekhov actually gives a kind of *ars poetica* of the possible function of using apparently insignificant mosaic units in the framework of a drama. When taking leave of Irina, immediately before going to his fatal duel with Solyony, in the presentiment of death, Tusenbach is overwhelmed by the intensity with which he experiences all the beauty and promise of life which are now at stake. His emotional concentration raises a trifle into a poetic image, which in turn becomes a lyrical symbol:

What trifles, what little things suddenly *à propos* of nothing acquire importance in life! One laughs at them as before, thinks them nonsense, but still one goes on and feels that one has not the power to stop. Don't let us talk about it! I am happy. I feel as though I were seeing these pines, these maples, these birch trees for the first time in my life, and they all seem to be looking at me with curiosity and waiting. What beautiful trees, and, really, how beautiful life ought to be under them! (*A shout of* "Halloo! Aa-oo!") I must be off; it's time. . . . See, that tree is dead, but it waves in the wind with the others. And so it seems to me that if I die I shall still have part in life, one way or another.[16]

Irina offers to accompany him, but Tusenbach will not let her, and goes off quickly in alarm. Yet he stops in the avenue and calls her name. Upon Irina's question his answer is simply: "I didn't have any coffee this morning. Ask them to make me some."[17] The sentences sound commonplace and trivial; and in this sense, they constitute a low-key counterpoint to the elevated poetic language he was using a moment before. At the same time, however, they represent such trifles as suddenly acquire importance in life. In the given dramatic context their bathetic tone expresses passionate questions such as why Irina cannot love him; when, if ever, they will meet again; what, if anything, they can tell one another at the crucial moment of their final farewell.

The dramatic significance of Chekhov's contrapuntal style unfolding in juxtaposed and confronted mosaic units lies in rendering his human and artistic credo authentic, which without his reservations and qualifications would seem merely an empty ostentation, an example of sentimental or dry didacticism: "A time will come when everyone will know what all this is for, why there is this misery; there will be no mysteries and, meanwhile, we have got to live . . . we have got to work",[18] Irina says. The play comes to an end, as it began, on a dual note. Thus in the last mosaic unit, in Olga's tragic and Chebutykin's comic utterances, the drama acquires a rondo form. His "Tarara-boom-dee-ay! . . . It doesn't matter, it doesn't matter"[19] and her "If we only knew, if we only knew!"[20] put a joint question about the meaning of a form of existence. The greatness of the play is manifest in its ability to question in this manner; its consistency lies in the fact that this very question is put with each of its scenes and mosaic pieces.

Chekhov's lyrical tragicomedy becomes fully developed in *The Cherry Orchard*. The drama partly continues, partly summarizes the playwright's earlier aspirations. Like so many of his former plays, *The Cherry Orchard* is also closely connected with a short story. The full elaboration of the dramatist's last play was preceded by the composition of his last short story, **"The Betrothed"** (1903). The story concerns a significant *peripeteia* in the life of a highly-born young lady, Nadya, who lives on the family estate, and is to be married to the bishop's son, Andrey. When, however, a poor, young lad, Sasha, enlightens her as to how dull, useless and worthless her idle life at Andrey's side would be, Nadya

escapes from home, flies to Petersburg, and enrolls at the university.

The juxtaposition of wealth, comfort, culture and their source—the toil of deprived servants living in utter misery, sleeping on the bare floor of the kitchen in filth, stench and among vermin—anticipates the contrast between the parasitic lives of the father and grandfather of Ranyevskaya (Lyubov Andreyevna) and the subjugation and deprivation of their serfs. Sasha's diatribes against Nadya's mother and grandmother, whose leisurely manner of living presupposes and requires the hard work of their servants, give a taste of Trofimov's views, just as his belief in the future foreshadows Trofimov's faith in the advent of a better life. And like Nadya, affected by Sasha's ideas and finding the very ceiling of her room lower and oppressive, Anya, too, comes under Trofimov's influence, and when he explains his position to her, she finds, somewhat to her own surprise, that she does not love the cherry orchard as she used to. Dreaming about the time when not a trace of Granny's house will remain, in which four servants must live in one dirty room in the cellar, Nadya outlines the fate of Ranyevskaya's house as well. Nadya's mother and grandmother also realize that they have lost their past position, authority, influence and rank.

Even if Sasha represents the ideal in the short story, Chekhov is far from idealizing him. When Sasha criticizes the outmoded way of life of the landed aristocracy, he is always right; and when expresses his belief in the future of mankind, he is invariably attractive, yet there is something tentative in his aims and awkwardly impractical in his performance. He has the reputation of being an excellent painter, and is sent to study at the Komisarov Institute in Moscow; but he leaves the place in two years and goes over to the Academy of Fine Arts where he spends almost fifteen years and, with great difficulty, finishes a course in architecture; nevertheless, he fails to become an architect and starts his career as a printer. Thus he prefigures Trofimov, the perennial student, who at the age of twenty-seven is as yet unable to complete his studies at Moscow University.[21] Sasha exposes the awful conditions the servants in Nadya's home are forced to live in, but his own room in Moscow is also filthy, slovenly and neglected, and after her return from St. Petersburg to Moscow, Nadya finds him much less interesting and intelligent than before. All the same, his death from consumption has a cathartic effect on her: she realizes that her life has changed in the direction Sasha meant it to change. His function was that of a catalyst; he precipitated Nadya's recognition of the truth. In this, too, Trofimov appears to be Sasha's successor. Refusing Lopakhin's money, Trofimov speaks, somewhat rhetorically, about humanity advancing towards the highest truth and his marching in the front ranks. Upon Lopakhin's question whether he will get there, Trofimov answers in the affirmative, then, after a pause, he adds a qualification: "I shall get there, or I shall show others the way to get there."[22] This is Sasha's role, too.

How reminiscences of *Three Sisters* and premonitions of *The Cherry Orchard* occupied Chekhov's mind while he was writing **"The Betrothed"** can be sensed in several motifs pointing backwards and forwards. The Andrey of the short story, who had graduated from the philological faculty of the university ten years before, but refused to undertake any kind of job, had no definite profession and liked to play his violin, is an echo of, and a variation on, the Andrey of *Three Sisters,* who had never even taken his degree, and tried to find consolation in playing his violin. The snapping of a string on Andrey Andreyevich's violin at midnight, causing general laughter, but in the given narrative context also suggesting the impracticability of his plans to marry Nadya, would seem to point forward to the mysterious sound of the breaking harpstring in *The Cherry Orchard,* so rich in symbolic overtones of the passing away of things.

The little boys banging the fence and teasing Nadya by calling her a bride prefigure the people who take Varya's betrothal to Lopakhin for granted.

Chekhov's mosaic technique, raised to a high level of perfection in his late plays and put to very effective use in *The Cherry Orchard,* also appears in **"The Betrothed."** Hinging on the central mosaic piece of Nadya's sudden change of mind, and subdivided into six small chapters, themselves almost reading like miniature short stories, the narrative of **"The Betrothed"** contains a number of minor but telling mosaic-like details. When Nadya realizes that her life is shallow and her fiancé is silly, and plucks up courage to say so to her mother, Nina Ivanovna, she, with an unexpected fit of temper, complains that Nadya and Granny torment her to death, and declares that she wishes to live and to be free. At first glance, her somewhat incongruous vehemence seems to be strange; after all, it was she who only a short while before was trying to convince Nadya that she must marry Andrey. All the same, Nina's reaction is psychologically perfectly understandable. As a mother, she wishes Nadya to marry the bishop's son. As a woman, she feels insulted at the thought that she has a marriagable daughter. Nadya's refusal to marry Andrey shocks her in her social function; her daughter's prospect of marriage upsets her body and soul; she abhors the idea of being made an elderly lady. The two insults intermingle since they threaten the same person, the psychic protests they elicit are but negative reactions of the same personality, and in this sense they are interchangeable. That is why Nina emphasizes with such passion that she is still young when Nadya speaks *against* marrying Andrey. The woman is speaking, as it were, through the mask of the mother. Nevertheless, even if the vexation is the same, yet the incongruity is there; the two contiguous mosaic pieces are deliberately and ingeniously ill-fitting.

Nadya is a rational being, she sees the incompatibility of Nina's attitude with the situation, and finds her crying and cuddling mother small, pathetic and silly; in fact, a further argument to leave home and go to university. Chekhov saves the reader the explanation; he is content to show the maladjustment of the two mosaic pieces and by implication reaches a true dramatic effect.

In their general psychology, the two short scenes in the story bear some resemblance to an equally—and equally unexpectedly—passionate exchange of words between Ranyevskaya and Trofimov in *The Cherry Orchard.* The conversation is also based on the mosaic principle. Ranyevskaya complains to Trofimov that her lover is a millstone about her neck, drawing her down, but she loves that stone, and cannot live without it. Trofimov displays a rational attitude, though it is emotionally motivated, stating that Ranyevskaya's lover has robbed her, is a worthless creature and a despicable wretch. Though Ranyevskaya admitted her lover was a savage creature only a moment before, Trofimov's words hurt her innermost feelings no less than Nadya's do Nina's, and she (Ranyevskaya) calls Trofimov a prude, a comic fool, a freak, who at twenty-seven still behaves like a schoolboy, and who at his age, were he a man, ought to have a mistress. A beautiful woman is talking, as it were, from behind the mask of a dutiful lady;[23] a personal offence is avenged by a personal affront; a rational remark causes an emotional eruption whose blast sends an outraged Trofimov down the stairs at a speed greater than he wished to go.

Another characteristic example of Chekhov's application of the mosaic principle of composition in **"The Betrothed"** is the seemingly innocent juxtaposition of a ponderous statement and a casual—and apparently inappropriate—question. Nina declares that lately she has been dealing with philosophy and makes a pronouncement to the effect that in her opinion the most important thing is that all life should flow, as it were, through a prism. Nadya, for her part, asks Nina about Granny's state of health. No long explanation is needed to express Nadya's (and the author's) opinion about the value of Nina's philosophizing.

Connected by numerous threads to the short story, and dramatizing various kinds of short-story-related motifs, *The Cherry Orchard* may be considered a summary of the main uses of the short story in Chekhov's dramatic art.

The technique of his mostly funny one-acters, especially those dramatizing an accidental yet telling story-like turn in a farcical manner, is recapitulated in Act III of *The Cherry Orchard.* In the scene in question, Varya becomes furious with Epikhodov, the counting-house clerk nick-named two and twenty misfortunes, who plays billiards, breaks the cue, goes wandering about the drawing-room like a visitor when there is a dancing party going on, protests against being taken to task, and further outrages Varya, who has expelled him from the room, by talking back from behind the door threatening to lodge a complaint against her. Thinking Epikhodov is coming back, Varya snatches a stick, and swings it heavily—at the very moment when Lopakhin is entering the room. He receives the blow, rapidly develops a bump and greets Varya with an ironical "very much obliged to you."[24]

If, however, the scene is viewed in a broader dramatic context, for all its farcical, indeed slapstick quality, it can be recognized as part and parcel of a more complex and grim situation characterized by tragicomic overtones. Before quarrelling with Epikhodov, Varya was teased by Trofimov as Madame Lopakhin, and since she takes Lopakhin quite seriously, while he only takes her lightly, Trofimov's tactless joke cuts deep. Varya considers Epikhodov a mere servant, and his awkwardly circumstantial courting of Dunyasha hardly serves to calm Varya's nerves. And, last but not least, the uncertainty surrounding the fate of the estate causes an increasing nervous tension which is soon exploded by Lopakhin's terse statement, appropriately expressed in a fearfully short, silence-provoking sentence, that he has bought the cherry orchard. The scene is rounded off by Varya taking the keys of the household from her waist-band, and flinging them on the floor in the middle of the drawing-room. Thus the scene she leaves with a broken heart is very different from the one she entered with comic anger.

The cascade connection of short-story-oriented dramatic units is also recognizable in the structure of the play. The framework of the drama is provided by the arrival (Act I) and departure (Act IV) of Ranyevskaya, which—like those of Arkadina and Trigorin in *The Sea-Gull,* of Elena and Serebryakov in *Uncle Vanya,* and of the soldiers in *Three Sisters*—upsets the semblance of naturalistic and impressionistic stasis and sets the action of the play into short-story-inspired capillary motion.

In Act II Ranyevskaya tells the story of her life: how she married a man who made nothing but debts, and drank himself to death; how she became the mistress of another man and lost her son, who was drowned in the river; how she fled to France, nursed her sick lover, was robbed and abandoned by him for the sake of another woman; how she tried to poison herself unsuccessfully and, yearning for her homeland, returned home to the old family nest, the cherry orchard. Although nobody seems to listen very attentively to her words, her narrative gives the pre-history of the dramatic plot, motivates her general attitude, subsequent deeds and even the lack of them (her inability to part with the orchard), and charges the atmosphere with dramatic tension.

Her past-oriented stance is counterpointed by the future-looking attitude of Trofimov, who also has a strong influence on Ranyevskaya's daughter, Anya. The truths expressed in the former plays by Treplev and Nina, Voynitsky and Astrov, Tusenbach, Vershinin and Irina, are proclaimed in *The Cherry Orchard* by Trofimov. If for Ranyevskaya the "all, all white"[25] orchard with its fairy-like radiance is the very image and symbol of beauty, purity, childhood and innocence beckoning from a faded past, for Trofimov the symbol changes its meaning, turns towards the future, becomes enlarged and is transsubstantiated:

> All Russia is our garden. The earth is great and beautiful—there are many beautiful places in it. . . . Think only, Anya, your grandfather, and great-grandfather, and all your ancestors were slave-owners—the owners of living souls—and from every cherry in the orchard, from every leaf, from every

trunk there are human creatures looking at you. Cannot you hear their voices? . . . We are at least two hundred years behind, we have really gained nothing yet, . . . we do nothing but theorise or complain of depression or drink vodka. It is clear that to begin to live in the present we must first expiate our past, we must break with it; and we can expiate it only by suffering, by extraordinary unceasing labour. . . . my soul was always, every minute, day and night, full of inexplicable forebodings. I have a foreboding of happiness, Anya. I see glimpses of it already. . . . Here is happiness—here it comes! It is coming nearer and nearer; already I can hear its footsteps.[26]

For the time being, however, only Varya, the narrow-minded, kopek-pinching housewife, is coming, putting an abrupt end to Trofimov's overflowing effusion and somewhat exaggerated vision of a bright future, and giving a short-story-like, ironic twist to the surging enthusiasm of the perennial student. The reminiscences from the short story **"The Betrothed"** are unmistakable. The irony is also fostered by the fact that Trofimov's ideal of a life of work is, for the moment, put into practice by the profiteering Lopakhin, just as Gregers Werle's idealist claims concerning mutual sincerity are realized by his father, the cynical merchant, and Mrs. Shörby in Ibsen's *The Wild Duck,* and like the way in which Hickey's aim to get rid of lying pipe-dreams is put into effect in his act of murdering Evelyn in O'Neill's *The Iceman Cometh.* All the same, Trofimov's idealism is not annihilated by the irony of his position; the idealism and the irony in the play only qualify but do not extinguish one another. Trofimov's credo may be impracticable in terms of its immediate implementation, but it is as imperishable as the social and moral trend it expresses.[27]

Act III represents an important narrative-dramatic unit in the action of the play. Against the background of a dancing party, which—for all its apparent casualness and merry-making—strikes the spectator as a dance of death, a strong tension is built up. While Ranyevskaya is dancing, her brother Gaev is attending an auction at which the cherry orchard is sold. The new owner of the orchard, Lopakhin, has good reasons to gloat: he has become sole master of an estate where his father and grandfather used to be slaves, where they were not even allowed to enter the kitchen. He loses no time in taking the axe to the cherry trees, turning a beautiful landscape into a lucrative business venture.

In Act IV the dramatic momentum of the play is enhanced by the energy of yet another short-story-slanted twist. Ranyevskaya is taking leave of her home, garden and friends, and starts back to Paris to squander what little money she has got left. Lopakhin is also leaving; he orders the house to be locked for the winter, and moves to Harkov to look after his business affairs. Neither the former nor the present owner of the house knows that Firs, the 87-year-old, seriously ill valet, has been left locked up in the house. Is this an accidental event?

It is certainly not a deliberate action. Before her departure Ranyevskaya is possessed by two major worries: she has to look after Firs, and she ought to find a husband for Varya. Looking at her watch five minutes before leaving the house, she actually asks Anya what has happened to the old valet, and Anya reassures her that the young valet, Yasha, took Firs to the hospital in the morning. Upon Ranyevskaya's further inquiry even Lopakhin gives her an encouraging answer: he seems to be willing to marry Varya—although later, in a scene finely and effectively understated, he avoids making a proposal. Varya also asks Anya whether Firs has been taken to the hospital, and when she is assured that Firs has been cared for, she warns Anya that the note for the doctor must also be sent. Before locking the door, even Lopakhin asks whether they have all assembled.

In spite of all this, leaving Firs behind and locking him up in the deserted house is a kind of accident which generalizes the relation of lord and servant, is dramatically necessary and socially typical. The universality of the scene is by no means impaired but rather increased by the fact that Firs served his lords most willingly, stayed on with his old master even after the emancipation of the serfs, is of the opinion that those were the happy times when both the peasants and the masters knew their places, and even in his last words grumbles anxiously that Gaev has not put his fur coat on and has gone off in his thin overcoat. The realistic depth and the neatly stratified objectivity of Chekhov's dramatic art are apparent in his ability to realize and represent with a tragicomic clarity the fact that the fundamental nature of the relationship between lord and servant is not changed by mutual goodwill, and the problem cannot be solved by the capitalist development represented by Lopakhin either.[28] It is this insight which gives an ironic quality to the tragically tinged elegiac words of Ranyevskaya as she is saying good-bye to her one-time home and to the disintegrated values of her life: "We are going—and not a soul will be left here."[29] Not a soul, save for the officious, helpful valet locked up by his well-meaning masters, left behind and condemned to slow death through long starvation by both his former and present lords. Chekhov's tragicomic view confronts Ranyevskaya's and Firs' patriarchal illusions with the essence of reality. It retains, magnifies, and even exaggerates them in the fancies of the characters, but disclaims, deflates and dispels them before the judgement of the audience. It is from the simultaneity of intuition and judgement that the Chekhovian unity of psychological portrayal and social representation is derived.

From these cascade connected short-story-like dramatic units it is the narrative-dramatic twist in Act III (the revelation of the sale by auction of Ranyevskaya's cherry orchard to Lopakhin) that has been given the greatest prominence. Here Chekhov's dramaturgy incorporates the third conspicuous use of the short story design: the coincidence of a short-story-oriented and a dramatically constructed turn at the apex of the play, usually at its penultimate structural division.

The presence of the mosaic composition is to be witnessed practically everywhere in *The Cherry Orchard.*

With sudden changes of emphasis, direction and evaluation, this strategy exposes the non-viability of a past turned into a beautiful but impracticable illusion. The result is usually a tragicomic interpretation of the fanciful and the real, the high and the low, the elegiac and the prosaic, the pathetic and the ridiculous.

After her return from Paris, Ranyevskaya greets her country, house and home, her people, relatives and servants with tears. Far from doubting in the slightest the subjective sincerity of her momentary feelings, Chekhov makes the audience feel their objective flimsiness. Ranyevskaya loves her country so tenderly that returning after her long absence, she could not look out of the window of the train: she kept crying; and when she is beside herself with joy that she finds Firs alive, the old and deaf valet's answer is simply: "the day before yesterday."[30] In Chekhov's early one-act plays utterances of this kind remained on the level of farcical situations or stereotype caricature. In *The Cherry Orchard,* however, they separate illusion from reality while maintaining the appearance of illusion. Since the characters are the captives of their illusions, they are not aware of the discrimination they are making themselves. The dramatist understands his *dramatis personae,* but he also takes an external view of them.

When Lopakhin suggests to Ranyevskaya that she should pay her debts by cutting the cherry orchard up into building plots and letting them for summer villas, his offer sounds reasonable. When Gaev calls Lopakhin's impassioned little speech "all rot",[31] and Ranyevskaya retorts that the only remarkable thing in the whole province is the cherry orchard, Lopakhin seems to be cut down to size; his offer implying the cutting down of the orchard appears in a vulgar light. When, however, Gaev addresses a rhetorical speech to the hundred-year-old bookcase, Yasha hands Ranyevskaya her medicine, and Pishchik, the boorish and impecunious landowner, takes the whole boxful of pills with a mouthful of kvass, it becomes obvious that the old form of life possesses an outmoded, outdated, old-fashioned, imbecile, sick and crude face as well. The mosaic technique produces an effect of light and darkness providing the onlooker with what might be termed the *pointillisme* of value judgements. Nevertheless, the illumination of the whole of the mosaic pattern from the direction of the future renders the *pointilliste* relativity of evaluation itself relative, and establishes a reliable, if distant, point of reference.

This point seems to give coherence to the mosaic design, no matter how incoherent its separate elements may be. Lepikhodov, the garrulous clerk, cannot "make out the tendency"[32] he is precisely inclined for; he does not know whether he wishes to live or to shoot himself. He always carries a revolver, but all the same, he appears to be no less cautious not to be overwhelmed by sorrow than Ranyevskaya, who actually attempted suicide but failed to kill herself. These figures already lack the intransigence of Ivanov, Treplev or even Voynitsky (in *The Wood Demon*). Anya talks from her heart of hearts when she comforts her mother, telling her she will work hard for her examination, and, having passed that, will set to work to be of help to her, but the spectator feels that Anya's promise remains unrealizable, and knows that while making it, Anya continues to build the kind of tragicomic conflict which burst out in **Uncle Vanya.** The mosaic pieces seem to be related to one another as much within as between the plays. Gaev making an ornate and sentimental speech to his old bookcase strikes the on-looker as a caricature of Ranyevskaya cherishing her dear old orchard; and when he becomes a bank clerk, calls himself with seeming reassurance and self-importance a financier, and—repeating one of his favourite billiard terms—immediately adds "cannon off the red",[33] he in-voluntarily caricatures himself. When Anya's former governess, Charlotta, who does not even know her moth-er, and with the loss of the orchard loses her job and income, picks up a bundle, nurses, dandles and fondles it like a baby, imitates its crying only to throw it back among the other packages, then she, anticipating the grotesque gestures of the absurd drama, expresses what Gaev, representing a recurring type of 19th century Rus-sian fiction and drama, formulates explicitly: "We have become of no use all at once."[34]

One of the most beautiful examples of the mosaic meth-od in the Chekhovian oeuvre is the enigmatic sound of a breaking string evoking rich overtones. It is heard at a long-abandoned old shrine, near a well in the open coun-try. Ranyevskaya and her company are sitting plunged in thought, perfectly silent. The general stillness is further increased by the monotonous muttering of Firs. *"Sud-denly there is a sound in the distance, as it were from the sky—the sound of a breaking harp-string, mournfully dying away."*[35] Is it simply a snapped string on Epik-hodov's guitar? The merchant-minded Lopakhin thinks it is a bucket fallen and broken in the pits somewhere very far away. His interpretation is practical, orientated towards everyday and industrial life; it is sober and ob-viously non-symbolic. The eccentric Gaev, who during lunch in a restaurant improvised an unsolicited lecture on decadent poetry for the waiters, still attempts to give a possible but more refined and imaginative explanation for the sound, guessing it might have come from a bird of some sort, possibly a heron. Trofimov, the truth-seek-ing perennial student supposes it must have been an owl. The sensitive and neurotic Ranyevskaya living in and from her past reaches out for an unreal cause suggesting a ghostly symbolic meaning when she shudders and finds the sound horrid. Firs, himself a ghost of the past haunt-ing the present, reinforces the ominously weird and ghast-ly impression: "It was the same before the calamity—the owl hooted and the samovar hissed all the time."[36] Upon Gaev's asking him before what calamity the signs had appeared, Firs is ready with the answer: "Before the emancipation."[37]

Considering that the emancipation involved the possibil-ity of Firs' liberation (even if the valet did not take the opportunity and continued serving his lords), his remark brings the tragic poetic symbol down to earth with an unexpected comic fall. Nevertheless, the symbol retains its elegiac—tragic, symbolic-lyric connotations as well.

Firs' comment is followed by a pause rather than laugh-ter on the stage: Chekhov's subtle humour based on a minor modification of the angle of vision is lost on Ranyevskaya's company; for them the emancipation was certainly not liberation, but rather a historical calamity indicating the decay of the old feudal order. Their inabil-ity to sense the comic incongruity of Firs' remark only strengthens the spectators' conviction that one of the functions of the mosaic technique is to relate the subjec-tively doleful to the objectively grotesque.

The establishment of a relationship of this kind, howev-er, is not an irrevocable single act; it is rather a polar-ization within fusion, counteracted by fusion despite polarization. The sound interpreted so differently by the various characters rings *in the distance,* it seems to have come *from the sky,* it reminds one of a *breaking harp-string, mournfully dying away,* and leaves behind what it emerged from: perfect stillness. Appearing in a stage direction, it makes the author's voice audible, too. And, last but not least, it is heard once more, in a structurally emphatic position, at the very end of the play, after the last words of the locked-up Firs and followed by deep silence in which nothing is heard but *"the strokes of the axe in the orchard."*[38] If the vegetation of the patriarchal illusion has an indelibly comic side to it, its death is not without elegiac and tragic overtones in the total pattern of the Chekhovian tragicomedy relying on so many uses of the short story design.[39]

. . . . .

Chekhov's great interest in short story techniques as dramatic devices was well-founded in his artistic out-look, his view of the world. On October 22, 1901, he wrote an enthusiastic letter to Maxim Gorky praising his first play *Smug Citizens* (or *The Petty Bourgeois*) of which he had read three acts. He would give, he stated, a great-er emphasis to Nil's figure and part, but he also suggest-ed to Gorky that he should render Nil more self-con-tained and modest:

> do not contrast him with Piotr and Tatyana, let him be by himself and them by themselves, all wonderful, splendid people independent of one another. When Nil tries to seem superior to Piotr and Tatyana, and says of himself that he is a fine fellow,—the element so characteristic of our decent working man, the element of modesty, is lost. He boasts, he argues, but you know one can see what sort of a man he is without that. Let him be merry, let him play pranks through the whole four acts, let him eat a great deal after his work—and that will be enough for him to conquer the audience with.[40]

Chekhov was certainly right in censuring Nil's rhetoric, as Gorky himself acknowledged by return of post. But the difference between Chekhov and Gorky is not only that of the experienced master and the talented beginner; there lurks a difference of outlook in Chekhov's lines as well. Chekhov did not appreciate the fact that in Nil's figure Gorky had portrayed a plebeian hero with poten-tially revolutionary energies, and not just a modest and merry lad playing pranks and eating a great deal. It is the plebeian drive of his new historical type which was destined to decrease the isolation of people around him. Nil in *Smug Citizens,* as Satin in *The Lower Depths,* or Sintsov, Ryabtsov and Akimov in *Enemies,* represents the force of integration and solidarity criticizing and attacking the old order of disintegration and fragmentation.[41]

The failure to see in Nil's type the unifying force capable of fighting against the social and moral deadweight of alienation and fragmentation, and the claim that Nil should not be contrasted with such characters as Piotr and Tatyana, inevitably lead to the concept that each of the characters ought to be left by himself or herself, i.e. "independent of one another". In the narrative structure of the play such a sort of "independence" results in a short-story-oriented dramatic strategy, and, in its most developed form, a mosaic design.

But even if Chekhov found Nil's level of consciousness, self-expression and dynamism exaggerated, he, too, like Tusenbach, had a presentiment of the promise of the future; he, too, fostered sometimes weaker, sometimes stronger hopes that "The time is at hand, an avalanche is moving down upon us, a mighty clearing storm which is coming, is already near and will soon blow the laziness, the indifference, the distaste for work, the rotten boredom out of our society."[42] This enabled him to see the independence and isolation of his figures as only relative, and to arrange the short-story-rooted fragments and mosaic traits of his characters in such a way that the total pattern, the dramatic design of a meaningful human truth is recognizable. The fragments may and do limit each other; they are not, however, mere splinters, unrelated chips, but interlocking parts of an emerging whole which they represent and present.

Besides the view of relative isolation, there is another feature of Chekhov's world concept which helps in understanding his preference for building up a drama out of short-story-shaped motifs. His manner of formulating a statement shows a conspicuous dichotomy.

He maintains that Russia is "an Asiatic country, where there is no freedom of the press and no freedom of conscience, where the government and nine-tenths of society regard the journalists as enemies, where life is so narrow and so abominable";[43] but he also censures I. L. Shcheglov for considering modern life a miserable bungling and for allowing this attitude to pass in sickly convulsions through all his writings rather than doing justice to contemporary life. "I am far from being enthusiastic about modern times", he adds, "but one should be objective as far as is possible. If things are not agreeable now, if the present is unpleasant, the past was simply abominable."[44]

He complains that in contemporary Russia "there is little hope for a better day";[45] but he also believes in individuals working for the future:

> I see salvation in a few people living their own private lives, scattered throughout Russia;—whether they be

intellectuals or *muzhiks,* the power is in them, though they are few. A man is never a true prophet in his own country; and the individuals of whom I speak play an obscure part in society; they are not domineering, but their work is apparent; whatever comes to pass, science keeps advancing, social self-consciousness increases, moral problems begin to acquire a restless character, etc. And all this is being done despite the procurators, the engineers, the teachers, despite the intelligentsia *en masse,* and despite everything.[46]

In Chekhov's condemnation of "doctors who own villas, greedy civil servants and bribe-taking engineers" that promising and honest students turn out to be as soon as they start their careers; in his indignation over a "hypocritical, false, hysterical, ill-bred, lazy" intelligentsia;[47] and in his praise of straightforward, self-sacrificing individuals weathering the general storm, appreciating, constituting and increasing human values, awaiting and promoting better days to come, it is not difficult to recognize the future-oriented views of Vershinin and a number of similar characters.

Chekhov records the facts of isolation, alienation and uncivilized backwardness with bitter precision:

> What is there to talk about? We have no politics, we have neither public life nor club life, or even a life of the streets; our civic existence is poor, monotonous, burdensome, and uninteresting. . . . We are stuck in our profession up to our ears, it has gradually isolated us from the external world. . . . In short, for our silence, for the frivolity and dullness of our conversations, don't blame yourself or me, blame the climate, the vast distances, what you will, and let circumstances go on their own fateful, relentless course;[48]

—but he ends the sentence with "hoping for a better future."[49] He declares unambiguously:

> It seems to me that the writer of fiction should not try to solve such questions as those of God, pessimism, etc. His business is but to describe those who have been speaking or thinking about God and pessimism, how, and under what circumstances. The artist should be, not the judge of his characters and their conversations, but only an unbiased witness.[50]

But he also points out no less unambiguously:

> Let me remind you that the writers who we say are for all time or are simply good, and who intoxicate us, have one common and very important characteristic; they are going towards something and are summoning you towards it, too, and you feel not with your mind, but with your whole being, that they have some object, just like the ghost of Hamlet's father, who did not come and disturb the imagination for nothing. Some have more immediate objects—the abolition of serfdom, the liberation of their country, politics, beauty, or simply vodka, like Denis Davidov; others have remote objects—God, life beyond the grave, the happiness of humanity, and so on. The best of them

are realists and paint life as it is, but through every line's being soaked in the consciousness of an object, you feel, besides life as it is, the life which ought to be, and that captivates you. And we? We! We paint life as it is, but beyond that—nothing at all. . . . Flog us and we can do no more! We have neither immediate nor remote aims, and in our soul there is a great empty space. We have no politics, we do not believe in revolution, we have no God, we are not afraid of ghosts, and I personally am not afraid even of death and blindness. One who wants nothing, hopes for nothing, and fears nothing, cannot be an artist.[51]

This is, clearly, an attitude fairly different from that of an unbiassed witness, even if partly seriously, partly humorously and politely, Chekhov includes himself in his cultural diagnosis.

Once he seems to accept the idea of specialization:

> . . . it is not the artist's business to solve problems that require a specialist's knowledge. It is a bad thing if a writer tackles a subject he does not understand. We have specialists for dealing with special questions: it is their business to judge of the commune, of the future, of capitalism, of the evils of drunkenness, of boots, of the diseases of women. An artist must judge only of what he understands, his field is just as limited as that of any other specialist . . . you confuse two things: *solving a problem* and *stating a problem correctly*. It is only the second that is obligatory for the artist;[52]

at another time he appears to reject it: "We write mechanically, merely obeying the long-established arrangement in accordance with which some men go into the government service, others into trades, others write";[53] and however much he is preoccupied in his works with stating his problems correctly, and refrains from didacticism or preaching, he certainly does not leave it to non-literary specialists "to judge of the future"; and he flatly condemns "the sluggish, apathetic, lazy, philosophizing, cold intelligentsia . . . who are unpatriotic, dreary, colourless . . . who grumble and hotly deny *everything,* because it is easier for a lazy brain to deny than to affirm".[54]

Throughout his career as a writer, Chekhov betrays an extraordinary and increasing ability to show the innermost feelings, desires, yearnings and illusions of his characters. Nevertheless, he often changes his perspective from the internal to the external view, and takes good care not to subjectify his figures: "to depict horse-thieves in seven hundred lines", he writes, "I must all the time speak and think in their tone and feel in their spirit, otherwise, if I introduce subjectivity, the image becomes blurred and the story will not be as compact as all short stories ought to be."[55] The objective, external, or even cold glance may furnish a comical antidote against sentimentality, but, most characteristically of Chekhov, it may also serve the purpose of throwing an emotion into relief. Commenting on L. A. Avilov's story "On the Road," by way of advice, he remarks: "when you depict sad or unlucky people, and want to touch the reader's heart, try to be colder—it gives their grief as it were a background, against which it stands out in greater relief. As it is, your heroes weep and you sigh. Yes, you must be cold."[56]

Then, with a gracefully sudden and graciously reassuring turn, he adds: "But don't listen to me, I am a bad critic. I have not the faculty of forming my critical ideas clearly. Sometimes I make a regular hash of it."[57]

Chekhov's statements and counter-statements are, sometimes, derived from the same period; in other cases they are separated by a gap in time, showing a modification of concepts and attitudes. In his last creative phase, at the preparatory stage of the 1905-7 bourgeois democratic revolution, his views became radicalized. But throughout his creative life, his attitude was characterized by a counter-balancing duality, the dichotomy of belief qualified by doubt, scepticism tempered by trust.[58] Such a stance involved constant changes of emphasis, attention and emotional disposition; presupposed incessant modifications in the direction of the argument, the thrust of the statement, and the outcome of the discussion; and resulted in repeated sparks flashed between the two intellectual and emotional poles of a case, the pros and cons of the matter.

It, therefore, created a very favourable climate for the short story which, with its pointed or more subdued turns in narrative or mood, transference of the artistic centre of gravity, and miniature dramatic *peripeteia,* is ideally suited for representing shifts of attitudes, modulations of moods, adjustments and readjustments of standpoints, or alterations in the angle of vision.

Where the outlook is marked by a careful deliberation of the various sides, merits and demerits of the given situation, the totality of the artistic view of the world, such as the genre of drama provides, is also bound to be composed of such units. This factor, besides the sense of relative isolation, goes a long way to explain why Chekhov transmitted his human, humane and dramatic message by incorporating the technique of the short story in his plays, and why in his hand this method, even the mosaic pattern, became a means to underline the complexity of objective reality in its full richness and variety, with its occasional stasis, uncertain direction, osmotic movements, resignation, fears and hopes.

NOTES

[1] *Letters on the Short Story, the Drama, and Other Literary Topics* by Anton Chekhov, selected and edited by Louis S. Friedland (New York, 1966), p. 171.
[2] Op. cit., p. 125.—Leo Tolstoy also identified Chekhov's mosaic technique, related it to impressionism, and considered Chekhov's method a new manifestation of realism: "His mastery is of a high order. I have reread his stories, and with great enjoyment. Several of them, for example, 'Kiddies', 'Sleepy', 'In Court', are true pearls. I have read absolutely everything in succession with great pleasure. Yet, it is a mosaic, there really is no main thread."
An unusual technique of realism has developed in Chekhov, and in contemporary writers generally. In Chekhov everything is so true, it's like an illusion, his works produce the impression of some sort of stereoscope. He throws down his words seemingly haphazardly and, like the impres-

sionist painter, he achieves surprising results with his brush strokes." See in Aleksandr Goldenveizer, *Vblizi Tolstogo* (Moscow, 1959), pp. 68-9. Tolstoy also realized that, when viewed from a proper perspective, the seemingly disparate parts come to form a picture: "As an artist, Chekhov cannot be compared with earlier Russian writers such as Turgenev, Dostoevsky, and myself. Chekhov has his own particular form, like that of the impressionists. You watch the man seemingly indiscriminately spread his paints, whichever come within his reach, and those paints seem to have no interrelationships whatsoever. But if you stand back at some distance and look, a harmonious impression opens up before you." See in Petr Sergeienko, *Tolstoy i ego sovremenniki* (Moscow, 1911), 228-9.—Analysing Chekhov's story "On the Road," Savely Senderovich establishes the presence of a mosaic design: "From the very outset the narration is constructed as a chain of momentary impressions. The switch from one impression to another is brought about by means of a change in the viewpoints. The brevity of every separate impression and the frequency of change in viewpoint create an original mosaic. . . . The poetic function of the mosaic of viewpoints described above is to break the continuity of time-flow, to reprogram the latter into a series of individually distinct quasi-spatial elements, and to transform a successive into a quasi-simultaneous system." Savely Senderovich, "Chekhov and Impressionism: An Attempt at a Systematic Approach to the Problem", translated by R. B. Mathison and T. Eekman. In Paul Debreczeny and Thomas Eekman (eds.), *Chekhov's Art of Writing: A Collection of Critical Essays* (Columbus, Ohio, 1977), pp. 140, 147, cf. p. 149.—For some other treatments of Chekhov's relationship to impressionism see: Petr M. Bitsilli, *Tvorchestvo Chekhova: Opyt stilisticheskogo analiza* (Sofia, 1942), pp. 38-52; Dmitri Chizhevsky, "Chekhov in the Development of Russian Literature", in Robert L. Jackson (ed.), *Chekhov: A Collection of Critical Essays* (Englewood Cliffs, 1967), p. 54; Charanne C. Clarke, "Aspects of Impressionism in Chekhov's Prose", in P. Debreczeny and T. Eekman, op. cit., pp. 123-33.

[3] Cf. M. Valency, *The Breaking String: The Plays of Anton Chekhov* (London, Oxford, New York, 1969), pp. 54, 62, 215, 298.

[4] M. Valency calls the action of *The Sea-Gull* "a complex tissue of interlaced stories", op. cit., p. 135, cf. pp. 167-8.

[5] M. Valency, op. cit., p. 238.

[6] Cf. M. Valency, op. cit., pp. 212-6; 222-3, 235, 237-8.

[7] Chekhov, *Three Sisters,* translated by Constance Garnett. *Nine Plays of Chekov* (New York, 1973), p. 99.

[8] Op. cit., p. 107.

[9] Op. cit., p. 113.

[10] The loneliness of the dramatic figures and the isolation of their aspirations (also often met with in Strindberg), and the fact that at the turn of the century dramatic characters tend to talk beside, rather than to, one another, sometimes expressing themselves in juxtaposed monologues rather than confronted dialogues, are parallel with the growing independence of musical voices in contemporary dramatic (operatic) and symphonic music (Debussy). The tendency is later intensified in both expressionist drama (Kaiser, the young O'Neill) and music (Schönberg, Berg, Webern). Chekhov's mosaic technique also implies an early manifestation of composing the drama in separate interlaced voices which, however, are ultimately related to, if contrasted with, one another, and are referred to both each other and to the possibility of a harmonious resolution of separation and dissonance by the promise of a distant and rather indistinct future. O'Neill's last plays are also characterized by the simultaneity of presenting and resolving isolation.

[11] *Nine Plays of Chekhov,* p. 119.

[12] Op. cit., p. 121.

[13] Op. cit., p. 133.

[14] Op. cit., p. 134.

[15] Op. cit., p. 138.

[16] Op. cit., pp. 140-1.

[17] Op. cit., p. 141.

[18] Op. cit., p. 145.

[19] Op. cit., p. 146.

[20] Ibid.

[21] It is partly the abstract nature of Sasha's and Trofimov's social and moral perspectives that is responsible for the slightly humorous way they are treated. It should, however, be borne in mind that Chekhov—as appears from one of his letters to his wife Olga Knipper—knew more about Trofimov than what he explicitly represented: one of the reasons why it took Trofimov so long to finish his studies was his having been sent down from university several times. Cf. M. Valency, op. cit., p. 264. For parallels between "The Betrothed" and *The Cherry Orchard* compare M. Valency, op. cit., pp. 257-60. For a discussion of the story see Thomas Winner's "Theme and Structure in Chekhov's 'Betrothed'", *Indiana Slavic Studies,* 3 (1963).

[22] Chekhov, *The Cherry Orchard,* translated by C. Garnett. *Nine Plays of Chekov* (New York, 1973), p. 89.

[23] The doubling of the personality into a role-playing and a vital part in Chekhov's plays implies a tentative pointer to O'Neill's full-fledged dual, divided personalities and direct or indirect (actual or quasi-) mask technique in plays like *The Reckoning, The Hairy Ape* (later production version), *The Ancient Mariner, All God's Chillun Got Wings, Marco Millions, The Great God Brown, Lazarus Laughed, Strange Interlude, Dynamo, Mourning Becomes Electra, Days Without End, More Stately Mansions, Long Day's Journey Into Night,* or *A Moon for the Misbegotten.*—Cf. O'Neill, "Memoranda on Masks", "Second Thoughts", "A Dramatist's Notebook", in O. Cargill et al. (eds.), *O'Neill and His Plays* (New York, 1970), pp. 116-22.—Eugene M. Waith, "Eugene O'Neill: An Exercise in Unmasking", in J. Gassner (ed.), *O'Neill: A Collection of Critical Essays* (Englewood Cliffs, 1964), pp. 29-41.

[24] *Nine Plays of Chekov,* p. 85. According to its sub-title, *The Cherry Orchard* is a comedy. In his letter of September 15, 1903, to Madame Stanislavsky, Chekhov also refers to the play as "a comedy, in parts a farce." *Letters on the Short Story . . . ,* p. 159. In fact, however, the total testimony of the drama proves it to be rather a tragicomedy with an added emphasis on the comic aspect, but certainly not without serious elegiac-tragic implications. In this, too, *The Cherry Orchard* sums up and develops further Chekhov's dramatic achievement.

[25] *Nine Plays of Chekov,* p. 66.

[26] Op. cit., pp. 77-8.—The vivid and tragic image of a lifegarden also crops up in a number of Chekhov's narrative works such as "The Black Monk" (1894), "The Teacher of Literature" (1894). "Ariadna" (1895), "The House with a Mezzanine" (1896), or "The Lady with the Little Dog" (1898). Cf. Z. Paperny, *A. P. Chekhov* (Moscow, 1960), Chapter 12.

[27] Cf. V. Ermilov, *Anton Pavlovich Chekhov* (Moscow, 1949), pp. 400-15.—E. Triolet, *L'histoire d'Anton Tchekhov* (Paris, 1954), pp. 189-203.—G. Berdnikov, *A. P. Chekhov* (Leningrad, 1970), pp. 468-94.—L. Speirs, *Tolstoy and Chekhov* (Cambridge, 1971), pp. 213-23. —J. L. Styan, *Chekhov in Performance: A Commentary on the Major Plays* (Cambridge, 1971), pp. 239-337.—G. Berdnikov, *Chekhov-Dramaturg* (Moscow, 1972), pp. 225-52.—M. L. Semanova, *Chekhov-Hudozhnik* (Moscow, 1976), pp. 186-223.—B. Hahn, *Chekhov: A Study of the Major Stories and Plays* (Cambridge, New York, Melbourne, 1977), pp. 12-36.

[28] Cf. Chapter 7 of *My Life.*

[29] *Nine Plays of Chekov,* p. 94.

[30] Op. cit., p. 62.

[31] Op. cit., p. 63.

[32] Op. cit., p. 70.

[33] Op. cit., p. 91.

[34] Ibid.

[35] Op. cit., p. 76.

[36] Ibid.

[37] Ibid.

[38] Op. cit., p. 95.

[39] Ultimately the breaking harp-string as a symbol is associated with the past, passing away, evanescence. The cherry orchard as a symbol also becomes charged with past properties, qualities and values which in the present have changed into impractical, if beautiful, illusions. But by way of Trofimov's generalization ("All Russia is our garden", op. cit., p. 77.) this symbol is also capable of enlargement and opening up towards the future. The two sets of symbols indicate their dramatic use: they are aligned according to the requirements of the conflict, the governing tension of the play.

[40] *Letters on the Short Story. . . ,* p. 179.

[41] When in Chekhov's long short story, "In the Ravine" the greedy Aksinya scalds the infant Nikifor, his mother Lipa shrieks and then the courtyard becomes silent. Nobody dares to go into the kitchen to find out what has happened. When in Gorky's *The Lower Depths* Vasilisa scalds Natasha, a rebellion of indignation breaks out, and Vasilisa's husband, Kostilyov, the owner of the night lodging, is killed.—Nevertheless, the claim of giving a true dramatic cross-section of contemporary society and its performance brought with it the adoption of a measure of the mosaic method even in Gorky's dramaturgy. This is true not only of the early plays written under Chekhov's influence, but also of the later dramas in which Gorky speaks fully in his own voice. This point of contact between Chekhov's and Gorky's dramatic art calls attention to the objective fragmentation of a social state which received an adequately realistic representation in the two playwrights' works conceived in different ideologies. With Gorky, however, the short-story-patterned, mosaic-like units of the dramatic action tend to unite into a more extensive and therefore more novel-oriented design than with Chekhov.

[42] *Nine Plays of Chekov,* p. 101.

[43] Letter to A. S. Suvorin, April 24, 1899. *Letters on the Short Story . . . ,* p. 278.

[44] Letter to I. L. Scheglov, Jan. 20, 1899. *Letters on the Short Story . . . ,* p. 222.

[45] Letter to A. S. Suvorin, April 24, 1899. *Letters on the Short Story . . . ,* p. 278.

[46] Letter to I. I. Orlov, Feb. 22, 1899. *Letters on the Short Story . . . ,* p. 287.

[47] Ibid., pp. 286-7.

[48] Letter to V. I. Nemirovich-Danchenko, Nov. 26, 1896. *Letters on the Short Story . . . ,* pp. 287-8.

[49] Op. cit., p. 288.

[50] Letter to A. S. Suvorin, May 30, 1888. *Letters on the Short Story . . . ,* p. 58. Cf. Chekhov's letter to A. N. Pleshcheyev, Oct., 1889. "I am afraid of those who look for a tendency between the lines, and who are determined to regard me either as a liberal or as a conservative. I am not a liberal, not a conservative, not a believer in gradual progress, not a monk, not an indifferentist. I should like to be a free artist and nothing more . . ." *Letters on the Short Story . . . ,* p. 63.

[51] Letter to A. S. Suvorin, Nov. 25, 1892. *Letters on the Short Story . . . ,* pp. 240-1.

[52] Letter to A. S. Suvorin, Oct. 27, 1888. *Letters on the Short Story . . . ,* pp. 59-60.

[53] Letter to A. S. Suvorin, Nov. 25, 1892. *Letters on the Short Story . . . ,* p. 241.

[54] Letter to A. S. Suvorin, Dec. 27, 1889. *Letters on the Short Story . . . ,* p. 263.

[55] Letter to A. S. Suvorin, April 1, 1890. *Letters on the Short Story . . . ,* p. 64.

[56] Letter to Madame Avilov, March 19, 1892. *Letters on the Short Story . . . ,* p. 97.

[57] Ibid.

[58] The interplay of belief and disbelief is well-founded in Chekhov's social experiences and therefore it can express the certainties and uncertainties of the time. But it is also motivated by the author-doctor's awareness of his incurable illness. He felt old when he was 35 (Letter to V. V. Bilibin, Jan. 18, 1895, *Letters on the Short Story . . . ,* p. 118), but one should bear in mind that he died at the age of 44.

Richard Peace (essay date 1987)

SOURCE: "Chekhov's 'Modern Classicism,'" in *The Slavonic and East European Review,* Vol. 65, No. 1, January 1987, pp. 13-25.

[*In this essay, Peace uncovers elements of Greek classical tragedy in* The Seagull *and* Three Sisters.]

Chekhov's real career as a dramatist may be seen as having begun with *The Seagull*: it marks the onset of the truly Chekhovian theatre. In this play the young writer Treplev issues something in the nature of a manifesto with his denunciation of the conventional theatre of his day and the staging of his own play, designed to impress (and to reproach) his mother—a pillar of that theatre, and her lover—the established writer Trigorin.

It is tempting to see in Treplev's demands for new forms in the theatre a manifesto launched by Chekhov himself. Indeed his fellow writer Potapenko (whose own life, as we know, provided material for Chekhov's plot) records that at the time of writing *The Seagull* Chekhov was himself constantly talking of the need for 'new forms'.[1] Nevertheless Treplev's playlet is obviously far removed from Chekhov's own innovatory achievements. But it is only, perhaps, a matter of degree: for if we consider that Chekhov's own revolutionary theatre was a subtle com-

bination of naturalism and symbolism, in which speech and poetic mood replaced overt action, then all these elements, but in a extreme and uncompromising form, also characterize the playlet staged by Treplev. Here, however, naturalism is that supposedly real background against which the piece is played, yet a naturalism which also turns out to be symbolic; for Treplev intends his audience to take the 'real' lake and the 'real' moon as eternal symbols. His playlet, too, emphasizes poetry and diction at the expense of action, yet the diction is artificial, elevated and anything but Chekhovian. The aborted playlet appeals to none of the other characters, with the possible exception of Dorn, the form is too 'new'—it is too *avant-garde.* Later in Act II his mother will hurl the epithet 'decadent' at her son.[2]

By an odd irony Chekhov's play itself suffered a similar fate on its opening night in St Petersburg, on 17 October, 1896. The audience reacted to *The Seagull* as though it, too, were *avant-garde,* decadent, rubbish and we are told that there was at least one voice from the pit which cried out 'C'est de Maeterlinck'.[3] Maeterlinck and the decadent movement often seem synonymous for Chekhov: both were in his mind as he worked on *The Seagull.* Thus, in a letter to Suvorin of 2 November 1895, he reports on the progress of his play: 'It is growing, but slowly', and he goes on to give Suvorin advice for his own theatre: 'Why do you not attempt to put on Maeterlinck in your own theatre? If I were the director of your theatre, I would make it a decadent one in two years, or would try to make it so. The theatre might, perhaps, seem strange, but it would nevertheless have a profile (*fizionomiya*)'.[4]

Two years later, Chekhov had not, of course, made Suvorin's theatre 'decadent', nor had he staged his own *avant-garde* play *The Seagull* with success, but he was nevertheless again writing to Suvorin to communicate his enthusiasm for Maeterlinck: 'I am reading Maeterlinck. I have read his *Les Aveugles, L'Intruse* and am reading *Aglavaine et Selysette.* All these are strange, weird things, but the impression is enormous, and if I had a theatre, I would definitely put on *Les Aveugles.* By the way there is wonderful scenery here, with the sea and a lighthouse in the distance.'[5]

Chekhov's interest in the play's natural background (which, of course, is also symbolic) seems to recall his own similar use of the lake and the moon in Treplev's playlet, but his own lack of success with *The Seagull* is obviously in Chekhov's mind; for he goes on to talk about the 'idiotic public' and the need to guard against the failure of his proposed production of *Les Aveugles* by giving the audience a synopsis of the play: 'the work of Maeterlinck, a Belgian writer, a decadent'.[6]

If 1896 is the year in which Treplev's 'decadent' playlet-cum-manifesto was first put before a Russian audience, it is also the year in which Maeterlinck himself published a manifesto for the theatre: *Le Tragique quotidien.* There is no evidence that Chekhov read it, but we do know of his great and continuing interest in Maeterlinck's theatre,[7] and *Le Tragique quotidien* proclaims an aesthetic

David Warner as Treplev, in a 1968 film adaptation of The Seagull *directed by Sidney Lumet.*

theory very close to Chekhov's own, not only in its title, but from its very opening sentence: 'There is a tragic element in the life of every day that is far more real, far more penetrating, far more akin to the true self that is in us than the tragedy that lies in great adventure.'[8]

Maeterlinck rejects violence and high drama on stage as merely superficial tragedy and is disillusioned by what he finds in the conventional theatre: 'I had gone thither, hoping that the beauty and grandeur and the earnestness of my humble day by day existence would, for one instant, be revealed to me . . .'.[9] This is a conception of theatre which is quite close to Chekhov's own:

> . . . in life people are not every minute shooting each other, hanging themselves, and making declarations of love. And they are not saying clever things every minute. For the most part, they eat, drink, hang about, and talk nonsense; and this must be seen on the stage. A play must be written in which people can come, go, dine, talk about the weather, and play cards, not because that's the way the author wants it, but because that's the way it happens in real life.

> Let everything on the stage be just as complex and at the same time just as simple as in life. People dine, merely dine, but at that moment their happiness is being made or their life is being smashed.[10]

In rejecting violent dramatic action on stage, Maeterlinck, in *Le Tragique quotidien,* is in search of its opposite extreme—the concept of 'static theatre': 'I do not know whether it be true that a static theatre is impossible. Indeed to me it seems to exist already. Most of the tragedies of Aeschylus are tragedies without movement.'[11]

Thus we see that this so-called 'decadent' is really an admirer of classical norms. A great part of his essay is devoted to an analysis of classical Greek tragedy which reveals where his own roots lie: his plays may be forward-looking and modern, but at the same time they are also backward-looking and classical in the basic concept of theatre which they express. As a recent Maeterlinckian scholar has said: 'Everything within Maeterlinck's plays works towards a cohesive whole. The drama is tightly structured, adhering to the formulas of French classical theatre: unity of time, place and action'.[12]

If we turn once more to Treplev's 'decadent' playlet, we can see that the static quality of its conception is one of its most striking features, set as it is in a cold, distant future when all life has ceased, but it also exhibits other elements of classicism, at however rudimentary a level— be it the simplicity of the set, the elevated diction or the sense of a subject dealing with eternal values.[13] It will be the argument of this article that classical elements, in that modern interpretation advanced by Maeterlinck, are present in at least one other of Chekhov's plays.

But first, let us look at Chekhov's own classical education. There was a thriving Greek community in his native town of Taganrog, and his father insisted on sending Anton and his brother Nikolay, as young boys, to the local Greek school. He hoped that this would provide an entrée for them into the Greek business community of the town. The instruction was entirely in modern Greek, and the first requirement was for them to learn this language, which they singularly failed to do because of the lack of any real tuition. After this dismal experience Anton was sent to the Taganrog *gimnaziya*—a type of institution often rendered in English as 'Classical School'. A large part of the curriculum was, in fact, devoted to the study of the classical languages, Latin and Greek. Indeed, after 1871, these subjects occupied more than forty per cent of a pupil's time in such schools.[14] The reasons for this were political; it was considered that Classical languages inculcated better attitudes, as opposed to the 'nihilism' often associated with the study of the natural sciences. The Latin master of the school was particularly despised; he acted as an informer, and he may well have served as a prototype for Belikov, the repressive teacher of Greek whom everybody fears, in Chekhov's story **"The Man in a Case"** (**"Chelovek v futlyare"**). There is perhaps a further reflection of the author's schooldays in the much milder portrait of a teacher of Latin, that toady to officialdom, Kulygin, in *The Three Sisters*.[15]

Teaching of these subjects in the Classical Schools concentrated on language and grammar, and there does not appear to have been much attention paid to classical literature. In any case, Chekhov was obviously not strong in Greek—he was kept down in the third and fifth forms for failing mathematics, geography, and ancient Greek. It seems doubtful, therefore, whether the future author derived much real benefit from his classical education.

Intellectual attitudes to the classics, however, began to change towards the end of the century, at least in a certain section of the intelligentsia. In Russia, as in the West in the case of Maeterlinck, it was figures associated with the growing symbolist movement who brought this about, in particular, D. S. Merezhkovsky and Vyacheslav Ivanov. The historian of Russian literature Prince D. S. Mirsky calls Merezhkovsky 'the principal figure of the "modern" movement during its first stages'.[16] He sees him as having developed what he calls 'a religion of

Greek antiquity', and thinks his chief merit lies in his popularization of the values of the ancient world and those of the Renaissance. He writes: 'After Merezhkovsky, Florence and Athens became something more than mere names to the Russian intellectual'.[17]

Merezhkovsky, although younger than Chekhov, was among the first to award him serious critical attention. His article 'An Old Question about a New Talent' appeared in the *Northern Courier* (*Severnyy vestnik*) in 1888 but was not entirely well received by Chekhov.[18] However, he got to know Merezhkovsky quite well. During a visit to Italy in 1891, he spent time with the Merezhkovskys in Venice,[19] he also corresponded with him, though, unfortunately, Chekhov's letters have been lost.[20] Nevertheless, from references to Merezhkovsky in other letters, he appears to have been prepared to give Merezhkovsky his due, but to have had reservations about some of his ideas and the way in which he constantly sought to propound them.[21]

One of Merezhkovsky's chief services to the cause of classical culture was his translations of Classical Greek tragedy, which between 1891 and 1896 inclusively appeared at the rate of one a year.[22] It was Merezhkovsky's translation of *Antigone* which was staged by the pupils of the L. F. Rzhevskaya classical school for girls (*Zhenskaya gimnaziya*), where Chekhov's sister Masha was a teacher. This took place in the hall of the Stroganov School on 18 April 1897,[23] and the following year, the Moscow Arts Theatre itself was preparing to put the play on. Nemirovich-Danchenko promised to send Chekhov a copy of the translation, and on 21 October 1898, Chekhov wrote to him: 'I am waiting for *Antigone.* I need it very much' (Zhdu *Antigonu.* Nuzhna ochen').[24] Four years later he had himself acquired a full set of Merezhkovsky's translations, for in 1902 he sent his six Greek tragedies, individually numbered, as a gift to the public library in Taganrog, as part of the regular donation of books he thought the library of his native town should have.[25] We may therefore assume that, whatever the shortcomings of his earlier classical education, Chekhov was aware of the achievements of Greek classical tragedy, not only from his personal contacts with Merezhkovsky but also from his translations.

What relevance has all this for Chekhov's own dramatic writing? We have seen Maeterlinck's championship of the classical theatre in *Le Tragique quotidien*; we have also seen the closeness of Maeterlinck's theories to the dramatic practices of Chekhov himself, and his interest in Maeterlinck at the time of writing *The Seagull,* and later. Yet one important qualification must be borne in mind. In *Le Tragique quotidien* Maeterlinck is discussing *tragedy,* and this is a designation for his own plays which Chekhov seems consciously to avoid. *The Seagull,* for all its tragic ending, he calls a 'comedy'. His next play, *Uncle Vanya,* is subtitled 'Scenes from Country Life'. Yet to call *Uncle Vanya* Chekhov's next play, in the true chronological sense, is very misleading, since it is a reworking of the earlier *Wood Demon.* When this reworking was undertaken is the subject of debate, but it cannot have been later than 1895.[26] ***The Three Sisters,*** begun in 1900, is the first play which could possibly show any influence of the aesthetic theories of Maeterlinck's *Le Tragique quotidien* of 1896. In fact, of all Chekhov's four major plays, ***The Three Sisters*** is the one that comes nearest to tragedy and, as if to make some concession in this direction, it bears the subtitle 'drama'.

Maurice Valency writes in his study, *The Breaking String*: 'Chekhov came very readily under the spell of Maeterlinck. In ***The Three Sisters,*** as much is conveyed symbolically as is expressed in words'.[27] This is undoubtedly true, but one should not assume that the symbolic expression of ideas in the theatre was in any sense new, nor the sole province of Maeterlinck. He, after all, had himself pointed to the symbolic qualities in classical Greek tragedy, and similar views were already being championed by Merezhkovsky. Writing in 1894, in his introductory article: 'In place of a Preface (to the tragedy *Oedipus Rex*)', Merezhkovsky calls *Oedipus Rex* a '*symbolic* tragedy', italicizing the word *symbolic,* and he claims: 'Indeed take away from it its symbolism and what will remain? Tragic chance'.[28] Merezhkovsky takes a sophisticated view of the play's symbolism, for him the chief symbol in *Oedipus Rex* is not even present on stage—it is the already banished sphinx: 'Over all the tragedy, like a symbolic statue over a shrine, there reigns the sphinx—the incarnation of fate'.[29] The manifestation of the sphinx in the play itself, he argues, is an inner one: 'The sphinx is no longer external, not in nature, but internal, in the soul of the conqueror.' The sphinx is 'the secret of life, the secret of every human conscience'.[30]

Let us now turn to ***The Three Sisters.*** From the outset, Chekhov presents his audience visually with a classical symbol—a row of columns. Their functional purpose is also symbolic for they divide the stage in two. In the front section, there are three women—the three sisters: in the rear—three men: Tuzenbakh, Chebutykin, and Solyonyy. The opening conversation of the women, which consists principally of the reminiscences and hopes of Olga and Irina, is punctuated at crucial moments from behind the columns by an apparently unrelated conversation carried on by the men. It is obvious that these snatches of conversation are to be taken by the audience as a commentary on the main conversation conducted by the sisters—a commentary on the theme of Moscow as a symbol of future hope, and as escape from the present. Chekhov, in this commentary from behind the columns, is introducing his audience to a device which is a modern, symbolic re-interpretation of the function of the chorus in Greek tragedy. The choric effect, of course, is not sustained in this form throughout the play, but having suggested it as a classical device from the very beginning, Chekhov will continue the 'indirect commentary' by a variety of means throughout his play. The characters on stage often speak apparently at random, uttering thoughts, or asking questions, which appear unconnected with what has gone before. On the one hand, this may be interpreted as 'naturalistic'—the way people speak in real life, but on the other hand, such randomness can also provide the suggestion of a commentary.

Maeterlinck, writing in *Le Tragique quotidien* about Sophocles' tragedy *Philoctetes,* makes a point which seems to bear on Chekhov's own use of dialogue:

> And, indeed, the only words in the play are those that at first seem useless, for it is therein that the essence lies. Side by side with the necessary dialogue will you almost always find another dialogue that seems superfluous, but examine it carefully, and it will be borne home to you, that this is the only one that the soul can listen to profoundly, for here alone is it the soul that is being addressed.[31]

Maeterlinck is obviously suggesting a metaphysical dimension behind the 'superfluous dialogue' of the true tragic poet, but at a less elevated level his analysis also suggests much that is consonant with Chekhov's dramatic practices. He goes on to ask: 'Is it the thing you say or the reply you receive that has the most value? Are not other forces, other words we cannot hear, brought into being, and do not these determine the event?'.[32]

Dialogue in ***The Three Sisters*** is permeated by 'words we cannot hear'. They are conveyed through a number of devices: indirect commentary, the use of pauses, and, perhaps most important of all, literary allusion. It is the 'unheard words' of literary allusion which can, in Maeterlinck's phrase, 'determine the event'. Thus the death of Tuzenbakh, the one overtly tragic event in the play, is conditioned by literature—Solyonyy's self-identification with the Lermontovian malevolent hero. Here, too, in a strange, roundabout way we seem to come back to the prototypes of classical Greek tragedy: Valency in his study on Chekhov makes the following point about Lermontov's troubled and trouble-seeking heroes: 'For all their theatricalism his characters foreshadow more or less clearly the neurotic hero of our time, the modern counterpart of the tragic protagonist of Sophocles'.[33]

The most striking literary allusion in ***The Three Sisters*** belongs to Masha: her enigmatic quotation from the Prologue to Pushkin's *Ruslan and Lyudmila.* These are the first actual words she utters in the play, and she feels compelled to recite them again towards the end of Act I, and finally in a slightly fuller, though garbled, version towards the end of Act IV. The reference contains 'words we cannot hear'. The full quatrain, to which her garbled quotation in Act IV relates, is as follows:

> Near the curved seashore is a green oak tree.
> On this oak tree is a golden chain,
> And day and night a learned tomcat
> Keeps going round and round on the chain.

These verses in their full form would be readily supplied by an educated Russian audience brought up on them from childhood. For Masha, they represent a riddle. They appear to baffle her (but perhaps only partly so). The riddle, however, has a solution: Masha herself is the 'green oak tree' (the oak is a symbol of strength, its greenery denotes youth),[34] but it is in a remote backwater and bound by a 'golden chain' (her marriage bond) to a 'learned tomcat'—the pedantic schoolmaster, Kulygin, who continually fusses round her. Thus Masha's perplexing quotation metaphorically refers to her own position at the opening of the play and to her reversion to this same position in Act IV on the departure of Vershinin. It is the riddle of her own 'tragic' situation.

Merezhkovsky's analysis of *Oedipus Rex* placed great emphasis on the concept of the riddle as the kernel of the play. Oedipus, he argued, having solved the riddle of the Sphinx, was confronted by an even greater riddle—that of his own being. The Sphinx was no longer external but inside himself. Masha, too, is confronted by a second and greater riddle: the mystery of being, of life itself. In Act II, she challenges Tuzenbakh's views on the predestined flight of migratory birds, which appears to make all philosophy irrelevant:

MASHA Isn't there some meaning?

TUZENBAKH Meaning? Look out there, it's snowing. What's the meaning of that? (*a pause*)

MASHA I think a human being has got to have some faith, or at least he's got to seek faith. Otherwise, his life will be empty, empty . . . How can you live and not know why the cranes fly, why children are born, why the stars shine in the sky . . . You must either know why you live, or else . . . nothing matters . . . everything's just wild grass . . . (*a pause*)[35]

We have here, surely, something akin to what Maeterlinck saw as the very essence of Greek tragedy: 'la situation de l'homme dans l'univers'.[36] This exchange between Masha and Tuzenbakh finds its final, despairing echo in the words which conclude the play, but now it is in the mouths of different characters.

CHEBUTYKIN . . . What does it matter? Nothing matters!

OLGA If only we knew, if only we knew![37]

Thus it is given to Olga, whose explanations of the sisters' position opened the play, to end it on a note of enigmatic pessimism, and here we come close to that metaphysical dimension of classical tragedy, hinted at in the Maeterlinckian formula: 'it is the soul that is being addressed'. We also come close to Merezhkovsky's view of *Oedipus Rex*: 'Perhaps in the poetry of the entire world, not excluding that of our own day, there has never been expressed more hopeless and terrifying pessimism'.[38]

Oedipus, Merezhkovsky argues, is a tragic figure because of the irony of fate: 'the wise man who saw through into the secrets of the Sphinx' (*Mudrets prozrevavshiy v tayny sfinksa*) is turned into a 'pathetic, blind man'.[39] Bearing this in mind we can see that there is irony too in the surname which Chekhov has given his sisters, for *Prozorov* is from the same root as Merezhkovsky's *prozrevavshiy* 'having seen through' (cf. *prozorlivyy*—'perspicacious'). For all the implications of their name, the

sisters are blind to what is going on around them. Even that embodiment of indifference, Chetbutykin, can chide them for it in Act III: 'Why are you staring at me? Natasha's having a nice little affair with Protopopov and you don't see it. You sit here seeing nothing, and meanwhile Natasha's having a nice little affair with Protopopov . . .'.[40]

'Perception' in the play, however, is not limited merely to 'sight'. The sisters' 'deafness' is also stressed in this same act Olga and Irina hide behind the screens in their bedroom and refuse to hear when Masha wishes to tell them of her illicit love for Vershinin. The process is repeated slightly later with Andrey, when he seeks to have a heart-to-heart talk with his sisters about the problems that are germane to their very existence in the house. Earlier in this same act Masha had herself indignantly raised the question of her brother's financial plight: he has mortgaged their house, and yet it is Natasha who has the money. She is silenced by Kulygin, who discourages his wife from speaking about it, and now when Andrey comes to have his heart-to-heart talk, Masha leaves, asking him to postpone the discussion. A similar combination of indignation, yet reluctance to speak up where it really matters characterizes Masha's attitude to the duel in Act IV. In fact, no one is prepared to say or do anything that would stop it, and so Tuzenbakh is needlessly killed.

It might seem from all this that the three sisters embody the characteristics exemplified in those three allegorical figures: 'Hear no evil', 'See no evil', and 'Speak no evil', but the allegorical suggestions which Chekhov himself appears to make are on quite a different plane. At the play's opening, he focuses attention on the sisters as a symbolic group of three, and again at the play's end. Their classical overtones are those of *Parcae*, the three weird sisters themselves, an identification strengthened by their 'perspicacious' surname—*Prozorovy*. Nevertheless, any such hint can only be ironical, for they are not the mistresses of fate, they are its victims. Indeed, it would be truer to see them as embodiments not of fate, but of fatalism. The Soviet scholar T. K. Shakh-Azizova in her book on Chekhov and the Western European theatre of his time (*Chekhov i zapadno-yevropeyskaya drama yego vremeni*) speaks of Maeterlinck's favourite paradox: 'Sighted people in his works are spiritually blind, and the blind are unusually perspicacious' (*prozorlivy*—again).[41] The motif of 'three sisters' who are also blind is a symbolic theme found in the poetry of Maeterlinck. In his *Quinze chansons* (Fifteen Songs) of 1896 there are two poems entitled: 'Les Trois Soeurs aveugles' (The Three Blind Sisters) and 'Les Trois Soeurs ont voulu mourir' (The Three Sisters Wanted to Die). Moreover, the first of these was used as a song in his play *Pelléas et Melisande* in its sixth edition which came out in 1898.[42]

The teleological symbol of Chekhov's play is Moscow. For the sisters it represents not only a happy future, but the lost happiness of the past. Yet it is not a goal to be attained by action, but rather through fervent wish, buoyed up by portent and omen. Thus, when Irina thinks that a game of patience has worked out, she takes this as a sign that they will be in Moscow. Fedotik, however, points to a card that has been misplaced. The good omen has been inverted.

In classical tragedy the workings of fate are also given expression through omen. Thus, Tiresias in *Antigone* draws a dire warning from the fighting of birds.[43] In *The Three Sisters,* birds not only form part of the symbolic argument of the riddle of life, they occur again in Act IV as a portent of departure. To the ancient Greeks the fate of Oedipus was seen to lie outside him: it was an external force beyond his control. Freud, in psychologizing the myth, pointed to the internal nature of Oedipus' fate, and Merezhkovsky, as we have already seen, made a similar suggestion, when he claimed that the Sphinx (the symbol of fate) was no longer outside Oedipus, in nature, but inside his own being. The allegorical overtones of Chekhov's three sisters are more in keeping with this modern view: the sisters can be identified with 'The Fates', only in as much as they are the embodiment of their own fates. At the same time, the past, as for Oedipus, seems to condition the present and the future. This is symbolically stated through the three sisters themselves at the opening of the play. Masha is wearing black, for the past, it is the anniversary of her father's funeral; Irina is wearing white, the day is also her name-day, and she is young and looking to the future; Olga (although it is Sunday) is in the dark blue of work, her schoolmistress's uniform, and is engaged in the present, the everyday routine of correcting schoolwork. Masha's dark mood is a cloud on a day which should be one of festivity. The past cannot be exorcised.

The father and the mother of the Prozorov family still exert an influence, as it were, from the grave. The father has been their driving force, making them learn foreign languages, forcing Irina to get up at seven o'clock, insisting on an academic career for Andrey. A year after his death the standards he set them remain, but they are drifting, unable either to see their meaning or to give them substance. As for the mother, to Chebutykin, at least, she still seems alive in Irina, and his old, unrequited love for her conditions his attitude both to Irina and, more ominously, to her fiancé, Tuzenbakh—it is yet another factor behind the ill-fated duel. As we have seen, Merezhkovsky saw the symbol of fate in *Oedipus Rex* to be embodied in the non-appearing figure of the Sphinx. In similar manner, *The Three Sisters* is remarkable for its fateful cast of non-appearing characters—the father, the mother, Protopopov, Kulygin's headmaster, Vershinin's wife and daughters—all of whom exert their baleful influence on the lives of those on the stage.

It is, of course, in its formal characteristics that Chekhov's *Three Sisters* most differs from classical tragedy: prose is substituted for verse; everyday conversation for elevated diction. Nor would we expect Chekhov to observe the three classical unities of action, place, and time. Yet, in a loose sense, Chekhov does observe them. Unity of action is preserved in as much as inchoate sub-plots, such as the affair between Natasha and Protopopov, or

the quarrel between Solyonyy and Tuzenbakh are not allowed to take on a separate dramatic life of their own, but are skilfully subordinated to the central dramatic line. The death of Tuzenbakh occurs out of sight and is reported to those on stage by Chebutykin: Chekhov's version of the classical device of the 'messenger'.

The unity of place is not infringed only in the sense that the action unfolds against the background of the same house (inside in two of its rooms and outside in its garden). Unity of time, however, is far more difficult to perceive in a play which with each act moves from one season to another. Nevertheless, there is a sort of stasis which Chekhov seeks to impose on the flow of time. Shortly after the opening of Act I, the clock on stage, in a very deliberate fashion, strikes twelve, and Olga links the sound to an event of exactly a year ago—the father's funeral: 'The clock struck twelve then, too'. The final act also begins at midday and brings with it a death. Thus, with a backward glance at a former sad midday, the play moves on from its own opening midday to a final noon of further tragedy.

The true form of the classical tragedy is obviously too rigid for the flexibility and sense of informality which Chekhov seeks in his modern theatre. Indeed, he mocks the ancients' veneration for form in the words of that absurd figure, the Latin master Kulygin, in whom Chekhov perhaps recalls something of his own classical schooling.

> The Romans enjoyed good health because they knew how to work and how to rest. They had *mens sana in corpore sano.* Their life had a definite shape, a form. The director of the school says that the most important thing about life is form . . . A thing that loses its form is finished. That's just as true in our ordinary everyday lives.[44]

In Chekhov's play itself, 'ordinary, everyday lives' are more in evidence than Kulygin's all important classical form. Nevertheless, beneath the surface flow of life there is a definite shape and form, and a sense of measure which ultimately derive from the spirit, if not the letter of Greek classical tragedy. As we have seen, *The Three Sisters* does exhibit certain characteristics of this tragedy, but in a more modern guise, as they were interpreted by Merezhkovsky and propounded by Maeterlinck.[45] In his modern classicism, Chekhov reveals the 'tragic element in the life of every day' rather than the 'tragedy that lies in great adventure'.

NOTES

[1] See R. Hingley, *A New Life of Chekhov,* London, 1976, p. 221.
[2] A. P. Chekhov, *Polnoye sobraniye sochineniy i pisem v tridtsati tomakh,* Moscow, 1974-83 (*Sochineniya*), XIII, p. 40 (hereafter referred to as *PSS*). See also A. P. Chekhov, *Plays* translated and with an introduction by Elisaveta Fen, Harmondsworth, 1959, p. 159 (this translation hereafter referred to as *Penguin*).
[3] As recorded in the diary of S. I. Smirnova-Sazonova. See *PSS (Pis'ma),* VI, p. 522.
[4] *PSS (Pis'ma),* VI, p. 89. The editor of this volume, N. I. Gitovich, suggests that it was perhaps under the influence of this advice that Suvorin

staged the first Maeterlinck play in Russia on 8 December 1895 in the Theatre of the Literary-Artistic Circle (*Teatr literaturno-artisticheskogo kruzhka*). The play is referred to as a one-act play *Tayny dushi* ('Secrets of the Soul'). This does not appear to correspond to the title of any Maeterlinck play. It may be the one-act play *Intérieur,* but the Bal'mont translation of this is *Tam vnutri* ('There inside'). In connection with the staging of this play, Chekhov wrote to Suvorin on 13 December 1895 'You are called in one newspaper a protector of decadence' (*PSS (Pis'ma),* VI, p. 108). The evidence of S. I. Smirnova-Sazonova suggests that Suvorin was sympathetic to the 'decadents': 'He began to argue with me about the decadents. He sympathizes with them because of their search for novelty and the unknown, he says that some genius or other will be brought up on this tendency'. Ibid., p. 451.

⁵ Letter of 12 July 1897, *PSS (Pis'ma)* VII, p. 26.

⁶ Loc. cit.

⁷ Thus he wrote to his wife on 17 December 1902: 'It would not be a bad thing to put on the three plays of Maeterlinck, as I said, with music' (*PSS (Pis'ma)* XI, p. 94). In October 1904 (after Chekhov's death) the Moscow Arts Theatre produced *Les Aveugles, Intérieur,* and *L'Intruse* in the translations of K. D. Bal'mont (ibid., p. 403). Stanislavsky records that in the spring of 1904, although Chekhov was already seriously ill, he was interested in the rehearsals of this production. Stanislavsky had to keep him informed on its progress, show him models of the scenery and explain his staging. See K. S. Stanislavsky, 'A. P. Chekhov v Moskovskom khudozhestvennom teatre', *Chekhov v vospominaniyakh sovremennikov (vtoroye dopolnennoye izdaniye),* Moscow, 1954, p. 391. There is, however, an account of Chekhov's negative attitude to Russian 'decadents' towards the end of his life, and his view that there was no place in Russian literature for these 'Russian Maeterlincks'. See Ye. Karpov, 'Dve posledniye vstrechi s A. P. Chekhovym', ibid., p. 576. See also *PSS (Pis'ma),* XII, pp. 231, 341.

⁸ See Maurice Maeterlinck, 'The Tragical in Daily Life', in *The Treasure of the Humble* (translated by Alfred Sutro), London, 1897, p. 97.

⁹ Ibid., p. 104.

¹⁰ Quoted in A. Skaftymov, 'Principles of Structure in Chekhov's Plays', in *Chekhov, A Collection of Critical Essays,* edited by R. L. Jackson, Englewood Cliffs, N. J., 1967, p. 73.

¹¹ Maeterlinck, op. cit., p. 106.

¹² Bettina Knapp, *Maurice Maeterlinck,* Boston, 1975, p. 175.

¹³ Balukhatyy has pointed to the influence of the writings of Marcus Aurelius on Treplev's playlet. See S. D. Balukhatyy, *Problemy dramaturgicheskogo analiza Chekhova,* Leningrad, 1927, p. 105.

¹⁴ See R. Peace, *Chekhov, A Study of the Four Major Plays,* New Haven and London, 1983, p. 170.

¹⁵ Hingley, op. cit., p. 14.

¹⁶ D. S. Mirsky, *A History of Russian Literature, Comprising a History of Russian Literature and Contemporary Russian Literature,* edited and abridged by F. J. Whitfield, New York, 1960, p. 421.

¹⁷ Ibid., p. 414.

¹⁸ See E. J. Simmons, *Chekhov, A Biography,* London, 1963, p. 166 and *PSS (Pis'ma),* II, pp. 53-54, 69.

¹⁹ See letter to I. P. Chekhov, 24 March/5 April 1891, *PSS (Pis'ma),* IV, p. 202.

²⁰ See *PSS (Pis'ma),* I, p. 312.

²¹ See letters to A. S. Suvorin of 7 March and 17 December 1892. *PSS (Pis'ma),* V, pp. 8, 143-44, 365. In his letter of 7 March, Chekhov refers disparagingly to Merezhkovsky's 'quasi-Goethe regime' apparently meaning his continual conversations on literature.

²² They appeared as follows:
1891 Aeschylus: 'Prometheus Bound' *Vestnik Yevropy,* No. 1
1892 Sophocles: 'Antigone' Ibid. No. 4
1893 Euripides: 'Hippolytus' Ibid. No. 1
1894 Sophocles: 'Oedipus Rex' *Vestnik inostrannoy literatury,* Nos. 1-2 (including Merezhkovsky's 'Preface')
1895 Euripides: 'Medea' *Vestnik Yevropy,* No. 7
1896 Sophocles: 'Oedipus at Colonus' Ibid. No. 7

²³ See *PSS (Pis'ma),* VII, p. 397.

²⁴ Ibid., p. 303.

²⁵ See Letter to P. F. Iordanov, 19 March 1902, *PSS (Pis'ma),* x, p. 216.

²⁶ For a discussion of this, see Hingley, op. cit., pp. 224-26.

²⁷ M. Valency, *The Breaking String, The Plays of Anton Chekhov,* New York, 1966, p. 244.

²⁸ D. S. Merezhkovsky, *Polnoye sobraniye sochineniy* (Reprint of Moscow 1914 edition), Hildesheim, New York, 1973, xx, p. 5.

²⁹ Ibid., p. 3.

³⁰ Ibid., p. 4.

³¹ Maeterlinck, op. cit., p. 111.

³² Ibid., p. 113.

³³ Valency, op. cit., p. 22.

³⁴ Cf. a similar symbolic use of an oak tree by Tolstoy in *War and Peace:* L. N. Tolstoy, *Polnoye sobraniye sochineniy,* Moscow, 1928-58, x, pp. 153-54, 156-57. See also Peace, op. cit., p. 79.

³⁵ *PSS (Sochineniya),* XIII, p. 147 (*Penguin,* p. 282).

³⁶ See Maurice Maeterlinck 'Le Tragique quotidien', *Le Trésor des humbles,* Paris, 1898, p. 190 (and translation Maeterlinck, op. cit., p. 108).

³⁷ *PSS (Sochineniya),* XIII, p. 188 (*Penguin,* p. 330) Senelick sees this ending as: 'a laconic equivalent of the final chorus in *Oedipus the King'.* See L. Senelick, *Anton Chekhov,* Basingstoke and London, 1985, p. 116.

³⁸ Merezhkovsky, op. cit., p. 8.

³⁹ Ibid., p. 6.

⁴⁰ *PSS (Sochineniya),* XIII, p. 162 (*Penguin,* p. 301).

⁴¹ T. K. Shakh-Azizova *Chekhov i zapadno-yevropeyskaya drama yego vremeni,* Moscow, 1966, p. 103.

⁴² See Maurice Maeterlinck, *Poésies complètes,* ed. J. Hanse, Brussels, 1965, pp. 183-84, 187-88, 207-09, 217-18, 284.

⁴³ Merezhkovsky, op. cit., XXI, p. 49.

⁴⁴ *PSS (Sochineniya),* XIII, p. 133 (*Penguin,* p. 265).

⁴⁵ For another view of Chekhov's debt to Maeterlinck see L. Senelick, 'Chekhov's Drama, Maeterlinck and the Russian Symbolists', in *Chekhov's Great Plays: A Critical Anthology,* ed. J. P. Barricelli, New York and London, 1981, pp. 161-80.

Laurence Senelick   (essay date 1987)

SOURCE: "Stuffed Seagulls: Parody and the Reception of Chekhov's Plays," in *Poetics Today,* Vol. 8, No. 2, 1987, pp. 285-98.

[*In the essay below, Senelick surveys works that caricature and satirize Chekhov's dramas.*]

Parody, the late Dwight Macdonald has declared, is "an intuitive kind of literary criticism, shorthand for what 'serious' critics must write out at length" (1969:xiii).¹ At its most refined, parody speaks to the in-crowd, those who are closely acquainted with the text being parodied, and who can best appreciate the accuracy of the parodist's hits. In its perception of an author's foibles and tics, parody must be as astute and as keen as any literary analysis; often, it is informed by a clear-sighted affection for its object of concern. The best parodist, at the level of a Max Beerbohm or a Marcel Proust, has so alert an ear for the idiosyncrasies of his author that his imitation may be all but indistinguishable from the original.

Generally, however, parody is normative, aiming to prune the excesses and eccentricities from a work of art. It is, in George Kitchin's definition, quoted by Macdonald, "the reaction of centrally-minded persons to the vagaries of the modes . . . [it is] inveterately social and anti-romantic" (p. 560). But it is only a step from anti-romanticism to philistinism and so, much of what passes for parody falls under the heading of heavy-handed travesty. Rather than subtly evoking the mannerisms of its victims, it wins laughs by transposing pathos to bathos, or by caricaturing the most obvious hallmarks of metre, imagery or diction. This commonly occurs when the parody is intended for a wide public, one to whom an author's name and a few salient traits are more familiar than a close acquaintance with his works. In this case parody is a means of neutralizing the uncomfortably novel, difficult or strange.

At such times parody becomes a useful gauge for the rate of cultural seepage, since it both derives from and contributes to the transmission of an easily assimilated image. An avant-garde artist wins common currency in the popular imagination through parody. Picasso, for example, is regularly associated with a jagged, geometric profile and two eyes nestled on the same side of the nose. Shakespearean style is summed up in improvisational comedy sketches by a couple of "I'faiths" and a sword-thrust. These hints are enough to trigger in the spectator's or reader's brain the sense that he knows what is being mocked and stimulates a laugh of superiority. The problem is that these generalized portraits linger in the cultural memory long after their inaccuracy has been demonstrated by the specialists.

Chekhov presents an excellent example of this low-level mythopoeia. His translucency as a writer enables him to be co-opted by those who explicate him: Stanislavsky's Chekhov is not Prince Mirsky's, and Mirsky's Chekhov is not Leo Shestov's. Yet ironically, it is essentially Shestov's view of the Chekhovian hero as a futile prisoner of life, and of Chekhovian words as sobs that has been transmitted to the imagination of those who never heard of Shestov or, for that matter, ever read a line of Chekhov.

Nowhere is this truer than with Chekhov's drama. When an American pop song alluded to "more clouds of grey / Than any Russian play could guarantee," the lyricist had in mind not Gorky or Artsybashev, but Chekhov and, more specifically, the pseudo-Art Theater productions on the New York stage. This cliché is of early origin, but it did not take shape until Chekhov the dramatist had become associated with the Moscow Art Theater.

From the start of his dramatic career, Chekhov was mercilessly attacked by various factions of critical opinion. The conservatives deplored his seeming inability to follow the rules of dramatic construction; the radicals complained that he did not go far enough in abandoning traditional structures. The "mystical anarchists" denounced him for his lack of spirituality and earthbound positivism, while non-partisan commentators referred to his dramas as "the most undramatic plays in the world," their dominant note one "of gloom, depression and hopelessness" (Mirsky 1927:292-304).[2]

These negative opinions, offered by intelligent and well-informed contemporaries, cannot be dismissed simply as a lack of sympathy or understanding. Modern culture, and the modern theater with it, have become so fragmented that few artists appeal to a majority, especially when their art is dense, ambiguous and low-keyed. For many, Chekhov is an acquired taste, like 12-tone music or Greek olives. But what has stood in the way of a broader acceptance of Chekhov's real qualities has been the caricature passed down since the 1890s. Just as "Dickensian" conjures up images of roast goose and exuberant

bonhomie, so "Chekhovian" has come to mean the twilight zone, a dim and moody penumbra peopled by feckless and maundering eccentrics. And Chekhov himself is seen as "the good doctor," quizzically but kindheartedly shaking his head over these vaporous emanations of his brain.

Chekhov's earliest full-length plays were subjected to satire from journalistic small-fry. Some of this was prompted by his political stance or lack thereof; some by his friendship with the arch-conservative publisher Suvorin; some by the seeming weakness of his dramatic carpentry. One humorist with the pseudonym "I. Grek" [*i.e.,* Y] summed up Chekhov's first performed play ***Ivanov*** as "A drama in four acts about a Jewess, a concertina, a count, virtue, an organ-grinder and a pistol." He was bemused by the fact that each act began with an incident that seemed trivial, and parodied it thus:

Act I (The Ivanov garden)

Ivanov feels a head-ache coming on. . . .

Act II (The Lebedev home)

Lebedev is showing his guests a way that he has invented to wash down vodka with water. . . .

Act III (The Ivanov home)

The curtain rises too soon and the spectator is unexpectedly presented a picture of Dalmatov, Varlamov and Svobodin [actors in the production] drinking vodka on stage. The actors retain their presence of mind and go on drinking vodka as if this were part of the play and talk about pickles and other hors d'oeuvre."

(1889:4-5).[3]

This last joke is particularly revealing. The scene that opens Act III of ***Ivanov*** is one of Chekhov's characteristic experiments. He shows Ivanov's study invaded by the banality of everyday life and submerges the hero's private anguish in a flood of apparently irrelevant chatter. As the Soviet critic Chudakov has noted, what puzzled the satirist was the seemingly "extraneous" elements "which many assumed to be Chekhov's attempt to reproduce real life" (1983:149-152). An ironic layering effect was mistaken as failed naturalism. Another typical reaction was that of the critic of *Artist* [*The Performer*] to Chekhov's next full-length comedy ***The Wood Demon***:

Such ordinary conversations over vodka and hors d'oeuvre have already bored everyone both at home and at friends', and there's no need to go to the theater and sit through four acts of "comedy" to hear ten times how people inquire after the health of some stranger and squabble (Ivanov 1890:124-125).

This misses the point that Chekhov was deliberately juxtaposing minutiae and matters of importance as co-equal in everyday life.

The failure of *The Seagull* at its St. Petersburg première in 1896 called forth a barrage of squibs and pasquinades. For several weeks, the *Peterburgskij listok* [*Petersburg Leaflet*] ran such poems as one that begins with the lines, "Ne zashchitnik on rutiny, novyx form pobornik on" ("He's no champion of routine, he's a defender of new forms"), thus identifying Chekhov with his character, the impotent writer Treplev (Realist 1896).[4] One wag, calling himself "Poor Jonathan," summed up *The Seagull* as "fantastical-lunatical scenes with a prologue, an epilogue, tomfoolery and a flop. (The plot borrowed from a mental hospital)" (Bednyj Ionafan 1896). Another, referring to the actor who played Treplev, summed up the last act as "Apollonsky's study. Ten or so performers, having nothing to do, have played a game of lotto and left" (Rylov 1896). But these fugitive attacks were directed at the plays as ephemeral phenomena; no notion of a specifically Chekhovian drama was under fire.

The gun-sights became more sharply focused when Chekhov was adopted by the Moscow Art Theater as its house playwright. Following the success of the MAT's revival of *The Seagull* in 1898, the Chekhovian ethos came to be perceived as synonymous with the theater's striving for *nastroenie* [mood or atmosphere]. The *bytovie* [true-to-life] productions masterminded by Stanislavsky, with their veristic behavior, elaborate sound effects, frequent and interminable pauses, and general air of muted despondency served to "sell" Chekhov's play to the intelligentsia and the cultivated merchant class that patronized that theater. Chekhov himself protested in vain that the Art Theater misinterpreted or thickened his intentions; it nevertheless provided his literary opponents and the theatrical rear-guard with artillery for their salvos. The more acclaimed the MAT's Chekhov productions, the more vehement were the caricatures of its style. Loudest among the mockers was Viktor Petrovich Burenin (1841-1926).

Burenin, a former colleague of Chekhov's at Suvorin's *Novoe Vremja* [*New Times*], was a well-established playwright and writer of light verse, whose historical dramas made up in technical expertise what they lacked in originality. Burenin stood for the conservative theatergoer who thought Chekhov a poor dramatist because he did not provide the standard peripeteias, *scènes à faire,* strong curtain-lines and messages [*pouchenie*] of the well-made play. At first, he and his faction sought to ignore Chekhov's success, but when the overwhelming kudos for *Three Sisters* had to be acknowledged, Burenin called it a "stupid success" (9280, Jan. 4, 1902), to be attributed to publicity which "hypnotized the public and especially the younger generation while obfuscating any wholesome meaning" (9301, Jan. 25, 1902). Granting Chekhov's talent as a short-story writer, Burenin discounted him as a dramatist for being quaint [*kur'eznyj*], vacuous, flaccid and monotonous, saved only by the Art Theater's stunts. "Chekhov," he declared, "is the minstrel of hopelessness" (10079, March 26, 1904).

Burenin's parodies of Chekhov are therefore not labors of love, but a polemical *reductio ad absurdum*. Under the

pseudonym Count Alexis Zhasminov, he published in *Novoe Vremja* in 1901 "Nine Sisters and Not a Single Fiancé or Talk about Bedlam! A symbolic drama in 3 acts with mood." (The title alludes to Treumann's operetta *Zehn Mädchen und kein Mann,* which was hugely popular on the Russian stage from 1864.) The identification of Chekhov as a symbolist is pertinent, since the stasis and inertia that Burenin loathed in his plays was more typical of Maeterlinck than of the naturalists. "Nine Sisters" is preceded by a cast list, which, in addition to the sisters themselves (Shura, Mura, Dura, etc.) includes "chickens, cocks, an old cow, a suckling pig, a trained maggot, a trained gnat, three trained spiders, a horse, Yid co-eds with sirens, wet rags, a drunken peasant and so forth." As epigraph he chooses the "tram-tam-tam" passage from *Three Sisters* as the most patent example of Chekhov's incoherence.

The opening stage direction, in agreement with Stanislavsky's sedulous procedures, goes on for pages and constitutes Act One in its entirety. After a very convincing rainstorm, the nine sisters, no muses they, enter "in matutinal house-coats, tousled, dishevelled, in down-at-heel slippers, their 'kissers' all made up, and deliberately cast from the worst possible actresses, so that 'realism,' 'truth,' and 'nature' will be all the greater." At first, they speak only in inarticulate sounds—E-e-ekh! A-a-akh! Ik-i-ik! U-ukh!—before launching into the more eloquent exchange of "Tram-tam-tam." When they do start to talk Russian it becomes clear that their state of perennial depression is not mourning for their parents or existential plight, but dismay at the lack of suitors. After a dance number performed by the trained gnat, who is met with "prolonged and friendly applause," they recite in unison "Lord, how boring-making and puke-making! [*Skuchishcha i toshishcha!*] This is what modern life in Russia is like! You could suck rags from boredom!" whereupon they all rush to suck the rags dangling from the prompter's box. The playlet ends with another extended stage direction, during which, in addition to the usual animal noises, the symbolist poet Gordy-Bezmordy [Proud-Faceless] recites lines from Konstantin Balmont's "The Burning Building," the Jewish co-eds blow into the sirens and throw galoshes from the wings, a factory whistle hoots, and a milkman and a herring-vendor peddle their wares. In short, "complete atmosphere" [*Polnoe nastroenie*].

Burenin's scatter-gun technique makes it clear that he was using Chekhov to stand for every tendency in modern drama that he detested. Except for the secondary attributes of staging and sound effects, there is no real comprehension of Chekhov's artistry. Burenin is, nonetheless, interesting as an early exponent of what might be called the "no-nonsense" approach to Chekhov, exemplified by Ivy Litvinov's remark that the three sisters are absurd to yearn for Moscow when they have the price of a ticket in their pocket. To Burenin's mind, the sisters (even Masha apparently) are suffering from terminal virginity: a vigorous love life will instantly dispel the vapors that assail them.

Burenin's later parody in the same vein, *Vishnevoe varenye,* "Cherry Jam on a Treacle Base. A white drama with mood. And not a single act," reduces the actors to playing birds who recite their dialogue entirely in bird-calls, until the Dramatist enters with a large jar of cherry jam and sits down between two stools to address the audience.

> Yes, on the whole life is, so to speak, a hole. What are human beings born for? To fall into the hole. Life has no other meaning. Here I sit in a room in an old, sort of baronial, aristocratic house, though in fact it's remarkably bourgeois. I sit and smear the table with treacly jam made from Vladimir cherries. There in the orchard, the actors and actresses, made up as birds, are chirping and cuckooing. There, beside the table, the property flies are flying on the strings which Messrs. Nemirovich-Danchenko and Stanislavsky are tugging with remarkable effort. The gramophone reproduces the buzzing of flies. What is all this for? Why is all this? For, so to speak, "mood" and the play's success, because without actors and actresses' chirping and cuckooing, without flies' buzzing, it would flop. . . . But in a thousand, in a million years new people will be born. And they too will smear treacly cherry jam on the table as I am now doing. But they, these people of a far-off day, will probably be more intelligent and will not create and present pseudo-realistic plays with mood, in which there is no meaning and in which over the course of four acts characters, for no reason at all, carry on dialogues like those in language primers for French and German. . . .

> (1917:V, 201-202)

Whereupon he quotes some *Bald-Soprano*-like phrases.

Burenin's unwitting premonition that Chekhov is a forerunner of Ionesco is, in retrospect, a happy hit; but nothing could be clearer than that the parodist is confusing the play with the production. The Art Theater's fondness for sound effects of birds and crickets, the "bourgeois" backgrounds of its founders and its audience, and its proneness to sentimentality are the prime targets of Burenin's snide remarks. He fails to see that the playwright may himself be ironizing over his characters and their self-pity, and so he does not manage accurately to burlesque the idiosyncrasies of Chekhovian dialogue.

More successful, because more attentive to linguistic detail, was the Chekhovian parody performed at St. Petersburg's popular "theater of miniatures," the Crooked Mirror. The brains behind the Crooked Mirror were the keen critical intelligence of A. R. Kugel, editor of *Teatr i Iskusstvo* [Theater and Art] and the theatrical flair of his director-in-chief Nikolay Evreinov. Kugel, himself an enemy of directorial excesses, had devoted his theater to satire of literary and artistic fashions familiar to his highly cultured audience. Evreinov the apostle of theatricality was personally dedicated to putting down what he saw as misguided attempts to reproduce real life on stage. Between them they were sympathetic to anti-Stanislavsky skits.

Boris F. Geyer's *The Evolution of the Theater,* performed at the Crooked Mirror in 1910, shows how commonplace

the characteristics of Chekhovian playwriting and the Art Theater approach had become in the public mind in the course of a decade. Geyer's play is a potted history of Russian drama. A love triangle is presented in four different styles, those of Gogol, Ostrovsky, Chekhov and Leonid Andreev. The Chekhovian pastiche, *Petrov,* is a clever intercutting of lines, situations and attitudes from Chekhov's major plays, spliced to create a hilarious portrait of woolly-mindedness. The Chekhovian quintessence that Geyer distilled was far more devastating than Burenin's hamfisted travesties because it was both more affectionate and more alert to the peculiar quirks of Chekhov's style.

The four characters of *Petrov* are Lidiya Petrovna, a black-clad moonstruck romantic; her father, Sklyanka, the typical buffoon with his catchphrases and pathetic memories; Petrov, eternally denouncing the boredom of life; and Semenov, the idealist. By putting only a few twists to Chekhov's own phrases, Geyer managed to reduce the poignancy of a situation to nonsense. Lidiya Petrovna enters to her *Leitmotiv.*

> All last night the old lindens were rustling in the garden . . . the old lindens. . . . That have seen so many tears and sorrows. . . . When we moved here, it seemed to me that we had been buried in a grave . . . a grave. . . . Moscow. . . . Oh, if only I might see Moscow again. . . . (*Sits, burying her head in her hands.*) Moskva . . . Moskve . . . Moskvoy. . . .

By having her inflect the grammatical forms of Moscow, Geyer undercuts any pathos that might adhere. Similarly, Semonov's hopes for the future are deflated: "In a hundred thousand years all of this will be gone, feelings will be so refined, so pure, so imperceptible. . . . There will be no dirty words." Petrov's disgust with mundane existence dwindles into a catalogue of derogatory adjectives: "But until then we shall rot and everything will be grey, disgusting, stupid. . . . I'd like to engrave in sounds all the foulness, all the vileness, all the nastiness, all the vulgarity, all the uselessness of our life." (*Exits, clutching his head.*) LIDIYA PETROVNA. "Poor Vanya. . . . He's yearning. . . . His talented nature is bored and inhibited here."

Because Geyer is more interested in Chekhov's dramatic style than in the Moscow Art Theater trappings (which would later be mocked by Evreinov in *The Fourth Wall* and *The Inspector General*), he includes only the kind of stage directions that are to be found on the page: the offstage gunshots, the watchman tapping, the grand piano playing in the distance. The final moments conflate **The Seagull** with **Uncle Vanya** to produce a masterpiece of bathos.

> (*Offstage a gunshot.*)
>
> LIDIYA PETROVNA. Ah . . .
>
> PETROV. What's that?
>
> (*SKLYANKA enters with a guitar.*)

Harry Andrews as Sorin, Simone Signoret as Arkadina, Alfred Lynch as Medvedenko, and Vanessa Redgrave as Nina, in Sidney Lumet's 1968 film adaptation of The Seagull.

LIDIYA PETROVNA (*rushes to him*). What? What happened? Tell me quickly. . . .

SKYLANKA (*quietly*). The cork popped on a bottle of Bavarian lager. . . .

LIDIYA PETROVNA. Yes? Oh, thank God, I thought. . . .

SKYLANKA (*quietly to Petrov*). Go at once, the doctor has shot himself for good. . . .

PETROV (*clutching his head*). God, how stupid this is . . . how uncivilized this is . . . how absurd, how nasty. . . . (*Exits.*)

SKLYANKA (*sits and plays the guitar*). Doublet off the cushion to the center. . . .

LIDIYA PETROVNA. All last night the old lindens rustled in the garden. . . . Father, I'm depressed, I'm incomprehensibly ill. . . . We shall die. . . .

Gradually, imperceptibly, without life, without motion. . . .

SKLYANKA. We shall doze. . . .

LIDIYA PETROVNA (*sobs*). Yes, yes, you speak the truth, Sklyanochka. . . . We shall doze. . . . (*Falls at his feet and, yawning, lays her head on his lap.*) (*The Watchman's rattle.*) We shall doze. . . .

SKLYANKA (*Yawns, weeps*). We shall doze, Lida . . .

LIDIYA PETROVNA (*weeps*). We shall doze . . .
(Geyer 1976:579-583).[5]

The significance of Geyer's *Petrov* is that it formulates once and for all the standard platitudes about Chekhovian drama, by refusing to recognize that Chekhov contains humor, irony and his own awareness of his characters' shortcomings. Chekhov's lack of popularity in the decades following the Revolution resulted more from this common consensus that he wrote only about gentrified morbidity and despondency than from any real understanding of his themes and methods.[5]

In the English-speaking world, from the very first, the characters in Chekhov's plays were taken to be neurotics and lunatics whose peculiar behavior was not uncommon in their homeland. The usual misapprehension of Chekhov's intent was compounded by the assumption that Russians are like that, that Chekhov inspissates in his writings a native Slavic melancholia or depression. Even the half-Russian William Gerhardi in his novel *Futility* has one character exclaim after a performance of *Three Sisters,* "Good God! How can there be such people? Think of it! They can't do what they want. They can't go off and commit suicide or something" (quoted in Woollcott 1923:10). The outlandishness was not ameliorated by awkward transliterations of Russian names into French or German forms, and the oddness of the patronymic complicated matters. The American critic George Jean Nathan had no patience with "Russian drama with a stage inscrutably occupied by Mishka Vaselenavitch Klooglosevtloff, a retired professor . . . and a heterogeneous and very puzzling assortment of Pishkins, Borapatkins, Sergius Vodkaroffs, Abrezkoffvitchs and Olthidors, all of them in whiskers" (1939:92).

Just as the early Russian audiences saw Chekhov's plays through the smoked glass of the Art Theater productions, in England and America, the incompetence and, later, the deliberate emphases of the first stagings created false impressions. In 1933 the Abbey Theater in Dublin presented Lennox Robinson's comedy *Is Life Worth Living? or Drama at Inish,* a benignly satirical look at the influence the "new drama" was having on provincial stages. In the course of this "exaggeration," as its author subtitled it, an acting troupe comes to a small Irish seaside resort with a repertoire of Ibsen, Strindberg, Tolstoy and, of course, Chekhov. As the actor-manager explains, "I now confine myself entirely . . . to psychological and introspective drama . . . because . . . they may revolutionize some person's soul" (1939:119, 123). A pall falls on the town and rain is incessant. The populace becomes addicted to this regimen of morbidity and is transformed from a pleasant assemblage of mediocrities to a hagridden set of depressives. They make suicide pacts, buy weedkiller to dispose of old relatives, leap off the pier; teetotalers take to drink and social drinkers go on the wagon; time-servers vote their conscience with disastrous results, and marriages begin to break up. As one sensible naysayer to the new drama remarks, "Sure you couldn't wear nice clothes going to that class of play; the best you could do would be a sort of half-mourning" (p. 145). Only with the forcible closure of the theater and the arrival of a circus does the town return to normal.

Chekhov gets off relatively lightly, mentioned by name in this exchange:

> LIZZIE [the maiden aunt]. . . . I lay awake all last night thinking of that play by—I never get the name right—it's like a cold in the head . . .

> CONSTANCE [the star]. I know who she means, darling. Tchekov, isn't it, Miss Twohig?

> LIZZIE. That's it, dear, Tchekov. Do you remember the woman in it? She had her chance and threw it away, and there she was drifting into middle age alone and neglected, just like myself.

> (p. 142)

For Robinson's satiric purposes, Chekhov can be lumped together with the other innovators of modern theater as propagandists for an unwholesome world view, long on introverted negativity and short on common sense.

"Introspection, morbidity, death and depression" were, according to the theatrical journalist A. E. Wilson the hallmarks of the Russian drama, and in his satirical primer *Theatre Guyed, The Baedeker of Thespia* (1935) he reiterated the common wisdom on "cheery Tchehov." The charge-sheet complains first that he provides no plot: "He simply assembles a lot of melancholy characters upon the stage, distributes a few grievances among them, adds a suicide or two and leaves them to worry the thing out to the bitter end" (p. 142).[6] The cast is invariably a group of failures, and Wilson enumerates them, giving them punning names like Sonia Marya Ileana Opushoff and Uncle Nikotin, General Epidemik and Lieutenant Nastikoff. Obviously many of his impressions are taken from actual performances, for he describes one wretch as "a dejected blonde who wears her hair screwed back" and another as a "a large, pale, tragic looking woman with red lips, a deep contralto voice and a *chevelure* that looks like a bird's nest" (pp. 144-145). This gives us some insight into the now standardized ways of playing Chekhov on the London stage.

Wilson then proceeds to provide sample dialogue, the usual droning and mooning that Geyer had already parodied, but without Geyer's awareness of *leitmotivs.*

> IVAN. Yes I am a failure. There is no doubt that I am a failure. (*He laughs hollowly.*) This morning I tried to shoot myself. I missed. At least the revolver was not loaded. I had forgotten to load it. But what does it matter? How unhappy I am. . . . For two roubles I would shoot myself. Will anyone lend me two roubles?

> (pp. 146, 148)

This is more redolent of bad translations than of Chekhov's own style, for all the characters are made to speak in this monotonous vein. Nevertheless, Wilson declares that "this is called Symbolism" and finds it remarkable that "people take pleasure in spending an evening listening to the maunderings of . . . such melancholy company" (p. 148).

Such an attitude is, in a nutshell, the Tired Businessman's idea of Chekhov, and only "high-brow" audiences could be attracted to his plays in Britain until the first truly popular productions were mounted by Theodore Komisarjevsky, a Russian emigre who decided that the English required a prettified and simplified Chekhov. He

had Trigorin, Tusenbach and Trofimov played as romantic leads; cut any ironic or obscure lines that detracted
from the love interest; drenched the stage in moonlight
or plunged it into shadowy silhouette; and stressed the
pauses and *longueurs,* supplying an almost under-water
atmosphere. This led to the notion that Chekhov the
dramatist wrote lyrical elegies, consonant with his image
as "the voice of twilight Russia."

Chekhov became so defined in England as lilac-tinted
and fragile that parodies addressed themselves to those
aspects. The first to capitalize on this was Peter Ustinov,
whose background was ideal for such an employment.
On his father's side an Ustinov, on his mother's a Benois
(his great-uncle was the Ballets Russes designer Alexandre Benois), he had imbibed the emigré notion that
Chekhov was a relic of paradise lost, those dear dead
days on the estate scanned through a roseate haze. Ustinov's first stage role as a student had been Waffles in
The Wood Demon, a production he characterized as "all
twilit impression." During World War II, he appeared in
the comic revue *Swinging the Gate* as a Russian professor jealous of Chekhov's success and "so academic that
the need for mystery totally escaped him." Confronted
with Nina's wish, "I want to be a seagull," he would
shrug and grumble, "For me . . . physical impossibility"
(1979:107-108, 122-123).

Ustinov's belief that Chekhov requires "mystery" informs
his personal definition of the playwright's qualities. In
his autobiography, he proclaims that,

> Chekhov set about showing up the false by a poetic
> mobilization of all that is inconsequential and wayward
> in human intercourse, with the result that his plays
> are not so much dialogues as many intertwined mono-
> logues, plays in which people talk far more than they
> listen, a technique which illuminated all the bitter-
> sweet selfishness and egotism in the human heart,
> and made people recognize, if not themselves, at least
> each other.
>
> (p. 113)

This attitude, with its emphasis on "poetic," "bittersweet,"
"monologues" had been nourished by the Komisarjevsky
approach and was to color Ustinov's parody.

His postwar comedy *The Love of Four Colonels* (the title
nods to Prokofiev and, through him, to Carlo Gozzi)
envisages the Palace of the Sleeping Beauty in Germany
administered by a four-power commission. The British,
American, French and Soviet colonels are tempted by the
Wicked Fairy Carabosse to seduce Sleeping Beauty and
thus realize the longings and aspirations that have been
beyond their grasp. Each man enacts a fantasy in which
his true self emerges to incarnate his ideal. The bland
Englishman turns into a full-blooded Elizabethan lecher;
the sincere Frenchman becomes a Molièrean marquis engaged in licentious badinage; the American, pill-popping
and psychiatrist-ridden, turns up as a Fighting Priest,
founder of "Girl's Town." Naturally, the Russian's tru-

culent and ursine paranoia melts into a maudlin Tsarist
officer.

This play-within-a-play puts a Chekhovian mask on the
Colonel's pursuit of his ideals. He sits on a swing, knitting a jumper, while the Beauty, as Aurora Petrovna,
plays croquet. Ustinov makes the most of what he conceives to be Chekhovian inconsequentiality. When Beauty scores a point, she looks directly at the Colonel, remarking, "And there was nobody here to see it." The by-
now obligatory shot rings out.

BEAUTY. What was that?

IKONENKO. A woodman felling a birch tree. . . .

BEAUTY. It sounded to me like . . .

IKONENKO. It was raining in Kharkov last Friday. I
know because Grischa left his umbrella at the barracks.

BEAUTY. Ever since Papa died, I have never carried
an umbrella. There were so many at the funeral . . .

IKONENKO. Was it raining?

BEAUTY. No. . . . (*Pause. Ikonenko looks at knitting.*)

IKONENKO. Now I have dropped a stitch, and must
undo it all. (*Does so.*)

BEAUTY (*rises, crosses D. a step or two*). I was so
looking forward to yesterday.

IKONENKO. Sadovsky's dance?

BEAUTY. Yes . . . but now that is over, I cannot look
forward to it any more

(1955:54).

This is as much Lewis Carroll as it is Chekhov, and the
set-ups and punchlines obviously derive from the caba-
ret-sketch format Ustinov had practiced. To get things
moving, the Wicked Fairy enters as an eccentric uncle
jollying them along.

> (*Pretends to shoot into the air with an imaginary
> gun.*) Piff! Paff! Pouf! (*Sits in armchair. Beauty kneels
> before him.*) I enjoy shooting seagulls, but it is less
> cruel without a gun. (*Looks at her.*) What pretty
> flowers. Stunted rhododendrons. You really should
> water your hat more often. (*Shot rings out*). . . . It is
> Uncle Mischa trying to shoot himself. It really is
> degrading how he fails at every thing he puts his
> hand to.
>
> (p. 55)

Ustinov's parody is a loving one, with specific gags (the
tree-chopping, the seagull) thrown in for the *cognoscen-
ti,* but it continues to disseminate the misconceptions
that Chekhov's plays are full of doleful non-happenings
and take place in the twilight zone. Although based on

the same premises, Paul Dehn's parody in *Punch* in 1956 was the first to use the mock-heroic or burlesque technique to reduce the so-called Chekhov atmosphere to absurdity. He considered what *The Seagull* might have been like had it been written by Rodgers and Hammerstein. *Kitty, Wake!* (or *Oklahomov*) satirizes the conventions of the American musical comedy with special reference to the way it inflates and coarsens the sources it adapts. At the same time, the skit sends up the ostensible delicacy and half-tones of Chekhov's plays, now smudged out of recognition by the garish exigencies of song-and-dance.

The characters are ruthlessly Americanized; Arkadina becomes Mrs Arkady Brown, a former burlesque artiste, saddled with a choreographer son, Con, and a gossip-writer lover, Trigger. This is bathos with a vengeance. Yakov the farmhand is easily transmogrified into Jake and Petr Sorin into Pete Sorenson, though both Doc Dorn and Masha get to keep their original names. The action takes place on Pete's farm by the shore of Lake Bogalusa, Mo. Essentially, Dehn stays close to the structure of Chekhov's play, eliminating one act; his comedy derives primarily from the characters' breaking into song at the drop of a Stetson and from trivializing the genteel Russian ambience into corn-fed Midwest. The exchange which follows the opening number is characteristic:

SEM. Whidja always wear black, Mash?

MASHA (*taking snuff*). I'm in mournin' fer my life.

SEM. O what a beautiful mournin',
Black as a Fishin' Crow's head
I gotta beautiful feelin'
Somebody oughta be dead
(1958:214).

Con has written a ballet for Nina, alias Kitty, which is performed as "(devised by Agnes de Mille from a Burmese translation of Nina's Act I speech) . . . with lions, eagles, partridges, antlered deer, geese, spiders, starfish, cranes, cockchafers, Alexander the Great, Caesar, Shakespeare, Napoleon, the meanest of leeches and Kitty." After twenty minutes of this, Mrs Arkady Brown is understandably fed up and explains, in song, "Oh I *do* like an ordi-nary play." The second act, down at the boathouse, opens with the Doctor's number "Take valerian drops" and Trigger's meditations on authorship have similarly been converted into a snappy ditty. When he insists that Kitty "Press the Trigger," a gunshot sends a Mandt's horn-gilled Guillemot dead at their feet as Con passes by with a smoking blunderbuss in hand.

Act Three, wherein lotto has become gin rummy, consists wholly of reprises of earlier songs whenever a character repeats a catchphrase. But in accordance with the musical's need to link up the juvenile leads in a happy ending, Con and Kitty run off together, leaving lovelorn Masha to commit suicide with Con's blunderbuss.

(*There is a deafening explosion. Trigger, notebook in hand, rushes to the window.*)

MRS A. Con O.K.?

TRIG. Yeah. Masha's shot herself. Make a note.

(*The wind dies down. From across the lake, through the open window, a distant chorus is heard singing:*)

CHORUS. Where the frozen lake is sleepin',
Hear that mournful sound.
All the Kittiwakes is weepin';
Masha's in the cold, cold ground.

(pp. 225-226)

Absurd this may be, but it is at least meant as a joke. Thomas Pasatieri's opera of *The Seagull,* of about the same vintage, was totally poker-faced in reducing the play's intricate motivations to a few romantic triangles.

On the whole, Chekhov has not been happy in his parodists. But that may be a token of his subtlety as a writer. An author of cruder contours, Dostoevsky, attracted the attention of such masters of parody as Alphonse Allais, Max Beerbohm and S. J. Perelman. Chekhov is more elusive: in his case, caricatures of his plays will tell us less about the refinements of his dramatic technique than about the distorted images of brooding dejection and meaninglessness that are conjured up in the popular imagination whenever his name is mentioned.

NOTES

[1] For parody as a major literary genre in the modern age, see Linda Hutcheon, *A Theory of Parody: The Teachings of Twentieth-Century Art Forms* (New York: Methuen, 1985).
[2] For a broader spectrum of this kind of criticism, see Simon Karlinsky, "Russian anti-Chekhovians," *Russian Literature* XV (1984), pp. 183-202.
[3] All translations in this paper are my own.
[4] See also Nos. 288, 293 (1896). For a list of contemporary Russian comic ephemera about Chekhov's plays, see I. F. Masanov.
[5] For further discussion of Russian literary parody, see B. Begak, N. Kravtsov and A. Morozov, *Russkaja literaturnaja parodija* (Moscow: Gos. Izd., 1980), esp. pp. 57, 94-95; and *Russische literarische Parodien*, herausg. von Dmitrij Tschiewskij und Johann Schröpfer (Wiesbaden: OHO Harrassowitz, 1957).
[6] Wilson later rewrote this parody as "The Fir Forest," as part of his collection *Playwrights in Aspic* (1950), in which a simple plot is presented as handled by twenty-one different dramatists.

WORKS CITED

Bednij Ionafan, 1896. "Fantasticheski-sumashedshie sceny s prologom, epilogom, beliberdoju i prolovom. . . ." *Peterburgskij listok* 290.

Burenin, V. P., 1901. "Devjat' sester i ni odnogo zhenixa," *Novoye vremja* 8991. Reprinted in Burenin 1917: V, 235-242.

1902 "Kriticheskie ocherki," *Novoye vremja* 9280 (4 Jan) and 9301 (25 Jan).

1904 "Kriticheskie ocherki," *Novoye vremja* 10079 (26 March).

1917 (1904) "Vishnevoe varenye," *Sochinenija V.P. Burenina. Tom pjatyj. Dramaticheskiye karikatury* (Petrograd), V, 201-202.

Chudakov, A. P., 1983 (1967). *Chekhov's Poetics*, trans. F.J. Cruise and D. Dragt (Ann Arbor: Ardis).

Dehn, Paul, 1958. "Oklahomov!" in: B. Lowrey, ed., *Twentieth Century Parody American and British* (New York: Harcourt, Brace).

Geyer, V. F., 1976. "Evoijucija teatra," in: M. Ja. Poliakov ed., *Russkaja teatral'naja parodia XIX nachala XX veka* (Moscow: Iskusstvo).

I. Grek (V.V. Bilibin), 1889. "Ivanov," *Oskolki* 7 (February 11).

Ivanov, Iv., 1890. "Teatr g-zhi Abramovy. *Leshij,* komediya v 40x d.g. Chekhova," *Artist* VL (February).

Macdonald, Dwight, ed., 1960. *Parodies. An Anthology from Chaucer to Beerbohm—and After* (New York: Random House).

Mirsky, Dmitry, 1927. "Chekhov and the English," *Criterion* VI, 292-304.

Nathan, G. J., 1939. *Since Ibsen: A Statistical Historical Outline of the Popular Theatre since 1900* (New York: Alfred A. Knopf).
Realist, 1896. "Listi iz 'alboma svistunov.' Tipy. I.," *Peterburgskij listok* 297.

Robinson, Lennox, 1939. *Killycreggs at Twilight and Other Plays* (London: Macmillan).

Rylov, K., (A. A. Sokolov), 1896. "Chajka, ili Podlog na Aleksandrinskoj scene. Komediya v 2-x vystrelax i 3-x nedorazumeniyax," *Peterburgskaja gazeta* 289 (October 23).

Ustinov, Peter, 1953. *The Love of Four Colonels* (New York: Dramatists Play Service). 1979 *Dear Me* (Harmondsworth: Penguin Books).

Wilson, A. E., 1935. *Theatre Guyed, The Baedeker of Thespia* (London: Methuen).

Woollcott, Alexander, 1923. *New York Herald* (January 31), 10.

Milton Ehre (essay date 1992)

SOURCE: "Introduction," in *Chekhov for the Stage,* Northwestern University Press, 1992, pp. 1-16.

[*In this essay, Ehre discusses Chekhov's efforts to "capture common reality" in his plays.*]

Anton Chekhov was born in the provincial town of Taganrog on the Sea of Azov in 1860. His father was a grocer; his grandfather had been a serf. A difficult childhood—poverty, an ambitious and tyrannical father, a long-suffering mother—left its scars: "In childhood I had no childhood." He was gregarious but had a streak of melancholy in his nature and fled from intimacy. "No one," his friend Ivan Bunin wrote, "not even those closest to him, knew what went on deep inside him. His self-control never deserted him." Neither did his good humor, his decency, his sense of personal dignity. In Chekhov's presence, Gorky remembered, "everyone involuntarily felt a desire to be simpler, more truthful, more oneself."

Chekhov reached maturity at the time when the Industrial Revolution finally hit Russia with full force. The social composition of Russian literature before the age of Chekhov can be summed up by the title of a Tolstoy story, "Master and Man"—or "Landowner and Serf." In Chekhov's works we find the full panoply of modern professions—lawyers, doctors, engineers, industrialists, traveling salesmen, factory workers. The new bourgeois ethos of "making it on your own" was beginning to influence people: Chekhov spoke of his lifelong battle to squeeze the slave out of himself drop by drop and be-

come a free man. He worked his way through medical school by writing humorous sketches about the quirks of ordinary people and the absurdities of daily life for the new popular press. Medicine, he said, was his wife; literature, his mistress. As he became successful, he spent more time with his mistress than with his wife. His journalism trained him to an economy of expression and a dispassionate observation of human foibles.

Around 1886 he began to attract the attention of the serious reading public. His work took on increasing maturity and depth, although the humorous side of his talent never left him. He wore his fame lightly, with the "spiritual modesty" he accused Dostoevsky of lacking. One of the ambitions of this descendant of serfs was to acquire an estate of his own, and when he did, he took an active interest in its management and in local affairs, giving medical treatment to peasants without charge. Aligning himself with no political party or group, he was socially progressive, religiously agnostic, an advocate of science and enlightenment, firm in his belief that individual freedom is a precious thing: "I am neither liberal, nor conservative, nor gradualist, nor monk, nor indifferent. I should like to be a free artist and nothing else. . . . I hate lies and violence in all their forms. . . . I look upon tags and labels as prejudices. My holy of holies is the human body, health, intelligence, talent, inspiration, love, and the most absolute freedom imaginable, freedom from violence and lies."

In 1890 he made an arduous journey across Siberia to the convict colony on Sakhalin Island ("to pay off some of my debt to medicine"), and his book-length study of local conditions led to reforms in the Russian prison system. In 1901, three years before his death, he married Olga Knipper, a leading actress of the recently formed Moscow Art Theater. They lived mostly apart—Olga, in Moscow because of the demands of her career, Anton, in the south at Yalta because of his illness. In 1884 he had shown the first symptoms of tuberculosis, and in 1897 massive hemorrhaging from his lungs compelled him to acknowledge his fatal disease publicly. It is impossible to pinpoint the moment when Chekhov knew he was doomed—though a doctor, he long denied the facts—but at least three of the plays were written by a man who knew his days were numbered. He died in Germany on July 2, 1904. The train car that brought his remains back to Russia bore the sign FOR OYSTERS. He would have enjoyed the joke.

Chekhov's plays were an important part of the revolution in the theater taking place at the close of the nineteenth century. The century had not been a good one for theater. Fluffy farces and overblown melodramas were dominating the stage when Chekhov began to write plays. Like Ibsen, Strindberg, Hauptmann, Maeterlinck, and other innovators, he was trying to break out of the straitjacket of the formulaic "well-made plays" of Scribe and Sardou. He complained about the "avowals of love, infidelities of husbands and wives, the tears of widows and orphans" that were the shopworn furniture of the contemporary stage. "Plays should be written badly and insolently"—

"the simpler the plot, the better." The action should be cumulative—"piled up, not polished and flattened out." Looser structures are necessary to capture common reality: "I would write of ordinary love and family life without angels or villains . . ., a life that is even, flat, ordinary, life as it really is."

Melodrama and farce are the fare of popular culture. Working for middle-brow weeklies, Chekhov cut his teeth on the very farces (usually in short-story form) that he was later to condemn. Although melodrama was less suited to his temperament, his first full-scale play, the juvenile *Platonov* (no later than 1879) is pure potboiler. His second effort, the more successful *Ivanov* (1889), shows psychological penetration but is still too talky and high-pitched—its subject, like that of *Platonov,* is a man who can find neither love nor an outlet for his talents— a "Russian Hamlet." While indulging in the melodramatic fashion, Chekhov parodied it. He continued to slap together farcical one-acters even after he had established a reputation as a serious writer, and some are still part of the repertoire.

Elements of farce and melodrama survive in his major plays, but they have become displaced from center stage or their conventions have been so deformed that they are barely recognizable. *The Sea Gull* turns on the stock formula of farce (and comedy)—A loves B who loves C who loves D; but instead of a resolution, in which the lovers find their proper partners, the young hero and heroine go their separate ways. *Uncle Vanya, The Three Sisters,* and *The Cherry Orchard* are all grounded on that recurrent plot of melodrama—the loss of property— which can be summed up by the old joke:

VILLAIN: Pay the rent!

HEROINE: I can't pay the rent!

VILLAIN: Pay the rent!

HEROINE: I can't pay the rent!

HERO: *I'll* pay the rent!

HEROINE: My hero!

But in Chekhov's plays no hero turns up to save the day and the victims seem curiously indifferent to impending disaster. In *Uncle Vanya* the crisis over the sale of the estate does not appear until act 3, and the conflict between Professor Serebryakov and Vanya, though the most dramatically tense moment of the play, quickly turns ludicrous. The three sisters are aware that the vicious Natasha is taking over their home, but they remain strangely passive. Although the threat of the loss of the cherry orchard hangs like an ominous cloud over Madame Ranevskaya and her brother, Gayev, they talk about it only occasionally and never confront their dilemma head on.

It is as if Chekhov's characters willfully ignore the plot that destiny and art have woven for them. They chat about the weather, their lives and loves, their disappointments and miseries, the meaning of life. They "philosophize"—a recurring word in Chekhov's plays (though rendered in different ways in these translations)—and in the meantime they forget about the matter at hand. Their blithe obliviousness to what threatens their lives can be frustrating to audiences who expect a neat package where an action is confronted and resolved: Chekhov's first audiences did not know what to make of his plays, though in time they learned to love them.

But it would be a mistake to dismiss Chekhov's characters as spoiled weaklings or jaded gentry of a bygone era simply because they don't do what we want them to do. Many of them are weak, almost all of them suffer, but in their refusal to be governed by a controlling plot they assert their freedom. They see their lives as larger than a particular circumstance: sticking to daily habits, observing common courtesies, loving and being loved, asking why one is alive are the kinds of things we do even in moments of crisis. His people insist on being themselves even in the face of disaster.

> After all, in real life, people don't spend every moment in shooting one another, hanging themselves, or making declarations of love. They do not spend all their time saying clever things. They are more occupied with eating, drinking, flirting, and saying stupidities. These are the things which ought to be shown on the stage. A play should be written in which people arrive, depart, have dinner, talk about the weather, and play cards. Life must be exactly as it is and people as they are. . . . Let everything on the stage be just as complicated, and at the same time just as simple, as in life. People eat their dinner, just eat their dinner, and all the time their happiness is taking form, or their lives are being destroyed.

Zola and other naturalists were talking about the need for such plays, but Chekhov actually wrote them. Instead of untying the knot of a single action, he gives us many actions. His major plays take shape around arrival and departure. Visitors interrupt the humdrum routine of a landowner's estate (in *The Three Sisters,* a bourgeois home), bearing the baggage of a different way of life—Arkadina and Trigorin with their loose bohemian ways in *The Sea Gull,* the urbane professor and his dazzlingly beautiful and indolent wife in *Uncle Vanya,* Colonel Vershinin from Moscow, to which the three sisters long to escape, Madame Ranevskaya from Paris in *The Cherry Orchard,* with her mixture of grief and frivolity. Hopes, dreams, anxieties, and conflicts are stirred up, and then simply die down as the intruders depart. *The Sea Gull* is somewhat different in that Arkadina and Trigorin return to witness the climax. It is the last play of Chekhov to end, like the earlier melodramas, on a strong dramatic note; still, the suicide takes place offstage. In *Uncle Vanya* and *The Three Sisters* the visitors simply leave and life returns to the ordinary. In *The Cherry Orchard* all (except the servant Firs) go off to continue their lives. Although the plays have their share of pain and sadness, the view of life depicted in them is essentially comic—disaster is seldom final: Treplev is destroyed but Nina survives; the cherry trees are chopped down but life goes on.

Chekhov not only made the stage freer by loosening speech from the dictates of a controlling plot, he also made it more democratic. After *Platonov* and *Ivanov* no single hero dominates a Chekhov play. Our interest is spread over a wide range of characters—almost everyone is given a story to tell, a life to recount. Chekhov's plays have often been described as studies in the failure to communicate, and it is true that his people, like most of us, are better at talking than listening. They can also be extraordinarily open about their feelings. If they sometimes take each other for granted, it may be because they know each other so well. They live in extended Russian families, where relatives, neighbors, and friends are drawn into the domestic circle. Except perhaps for Tolstoy, no modern writer has been better at depicting the tensions, affections, and profound loyalties of familial life. In Chekhov's view, we are, for better or worse, social animals inextricably bound to each other.

Americans know Chekhov primarily through his plays; for Russians he is to this day a writer of short stories who digressed into the theater to produce a handful of masterpieces. He wrote hundreds of stories, many of them extraordinarily beautiful. Taken together, they comprise a Balzacian *comédie humaine* of Russian life at the turn of the century. His stories ferret out with a dispassionate eye every layer of Russian society—peasants, workers, professionals, emergent capitalists, the state bureaucracy. The plays have a narrower focus, concentrating on the declining gentry (and, in *The Three Sisters,* the upper middle class). The landowner's estate provided him a place where he could plausibly bring together a large cast of characters.

The Russian dramatic tradition had long emphasized character over plot. Gogol may have been the source of some of the slapstick that occurs in Chekhov's plays (especially *The Cherry Orchard*), though he had more than enough French farces, and their Russian imitations, to draw upon. Chekhov much admired Alexander Ostrovsky, Russia's first full-time playwright—most of the important plays of the nineteenth century, like Chekhov's, were also written by writers of prose fiction. Ostrovsky may have inspired his aim to show "life as it is," though Ostrovsky's plays, for all their marvelous fidelity to actual life and their extraordinary richness of language, are too high-keyed to have left a mark on Chekhov's softer music. Through Treplev of *The Sea Gull,* he showed his scorn for the second-rate followers of Ostrovsky, mere ethnographers who were content to show how people "eat, drink, love, walk about, wear their jackets." A more likely influence is Turgenev's masterpiece, *A Month in the Country,* which, like Chekhov's plays, concentrates its energies on psychological nuance. The action of Turgenev's play, however, is more carefully ordered, its speech more rationally constructed, than Chekhov's casual flow.

The glory of Russian literature after the age of Pushkin and until the end of the nineteenth century is, of course, the novel. The novel as a genre broke with classical views of character as fixed identity: in tragedy, to be revealed in a moment of crisis; in comedy, to be shown naked as the mask of pretension is ripped away. In the nineteenth century the disciplines of biology and history came into their own, and from Hegel through Marx and Darwin the emphasis was on development, growth, change, progress (even Darwin's natural selection was interpreted as a process of the gradual evolution of higher forms promising future perfection). Chekhov drew on his own short stories for his plays, often spoke of his plays as short stories or novellas (as did the critics), and, indeed, their structure is more novelistic than dramatic. There are no sudden revelations of "true" character ("Ah, so *that's* what X is like!"). He applies to drama the studied artlessness of the short story. His people reveal themselves slowly and incompletely, like neighbors or friends we get to know step by step but never know fully. There is always a shadow of mystery about his characters, some corner of their being we have not been able to dig into. We are touched by their sufferings, amused by their foolishness, and yet puzzled. Chekhov, in praising *Anna Karenina,* said that Tolstoy had done what an artist ought to do: he gave no answers, though he raised all the right questions. Chekhov wanted us to leave the theater mulling over the enigmas of human personality.

Chekhov wrote his major plays at a time when Russian poetry was enjoying a revival. Russian decadence and symbolism (the terms were used interchangeably) dominated the scene roughly from 1894 to 1910. Chekhov rejected the aestheticism of decadence and the mysticism of Russian symbolism. A physician by training, a journalist in his apprentice years, he always held to the naturalist's insistence on impartiality—"the writer must be as objective as a chemist." He also felt that art must serve some purpose. The great writers are "realists" but make us feel "life as it should be in addition to life as it is." In *The Sea Gull* he even parodied the decadent manner.

However, naturalism and symbolism, opposed to each other at the time, had something in common: they both turned their backs on realism's attempt to embrace all of life in the broad expanse of the novel. Life seemed too chaotic, too fragmented, to be caught whole. The naturalists turned to "a slice of life"; the symbolists, to a poem of mysterious allusion. By the 1880s the Russian realistic novel had passed from the scene. Short forms, like Chekhov's stories or symbolist lyrics, were the order of the day. Artists were trying to capture the fleeting moment, the impression of the surface, ripples in the stream of life that might suggest richer meanings. French impressionist painting had been introduced to Russia by *The World of Art* journal, one of the major organs of the new aestheticism. Despite Chekhov's professions of reportorial neutrality, there is a moving lyricism and suggestive symbolism in the best of his stories and plays. He was among the first to employ evocative silences on the stage. Chekhov did not remain untouched by the symbolist movement and may in turn have influenced it—indeed, the symbolists claimed him as one of their own. Theater critics, not knowing what to make of his peculiar mixture of comedy and pathos, often called his plays "plays of mood," "poems," or compared them to music.

His lyricism is sometimes nostalgic: his characters look back longingly to a time when life was better, or at least *seemed* better (the ironist in Chekhov is always lurking around the corner). Nature is often perceived poetically—the lake and the sea gull, the forest of *Uncle Vanya*, the birds Masha sees crossing the sky in *The Three Sisters*, the cherry orchard. Chekhov's lyrical apprehension of nature grew out of his sense that our human dramas are played out in a setting much larger than ourselves, that our lives are but ephemeral moments in the vast expanses of space and time, that if we fail and when we die, something will survive us.

Chekhov's Russia was acutely conscious of historical change. Urbanization and industrialization brought the social dislocation and alienation that are still with us. Railroads fill the pages of Chekhov's stories and provide a metaphor for a world in flux—his art has been described as life seen from a moving railway car. A large city forms the backdrop of act 2 of *The Cherry Orchard*; Dr. Astrov of *Uncle Vanya* worries about the ravaged countryside. The gentry as a class was dying, and its death provoked the themes of loss and waste that are at the heart of Chekhov's plays. Rapid historical change is a cause of both anxiety and hope. Both were intensified in Russia by the widespread sense that the days of the prevailing political order were numbered; the regimes of Alexander III (1881-94) and Nicholas II (1894-1917) were reactionary, corrupt, and stupid. The yoke of the imperial state weighed heavily, the revolutionary movement was in temporary disarray, and the generation of the 1880s felt itself lost. Liberal intellectuals contented themselves with a program of "little deeds"—cultivating one's own garden, as Dr. Astrov cultivates his forest, so as to add a drop of improvement to the world's ocean of misery. In the 1890s revolutionary expectations revived, and we find premonitions of a radical transformation in Chekhov's last two plays, written on the eve of the upheaval of 1905. Baron Tuzenbach of *The Three Sisters* speaks of an "impending powerful, invigorating storm" that will blow away all the vices of the old order; Trofimov, in *The Cherry Orchard,* is confident that a "new life" is around the corner.

Change makes men and women aware of the passage of time—time is almost the hero of *The Three Sisters* and *The Cherry Orchard.* When Chekhov's people are not gazing nostalgically backward to the past, they look forward to the future with hope—which he continually undercuts. The character speaks confidently of how the world will be better, even perfect, in two or three hundred years, but we know him (the bombast belongs to the men) to be weak, passive, lazy. In Chekhov there is often no symmetry between word and action (or between the speech of one character and that of another), a discordance that is comic and ironic, and also quite "modern." This debunking of the rhetoric of progress

has led some critics to interpret his message as saying that we must live only in the present. But Chekhov's letters express the same faith in progress that sounds so hollowly in the mouths of his heroes. He believed that "he who wants nothing, hopes for nothing, and fears nothing, cannot be an artist." A life lived for the present can only result in hedonistic despair. Perhaps the most poignant moment in all Chekhov's plays is the conclusion of *The Three Sisters,* when the sisters, in counterpoint to the nihilism of Dr. Chebutykin, insist upon continuing to hope when all the grounds of their hope have evaporated. As Dr. Astrov puts it, to give meaning to our lives, we have to have a sense of purpose, a destination, see "a light shining in the distance," even if it proves to be illusory. Characteristically, Astrov is drunk when he says this. Chekhov's men are caught in a web of abstraction. Even when they are mouthing their author's ideas, they are slightly comic. His women, fragile as they may be, seem closer to the pulse of life. Nina of *The Sea Gull* and Sonya of *Uncle Vanya,* like the three sisters, tell us that the important thing is "to endure."

In October of 1895, when Chekhov began work on *The Sea Gull,* he wrote to a friend, "I am sinning terribly against the conventions of the stage. It is a comedy with three female parts, six male, a landscape (a view of a lake), much talk of literature, little action and tons of love." He finished in November, though, as was his custom, he later made changes for production and publication. The play opened at the state-run Alexandrinsky Theater in St. Petersburg on October 17, 1896. It flopped badly. Despite Chekhov's anxious instructions, the actors insisted upon playing it tragically, in the nineteenth-century style of broad theatrical gestures, grand entrances and exits, heightened dramatic points. Audiences were bewildered by the commonplace characters, the absence of explicit motivation for their behavior, and the paucity of action—"Why do they play lotto and drink beer?" one viewer asked. (Complaints about the randomness of Chekhov's world dogged all of his plays.) The fashionable opening-night crowd booed after the first act, and though subsequent evenings were a bit better, the play closed after five performances.

In contrast, after December 17, 1898, the date of the first performance of *The Sea Gull* at the newly established Moscow Art Theater under the leadership of Konstantin Stanislavsky and Vladimir Nemirovich-Danchenko, Russians spoke of the dawn of a new era in the history of the theater. As the curtain descended on the last act, the theater was strangely silent. The actors, who this time had played it as Chekhov wanted, simply and without affectation, walked off the stage certain that they had failed; and then, after a long pause, the audience burst into resounding applause and shouts of praise. A creative collaboration of the greatest dramatist and greatest director of the age had begun. *Uncle Vanya* opened at the Moscow Art Theater on October 26, 1899 (though it had been shown earlier, in the provinces). *The Three Sisters* and *The Cherry Orchard* were written expressly for Stanislavsky's theater.

Relations between Chekhov and Stanislavsky were often strained. Chekhov complained about excessive stage effects—too much chirping of crickets, croaking of frogs, barking of dogs. Stanislavsky frankly admitted that he did not understand *The Sea Gull*; later they argued over *The Three Sisters* and *The Cherry Orchard,* Stanislavsky viewing them as a tragedies, Chekhov insisting they were comedies. Yet the two men complemented each other well. Stanislavsky's revulsion at the star system and introduction of ensemble acting, his insistence on naturalness of speech and gesture, his fervent, almost religious, dedication to the craft of acting, were all tailor-made for plays where almost everyone is a protagonist and psychological nuance conveys more than overt dramatic action. Without surrendering his naturalistic bias, Stanislavsky highlighted the lyrical dimension of Chekhov's plays. To achieve his goal of having actors live through a part, he wanted them to be in character before and after walking on and off stage, and Chekhov's plays do seem to commence in the midst of ongoing life that will continue after the curtain falls. They make extraordinary demands upon the actor—few things are as deadly as a Chekhov play played badly. The actor must be completely at ease and yet intensely alert to the subtle gradations of emotion in his own role and that of everyone else on stage. Stanislavsky's dedicated professionalism and Chekhov's lifelike plays made for a rare combination in the history of the stage. A sea gull was chosen as the logo for the Moscow Art Theater.

Chekhov was not entirely accurate when he implied that he had tossed overboard all the commonplaces of the stage in *The Sea Gull.* The conventional love triangles are there, even to surplus—almost everyone on stage is involved in one—and the play ends with the shock of a suicide. "Tons of love," is right, though the loves of *The Sea Gull* never find their true objects. To construct a play around unsatisfied longing was something new in the theater. So was the uncertainty of response the play seems to call for. "I'm in mourning for my life," Masha says as she opens act 1, and so is almost everyone else. The line is funny, but Masha is sad. Are wc meant to be amused by her self-pity? Feel sorry for her? What the conventional theater considered important is given second place; what it considered trivial is brought to the forefront. Trigorin's love for Nina is played out with a coy reference to a line in one of his books (and then recounted retrospectively by Treplev, a theatrical device Chekhov dropped from his later plays). Arkadina changing the bandage of her son, Treplev, is given an entire scene. Of course, we learn much about Trigorin from the casual way in which he becomes enamored of the young and dreadfully naive Nina; the bandaging scene shows us the complex relations between mother and son. Chekhov's insight was that we reveal ourselves in the ordinary moments of our daily living.

The Sea Gull is a play about youth—hence its tons of love—and the deep divide between the generations. Mother and son, older successful writer and young aspiring writer, the aging star and the hopeful ingenue, find no common ground. But there are no victims, unless we see Treplev as his own victim. Chekhov wrote about *Ivanov* words that he might have used of all his major plays: "I wanted to be original—there is not a single villain or angel in my play (though I could not resist the temptation of putting in a few buffoons). I have not found anyone guilty, nor have I acquitted anyone." Yet we have more sympathy for Nina and Treplev than for Trigorin and Arkadina. The young are entitled to be foolish; those with experience ought to know better.

Uncle Vanya, on the other hand, is a play about middle age. It grew out of an earlier effort, *The Wood Demon,* which was first performed—and flopped—in 1889. Chekhov, stung by its failure, abandoned the theater for six years (until he wrote *The Sea Gull*) and reworked it, in 1896, into the masterpiece that is *Uncle Vanya. The Wood Demon* has too many characters to keep track of, they talk too much, everything ends cheerily as the assorted lovers are reconciled, and the character who was to become Vanya takes his own life and is quickly forgotten. To go from *The Wood Demon* to *Uncle Vanya* is to move from speechifying to conversation, from stereotypes to realized individuals, from argument to poetry.

The major characters of *Uncle Vanya,* like those of the other major plays, can be placed on a scale of age. Professor Serebryakov is old and whines. Sonya is young and hopes. Vanya and Astrov are middle-aged and worry that their lives have been failures. Vanya is angry and Astrov resigned. The "mermaid" Yelena (Russian for Helen) shows up, stoking a fire in these tired men, though she herself is cold. For Chekhov, as for Dostoevsky before him, beauty has a moral quality. In his story **"The Beauties"** (1888), the sight of beauty fills men with sadness, as it reminds them of their own imperfections, of what is missing from their lives. Perhaps what is wrong with Yelena is that her beauty is untouched by moral grace—she is indolent and as unhappy as the men.

There is something mysterious about the misery of Chekhov's people. Is Sonya really so ugly that Astrov could not be happy with her? Why can't Vanya feel at least some contentment about his very real achievement in holding the estate together? It is as if they are determined to make the wrong choices or are possessed of a will to suffer. The play turns in a circle, with the leavetaking of the ending repeating gestures and words of the opening—"nothing has changed," Vanya tells us. Then Sonya adds a memorable coda of hope as mysterious as the play's despair. Critics have been divided. Is it meant to be taken straight or is it ironic? Perhaps both. Chekhov certainly wanted us to feel the dignity of her refusal to surrender to despair, although he did not want us to abandon our critical detachment. His plays bring us too close to his characters for us to dismiss them, while a comic tone concurrently sets them at a distance. We watch them with what Shakespeare called a "parted eye": one part sees Vanya stumbling across the stage, revolver in hand, crying "Bang!" as he shoots at the hated professor, and we laugh; the other has not lost sight of his very real suffering.

Scene from a 1970 Russian film adaptation of Uncle Vanya.

The Three Sisters gave Chekhov a good deal of trouble—he worried about the difficulties of handling such a large cast of characters and three heroines. It was written from August through December of 1900 and opened at the Moscow Art Theater on January 31, 1901. During rehearsals Stanislavsky felt stuck, until it dawned on him that Chekhov's characters "don't at all wear their melancholy like a badge; to the contrary, they seek gaiety, laughter, cheerfulness; they want to live, not vegetate."

The Sea Gull describes a summer of love's infatuations and confusions, then, after a gap of two years, events are summarized and act 4 takes place in autumn—as do all the last acts of Chekhov's major plays. The others unfailingly show life in process. They are plays of loss: *Uncle Vanya* moves from summer to autumn, *The Cherry Orchard* from May to October. In *The Three Sisters* the process of loss takes place over a number of years, long enough for Natasha to bear two children. Again the movement is from spring to fall, with dark winters interspersed in acts 2 and 3, and another on its way at the end.

The Three Sisters opens with remembering, but it is really about forgetting. When they first meet, Vershinin cannot remember the sisters, nor they him. Chebutykin has forgotten medicine. Irina has forgotten Italian. Masha has forgotten her mother, how to play the piano, and eventually the lines of the Pushkin poem that obsess her throughout the play. By act 3 the party of act 1 has become a dim memory in Tuzenbach's mind; at the end, the sisters have apparently forgotten their dream of escape to Moscow. "People won't remember us too. We'll be forgotten," Masha laments. As time strips them of memory, Natasha dispossesses them of the space they inhabit. Acts 1 and 2 take place in a large living room with a ballroom in the background; act 3, in the bedroom Olga and Irina are sharing now that Natasha has taken over Olga's room. In act 4 they are out of the house altogether, and Natasha rules the roost. Life is remorseless, everything passes, almost nothing holds firm against the stream of time—"almost" because the sisters' deep affection for each other survives their losses.

The Three Sisters may be Chekhov's supreme achievement (some would vote for **The Cherry Orchard**). Here his art of suggesting the undercurrents of life is at its height. It is the only one of his four major plays to be subtitled "drama"—he called **The Sea Gull** and **The**

Cherry Orchard "comedies," *Uncle Vanya* "scenes"— but its dramatic moments are mere eddies on the stream of time. Yet there is a drama submerged beneath time's inexorable course, one present in all of his plays but most powerfully felt in *The Three Sisters*—the struggle of men and women to extract meaning from a world beyond their control.

By 1901 the Russian public was moving away from the fashionable pessimism of the 1880s and demanding a more affirmative art. Critics, though they praised the "poetry" of *The Three Sisters,* objected to its dark view of life and accused Chekhov of repeating himself. Chekhov worried that his "manner was out of date." His next play, he promised, would be "definitely funny, very funny. . . ." At times he spoke of *The Cherry Orchard* as a "vaudeville." When he finished, he wrote his wife, "It is not a drama, but a comedy, in places even a farce." The writing was even tougher going than *The Three Sisters.* It is unclear just when he conceived the play; the traditional dating is the spring of 1901. It was completed in the fall of 1903 and opened at the Moscow Art Theater on January 17, 1904, in conjunction with a celebration of Chekhov's twenty-fifth year of literary activity; he died a mere five and a half months later.

The Cherry Orchard does have many elements of farce. Ranevskaya, the grande dame; Gayev, the effete nobleman; perpetually astonished Pishchik; clumsy and incoherent Yepikhodov; the Frenchified valet, Yasha; the lovestruck soubrette Dunyasha, the odd-speaking "German" governess, Charlotta; Anya the ingenue; the faithful retainer, Firs (who has his counterpart in Ferapont of *The Three Sisters*) are stock figures of the kind of light comedy Russians called vaudeville. Yepikhodov takes his pratfalls; Varya swings a cue at him and almost hits her reluctant suitor; pompous Trofimov goes flying down a staircase. But again, too many of them are too fully realized as complex human beings to be entirely funny. If *The Three Sisters* is Chekhov's most moving play, *The Cherry Orchard* shows an extraordinary lightness of touch, an uncanny blend of comedy and pathos.

"It seems to me that in my play, no matter how boring it is, there is something new. In the entire play there is not one gun shot." Chekhov might have added that also new was the absence of an unfolding love affair. In the other plays the characters desire—Sorin of *The Sea Gull* would entitle the story of his life "The Man Who Wished," a title most of Chekhov's characters might accept for their life stories. Desire leads to some kind of action, however displaced from center stage, and results in the anguish of unfulfillment. In *The Cherry Orchard* Lopakhin and Varya spend most of their energy avoiding each other; Trofimov, who sees himself as "above love," is more of Anya's chum than her lover; Ranevskaya agonizes over past affairs. The loss of the cherry orchard is always in the background, giving the play unity—at least we know what it's *about*. But it does not provide much action either, since its owners, no matter how much Lopakhin insists that they do something about it, do nothing. They would rather talk about themselves. More

than in any other of Chekhov's plays, the spotlight is on the comedy of daily life.

In a passage Chekhov omitted in order to get the play through the censors, it is clear that Trofimov, the "eternal student," is a radical belonging to what Russians called the "intelligentsia"—a type Chekhov always mocked. He could never abide anyone who pretended to have the answers to the riddles of life. Yet Trofimov expresses many of Chekhov's own views—on the need to work, on social amelioration, on the necessity to envision a future. He may touch the heart of the play when he says, "To live in the present we first have to make up for our past, to have done with it once and for all." He is referring to the central ill of Russian history—its legacy of serfdom. But there are also personal histories the characters are struggling to come to terms with. Ranevskaya suffers painful guilt over the death of her child and her various love affairs, and the supporting cast echoes, even if in a comic mode, the theme of guilt for a misspent life—"They say I've eaten up my fortune in candy," Gayev quips. At the other end of the social scale, Lopakhin, the son of a serf, has not gotten over the loveless brutality of his peasant childhood. Perhaps Gayev and Ranevskaya cannot focus on the loss of their estate because, much as they love it, salvaging it will not solve their essential problem—to discover who they are. On the other hand, Lopakhin is obsessed by its acquisition because he is under the illusion that it will solve all his difficulties. *The Three Sisters* concluded with Olga's cry for self-knowledge—"if we only knew." In *The Cherry Orchard* Charlotta, in a voice half-pathetic, half comic, asks the question that nags all of us: who am I?

If *The Cherry Orchard* is vaudeville, it is so in the manner of *Waiting for Godot*—comic characters are adrift in a voiceless cosmos. "Suddenly a distant sound is heard, as if coming from the sky, the mournful dying sound of a breaking string" is the stage direction in the middle of lovely act 2. It is sunset, the characters are in a darkening meadow, the cherry orchard is nearby, and faraway on the horizon is the faint outline of a large city—symbols of the old ways and the new. Everyone onstage falls silent, in fear and awe. The stage has opened up upon the universe, upon some dark mystery at the heart of things. A tramp appears, and Ranevskaya gives him a gold coin, as if to propitiate the gods. As space opens to infinity, the characters contract, undergoing a diminution that lies at the heart of comedy. Gayev and Ranevskaya grieve over their loss; Lopakhin revels in his triumph, though he senses that his victory may be hollow. But their mourning and joy, their failure and success, are only things of a moment in the great scheme of things—if there is one. They pack their bags in yet another final scene of leavetaking. The pathos of tragedy has been robbed of its finality. Somewhere out there, the middle-aged Gayevs and Ranevskayas of the world are still grieving that their lives haven't turned out as they wished, the youthful Anyas are hoping that theirs will be different, old men like Firs are dying, and the human comedy rolls on.

Laurence Senelick   (essay date 1994)

SOURCE: "Chekhov and the Bubble Reputation," in *Chekhov Then and Now: The Reception of Chekhov in World Culture,* edited by J. Douglas Clayton, Peter Lang, 1997, pp. 5-18.

[*The following is the text of an address Senelick delivered at a 1994 symposium on Chekhov's reception. Senelick traces shifts in the author's reputation over the years.*]

When Douglas Clayton asked me to deliver the keynote address to this illustrious assemblage, my first impulse was to entitle it "Confessions of an Inveterate Chekhovian." From my earliest memories, as the grandchild of Russian émigrés and in particular of an *ochen' kul'turnaia babushka,* as a child playgoer and a child actor in a company based on the Method, I was surrounded by people who venerated Chekhov, and who thought nothing in the world more fulfilling than to be associated with a production of his plays. "Hallowed awe" is the term Ivan Voinitsky applies to his mother's infatuation with Professor Serebriakov, and it seems equally applicable here. This veneration persisted in college, three years of Russian classes culminating in the translation of *Vishnevy sad.* It led me, as a graduate student at Harvard, to learn from Nils Åke Nilsson a more objective, more technical approach to the works. For nearly forty years, I have translated Chekhov, written about him from the standpoint of a theatre historian, a literary critic, a biographer, taught him to undergraduate and graduate students alike, lectured on him at conferences and congresses in several languages, directed my own productions of his plays and acted in other people's, and served as advisor, dramatist or reviewer on still others. In the course of this time, I have traversed acres of cherry orchards, met whole dynasties of uncle Vanias, hearkened to the longings of endless sororal trios, and been the sitting target for flocks of transitory seagulls.

I elaborate on my *bona fides* simply to attest to the fact that after all this study I continue to find Chekhov inexhaustible. Wherever one plunges the probe, it meets solid matter: the texture of a Chekhov work is so tightly interwoven, so devoid of the extraneous, that it always yields gratifying results to the assiduous student. However, at the risk of offending my learned colleagues here assembled, I have to state that, when it comes to Chekhov's drama, I have usually found the plays in production and the remarks of directors, designers and actors more illuminating than most academic critical studies. This is even the case when the production is, necessarily, partial and poorly realized. The pressures of the rehearsal room, the actual configuration of bodies in space, the adventitious discoveries of a performer's imagination can force insights unavailable in the closest reading. The only comparable experience is to translate a play, paying close attention to such things as lexical repetition, sentence structure and levels of discourse. Watching even the most hopeless staging of Chekhov, I have come upon connections and insights that eluded me in years of poring over texts.

Let me give one recent, unvarnished example, still fresh in my mind. Ron Daniel's production of *The Cherry Orchard* at the American Repertory Theatre in Cambridge, Mass. was not very good: he had set it amid geometric shapes in primary colours, evocative of Kazimir Malevich but signifying nothing. Claire Bloom's Ranevskaia was a brisk, business-like woman getting on with her life, amid a very uneven cast, ranging from hammy veterans of British rep to raw tyros straight from the acting class. There was a certain amount of what I call "post-modern" speaking of the dialogue, in which any line reading will do, divorced from any connection with character psychology or a directorial intention. And yet—at the beginning of the party scene, when Simeonov-Pishchik felt for his borrowed money, he went through the most genuine and detailed agonizing over its possible loss that I have ever seen. It stuck in the memory. Then, at the top of Act IV, when Lopakhin offers Trofimov a loan, and Trofimov proudly refuses it, the actor playing Trofimov, a black youth in dreadlocks, felt for the money he claimed he had received for a translation, and a brief flash of panic crossed his face. Not that he had lost any money: his claim was a lie enforced by vanity, but he had no way of proving it to Lopakhin, and Lopakhin knew it. The complexity of their relationship was lit up, forgive the jargon, paratextually. Moreover, the visual association with Pishchik, instantaneous though it was, efficiently sustained the obbligato of money matters and impecuniousness that that previously dominated the play; it also stressed the theme of fortuity (on which Peter Brook had based his whole production) by aligning Trofimov, buffetted by fate, with the clownish Pishchik, always waiting for something to turn up. These aperçus were fleeting, possibly fortuitous themselves, undetermined by directorial choice, but nonetheless enlightening.

Some years ago at a round-table discussion in Moscow, one scholar/apparatchik proposed a conference whereat it would be determined which method of staging Chekhov was the correct one. I rounded on her with the objection that if such a thing were possible, it would mean that Chekhov was the least of dramatists, of no relevance or resonance to posterity whatever. In fact, he has in a mere hundred years shifted shapes and taken on the form and impress of the times to a remarkable degree.

I am now completing a cross-cultural history of Chekhovian *mises-en-scène* over the past century and throughout the world, which will be published by Cambridge University Press. In part *Rezeptionsgeschichte,* in part the tracing of fashion and concept in directing, it treats the oscillation of Chekhov's reputation and the metamorphoses his dramatic work has undergone in the theatre. The fact that we are drawn here from across the globe to examine his creativity bespeaks the present high-water mark of estimation for Chekhov. But let us not forget that this high estimation is essentially an acquired taste and that he remains caviare to the general.

The attitudes towards Chekhov held by the present age can be summed up by two newspaper cartoons I have pinned to the corkboard in my study. One, by Ben Sargent, showed a wild-haired professor erupting into the office of the president of Enormous State University. "I've tolerated the state of affairs around here long enough, sir," he protests. "I finally realized I had to speak out! Sir, we're turning out graduates who don't know anything! They've got diplomas but they can't read! They can't write! They can't think!" The president interjects a curt "Outrageous!" "I realized, sir," the professor thunders on, "the humanities had hit bottom when one of my students identified Anton Chekhov as a defensive guard for Indiana!!" "Appalling", responds the president and then, leaning across his desk, "Uh—who did he play for?"

This cartoon, in addition to feeding our contempt for our administrative masters, should remind us that, to the world at large, Chekhov is at best a name, perhaps a character in *Star Trek,* but certainly not a household word. In the literary world, however, his name remains one to conjure with, as the other cartoon, "Influences" by S. Harris, sardonically illustrates. The three boxes depict an author at his desk, a mechanic in his garage, and a baseball player leaning on his bat. The bespectacled writer is speaking to an invisible interviewer, saying "Mainly the short-story writers—Hemingway, Eudora Welty, and, of course, Chekhov." Then comes the mechanic: "There was a teacher in high school, and the owner of the first garage I worked in. Then, of course, Chekhov." And finally, the ball player: "I had a great batting coach in the minors, and I try to emulate the great outfielders, like DiMaggio and Mays. And, of course, there's Chekhov."

This is the inevitable Chekhov, the Chekhov who pervades any discussion of modernism in fiction or theatre, the Chekhov who has become a graven image on the Mt Rushmore of contemporary aesthetic sensibilities. I would like to devote the remainder of this address to surveying the shifts in his reputation which have preceded and led up to this state of affairs. Here I limit myself to Chekhov the dramatist, because I believe that it is as a dramatist that Chekhov has persisted most indelibly in the collective consciousness. While his fiction still exercises an influence on the literati and is still fodder for academic dissection, he is thought of first and foremost as a playwright. And the ordinary citizen is more likely to encounter him in a theatre than in a library.

Shortly before Chekhov's death, if you asked anyone who was the greatest living Russian writer, the answer would no doubt have been, "Lev Tolstoy." Tolstoy's imposing position as a moralist and reformer, his eminence at the panoramic novel, the genre most honoured by the nineteenth century, which preferred monumentality, his political stance as the unassailable opponent of autocracy— these and other features made the sage of Yasnaia Poliana the voice of humanitarian culture to the world at large.

Chekhov, on the other hand, was regarded as a purely local phenomenon. Within the Russian Empire, his reputation was fragmented among various publics. The common reader remembered him chiefly as the author of a number of funny stories. The intelligentsia regarded him

as a chronicler of its own malaise, particularly in the plays staged by the Moscow Art Theatre. Factions on the right and left dismissed him as a fence-sitter, what American politics called a "mugwump," too cowardly to take sides in the ideological battles that dominated the pre-revolutionary scene. Outside Russia, he was viewed at best as an exotic *petit-maître,* trading in doom and gloom. The Poles patriotically neglected him, the Germans interpreted him as another exponent of doleful *Schicksalstragödie,* and the Georgians noted sarcastically of his characters that only ethnic Russians would fritter away their lives so trivially. In France, the standard works on Russian literature in 1900 dismissed Chekhov: Waliszweski described his drama as "completely devoid of action and psychological differentiation of characters," while Melchior de Vogüé declared the full-length plays too pessimistic for the French, full of impotent heroes with "enigmatic Slavic souls."[1] (This may signal the first time that deadly but undying remark was made.) In the first two English-language reference books to gloss Chekhov, both published the year before his death, those same dramatic characters were cited as "fit subjects for the psychiatrist" and "a strange assemblage of neurotics, lunatic and semi-lunatic," obsessed with solving the problem of life.[2]

Whatever respect and affection were bestowed on Chekhov, due in part to his untimely demise, began to evaporate almost immediately. At the jubilee celebrations in 1910, dissenting voices could be heard above the chorus of praise. At a meeting of the St Petersburg Literary Society, the prominent feminist author Olga Shapir renewed the charge that he was a poet of gray, humdrum depressives, and added the complaint that his women especially lacked clear outlines or strong emotion, despite the fact that since the 1880s women had been in the forefront of political reform movements.[3] In a period of activism and engagement, Chekhov's deliberately peripheral stance grew increasingly distasteful. It would culminate in the Bolshevik rejection of Chekhov after the October Revolution.

That rejection was due in part to Chekhov's inextricable association with the Moscow Art Theatre, a symbiosis rich in ironies. It was ironical that Chekhov, who deeply admired professional acting technique, should have been imposed on the cultural consciousness of his times by a troupe of amateurs and semi-pros. (Shortly before his death, when asked whom he considered the best actors in his plays, Chekhov provocatively left out the Art Theatre and named only three members of the Imperial Alexandra troupe: Komissarzhevskaia as Nina, Davydov as Ivanov, and Sazonov as Shabelsky.[4]) It was ironical that Stanislavsky, who had trained in Shakespeare, Schiller and musical comedy and whose dearest ambition was to stage historically veristic productions of the classics, should find his most important challenge and success in recreating the dreary world of his contemporaries, and, along the way, inevitably ennoble Chekhov's characters. It was ironical that a theatre whose founders intended to it to be a school for a mass public should find itself explicating the intelligentsia to the intelligentsia. It is perhaps the irony of ironies that the Art Theatre, having discovered its most successful *modus operandi* in its staging of Chekhov, tried to apply it to all sorts of unlikely authors with the to-be-expected failure; while Chekhov himself chafed at what he felt were willful departures from his meaning and technique.

Whatever the discrepancy between Chekhov's vision and that of the Art Theatre, what struck the spectators of the original productions most forcefully was that, like the Maly Theatre in the palmy days of its Ostrovsky premieres, company and author seemed to be totally and intimately amalgamated, the plays seemed to be written and staged by the same person. When the actors at provincial theatres simple-mindedly played Chekhov in a dismal tone, the result was boredom; whereas the Art Theatre revealed the covert, repressed feelings underlying the bad jokes and banal conversation. What distinguished Chekhov's drama from all other plays at the time was what Stanislavsky called the "submarine" course of the through action, which renders the dialogue nearly allegorical. Every individual scenic moment was carefully worked out in terms of the integrality of the entire production, to create a seamlessness. Quotidian or material reality went beyond mere naturalism to achieve the famous *nastroenie* (mood). Stanislavsky's layering of "mood" or "atmosphere" is essentially a symbolist technique: just as the words "Balzac was married in Berdichev" overlay another, more profound emotional reality, so the tableaux of everyday-life, abetted by sound and lighting effects, conduced to an emotional *au-delà,* another realm of more intense reality.

To paraphrase a remark of von Clausewitz, the Art Theatre approach was the carrying-on of literature by other means. This scenic extension of the Russian realistic literary tradition enabled the intelligentsia to behold its hopes and fears on stage in terms it readily adopted. As Osip Mandelshtam wrote in 1923,

> For the intelligentsia to go to the Moscow Art Theatre was almost equal to taking communion or going to church . . .

> Literature, not theatre, characterized that entire generation . . . They understood theatre exclusively as an interpretation of literature . . . into another, more comprehensible and completely natural language.

> . . . The pathos of the generation and of the Moscow Art Theatre was the pathos of Doubting Thomas. They had Chekhov, but Thomas the intellectual did not trust him. He wanted to touch Chekhov, to feel him, to be convinced of his reality.[5]

The illusion of life created by Stanislavsky, his emphasis on subtext and context, provided that reality, and gave Chekhov a novel-like amplitude that satisfied the intelligentsia's need for theme and *Tendenz.*

The Bolsheviks had extra-literary uses for the theatre. No less tendentious, they fomented performance that was stark, immediate and viscerally compelling. The new demands made on art in the aftermath of the October Revolution had a Medusa-like effect on the Art Theatre: it froze in place. Locked into its aging repertory, it found itself and Chekhov both repudiated as irrelevant excrescences of an obsolete bourgeois culture. Sailors at special matinees for workers shouted, "You bore me, Uncle Vania!" while ideologues and the press called for his suppression in favour of a vital, swashbuckling, romantic drama. Although it would later become an article of faith that Lenin had attended the Art Theatre *Vania* and endorsed it (quoth Krupskaia laconically, "He liked it"), at the time émigrés spread the tale of his dissatisfaction: "Is it really necessary to stir up such feelings?" Lenin is reported to have complained. "One needs to appeal to cheerfulness, work, joy."[6] Such vital *animateurs* of Bolshevik theatre as Vakhtangov and Meyerhold turned to the vaudevilles when they sought to stage Chekhov, and the only full-length play of his to be regularly performed was *The Cherry Orchard,* treated as a satiric farce mocking the estate owners and their parasites. In Lobanov's version of 1934, Act II was set in a seedy restaurant; a tipsy Trofimov was thrown out by the waiters in the course of his harangue, which he continued in a bathhouse packed with gymnasium students of both sexes.

While Chekhov languished at home, abroad he was promulgated by a diaspora. The 1920s and '30s are the decades of the émigrés' Chekhov; fugitives from the Revolution saw themselves as Ranevskaias and Gaevs, expelled from a tsarist Eden. The tours of the Moscow Art Theatre and its offshoot the Prague Group disseminated the style and look of the original, now aging, productions, while defectors from the Art Theatre, such as Peter Sharoff and Richard Boleslavsky, perpetuated a Stanislavskian approach in Europe and America. But émigrés tend to preserve their abandoned culture in amber: we should ask, in imitation of Ancient Pistol, "under which Stanislavsky, Bezonian, speak or die?" At what point the *émigré* director had encountered Stanislavsky in the restless evolution of his system determined which phase of Stanislavskianism was promulgated.

Even those refugees who had either rejected the Art Theatre approach or had never practiced it carried on under its banner—Theodore Komisarjevsky in England and Georges Pitoëff in France, who was lyrical, enigmatic, moonstruck and, above all, steeped in romantic nostalgia. If Stanislavsky's *nastroenie* had been that of a *fin-de-siècle* symbolist, evoking psychic states through physical means, the émigré's *nastroenie* hearkened back to a paradise lost. Chekhov, a man of sorrows acquainted with grief, took on, in the eyes of European spectators, a tinge they held to be peculiarly "Russian." Émigré Chekhov was, above all, elegiac, wistful and, like Noel Coward's white elephants, "terribly, terribly sweet."

After the Second World War, Chekhov suffered, in Central and Eastern Europe, from being imparted as a basic cultural ingredient of the Soviet hegemony: he and the Art Theatre interpretation, now heavily adulterated by Socialist Realism, were thrust down the throats of Czech,

Polish, East German and Hungarian audiences. Little wonder if, left to their own devices, they spewed him out again and sought to discredit and supplant the Stanislavsky legacy.

Chekhov's revivification in Europe is due to a Czech and an Italian—Otomar Krejča and Giorgio Strehler, both leftists, but of quite different stripe. At the Divadlo za Brano in Prague, Krejča worked in collaboration with his actors to realize what Gorky had called the cold and cruel Chekhov, an impassive creator who flung his characters into an absurd world. There they beat their wings futilely against the meaninglessness of existence. Without being either a programmatic existentialist or a doctrinaire absurdist, Krejča distilled his own experience as a victim of post-war Soviet domination into an interpretation of Chekhov that administered the shock of recognition to audiences in Prague, Düsseldorf, Louvain and London.

Strehler, for his part, employed elegance and metaphor in his 1956 *Cherry Orchard*, arguably the most influential Chekhov production of modern times. His white-on-white décor with its overhead membrane of petals in a diaphanous veil, breathing with the actors and audience, has influenced everyone from Andrei Serban to last year's staging at the Indiana Rep. Whereas Krejča proclaimed that every decision made in a production automatically gave it a bias that compromised the author's intention, Strehler sought to conflate all the levels of meaning in the play: the narrative, the socio-historical and the universally metaphoric. The toys in the nursery, for instance, went beyond veristic props to become emblemata of the characters' lost innocence and their retarded world. Strehler universalized the nostalgia of Komisarjevsky and Pitoëff by enlarging it beyond the private sphere, while Krejča's productions grew ever more schematic, insisting on the collective grotesque of the Chekhovian ethos.

In the Soviet world of the 1960s, Chekhov was co-opted by those actors and directors who revelled in the conflicts of Arbuzov, Rozov and Volodin. The opposition of a generation of idealists against one of cynics was read into Chekhov's plays, particularly *Ivanov,* which was revived on a regular basis. Echoes from the contemporary stage reverberated in works of Tsarist vintage: Oleg Efremov, for instance, within a three-year span, played Turgenev's Rudin in the movies, Vampilov's anti-hero Zilov on stage and directed *Ivanov* at the Art Theatre, all of them as variations on Lermontov's hero of our times. Antidomesticity was proclaimed by scenery that lacked walls and doors; manor-houses were made to look like skeletal prisons and the branches of the cherry orchard became sterile and gnarled.

The English-speaking world has been most resistant to extremist reforms in the presentation of Chekhov. Psychologized realism remains the preferred format, and the Chekhovian estate has been familiarized as the old homestead or the derelict country house. "Chekhov has been ennobled by age," says Spencer Golub. ". . . He is as soothing and reassuring as the useless valerian drops

dispensed by the doctors in all his plays . . . an article of faith, like all stereotypes . . . the Santa Claus of dramatic literature."[7] This may account for the large number of American plays about Chekhov's own life, in which he turns into Drs Dorn, Astrov or Chebutykin, depending on the playwright's bent. But it is also the case that the English-speaking theatre has, until very recently, been one dominated by playwrights rather than directors. The Chekhovian influence is to be sought more in the plays of N. C. Hunter and Rodney Ackland, Robert Anderson and Tennessee Williams, than in extraordinary *mises-en-scène*. Which means that in the English-speaking world, the treatment of Chekhov is rather backward.

For, whether we look at the development of Chekhovian interpretation inside Russia under Efremov, Tovstonogov, Efros, Liubimov, Nekrosius, and more recently Ianovskaia and Pogrebnichko, or, in the Western world, under Brook, Pintiliè, Bergman, Sturua, Vitez, and Stein, we are looking at the work of directors. At least until the end of the nineteenth century, one could trace the stage history of Shakespeare or Molière through the actors and their treatment of individual roles. But Chekhov's career as a dramatist coincides with the rise of the director as prime mover in the modern theatre; and the integrality of his last plays derives in part from his awareness of what a director's theatre was capable of. Following the Wagnerian notion of *Gesamtkunstwerk,* it required the integration of every component; the actors had to become an ensemble led by a virtuoso conductor. We can compare the Hamlets of Kean and Mochalov to some advantage and understanding; but to compare the Ranevskaias of Irene Worth and Jutta Lampe makes no sense outside the context of the visions of Andrei Serban and Peter Stein.

But even that directorial dominance, or rather imposition of unity, is breaking down under the pressure of post-modernism and deconstruction. The acceptance of Chekhov as a readily recognizable cultural totem makes him available for all sorts of cooptation. Writing in 1960, the late Harry Levin pointed out that the opening of a New York apartment building called The Picasso signalled the domestication and hence end of modernism.[8] When the *enfant terrible* becomes the elder statesman and new coinages have turned into clichés, efforts have to made to recapture the original shock effect. In the 1970s, the process of dismantling the Soviet Chekhovian icon continued: Efros converted *The Cherry Orchard* to a graveyard and Iury Liubimov flung open the wall of the Taganka Theatre during his *Three Sisters,* to reveal the Moscow streets outside: "You yearn for Moscow?" he seemed to be saying. "Well there it is, in all its noise, grubbiness and squalor." Fifty years of false aspiration were debunked in one moment.

Currently Pogrebnichko recreates *Three Sisters* behind a velvet rope as a museum exhibit, cluttered with the detritus of the past, forcing the post-Soviet spectator to come to terms with a culture that has left him washed up on the shoals of the present; while Henrietta Ianovskaia puts her *Ivanov* on roller-skates to show how he attempts to evade the responsibilities of his own sordid situation.

In the United States, the experimental Wooster Group deconstructs *Three Sisters* by means of video screens and improvisations to deconstruct in turn the modern world of mass media and create a hybrid theatrical language. The seamless web of the Stanislavskian simulacrum is fragmented into jagged shreds of interrupted meaning and faulty recollection. Dramatists remote from both Chekhov's sensibility and his language, such as Pam Gems, Edward Bond, David Mamet and Trevor Griffiths, transmogrify him in new versions, refracting their own preoccupations: the Chekhov of Mamet is obsessed with sex, the Chekhov of Griffiths is an angry member of a British labour union. This need of English-speaking playwrights to wrestle Chekhov to the mat has become a rite of passage. There is something primitive and Oedipal in the recurrent cannibalizing of the one universally-admitted patriarch of the modern stage.

Chekhov as patriarch is a jarring image. To explain it, let me return to my earlier remarks about the replacement of Tolstoy by Chekhov as the man of letters *par excellence*. Even as late as the 1940s, György Lukács could emblazon Tolstoy as the *bel idéal* of the universal genius who transcended his otherwise hampering bourgeois milieu by the power of his demiurge-like creativity. In our less heroic age, however, Tolstoy seems unsympathetic at best; like Blake's Old Nobodaddy, he glowers at us disapprovingly from beneath his beetling brows. Tolstoy's creative attainments and his moral demands on us seem the titanic labours of a Golden Age, impossible for us puny mortals to achieve. They also exude a kind of confidence and self-righteousness which are luxuries too costly for the spiritually impecunious survivors of the twentieth century. Even his death was exemplary: Tolstoy's isolated expiration in the railway station at Astapovo is the stuff of tragedy, Lear succumbing on the heath, unreconciled with Cordelia.

Chekhov's death, which has so bemused his successors and been so often retold and reworked as fiction, is, in contrast, a comedy of errors. In a farcical mode, it too is exemplary, from his reported last words "It's a long time since I've had champagne," to his corpse being transported in the goods car marked "Oysters," to the military band straying from a general's funeral to double in brass at his graveside. Chekhov is the more accessible and more familiar figure. His irony has greater appeal than does Tolstoy's moral absolutism. His vaunted objectivity, not all that objective under scrutiny, is nevertheless more welcoming, less judgemental. His inability to write a novel, his preference for small forms, open endings, ethical ambiguities appeal to our post-modern fondness for the marginal, our wary distrust of the grand gesture. Tolstoy the schoolmaster stands over his text, ferule in hand, to make sure we have learned the lesson; Chekhov endears himself to the New Critic, the structuralist and the deconstructionist by modestly bowing himself out, protesting that it's all in the words.

Yet, for all this modesty, over the course of a mere century Chekhov has reached the rank of Shakespeare. They are bracketed together as the greatest playwrights of all time. To cite only one such statement, Andrzej Wajda remarked, "Theatre in our European tradition derives from the word, from literature, the Greeks, Shakespeare, Chekhov."[9] To depict the history of Western theatre as a mountain-range made up of three Everests, the Greeks, Shakespeare and Chekhov, is a breathtaking risk; but it is commonly attempted. Note the absence of Ibsen, who might deserve better, with his ambitious historical dramas and his endeavours to raise everyday experience to the heights of tragic treatment. Chekhov sedulously avoided the grandiose, the overtly poetic, the tragic pose; or else, he undercut them when they arose inadvertently.

Shakespeare, moreover, does put it all in the words. This is all ye know and all ye need to know. But Chekhov's special appeal comes from what he leaves out, another legacy from the symbolists, the pregnant pause. Of course, Stanislavsky, who distrusted the understated, amplified and multiplied the Chekhovian pause, turning it into a pretext for veristic stage effects; an actor who worked at the Art Theatre for one season in 1908/9 recalled that the pauses "were held precisely by the numbers and the actors were recommended to count the seconds mentally during the duration of the pauses."[10] This mechanical rendition loses touch with the essence of the Chekhovian pause, itself a precursor of what Beckett, in his essay on Proust, refers to as the transitional zone in which being makes itself heard. Stanislavsky never succeeded with Shakespeare because he never realized that the playing must be done on the lines and not in-between them.

What then justifies the modern coupling of Chekhov and Shakespeare? I would suggest that Keats, in his famous 1818 letter on "negative capability," put his finger on it. Reacting to a performance of Edmund Kean as Richard III, he mused on Shakespeare's protean brilliance: ". . . at once it struck me, what quality went to form a Man of Achievement especially in Literature & which Shakespeare possessed so enormously—I mean Negative Capability, that is when man is capable of being in uncertainties, Mysteries, doubts, without any irritable reaching after fact & reason."[11] Walter J. Bate paraphrases this to mean, "in our life of uncertainties, where no one system or formula can explain everything . . . what is needed is an imaginative openness of mind and heightened receptivity to reality in its full and diverse concreteness."[12] Or to put it another way, Shakespearean mastery requires a negation of the writer's own ego, a sympathetic absorption in the essential significance of the writer's object. Chekhov seems to have attained that state of authorial absence.

For Keats, as for the English Romantics as a whole, Shakespeare's brilliance at negative capability was exhibited by his extensive gallery of characters, all equally vivid, multi-faceted and imbued with idiosyncratic opinions, speech-patterns, behaviour. Chekhov can hardly exhibit such variety or plenitude in his plays; the narrow, seemingly repetitive nature of his dramatic world was a ready target for satire and parody even in his lifetime. But another, earlier letter of Keats comes to our aid: in it he divided ethereal things into three categories: "Things real—things semireal—and no things—Things real—such as existences of Sun Moon & Stars and passages of Shakspeare—Things semireal such as Love, the Clouds &c which require a greeting of the Spirit to make them wholly exist—and Nothings which are made Great and dignified by an ardent pursuit."[13]

Chekhov admits the existence of real things in his writings, but takes them for granted; however, his spirit is not so ready to greet semireal things such as love. Their existence remains problematic and nebulous for his characters. But the confines of the Chekhovian world teem with Keats's "Nothings" to be made great and dignified by an ardent pursuit. As Stanislavsky intuitively perceived, a samovar in Chekhov was not the same as a samovar in Ostrovsky: it, along with the pauses and sound effects and changeable weather, bespoke the overall tone, reflected the inner life of the characters. Leonid Andreev named this interrelationship of everything in Chekhov "panpsychism." The same soul animates whatever appears on stage:

> On the stage Chekhov must be performed not only by human beings, but by drinking glasses and chairs and crickets and military overcoats and engagement rings . . . it all comes across not as items from reality or true-to-life sound and its utterances, but as the protagonists' thoughts and sensations disseminated throughout space.[14]

This goes beyond the sympathetic fallacy; it creates a distinctive microcosm, instantly recognizable whatever the vagaries of directors. It is the unifying factor that ties together even the most seemingly non-communicative dialogue and solipsistic yearnings.

In his book *The Theatrical Event*, David Cole refers to *illud tempus,* an archetypal realm which the theatre must depict, "not so much when it first occurred as where it is always happening."[15] Whatever reality the estates and garrison towns of Chekhov's plays held for its original audiences, they have now taken on a wider semiotic function. They transcend a specific society to become archetypal realms. The spell-binding lake of **The Seagull** has more in common with the island of *The Tempest* than with a similar landscape in Turgenev; the rooms in the Prozorovs' home can expand to the dimensions of Agamemnon's palace or dwindle to the claustrophobic cells of Samuel Beckett. The first foreign critics of Chekhov could not have been more wrong when they condemned him as the poet of an obsolescent set, circumscribed by its own eccentricity. Just as the Shakespearean *illud tempus* shines through modern-dress and tendentious transpositions, the Chekhovian *illud tempus* gains in eloquent meaning from its disguises, even when Thomas Kilroy transfers **The Seagull** to the Ireland of the Celtic Twilight or Tadashi Suzuki plunges the officers of **Three Sisters** into Beckettian baskets or the Irondale Ensemble Project turns **Uncle Vania** into a 1940s radio announcer in Charlevoix, Michigan. Without shedding its specificity, the world of the Chekhovian *intelligent* has become as remote as Camelot and as familiar as Grover's Corners, as exotic as Shangri La and as homely as Bellow's

Falls. It instantly conjures up a long vanished way of life that nevertheless compels us to adduce current counterparts. The persistence of this identifiable and idiosyncratic world suggests that he never stopped being Chekhov our contemporary.

NOTES

[1] K. Waliszewski, *Littérature russe* (Paris, 1900): 426; de Vogüé quoted in Iu. Felichkin, "Rol' teatra v vospriiatii tvorchestva Chekhova vo Frantsii," in *Literaturnyi Muzei A. P. Chekhova: Sbornik statei i materialov,* vypusk V (Rostov, 1969): 155.
[2] Leo Wiener, *Anthology of Russian Literature* (New York, 1903): II; A. Bates, *The Drama* (London, 1903): 73.
[3] "V Peterburge," *Chekhovskii iubileinyi sbornik* (Moscow, 1910): 530.
[4] A. Ia. Al'tshuller, "Chekhov i Aleksandrinskii teatr ego vremeni," *Russkaia literatura,* 3 (1968): 169.
[5] Osip Mandel'shtam, *Teatr i muzyka,* 36 (6 November 1923).
[6] Krupskaia quoted in *Moskovskii Khudozhestvennyi teatr v sovetskuiu epokhu: Materialy i dokumenty,* 2nd ed. (Moscow, 1974): 124; V. A. Nelidov, *Teatral'naia Moskva (sorok let moskovskikh teatrov)* (Berlin-Riga, 1931): 426.
[7] Spencer Golub, in *Newsnotes on Soviet and East European Drama and Theatre,* III, 3 (Nov. 1983): 2-3.
[8] Harry Levin, "What Was Modernism?" (1960) in *Varieties of Literary Experience,* ed. S. Burnshaw (New York, 1962): 307.
[9] Quoted in Maciej Karpinski, *The Theatre of Andrzej Wajda,* tr. C. Paul (Cambridge, 1989): 124.
[10] A. A. Mgebrov, *Zhizn' v teatre,* ed. E. Kuznetsov, I (Leningrad, 1920): 224-5.
[11] *The Letters of John Keats,* ed. H. E. Rollins, I (Cambridge, Mass., 1958): 184.
[12] W. J. Bate, *John Keats* (New York, 1966): 249.
[13] Keats, letter to Benjamin Bailey (13 Mar. 1818).
[14] Leonid Andreev, *Pis'ma o teatre* (1912), trans. as "Letters on Theatre," in *Russian Dramatic Theory from Pushkin to the Symbolists,* ed. and trans. L. Senelick (Austin, 1981): 240-1.
[15] D. Cole, *The Theatrical Event: a Mythos, a Vocabulary, a Perspective* (Middletown, Conn., 1975): 8.

One-Act Plays

Eric Bentley (essay date 1958)

SOURCE: "Apologia," in *The Brute and Other Farces,*
by Anton Chekhov, edited by Eric Bentley, translated by
Eric Bentley and Theodore Hoffman, Applause Theatre
Book Publishers, 1958, pp. i-vii.

[*In the following excerpt, Bentley discusses Chekhov's
short comic plays and declares that the writer's "greatest
plays have a farcical component, and his slightest farces
have something in them of the seriousness, pathos, and
even subtlety of the greatest plays."*]

1.

Except for some later revisions in the dialogue, Chekhov's seven one-act farces belong to the years 1886-1891,
which immediately precede the 'major phase' when the
famous full-length plays were written. Like the funny stories which he signed 'Chekhonte' because he was a little
self-conscious about them, these little plays are admittedly 'minor Chekhov,' though one makes the admission with
a sinking heart in an age which makes a cult of the 'major'—the notion of the major, anyway—in order to excuse
its lazy reluctance to read any man's collected works. One
would not deny that 'The Best Plays of Chekhov' contains
just what it says it does, but one might assert that a reader
should no more be content to sit down with that book than
a parent should be content to sit down to dinner with only
his best children.

Chekhov in 1888.

It is never wise for an author to give a modest account of
himself: the critics accept it. The lighthearted Chekhonte
was discounted long ago. Anton Chekhov is played on
Broadway and in the West End in a vein of soulful som-
nolence. The adjective 'Chekhovian' can convey any shade
of mournful emotionality from the wistful to the lugubrious; it never suggests the sunny, the zany, the skittish, the
wildly destructive, though Chekhov in fact was famous for
these qualities even before the others showed themselves.

In a recent collection designed to modify and correct the
prevailing view of Chekhov, Mr. Edmund Wilson finds
'his true weight and point' in his last, most sombre, and
most sociological works. It is high time, I conclude, to
protest against the tendency of modern critics to overlook
the obvious. Mr. Wilson did exactly the same thing in his
study of Dickens years ago. His new Dickens was to interest us as a man involved in psychoneurotic conflict.

And today there is a fairly widespread assumption that a
writer of funny stories—or melodramatic ones—is scarcely worth a critic's attention. Farce and melodrama have
come to be valued, if at all, as embellishments of more

earnest and more tortured books. One critic makes a
favourite of *Hard Times,* ostensibly because of its superior (that is, more Jamesian) structure. One cannot resist the conclusion, however, that he prefers dark moods
to more frivolous ones as more becoming to the serious
business of Literature, not to mention Criticism. This is
to be seduced by *l'esprit sérieux. The Pickwick Papers*
may be incommensurable with *Hard Times,* but surely
is no more inferior to it than *Don Quixote* is inferior to
Madame Bovary?

Even in the most serious works of Chekhov, as of Dickens, farce and melodrama are not embellishments added
later to a structure of more 'literal' substance. One might
plausibly maintain, on the contrary, that the structure itself is farcical and melodramatic and that it is the seriousness which is superadded. But at this point the notion
of addition is itself misleading, for, in a fully realized
masterpiece, nothing is merely stuck on; all is, finally, of
a piece. At any rate, once we see that the role of farce in

certain non-farcical masterpieces—from Molière and Dickens to Shaw and Chekhov—is a large and reputable one, we are free at last to view farce in its pure state as a large and reputable phenomenon.

2.

Not that its state often *is* pure. Labiche has kept French schoolteachers busy for a long time now distinguishing between his 'true farces' and his 'comedies of character'. The poor man himself seems to have been terribly confused on the point. And Chekhov takes no greater pains to stay within boundaries staked out by pedagogues. In the latest of the plays printed, here, **"The Celebration,"** he is taking his leave of farce forever and launching out, as we sense in reading it, towards his masterworks. He made six versions of **"The Harmfulness of Tobacco,"** the earliest of our plays, each one more serious than the last. Even **"The Brute"** and **"Marriage Proposal"** are a mass of psychological details such as no average farceur would use.

How far Chekhov's individuality carried him from the regular article can be demonstrated by comparing **"The Brute"** with its 'source'. The play was suggested to Chekhov by a performance of a French one-act farce: "Les Jurons de Cadillac" by Pierre Berton (1865). Here the principal joke is that the man—already a suitor for the lady's hand at the outset—can't refrain from swearing for more than a few seconds at a time. The action of the play consists of the lady's offering to marry him if only he can hold himself in for one hour. The climactic twist in the action comes when the man fails to meet the demand in such an amiable way that the lady is charmed by him, and the curtain comes down as she herself swears one of his great oaths. The jest seems almost simpleminded compared with Chekhov's. And to tell a less simple story, Chekhov has recast the dramatic action entirely, and placed it in a different, more actual social setting. He has, as we say, 'made more of it', and that 'more' includes a good deal that, by any standard, is serious.

Yet, if it is possible to overlook the serious elements in a Chekhov farce, it is also possible to be obsessed with them. Actors are sometimes tempted to play **"Swan Song"** or **"The Harmfulness of Tobacco"** as wholly pathetic outpourings. The wrongness of the interpretation is proved by the fact they find themselves forced into making cuts. When the lecturer in **"Tobacco"** is exclusively pathetic, the actor has to omit 'business' that is inevitably grotesque, such as his stamping on his jacket and showing the audience the rents in the back of his waistcoat. To be consistent he should also omit parts of the text too, for only the license of farce permits—for example—the number thirteen to recur so madly.

In some ways, **"Swan Song"** is an even subtler case. Here the pathos is more unabashed. Yet a touch of the utterly ridiculous is necessary not merely to the texture but to the characterization. Those who think that farce always coarsens and simplifies should note that it is farce, in this play, that makes the characterization complex.

Chekhov's skill in the mixing of the elements is nowhere more remarkably apparent than in his *re*-mixing of them when he makes over one of his own stories into a play. Perhaps the most interesting instance is **"Summer in the Country,"** which was made out of a story called **"One of Many."**[1] Mr. Magarshack interprets the changes as an attempt to 'preserve the decencies of the stage', for, in the story, Tolkachov's load includes a child's coffin, and the poor fellow grumbles that he will probably never get paid for it. But there are reasons for omitting this which go far beyond the matter of moral propriety. A child's coffin on stage, Chekhov must rightly have felt, would carry a higher charge of painful emotion than a farce can stand. Chekhov also knew his stagecraft, and might have concluded that no actor could manage a coffin in addition to half a dozen other impedimenta.

On one point, however, I agree with the Magarshack interpretation. In the story, as a climax to her various persecutions, the wife presents her lawful claim to Tolkachov's person at four in the morning. Chekhov's omission of this poignant incident in the play can surely be taken as a concession to the squeamishness of nineteenth-century audiences. I have smuggled it into the script printed here. And I will report an experience that would have no public importance except that it shows rather vividly how Chekhovian work depends upon a balance that is very easily upset: re-instating this single 'point', I was tempted to put back other things as well, but I soon found myself in danger of destroying the farcical tone of the play without substituting any other.

Chekhov's whole life in the theatre might be seen, not as an exercise in tragi-comedy as traditionally conceived, but as a search for a kind of drama in which tragic and comic elements lose their separate identities in a new, if nameless, unity. Even a title may vibrate with the energy of this search. The play now under discussion is called in the Russian original: **"The Tragedian in Spite of Himself,"** on the pattern of *Le médecin malgré lui*. Farce is here the form imposed on a potentially tragic situation. But only potentially tragic. The play does not resemble one of Eugène Ionesco's tragic farces in which the despair is deeper than the humour or the love. It is not a tragedy 'in spite of' the farcical form, for Tolkachov is not a tragic figure but a tragedian, a play actor, one who sees himself as tragic, a victim of self-dramatization and self-pity, a comic figure. (With all this in mind, I very much wanted to keep the original title. But, since there has never been a plausible translation of Molière's title, it seemed foolish to follow one of the implausible ones in translating Chekhov. My title is derived from Chekhov's subtitle, and my subtitle is more or less a quotation from Tolkachov, the play being, in reality, not a tragedy but a farce.)

In fine, Chekhov's farces, if they are minor, cannot, as such, be dismissed. His greatest plays have a farcical component, and his slightest farces have something in them of the seriousness, pathos, and even sublety of the greatest plays. In some ways simple, they are not one-sided but dialectical. The critic who judges them and the director who stages them must have a dialectical mind in order to grasp the constant conflict and synthesis of elements. In its fine balance of contrasts—particularly of the pathetic and the ridiculous—a Chekhov farce might be regarded as a full-fledged Chekhov drama in miniature.

NOTE

[1] *Swan Song* and *The Celebration* are also adaptations of Chekhov stories—*Kalkhas* and *A Helpless Creature*, respectively. In *The Wedding* he draws on two stories (*A Marriage of Convenience* and *A Wedding with a General*) and a sketch (*The Marriage Season*). For further particulars, see David Magarshack's two books on Chekhov: *Chekhov the Dramatist* and *Chekhov: A Life*.

Vera Gottlieb   (essay date 1982)

SOURCE: "The Farce-Vaudevilles," in *Chekhov and the Vaudeville: A Study of Chekhov's One-Act Plays,* Cambridge University Press, 1982, pp. 46-109.

[*In the essay below, Gottlieb closely examines several of Chekhov's short comic plays, including "The Bear," "The Proposal," and "The Anniversary," uncovering dramatic techniques similar to those employed in the author's full-length works.*]

> Chekhov's language is as precise as 'Hullo!' and as simple as 'Give me a glass of tea'. In his method of expressing the idea of a compact little story, the urgent cry of the future is felt: 'Economy!'
>
> It is these new forms of expressing an idea, this true approach to art's real tasks, that gives us the right to speak of Chekhov as a master of verbal art.
>
> Behind the familiar Chekhovian image created by the philistines, that of a grumbler displeased with everything, the defender of 'ridiculous people' against society, behind Chekhov the twilight bard we discern the outlines of the other Chekhov: the joyous and powerful master of the art of literature.[1]
>
> Vladimir Mayakovsky,
> *The Two Chekhovs* (1914)

On 12 December 1900, Tolstoy was present at a rehearsal of a 'Chekhov evening' arranged by the Society for Art and Literature. Not wishing to be stared at in the auditorium, Tolstoy asked the producer, Nikolai Arbatov, to seat him somewhere in the wings. The vaudevilles *The Bear* and *The Wedding* were being performed and, as an eye-witness reports, 'Tolstoy watched, and all the time a pleased, joyful smile never left his face. At times he roared with laughter as he listened to the incredibly funny lines.' During the interval Tolstoy talked to the actors, and expressed his enthusiasm and amazement over Chekhov's humour: 'After Gogol,' he is reported to have said, 'we don't have such a brilliant, powerful humorist as Chekhov. Sound and powerful humour is absolutely necessary for us. And Chekhov's stories are pearls of beauty.'

It is, of course, scarcely surprising that Tolstoy immediately responded to the social value of Chekhov's one-act comedies, but, in addition, Tolstoy was apparently fully aware of the innovatory nature of Chekhov's dramatic form. After the performance, he went to see Arbatov and began to talk enthusiastically about the virtues of the Russian vaudeville: 'I love the vaudeville, and I think a real Russian vaudeville—and the best I know—is Chekhov's **Wedding**.' Valuing Chekhov's 'dramatic jokes' highly (though none of the full-length plays),[2] Tolstoy noted the way they differed from the traditional vaudeville, and he pointed out the 'causal' comedy which motivated the action and served as the main driving force of the plays. In addition, Tolstoy praised *The Proposal* for the absence in it of what he called 'the French nonsensical surprises'.[3]

Implicit in Tolstory's reported remark about the lack of 'the French nonsensical surprises' is an awareness of the different nature of action and plot in Chekhov's one-act plays, a difference which, in turn, opens up further innovatory features. Tolstoy recognised and valued a characteristic of Chekhov's vaudevilles which was significantly lacking in the conventional vaudevilles: 'realism'. This 'realism' relates to the depiction of a milieu and to the credibility of Chekhov's characters, to a particular comic characterisation which prompted Vakhtangov to talk not of caricature but of 'broader realism'.[4] It is to this 'broader realism' that Tolstoy's remark about Gogol and Chekhov may be related: the 'realism' of Chekhov's one-act plays has room for the grotesque and the exaggerated, elements which were heightened to varying degrees by both Vakhtangov in his production of *The Wedding* (1920), and Meyerhold in his programme composed of *The Bear, The Proposal* and *The Anniversary* which he called *33 Swoons* (1935). 'Realism' was substantially lacking in the traditional vaudevilles given that the content was dictated by the conventions of the genre, whereas in Chekhov's vaudevilles the content demands and dictates a new form.

This new form manifests itself in all of the one-act plays, whether in the farce-vaudevilles *The Bear* (1888), *The Proposal* (1888-9), *A Tragic Role* (1889), *The Anniversary* (1891), or the unfinished *Night before the Trial* (1890s); in the 'dramatic studies' *On the High Road* (1885), *Swan Song* (1887) or *Tatyana Repina* (1889); in the one-act play *The Wedding* (1889-90), or the one-act monologue *Smoking is Bad for You* (1886-1903). All of these short plays are often referred to as 'vaudevilles', but it is important to note that Chekhov gave each of the plays a precise subtitle indicating the form and, up to a point, the mood, a practice he was to follow in his full-length plays. . . .

THE BEAR (1888)

In a letter to Yakov Polonsky on 22 February 1888, Chekhov wrote: 'Just to while away the time, I wrote a trivial little vaudeville in the French manner, called *The Bear* . . . Alas! when they find out on *New Times* that I write vaudevilles they will excommunicate me. What am I to do? I plan something worthwhile—and—it is all tra-la-la! In spite of all my attempts at being serious the result is nothing; with me the serious always alternates with the trivial'.

According to Magarshack,[5] Chekhov had, in fact, followed the practice of so many of his predecessors and his contemporaries in 'borrowing' a French play as the source for *The Bear*: *Les Jirons de Cadillac* by Pierre Berton. The version Chekhov may have seen at Korsh's Theatre, however, had already been adapted from a French to a Russian vaudeville and was performed under the title of *Conquerors are Above Criticism* by a friend of Chekhov's, Solovstov, the actor to whom Chekhov dedicated *The Bear* and who subsequently played the part of Smirnov, Chekhov's 'bear'. The part of Popova was taken by Natalya Rybehinskaya, the actress with whom Solovstov had appeared in *Conquerors are Above Criticism*. Both the French original and the Russian adaptation are conventional comedies of situation: a beautiful society woman tames a vulgar but good-natured sea-dog. The situation is funny, but the characters are stereotypes, and the 'transitions' as unlikely and incredible as those of so many vaudevilles. The only similarity, in fact, between the plot of the original and that of Chekhov's *The Bear* is in the idea of the 'bear' himself, since it is debatable whether Popova does 'tame' Smirnov; she is certainly not a beautiful society woman, and Smirnov is nothing as exotic as a seaman, but simply (and this follows a convention) a rival landowner. Chekhov does, however, replace one convention with another: Popova, though not a society lady, and not a beautiful woman, is a young widow—our first image of her is as she sits 'in deep mourning'—but (and this is crucial to an understanding of Chekhov's technique) she has 'dimpled checks'. Chekhov thus immediately sets up the apparently conventional image of a young grieving widow, and simultaneously raises a question as to either the depth and sincerity of her grief, or the 'naturalness' of it. In other words, he is, in a sense, 'under-cutting' his own image.

At first glance, however, this one-act 'joke' appears little other than an extremely funny conventional vaudeville of situation or, in terms of the vaudevilles of the 1880s, 'a comedy-joke': a cast list of three characters composed of a widowed landowner called Popova, a landowner called Smirnov who is in early middle age, and an old manservant who is called Luka. The names of the characters are common Russian names. Thus Chekhov's audience might well have expected a conventional amorous vaudeville: a man, a woman, a servant who might be there as a source of intrigue and obstacle, and the resulting tangle. Moreover, there *are* obstacles in the play: the woman is in mourning for her husband, and has shut herself off from life, while the man has come to claim his debts, and has no respect for the grieving widow. The play reaches a climax in which a duel is nearly fought, but suddenly Smirnov and Popova are in love and the play appears to end happily.

But even when considering the play on the level of plot, a discordant note is sounded: the duel. A duel on-stage was a completely conventional climactic device and source of tension, and invariably involved the rival lovers fighting over the hand of a woman; in *The Bear,* however, the convention of a duel is maintained by Chekhov, but only to be turned inside out given that the participants are Smirnov and Popova herself. Popova's acceptance of Smirnov's furious challenge, and subsequent insistence on fighting are both a reversal of the convention and a parody. As a result, the woman over whom men conventionally fought a duel is no longer the conventionally romantic, passive figure in the background of the action but an active participant in the action. In addition, Chekhov 'plays' with a further device which is implicit in the stock situation of a duel: a love triangle. Here, if there is a 'triangle' at all, it is between Smirnov, Popova and her dead husband, Nikolai. However, any rivalry offered by the dead Nikolai decreases in the course of the play, is in itself a source of irony, and in any case only exists in the mind of Popova; there is, therefore, no impediment to the action of the play except the characters themselves, and no source of action except their attitudes and behaviour. Thus Luka, instead of furthering or impeding the action, cannot, in fact, cope with the clash of characters and becomes an impotent, though sometimes sensible, witness. In the conventional 'comedy-joke' the servant was often at the source of the play's comic structure, and also used to supply exposition for the audience; in *The Bear,* however, Chekhov makes Luka not so much a structural part of the comic action as a witness of the comedy, who thus serves more as a 'norm' or 'touchstone' for the audience. Again, Chekhov's technique is to set up a 'tone' which is then commented on by someone or something within the same structure. But what in the last four full-length plays becomes a complex use of juxtaposition and counterpoint, may, in the early plays, be seen working very simply: Luka, in *The Bear,* provides a sense of proportion.

This 'sense of proportion' is evident at the very beginning of the play, in that what Luka says to Popova is juxtaposed with what the audience sees in the opening *tableau*: Popova, 'in deep mourning, with her eyes fixed on a snapshot', forms an exaggerated visual statement of 'grief'. An audience has no sooner accepted this *tableau* than Luka provides both exposition and exposure:

> This won't do, madam, you're just making your life a misery. Cook's out with the maid picking fruit, every living creature's happy and even our cat knows how to enjoy herself—she's parading round the yard trying to pick up a bird or two. But here you are cooped up inside all day like you was in a convent cell—you never have a good time. Yes, it's true. Nigh on twelve months it is since you last set foot outdoors.
>
> (H.1.51)

With the opening lines of the play, Luka simultaneously sets up the situation, and exposes the ridiculous: he compares Popova, unfavourably, with the cat. Thus, just as Popova's 'dimpled cheeks' work against her mourning dress, so Luka's opening words work against the opening visual statement. Luka does, therefore, serve his traditional purpose in explaining matters to the audience weather, time of day, off-stage dramatic world, and so on; but on an innovatory level, Chekhov uses him to indicate to the audience exactly how ludicrous the situation is, an indication which works implicitly through contrasts. The effect, though comic, is immediately three-dimensional, since the ludicrous aspect of the situation rests entirely on Popova's attitude and behaviour: the cat lives normally, but Popova gazes soulfully at a snapshot—not, significantly, a large, dominating oil-painting of the dead husband, but a little snapshot which, in turn, makes its own 'proportional' comment. Popova has abdicated from life: 'My life's finished. He lies in his grave, I've buried myself inside these four walls. We're both dead.' She, to paraphrase Masha in *The Seagull,* is 'in mourning for her life':[6] both Popova and Masha are young women, both are 'role-playing' and self-dramatising, but whereas Popova drops her romantic image and thus remains a comic character, Masha increasingly lives out her role until, with the frustration and pointlessness of her own unrealised, even ill-defined, aspirations, she becomes a tragicomic figure. Masha never recognises her own initially ridiculous stance, whereas Popova, even before meeting Smirnov, is able to appraise her self-imposed role as the grief-stricken widow, and its value:

LUKA: . . . You're young, and pretty as a picture with that peaches-and-cream look, so make the most of it. Them looks won't last for ever, you know. If you wait another ten years to come out of your shell and lead them officers a dance, you'll find it's too late.

POPOVA: (*decisively*) Never talk to me like that again, please. When Nicholas died my life lost all meaning, as you know. You may think I'm alive, but I'm not really. I swore to wear this mourning and shun society till my dying day, do you hear? Let his departed spirit see how I love him!

But then Popova explodes her own romantic image as she continues:

Yes, I realize you know what went on—that he was often mean to me, cruel and, er, unfaithful even, but I'll be true to the grave and show him how much I can love. And he'll find me in the next world just as I was before he died.

(H.1.51-2)

In this way, Popova, through self-revelation, deflates her own romantic act, but the pattern of meaning is complex and, correspondingly, psychologically accurate: partly because Nikolai was unfaithful, Popova is determined to play the grieving widow to the hilt, but her realisation of her own role-playing and of the true nature of relations between herself and her dead husband makes her ripe for deflation by the outside world. The situation is therefore set up in which Popova must be exposed; with the arrival of Smirnov the clash between romanticism and vulgarity begins. But this need for 'deflation' also places the situation clearly in the world of comedy. If, in the course of the play, Popova had been led to the realisation of Nikolai's infidelity the play would, at the very least, have been a drama, not a comedy. As it is, Chekhov presents Popova as playing out a drama in a play which is resolutely a comedy. Popova is one of many characters in Chekhov's plays who, intent on playing out a drama, find themselves in a comedy of their own making.

This feature of the play was clearly brought out by Meyerhold's interpretation of *The Bear* in his production: *33 Swoons.* The actress Zinaida Raikh played Popova, a performance described by Yuzovsky:

Recently we saw her in *The Lady of the Camellias.* The dramatic character of Marguerite Gautier which had been revealed by her lyrically—all those half-shades, pauses, the sad play of glances, the voice full of feeling, the hidden feelings—the more hidden, the dearer they were to her. And lo and behold!—maybe it is a risky comparison—but there appeared Marguerite's younger sister. The very same lyricism: half-shades, pauses, play of glances, hidden feelings. But only within the plane of a comedy. It is as if the younger sister were teasing the older one. And the similarity is intensified also because they are both Frenchwomen. Popova-Raikh is, of course, a Frenchwoman—or wants to resemble a Frenchwoman. Everything that there is of a French element, of a Maupassant element, of 'winking', of the slyly ironical in the words 'young widow' opens up in the presentation of Popova. 'The young widow!' . . . this is a whole culture . . . a real social type . . . She hides [vice], but she hides it gracefully, which means she is hiding and showing it, and in this is the whole art: to hide so that it can be seen, otherwise there is no play. What kind of young widow is she? She is also a hypocrite, but hypocrisy is here playing with open cards, that is to say—the revealing of the method.[7]

Meyerhold did not distort the play in casting and interpreting Popova in this way, as a younger sister to Marguerite Gautier. Instead, he heightened the parody in the play, and made a total interpretation which was justified also by Smirnov's realisation of Popova's 'act':

POPOVA: . . . I've buried myself alive inside these four walls and I shall go round in these widow's weeds till my dying day.

SMIRNOV: (*with a contemptuous laugh*) Widow's weeds! Who do you take me for? As if I didn't know why you wear this fancy dress and bury yourself indoors! Why, it sticks out a mile! Mysterious and romantic, isn't it? Some army cadet or hack poet may pass by your garden, look up at your window and think: 'There dwells Tamara, the mysterious princess, the one who buried herself alive from love of her husband.' Who do you think you're fooling?

POPOVA: (*flaring up*) *What!* You dare to take that line with me!

SMIRNOV: Buries herself alive—but doesn't forget to powder her nose!

(H.1.59)

Smirnov, a man who 'calls a spade a spade', sees through Popova, and considers himself wise to all feminine wiles. But if Popova must be brought down to earth and shocked out of her 'romanticism', Smirnov must be tamed. No intrigue, no 'misunderstandings', are required: the source of the action lies in the characters and the clash of characters; equally, the source of the comedy lies in the clash between Popova's 'refinement' and Smirnov's 'vulgarity'. The worse he behaves, the greater her air of refinement, and vice versa. The exaggeration of these characteristic features was not Meyerhold's distortion of the play, but Chekhov's method of characterisation. The effect, though exaggerated, is nonetheless three-dimensional. Thus, although the conflict is set in motion by the fact that Popova is 'in no fit state to discuss money', while Smirnov, if he does not get the money, 'will be in a fit state to go bust with a capital B', the psychological motivation for the conflict arises exactly because of Popova's 'state' and Smirnov's use, so to speak, of 'capitals'.

Smirnov is, in fact, almost disarmingly aware of his own character: whereas Popova is full of guile, Smirnov is blunt to the point of rudeness, but, again, Chekhov allows the characters to reveal themselves. There is no exposition, in the conventional sense, of Smirnov's character—only self-revelation:

> And people expect me to be cool and collected! I met the local excise man on my way here just now. 'My dear Smirnov,' says he, 'why are you always losing your temper?' But how can I help it, I ask you? I'm in desperate need of money! Yesterday morning I left home at crack of dawn. I call on everyone who owes me money, but not a soul forks out. I'm dog-tired. I spend the night in some God-awful place—by the vodka barrel in a Jewish pot-house. Then I fetch up here, fifty miles from home, hoping to see the colour of my money, only to be fobbed off with this 'no fit state' stuff! How *can* I keep my temper?
>
> (H.1.54)

Following the same tack in a monologue in Scene V, Smirnov also helps to create the off-stage dramatic world and the milieu of the play, and continues, comically, to reveal himself. The monologue itself, with Popova hurrying out to leave Smirnov on his own, is credibly motivated by the inevitable explosion of Smirnov's temper, but the relationship with the audience at this point is multifaceted. Chekhov's use of the artificial device of the monologue is interesting: on the one hand, an element of confidentiality with the audience is very much present in Smirnov's movement, attitude, and sometimes rhetorical questions; on the other hand, this outburst seems both natural and inevitable, given Smirnov's character and behaviour; but, in addition, Smirnov seems initially to continue his conversation with the absent Popova:

> Well, what price that! 'In no fit state'! Her husband died seven months ago, if you please! Now have I got my interest to pay or not? I want a straight answer—yes or no? All right, your husband's dead, you're in no fit state and so on and so forth, and your blasted manager's hopped it. But what am I supposed to do? Fly away from my creditors by balloon, I take it! Or go and bash the old brain-box against a brick-wall?! I call on Gruzdev[8]—not at home. Yaroshevich is in hiding. I have a real old slanging-match with Kuritsyn and almost chuck him out of the window. Mazutov has the belly-ache, and this creature's 'in no fit state'. Not one of the swine will pay. This is what comes of being too nice to them and behaving like some snivelling no-hoper or old woman. It doesn't pay to wear kid gloves with this lot! All right, just you wait—I'll give you something to remember me by! You don't make a monkey out of me, blast you! I'm staying here—going to stick around till she coughs up. Pah! I feel well and truly riled today. I'm shaking like a leaf, I'm so furious—choking I am. Phew, my God, I really think I'm going to pass out!
>
> (H.1.54-5)

It is the physical manifestation of the characters' emotional state in the farce-vaudevilles which gave Meyerhold his title: *33 Swoons.* In **The Bear,** in **The Proposal** and **The Anniversary** there are, in total, 33 occasions in which one character or another 'swoons'; situations, other people, or emotions cause a physical reaction which, invariably, is out of all proportion to cause. The discrepancy between the extreme physical reaction and the situation causing it, is a source of farce and slapstick but, as always with Chekhov, it too makes its own ironic point: the very discrepancy between cause and effect heightens the ridiculous in character and situation. This, too, relates to the 'hiding of the method—and showing it'. The audience thus accepts the straight farce (and correspondingly increased rhythm and tempo) of what is witnessed, but simultaneously recognises the ridiculous. In *The Bear,* Chekhov uses a 'swoon' to make *unconventional* the servant's reaction to the climactic mood around him:

> SMIRNOV: (*jumping up*). You hold your tongue! Who do you think you're talking to? I'll carve you up in little pieces.

> LUKA: (*clutching at his heart*). Heavens and saints above us! (*falls into an armchair*) Oh, I feel something terrible—fair took my breath away, it did.

and, as the tension builds:

> I feel faint. Fetch water.

> (H.1.60)

In this way, the 'heroes' are made thoroughly unheroic, and the servant as human in his physical reactions as his masters. In the one-act plays this extreme physical reaction is primarily farcial, but in *Ivanov* or in the four last full-length plays, the physical state of many of the characters expresses a deeper psychological and sociological malaise. Thus, in *The Three Sisters,* for example, Andrey says to Chebutykin: 'I shan't play cards tonight, I'll just sit and watch. I feel a bit unwell. I get so out of breath, is there anything I can do for it, Doctor?'[9] The cure would be a different life-style and attitude. In *Uncle Vanya* the constant physical malaise of the characters says much about the way of life and the characters' ability or inability to cope with life. And, at other times, Chekhov conveys a character's inability to cope with reality not only by means of a physical *reaction* but also by an *action* expressive of an inner malaise: in *The Seagull,* for instance, Masha takes snuff and secret drinks as 'drugs' to insulate herself from reality; and similarly, in *The Cherry Orchard,* Gaev comforts and distracts himself with sweets and imaginary games of billiards. But where Chekhov retains an extreme physical reaction from his characters, it is not only to show a character's lack of a sense of proportion but develops in the later plays into a means of showing a character's inability to cope, and the effect is thus no longer necessarily farcial. In *The Three Sisters,* Olga feels faint and has to have a drink of water after Natasha has shouted at Anfisa; Olga cannot cope with unpleasantness, and reacts physically. Serious, or tragi-comic, techniques of the later plays may be seen as initially farcial in the earlier one-act plays.

This may be seen in *The Bear* where Smirnov's reaction to women expresses itself physically:

> Talk to a woman—why, I'd rather sit on top of a powder magazine! Pah! It makes my flesh creep, I'm so fed up with her, her and that great trailing dress! Poetic creatures they call 'em! Why, the very sight of one gives me cramp in both legs, I get so aggravated.

> (H.1.55)

Thus the constant request for water or vodka, the complaints of headaches, cramps, pains in the heart, and a rage which makes Smirnov feel ill, all serve as a farcical 'running-gag' throughout the action of the play, but also relate to an extremity of behaviour and thinking which will have to be reversed: significantly, at the very moment when Smirnov stops feeling angry and becomes enamoured of Popova, all aches and pains are forgotten, and Popova's fury makes her completely forgetful of her role as the grieving widow. The characters' interaction first intensifies and then modifies their behaviour.

There are, therefore, two sources of fury in Smirnov (and of comedy in the play): his money and women. And the moment at which the one takes over from the other is psychologically accurate—Popova tries to use her sex as a means of getting rid of Smirnov:

> POPOVA: Kindly don't raise your voice at me, sir— we're not in the stables.

> SMIRNOV: I'm not discussing stables, I'm asking whether my interest falls due tomorrow. Yes or no?

> POPOVA: You don't know how to treat a lady.

> (H.1.57)

It is this—one of many challenges which Popova issues to Smirnov—which starts to increase the rhythm which climaxes in the duel, and which provokes Smirnov into exposing Popova's role-playing, into tearing down her pretence at refinement, and into exploding with fury against women. And the climax of Smirnov's outburst against women expresses itself in the most physical and farcical stage action: he 'clutches the back of a chair, which cracks and breaks'. This same stage action is repeated by Smirnov when he has reached the height of emotional confusion after refusing to fight the duel:

> SMIRNOV: . . . (*Shouts.*) Anyway, can I help it if I like you? (*Clutches the back of a chair, which cracks and breaks.*) Damn fragile stuff, furniture! I like you! Do you understand? I, er, I'm almost in love.

> (H.1.63)

This, the kind of physical stage action accepted in slapstick and farce is, however, in keeping with Smirnov as a character—behaviour which is to be expected, and accepted, of a 'bear'.

The progression from comedy of situation to comedy of character is seen very clearly when Popova accuses Smirnov of not knowing how to treat a lady: what started as a situational comedy in which Smirnov simply wanted his money, increasingly develops into a clash between a man who is driven mad by women and considers them faithless, and a woman who is determined to remain faithful even in the face of her dead husband's infidelity. The conflict broadens out to generalise about men and women, and then focuses on one man, Smirnov, and one woman, Popova. In this way, Chekhov presents a shifting perspective which increases the audience's objective response to what is witnessed.

The form which Smirnov's outburst takes, however, is almost that of a dance: Smirnov starts by mimicking Popova, and proceeds to mimic and parody romantic love in general, but in such terms as vividly to suggest the accompanying movement:

> 'Silly, not very clever.' I don't know how to treat a lady, don't I? Madam, I've seen more women in my time that you have house-sparrows. I've fought three duels over women. There have been twenty-one women in my life. Twelve times it was me broke it off, the other nine got in first. Oh yes! Time was I made an ass of myself, slobbered, mooned around, bowed and scraped and practically crawled on my belly. I loved, I suffered, I sighed at the moon, I languished, I melted, I grew cold. I loved passionately, madly, in every conceivable fashion, damn me, burbling nineteen to the dozen about women's emancipation and wasting half my substance on the tender passion. But now—no thank you very much! I can't be fooled any more, I've had enough. Black eyes, passionate looks, crimson lips, dimpled checks, moonlight, 'Whispers, passion's bated breathing'—I don't give a tinker's cuss for the lot now, lady. Present company excepted, all women, large or small, are simpering, mincing, gossipy creatures. They're great haters. They're eyebrow-deep in lies. They're futile, they're trivial, they're cruel.
>
> (H.1.58)

In the midst of this tirade Smirnov, dancing about, breaks a chair, an action of which he seems totally unaware. And he ends up with a challenge to Popova:

> You must know what women are like, seeing you've the rotten luck to be one. Tell me frankly, did you ever see a sincere, faithful, true woman? You know you didn't. Only the old and ugly ones are true and faithful. You'll never find a constant woman, not in a month of Sundays you won't, not once in a blue moon!
>
> (H.1.58)

Popova picks up the challenge immediately—she proves men's infidelity by telling Smirnov about Nikolai's deceit, and refutes the argument against women by telling of her own constancy. It is this which Smirnov explodes, with the result that after the two 'set speeches' by Smirnov and Popova, the situation and the clash of characters and attitudes reach an apparent impasse:

> POPOVA: Just to be awkward, you won't get one single copeck. And you can leave me alone.
>
> SMIRNOV: Not having the pleasure of being your husband or fiancé, I'll trouble you not to make a scene. (*Sits down.*) I don't like it!

> POPOVA: (*choking with rage*) Do I see you sitting down?
>
> (H.1.60)

Again, it is psychologically accurate that the clash should take on a renewed force after each has revealed much to the other about attitudes, previous experiences, and views of the opposite sex, but it is now that the insults and the tempo build, until Smirnov can bear the insults no longer:

> SMIRNOV: Just because you look all romantic, you can get away with anything—is that your idea? This is duelling talk!
>
> LUKA: Heavens and saints above us! Water!
>
> SMIRNOV: Pistols at dawn!
>
> POPOVA: Just because you have big fists and the lungs of an ox you needn't think I'm scared, see? . . .
>
> SMIRNOV: We'll shoot it out! No one calls me names and gets away with it, weaker sex or no weaker sex.
>
> POPOVA: (*trying to shout him down*). You coarse lout!
>
> SMIRNOV: Why should it only be us men who answer for our insults? It's high time we dropped that silly idea. If women want equality, let them damn well have equality! I challenge you, madam!
>
> POPOVA: Want to shoot it out, eh? Very well.
>
> SMIRNOV: This very instant!
>
> POPOVA: Most certainly! My husband left some pistols. I'll fetch them instantly (*Moves hurriedly off and comes back.*) I'll enjoy putting a bullet through that thick skull, damn your infernal cheek! (*Goes out.*)
>
> SMIRNOV: I'll pot her like a sitting bird. I'm not one of your sentimental young puppies. She'll get no chivalry from me!
>
> (H.1.61)

Ironically, in the heat of her fury, Popova is able to talk of her husband's pistols and the use she will make of them without a thought for the dead Nikolai, whereas at the beginning of the play the mere mention of Toby the horse brought tearful associations and the corresponding sentimentality which ensured that at every reference to Toby, Popova requested an extra bag of oats for the horse—oats provided, again ironically, by Smirnov. This was the cause of the debt. But by this time Popova has completely discarded her role as the grieving widow, and in the same moment Smirnov discovers the gentleman in himself. Smirnov starts to behave like a gentleman because Popova stops behaving like a lady:

> SMIRNOV: There's a regular woman for you, something I do appreciate! A proper woman—not some namby-pamby, wishy-washy female, but a really red-hot bit

of stuff, a regular pistol-packing little spitfire. A pity to kill her, really.

(H.1.62)

By the time Popova returns with the pistols, the situation has changed to that of dramatic irony: Popova does not know that Smirnov no longer wants to fight; that her acceptance of his challenge has made him reverse his opinion of her completely. This reversal of roles relates very clearly to the Chekhovian parody and reversal of dramatic conventions: first, a man and a woman fighting a duel; second, a duellist (Popova) who does not even know how to use a gun; and third, the eventual refusal by Smirnov to accept the challenge even in the face of insults from Popova when she accuses him of having 'cold feet' and having the 'wind up', insults which, if made by a man, would traditionally result in a fight to the death.

But in the interim, Smirnov has had to show Popova how to use her husband's 'Smith and Wessons, triple action with extractor, centre-fired',[10] and in the course of showing her, he no doubt has to have his arms round her, and becomes, as does the audience, fully aware of her physical proximity: 'Now, you hold a revolver like this. (*Aside.*) What eyes, what eyes! She's hot stuff all right!' This comic visual picture begins to prepare for the subsequent *dénouement,* but, both unconventionally and ironically, Popova does not acknowledge that she is in the arms of the man she hates; and the ostensible reason for being there is, in any case, to ensure equal ability to kill each other. There is a comic discrepancy between the nature and *ostensible* motive for the stage action done by Smirnov and the feelings which he brings to this stage action: a discrepancy between action and thought which, in turn, relates to the use of the aside and, ultimately, to subtext. The subtext becomes clear because of the dramatic irony. Irony, however, is increased by the very nature of that particular stage action: Smirnov, at home at last in a subject he understands as a man and as a retired lieutenant of artillery, can afford to be expansive as he shows 'the little woman' how a gun works. He achieves dominance by virtue of being a man in this situation, but, equally, is made vulnerable and susceptible by his proximity to Popova.

It is, however, still as a 'bear' that Smirnov proposes to Popova: he clutches her hand so violently that she shrieks with pain (while she is also still holding the revolver), and his words are the complete opposite of romantic:

> SMIRNOV: (*going up to her*). I'm so fed up with myself! Falling in love like a schoolboy! Kneeling down! It's enough to give you the willies! (*Rudely.*) I love you! Oh, it's just what the doctor ordered, this is! There's my interest due in tomorrow, haymaking's upon us— and *you* have to come along! (*Takes her by the waist.*) I'll never forgive myself.

> POPOVA: Go away! You take your hands off me! I, er, hate you! We'll sh-shoot it out! (*A prolonged kiss.*)

(H.1.64)

In a conventional vaudeville, the curtain would have descended after the 'prolonged kiss', the *dénouement* has taken place, and everything has been happily resolved, but Chekhov's ending of the play is quite different. He parodies the convention of the 'interrupted love scene' to end the play unconventionally with both an anti-climatic 'proportional statement' and a psychological curtain-line. The 'proportional statement' is made by the prepared and motivated entry of Luka with an axe, the gardener with a rake, the coachman with a pitchfork, and some workmen with sundry sticks and staves; this 'army' is no longer required, but it makes its own comment in contrast to the embracing couple, a comment which is enhanced by the physical debris around them from two broken chairs. Thus the visual makes its own superbly comic statement. But Chekhov, having slowed the tempo with the 'prolonged kiss', ensures a slow ending—the *true dénouement,* so to speak, which is also psychologically accurate and much more indicative of the *real* Popova:

> LUKA: (*seeing the couple kissing*) Mercy on us! (*Pause.*)

> POPOVA: (*lowering her eyes*) Luka, tell them in the stables—Toby gets no oats today.

(H.1.64)

Reality asserts itself.

The duel as such does not take place; yet, nonetheless, Smirnov and Popova fight a duel throughout the whole play. This becomes evident when looking at the structure of the play: it moves through a complex succession of movements which could be compared to the 'parry' and 'riposte' of a fencing match; or, equally, the structure could be compared to a dance in which, in turn, Popova or Smirnov advances and retreats. That the movement must be choreographed is made evident, for example, towards the end of the play:

> SMIRNOV: . . . Take it or leave it. (*Gets up and hurries to the door.*)

> POPOVA: Just a moment.

> SMIRNOV: (*stops*) What is it?

> POPOVA: Oh, never mind, just go away. But wait. No, go, go away. I hate you. Or no—don't go away. Oh, if you knew how furious I am! (*Throws the revolver on the table.*) My fingers are numb from holding this beastly thing. (*Tears a handkerchief in her anger.*) Why are you hanging about? Clear out!

> SMIRNOV: Good-bye.

> POPOVA: Yes, yes, go away! (*Shouts.*) Where are you going? Stop. Oh, go away then . . .

(H.1.64)

The rhythm and movement of the play are farcial, but farce never detracts from the psychological validity of the characters. Thus, although the situation of the duel may be seen as improbable, the reality of it is such that the appearance of the revolvers after the challenge is inevitable. The entrances and exits also indicate the farcical nature of the stage movement: does Luka, for example, always come from the same place? These must be 'geographically' accurate given the dramatic world and milieu which Chekhov creates, but the *use* made of entrances and exits, of furniture, of the window in the room, all indicate the farcical nature of stage business, and also extend their functional use to make a credible dramatic world. Equally, the climax of a conventional vaudeville, namely the 'prolonged kiss', is made anti-climatic by Chekhov's very characteristic psychological curtain-line. Much is implied about the future life of Smirnov and Popova in Popova's last line. Throughout the play, in fact, the rhythm builds to a climax only to become anti-climactic, as is evident in the number of times Smirnov sits down, refusing to budge, or the number of times the argument reaches an apparent impasse:

POPOVA: You'll get your money the day after tomorrow.

SMIRNOV: I don't want it the day after tomorrow, I want it now.

POPOVA: I can't pay you now, sorry.

SMIRNOV: And I can't wait till the day after tomorrow.

POPOVA: Can I help it if I've no money today?

SMIRNOV: So you can't pay then?

POPOVA: Exactly.

SMIRNOV: I see. And that's your last word, is it?

POPOVA: It is.

SMIRNOV: Your last word? You really mean it?

POPOVA: I do.

(H.1.54)

Thus, to sum up, the play *is* an amorous 'comedy-joke' similar in a number of crucial respects to the conventional farce-vaudevilles of the 1880s: a small cast, amorous entertainment (with a sudden transition), tension, brisk tempo, a happy ending, monologues, asides, running gags, a duel, a love triangle (of a kind), the observance of the unities, the division of the play into scenes according to the entrances and exits of each character,[11] and the use of farce and slapstick. But it is essentially a comedy of three-dimensional characters—without 'intrigue', without heroes and heroines, with the surprising appearing natural, with tension arising organically from the characters—and not the plot or intrigue, and with the use of comic techniques and forms ranging from pure slapstick to parody and irony. The inter-relationship of the visual with the verbal is equally complex.

This was the play, however, which was regarded by some critics on its first performance in 1888 as 'trivial', and to which the dramatic censor initially gave an adverse report:

The unfavourable impression produced by this highly peculiar theme is increased by the coarseness and impropriety of the tone throughout the play, so that I would have thought it quite unsuitable for performance on the stage.[12]

THE PROPOSAL (1888-1889)

The Proposal, written only a few months after *The Bear,* may at first glance seem a more conventional farce-vaudeville than its predecessor: there are more farcical scenes than in any other play by Chekhov, the situation of the play is suggested by its title, the cast size is small (a landowner, his daughter, and a neighbouring landowner), and the play ends with an engagement of marriage. Given the title and the list of characters, it would be a natural assumption for Chekhov's contemporary audience that the play must be an amorous vaudeville with a 'stock' situation and 'stock' characters. The 'stock' situation does not, however, materialise; Chekhov seems to extend the idea of *The Bear* in which *the* duel does not finally take place although the whole play is *a* duel, so that in *The Proposal,* Lomov, who has come to propose to Natasha, never actually does so, although at the end of the play the couple are engaged. In this way, Chekhov denies the event which belongs to the convention and presents instead the characters who themselves impede the event. In *The Proposal* it is, once again, evident that the characters of Chekhov's farce-vaudevilles are not created by or for the situation but create a situation simply by being themselves. The engagement of Lomov and Natasha starts off by design and ends, as it were, by accident, almost incidentally.

As in *The Bear,* it is possible to see where comedy of character takes over from comedy of situation or, to put it another way, where innovation takes over from convention: Lomov comes to propose, receives support (unimpeded by the usual obstacles) from his prospective father-in-law, and is left alone with Natasha. In his struggle to get the proposal off his chest, he mentions, fatally, an adjoining property: Oxpen Field. It is at this point that character takes over decisively from situation, and the clash begins:

LOMOV: I'll try to cut it short. Miss Chubukov, you are aware that I have long been privileged to know your family—since I was a boy, in fact. My dear departed aunt and her husband—from whom, as you are cognizant, I inherited the estate—always entertained the deepest respect for your father and dear departed mother. We Lomovs and Chubukovs have always been on the friendliest terms—you might say we've been pretty thick. And what's more, as you are also aware, we own closely adjoining properties. You may recall that my land at Oxpen Field is right next to your birch copse.

NATASHA: Sorry to butt in, but you refer to Oxpen Field as 'yours'? Surely you're not serious!

LOMOV: I am, madam.

NATASHA: Well, I like that! Oxpen Field is ours, it isn't yours.

LOMOV: You're wrong, my dear Miss Chubukov, that's my land.

(H.1.71)

Oxpen Field, and the comparative merits and demerits of the dogs Tracker and Rover, both serve as the ostensible cause of the clash between Lomov and Natasha, but the real reason for the clash lies in the personality of the two characters: their respective personalities take over from the 'plot' of the proposal, and consistently thwart the very situation in which they are participants. But Chekhov also makes use of dramatic irony: Natasha does not know that Lomov has come to propose. Thus the audience's knowledge of a situation as yet unknown to Natasha allows of a degree of objectivity which throws the emphasis on behaviour, rather than on mystery of plot. By understanding the situation immediately, an audience is able to observe the characters' inter-relationship, and, implicitly, draw conclusions about the suitability of a match which in any case consistently fails to take place.

The title of the play is therefore the first of many 'ironies' in the play: 'the proposal' does not form the action of the play, whereas all the impediments to the proposal *are* central to the action; an amorous vaudeville, dependent on intrigue, does not take place—yet much of the play *is* an amorous vaudeville, dependent on a comic misunderstanding (namely, Natasha's ignorance of Lomov's intentions). There is, in fact, a crucial contradiction between the characters and their situation: a discrepancy between behaviour and intention which makes *The Proposal* by title, by structure, by situation, and by conventional criteria, comically ironic. And the irony is achieved by Chekhov's particular use of the conventional, a use which relates to parody on the one hand and, on the other, to what Tolstoy called 'the lack of French nonsensical surprises'.

Thus the play does not move, as would a traditional vaudeville, from 'complication' to 'unravelling', with intrigue preceding a *dénouement;* it is not structured through a series of incredible twists of plot—it is motivated, in a sense credibly, by the characters. As Chekhov wrote in a letter in the same year: 'One has to write nonsense in one-act plays—that is their strength. Go on in such a way that the wife in earnest wants to run away—she has become bored and wants new sensations; he—in earnest—threatens to make a cuckold of her second husband.'[13] From one point of view, it is incredible that a 'hefty and well-nourished' man should collapse as frequently as does Lomov but Ivan Lomov is a 'hypochondriac', and this characteristic of Lomov's makes his collapses, or swoons, both natural and inevitable. Thus, even in the list of characters preceding the play, Chekhov indicates the main feature of Lomov an indication which suggests the apparent contradiction in Lomov between his physique and his temperament, a discrepancy between his physical appearance and his nervous disposition: 'hefty and well-nourished, but a hypochondriac'. The same technique may be found in *The Bear,* in which Popova's widow's weeds contrast with her 'dimpled cheeks', and the effect is much the same: an audience need have no real fear of danger to Lomov's health; his hefty physique constantly makes a visual comment on his hypochondriacal behaviour, and keeps even the most extreme of 'swoons' in proportion, and well within the bounds of comedy.

This method of characterising—through apparent contradictions—may be seen, albeit in a more subtle form, in much of Chekhov's later dramatic work: in *The Seagull,* Trigorin is a famous and successful writer but, in Chekhov's view, 'he wears check trousers and his shoes are in holes . . . and he does not even know how to smoke a cigar properly';[14] in Act 2 of *The Cherry Orchard,* the governess Charlotte Ivanovna wears a man's peaked hat, and sits with a shotgun in her lap, and in the same play, Lopakhin 'waves his arms about' but, as Trofimov says, he also has 'fine sensitive fingers, like an artist's'. These apparently contradictory features of the visual appearance and of gesture relate, in fact, to the contradictory nature of credible human beings, and it is this kind of characterisation in-the-round which is normally related to Chekhov's 'naturalism'; in the one-act plays, however, where this feature of character is heightened and exaggerated, it may be seen in terms of what Vakhtangov called 'broader realism'. A student of Vakhtangov's, and the subsequent director of the Vakhtangov Theatre, Ruben Simonov, wrote:

> Chekhov's one-act plays afford the possibility of creating characters on the basis of rather short text material . . . Plays with a number of acts portray the development of the characters in a much slower tempo. The central characters in a three- or four-act play show the beginning, growth, and conclusion of action; in this way the characters are revealed gradually. The characters in a one-act play must be immediately revealed by the actor and the regisseur; all exposition must be omitted and the characters shown fully defined in both their inner and outer design. Plays with several acts may be compared to a large river; plays in one act to a rushing torrent.[15]

And earlier in the same book, describing Vakhtangov's production of *The Wedding*:

> At the basis of apparent eccentricity lies the truth of life. But whereas an actor in dramatic presentation has three or four hours in which to reveal the character and psychology of his hero, the actor-eccentric has at his disposal only five or six minutes. In these he must live through a rich scenic life, filled with brilliant events, and create an impressive living image. An actor-eccentric must go through all the psychological transitions thoroughly in order to be convincing. Where the dramatic actor has a number of pages of text, an actor-eccentric (in vaudeville, for example) has just a few words—and sometimes no words—with which to communicate to his audience a complex psychological state of mind.

How does a talented actor-eccentric accomplish his peculiar scenic truth? He does it by selecting the most typical and expressive details of that which he wants to convey to the audience and building them up to the fullest scenic expressiveness. Proportion and correlation between a canvas painted in oil and a laconic, graphic design is similar to that between the dramatic actor and the eccentric actor or clown. The exceptionally difficult art of an eccentric demands extraordinary skill and certainly could not be considered a second-rate art.[16]

These words might well serve as directions to the actress playing the part of Charlotte Ivanova in *The Cherry Orchard,* or to 'Waffles' in *Uncle Vanya,* to Yepikhodov and Simeonov-Pishchik in *The Cherry Orchard,* or to Shamrayev and Medvedenko in *The Seagull*—to all the characters, in fact, who in the full-length plays might quite inappropriately be regarded as 'minor' characters. It is, perhaps, a commonplace to say that there are no 'minor' characters in Chekhov's plays.

In Simonov's terms, however, given the brevity of the one-act plays, the approach of the 'actor-eccentric' might first and foremost be related to characters such as Smirnov and Popova, or Natasha, Chubukov and Lomov. And in *The Proposal* it could be argued that Chekhov retains certain short-cuts to characterisation which were traditional in vaudeville and to comedy as a whole: the use of 'meaningful' names. Thus Lomov's name may be translated as 'breaker', while Chubukov's name derives either from 'pipe' or from 'forelock'. In Chubukov's case, therefore, his name may be taken in several ways, possibly as a guide to his appearance or, if translated as 'forelock', he may be seen in opposition to Lomov 'the breaker', as a 'wedge'. In the case of neither Lomov nor Chubukov, however, is this an indication of 'type'; Chekhov also characterises immediately by the visual effect of Lomov and Chubukov and, again, this is largely achieved through the use of discrepancy and contrast. Lomov enters 'wearing evening dress and white gloves':

CHUBUKOV: (*going to meet him*). Why, it's Ivan Lomov—or do my eyes deceive me, old boy? Delighted. (*Shakes hands.*) I say, old bean, this is a surprise. How *are* you?

LOMOV: All right, thanks. And how might you be?

CHUBUKOV: Not so bad, dear boy. Good of you to ask and so on. Now, you simply must sit down. Never neglect the neighbours, old bean—what? But why so formal, old boy—the tails, the gloves and so on? Not going anywhere, are you, dear man?

LOMOV: Only coming here, my dear Chubukov.

CHUBUKOV: Then why the tails, my dear fellow? Why make such a great thing of it?

(H.1.69)

The 'great thing' is the proposal, and Lomov had dressed in the most formal clothes he could think of, namely evening dress, even though it is lunchtime. There is, therefore, an immediate visual anachronism between Lomov and Chubukov,[17] and, crucially and comically, between Lomov and his bride-to-be: Natasha is wearing an apron:

NATASHA: Excuse my apron, I'm not dressed for visitors. We've been shelling peas—we're going to dry them. Why haven't you been over for so long? Do sit down. (*They sit.*) Will you have lunch?

LOMOV: Thanks, I've already had some.

NATASHA: Or a smoke? Here are some matches . . . But what's this I see? Evening dress, it seems. That *is* a surprise! Going dancing or something?

You're looking well, by the way—but why on earth go round in that get-up?

(H.1.71)

It is ironic that Lomov, who had clearly 'dressed up' in order to give himself confidence and to formalise the 'great event', is, in fact, undermined by his appearance. The comic visual effect of Lomov in black tails and white gloves in contrast to Natasha in her apron, is also paralleled by the psychological effect: both Lomov and Natasha are at a disadvantage because of what each is wearing. Lomov has 'over-done', while Natasha is, correspondingly, 'under-done'. The effect, then, is manifold: by showing Lomov inappropriately 'dressed to kill' in a ridiculous light, the audience clearly keeps 'the great event' in proportion, and is forced into an objective awareness both of Lomov and of 'the proposal'; much is expressed about Lomov's personality and his attitude through his physical appearance, and an audience is forced—in the same 'frame', so to speak—to take stock of Lomov in relation to Natasha; moreover, Natasha (dressed in her apron and talking about shelling peas) may invite a domestic conversation, but scarcely a romantic one. Turning up, without warning, at lunchtime and dressed in evening clothes scarcely encourages a situation conducive to a marriage proposal. Lomov makes his task more difficult (even before any mention of Oxpen Field) and diffuses any 'romance' by being excessive, and therefore ridiculous.

Chekhov's parody of a 'marriage proposal' is made evident when Lomov's motives and attitude are expressed in his monologue (Scene 2) immediately preceding Natasha's entrance:

LOMOV: I feel cold, I'm shaking like a leaf. Make up your mind, that's the great thing. If you keep chewing things over, dithering on the brink, arguing the toss and waiting for your ideal woman or true love to come along, you'll never get hitched up. Barr! I'm cold. Natasha's a good housewife. She's not bad-looking and she's an educated girl—what more can you ask? But I'm so jumpy, my ears have started buzzing. (*Drinks water.*) And get married I must. In the first place, I'm thirty-five years old—a critical age, so to speak. Secondly, I should lead a proper, regular life. I've heart trouble and constant pal-

Chekhov with family and friends, 1890.

pitations, I'm irritable and nervous as a kitten. See my right eyelid twitch? But my nights are the worst thing . . .

(H.1.70)

Lomov then continues to give a graphic description of his nights—nights which, unless improved by the presence of a wife, would almost certainly lead to the separation of the couple. This monologue serves the usual purpose of exposition: an audience is informed about Lomov's motivation for marriage, his view of his intended, and about Lomov himself. What is not conventional, however, is the anti-romantic and unheroic posture of the prospective bridegroom: he is not in love with Natasha, but because she is a good housewife, 'not bad-looking' and 'an educated girl' he has finally, after much dithering, decided to take the plunge. In effect, however, what he really requires is a nurse or a nanny, not a young wife. Chekhov therefore uses the device of the monologue to expose Lomov's hypochondria, to prepare an audience for the physical reactions which Lomov has to any kind of situation, particularly emotional ones, and as a means of characterising this unprepossessing suitor.

It is interesting that when Natasha first enters she does not expect to see Lomov:

> NATASHA: Oh, it's you. That's funny, Father said it was a dealer collecting some goods or something. Good morning, Mr Lomov.

(H.1.70)

Had Lomov been passionately declaring his love for his intended, Natasha's opening remark might well have stopped him dead in his tracks; as it is, Chubukov's 'joke' in pretending to Natasha that a 'dealer' has come to collect goods is not acknowledged by the self-absorbed Lomov, but it does have an effect (albeit unconscious) on an audience. First, without realising it, Natasha 'deflates' Lomov and his purpose, by reducing his arrival to a mundane business; second, it indicates Chubukov's role in the background, a role which is not that of conventional vaudeville intriguer, nor of the parent placing obstacles in the path of a young couple, but that of a parent fully in support of the engagement who is just having a 'joke'. This 'joke' is, however, ironic: from Lomov's monologue, it is clear that in a way he *is* 'a dealer' who has come to collect 'goods', namely Natasha. This, the first comic misunderstanding in the play, sets in motion the major comic misunderstanding: it enables Natasha to enter without any knowledge of Lomov's presence or his intentions.

In fact, Chubukov's 'joke' about Lomov turns sour: Lomov is too much of a 'dealer' to avoid the fatal mention of their 'adjoining property', and from this Chekhov develops a theme to be found in Pushkin, Gogol, and Turgenev,[18] and often in the vaudeville—arguments over property leading to litigation between rival landowners:

> LOMOV: But you have only to look at the deeds, my dear Miss Chubukov. Oxpen Field once *was* in dispute, I grant you, but it's mine now—that's common knowledge, and no argument about it. If I may explain, my aunt's grandmother made over that field rent free to your father's grandfather's labourers for their indefinite use in return for firing her bricks. Now, your great-grandfather's people used the place rent free for forty years or so, and came to look on it as their own. Then when the government land settlement was brought out—

> NATASHA: No, that's all wrong. My grandfather and great-grandfather both claimed the land up to Burnt Swamp as theirs. So Oxpen Field was ours. Why argue? That's what I can't see. This is really rather aggravating.

> LOMOV: I'll show you the deeds, Miss Chubukov.

(H.1.72)

The argument (over land with the unprepossessing names of 'Burnt Swamp' and 'Oxpen Field') continues in a completely farcical manner; long-deceased relatives on both sides are brought in as 'proof' or justification (as Natasha says: 'Grandfather, grandmother, aunt—it makes no sense to me. The field's ours and that's that'); and—perhaps most revealing of all—both Natasha and Lomov separately claim that the argument is over *principle,* not the land itself.

> NATASHA: . . . I don't mind about the field—it's only the odd twelve acres, worth the odd three hundred roubles. But it's so unfair . . . It's ours! Argue till the cows come home, put on tail-coats by the dozen for all I care—it'll still be ours, ours, ours! I'm not after your property, but I don't propose losing mine either, and I don't care what you think!

> LOMOV: My dear Miss Chubukov, it's not that I need that field—it's the principle of the thing. If you want it, have it. Take it as a gift.

> NATASHA: But it's mine to give *you* if I want—it's my property.
>
> (H.1.72-3)

The pointless argument builds in tempo and vehemence, until, in a clear parody of the 'interrupted love scene', Chubukov is drawn by the sound of the row. With his entrance, the rhythm drops slightly, but only to reach renewed force in the argument now involving all three: prospective suitor, would-be father-in-law, and the ferocious and unknowing bride-to-be. It is with Chubukov's entrance that the theme of litigation comes to a head:

> LOMOV: We'll see about that! I'll have the law on you!

> CHUBUKOV: You will, will you? Then go right ahead, sir, and so forth, go ahead and sue, sir! Oh, I know your sort! Just what you're angling for and so on, isn't it—a court case, what? Quite the legal eagle, aren't you? Your whole family's always been litigation-mad, every last one of 'em!

> LOMOV: I'll thank you not to insult my family. We Lomovs have always been honest, we've none of us been had up for embezzlement like your precious uncle.
>
> (H.1.75)

With that, Lomov starts off a succession of insults—neatly reciprocated by Chubukov—involving near and distant, living and deceased relatives on both sides; the fury of the argument is such that each completely forgets the reason for Lomov's visit. The situation is not so much that of a comic misunderstanding as of an argument in which the 'heat' and subject causes both parties to forget what is important. Eventually the severity of Lomov's palpitations drives him away and Chubukov—again, ironically—shouts after him that he need never return to his house. The irony lies in the fact that seconds later Natasha, having at last learnt the real reason for Lomov's visit, hysterically sends her father to bring Lomov back. And the moment of truth comes not as an artificial, conventional revelation, but as a totally motivated and almost incidental comment:

> CHUBUKOV: And this monstrosity, this blundering oaf, has the immortal rind to come here with his proposal

and so on, what? A proposal! I ask you!

> NATASHA: A proposal, did you say?

> CHUBUKOV: Not half I did! He came here to propose to you!

> NATASHA: Propose? To me? Then why didn't you say so before?
>
> (H.1.76)

As it turns out, Natasha's knowledge of Lomov's intentions makes very little difference to her behaviour—Natasha behaves with as little self-control and discipline in the second argument, over the dogs Tracker and Rover, as she did in the argument over Oxpen Field. But perhaps the greatest irony in the play lies, as Vladimir Lakshin points out in his book *Tolstoy i Chekhov,*[19] in the fact that all property would, in any case, be shared and jointly owned after the marriage.

The greatest obstacle in the play is, therefore, the basic incompatibility of the characters; Natasha and Chubukov even argue about which of them was responsible for arguing with Lomov. And the subjects of the arguments—Oxpen Field, the two dogs, who started a row, and so on— are made deliberately absurd and petty both as expressive of the characters, and as a comment on them. Much the same technique and dramatic effect may be seen in Act 2 of *The Three Sisters,* in the argument between Chebutykin and Solyony:

> CHEBUTYKIN: (*coming into the drawing-room with Irina*). They gave us real Caucasian food too—onion soup followed by a meat dish, a kind of *escalope.*

> SOLYONY: A shallot isn't meat at all, it's a plant rather like an onion.

> CHEBUTYKIN: You're wrong, my dear man. *Escalope* isn't an onion, it's a sort of grilled meat.

> SOLYONY: Well, I'm telling you a shallot is an onion.

> CHEBUTYKIN: Well, I'm telling you *escalope* is meat.

> SOLYONY: Well, I'm telling you a shallot is an onion.

> CHEBUTYKIN: Why should I argue with you? You've never been to the Caucasus or eaten *escalope.*

> SOLYONY: I've never eaten them because I can't stand them. Shallots smell just like garlic.
>
> (H.3.104)

In this scene, the argument manufactured by Solony is not even over the same thing, the argument is a misunderstanding: Chebutykin fails to understand that Solyony is talking about *cheremsha,* not *chekhartma,* and they are not even listening to each other, Solyony arguing for the sake of it, Chebutykin reacting only out of irritation. And a few minutes later, in the same act, Solyony's latest source of argument, over whether there are one or two universities in Moscow, simply peters out when Andrey, characteristically, refuses to join in: 'Three if you like. So much the better.' In the later plays, such arguments over petty and unimportant matters are deeply expressive of character and clash of character but, perhaps more important, these 'flash-points' relate to Chekhov's method of expressing a way of life: often an argument is only the outward manifestation of a different subtextual tension, as in the argument in Act I of *Uncle Vanya* between Vanya and his mother Maria Vassilyevna over her pamphlets. In the later plays, as in many of the short stories, petty arguments spring out of boredom, unhappiness, dissatisfaction, and invariably mask something far from petty; in *The Three Sisters,* Solyony's posturing unhappiness and boredom result in the death of Tuzenbakh. The argument may be petty, but the way of life which breeds such pettiness is destructive.

It was perhaps with this pettiness and destructiveness in mind that Meyerhold determined on his interpretation and emphasis in his *Proposal* which formed part of *33 Swoons,* a production interpretation which must be understood in the context of its time, namely 1935:

> The image created by Ilinsky [who played Lomov] does not fit into a vaudeville: the comic nervousness of Ilinsky's interpretation has grown to the scale of pathology. This is already a disease. One could say: a social disease. In Ilinsky's Lomov the spectator could see the Metrofanushka of Fonvizin's *The Minor*—but not the ignoramus of *that* period. That was a Metrofanushka who was bursting with health and strength; the future was standing before him. But now Metrofanushka has completed a historical circle . . . a degeneration, the finale. Now this Metrofanushka is of the period of decay, of the eve of the revolution, when—in all corners of the country, they chop down the cherry orchards. He is ill, incorrigibly sickly . . . whenever there is the smallest occurrence in his life—a trifle, a draught, unpleasantness—he has heart spasms—any moment he will die. This is the meaning of Lomov's hypo-chondria.[20]

According to Yuzovsky, the author of the above, Meyerhold's interpretation of Lomov was that of the down-trodden, pathetic 'little man', an Akaky Akakeyevich, 'an unfortunate one, insulted and injured', a 'ludicrous person'. Thus Meyerhold interpreted Lomov not as a 'comic' character but as a 'dramatic' character:

> this Lomov is, in fact, a lonely man of thirty-five, who has shut himself up on his estate, who has not known women, but is always thinking of them . . . this Akaky Akakeyevich element . . . This Lomov, is lonely, defenceless, and faint-hearted. When among people he wishes by his behaviour to hide these characteristics—he wears camouflage.[21]

Meyerhold expanded the significance of Lomov's evening dress, and provided him with an everyday hat, in addition to his top-hat: when wearing the top-hat, Lomov was the prospective suitor; when arguing or 'swooning', Lomov wore his everyday hat: hats, gloves, and tails were used not merely as 'props' but as physical extensions of Lomov's mood and behaviour, as masks, and camouflage.

By all accounts,[22] Meyerhold's production of *The Proposal* was not well received—in order to play Lomov dramatically, the fast tempo of a vaudeville was lost: and although Meyerhold's interpretation of Lomov was a strong one, it did not work well with Chekhov's Natasha. But even in this less successful production, there is much to be learnt, and in the extremity of this interpretation there is a crucial aspect which should not be overlooked: Chekhov's play *is* farcical, but it is also exposing a social milieu at a particular time, a time in which money, mortgages, and the upkeep of the estates were an increasing preoccupation. Lomov and Chubukov, individualised and three-dimensional, are also landowners (as are Smirnov and Popova in *The Bear*); it is important to note that when Lomov is 'the suitor', he is at his most nervous and agitated, but he has enough energy and strength to protect 'his' property against Natasha. In fact, his nervousness is initially attributed to only one thing by Chubukov:

> LOMOV: . . . I came to ask a favour, my dear Chubukov, if it's not too much bother. I have had the privilege of enlisting your help more than once, and you've always as it were—but I'm so nervous, sorry. I'll drink some water, my dear Chubukov. (*Drinks water.*)
>
> CHUBUKOV: (*aside*). He's come to borrow money. Well, there's nothing doing! (*To him.*) What's the matter, my dear fellow?
>
> (H.1.69)

Money, or the lack of it, forms either background or a major aspect of most of Chekhov's plays—in *The Bear,* in *The Anniversary,* in *The Wedding,* in *On The High Road,* in the unfinished *Night Before the Trial, Ivanov, The Wood Demon* (and in *Uncle Vanya*), in *The Seagull, The Three Sisters,* and, of course, in *The Cherry Orchard.* In *The Proposal,* Chubukov's mistaken assumption is comic but it is also mean; and this meanness and greed is also very evident in Natasha's opening chatter:

> It's lovely weather, but it rained so hard yesterday— the men were idle all day. How much hay have you cut? I've been rather greedy, you know—I mowed all mine, and now I'm none too happy in case it rots. I should have hung on.
>
> (H.1.71)

In the same way, old grievances come out in the row, as when Natasha says: 'We lent you our threshing-machine last year, and couldn't get our own threshing done till November in consequence'. Or there is the new argument over the money paid for the two 'rival' dogs:

> LOMOV: . . . Do you know, I gave Mironov a hundred and twenty-five roubles for him?
>
> NATASHA: Then you were had, Mr Lomov.

LOMOV: He came very cheap if you ask me—he's a splendid dog.

NATASHA: Father only gave eighty-five roubles for Rover. And Rover's a jolly sight better dog than Tracker, you'll agree.

(H.1.78)

There is much in **The Proposal** which is farcical, but there is also much which verges on the grotesque: Lomov's hypochondria motivates many of his physical complaints and physical reactions, but, even more than in **The Bear,** Chekhov again uses the extremity of physical reactions to 'deflate' his characters, and demonstrate their lack of a sense of proportion. Towards the end of the play, first Lomov, then Chubukov, and then Natasha collapse in a 'swoon', a comic visual picture of one after the other collapsing in a chair, which appears to reach a climax, only to become anti-climactic:

LOMOV: Oh, oh! My heart's bursting. My shoulder seems to have come off—where is the thing?[23] I'm dying. *(Falls into an armchair.)* Fetch a doctor. *(Faints.)*

CHUBUKOV: Why, you young booby! Hot air merchant! I think I'm going to faint. *(Drinks water.)* I feel unwell.

NATASHA: Calls himself a sportsman and can't even sit on a horse! *(To her father.)* Father, what's the matter with him? Father, have a look. *(Screeches.)* Mr Lomov! He's dead!

CHUBUKOV: I feel faint. I can't breathe! Give me air![24]

NATASHA: He's dead. *(Tugs Lomov's sleeve.)* Mr Lomov, Mr Lomov! What have we done? He's dead. *(Falls into an armchair.)* Fetch a doctor, a doctor! *(Has hysterics.)*

CHUBUKOV: Oh! What's happened? What's the matter?

NATASHA: *(groans)* He's dead! Dead!

CHUBUKOV: Who's dead? *(Glancing at Lomov.)* My God, you're right! Water! A doctor! *(Holds a glass to Lomov's mouth.)* Drink! No, he's not drinking. He must be dead, and so forth. Oh, misery, misery! Why don't I put a bullet in my brain? Why did I never get round to cutting my throat? What am I waiting for? Give me a knife! A pistol![25] *(Lomov makes a movement.)* I think he's coming round. Drink some water! That's right.

(H.1.81)

The borderline between three-dimensional farce and the grotesque is a narrow one.

It is in the anti-climactic aftermath of Lomov's 'return from the grave' that the couple finally became engaged, and it is not Lomov but Chubukov, again as a reversal of the 'stock parent' in a vaudeville, who announces the engagement. The ending of the play is a complete parody of the traditional finale of the vaudeville since the couple's reconciliation only takes place when they are completely exhausted from their quarrels and, in any case, after the engagement the rows begin again with renewed vigour. The ending of the play not only does not resolve the 'obstacles', but in fact emphasises the obstacles even more clearly. In the sense that the couple *are* engaged, the play has a happy ending, but equally it must be seen as an unhappy beginning. Chekhov has written a comedy of character, not of situation: external obstacles or difficult and unpleasant situations may be overcome, but Lomov and Natasha do not suddenly change their nature. In this sense, there is no *dénouement,* only a renewed outbreak of argument between Lomov and Natasha; and the final irony is in Chubukov's direct comment and address to the audience: 'You can see those two are going to live happily ever after! Champagne!' Any witness of this comedy is only able to regard Lomov and Natasha as welcome to each other, an objective assessment which comes from the balanced presentation of all the characters and from their clearly expressed view of each other: Lomov is a hypochrondriac, although well-fed and healthy; Natasha is greedy, argumentative, and shrewish; Chubukov is bad-tempered and, a nice reversal, was beaten by his wife.

The depth of characterisation is partly achieved by Chekhov's particular use of speech peculiarities and individualised speech patterns—Chubukov's catch-phrase is 'and so forth', and all of his speech is larded with phrases like 'dear man', 'old boy', 'old bean', an individualised manner of speech which emphasizes Chubukov's *apparent* bluff heartiness; Natasha is characterised by her frequent ability to speak her mind, and by short, sharp sentences, often composed of derogatory synonyms, while Lomov's speech is, of course, most characterised by the interruption of his own train of thought and argument by his physical ailments:

NATASHA: What a rotten, beastly, filthy thing to say.

CHUBUKOV: You're a thoroughly nasty, cantankerous, hypocritical piece of work, what? Yes, sir!

LOMOV: Ah, there's my hat. My heart—. Which way do I go? Where's the door? Oh, I think I'm dying. I can hardly drag one foot after another. *(Moves to the door.)*

CHUBUKOV: *(after him)* You need never set either of those feet in my house again, sir.

NATASHA: Go ahead and sue, we'll see what happens.

(H.1.75)

The play is full of phrases relating to hunting (although it clearly emerges that neither Lomov nor Chubukov are exactly 'sportsmen'), a requirement which Chekhov listed in his notes on **Things Most Frequently Encountered in Novels, Stories and Other Such Things**: 'an endless number of interjections, and attempts to use an appropriate technical term', and which he itemised as a requirement of the vaudeville: 'each character must possess individual features and idiosyncrasies and must speak in a language of his own'. It is, of course, partly the language which so strongly depicts and creates the milieu of the play.[26]

The structure of the play is also a parody: Lomov comes to propose—twice; Natasha and Lomov have a row—twice, and twice Chubukov's entrance parodies the 'interrupted love scene' and increases the ferocity of the argument; on each occasion, Lomov's 'swoon' results in an anti-climax. Thus, just as Beckett's *Waiting for Godot* requires two acts to make probable the continuation of another and another, so in *The Proposal* the 'ending' of the play serves to indicate the likely continuation of the action. The play is therefore appropriately structured according to the arguments which form the 'action': initiated by a comic misunderstanding, but subsequently carried by the momentum of the characters. In the 'repeat' action of the play (from Scene VI onwards), it is evident that these people can row even without a 'misunderstanding'. But Chekhov does introduce a new element of dramatic irony with Lomov's reappearance: Natasha now knows Lomov's intentions, but he does not know that she knows!

The Proposal is, therefore, a fascinating 'mixture': Chekhov takes over the 'stock' situation of an 'amorous vaudeville', and parodies it; he retains aspects such as the monologue and asides; the scene divisions and small cast of identifiable vaudeville figures, and the unity of time, place and action, but by substituting misunderstanding and character for intrigue and plot, and introducing the convention of 'rival landowners', 'the proposal' becomes subsidiary to what, in effect, is closer to social satire.

A TRAGIC ROLE (1889)

By the time Chekhov wrote his one-act farce *A Tragic Role* in May 1889, he had already written *Platonov, On the High Road,* three versions of *Smoking is Bad for You, Swan Song (Calchas), Ivanov, The Bear, The Proposal,* and *Tatyana Repina,* and was in the middle of writing *The Wood Demon*:

> Can you believe it? I've got the first act of *The Wood Demon* ready. It's turned out all right, though a bit long. I have a greater sense of my own strength than when I was writing *Ivanov*. The play will be ready by the beginning of June . . . Last night I remembered I'd promised Varlamov[27] to write a farce for him. Today I wrote it, and I've already sent it off. You see how fast I turn things out![28]

This letter to Suvorin was followed, two days later, by a letter to Leontyev, to whom Chekhov wrote:

> A day or two ago I remembered promising Varlamov last winter to turn one of my novels [sic] into a play. I sat straight down and did so, making a pretty bad job of it. A novel on a stale and hackneyed theme produced a stale farce that falls flat. It's called *A Tragic Role*.[29]

Chekhov's diffident, not to say derogatory, view was not shared by contemporary audiences, the play was revived again and again in Chekhov's lifetime, but today it is virtually ignored by producers and dismissed as unworthy of analysis by critics. But although it cannot be claimed that *A Tragic Role* rates amongst the highest of Chekov's dramatic works, there are a number of features of the play which relate crucially to an understanding of his dramatic method, and to the use he makes of stock situations and stock techniques.

The title of the play in itself brings translator and critic face to face with an important aspect of the play as a whole: like Molière's *Le Médecin malgré lui (A Doctor in Spite of Himself),* Chekhov's title conveys a meaning which a translator finds hard to capture. The play is normally referred to as *A Tragic Role,*[30] but a more literal translation is, in fact, like Molière's, *A Tragedian in Spite of Himself.* The title has also been translated as *The Reluctant Tragedian,* and in Eric Bentley's version as *Summer in the Country—Not a Farce But a Tragedy.* Thus the actual name of the play raises the question as to whether 'the role' is, in fact, a 'tragic' one, a question reinforced by the apparent disparity of the subtitle: Chekhov calls the play 'a farce'. But 'the reluctant tragedian' raises the question himself: reaching the end of his frenzied tirade, Tolkachov says, 'This isn't funny, it's downright tragic' or, to translate it another way, 'This isn't farce—it's tragedy.' In this play, Chekhov extends the meaning of the word 'farce' to encompass an attitude, an approach to life—a philosophy as well as a dramatic genre.

Chekhov's treatment of the 'hackneyed' situation of the henpecked, harassed, commuting husband is multifaceted: the play *is* a farce, and partly so by virtue of Tolkachov's extreme reaction to a commonplace situation; he insists on seeing himself as a tragic figure, but in a situation at which everyone laughs; at the same time, however, it is in fact the very banality of the situation which is driving him into a frenzy. There is, therefore, a conflict within the play between Tolkachov's situation and his reaction to it: he is an *unwilling* participant who none the less dramatises his role. Thus, whereas in *The Bear* or *The Proposal* the characters create their own situation and so the action of the play, the action of *A Tragic Role* is largely Tolkachov's reaction to his situation. Tolkachov's reaction is extreme and therefore comic; his insistence on seeing himself as a tragic figure is disproportionate and misplaced and therefore comic; the situation itself is as commonplace as somebody's 'mother-in-law', and therefore comic; but in the extremity of his reaction lies a real despair; in his 'martyrdom' to the mundane there is a serious protest; and in the very banality of the situation there is potential for tragedy. It is exactly the petty and trivial nature of the commonplace which provokes Tolkachov into an assessment of his life—at the end of his tether, at the mercy of the mundane and the trivial, Tolkachov wants to find some meaning:

> A family man? A martyr, more like—a complete drudge, a slave, a chattel, the lowest thing that crawls.

Why don't I end it all—what am I waiting for, like some benighted idiot? I'm a regular doormat. What have I to live for? Eh? (*Jumps up.*) Come on, tell me what I have to live for, why this unbroken chain of moral and physical tortures? Certainly I can understand a man who sacrifices himself for an ideal, but to martyr yourself to women's petticoats, lampshades and that sort of damn tomfoolery—no, thank you very much. No, no, no! I've had enough! Enough, I tell you!

(H.1.109)

As part of his tirade against his way of life, Tolkachov describes how at last, exhausted, he is able to go to bed:

Wonderful! Just shut your eyes and sleep. Nice and snug isn't it—like a dream come true? The children aren't screaming in the next room, the wife isn't there, and you've nothing on your conscience—what could be better? You drop off. Then, all of a sudden—bzzzzz! Gnats! (*Jumps up.*) Gnats! Damn and blast those bleeding gnats! (*Shakes his fist.*) Gnats! The Plagues of Egypt aren't in it—or the Spanish Inquisition! Buzz, buzz, buzz! There's this pathetic, mournful buzzing as if it were saying how sorry it was, but you wait till the nipper gets his fangs in—it means an hour's hard scratching. You smoke, you lash out, you shove your head under the blankets—but you're trapped. You end by giving yourself up like a lamb to the slaughter.

(H.1.112.)

This completely realistic 'torment' of summer in the country becomes, however, also an image of Tolkachov's situation: because gnats are basically harmless, a violent reaction to them may be seen as comically out of proportion; by being both harmless and commonplace, gnats may be treated as a joke; but although not fatal, they first drive one into a frenzy, and then into passive exhaustion. The action of the play captures Tolkachov in such a frenzy, and possibly before passive exhaustion about his way of life finally sets in. Chekhov achieves this exactly by using the commonplace, the apparently harmless, and the apparently undramatic. In Chekhov's terms, the majority of people are more likely to be 'martyrs' to lampshades, petticoats and gnats than to abstract ideas or dramatic actions:

Why write that someone boards a submarine and sails to the North Pole to seek some sort of reconciliation with people, and at the same time his beloved, with a dramatic wail, throws herself from a belfry? All that is false, and does not happen in reality. One must write simply: about how Peter Semeonovich married Maria Ivanovna. That is all.[31]

Part of what the play shows is the result of one such marriage; the play is an adaptation of a story written by Chekhov in 1887 and significantly titled: *One of Many*. The story describes the unhappy plight of a thoroughly married man who travels to town every day to work from his country cottage where his wife and children have moved for the summer. This 'hackneyed' situation has been treated by Chekhov in a number of short stories, in particular *Not Wanted, A Nest of Kulaks, Gone Astray,* or *The*

Grasshopper. In *Not Wanted,* Chekhov describes a June evening at seven o'clock, and:

a crowd of dacha dwellers who had just come out of the train at the small station Khilkovo and were making their way towards the dacha colony, most of them fathers of families, burdened with shopping bags, briefcases and hat-boxes. They all looked worn out, hungry and in a bad temper, as though the sunshine and the green grass meant nothing to them.

In the same story, Zaikin describes life in town once the family have moved to the country for the summer:

Back in town you have no furniture, no servants— everything is at the decha. You feed on the devil knows what, have no tea to drink because there's no one to heat the samovar, you can't get a proper wash, and when you come out here, into the lap of nature, you have to walk from the station in the dust and heat . . . It's a miracle we're still alive.

And in *Gone Astray,* one such unhappy husband tries to get into the wrong dacha—they all look alike.

In *A Tragic Role* Chekhov retains the basic point of the story from which the play derives: the family man is over-burdened with demands from his wife and friends who take advantage of his daily commuting into town. In the story, *One of Many,* one of the burdens which he carries is a child's coffin, a 'prop' which Chekhov omitted from the stage adaptation not, as Magarshack explains, to 'preserve the decencies of the stage'; nor, as Bentley puts it, because 'a child's coffin on stage . . . would carry a higher charge of painful emotion than a farce can stand', but because Chekhov did not automatically lift the story from page to stage. He was clearly well aware of the physical limits of farce: in addition to all of Tolkachov's other burdens, it would be virtually impossible for any actor to carry a coffin as well; moreover, in stage terms, that particular 'prop' would be much cruder, much more grotesque as a visual statement than it is when merely described in a narrative; finally, its existence on stage would raise questions irrelevant to the action and point of the play. The actual list of Tolkachov's 'props' is, therefore, carefully contrived to suggest both credible purchases and yet objects of varying shapes, sizes, textures, and uses which immediately create, purely through visual effect, a farcical entrance:

Tolkachov comes in. He carries a glass lamp-globe, a child's bicycle, three hat-boxes, a large bundle of clothes, a shopping-bag full of beer and a lot of small parcels.

(H.1.109.)

Like a clown, Tolkachov enters balancing 'hostile' objects, all of which might well conspire to plague him: it is vital to this visual image that the objects should be commonplace—and yet potential hazards. Tolkachov's entrance introduces the audience into a world where the glass lamp-globe might break; the child's bicycle might trip him up;

the hat boxes, piled one on top of the other, might slide off; the bottles of beer might burst; and the small parcels—of which there are many—might slip from under Tolkachov's arms and chin. The opening statement of the play, expressed purely through the visual, is an apparently commonplace one of a man over-burdened by daily objects: Tolkachov's entrance therefore operates on a literal, credible and comic level, and, simultaneously, as an image of his situation. A similar effect is found in **The Cherry Orchard** in which Yepikhodov, nicknamed Twenty-Two Calamities, lives in a world in which a new pair of boots, a billiard cue, even a glass of water, all conspire against him. Thus Tolkachov's burdens, like Yepikhodov's calamities, are farcical—and an image of a situation, a combination which may be seen, albeit in a more abstract context (and therefore perhaps as a more explicit image) in, for example, Lucky's first entrance in Beckett's *Waiting for Godot:*

> Enter Pozzo and Lucky. Pozzo drives Lucky by means of a rope passed round his neck, so that Lucky is the first to appear, followed by the rope which is long enough to allow him to reach the middle of the stage before Pozzo appears. Lucky carries a heavy bag, a folding stool, a picnic basket and a greatcoat . . . Noise of Lucky falling with all his baggage.

The communication of meaning through a visual image is familiar to a twentieth-century audience, but the communication of meaning through a visual image within the context of a farce-vaudeville in 1889 clearly demonstrates Chekhov's unique extension of the farcical into the metaphorical. To Chekhov's contemporary audience, however, there was little particularly innovatory about the form: it relates clearly to the other two 'types' of farce-vaudeville popularised in the 1880s: the 'comic scene' and a version of the comic scene, the 'scene monologue'.

Thus whereas **The Bear** and **The Proposal** are 'amorous vaudevilles', **A Tragic Role** bears a clear generic resemblance both to the 'comic scene'—which employed more static action, the absence of an ending as such, and the portrayal of everyday life and everyday types—and to the 'scene monologue', which employed a comic situation narrated by a comic stereotyped character. But in particular, Chekhov employs the convention of the 'false monologue' in which other characters are present but do not interrupt or respond. Viewed in that way, it may be seen that Chekhov uses an artificial and conventional form in **A Tragic Role,** but it must also be seen that Tolkachov's monologue is, in fact, significantly modified and influenced by the 'control' presence of his friend Murashkin. Alexis Murashkin (whose name might be translated as 'Shivers') has a crucial function in the play which goes beyond the purely conventional one of reducing the artificiality of a monologue by providing a passive on-stage listener: Tolkachov has come to Murashkin to borrow a revolver in order to 'end it all'. Murashkin's presence thus serves as the ostensible motivation for Tolkachov's tirade—both Murashkin and the audience are recipients of Tolkachov's lengthy exposition of his situation—but Chekhov

then reverses the conventional *dénouement* by means of Murashkin. The action of the play does not arise out of a comic misunderstanding which is then resolved; instead the comic misunderstanding comes at the end of the play and in fact *provides* the *dénouement* and, in effect, the anti-climax which virtually ends the play. This, in turn, is achieved by Chekhov's particular use of a form of comic misunderstanding: the 'conversation-of-the-deaf'. Murashkin, like the audience, has heard Tolkachov's frenzied exposition, but he has not listened to it, and therefore not taken it seriously:

> TOLKACHOV: . . . Look here, if you won't lend me a revolver, at least show a spot of fellow-feeling.
>
> MURASHKIN: But I do feel for you.
>
> TOLKACHOV: Yes, I can see how much you do. Well, good-bye. I'll get some sprats and salami, er, and I want some toothpaste too—and then to the station.
>
> MURASHKIN: Whereabouts are you taking your holiday?
>
> TOLKACHOV: At Corpse Creek.
>
> MURASHKIN: (*joyfully*). Really? I say, you don't happen to know someone staying there called Olga Finberg?
>
> TOLKACHOV: Yes. In fact she's a friend of ours.
>
> MURASHKIN: You don't say! Well, I never! What a stroke of luck and how nice if you—
>
> TOLKACHOV: Why, what is it?
>
> MURASHKIN: My dear old boy, could you possibly do me a small favour, there's a good chap? Now, promise me you will.
>
> TOLKACHOV: What is it?
>
> MURASHKIN: Be a friend in need, old man—have a heart! Now, first give my regards to Olga and say I'm alive and well, and that I kiss her hand. And secondly, there's a little thing I want you to take her. She asked me to buy her a sewing-machine and there's no one to deliver it. You take it, old man. And you may as well take this cage with the canary while you're about it— only be careful or the door will break. What are you staring at?
>
> TOLKACHOV: Sewing-machine—. Cage—. Canary—. Why not a whole bloody aviary?
>
> (H.1.113.)

For Tolkachov, the irony of his friend's reaction is the last straw, but for the audience the effect of this ironic twist is mixed: on the one hand, Murashkin's attitude and response confirms the objective view that Tolkachov is over-reacting and self-dramatising but, simultaneously, Murashkin's failure to listen, and his casual response, justifies Tolkachov in his view that the situation is tragic, not farcical.

In addition, Murashkin finally pushes his friend 'over the edge'. The dramatic effect of this, following immediately after Tolkachov's frantic monologue, is initially anti-climactic but then provides the climax on which the play ends: a climax which utilises a 'stock' technique but one usually used earlier in a play: the chase. The play ends as Murashkin frantically tries to get out of the way of the incensed Tolkachov. Again, the comedy is visual, farcical and psychologically apt: Murashkin is both literally and metaphorically adding to Tolkachov's 'burden'. Murashkin therefore provides a sense of proportion in a double-edged way: he points the extremity of Tolkachov's reaction but, by the inadequacy and even insensitivity of his response, he *justifies* Tolkachov's view of the situation.

A further crucial feature of the play is the realism of the milieu depicted; Tolkachov—'a family man, high up in the civil service'—exposes a whole way of life: the nature of his work in the office, the nature of life on the dacha surrounded by his immediate family (Sonya, Misha, Vlasin, his sister-in-law), Colonel Vikhrin's pregnant wife, and the French governess Mademoiselle Chanceau. He depicts the task of shopping in the city 'from draper's to chemist's, from chemist's to dressmaker's, from dressmaker's to sausage-shop, then back to the chemist's again'. Then there is the physical problem of carrying everything, the crowded train journey into the country with piles of packages, the exhausted arrival, only to be greeted by the wife's request for social events such as a dance or—a nice ironic touch—a visit to an amateur performance of a play called *A Scandal in a Respectable Family*. This is followed by dancing, by gnats, and then by the wife practising songs with amateur tenors who 'sleep all day and spend their nights getting up amateur concerts'. And then the dash in the early morning mist for the train to town, and 'the whole ruddy rigmarole starts all over again'. It is not by chance that Chekhov called this particular place in the country Corpse Creek. Moreover, all this takes place in a heat wave which generates exhaustion and irritation, a 'naturalistic' element characteristic of much of Chekhov's dramatic work in which mood and behaviour are closely related to the weather and season, or the time of day or night.

Tolkachov's monologue serves, therefore, both as self-exposition and as the exposure of a way of life, an exposé which extends to other people who never appear on stage although they become very real to an audience. Tolkachov's wife, Mademoiselle Chanceau and her 'eighty-two' corset-size, the sister-in-law, the children and the Colonel are all graphically created through the nature of their requirements and demands; in this way, Chekhov creates off-stage characters and a credible off-stage dramatic world. In a similar way, the three-dimensionality of certain characters in the later plays is enhanced: in *The Three Sisters,* Natasha's admirer, Protopopov is heard, but not seen, a factor which does not inhibit an audience's awareness of the situation and of Natasha's behaviour; equally, Simeonov-Pishchik's life and character are made more real by his constant reference to his daughter, Dashenka, a character well-known by the end of the play, but one who never appears; the same is true of Vershinin's wife, and

children. In *A Tragic Role,* the character of Murashkin, who *is* present on-stage, is presented in much the same light as the off-stage characters: by his demands and requirements, he joins the ranks of Tolkachov's tormentors.

The beginning and conclusion of the play are farcical, whilst the central part of the play—the 'false monologue'—is a satirical exposure of a way of life and a milieu, or, to put it another way, an indirect comedy of manners. Tolkachov is the 'stock' figure of the henpecked husband and frenzied commuter, but his state of mind is clearly communicated partly through the disproportionate physical reaction: Tolkachov wants to kill himself, dreams of crocodiles, and is made ill by his situation:

> It's a rotten life, I can tell you—I wouldn't wish it on my worst enemy. It's made me ill, you know—I've asthma, I've heartburn, I'm always on edge, I've indigestion and these dizzy spells. I've become quite a psychopath, you know! (*Looks about him*). Keep this under your hat, but I feel like calling in one of our leading head-shrinkers.
>
> (H.1.112-13.)

The movement of the play follows his mood: from a suicidal Tolkachov to a murderous Tolkachov. But underneath this stereotyped figure in a commonplace situation is a human being struggling comically towards something more valuable—as Tolkachov puts it at the end of his monologue:

> And you get no sympathy or pity, either, everyone takes it so much for granted. You even get laughed at. But I'm alive, aren't I? So I want a bit of life! This isn't funny, it's downright tragic.
>
> (H.1.113.)

Implicit in this play, as in many of Chekhov's short stories and in his dramatic works, is the sense that there is tragedy in the banal, the petty, but in that it *is* banal and petty, there is also farce.

THE ANNIVERSARY (1891)

In his book on Chekhov, William Gerhardi writes:

> Chekhov does not give us a cross-section of a lump of life, taken as it were, at random, by merely registering the irrelevant perceptions which make it up. Chekhov—because he is an artist as well as a psychologist—discriminates in his choice of those seeming irrelevancies which in literature go to the making of the illusion of real life . . .
>
> Thus when he introduces an irrelevancy, it is always one of those seeming irrelevancies which are, in point of actual result, significant relevancies. For he charges each with several tasks. (*a*) To connote by its apparent irrelevancy the illusion of real life: it is so in real life, we think of one thing and then our thought goes off at a tangent. (*b*) To be in itself amusing, delightful, pathetic, tragic, or otherwise beautiful. (*c*) To be

always significant, that is psychologically true, throwing additional light on the character as well as on his subjective existence. (*d*) To consolidate the form of the story by bringing in, if possible, the same apparent irrelevancy more than once—by making it characteristic of a person. And, above all (*e*), by emphasizing some irrelevancies at the expense of others to bring the reader to a point at which he can see where these more prominent irrelevancies . . . touch upon the fading threads of others in the background.[32]

The one-act farce *The Anniversary* (adapted from the short story written in 1887, *A Defenceless Creature*) relies for its comic action on a number of 'irrelevancies', some of which take the form of 'comic misunderstandings'.

In the midst of the hectic preparations for the anniversary celebrations of a private bank, the Chairman's wife, Tatyana Shipuchina, arrives in the bank fresh from the country, full of gossip and irrelevant information which distracts her husband and his elderly bank clerk; the 'action' is further interrupted by the arrival of a complete stranger—an old woman, Mrs Merchutkina—who has, in fact, come to the wrong address in the hope of getting money from the War Office medical department for her sacked and sick husband. This comic misunderstanding (which is partly achieved through the conventional 'conversation-of-the-deaf') results in such complete chaos that the clerk, Khirin, 'misunderstands' the Chairman's request, and tries to throw out the wrong woman, the Chairman's wife instead of Mrs Merchutkina. In this way, the farcical elements of the play (and the action) are set in motion by the arrival of the two women both of whom, by their interruption, create action seemingly irrelevant to the intended action of the play. This same technique may be seen in *The Proposal* in which Lomov's apparently irrelevant mention of Oxpen Field throws the intended action of 'the proposal'. The 'irrelevancies' of *The Proposal* become, in fact, the true action of the play, and in the same way in *The Anniversary* both Mrs Shipuchina and Mrs Merchutkina, by interrupting the 'action' of the play in effect create the real action. Part of the farce arises from the conflict between the intended action, namely the anniversary celebrations, and the resulting action, namely the interruptions. These interruptions also take the form of totally irrelevant information which simultaneously creates comedy and reveals character:

TATYANA: (*coming in after her husband*) We went to a party at the Berezhnitskys'. Katya was wearing a dear little blue silk frock with an open neck, and trimmed with fine lace. She does look nice with her hair up, and I arranged it myself. Her dress and hair were quite devastating!

SHIPUCHIN: (*who now has migraine*) Yes, yes, I'm sure. Someone may come in here at any moment.

MRS MERCHUTKINA: Sir!

SHIPUCHIN: (*despondently*) What now? What do you want?

MRS MERCHUTKINA: Sir! (*Points to Khirin.*) This man here, this creature—he taps his forehead at me and then on the table. You tell him to look into my case, but he sneers at me and makes nasty remarks. I'm a weak, defenceless woman, I am.

SHIPUCHIN: Very well, madam, I'll see about it. I'll take steps. Now do go, I'll deal with it later. (*Aside.*) My gout's coming on.

KHIRIN: (*goes up to Shipuchin, quietly*) Mr Shipuchin, let me send for the hall-porter and have her slung out on her ear. This beats everything.

SHIPUCHIN: (*terrified*) No, no! She'll only raise Cain and there are a lot of private apartments in this block.

MRS MERCHUTKINA: Sir!

KHIRIN: (*in a tearful voice*). But I have a speech to write. I shan't get it done in time. (*Goes back to the desk.*) I can't stand this.

MRS MERCHUTKINA: Please sir, when do I get my money? I need it at once.

(H.1.146.)

Much of *The Anniversary* is structured (as are the later full-length plays) by means of several different rhythms taking place simultaneously: Shipuchina trying to fill her husband in on family events and gossip; Mrs Merchutkina trying to get her money; Khirin trying to finish writing the speech in time, thwarted by his pet hate—women; and Shipuchin himself trying to keep up appearances, maintain a formality, while expecting the delegation to arrive at any minute for the celebration. These different rhythms are composed of a mixture of the 'relevant' and the apparently 'irrelevant', and the apparently irrelevant rhythms in fact alter the action and, by so doing, become the relevant action of the play. Each of these different rhythms is completely expressive of one or other of the characters.

In the later full-length plays the same basic technique is used, but in such a way that the interruption or the interjection of the irrelevant does not alter the action: instead, it alters audience perception and sometimes stage mood. Such interruptions of the seemingly irrelevant become, in fact, relevant in their own right, are often a source of the comic, and—as in *The Anniversary*—simultaneously reveal character and thought-process. An example of this may be seen in Act 2 of *The Three Sisters* in which Fedotik and Rodé softly strum a guitar in the background; Vershinin, Tuzenbakh and Masha are talking; Irina is playing patience, and Chebutykin reads the paper:

MASHA: I feel that man should have a faith or be trying to find one, otherwise his life just doesn't make sense. Think of living without knowing why cranes fly, why children are born or why there are stars in the sky. Either you know what you're living for, or else the whole thing's a waste of time and means less than nothing. (*Pause.*)

VERSHININ: Still, I'm sorry I'm not young any more.

MASHA: As Gogol said, 'Life on this earth is no end of a bore, my friends.'

TUZENBACH: What I say is, arguing with you is no end of a job, my friends. Oh, I give up.

CHEBUTYKIN: (*reading the newspaper*) Balzac got married in Berdichev. (*Irina sings softly.*)

CHEBUTYKIN: I really must put that down in my little book. (*Makes a note.*) Balzac got married in Berdichev. (*Carries on reading the newspaper.*)

IRINA: (*playing patience, thoughtfully*) Balzac got married in Berdichev.

(H.3.100.)

This interruption by Chebutykin of the seemingly irrelevant achieves several distinct results: first, it expresses the apparently random which creates 'a slice of life'; second, it is expressive of Chebutykin as a character; and third, juxtaposed with what has been said (yet maintaining the mood of the scene), it raises a question: if Balzac could be married in a place like Berdichev, then perhaps it is not the *place* which is significant, but the activity? As such, the dramatic technique here relates crucially to the 'action' of the play, to the discussion taking place, and to an audience, in that it shifts perspective and alters the focus and perception of the audience view. It takes the audience 'out' of the Prozorov household, out of the small garrison town—not 'to Moscow', but to a place like Berdichev. A further example may be seen in Act 4 of *Uncle Vanya* at the point just prior to his departure when Astrov accepts a glass of vodka from Marina:

MARINA: A little vodka then?

ASTROV: (*hesitantly*) Well, perhaps— (*Marina goes out.*)

ASTROV: (*after a pause*) My trace horse has gone a bit lame. I noticed it yesterday when Petrushka was taking him to water.

VOYNITSKY: You'll have to get him reshod.

ASTROV: I'd better call at the blacksmiths' in Rozhdestvennoye. There's nothing else for it. (*Goes up to the map of Africa and looks at it.*) Down there in Africa the heat must be quite something. Terrific!

VOYNITSKY: Very probably.

(H.3.66.)

The mention of Africa seems completely irrelevant, and is only prompted by what is, in fact, a stage 'prop', but again, it draws an audience back from the scene immediately witnessed to a wider world beyond; it reminds them of Vanya's aspirations and previous illusions, and it serves—comically—to express Astrov's awkwardness

and embarrassment at this point of his departure: the inconsequential takes on a relevance and depth. In the later full-length plays, the inconsequential or the seemingly irrelevant may take many different forms: whether the form of a remark, music or a sound effect, reference to a stage object, an action, or the physical form of an entrance which 'interrupts' the action. This last may be seen in Act 2 of *The Cherry Orchard* where the unexpected arrival of the tramp vitally *affects* the play, but does not alter the action. The tramp's arrival is basically irrelevant to the discussion preceding his entrance; he is seemingly irrelevant to the characters' lives, but his entrance has a crucial effect on the meaning of the play, on the mood of the scene, and, again, on the audience's perception. Examples of such 'irrelevancies' may be found in all of Chekhov's later dramatic works.

These apparently random or irrelevant comments or actions are generally attributed to Chekhov's 'naturalism', but when seen in embryo, so to speak, and on a more overt level in the one-act plays, this technique may also be seen as a vital ingredient of Chekhov's farces. Thus in *The Anniversary* such interruptions and irrelevancies are only more overt because they do actually alter the action of the play and, given the resulting chaos, serve as an element of farce. But, as in the later plays, a multiple rhythmic structure is created, and character is revealed by the nature of the particular 'irrelevance'.

In both *The Anniversary* and, for example, *The Cherry Orchard*, the use of irrelevancies also results in, and relates to, the characters' failure or inability to communicate with each other:

ANYA: (*quietly embracing Varya*) Has he proposed, Varya? (*Varya shakes her head.*) But he does love you. Why can't you get it all settled? What are you both waiting for?

VARYA: I don't think anything will come of it. He's so busy he can't be bothered with me, he doesn't even notice me. Wretched man, I'm fed up with the sight of him. Everyone's talking about our wedding and con-gratulating us, when there's nothing in it at all actually and the whole thing's so vague. (*In a different tone of voice.*) You've got a brooch that looks like a bee or something.

ANYA: (*sadly*) Yes, Mother bought it. (*Goes to her room, now talking away happily like a child.*) Do you know, in Paris I went up in a balloon.

(H.3.149.)

From Varya's unhappiness, to a brooch, to a balloon in Paris—Anya is no longer listening to Varya, and each continues her own train of thought. In *The Anniversary,* Merchutkina resolutely fails to listen to anyone else and, following her own train of thought, introduces complete irrelevancies, meaningful to nobody but herself:

SHIPUCHIN: . . . As I've said already, madam, this is a bank—a private business establishment.

MRS MERCHUTNINA: Have mercy, kind sir. Think of yourself as my father. If the doctor's certificate isn't enough, I can bring a paper from the police too. Tell them to pay me the money.

SHIPUCHIN: (*sighs heavily*) Phew!

TATYANA: (*to Mrs Merchutkina*) I say, old girl, you're in the way, do you hear? This won't do, you know.

MRS MERCHUTNINA: Pretty lady, I've no one to stick up for me. Food and drink don't mean a thing, dearie, and I've had some coffee this morning, but it didn't go down well at all, it didn't.

(H.1.146-7.)

In the above scene from *The Cherry Orchard,* the context, the mood, and the effect are subtly different from the scene quoted from *The Anniversary,* but the technique is similar. And the technique is a well-known characteristic of comedy relating, in particular, to Gogol's 'comic illogic'. Thus 'speech flow through association', relying heavily on the apparently illogical or irrelevant, is used by Chekhov both as a source of the comic and as a means of creating 'a slice of life'. The comic convention becomes, in Chekhov's later dramatic work, a feature of realism which is different because of the context within which it is utilised.

This realism and the farce in *The Anniversary* emanate largely from the characterisation, and it is in the characterisation that further examples are found to justify Vakhtangov's 'broader realism': the characters in the play combine elements of 'stock' characterisation, of the three-dimensional, and of the grotesque. As in *The Bear* and *The Proposal,* certain characteristics are heightened and exaggerated. The use of 'stock' or 'type' characters relates to the harassed husband, Shipuchin, with his overbearing young wife, Shipuchina; the elderly bank clerk, Khirin, who is a complete misogynist; and the old woman Merchutkina who, far from being 'a defenceless creature' is, in fact a perfect pest. And as in the case of Lomov ('Breaker') in *The Proposal,* the names of the male characters may also relate to their distinctive features: Shipuchin may be translated as 'Hissing', and Khirin as 'Sickly'.

The Anniversary was the last of the three one-act Chekhov farces which formed Meyerhold's production *33 Swoons,* and as with *The Bear* and *The Proposal,* the interpretation was partly governed by certain distinctive features of the characters—Meyerhold isolated certain 'crazy features' of each character, and exaggerated them to create a grotesque farce:

The Anniversary in Meyerhold's programme carries Chekhov's title, but Meyerhold could daringly re-name it, and call it, for example, as follows: *A Mad Day or Chekhov's Anniversary,* or simply *A Mad Day* or even *Crazy People.* In Chekhov's vaudeville there walk about strange, odd people—in Meyerhold's production there run about lunatics. (Nine Swoons of the vaude-

ville—there are nine points where the madness reaches its climax.) The madness of each character or hero climbs to a crescendo until he completely loses consciousness, and falls flat on his back to the accompaniment of Strauss's music. In Chekhov's vaudeville they are simply funny people; Meyerhold exaggerates this comic feature. And so one has on stage crazy people. Every one of them has his/her special point of craziness: Shipuchin has gone mad over his grandeur; Merchut-kina over the need to get her 'Twenty-four roubles, Thirty-six kopecks'; Khirin has his point of madness-suspicion, while Tatyana Alexeyevna has gone crazy through eroticism.[33]

This farce-vaudeville was turned, by Meyerhold, into a farce-grotesque, but although Meyerhold was himself subsequently highly critical of his own production and interpretation[34] it is not necessarily without valid justification from Chekhov's script. Thus Yuzovsky's description of Meyerhold's treatment of Khirin, for example, is revealing of the character as created by Chekhov:

About Khirin it is known that at home he chases his wife and sister-in-law with a knife. And that is sufficient. We have in front of us a lunatic who is looking around him suspiciously; he wraps himself in a shawl because he regards himself as ill, but this helps the actor in performance [Kel'berer] to keep his head bowed all the time as if suspecting, as if looking out for all kinds of tricks that may arise. It seems he talks to himself, he smiles a crazy smile; any moment—just wait—and he will do something crazy. In the play, Khirin shouts to Tatyana Shipuchina furiously: 'Clear out!'—in this performance he does this with obvious pleasure. He produces a revolver—which is not in Chekhov's play—and with a blissful smile he loads it bullet by bullet, and he does it slowly, enjoying himself. He chases the others present with the gun, and his eyes shine with joy. It is as if he has waited for this possibility for a long time . . . And if, suddenly, without any special reason he would have set fire to the bank, hardly anyone would have been surprised.[35]

Much of this may be seen as justified, if exaggeratedly so, by Khirin's own words in the opening monologue of the play. Khirin makes it clear that he is not writing Shipuchin's speech for him out of loyalty, or the desire to be helpful, but because he will gain by it:

KHIRIN: . . . He's promised to see I don't lose by it. If all goes well this afternoon and he manages to bamboozle his audience, he's promised me a gold medal and a three-hundred-rouble bonus. We shall see. (*Writes*) But if I get nothing for my pains, my lad, then you can watch out—I'm apt to fly off the handle! You put my back up, chum, and you'll find yourself in Queer Street, believe you me!

(H.1.137)

Thus Khirin has a vested interest in ensuring that the proceedings do pass off satisfactorily; in addition, Khirin dislikes 'messes and muddles' which, in his terms, means the presence of women! By introducing Shipuchina and

Merchutkina onto the scene, Chekhov has mixed 'a witch's brew': when an old misogynist meets a simpering, gossipy and flirtatious young woman, and an obstinate pest in the shape of an old woman, a clash is bound to occur. A situation will arise simply because of the interaction of these characters. And the possible result is carefully plotted in by Chekhov before the arrival of the women:

> SHIPUCHIN: . . . Your wife was here this morning, complaining about you again—said you ran after her with a knife last night, and your sister-in-law too. Whatever next, Khirin! This won't do.

> KHIRIN: (*sternly*) Mr Shipuchin, may I venture to ask you a favour on this anniversary occasion, if only out of consideration for the drudgery I do here? Be so good as to leave my family life alone, would you mind?

> SHIPUCHIN: (*sighs*) You're quite impossible, Khirin. You're a very decent, respectable fellow, but with women you're a regular Jack the Ripper. You are, you know, I can't see why you hate them so.

> (H.1.138-9)

This sickly misogynist (or Jack the Ripper) is forced to witness the endless little kisses which Tatyana Shipuchina bestows on her husband, and much is comically revealed by his reaction, repeated several times: 'Khirin gives an angry cough', a brilliantly appropriate and economical sound which indicates both his hypochondria and his irritation. He is also forced to listen to Tatyana's gossip, her vanities, and her little song from *Eugene Onegin,* all while he is trying to finish Shipuchin's speech and meet a deadline. Merchutkina's arrival increases an explosive situation and, in effect, everything that the two women do and say only serves to motivate and justify Khirin's fears and fury. And to make matters worse, Tatyana starts to talk directly to him when Shipuchin's attention is taken up by Merchutkina, and her behaviour with Khirin is like a 'red flag to a bull':

> TATYANA: (*to Khirin*) Well, I must begin at the beginning. Last week I suddenly get a letter from Mother. She writes that my sister Katya's had a proposal from a certain Grendilevsky—a very nice, modest young man, but with no means or position at all. Now, by rotten bad luck Katya was rather gone on him, believe it or not. So what's to be done? Mother writes and tells me to come at once and influence Katya.

> KHIRIN: (*sternly*) Look here, you're putting me off. While you go on about Mother and Katya, I've lost my place and I'm all mixed up.

> TATYANA: Well, it's not the end of the world! And you listen when a lady talks to you! Why so peeved today? Are you in love? (*Laughs.*)

> SHIPUCHIN: (*to Mrs Merchutkina*) I say, look here, what's all this about? I can't make sense of it.

Chekhov (seated) with his brother Nikolai (standing), 1880.

> TATYANA: In love, eh? Aha—blushing, are we?
> (H.1.142-3.)

Significantly—and dangerously—Khirin makes no reply, but his facial reaction, or the visually comic reaction which must follow, is such that seconds later Tatyana rather meekly and readily agrees to her husband's request to wait in the office outside. Ironically, however, Khirin seems to meet his match in Merchutkina—left by Shipuchin to deal with her, Khirin tries to frighten her into at last understanding that she has come to the wrong place:

> KHIRIN: I don't think I've ever seen anything nastier in my life. Ugh, what a pain in the neck. (*Breathes heavily.*) I repeat, do you hear? If you won't clear out, I'll pulverize you, you old horror. I'm quite capable of crippling you for life, that's the sort of man I am. I'll stop at nothing.

> (H.1.145)

Merchutkina's response is both anti-climactic and virtually unanswerable:

MERCHUTKINA: You're all bark and no bite. You don't scare me, I know your sort.

Each thinks that the other is 'crackers', but when Mrs Merchutkina, having received some money, then starts asking for her husband's job to be returned, and when Tatyana returns still gossiping, Shipuchin can take no more; he appeals to Khirin to get rid of Mrs Merchutkina, and chaos (that crucial ingredient of farce) is the result. Either deliberately misunderstanding in order to get his revenge on Tatyana, or because he is too far gone in his rage to listen properly, Khirin first chases the wrong woman, and only then goes after Mrs Merchutkina. As a result, first one woman, and then the other 'swoons'. The extremity of Khirin's reaction is farcical, but it has been so carefully motivated that it becomes inevitable.

Until this moment, however, Shipuchin has tried to remain calm although—as so often with the characters of Chekhov's farce-vaudevilles—he is reacting by suffering increasing physical ailments. The play begins with Shipuchin feeling exhausted:

> SHIPUCHIN: . . . I say, I'm getting as nervous as a kitten. I'm so on edge, I feel I'll burst into tears at the slightest provocation.
>
> (H.1.140.)

The provocation is, in fact, considerable: a few minutes of trying to cope with Mrs Merchutkina sends Shipuchin dizzy; coping with his wife, who is gossiping with the clerks in the outer office, brings on a migraine, and then his gout starts to come on. But his outward calm is for one crucial, comic, and psychologically accurate reason: he is desperate to keep up appearances. This factor, combined with his pretentiousness and vanity, is exactly what makes him—in terms of a comedy—ripe for deflation:

> SHIPUCHIN: The clerks have just given me an album, and I hear the shareholders want to present me with an address and a silver tankard. (*Playing with his monocle.*) Very nice, or my name's not Shipuchin— no harm in it at all. A little ceremony's needed for the sake of the Bank's reputation, damn it. You're one of us, so you're in the know, of course. I wrote the address myself—and as for the tankard, well, I bought that too. Yes, and it set me back forty-five roubles to have the address bound, but there was nothing else for it. *They'd* never have thought of it. (*Looks around*) What furniture and fittings! Not bad, eh? They call me fussy—say I only care about having my door-handles polished, my clerks turned out in smart neck-ties and a fat commissionaire standing at my front door. Not a bit of it, sirs. Those door-handles and that commis-sionaire aren't trifles. At home I can behave like some little suburban tyke—sleep and eat like a hog, drink like a fish—

> . . . at home I can be a jumped-up little squirt with my own nasty little habits. But *here* everything must be on the grand scale. This is a bank, sir! Here every detail must impress and wear an air of solemnity, as you might say. (*Picks up a piece of paper from the floor and throws it on the fire.*) My great merit is simply that I've raised the Bank's prestige. Tone's a great thing. A great thing is tone, or my name's not Shipuchin.

> (H.1.139.)

This characteristic catch-phrase—'or my name's not Shipuchin'—is one feature which Meyerhold emphasised; and, in addition to the monocle specified by Chekhov, Meyerhold also gave the actor playing Shipuchin (Chikul) 'a furcoat which hangs down from one shoulder which he holds with his other hand, and this gives him a special lightness, airiness, dandyism, chic'.[36] But the main feature which Meyerhold exaggerated was the image that Shipuchin has of himself as a 'firework': 'I'm hoping for a lot from this speech. It's a statement of faith—a firework display, rather. There's some pretty hot stuff in this, or my name's not Shipuchin.' The comic deflation, however, results in the firework 'hissing' but not taking off. Shipuchin's pretensions result in a final *tableau* which is contrary to everything for which he had hoped.

In his introduction to *The Oxford Chekhov* Hingley describes the women in the play as the chief culprits, implying what today might be called anti-feminism on Chekhov's part, but, in fact, both men are ripe for deflation: Shipuchin because 'Tone's a great thing' and because of his pretentiousness, and Khirin because he does not like 'messes and muddles' and also—given the structure and situation of a farce-vaudeville—because the challenge of a misogynist must be met.

There is no doubt, however, that Tatyana meets this 'challenge': her entire conversation is about love, men, and romantic affairs, and—like her husband—she is very vain. Describing her train journey down to the country, Tatyana seems blissfully unaware that she is describing events which are not conventionally narrated to a husband:

> TATYANA: . . . There was this dark-haired young fellow sitting opposite me—not bad-looking, quite attractive, actually. Well, we got talking. A sailor came along and some student or other. (*Laughs.*) I told them I wasn't married. Oh, they were all over me! We chattered away till midnight—the dark young man told some screamingly funny stories and the sailor kept singing! I laughed till my sides ached. And when the sailor—oh, those sailors!—when it came out that I was called Tatyana, do you know what he sang? (*Sings in a bass voice.*)
>
> 'Onegin, how can I deny
> I'll love Tatyana till I die?'[37]
>
> (*Roars with laughter. Khirin coughs angrily.*)
> (H.1.141-2.)

Tatyana Shipuchina is vulgar, an outrageous flirt, and utterly insensitive to other people and her surroundings; dangerously, she tries her feminine charms on Khirin, and even when sent into outer office to wait she distracts the clerks by flirting with them—as the stage direction reads: 'Tatyana's laughter is heard off-stage, followed by a man's laughter.' Her conversation is almost exclusively about men, their attentions to her, and her sister's love affair. But by means of Tatyana's ridiculous prattle, Chekhov—in her narrative—is in effect parodying 'romantic love' and a 'stock' situation from an amorous vaudeville. Describing how, finally, due to her influence, her sister Katya turned down young Grendilevsky, Tatyana continues:

TATYANA: . . . Katya and I are walking in the garden just before supper, when suddenly—. (*Excitedly.*) When suddenly we hear a shot! No, I can't talk about it calmly. (*Fans herself with her handkerchief.*) It's too much for me! (*Shipuchin sighs.*)

TATYANA: (*weeps*) We rush to the summer house, and there—there lies poor Grendilevsky with a pistol in his hand.

SHIPUCHIN: Oh, I can't stand this—can't stand it, I tell you! (*To Mrs Merchutkina.*) What more do you want?

MRS MERCHUTKINA: Please sir, can my husband have his job back?

TATYANA:(*weeping*) He shot himself straight through the heart, just here. Katya fainted, poor dear. And he got the fright of his life. He just lies there and asks us to send for the doctor. The doctor turns up quite soon and—and saves the poor boy.

(H.1.147.)

It is Tatyana's ridiculous hyperbole which creates the anti-climax to this melodramatic 'stock' situation of unrequited love and attempted suicide. Tatyana's probable accompanying mime, and her obvious enjoyment of this country drama both help to create the parody and reveal her character. Extending her 'point of craziness', namely love, Meyerhold produced all the scenes with Tatyana (played by Tyapkina) as 'some kind of completely exotic can-can.' In this, however valid as one feature of the character, Meyerhold's interpretation excluded other aspects. In the character of Tatyana, Chekhov creates a different type of misunderstanding: Tatyana is completely incapable of understanding that a married woman is expected to behave with propriety, and that the wife of the Bank's Chairman does not gossip about his business affairs. Her insensitivity and lack of awareness to situation and people is illustrated by her inability to leave: like Medvedenko in the last act of *The Seagull,* Tatyana several times states that she will 'only be a minute, and then leave', and—again like Medvedenko—consistently fails to go.[38] But whereas Medvedenko fails to leave because he is unhappily torn between leaving Masha or leaving the baby, Tatyana fails to go because she is too full of her own gossip, and too insensitive to realise when she is not wanted. She is incapable of understanding because she is incapable of listening. The convention of 'the conversation-of-the-deaf' has become a means of psychological characterisation.

It is this feature—perhaps above all others—which characterises Merchutkina: she is almost a physical embodi-

ment of a 'comic misunderstanding', of the failure to communicate given a 'conversation-of-the-deaf'. In Meyerhold's production:

she appears unexpectedly, she 'arises'—a pale bird-like face, the eyes set fixedly on Shipuchin; the voice monotonous, colourless. She has got used to her own voice so she doesn't hear it herself. It seems to her that merely by her appearance, everyone will understand what she needs: that all understand, all know, all are preoccupied with that one and only thing—to give or not to give 'twenty-four roubles, thirty-six kopecks'.[39]

Ironically, given the title of the story from which the play derives, Mrs Merchutkina is not 'a defenceless creature': her total inability to listen insulates her from the world, and by remaining unmoved by Shipuchin's explanations, and Khirin's threats, she finally gets what she has come for, albeit to the wrong place, and from the wrong people:

SHIPUCHIN: I repeat, madam. Your husband was employed by the War Office medical department, but this is a bank, a private business.

MRS MERCHUTKINA: Quite so, quite so. I understand, mister. Then tell them to give me fifteen roubles, say. I don't mind waiting for the rest, sir.

(H.1.144)

The balance of sympathy for this character is carefully maintained by Chekhov: she is initially characterised as 'an old woman who wears an old-fashioned overcoat', and her speech is distinguished as of a lower social order, and as such, she conjures up images of 'the insulted and humiliated', endlessly sitting in the anteroom of some petty official, waiting for justice:

MRS MERCHUTKINA: Pity a helpless orphan, sir. I'm a weak, defenceless woman. Fair worried to death I am, what with lodgers to have the law on, my husband's affairs to handle, a house to run—and my son-in-law out of work as well.

(H.1.144.)

But Merchutkina's defencelessness is qualified by the fact that she is going to have the law on her lodgers, that she *has* come to the wrong place, without her husband's knowledge, to get his money and job back, and that she does not listen to anything said to her. As far as she is concerned, she is 'not asking for what isn't mine', she has a medical certificate to prove her husband's illness, and, as she characteristically keeps repeating: 'I'm a weak, defenceless woman, I am.' Ironically, however, this comic misunderstanding is only deepened when Shipuchin—out of exhaustion and despair—finally gives her the money: seemingly justified in her insistence and assumption that she has come to the right place, she starts a new plea: 'Please sir, can my husband have his job back?'

Significantly, Merchutkina gets her money through pestering, and not through justice. As she says: 'I've been in half a dozen different places already, mister, and they wouldn't even listen.' In this way, the comic misunderstanding has its serious side: the appeal of 'the little man' to an 'Excellency', the respect for 'authority' (even an inappropriate one) are crucial themes in Russian literature, whether in Gogol's *The Government Inspector* and *The Greatcoat,*[40] Dostoyevsky's *Poor Folk,* or Chekhov's short story, *The Death of a Government Clerk.* This same (misplaced) respect for authority may be seen in *The Wedding* in which 'a general' is invited simply because that adds tone and class to the event. Chekhov was therefore using a conventional theme or situation, and one which may be found in several vaudevilles of the period, but these 'comic scenes' of the conventional vaudeville used 'the little man' to laugh and sneer at him, while Chekhov treats such characters—whether Merchutkina or Nyukhin in *Smoking is Bad for You*—with objective, comic compassion. Merchutkina is irritating, a perfect pest, deaf to all reason, but she needs the money. Thus Chekhov's characterisation is completely devoid of sentimentality: Merchutkina's 'deafness' and self-pity create objectivity in an audience.

In one of his letters, Chekhov wrote that in the one-act 'miniature joke'—'every character must be three-dimensional, and must speak his own language'.[41] The characterisation of *The Anniversary* is indeed three-dimensional, but it is also heightened and exaggerated: Chekhov creates a character 'in-the-round', but then singles out the main features and emphasises the basic and typical traits and 'speech peculiarities'.

The structure of *The Anniversary* is more complicated than that of *The Bear* or *The Proposal*: there are more characters all of equal importance, and the interaction of each character's different 'rhythm' provides the source of conflict and a multiple rhythmic structure which enables one to 'comment' on the other. In addition, it is the interaction of the characters which creates the comic misunderstandings and the chaos or confusion necessary to a farce-vaudeville. But the situation and the setting provide this interaction with an 'external' tension and time-limit: the anniversary celebration and its imminence motivates Shipuchin and Khirin in their actions and reactions. The setting, namely the Bank, is a public one in which formality is expected and respectability maintained; both Shipuchin's position and the nature of the setting are conveyed partly by other characters who, at regular intervals, come in and go out of Shipuchin's office—other characters who add to the realistic yet grotesque element in the play: 'While he [Shipuchin] is on stage, clerks come and go from time to time with papers for him to sign.' The 'off-stage' world of the Chairman's office is credibly created and maintained largely by off-stage sound effects and the to-ing and fro-ing of the clerks, while the setting of Shipuchin's office is given an individuality significant in its relevance to the action, characters and point of the play: 'The Chairman's office. A door, left, leading into the main office. Two desks. The furnishings have pretensions to extreme luxury: velvet-upholstered furniture, flowers, statues, carpets and a telephone.'

This visual pretentiousness is apparent at the opening of the play but, in addition, an immediate visual comic disparity is evident between the setting, and Khirin—in the midst of these 'posh' surroundings, Khirin wears felt boots, something which even Merchutkina notices and knows is not done: 'Sits around in the office with his felt boots on! Cheek! Where was you brought up?' But not content with that, Khirin has made no concession to the celebration, and his clothes are quite unsuitable even for a normal working day:

> SHIPUCHIN: . . . (*looking Khirin over*) My dear fellow, a shareholders' deputation may come in any moment, and here you are in those felt boots and that scarf and, er, that jacket thing—what a ghastly colour! You might have worn tails or at least a black frock-coat—
>
> KHIRIN: My health matters more to me than your shareholders. I feel sore all over.
>
> SHIPUCHIN: (*excitedly*) Well, you must admit you look an awful mess. You're spoiling the whole effect.
>
> (H.1.139)

The 'whole effect' is also spoilt by Tatyana when she enters 'wearing a mackintosh, with a travelling handbag slung over her shoulder'. This provides one of the reasons for Shipuchin's desire to send her home: 'My dear, we're celebrating our anniversary today, and a shareholders' deputation may turn up any moment. And you're not properly dressed.' Merchutkina's entrance, however, provides a further visual anachronism (and comic discrepancy): in her old-fashioned overcoat she is immediately out of place in her surroundings. In this way, the conflict and the farce of the play are conveyed visually: the characters do not fit their surroundings. Only Shipuchin, in his evening dress, is in tune with the pretentiousness of the setting, and only at the end do others enter who are appropriately dressed for this event: 'Enter a deputation of five men, all in evening dress . . .'. These five men, dressed in evening dress at noon,[42] reinstate the pretentious formality of this celebration—but at the most critical, climactic and most farcical moment in the play. The deflation (and the farce) are conveyed through the visual clash between the pretentious and the comically inappropriate. This technique may be seen in Chekhov's later dramatic work in, for example, the treatment of Natasha in Act I of *The Three Sisters,* or in Masha's black dress in Act I of *The Seagull* or—though to different effect—in Charlotte Ivanovna's appearance in *The Cherry Orchard.*

The climax of the play—and the most farcical moment—is carefully prepared by Chekhov, and used by him to explode the pretensions of the anniversary celebrations and Shipuchin's façade. The technique used—while credibly motivated—utilises a number of conventional devices. First, the chase: the farcical situation of Khirin the misogynist chasing a woman—and the wrong woman, namely Tatyana the flirt; the confused husband joins in the chase to protect his wife; Khirin then switches his enraged attentions to the old woman in her long over-coat; Tatyana, trying to get out of Khirin's way, jumps on a chair and then—feeling faint—collapses on to the sofa; while Merchutkina, also feeling faint, collapses in Shipuchin's arms. The *tableau* which therefore meets the eyes of the shareholders' deputation, and of the bank employees who crowd in after them, is the frozen *tableau* of farce: Khirin frozen in an attitude of ferocity, with his sleeves rolled up and in his felt boots; Mrs Merchutkina in the arms of the Chairman who is apparently unaware that he has a strange old woman in his arms while his wife lies groaning on the sofa. Inevitably, the office must be in some disarray given the chase around the room.

This climactic *tableau* is held while one of the sharehold-ers loudly reads the address—bound in velvet—which had been so carefully prepared by Shipuchin, in a falter-ing attempt not to notice that anything is amiss. The speech itself is a mixture of the pretentious and the iron-ic: the pretentiousness comes over in the style of the speech, and, comically, in the totally inappropriate quo-tation from *Hamlet*; the irony comes from the comic disparity between what is seen and what is said. Thus the Shareholder's unfortunate mention of Shipuchin's 'natu-ral tact', and his several times repeated phrase, 'the rep-utation of the Bank', creates a bizarre contrast to what the audience both on and off the stage are actually wit-nessing. This irony is further increased by Shipuchin's glassy-eyed reaction: in a complete daze, he utters a poetic verse of apparently comic irrelevance, from Krylov's *The Passers-by and the Geese*. 'Under the circumstances' the shareholders can only mumble that they will return later, and they retreat in embarrassment.

Thus the ludicrous formality of the celebratory event is reasserted in the play at the most farcical moment to create a natural climax—a climax which simultaneous-ly serves as a deflatory device. It is significant that Chekhov did not end the play with the frozen *tableau*: by extending the play to include the Shareholder's speech, Chekhov underlines the pretentions, *and* slows the action down; by Shipuchin's dazed irrelevancies, and the shareholders' and employees' embarrassed exit, a different tone is asserted. Thus the slower pace, the down-beat, the anti-climax, create a more thoughtful ending. The play comes to an end not with the usual conventional happy ending, but with what is undoubt-edly a scandal.

This farce-vaudeville is not an 'amorous vaudeville' (al-though 'love' and 'romance' are parodied by means of both Tatyana and Khirin); it is not, of course, a 'scene-monologue' (although the play begins with Khirin's monologue); it is not simply 'a biting exposure of the private banks in Russia';[43] it is an innovatory 'comic scene of daily life' which is also in the tradition of Gogol: a satire on the pretentious, the petty, and the philistine. It combines comedy of situation and comedy of character, but the play is a comedy of the characters' own making.

THE NIGHT BEFORE THE TRIAL (1890s)

The unfinished, posthumously published **The Night be-fore the Trial** is not subtitled by Chekhov, but the situa-tion, characterisation and dramatic techniques place the play clearly within the context of a farce-vaudeville, and the story of the same title, written in 1886, indicates the probable and farcical continuation of the play. With the exception of some of the little known or early parodies,[44] **The Night before the Trial**—although unfinished—is po-tentially one of Chekhov's most overt parodies: it utilises the most conventional, even traditional, comic situation, stock 'types', action and probable *dénouement*. It is, per-haps, for this reason that the play remained unfinished. Speculation is, of course, idle, but when the play is seen in the context of Chekhov's other work of the 1890s, it is probable that the play had out-grown its usefulness; it is, however, interesting for the light it throws on Chekhov's use—albeit unfinished—of traditional comic devices and situations.

The play relies for its comic plot on a succession of misunderstandings which arise from mistaken, and as-sumed, identity: a dissolute young man, Zaytsev, assumes the identity of a doctor in order to make love to a lovely young woman—apparently unaccompanied—whom he meets in the middle of the night in an inn, while a blizzard howls outside. The young lady is, however, accompanied by none other than her husband—an ugly old man—called Fred Gusev ('Goose'). Rapidly improvising a respectable 'motive' for his advances to the young wife, Zaytsev con-tinues to play the part of a doctor, only to be asked by the old husband to examine the young wife, Zina. This Zay-tsev does, and uses his medical disguise as a means of continuing his flirtation, aided by Zina herself. At the beginning of the play, however, Zaytsev tells the audience that he is on his way to town, to be tried at the assizes for 'attempted bigamy, forging my grandmother's will to the tune of not more than three hundred roubles, and the attempted murder of a billiards-marker'. And, as the orig-inal story makes clear, the prosecuting counsel turns out to be none other than Fred Gusev:

> As readers of this unfinished play can easily deduce for themselves, the dénouement would have involved Zaytsev facing Zina's husband as his prosecuting counsel in court next day. Such, at any rate, is the ending of Chekhov's short story with the same title, where the hero comments: 'Looking at him [the prosecutor], I remembered the bugs, little Zina and my diagnosis, whereupon a chill—nay a whole Arctic Ocean—ran down my spine.'[45]

In this way, presumably, the 'cuckolded husband' is able to get his revenge on the young imposter.

This is the only one of Chekhov's plays which uses the device of assumed identity to enable a character to prac-tise a comic deception, but it is a device which goes back, through Moliére, to the commedia dell'arte. This assump-tion of a 'respectable' identity was—equally traditional-ly—often utilised in order to make a cuckold of a husband, and this, in turn, was conventionally applied to the marital situation of an ugly old husband and a young, beautiful wife. Variations may be seen in Molière, whether in *Le Médecin malgré lui,* or in *Le Malade imaginaire,* or *L'Amour médecin,* or in the early play generally attributed to Molière, *Le Médecin volant.* Again, it was traditional for the 'respectable disguise' to be that of a doctor: first, because it allowed access to the young wife, which the husband would never normally permit, let alone encourage; secondly, because the joke was increased by the husband actually inviting the 'doctor' to examine his wife; and third, because (certainly in the case of, for example, Molière's *Monsieur de Pourceaugnac*), it motivates and justifies a parody of medical terminology and practice, a source of parody to which Chekhov, as a doctor himself, was not averse.[46]

All of these traditional sources of comedy are found in **The Night before the Trial**: 'stock' or 'type' characters, a 'stock' situation, and a greater emphasis on plot as such than on psychological depth of character. The stock characterisation may be seen in the figures of the charming scoundrel of a lover, the beautiful young wife, and the ugly old husband; the landlord of the inn scarcely figures in this fragment—unlike for example, Luka in **The Bear,** no attempt is made to create anything more than the functional with this character. It is, however, exactly in Chekhov's particular use of the conventional that parody may be seen: Gusev is *excessively* ugly, while Zina is excessively young and beautiful; equally, Zaytsev has committed an excessive variety of crimes—thus the element of parody is contained in the 'excess' of all the conventionalised facets of the play.

Zaytsev's character is established partly by his opening monologue—a monologue which serves the usual purpose of exposition—and through it his attitude to women and his comically exaggerated mixture of crimes are revealed to an audience: 'It's here today, in jug tomorrow—and Siberia's frozen wastes in six months' time. Brrr.' The tone is light, and so is Zaytsev's casual and conventional solution to his problems: suicide.

> ZAYTSEV: . . . If the jury finds against me, I'll appeal to an old and trusty friend. Dear, loyal old pal! (*Gets a large pistol out of his suitcase.*) This is him! What a boy! I swapped him with Cheprakov for a couple of hounds. Isn't he lovely! Why, just shooting yourself with this would be a kind of enjoyment. (*Tenderly.*) Are you loaded, boy? (*In a reedy voice, as if answering for the pistol.*) I am that. (*In his own voice.*) I'll bet you'll go off with a bang—one hell of a ruddy great bang! (*In a reedy voice.*) One hell of a ruddy great bang! (*In his own voice.*) Ah, you dear, silly old thing. Well, lie down and go to sleep. (*Kisses the pistol and puts it in his suitcase.*)

(H.1.163)

The tone is such that no audience would take this threatened suicide in any way seriously: the parody, however, is evident in lines such as 'Why, just shooting yourself with this would be a kind of enjoyment'; through the emphasis on the size of the pistol, and through the 'char-

acterisation' of the pistol by ventriloquism, all of which removes Zaytsev's threat from both depth motivation, and the realistic or serious consequences of suicide.

The use of ventriloquism in this play contrasts vividly with the use made of it—to totally different effect—in **The Cherry Orchard.** The governess, Charlotte Ivanovna, is renowned for her party tricks, but on several occasions Chekhov uses her tricks to express her unhappiness and loneliness, and thus ventriloquism as practised by Charlotte Ivanovna is one of the subtly appropriate means of communicating the psychological depth of this character:

> (*Lopakhin comes in. Charlotte quietly hums a tune.*)
>
> GAYEV: Charlotte's happy, she's singing.
>
> CHARLOTTE: (*picking up a bundle which looks like a swaddled baby*) Rock-a-bye, baby. (*A baby's cry is heard.*) Hush, my darling, my dear little boy. (*The cry is heard again.*) You poor little thing! (*Throws the bundle down.*) And please will you find me another job? I can't go on like this.

(H.3.193)

In the characterisation of Charlotte Ivanovna, her comedy 'turns' serve to mask her despair—comedy is used to comment on the serious. In the case of Zaytsev, however, comedy is purely conventionalised, and neither creates nor implies hidden, serious depths. This is also emphasised by his actions, he kisses the pistol before 'putting it to bed', and readily maintains the comic mood by immediately proceeding to do physical jerks to warm himself up. Thus the monologue is in no way introspective, self-revelatory, or disturbing—it serves as exposition of situation, rather than revelation of character.

The frivolity of tone is continued when Zaytsev, hearing a noise, realises that he has neighbours, and then muses that this might result in a round of bridge, or, better still, a 'wayside romance' and 'an affair better than any in Turgenev's novels'.[47] And he starts to remember a previous affair at a post-house 'down Samara way' when, one night, 'The door opens and . . .' . His reminiscences are interrupted by the entrance of Zina, a comic coincidence in timing which, although absurd, is also purely conventional. But the reason for Zina's disturbed night is not, as it turns out, even remotely romantic: she has been bitten by bed-bugs! Zaytsev, however, responds romantically; like a real gallant, he ventures to offer his services as 'a gentleman and man of honour', wishes to aid the lady in her distress, and offers help—an offer, made from the bottom of his 'heart', which takes the prosaic form of insect-powder. Sensing an affair, Zaytsev offers to put the powder down in her room, and it is then that he starts to pretend that he is a doctor: 'From their doctors and hairdressers ladies have no secrets.'[48] Zaytsev is confirmed as a scoundrel and the 'villain' when he swears, on his word of honour, that he really is a doctor; and equally 'villainous' is his—characteristically—excessive reaction to the discovery that Zina's husband is present. The would-be lover turns the husband into the villain:

ZAYTSEV: . . . What a ghastly old frump! I'd bury him alive in insect-powder if I had my way. I'd like to beat the swine at cards and clean him out good and proper a dozen times over. Better still, I'd play him at billiards and accidentally fetch him one with a cue that would make him remember me for a whole week.

(H.1.166)

Zaytsev's contempt for the old man is increased when Gusev, accepting that he is a doctor, asks him to examine his wife, and Zaytsev is quick to take advantage of what is both gullibility and a very real concern over Zina's health. In the true tradition of a farce-vaudeville and a comedy of situation, Zaytsev will, inevitably, receive his just deserts when he meets Gusev in court the next day.

The conventional nature of the characters is also evident—as so often in Chekhov's work—in their names: Zaytsev—a common name—means 'Hare', while Gusev—appropriately—is associated with 'Goose'. But in this case, the use of 'meaningful names' may also have another purpose: it introduces the element of the proverb, or fable. Relevant to Zaytsev's treatment of Gusev (and, no doubt, Gusev's treatment of Zaytsev the next day), is the Russian proverb: 'First catch your hare—and then cook him.' Equally relevant to the play is Krylov's famous fable *The Hare A-Hunting* in which the boastful hare is given a share of the spoils simply because his boasting is amusing, and the fable ends: 'We mock the boaster: all the same / In sharing up the spoils, he often gets his claim.' There is no evidence, however, that Chekhov necessarily had this fable in mind.

Gusev 'the goose' is characterised by Zaytsev with typical excess:

With that blob of a nose, those blue veins all over his face and that wart on his forehead, he—he has the nerve to be married to a woman like that! What right has he? It's disgusting!

(H.1.166)

In this way, Gusev is made the epitome of the ugly old husband of the commedia dell' arte, while Zaytsev justifies the view of himself as a young fop:

And then people ask why I take such a jaundiced view of things. But how can you help being pessimistic under these conditions?

(H.1.166)

With one stroke, Chekhov simultaneously maintains the comedy of Zaytsev's philosophy and morality, and satirises pessimism and a 'jaundiced view' of life, by providing a ridiculous motivation and justification for it. But the joke of the whole situation is continued by Gusev's zest in pushing Zina into Zaytsev's arms:

GUSEV: (*shouts*) Zina! Oh really, you are silly. (*To him.*) She's shy—quite the blushing violet, same as me. Modesty's all very well in its way, but why overdo

things? What—stand on ceremony with your doctor when you're ill? That really is the limit.

(H.1.167)

The joke is in the 'persuasion' by the husband—a 'stock' example of dramatic irony, but also in the fact that Zina is no more ill than any other traditional young lady in a similar situation (such as Lucinde in *L'Amour médecin*), and, finally, in what Gusev sees as Zina's 'modesty' and shyness: the husband is deceived not only by the wife's actions, but also by her character. A further source of the comic is Gusev's excessive respect for medicine, combined with an experienced lack of respect for certain doctors. It becomes clear that Zina has already carried on an affair with a certain Dr Shervetsov; Gusev, therefore, has cause for his jealousy, but still entertains no doubts as to Zaytsev's qualifications:

ZAYTSEV: . . . One more question—when do you cough more, on Tuesdays or on Thursdays?

ZINA: On Saturdays.

ZAYTSEV: I see. Let me take your pulse.

GUSEV: (*aside*) It looks as if there's been kissing—it's the Shervetsov business all over again. I can't make any sense of medicine. (*To his wife.*) Do be serious, Zina—you can't go on like this, you can't neglect your health. You must listen carefully to what the doctor tells you. Medicine's making great strides these days, great strides.

(H.1.168)

Chekhov is satirising the inflated, exaggerated respect for medicine—a respect which was invariably divorced from the morality and worth of its practitioners. The 'Goose' therefore puts both Shervetsov's and Zaytsev's behaviour down to some strange mystery of medicine, and carries on ignoring 'the great strides' which 'medicine' has been making under his nose. Thus, only in a conventional farce situation of this kind is it acceptable that Gusev does not penetrate Zaytsev's improvised medical 'mumbo-jumbo'.

ZAYTSEV: . . . Your wife's in no danger as yet, but if she doesn't have proper treatment she may end up badly with a heart attack and inflammation of the brain.

(H.1.168)

Gusev swallows this diagnosis without question, and then proceeds—unwittingly—to help Zaytsev improvise the cure:

ZAYTSEV: I'll write a prescription at once. (*Tears a sheet of paper out of the register, sits down and writes.*) *Sic transit* . . . two drams. *Gloria mundi* . . . one ounce. *Aquae dest*— . . . two grains. Now, you take these powders, three a day.

GUSEV: In water or wine?

ZAYTSEV: Water.

GUSEV: Boiled?

ZAYTSEV: Boiled.

(H.1.169)

Again, it was traditional for the 'mock doctor' to improvise in pidgin Latin in order to maintain the disguise, and gain respect, and—as in all such scenes—the 'Latin' is complete nonsense. The parody of medicine is obvious—as is the satire on its practitioners—but in that Chekhov uses conventional, even traditional, comic situations and forms, the play may be seen as, in fact, parodying a parody. And, in addition, Chekhov parodies those comedies, and farce-vaudevilles, which centre on the cuckolded husband and his young wife. Perhaps for this reason Gusev remains a 'stock' character, while very little is done with the character of Zina: she is twenty-two, attractive—and a flirt: 'My husband's coming now, I think. Yes, yes, he's coming. Why don't you speak? What are you waiting for? Come on, then—kiss me, can't you?' Zaytsev receives all the co-operation he requires from Zina, but she remains a character 'by function' rather than developed as an individual.

Chekhov employs the same setting as that of **On the High Road,** but once this is clearly established, once the bedbugs have set the plot in motion, it plays very little part: true to the convention, the setting is not used for mood or atmosphere, but only to motivate the characters' transient relationship with the location. Equally conventional are the monologue and the extensive use of 'the aside', both of which—given the style of the play—are completely acceptable.

This unfinished comedy is strangely overt: the parody emerges through the exaggeration of the conventional, rather than by means of the 'counterbalancing' techniques which Chekhov employs in all the other farce-vaudevilles—techniques involving the parody, reversal, or extension of conventions. But it is, of course, impossible to draw any conclusions about what is an unfinished—and therefore unrevised—fragment. It is idle to speculate what the play might have become, but in its unfinished state, it demonstrates very clearly Chekhov's familiarity with conventional comedy techniques and situations; moreover, it serves as an interesting contrast to similar situations in Chekhov's dramatic work in which the 'stock' and the obvious are apparently established, only to be completely avoided subsequently. Thus, Dr Lvov in **Ivanov** treats Sara—but it is Ivanov who is unfaithful, not Sara and her doctor, or, in **Uncle Vanya,** both Astrov and Vanya are attracted by the young and beautiful wife of a garrulous old man, but everyone's expectations of infidelity are disappointed—

VOYNITSKY: . . . she married him when he was already an old man and gave him her youth, her beauty, her freedom, her radiance. Whatever for?—Why?

ASTROV: Is she faithful to him?

VOYNITSKY: Yes, I'm sorry to say.

ASTROV: Why sorry?

VOYNITSKY: Because she's faithful in a way that's so thoroughly bogus. Oh, it sounds impressive enough, but it just doesn't make sense. To be unfaithful to an elderly husband you can't stand, that's immoral. But if you make these pathetic efforts to stifle your own youth and the spark of life inside you, that isn't immoral at all.

(H.3.23)

Here the expectations of fidelity are given a new—philosophical—twist: convention can be stultifying, a sin against life rather than society. Equally, Chekhov reverses the situation of the cuckolded husband in his treatment of Andrey in **The Three Sisters**: Natasha's affair with Protopopov makes Andrey not a comic figure of fun, but a tragi-comic figure pretending not to see what is going on in front of him. Thus, what is treated as a joke and as farce in **The Night before the Trial,** may well have served as an experiment in situations and techniques which are reversed, modified, and then treated in an innovatory way in the later full-length plays. Perhaps relevant both to **The Night before the Trial,** and Chekhov's other dramatic works, is Strindberg's comment made in relation to **The Father** (1887):

A deceived husband is a comic figure in the eyes of the world, and especially to a theatre audience. He must show that he is aware of this, and that he too would laugh if only the man in question were someone other than himself. This is what is *modern* in my tragedy, and alas for me and the clown who acts it if he goes to town and plays an 1887 version of the Pirate King! No screams, no preachings! Subtle, calm, resigned!—the way a normally healthy spirit accepts his fate today.[49]

NOTES

[1] V. Mayakovsky, 'Dva Chekhova', in *Polnoe sobranie sochineniy v trinadtsati tomakh,* Moscow, 1955, Vol. 1, p. 301.
[2] After seeing a performance of *Uncle Vanya* at the Moscow Art Theatre on 24 January 1900, Tolstoy is reported to have said to Chekhov: 'You know I cannot stand Shakespeare, but your plays are even worse than his.' Quoted in S. Karlinsky, *Letters of A. Chekhov* London, 1973, p. 375.
[3] Quoted in V. Lakshin, *Tolstoy i Chekhov,* Moscow, 1975, pp. 104-5.
[4] Quoted in Simonov, *Stanislavsky's Protégé: Eugene Vakhtangov,* New York, 1969, p. 22.
[5] Magarshack, *Chekhov the Dramatist,* New York, 1960, p. 59.
[6] *The Seagull,* Act 1, H.2.233.
[7] Yu. Yuzovsky, 'Chekhov u Meyerkholda', *Razgovor zatyanulsya za polnoch,* Moscow, 1966, p. 252.
[8] The choice of names here serves as an example of Chekhov's employment of 'meaningful names'. While there is an obvious danger in sometimes 'reading in' a significance which may not have been intended, in this case the association of the names is part of the comic effect: Gruzdev's name is associated with the Russian word for 'mushroom'; Yaroshevich with 'spring wheat', and Kuritsyn with 'chicken'.
[9] *The Three Sisters,* Act 2, H.3.106.
[10] See Chekhov's 1880 list of clichés and conventions, Chapter 2, p. 17.
[11] See Chapter 2, p. 35, and H.1.175.
[12] Quoted in H.1.174.
[13] Letter to Suvorin, 6 January 1889.
[14] See C. Stanislavski, *My Life in Art,* London, 1962, p. 358.
[15] Simonov, *Stanislavsky's Protégé,* p. 55.
[16] *Ibid.* pp. 24-5.

[17] Similarly, Serebryakov's first entrance in Act 1 of *Uncle Vanya* tells the audience a great deal about him—as Vanya says: 'It's hot and stuffy today, but the great sage is complete with overcoat, galoshes, umbrella and gloves' (H.3.21). The extremity and disparity of dress is comic and telling.

[18] Such as Pushkin's *Dubrovsky, or Tales of Belkin;* Gogol's *The Two Ivans,* or in several of Ostrovsky's plays.

[19] Lakshin, *Tolstoy i Chekhov,* p. 105.

[20] Yuzovsky, *Razgovor zatyanulsya za polnoch,* pp. 256-7.

[21] *Ibid.* p. 259.

[22] See K. L. Rudnitsky, *Rezhissyor Meyerhold,* Moscow, 1969, pp. 473-81, and E. Braun, *Meyerhold on Theatre,* London, 1969, p. 248.

[23] Lomov is looking for his own shoulder!

[24] In *The Wedding,* Zmeyukina keeps asking for air: 'Give me air, do you hear?'; and in *Uncle Vanya,* Astrov says: 'You know, I don't think I should survive a single month in your house, this air would choke me' (H.3.38). The demand for air invariably relates to atmosphere and situation, and is rarely simply a comment on the weather.

[25] In Meyerhold's production, Chubukov's plea was answered—a giant knife and pistol appeared, and no doubt motivated a 'relapse' from the reviving Lomov.

[26] See G. P. Berdnikov, *Chekhov-dramaturg,* Mowscow, 1972, pp. 38-9.

[27] Konstantin Varlamov, a well-known Petersburg actor.

[28] Letter to Suvorin, 4 May 1889. Karlinsky, *Letters of Chekhov,* p. 140.

[29] Letter to Leontyev, 6 May 1889. Quoted in H.1.180.

[30] H.1.105-14.

[31] Quoted in B. Eichenbaum, 'Chekhov at Large', an essay in R. L. Jackson, ed., *Chekhov: A Collection of Critical Essays,* Englewood Cliffs, N.J., 1967, p. 28.

[32] W. Gerhardi, *Anton Chekhov: A Critical Study,* London, 1974, pp. 100-1.

[33] Yuzovsky, *Razgovor zatyanulsa za polnoch,* p. 248.

[34] See Rudnitsky, *Rezhissyor Meyerhold,* pp. 473-81.

[35] Yuzovsky, *op. cit.,* pp. 248-9.

[36] *Ibid.* p. 250.

[37] From the aria in the final act of Tchaikovsky's opera, *Eugene Onegin.* Significantly, the aria is sung by Tatyana's *husband.*

[38] A similar comic technique was used by Gogol in *How Ivan Ivanovich Quarrelled with Ivan Nikiforovich:* '"*Please* have some more, Ivan Ivanovich." "I can't stop, thank you very much." With these words Ivan Ivanovich bowed and sat down again.' Gogol, *Diary of a Madman and Other Stories,* ed. R. Wilks, Harmondsworth, 1972, p. 132.

[39] Yuzovsky, *op. cit.,* p. 249. The part of Merchutkina was played by Serebryannikova.

[40] See Gogol, *Diary of a Madman and other Stories,* pp. 96-7.

[41] Chekhov, *Works,* Moscow, 1944-51, vol. 13, p. 391. For a similar view expressed by Ibsen, see his letter of June 1883 to August Lindberg, quoted in M. Meyer, *Henrik Ibsen,* vol. 3, p. 26.

[42] Like Lomov in *The Proposal.*

[43] Magarshack, *Chekhov the Dramatist,* p. 65.

[44] Such as *Tatyana Repina,* the two little-known sketches, *Dishonourable Tragedians and Leprous Dramatists* and *A Forced Declaration* (see Appendices 1 and 2), and some of Chekhov's early parodies on the work of Gaboriau, Jules Verne, Victor Hugo, Alphonse Daudet, and others.

[45] H.1.201.

[46] In a letter to Leykin on 20 May 1884, Chekhov wrote: 'I would now enjoy writing a satirical medical text in two or three volumes.'

[47] Possibly a reference to Turgenev's *Asya.*

[48] It was exactly because of this 'access' that hairdressers, barbers, and chambermaids were well-placed to create intrigue—as in *The Barber of Seville, The Marriage of Figaro,* or many vaudevilles.

[49] Letter to Axel Ludegård, October 1887, quoted in M. Meyer, *Strindberg: The Father, Miss Julie and The Ghost Sonata,* London, 1976, pp. 17-18.

The Seagull

Ellen Chances (essay date 1977)

SOURCE: "Chekhov's *Seagull:* Ethereal Creature or Stuffed Bird?" in *Chekhov's Art of Writing: A Collection of Critical Essays,* edited by Paul Debreczeny and Thomas Eekman, Slavica Publishers, 1977, pp. 27-34.

[*In the following essay, Chances views the seagull as a symbol that Chekhov ridicules; in fact, the critic asserts, "the entire play might, perhaps, be considered a parody of symbolism."*]

When discussing Chekhov's play **The Seagull,** one can divide criticism into two schools. There are those interpretations, set forth in excellent articles and excellent productions, which belong to the "ethereal creature" school. Nina is seen as a poor, naive, young girl who, like a seagull, strives to spread her wings and be free. The play within the play, according to "ethereal creature" proponents, represents the efforts of a struggling young playwright in his search for new art forms. The seagull image itself has been plucked bare. Leonid Grossman has stated that the seagull is a symbol of Nina's unhappy fate and of human fate in general. Nina is said to be like the wounded bird who silently watches the cruelties of life unfold before its eyes.[1] Or, the seagull is said to symbolize the fate of Treplev.[2] Or, the seagull is made to represent the beauty of all living things.[3] Or, it is interpreted as a representation of Nina's own personal struggle and of her ability to triumph, and as a symbol of the destruction of beauty.[4]

There are also those interpretations which belong to the "stuffed bird" school. The exponent of this school (the author of this article) certainly does not deny the perceptivity of other interpretations. It is, however, important to bear in mind that the play can be given a less serious reading as well. After all, Chekhov did entitle the play **Chaika. Komediia *v chetyrekh deistviiakh*** (Emphasis mine—E. C.). In addition, Chekhov's use of symbols in the play is, to a certain extent, ironic.

Let us examine the evidence. Take Nina, for example. What is she? She is far from the beautiful, fragile, poetic being which she and others consider her. Rather, she is a plain, talentless girl, mesmerized by the vacuous notion of fame. One has only to count the number of times she repeats the word "famous" (*izvestnyi*). She casts aside the unknown author Treplev in order to chase the double rainbows of fame and Trigorin, and she ends up as a mediocre provincial actress in a cold, empty hotel room in Elets.

Consider the play within the play as another telling piece of evidence. Treplev's creation, with its Eternal Matter, red devil eyes, and new forms, can hardly be treated in a

serious manner. Although Arkadina the actress has no role in her son's play, Chekhov has given her a key role in the scene—that of discrediting the performance of the play. Her mocking comments, first that the play belongs to the Decadent School, and later, that the Devil with his blood-red eyes is merely sulphur, create in the real audience the sceptical attitude toward symbolism which cannot easily be dispelled when applied to other symbolic elements in **The Seagull.** In a way, one can even speak of elements of parody in the treatment of symbolism here.

Minor incidents of an episodic nature also contribute to the theory of **The Seagull** as a "stuffed bird" play. There is, for example, the exchange in which Treplev speaks to Nina of a Romeo-and-Juliet-like scene. He will follow her home, he says, and will stand in the garden all night, watching her window. Nina shatters this romantic illusion by answering: "You can't. The watchman will notice you. Tresor still isn't used to you; he'll bark" (XI. 148).

The very beginning of Act One serves as still another example. Chekhov blows up many a romantic balloon, only to stick pins in them. In fact, he uses this technique in the very first lines of the play. Medvedenko asks Masha why she always wears black. When she explains that she is in mourning for her life, Medvedenko injects the everyday world of rubles into her misty spheres of poetry: "I don't understand . . . You're healthy. Although your father isn't rich, he's well-off. My life is much more difficult than yours. I get only twenty-three rubles a month. In addition, they deduct my superannuation from that. All the same, I don't wear mourning" (XI. 144).

Masha tries again: "The money doesn't matter. Even a poor man can be happy" (XI. 144). Yet again Medvedenko responds to Masha's starry-eyed world with a lesson in economics. "That's in theory, but in practice, it works out like this: there's me, my mother, two sisters and my little brother, and my salary is only twenty-three rubles. After all, one has to eat and drink, right? And one needs tea and sugar, right? And tobacco, right? Try to get by on that" (XI. 144).

And what about the role of the seagull image, according to the "stuffed bird" school? The image does, of course, play a very important part in the play. We human beings observe birds as they drift gently, always beyond our grasp, in the blue expanses above. In "To a Skylark," Shelley, for instance, places the skylark on a romantic pedestal—"Hail to thee blithe spirit! . . . and singing still dost soar, and soaring ever singest." Chekhov endows his own bird image with a great number of dimensions. Already in Act One, Chekhov sets up the association between the seagull and Nina, who says she's drawn to the lake as if she were a seagull. Later, when Treplev lays a dead seagull at her feet and identifies himself with it, she mocks the very symbol which she had chosen for herself and which she later uses again. At the end of Act Four, the seagull makes a last entrance—stuffed, its poignant symbolic value underlined. Trigorin has forgotten that he ordered the stuffing of the very bird of which he had once spoken: "A subject for a short story: a young girl like you [Nina] has lived by a lake since childhood. She loves the lake as does a seagull, and she is happy and free as a seagull. But a man happens to come by who sees her; and to while away the time, he destroys her, just like this seagull" (XI. 168).

The seagull image, as we have seen, is usually interpreted in a serious way. Although to do so is valid, it is, I believe, just as appropriate to consider it in another light. Just as thematically and stylistically Chekhov was puncturing illusions, so too he brings the poetic bird down from its soaring heights. In his hands, the seagull becomes, by the final act, nothing more than a stuffed bird, a delight for taxidermists. The seagull has become a symbol, not only of destroyed lives or of Nina's or Treplev's fate, but of the overriding theme of the play, the stripping away of the many layers of artificiality. And the way Chekhov has done this is to laugh at the very image. After the tremendous build-up during the play, it is laughable that Trigorin cannot even remember that he has

ordered the bird to be stuffed. The fact that Chekhov chooses a scavenger bird (although the seagull is, of course, also evocative of romantic visions of freedom and the restless sea) contributes to the touches of comedy. In addition, Chekhov's pounding the reader on the head with references to the seagull adds to the comic effect. Chekhov, master of subtlety and suggestion, creator of the half-statement, painter of an entire mood with but a few strokes of the pen, knew full well what he was doing as he repeatedly dragged the seagull image before his audience in this play. Really, then, in many ways, the entire play might, perhaps, be considered as a parody of symbolism.

Chekhov's method can fruitfully be described as that which was first attributed to Gogol, *smekh skvoz' slezy* ("laughter through tears"). This feature runs throughout his short stories, even in his so-called "comic" pre-1886 period. In this respect one has only to think, for example, of **"Death of a Government Clerk."** The story is funny, but at the same time, there is a real sense of pathos, too.

The aftertaste—and not even the aftertaste, but an integral effect—of the play under consideration is not at all funny. What one is left with is the sad, melancholy, minor key. Chekhov's sad "message" is contained even in the small cues that he throws to his audience. At the beginning of Act Two, for instance, as Arkadina is reading aloud, Nina wanders by and asks what she is reading. The answer is Maupassant's *Sur l'eau*. It is indeed surprising that critical literature has hitherto failed to pick up the obvious connection between the two works.[5]

The passage which Arkadina reads from *Sur l'eau* concerns the practice in society for women, by means of flattery, to capture that much sought-after creature, the writer. The practice is compared to corn merchants' breeding of rats in their granaries. Arkadina emphatically denies the applicability of the statement to Russians. Citing herself and Trigorin, she insists that Russian relationships are based on love. The audience, however, readily sees that her relationship with Trigorin does fit the Maupassant description. She continues to read to herself, then abruptly closes the book after saying, "Oh, well, the next part isn't interesting and isn't true" (XI. 159).

Just what *is* this "next part"? Maupassant's narrator writes:

> When, therefore, a woman has fixed her choice on the writer she intends to adopt, she lays siege to him by means of every variety of compliments, attractions, and indulgence. Like water which, drop by drop, slowly wears away the hardest rock, the fulsome praise falls at each word on the impressionable heart of the literary man. Then, when she sees that he is moved, touched, and won by the constant flattery, she isolates him, severing, little by little, the ties he may have elsewhere, and imperceptibly accustoms him to come to her house, make himself happy, and there enshrines his thoughts. In order the more thoroughly to acclimatize him in her house, she paves the way for his success, brings him forward, sets him in relief, and displays for him, before all the old

habitués of the household, marked consid-eration and boundless admiration.

> At last, realizing that he is now an idol, he remains in the temple. He finds, moreover, that the position offords him every advantage, for all other women lavish their most delicate favors upon him to entice him away from his conqueror.[6]

Although this is the only place where the Maupassant work is mentioned, knowledge of the novel reveals its immense significance for the Chekhov play as a whole. The narrator of *Sur l'eau* is on a small boat, the Bel-Ami, which sails from port to port along the French Mediterranean coast. Each chapter of the book is constructed around the narrator's observations as he wanders through a town. In the second chapter, "Cannes," the one which is quoted in **The Seagull,** Maupassant's narrator takes note of the preponderance of princes and prince worshippers. He describes those who eagerly encircle the prince and then tell you what the princess answered or the Grand Duke replied. "One feels, one sees, one guesses," continues the narrator, "that they frequent no other society but that of persons of Royal blood, and if they deign to speak to you, it is in order to inform you exactly of what takes place on these heights."[7] The narrator then delineates the ". . . various races of heroworshippers."[8]

He continues his discourse on Cannes by writing that he is certain that he can predict the topic of conversation at parties, at villas and hotels: ". . . people were gathered together this evening, as they will be tomorrow and . . . they are talking. Talking! about what? The Princes! the weather! And then?—the weather!—the Princes!—and then—about nothing! . . . I have lived in hotels, I have endured the emptiness of the human soul as it is there laid bare."[9]

A similar undercurrent of the phoniness of life runs through the Chckhov play. Nina, as we have observed, serves as a prime example. Sorin, at one point, comments that his appearance is the tragedy of his life. Because he *looked* as if he drank, women were never attracted to him, he tells Treplev. Appearance was more important than substance. Maupassant's narrator informs us that there is a promenade which goes along the coast. Roses and orange blossoms line the walks. Yet the fragrant aromas are merely covering the odors of death, for this is also the location of a cemetery, filled with aristocratic victims of tuberculosis from all over Europe.

It would almost seem worthwhile to reproduce the entire Cannes chapter, so much of which is crucial to the understanding of **The Seagull.** After a few more emphatic statements about the stupidity and false pride of the human animal, our visitor to Cannes philosophizes on the nature of happiness. Some people are happy, he writes, because they envision life as a light play in which they themselves are the actors. Life, or the play, amuses them although it offers nothing of substance. Arkadina, who plays equally insipid roles on stage and in life, seems to fit well into this category. Even if she herself lives be-

hind a wall of illusion, the audience cannot bc kidded about the true nature of her life. She is shown as a flighty creature who acts in second-rate plays and is concerned mainly with facades. She rejects her son, for he reminds her of the fact that time does not stop. She clings to Trigorin, the Very Famous Person, even in the face of his infatuation with Nina.

Technical as well as thematic considerations bind the two works. In one chapter, Maupassant's narrator speaks about the mysterious influence which the moon exerts on human beings. The poet, he says, promotes romantic illusions about the moon. "When it rises behind the trees, when it pours forth its shimmering light on the flowering river . . . are we not haunted by all the charming ruses with which it has inspired great dreamers?"[10] However, the narrator quickly disperses any illusion. The moon, he says, like any other woman, needs a husband. Disdained by the sun, this heavenly body is nothing more than a cold virgin, an old maid.

In similar fashion, the narrator deflates any notion which considers war a noble pursuit. "Civilized" man should not look down haughtily at cannibals, he maintains. After all, who is the real savage, the person who fights to eat or the person who kills for no purpose other than to kill? From all these descriptions of the Maupassant work, one can readily see that the French author in *Sur l'eau* is doing exactly the same thing as Chekhov is doing in **The Seagull**: both constantly puncture illusions, constantly remove the veneered cover of falsity to expose the deflated reality.[11]

What Chekhov does throughout the play leads to a sad commentary on life. Yet, it seems to me that in coming to grips with the play, people have placed more emphasis on the tears than on the laughter, which is certainly there. Yes, Chekhov's seagull can mean one thing, an ethereal creature, but at the same time it is very much to be seen as a stuffed bird, too.

NOTES

[1] Leonid Grossman, "The Naturalism of Chekhov," in *Chekhov. A Collection of Critical Essays,* ed. Robert Louis Jackson (Englewood Cliffs, N.J.: Prentice-Hall, 1967), 34, 35.
[2] V. V. Ermilov, *"Chaika." Materialy i issledovaniia* (Moscow: Vserossiiskoe teatral'noe obshchestvo, 1946), 46.
[3] Maurice Valency, *The Breaking String: The Plays of Anton Chekhov* (New York: Oxford U. Press, 1966), 154.
[4] David Magarshack, *Chekhov the Dramatist* (London: John Lehmann, 1952), 192.
[5] In a footnote (p. 177) in *Problemy dramaturgicheskogo analiza. Chekhov* (Leningrad: Academia, 1927), S. D. Balukhatyi mentions the Maupassant passage which is quoted in Chekhov's play. Balukhatyi does write that the passage is a reflection of Arkadina's relationship with Trigorin. This is as far as he goes, though.
[6] Guy de Maupassant, *Sur l'eau or On the Face of the Water* (New York: M. Dunne, 1903), 20-21.
[7] Ibid., p. 16.
[8] Ibid.
[9] Ibid., p. 25.
[10] Ibid., pp. 49-50.
[11] In fact, a study of the Maupassant work would indicate that Maupassant was Chekhov's spiritual father in drama as well as in the short story.

Vladimir Nabokov (essay date 1977?)

SOURCE: "Notes on *The Seagull* (1896)," in *Vladimir Nabokov: Lectures on Russian Literature*, edited by Fredson Bowers, Harcourt Brace Jovanovich, 1981, pp. 282-95.

[The excerpt below is taken from a posthumous publication of Nabokov's notes for lectures delivered to literature classes. The year of Nabokov's death has been used to date the essay. Here, he provides scene-by-scene comments on Chekhov's art and stagecraft as demonstrated in The Seagull.]

In 1896 *The Seagull* (*Chaika*) was a complete failure at the Alexandrine Theatre in St. Petersburg, but at the Moscow Art Theatre in 1898 it was a tremendous success.

The first exposition—talk between two minor characters, the girl Masha and the village teacher Medvedenko—is thoroughly permeated by the manner and mood of the two. We learn about them and about the two major characters, the budding actress Nina Zarechny and the poet Treplev, who are arranging some amateur theatricals in the alley of the park: "They are in love with each other and to-night their souls will unite in an effort to express one and the same artistic vision," says the teacher in the ornate style so typical of a Russian semi-intellectual. He has his reasons to allude to this, being in love too. Nevertheless, we must admit that this introduction is decidedly blunt. Chekhov, like Ibsen, was always eager to get done with the business of explaining as quickly as possible. Sorin, the flabby and good-natured landowner, drops by with Treplev, his nephew, who is nervous about the play he is staging. The workmen who have built the platform come and say, we are going for a dip. And meanwhile old Sorin has asked Masha to tell her father (who is his own employee on the estate) to have the dog kept quiet at night. Tell him yourself, she says, rebuffing him. The perfectly natural swing in the play, the association of odd little details which at the same time are perfectly true to life—this is where Chekhov's genius is disclosed.

In the second exposition Treplev talks to his uncle about his mother, the professional actress, who is jealous of the young lady who is going to act in his play. Nor can one even mention Duse in her presence. My goodness, just try, exclaims Treplev.

With another author the complete picture of the woman in this expository dialogue would be a dreadful piece of traditional technique, especially seeing that it is to her own brother that the young man is speaking; but by sheer force of talent Chekhov manages to pull it through. The details are all so amusing: she has seventy thousand in the bank, but if you ask her for a loan she starts crying. . . . Then he speaks of the routine theatre, of its smug household morals and of the new thing he wants to create; and he talks about himself, about his sense of inferiority because his mother is always surrounded by famous artists and writers. It is quite a long monologue. By a judiciously placed question he is further made to speak of Trigorin, his mother's friend, the author. Charm, talent,

but—but somehow after Tolstoy and Zola one does not want to read Trigorin. Note the placing of Tolstoy and Zola on one level—typical for a young author like Treplev in those days, the late nineties.

Nina appears. She was afraid her father, a neighboring squire, would not let her come. Sorin goes to call the household, for the moon is rising and it is time to start Treplev's play. Note two typical Chekhov moves: first, Sorin sings a few bars of a Schubert song, then checks himself and tells with a laugh the nasty thing somebody once said about his singing voice; second, then when Nina and Treplev are left alone they kiss and immediately after she asks, "What's that tree there?" The answer, an elm. "Why is the tree so dark?" she goes on. These trifles disclose better than anything invented before Chekhov the wistful helplessness of human beings—the old man who made a mess of his life, the delicate girl who will never be happy.

The workmen come back. It is time to begin. Nina refers to her stage-fright emotion—she will have to be acting in front of Trigorin, the author of those wonderful short stories. "Dunno, haven't read them," Treplev says curtly. It has been pointed out by critics, who like noting such things, that while the elderly actress Arkadina is jealous of the amateur Nina who as yet is only dreaming of a stage career, her son, the unsuccessful and not very gifted young writer, is jealous of a really fine writer, Trigorin (incidentally, a kind of double of Chekhov the professional himself). The audience arrives. First Dorn, the old doctor, and the wife of Shamraev, the manager of Sorin's estate, who is an old flame of Dorn. Then Arkadina, Sorin, Trigorin, Masha, and Medvedenko flock in. Shamraev asks Arkadina about an old comic he used to applaud. "You keep asking me about antediluvian nobodies," she replies, rather testily.

Presently the curtain rises. There is a real moon and a view of the lake instead of a backdrop. Nina sitting on a stone makes a lyrical speech in a Maeterlinck style, mystically commonplace, obscurely trite. ("It is something in the decadent manner," whispers Arkadina. "Mother!" says her son in pleading tones.) Nina goes on. The idea is that she is a spirit talking after all life has ceased on earth. The red eyes of the devil appear. Arkadina makes fun of it and Treplev loses his temper, shouts for the curtain, and goes away. The others rebuke her for having hurt her son. But she feels insulted herself—that bad-tempered, vain boy . . . wants to teach me what the theatre ought to be. . . . The subtle point is that though Treplev has a real desire to destroy the old forms of art, he has not the talent to invent new ones to take their place. Note what Chekhov does here. What other author would have dared to make his main character—a positive character, as they say, that is, one which is expected to win the audience's sympathy—who else would have dared to make him a minor poet, at the same time giving real talent to the least pleasant persons of the play, to the nasty self-sufficient actress and the egotistical, supercritical, emphatically professional writer?

Some singing is heard on the lake. Arkadina recalls the days when youth and gaiety filled the place. She regrets having hurt her son. Nina appears and Arkadina introduces her to Trigorin. "Oh, I always read you." Now comes a delightful little parody of Chekhov's own method of contrast between poetry and prose. "Yes, the setting was beautiful," says Trigorin, and adds after a pause, "That lake must be full of fish." And Nina is puzzled to learn that a man who, as she says, has experienced the delights of creative work, can be amused by angling.

Without any special connection (again a typical device with Chekhov and beautifully true to life), but evidently continuing the line of thought of his previous conversation, Shamraev recalls a certain funny incident in a theatre years ago. There is a pause after this when the joke falls flat and nobody laughs. Presently they disperse, with Sorin complaining without effect to Shamraev about the dog barking at night, Shamraev repeating an earlier anecdote about a church singer, and Medvedenko, the socialist-minded, needy village teacher, inquiring how much such a singer earns. The fact that the question is unanswered shocked many critics who required facts and figures from plays. I remember reading somewhere the solemn statement that a playwright must tell his audience quite clearly the income of his respective characters, for otherwise their moods and action cannot be understood in full. But Chekhov, the genius of the casual, attains in the harmonious interplay of these trivial remakrs much greater heights than the ordinary slaves of cause and effect.

Dorn tells Treplev, who now appears again, that he liked his play—or what he heard of the play. He goes on expounding his own views about life, ideas, and art. Treplev, who was at first touched by his praise, now interrupts him twice. Where is Nina? He rushes away almost in tears. "Oh, youth, youth!" sighs the doctor. Masha retorts, "When people can't find anything else to say, they say, Oh youth, youth." She takes a pinch of snuff to the vast disgust of Dorn. Then she becomes suddenly hysterical and tells him she is desperately and hopelessly in love with Treplev. "Everybody is so nervous," the doctor repeats. "So very nervous. And everybody is in love. . . . This magic lake. But how can I help you, my poor child, how?"

So ends the first act, and we may well understand that the average audience in Chekhov's time, as well as the critics—those priests of the average—were left rather irritated and puzzled. There has been no definite line of conflict. Or rather there have been several vague lines and a futility of conflict, for one cannot expect any special conflict from a quarrel between a quick-tempered but soft son and a quick-tempered but equally soft mother, each always regretting his or her hasty words. Nothing special further is suggested by Nina meeting Trigorin, and the romances of the other characters are blind alleys. Finishing the act with an obvious dead end seemed an insult to people eager for a good tussle. But notwithstanding the fact that Chekhov was still tied up by the very traditions he was flaunting (the rather flat expositions, for instance), what seemed nonsense and faults to the average critic are really the grain from which some day a really great drama will grow, for with all my fondness for Chekhov I cannot hide the fact that in spite of his authentic genius he did not create

the perfect masterpiece. His achievement was that he showed the right way to escape the dungeon of deterministic causation, of cause and effect, and burst the bars holding the art of drama captive. What I hope of future playwrights is not that they will merely repeat the actual methods of Chekhov, for these belong to him, to his type of genius, and cannot be imitated, but that other methods tending with even more power to the same freedom of drama will be found and applied. This said, let us turn to the next act and see what surprises it reserved for an irritated and puzzled audience.

Act II. A croquet lawn and part of the house and lake. Arkadina is giving Masha a few hints as to how a woman keeps fit. From a chancc rcmark we learn that she has been Trigorin's mistress for quite a while. Sorin comes, together with Nina who has the opportunity of being here because her father and stepmother have gone away for three days. A rambling conversation is set rolling about Treplev's low spirits, about Sorin's poor health.

> MASHA. When he reads something aloud, his eyes burn and his face becomes pale. He has a beautiful sad voice and his manners are those of a poet.
>
> (SORIN *reclining in a garden chair is heard snoring.*) [*The contrast!*]
>
> DR. DORN. Good night, baby.
>
> ARKADINA. Hello Peter!
>
> SORIN. Eh? What's that? (*Sits up.*)
>
> ARKADINA. You are sleeping?
>
> SORIN. Not at all.
>
> (*A pause.*) [*Great master of pauses, Chekhov.*]
>
> ARKADINA. You do nothing for your health—that's bad, brother.
>
> SORIN. But I'd like to—only the doctor here is not interested.
>
> DR. DORN. What's the use of seeing a doctor at sixty.
>
> SORIN. A man of sixty wants to live, too.
>
> DR. DORN (*testily*). Oh, all right. Try something for the nerves.
>
> ARKADINA. I keep thinking that he ought to go to some German watering place.
>
> DR. DORN. Well. . . . Well, yes, he might go. And then he might not.
>
> ARKADINA. Do you see what he means? I don't.
>
> SORIN. There is nothing to see. It is all perfectly clear.

That's the way it goes. The wrong audience may get the impression that the author is frittering away his precious twenty minutes, his second act, while conflict and climax are fretting in the wings. But it is quite all right. The author knows his business.

> MASHA (*gets up*). Time for lunch, I think. (*Moves indolently.*) My foot is asleep. (*Exit.*)

Presently Shamraev turns up and is annoyed that his wife and Arkadina want to go to town when the horses are needed for the harvest. They quarrel; Shamraev loses his temper and refuses to manage the estate any longer. Can this be called a conflict? Well, there has been something leading up to it—that little thing about refusing to stop the dog barking at night—but really, really, says the smug critic, what parody is this?[1]

Here quite simply and with great aplomb Chekhov, the novator, reverts to the old old trick of having Nina, the heroine (who now remains alone on the stage) speaking her thoughts aloud. Well, she is a budding actress—but not even that can be an excuse. It is rather a flat little speech. She is puzzling over the fact that a famous actress weeps because she cannot have her own way and a famous writer spends the whole day fishing. Treplev comes back from hunting and throws a dead sea gull at Nina's feet. "I was a cad to kill this bird." Then he adds, "Soon I shall kill myself in the same way." Nina is cross with him: "These last few days you talk in symbols. This bird is apparently a symbol, too. (*She removes it onto a bench.*) But excuse me, I am too simple; I don't understand symbols." (Note that this line of thought will have a very neat ending—Nina herself will turn out to be the live subject of this symbol, which she does not see and which Treplev applies wrongly.) Treplev raves at her for becoming cold and indifferent to him after the flop of his play. He refers to his own oafishness. There is a faint hint at a Hamlet complex, which Chekhov suddenly turns inside out by Treplev applying another Hamlet motive to the figure of Trigorin, who stalks in with a book in his hands. "Words, words, words," Treplev shouts and exits.

Trigorin jots down in his book an observation about Masha: "Takes snuff, drinks strong liquors. . . . Always in black. The schoolteacher is in love with her." Chekhov himself kept such a notebook for jotting down characters that might come in handy. Trigorin tells Nina that he and Arkadina are, apparently, leaving (because of the quarrel with Shamraev). In reply to Nina, who thinks "it must be so wonderful to be a writer," Trigorin delivers a delightful speech, almost three pages long. It is so good and so typical for an author who finds a chance to talk about himself that the general aversion to long monologues in the modern theatre is forgotten. All the details of his profession are remarkably well brought out: ". . . Here I am, talking to you and I am moved, but at the same time I keep remembering that an unfinished long short story awaits me on my desk. I see, for instance, a cloud; I see it looks like a piano, and immediately I tell myself, I must use that in a story. A passing cloud that had the form of a piano. Or, say, the garden smells of heliotrope. Straightway I collect

it: a sickly sweet smell, widow blossom, must mention it when describing summer dusk. . . ." Or this bit: "When in the beginning of my career I used to have a new play staged, it always seemed to me that the dark spectators were opposed to me and that the blond spectators were coldly indifferent. . . ." Or this: "Oh, yes, it is pleasant to write, while you write . . . but afterwards. . . . The public reads and says: Yes, charming, talented. . . . Nice—but so inferior to Tosltoy; . . . yes, a beautiful story—but Turgenev is better." (This was Chekhov's own experience.)

Nina keeps telling him that she could readily undergo all such troubles and disappointments if she could have fame. Trigorin glancing at the lake and taking in the air and the landscape, remarks that it is such a pity he must leave. She points out to him the house on the opposite bank where her mother had lived.

> NINA. I was born there. I spent all my life near that lake and know every little island on it.
>
> TRIGORIN. Yes, it's beautiful here. (*Noticing the sea gull on the bench.*) And what's that?
>
> NINA. A sea gull. Treplev killed it.
>
> TRIGORIN. A fine bird. Really, I don't want one bit to go. Look here, try and persuade Madame Arkadin to stay. (*He proceeds to note something down in his book.*)
>
> NINA. What are you writing?
>
> TRIGORIN. Oh, nothing. . . . Just an idea. (*He puts the book into his pocket.*) An idea for a short story: lake, house, girl loves lake, happy and free like a sea gull. Man happens to pass, a glance, a whim, and the sea gull perishes. (*Pause*)
>
> ARKADINA (*from window*). Hullo, where are you?
>
> TRIGORIN. Coming!
>
> ARKADINA. We remain.
>
> (*He goes into the house*)
>
> (*NINA is left alone and broods awhile on the stage-front.*)
>
> NINA. A dream. . . .
>
> *Curtain.*

Now three things must be said about the ending of this second act. First of all, we have already noticed Chekhov's weak point: the featuring of young poetical women. Nina is slightly false. That last sigh over the footlights dates, and it dates just because it is not on the same level of perfect simplicity and natural reality as the rest of the things in the play. We are aware, certainly, that she is actressy and all that, but still it does not quite click.

Trigorin says to Nina, among other things, that he rarely happens to meet young girls and that he is too far gone in life to imagine clearly the feelings of sweet eighteen, so that in his stories, he says, his young girls are generally not true to life. (We may add, something wrong about the mouth, as Sargent the painter used to say the family of his sitters invariably observed.) What Trigorin says may be curiously enough applied to Chekhov, the playwright; for in his short stories, as for instance **"The House with the Mezzanine,"** or **"The Lady with the Little Dog,"** the young women are wonderfully alive. But that's because he does not make them talk much. Here they talk, and the weak spot is felt: Chekhov was not a talkative writer. That's one thing.

Another thing to be remarked is this. To all appearances, and judging by his own subtle approach to the writer's trade, his power of observation, and so on, Trigorin is really a good writer. But somehow the notes he takes about the bird and the lake and the girl do not impress one as the making of a good story. At the same time, we already guess that the plot of the play will be exactly that story and no other. The technical interest is now centered on the point: will Chekhov manage to make a good story out of material which in Trigorin's notebook sounds a little trite. If he succeeds, then we were right in assuming that Trigorin is a fine writer who will succeed in making of a banal theme a fine story. And finally a third remark. Just as Nina herself did not realize the real import of the symbol when Treplev brought the dead bird, so Trigorin does not realize that by remaining in the house near the lake he will become the hunter who kills the bird.

In other words, the end of the act is again obscure to the average audience because nothing can be expected yet. All that has really happened is that there has been a quarrel, a departure settled, a departure put off. The real interest lies in the very vagueness of the lines, and in artistic half-promises.

Act III, a week later. A dining room in Sorin's country house. Trigorin is breakfasting and Masha is telling him about herself so that "you, a writer, can make use of my life." From her very first words it transpires that Treplev has attempted to commit suicide but his wound is not serious.[2]

Apparently Masha's love for Treplev goes, for now she decides to marry the school teacher in order to forget Treplev. We learn further that Trigorin and Arkadina are about to leave for good now. A scene between Nina and Trigorin follows. She makes him a present, a medallion with, engraved, the title of one of his books and the number of a page and line. As Arkadina and Sorin come in, Nina hurriedly leaves, asking Trigorin to grant her a few minutes before he goes. But note, not a word of love has been spoken, and Trigorin is a little obtuse. As the play proceeds, Trigorin keeps muttering under his breath, trying to remember what was that line on that page. Are there any books of mine in this house? There are, in Sorin's study. He wanders off to find the required volume, which is the perfect way of getting him off the stage. Sorin and Arkadina discuss the reasons for Treplev's attempted

suicide: jealousy, idleness, pride. . . . When he suggests she give him some money she starts crying, as her son has predicted she does in such cases. Sorin gets excited and has a fit of dizziness.

After Sorin is led away, Treplev and Arkadina talk. This is a slightly hysterical and not very convincing scene. First move: he suggests to his mother that she lend some money to Sorin and she retorts that she is an actress and not a banker. A pause. Second move: he asks her to change the bandage on his head and as she does so very tenderly he reminds her of an act of great kindness which she once performed, but she does not remember. He tells how much he loves her but—and now the third move: why is she under the influence of that man? This makes her cross. He says that Trigorin's literature makes him sick; she retorts, you are an envious nonentity; they quarrel fiercely; Treplev starts crying; they make up again (forgive your sinful mother); he confesses he loves Nina but she does not love him; he cannot write any more, all hope is lost. The undulation of moods here is a little too obvious—it is rather a demonstration—the author putting the characters through their tricks. And there is a bad blunder directly afterwards. Trigorin comes in, turning the pages of the book, looking for the line, and then he reads, for the benefit of the audience: "Here it is: '. . . if any time you need my life, just come and take it.'"

Now it is quite clear that what really would have happened is that Trigorin, hunting for the book in Sorin's study on the lower shelf and finding it, would, normally, crouch and there and then read the lines. As often happens, one mistake leads to another. The next sentence is very weak again. Trigorin thinking aloud: "Why do I seem to hear such sadness in the call of this pure young soul? why does my own heart sink so painfully?" This is definitely poor stuff, and a good writer like Trigorin would hardly indulge in such pathos. Chekhov was faced with the difficult task of making his author suddenly human, and he bungled it completely by making him climb up on stilts so that the spectators might see him better.

Trigorin tells his mistress very bluntly that he wants to remain and have a go at Nina. Arkadina falls on her knees and in a very well imagined speech pleads with him: My king, my beautiful god. . . . You are the last page of my life, etc. You are the best contemporary writer, you are Russia's only hope, etc. Trigorin explains to the audience that he has no will-power—weak, slack, always obedient. Then she notices him writing something in his notebook. He says: "This morning I happened to hear a good expression—the pine grove of maidens. It may come in useful. . . . (*He stretches himself.*) Again railway carriages, stations, station-meals, cutlets, conversations. . . ."[3]

Shamraev who comes in to say that the carriage is ready speaks of an old actor he used to know. This is his being true to type, as in the first act, but a curious thing seems to have happened here. We have noted that Chekhov found a new device for making his characters live by giving them some silly joke or foolish observation or casual recollection instead of making the miser always talk of his

Chekhov reading The Seagull *to the Moscow Art Theater company, 1899.*

gold and the doctors of their pills. But what happens now is that the thwarted goddess of determinism takes her revenge, and what seemed to be a delightful casual remark indirectly disclosing the nature of the speaker now becomes as unescapable and all-powerful a feature as the miser's stinginess. Trigorin's notebook, Arkadina's tears when money questions are raised, Shamraev's theatrical recollections—these become fixed labels as unpleasant as the recurring oddities in traditional plays—you know what I mean—some special gag which a character repeats throughout the play at the most unexpected or rather expected moments. This goes to show that Chekhov, though he almost managed to create a new and better kind of drama, was cunningly caught in his own snares. I have the definite impression that he would not have been caught by these conventions—by the very conventions he thought he had broken—if he had known a little more of the numerous forms they take. I have the impression that he had not studied the art of drama completely enough, had not studied a sufficient number of plays, was not critical enough about certain technical aspects of his medium.

During the bustle of departure (with Arkadina giving a ruble, then worth about fifty cents, for the three servants, and repeating that they should share it) Trigorin manages to have a few words with Nina. We find him very eloquent

about her meekness, her angel-like purity, etc. She tells him she has decided to become an actress and to go to Moscow. They fix a date there and embrace. Curtain. There can be no question that though this act has a few good things in it, mainly in the wording, it is far below the two first ones.[4]

Act IV. Two years pass. Chekhov quietly sacrifices the ancient law of unity of time to secure unity of place, for in this last respect there is something quite natural in going over to next summer when Trigorin and Arkadina are expected to come again to stay with her brother in his country house.

A drawing room converted by Treplev into his den—lots of books. Masha and Medvedenko enter. They are married and have a child. Masha is concerned about Sorin, who is afraid to be alone. They refer to the skeleton of the theatre standing in the dark garden. Mrs. Shamraev, Masha's mother, suggests to Treplev that he be nicer to her daughter. Masha still loves him but now hopes that when her husband gets transferred to another place she will forget. Incidentally we learn that Treplev writes for magazines. Old Sorin has his bed made here in Treplev's room. This is a very natural thing for a man suffering from asthma to want, a craving for some change—it must not be confused with the "keeping on the stage" device. A delightful conversation ensues between the doctor, Sorin, and Medvedenko. (Arkadina has gone to the station to meet Trigorin.) For instance, the doctor alludes to his having spent some time and a lot of money in foreign countries. Then they speak of other things. There is a pause. Then Medvedenko speaks.

MEDVEDENKO. May I inquire, Doctor, what foreign town did you like best?

DORN. Genoa.

TREPLEV. Why Genoa—of all towns?

The doctor explains: just an impression, lives there seemed to meander and fuse—rather in the ways, he adds, as the world-soul in your play—by the way where is she now, that young actress? (A very natural transition.) Treplev tells Dorn about Nina. She had a love affair with Trigorin, had a baby, the baby died; she is not a good actress though quite a professional one by now, plays big parts but acts them coarsely, no taste, gasps, gesticulates. There are moments when one feels talent in some outcry of hers, as in the way she dies, but these are but moments.

Dorn inquires whether she has talent and Treplev answers that it is difficult to say. (Note that Nina is much in the same position as Treplev in their artistic achievements.) He goes on to tell that he has followed her from town to town wherever she played, but she never let him come near. Sometimes she writes. After Trigorin left her she has seemed a little wrong in the head. She signs her letters sea gull. (Note that Treplev has forgotten the connection.) He adds that she is here now, roams about, does not dare come, not does she want anyone to speak to her.

SORIN. She was a charming girl.

DORN. What's that?

SORIN. I said she was a charming girl.

Then Arkadina comes back from the station with Trigorin. (Intertwined with these scenes we are shown the pitiful plight of Medvedenko whom his father-in-law bullies.) Trigorin and Treplev manage to shake hands. Trigorin has brought a copy of a monthly review from Moscow with a story by Treplev, and with the flippant geniality of a famous writer to a lesser star tells him that people are interested, find him mysterious.

Presently all of them but Treplev sit down to play a game of lotto as they always do on rainy evenings. Treplev to himself, looking through the monthly: "Trigorin has read his own stuff but has not even cut the pages of my story." We follow the lotto game, and this is a very typical and beautiful Chekhov scene. It seems that in order to attain the heights of his genius he must put his people at ease, make them feel at home, make them comfortable, though this does not preclude slight boredom, gloomy little thoughts, stirring recollections, etc. And though here again

the characters are shown in their oddities or habits—Sorin again dozes, Trigorin talks of angling, Arkadina recalls her stage successes—this is much more naturally done than in the false dramatic background of the preceding act, because it is quite natural that in the same place, with the same people collected, two years later, the old tricks would be gently and rather pathetically repeated. It is hinted that critics have handled Treplev, the young author, very roughly. The numbers of the lotto are called out. Arkadina has never read a line of her son's stuff. Then they interrupt the game to go and have supper, all except Treplev, who remains brooding over his manuscripts. A monologue—it is so good that we do not mind the convention: "I have talked so much about new forms—and now I feel that little by little I myself slip into routine." (This may be applied—like most of the professional observations in the play—to Chekhov himself, in a way certainly, but only when he has lapses as in the previous act.) Treplev reads: "'Her pale face framed by her dark hair.' That's rotten, that 'framed,'" he exclaims and strikes it out. "I shall begin with the hero being awakened by the sound of rain—and to hell with the rest. The description of the moonshine is much too long and elaborate. Trigorin has created his own tricks; for him it is easy. He will show the neck of a broken bottle glistening on a river-dam and the black shadow under the mill-wheel—that's all and the moonlight is ready; but with me it is all the 'tremulous light' and 'softly twinkling stars' and the distant sounds of a piano, which 'dissolved in the soft intoxicating night air.' It is horrible, awful. . . ." (Here we get, incidentally, a beautifully defined difference between Chekhov's art and that of his contemporaries.)

Next follows the meeting with Nina, which from the point of view of the traditional stage may be considered the main and what I called satisfying scene of the play. Actually it is very fine. Her way of talking is much more in Chekhov's line here, when he is no more concerned with depicting pure, eager, romantic maidens. She is tired, upset, unhappy, a jumble of recollections and details. She loves Trigorin still and ignores the tremendous emotion of Treplev, who tries for the last time to make her consent to stay with him. "I am a sea gull," she says without any special connection. "Now I'm mixing things up. You remember you once shot a sea gull? A man happened to pass, saw the bird, and killed it. Idea for a short story. No . . . I'm getting mixed up again." "Stay a bit, I shall give you something to eat," says Treplev, clinging at a last straw. It is all very finely done. She refuses, speaks again of her love for Trigorin who has so grossly dropped her, then switches to the monologue of Treplev's play, in the beginning of the first act, and hurriedly departs.

The end of the act is magnificent.

TREPLEV (*after a pause*). Pity if somebody meets her in the garden and then tells mamma. It may distress mamma. [Note these are his last words, because now after coolly destroying his writings he opens the door on the right and goes out into an inner room, where presently he will shoot himself.]

DORN (*struggling to push open the door on the left [against which a few moments ago TREPLEV had moved* an armchair so as not to be disturbed while talking to *NINA*]). Queer. . . . The door seems locked. (*At last he comes in and pushes away the armchair.*) Hm. . . . Kind of a steeplechase.

[The others too come back from supper] (*ARKADINA, the SHAMRAEVS, MASHA, TRIGORIN, the servant with the wine and beer.*)

ARKADINA. Place it here. The beer is for Trigorin. We shall drink and go on with the game. Let us sit down.

[*Candles are lighted.*] (*SHAMRAEV leads TRIGORIN toward a chest of drawers.*)

SHAMRAEV. Look, here's the bird you asked me to stuff last summer.

TRIGORIN. What bird? I don't remember. (*Thinks it over.*) No, really, I don't remember.

(*A shot is heard on the right. They all start.*)

ARKADINA (*frightened*). What was that?

DORN. I know. Something has probably exploded in that medicine chest of mine. Don't worry. (*He goes out and half a minute later [while the rest are settling down to their game] comes back.*) Yes, I was right. A bottle of ether has burst. (*He hums*) "Oh, maiden, again I am bound by your charms. . . ."

ARKADINA (*as she sits down at the table*). Ugh, it gave me a fright. It reminded me of that time when. . . . (*She covers her face with her hands.*) It has made me quite faint.

DORN (*perusing the review, to TRIGORIN*). A month or two ago there was an article here . . . a letter from America . . . and I wanted to ask you . . . (*He leads TRIGORIN [gently] toward the front of the stage.*) . . . because, you see, I am very much interested in the question. (*In a slightly lower voice*)—Will you, please, take Mrs. Arkadin to some other room? The fact is that her son had shot himself.

Curtain.

This is, I repeat, a remarkable ending. Note that the tradition of the backstage suicide is broken by the chief character concerned not realizing what has happened but imitating, as it were, the real reaction by recalling a former occasion. Note, too, that it is the doctor speaking, and so there is no need to call one in order to have the audience quite satisfied. Note, finally, that whereas before his unsuccessful suicide Treplev spoke of doing it, there has not been a single hint in the scene—and still it is perfectly and completely motivated.[5]

NOTES

[1] Not even could a moralist note here the paradox, typical, one might say, of a decaying class: the employee bullying his master—

for this was *not* typical of Russian country life: it is a mere incident based on such and such characters, who may crop up and who may not. (VN deleted marginal note. Ed.)
[2] Note that according to the rules, which I dislike so intensely, you cannot make a man kill himself between the acts, but you can make him make the attempt if he does not die; and vice-versa, you cannot have a man bungle his shot in the last act when he retires behind the scenes to make an end of it. (VN in a deleted passage. Ed.)
[3] Note again, that just as in the demonstration of changing moods in the scene between mother and son, we get here the demonstration of the man reverting to the professional author—a little too obvious. There follows another demonstration: Shamraev . . . (VN in a deleted passage. Ed.)
[4] Note very carefully, please, the queer revenge which I have just described [of the goddess of determinism]. There is always such a devil awaiting the unwary author just as he thinks he has succeeded. And most important, it is just now when from the point of tradition the author has come back to the fold and when something like a climax looms and the audience expects if not *the* obligatory scene (which would be too much to ask of Chekhov), at least *some* obligatory scene; (which queerly enough is much the same thing—what I mean is, such a scene that, though not consciously defined in the expectancy, is felt to be satisfying the "just what we wanted" when it comes—we may call it the satisfying scene), it is just at this moment that Chekhov is at his worst. (VN deleted passage. Ed.)
[5] This final paragraph was deleted by VN. Ed.

Carol Strongin (essay date 1981-82)

SOURCE: "Irony and Theatricality in Chekhov's *The Sea Gull*," in *Comparative Drama*, Vol. 15, No. 4, Winter 1981-82, pp. 366-80.

[*In this essay, Strongin contends that* The Seagull *parodies "the artificial and melodramatic conventions of so much of the theater of its day."*]

The play's ending suggests melodrama: Nina, the innocent country girl seduced and abandoned by the worldly writer Trigorin, delivers an emotional speech about faith and endurance and bearing her cross before she runs out into the stormy autumn night. Treplev, the sensitive young man who loves her and has lost her as he has also failed in his attempt to become a great writer, tears up his manuscripts, throws them under his desk, and leaves the stage. Now, as Treplev's mother, the actress Irina Nikolayevna Arkadina, and her companions enter and resume their game of lotto, the sound of a gunshot is heard off-stage. Dr. Dorn leaves to see what has happened and *"returns in half a minute"* to report that a bottle of ether has exploded in his medicine bag. Arkadina breathes a sigh of relief as she remembers her son's suicide attempt of two years before. The lotto players resume their game and Dorn casually leads Trigorin, Treplev's successful rival in love and art, toward the front of the stage, drops his voice, and speaks the last lines of the play: "Somehow get Irina Nikolayevna away from here. The fact is, Konstantin Gavrilovich has shot himself. . . ."[1] The curtain falls and the audience, as well as the many directors, actors, and critics of *The Sea Gull,* all assume that Treplev is dead. But what if Chekhov has himself left the actual success of Treplev's second suicide attempt ambiguous?

To assume that Treplev is successful in that attempt is, of course, to go along with the traditional view of the play and its place in the development of Chekhov's dramatic art, for according to that view, as it is expressed by a critic like J. L. Styan, *The Sea Gull* is Chekhov's

> compromise with nineteenth-century theatre practice in many respects. Although we see neither event, the young female lead is seduced and the young male lead does commit suicide. The play is still built upon several intense and potentially melodramatic relationships. . . . Chekhov has not yet fully managed to arrange his characters to undercut melodrama. . . . Although Treplev shoots himself offstage rather than in full view like Ivanov, the effect of an over-strong theatrical statement remains as potent. . . . [2]

However, as Styan goes on to say, "When in 1900 Chekhov saw Hedda Gabler's theatrical suicide, he declared to Stanislavsky, 'Look here, Ibsen is really not a dramatist',," a remark which Styan interprets as Chekhov's declaration "against the artificial in drama."[3] Yet it may be possible that Chekhov had already made that declaration in 1896 with the writing of *The Sea Gull,* a play which itself deals with the nature of art, particularly in terms of the theater. Chekhov called *The Sea Gull* a "comedy in four acts," and it may very well be that Nina's final speeches are implicitly undercut, while the success of Treplev's second attempt at suicide is left deliberately ambiguous. The evidence for such a reading rests not only on Chekhov's use of the word "comedy," itself the subject of years of interpretation and debate, but, more importantly, on the structure of the play—a structure which is essentially circular, grounded as it is on the continual ironic parodying of the characters' self-conscious poses which undercut the authenticity of their words and actions.

To begin to establish the possibility of a more deeply ironic reading of *The Sea Gull,* it is helpful to recall Chekhov's well-known pronouncement on what he thought the task of the modern theater should be:

> The demand is made that the hero and the heroine should be dramatically effective. But in life people do not shoot themselves, or hang themselves, or fall in love, or deliver themselves of clever sayings every minute. They spend most of their time eating, drinking, or running after women or men, or talking nonsense. It is therefore necessary that this should be shown on the stage.[4]

Although implicit in this statement, made while Chekhov was working on *The Wood Demon* (1889-90), the play which immediately preceded *The Sea Gull,* is the rejection of all the excesses of nineteenth-century dramaturgy, it cannot be denied that in *The Sea Gull* the "hero" shoots himself twice (albeit off-stage), the "heroine," as well as many of the other characters in the play, suffers the ecstacy and the agony of falling in love, and almost all the characters are given to delivering clever or grand speeches at every opportunity. What is important, however, is that these excesses of speech and behavior are self-con-

scious to the point at which each character sees himself or herself through a kind of third eye and so becomes the hero of a drama of his or her own making.[5]

For a character like Trigorin, for example, the dispassionate collector of the facts of other people's lives, his own involvement with Nina arises itself out of an idea for a story, for what is essentially a melodrama of his own making. For Sorin, on the other hand, the drama he has created for himself would be titled, as he says, *"L'homme qui a voulu"* (p. 165), a kind of tragicomedy of unfulfilled dreams and aspirations. For Nina, as for Treplev, Masha, and Polina, the self-created role is that of the tragic figure forced to suffer by a cruel fate which has made their lives a torment to them. And for Arkadina, who sees herself as the great actress surrounded by worshipping admirers, hers is a melodrama for which the script has been provided by her reading of de Maupassant's *On the Water* in Act II; for in the third act, worried about Trigorin's growing infatuation with Nina, Arkadina throws herself on her knees before him and, as de Maupassant's words have already described it for her, "besieges him with compliments, flattery, and favors" (p. 141), so that, like the "conquered" writer in the passage which Arkadina so pointedly does not read out loud, Trigorin agrees to stay with her, "to yield up his mind to her."[6] Only Dorn, the sympathetic, though detached observer, himself cast in the role of savior and torturer by the lovelorn Polina in her own drama, is not a "star" but a self-conscious chorus character who can do little more than comment on the dramas being acted out around him—"How upset everyone is! How upset! And everybody seems to be in love . . ." (p. 140)—while not really being able to participate in any of them, for as he tells Masha, "But what can I do, my child? What can I do?" (p. 140).

If there are any characters in *The Sea Gull* who are authentically themselves rather than their visions of themselves, they are Medvedenko, the school teacher who loves Masha to the point of his own self-abnegation, and Shamraev, Polina's boorish husband and the manager of Sorin's estate. Given the presence of Medvedenko and Shamraev, the first too beaten down by the daily grind of his life to star in it—though, interestingly enough, he does tell Trigorin that "someone ought to write a play about how teachers live. That ought to be put on the stage!" (p. 136)—and the second too concerned with running the estate to spend much time constructing a personal drama, the posturings of the other characters are thrown into ironic relief. Thus to take these characters' views of themselves as Chekhov's view of them may be to miss that very irony which makes *The Sea Gull* a parody of so much of nineteenth-century drama as well as a satiric comment on the sort of people who live life as though they are characters in books and whose words and actions are, therefore, essentially inauthentic. In calling his play a "comedy," Chekhov may be pointing to the possibility that much of the suffering of his characters is not so much authentically felt as it is acted, or, when it is felt, is continually projected in self-consciously theatrical terms that make the sufferer both the performer of and the audience to his or her own suffering.

In this play, then, concerned so much with artists and the nature of art, the key to what Chekhov may be doing can be found in the sea gull itself, that theatrically rather clumsy—looking all too often like a dead duck or an overgrown pigeon—stage prop. It is the characters who, much like Gregers and Hedvig of Ibsen's *Wild Duck*—a play at which Chekhov may be aiming some satiric jabs[7]—make the bird into a symbol of youthful innocence and aspiration and hope gratuitously destroyed. Nina is the first of the characters to compare herself to the bird as she speaks of being "pulled" to the Sorin estate, "to this lake, as if I were a sea gull" (p. 130); but it is Treplev who shoots the literal bird and lays it at Nina's feet. Though Nina can only ask, "What does this mean?" (p. 146) since Trigorin has not yet presented Nina with the script of what will become her own drama, it is Treplev who takes the first turn at making the dead sea gull into a symbol, in this case a symbol of himself and what he sees as the tragedy that is his life:

TREPLEV I was rotten enough to kill this sea gull today. I lay it at your feet.

NINA What's wrong with you? *Picks up the sea gull and looks at it.*

TREPLEV, *after a pause.* And soon I'm going to kill myself in the same way.

NINA What *is* wrong with you? This isn't like you at all!

TREPLEV That's true! I began to change when you did. You've changed towards me and you know it. . . . You're cold to me, and my very presence bothers you.

NINA You've been so irritable lately, and most of the time you talk in riddles and I don't understand a word you're saying.

And I suppose now that this sea gull, here, is some kind of symbol too. Well, forgive me, I don't understand that either. . . . *Putting the sea gull down on the seat.* I'm too simple-minded to understand you.

(p. 146)

It is interesting to suggest that there may be a kind of parodic echo in this conversation of the exchange between Ibsen's Gina and Hedvig in their response to Gregers' desire to be the "clever dog" that drags the wild duck up from the "ocean's depths":

GINA. . . . A funny idea, to want to be a dog!

HEDVIG. Do you know, mother—I believe he meant something quite different by that.

GINA. What else could he mean?

HEDVIG. I don't know; but I thought he seemed to mean something quite different from what he said—all the time.

GINA. Do you think so? It certainly was queer.[8]

Yet unlike the mysterious wild duck which is never seen on stage in Ibsen's play, Chekhov's sea gull is all too visually present, and unlike the enigmatic Gregers, Treplev provides the gloss for his symbolism. And if Gina, the simple-minded literalist, remains mystified by Gregers' emblematic language, while Hedvig goes on to read or invent a subtext which makes the wild duck the symbol of herself and so dictates her suicide, Nina's response to Treplev here is closer to that of Gina than it is to Hedvig, though, like Hedvig, Nina will go on to act out a script of someone else's invention as she comes to make the sea gull into the emblem of herself.

It is, of course, ironic that Nina fails to understand Treplev's meaning here, since he tells her outright that he will soon kill himself "in the same way" as he has killed the sea gull, though what is even more ironic is the fact that he fails in his first suicide attempt and so, in essence, is wrong. Yet Treplev's problem is that he is never given the attention he craves and, therefore, in his own mind at least, is never understood or valued or, even more important for him, applauded.

Treplev, whose play within the play has begun *The Sea Gull* and launched Nina's acting career, is, as that play so clearly demonstrates with its references to the "common soul of the world," the "Prince of Darkness . . . father of Eternal Matter," and the "Kingdom of the Cosmic Will" (p. 134), a writer of the kind of self-indulgent, heavy-handed symbolist school which Chekhov is lampooning here. As Nina says of Treplev's play, "There aren't any living characters in it" (p. 131), and, as Trigorin will say about Treplev's writing two years later, "none of his characters seem to have any life" (p. 170), a statement which points to Treplev's lack of development as a writer just as it also points to the circular structure of Chekhov's play. Yet the self-indulgent symbolist Treplev, in killing the sea gull, has self-consciously projected his life in terms of art as he takes on the role of suicidal genius literally shot down by the insensitivity of the people around him. Having lost her adolescent crush on Treplev in her equally adolescent infatuation with Trigorin, Nina cannot respond to Treplev's symbolism, though he has, in fact, cast her in one of the chief supporting roles in his life as drama.

Like everyone else in this play, Nina does not want to perform a secondary role in someone else's drama; she wants to star in a drama of her own. Having already indentified herself with a sea gull, Nina is fully prepared to respond to the romantically tragic story of her life as it is about to be created for her by Trigorin. Ever ready with notebook and pen in hand to jot down the details of real life to be used in the service of ideas for new stories, Trigorin paves the way for Nina's own taking over of the sea gull as the symbol of herself:

TRIGORIN . . . *Seeing the sea gull.* What's that?

NINA A sea gull. Kostya killed it.

TRIGORIN What a beautiful bird! . . . *Writes in his notebook.*

NINA What are you writing?

TRIGORIN Just making a note . . . An idea for a story suddenly came into my head. A young girl, like you, has lived in a house on the shore of a lake since she was a little girl; she loves the lake like a sea gull, and she's free and happy as a sea gull. Then a man comes along, sees her, and having nothing better to do, destroys her, like this sea gull here. *A pause. . . .*

(pp. 150-51)

It does not matter that Nina, as we have heard about her and as she has described herself, is neither "happy" nor "free," subject as she is to the tyrannical dictates of her father and stepmother from whom she must sneak away in order to come to the Sorin estate. What is important is that Nina is in love with her romantic vision of Trigorin as a "great and wonderful person" (p. 150) and that, as Chekhov's direction for a pause here suggests, she has, in a sort of metatheatrical moment, identified herself with the gratuitously murdered sea gull at the very instant in which the audience has made that same indentification.

For Nina, as for himself, Trigorin has projected future experience in terms of future art as he outlines the script of the affair that he will play out with her during the two years' time that separates the last two acts of *The Sea Gull.* Trigorin has given Nina the plot of her drama and the symbol of herself as its heroine, a point that Chekhov will stress again in Act III when Trigorin tells Nina: "I'll think of you as you were on that sunny day . . . when you were wearing that white dress . . . there was a white sea gull lying on the seat"; and Nina replies, *"pensively . . . Yes, a sea gull"* (p. 153). Now it is only left to Nina to embellish that drama, which she very quickly does by handing Trigorin a medallion inscribed with the title of one of his books and the pertinent page and line numbers. Those lines are, of course, blatantly romantic, as befits the personal context in which Nina can now place them: "If you ever need my life, come and take it" (p. 157). But what is ironic is that those lines, like the plot of her drama itself, are not Nina's creation, just as her final use of the sea gull as personal emblem will not merely be taken from Trigorin's idea for a story, but will be cribbed, both clumsily and imprecisely as we shall see, from Pushkin's play *The River Nymph* (p. 166). Nina may indeed suffer as the star of a rather shabby melodrama of seduction and betrayal, but the ironic part of that suffering is that, like the suffering of Treplev, it is not completely authentic, projected as it is in terms of Trigorin's story and Pushkin's play. The point, then, is not so much that Nina suffers and endures, but that she at once acts out that suffering and is the audience held enraptured by her own acting.

This situation of characters who are self-consciously their own audience and who use others as an audience for themselves suggests yet another ironic facet of Chekhov's play: although Treplev, Trigorin, and Nina all see the dead sea gull as a symbol of purity and freedom, innocence, youth, and hope gratuitously destroyed, the fact is that live sea gulls, welcome harbingers of land that they may be for weary sailors, are themselves scavengers and birds of prey. Sea gulls live off the refuse along coast lines and dive into the water to pull out the fish they devour. What is more, this particular sea gull, whose freedom everyone in the play is romanticizing, did not live on the ocean, but was itself trapped on a lake, an inland body of water with no outlet to the sea. Thus the sentimentalized symbol which Treplev applies to himself, Trigorin applies to the heroine of his story, and Nina takes over as her own, though none of them realizes it, is, in fact, the authentic emblem that suggests the real, unvarnished activities of them all; for all of them, as well as most of the other characters in the play, are essentially trapped by the dynamics of their relationships with each other, feeding off each other, scavenging bits and pieces of each other's lives, either to turn them into art, as Trigorin does, or to fill out the plot of a private drama.

That scavenging continues from the beginning of the play to the end and points to the fact that nothing really changes for the characters, that they have, in essence, done no more than go around in a circle. Thus *The Sea Gull* opens with Masha's self-conscious response to Medvedenko's question about why she "always wear[s] black": "I'm in mourning for my life," she replies. "I'm unhappy." But Masha continues to play her role of "mourner" as she keeps on projecting her identity in terms of her unrequited love for Treplev, attaching herself to him like a kind of lichen even after she has married Medvedenko in order to "tear this love out of my heart by the roots" (p. 151), itself a rather affected theatrical statement. Similarly, Polina keeps hounding Dorn, ironically living off his frustrating lack of attention to her in order to keep on playing her own role of tragic heroine. It is, therefore, no wonder that when, in Act IV, the sound of a *"melancholy waltz"* is heard being *"played two rooms away,"* it is Polina who knows how to interpret it: "Kostya's playing again," she says. "He must be very sad" (p. 163). Self-conscious sufferer that she is herself, Polina knows very well what Treplev's piano playing is all about, for he, too, is performing for an audience. And indeed, one cannot help wondering if Treplev, so consciously acting the role of tortured romantic hero, would play his melancholy waltz were there no one in the other room to respond to the angst it objectifies for him.

Perfectly willing to play the role of such an audience is, of course, Dorn who, from the beginning of the play to the end, comments on the lives going on around him as he sings snatches of opera and sentimental songs in keeping with the mood of the poseurs and sentimentalists, the self-conscious "actors" whose "dramas" he is observing. As for the most polished of those "actors," Arkadina, she continues to play the role of eternally young, eternally glamorous star, belittling her son to flatter Trigorin, the younger lover upon whom her image of youth and desirability depends, while Trigorin, whose love of fishing itself suggests a sea gull, continues for his part to scavenge the details of the lives of the people around him to be used as material for his stories. And, finally, Treplev, writing stories of his own and playing melancholy waltzes on the piano, ironically keeps feeding off the very insensitivity of the others around him in order to play out his role of suffering artist, just as Nina seems almost to revel in Trigorin's shabby treatment of her so that she may act the tragic heroine who comes to perform her grand exit scene before Treplev.

Yet in this play where characters move only in circles, it is all too possible that Nina performs that grand exit scene rather badly, for such a possibility is not only suggested by the structure of the play itself, but also by the comparison implicitly drawn between Nina and Treplev, the two aspiring artists in the play, and Arkadina and Trigorin, the two successful, though essentially second-rate, "artists." Famous as she may be, particularly from the perspective of the people out in the backwater of the country estate, the irony is that Arkadina, as her son describes her, acts in plays that are nothing but "clichés and shopworn conventions," "parad[ing] about in . . . costumes in front of footlights . . . try[ing] to squeeze a moral out of commonplace phrases and meaningless events—some cliché that everyone knows and is suitable for home consumption . . . a thousand variations of the same old thing over and over again . . ." (p. 129). And though Treplev has described his mother as "talented and intelligent" (p. 128), given the quality of her "performance" for Trigorin in the third act, a performance which gives us some sense of what her professional acting must be like, Arkadina is not so much talented as she is shameless and not so much intelligent as she is shrewd.

That performance, staged by Arkadina to keep Trigorin from dropping her for Nina, would be dismissed by anyone other than the egoist whom it flatters as a flagrant piece of overacting, for Arkadina "[f]alls on her knees" before Trigorin and speaks lines that could come straight out of what Treplev has called the "lousy third-rate plays" (p. 157) in which Arkadina stars:

> My joy, my pride, my happiness! . . . *Embraces his knees.* If you leave me even for a single hour I won't survive it, I'll go out of my mind—my wonderful, marvelous, magnificent man, my master . . . I'm not ashamed of my love for you. *Kisses his hands.* My darling reckless boy, you may want to be mad, but I won't let you . . . *Laughs.* You're mine . . . mine . . . This forehead is mine, and these eyes, and this lovely silky hair. . . . All of you is mine. . . .
>
> (p. 159)

And as for Trigorin himself, the audience to all this, he is in his way one of the more honest characters in *The Sea Gull*, for though Arkadina goes on to call him "the best of all modern writers, Russia's only hope" (p. 159), he has told Nina that he "can't stand" the things he writes, that, as he says, "until my dying day . . . everything [I write] will be charming and well done—and nothing more. And after I'm dead my friends will pass by my grave and say: 'Here lies Trigorin. He was a good writer, but no Turgenev'" (p. 149).

Thus if Arkadina and Trigorin, viewed with awe though they may be by the people on the estate, are in reality no more than second-rate artists, the fact is that Nina and

Treplev rank even lower. And if Treplev's ponderously symbolic play of the first act has found its perfect expression in Nina's clumsy acting, in Chekhov's own play—where situations and people are, in essence, very much the same at the end as they were at the beginning—there is no reason to assume that either Treplev or Nina has improved as an artist. Treplev, as noted above, is still writing pieces in which "none of" the "characters seem to have any life," for, as Trigorin also says of him, "There's [still] something vague and mysterious about his style; it's like the ravings of a madman" (p. 170). And even Treplev himself, in a rare moment of insight, can finally say about his writing, "It's terrible" (p. 171). Yet Nina cannot go that far when talking about her acting; though, in her final scene with Treplev, she can admit that her "acting was very bad" when she began (p 174), Nina goes on from here to insist: "I've become a real actress. I enjoy acting! I revel in it! The stage intoxicates me . . ." (p. 174).

The stage, however, has always intoxicated Nina, for as she says at the beginning of the play, her "one and only dream" is to become an actress (p. 136). And while it is true that in this final scene she can tell Treplev, "I know now . . . that what matters most for us, whether we're writers or actors, isn't fame or glamor, or any of the things I used to dream of. What matters most is knowing how to endure, knowing how to bear your cross and still have faith" (p. 174), it is also possible—and it would be interesting to see a production of *The Sea Gull* in which the director and the actress have made this choice—that Nina is delivering these lines like the bad actress she still may be; for the authenticity of almost every word she says here is ironically undercut by the self-conscious theatricality with which those words are declaimed. Throughout her final speeches Nina not only quotes from Turgenev, to whom she gives credit (p. 172), but lifts her repeated line, "I am a sea gull . . . No, that's not it," from Pushkin's play *The River Nymph.*

We have been prepared for Nina's use of Pushkin by the earlier conversation between Treplev and Dorn in which Treplev, recounting the events that Dorn has missed during his trip abroad, tells him about Nina's unfortunate affair with Trigorin. "She never complained," Treplev says,

> but I could tell [from the letters she wrote] that she was unhappy, every line showing that her nerves were on edge. And then her mind seemed to be a little unbalanced. She always signed herself 'Sea Gull.' You remember, in Pushkin's *The River Nymph* the miller calls himself a raven.
>
> (pp. 166-67)

It is, however, the miller's daughter who, like Nina herself, has been seduced, become pregnant, and then abandoned by a man outside her sphere, in this case a prince who, rather like Trigorin on holiday at the country estate, happens just to be passing through. Yet though Treplev has said that Nina's mind "seemed a little unbalanced" and though Pushkin's miller goes mad with grief, the fact is that Nina's identification is obviously with the miller's daughter, while the lines she speaks, allowing for the necessary change from "raven" to "sea gull," belong to the miller. Thus the pathos of Nina's last speeches is balanced by irony, for when Nina calls herself a sea gull and immediately follows this with "No, that's not it," that line, coming itself from Pushkin's *River Nymph,* turns into a kind of joke as it takes on a double meaning in Chekhov's play and calls attention to Nina's bad acting: although the role she is so self-consciously playing is that of the miller's daughter in Pushkin's play, the lines Nina is speaking are, in fact, "not it," for they belong to the miller.

Even more ironically, however, that pathos is also undercut by Chekhov's own final treatment of the literal sea gull itself. Now in the keeping of the character least likely to respond to its romantic symbolism—the boorish Shamraev—the bird has been stuffed and put away in a cupboard. When Shamraev "leads TRIGORIN to the cupboard . . . Takes [out] the stuffed sea gull," and says, jovially, "This is what you ordered," Trigorin can only look at the rigid, preserved bird and reply, "I don't remember. *Musing.* No, I don't at all!" (p. 175) And there is no time to determine whether Trigorin's response is truthful or the result of guilt, for at this point "[t]here is a sound of a shot off-stage" (p. 175).

The sound of that gunshot, coming when it does, is placed in a context in which ironies are in the process of being piled on top of ironies, for the sea gull, now stuffed and stuck away in a cupboard, has become a grotesque parody of itself, just as Nina's repetition of Pushkin's lines has not only become a kind of parody of Pushkin's play, but also a parody of the very authenticity of her own experience and emotions. And it is, therefore, also interesting to suggest here that given any literate Russian's knowledge of Pushkin, Chekhov may be pointing to what is, in effect, Trigorin's act of plagiarism, for scavenger and second-rate writer that he is, Trigorin may very well have lifted the idea for his own story of seduction and betrayal as well as his use of the sea gull as a symbol from Pushkin's play.

In light of all these ironies, the self-parody and lack of authenticity, it is no wonder that the sound of Treplev's gunshot comes at the moment at which we see the romantic symbol turned into a stuffed bird, the moment at which Trigorin's faulty memory (or outright guilt or dismissal) comes together with Nina's projection of herself as a character in a play. Because the sound of that gunshot recalls Treplev's suicide attempt of two years before, it is possible to suggest that the present situation, like the one two years ago, finds Treplev again upstaged by his mother's vanity and the presence of his successful rival Trigorin, whom Nina still loves "passionately . . . desperately" (p. 175). As also happened two years ago, Nina has again not managed to complete her performance of Treplev's symbolist play, using its lines this time in order to make her own theatrical exit (p. 175) and leaving Treplev reduced once more from lead player in his own drama to supporting actor and finally audience to a drama that stars someone else.

Thus it is finally Nina's second rejection of him, coupled with his mother's insensitivity and Trigorin's success as writer and lover, that inspires Treplev to play out what he

intends to be his own final scene. He proceeds to spend *"the next two minutes silently tearing up all his manuscripts and throwing them under the table"* (p. 175), believing, no doubt, that they will be discovered as a symbol of his despair, though, ironically enough, they go unnoticed by the returning lotto players. Having been given the cue for his final performance by Nina's reference to Turgenev's *Rudin* (p. 172), Treplev, self-consciously projecting himself now as Rudin, can also see all his dreams and aspirations as having ended in failure, and the storm raging outside becomes for him, as it is in Turgenev's novel,[9] the perfect setting for the death of the "hero."

Yet the irony here may be that though Treplev has his stormy night on which to recognize his failure, both in the final loss of Nina and in his own realization that everything he "write[s] turns out lifeless and gloomy and bitter" (p. 173), the success of his second suicide attempt may be left ambiguous. When Dorn returns to report on the source of the explosion heard off-stage, it is all too fitting that he says that a bottle of ether has blown up in his medicine bag, for his statement places Treplev and his posturings in the context of a vessel filled with no more than a lot of volatile gas which blows up and leaves no trace.

Treplev playing Rudin, like Nina playing Pushkin's miller's daughter while speaking the wrong lines, has undercut the authenticity of his emotions and his actions, for they seem to have come not so much out of a genuine sense of despair as out of despair seen through a third eye and so, in essence, removed from him. What is more, in the English versions of **The Sea Gull,**[10] Dorn's line to Trigorin, traditionally viewed by directors and critics as Chekhovian understatement[11] and translated as "Konstantin Gavrilovich has shot himself" implicitly casts doubt on the success of that suicide attempt in the choice of the word "shot," as opposed to "killed"; for in English at least, to shoot oneself is not necessarily to succeed in killing oneself, particularly in light of the fact that Treplev has shot himself once before and did not die as a result.

In Russian, of course, that ambiguity is reduced, since the line reads *"Konstantin Gavrilovich zastrelilsja"*—the perfective form of the verb *"zastrelit'sja,"* to shoot oneself, implying a completed action and, therefore, the probability of death. Yet it is interesting that Chekhov's choice of words here is still not as unambiguous as it could have been, even when one accounts for the effect of understatement, since Chekhov could have written, *"Konstantin Gavrilovich zastrelilsja na smert'"*—"Konstantin Gavrilovich has shot himself to death"—and thereby removed all doubt.[12]

Given the fact that in **The Sea Gull** the more things appear to have changed, the more they have, in essence, remained the same, it is quite possible that Chekhov has deliberately cast a certain degree of doubt on the success of Treplev's second attempt at suicide, for if this play is seen as Chekhov's break with the conventional, melodramatic dramaturgy of his day, he may indeed be parodying that dramaturgy through his creation of characters who not only consider themselves to be artists, but who self-

consciously go about their lives as though they are characters in novels and plays. Thus in *The Sea Gull* Chekhov
may not simply be taking a step beyond the on-stage
suicide of his own melodramatic Ivanov, for again to recall
Ibsen's *Wild Duck,* Hedvig, like Treplev, also shoots
herself off-stage and of that play Chekhov said, "Ibsen
does not know life. It is not so in life."[13] Instead, if Chekhov is indeed parodying the artificial convention of suicide itself, Treplev, not suffering authentically—that is,
not suffering as himself, but projecting that suffering in
terms of the fictional Rudin—can perhaps literally not die
authentically: having remained a failure as a writer, the
final irony may be that Treplev also remains a failure as a
marksman. Because he has not succeeded in killing himself
once before in the play, it is all too possible that Treplev
has missed a second time, and in such failure lies the true
Chekhovian balance of pathos and farce.

As Chekhov himself said of *The Sea Gull,* "I began it
forte and ended it *pianissimo*—contary to all the rules of
dramatic art."[14] And contrary to all the rules of dramatic
art of his time, Chekhov may also have left the fate of his
"hero" in doubt, particularly when it is remembered that
in the plays that follow *The Sea Gull* intentions do not
result in their desired ends, since Vanya misses shooting
the hated Professor at pointblank range, while Solyony,
in *The Three Sisters,* succeeds in killing Tusenbach only
because he had intended to do no more than wound him.
Like these later plays, *The Sea Gull,* too, is continually
exposing the ironic gap between aspiration and fulfillment of aspiration, the pose and the person, the wish to
be the star of one's own drama and the reality of finding
oneself to be, as T. S. Eliot's Prufrock will put it, no more
than "one that will do / To swell a progress, start a scene
or two. . . . At times, indeed, almost ridiculous— / Almost, at times, the Fool." And finally, parodying as it
does the artificial and melodramatic conventions of so
much of the theater of its day, Chekhov's *Sea Gull* be-

comes, as Styan has said of all of Chekhov's mature
drama, the kind of play in which the "fundamental concern
is to give us the feel of life by showing us the balance of
life," as "[e]very character and every attitude . . . [is] seen
from two sides or more; every posture of body or mind is
its own critic."[15]

NOTES

[1] Anton Chekhov, *The Sea Gull,* trans. Robert W. Corrigan, in *Six
Plays of Chekhov* (San Francisco: Rinehart Press, 1962), p. 176.
All further citations refer to this edition.
[2] J. L. Styan, *Chekhov in Performance: A Commentary on the
Major Plays* (Cambridge: Cambridge Univ. Press, 1978), p. 13.
[3] Styan, p. 14.
[4] Corrigan, p. xxvii.
[5] See Styan, p. 16.
[6] Paul Schmidt, "Textual Notes," in *The Sea Gull,* trans. Jean-
Claude Van Italie (New York: Harper and Row, 1974), p. 94.
[7] See Dorothy U. Seyler, "*The Sea Gull* and *The Wild Duck:* Birds
of a Feather," *Modern Drama,* 8 (September 1965), 167-73.
[8] Henrik Ibsen, *The Wild Duck,* trans. R. Farquharson Sharp, in *Four
Great Plays by Ibsen* (New York: Bantam Books, 1978), p. 251.
[9] Schmidt, pp. 101-02.
[10] See Corrigan; Constance Garnett (London: Modern Library,
1923); Stark Young (New York: Random House, 1950); Jean-
Claude Van Italie (New York: Harper and Row, 1974); Ronald
Hingley (New York: Oxford Univ. Press, 1977); Eugene K. Bristow
(New York: W. W. Norton, 1977).
[11] See Styan, p. 88.
[12] I am indebted to Olga Markof-Belaeff, Oberlin College, for her
help with the Russian.
[13] Nicholas Moravcevich, "Chekhov and Naturalism: From Affinity
to Divergence," *Comparative Drama,* 4 (1970-71), 226.
[14] Daniel Gillès, *Chekhov: Observer Without Illusion,* trans. Charles
Lam Markmann (New York: Funk and Wagnalls, 1967), p. 216.
[15] J. L. Styan, *The Dark Comedy: The Development of Modern
Comic Tragedy* (Cambridge: Cambridge Univ. Press, 1968), p. 74.

Zinovii S. Paperny (essay date 1982)

SOURCE: "Microsubjects in *The Seagull*," in *Critical
Essays on Anton Chekhov,* edited by Thomas A. Eekman,
G. K. Hall & Co., 1989, pp. 160-69.

[*In the following essay, which was originally published
in Russian in 1982, Paperny maintains that* The Seagull
*comprises "a mosaic of disparate bits," or microsubjects,
in which "characters not only advance opinions, make
confessions, argue, and act, they also offer each other
various subjects for literary works, which express their
understanding of life, their point of view, their basic
'idea.'"*]

The study of Chekhov's text can be compared to the history of the investigation of matter, where researchers have
come to employ smaller and smaller units of magnitude.
What formerly seemed indivisible has proved a complicated
structure consisting of interconnected microparticles.

Something similar is taking place in Chekhov studies. From
general formulations investigators delving more deeply
into the text have become increasingly convinced that the
tissue of poetic narration displays a structure. Along with
the main actors, there are also "microparticles" of a sort,

and all these "macros" and "micros" are interconnected and subordinated one to the other.

In *The Seagull* the movement of the main subject—the history of the characters' development and their mutual relations—is complicated by microsubjects. The characters not only advance opinions, make confessions, argue, and act, they also offer each other various subjects for literary works, which express their understanding of life, their point of view, their basic "idea."

This is an important feature of the play. Almost every character has not only his own personal drama or tragedy, but also a literary subject, a project that he intends to carry out himself or offers to someone else.

Let us recall the schoolteacher Medvedenko. He says to Trigorin, "Or how about writing and then staging a play that describes the life of teachers like me? Our life is hard, very hard!"

Fictive invention is totally foreign to this subject. Medvedenko proposes to "describe," that is, to tell everything as it really is, to reveal life in its reality. His subject betrays the single idea that runs through his every speech: material need, his difficulty in making ends meet.

Trigorin, the practiced literary master, has his subject:

NINA: What's that you're writing?

TRIGORIN: Just making a note. I had the glimmer of a subject. (*Putting away his notebook*) A subject for a little story: a young girl has lived on the shore of a lake since childhood, someone like you. She loves the lake the way gulls do, and she's happy and free like them. But a man happens by, sees her, and for lack of anything better to do, destroys her life—like this gull here.

This subject does not go to waste in Trigorin's literary economy. In the fourth act he will say to Treplev: "Tomorrow morning, if it's calm, I'm going fishing at the lake. By the way, I want to look over the garden and the place where your play was staged—remember? A motif has taken shape in my mind, and all I need now is to refresh my memory of the scene."

Everything that Trigorin sees and feels is skillfully and efficiently fashioned into subjects for novels, stories, and plays. His interest in life is above all professional. Even Nina interests him not only in herself but also as a kind of literary "raw material." "I don't often meet young girls—young and attractive," he tells her. "I've forgotten how it feels to be eighteen or nineteen and can't imagine it clearly, so young girls in my novels and stories generally don't ring true. I'd like to change places with you, even for an hour, to find out how your mind works and just what you're like." There is a certain cruelty in Trigorin's "subject-creation," his tireless reworking of life into literature. He leaves Nina calmly and easily; nothing is left of his affair with the beginning actress but a literary project that, we may be quite certain, he will successfully carry out.

At the end of the play, Nina confesses to Treplev that she still loves Trigorin. But she does not want to be merely the occasion for one of Trigorin's subjects and argues with him, as if trying to free herself from painful chains: "I'm a seagull. No, that's not it. . . . You once shot a gull, remember? A man happened by, saw it, and for lack of anything better to do, killed it. A subject for a little story. . . . That's not it. . . ."

Here it is particularly clear how active the microsubjects are in *The Seagull* and how tellingly they touch, move, and disturb the characters. What for Trigorin is merely a theme that has taken shape, a subject for a little story, is for Nina her fate, her vocation.

The microsubjects in *The Seagull* are like little periscopes that connect what is happening on the surface with the very depths. Only here the direction is reversed, running not from the surface to the depths, but the other way around.

Treplev has his subject, and not just one, but two. The first is the one that formed the basis of his unfortunate play, whose performance was such a disaster. The second is the subject, vaguely and incompletely sketched, of the story he is working on in the fourth act, before Nina's arrival.

At the end of the play Nina takes issue with Trigorin's "subject for a little story," which assigns her the role of a defenseless victim and, as it were, returns to Treplev's play.

We see that Trigorin's and Treplev's subjects are profoundly connected to the general development of the action and the fortunes of the characters. They appear and reappear like leitmotivs throughout the entire narration, and this intermittent but insistent repetition of motifs and details is one of the most characteristic features of the play.

Both these subjects are present in the ending. But while Nina rejects Trigorin's, Treplev's subject becomes accessible to her once more. And when she runs off at the end, it is as if she takes it with her.

Old Sorin has a literary idea to propose: "I want to give Kostya Treplev a subject for a story," he says. "It is to be called 'The Man Who Wished,' 'L'Homme qui a voulu.' When I was young at one point I wanted to become a writer, but never did; I wanted to be a good speaker, but I spoke terribly . . . I wanted to marry, but I didn't; I always wanted to live in the city, but here I am ending my days in a village, and everything."

His life is drawing to a close, and he still has not started to live. Fortune has passed him by; it has not provided him what he sought or what he hoped to achieve.

The subject that he offers Treplev is not merely autobiographical. Do we not sense Masha's fate in it as well? Or that of her mother, the manager Shamraev's wife? It can be said that Sorin's microsubject helps a great deal in understanding Chekhov's larger subject.

Act I of a 1905 Moscow Art Theater production of The Seagull.

At the beginning of the third act Masha says to Trigorin: "I'm telling you all this so that you can use it in your writing." And then: "In all honesty, if he had wounded himself seriously, I wouldn't have lived another minute."

What Masha tells Trigorin he can use is the story of her love for Treplev, the love she tries so assiduously and so vainly to tear out of her heart during the course of the whole play, the hopeless and ineradicable love that swallows up all her feelings and desires.

Thus in *The Seagull* the main subject unfolds before our eyes, performed by Chekhov's characters; and simultaneously this represented reality appears twisted, foreshortened, and brokenly reflected, as it is seen by different characters. The microsubjects of Medvedenko, Trigorin, Treplev, Sorin, and Masha are, as it were, micromodels of life that contend among themselves and contradict each other. In this peculiarity of the play's construction is crystallized an important aspect of its content: that attention to secondary characters that so struck sensitive early readers.

At the same time the microsubjects of the five characters reflect various relationships between art and life, from Medvedenko's despondency in the face of prosaic everyday demands, to Treplev's aspirations beyond the bounds of reality.

It is most significant that not only the writers propose subjects, but also the schoolteacher Medvedenko, Masha, and Sorin. Chekhov seems to imply that the boundary between art and life is elusive. Not everyone in *The Seagull* writes, but they are all as it were surrounded by waves of art, and nearly every character tries to make sense of life in his own way. Even if a character does not write himself, he takes his literary "commission" to a professional.

One can speak of a large and a small subject in Chekhov. This aspect of his plays, which has escaped scholarly attention, appears not only in the form of literary subjects proposed by the characters.

The principle of large and small subjects makes itself felt in the overall construction of *The Seagull* as well. We have a rather rare example of theater within theater, a play within a play, and even (if we recall the fate of the original Aleksandrinski Theater production) a failure within a failure: Treplev's play is ridiculed as was Chekhov's own.

The reader is confronted with two theaters. One is firmly established, the one that the actress Arkadina and the playwright Trigorin serve, and in which Treplev feels stifled (". . . the contemporary theater is convention, prejudice"). The second is Treplev's own, set up at the beginning of the first act. It does not look like a stone box, and nature itself and the real moon form the scenery. This theater will be misunderstood. At the conclusion it "stands naked, ugly as a skeleton, the curtain flapping in the wind." But after many wanderings, afflictions, and quests Nina will return here and weep as she remembers everything youthful, innocent, and pure connected with this stage.

In *The Seagull* the very word "theater" seems to split up. The play's microsubjects create a distinctive system of poetic mirrors that register various clashing "reflections."

Thus the constant, unitary symbolic image of the seagull seems to shatter and take the form of various "fragments," one of which reflects Treplev's fate, another Trigorin's, and a third Nina's.

During Chekhov's lifetime critics more than once resorted to such a simile: his works reflect reality not like a large, intact poetic mirror but rather like the broken pieces of a mirror that was once intact. Only taken as a whole do Chekhov's stories create a total impression. In reading *The Seagull* we see that the principle of "multimirrored" construction makes itself felt in the structure of the play as well, where microsubjects enter into complicated and tension-filled relations with each other.

A special type of microsubject consists of references to the classics, quotations that far from seeing mere anthological snippets, start to take on new life in their new context.

Three writers are mentioned in *The Seagull*—Shakespeare, Maupassant, and Turgenev—each of them not once but two or three times.

Just before the performance of Treplev's play begins, Arkadina suddenly and apparently without the slightest motivation, recites from *Hamlet:*

> O Hamlet, speak no more:
> Thou turn'st mine eyes into my very soul,
> And there I see such black and grained spots
> As will not leave their tinct.

Treplev answers with a quotation from the same source:

> Nay, but to live
> In the rank sweat of an enseamed bed,
> Stew'd in corruption, honeying and making love
> Over the nasty sty,—

Then a horn sounds and Treplev's play begins. The quotation from Shakespeare is like an overture.

From the very beginning of the first act one senses the tension in the relationship between Arkadina and her son, his dissatisfaction with her, his sense of injury, his jeal-

ous, unfriendly feelings toward her lover, Trigorin. The exchanges of speeches from *Hamlet,* in itself half-joking and playful, at the same time lends an unexpectedly tragic coloration to all that follows. Associations develop between Treplev and Hamlet, Arkadina and the Queen, and Trigorin and the King who has no right to his throne.

Of course in so putting it we coarsen Chekhov's meaning to some extent; in the play everything is put less definitely and is less "spelled out."

Shakespeare is mentioned next in Nina's monologue from Treplev's play ("I am the universal world soul, I! The soul of Alexander the Great is in me, and of Caesar, and of Shakespeare . . ."). And finally Shakespeare is mentioned for the third time (again it is *Hamlet*) in Treplev's conversation with Nina after the collapse of his play. Catching sight of Trigorin who is approaching, he says sarcastically, "Here comes real talent; he strides along like Hamlet and is even reading, too. (*Mockingly*) 'Words, words, words. . . .'"

It is not simply a matter of references and quotations, but of deeper correspondences between *The Seagull* and *Hamlet.*

A. I. Roskin accurately observed that "the lines from *Hamlet* in *The Seagull* sound not like quotation but like a leitmotive, one of the play's leitmotivs."[1]

Much in Chekhov's plays goes back to Shakespeare's *Hamlet,* in subject and in the development of the action where the main event is postponed.

The source of tension in Shakespeare's subject is not that the Prince of Denmark kills the false King, but rather the opposite, that for so long he does not.

The "Shakespearean" enters into the very nature and most essential character of Chekhov's subject.

Another link between *The Seagull* and *Hamlet* is the theater within a theater. The Prince arranges a performance that ends in an uproar and is broken off. The fate of Treplev's production seems in a way similar. Particularly interesting are the parallels between the conversations of the Prince with the Queen and Treplev with Arkadina in the third acts of both plays. It is lines from precisely this act that are quoted in *The Seagull.*

In *Hamlet* while the Prince is castigating his mother who has fallen into vice, the Ghost appears; and Hamlet's tone of voice alters and he begins to sound more sympathetic toward his mother, whom the Ghost of his father the King seems to defend.

A similarly abrupt transition takes place in *The Seagull* when after mutual insults mother and son cry, are reconciled, and embrace.[2]

Chekhov studies Shakespeare's art of abrupt reversals, discontinuities in the character's states of mind, and sharp transitions from anger to remorse or from apparently irreconcilable quarreling to unexpected tranquillity.

In **The Seagull** Shakespeare is not merely a quoted classic. Like the ghost of Hamlet's father he appears in the play and exercises an unseen influence on the course of the action and on its character. Associations with *Hamlet* enrich our perception of **The Seagull** and enter into the very structure of Chekhov's play.

Guy de Maupassant is mentioned twice. Treplev speaks of him at the beginning of the play (". . . when I am served up the same stuff again and again and again, I run and run, as Maupassant ran from the Eiffel Tower which was crushing his brain with its vulgarity). At the beginning of the second act Arkadina, Dorn, and Masha are reading aloud from Maupassant's *Sur l'eau.* Arkadina opens the book at a passage about a society woman who is trying to attract a writer: "She lays siege to him by means of every variety of compliments, attractions, and indulgence."[3] Arguing against Maupassant, Arkadina points to the example of herself and Trigorin.

Maupassant's *Sur l'eau* appeared in 1888. It consists of the description of a week's cruise on the yacht "Bel-Ami." It is a bitter book, full of skepticism and mockery of deceitful human society, particularly fashionable society.

Treplev in **The Seagull** attacks convention, banality, and vulgarity. For Maupassant, however, vulgarity is a synonym for life: "Happy are those whom life satisfies, who are amused and content."[4]

Upset by his mother's ironic remarks, Treplev, at the performance of his play, cries "Enough! Curtain!"

In *Sur l'eau* Maupassant directs this cry against life as a whole, for him a cheap and deceitful spectacle. "How is it that the worldly audience has not yet called out, 'Curtain,' has not yet demanded the next act, with other beings than mankind."[5]

A comparison of *Sur l'eau* with **The Seagull** helps us to feel more sharply the differences in world outlook of the two writers and lets us grasp the distinction between the total pessimism of the one and, as it were, the imperfect skepticism of the other.

Echoes of Maupassant's novel are to be heard in other parts of Chekhov's play as well. In one of the chapters of *Sur l'eau* Maupassant expresses disagreement with those who envy writers and says that writers are to be pitied, not envied. Reading these lines, it is hard not to be reminded of Trigorin's monologue:

> For (the writer) no simple feeling any longer exists. All he sees, his joys, his pleasures, his suffering, his despair, all instantaneously become subjects of observation. . . . If he suffers, he notes down his suffering, and classes it in his memory. . . . He has seen all, noticed all, remembered all, in spite of himself, because he is above all a literary man, and his intellect is constructed in such a manner that the reverberation in him is much more vivid, more natural, so to speak, than the first shock—the echo more sonorous than the original sound.[6]

And a little further on he compares the writer to "a terribly vibrating and complicated piece of machinery, fatiguing even to himself."[7]

Thus Treplev, Arkadina, and Trigorin unexpectedly intersect with Manupassant. And each of them approaches him from his own angle. It is true that in Trigorin's monologue there is no mention of Maupassant, but traces of *Sur l'eau* are none the less discernible.

Turgenev's presence in the play is equally varied. Trigorin feels mocked by Turgenev's unattainable eminence as a writer, of which people constantly remind him: "'A marvelous piece, but Turgenev's *Fathers and Sons* is better.' . . . and when I die my friends will say as they go past my grave, 'Here lies Trigorin. He was a good writer, but not as good as Turgenev.'"

And at the end of the play it is as if Turgenev extends a hand to Nina: "Listen—do you hear the wind? Turgenev says somewhere, 'A man's all right if he has a roof over his head on nights like these, some place where it's warm.' I'm a seagull. No, that's not it. (*She rubs her forehead*) What was I saying? Yes, Turgenev. 'And God help all homeless wanderers.' It's nothing. (*She sobs*)"

Turgenev's words in the context of Nina's monologue lose their "quotedness" and become Chekhov's. The actor V. A. Podgorny, who performed with Kommissarzhevskaya and knew her well, tells this story about her last days, when she was rehearsing **The Seagull** with her company in Tashkent: "'And God help all homeless wanderers,' said Kommissarzhevskaya in the sad words of Nina Zarechnaya, and looked at the actors with a smile. We really are those homeless wanderers! Here in the middle of nowhere we are rehearsing and acting and living, and in a few days it will be time to go on and rehearse and act and live some more. . . ."[8]

Whom is she quoting? Formally, Turgenev; but actually it is Chekhov.

This example makes it particularly clear how a literary source changes on entering into Chekhov's text, and becomes no longer someone else's, but Chekhov's own.

Microsubjects in **The Seagull** are of various sorts. There are the literary subjects of the characters, both professional writers and people who have nothing to do with literature, and there are associations with classical works such as the quotations from Shakespeare, Maupassant, and Turgenev. There is still another variety: the anecdotes and funny stories that Shamraev and Sorin tell.

A few minutes after the end of Treplev's play, Nina steps down from the stage, Arkadina praises her and introduces her to Trigorin. They begin their first conversation.

On making the acquaintance of her idol Trigorin, Nina immediately starts talking about what pains her most: those who live for art, the chosen ones of fame who taste the higher pleasures. Arkadina, laughing, intervenes (she does not leave Trigorin alone for a minute). And at this dramatic moment, when conversation is starting up among the three characters who are to cause each other so much suffering-becoming close, separating, coming back together—at this point Shamraev begins telling his old story about a synodal cantor:

> SHAMRAEV: I remember one time at the Opera House in Moscow, the famous Silva hit a low C. As luck would have it one of our synodal cantors happened to be in the gallery and—you can imagine our astonishment—we heard booming out of the gallery, "Bravo, Silval," a whole octave lower. Like this: (*in a low approximation of a bass voice*) Bravo, Silva! The whole theater just died. (*pause*)
>
> DORN: A quiet angel flew by—we are sitting here in silence.
>
> NINA: It's time for me to go. Good-by.

This anecdote, perhaps amusing in itself, is totally out of place here, at this moment. No one is listening to Shamraev, and when he finishes, they do not know what to say.

Shamraev's anecdote is funny less because of its intrinsic humor than because it is totally unexpected and unmotivated.

Shamraev's second anecdote is even more at odds with its context ("We're twapped!" instead of "We're trapped!"). Shamraev enters as the scene between Trigorin and Arkadina has just concluded, where she tries to take him away from Nina. At this moment he enters and "with regret" announces that the horses are ready and tells his story about "twapped."

At first glance all these little anecdotes are pointless and only interrupt the course of the narration. However the stories told by Shamraev and Sorin ("Your voice, your Excellency, is powerful . . . but unpleasant"), are at once inappropriate and essential. Their very lack of harmony with the context makes them deeply organic elements of a play where everything is built on conflicts, contrasts, and discontinuities. One may say that these half-humorous microsubjects let us perceive life's lack of harmony, refracted by the play as if by a magnifying glass, and not only in the twists and turns of the larger subject, but on a smaller scale as well.

Shamraev's and Sorin's anecdotes play an important role in intensifying the play's polyphonic sound quality, in which tragedy and comedy merge into one.

Some readers, viewers, and interpreters of *The Seagull* have unintentionally tried to reduce the amplitude of oscillation from large to small, from tragic to comic. A curious example is provided by N. M. Ezhov's letter to Chekhov of 29 January 1899: ". . . there are things in *The Seagull* which I find most unattractive. The first is Sorin's singing and what he says about some gentleman's witticism, that the general's voice is powerful but repulsive [for "unpleasant"]. This is so jarring to the viewer that it is a shame! The second thing is the manager's story about 'trapped' and 'twapped.' I can't explain ex-

actly why, but these two passages seem to me for some reason impossible in *The Seagull*."[9]

What seemed to Ezhov an unjustified and impermissible violation of the style and tonality of the play is actually the bold introduction of counterpoint, creating a sort of disharmonic structure with constant interruptions in the development of the subject, a lack of mutuality in the sympathies of the characters, and clashes between the tragic "Hamletic" impulse and the anecdotal.

As we have seen, Chekhov's microsubjects are least of all illustrations. They have various sources, ranging from the literary "claim checks" of the characters themselves, to quotations from the classics, to anecdotes. In their many-colored mosaic there is a whole range of transitional tints and shades.

"Thou turnst mine eyes into my very soul" and "We're twapped!" are equally microsubjects.

Chekhov did not immediately achieve so rich and complicated a palette of colors, of transitions from high to low, from tragic to laughable.

In his first play *Platonov* we do not find microsubjects at all.

In *Ivanov* the main character tells about the workman Semyon who heaved two sacks of rye up on his back and strained something: "I think I've strained something, too." Here the microsubject simply illustrates what is going on with the main character. The unexpectedness that characterizes the microsubject in *The Seagull* is lacking and there is no contradiction between the large and small subjects.

In Chekhov's third play *The Wood Demon* the situation is just about the same as in *Ivanov*. With *The Seagull* he first attains multimirrored reflections of reality. They form a complicated system that at first glance seems a mosaic of disparate bits, but which in reality is profoundly consistent in affirming through images on various levels the disharmony of life, its conflicts and contradictions, and the agonizing discrepancy between dream and reality.

NOTES

[1] A. Roskin, *A. P. Chekhov; stat'i i ocherki* (Moscow: GIKhL, 1959), 131.
[2] Chekhov was particularly fond of the scene between the Queen and her son in *Hamlet*. There is much evidence of this. One example is the review "*Hamlet* on the Stage of the Pushkin Theater," where, in discussing the performance of M. Ivanov-Kozlovsky, the twenty-two-year-old Chekhov notes that "the scene with the mother was done beautifully" (A. P. Chekhov, *PSSP,* 16:21).
[3] *A Selection from the Writings of Guy de Maupassant,* vol. 4: *Sur l'eau and Other Tales* (New York: Review of Reviews Co., 1903), 20.
[4] Maupassant, *Writings,* 26.
[5] Ibid., 28.
[6] Ibid., 56.
[7] Ibid., 58.
[8] V. A. Podgorny, *Pamiati* [Memories], in *Sbornik pamiati V. F. Komissarzhevskoi* (Moscow: GIKhL, 1931), 99.
[9] In the archive of the Lenin State Library, Moscow, 331.43.11.

James M. Curtis (essay date 1985)

SOURCE: "Ephebes and Precursors in Chekhov's *The Seagull*," in *Slavic Review,* Vol. 44, No. 3, Fall 1985, pp. 423-37.

[*In the essay below, Curtis offers a psychoanalytic reading of* The Seagull, *in which he argues that the play "represents a successful working through of Chekhov's anxiety of influence" from Turgenev and Shakespeare.*]

Harold Bloom's *The Anxiety of Influence* takes the Freudian concept of an oedipal relationship between father and son as a model for the relationship that exists when one artist, the father figure (or precursor, as Bloom calls him), influences another artist (the ephebe, in Bloom's terminology). Bloom's work provides a desirable redefinition of standard treatments of influence and stylistic change in that it offers a dynamic, rather than a static, paradigm, and denies any simplistic dissociation of the artist as historical figure from the poet as poet. Furthermore, it denies that literary influences can occur as purely verbal processes, and it affirms that the creative process is emotionally charged, like so many other important human experiences.

In *Anxiety of Influence* Bloom states, in typically absolute terms, "Poetic Influence—when it involves two strong, authentic poets,—always proceeds by a misreading of the prior poet, an act of creative correction that is actually and necessarily a misinterpretation."[1] If poets necessarily misread other poets, then it follows that critics necessarily misread other critics as well. And indeed, for those of us who lack Bloom's unique sensibility and rhetorical mannerisms, his paradigm for literary influence requires some misreading, some revision, before we can use it to write practical literary history. That is to say, we must misread Bloom in a creative way—which is what he would expect us to do.

Among other things, I wish to revise Bloom's opposition of precursors and ephebes, which strikes me as too absolute. He rarely, if ever, treats the process by which an ephebe becomes a precursor, nor does he deal with the stylistic evolution that this process entails. Moreover, he seems to think of precursors as possessing a godlike serenity, but what we know about the lives of many poets makes this view untenable.

Another necessary revision of Bloom's theory involves the historical context of creativity. Steve Polansky has referred to "one of the central weaknesses of Bloom's theory of influence: the lack of sense of historical perspective."[2] Bloom writes as though nothing existed except the oedipal struggle between writer A and writer B. Although he is not interested in the specifics of literary history—as major theorists usually are not—he at least allows for it when he comments that "no strong poet can choose his precursors, any more than any person can choose his own father."[3] Critics who are interested in practical literary history and who refuse to think of precursors as doled out by the gods may revise this statement to read that the sociocultural circumstances into which artists are born

determine their precursors. Loy D. Martin makes just such a connection between artists and their milieus when he speaks of the poet as "the well-instructed missionary of the language which constitutes both his own subjectivity and that of his culture."[4] But since stylistic change and social change are always interrelated, Martin's comments can be generalized: social change can make a certain style obsolete and thus render it incapable of expressing an artist's meaning. The artist then has to create a new style that can express the new historical situation.

In this process of social and stylistic change the artist may juxtapose the old style with the new for the sake of contrast. To notice the importance of such quotations as clues to the anxiety of influence is not to indulge in the pedantry of what the Germans call *Quellenforschung,* for which Bloom has such disdain. Clearly, any theory of creativity that makes general claims cannot confine itself to the study of sources, because we do not have sources for everything we wish to study. Even Bloom would concede, however, that when an ephebe quotes his precursor in his own work, something is afoot. An ephebe takes a great risk by opening his work to the precursor—the risk that the precursor's words will overwhelm his own.

Such a misreading of Bloom provides a paradigm for a nonreductionist interpretation of Chekhov's *The Seagull* combining biography, history, and stylistics into a kind of psychohistory of creativity. In *The Seagull,* and only in *The Seagull,* his first dramatic masterpiece, Chekhov creates characters who are themselves artists: Trigorin and Treplev are writers, and Arkadina and Nina are actresses. Their professions are significant because these four characters suffer from, and in various ways come to terms with, the anxiety of influence. *The Seagull* may be called the first masterpiece of modern literature that has the anxiety of influence as its proper subject. The play thus offers us an opportunity to study the relationships between ephebes and precursors both in the text itself and in Chekhov's life cycle as an artist, as that life cycle incorporated the sociocultural circumstances into which he was born. (Of course, I acknowledge a debt to a precursor for everyone interested in psychohistory, Erik Erikson, the author of *Young Man Luther.*)

Applying the paradigm suggested here to Chekhov's life and work, we find that the crucial fact about his sociocultural situation is that he was the first great nonaristocratic writer who became influential outside Russia. As ephebes often do, he had an intense sense of coming after great figures. These great figures—Tolstoi, Goncharov, and most especially Turgenev—were aristocrats. They did not know what it was like to have to support themselves, as Chekhov did, or to have to work their way through school, as Chekhov did. The dermatologist Mikhail Chlenov, who knew Chekhov in his later years, wrote in his memoirs: "'It was very difficult for me to break out,' Chekhov told me several times, 'after all I am a peasant; my grandfather was a serf.'"[5] More than any other European writer of comparable stature in his time, Chekhov was a self-made man. He defined himself against what had gone before, and in doing so he claimed Russian literature from the aristocrats—from Pushkin to Tolstoi and Turgenev—who had created it. In making himself, Chekhov also revolutionalized modern theater.

Chekhov was not, however, alone in creating a nonaristocratic Russian art, for he found in Stanislavskii, a scion of the Moscow merchant family the Alekseevs, a director who could bring his plays to life. And in the 1880s the railroad magnate Savva Mamontov, Fedor Shaliapin's patron, founded the Private Opera in Moscow. Indeed, the beginning of the *Verbürgerlichung* of Russian culture may be dated to 1870, the year when Momontov bought Abramtsevo, the Aksakovs' estate, and turned it into an artists' colony. As is often the case with major artists, Chekhov's personal concerns had more general meaning.

After the disastrous premiere of *The Seagull* on October 19, 1896, Chekhov wrote to his publisher Aleksei Suvorin, explaining his sudden departure from St. Petersburg: "The problem is not that my play failed; after all, the majority of my plays failed in the past, too, and it was like water off a duck's back. On the 19th of October, it wasn't my play that failed, it was my personality."[6] Although there was more involved in the failure of the premiere than Chekhov's personality, this letter confirms that the play had personal meaning for him. I interpret Chekhov's extreme reaction as an expression of his anxiety that in his confrontation with Turgenev, Turgenev had won, and I see in *The Seagull* the culmination of Chekhov's struggle with Turgenev, which had begun in the early 1880s. In saying this, I am assuming that the anxiety of influence transcends genre, for in the 1870s and 1880s Turgenev was known as a prose writer, not as a playwright.[7] It was his stature as a prose writer that engendered the anxiety of influence in the young Chekhov, the writer of short prose sketches. But if writers do not choose their precursors, why did Turgenev serve as Chekhov's principal precursor? Why not Tolstoi and Dostoevskii?

The fact that Tolstoi and Dostoevskii were best known for their long novels is part of the answer; the long form did not suit Chekhov's genius. But both Tolstoi and Dostoevskii wrote short stories as well. The crucial issue here is one of class. Although Dostoevskii was technically a nobleman, and Tolstoi was of course Count Tolstoi, both of them had ambiguous feelings about the nobility. Only a few nobles appear in Dostoevskii's writings, and most of those few are melodramatic villains; and Tolstoi's idiosyncratic populism dominated his life, as well as his public image, throughout Chekhov's adult years. Turgenev, however, expressed no such ambiguity. Reared on his family's estate (to which he was later exiled) and educated abroad, he was the archetypal aristocratic writer. His best-known works—*Rudin, A Nest of Gentle Folk,* and *Fathers and Sons,* for instance—deal with the crisis in the socioeconomic position of the nobility. In "breaking out," as he put it, Chekhov defined himself against Turgenev, and we may interpret a great deal of his career as a misreading of Turgenev as mannered and passé.

But if *The Seagull* represents a successful working through of Chekhov's anxiety of influence from Turgenev that had

been building up over a fifteen-year period, as I believe it does, the play itself cannot serve as the starting point for a study of the anxiety of influence. The short sketches with which Chekhov began his career must be considered as well. Chekhov's contemporaries very early recognized those sketches as reactions against Turgenev and made some revealing comments to that effect. Chekhov himself provided an introduction to the subject of his anxiety of influence from Turgenev in his correspondence.

On August 15, 1894, by which time he had already started thinking about *The Seagull,* Chekhov again wrote to Suvorin. He had this to say about the then popular Polish writer Kazimierz Barancewicz:

> This is a bourgeois writer writing for the well-dressed public that rides in the third class. For this public Tolstoi and Turgenev are too luxurious, aristocratic, and a little foreign and indigestible. The public that enjoys eating salted beef with horseradish doesn't recognize artichokes and asparagus. Take its point of view, imagine a gray, boring courtyard, intellectual ladies who look like cooks, the smell of kerosine, the paucity of interests and tastes—and you will understand Barancewicz and his readers. He is not colorful; this is partially because the life which he draws on is not colorful. He is false ("good little books") because bourgeois writers cannot help being false. These are highly developed bourgeois writers. Boulevard writers sin together with their public, and bourgeois writers sin together with it and flatter its narrow virtue.[8]

The gray courtyards, the middle-class intellectuals, and the lack of color remind us immediately of the qualities of Chekhov's own work. One hardly has to be a Freudian to misread this passage as a projection onto Barancewicz of Chekhov's own inner doubts about the validity of bourgeois literature, which is to say about what he himself was writing. We may interpret historically the statement which sounds so absolute: "Bourgeois writers cannot help being false." They cannot help being (read: "feeling") false because they come after the great writers of the nobility who grew up with an unselfconscious confidence about their place in the social order. Bourgeois writers like Chekhov, on the other hand, had to make a place for themselves and consequently suffered from the identity crises endemic to the middle classes all over Europe and America.

Thus the gray courtyards and provincial towns of Chekhov's short stories, as well as the deliberately prosaic, deliberately understated qualities of his plays which make him so demanding for actors, make historical sense as Chekhov's reaction against his "luxurious, aristocratic" precursor.

Thus, Chekhov's stylistic reaction to Turgenev corresponds to kenosis, the third of the six revisionary ratios which Bloom defines in *The Anxiety of Influence.*

> *Kenosis,* which is a breaking-device similar to the defense mechanisms our psyches employ against repetition compulsions; *kenosis* then is a movement towards discontinuity with the precursor. I take the

word from St. Paul, where it means the humbling or emptying-out of Jesus by himself, when he accepts reduction from divine to human status. The later poet, apparently emptying himself of his own afflatus, his imaginative godhood, seems to humble himself as though he were ceasing to be a poet, but this ebbing is so performed in relation to a precursor's poem-of-ebbing that the precursor is emptied out also, and so the later poem of deflation is not as absolute as it seems.[9]

Chekhov "humbles himself" or "empties himself out" by means of his stylistic differences from Turgenev. In contrast to the lush imagery and complex, participle-filled syntax of *A Sportsman's Sketches,* Chekhov writes a restrained, non-poetic prose; he has "ceased to be a poet" stylistically. In contrast to Turgenev's late-blooming Romantics who die romantic deaths in the name of the revolution, like Rudin, Chekhov's more modest characters rarely die symbolic deaths. Indeed, except for Treplev and Tuzenbakh in **The Three Sisters,** none of the major characters die at the end of the plays. His masterpieces thus have the effect of emptying Turgenev's grandiloquence of its elan. Trofimov, in **The Cherry Orchard,** offers the clearest specific instance of the way Chekhov empties out Turgenev when he writes against him. In the tradition of Rudin and Turgenev's other revolutionaries, Trofimov spouts revolutionary rhetoric about "the bright future" and a "new life," but his head is so lost in the clouds of his verbiage that he falls down the stairs in act 3 and loses his galoshes in act 4.

Significantly, Chekhov's contemporaries perceived this kenosis as early as 1888, although they did not articulate it in this way. In early March of that year, Vsevolod Garshin read Chekhov's **"The Steppe"** aloud to some guests, including the artist Il'ia Repin. Repin recorded the reactions of those present in his autobiography:

> Chekhov was still a quite unknown, new phenomenon in our literature. The majority of the listeners—including me—attacked Chekhov and his new manner of writing "subjectless" and "contentless" pieces. . . . Our men of letters at that time still lived by Turgenev's canons.[10]

At a similar gathering later in the same month, the minor writer Vladimir Tikhonov informed his diary that Nikolai Albov "rejected An. Chekhov and considers him an image of the degeneration of our literature. . . . He says that it is a sign of our depraved times."[11] The belief that art has degenerated usually bespeaks an unconscious awareness of a precursor's power, because it so obviously indicates a felt perception of the difference between the dead precursor and the living ephebes. In the 1880s Turgenev was a more threatening precursor for second- and third-rate writers than either Tolstoi, whose epic power was beyond them, or Dostoevskii, whose dramatic intensity could not be matched. Lidiia Nazarova quotes a most revealing comment by Dmitrii Mamin-Sibiriak, to the effect that at first he had tried to write like Gogol', and then he "carefully assimilated a manner of beautiful descriptions à la Turgenev."[12]

Chekhov himself was not without Turgenev's influence in the usual sense of the word in the 1880s, as Nazarova points out. She cites, for instance, his story **"Agafia"** (1886) as resembling stories from *A Sportsman's Sketches,* even to the use of the hunter-narrator.[13] But by then Chekhov had also begun the process of kenosis, of emptying out Turgenev. Chekhov's kenosis begins in a primarily verbal, not stylistic, sense in such early sketches as **"In the Landau,"** written just after Turgenev's death in 1883.

Chekhov published **"In the Landau"** in *Fragments,* a satirical journal. Its editor Nikolai Leikin excised the ending, which is now lost. A certain Baron Dronkel' is riding in a landau with two young girls, Katia and Zina, and their sixteen-year-old cousin from the provinces, Marfusha. The baron comments that he has missed a funeral mass for Turgenev that day, and asks the girls if they like him. When they say that they do, he comments:

> No matter whom you ask, everyone likes him, but I . . . I don't understand! Either I don't have a brain, or I am such a desperate sceptic, but all the hoopla raised about Turgenev seems exaggerated, if not absurd, to me! I don't deny that he is a good writer. . . . He writes smoothly, the style is even lively in places, there's humor, but . . . nothing special. . . . He writes like all Russian writers. . . . Like Grigorovich, like Kraevskii. . . . I deliberately got a copy of *A Sports-man's Sketches* from the library, read it from cover to cover, found absolutely nothing special. . . . [It has neither] self-consciousness, nor [anything] about the freedom of the press . . . no idea! And there's nothing at all about hunting. It's not badly written, though![14]

When Kitty sighs, "How he wrote about love!" Dronkel' replies, "He wrote well about love, but there are some who wrote better. Jean Richepin, for example." (He is presumably referring here to *Les Caresses* [1877], a collection of erotic stories by this late French Romantic.) Predictably, one of the girls then defends Turgenev's descriptions of nature, and Dronkel' has a reply to that as well:

> I don't like to read descriptions of nature. It drags on and on. . . . "The sun set. . . . The birds began to sing. . . . The forest rustles. . . ." I always skip these charms. Turgenev is a good writer, I don't deny it, but I don't recognize in him the capacity to create miracles, as people shout about him. Supposedly he gave an impetus to self-consciousness, and touched to the quick some political conscience in the Russian people . . . I don't see all this . . . I don't understand. . . .

But Chekhov saves the unkindest cut of all for last: "'But have you read his *Oblomov?*' asked Zina. 'There he's against serfdom!'" These devoted admirers of Turgenev do not even remember that it was Goncharov who wrote *Oblomov.* Chekhov is not ready to make a class distinction between himself and Turgenev, so he uses a baron as a spokesman. But we can hardly mistake the *Schadenfreude* at the death of a precursor in the baron's remarks about Turgenev on the very day of a funeral mass for him.

The character who attracts the reader's attention in this tendentious piece, the first sign that Chekhov had begun to work through his anxiety of influence from Turgenev, is not Baron Dronkel' but Marfusha, who has come to St. Petersburg for the first time to see the sights. Marfusha reacts intensely to Dronkel's denunication of Turgenev:

> "Ask him to shut up! For God's sake!" Marfusha whispered to Zina. Zina looked with amazement at the naive, shy girl. The provincial girl's eyes were going frantically about the landau, from face to face, aglow with an evil feeling, and were apparently searching for someone to pour out her hatred and contempt on. Her lips trembled with rage.

When we recall that Nina quotes Turgenev in her magnificent last scene with Treplev, we realize that she and Marfusha are distant cousins. Chekhov's misreading of Turgenev as a Romantic imputes to Turgenev a capacity to attract weak readers, young provincial girls who live out their fantasies which they have acquired from books. (Obviously, Marfusha and Nina count Tatiana Larin and Emma Bovary among their predecessors.) Since Chekhov's ending has been lost, we will never know what, if any, resolution he supplied for Marfusha's outrage, but it strikingly anticipates Nina's confusion in act 2 of *The Seagull* when she finds out that Trigorin does not think of his life as glamorous and exciting, and that Arkadina can be petty and self-centered when Shamraev denies her horses. In 1883 Chekhov was not yet capable of creating so complex a character as Nina, but he understood the attitudes of the Nina we see in act 2 of *The Seagull*.

One final comment about **"In the Landau."** In the story without Chekhov's original ending, Baron Dronkel' has the next to last line. Speaking of Turgenev, he says, "He hasn't had the slightest influence on me, for example." Even as he began to work through his anxiety, Chekhov denied the influence. At the age of twenty-three he probably had to deny it in order to summon the courage to work through it.

The following statement by Trigorin to Nina in act 2 may thus be understood as a culmination of Chekhov's anxiety of influence from Turgenev: "And when I die, and people who know me pass by my grave, they will say, 'Here lies Trigorin. He was a good writer, but he didn't write as well as Turgenev.'"[15] This is not hostility, as in the early sketches, but simply anxiety. I believe that the capacity to express, to admit, one's anxiety of influence in a masterpiece that is coherent to the reader who has no knowledge of the artist's anxiety represents a working through of that anxiety. I disagree with Bloom's assertion that "a poem is not an overcoming of anxiety, but is that anxiety."[16] This formulation, meant as absolutely as it appears to be here, does not seem to allow for change and evolution.

In *The Seagull* Treplev does not wish to recognize Trigorin's accomplishment and says of his writing, "It's nice, it's talented . . . but . . . after Tolstoi or Zola you don't want to read Trigorin" (p. 9). In this remark Treplev is both

revealing his own anxiety of influence by denying it, as Baron Dronkel' had done, and saying what Trigorin says that everybody else says about him. In act 2 Trigorin says that people read reviews about him which say, "Yes, it's nice, it's talented . . . Nice, but far from Tolstoi," or "It's a marvelous piece, but Turgenev's *Fathers and Sons* is better" (p. 30). This, too, is autobiographical. In a letter he wrote to an aspiring writer, one Aleksandr Zhirkevich, on April 2, 1895, Chekhov commented ironically about the short story that Zhirkevich had asked him to evaluate: "'It's talented, intelligent, and noble.'" In a footnote, he explained the quotation marks: "This is from one of my stories ['**A Boring Story**']; when I am being reviled, people usually cite this phrase with 'but.'"[17]

The biographical elements in Trigorin require no special research. Chekhov's contemporaries perceived them even while Chekhov was still alive. When Chekhov has Nina give Trigorin a medallion with the words, "If you ever need my life, come and take it," engraved on it (p. 40), he is citing himself. As Petr Bitsilli pointed out long ago, these words occur in Chekhov's short story **"Neighbors,"**[18] Similarly, when Treplev comes finally to his grudging, agonizing recognition of Trigorin's talent, he refers to the way Trigorin creates the effect of a moonlit night by mentioning the gleam of the neck of a broken bottle. This very image appears in Chekhov's short story **"The Wolf"** (1888).

Critics who draw on biographical evidence usually content themselves with matching textual and extra-textual passages in this way. But Chekhov's anxiety of influence also affected the form of the work, which is unique among his four major plays. *The Seagull* is the only one that contains a play within the play, and the only one in which artists appear as characters. And in act 2 Trigorin makes several speeches to Nina that are longer than any other speeches in any of the other plays. In fact, when Trigorin responds to Nina's breathless outburst, "Your life is beautiful!" (p. 28), he delivers the longest speech Chekhov ever wrote. (It runs to about a page and a half.) Toward the end of it, Trigorin vividly recalls what it was like to be an ephebe.

> And in those years, in my young, best years, when I began, my writing activity was nothing but torture through and through. A minor writer, especially when he is not successful, seems awkward to himself, awkward, superfluous; his nerves are strained, and frazzled; he compulsively wanders about in the presence of people privy to literature and to art, unrecognized, unnoticed by anyone, afraid to look people directly in the eyes, like a passionate gambler who has no money (pp. 29-30).

This clearly autobiographical passage creates an anomaly in the form of the play. But Chekhov is not giving in to self-indulgence here, for he is using his own life experience to create a character. Once we know that Trigorin's pain is still with him, we may surmise that it is this pain which he senses in Treplev, and which causes him to be generous toward him.

Playbill for the Moscow Art Theater production of The Seagull.

In Act 3 of *The Seagull,* Trigorin writes something down in his notebook; when Arkadina asks him what he is doing, he replies, "This morning I heard a good expression: 'A virginal pine forest. . . .' It'll do" (p. 43). By having Trigorin keep a notebook, Chekhov is endowing him with one of his own writing practices. The editors of Chekhov's notebooks comment that "in the recollections of his contemporaries there is a lot of talk about how he himself would show his acquaintances among men of letters his notebook (usually not opening it), would give advice on how to use it, what kind of notes to enter, and would remind them that an artist must work constantly."[19] Not only did Chekhov keep a notebook as Trigorin does, he wrote in it what Trigorin writes. In the notebook that Chekhov kept while working on *The Seagull* there occurs the entry, "A Virginal, or Mashka's Pine Forest."[20] Clearly he found no way to work this phrase into a play or a story, so he gave it to Trigorin as a random notebook entry.

But just as it is inadequate to note that Trigorin is an autobiographical character without giving a more general interpretation of that fact, so it is inadequate to say that Trigorin represents Chekhov, because he also represents Turgenev. In the crucial scene with Nina in act 2, he tells her: "I don't often have a chance to meet young girls, young and interesting ones; I've already forgotten and can't clearly imagine how they feel at eighteen or nine-

teen, and so in my novellas and stories the young girls are usually false" (p. 28). This attitude surely expresses Chekhov's judgment of Turgenev's ingenues. Indeed, two of Chekhov's short stories, **"Late-Blooming Flowers"** (1882) and **"The Story of an Unknown Man"** (1893) also take issue with Turgenev's treatment of his heroines.

Moreover, Trigorin's relationship with Arkadina does not resemble any of Chekhov's relationships with women, but it strongly resembles Turgenev's relationship with another self-centered performer, Pauline Viardot. At the end of act 2, when Arkadina, jealous of Nina, tells Trigorin that they must go, he says, "I don't have a will of my own . . . I have never had a will of my own" (p. 42). One cannot imagine a man of Chekhov's strength and determination saying this to a woman, but one can readily imagine Turgenev saying it to Viardot.

Finally, for all his anxieties, Trigorin is an accomplished writer (Arkadina refers to him as a "celebrity") and plays the role of a precursor to Treplev. Trigorin represents as much of a threat to Treplev as Turgenev himself represented to Chekhov. As a character Trigorin expresses neither Chekhov's self-pity because of his difficulties in life, nor Chekhov's self-aggrandizement in giving an autobiographical character some of Turgenev's traits. In writing this groundbreaking play, Chekhov drew on both the ephebe which he had been and the precursor which he was becoming. It is this tension which characterizes the play.

By failing to understand the ambiguity of Trigorin's role as both ephebe and precursor, as both Chekhov and Turgenev, critics have also failed to understand Trigorin's evolution. As I interpret the play, it is Trigorin's affair with Nina that allows him to work through his anxiety of influence. In their initial conversation he expresses his interest in her in artistic terms. Trigorin has had to make his way in the world and recognizes that he is incomplete as an artist because of it, and he gains confidence in himself during his affair with Nina. This does not mean that he is not sexually attracted to her but that the sexual and the artistic attractions are indistinguishable, just as the personal and professional rivalries in general are indistinguishable in the play.

Although Trigorin's affair with Nina takes place offstage, between act 3 and act 4, we find evidence for its effect in act 4, when Trigorin honestly cannot remember asking Shamraev to have the gull stuffed, for it represents Nina as a stage of his artistic evolution which he has completed. We also notice that in act 4 he is consistently cheerful and no longer complains about having to write all the time. He recognizes, and accepts, his life for what it is. When Treplev asks Trigorin about his plans, Trigorin mentions his current projects and adds, "In a word, it's the old story" (p. 52).

But it is inadequate to say, "Trigorin is an autobiographical character," because Treplev is equally autobiographical. If in Trigorin Chekhov presents himself as a precursor who remembers what it was like to be an ephebe, in Treplev he presents himself as an ephebe acutely aware of his social position as a middle-class outsider who dreams of becoming a precursor. With Treplev's suicide Chekhov is killing off the ephebe in himself; but this purgation presupposes that the work in which the suicide occurs has coherence without that autobiographical meaning. Such an understanding of autobiographical meaning resolves a major difficulty of most criticism that establishes a relationship between the author's life and the work, for this criticism allows no valid criterion for evaluation. The presence of autobiographical material in a work clearly does not ensure its quality—more often than not quite the reverse is true. Once one realizes that Chekhov the ephebe in the process of becoming a precursor split these two roles into two very different characters, one begins to have some sense of the complexity of a creative process that draws on the author's life experiences.

By the spring of 1895, when he wrote the letter to Zhirkevich, Chekhov was beginning to formulate some views that were later expressed in *The Seagull.* He said of Zhirkevich's style that "the devices in the descriptions of nature are routine,"[21] and that there was a "routineness of the devices in general in descriptions."[22] And it is just this quality of "routineness" (*rutinnost'*) that Treplev finds characteristic of the theater of his day. But since he is a character in a play, his aesthetic judgments merge with his personal feelings. In act 2 he says of his mother that "she loves the theater; it seems to her that she is serving humanity, and holy art, but in my opinion the contemporary theater is routine and prejudice" (p. 8). Like Treplev's play, Chekhov's play offered radical innovations in the theater, and Chekhov knew it. In a letter of October 21, 1895 he wrote Suvorin that he was working on a play. "I am writing not without satisfaction, although I am frightfully going against the conventions of the stage."[23] A month later he again wrote to Suvorin. "Well, sir, I've already finished the play. I began it forte and ended it pianissimo—despite all the rules of dramatic art."[24]

If in *The Seagull* Chekhov shows himself as Trigorin in the process of writing a short story, a form which he had mastered, he also shows himself as Treplev, who presents a new form, a radically innovative play, to an audience that fails to appreciate it. After the debacle of the premiere, he must have felt his affinity with Treplev very intensely; he uncannily anticipates, in the hostile reaction of Treplev's mother to her son's play, the reaction of the audience at the Aleksandrinskii Theater that fateful night. In effect, the audience said to him what Nina says to Treplev: "There's too little action in your play; it's just recitation" (p. 11). Thus both Treplev and Chekhov are carrying out kenosis, an emptying out of the precursor's work.

Treplev's play amounts to an extreme example of kenosis in that it empties drama of character, conflict, imagery, and theme, leaving only despair. But Treplev is not Samuel Beckett, and instead of emptying out his precursor, he empties out only himself. Treplev has cut himself off from potential sources of strength and creativity by cutting himself off from Trigorin, as when he lies to Nina by telling her that he has not read Trigorin's work.

Just as Chekhov distances himself from Trigorin by giving him some of Turgenev's traits, so he distances himself from Treplev by giving his writing some traits of what he considered inferior literature. In the letter to Zhirkevich he had commented scornfully that "nowadays only ladies write 'the poster announced,' 'a face framed by hair.'"[25] And it is, of course, just these phrases that he gave to Treplev in the moving scene in act 4 during which he realizes that his own writing has become as cliché-ridden as the works which he had denounced.

> I've talked so much about new forms, but now I feel that I myself am slipping little by little toward a routine. (He reads.) "The poster on the fence announced. . . . The pale face framed by dark hair. . . ." Announced, framed. . . . This is untalented (p. 55).

Only after Treplev understands his own work for what it is can he understand Trigorin's work for what *it* is. It seems to him that Trigorin has taken both his beloved and his work, but in fact he has weakened his own work by denying it a relationship with Trigorin's, and denounced Nina while she still loved him. He has nothing left but suicide.

The assumption that the anxiety of influence gives thematic unity to the play has important implications for the dialogue as well as for the characters. Chekhov's characters notoriously do not talk to each other but past each other. They do so, it now seems, because they are addressing the theme of the play.

By letting these tensions between ephebes and precursors shape *The Seagull,* Chekhov was beginning a middle-class, as opposed to aristocratic, literary tradition in Russian, and Bloom has this to say about the beginning of literary tradition:

> Literary tradition begins when a fresh author is simultaneously cognizant not only of his own struggle against the forms and presence of a precursor, but is compelled also to a sense of the precursor's place in regard to what came before him.[26]

For Chekhov, what came before the aristocratic literature that Turgenev represented was Western literature, and the most important single work of foreign literature for Russians is and always has been *Hamlet.* In her book *Hamlet: A Window on Russia,* Eleanor Rowe quotes a Russian critic: "We can almost say that in Russia alone Hamlet is sincerely loved and understood."[27] The play strikes home so much in Russia because it deals with the very Russian theme of conflict between civic duty and personal desire. But *Hamlet* also embodies the father-son tension which Bloom takes as the mode for the precursor-ephebe relationship. As the dead precursor is more alive than the living ephebe, so the ghost of Hamlet's father is more alive than Hamlet.

In *The Seagull* Chekhov achieves a kenosis with regard to Shakespeare that is of the same nature as his kenosis with regard to Turgenev. Chekhov's prosaic diction contrasts with Shakespeare's florid Elizabethan rhetoric even more than with Turgenev's nature descriptions, and Chekhov's open endings do not restore order in the kingdom, as the endings of Shakespeare's history plays and tragedies do. If Shakespeare (as well as Turgenev) engages his characters in historical events, Chekhov places his characters in isolated settings, which reflect their isolated psyches.

In a previous article I have shown that the four principal characters of *Hamlet* correspond to the four principal characters of *The Seagull*.[28] Claudius corresponds to Trigorin, Gertrude to Arkadina, Ophelia to Nina, and Treplev to Hamlet. But Chekhov creates what Bloom calls a clinamen, or swerve, with Shakespeare by reversing the significance of the characters. It is as though Chekhov had asked, "What if Claudius were a legitimate king, and what if Hamlet made the other choice in the 'To be or not to be' soliloquy?" This reversal becomes most apparent when Treplev sees Trigorin walking along with his notebook in hand and jeers, "'Words, words, words'" (p. 449). He is using the words of Hamlet's reply to Polonius when Polonius sees him, book in hand, and asks him what he is reading. In using Hamlet's words, Treplev expresses his awarenesss of his affinities with Hamlet, of course, but he is also unconsciously expressing something else. Treplev thinks he is jeering at Trigorin, but in fact he is admitting that Trigorin has what he does not have: words.

In 1882 Chekhov reviewed a production of *Hamlet* at the Pushkin Theater in Moscow and noted that "the scene with the mother is beautifully carried through."[29] It is probably not coincidental that the so-called closet scene (act 3, scene 4) from *Hamlet* to which he is referring here reappears in *The Seagull.* Before the beginning of the play within the play, *The Seagull*'s most obvious reference to *Hamlet,* Treplev asks for his mother's patience, and thus for her respect. She refuses it by quoting Gertrude's reply from the closet scene when Hamlet reproaches her for her hasty marriage to Claudius:

> Thou turn'st mine eyes into my very soul;
> And there I see such black and grained spots
> As will not leave their tinct.[30]

She cannot openly admit that she feels hostile toward her son because he reminds others of her true age (as Treplev accurately points out in act 1), nor can she deal with his oedipal hostility toward Trigorin, which has both personal and professional origins. In *The Seagull* Chekhov used Nikolai Polevoi's translation of *Hamlet,* which significantly abbreviates Hamlet's outburst:

> Nay, but to live
> In the rank sweat of an enseamed bed
> Stewed in corruption, honeying and making love
> Over the nasty sty,—

Stripped of their vivid imagery in Polevoi's version, these lines become a question which Treplev asks his mother, both as her son and as Hamlet: "Why have you given in to vice, Why have you sought love in the abyss of transgression?" (p. 12). But then a horn sounds to signal the beginning of his play, so Arkadina does not have to reply.

In act 3 Chekhov gives his own version of the closet scene when Treplev asks his mother to change the bandage that covers the wound which he inflicted on himself when he tried to commit suicide. In this, the most tense scene of the play, the hostility between mother and son comes out, but it is couched only in professional terms, as when Treplev denounces his mother and Trigorin in a line which Chekhov must have enjoyed writing: "You, the creatures of routine, have taken primacy in art, and you consider legal and real only what you yourselves do, and you repress and choke the rest" (p. 40).

Since Treplev and his mother cannot discuss or resolve their hostility, they mask it by the use of quotation—the literal quotation from the closet scene in act 1, and the compositional quotation in act 3. In doing so they are also allowing Chekhov to work through his own anxiety of influence, for he cannot express it openly, either. For Chekhov, however, the question whether he could articulate it, even to himself, is not the point. As an artist he could not openly express his anxiety of influence from Shakespeare, if he ever wanted to work through it, for resolution of an ephebe's anxiety of influence comes about only when the ephebe embodies that anxiety in a coherent structure. And that is what Chekhov did in *The Seagull.*

Thus, Chekhov in his quietly courageous way takes on two threatening precursors in the same play, with the same set of characters. This remarkable fact suggests a relationship between Shakespeare and Turgenev, and indeed such a relationship exists, in "Hamlet and Don Quixote," the famous essay that Turgenev published in the January 1860 issue of *The Contemporary* and which he delivered as a lecture in St. Petersburg on January 22 of that year. Chekhov read "Hamlet and Don Quixote" in 1879, and in a letter from April 6-8 he recommended that his older brothers read it.[31]

In the nineteenth-century manner, Turgenev interpreted Hamlet and Don Quixote as types who recurred throughout world literature. In his conclusion Turgenev commented that "a certain English lord (a good judge in this matter) in our presence called Don Quixote the model of a real gentleman."[32] In contrast, he says that Hamlet had *"des airs de parvenu,"* and continues: "But he is given the force of unique and precise expression, a force characteristic of any personality that thinks and develops itself—and therefore is inaccessible to Don Quixote."[33] Don Quixote as "the model of a real gentleman," and Hamlet as a parvenu; Don Quixote as a "true *hidalgo*" and Hamlet as a forceful personality that "thinks and develops itself." Significantly, these contrasts correspond well enough to the difference between Turgenev and Chekhov. Turgenev was certainly a model of a genteel man of letters, and Chekhov was certainly a parvenu. Turgenev—so it must have seemed to Chekhov—had European culture given to him as a birthright. Nobody ever gave Chekhov anything; he worked for everything he got.

In the sense in which Turgenev treated Hamlet and Don Quixote as polar opposites, Chekhov played Hamlet the outsider struggling against the established order to Turgenev's Don Quixote, "the model of a real gentleman." And if Hamlet acts as he does because his father imposed on him an obligation which, he fears, may be beyond his powers, then Chekhov struggled with the prestige and the authority of Turgenev, and he must have felt, after the premiere of *The Seagull,* that he had been unable to overcome Turgenev. A holistic treatment of *The Seagull* in Chekhov's creative life cycle therefore yields the following chain of associations: Chekhov as ephebe; Treplev as ephebe; the ephebe as parvenu; the parvenu as Hamlet; Hamlet as opposed to Don Quixote; Don Quixote as Turgenev; Turgenev as Trigorin; and Trigorin as Chekhov. I choose to state the matter in this way, rather than as a set of declarative statements, for I believe that any such set of statements has a reductionist quality.

Chekhov's relationship with Shakespeare as well as with Turgenev poses more general issues than those of an isolated struggle between an ephebe and his precursors. If Chekhov's confrontation with Turgenev meant the opposition of the middle class to the aristocracy, then in his confrontation with Shakespeare we have the age-old confrontation between Russia and the West. If Chekhov was a parvenu in the aristocratic milieu of Russian letters, then Russian literature as a whole was a parvenu in the aristocratic milieu of European letters, which had a far longer and far richer tradition. And since both confrontations, and their implications, thus have clear analogies, Chekhov deals with them in the same way.

Hence a revised version of Bloom's theory of the anxiety of influence creates a paradigm for interpreting *The Seagull* in terms of its biographical and historical context. This interpretation avoids both formalistic and biographical reductionism; it depends, furthermore, on avoiding Bloom's own reductionism, a reduction of all literary history to an oedipal struggle between an isolated son and an isolated father. Assuming that strong writers incorporate in their psyches the social processes of their times in ways which they cannot possibly understand or articulate, I have argued that the relationship between Turgenev and Chekhov involves an encounter between a father and a son who represent two different social classes. By overcoming his anxiety of influence from Turgenev, Chekhov was also working out the characteristics of a middle-class art, something no one in Russia—not even Ostrovskii—had done in a satisfactory way. If the great novelists of the generation before him had used the novel, which was historically a middle-class form, to deal with the plight of the aristocracy to which they belonged, then Chekhov had the task of reversing what they had done. He created a middle-class style that dealt with the appearance of a significant middle class in Russia. In the process of doing so he transformed himself from an ephebe into a precursor. Specifically, he became a precursor in America and in England after World War II, where the democratic middle-class social structure of society made his work a model, a model to be revised by such dramatic talents as Lillian Hellman in America and Harold Pinter in England. But that, as the Russian saying goes, is from another opera.

NOTES

1 Harold Bloom, *The Anxiety of Influence* (New York: Oxford University Press, 1973), p. 30.
2 Steve Polansky, "A Family Romance—Northrop Frye and Harold Bloom: Study of Critical Influences," *Boundary* 2, vol. 9, no. 2 (Winter 1981): 238.
3 Harold Bloom, *A Map of Misreading* (New York: Oxford University Press, 1975), p. 12.
4 Loy D. Martin, "Literary Invention: The Illusion of the Individual Talent," *Critical Inquiry,* 6, no. 4 (Summer 1980): 667.
5 Quoted in Anatolii Kotov, ed., *Chekhov v vospominaniiakh sovremennikov,* 2nd ed. (Moscow, 1954), p. 55.
6 Anton Chekhov, *Polnoe sobranie sochinenii i pisem v tridtsati tomakh* (hereafter *PSS*), I:2, V. V. Ermilov et al., eds. (Moscow, 1964), p. 148.
7 Turgenev's *A Month in the Country* (1850), the most important play written in any European language in the middle of the nineteenth century, had its premiere only on January 13, 1872 and was staged only occasionally during the 1870s and 1880s. Chekhov does not seem to have seen a performance; on March 23, 1903, just over a year before his death, he wrote to his wife Ol'ga Knipper, "I've read almost all of Turgenev's plays. I've already written you, I didn't like *A Month in the Country*" (Chekhov, *PSS,* I:12, p. 487). Chekhov did not like *A Month in the Country* because he recognized in it some of the elements of his own work which derive from Turgenev, such as the atmospheric quality and the delicate psychological tensions.
8 Chekhov, *PSS,* I:12, p. 52.
9 Bloom, *The Anxiety of Influence,* pp. 14-15.
10 Quoted in Nikolai Gitovich, *Letopis' zhizni i tvorchestva A. P. Chekhova* (Moscow, 1955), p. 186.
11 Quoted in ibid., p. 187.
12 Liudmila Nazarova, *Turgenev i russkaia literatura kontsa XIX-nachala XX v.* (Leningrad, 1979), p. 35.
13 Ibid., p. 41.
14 Chekhov, *PSS,* II:2, p. 243. All quotations from "In the Landau" come from this page except the last one, which is on p. 244.
15 Page numbers after quotations from *The Seagull* refer to Chekhov, *PSS,* II:12-13 (Moscow, 1978).
16 Bloom, *A Map of Misreading,* p. 94.
17 Chekhov, *PSS,* I;12, p. 79.
18 Petr M. Bicilli, *Anton echov. Das Werk und sein Stil* (Munich: Wilhelm Fink Verlag, 1966), p. 28.
19 Chekhov, *PSS,* II:17, p. 243.
20 Ibid., p. 34.
21 Chekhov, *PSS,* I:12, p. 78.
22 Ibid., p. 79.
23 Ibid., p. 86.
24 Ibid., p. 90.
25 Ibid., p. 79.
26 Bloom, *A Map of Misreading,* p. 32.
27 Quoted in Eleanor Rowe, *Hamlet: A Window on Russia* (New York: New York University Press, 1976), p. viii.
28 See James M. Curtis, "Spatial Form in Drama: *The Seagull,*" Canadian-American Slavic Studies, 6, no. 1 (Spring 1972): 13-57.
29 Chekhov, *PSS,* II:16, p. 21.
30 I have used the Cambridge Edition text of *Hamlet* as it appears in *The Complete Works of Shakespeare* (Garden City: n.p., n.d.)
31 See Gitovich, *Letopis' zhizni,* pp. 36-37.
32 Ivan Turgenev, *Polnoe sobranie sochinenii i pisem v dvadtsati vos'mi tomakh,* I:8 (Moscow-Leningrad, 1964), p. 187.
33 Ibid.

Michael Frayn (essay date 1986)

SOURCE: Introduction to *The Seagull: A Comedy in Four Acts,* translated by Michael Frayn, Methuen, 1986, pp. ix-xx.

[*In the following essay, Frayn provides an overview of* The Seagull, *focusing on its initial spectacular failure in*

St. Petersburg and its equally spectacular success in Moscow a month later.]

'A comedy—three f., six m., four acts, rural scenery (a view over a lake); much talk of literature, little action, five bushels of love.'

Chekhov's own synopsis of the play, in a letter to his friend Suvorin written a month before he finished it, is characteristically self-mocking and offhand. (His cast-list is even one f. short, unless he added the fourth woman only during that last month, or when he revised the play the following year). He says in the same letter that he is cheating against the conventions of the theatre, but no one could have begun to guess from his flippant resumé how extraordinary an event was being prepared for the world. No doubt Chekhov took the play more seriously than the letter suggests, but even he can scarcely have realised quite what he had on his hands: a catastrophe so grotesque that it made him swear never to write for the theatre again; a triumph so spectacular that it established him as a kind of theatrical saint; and the first of the four masterpieces that would change forever the nature and possibilities of drama.

Chekhov wrote *The Seagull* in 1895. He was 35 years old, and already an established and celebrated writer who had known almost nothing but success. But the success was on the printed page, as a writer of short stories, and the leap he was trying to make now, from page to stage, was one which few major writers have managed. He had written for the theatre before, of course. He had done a number of short plays, all but one broadly comic, and related to his humorous journalism rather than to his more serious work. He had also written at least three full-length plays with more serious intentions—the untitled piece of his student days, *Ivanov*, and *The Wood Demon*—and with these he had encountered almost the only setbacks of his career so far. Now, as he finished *The Seagull* and read it through, he had a moment of fundamental doubt about the direction he was trying to take. 'I am once again convinced', he wrote to Suvorin, 'that I am absolutely not a dramatist.'

There were prolonged difficulties in getting the play past the theatrical censor, which almost made him despair of the whole enterprise, but once this hurdle was behind him Chekhov's apparently offhand mood returned. The play was to be performed at the Alexandrinsky Theatre in St. Petersburg, where *Ivanov* had been well received seven years earlier after a highly disputed opening in Moscow, and his letters in September 1896, as rehearsals approached, have the same cheerful flippancy as his original account of the play to Suvorin. They read with hindsight as ironically as the banter of some doomed statesman as he goes all unknowing towards his assassination. To his brother Georgi: 'My play will be done in the Alexandrinsky Theatre at a jubilee benefit [for the actress Levkeyeva]. It will be a resounding gala occasion. Do come!' To his friend Shcheglov: 'Around the 6th [of October] the thirst for glory will draw me to the Palmyra of the north for the rehearsals of my *Seagull*.' To his brother Alexander: 'You are to meet me at the station, in full parade uniform (as laid down for a customs officer retd.) . . . On the 17th Oct my new play is being done at the Alexandrinsky. I would tell you what it's called, only I'm afraid you'll go round boasting you wrote it.'

The seventeenth, when it came, was indeed a resounding gala occasion. 'I have been going to the theatre in St. Petersburg for more than twenty years,' wrote a correspondent in a theatrical journal afterwards, 'and I have witnessed a great many "flops" . . . but I can remember nothing resembling what happened in the auditorium at Levkeyeva's 25th jubilee.' The trouble started within the first few minutes of Act One. Levkeyeva was a popular light comedy actress, and even though she had no part in the play the audience were minded to laugh. The first thing that struck them as funny was the sight of Masha offering a pinch of snuff to Medvedenko, and thereafter they laughed at everything. Konstantin's play, Konstantin with his head bandaged—it was all irresistible. By Act Two, according to the papers next day, the dialogue was beginning to be drowned by the noise and movement in the audience; by Act Three the hissing had become general and deafening. The reviewers struggled for superlatives to describe 'the grandiose scale' of the play's failure, the 'scandalous' and 'unprecendented' nature of 'such a dizzying flop, such a stunning fiasco.' The author, they reported, had fled from the theatre.

According to his own accounts of the evening Chekhov escaped from the theatre only when the play ended, after sitting out two or three acts in Levkeyeva's dressing-room, had supper at Romanov's, 'in the proper way', then slept soundly and caught the train home to Melikhovo next day. Even Suvorin accused him of cowardice in running away. All he had run away from, he protested in a letter to Suvorin's wife, was the intolerable sympathy of his friends. He told Suvorin: 'I behaved as reasonably and coolly as a man who has proposed and been refused, and who has no choice but to go away . . . Back in my own home I took a dose of castor oil, had a wash in cold water—and now I could sit down and write a new play.'

But Suvorin, with whom he was staying, recorded in his diary that Chekhov's first reaction had been to give up the theatre. He had not come back until two in the morning, when he told Suvorin that he had been walking about the streets, and that 'if I live another seven hundred years I shan't have a single play put on. Enough is enough. In this area I am a failure.' When he went home next day he left a note telling Suvorin to halt the printing of his plays, and saying that he would never forget the previous evening. He claimed to have slept well, and to be leaving 'in an absolutely tolerable frame of mind'; but he managed nevertheless to leave his dressing-gown and other belongings on the train, and the accounts he subsequently gave of the evening in various letters to friends and relations make it clear how painful the experience had been. 'The moral of all this', he wrote to his sister Masha, 'is that one shouldn't write plays.'

And yet, not much more than a month later, in another letter to Suvorin, he was mentioning the existence of a play 'not known to anyone in the world'—*Uncle Vanya.* By this time, too—in fact from the very next performance—the tide had turned at the Alexandrinsky. 'A total and unanimous success', wrote Komissarzhevskaya, who was playing Nina, in a letter to Chekhov after the second performance of *The Seagull,* 'such as it ought to be and could not but be.' And two years later, in a stunning reversal of fortune of the kind that occurs in plays (though never in Chekhov's own), it triumphed in Moscow as noisily as it had failed in Petersburg.

In fact the event went rather beyond anything one might find in a play; it was more like something out of a back-stage musical—particularly as recounted by Stanislavsky (who was both directing and playing Trigorin) in his memoir of Chekhov. For a start the fate of the newly-founded Moscow Arts Theatre depended upon it. The other opening productions had mostly either failed or been banned by the Metropolitan of Moscow, and all hopes were now riding aboard this one salvaged wreck. There was a suitable love interest depending upon the outcome of the evening—the leading lady (Olga Knipper, playing Arkadina) and the author had just met, and were to marry two plays later—provided there *were* two more plays to allow their acquaintance to develop. Moreover, the author had now been diagnosed as consumptive and exiled to Yalta. The dress rehearsal was of course a disaster. At the end of it Chekhov's sister Masha arrived to express her horror at the prospect of what another failure like Petersburg would do to her sick brother, and they considered abandoning the production and closing the theatre.

When the curtain finally went up on the first night the audience was sparse, and the cast all reeked of the valerian drops they had taken to tranquillise themselves. As they reach the end of Act One Stanislavsky's paragraphs become shorter and shorter:

> 'We had evidently flopped. The curtain came down in the silence of the tomb. The actors huddled fearfully together and listened to the audience.

> 'It was as quiet as the grave.

> 'Heads emerged from the wings as the stage staff listened as well.

> 'Silence.

> 'Someone started to cry. Knipper was holding back hysterical sobs . We went offstage in silence.

> 'At that moment the audience gave a kind of moan and burst into applause. We rushed to take a curtain.

> 'People say that we were standing on stage with our backs half-turned to the audience, that we had terror on our faces, that none of us thought to bow and that someone was even sitting down. We had evidently not taken in what had happened.

> 'In the house the success was colossal; on stage it was like a second Easter. Everyone kissed everyone else, not excluding strangers who came bursting backstage. Someone went into hysterics. Many people, myself among them, danced a wild dance for joy and excitement.'

The only person who remained completely calm seems to have been Chekhov himself, since he was 800 miles away in the Crimea. But when after Act Three the audience began to shout 'Author! Author!', as audiences do in this kind of script, and Nemirovich-Danchenko explained to them that the author was not present, they shouted 'Send a telegram!' In the event he was informed of his triumph not only by telegram, but in shoals of letters from everyone present. But, judging by how rarely he referred to it either beforehand or afterwards in his own letters from Yalta, he had kept this production at a distance emotionally as well as geographically, and the Moscow success was considerably more remote from him than the Petersburg failure.

There were of course external reasons for the play's extraordinarily different reception in the two capitals. The choice of Levkeyeva's benefit night in St. Petersburg, on the one hand, and the fact that it had been produced there at nine days notice; the thorough preparation in Moscow on the other hand, with twelve weeks' rehearsal. The Moscow audience may also have been impressed by the sheer weight of Stanislavsky's production. At the beginning of Act One, for example, his prompt copy notes: 'Glimmer of lantern, distant singing of drunk, distant howling of dog, croaking of frogs, cry of corncrake, intermittent strokes of distant church bell . . . summer lightning, barely audible far-off thunder . . .' —All this before the first two characters have even got on stage. Chekhov, grateful as he was for the success, was ungratefully cool about the production when he finally saw it. He greatly disliked the slowness of Stanislavsky's tempo, and according to Nemirovich-Danchenko he threatened to put a stage-direction in his next play saying: 'The action takes place in a country where there are no mosquitoes or crickets or other insects that interfere with people's conversations.'

Even without Levkeyeva or the corncrakes, though, the play would almost certainly have elicited a passionate response of one kind or another. Its influence has been so widespread and pervasive since that it is difficult now to realise what a departure it was. The traditional function of literature in general, and of drama in particular, has always been to simplify and formalise the confused world of our experience; to isolate particular emotions and states of mind from the flux of feeling in which we live; to make our conflicts coherent; to illustrate values and to impose a moral (and therefore human) order upon a non-moral and inhuman universe; to make intention visible, and to suggest the process by which it takes effect. *The Seagull* is a critical survey of this function. For a start two of the characters are writers. One of them is using the traditional techniques without questioning them, one of them is searching for some even more formalised means of expression; and what interests Chekhov is how life eludes the efforts of both of them. Konstantin cannot even begin to

Chekhov recalls the opening night of *The Seagull*:

To A. F. Koni

Melikhovo. Nov. 11, 1896.

You cannot imagine how your letter rejoiced me. I saw from the front only the first two acts of my play. Afterwards I sat behind the scenes and felt the whole time that **The Sea-Gull** was a failure. After the performance that night and next day, I was assured that I had hatched out nothing but idiots, that my play was clumsy from the stage point of view, that it was not clever, that it was unintelligible, even senseless, and so on and so on. You can imagine my position—it was a collapse such as I had never dreamed of! I felt ashamed and vexed, and I went away from Petersburg full of doubts of all sorts. I thought that if I had written and put on the stage a play so obviously brimming over with monstrous defects, I had lost all instinct and that, therefore, my machinery must have gone wrong for good. After I had reached home, they wrote to me from Petersburg that the second and third performances were a success; several letters, some signed, some anonymous, came, praising the play and abusing the critics. I read them with pleasure, but still I felt vexed and ashamed, and the idea forced itself upon me that if kind-hearted people thought it was necessary to comfort me, it meant that I was in a bad way. But your letter has acted upon me in a most definite way. I have known you a long time, I have a deep respect for you, and I believe in you more than in all the critics taken together—you felt that when you wrote your letter, and that is why it is so excellent and convincing. My mind is at rest now, and I can think of the play and the performance without loathing. Kommissarzhevskaya is a wonderful actress. At one of the rehearsals many people were moved to tears as they looked at her, and said that she was the first actress in Russia to-day; but at the first performance she was affected by the general attitude of hostility to my **Sea-Gull,** and was, as it were, intimidated by it and lost her voice. Our press takes a cold tone to her that doesn't do justice to her merits, and I am sorry for her. Allow me to thank you with all my heart for your letter. Believe me, I value the feelings that prompted you to write it far more than I can express in words, and the sympathy you call "unnecessary" at the end of your letter I shall never forget, whatever happens.

Letters of Anton Chekhov, in *Letters on the Short Story, Drama and Other Literary Topics,* by Anton Chekhov, edited by Louis S. Friedland, Minton, Balch, 1924, pp. 115-63.

plification and formalisation by which the world is represented in art and to show the raw, confused flux of the world itself, where nothing has its moral value written upon it, or for that matter its cause or its effect, or even its boundaries or its identity.

The most obvious characteristic of this approach is the play's ambiguity of tone. The author does not give us any of the customary indications as to whether we are to find these events comic or tragic. Indeed, what we are watching has not even been clearly organised into *events*; a lot of it bears a striking resemblance to the non-events out of which the greater part of our life consists. Then again, the play is to a quite astonishing extent morally neutral. It displays no moral conflict and takes up no moral attitude to its characters. Even now, after all these years, some people still find this difficult to accept. They talk as if Arkadina and Trigorin, at any rate, were monsters, and as if the point of the play were to expose her egotism and his spinelessness. It is indeed impossible not to be appalled by Arkadina's insensitivity towards her son, or by the ruthlessness with which she attempts to keep Trigorin attached to her; moral neutrality is not moral blindness. But Konstantin continues to find good in her, for all his jealousy and irritation, and she remains capable of inspiring the love of those around her. Konstantin's assessment is just as valid as ours; the devotion of Dorn and Shamrayev is just as real and just as important as our outrage. There is moral irony, too, in her manipulation of Trigorin; had she succeeded more completely in blackmailing him to remain with her she might have saved Nina from the misery that engulfs her. It is hard to respect Trigorin as we see him crumble in Arkadina's hands, harder still to like him when we know how he has treated Nina. But Masha likes and respects him, and for good reason—because he listens to her and takes her seriously; no grounds are offered for discounting her judgment. And when Trigorin wanders back in the last act, makes his peace with Konstantin, and settles down to lotto with the others, he is once again neither good nor bad in their eyes, in spite of what he has done; he is at that moment just a man who always seems to come out on top, whether in lotto or in love. We are perfectly entitled to find against him, of course—but that is our own verdict; there has been no direction to the jury in the judge's summing-up; indeed, no summing-up and no judge.

But then nothing is fixed. Everything is open to interpretation. Are we, for instance, to take Konstantin seriously as a writer? Impossible, after Nina's complaint that there are no living creatures in his work. But then it turns out that Dorn likes it, and he is a man of robust good sense (though not good enough to prevent his ruining Polina's life). And in Act Four we discover that Konstantin is at any rate good enough to be able to make a career as a professional writer. But even then Trigorin's judgment remains the same as Nina's, and Konstantin comes round to much the same view himself.

No one is valued for us; nothing is firmly located or fully explained. Why is Arkadina called Arkadina? She is Sorina by birth and Trepleva by marriage. It could be a stage-

capture it, for all the seriousness of his intentions; Trigorin feels that in the end all he has ever managed to do without falsity is landscapes, while his obsessive need to write drains his experience of all meaning apart from its literary possibilities. The extraordinary trick of the play is that all around the two writers we see the very life that they are failing to capture. What Chekhov is doing, in fact, is something formally impossible—to look behind the sim-

name, of course, or she could have married more than once. The people around her presumably know. They do not trouble to tell us. Has Dorn had an affair with Arkadina in the past? Is this why Polina is so relentlessly jealous of her? Is it what Arkadina is referring to when she talks about how irresistible he had been in the past? (In an earlier draft Polina begins to weep quietly at this point; but that may of course be for the lost early days of her own love.) In an astonishing moment at the end of Act One we do in fact stumble across one of the unexplained secrets of this world, when Dorn snatches Masha's snuff-box away from her, admonishes her for her 'filthy habit', and flings it into the bushes. From that one gesture of licensed impatience, without a word being said, we understand why Masha feels nothing for her father, why she sees herself as being 'of dubious descent', and why she feels so close to Dorn; because Dorn is her father, not Shamrayev. But who knows this, apart from us and Dorn? Not Masha herself, apparently. Does Shamrayev? Arkadina? Medvedenko? We are not told; the clouds that have parted for a moment close in again.

But then which of them knows about Dorn's relationship with Masha's mother in the first place? Perhaps everyone; or perhaps no one. We can only speculate. In any case it is characteristic of the relationships in the play; overt or covert, they are all one-sided, unsatisfactory, anomalous, and unlikely ever to be resolved. Medvedenko loves Masha who loves Konstantin who loves Nina who loves Trigorin who is supposed to love Arkadina, but who doesn't really love anyone, not even himself. No one's life can be contained in the forms that marriage and family offer. Konstantin's dissatisfaction with the existing dramatic forms is only a special case of this general condition. Plainly Chekhov is not advocating new social forms, in the way that Konstantin is calling for new literary ones. In the end even Konstantin comes to think that it is not a question of forms, old or new—the important thing is to write from the heart; nor are there any social forms suggested in the play which could ever contain the great flux of life itself.

We cannot help wondering, of course, if in this play we for once catch a glimpse of its elusive author. Chekhov is astonishingly absent from his works. Even the most intimately understood of his characters is unlike him—from quite different backgrounds, most of them, with quite different feelings and outlooks. But here is a play about two professional writers; it is unlikely that it does not reflect his own experience in some way. Konstantin is scarcely a plausible candidate, overwhelmed as he is by an artistic family, obsessed by questions of literary theory, and unable to create a living character; Chekhov's parents, after all, ran a provincial grocery, he displayed no interest in theory, and life is the very quality in which his stories and plays abound. But Trigorin is another matter. He is a celebrated and successful author, in much the same way that Chekhov was. His passion is fishing; so was Chekhov's. His modest estimate of his place in Russian letters is very much the kind of thing that Chekhov might have said mockingly about himself. More importantly, it seems at any rate plausible that his painful memories of beginning his career, and the terrible compulsion to write which

is eating his life, reflect something that Chekhov felt about himself—particularly since the only palliative for his obsession is fishing. But this is about as far as we can push the parallel. David Magarshack, in his book *The Real Chekhov*, goes on to suppose that Trigorin is Chekhov's spokesman, and that when he tells Nina about the need he feels to pronounce on social questions he is making some kind of declaration of social commitment on Chekhov's behalf. This is preposterous. Trigorin is not even issuing a manifesto on his own behalf—he is making a confession of helplessness and ineptitude. Chekhov was notorious for refusing to pronounce on social questions, and if there is any manifesto in *The Seagull* it is plainly its general orientation *against* the imposition of the author's own interpretations and views upon his material.

Any biographical parallel has in any case clearly broken down by this point. There would be something characteristically self-mocking in choosing a second-rate author to represent himself, but when Trigorin says finally that all he can write is landscapes we realise that the picture which has been built up deliberately excludes the very essence of Chekhov's literary identity. Nor do any of the other biographical details fit. Arkadina is indeed based in part upon an actress, Yavorskaya, who seems from her letters to have been very briefly his mistress. But Chekhov, unlike Trigorin, had no difficulty in disentangling himself from her, and in keeping women at arm's length generally. One of the women who were in love with Chekhov, Lika Mizinova, he kept at bay so successfully that she provided a model for not one but two of the characters in *The Seagull*: first Masha, with her life ruined by the unquenchable but unreciprocated love she has for Konstantin, and then Nina. To forget the Masha-like feelings she had for Chekhov, Lika threw herself into a disastrous affair with a friend of his, the Ukrainian writer Potapenko, who left his wife and went off to Paris with Lika, where he made her pregnant and then abandoned her. Potapenko, ironically, having provided Chekhov with a model for the more dubious aspects of Trigorin, was then called upon by him, after the play was finished, to undertake all the endless negotiations with the censor for him.

Nina was also contributed to by another of Chekhov's admirers, the writer Lidia Avilova, whom he treated even more high-handedly. She gave him a charm for his watch-chain with a page reference inscribed upon it, exactly as Nina does Trigorin with the medallion, and referring to a passage in one of Chekhov's stories which is exactly the same as the passage in Trigorin's works referred to by Nina's present—'If ever you have need of my life, then come and take it'. Meeting her later at a masked ball, Chekhov promised to give her the answer to this from the stage in his new play. Ronald Hingley, in his biography of Chekhov, recounts how she went to the catastrophic first night in St. Petersburg and struggled to hear the promised answer through the uproar all around her. She noted the page-reference given by Nina to locate the passage in Trigorin's works, and when she got home looked up the same page and line in a volume of her own stories. It read: 'Young ladies should not attend masked balls.' By this time, anyway, says Hingley, Chekhov had passed Avilova's fervently inscribed charm on to Komissarzhevskaya, the actress playing Nina, and it was being used on stage as a prop. If Chekhov had modelled Trigorin's behaviour with women on his own the play would have been deprived of Acts Three and Four.

It has to be recognised, I think, that there are some elements in the play which Chekhov has not completely succeeded in accommodating to his new aesthetic. Arkadina's aside after she believes she has broken Trigorin's will to leave her, 'Now he's mine,' (at any rate if played 'to herself', as written) seems to stem more from nineteenth-century dramatic convention than from life. Still, she is an actress by profession; it may be she rather than Chekhov who has imported the line from the theatre. Then again, Konstantin's account in Act Four of what has happened to Nina over the past two years seems to me awkwardly and belatedly expository, dramatically inert, and curiously old-fashioned in tone. Again, though, a similar justification might be offered—that it is only natural for Konstantin, as a writer of the time, to talk like a nineteenth-century short story. The soliloquies, too, seem to me a breach of the convention that Chekhov has established. If we are elsewhere left, as we are in life, to work out for ourselves what people are thinking and feeling from what they actually choose or happen to say to each other, why should we suddenly be given direct access, by means of a traditional stage convention, to Dorn's actual thoughts about Konstantin's play, or to Konstantin's assessment of his own stories? I was tempted to reorganise the scenes a little to avoid the need for soliloquy (it could be done fairly easily). It is true that Chekhov was still relying on soliloquy in **Uncle Vanya,** but by the time he came to write the last two plays he had abandoned it. The only apparent exception is Firs, locked into the house alone at the end of **The Cherry Orchard.** But he is not really soliloquising; he is an old man talking to himself, as he has earlier even in other people's presence.

These are small points. The other complaints which are sometimes made against the play seem to me to stem from misunderstandings. The symbolism, for instance, is occasionally disparaged as a portentous device to be outgrown by Chekhov in the three later and even greater plays. There is in fact only one piece of symbolism—though it recurs throughout the play—and that is the motif of the seagull itself. Now for a start it is not true that symbolic images of this sort do not occur in the last three plays. Moscow plainly stands for much more than its geographical self in **Three Sisters**; so does Natasha's colonisation of the Prozorovs' house; while the cherry orchard and its destruction must be one of the most suggestive and powerful symbols ever used on the stage. In the second place the symbolism of the dead seagull is set up not by Chekhov but by Konstantin, as Nina immediately recognises when he lays the bird accusingly at her feet. It is part of the portentousness and inertness of Konstantin's art, not of Chekhov's—and it is then taken up by Trigorin and absorbed into the machinery of *his,* when he discovers the dead bird and outlines his story of the girl who is destroyed with the same wilfulness and casualness. Between them they burden Nina with an image for

herself and her fate that comes to obsess her. One of the themes of the play, as I have argued, is the way in which art warps and destroys the life that it draws upon. The message of the seagull, as it stands there stuffed and forgotten at the end of the play, is precisely of the deadness of the symbolic process.

Many people, too, have had difficulty in the past with the scene in the last act between Nina and Konstantin. The difficulty has arisen because it has often been regarded, and played, as a version of the traditional mad scene, where the pathos of the heroine who has lost or been rejected by her love is demonstrated by her retreat from reality into a world of illusion. This is plainly not the case with Nina for the greater part of the scene; she gives an entirely clear, calm, and sane account of her experiences. The problem comes when she says, as she does in all the English translations of the play that I have come across, 'I am a seagull'. The poor girl thinks she is a bird; her mind in plainly going. Now, there is a much more reasonable construction to place upon her words here—and if there is a choice then a reasonable construction must surely always be preferred in interpreting a character's behaviour—but it is obscured by a difficulty in the translation of the Russian that may at first sight seem quibbingly small. In the Russian language there is no such thing as an article, either definite or indefinite. No distinction can be made, in speech or thought, between what English-speakers are forced to regard as two separable concepts—'a seagull' and 'the seagull'. So when Nina signs her letters *'Chaika'* (Seagull), it is perfectly open to Konstantin to regard this as a sign of distraction, of the sort suffered by the grief-stricken miller in Pushkin's *Rusalka,* who tells people he is a raven. But what Nina herself means, surely, when the distinction has to be made in English, is not that she is *a* seagull but that she is *the* seagull. In other words, she is not identifying with the bird but with the girl in Trigorin's story, who is the Seagull in the same way that Jenny Lind was the Swedish Nightingale, or Shakespeare was the Swan of Avon. This is the idea that has seized hold of her—not that she has white wings and a yellow beak—but that she has been reduced to the status of a manipulated character in Trigorin's fiction—a character whose fate can be summed up in a single image. This is an obsessive thought, and she makes repeated efforts to throw it off, but it is not in any sense a deluded one. She *has* been manipulated; she is another victim of the distorting and deadening process of art. One can't help wondering if Avilova and Lika Mizinova ever came to feel that they had this in common with Nina, as well as everything else.

If her picture of herself as being the seagull of Trigorin's projected story is sane and sober, so is her claim to have found her way at last as an actress. We have no way of judging whether her hopes are well-founded; but her feeling that she is on the right path at last is an entirely rational one. Konstantin takes it seriously, anyway—seriously enough to realise that he by comparison is still lost, and to shoot himself in despair as a result. Faced with that testimony to the seriousness of his judgment we are scarcely in a position to dissent.

And this in fact is the final irony of the play—that in the end the Seagull herself escapes, wounded but still flying. It is the shooter who is shot, the writer who is written to death. Konstantin, not Nina, turns out to be the real victim of Trigorin's story, the true Seagull; Konstantin, who first brought the creature down to earth and declared it to be a symbol, is the one who ends up symbolised, lying as inert and irrelevant in the next room as the poor stuffed bird is in this. Perhaps Mizinova and the others found some symbolic comfort in that.

Richard Gilman (essay date 1992)

SOURCE: "*The Seagull*: Art and Love, Love and Art," in *Chekhov's Plays: An Opening into Eternity,* Yale University Press, 1995, pp. 70-100.

[*In the essay below, which was first published in 1992, Gilman asserts:* "The Seagull *is about art and love not so much in the sense that they are its topics but in the sense that the entire play quite literally surrounds them, providing those abstractions with the dramatic context or field in which they can come to life, working themselves out as motifs.*"]

Some preliminary notes, ideas, observations, questions, and reminders for an essay on the play.

Its title is the most nearly symbolic of those for any Chekhov play but, like its closest rival, *The Cherry Orchard*'s trees, the bird isn't symbolic in any pseudopoetic or culturally anxious way.

The Russian word for the title, *chaika,* is used for both "gull," the genus, and the particular species "seagull."

The play's chief subjects are art and love, never far from each other thematically. Or perhaps a better way of putting this is in the form of questions: What does it mean to be in love? What does it mean to be an artist? And to be both in love and an artist?

This is Chekhov's first play that doesn't have a dominant figure, a protagonist whose fate, and our interest in it, dwarfs all others, and so his first thoroughly to disperse action and sentience among a considerable number of people of whom, in this instance, four can be thought of as major characters, dramatically equal; four protagonists then.

Though it ends with the suicide of one of the main characters, Chekhov made a point of calling the play a "comedy."

Its architectonics or musical structure is easily discernible, more surehandedly laid out than in *Ivanov* yet not so finely balanced as this quality of composition will become in the three plays that will follow. Another artistic advance over *Ivanov* . . . is that the earlier play's melodramatic disfigurations are mostly gone.

The Seagull stands in relation to its successors in an even more nourishing position than its predecessor does to it. How does this show itself? Obviously that will have to wait until we come to the later plays, but a few ropes into the future can be thrown out in this section.

Some commentators on the play, including Vladimir Nabokov, have chosen to dwell on the things they think faulty. Ronald Hingley, the Chekhov translator and biographer, perversely considers *The Seagull* inferior to *Ivanov.*

In his pioneering but now somewhat out-of-date study, David Magarshack accounted for Chekhov's arrival at artistic maturity in *The Seagull* by drawing a distinction between his earlier "scientific" approach to writing and a new spirit of humanistic concern, and saw an even more important differentiation between his old method of "direct" action and a new "indirect" mode of composition. How useful are these distinctions now? Do they go far enough, or too far?

My favorite critical observation about the play is from an originally unsigned review by H. de W. Fuller in the *Nation* in 1916: "If the boy [Konstantin] had had the advantage of some athletic sport, he would doubtless have worked off most of the vague feelings which he mistook for the stirrings of genius."[1]

I think the reigning spirit of *The Seagull* is that of anti-romanticism.

To write about any Chekhov play, or story for that matter, is to risk going off on digressions, the homeopathic reason for this, or the imitative fallacy involved, being his own digressive procedures, his continual deviations from an expected narrative line. Is the temptation to wander off on side-trips especially strong when writing about *The Seagull*? One reason it may be is just that relationship to the previous and ensuing plays I've mentioned. This one is so full of ripening method, archetypal situation, that one wants to seize those things for light on the whole of Chekhov's theater. Not that *The Seagull* doesn't have its own substantiality, independence, and artistic specificity; but as a storehouse of things to come it continually presses you to think ahead.

Another reason for the mind's being led afield by Chekhov is the way his writing so often suggests so much more than it directly says. All good writing does this, of course, but in his case the unstated has an especially rich life. You want to hunt down his implications, gathering them as fuel and instigation, his very reticence setting in motion the loosening of your own tongue.

I'll save the question of the title until near the end of this chapter, since by then the text, explored and meditated upon, should have something to say about its own name, and I'll look now at the words Chekhov used to describe the play, "A Comedy in Four Acts." We can assume that he knew exactly what he was doing, for he most likely chose the subtitle with the same care he exercised on those for all his other plays. *Ivanov* is a "drama," *Uncle Vanya*

Scene from the 1898 Moscow Art Theater production of The Seagull.

"Scenes from Country Life," **Three Sisters** is another "drama," and **The Cherry Orchard** is another "comedy."

All these terms or descriptive phrases are to one degree or another tactical alerts to audiences and readers. In effect they tell us not to bring to these works preconceptions about types of drama, they ask us to be supple in the way we wield artistic categories and to be open in our anticipations. The extreme flatness and neutrality of "Scenes from Country Life," for example, have an ironical quality in the light of the text, which is scarcely a pastoral idyll, but they also warn us not to expect or look for a "high" theatrical experience, one that will induce in us what we think of as pity and terror in the classical sense. On another level the subtitles would seem to indicate the relationship of the plays to each other in Chekhov's mind: lighter, graver, more subject to misinterpretation, less so, and the like.

The most notorious instance of his gentle advice being ignored was Stanislavsky's staging of **The Cherry Orchard** for its première at the Moscow Art Theater in January 1904. We will take this up again, but for now it should be noted that Stanislavsky was a most serious man; his own writings and the accounts of others tell us that wit and humor weren't his strong points. And so it isn't surprising that he directed Chekhov's last play as something of a tragedy, with a wide strain of melancholy the text does not support. Like a number of directors after him, and performers and critics for that matter, Stanislavsky wasn't able to see that for all the losses some of its characters sustain, others are given accessions, so that

The Cherry Orchard is far from being a heavy or in any way depressing play. For its mood of recognition and reconciliation, it can even be thought of as making up something like Chekhov's *Tempest.*

In much the same way **The Seagull** is also a comedy, not in spite of the suicide and other painful events but in part because of them, in a quietly original way that at the same time has classical precedents. To discuss that now would be to run far ahead of myself, but to talk more generally about "comedy" as a designation for a work it might not seem to fit wouldn't be inappropriate. And so a digression.

The two towering examples that come immediately to mind are of course *La divina commedia* and *La comédie humaine.* In both cases the word clearly isn't being used to denote a conventional genre or to describe the main substance of the works; both, after all, enclose more than enough suffering, evil, and death, everything grievous, somber, and cruel. Instead it points to or controls a final, governing response. The word "comedy" suggests the answers to the following questions: What is our state of mind or spirit supposed to be after we finish these works? How are we to understand them, to "take" them, as we like to say?

With Dante the matter is comparatively clear. Because the movement of his great poem is from suffering to rejoicing, hell to heaven, it ends happily, that much is obvious. Not so obvious, we might think, is why this outcome should earn for the entire work the description of comedy. After a little reflection we can see that it does so because such is the state of morale, the lasting attitude, wrung from the whole arduous yet ultimately successful journey "upwards," that Dante has toward his creation and that we are meant to share.

For beyond its ordinary function of making us laugh or smile, comedy has a wider and deeper action, as formal comedies like Shakespeare's have always made evident: to restore, to heal, to embolden. Just as there are "thoughts that lie too deep for tears," so there are those that lie beyond the relative simplicity of laughter. In Dante's universe, comedy is a lightness retroactively at work for those who qualify, the potentially saved (and, by analogy, for nonbelievers of goodwill, as T. S. Eliot pointed out); it's a relief from spiritual anxiety, a reminder of redemption, a restoration and a new existence of hope; it's God's difficult yet loving "joke."

Balzac uses the word in a different, much more problematic sense, deliberately and more than half-mockingly adapting his title from Dante yet in the end retaining some portion of the poet's meaning. The new title suggests a God-like perspective, with the novelist's eye replacing the divinity's omniscience. In this secular world life is comic in a negative sense because it lacks the dignity of tragedy as well as the metaphysical structure to sustain a tragic view, and in a positive one, which is to say one it does deserve, because it contains its own principle of redemption.

Forever defeating itself, like a haplessly suffering circus clown, it roughly resembles what we call a "comedy of errors," rather more grave and consequential than in customary in such a genre, no doubt, but still full of endless deviations from or betrayals of the ideal, perpetual failures of understanding, slip-ups, workings at cross-purposes, and gaffes—some of them, to be sure, with fatal outcomes. But though it may be a black farce at times, a comedy we sigh over, whose humor is often of the gallows variety, it isn't in the end conducive to despair.

This is because the imaginative act has intervened. Simply to see this roiling series of mistakes, miscalculations, and failings, this burlesque of the ideal, to observe its inexhaustible variety—comedy is always much more multifarious than tragedy—and to organize all that in the creating mind as a sort of failed *Divine Comedy,* is paradoxically enough to bring some of the relief Dante gives us. It's to offer hope through privileged perception, a "cure" through a well-wrought description of the disease. Even the darkest moments in Balzac, the particular novels or sequences within them that recoil most strongly from being called comic, take their places in the general easing of anxiety which occurs whenever experience is recovered from shapelessness and made less inexplicable.

Chekhov, it goes without saying, is much closer to Balzac than to Dante. Like the French writer, he hasn't any religious convictions that can make for comedy in a sublime sense, he isn't dealing in salvation. Like Balzac, he gives us nothing that resembles a conventional "happy ending" either. But Chekhov has an even more wry

and rueful appreciation of human folly and frailty than Balzac, and he is far less disposed to draw moral conclusions—he isn't disposed that way at all—or to impose his own views. He doesn't try to substitute for God, as Balzac often seems to be doing, nor does he claim knowledge of *everything* or wish to extend his artistic dominion over it all. His comedies aren't part of any broad "canvas" but the products of alternations in his moods or in particular visions.

When Chekhov is engaged in writing a comedy the situations he invents receive their identifying energy and shape from his decision to keep them open, not yet determined; something can be done about what otherwise would be taken as inescapable fate. Clearly the comedic aspect of *The Seagull* (and of *The Cherry Orchard* too) lies in its attitude or point of view, not in its literal series of events or despite any of them. This is so obviously true that I hesitate to make anything of it. Yet misunderstandings abound of how these things work, especially in regard to Chekhov, whose subject matter is so often seen to dictate his manner, instead of the other way round.

Attitude shows itself, of course, not declaratively but in structure, design, and tone. One thing we will see in *The Seagull* is that Chekhov constantly deflects matters away from being taken too seriously, which in this context means either tragically or in too absolute a way. This is true even in the plays he didn't call comedies, as we saw with *Ivanov* and will see again. In the more "serious" works there is still an openness to the idea that destiny may not be fatal, though physical ways out of disaster or dilemma have been closed off.

The resulting "lightness" in the noncomedies is nothing like a diminution of seriousness, and in the comedies it's nothing like frivolity. In their different ways both kinds of play offer us something like breathing room, space in which we can maneuver, take emotional or intellectual steps of our own, set matters in order, compare, *recognize.* All this is an act of freedom from what deconstructionists would call a programed response. As a corollary of this, or as its executive means, Chekhov's tone in *The Seagull* is bantering, excited, matter-of-fact, or affectionate, but never somber and never cold. He'd enjoyed writing the play, he let it be known, something rather rare for him, and the pleasure permeates the text.

In a much quoted letter of October 21, 1895, Chekhov wrote to Alexei Suvorin that he was at work on a new long play, his first since *The Wood Demon* of five or six years earlier.[2] During that interval he had several times expressed his disgust with the condition of the theater in Russia; a representative, if rather elaborate, comment was this: "We must strive with all our power to see to it that the stage passes out of the hands of the grocers and into literary hands, otherwise the theater is doomed."[3] Yet he had also given voice to those by now familiar doubts as to his own talent for writing plays; "as far as my dramaturgy is concerned, it seems to me that I was not destined to be a playwright"[4] is a comparatively mild expression of those misgivings. But now he told his friend and publisher, "I can't say I'm not enjoying writing it, though [it would have been more accurate for him to have said 'because'] I'm flagrantly disregarding the basic tenets of the stage. The comedy has three female roles, six male roles, four acts, a landscape (a view of a lake), much conversation about literature, little action and five tons of love."[5] (The Russian text actually reads five "poods" of love; a *pood* is a unit of approximately thirty-six pounds.)

Chekhov had some way to go before he finished writing it, but *The Seagull* would turn out to be almost exactly as he had described it, with the addition of a fourth, minor female character and rather more action than he had suggested. Later on I'll take up the supremely important nature of this action.

Chekhov wasn't exaggerating the weight of love in his play. It announces itself almost immediately and by the end of the first act a character will remark, "What a state they're in and what a lot of loving." As we'll see, what a cross-hatching too of amorous relationships and would-be liaisons! He wasn't over-stating, either, the prominence of what he had called "conversation about literature." Actually, the conversation—and not just that but also monologues, interjections, spoken thoughts, and private murmurings—is about fiction and writing it, plays and writing them, the state of the theater in Russia, the nature and profession of acting and, most widely and pertinently, the life of both art and the artist.

The Seagull, then, is a play, a comedy, largely "about" art and love, creativity and the erotic. I put "about" in quotation marks so as to make what I think is an important point, the one Beckett was making when he said of Joyce that "his writing is not *about* something; *it is that something itself.*"[6] This is to say that the subjects of imaginative literature—in which for my present purposes and while recognizing the difference I include plays both as texts and in performance—don't exist independently of the writing itself. They're not like prey waiting to be pounced upon by a verbally gifted hunter or seedy rooms needing to be refurbished by a painter in words. In turn writing isn't the expression or treatment of a preexisting reality but an act that discovers and gives life to a "subject" within itself.

Ibsen once said that "I have never written because I had, as they say, a 'good subject'" but out of what he called "lived-through" experience.[7] And Picasso, to turn to another art to which Beckett's observation is every bit as pertinent, said once, "Je ne cherche pas, je trouve." By which he certainly didn't mean that he found promising things to paint—just imagine him coming upon a woman with three noses or legs like giant sausages and crying "Aha!"—but that he found aesthetic reality of a visual order in the making of the painting.

Following on this *The Seagull* is about art and love not so much in the sense that they are its topics but in the sense that the entire play quite literally surrounds them, providing those abstractions with the dramatic context or field in which they can come to life, working themselves out as motifs; or rather it might be more useful to think of

them as something like "notional presences," ideas attached to bodies and impregnating them. Chekhov takes art and love *into* his writing, turning them from their disembodied state into dramatic energies. These are then deployed throughout the play, and in the process art and love necessarily assume new identities, since they are being written, not being written *about.* This is what happens whenever we encounter something in an imaginative work and say, I never saw it that way before; you couldn't have, because it wasn't that way before.

But this isn't all of it. What his characters say or think about love or art has to be revelatory of what they are, of their natures, not discrete attitudes or a series of opinions (although having more opinions than passions is itself a revelation of character). Which is only to say that themes have to be active, incarnate, endowed with physiognomies we might almost say, or else they plague us as inert, gaseous thought.

Who are these characters in so many of whom love and art have lodged or taken over like an infection? An anatomy of the dramatis personae seems in order at this point.

Irina Arkadina is a famous or at least a well-known actor. (In accordance with current tendencies and common sense, I intend from now on to use "actor" when I refer to a performer of either sex; "actress" has become silly and demeaning and ought to be buried along with "authoress" and "aviatrix." Of course Chekhov was committed to the usage of his own day, so that we'll find "actress" in the text and I'm not about to tamper with that.) Vain, voluble, a "foolish, mendacious, self-admiring egoist," Chekhov said about Arkadina, which on the play's balance might be just a bit strong; she's concerned about her son Konstantin Treplev, yet constantly forgetful of him or actively hostile, and she's in love with her companion, Boris Trigorin. Treplev is in his early twenties when the play begins, at the outset of a career as a playwright and writer of fiction; he's self-absorbed and self-pitying, with, one suspects, something of an oedipal fixation on his mother, and he's romantically in love with Nina Zarechnaya.

Trigorin is a famous writer, possibly modeled on someone Chekhov knew and containing elements of his own self (by which I mean something more specific than the usual generalities playwrights take from their own biographies for their characterizations). He's absorbed in his craft but indifferent to his celebrity. An essentially selfish man, he'll leave Arkadina for a while when he falls in love with Nina. She's an aspiring actor, sensitive, impulsive, someone we might in today's debased vocabulary call "vulnerable." She's in love with Treplev at first, then falls violently for Trigorin.

These are the four principals. It's more than interesting to note that all are actively in love and all are practicing artists in one way or another.

A few degrees below them in significant presence are Pyotr Sorin and Evgenii Dorn. Sorin is Arkadina's brother, a retired civil servant, self-deprecating, genial, yet also fussily melancholy over the imminent prospect of old age;

he's rather reminiscent of Shabelsky in *Ivanov* and somewhat of a characterological ancestor of Gayev in *The Cherry Orchard.* Dorn is one of the five doctors in Chekhov's full-length plays (only *The Cherry Orchard* lacks one); an intelligent wryly sceptical man with an impulse toward lyricism and a mild philosophical bent, he might be thought of as the only "balanced" person in the play.

The other four characters occupy with varying bulk the remainder of the dramatic space. We can think of them as participants in subplots or as secondary agencies for the working out of perception, but they are never simply functional, never purely instrumental figures like the servants, guards, and messengers of classical drama.

Ilya Shamrayev, Sorin's estate manager, is a brusque, officious, somewhat despotic man and the only character apart from Sorin who isn't either in love or the object of someone else's carnal, or at least amorous, desire. His daughter Masha is an intelligent, self-dramatizing young woman hopelessly in love with Treplev (in an early draft she turns out to be Dorn's daughter), and her mother, Polina, is an efficient, loyal family retainer lifted from a merely functional status by being unrequitedly in love with Dorn. And Simon Medvedenko, a schoolmaster both long-suffering and pedantic, pathetically desires Masha, who treats him contemptuously for his pains, though she'll later with unchanged contempt agree to marry him; he's a direct forerunner of Kulygin in *Three Sisters,* though he lacks the latter's redeeming kindness.

The setting for the comedy they enact, Sorin's estate in the country, is similar to those for all of Chekhov's major plays with the apparent exception of *Three Sisters,* which has an urban milieu; still, that play is linked to the other mises en scène by the extreme provincial dullness and isolation of the town. These settings provide Chekhov with dramatic conditions, or conditions for a drama, that wholly suit his artistic intentions; and thinking about that irresistibly compels a digression at this point.

The places are isolated, at a considerable distance from the hurly-burly and multiple distractions of big cities, from "culture," careers, formal amusements, professional entanglements, politics, ideas, the sway and clutch of complicated, often abstract associations. In his long story **"The Duel,"** written in 1891, Chekhov has a character "stuck" in the Caucasus and ardently (if a bit journalistically!) longing for the pleasures of Moscow and St. Petersburg. People in those places, he says to himself, "discuss trade, new singers, Franco-Prussian accord. Everywhere life is vigorous, cultured, intelligent, brimming with energy." And in a story written as early as 1886, **"Difficult People,"** someone is "reminded . . . of . . . Moscow, where streetlamps were burning and carriages were rattling in the streets, where lectures were being given." And then of course we will hear the Prozorov sisters' repeated "Moscow! To Moscow!" in *Three Sisters.*

In the settings Chekhov chooses, the characters, deprived of the stimulation the metropolis affords, are pressed back on themselves and on each other. Some of them—Arkadina,

Trigorin, and, at the end, Nina of **The Seagull,** Ranevskaya and some of her extended family of **The Cherry Orchard,** and the Prozorovs and army officers of *Three Sisters*—have known or will come to know what the larger world, the great world, is like. In his two comedies Chekhov offers that kind of relief from the narrowness of provincial or rural life—this is one reason they're comedies—but even so the alternative is given to us indirectly, talked about, offered as a possibility but not lived visibly on the stage.

On these isolated estates people gaze, speak, gesture, kiss, think, and weep in a severely limited atmosphere. They're enclosed in an enclave, tiny, burdensomely self-sufficient, stifling at times yet also, for the purposes of Chekhov's art, in a very special way "pure," reduced to essentials. They are far from the vast sprawling human country whose distant voices they hear, speaking of another, richer life. And they're there because Chekhov has put them there, as part of a design, so as to exist in one kind of play rather than another, not, as those who see him fundamentally as a concerned social observer think, because he looked around and there they were, leading "deprived" lives and so making up fitting objects for his famous brooding, pitying, humane, and mournful glance.

In the way he *chooses* to circumscribe the situations his characters inhabit, he is closer to Beckett than to any of his contemporaries, or to any other Russian writer for that matter; Gorky put many of his people into a romanticized poverty, Tolstoy put some of his in a romanticized asceticism. The restricted circumstances Beckett and Chekhov fashion for their plays are of another order; beneath their enormous physical differences they greatly resemble each other, for the artistic purpose of the confinement is very much the same for both.

In their plays—so much straitening, so much absence! In *Endgame* as in **Uncle Vanya,** in *Waiting for Godot* as in **Three Sisters,** the inescapable fact is that there's nothing much to do. Beckett's plays are of course far more radically denuded than Chekhov's, though they're certainly not better on that account, but the surprisingly dramatic result of the scarcity and want in the lives both playwrights invent, so unpropitious for drama, one would think, is nearly the same.

For what *is* done is closer to fundamental life than the seductions toward activity, toward choice and mobility as the very essence of meaningful existence, ever allow us to come in the conventional theater or to see in our own lives. Deprived of distractions or having to rely on their own primitive, sadly provincial, or solipsistic ones—all that keeping "the ball rolling" or fussing with the bag in Beckett, all those card or lotto games or musical evenings in Chekhov—bereft of the consolations of staying busy, on the road neither to "fulfillment," that fictive aim or shibboleth, nor to wisdom, nor even in most cases to understanding, all of Beckett's characters and nearly all of Chekhov's are reduced to the essential tasks of getting through the days and nights, making their way, with what is left to them, through time. Once again, we remember that in Chekhov's comedies more is left to them, but even so such a residue is on hold, so to speak, reserved for the future, which in both dramatists, for highly significant reasons (which in Chekhov's case we'll take up later), has no status, is simply a fiction.

And then, or rather along with this, they go off in that quintessential human way of holding back the darkness, they talk; they tell their lives, they ad lib their hopes, joys and sorrows, creating their fates in language as they go, more precisely our recognition of their fates. These outwardly minimal existences come to us with all the freshness, peculiar as the word may sound in this context, of the root, of the way it is at bottom, Beckett's *comme c'est ça.* "Oh what a curse, mobility," Winnie cries out in *Happy Days.* The artistic undoing of the curse, the blessing, makes itself felt in the characters having to stay still; this is the condition in which we can see "how it is."

And so the characters of *The Seagull* talk. Naturally, there are physical events too, but nearly all of the decisive ones take place off stage. This is one of the things Chekhov meant when he spoke of consciously ignoring the fundamental tenets of the stage, and it is at the center of David Magarshack's argument about Chekhov's emergent mastery. The subject is so dense and important that I'm tempted to go off in full pursuit right now, but I'll content myself with simply saying here that among the theatrical principles, pieties we might better call them, he was challenging was the notion that off stage is only for actions which for reasons of propriety or mechanical impossibility can't be shown directly. In Greek and Roman drama, of course, important events took place off stage, as they did in Shakespeare and other classical writers, but for the most part these were events inconvenient or impossible to show, and in any case for a long time off stage had been chiefly where the stagehands waited.

ART

As he does in every one of his full-length plays after *Ivanov,* Chekhov quickly brings on all the persons of the drama. From *The Seagull* on no play will fail to introduce well before the end of the first act everyone of any significance—which is to say nearly everyone, since almost no Chekhov character, however "minor," lacks dramatic weight. The strategic point of this is that it can work against the linear or accumulating movement of the usual play. Nobody will come on stage later, bringing important news or actively furthering developments and so extending a line of more or less strictly unfolding narrative. The quietly revolutionary effect of this is that characters take their places almost like players in a game such as basketball or soccer, occupying a field and ready for whatever will happen.

The very first stage direction informs us that art, in the form of the theater itself, is going to figure in *The Seagull.* Setting the scene, Chekhov writes of a stage "hastily put together for an amateur performance" and of "workmen . . . coughing and hammering . . . behind the lowered curtain." Then in the first lines of dialogue "love" also makes its first appearance, in intimate if a little ludicrous connection to art.

Medvedenko and Masha are on and, glancing at the crude stage, she says, "The Play will start soon." "Yes," Medvedenko says, "Konstantin Gavrilovich wrote it, and Nina Zarechnaya will act in it. They're in love, and tonight their souls will merge in the creation of a single artistic symbol." After this banality he goes on to complain that unlike Nina and Konstantin "my soul and yours don't share a common ground." Masha has a moment earlier indicated her own lovesickness in the play's wonderful second line, the dourly cryptic "I'm in mourning for my life," after Medvedenko's opening "How come you always wear black?"

After a few more exchanges they're soon joined by all the other characters, who lay out for us, offhandedly and in some respects unconsciously, most of their ruling qualities and idiosyncracies, as well as what binds them factually and emotionally to one another. Little signatures show themselves—Sorin's self-deprecating laugh and his habit of finishing his remarks with "and that sort of thing" or "and so on," Dorn's bemused singing of snatches of songs—the kind of thing that so unaccountably irritated Nabokov. And we hear the first mention of a seagull when Nina says that she feels drawn to the lake as though she were one of those birds.

They've gathered for the performance of Konstantin's play. They're mostly in an amiable mood, except for Masha, who's almost never amiable, Treplev, who's nervous, and Arkadina, who's clearly disgruntled by her son's having dared to step onto her territory. "When is this thing ever going to start?" she asks and then breaks out in a pointed, only partially accurate quote from Shakespeare—"My son! Thou turn'st mine eyes into my very soul . . . ," to which Konstantin replies with another (paraphrased) speech from *Hamlet* that in the most literary way reveals his oedipal rivalry with Trigorin (he's already revealed his envy of him as a writer): "Nay, but to yield to wickedness, to seek [out] love in the depths of sin."

The inner play begins with a prologue by Konstantin, who "loudly" orates: "Oh, you venerable old shadows that linger above this lake at night. . . ." The curtain parts to reveal Nina, in white, sitting on a large rock. "People, lions, eagles and partridges, horned deer, geese, spiders, silent fish dwelling in the water," she begins, launching into a long futuristic monologue that speaks of a time when everything in the world is dead except for some vague spirit that will do battle with the Devil and, victorious, will bring "matter and spirit . . . together in perfect harmony."

The "decadent gibberish," as Arkadina so cruelly yet not without reason will call it, suggests the worst of German expressionist drama of a generation later, in its whole tone and in specific lines like "I am that great World Spirit." Still, it does give some evidence of anarchic talent and urgent ambition and this, rather than any reasoned scornfulness, lies behind Arkadina's jibes, so jealous is she of what she considers her own fiefdom. After she's interrupted Nina several times, Konstantin abruptly stops the performance, saying bitterly, "I'm sorry. I forgot that writing plays and acting in them was only for the chosen few. I intruded on your domain!" Everyone is left buzzing.

In a generally most perceptive essay on *The Seagull,* Robert Louis Jackson makes an ingenious case for Konstantin's play as being highly significant in its own right.[8] He offers a detailed reading of it in terms of a creation myth, a metaphor for the artist's journey and a disguised oedipal confession, and then extends his findings beyond their source and into the main text. I owe a great deal to Jackson's other ideas and will make grateful use of them in this section, but I think he makes too much of this one.

Whatever the literary motifs of Konstantin's little play, they seem to me less important in themselves than what, among other things, they tell us about Konstantin himself, which, to be sure, Jackson partly acknowledges. Yet he pushes his interpretation a little too far, somewhat over-loading with abstract ideas a relatively uncomplicated if subtle comedy, and in the process losing sight of a very concrete function of the inner play, which, as I see it, is to set going talk about art and the artist. We can be sure that Chekhov didn't provide Konstantin with any old overblown piece of writing in an effort to discredit him, but he didn't give him such an arcane and ponderously philosophic one as Jackson thinks either. (I don't want to leave this point without stressing how enormously useful Jackson's insights are in general; his ideas about *The Seagull* as a play about what being an artist means are some of the main sources of my own thinking.)

The talk set in motion by the inner play, Chekhov's "conversation about literature," which as I said earlier is about other things as well, begins even before the aborted performance. "It's hard to act in your play," Nina tells Konstantin as they wait for the others to take their places, "it has no living characters." "Living characters!" Konstantin explodes. "We must represent life not as it is, and not as it should be, but as it appears in our dreams." Nina calmly ignores this, going on to say, "There's so little action, it's just one long monologue. And I think every play really ought to have some love interest."

The exchange tells us a good deal about where they are in relation to their art at this point and obliquely suggests their eventual destinations in the comedy. Treplev's ideas are vague, soft, *inexperienced,* making up a young man's aesthetic, and they're peculiarly belligerent. He'll drop the programmatic aspect later on, but for tactical reasons, not out of conviction, when he turns into a technician in the fiction he comes to write. But he won't overcome the absence of life from his work, and by continually trying to justify his writing on one basis or another, most often by attacking other people's, he reveals something dangerously defensive, polemical, and theoretical in his approach to art.

As for Nina, she's basically right in her criticism but she too betrays a weakness, provisional in her case, as it happens; her remark about a play needing "love interest" indicates that she's not yet a serious actor, or artist, but is in the preliminary phase of being stage-struck. We should notice that in a delicious piece of irony Chekhov has written her into a play with an abundance of what might be called love interest, only of a kind whose weight

and dramatic implications are as far as they can be from what she means here.

Treplev's play provokes other responses besides Nina's and Arkadina's and each provides a little revelation of character. Trigorin is neutral, evasive in his "Every person writes what he wants to and can" and Medvedenko adds to his reputation for boring pedantry with "No one has the right to separate spirit from matter, since perhaps spirit itself is the sum total of material atoms." Dorn's surprising approval—"I liked the play. There's something to it"—can be ascribed to his usual kindness but is better explained by his confession to Konstantin after praising him that if "I could have experienced thc lift of the spirit that artists feel when they create something, it seems to me . . . I'd have flown away from earth and into the sky." And the play also inspires Sorin to confess to having in his youth had aspirations to being a writer.

Understandably, the talk about art and the artist has as its chief participants Treplev, Trigorin, Arkadina, and, with especially great consequence at the end, Nina. They are the artists and each has something to elucidate, press for, or defend. In everything they say we can feel Chekhov's presence, in more than the obvious sense of his having written the dialogue; the points of view and attitudes he presents touch, often intimately, on his own concerns as a writer. He doesn't necessarily endorse any of them, he clearly disapproves of some, but he anchors the "debate" in animate personalities who have a stake in its outcome, and so keeps it from becoming abstract.

As we would expect, Treplev is most vociferous. Besides the conversation with Nina before his play begins he also talks to Sorin about his mother and the theater, the two "topics" merging into one argument. "She loves the theater," he says of Arkadina, "she thinks she's serving humanity, the sacred art, but in my opinion the contemporary theater is stuck in a rut. . . . These great talents, high priests of . . . art . . . they try to dig up a moral from banal pictures and phrases . . . a thousand variations [of] the same old thing."

To this point his views would certainly have been echoed by Chekhov (except for the note of envy they contain), as would his remark about needing a new kind of theater. But when he adds, "We need new forms . . . and if we can't have them, we're better off with nothing," an alarm ought to go off.

As we know, Chekhov never spoke of "new forms." He wanted changed morale, a theater of truthfulness and re-siliency instead of dead mechanics, but he never con-sciously or avowedly aspired to technical change or pur-sued it as an end in itself, as Konstantin seems to do. When Trigorin says of him that "he grumbles, snorts and preaches about new forms," the verbs suggest that Kon-stantin's quest for originality has something inorganic and inauthentic about it, in large part because it's a mis-sion too conscious by far.

At the end of the play, after he's achieved an empty success as a writer of fiction, Konstantin will partly recognize his own condition. "I've talked so much about new forms," he tells himself, "and now I feel that I'm gradually falling into a rut." He unhappily ponders Trigorin's "easy" methods for a while, quoting some images from one of Trigorin's stories (actually they're from a Chekhov story, **"Wolf"**), comparing them to his own stressful, slick, and brittle style (qualities we identify from his own and others' comments), and then says, "This is agony. (Pause.) Yes, I'm coming to believe more and more that what's important isn't old and new forms at all, but the fact that one writes without thinking of any forms. A person writes because it flows freely from his soul."

Chekhov isn't advocating, through Treplev, any naive or primitive aesthetic; he's not saying anything so simple-minded as "The hell with how you write, it's what you write that counts." But for him technique was always in the service of vision and experience, not the other way round, just as originality was a possible outcome and never a goal. Konstantin's "agony" is spiritual, not the result of wrong methods. Dorn, who admires him, says near the end, "It's a pity . . . that he doesn't have any particular mission." (This is an observation Chekhov had made in his preliminary notes on the Treplev character; for "mission" or, another possible translation, "aims" we can read "intentions beyond the ego.") "He conveys an impression and nothing more. And impressions alone won't get you . . . far." Trigorin sums it up: "There's something strange and vague about his work. . . . He doesn't have a single living character." A most subtle point Chekhov is making about Konstantin is that in the dominion of art, ideas, no matter how "correct," don't guarantee anything.

Trigorin talks even more about writing than does Konstantin, but never aggressively and never as a matter of theory. Quite the contrary: in the play's longest speeches he tells Nina about the writer's, or artist's, life, countering with prosaic, deflating comments her breathlessly romantic notions of what it must be like. When she speaks of "fascinating, brilliant lives full of meaning," he replies, "All these nice words—forgive me—remind me of . . . candy, which I never eat." When she insists that his "life must be wonderful," he says, "What's so good about it?" and goes on to tell her that writing for him is compulsive, not a matter of inspiration. "I write without a break, like a runaway train. . . . I can't help it. What's so wonderful and brilliant about that?"

In her infatuation with him or at least as much with the life he seems to inhabit, Nina continues to press him. When he keeps denying that his vocation is glamorous, she tells him, "You're simply spoiled by success." Trigorin's reply is crucial to an understanding of Chekhov's idea of the artist in *The Seagull,* as are also some balancing things Nina will say at the end. "What success?" he asks. "I've never pleased myself. I don't like myself as a writer. Worst of all, I'm in a kind of stupor and often don't understand what I write."

The words may not precisely represent Chekhov's feelings and attitude in every respect, but the self-critical position does. He once wrote in his notebook that "dis-

satisfaction with oneself is one of the fundamental qualities of every true talent," and this, among other things, is what distinguishes Trigorin from Treplev, whose later self-depreciation is a matter of injured ego, not creative modesty. Moreover, Trigorin's scoffing at Nina's immature idea of success—acclaim by the world—echoes Chekhov's often expressed and passionately held opinion that success defined in that way is more than contemptible. Though he wasn't without a reasonable interest in his own reputation, he hated the sort of celebrity which produced followers, a cult. In 1898 he wrote to Lydia Avilova, an erstwhile fiction writer who was in love with him, that "writing itself is not what repels me but this literary entourage, from which one has no escape."[9]

There are other connections between Trigorin and Chekhov, including, on a minor note, their both being avid fishermen. When, for example, Trigorin tells Nina that early in his career, when he was a playwright, he was afraid of the public, he says, "When I had to stage a new play, it always seemed to me that the dark-haired people in the audience were hostile and the light-haired people were cool and indifferent."[10] This is an immediate reminder of a well-known letter of Chekhov's to Suvorin in which he says that before performances of *Ivanov* he was sure that "the dark-haired men" among the onlookers would be "hostile." None of this is to say that Trigorin is anything like Chekhov's alter ego; there are extremely important differences between them, which I'll take up later. But the connections are clear.

If Trigorin isn't an egotist about his work, he's not free from one occupational disease of the writer, which is to exploit others for the sake of one's art. "I try," he tells Nina, "to catch you and myself in every sentence—every word—and I rush off . . . to lock up all those sentences and words in my literary storehouse on the off-chance they might come in handy." And indeed we see him at this work of plucking what he calls the living "flowers" for imaginative use. Into his ever-present notebook go jottings about Masha—"Takes snuff and drinks vodka. . . . Always wears black. Loved by the school teacher"—and Nina too: "A plot for a short story," a story about her and a seagull, he says of one note she sees him making.

Dangerous as it is to interpolate from a writer's life to the work, it seems justified at times and this is one of those cases. On several occasions, most notably concerning a short story of 1891, **"The Butterfly,"** Chekhov was accused of having exploited for literary purposes some embarrassing facts about friends of his. He denied any conscious intention of doing it and there is no reason not to believe him, but the matter must have remained vaguely oppressive to him. We're put in mind of how Ibsen tried to expiate in his last plays his guilt for having "sacrificed" to his art the people closest to him, his wife and son. While Chekhov is nowhere near such moral anguish, he does, I think, render Trigorin in part as a cautionary figure and a delegate from his own conscience.

Arkadina doesn't talk so much about art as about the artist—herself, as it happens. Chekhov called her an "egoist" and many touches contribute to a portrait of the actor as Narcissus. We've seen Arkadina attack her son for his own artistic ambitions; later she'll announce that she's never read his published stories, "I just don't have the time." In their famous quarrel as she bandages his self-inflicted head wound, she tells him that he has "no talent—just pretensions" and he in turn calls her a "hack." Though it's not quite fair, Konstantin's epithet is rather more accurate. Fame, éclat, position are what his mother wants. When she does speak about acting, it's to call attention to her successes: "They gave me the warmest reception in Kharkov, my dears. My head is still spinning! . . . I wore a gorgeous gown."

There's fine irony and splendidly deft characterization in her reaction to a Maupassant story they've been reading aloud at the beginning of Act Two. Arkadina reads from "On the Water": "When a woman has chosen a writer whom she wishes to captivate, she bombards him with compliments, kindnesses and favors." She breaks off reading to say, "Well, that may be true for the French, but we're not like that at all" and then reads some more lines to herself and tells Nina that "the rest isn't interesting or . . . accurate."

She speaks highly of Trigorin's stories, but we suspect that, as was true of her son's work, she hasn't read them, having instead captured him and his name. She's a miser who gives three servants a ruble to split among themselves; she's a prima donna in almost every respect. But though she clearly incarnates Chekhov's deep dislike for the artist or practitioner consumed by self, something a little more positive about her, a few bases for redemption, escapes his authorial vigilance. She does love her brother and in a beleaguered way her son, and is generous enough to encourage Nina to go on the stage.

Whether or not she is a really bad actor, a fake in other words, as some commentators think she is, seems to me not to be the point. We've only Treplev's assertion that she's a "hack" (or "drone," as the Russian word *rutinyor* can also be translated); in his screed against her, Chekhov never even hints that she's untalented. No, her presence in the play is as a specimen of existence and behavior in whom self-absorption is a deep coloration. She should never be played on a single strident note, for she isn't a villain but the occupant of one end of a spectrum covering the variations of selves as they engage with love and art, the way Nina stands at the other end.

Nina. I wrote earlier of how she begins as stage-struck and of her infatuation with some presumedly thrilling elements of artistic life; as an aspect of that phase we see her also as "star-struck." When Shamrayev rudely tells Arkadina that no horses are available to take her to the station, Nina says to Polina, "To refuse . . . a famous actress! Surely her slightest wish, her merest whim, is more important than your farm? Simply incredible!" The evolution, or education, that carries her far past these immature conditions of mind and spirit lies behind Chekhov's having written, "To me, Nina's part is everything in the play."[11] But I have to defer my consideration of how this "everything" accumu-

lates and decisively asserts itself, until we have the rest of *The Seagull*'s substance in our grasp.

LOVE

If we were to imagine a piece of music inspired by some aspect of *The Seagull*, a likely one might be called "The Love Variations" or maybe, borrowing from Bach, "Chaconne for Violin Solo on an Amorous Theme." "Five tons of love," Chekhov had jestingly said the play contained, but of course the real point isn't such undifferentiated heft but the diversity on display, and the intermeshings. In that last regard there are moments when we're reminded of Arthur Schnitzler's play *Reigen* or, as it's better known to us, *La ronde*, written five years later out of a very different, far narrower sensibility and idea but somewhat resembling Chekhov's play in the way its characters link up in a chain of carnality or carnal aspiration, as well as in a skein of romantic longing.

I'll begin with the lesser characters' desires, all of them, as it happens, unsatisfied. I say "as it happens," but Chekhov never lets things simply happen, for he's always and wholly the deliberate artist. Not to have your cravings fulfilled is as instructive and dramatic as to attain satisfaction, especially in light of the fact that for the major characters satisfaction is always partial, temporary, or fugitive. What love *doesn't* do or bring is a central "action" of *The Seagull,* and how it affects other aspects of life, most pointedly the morale of artistic practice, is another and even more important one.

Medvedenko loves Masha, Masha loves Konstantin, Polina loves Dorn. None of these lovers is, in the old-fashioned term, requited, and much of the play's lower level or integumentary buzz and hum of conversation and musings is made up of their sense of injury or deprivation. Medvedenko is the first to declare his emotion, to which Masha's response is, "I'm touched by your love but I can't love you back and that's that." Then, in a fine example of how Chekhov, beginning with *The Seagull,* will often have his characters change the subject whenever it threatens to become too ponderous—or, at times, too disturbing—she adds, "Have some [snuff]." Later, in despair over Konstantin's indifference to her, she consents to marry Medvedenko, rationalizing her decision to Trigorin: "To love without hope, to wait whole years for something. . . . But when I get married I won't have time for love."

She's lying or deceiving herself. When she does marry Medvedenko she continues to treat him with brutal scorn and keeps the torch burning for Treplev, to the point where her mother Polina embarrassingly pleads with him on her behalf: "All a woman needs, Kostya, is to be looked on kindly. I know for myself." For her part Polina "imploringly" says to Dorn, "Evgenii, my dear, my beloved, let me come and live with you." Dorn, who earlier had made the remark about the "lot of loving" going on, tells her, "I'm fifty-five . . . it's too late for me to change my life." The most sceptical of all the characters, as well as the most detached, Dorn moves to deflect and disarm the passions swirling

Act I of the 1898 Moscow Art Theater production of The Seagull.

around him with bits of balladry, half-mocking commentary on the love-charged atmosphere: "Tell me not your young life's ruined" and "Oh, speak to her, you flowers."

These three minor characters in love aspire to an "other" as an agency of deliverance: Medvedenko from his material and emotional impoverishment and the lack of self-esteem his sententiousness masks; Polina from her unhappy marriage to the cold-spirited Shamrayev; Masha from the emptiness of a life without any man she thinks equal to the high estimate she's made of her own worth—Medvedenko clearly doesn't fill the bill. And motivations or dispositions like these are present in the major characters too, only with greater complication and weightier consequences.

Arkadina needs Trigorin for her own amour propre and as a shield against the loneliness or, more deeply, the solipsism her selfish, brittle life creates. In turn Trigorin stays placidly with her, out of what he calls his "flabby, spineless" nature (one way he doesn't resemble Chekhov!), until his writer's quest for new material and his need for emotional replenishment, or rejuvenation, encounter Nina. She begins by being in love with Konstantin, mildly, as a kind of early habit, we suspect, then falls for Trigorin, who seems to beckon with the promise of a glamorous new life. And Konstantin needs Nina for reasons of ego as well as for a muse, a reliable source of inspiration.

And so for all the characters-in-love the common condition is need. This sometimes displays itself directly, but more often it makes its way to everyone's consciousness through speech whose excessiveness and rhetorical zeal betray a disjunction between feeling and fact, emotion and its object. I said at the beginning that I think the prevailing spirit of *The Seagull* is one of "antiromanticism." This negative quality is grounded precisely on repeated expressions of romantic desire itself, flowery outbursts about the wonders of the other and dirges on love's absence. The characters lay bare their hearts and in so doing reveal their dreamy or febrile overvaluation of love.

Listen to the twittering eloquence of the love birds, along with some harsher notes:

> Konstantin on Nina: "I can't live without her. . . . Even the sound of her footsteps is wonderful. . . . My enchantress, my dream. . . ."

> Masha (talking to Dorn) on Konstantin: "I'm suffering. No one, no one knows how I suffer! (Puts her head on his breast, quietly.) I love Konstantin."

> Trigorin on Nina: "Young love . . . delightful and poetic—that carries you off to a world of daydreams— only such love can give one happiness on this earth." And to her: "You're so wonderful . . . your marvelous eyes . . . your indescribably . . . tender smile . . . that expression of angelic purity. . . ."

> Nina to Trigorin: "If you should ever need my life, then come and take it," a line from a short story, ostensibly by him but actually from Chekhov's **"The Neighbors,"** which Nina has had engraved on a medallion. And to herself: "It's a dream."

Arkadina to Trigorin: "My wonderful, marvelous man.
. . . My happiness, my pride, my joy. . . . If you
leave me, even for one hour, I won't survive. I'll go
out of my mind."

A few notes on these urgencies and avowals. One of
Chekhov's purposes throughout his writing is to expose
or, if that's too harsh, to bring out the ways we fashion
our feelings out of culture, articulating them along literary—that is to say borrowed—lines. Konstantin's "I can't
live without her" is just such an appropriation; the point
is we do live without "her" or "him," or ought to be able
to if it becomes necessary and, in the way *The Seagull*
unfolds, Konstantin's incapacity to do this, his making an
almost literal condition out of a stock phrase will become
part of a cautionary tale.

The line on the medallion Nina gives to Trigorin, from
Chekhov's story **"The Neighbors,"** was actually engraved
on a medallion by Lydia Avilova; on the back were the
words "Short Stories by Anton Chekhov." Avilova evidently hoped to stir his passion, but Chekhov wasn't to
be moved by such a literary solicitation, not even of his
own authorship.

ART AND LOVE

Those two themes or motifs or subjects—better to go
back to a term I coined earlier, "notional presences"—
begin to converge as the play moves toward its close. In
a brilliant stroke of the dramatic imagination, which I'll
discuss more fully a little later on, Chekhov prepares the
way for the final fusion of these presences—the confrontation at the end between Konstantin and Nina—by having some of the narrative's central pieces of action occur
off stage.

At the end of Act Three, which closes on a "prolonged"
kiss between Nina and Trigorin, a stage direction reads,
"Two years pass between the third and fourth acts." The
events of this period include Masha's marriage to
Medvedenko, Treplev's unexpected literary success and,
most important, Nina's affair with Trigorin and the subsequent start of her career on the stage. All this news
reaches us almost entirely through apparently casual conversations; one in particular, concerning Nina, is between
Dorn and Konstantin, who has kept up with her life, even
"follow[ing] her" secretly for a time.

The facts, as he knows them, are these: Nina had a baby,
who died, Trigorin "fell out of love with her" and went
back to Arkadina, and the "disaster" of Nina's life, as
Konstantin sees it, extended to her acting stints in provincial theaters. He saw some of her performances and tells
Dorn that her acting was "crude . . . with a good deal of
ranting and raving," though with a few high histrionic
notes too—"she screamed . . . and died brilliantly." Later
he'd had some letters from her, "intelligent . . . warm and
interesting" ones, but he had "felt that she was deeply
unhappy." She'd seemed to him "slightly unhinged" and
had strangely signed the letters "Seagull."

Chekhov drew most of his material for Nina's life away
from our gaze from a longish piece of fiction of his own
called **"A Boring Story,"** written in 1889. In the story a
stage-struck young woman runs away with an actor, has
a child who dies in infancy, is jilted by her lover, and then
goes on the stage, although she has severe doubts about
her talent. To this point her story is almost exactly Nina's,
but the moral and intellectual consequences of these
material details are wholly different for Katya of the fiction
and Nina, as we'll see in a moment.

The Seagull's climactic actions, some of the most passionately unfolding and swiftly revelatory in all of Chekhov, begin with Konstantin in his room, meditating on
writing, technique, his own feeling of sterility. The others
are playing lotto in an adjoining room. Nina knocks on the
French window and when Konstantin brings her in she
"puts her head on his breast and sobs quietly," reminding
us of Masha's having done the same thing earlier with
Dorn.

But once again, as so often in Chekhov, material actions
that resemble each other have entirely different aftermaths.
From this point on, in Konstantin's and Nina's agitated,
discordant, and ultimately "failed" conversation, everything having to do with art and love, talent and the ego,
is brought together and we witness what can best be
described as the exposure and testing of the two characters' deepest—or rather, since Chekhov isn't interested in
depth psychology, their most dramatically representative—
selves.

For Konstantin, Nina's reappearance seems to be a miracle; she's come back to save him, he thinks. Earlier he had
told his mother, "She doesn't love me and I can't write
any more," but now his hope springs up. Nina is at first
bewildered, almost incoherent at times, struggling to express the hard wisdom her recent life has taught her and
about which Konstantin knows nothing, despite his possession of the "facts."

"I'm a seagull," she says several times, identifying herself
with the bird as victim and with her youth at the lake, and
then, "No, that's not right," quickly taking on a real description, not a fictive one—"I'm an actress." And she
says to him, still partly under the sway of their easy
youthful romance and shared ambitions, "So, you've become a writer. You're a writer, and I'm an actress." Then,
in a prologue to the rapid, violent change in attitude she
will soon have to him, a movement away from the way-
wardness of memory and the pull of early desire, she tells
him, "I loved you and dreamed of being famous. But
now—." The "now" indicates that neither of these things
is any longer true and the break leads her to recite a few
details of her physical life as an actor. She thus unwittingly baits a trap into which Konstantin will immediately fall.

Ignoring her words and so revealing that his interest in
her is selfish and instrumental, a function of his need,
Konstantin pours out his misery and persisting desire,
telling her that since she left him "life's been unbearable"
for him. Then, in the most fateful line in the play, he says

to her, "I call out to you, kiss the ground you walked on." To which Nina, "taken aback," responds, "Why does he talk this way?" emphasizing the crisis by saying it again, "Why does he talk this way?"

Nina's use of the impersonal "he" instead of "you" beautifully indicates her sudden understanding of Konstantin's character, so that her "why"s aren't really questions but a recognition and an expression of regret. He has in effect hanged himself by the romanticism that coats her in such sentimental language and by his having pinned his sense of himself as a writer, his vocational ego, to her erstwhile and potential love for him. Early in the play he had engaged in the "she loves me, she loves me not" game with the petals of a flower (in relation to his mother), and this seemingly innocuous activity can be seen in retrospect as a foreshadowing of his fatal lack of emotional maturity.

What Nina regrets or fleetingly mourns is, I think, her loss of innocence in regard to Konstantin, the death of their shared values and beliefs. She has already lost her larger, more comprehensive innocence. In several long, beautifully modulated speeches she traces the course of her spiritual growth. Because of "the worries of love, jealousy" and his "always laugh[ing] at my dreams," her life with Trigorin had made her "petty and small-minded" and her acting had "lost all meaning" and suffered "terribly." But now, she says, "I'm not like I was." Through a process of maturation that Chekhov doesn't describe, and doesn't have to, she has learned to esteem herself and "delight in" her work. Most significant for *The Seagull*'s pervasive themes, she has learned what it means to be an artist.

"I know now, I understand," she tells Konstantin, "that in our work—it doesn't matter whether we act for the stage or write—the most important thing isn't fame or glory, or anything I had dreamed about, but the ability to endure. To know how to bear your cross and have faith . . . when I think about my vocation, I'm not afraid of life."

For all their differences, Nina has come to share with Trigorin an attitude towards what it means to be an artist, or rather towards what it ought not mean. It isn't "fame or glory" that one should be after, it's not narrow egoistic satisfaction but something strangely "impersonal," worked at with a kind of detached love or at least a freedom from self-importance. Nina is more "advanced" than Trigorin, we might say, more "positive"; but both are better equipped to go on, to survive, than Konstantin, whose sick ego is lost in conflicting realms of types of satisfaction.

We'll remember that Nina's education began with Trigorin's deflation of her romantic view of the artist's life, in those speeches of his about how unglamorous it really is. And now her speech to Konstantin completes the process of maturation, or is its sign. In various ways Nina's idea of "enduring," spiritual stamina, will be active in every Chekhov play to come; the great difference between Katya of **"A Boring Story"** and Nina is that the girl of the story gives up in the face of adversity.

In profound contrast to Treplev's having allowed his romantic hunger for Nina to ruin his self-possession, she neither denounces Trigorin nor pines for him, as a lesser dramatist would certainly have made her do; instead she confesses to still loving him, "passionately, desperately," yet without allowing this to at all weaken her resolve to forge her own life as an artist or in any way diminish her determination to endure. She has been able to separate the realms of love and work, the *Lieben und Arbeit* of Freud's prescription for a happy life, those two central components, of which most often it's only given us to possess one.

When she leaves she allows herself a moment of fond remembrance, quoting from Konstantin's little play, something from their mutual past. Along the way she has exorcised the image of the seagull with which both Trigorin, for whom she and the bird had been material for a story, and Konstantin, stuck in barren literary imaginings, continue to identify her.

Left to himself, Konstantin offers one last revelation of his weakness and immaturity. If his mother were to learn of Nina's visit, he thinks, "It might upset her." A few minutes later, from behind his closed door, we hear the shot.

THE ART OF *THE SEAGULL*

"I'm flagrantly disregarding the basic tenets of the stage."[12] In that famous high-spirited letter I quoted from earlier, Chekhov, for one of the few times we know about, spoke of, or at least alluded to, matters of technique in his work, the methods he was choosing to make his plays take the shapes he wanted them to have. Uncharacteristically, he had claimed originality for *Ivanov,* but that was in regard to its plot, which, we'll remember, he had called "unprecedented" because it had broken with the long tradition of plays as moral struggles, pitched between heroes and villains. And though *Ivanov* had exhibited a number of innovative dramaturgical steps, they were uncertain or incomplete and were surrounded by elements of a not yet fully superseded practice; nor, in any case, did Chekhov make mention of any of them.

The most basic theatrical "tenet" he was ignoring in the composition of *The Seagull* was that of the nature of *action,* as this was conceived by the largely melodramatic or farcical imagination out of which at the time proceeded nearly all the plays of the reigning French style and its Russian imitations. But this principle he was spurning or sidling around had energized most classical drama too, though much more subtly.

A play has to be materially active, it was thought, full of incidents or built around one or two really big ones, and what physically happens on the stage is of a different order from, and almost always more decisive than, what is said. Chekhov's implicit reply to this was that speech can be a good part, perhaps even most, of what "happens" in a play, as much an action as any sword thrust or discovery of a lover in a closet or arrival of a letter with fateful news.

Eugène Scribe, the high priest of *les drames des boule-vardes,* those well-made plays of French popular theater, once wrote that "when my story is right, when I have the events of my play firmly in hand, I could have my janitor write it." How can you not be impressed by the magnif-icent shamelessness of this assertion, which stands as the polar opposite of Chekhov's method, indeed of his entire sense of drama as an art?

For him events don't dictate the writing but very nearly the other way round. Speech is action, something taking place. Dialogue can therefore be much more than comment on physical activity, or an environment for it, an instiga-tion toward it, or its verbal counterpart. Beginning with *The Seagull* things *said* in Chekhov's theater constitute most of the drama. Material occurrences have their own necessity and integrity, but in a shift with enormous con-sequences for the future of the stage, they mainly serve now to spring speech—the executive instrument of thought—into life, behaving as language's outcomes more than its causes. Or events accompany language as a sort of ballast, preventing words from flying off like balloons, the way they do in the sort of sterile dramas we discon-solately call "talky," of which Konstantin's little play at the beginning of *The Seagull* is an example.

That the play's chief physical eventfulness—Nina's flight with Trigorin, her baby's birth and death and her early career as an actor; Masha's marriage to Medvedenko; the shooting of the gull; and Konstantin's suicide—that all this takes place off stage, out of view, with most of the events not even made known until time has passed, has several powerful effects. It deeply undercuts if it doesn't entirely eliminate the possibility of melodramatic excess; it "cools" the play down and so allows reflectiveness to control sensation; and it therefore enables us to experi-ence the play more as a pattern of animate consciousness, a set of moral and psychic rhythms and discoveries, than as a narrow, emotionally overwrought tale.

This shift from the explicit to the implied or reported on, from activity before our eyes to that which reaches us through language, is the movement David Magarshack so usefully if incompletely and programatically described as being from "direct" action to "indirect." For all its basic accuracy the formulation is too neat; it tends to blur the relationship between physicality and speech and gives insufficient weight to language's own directness, the way it can exist as action in its own right. In his effort to account for the radical change in Chekhov's dramaturgy, Magarshack saw the process in too formulaic a way, but his fundamental argument—that at some point Chekhov stopped building his plays around large physical scenes in favor of a dispersal of action and the replacement of statement by suggestion—was a greatly original percep-tion at the time and remains essentially sound.

Whatever its nature, the "indirect" has the great and mysterious virtue of freeing us from the tyranny of a priori assumptions, the ones on which sentimental drama, or any heavily plotted kind, is based. Melodrama, I once wrote, "may be defined as physical or emotional action for its

own sake, action without moral or spiritual consequences or whose consequences of those kinds have atrophied and turned into cliché precisely by having been the sta-ples of previous 'high' drama." Theater—this is as good a time as any to say it—is the most cannibalistic of the arts, forever chewing on its own history.

The a priori assumptions—amorous passion can be fatal, murder is detestable, a cuckold is ridiculous, and the like—move us in the direction of the already known; they create a stasis of imagination, its defeat, really, by sensation, habit, cliché. On the most trivial level physicality tends to carry its own fixed meanings; to scratch one's head is to indicate bewilderment, to shake one's fist, anger. In regard to the theater, where the connections between inner and outer reality are of course paramount, these correspon-dences have always been present and were more than once codified, perhaps most notably by Goethe, who composed a manual for actors in which a great range of emotions and states of being were given their "correct" physical equivalents or objective correlatives.

We may be more sophisticated than that, yet so strong is our compulsion to read things this way, so thorough has been our indoctrination in it, that one secret of good acting, *pace* Goethe, is to make gestures that are unex-pected, unpredictable, yet that feel exactly right in the *aesthetic* context—to scratch one's head in anger, it might be, for the purposes of this argument, or to shake one's fist in bewilderment.

The larger point about this in relation to *The Seagull* is that had we witnessed any crucial parts of Nina's life between the acts (to take one large part of what Chekhov moved "off"), had it been given to us unmediated, we would have been swayed toward emotions too inelastic and circumscribed for the play's amplitude, too small, paradoxical as that might sound in light of the broad material scope, because fixed and conventional. Pity for the infant's death, sympathy for the abandoned lover, perhaps contempt for Trigorin: such "natural" feelings would have flattened out the subtleties of Chekhov's scheme and converted the truest action—Nina's move-ment into spiritual and psychological maturity against a frieze of other characters more or less arrested within their situations and personalities—into the story of an ill-treat-ed, doggedly ambitious young woman who somehow man-ages to survive.

As the play is constructed, Nina's inner change takes place away from our awareness; what we do see are the crystal-lization and articulation of her new self. We get the "facts" about her interim life first from Konstantin, who wholly misinterprets them because he sees them conventionally, and then the truth from her own lips. The contrast, which is at the same time the difference in their natures, is superb-ly dramatic, unfolding as a *coup de théâtre* in the realm of consciousness such as an ordinary drama of highlighted physical events could not have given us.

Except for Anna's death *Ivanov* had offered its chief physical particularities to our direct gaze. And surely the most instructive demonstration of Chekhov's growth from that play to ***The Seagull*** is in the suicides with which both dramas end. Nikolai shoots himself before our eyes, Konstantin away from them. The obvious difference is that the latter suicide is at a distance, reaching us obliquely—the sound of the shot, Dorn's whispered words to Sorin—and that this greatly diminishes the emotional impact of the event. But this is an accession to the imagination, not a loss, for the assault on the senses of the suicide on stage, no matter how discreetly done, leaves no space for reflection, specifically about the significance of the act, in itself and, more important, in relation to other things. No space for reflection and not much material for it.

Ivanov's shooting himself is essentially solipsistic, isolated from the rest of the drama, or, more pertinently, from any large pattern of consciousness, the way such melodramatic actions tend to be. We've interpreted the suicide, relying on the character's own words, as in part an attempt to recapture his "old self," through a last catastrophic but at least decisive act. It's also of course simply a way out of his untenable situation and a device by which Chekhov can end the play. Missing from it is any significant connection to other lives.

Suicide is always carried out in the moral and psychic neighborhood of other people, directed toward them ("See what you've made me do!") or implying something about them, so that taking one's own life invariably poses questions about those who don't take theirs, those who continue to live. Camus called suicide "the one serious philosophical problem,"[13] and this dimension of thoughtfulness, of ontological query, is just what's lacking in Ivanov's shooting himself. By contrast, it's abundantly present in the circumstances and aftermath of Konstantin's self-destruction.

His suicide exists at the imaginative center of ***The Seagull***'s concerns, which are chiefly the different ways people confront themselves in situations of love and vocation or, if they lack a calling, like Sorin and Masha, in whatever niches they do occupy. Especially being tested is the relationship between love and talent, with Nina and Konstantin as the exemplary figures, while most of the other characters circle at various distances from this thematic center.

When Konstantin kills himself, it's squarely in the light of Nina's stamina, her *going on.* Her strength has revealed to him his own weakness in two connected ways. She has taught him in an instant how pallidly romantic and compensatory is his desire for her, and he has learned (we sense rather than are told this) that he lacks the courage—a clear-headed capacity to continue on through vicissitudes and setbacks, on the most profound level through *complexity*—that she incarnates. Her visit and its words hover in the air of the final scene, as the lotto game so casually goes on and behind the closed door Konstantin, brooding about what she has shown him, "defeated" by her example, prepares his pathetic counterstatement. A remarkably shrewd analysis of the play and especially of the ending was made by a famous contemporary jurist and friend of the arts, Anatoly Koni. "How good the ending

is," he wrote to Chekhov. "It is not . . . she, the seagull, [who] commits suicide (which a run-of-the-mill playwright, out for his audience's tears, would be sure to have done) but the young man who lives in an abstract future and has no idea of . . . what goes on around him."[14]

This is why the play is a comedy, in one of the ways I defined the genre earlier, why the suicide is neither tragic nor bathetic. For Konstantin's death is the result neither of some fatal crack in existence nor of an attempt to pass beyond limits; its "reality" is brilliantly seen against a contrasting one, a choice of life that will be lived bravely and with honor. Something essential has been saved out of the entire human substance of the play, the principle of relief from fatality that governs all comedy is now in place, so that the imaginative balance is toward what remains, not what has been lost. Konstantin is the cautionary figure in this dramatic positioning of selves and self-questioning, as Nina is its force of redemptive acceptance.

The mainsprings of its plot having been moved off stage, ***The Seagull*** presents a surface without any visible peaks, the landscape of a remarkably flat terrain. But this flatness is of a physical order, not an aesthetic or intellectual one. On those levels ceaseless activity goes on, usually small, often casual seeming, an intricate meshing of gesture, speech, and idea. And something else becomes apparent when we have adjusted our sights to the newness of the dramaturgy.

For the first time in Chekhov we see the drama proceeding as though its language and actions are gradually filling in a field, not moving in any sort of conventional straight line, the usual unfolding of exposition, development, and dénouement. The energy thus released, the force of locomotion turned into presence, is exactly the principle of "newness" in Chekhov's theater, Magarshack's idea of the "indirect" but more accurately formulated this way, I think.

Ivanov had begun this transformation, but stumblingly and, as I wrote earlier, with an incompleteness that came from Chekhov's inability at that point fully to shake off the past, the seductions toward melodrama, the mechanical deference given to physical sensation. Resisting these, Chekhov could greatly extend, by freeing them from their surrounding narrative pressures, all those kinds of scene without preamble or immediate aftermath, without *plotted logic,* that had constituted the rough technical originality of the earlier play.

In ***The Seagull*** characters move in and out of our sight and of each other's, in a constant traffic of direct encounters, glancing meetings, conferences, interruptions, breakings up, and reassemblings, all of it governed sometimes by mutual understanding and sometimes by its lack. A seemingly structureless drama, it's really all structure, if by that we mean, as we should, something inseparable from texture and pattern. The play isn't an edifice laid horizontally yet rearing its "meanings" skyward, but a meshing of revelations, withholdings, recognitions, everything serving as clues to the whole.

The entire substance is somewhat thinner than it will become in Chekhov's next plays; its characters' destinies, Nina's most saliently, are a little too *predicted* beyond the play instead of being fates wholly within it; but the ground for the full flourishing of Chekhov's imagination has been prepared. His vision will darken in *Uncle Vanya* and even more in *Three Sisters,* to lighten again in *The Cherry Orchard,* but here in *The Seagull* for the first time vision and method have largely fused.

NOTES

[1] Victor Emeljanow, ed., *Chekhov: The Critical Heritage* (London: Routledge and Kegan Paul, 1981), 139.
[2] *Anton Chekhov's Life and Thought: Selected Letters and Commentary,* translated by Michael Henry Heim in collaboration with Simon Karlinsky; selection, commentary and introduction by Simon Karlinsky (Berkeley: University of California Press, 1975), 277.
[3] Ernest J. Simmons, *Chekhov: A Biography* (Boston and Toronto: Little, Brown, 1962), 172.
[4] Ibid., 353.
[5] *ACLT,* 277.
[6] "Dante . . . Bruno. Vico . . . Joyce," *Our Exagmination Round His Factification for Incamination of Work in Progress* by Samuel Beckett et al. (London: Faber and Faber, 1961), 14.
[7] *Ibsen: Letters and Speeches,* ed. Evert Sprinchorn (New York: Hill and Wang, 1964), 100.
[8] Robert Louis Jackson, "Chekhov's *Seagull:* The Empty Well, the Dry Lake, and the Cold Cave," in *Chekhov: A Collection of Critical Essays,* ed. Robert Louis Jackson (Englewood Cliffs, N.J.: Prentice-Hall, 1967), 99-111.
[9] Avram Yarmolinsky, ed., *Letters of Anton Chekhov* (New York: Viking, 1968), 310.
[10] David Magarshack, *Chekhov the Dramatist* (New York: Hill and Wang, 1960), 177.
[11] Ibid., 190.
[12] *ACLT,* 277.
[13] Albert Camus, *The Myth of Sisyphus and Other Essays* (New York: Knopf, 1955), 3.
[14] *ACLT,* 285.

Uncle Vanya

Eric Bentley (essay date 1946)

SOURCE: "Craftsmanship in *Uncle Vanya*," in *In Search of Theater*, Alfred A. Knopf, 1953, pp. 342-64.

[*In the following essay, which was written in 1946, Bentley examines Chekhov's modifcations of* The Wood Demon *to create* Uncle Vanya *and explores the author's manipulation of mundane details in the latter play to achieve "a drama of imagination and thought."*]

The Anglo-American theater finds it possible to get along without the services of most of the best playwrights. Æschylus, Lope de Vega, Racine, Molière, Schiller, Strindberg—one could prolong indefinitely the list of great dramatists who are practically unknown in England and America except to scholars. Two cases of popularity in spite of greatness are, of course, Shakespeare and Shaw, who have this in common: that they can be enjoyed without being taken seriously. And then there is Chekhov.

It is easy to make over a play by Shaw or by Shakespeare into a Broadway show. But why is Chekhov preserved from the general oblivion? Why is it that scarcely a year passes without a major Broadway or West End production of a Chekhov play? Chekhov's plays—at least by reputation, which in commercial theater is the important thing—are plotless, monotonous, drab, and intellectual: find the opposites of these four adjectives and you have a recipe for a smash hit.

Those who are responsible for productions of Chekhov in London and New York know the commodity theater. Some of them are conscious rebels against the whole system. Others are simply genuine artists who, if not altogether consciously, are afflicted with guilt; to do Chekhov is for them a gesture of rebellion or atonement, as to do Shakespeare or Shaw is not. It is as if the theater remembers Chekhov when it remembers its conscience.

The rebels of the theater know their Chekhov and love him; it is another question whether they understand him. Very few people seem to have given his work the careful examination it requires. Handsome tributes have been paid Chekhov by Stanislavsky, Nemirovich-Danchenko, and Gorky, among his countrymen; and since being taken up by Middleton Murry's circle thirty years ago, he has enjoyed a high literary reputation in England and America. The little book by William Gerhardi and the notes and *obiter dicta* of such critics as Stark Young and Francis Fergusson are, however, too fragmentary and impressionistic to constitute a critical appraisal. They have helped to establish more accurate general ideas about Chekhov's art. They have not inquired too rigorously in what that art consists.

I am prompted to start such an enquiry by the Old Vic's engrossing presentation of **Uncle Vanya** in New York. Although **Vanya** is the least well known of Chekhov's four dramatic master-pieces, it is—I find—a good play to start a critical exploration with because it exists in two versions—one mature Chekhov, the other an immature draft. To read both is to discover the direction and intention of Chekhov's development. It is also to learn something about the art of rewriting when not practiced by mere play-doctors. There is a lesson here for playwrights. For we are losing the conception of the writer as an artist who by quiet discipline steadily develops. In the twentieth century a writer becomes an event with his first best-seller, or smash hit, and then spends the rest of his life repeating the performance—or vainly trying to.

Chekhov's earlier version—**The Wood Demon**—is what Hollywood would call a comedy drama: that is, a farce spiced with melodrama. It tells the story of three couples: a vain Professor[1] and his young second wife, Yelena;

243

Astrov, the local doctor, who is nicknamed the Wood Demon because of his passion for forestry, and Sonya, the Professor's daughter by his first marriage; finally, a young man and woman named Fyodor and Julia. The action consists to a great extent in banal comedic crisscrossing of erotic interests. Julia's brother seems for a time to be after Sonya. Yelena is coveted rather casually by Fyodor and more persistently by Uncle Vanya, the brother of the Professor's first wife. Rival suitors, eternal triangles, theatric adultery! It is not a play to take too seriously. Although in the third act there is a climax when Uncle Vanya shoots himself, Chekhov tries in the last and fourth act to re-establish the mode of light comedy by pairing off all three couples before bringing down the curtain on his happy ending.

Yet even in *The Wood Demon* there is much that is "pure Chekhov." The happy ending does not convince, because Chekhov has created a situation that cannot find so easy an outcome. He has created people who cannot possibly be happy ever after. He has struck so deep a note that the play cannot quite, in its last act, become funny again.

The death of Vanya is melodrama, yet it has poignancy too, and one might feel that, if it should be altered, the changes should be in the direction of realism. The plot centers on property. The estate was the dowry of Vanya's sister, the Professor's first wife. Vanya put ten years' work into paying off the mortgage. The present owner is the daughter of the first marriage, Sonya. The Professor, however, thinks he can safely speak of "our estate" and propose to sell it, so he can live in a Finnish villa on the proceeds. It is the shock of this proposal, coming on top of his discovery that the Professor, in whom he has so long believed is an intellectual fraud—coming on top of his infatuation with Yelena—that drives Vanya to suicide. And if this situation seems already to be asking for realistic treatment, what are we to say to the aftermath? Yelena leaves her husband, but is unable to sustain this "melodramatic" effort. She comes back to him, defeated yet not contrite: "Well, take me, statue of the commander, and go to hell with me in your twenty-six dismal rooms!"[2]

The Wood Demon is a conventional play trying, so to speak, to be something else. In *Uncle Vanya,* rewritten, it succeeds. Perhaps Chekhov began by retouching his ending and was led back and back into his play until he had revised everything but the initial situation. He keeps the starting-point of his fable, but alters the whole outcome. Vanya does not shoot himself; he fires his pistol at the Professor, and misses. Consequently the last act has quite a different point of departure. Yelena does not run away from her husband. He decides to leave, and she goes with him. Astrov, in the later version, does not love Sonya; he and she end in isolation. Vanya is not dead or in the condemned cell; but he is not happy.

To the Broadway script-writer, also concerned with the rewriting of plays (especially if in an early version a likable character shoots himself), these alterations of Chekhov's would presumably seem unaccountable. They would look like a deliberate elimination of the dramatic element. Has

not Prince Mirsky told us that Chekhov is an undramatic dramatist? The odd thing is only that he could be so dramatic *before* he rewrote. The matter is worth looking into.

Chekhov's theater, like Ibsen's, is psychological. If Chekhov changed his story, it must be either because he later felt that his old characters would act differently or because he wanted to create more interesting characters. The four people who emerge in the later version as the protagonists are different from their prototypes in *The Wood Demon,* and are differently situated. Although Sonya still loves Astrov, her love is not returned. This fact is one among many that make the later ending Chekhovian: Sonya and Astrov resign themselves to lives of labor without romance. Vanya is not resolute enough for suicide. His discontent takes form as resentment against the author of his misery. And yet, if missing his aim at such close quarters be an accident, it is surely one of those unconsciously willed accidents that Freud wrote of. Vanya is no murderer. His outburst is rightly dismissed as a tantrum by his fellows, none of whom dreams of calling the police. Just as Vanya is the kind of man who does not kill, Yelena is the kind of woman who does not run away from her husband, even temporarily.

In the earlier version the fates of the characters are settled; in the later they are unsettled. In the earlier version they are settled, moreover, not by their own nature or by force of circumstance, but by theatrical convention. In the later, their fate is unsettled because that is Chekhov's view of the truth. Nobody dies. Nobody is paired off. And the general point is clear: life knows no endings, happy or tragic. (Shaw once congratulated Chekhov on the discovery that the tragedy of the Hedda Gablers is, in real life, precisely that they do *not* shoot themselves.) The special satiric point is also familiar: Chekhov's Russians are chronically indecisive people. What is perhaps not so easy to grasp is the effect of a more mature psychology upon dramaturgy. Chekhov has destroyed the climax in his third act and the happy consummation in his fourth. These two alterations alone presuppose a radically different dramatic form.

II.

The framework of the new play is the attractive pattern of arrival and departure: the action is what happens in the short space of time between the arrival of the Professor and his wife on their country estate and their departure from it. The unity of the play is discovered by asking the question: what effect has the visit upon the visited—that is, upon Vanya, Sonya, and Astrov? This question as it stands could not be asked of *The Wood Demon,* for in that play the Professor and Yelena do not depart, and Vanya is dead before the end. As to the effect of the Professor's arrival, it is to change and spoil everything. His big moment—the moment when he announces his intention to sell the estate—leads to reversal in Aristotle's sense, the decisive point at which the whole direction of the narrative turns about. This is Uncle Vanya's suicide. Vanya's futile shots, in the later version, are a kind of mock reversal. It cannot even be said that they make the

Professor change his mind, for he had begun to change it already—as soon as Vanya protested. Mechanical, classroom analysis would no doubt locate the climax of the play in the shooting. But the climax is an anticlimax. If one of our script-writers went to work on it, his "rewrite" would be *The Wood Demon* all over again, his principle of revision being exactly the opposite of Chekhov's. What Chekhov is after, I think, is not reversal but recognition—also in Aristotle's sense, "the change from ignorance to knowledge." In Aristotle's sense, but with a Chekhovian application.

In the Greeks, in much French drama, and in Ibsen, recognition means the discovery of a secret which reveals that things are not what all these years they have seemed to be. In *Uncle Vanya,* recognition means that what all these years seemed to be so, though one hesitated to believe it, really is so and will remain so. This is Vanya's discovery and gradually (in the course of the ensuing last act) that of the others. Thus Chekhov has created a kind of recognition which is all his own. In Ibsen the terrible thing is that the surface of everyday life is a smooth deception. In Chekhov the terrible thing is that the surface of everyday life is itself a kind of tragedy. In Ibsen the whole surface of life is suddenly burst by volcanic eruption. In Chekhov the crust is all too firm; the volcanic energies of men have no chance of emerging. *Uncle Vanya* opens with a rather rhetorical suggestion that this *might* be so. It ends with the knowledge that it certainly *is* so, a knowledge shared by all the characters who are capable of knowledge—Astrov, Vanya, Sonya, and Yelena. This growth from ignorance to knowledge is, perhaps, our cardinal experience of the play (the moment of recognition, or experimental proof, being Vanya's outburst *before* the shooting).

Aristotle says that the change from ignorance to knowledge produces "love or hate between the persons destined by the poet for good or bad fortune." But only in *The Wood Demon,* where there is no real change from ignorance to knowledge, could the outcome be stated in such round terms. Nobody's fortune at the end of *Uncle Vanya* is as good or bad as it might be; nobody is very conclusively loving or hating. Here again Chekhov is avoiding the black and the white, the tragic and the comic, and is attempting the halftone, the tragicomic.

If, as has been suggested, the action consists in the effect of the presence of the Professor and Yelena upon Sonya, Vanya, and Astrov, we naturally ask: what *was* that effect? To answer this question for the subtlest of the characters—Astrov—is to see far into Chekhov's art. In *The Wood Demon* the effect is nil. The action has not yet been unified. It lies buried in the chaos of Chekhov's materials. In *Uncle Vanya,* however, there is a thread of continuity. We are first told that Astrov is a man with no time for women. We then learn (and there is no trace of this in *The Wood Demon*) that he is infatuated with Yelena. In *The Wood Demon,* Sonya gets Astrov in the end. In *Uncle Vanya,* when Astrov gives up Yelena, he resigns himself to his old role of living without love. The old routine—in this as in other respects—resumes its sway.

The later version of this part of the story includes two splendid scenes that were not in *The Wood Demon,* even embryonically. One is the first of the two climaxes in Act III—when Yelena sounds out Astrov on Sonya's behalf. Astrov reveals that it is Yelena he loves, and he is kissing her when Vanya enters. The second is Astrov's parting from Yelena in the last act, a scene so subtle that Stanislavsky himself misinterpreted it: he held that Astrov was still madly in love with Yelena and was clutching at her as a dying man clutches at a straw. Chekhov had to point out in a letter that this is not so. What really happens is less histrionic and more Chekhovian. The parting kiss is passionless on Astrov's side. This time it is Yelena who feels a little passion. Not very much, though. For both, the kiss is a tribute to the Might-Have-Been.

Astrov's failure to return Sonya's love is not a result of the Professor's visit; he had failed to return it even before the Professor's arrival. The effect of the visit is to confirm (as part of the general Chekhovian pattern) the fact that what seems to be so *is* so; that what has been will be; that nothing has changed. How much difference has the visit made? It has made the case much sadder. Beforehand Astrov had maintained, and presumably believed, that he was indifferent to women. Afterward we know that it is Sonya in particular to whom he is indifferent. The "wood demon," devoted to the creative and the natural, can love only Yelena the artificial, the sterile, the useless. To Sonya, the good, the competent, the constructive, he is indifferent.

The Professor's visit clarifies Astrov's situation, indeed, his whole nature. True, he had already confessed himself a failure in some of the opening speeches of the play. The uninitiated must certainly find it strange (despite the august precedent of *Antony and Cleopatra*) that the play starts with a summary of the whole disaster. Yet the rest of the play, anything but a gratuitous appendix, is the proof that Astrov, who perhaps could not quite believe himself at the beginning, is right after all. The action of the play is his chance to disprove his own thesis—a chance that he misses, that he was bound to miss, being what he was. What was he, then? In the earlier version he had been known as the Wood Demon or Spirit of the Forest, and in *Uncle Vanya* the long speeches are retained in which he advances his ideal of the natural, the growing, the beautiful. Because he also speaks of great ennobling changes in the future of the race (not unlike those mentioned in the peroration of Trotsky's *Literature and Revolution*), he has been taken to be a prophet of a great political future for Russia in the twentieth century. But this would be wrenching his remarks from their context. Astrov is not to be congratulated on his beautiful dreams; he is to be pitied. His hope that mankind will some day do something good operates as an excuse for doing nothing now. It is an expression of his own futility, and Astrov knows it. Even in the early version he was not really a Wood Demon. That was only the ironical nickname of a crank. In the later version even the nickname has gone,[3] and Astrov is even more of a crank. When Yelena arrives, he leaves his forest to rot. Clearly they were no real fulfillment of his nature, but an old-maidish hobby, like

Persian cats. They were *ersatz;* and as soon as something else seemed to offer itself, Astrov made his futile attempt at seduction. Freud would have enjoyed the revealing quality of his last pathetic proposal that Yelena should give herself to him in the depth of the forest.

The actor, of course, should not make Astrov *too* negative. If one school of opinion romanticizes all Chekhov characters who dream of the future, another, even more vulgar, sees them as weaklings and nothing else. Chekhov followed Ibsen in portraying the average mediocre man—*l'homme moyen sensuel*—without ever following the extreme naturalists in their concern with the utterly downtrodden, the inarticulate, the semihuman. His people are no weaker than ninety-nine out of every hundred members of his audience. That is to say, they are very weak, but there are also elements of protest and revolt in them, traces of will-power, some dim sense of responsibility. If his characters never reach fulfillment, it is not because they were always without potentialities. In fact, Chekhov's sustained point is precisely that these weeping, squirming, suffering creatures *might have been men.* And because Chekhov feels this, there is emotion, movement, tension, interplay, dialectic, in his plays. He never could have written a play like Galsworthy's *Justice,* in which the suffering creature is as much an insect as a man.

The Might-Have-Been is Chekhov's *idée fixe.* His people do not dream only of what could never be, or what could come only after thousands of years; they dream of what their lives actually could have been. They spring from a conviction of human potentiality—which is what separates Chekhov from the real misanthropes of modern literature. Astrov moves us because we can readily feel how fully human he might have been, how he has dwindled, under the influence of "country life," from a thinker to a crank, from a man of feeling to a philanderer. "It is strange somehow," he says to Yelena in the last scene, "we have got to know each other, and all at once for some reason—we shall never meet again. So it is with everything in this world." Such lines might be found in any piece of sentimental theater. But why is it that Chekhov's famous "elegiac note" is, in the full context, deeply moving? Is it not because the sense of death is accompanied with so rich a sense of life and the possible worth of living?

III.

Chekhov had a feeling for the unity of the drama, yet his sense of the richness of life kept him clear of formalism. He enriched his dramas in ways that belong to no school and that, at least in their effect, are peculiar to himself. While others tried to revive poetic drama by putting symbolist verse in the mouths of their characters, or simply by imitating the verse drama of the past, Chekhov found poetry within the world of realism. By this is meant not only that he used symbols. Symbolism of a stagy kind was familiar on the boulevards and still is. The Broadway title *Skylark* is symbolic in exactly the same way as *The Wild Duck* and *The Seagull.* It is rather the use to which Chekhov puts the symbol that is remarkable. We have seen, for instance, what he makes of his "wood demon." This is not merely

a matter of Astrov's character. Chekhov's symbols spread themselves, like Ibsen's, over a large territory. They are a path to the imagination and to those deeper passions which in our latter-day drama are seldom worn on the sleeve. Thus if a symbol in Chekhov is explained—in the manner of the *raisonneur*—the explanation blazes like a denunciation. Yelena says:

> As Astrov was just saying, you are all recklessly destroying the forests and soon there will be nothing left on the earth. In the same way you recklessly destroy human beings, and soon, thanks to you, there will be no fidelity, no purity, no capacity for sacrifice left on the earth either! Why is it you can never look at a woman with indifference unless she is yours? That doctor is right: it's because there is a devil of destruction in all of you. You have no mercy on woods or birds or women or one another.

What a paradox: our playwrights who plump for the passions (like O'Neill) are superficial, and Chekhov, who pretends to show us only the surface (who, as I have said, writes the tragedy of the surface), is passionate and deep! No modern playwright has presented elemental passions more truly. Both versions of *Uncle Vanya* are the battleground of two conflicting impulses—the impulse to destroy and the impulse to create. In *The Wood Demon* the conflict is simple: Vanya's destructive passion reaches a logical end in suicide, Astrov's creative passion a logical end in happiness ever after. In *Uncle Vanya* the pattern is complex: Vanya's destructive passion reaches a pseudo-climax in his pistol-shots, and a pseudo-culmination in bitter resignation. Astrov's creative passion has found no outlet. Unsatisfied by his forests, he is fascinated by Yelena. His ending is the same as Vanya's—isolation. The destructive passions do not destroy; the creative passions do not create. Or, rather, both impulses are crushed in the daily routine, crushed by boredom and triviality. Both Vanya and Astrov have been suffering a gradual erosion and will continue to do so. They cry out. "I have not lived, not lived . . . I have ruined and wasted the best years of my life." "I have grown old, I have worked too hard, I have grown vulgar, all my feelings are blunted, and I believe I am not capable of being fond of anyone." Chekhov's people never quite become wounded animals like the Greek tragic heroes. But through what modern playwright does suffering speak more poignantly?

At a time when Chekhov is valued for his finer shades, it is worth stressing his simplicity and strength, his depth and intensity—provided we remember that these qualities require just as prodigious a technique for their expression, that they depend just as much on details. Look at the first two acts of *Uncle Vanya.* While the later acts differ from *The Wood Demon* in their whole narrative, the first two differ chiefly in their disposition of the material. Act I of *The Wood Demon* is a rather conventional bit of exposition: we get to know the eleven principals and we learn that Vanya is in love with Yelena. In *Uncle Vanya* Chekhov gives himself more elbow-room by cutting down the number of characters: Julia and her brother, Fyodor and his father are eliminated. The act is no longer mere exposition in the naturalistic manner (people meeting and asking questions like "Whom did you write to?" so that the reply can be given: "I wrote to Sonya"). The principle of organization is what one often hears called "musical." (The word *poetic* is surely more accurate, but music is the accepted metaphor.) The evening opens, we might say, with a little overture in which themes from the body of the play are heard. "I may well look old!" It is Astrov speaking. "And life is tedious, stupid, dirty. Life just drags on." The theme of human deterioration is followed by the theme of aspiration: "Those who will live a hundred or two hundred years after us, for whom we are struggling now to beat out a road, will they remember and say a good word for us?" The overture ends; the play begins.

Analyses of the structure of plays seldom fail to tell us where the climax lies, where the exposition is completed, and how the play ends, but they often omit a more obtrusive factor—the *principle of motion,* the way in which a play copes with its medium, with time-sequence. In general, the nineteenth-century drama proceeded upon the principles of boulevard drama (as triumphantly practiced by Scribe). To deal with such a play, terms like *exposition, complication,* and *denouement* are perfectly adequate because the play is, like most fiction, primarily a pattern of suspense. The "musical" principle of motion, however, does not reflect a preoccupation with suspense. That is why many devotees of popular drama are bored by Chekhov.

Consider even smaller things than the use of overture. Consider the dynamics of the first three lines in *Uncle Vanya.* The scene is one of Chekhov's gardens. Astrov is sitting with the Nurse. She offers him tea. She offers him vodka, but he is not a regular vodka-drinker. "Besides, it's stifling," he says; and there is a lull in the conversation. To the Broadway producer this is a good opening because it gives latecomers a chance to take their seats without missing anything. To Chekhov these little exchanges, these sultry pauses, are the bricks out of which a drama is built.

What makes Chekhov seem most formless is precisely the means by which he achieves strict form—namely, the series of tea-drinkings, arrivals, departures, meals, dances, family gatherings, casual conversations, of which his plays are made. As we have seen, Chekhov works with a highly unified action. He presents it, however, not in the centralized, simplified manner of Sophocles or Ibsen, but obliquely, indirectly, quasi-naturally. The rhythm of the play is leisurely yet broken and, to suspense-lovers, baffling. It would be an exaggeration to say that there is no story and that the succession of scenes marks simply an advance in our knowledge of a situation that does not change. Yet people who cannot interest themselves in this kind of development as well as in straightforward story-telling will not be interested in Chekhov's plays any more than they would be in Henry James's novels. Chekhov does tell a story—the gifts of one of the greatest raconteurs are not in abeyance in his plays—but his method is to let both his narrative and his situation leak out, so to speak, through domestic gatherings, formal and casual. This is his principle of motion.

The method requires two extraordinary gifts: the mastery of "petty" realistic material and the ability to go beyond sheer *Sachlichkeit*—materiality, factuality—to imagination and thought. (Galsworthy, for example, seems to have possessed neither of these gifts—certainly not the second.) Now, the whole Stanislavsky school of acting and directing is testimony that Chekhov was successfully *sachlich*—that is, not only accurate, but significantly precise, concrete, ironic (like Jane Austen). The art by which a special importance is imparted to everyday objects is familiar enough in fiction; on the stage, Chekhov is one of its few masters. On the stage, moreover, the *Sachlichkeit* may more often consist in a piece of business—I shall never forget Astrov, as played by Olivier, buttoning his coat—than in a piece of furniture. Chekhov was so far from being the average novelist-turned-dramatist that he used the peculiarly theatrical *Sachlichkeit* with the skill of a veteran of the footlights. The first entrance of Vanya, for instance, is achieved this way (compare it with the entrance of the matinee idol in a boulevard comedy):

VANYA (comes out of the house; he has had a nap after lunch and looks rumpled; he sits down on the garden-seat and straightens his fashionable tie): *Yes.* . . . (Pause.) *Yes.* . . .

(Those who are used to the long novelistic stage-directions of Shaw and O'Neill should remember that Chekhov, like Ibsen, added stage-directions only here and there. But the few that do exist show an absolute mastery.)

How did Chekhov transcend mere *Sachlichkeit* and achieve a drama of imagination and thought? Chiefly, I think, by combining the most minute attention to realistic detail with a rigorous sense of form. He diverges widely from all the Western realists—though not so widely from his Russian predecessors such as Turgenev, whose *Month in the Country* could be palmed off as a Chekhov play on more discerning people than most drama critics—and his divergences are often in the preservation of elements of style and stylization, which naturalism prided itself it had discarded. Most obvious among these is the soliloquy. Chekhov does not let his people confide in the audience, but he does use the kind of soliloquy in which the character thinks out loud; and where there is no traditional device for achieving a certain kind of beginning or ending, he constructs for himself a set piece that will do his job. In *Uncle Vanya,* if there may be said to be an overture, played by Astrov, there may also be said to be a finale, played by Sonya. For evidence of Chekhov's theatrical talents one should notice the visual and auditory components of this final minute of the play. We have just heard the bells jingling as the Professor and his wife drive off, leaving the others to their desolation. "Waffles"—one of the neighbors—is softly tuning his guitar. Vanya's mother is reading. Vanya "passes his hand over" Sonya's hair:

SONYA: We must go on living! (*Pause.*) We shall go on living, Uncle Vanya! We shall live through a long, long chain of days and weary evenings; we shall patiently bear the trials that fate sends us; we shall work for others, both now and in our old age, and have no rest; and when our time comes we shall die without a murmur, and there beyond the grave we shall say that we have suffered, that we have wept, that our life has been bitter to us, and God will have pity on us, and you and I, uncle, dear uncle, shall see a life that is bright, lovely, beautiful. We shall rejoice and look back at these troubles of ours with tenderness, with a smile—and we shall have rest. I have faith, uncle, fervent, passionate faith. (*Slips on her knees before him and lays her head on his hands; in a weary voice*) We shall rest! (*"Waffles" softly plays on the guitar.*) We shall rest! We shall hear the angels; we shall see all heaven lit with radiance, we shall see all earthly evil, all our sufferings, drowned in mercy, which will fill the whole world, and our life will be peaceful, gentle, sweet like a caress. I have faith, I have faith. (*Wipes away his tears with her handkerchief.*) Poor, poor Uncle Vanya, you are crying. (*Through her tears*) You have had no joy in your life, but wait, Uncle Vanya, wait. We shall rest. (Puts her arms around him.) We shall rest! (*The watchman taps; Waffles plays softly; Vanya's mother makes notes on the margin of her pamphlet; the Nurse knits her stocking.*) We shall rest! (*Curtain drops slowly.*)

The silence, the music, the watchman's tapping, the postures, the gestures, the prose with its rhythmic repetitions and melancholy import—these compose an image, if a stage picture with its words and music may be called an image, such as the drama has seldom known since Shakespeare. True, in our time the background music of movies and the noises-off in radio drama have made us see the dangers in this sort of theatricality. But Chekhov knew without these awful examples where to draw the line.

A weakness of much realistic literature is that it deals with inarticulate people. The novelist can of course supply in narrative and description what his milieu lacks in conversation, but the dramatist has no recourse—except to the extent that drama is expressed not in words but in action. Chekhov's realistic milieu, however, is, like Ibsen's, bourgeois and "intellectual"; a wide range of conversational styles and topics is therefore plausible enough. But Chekhov is not too pedantic about plausibility. He not only exploits the real explicitness and complication and abstractness of bourgeois talk; he introduces, or reintroduces, a couple of special conventions.

The first is the tirade or long, oratorically composed speech. Chekhov's realistic plays—unlike Ibsen's—have their purple patches. On the assumption that a stage character may be much more self-conscious and aware than his counterpart in real life, Chekhov lets his people talk much more freely than any other modern realist except Shaw. They talk on all subjects from book-keeping to metaphysics. Not always listening to what the other man is saying, they talk about themselves and address the whole world. They make what might be called self-explaining soliloquies in the manner of Richard III—except for the fact that other people are present and waiting, very likely, to make soliloquies of their own.

This is the origin of the second Chekhovian convention: each character speaks his mind without reference to the others. This device is perhaps Chekhov's most notorious idea. It has been used more crudely by Odets and Saroyan; and it has usually been interpreted in what is indeed its primary function: to express the isolation of people from one another. However, the dramaturgic utility of the idea is equally evident: it brings the fates of individuals before the audience with a minimum of fuss.

In Chekhov, as in every successful artist, each device functions both technically and humanly, serves a purpose both as form and as content. The form of the tirade, which Chekhov reintroduces, is one of the chief means to an extension of content; and the extension of content is one of the chief means by which Chekhov escapes from stolid naturalism into the broader realities that only imagination can uncover. Chekhov's people are immersed in facts, buried in circumstances, not to say in trivialities, yet—and this is what differentiates them from most dramatic characters—aware of the realm of ideas and imagination. His drama bred a school of acting which gives more attention to exact detail than any other school in history; it might also have bred a school of dramaturgy which could handle the largest and most general problems. Chekhov was a master of the particular and the general—which is another sign of the richness and balance of his mind.

IV.

Obviously Chekhov is not a problem playwright in the vulgar sense. (Neither is Ibsen; neither is Shaw. Who is?) Nor is his drama *about* ideas. He would undoubtedly have agreed with Henry Becque: "The serious thing about drama is not the ideas. It is the absorption of the ideas by the characters, the dramatic or comic force that the characters give to the ideas." It is not so much the force Chekhov gives to any particular ideas as the picture he gives of the role of ideas in the lives of men of ideas—a point particularly relevant to **Uncle Vanya.** If Vanya might be called the active center of the play (in that he precipitates the crisis), there is also a passive center, a character whose mere existence gives direction to the action as a whole.

This is Professor Serebryakov. Although this character is not so satisfactory a creation as the professor in Chekhov's tale **"A Tiresome Story,"** and though Chekhov does too little to escape the cliché stage professor, the very crudeness of the characterization has dramatic point. Serebryakov is a simple case placed as such in contrast to Vanya and Astrov. His devotion to ideas is no more than a gesture of unearned superiority, and so he has become a valetudinarian whose wife truly says: "You talk of your age as though we were all responsible for it." Around this familiar and, after all, common phenomenon are grouped the others, each of whom has a different relation to the world of culture and learning. The Professor is the middle of the design; characters of developed awareness are, so to say, above him; those of undeveloped awareness below him. Above him are Vanya and Astrov, Yelena and Sonya—the men aware to a great extent through their superior intellect, the women through their finer feeling. Below him are three minor characters—Waffles, Vanya's mother, and the Nurse.

The Nurse, who is not to be found in *The Wood Demon,* stands for life without intellectuality or education. She sits knitting, and the fine talk passes her by. She stands for the monotony of country life, a monotony that she interprets as beneficent order. One of the many significant cross-references in the play is Vanya's remark at the beginning that the Professor's arrival has upset the household routine and the Nurse's remark at the end that now the meals will be on time again and all will be well.

Vanya's mother stands on the first rung of the intellectual ladder. She is an enthusiast for certain ideas, and especially for reading about them, but she understands very little. Less intelligent, less sensitive than Vanya, she has never seen through the Professor. Her whole character is in this exchange with her son:

> MOTHER: . . . he has sent his new pamphlet.
>
> VANYA: Interesting?
>
> MOTHER: Interesting but rather queer. He is attacking what he himself maintained seven years ago. It's awful.
>
> VANYA: There's nothing awful in that. Drink your tea, maman.
>
> MOTHER: I want to talk.
>
> VANYA: We have been talking and talking for fifty years and reading pamphlets. It's about time to leave off.
>
> MOTHER: You don't like listening when I speak; I don't know why. Forgive my saying so, Jean, but you have so changed in the course of the last year that I hardly know you. You used to be a man of definite convictions, brilliant personality. . . .

On a slightly higher plane than the tract-ridden Mother is the friend of the family, Waffles. If Vanya is the ruin of a man of principle, Waffles is the parody of one. Listen to his account of himself (it is one of Chekhov's characteristic thumbnail autobiographies):

> My wife ran away from me with the man she loved the day after our wedding on the ground of my unprepossessing appearance. But I have never been false to my vows. I love her to this day and am faithful to her. I help her as far as I can, and I gave her all I had for the education of her children by the man she loved. I have lost my happiness, but I still have my pride left. And she? Her youth is over, her beauty, in accordance with the laws of nature, has faded, the man she loved is dead. . . . What has she left?

Just how Waffles is able to keep his equilibrium and avoid the agony that the four principals endure is clear enough. His "pride" is a form of stupidity. For him, as

for the Professor, books and ideas are not a window through which he sees the world so much as obstacles that prevent him seeing anything but themselves. The Professor's response to the crisis is a magnanimity that rings as false as Waffles's pride:

> Let bygones be bygones. After what has happened. I have gone through such a lot and thought over so many things in these few hours, I believe I could write a whole treatise on the art of living. . . .

Waffles also finds reflections of life more interesting than life itself. In *The Wood Demon* (where his character is more crudely drawn), having helped Yelena to run away, he shouts:

> If I lived in an intellectual center, they could draw a caricature of me for a magazine, with a very funny satirical inscription.

And a little later:

> Your Excellency, it is I who carried off your wife, as once upon a time a certain Paris carried off the fair Helen. I! Although there are no pockmarked Parises, yet there are more things in heaven and earth, Horatio, than are dreamt of in your philosophy!

In the more finely controlled *Uncle Vanya* this side of Waffles is slyly indicated in his attitude to the shooting:

> NURSE: Look at the quarreling and shooting this morning—shameful!
>
> WAFFLES: Yes, a subject worthy of the brush of Aivazovsky.

Aside from this special treatment of the modern intellectual and semi-intellectual, aside from explicit mention of various ideas and philosophies, Chekhov is writing "drama of ideas" only in the sense that Sophocles and Shakespeare and Ibsen were—that is to say, his plays are developed thematically. As one can analyze certain Shakespeare plays in terms of the chief concepts employed in them—such as Nature and Time—so one might analyze a Chekhov play in terms of certain large antitheses, such as (the list is compiled from *Uncle Vanya*) love and hate, feeling and apathy, heroism and lethargy, innocence and sophistication, reality and illusion, freedom and captivity, use and waste, culture and nature, youth and age, life and death. If one were to take up a couple of Chekhov's key concepts and trace his use of them through a whole play, one would find that he is a more substantial artist than even his admirers think.

Happiness and work, for instance. They are not exactly antitheses, but in *Uncle Vanya* they are found in by no means harmonious association. The outsider's view of Chekhov is of course that he is "negative" because he portrayed a life without happiness. The amateur's view is that he is "positive" because he preached work as a remedy for boredom. Both views need serious qualification.

Act I of the 1899 Moscow Art Theater production of Uncle Vanya.

The word *work* shifts its tone and implication a good deal within the one play *Uncle Vanya.* True, it sometimes looks like the antidote to all the idleness and futility. On the other hand, the play opens with Astrov's just complaint that he is worked to death. Work has been an obsession, and is still one, for the Professor, whose parting word is: "Permit an old man to add one observation to his farewell message: you must work, my friends! you must work!"[4] Vanya and Sonya obey him—but only to stave off desperation. "My heart is too heavy," says Vanya. "I must make haste and occupy myself with something. . . . Work! Work!" To Sonya, work is the noblest mode of self-destruction, a fact that was rather more than clear in *The Wood Demon*:

ASTROV: Are you happy?

SONYA: This is not the time, Nikhail Lvovich, to think of happiness.

ASTROV: What else is there to think of?

SONYA: Our sorrow came only because we thought too much of happiness. . . .

ASTROV: So! (*Pause.*)

SONYA: There's no evil without some good in it. Sorrow has taught me this—that one must forget one's own happiness and think only of the happiness of others. One's whole life should consist of sacrifices. . . .

ASTROV: Yes . . .(*after a pause*). Uncle Vanya shot himself, and his mother goes on searching for contradictions in her pamphlets. A great misfortune befell you and you're pampering your self-love, you are trying to distort your life and you think this is a sacrifice. . . . No one has a heart. . . .

In the less explicit *Uncle Vanya* this passage does not appear. What we do have is Sonya's beautiful lyric speech that ends the play. In the thrill of the words perhaps both reader and playgoer overlook just what she says—namely, that the afterlife will so fully make up for this one that we should learn not to take our earthly troubles too seriously. This is not Chekhov speaking. It is an overwrought girl comforting herself with an idea. In *The Wood Demon* Astrov was the author's mouthpiece when he replied to Sonya: "You are trying to distort your life and you think this is a sacrifice." The mature Chekhov has no direct mouthpieces. But the whole passage, the whole play, enforces the meaning: work for these people is not a means to happiness, but a drug that will help them to forget. Happiness they will never know. Astrov's yearnings are not a radical's vision of the future any more than the Professor's doctrine of work is a demand for a workers' state. They are both the daydreams of men who Might Have Been.

V.

So much for *The Wood Demon* and *Uncle Vanya.* Chekhov wrote five other full-length plays. Three—*Ivanov, That Worthless Fellow Platonov,* and *The Wood Demon*—were written in his late twenties, and are experimental in the sense that he was still groping toward his own peculiar style. Two plays—*The Seagull* and *Uncle Vanya*—were written in his middle thirties; the last two plays—*The Three Sisters* and *The Cherry Orchard*—when he was about forty.

Chekhov's development as a playwright is quite different from that of Ibsen, Strindberg, or any of the other first-rate moderns. While they pushed tempestuously forward, transforming old modes and inventing new ones, perpetually changing their approach, endlessly inventing new forms, Chekhov moved quietly, slowly, and along one straight road. He used only one full-length structure: the four-act drama; and one set of materials: the rural middle class. For all that, the line that stretches from *Ivanov* (1887-9) to *The Cherry Orchard* (1903) is of great interest.

The development is from farce and melodrama to the mature Chekhovian *drame.* The three early plays are violent and a little pretentious. Each presents a protagonist (there is no protagonist in the four subsequent plays) who is a modern variant upon a great type or symbol. Ivanov is referred to as a Hamlet, Platonov as a Don Juan, Astrov as a Wood Demon. In each case it is a "Russian" variant that Chekhov shows—Chekhov's "Russians" like Ibsen's "Norwegian" Peer Gynt and Shaw's "Englishman" representing modern men in general. Those who find Chekhov's plays static should read the three early pieces: they are the proof that, if the later Chekhov eschewed certain kinds of action, it was not for lack of dramatic sense in the most popular meaning of the term. Chekhov was born a melodramatist and farceur; only by discipline and development did he become the kind of playwright the world thinks it knows him to be. Not that the later plays are without farcical and melodramatic elements; only a great mimic and caricaturist could have created Waffles and Gaev. As for melodrama, the pistol continues to go off (all but the last of the seven plays have a murder or suicide as climax or pseudo-climax), but the noise is taken further off-stage, literally and figuratively, until in

The Three Sisters it is "the dim sound of a far-away shot." And *The Cherry Orchard,* the farthest refinement of Chekhov's method, culminates not with the sharp report of a pistol, but with the dull, precise thud of an ax.

These are a few isolated facts, and one might find one hundred others to demonstrate that Chekhov's plays retain a relationship to the cruder forms. If, as Jacques Barzun has argued, there is a Balzac in Henry James, there is a Sardou in Chekhov. Farce and melodrama are not eliminated, but subordinated to a higher art, and have their part in the dialectic of the whole. As melodrama, *The Seagull,* with its tale of the ruined heroine, the glamorous popular novelist, the despairing artist hero, might have appealed to Verdi or Puccini. Even the story of *The Cherry Orchard* (the elegant lady running off to Paris and being abandoned by the object of her grand passion) hardly suggests singularity, highbrowism, or rarefaction.

In the later plays life is seen in softer colors; Chekhov is no longer eager to be the author of a Russian *Hamlet* or *Don Juan.* The homely Uncle Vanya succeeds on the title page the oversuggestive Wood Demon, and Chekhov forgoes the melodrama of a forest fire. Even more revealing: overexplicit themes are deleted. Only in *The Wood Demon* is the career of the Professor filled in with excessive detail (Heidelberg and all) or Astrov denounced as a socialist. Only in the early version does Vanya's mother add to her remark that a certain writer now makes his living by attacking his own former views: "It is very, very typical of our time. Never have people betrayed their convictions with such levity as they do now." Chekhov deletes Vanya's open allusion to the "cursed poisonous irony" of the sophisticated mind. He keeps the substance of Yelena's declaration that "the world perishes not because of murderers and thieves, but from hidden hatred, from hostility among good people, from all those petty squabbles," and deletes the end of the sentence: ". . . unseen by those who call our house a haven of intellectuals." He does not have Yelena explain herself with the remark: "I am an episodic character, mine is a canary's happiness, a woman's happiness." (In both versions Yelena has earlier described herself as an "episodic character." Only in *The Wood Demon* does she repeat the description. In *The Wood Demon* the canary image also receives histrionic reiteration. In *Uncle Vanya* it is not used at all.)

Chekhov does not tone things down because he is afraid of giving himself away. He is not prim or precious. Restraint is for him as positive an idea as temperance was for the Greeks. In Chekhov the toned-down picture—as I hope the example of *Uncle Vanya* indicates—surpasses the hectic color scheme of melodrama, not only in documentary truth, but also in the deeper truth of poetic vision. And the truth of Chekhov's colors has much to do with the delicacy of his forms. Chekhov once wrote in a letter: "When a man spends the least possible number of movements over some definite action, that is grace"; and one of his critics speaks of a "'trigger' process, the release of enormous forces by some tiny movement." The Chekhovian form as we find it in the final version of

Uncle Vanya grew from a profound sense of what might be called the *economy* of art.

We have seen how, while this form does not by any means eliminate narrative and suspense, it reintroduces another equally respectable principle of motion—the progress from ignorance to knowledge. Each scene is another stage in our discovery of Chekhov's people and Chekhov's situation; also in their discovering of themselves and their situation (in so far as they are capable of doing so). The apparent casualness of the encounters and discussions on the stage is Chekhov linking himself to "the least possible number of movements." But as there is a "definite action," as "large forces have been brought into play," we are not cheated of drama. The "trigger effect" is as dramatic in its way as the "buried secret" pattern of Sophocles and Ibsen. Of course, there will be people who see the tininess of the movements and do not notice the enormousness of the forces released—who see the trigger-finger move and do not hear the shot. To them, Chekhov remains a mere manufacturer of atmosphere, a mere contriver of nuance. To others he seems a master of dramatic form unsurpassed in modern times.

NOTES

[1] In cases where Chekhov changed the name of a character for his later version, I have used the later name only, to avoid confusion. And I have called each person by the designation that non-Russians most easily remember: "the Professor," "Waffles," "Astrov," "Sonya."
[2] In general I quote from published translations of Chekhov: the English of *The Wood Demon* is S. S. Koteliansky's; of *Uncle Vanya*, Constance Garnett's. But I have altered these versions, consulting the Russian original wherever alteration seemed desirable.
[3] From the title as well as from the dialogue. For not only does the center of interest shift from Astrov to Vanya, but Chekhov deliberately drops from his masthead the evocative *demon* in favor of the utterly banal *uncle*. If the name Vanya sounds exotic to non-Russian ears, one has to know that it is the equivalent of Jack.
[4] So Constance Garnett. Actually Chekhov does not here use the Russian word for "to work" (*rabotat*), which is his leitmotiv; he uses an idiom meaning "you must do something!" (*"Nado delo delat!"*)

Philip Bordinat (essay date 1958)

SOURCE: "Dramatic Structure in Chekhov's *Uncle Vanya*," in *Slavic and East European Journal*, Vol. 16, 1958, pp. 195-210.

[*In the essay below, Bordinat contends that* Uncle Vanya *has no single protagonist but that four characters collectively comprise "the individual," who fills the role. The critic maintains that the play is structured around a "series of bids by 'the individual,' whichever character it might be, for some kind of value or happiness in the provincial Russian 'wasteland' that Chekhov pictures for us."*]

Anton Chekhov's *Uncle Vanya* has often been criticized as being aimless, implying a lack of sound dramatic structure. Yet the play confounds these formalist critics by continuing to be successful on the stage. My view is that the play is built on a rigid structural framework and that the play does possess specific direction.

Chekhov was certainly conscious of the need for a basic framework for his plays. The following statement from one of his letters indicates his realization of the importance of climax in a play:

> The first act can go as long as an hour, but the others must not take longer than thirty minutes. The climax of the play must occur in the third act, but it must not be too big a climax to kill the fourth act.[1]

In addition to Chekhov's concern with climax, this passage suggests his interest in proportion. Yet this passage, though it suggests a consciousness of some of the structural problems of the playwright, tells us little about *Uncle Vanya.* It is in the examination of the play in the light of some of the basic rules for constructing a play that the structure becomes clear. We can see, then, that there is an aim and that *Uncle Vanya* adheres to the conventional structural pattern of exposition, dramatic incident, rising action (through a series of complications), climax, and resolution.

For these formal qualities to become evident, however, the reader must accept a unique idea of protagonist in *Uncle Vanya.* The suggestion is here advanced that there is no single protagonist in the play; rather, the protagonist is "the individual." Thus, the protagonist is no one character throughout the play, but each character during the time when he is attempting to find some value in Chekhov's Russian "wasteland." In other words, the protagonist is "the individual" in the abstract.

The question may be raised at this point: "But what about Vanya? Surely he is the protagonist." It is true that Vanya is onstage for a major portion of the play; it is also true that, when he is not onstage, he is often kept before us through the conversations of the other characters. On the other hand, there are extended periods when the audience is far more concerned with the fate of Astrov, Yelena, or Sonya than they are with Vanya. It is a rule of the drama that the fate of the central character should always be paramount in the minds of the audience. Such is not the case in our reactions to Vanya nor to any other single character in the play. Rather, we are concerned with the series of bids by "the individual," whichever character it might be, for some kind of value or happiness in the provincial Russian "wasteland" that Chekhov pictures for us.

It is well to remember that *Uncle Vanya* is a revision of his early, less controlled play, *The Wood Demon.*[2] Chekhov, in his revision, supports the idea of no single protagonist by, in a sense, leveling the characters relative to their respective interest value for an audience. The fact that the name of the play was changed from *The Wood Demon,* which refers to Khrushchev, Doctor Astrov's counterpart, to *Uncle Vanya* reflects such a change of thinking on the part of the playwright. Consistent with this change of thinking is the omission of Yegor Voynitskiy's (Vanya in *Uncle Vanya*) suicide. Thus, Vanya is carried through to the final curtain. Furthermore, in *Uncle Vanya* Chekhov makes Sonya much more appealing and Yelena more cowardly than either was in *The Wood Demon*. All of these changes suggest that Chekhov was bringing these characters to the level of protagonist, thus enabling each to be "the individual" during a part of the play.

Let us now consider dramatic structure. A basic structure test that is often applied by playwrights to a new play idea is that of the *fighting triad*. Samuel Seldon describes the fighting triad in this way:

> Nearly all successful plays are built around a triad so arranged as to imply a conflict.

PRINCIPAL FORCE	OPPOSING FORCE	DECIDING AGENT

The Principal Force is that driving desire of the central character which motivates the action. It is his desire for an object or person, or for a change of condition. The Opposing Force is the desire of someone else—a rival, foe, or other inimical presence—to block the fulfillment of the first character's want. And the Deciding Agent is that thing which finally turns the course of the conflict to the advantage of the first or the second force. The age-old plot involving two men and a girl is a perfect example of the triad.

Principal Force	Opposing Force	Deciding Agent
The desire of the man for the girl.	The desire of the rival for the same girl.	The mind of the girl.[3]

If the fighting triad is applied to *Uncle Vanya* with Vanya or any single character as the central character, the term "principal" could hardly be used because there are similar forces in the other characters which often occupy audience interest for significant periods of the play. On the other hand, if "the individual" is considered as the central character, the triad applies.

Principal Force	Opposing Force	Deciding Agent
The individual's desire for happiness.	The Provincial Russian "wasteland."	The overpowering quality of the Russian "wasteland."

Through the use of "the individual" as protagonist, the playwright avoided the impossible task of having to create an all-encompassing, everyman character to give his play universal significance. Instead, he achieved this appeal through four characters. Two are men, one a doctor and the other a gentleman farmer; and two are women, one married, physically beautiful and spiritually ugly, and the other unmarried, physically unattractive and spiritually beautiful. However, though the introduction of "the individual" as protagonist simplified one problem it intensified another, the problem of exposition.

The major exposition of any play is difficult; but in *Uncle Vanya,* in addition to the usual details of time, place, and situation, four major characters had to be developed in enough detail to make each one of them of central interest to an audience during that portion of the play in which he would represent "the individual."[4] In a sense, it was the problem of introducing four protagonists. In accomplishing this huge task, Chekhov violated a number of fundamental rules; yet the results are rewarding. In the opening scene of the play, Chekhov violated a cardinal rule of dramatic exposition in that he introduced two characters who both know all of the information that must be imparted to the audience. Thus, the questions which Doctor Astrov puts to Marina, the nurse, are unnatural in that he already knows the answers to them:

> MARINA *pours out a glass of tea:* Here, drink it dearie.
>
> ASTROV *reluctantly accepting the glass:* I don't feel like it somehow.
>
> MARINA: Perhaps you'd like a drop of vodka?
>
> ASTROV: No. I don't drink vodka every day. It's too close anyway. *A pause.* By the way, Nanny, how many years is it we've known each other?
>
> MARINA *pondering:* How many? The Lord help my memory. . . . You came to live around here . . . well, when was it? . . . Sonechka's mother, Vera Petrovna, was still living then. You came to see us for two winters when she was alive. . . . That means that at least eleven years have gone by. . . . *After a moment's thought.* Maybe more. . . .
>
> ASTROV: Have I changed a lot since then?
>
> MARINA: Yes, a lot. You were young and handsome then, but you've aged now. And you're not as good looking as you were. There's another thing too—you take a drop of vodka now and again.
>
> (I, 93)[5]

At this point, Astrov takes up the story and proceeds to give an extended answer to his own question. In most plays having a major character put two such contrived questions about himself to another character and then having him launch into an extended, inadequately motivated self-analysis in arswer to his own question would be the worst kind of dramaturgy. However, in *Uncle Vanya,* Chekhov's violation of convention seems to fit into context, in that he was attempting to create an atmosphere of boredom in which people act without reason. Here people talk about the past because there is little meaning in the present or hope for the future; there is only the past when there was still hope for a good life.

The entrance of Uncle Vanya illustrates another break with dramatic convention, for there is absolutely no preparation for his entrance. He simply appears, yawning, upon the stage, having just awakened from a nap. Then, in answer to the question "Had a good sleep?" he proceeds to give an extended treatment of the upset in his living routine since the professor and his wife came to live with them, thus for the first time mentioning the dramatic incident. The effect of this speech on the audience is much like the feeling produced on an individual who has politely asked another "How are you?" and is forced to listen to an extended analysis of that person's medical history. The information is hardly interesting in itself, but the surprise of the reply holds the audience. In both cases, we have a bore; yet we are compelled to listen. Vanya's speech, in addition to accentuating the utter boredom of the situation, initiates the preparation for the entrance of Professor Serebryakov and his wife, Yelena.

A brief discussion of the professor's upsetting habits precedes his and Yelena's entrance. The entrance seems to come too soon, for we have learned nothing about Yelena. The audience can only assume that she is the right age and type for the professor. Chekhov outraged dramatic convention in getting them onstage, for he had the couple enter with Sonya and Telegin. Vanya (Voynitskiy) draws the attention of the audience to the entrance when he says:

> VOYNITSKIY: They're coming, they're coming! Don't fuss!
> *Voices are heard.* SEREBRYAKOV, YELENA ANDREYEVNA, SONYA, *and* TELEGIN *approach from the farther part of the garden, returning from their walk.*
> SEREBRYAKOV: It was beautiful, beautiful! . . . Wonderful scenery!
>
> TELEGIN: Yes, Your Excellency, the views are remarkable.
>
> SONYA: To-morrow we'll go to the plantation, Papa. Would you like to?
>
> VOYNITSKIY: Tea's ready, my friends!
>
> SEREBRYAKOV: My friends, will you be good enough to send my tea to my study? I've something more I must do to-day.
>
> SONYA: I'm sure you will like it at the plantation.
>
> YELENA ANDREYEVNA, SEREBRYAKOV, *and* SONYA *go into the house.* TELEGIN *goes to the table and sits down beside* MARINA.
>
> VOYNITSKIY: It's hot and close, but our great man of learning has got his overcoat and goloshes on, and he's carrying his umbrella and gloves.
>
> ASTROV: He's obviously taking care of himself.
> (I, 95-96)

This apparently premature entrance seems to serve the function of a preview, for three important characters merely pass through. Yet, the brief conversation identifies Professor Serebryakov and his daughter, Sonya, while Telegin stops on stage to contribute to the ensuing dis-

cussion. Yelena crosses the stage and exits. Yet, with Sonya identified through her reference to "Papa," the audience would realize that the other woman is Yelena, the professor's wife. This realization would come as a shock to the audience, for she is much too young for the professor, and she is beautiful. Audience curiosity regarding Yelena would be aroused at this point, and Vanya's comments would accentuate this curiosity:

> VOYNITSKIY: But how lovely *she* is! How lovely! I've never seen a more beautiful woman in all my life.

Then he adds:

> Her eyes . . . a wonderful woman!
> (I, 96)

These two utterances by Vanya would create a desire in the audience to have another look at the woman, seen only briefly, who could motivate such comments.

The four characters representing "the individual," or the protagonist, have been presented to the audience during the first quarter of the first act. The remainder of the exposition consists of dialogues which elaborate on these characters and on the antagonist, Serebryakov. Some of these speeches are long and often about the speaker, himself. Here again Chekhov reinforced the utter boredom and hopelessness of the situation, for the boring situation is often characterized by people talking at length about themselves and what they might have been. The following speech by Vanya is typical:

> Oh, yes! I used to be an inspiring personality who never inspired anybody! . . . *A pause.* I used to be an inspiring personality! . . . You could hardly have made a more wounding joke! I'm forty-seven now. Up to a year ago I tried deliberately to pull the wool over my eyes—just as you do yourself with the aid of all your pedantic rubbish—so that I shouldn't see the realities of life . . . and I thought I was doing the right thing. But now—if you only knew! I lie awake, night after night, in sheer vexation and anger—that I let time slip by so stupidly during the years when I could have had all the things from which my age now cuts me off.
> (I, 100-101)

Reflected here is both the boredom and the hopelessness of Vanya's and, for that matter, the provincial Russian's situation. A desert much like T. S. Eliot's "Wasteland" is suggested when Astrov comments on wanton waste, later in the first act:

> You can burn turf in your stoves and build your barns out of stones. . . . Well, I would consent to cutting wood when people really need it, but why destroy the forests? The Russian forests are literally groaning under the axe, millions of trees are being destroyed, the homes of animals and birds are being laid waste, the rivers are getting shallow and drying up, wonderful scenery is disappearing for ever—and all this is happening just because people are too lazy and stupid to stoop down and pick up the fuel from the ground. *To* YELENA. Isn't it so, Madam? Anyone

who can burn up all that beauty in a stove, who can destroy something that we cannot create, must be a barbarian incapable of reason. Man is endowed with reason and creative power so that he can increase what has been given him, but up to the present he's been destroying and not creating. There are fewer and fewer forests, the rivers are drying up, the wild creatures are almost exterminated, the climate is being ruined, and the land is getting poorer and more hideous every day.

(I, 103-4)

Here we have a Russian "wasteland" characterized by boredom, hopelessness, destruction, and lack of creativity. The intellectual sterility is evidenced by the professor, who is described as "a dull old stick, a sort of scholarly dried fish." The reference to dryness is significant in this and in the reference to "the rivers . . . getting shallow and drying up . . ." in the above quotation. Both augment the impression of a "wasteland."

Thus Chekhov effectively acquainted the audience with the major characters, the mood, the setting, and the dramatic incident of the play.[6] It is true that he violated certain dramatic conventions, but he seems to have gained rather than lost from these violations.

Early in the first act, Chekhov began to develop suspense according to the fighting triad, through three dramatic situations each involving an attempt by "the individual" to find a measure of happiness in the provincial Russian milieu. The three situations are as follows:

1. The attempt of Vanya to secure the love of Yelena.
2. The attempt of Astrov to secure the love of Yelena.
3. The attempt of Sonya to secure the love of Astrov.

Each of these situations holds our attention for a part of the play, but no one of them dominates throughout.

The first hint we have of Vanya's desire for Yelena occurs early in the first act when he comments on her loveliness as she is leaving the stage for the first time (I, 96). The situation is finally resolved in the fourth act. Coming between these passages are three other scenes involving Vanya and Yelena, one in each of the first three acts. Each of these scenes ends in complete frustration for Vanya. The scene at the end of the first act is typical:

YELENA: . . . Perhaps, Ivan Petrovich, you and I are such good friends just because we both are such tiresome and boring people. Tiresome! Don't look at me like that, I don't like it!

VOYNITSKIY: How else can I look at you if I love you? You are my happiness, my life, my youth! I know the chances of your returning my feelings are negligible, just zero—but I don't want anything—only let me look at you and hear your voice. . . .

YELENA: Hush, they might hear you! *They go into the house.*

VOYNITSKIY *following her:* Let me talk of my love, don't drive me away—that in itself will be such great happiness to me. . . .

YELENA: This is a torture. . . .

(I, 105-6)

The suspense generated during a scene of this kind is considerable. The same may be said of the scenes between Astrov and Yelena.

The Astrov–Yelena situation develops possibly more suspense than the Vanya–Yelena situation because the characters are attracted to each other. Once more Chekhov initiated suspense by a subtle hint when Yelena says to Vanya in the first act:

The doctor has a tired, sensitive face. An interesting face. Sonya is obviously attracted by him; she's in love with him, and I understand her feelings. He's visited the house three times since I've been here, but I'm shy and I haven't once had a proper talk with him or been nice to him. He must have thought me bad-tempered.

(I, 105)

In the second act, Astrov describes Yelena as "an exceptionally attractive woman!" (II, 113). Later in the act, he says to Sonya:

What still does affect me is beauty. I can't remain indifferent to that. I believe that if Yelena Andreyevna wanted to, for instance, she could turn my head in a day. . . . But that's not love, of course, that's not affection.

(II, 118)

Shortly after this speech, Astrov and Yelena are bracketed together. Sonya says to Yelena:

Tell me honestly, as a friend. . . . Are you happy?

YELENA: No.

SONYA: I knew that. One more question. Tell me frankly—wouldn't you have liked your husband to be young?

YELENA: What a little girl you are still! Of course I should. *Laughs.* Well, ask me something else, do. . . .

SONYA: Do you like the doctor?

YELENA: Yes, very much.

(II, 120)

Then Yelena speaks at length in praise of Astrov. Finally, the preparation for the big scene between Astrov and Yelena is complete. The lines immediately preceding the scene reflect the playwright's skill in bringing his audience up to a high level of expectation. Yelena soliloquizes first about Sonya, and then she continues about Astrov:

. . . To fall under the fascination of a man like that, to forget oneself. . . . I believe I'm a little attracted myself. . . . Yes, I'm bored when he's not about, and here I am smiling when I think of him. . . . Uncle Vanya here says I have a mermaid's blood in my veins, "Let yourself go for once in your life." . . . Well, perhaps that's what I ought to do. . . . To fly away, free as a bird, away from all of you, from your sleepy faces and talk, to forget that you exist at all—everyone of you! . . . But I'm too timid and shy. . . . My conscience would torment me to distraction. . . . He comes here every day. . . . I can guess why he comes and already I feel guilty. . . . I want to fall on my knees before Sonya, to ask her forgiveness and cry. . . .

(III, 126-27)

At this moment, when Yelena's mind is full of her feelings for Astrov, he shocks her from her thoughts:

ASTROV *comes in with chart:* Good-day to you! *Shakes hands.* You wanted to see my artistic handiwork?

(III, 127)

From this point, Chekhov increases the suspense by having Astrov bore her with talk about the maps of his reforestation projects. Then, when she admits to being bored, the playwright once more delayed the intimate scene that must come by shifting the conversation to Sonya's love for Astrov. Finally, he shifted the discussion to their own relationship:

ASTROV: . . . There's only one thing I don't understand: Why did you have to have this interrogation? *Looks into her eyes and shakes his finger at her.* You're a sly one!

YELENA: What does that mean?

ASTROV *laughs:* Sly! Suppose Sonya is suffering— I'm prepared to think it probable—but what was the purpose of this cross-examination? *Preventing her from speaking, with animation.* Please don't try to look astonished. You know perfectly well why I come here every day. . . . Why, and on whose account— you know very well indeed. You charming bird of prey, don't look at me like that, I'm a wise old sparrow. . . .

YELENA *perplexed:* Bird of prey! I don't understand at all!

ASTROV: A beautiful, fluffy weasel. . . . You must have a victim! Here I've been doing nothing for a whole month. I've dropped everything, I seek you out hungrily—and you are awfully pleased about it, awfully. . . . Well, what am I to say? I'm conquered, but you knew that without an interrogation! *Crossing his arms and bowing his head.* I submit. Here I am, devour me!

YELENA: Have you gone out of your mind?
ASTROV *laughs sardonically:* You are coy. . . .

YELENA: Oh, I'm not so bad, or so mean as you think! On my word of honor! *Tries to go out.*

(III, 130-31)

In spite of Astrov's persistence, Yelena continues to resist him. Thus Yelena's lack of courage, which keeps her from defying convention, forces Astrov back into the utter boredom of his life as a country doctor and dooms her to the boredom of her marriage with the professor. Their bids for happiness are frustrated.

Sonya's attempt at happiness with Astrov is also frustrated. The doctor, who despite his submission to his environment could react to the superficial beauty of Yelena, is dulled to the point of being incapable of reaction to the less obvious but more substantial beauty of Sonya. Chekhov made this situation more poignant by having Sonya confess her love for Astrov to Yelena, who in turn acts as an unsuccessful emissary to Astrov. Chekhov here achieved added suspense, for the audience is concerned not only with Astrov's reaction to Yelena's mission but also with Sonya's reaction to the disappointing news. Here is one of the most emotionally moving scenes in the play, for the playwright arranged to have Sonya learn the unhappy news at the professor's meeting. Thus, she must suffer while in the group rather than alone:

SEREBRYAKOV: But where are the others? I don't like this house. It's like a sort of labyrinth. Twenty-six enormous rooms, people wander off in all directions, and there's no finding anyone. *Rings.* Ask Mar'ya Vasil'yevna and Yelena Andreyevna to come here!

YELENA: I'm here.

SEREBRYAKOV: Please sit down, my friends.

SONYA *going up to* YELENA, *impatiently:* What did he say?

YELENA: I'll tell you later.

SONYA: You're trembling? You're upset? *Looks searchingly into her face.* I understand. . . . He said he wouldn't be coming here any more . . . yes? *A pause.* Tell me: yes? YELENA *nods her head.*

SEREBRYAKOV *to* TELEGIN: One can put up with ill health, after all. But what I can't stomach is the whole pattern of life in the country. I feel as if I had been cast off the earth on to some strange planet. Do sit down, friends, please! Sonya!

SONYA *does not hear him; she stands and hangs her head sadly.* Sonya! *A pause.* She doesn't hear. *To* MARINA. You sit down too, Nanny.

(III, 132-33)

At this point, shortly before the climax of his play, Chekhov introduced a flash of humor. The professor facetiously informs the group that "the Inspector General is coming." This attempt at humor, coming while the audience is still reacting to Sonya's suffering and contrasting with the mood pervading the theater at the moment, helps to emphasize Sonya's suffering. The laugh evoked is a cruel trespass upon Sonya in her grief.

The professor's proposal brings our attention back to Vanya and, therefore, justifies the name of the play. The professor, in an effort to escape completely from the discouraging provincial atmosphere by selling this Russian country estate, endangers the material security of Vanya and Sonya. Furthermore, there is the danger of Vanya's having Yelena drift completely out of his life. This danger, however, relates only to the first of the three dramatic situations mentioned earlier in the discussion. Yet, the professor's proposal is a threat to "the individual" in each of the other two dramatic situations, as well; for Yelena would also be removed from Astrov's life; and Astrov, without a place to visit, would be removed from Sonya's life. Furthermore, Astrov would have no escape from his day-to-day routine and, as a result, no one with whom to discuss his theories of lost opportunity. However, it is Vanya who protests indignantly and then accuses the professor of ruining him:

> I will not be silent! *Barring* SEREBRYAKOV'S *way.* Wait, I haven't finished yet! You've ruined my life! I haven't lived. I have not lived! Thanks to you I've destroyed, I've annihilated the best years of my life! You've been my worst enemy! . . . My life is ruined! I have talent, courage, intelligence. . . . If I had had a normal life, I might have been a Schopenhauer, a Dostoyevskiy. . . . Oh, I'm talking rubbish! . . . I'm going out of my mind. . . . Mother, I'm in despair! Mother!
>
> (III, 136-37)

Yet, in his protest, Vanya is outlining not only his own lost opportunities but those of "the individual"—Sonya, Astrov, Yelena, and even the professor—all whose hopes are crushed in the Russian provinces. The climax, which follows immediately with Vanya's abortive attempt to shoot his "worst enemy," symbolically reflects the frustration of "the individual," his inability to carry through to completion any plan requiring decisive action.

In the final act, Chekhov resolved each of the three dramatic situations in a way that shut out hope for value or happiness for "the individual." First, Astrov and Yelena say good-bye forever:

> ASTROV: It is strange somehow. . . . Here we've known one another, and all at once for some reason . . . we shall never see each other again. That's the way with everything in this world. . . . While there's no one here—before Uncle Vanya comes in with a bunch of flowers, allow me . . . to kiss you . . . good-bye. . . . Yes? *Kisses her on the cheek.* There . . . that's fine.
>
> YELENA: I wish you every happiness . . . *Looks around.* Well, here goes—for once in my life! *Embraces him impulsively, and both at once quickly step back from each other.* I must be off.

Stanislavsky as Astrov, in the 1899 Moscow Art Theater production of Uncle Vanya.

> ASTROV: Go as soon as you can. If the horses are ready, you'd better be off!
>
> YELENA: I think someone's coming. *Both listen.*
>
> ASTROV: Finita!
>
> (IV, 146-47)

Following this exchange, Vanya bids farewell to Yelena:

> VOYNITSKIY *warmly kisses* YELENA'S *hand.* Good-bye. . . . Forgive me. . . . We shall never see one another again.
>
> YELENA *moved:* Good-bye, dear Ivan Petrovich. *Kisses him on the head and goes out.*
>
> (IV, 147-48)

Finally, Sonya and Astrov part:

> SONYA: When shall we see you again?
>
> ASTROV: Not before next summer, I expect. Hardly in the winter. . . . Naturally, if anything happens you'll let me know and I'll come. *Shakes hands with them.* Thank you for your hospitality, your kindness . . . for everything, in fact. *Goes to the nurse and kisses her on the head.* Good-bye, old woman!
>
> MARINA: So you're going before you've had tea?
>
> ASTROV: I don't want any, Nurse.

MARINA: Perhaps you'll have a drop of vodka?

ASTROV *irresolutely:* Perhaps. . . .

                            (IV, 149)

Chekhov quickly resolved the three dramatic situations and, at the same time, brought his play back to the point where it opened, that is, with Marina's offering Astrov "a drop of vodka." It is as if nothing has happened; yet something has happened. "The individual," represented by Vanya, Astrov, Sonya, and Yelena, has been defeated; nor is there hope for "the individual," whether it be Yelena committed to a life of boredom with the professor or the others doomed to the unrelieved lethargy of the Russian provinces. Astrov has already spoken the epitaph:

> The people who come a hundred years or a couple of hundred years after us and despise us for having lived in so stupid and tasteless a fashion—perhaps they'll find a way to be happy. . . . As for us. . . . There's only one hope for you and me. . . . The hope that when we're at rest in our graves we may see visions—perhaps even pleasant ones. *With a sigh.* Yes, my friend! In the whole of this province there have only been two decent, cultured people—you and I. But ten years of this contemptible routine, this trivial provincial life has swallowed us up, poisoned our blood with its putrid vapors, until now we've become just as petty as all the rest.
>
>   (IV, 143)

Chekhov has, in *Uncle Vanya,* written a play that obeys the rules of dramatic construction if the reader will accept the idea of the protagonist's being "the individual." Without the idea of "the individual" in *Uncle Vanya,* our interest shifts from one character to another in a way that implies not a single motivating force, but a separate force for each of the three important dramatic situations in the play. Thus, these three situations seem unrelated dramatically. However, when "the individual" is accepted, the "individual's" desire for happiness becomes the central motivating force in the play. At this point it can be seen that the three important dramatic situations are related dramatically to each other; and the structural framework of exposition, dramatic incident, rising action, climax, and resolution becomes clear.

NOTES

[1] David Magarshack, *Chekhov the Dramatist* (New York: Hill and Wang, 1952), p. 46.
[2] *The Wood Demon* was completed in October 1889 and first produced on December 27 of the same year. *Uncle Vanya* was completed before the end of 1896 and first produced on September 30, 1899. Chekhov achieved far greater economy and polish in *Uncle Vanya* than he had in *The Wood Demon.* In characterization, for example, he secured greater concentration by cutting the number of characters from thirteen in *The Wood Demon* to nine in *Uncle Vanya.*
[3] Samuel Seldon, *An Introduction to Playwriting* (New York, 1946), p. 41.
[4] In 1900 Chekhov was faced with a similar problem of exposition in *Three Sisters.* He says in a letter to Gor'kiy, dated October 16, 1900, "It has been very difficult to write *Three Sisters.* Three heroines, you see, each a separate type and all the daughters of a general." See Constance Garnett, trans., Letters of Anton Chekhov (New York: Macmillan, 1920), p. 400.

[5] All quotations from *Uncle Vanya* have been taken from Elisaveta Fen, trans., *The Seagull and Other Plays* (London: Penguin Classics, 1954).
[6] The dramatic incident is the entrance of Professor Serebryakov and his wife, Yelena. The impact of the professor and Yelena upon the several protagonists of the play causes each of these protagonists to make one last attempt to find happiness. The suspense of the play depends upon audience concern as to the outcome of these attempts.

Tyrone Guthrie (essay date 1969)

SOURCE: "A Director's Introduction," in *Uncle Vanya: Scenes from Country Life in Four Acts,* by Anton Chekhov, translated by Tyrone Guthrie and Leonid Kipnis, The University of Minnesota Press, 1969, pp. 3-8.

[*In the essay below, Guthrie underscores the ironic tone of* Uncle Vanya.]

The impression made by Chekhov's plays depends a great deal upon the period of time from which they are viewed.

In the first decade of this century, when they were new, it was their lack of event which seemed so very noticeable. A group of characters compelled the attention, because they were so lifelike, so interesting, and so various; but, compared to the characters in other plays of the epoch, they *did* nothing. A milieu was created, but there was scarcely any activity—no big scenes, no strong situations, as in the still popular plays of Scribe and Sardou; no great rhetorical set pieces, as in Shakespeare, Racine, Goethe, or Schiller; no problems were debated, as in the theatre of Ibsen or Shaw.

Chekhov's plays, even in Russia, in Stanislavsky's productions for the Moscow Art Theatre, which were also shown in St. Petersburg and Kiev, seemed strangely lacking in the qualities which audiences had learned to regard as "dramatic." Abroad, with the barrier of translation imposed upon the original texts, they were even harder to understand.

In the English-speaking theatre it was many years before any translations appeared other than those of Mrs. Constance Garnett. Her versions have many splendid virtues, and in some ways have never been surpassed, but they do, in my estimation, lack humor and lightness. All the characters seem to be melancholy, tearful eccentrics; and for a generation Chekhov was regarded as an arch-apostle of Russian Gloom.

Gradually it began to be apparent that the emotion of Chekhov's characters is strongly tempered by humor; that the general tone of his major works is absolutely not tragic or heavily emotional; it is affectionately ironic. It is ironic that the beautiful old cherry orchard is going to be cut down to make way for a suburban real-estate development—ironic, not tragic; and Madame Ranevskaya is not, though many leading ladies have tried to make her so, a Tragedy Queen; she is a charming birdbrain. It is ironic that the three sisters never reach Moscow; but their yearning is predominantly sentimental; there is no reason to suppose that, had Moscow been achieved, they would have been any happier. Tusenbach dies in a silly, meaningless duel with a psychopath; it is ironic but not tragic; there is no reason to suppose that Irina's married life with him would have been more successful than Masha's with her schoolmaster.

Finally, *Uncle Vanya*: the formula is very similar to that of *The Three Sisters* and *The Cherry Orchard*. A group of characters is presented in a situation which, while potentially tragic, is treated ironically. In *Uncle Vanya* the situation between Vanya and the Professor is developed into a big scene; but, when the crisis occurs, it is not the tragic clash of incompatibles as Sophocles might have presented it; not the blood-orgy of Seneca, nor the noble mind o'erthrown of Shakespearean tragedy; it is not a thrillingly dramatic "curtain," such as Dumas, Sardou, Pinero, even Ibsen would have been unable to resist. It is farce. The climax of *Uncle Vanya* takes place at the end of Act Three. The men exchange angry words; Vanya flourishes a gun; the women scream; the Professor flies in terror; a shot is fired. But since Vanya is the trigger-man the bullet is far off the mark. The scene ends with the protagonist collapsing in a flood of angry, frustrated, pathetic, but essentially absurd tears.

As always, Chekhov offers marvelous acting opportunities, not merely to the actors who have the longest parts, but also to those whose characters appear to be less fully developed: the nurse, the old bluestocking Maman, Waffles are all rewarding parts. In Laurence Olivier's excellent and enormously successful production with the British National Theatre Company, these three parts were taken by three senior players of the utmost celebrity and eminence. Immediately they became not one-dimensional decorations on the fringe of the play. They took their place, as intended, as essential parts of the pattern, essential voices in a piece of intricate, but beautifully intelligible, chamber music.

What of Astrov? It is my view that this part should not be played romantically. Although Sonia is deeply in love with him and Yelena too feels his charm, it is not intended, I think, that he should charm the audience. In this play he expresses the sort of sentiment which in *The Cherry Orchard* is uttered by Trofimov, the perennial student; in *The Three Sisters* similar sentiments are scored for two voices, those of Vershinin and Tusenbach. In each of these cases high-flown sentiment is put into the mouths of characters whom Chekhov, in his affectionate-ironic way, clearly did not regard as high-flyers. I believe that the same sort of irony is intended in the case of Astrov.

He *is* noble; he *is* attractive; but he is running away from his personal problems, taking refuge in overwork and alcohol. The inference, I suggest, is that he is no less perceptively aware of the personal problems which beset him than of the ecological problems which surround him. And in both cases he is incapable of following up a correct diagnosis with an effective treatment. I think that the actor who plays Astrov must avoid the stereotype of

the handsome, lonely hero fighting insuperable odds. That performance can be left for the movie version.

Nowadays I do not think that audiences regret the lack of event, the lack of obvious drama in Chekhov. Compared to those of, for example, Harold Pinter, his plays seem positively action-packed and their dialogue develops a theme almost as relentlessly as that of Sophocles.

This means that a production of Chekhov today can afford to be less explicit both in storytelling and in the expression of character than was necessary thirty or forty years ago. It is no longer expected that every picture should "tell a story." Indeed it is becoming rather old-fashioned to do so. The movies have pulled the rug from under the sort of painting in which a Lady (in full evening dress) is depicted face down on the hearthrug, what time a Gentleman (in full evening dress) "registers" stern feeling by biting his lips, while he stands at the chimney-piece with a packet of letters in his hand. A similar change has occurred in drama. Movies and television supply the public demand for narrative. With plots unraveling every hour, from breakfast till bedtime of every day, from cradle to grave, we no longer need go to the theatre to see one more plot unravel.

The greatest drama has never, I guess, depended very much upon plot; comment has always been more important than narrative. This is not to say that none of the great dramatic masterpieces have good plots; *Oedipus Rex,* for instance, has a plot as thrilling, far more simple, and rather more coherent than *The Perils of Pauline.* But many of the great masterpieces are distinctly weak in the plot department. No one can be very much interested in the story development or surprised at the denouement of *Prometheus Bound*; it is more than its strange yet conventional story which makes *Phèdre* as great as it is; *Hamlet* certainly has a complex, but hardly a tidy, plot; Molière's plots are tidy enough but as stylized as ballad poetry, as predictable as the multiplication table, while Congreve's are barely intelligible and suffocatingly tedious; Ibsen told some good stories, but no better than many a lesser playwright; *The Importance of Being Earnest* is a masterly comedy, but *what* would one make of a synopsis of its plot?

Chekhov stands at the close of an era when narrative was an important ingredient of drama. It may, almost certainly will, become so again. But not yet. Now, and for a while, the so-called well-made play seems a dated and obvious formula. But it does not yet appear so to the audience, which, naturally, is a little behind the playwrights, actors, directors, and so on, whose business it is to be concerned with these matters.

I was interested when, a few years ago, I was connected with a production of *The Three Sisters* which its audiences gradually turned into the sort of performance to which they were accustomed and which they wanted. Without their conscious intention, the actors were pushed by the audience in the direction of big scenes, strong situations, comedy routines, emotional confrontations.

After about eight or ten performances the production had become subtly but unmistakably distorted. The comedy was louder and funnier, the pathos had become sentimental, moments of delicate tension had broadened into theatricality.

Absolutely this was not the fault of the actors; there was no indiscipline, no cheap playing for personal glory or obvious applause. I could not—and as its director I was familiar with every phrase, every gesture—detect any departure from the agreed routine of the production. It was all the fault of the people "out front." They were intelligent, eagerly sympathetic, alertly aware that the play was both funny and sad, but they were reacting as they were accustomed to react when "at the theatre," looking for and evoking big scenes, strong situations, heroes, heroines, and all the familiar claptrap of the well-made play.

I guess they were only able to evoke the claptrap because the seeds of it were already in the production. Our performance was too like A Play and not sufficiently like Real Life.

With Chekhov a happy medium needs to be sought. The performance must be just sufficiently theatrical to "hold" an audience in a large, though not very large, house; not so theatrical that an intelligent spectator says "How theatrically effective" instead of "How true."

Ieva Vitins (essay date 1978)

SOURCE: "Uncle Vanja's Predicament," in *Slavic and East European Journal,* Vol. 22, No. 4, Winter 1978, pp. 454-63.

[*In this essay, Vitins argues that Vanya's family ties are the source of his passivity and impotence.*]

Overlooked in discussions of Uncle Vanja's ineffectuality as a male protagonist is a textual network of emotional ties which bind him to his dead sister, her family, and his mother. To a great degree these ties serve to repress his masculinity and prevent him from establishing a family of his own or making an imprint on the outside world.[1] Vanja has become a peripheral male figure, a veritable "Uncle Johnnie" who proudly supports his sister Vera's family and experiences the role of husband vicariously. It is only years after Vera's death and the recent remarriage of her husband that he becomes dissatisfied with his secondary role in life.[2] He ceases temporarily to act the uncle and family provider; instead, he vents his hatred for the brother-in-law he formerly admired and assumes the role of self-dramatized suitor of the new wife Elena. Querulous and aggressive, he suggests a man painfully out of character, whose impotence reflects the sterility of the dying gentry class. This seemingly sudden change was criticized by early readers for its lack of motivation within the play and has been inadequately treated by later critics.[3] When considered within the context of the

play's underlying family drama, however, it is psychologically convincing and justified.

Until recently, Vera has been the sole love-object in her brother's life, displacing an unresponsive mother in his affections.[4] Idealized in his memory, she emerges as "a beautiful, gentle creature as pure as the blue sky above us, a fine, generous girl" (Act III).[5] When she leaves home to marry the son of a common priest, Serebrjakov, who subsequently becomes a respected professor of art history, Vanja not only gives up his inheritance but also pays the debts on her estate. For twenty-five years he has devoted his energy to its management in order to provide her family with a steady income. Even after Vera's death, ten years before, he continued to send money to Serebrjakov, in whose scholarship he took great pride: "I was proud of him and his great learning. I lived, I breathed by him! It seemed to me that everything he wrote and uttered was inspired" (Act II).[6] Vanja's role as self-sacrificing brother so absorbs him that it stifles his desire for other women; he is at a loss to understand why he did not fall in love with Elena when his sister was still alive:

> . . . To think that ten years ago I used to meet her at my sister's when she was only seventeen and I was thirty-seven. Why didn't I fall in love then and ask her to marry me? It would have been the most natural thing in the world. And she'd be my wife now. Yes. And tonight the storm would have woken us both. She'd be scared of the thunder and I'd hold her in my arms and whisper, "Don't be afraid. I'm here."

(Act II)

It appears that even Vanja's high regard for Serebrjakov was determined more by Vera's feelings for her husband than by objective considerations of intellectual worth. Since Vera loved the professor "as only angels in heaven can love beings as pure and lovely as themselves," Vanja, by extension, also came to worship him, investing him with the authority and respect due to a father figure. Fear of losing Vera's love and a son's fear of the "castrating" father no doubt also motivated Vanja's unquestioning devotion to the man.[7]

In the past year, however, Vanja has become disillusioned with the now retired professor, and it is the latter's arrival on the estate, accompanied by Elena, that precipitates the events which bring about the temporary breakdown in the pattern of Vanja's existence. For by remarrying, Serebrjakov has abrogated his bond to Vera and set Vanja free from emotional obligation. This in turn triggers long repressed hostility, part of the price of the brother's unrealized love of his sister; the formerly passive uncle displays belligerent qualities suggested in his family name, Vojnickij (from the Russian word for "war," *vojna*). He openly admits to the envy behind his admiration of the man who, in his "Don Juanish" success with women, has been the victorious rival for his sister's, mother's, and Elena's love. He no longer regards Serebrjakov with the blind worshipping eyes of the sister and mother, but with the equally subjective lenses of the brother-avenger facing his "worst enemy." The professor's contributions as a scholar, though flashy like his name ("silver," *serebro*), now strike Vanja as shallow and insignificant: "Now he's retired you can see exactly what his life is worth. Not a page of his work will survive him. He's totally obscure, a nonentity. A soap bubble! And I've made a fool of myself, I see it now, a complete fool" (Act II).

The boldness of Vanja's attacks on the professor stems not only from his conviction that the man is an impostor, but also because he is no longer an effective sexual rival. Physically moribund, "a man in a shell," Serebrjakov is now instinctively afraid of the physical threat behind Vanja's hatred, and even refuses to be left alone with him: "No, no! Don't leave me alone with him! No. He'll talk my head off" (Act II). Most importantly, Serebrjakov's success as a ladies' man has become suspect, for Vanja is aware that the beautiful Elena no longer loves her husband and that she too has been blinded by the professor's fame.

When considered against the background of his feelings for Vera and his desire for revenge, Vanja's sudden infatuation and pursuit of Elena suggest the emergence of a hitherto suppressed and forbidden aspect of his love for his sister. By occupying Vera's position as Serebrjakov's wife, Elena becomes, in effect, Vanja's "foster" sister. But whereas in Vera he recognized only spiritual beauty (as implied by her very name, the Russian "Faith"), Elena (Helen), the lovely disrupter of tranquility and home, appeals to him physically: ". . . but isn't she lovely? Lovely! She's the most beautiful woman I've ever seen" (Act I). Before her, the brother-protector succumbs to the brother as would-be seducer, one who defies the rival he no longer deems worthy of the sister. (See Valency, 196; Irwin, 28.) Čexov did not ignore the implied incestuous overtones in the situation; although not stated in *Uncle Vanja,* they are alluded to in the earlier play *Wood Demon* where rumor links the uncle in an affair with Elena.

> Is nothing sacred to you? You might remember, you and the dear lady who's just gone out, that her husband was once married to your sister. And that you have a young girl living under the same roof. Your affair's already the talk of the whole country. You should be thoroughly ashamed of yourselves.
>
> (Act III)

Although Vanja professes a strong physical desire for Elena, psychologically, he is incapable of attaining his goal. Like Vera, Elena is a woman to behold, worship, and protect, but never possess. The "sister," in both her spiritual and physical aspects, remains inviolate:

> VOJNICKIJ: You are my happiness, my life, my youth. I know there's little or no chance of your loving me, but I don't want anything from you. Only let me look at you, listen to your voice—
>
> ELENA: Sh! Someone might hear you.

> VOJNICKIJ: Let me speak of my love. So long as you don't drive me away, that's all I need to be the happiest man on earth.
>
> (Act I)

Vanja remains "prisoner of his passivity, the lack of vigor from which he has always suffered" (Valency, 184).

If Vera gave the household a reason for its existence and cohesiveness, Elena upsets its established order and refuses to contribute to its proper functioning, admitting that domestic concerns completely bore her. She sees herself accurately as an episodic figure in the house; inevitably she vitiates every family role she undertakes. Her beauty and sexuality endow her with an energy that lends an element of vitality to the monotonous daily life on the estate and threatens to destroy its very core by exposing and exacerbating family tensions:

> We are in a bad way in this house. Your mother hates everything except her pamphlets and the professor. The professor's overwrought, he doesn't trust me and he's afraid of you. Sonja's annoyed with her father and with me too. She hasn't spoken to me for a fortnight. You loathe my husband and openly sneer at your mother, and I'm so much on edge I've been on the verge of tears a dozen times today. We are in a bad way, aren't we?
>
> (Act III)

Elena finds a certain similarity in character between Vanja and herself—both are "abysmal bores." She regards him more as a brother-confidant than a suitor; his declarations of love and physical attentions clearly exasperate her. By telling him that he should not participate in petty squabbles but mend them, she urges him to resume his role as uncle. At the same time, she prevents him from doing so; her idleness is infectious, and her paralyzing beauty unmans him.

Appropriately, it is a glance from his niece Sonja, reminding him of her dead mother, that brings to the foreground Vanja's guilt about his changed behavior:

> SONJA: The hay's cut, there's rain every day, and it's rotting. And you spend your time on illusions. You've completely abandoned the farm. I do all the work myself and I'm about at the end of my tether. Uncle, you have tears in your eyes.

> VOJNICKIJ: The way you looked at me just now, your dead mother used to look like that. My darling—. (*Eagerly kisses her hands and face.*) My sister, my darling sister—. Where is she now? *If she only knew! Oh, if she only knew!*

> SONJA: Knew what? What do you mean, Uncle?

> VOJNICKIJ: It's so painful, such a wretched business. Never mind. I'll tell you later. It doesn't matter. I'll go.
>
> (Act II)

In one of his outlandish yet revealing bits of hyperbole, the household hanger-on Telegin provides an insight into the nature of the "wretched business" alluded to by Vanja. Upset by Vanja's insistence that Elena should be unfaithful to Serebrjakov because she does not love him, Telegin protests that unfaithfulness in marriage is the same as treason to one's country. Vanja immediately squelches him, as if realizing that he himself has committed a kind of "treason" by surrendering his earlier way of life to the pursuit of Elena, thereby betraying his sister and the lifestyle he maintained out of loyalty to her. Yet he is at the same time aware that such unfaithfulness is perhaps his and Elena's only escape from the emptiness of their personal lives to some measure of freedom. (See Gurvič, 114.)

In contrast to Vanja, Sonja (the Russian Sophia) has been endowed with a nature which might have enabled her to move outside the narrow confines of the immediate family and establish a life of her own. From her mother she has inherited spiritual strength, from her father, a sense of purpose, and with Vanja she shares her industriousness. Yet like her uncle, she is sexless, lacking in beauty, and "as a woman" fails to attract the doctor, Astrov, whom she loves "more than my own mother." Astrov claims that he might have considered marriage to Sonja, but Elena's beauty quickly turns his thoughts to seduction. Sonja is blind to the threat presented by Elena; at first she distrusts her, for she has taken her mother's place, but eventually the stepmother wins her over (ironically, they even drink a *Bruderschaft*), and Sonja confides in her as she would her mother, confessing her love for Astrov. By accepting the role of confidante and even volunteering to serve as matchmaker, Elena further injures her family image. In truth she acts as Sonja's rival, not mother, and foils whatever chances her stepdaughter might have had with Astrov, thereby destroying the family's sole hope for a future generation.

Just as Sonja fails to see in her beautiful stepmother a rival for Astrov's attentions, Vanja fails to see that Astrov has replaced Serebrjakov as his sexual rival. The two men have been longtime friends; they share intelligence, a life of sacrifice and hard work. If Vanja's concern is for his immediate family and the estate, Astrov, a doctor, concerns himself with the larger community and the forest which he admits is his true love. The "family" gratification which Vanja earlier derived from providing for the future of his kin, Astrov finds in planting trees: "When I plant a young birch and later see it covered with green and swaying in the breeze, my heart fills with pride and I—" (Act I). Both men are infected by Elena's beauty, but for Vanja it is a beauty to behold, whereas for Astrov, feminine beauty is to be savored and enjoyed. Women for Vanja are fated to be sister-friends; for Astrov, friendship between the sexes can be established only after the woman has been the man's mistress. In some sense, the sexually aggresive Astrov realizes in Vanja's stead his would-be aspect as seducer: he is desired by both his friend's "foster" sister and his niece. There is even a vague hint that the relations between Vera and Astrov were not indifferent: the doctor marks

the beginning of his physical decline from about the time of her death. Vanja's disillusionment, on the other hand, appeared the previous year, after Serebrjakov's remarriage. The difference in the manner of the two rival-friends is highlighted when Vanja, by way of an apology, pleads Elena's favor with a bouquet of fall flowers, while Astrov, weary of a verbal game of sexual innuendoes, embraces her. As Čexov himself noted, "Uncle Vanja cries, Astrov—whistles."[8]

The final shattering of Vanja's male ego in the play comes not when he discovers Elena in Astrov's arms, but immediately following, at the unprecedented family gathering called by Serebrjakov. Significantly, both Vanja and Sonja, the most family-conscious members present, are at the outset reluctant to participate in the event. Vanja is stunned by what he has just witnessed, and Sonja, by Astrov's rejection. The meeting does not bring the family its much-needed unity but hastens its disintegration.

In his proposal to sell the family estate, Serebrjakov implements his patriarchal authority to bring about the dissolution of the family hearth. Despite his "fall" from favor in the eyes of all but the mother Marija Vasil'evna, he continues as head of the household. "No one questions your rights," Elena tells him earlier, and she submits when he denies her permission to play the piano. Unfeelingly, Serebrjakov equates his brother-in-law's life of labor with the amount of cash that the property will bring for Elena and himself in the city. Since Vanja's remaining identity is so inextricably bound up with the estate, the proposal that it be taken from its lawful owner, Sonja, the last member of the Vojnickij line, is tantamount to his emasculation. Nor can he tolerate the humiliating prospect of being reduced to the position of Telegin who, deprived of all family rights, is obliged to live out the rest of his days as a sponger on the estate that formerly belonged to his uncle.[9] Consequently, Vanja's dramatic attempt to assert himself by shooting at the professor is as understandable (even in its choice of weapons) as its abortive outcome.[10] At long last the son openly challenges the father, in this case, an impostor; yet as always, from "a habit of missing" (Valency, 190), he is doomed to remain ineffectual before him. And tellingly, it is Elena who tries to wrest the pistol from him after shooting (from Astrov, however, she takes a pencil as a memento). He even blunders his suicide attempt by failing to keep his new rival Astrov from discovering the morphine he has taken from him. (Suicide by morphine would have enabled Vanja to take posthumous revenge on the doctor by implicating him in the act.)

Vanja's failure as a man extends even to his unsuccessful bid for maternal love. When overwhelmed by the import of Serebrjakov's plan, he turns in desperation to his mother for comfort; she not only rejects him,[11] but tells him to heed the professor's advice:

> VOJNICKIJ: My life's ruined. I'm gifted, intelligent, courageous. If I'd had a normal life I might have been a Schopenhauer or a Dostoevsky. . . . But I'm talking

nonsense, I'm going mad. Mother dear, I'm desperate. Mother!

MRS. VOJNICKIJ: (*sternly*) Do as Alexander says.

(Act III)

She alone continues to idolize her ex-son-in-law and prefers him to her own son. Her empty and impassioned pre-occupation with liberalism and women's emancipation has deprived the family of a viable mother. Instead, the old nanny, Marina, fills the vacuum by answering the family's need for a nurturing and comforting mother figure. She provides a link between the present and the seemingly happier past. Throughout, she is associated with food and drink.[12] The play opens as she urges Astrov to eat and reassures him with her faith in God. Astrov recognizes her as the only being of whom he is fond: "I don't want anything, I don't seem to need anything, and there's no one I'm fond of. Except just you perhaps. . . . I had a nanny like you when I was a little boy" (Act I). The demanding professor responds to her alone when he is ailing, for she sympathizes with his pain and attends to him as she would a child:

> MARINA: . . . Old folks are like children, they want a bit of affection, but who feels sorry for old folks? . . . Come along to bed, my dear. Come on, my lamb, I'll give you some lime-flower tea . . . I'll say a prayer for you.
>
> SEREBRJAKOV: (*very touched*) Come on then, Marina.
>
> (Act II)

Sonja, too, runs to Marina for solace, not to her maternal gradmother; the nanny is the only person who senses her vulnerability as an orphan:

> SONJA: (*pressing to the nurse*) Nanny, nanny!
>
> MARINA: It's all right, my child. The geese will cackle for a while and then they'll stop. . . . They'll cackle a bit and then they'll stop their cackling.
>
> SONJA: Nanny!
>
> MARINA: (*stroking her head*) You're shivering as if you'd been out in the cold. There, there, little orphan. God is merciful. A cup of lime-flower tea or tea with raspberrry jam and it will all pass. . . .
>
> (Act III)

Because she represents order and domestic tranquility, Marina complains most about the Serebrjakovs' effect on the household. With a few well-chosen remarks she ridicules and deflates Vanja's emotional outbursts and flights of self-dramatization. She compares both his and the professor's antics to those of barnyard animals.

By the end of the play, however, Sonja has taken over the central female role in the family. Like Marina, she offers food (by contrast, Astrov offers himself to Elena to be eaten!) but never acquiesces, like the nanny, to

serving vodka in order to mask life's realities. In a play which abounds with imagery of seeing and non-seeing, Sonja initially opts for clarity of vision. Even when "it's easier when you don't see," she chooses to learn Astrov's true feelings for her. She refuses to tolerate her father's silliness, criticizes her uncle's recent drinking habit which he treats as a substitute for his earlier illusions in regard to Serebrjakov ("When one has no real existence, one lives by illusions"), and she entreats Astrov not to drink. For the moment, he complies with her request, but his acceptance of vodka and refusal of bread from Marina before departure punctuate his estrangement.

Denied her dream of becoming Astrov's wife, however, Sonja also seeks an alternative to emotional realities. She becomes surrogate wife, mother, and sister to her uncle. He, in turn, will be her sole male companion and loving mate. She embraces and comforts him, urges him to work, and creates a new illusion, turning his thoughts away from the frustrations of this world to work and the peace of an afterlife, much as Marina had earlier done for Astrov. Her concluding words to Vanja after the Serebrjakovs and the doctor have fled the estate incorporate Marina's faith in God and Astrov's reliance on a better future.[13]

Despite his numerous failures, Vanja ultimately manages to keep the estate intact and successfully defends his right to resume his role as uncle and family provider. Because the others have always seen him in that role and have chided him for abandoning it, it is not surprising that they readily forgive his violent aberration: "I've just tried to murder somebody, but no one thinks of arresting me or putting me on trial. So they must think I'm mad". (Act IV). He becomes reconciled with the professor and states his intention to return to the *status quo*:

> SEREBRJAKOV (*to* VOJNICKIJ): We'll let bygones be bygones. So much has happened and I've been through so much and thought so many thoughts these last few hours, I could probably write a whole treatise on the art of living for the benefit of posterity. I gladly accept your apologies and beg you to accept mine. Good-bye.
>
> VOJNICKIJ: You'll be receiving a regular amount as before. Everything will be just as it was.
>
> (Act IV)

Yet Vanja has been deeply shamed by his brief interlude on center stage, and he will never regain his former pride, aware as he now is of his own impotence and the falsity of the man he serves. If by the end of *The Wood Demon* Vanja's predecessor commits suicide, thereby neatly bringing to a close the old gentry line, and Sonja, there an attractive woman, is to marry the play's democratic hero, in *Uncle Vanja* both niece and uncle are doomed to live out a sterile existence on the estate. This sterility is underlined in the stage directions for the fourth act: in the rambling twenty-six room house, Vanja's room "serves as his bedroom and the estate office." He is, in effect, "married" to the family hearth, unable to leave.[14] Astrov,

Chekhov's reaction to the failure of *Uncle Vanya*:

To A. S. Suvorin

Melikhovo. Dec. 14, 1896.

I received your letters about *Uncle Vanya*,—one in Moscow, and the other at home. Not long ago I received another letter from Koni who saw *The Sea-Gull.* You and Koni gave me in your letters more than one happy moment, but still, my spirits are quite unrelieved; I feel for my play nothing but aversion, and read the proofs only by force of will. You will say again that this is not wise, that it is stupid self-love, pride, etc., etc.,—but what am I to do? I would gladly free myself of the torpid feeling, but I cannot, cannot. It is not because the play failed; most of my plays went the same way, and each time it is like so much water on a duck's back. On the seventeenth of October it was not my play that failed, but myself. I was, even during the first act, struck by one circumstance, namely:—those with whom, before the seventeenth of October, I had been frank, as with friends and comrades, with whom I had joyously dined, for whom I broke a lance (as, for example, Y.),—all of them bore a strange expression, terribly strange. . . . In a word, there took place that which gave Leikin occasion to say, in his consoling letter, that I have so few friends, and *The Week* to ask: "What has Chekhov done to them?" and *The Theatre-Goer* to give space to a lengthy correspondence (No. 95) about the writing fraternity's having shown scandalous ill-will toward me in the theatre. I am now calm; my mood is as usual, but I cannot forget what happened, as I could not forget it if I had been struck.

You classify plays into those which can be performed, and those which can be read. Into which class would you put "Bankrupt," particularly the act during the whole of which Dalmatov and Mikhailov carry on a conversation about book-keeping, and nothing else, and do this successfully? I think that when a good actor plays a closet-drama, the play becomes one that can be performed.

Letters of Anton Chekhov, in *Letters on the Short Story, Drama and Other Literary Topics,* by Anton Chekhov, edited by Louis S. Friedland, Minton, Balch, 1924, pp. 115-63.

it is noted, has a table in Vanja's room, but significantly, he is an infrequent visitor to the house. For he finds the atmosphere stifling, as do the other "outsiders." Elena refers to the house as a crypt, a place of exile, while Serebrjakov calls it a labyrinth. All three abandon it at the end of the play.

Vanja is perhaps the most poignant example in Čexov's plays of a man whose lasting attachment to a sister or mother has decisively affected his desire and ability to lead an independent life, but he is only one of several such ineffectual brothers and sons. Treplev's troubled relationship to his mother in *The Seagull* is recognized as a salient factor in his inability to cope with life and offers striking parallels to the family situation in *Uncle Vanja.*[15] Andrej, in *Three Sisters,* is loved and looked up to by his sisters, but is cuckolded soon after his marriage and turns out to be a disastrous *pater familias.* Finally, the tearful Gaev in *The Cherry Orchard* (Lopaxin refers to him as "an old woman") adores his sister but can do nothing to save the family estate, nor lead a productive life. Each of these men, in his over-refined sensitivity and lack of physical and intellectual vigor, is somewhat of an "old woman," or perhaps an affable and harmless "uncle."

NOTES

[1] Maurice Valency, *The Breaking String: The Plays of Anton Chekhov* (New York: Oxford Univ. Press, 1966), 181-203, dwells on the neurotic and masochistic aspects of Vanja's character. Harvey Pitcher, *The Chekhov Play: A New Interpretation* (New York: Barnes and Noble, 1973), 75-78, identifies frustration as the "keynote" of the play, but does not focus on the role of the family in determining Vanja's behavior. V. Lakšin, *Tolstoj i Čexov* (M.: Sov. pisatel', 1975), 413, is sensitive to the play's text, but mentions the family only in passing. Daniel Gillés, *Chekhov: Observer Without Illusion,* tr. C. L. Markman (New York: Funk and Wagnalls, 1967), 295, recognizes the family as a source of Vanja's dilemma, but barely touches on this line of thought: "(Vanja) begins to wonder whether he himself has been the dupe of family feeling." See also V. Ermilov, *Dramaturgija Čexova* (M.: GIXL, 1954), 138-39.
[2] Isaak Gurvič, *Proza Čexova: čelovek i dejstvitel'nost'* (M.: GIXL, 1970), 38-39, observes that number of Čexov's heroes and heroines of the 1890s suffer from disenchantment with their "calling": ". . . at times the juxtaposition of a person as he is with his name becomes the vehicle of a story, gives rise to a special plot interest." In this regard Z. Papernyj, "Sjužet dolžen byt' nov . . . ," *Voprosy literatury,* 1976, No. 5, 182-83, notes that Čexov's titles tend to be pivotal for a work; thus, the change of the play's title from that of the earlier version, *The Wood Demon,* to *Uncle Vanja* points to the new significance that attaches to Vanja and his family role. It ironically underlines the hero's ill-fated attempt to assume a more central role in life (and on stage). G. Berdnikov, *Čexov-Dramaturg* (M.: Iskusstvo, 1972), 173, ignores this important shift in emphasis by dismissing the title change as irrelevant and stressing Astrov as the central character.
[3] The literary-theatrical committee of the Maly Theater which first reviewed the play found among its shortcomings that "the change in Vojnickij's attitude toward the professor, whom he previously worshipped, is incomprehensible" and that it is inexplicable how Vojnickij could go after Serebrjakov with a pistol. See the notes to A. P. Čexov, *Sobranie sočinenij* (12 vols.; M.: GIXL, 1963), IX, 689-90. Later critics, including Valency, Pitcher, Ermilov, Lakšin, and Berdnikov, tend to ignore the impact that the disruption of the family circle by the remarriage has had on Vanja, disregarding the information that his disillusionment begins not with the arrival of the Serebrjakovs but further back. Vanja has been "different" and "unrecognizable" for a year already, from about the time of the marriage.
[4] Otto Rank, *Das Inzest-Motiv in Dichtung und Sage* (Wien: Franz Deuticke, 1926), 407, writes of the close connection between the sibling-complex and the parent complex: ". . . sie (die Schwester) zuerst als Konkurrentin um die Mutter gilt, bald aber als idealer Ersatz an ihre Stelle treten kann. Sie übernimmt in den Phantasien dann die Rolle des reinen Frauenideals, welcher die Mutter durch ihre Angehörigkeit an den Vater in den Augen des Knaben meist unwürdig geworden ist."
[5] I have used the English version in Anton Chekhov, *Uncle Vanja,* in *The Oxford Chekhov,* tr. Ronald Hingley (London: Oxford Univ. Press, 1961). The canonical Russian text of *Djadja Vanja* is in *Sobranie Sočinenij,* IX, 482-532.
[6] An echo of Vanja's dilemma, one which underscores the relevance of the dead sister in his life, is heard in the fate of Telegin, godfather of Vanja's niece Sonja. Because of his unappealing appearance, Telegin's wife abandons him the day after their wedding; yet he remains true to her and gives up his property to support her children by another man. When this man dies, the wife, as Telegin understands it, is left with nothing, whereas he himself still has his pride. The parallel between Vanja's devotion to Vera

and that of Čexov's sister to Čexov is striking. Their relationship is discussed at length by Virginia Llewellyn Smith, *Anton Chekhov and the Lady with the Dog* (London: Oxford Univ. Press, 1973), 165-72. Surprisingly, she says almost nothing about *Uncle Vanja,* although it seems highly relevant for her study.

[7] See John T. Irwin, *Doubling and Incest/Repetition and Revenge: A Speculative Reading of Faulkner* (Baltimore: John Hopkins Univ. Press, 1975), 47: "On the one hand, there is an aggressive reaction of the son toward the castrating father, a desire for the father's death, a desire to kill him. But on the other hand, there is a tender reaction, a desire to renounce the object that has caused the father's anger by assuming a passive, feminine role in relation to him—in short, to become the mother in relation to the father."

[8] Konstantin S. Stanislavskij, *Sobranie sočinenij,* (3 vols.; M.: Iskusstvo, 1954), I, 232.

[9] Karlinsky notes that the loss of the family homestead, a recurring theme in Čexov's work, has a basis in the writer's own biography. See Simon Karlinsky and Michael Heim, *Anton Chekhov's Life and Thought: Selected Letters and Commentary* (Berkeley, Cal.: Univ. of California Press, 1975), 441.

[10] An illuminating discussion of the shooting incident and Vanja's failure to commit suicide is to be found in Z. Papernyj, "Roždenie sjužeta," in *Čexovskoe čtenie v Jalte* (M.: 1973), 39-51.

[11] Her behavior suggests that of the "terrible," "denying" mother discussed by Erich Newmann, *The Great Mother: An Analysis of the Archetype,* tr. Ralph Manheim (Princeton, N.J.: Princeton Univ. Press, 1972), 66-68.

[12] Styan, 102, takes a harsher view of Marina, referring to her comfort as "dried religious fatalism" and her offer of food as a "comical greeting" to Astrov's longing for human affection.

[13] One hardly need view Sonja's resignation as an indication of "deep religiosity," as does David Magarshak, *Chekhov the Dramatist* (New York: Hill and Wang, 1960), 224. Nor does the "weight" of the play deny Sonja "her faith before she opens her mouth" (Styan, 98). For a summary of J. J. Moran's "poll" of readings of the play's ending, see Styan, 140-41.

[14] "From the time of puberty onward the human individual must devote himself to the great task of *freeing himself from the parent:* and only after this detachment is accomplished can he cease to be a child and so become a member of the social community. For a son, the task consists in releasing his libidinal desires from his mother, in order to employ them in the quest of an external love-object in reality. . . . In neurotics, however, this detachment from the parents is not accomplished at all; the son remains all his life in subjection to the father and incapable of transferring his libido to a new sexual object." Sigmund Freud, *A General Introduction to Psychoanalysis,* tr. Joan Rivière (1924; rpt. New York: Pocket Books, 1975), 345-46.

[15] For a discussion of Treplev's relationship to his mother, See Thomas G. Winner, "Chekhov's *Seagull* and Shakespeare's *Hamlet:* A Study of a Dramatic Device," *American Slavic and East European Review,* 15 (1956), 103-11, and Robert L. Jackson, "Chekhov's *Seagull,*" in *Chekhov: A Collection of Critical Essays,* ed. Robert L. Jackson (Englewood Cliffs, N.J.: Prentice Hall, 1967), 99-111. Of note also is Pitcher's treatment, 51-52, and Valency, 195.

Michael Frayn (essay date 1987)

SOURCE: Introduction to *Uncle Vanya,* by Anton Chekhov, translated by Michael Frayn, Methuen, 1987, pp. ix-xxii.

[*In the following, Frayn surveys the genesis and development of* Uncle Vanya.]

No one knows exactly when *Uncle Vanya* took its present form. It was most probably in 1896, between the completion of *The Seagull* in the spring of that year and its disastrous première in St. Petersburg that October. It was first produced in the following year, as the second of Chekhov's four last great plays. But in its origins it goes back to a much earlier period than any of them. It is substantially a reworking of *The Wood Demon,* which was conceived nearly a decade before, when Chekhov was twenty-eight, and still only just emerging as a serious writer. Its development into its final form was tortuous and painful, and it is the story of Chekhov's own development as a dramatist. It was many times nearly abandoned; so was Chekhov's new career. At an early point both play and career nearly took off in a startlingly different direction, when Chekhov proposed changing the subject to the story in the Apocrypha of Holofernes and his decapitation by Judith, or else Solomon, or alternatively Napoleon on Elba, or Napoleon III and Eugénie. The possibilities are as extraordinary to consider as Vanya's own missed alternative career as a Schopenhauer or a Dostoyevsky.

Chekhov's original conception was bizarre enough. It was for a collaboration between himself and Suvorin, the wealthy publisher who was, somewhat improbably, his closest friend. Suvorin had literary ambitions of his own, and wrote stories which he submitted to Chekhov's practical and often devastating criticism, and a play, *Tatyana Repina,* which Chekhov parodied. The first work on the proposed collaboration seems in fact to have been done by Suvorin rather than Chekhov. In a letter written in November 1888—the earliest reference to the joint venture—Chekhov acknowledges receipt of 'the beginning of the play', and congratulates Suvorin on the creation of one of the principal characters—Blagosvetlov, who was to become Serebryakov in the final version. 'You've done him well: he's tiresome and irritating from the very first words, and if the audience listens to him for 3-5 minutes at a stretch, precisely the right impression will be produced. The spectator will think: "Oh, dry up, do!" This person, i.e. Blagosvetlov, should have the effect on the spectator of both a clever, gouty, old grouser and a dull musical comedy which is going on for too long.' It was a little ironical that this tedious character was Suvorin's contribution to the enterprise, because some people thought later that Chekhov had *based* him on Suvorin.

In the same letter Chekhov goes on to remind Suvorin of 'the bill of our play'—a list of eleven characters, with a description of each of them. Of these eleven, four can be recognised as the precursors of characters in the final version of *Uncle Vanya.* One of them, Blagosvetlov's daughter, bears little resemblance to the plain, hard-working Sonya she eventually became, and is more like Yelena, her lethargic and beautiful stepmother. But the other three are already the substantial originals of Serebryakov, Astrov, and Vanya himself. Blagosvetlov is a retired government official, not an academic, but he is 'of clerical origins, and was educated in a seminary. The position he occupied was achieved through his own efforts . . . Suffers from gout, rheumatism, insomnia, and tinnitus. His landed property he got as a dowry . . . Can't abide mystics, visionaries, holy fools, poets, or pious Peters, doesn't believe in God, and is accustomed to regard the entire world from the standpoint of practical affairs. Practical affairs first, last, and foremost, and everything else—nonsense or humbug.' Astrov, at this stage, is still a landowner rather than a doctor. But he already has his amaz-

Stanislavsky as Astrov and Olga Knipper as Elena Andreievna, in a scene from a Moscow Art Theater production of Uncle Vanya, *1904.*

ingly prescient concern for the ecology (and is already nicknamed the Wood Demon because of it). He already believes that 'the forests create the climate, the climate influences the character of the people, etc etc. There is neither civilisation nor happiness if the forests are ringing under the axe, if the climate is harsh and cruel, if people are harsh and cruel as well . . .' Blagosvetlov's daughter is attracted to him, as Yelena is in *Vanya,* 'not for his ideas, which are alien to her, but for his talent, for his passion, for his wide horizons . . . She likes the way his brain has swept over the whole of Russia and over ten centuries ahead . . .'

His account of the proto-Vanya is brief, and contains characteristics which were later discarded ('Drinks Vichy water and grouses away. Behaves arrogantly. Stresses that he is not frightened of generals. Shouts.') But in outline Uncle Vanya is already there—and in describing him Chekhov is also laying down the first outline of the plot: 'The brother of Blagosvetlov's late wife. Manages Blagosvetlov's estate (his own he has long since run through). Regrets he has not stolen. He had not foreseen that his Petersburg relations would have such a poor appreciation of his services. They don't understand him—they don't want to understand him—and he regrets he has not stolen.'

Chekhov says in his letter he will sketch out the rest of Act One himself and send it to Suvorin. He undertakes not to touch Blagosvetlov, and suggests sharing the work on Blagosvetlov's daughter, because 'I'll never be able to manage her on my own.' The great arborealist will be Chekhov's up to Act Four, then Suvorin's up to a certain

scene where Chekhov will take over because Suvorin will never manage to catch the right tone of voice. Then he will leave Suvorin to start Act Two, as he did Act One.

It is difficult to believe that this strange two-headed beast would have been any substitute for the *Vanya* it would presumably have displaced. Fortunately, perhaps, Suvorin seems to have backed down, and left Blagosvetlov as his sole contribution, because a month later Chekhov was writing to ask him why he was refusing to collaborate on *The Wood Demon* (as it was by this time called), and offering to find a new subject altogether if Suvorin would prefer it. This was when he proposed switching to Holofernes or Solomon, or one of the two Napoleons.[1] But not even the attractions of a biblical or historical subject could tempt the literary-minded magnate back into harness, and the following spring Chekhov reluctantly began to struggle with the material on his own.

There were some moments of elation in the weeks that followed, judging at any rate from the bulletins to Suvorin. 'Act III is so scandalous that when you see it you'll say: "This was written by a cunning and pitiless man" . . .' 'The play is terribly strange, and I'm surprised that such strange things are emerging from my pen.' There were also more or less simultaneous moments of discouragement, when he informed other correspondents that he was not going to write plays, and that he was not attracted by the idea of fame as a dramatist. By the end of May, with only two acts written, he had given up, and in September he had to start all over again from the beginning.

Then, when it was at last finished, the play was rejected out of hand by both the Alexandrinsky Theatre in St. Petersburg, which had just successfully staged *Ivanov,* and by the Maly in Moscow. An unofficial meeting of the Petersburg section of the Theatrical-Literary Committee, which vetted all the plays submitted for production in the imperial theatres, judged it 'a fine dramatised story, but not a drama.' Lensky, the actor for whose benefit performance the play had been offered to the Maly, returned the manuscript to Chekhov with a particularly crushing dismissal. 'I will say only one thing: write a story. You are too contemptuous of the stage and of the dramatic form, you have too little respect for them, to write drama. This form is harder than that of the story, and you—forgive me—are too spoiled by success to study as it were the basic ABC of the dramatic form, and to learn to love it.' Even Nemirovich-Danchenko, another member of the committee, who was later of course to be a co-founder with Stanislavsky of the Moscow Arts Theatre and one of Chekhov's most important patrons, thought that Lensky was right in diagnosing ignorance of the demands of the stage (though he thought Chekhov could easily master them). 'Say what you like,' he wrote, 'clear, lifelike characters, an interesting conflict, and the proper development of the plot—these are the best guarantee of success on the stage. A play cannot succeed without a plot, but the most serious fault is lack of clarity, when the audience can't possibly grasp the essence of the plot. This is more important than any stage tricks or effects.' Chekhov swore again—not for the last time—to give up playwriting. But in the end he rewrote once more, and did a completely new version of the last act, with which he had been having difficulties from the beginning. The play was then produced, in December 1889, by a Moscow commercial management. It was dismissed by the critics not only as untheatrical, but also as 'a blind transcription of everyday reality,' and was taken off after three performances.

With hindsight, the most remarkable thing about *The Wood Demon* is how much of *Uncle Vanya* is already there—often word for word. All the essential material of Act One, including most of the big speeches; almost the whole of Act Two; and in Act Three the entire scene in which Serebryakov proposes to sell the estate. It seems amazing that this wealth of brilliant scenes was not enough to alert even the most sluggish producer and the most jaded critic to Chekhov's powers in the theatre. But it is true that they fail to make the impact they should because he had not yet overcome certain faults recognisable from his two earlier full-length plays, *Ivanov* and the one written when he was a student (untitled, but called *Platonov* in some versions and *Wild Honey* in mine). The characters are too simple; too noble and Tolstoyan in the case of the Wood Demon himself, too coarsely comic in the case of Orlovsky, the debauched son of a local landowner. The setting of the first and last acts has wandered in pursuit of the picturesque; and there is something unsettling about the tone of the whole. It may have seemed offensively naturalistic to contemporary critics, but to the modern reader it veers more towards the facetiousness of Chekhov's early comic journalism, and towards a certain bucolic jollity, which sit oddly with the story that is beginning to emerge. At the end of Act Three all resemblance to the later version ceases. Vanya attempts to shoot not Serebryakov but himself, and succeeds. So the last act is left without a Vanya, and instead proceeds by way of a sunset picnic alongside an old watermill to a happy ending, with the Serebryakovs more or less reconciled, the Wood Demon and Sonya paired off, and even the debauched Orlovsky settling down with a nice girl. Nemirovich-Danchenko's assessment of the play is shrewd; the story is not clear. And the reason is that Chekhov has not yet recognised the story he is trying to tell.

After its failure in Moscow the play was abandoned again, and might well have remained so for good. It seems to have been Prince Urusov, a jurist and well-known literary figure, who provoked Chekhov into starting work on it again—somewhat ironically, because Urusov admired the earlier version so much that he persisted to the end in believing that Chekhov had ruined it by turning it into *Uncle Vanya.* It was Urusov's request for permission to reprint the text of *The Wood Demon,* in fact, that made Chekhov re-read it. He evidently did not like what he saw (years later he was still telling the loyal Urusov: 'I hate that play and I try to forget about it') and it was presumably this reawakened dissatisfaction that made him set to work on it again. The internal evidence, at any rate—the dates of the diaries and notebooks which were the provenance of some of the material in the new version—suggests that the reworking was done the following year, in 1896; and in a letter to Suvorin written that December is the first reference to *Uncle Vanya*—already, apparently, a finished text. If this dating is correct then the project was probably only just completed in time, because after the débâcle with the St. Petersburg opening of *The Seagull* in October he once again swore off playwriting.

The play in its new form still faced one final rebuff. The Maly Theatre asked for it, which gave the Theatrical-Literary Committee the chance to produce an even more magisteral rejection and scheme of improvement than before. Its report identified a number of 'unevennesses or lacunae' in the play, and complained of 'longeurs', such as 'the extended eulogy of forests, shared between Sonya and Astrov, and the explanation of Astrov's theory of arboriculture.' The committee was worried about the distressing frequency with which it believed Vanya and Astrov were shown suffering from hangovers, and the unfortunate effect that would be produced if this were thought to be the cause of Vanya's attempt to shoot Serebryakov. It felt that Vanya and Astrov 'as it were merge into a single type of failure, of superfluous man', and it complained that 'nothing prepares us for the powerful outburst of passion which occurs during the conversation with Yelena.' It reserved its greatest concern, though, for Vanya's treatment of Serebryakov. 'That Vanya could take a dislike to the professor as Yelena's husband is understandable,' it conceded; 'that his sermonising and moralising cause irritation is also natural, but the disillusionment with Serebryakov's academic stature, and indeed more precisely with him as an art historian, is somewhat strange . . . nor is it a reason for his being pursued with pistol shots, for his being hunted down by someone who is no longer responsible for his actions.' The unfairness of shooting professors because you have a low opinion of their academic achievements seems to have spoken deeply to the committee's learned members.

This time, however, Chekhov declined all suggestions for rewriting. By now, in any case, the play had been successfully produced in a number of provincial theatres, and it was finally established in Moscow by being produced at the Arts Theatre—though its reception there was initially more muted than the hysterical success which *The Seagull* had just enjoyed in the same place. With hindsight we can see that Chekhov's reworking of the material from *The Wood Demon,* whenever it was done, has shifted it across the crucial divide that separates the four last plays from all his earlier ones—from all the earlier ones in the world.

Some of the changes he has made are straightforward improvements in dramatic technique. He has concentrated the setting of the play on the place where the real events of the story actually happen—the Serebryakovs' estate—and he has stripped out the superfluous characters. But in the course of doing this he has had an idea of genius. He has elided the debauched young neighbour, Orlovsky, with the Wood Demon. The most upright and selfless character in the original play is now the one who also indulges in periodic drinking bouts; instead of being in love with Sonya he is now, like Orlovsky, first coarsely knowing about Vanya's relations with Yelena, and then ready to propose a passing liaison with her himself; he has become Astrov in all his dark, self-contained complexity. And Yelena, a figure of uncompromised virtue in the original version, has become fascinated by him, so that, engaged as she is to advance poor Sonya's cause with him, she has become touched by the same characteristic ambiguity.

With these changes the whole tone of the play has been modified. The bucolic geniality and the facetiousness have gone, and left exposed the sense of wasted life at the heart of the story. By the same token the mood has changed from one of comfortable idleness to one of uncomfortably interrupted work. The importance of work in these last four plays is not always grasped. An impression lingers that they are about impoverished gentry with nothing to do all day but watch their fortunes decline; 'Chekhovian' is a synonym for a sort of genteel, decaying, straw-hatted ineffectualness. There are such characters, it's true—Telegin, the ruined neighbour who is living on Vanya's charity, Gayev and his sister in *The Cherry Orchard*—but they are few in number. Why do we tend to pick on them when we think about these harsh plays? A bizarre combination of nostalgia and condescension, perhaps—nostalgia for a lost world of servants and rural leisure, easy condescension from the moral superiority of our own busy lives. What we forget, when we are not face to face with them, is that most of the people in these plays are not members of the leisured class at all. They have to earn their living, and earn it through hard professional work. We catch them at moments of leisure, because this is when they can stand back and look at their lives, but their thoughts are with their jobs. The memory that remains with us from *The Seagull* is of people sitting in a garden and enjoying their 'sweet country boredom'. Who are these idle folk? They are two actresses, two writers, a doctor, a teacher, a civil servant, and a hardpressed estate manager. Some of them have time to sit down because they are only at the beginning of their careers, some because they are at the end; the others are simply on holiday. The idleness of Masha and Andrey, in *Three Sisters,* is remarkable because it is in such contrast to the drudgery of Masha's husband and her other two sisters; the idleness of the fading landowners in *The Cherry Orchard* is being swept aside by the industrious energy of the new entrepreneurs and activists. At the centre of *Vanya* is a woman so drugged with idleness that she can't walk straight; but the corrupting effects of this are felt in the lives around her, and they are lives of hitherto unceasing toil—whether the pedantic labours of her husband, or the agricultural stewardship of Vanya and Sonya, or the sleepless rural medicine of Astrov. These working lives are already the background of *The Wood Demon,* but there they remain offstage, somewhat secondary to the picnicking and moralising. In the final version, Vanya's bitterness over his years of misdirected sacrifice has become the centre of the action, and its culmination is now the resumption by Vanya and Sonya of their labours. In fact they resume them on stage, in front of our eyes. This is not the first time that work has been shown on stage. In *The Weavers,* first produced in Berlin three years earlier, Hauptmann had shown the wretched weavers labouring at their looms. For that matter we see the gravediggers briefly at work in *Hamlet,* and we have seen plenty of servants serving, soldiers soldiering, and actors rehearsing. But this is surely the first great theatrical classic where we see the principals set about the ordinary, humdrum business of their lives. In fact work is one of the central themes in Chekhov. Work as the longed-for panacea for all the ills of idleness; work as obsession and drudgery and the destruction of life; work as life, simply. What Sonya looks forward to in heaven for herself and her uncle at the end of the present play is not finding peace, as some translations have it; what she says, five times over, in plain everyday Russian, is that they will *rest.*

Chekhov's second masterstroke in the rewriting, even more fundamental and consequential than the new ambiguity of the characters, is his alteration to the aim of Vanya's revolver. All his full-length plays up to this point have resolved with the death of one of the central characters. Now, instead of letting Vanya likewise tidy himself away after his confrontation with Serebryakov, he has had the idea of making him turn murderer instead of suicide—and of failing.

In the first place this is simply a more interesting development. For the pacific and long-suffering Vanya to have been driven to attempt murder tells us much more about the intensity of his anger and of his sense of betrayal; and his missing the target is something he at once recognises as bitterly characteristic. This is slightly obscured by the traditional translation of his line. 'Missed again!' sounds as if it refers only to the two shots. The word he uses in Russian, however, refers not only to a missed shot but to any kind of mistake. What he is thinking of is surely all the missed opportunities in his life, and in particular his failure to have made advances to Yelena when she was still free. Then again, the fact that he misses at point-blank range opens up a whole series of questions about the nature of these mistakes. Perhaps they are not serious attempts at all; even as he pulls the trigger he *says* 'bang!', like a child with a toy revolver. And even if he sees them as seriously intended, are they examples of what a modern psychiatrist would call self-sabotage? And if they are, is the unconscious objective to protect himself from the consequences of success? Not only from being tried for murder, but from being tested as a lover and husband, from having the chance (as he at one moment believes he could have done if only he had lived 'normally') to become a Schopenhauer or a Dostoyevsky—and *then* failing, with no possibility of concealing his own responsibility for it?

In the second place, the failure of this dramatic gesture to have dramatic consequences destroys the drama; or rather it destroys the neatness with which the slow and confused changes of the world we inhabit are concentrated theatrically in simple and decisive events. The world of *Vanya* is the ambiguous and unresolved world of *The Seagull*—stripped of even the final note of resolution suggested by Konstantin's suicide. Most of the relatively few notes Chekhov gave to the director and actors were to do with this dislocation and diffusion. He missed the production in Moscow, because he had been exiled to Yalta for his consumption, but when he saw the play, on a tour the Arts Theatre made in 1900 to the Crimea, one of the actresses in the company remembered his telling them afterwards that Sonya shouldn't kneel and kiss her father's hand on the line 'You must be merciful, father' at the end of Act Three, because 'after all that wasn't the drama. All the sense and all the drama of a person is on the inside, and not in external appearances. There was drama in Sonya's life up to this moment, there will be drama afterwards—but this is simply something that happens, a continuation of the shot. And the shot, in fact, is not drama—just something that happens.'[2] In a similar spirit he deprecated Stanislavsky's direction that Astrov should make his pass at Yelena, in Act Four, 'like a drowning man clutching at a straw.' By then, says Chekhov in a letter to Olga Knipper, who was playing Yelena, Astrov knows that nothing is going to come of his attraction to her, 'and he talks to her in this scene in the same tone of voice as he does about the heat in Africa, and kisses her in the most ordinary way, quite idly.' Stanislavsky remembered him as saying, after the performance in the Crimea, '"He kisses her like that, though."—And here he planted a brief kiss on his own hand.—"Astrov has no respect for Yelena. In fact when he leaves the house afterwards he's whistling."'

More important even than the nature of the failed murder are the consequences it has for the last act. Chekhov, as we have seen, had already tried various versions of

this. What had caused the problem was his odd insistence, in all the variants of *The Wood Demon,* on placing Vanya's suicide at the end of Act Three, so that this traditional dramatic resolution still left everything unresolved for everyone else. But he had been feeling his way towards *something* with this arrangement, and now that Vanya remains alive it becomes clear what it is: precisely that—remaining alive. It is survival itself, the problem of going on with life *after* it has been robbed of hope and meaning. 'The ability to endure' had already been identified by Nina at the end of *The Seagull* as the most important quality in life. Now Sonya takes it up as her watchword—'Endure, uncle! Endure!'—as she coaxes Vanya through his despair at the prospect of living for another dozen years, and as the future dwindles to a 'long, long succession of days and endless evenings' unilluminated by either any sense of purpose or any prospect of alteration. From now on the tragedy in Chekhov's plays will be not death but the continuance of life; the pain of losing the past, with all the happiness and wealth of possibilities it contained, will always be compounded by the pain of facing the future in all its emptiness. Two more characters will die, it is true. Tusenbach's death in *Three Sisters,* though, is shown not as *his* tragedy—the imminence of it gives him his first real awareness of the world and his first real pleasure in it—but as one more of the losses which empty the sisters' future of meaning. Firs is left dying at the end of *The Cherry Orchard,* but the sale of the estate, which finally destroys any hopes the Gayevs have had in life, has already occurred, like the attempted murder of Serebryakov, at the end of Act Three, so that the last act is left once again to show life continuing, and Gayev and his sister facing—with in this case what one might think to be an ironically misplaced insouciance—even grimmer futures still.

The insistence upon endurance is connected with another idea which first emerges in *Vanya,* and which will dominate *Three Sisters* as well—the conviction felt by some of the characters that the sufferings which stretch to the visible horizon of the future are in some way to be redeemed by a happiness lying beyond that horizon. Some of this optimism plainly has a quality of desperation about it; it is easy to recognize the obsessiveness with which Vershinin keeps returning to the idea that life on earth will be 'astonishingly, unimaginably beautiful' in two or three hundred years time, or perhaps a thousand, particularly since it doesn't seem to matter to him exactly when, provided only the prospect exists. But the two passionate and heartbreaking speeches with which these plays end, by Sonya in the present play and by Olga in *Three Sisters,* are something else again. The forms of redemption that the two women expect are different; Sonya sees it as coming only in the next world, but does see it as some kind of personal recompense to herself and her uncle. Olga expects the sufferings of the present to purchase happiness in this world—but a happiness which will be experienced only 'by those who live after us'. Both speeches, though, are so eloquent, and so powerfully placed, that we cannot help wondering whether they reflect some deep beliefs of this nature in Chekhov himself.

Stanislavsky as Astrov and Olga Knipper as Elena Andreievna, in a scene from the 1899 Moscow Art Theater production of Uncle Vanya.

The external evidence in favour of this reading is slight. In his notebooks he once expressed the hope that 'Man will become better when we have shown him to himself as he is,' and the writer Vladimir Tikhonov remembered him as saying that once people had seen themselves as they were 'they will surely by themselves create a different and better life. I shall not see it, but I know that everything will be changed, that nothing will be like our present existence.' There is an echo of Vershinin here, if Tikhonov has quoted him correctly, but it is a rare one. His notes make it clear that the only unconditional prediction he made for the future was that people would continue to think the past was better. He had no utopian political views of any sort, as his famous letter to another writer, Aleksei Pleshcheyev, makes clear. In a letter to a third writer, Shcheglov, he states categorically that he had no religion, which would rule out any possibility of his entertaining the sort of hopes that Sonya does. And on a number of occasions he specifically dissociated himself from the ideas of his characters. 'If you're served coffee,' he says in a letter to Suvorin, 'then don't try looking for beer in it. If I present you with a professor's thoughts, then trust me and don't look for Chekhov's thoughts in them.' For him as author, he says in the same letter, his characters' ideas 'have no value for their content. It's not a question of their content; that's changeable and it's not new. The whole point is the nature of these opinions, their dependence upon external influences and so on. They must be examined like objects, like symptoms, entirely objectively, not attempting either to agree with them or to dispute them. If I described St. Vitus' dance you wouldn't look at it from the point of view of a choreographer, would you? No? Then don't do it with opinions.' In another letter to Suvorin he took up the latter's complaint that one of his stories had not resolved the question of pessimism. 'I think that it's not for novelists to resolve such questions as God, pessimism, etc. The novelist's job is to show merely who, how, and in what circumstances people were talking or thinking about God or pessimism. The artist must be not the judge of his characters and what they are talking about, but merely an impartial witness. I heard a confused conversation, resolving nothing, between two Russian people about pessimism, and I have to pass on this conversation in the same form in which I heard it, but it will be evaluated by the jury, i.e. the readers. My job is merely to be talented, i.e. to be able to distinguish important phenomena from unimportant, to be able to illuminate characters and speak with their tongue.'

We do not have to suppose the author shares the beliefs expressed in these two speeches to find them moving, any more than we have to share the beliefs ourselves. The very remoteness, the very impossibility, of that sky dressed in diamonds, of that peace and happiness on earth, is what makes the speeches so poignant. And yet the force and insistence of the idea, in the two successive plays, is very striking. Even if they do not express beliefs which Chekhov shared, they may reveal a similarly poignant yearning of his own for a future whose unattainability he was just beginning to grasp. It is a common experience for people in early middle age, which is where Chekhov was when he wrote these plays, to come over the brow of the hill, as it were, and to see for the first time that their life will have an end. But the end with which Chekhov came face to face in mid-life was suddenly much closer still. It was not until six months after he had finished *Vanya* that he had his first major haemorrhage, and that his tuberculosis was finally diagnosed. But he had been spitting blood for a long time. He insists over and over again in his letters that this is the most normal thing in the world; but the more he insists the more one wonders. As Ronald Hingley puts it in his biography: 'Can Anton really have been unaware, still, that he suffered from tuberculosis? It seems incredible that a practising doctor could continue to ignore symptoms of which the possible purport might have struck any layman. On the other hand, as Chekhov's own works richly illustrate, human beings have an almost infinite capacity for self-deception. Did the man who deluded others about the desperate condition of his health also delude himself? Or did he hover between self-deception and self-knowledge?'

It was at some point in that final year before the diagnosis was made that he was writing *Vanya* in its definitive form and giving up the idea of death as a dramatic resolution. Perhaps somewhere inside himself he had begun to recognize what was happening to him. Perhaps, now that he was suddenly so close to it, death seemed a little less neat, a little less of an answer to the equation; perhaps it began to seem more like something you could look as far as, or beyond, but not at. And even if Chekhov hadn't yet seen the truth about his condition, perhaps Sonya and the others had in a sense seen it for him. A writer's characters, particularly when they are not forced to represent his conscious thoughts, can be appallingly well-informed about his unconscious ones. It is ironical. Chekhov most sedulously absented himself from his works. Sonya's passionate invocation of an after-life in which he didn't believe may be one of our rare glimpses of him—and of an aspect of him that he couldn't even see himself.

NOTES

[1]Chekhov himself did in fact start on the Solomon project, and the following fragment was found among his papers. The metaphysical anguish which the king expresses in this monologue appears to derive not from the figure of wealth and wisdom in Chronicles but from the author of Ecclesiastes. The ascription to Solomon in the first verse of Ecclesiastes ('The words of the Preacher, the son of David, king in Jerusalem') was once taken literally, but is now thought to be conventional. The book is now considered

to be the work of a much later author, and its wonderful melancholy Epicurean charm more Hellenistic than Judaic.

> SOLOMON (*alone*). O, how dark life is! No night in all its blackness when I was a child struck such terror into me as does my unfathomed existence. My God, to my father David Thou gavest but the gift of bringing words and sounds together as one, of singing and praising Thee with plucked strings, of sweetly weeping, of wresting tears from the eyes of others and of finding favour with beauty; but to me why gavest Thou also a languishing spirit and unsleeping hungry thought? Like an insect born out of the dust I hide in darkness, and trembling, chilled, despairing, fearful, see and hear in all things a fathomless mystery. To what end does this light of morning serve? To what end does the sun rise from behind the Temple and gild the palm-tree? To what end is the beauty of women? Whither is younder bird hastening, what is the meaning of its flight, if it and its fledglings and the place to which it hurries must come like me to dust? O, better I had never been born, or that I were a stone to which God had given neither eyes nor thoughts. To weary my body for the night I yesterday like a common workman dragged marble to the Temple; now the night is come, and I cannot sleep . . . I will go and lie down again . . . Forses used to tell me that if one imagines a flock of sheep running and thinks hard about it then one's thoughts will dissolve and sleep. This will I do . . . (*Exit.*)

[2] There is something askew—and perhaps this is in keeping with the obliqueness of the play—about either Chekhov's note or the actress's memory of it, because his own stage direction calls for Sonya to kneel, if not to kiss her father's hand, while the line can hardly be construed as a 'continuation of the shot' because it occurs before it.

Gary Saul Morson   (essay date 1993)

SOURCE: "*Uncle Vanya* as Prosaic Metadrama," in *Reading Chekhov's Text*, edited by Robert Louis Jackson, Northwestern University Press, 1993, pp. 214-27.

[*In the following essay, Morson reads* Uncle Vanya *as a "metaliterary satire of histrionics and intelligentsial posing."*]

> SOLYONY: I have never had anything against you, Baron. But I have the temperament of Lermontov. [*Softly*] I even look like Lermontov . . . so they say . . .
>
> —Chekhov, *The Three Sisters*

THEATER OF THEATRICALITY

It might be said that the fundamental theme of Chekhov's plays is theatricality itself, our tendency to live our lives "dramatically." In Chekhov's view, life as we actually live it does not generally conform to staged plots, except when people try to endow their lives with a spurious meaningfulness by imitating literary characters and scenes. Traditional plays imitate life only to the extent that people imitate plays, which is unfortunately all too common. There are Hamlets in life primarily because people have read *Hamlet* or works like it. The theater has been realistic only when people have self-consciously reversed mimesis to imitate it.

Such reverse mimesis is typical of Chekhov's major characters. His plays center on histrionic people who imitate theatrical performances and model themselves on other melodramatic genres. They posture, seek grand romance, imagine that a tragic fatalism governs their lives, and indulge in utopian dreams while they neglect the ordinary virtues and ignore the daily processes that truly sustain them. Such virtues—the prosaic decencies in which Chekhov deeply believed—are typically practiced by relatively undramatic characters who do not appreciate their own significance.[1] In the background of the play and on the margins of its central actions, truly meaningful prosaic life can be glimpsed.

Because histrionics is Chekhov's central theme, his plays rely to a great extent on metatheatrical devices. Those devices show us why the world is *not* a stage and why we should detect falsity whenever it seems to resemble a play. Metatheatricality is most obvious in **The Sea Gull,** Chekhov's first major dramatic success. Indeed, Chekhov's use of the technique in this play borders on the heavy-handed. We have only to recall that one major character, an actress, behaves as theatrically with her family as she does on the stage; that her son is a playwright who devotes his life to romantic longing and *ressentiment;* that an aspiring young actress tries to reenact the romance of a famous novel by sending its author a quotation from it; that citizens from *Hamlet* suffuse the action; and, of course, that a play-within-a-play provides the point of reference for all other events. **Uncle Vanya** dispenses with much of this overt machinery while still maintaining the metatheatrical allusions it was designed to create. In effect, the internal play expands to become the drama itself. Like a committee of the whole, **Uncle Vanya** becomes in its entirety a sort of play-within-a-play.

As a result, the work reverses the usual foreground and background of a drama. In most plays, people behave "dramatically" in a world where such behavior is appropriate. The audience, which lives in the undramatic world we all know, participates vicariously in the more interesting and exciting world of the stage. That, indeed, may be one reason people go to the theater. In **Uncle Vanya** the characters carry on just as "dramatically" as anyone might expect from the stage, but they do so in a world that seems as ordinary and everyday as the world of the audience. Consequently, actions that would be tragic or heroic in other plays here acquire tonalities of comedy or even farce. Chekhov never tired of reminding Stanislavsky and others that his plays were not melodramas but precisely (as he subtitled **The Sea Gull** and **The Cherry Orchard**) comedies. Chekhov gives us dramatic characters in an undramatic world in order to satirize all theatrical poses and all attempts to behave as if life were literary and theatrical. Histrionics for Chekhov was a particularly loathsome form of lying, which truly cultured people avoid "even in small matters."[2]

Chekhov's toying with the dramatic frame may be seen as a particularly original use of a traditional satiric technique. Like his great predecessors in parody, he transforms his main characters into what might be called "generic refugees."[3] That is, he creates characters who would be at home in one genre but places them in the world of another. So Don Quixote, Emma Bovary, and Ilya Ilych Oblomov become comic when forced to live in a realistic world rather than the chivalric adventure story, the romantic novel, or the idyll of which they dream. *War and Peace* places its epic hero, Prince Andrei, in a novelistic world where epic heroism is an illusion; *Middlemarch* confers refugee status on Dorothea in its Prelude about how she, like Saint Theresa, needed an "epic life" to realize her potential but, in the nineteenth century, could find only prosaic reality. As these examples show, this technique does not preclude an admixture of sympathy in the satire.

Chekhov's main characters think of themselves as heroes or heroines from various genres of Russian literature, which is ironic, of course, because they are characters in Russian literature. Having read the great authors, they, like many members of the *intelligentsia,* plagiarize significance by imitating received models. Here it is worth observing that the Russian term *intelligentsia* does not mean the same thing as the English word *intelligentsia,* which underwent a shift in meaning when borrowed from the Russian. In Russian, an *intelligent* (member of the intelligentsia) was not necessarily an intellectual, and not all intellectuals were *intelligenty.* A member of the *intelligentsia* was identified as such by a particular way of living—bad manners of a specified sort were important—and above all by a complex of attitudes, including militant atheism, an opposition to all established authority, socialism, and a mystique of revolution. Prosaic virtues were regarded as unimportant, if not harmful, and a taste for the grand and dramatic was cultivated. *Intelligenty* were expected to adopt one or another grand system of thought that purported to explain all of culture and society and promised an end to all human suffering if a given kind of revolution should take place; the function of the *intelligentsia* was to adopt the right system and make sure its recommendations were put into practice. To do so, solidarity—what Chekhov despised as intellectual conformism—was needed. If by *intellectual* we mean someone characterized by independence of thought, we can see how it was easily possible for an intellectual to be an "antiintelligentsial" and for an *intelligent* to be antiintellectual. A member of an *intelligentsia* "circle," even if he never read a book, would be considered an *intelligent* more readily than Leo Tolstoy, who expressed utter contempt for this whole complex of beliefs and lived a manifestly nonintelligentsial life.

Not surprisingly, this dominant tradition of the *intelligentsia* generated a countertradition of thinkers who rejected its fundamental premises. Tolstoy's masterpieces, *War and Peace* and *Anna Karenina,* explicitly attack all grand systems of thought, all attempts to find hidden laws of history, and, consequently, all prescriptions for universal salvation. For Tolstoy, and the countertradition generally, it is not the dramatic events of life that matter, either for individuals or for societies, but the countless small, prosaic events of daily life.

It was above all this aspect of Tolstoy's thought that had the most profound influence on Chekhov, who, as we have seen, constantly expressed the deepest skepticism about the intelligentsial mentality and valued everyday virtues.

Invited to join one *intelligentsia* circle, Chekhov responded with an accusation of hypocrisy and a restatement of his most cherished values—honesty and simple acts of kindness, for which "you've got to be not so much the young literary figure as just a plain human being. Let us be ordinary people, let us adopt the same attitude *toward all,* then an artificially overwrought solidarity will not be needed."[4] In the twentieth century this countertradition—the kind of thought I call prosaics—has been represented by that remarkable anthology of essays by disillusioned *intelligenty, Landmarks: A Collection of Essays on the Russian Intelligentsia* (1909); by Mikhail Zoschenko; and by the literary and cultural critic Mikhail Bakhtin.[5]

Both Chekhov and Tolstoy understood that the prestige of the *intelligentsia* cast a shadow on educated society as a whole and predisposed people to adopt grand roles drawn from literature. Chekhov's characters imagine that they are heroes or heroines in a genre suffused with romance, heroism, great theories, and decisive action, or else they try to play the lead roles in tragic tales of paralyzing disillusionment and emptiness. They consider themselves to be either heroes or "heroes of our time." But their search for drama unfolds in Chekhov's universe of prosaics.

In its examination of histrionics, **Uncle Vanya** is in a position to exploit metatheatrical devices. **Uncle Vanya** is theater about theatricality, and so its main characters are continually "overacting." One reason the play has proven so difficult to stage in the right tonality—as critics and directors have constantly noted—is that the actors must overact and call attention to their theatrical status but without ceasing to play real people who truly suffer. They must not over-overact. Their performance must allude to but not shatter the dramatic frame.

When we watch **Uncle Vanya,** we do not see actors playing characters. We see characters playing characters. They labor under the belief that this role-playing brings them closer to "true life," but in fact it does the opposite. The audience contemplates real people—people like themselves—who live citational lives, that is, lives shaped by literary role-playing, lives consisting not so much of actions as of allusions. We are asked to consider the extent to which our own lives are, like the title of this play, citational.

TURGENEV'S GOUT

If criticism, the authority of which you cite, knows what you and I don't, why has it kept mum until now? Why doesn't it disclose to us the truth and immutable laws? If it had known, believe me, it would long ago have shown us the way and we would know what to do. . . . But criticism keeps pompously quiet or gets off cheap with idle, worthless chatter. If it presents itself to you as influential, it is only because it is immodest, insolent, and loud, because it is an empty barrel that one involuntarily hears. Let's spit on all this.

—Chekhov, letter to Leontiev-Shcheglov,
March 22, 1890

Chekhov places members of the *intelligentsia* at the center of his play because they are especially given to self-dramatization and because they love to display their superior culture. As they cite novels, criticism, and other dramas, Chekhov shapes his metaliterary satire of histrionics and intelligentsial posing.

Old Serebryakov, we are told at the very beginning of the play, was a former theology student and the son of a sexton. These are just the roots one would choose if one's goal was to display a typical member of the *intelligentsia.* A professor of literature, he peevishly demands that someone fetch his copy of the poet Batyushkov, looks down on those with fewer citations at their disposal, and tries to illuminate his life with literary models.

He makes even his illness allusive: "They say that Turgenev developed angina pectoris from gout. I'm afraid I may have it."[6] At the beginning of his speech to the assembled family in act III, he first asks them "to lend me your ears, as the saying goes [*Laughs*]." As is so often the case in Chekhov's plays, the line is more meaningful than he knows, for the speech he has prepared, like that of his Shakespearean model, is made under false pretenses. Appropriately enough, he continues his game of allusions by citing Gogol's famous play—"I invited you here, ladies and gentlemen, to announce that the Inspector General is coming"—evidently without having considered that its action concerns confidence games. Like **Uncle Vanya,** *The Inspector General* involves multiple layers of role-playing, mutually reinforcing poses, and self-induced self-deceptions. In his last appearance of the play, the professor proposes to transform its action into yet another occasion for professional criticism: "After what has happened, I have lived through so much, and thought so much in the course of a few hours, that I believe I could write a whole treatise for the edification of posterity." It is hard to decide whether to call this line pathetic or repulsive, but in either case it ought to disturb us professionals more than it has.

If the old professor projects ill-considered confidence in his merely citational importance, then Voinitsky, who has at last understood such falsities, can only create new ones. He realizes that for most of his life he has been content with a vicarious connection to the professor's vicarious connection to literature, but all he learns from his disillusionment is that the professor was the wrong intermediary.

Given our own views of the professor, we may take at face value Voinitsky's denunciation of his work as an uncomprehending and momentarily fashionable deployment of modish but empty jargon. But that only makes Voinitsky's desire for a better connection with literature even more misguided. Filled with all the self-pity, impotent rage, and underground *ressentiment* of a disappointed member of the *intelligentsia,* he regrets that he is too old to surpass the professor at his own game. Chekhov brilliantly merges despair and slapstick humor—we seem to check ourselves in midlaugh—when Voinitsky declares: "My life is over! I was talented, intelligent, self-confident . . . If I had had a normal life, I might have been a Schopenhauer, a Dostoevsky . . ." To put it mildly, the choice of Dostoevsky as an example of someone who lived "a normal life" suggests a rather odd (but intelligentsial) understanding of normality. And we are aware of Dostoevsky's penchant for describing the very mixture of megalomania and self-contempt that Vanya so pathetically displays.

As if to mock both Voinitsky's precarious connection to literature and his self-indulgent pleas for pity, Chekhov has the ridiculous and truly pitiful Telegin interrupt the scene of confrontation. Telegin insists on his own incredibly vicarious link to scholarship:

> TELEGIN [*embarrassed*]: Your Excellency, I cherish not only a feeling of reverence for scholarship, but of kinship as well. My brother Grigory Ilych's wife's brother—perhaps you know him—Konstantin Trofimovitch Lakedomonov, was an M.A. . . .

> VOINITSKY: Be quiet, Waffles, we're talking business.

In Telegin's pathetic "perhaps you know him" and in the truly Gogolian name Lakedomonov we may perhaps detect another allusion to *The Inspector General*. In Gogol's play, Pyotr Ivanovich Bobchinsky would feel his life were worthwhile if the powers that be knew of his mere existence:

> BOBCHINSKY: I humbly beg you, sir, when you return to the capital, tell all those great gentlemen—the senators and admirals and all the rest—say, "Your Excellency or Your Highness, in such and such a town there lives a man called Pyotr Ivanovich Bobchinsky." Be sure to tell them, "Pyotr Ivanovich Bobchinsky lives there."

> KHLESTAKOV: Very well.

> BOBCHINSKY: And if you should happen to meet with the tsar, then tell the tsar too, "Your Imperial Majesty, in such and such a town there lives a man called Pyotr Ivanovich Bobchinsky."

> KHLESTAKOV: Fine.[7]

Telegin is a Bobchinsky for whom professors have replaced admirals. Voinitsky seems unaware that he treats Telegin with the same disregard that he so resents in the professor's treatment of him.

Voinitsky is undoubtedly correct that his mother's "principles" are, as he puts it, a "venomous joke." As he now sees, she can only repeat received expressions "about the emancipation of women," without being aware that her own behavior verges on an unwitting counterargument. Her actions also suggest unconscious self-parody as she, presumably like so many shallow members of the *intelligentsia,* constantly "makes notes on the margins of her pamphlet." This stage direction closes act I, and the phrase is repeated by a number of characters, so by the time the stage directions repeat it again at the very end of the play, we are ready to apply Voinitsky's phrase about the professor—*perpetuum mobile*—to her as well. Her first speech

concerns these insipid pamphlets that she imagines to be, in Voinitsky's phrase, "books of wisdom."

Her devotion to intelligentsial concerns has led her to idolize the old professor; she alone remains unaware that he is not what he pretends to be. But it is not so much her vacuity as her small, incessant acts of cruelty to her son that deprive her so totally of the audience's sympathy. As her son regrets his wasted life, she reproaches him in canned phrases for not caring more about the latest intellectual movements: "You used to be a man of definite convictions, an enlightened personality." We may imagine that Voinitsky's rage at the professor's proposal to deprive him of the estate is fueled to a significant extent by resentment of his mother, who repeats, as she has evidently done so often, "Jean, don't contradict Aleksandr. Believe me, he knows better than we do what is right and what is wrong." Even the professor, who has utter contempt for her, is not so intolerable as she is. Perhaps he senses, as we do, that as Telegin is a paltry double of Voinitsky, so Maria Vasilievna farcically duplicates him.

IDLENESS AND THE APOCALYPSE OF SQUABBLES

Elena Andreevna, the professor's young wife, and Astrov, the doctor who is summoned to treat him, each combine prosaic insight with melodramatic blindness. Though they often fail to live up to the standards they recommend, they do glimpse the value of everyday decency and ordinary virtues. They even understand, more or less, the danger of histrionic behavior, cited self-pity, and grand gestures, all of which nevertheless infect their own speeches. For this reason, Chekhov can use these speeches to enunciate the play's central values while simultaneously illustrating the consequences of not taking these values seriously enough.

Elena comes closest to a Chekhovian sermon as she fends off Voinitsky in act II:

> ELENA ANDREEVNA: Ivan Petrovich, you are an educated, intelligent man, and I should think you would understand that the world is being destroyed not by crime and fire, but by hatred, enmity, all these petty squabbles . . . Your business should be not to grumble, but to reconcile us to one another.

> VOINITSKY: First reconcile me to myself! My darling . . .

Elena is absolutely right: life is spoiled not by grand crises or dramatic disappointments but by "petty squabbles." It is all the more ironic, then, that in praising prosaic virtues she cannot avoid images of catastrophe and the rhetoric of apocalypse. Characteristically, her choice of words strikes Voinitsky most: "All that rhetoric and lazy morality, her foolish, lazy ideas about the ruin of the world—all that is utterly hateful to me."

Perhaps Chekhov intended Elena as an allusion to Dorothea Brooke, although Elena lacks Dorothea's unshakable integrity. Elena married the professor, just as Voinitsky worked for him, out of an intelligentsial love. Her speech about petty squabbles suggests that she has reflected on his daily pettiness and self-centered petulance, which he explicitly justifies as a right conferred by his professorial status. And so Elena, who has studied music at the conservatory, requires and does not receive permission to play the piano.

Elena understands that something is wrong, but not what would be right. We first see her in act I ignoring, almost to the point of the grotesque, the feelings of Telegin:

> TELEGIN: The temperature of the samovar has fallen perceptibly.
>
> ELENA ANDREEVNA: Never mind, Ivan Ivanovich, we'll drink it cold.
>
> TELEGIN: I beg your pardon . . . I am not Ivan Ivanovich, but Ilya Ilych . . . Ilya Ilych Telegin, or, as some people call me because of my pockmarked face, Waffles. I am Sonichka's godfather, and His Excellency, your husband, knows me quite well. I live here now, on your estate . . . You may have been so kind as to notice that I have dinner with you every day.
>
> SONYA: Ilya Ilych is our helper, our right hand. [*Tenderly*] Let me give you some more tea, Godfather.

If these lines are performed as I think Chekhov meant them, one will detect no reproach, no irony, in Telegin's voice. He has so little self-esteem that he expects to be overlooked, and so he reminds people of his existence—or of his brother's wife's brother's existence—sincerely, out of a sense that he is too insignificant to be remembered even when he is constantly present. Chekhov uses Telegin as a touchstone for the basic decency of other characters: is it worth their while to be kind to someone who is obviously of no use to anyone? In this scene, Elena fails the test, and Sonya, who calls him Godfather, passes it. Voinitsky, we remember, calls him Waffles, a nickname that only the pathetic Telegin could possibly accept and even repeat.

Elena does not work but, rather, as Astrov observes, infects everyone around her with her idleness. The old nurse speaks correctly when she complains that many of the household's ills derive from the visitors' disruption of old habits, habits related to work. A schedule, arrived at over the course of decades and carefully calibrated so that the estate can be well managed, has been replaced by a purely whimsical approach to time: Marina is awakened to get the samovar ready at 1:30 in the morning.

The *intelligentsia* may view habits as numbing, but from the standpoint of prosaics, good or bad habits more than anything else shape a life. Attention, after all, is a limited resource, and most of what we do occurs when we are concentrating on something else or on nothing in particular, as the sort of action and dialogue in Chekhov's plays makes clear. And yet it is the cumulative effect of all those actions, governed largely by habit, that conditions and indeed constitutes our lives. Moreover, habits result from countless earlier decisions and therefore can serve as a good index to a person's values and past behavior. That, indeed, is one reason Chekhov emphasizes them so much and one way in which he makes even short literary forms so resonant with incidents not directly described. Chekhov's wiser characters also understand that attention can be applied to new problems that demand more than habit only if good habits efficiently handle routine concerns. They keep one's mental hands free.

Relying on beauty, charm, and high ideals—she really has them—Elena does not appreciate the importance of habits, routine, and work. For her, life becomes meaningful at times of high drama, great sacrifice, or passionate romance. That is to say, it can be redeemed only by exceptional moments. Consequently, when those moments pass, she can only be bored. Sonya tries to suggest a different view. She values daily work and unexceptional moments, but Elena cannot understand:

> ELENA ANDREEVNA [*in misery*]: I'm dying of boredom, I don't know what do do.
>
> SONYA [*shrugging her shoulders*]: Isn't there plenty to do? If you only wanted to . . .
>
> ELENA ANDREEVNA: For instance?
>
> SONYA: You could help with running the estate, teach, take care of the sick. Isn't that enough? When you and Papa were not here, Uncle Vanya and I used to go to market ourselves to sell the flour.
>
> ELENA ANDREEVNA: I don't know how to do such things. And it's not interesting. Only in idealistic novels do people teach and doctor the peasants, and how can I, for no reason whatever, suddenly start teaching and looking after the peasants?
>
> SONYA: I don't see how one can help doing it. Wait a bit, you'll get accustomed to it. [*Embraces her*] Don't be bored, darling.

Elena significantly misunderstands Sonya. Given her usual ways of thinking in literary terms, she translates Sonya's recommendations into a speech from an "idealistic novel." That, presumably, is why she ignores the possibility of helping with the estate and singles out teaching or doctoring the peasants. She imagines that Sonya offers only a ridiculous populist idyll.

If that were what Sonya meant, Elena's objections would be quite apt. Her misunderstanding allows Chekhov to make a characteristically prosaic point about meaningful activity. In the Russian countertradition, the dynamics and significance of work—daily, ordinary work—figure as a major theme. Elena's only idea of work corresponds to a view that Levin learns to reject in *Anna Karenina*—work "for all humanity"—and she correctly rejects that choice as work "for no reason whatever." What she cannot understand is the possibility of a different sort of work that would be meaningful: prosaic work.

Thinking like a member of the *intelligentsia,* she believes that either meaning is grand and transcendent or else it is absent. Her mistake in marrying the professor has convinced her that transcendent meaning is an illusion, and so she, like Voinitsky, can imagine only the opposite, a meaningless world of empty routine extending endlessly. But Sonya's actual recommendation, like the sort of daily work Levin describes as "incontestably necessary," implicitly challenges the very terms of Elena's, and the *intelligentsia*'s, dialectic.

Sonya recommends taking care of the estate *because it has to be done.* She can draw an "incontestable" connection between getting the right price for flour and making the estate operate profitably or between not allowing the hay to rot and not indulging in waste, which is troubling in itself. Like Tolstoy, Chekhov had utter contempt for the *intelligentsia*'s (and aristocracy's) disdain of efficiency, profitability, and the sort of deliberate calculation needed to avoid waste. That is one reason the play ends with the long-delayed recording of prices for agricultural products.

When Elena characterizes caring for peasants as a purely literary pose, Sonya replies that she does not see "how one can help doing it." For Sonya, it is not a literary pose, and it serves no ideology but is part of her more general habits of caring for everyone. High ideals or broad social goals have nothing to do with her efforts on behalf of others, as we see in this very passage when she responds not with a counterargument but with a sympathetic embrace of the despairing Elena.

Sonya understands that both work and care require habits of working and caring. One has to know how they are done, and they cannot just be picked up "suddenly," as Elena correctly observes. Elena has the wrong habits, and that is her real problem. What she does not see is that she needs to being acquiring new ones, which is what Sonya is really recommending.

WASTE BY OMISSION

those graceful acts,
Those thousand decencies that daily flow.
—Milton, *Paradise Lost*

Least of all does Elena need romance, which is what Astrov offers. Like Elena and Voinitsky, he is obsessed with the vision of a brief, ecstatic affair in a literary setting. You are bound to be unfaithful sometime and somewhere, he tells Elena, so why not here, "in the lap of nature . . . At least it's poetic, the autumn is really beautiful . . . Here there is the plantation, the dilapidated country houses in the style of Turgenev." He might almost have said in the style of Chekhov. When this pathetic attempt at seduction fails, Astrov intones "Finita la commedia," a line that,

interpreted literally, does correctly characterize his desire for romance as comic, if not farcical. When he repeats "Finita!" soon afterward, the possibility of farce grows stronger.

Astrov constantly looks for literary or theatrical images to explain his life. "What's the use?" he asks at the beginning of the play. "In one of Ostrovsky's plays there's a man with a large moustache and small abilities. That's me." In fact, these self-pitying allusions make him a good example of the "more intelligent" members of the *intelligentsia* as he describes them:

> ASTROV: . . . it's hard to get along with the intelligentsia—they tire you out. All of them, all our good friends here, think and feel in a small way, they see no farther than their noses: to put it bluntly, they're stupid. And those who are more intelligent and more out-standing, are hysterical, eaten up with analysis and introspection . . . They whine. . . . [*He is about to drink*]
>
> SONYA [*stopping him*]: No, please, I beg you, don't drink any more.

Of course, this very speech examplifies the *intelligentsia*'s indulgence in self-pitying self-analysis. Astrov whines about whining, and what's more, he knows it. But this self-knowledge does him no good for reasons that Chekhov frequently explores.

Some self-destructive behavior can be modified by an awareness of what one is doing, but not the sort of introspection that Astrov describes. On the contrary, the more one is aware of it, the more that awareness becomes a part of it. (Perhaps that is what Karl Kraus meant when he said that psychoanalysis is the disease that it purports to cure.) The more Astrov blames himself for whining, and for whining about whining, the more he whines about it. This sort of introspective self-pity feeds on itself; so does alcoholic self-pity, which is why Chekhov has him drink while complaining.

To persuade him not to drink, Sonya reproaches Astrov for contradicting himself. "You always say people don't create, but merely destroy what has been given them from above. Then why, why, are you destroying yourself?" And in fact, Astrov has spoken powerfully about waste and the need for prosaic care; his speeches are the closest Chekhov comes to a Tolstoyan essay or to one of Levin's meditations.

Astrov's lectures on what we would now call "the environment" sound so strikingly contemporary that it is hard to see them in the context of Chekhov's play. In a way not uncommon in literary history, their very coincidence with current concerns provokes critical anachronism or the interpretation of them as detachable parts. It is worth stressing, therefore, that Astrov does not object to any and all destruction of trees. "Now I could accept the cutting of wood out of need, but why devastate the forests?" he says. "You will say that . . . the old life must naturally give place to the new. Yes, I understand, and

if in place of these devastated forests there were high-
ways, railroads, if there were factories, mills, schools,
and the people had become healthier, richer, more intelligent—but, you see, there is nothing of the sort!" The
chamber of commerce might well concur.

What bothers Astrov, what bothers Chekhov, is waste.
And waste results from the lack not of great ideals but of
daily care. The forests disappear for the same reason that
the hay rots. After Sonya offers her breathless paraphrase
of Astrov's ideas, Voinitsky, with his clothes still rumpled
and his bad habits showing, refuses to see the point:

> VOINITSKY [*laughing*]: Bravo, bravo! . . All that is
> charming, but not very convincing, [*to Astrov*] and so,
> my friend, allow me to go on heating my stoves with
> logs and building my barns with wood.

> ASTROV: You can heat your stoves with peat and build
> your barns with brick. . . . The Russian forests are
> groaning under the ax . . . wonderful landscapes vanish
> never to return, and all because lazy man hasn't sense
> enough to stoop down and pick up fuel from the ground.

What destroys the forests, and what destroys lives, is not
some malevolent force, not some lack of great ideas, and
not some social or political evil. Trees fall, and lives are
ruined, because of thoughtless behavior, everyday laziness, and bad habits, or, more accurately, the lack of
good ones. Destruction results from what we do not do.
Chekhov's prosaic vision receives remarkably powerful
expression in these passages.

Astrov and Sonya also give voice to that vision when they
describe how the ruin of forests is not just an analogue for
but also a cause of needlessly impoverished lives. To
paraphrase their thought: the background of our lives
imperceptibly shapes them, because what happens constantly at the periphery of our attention, what is so familiar that we do not even notice it, modifies the tiny alterations of our thoughts. Literally and figuratively, our surroundings temper the "climate" of our minds. Like good
housekeeping and careful estate management, unwasted
forests subtly condition the lives unfolding in their midst.

Where Sonya, and especially Astrov, go wrong is in their
rhetoric, which, like Elena's, becomes rapidly apocalyptic
or utopian. They intone lyrical poetry celebrating prosaic
habits and praise undramatic care with theatrical declamation:

> SONYA: If you listen to him [Astrov], you'll fully
> agree with him. He says that the forests . . . teach
> man to understand beauty and induce in him a
> nobility of mind. Forests temper the severity of the
> climate. In countries where the climate is mild, less
> energy is wasted in the struggle with nature, so man
> is softer and more tender; in such countries the people
> are beautiful, flexible, easily stirred, their speech is
> elegant, their gestures graceful. Science and art
> flourish among them, their philosophy is not somber,
> and their attitude toward women is full of an
> exquisite courtesy . . .

. . . . .

> ASTROV: . . . maybe I am just a crank, but when I
> walk by a peasant's woodland which I have saved
> from being cut down, or when I hear the rustling of
> young trees which I have planted with my own hands,
> I realize that the climate is somewhat in my power,
> and that if, a thousand years from now, mankind is
> happy, I shall be responsible for that too, in a small
> way. When I plant a birch tree and then watch it put
> forth its leaves and sway in the wind, my soul is
> filled with pride, and I . . . [*seeing the workman who
> has brought a glass of vodka on a tray*] however . . .
> [*Drinks*]

They expect a lot from trees. The doctor and his admirers show enthusiasm in the sense Dr. Johnson defined
the word: a vain belief in private revelation. Sonya's
enthusiasm reflects her love for Astrov, but what does
Astrov's reflect? In his tendency to visionary exaggeration, in his millenarian references to the destiny of all
mankind, we sense his distinctly unprosaic tendency, in
spite of everything, to think in the terms of drama, uto-
pias, and romance—and to drink.

NOTES

[1] Chekhov's belief in the prosaic virtues and skepticism of the grandiose and dramatic, in which he detected falsity, is often expressed explicitly in his correspondence. Consider, for instance, his famous letter of
March 1886 to his wayward and talented brother Nikolai. "In my opinion," Chekhov wrote, "people of culture must fulfill the following conditions":
> 1. They respect the human personality and are therefore forebearing,
> gentle, courteous, and compliant. They don't rise up in arms over a
> misplaced hammer or a lost rubber band. They do not consider it a favor
> to a person if they live with him, and when they leave, they do not say:
> "It is impossible to live with you!"

> 2. They are sympathetic not only to beggars and cats. . . .

> 3. They respect the property of others and therefore pay their debts.

> 4. They are pure of heart and fear lying like fire. They do not lie even
> in small matters. . . . They don't pose. . . .

> 5. They do not humble themselves in order to arouse sympathy in oth-
> ers. They do not play upon the heartstrings in order to excite pity. . . .
> They don't say, "I'm misunderstood!" . . .

> 8. They develop an aesthetic taste. They cannot bring them-selves to fall
> asleep in their clothes, look with unconcern at a crack in the wall with
> bedbugs in it, breathe foul air, walk across a floor that has been spat on,
> or feed themselves off a kerosene stove. . . . What they, and especially
> artists, need in women is freshness, charm, human feeling, and that
> capacity to be not a . . . [whore] but a mother. . . .

> . . . Such are cultured people. It is not enough to have read only *Pickwick
> Papers* and to have memorized a monologue from *Faust*. . . .

> What you need is constant work (Ernest J. Simmons, *Chekhov: A Bi-
> ography* [Boston, 1962], 111-13).

[2] Simmons, 111.
[3] For a more extensive discussion of "generic refugees," see Gary Saul
Morson, "Genre and Hero / *Fathers and Sons*: Inter-generic Dialogues,
Generic Refugees, and the Hidden Prosaic," in *Literature, Culture, and
Society in the Modern Age*, ed. Edward J. Brown, Lazar Fleishman, Gregory Freidin, and Richard Schupbach, Stanford Slavic Studies 4.1 (Stanford
Calif., 1991), 336-81.
[4] Letter to Leontiev-Shcheglov, May 3, 1888, Simmons, 165.
[5] I have discussed the concept of "prosaics" in a number of articles, includ-

ing "Prosaics: An Approach to the Humanities," *The American Scholar* (Autumn 1988):515-28; "Prosaics and *Anna Karenina*," *Tolstoy Studies Journal* 1 (1988):1-12; "Prosaics, Criticism, and Ethics," *Formations* 5, no. 2 (Summer-Fall 1989):77-95; and "The Potentials and Hazards of Prosaics," *Tolstoy Studies Journal* 2 (1989):15-40. The concept is also mentioned in my book *Hidden in Plain View: Narrative and Creative Potentials in "War and Peace"* (Stanford, Calif., 1987). It is central to the argument of the book I coauthored with Caryl Emerson, *Mikhail Bakhtin: Creation of a Prosaics* (Stanford, Calif., 1990).

[6] Citations from Chekhov's plays are from *Chekhov: The Major Plays*, trans. Ann Dunnigan (New York, 1964).

[7] Milton Ehre, ed., *The Theater and Plays of Nikolay Gogol: Plays and Selected Writings*, trans. Milton Ehre and Fruma Gottschalk (Chicago, 1980), 104.

Donald Rayfield   (essay date 1995)

SOURCE: "The Reception of *Uncle Vania*," in *Chekhov's* Uncle Vania *and* The Wood Demon, Bristol Classical Press, 1995, pp. 61-72.

[*In the essay below, Rayfield offers an overview of the reception of* Uncle Vanya, *emphasizing critics' reactions to Chekhov's reworking of* The Wood Demon.]

Our own critical interpretation of *Uncle Vania* can only build on the Russian public's reception, at first bemused, then enthusiastic, of the work. Three factors inhibited the response: firstly the play was published two years before it was first performed in Moscow 26 October 1899 (even though it had had a number of provincial performances from 1897); secondly, although *The Wood Demon* had been read and seen by only a few hundred people, it was widely known that the new play was a reworking of its lame prototype; thirdly *The Seagull,* which was published in the same 1897 edition of Chekhov's collected plays, was still recovering its reputation from its disappointing first staging in St Petersburg. It was not until the triumphant Moscow Arts Theatre performance of autumn 1898 that Chekhov's reputation as a great playwright became permanently unassailable.

The first critics responded to the written text, which they found far less interesting than such controversial stories as **"Peasants."** They were sceptical about its viability on the stage: 'Seven or eight years ago the same play, as *The Wood Demon,* was performed on one of the Moscow private stages [. . .] Now the drama, or as the author modestly calls it, "Scenes from country life" has been significantly reworked [. . .] The impression from reading the play is very great and very depressing, oppressive. It is difficult to predict its success on the stage. Even after reworking it is unlikely to find success with the average spectator [. . .] Much is vaguely sketched, the whole action seems to be wrapped in mist, perhaps deliberately. You have to give it a lot of thought to understand the motives behind the heroes' actions and evaluate all the truth in them. But spectators like clarity, precision, definition, firm, even sharp contours. So-called "mood" (and there is no end to the mood in the play!) is valued very little in the auditorium.' (*Novosti dnia,* 5 June 1897).

Such opinions kept *Uncle Vania* off the metropolitan stage. In May 1897 Chekhov's friend Sumbatov-Iuzhin offered to have it or *The Seagull* staged by the Moscow Maly Theatre: but it was not until February 1899 that the acting director of the Maly formally asked for the performing rights and only then did the Theatrical-Literary Committee meet at the home of the director of the Moscow office of Russia's Imperial Theatres for a reading. The actors present loved the play; the bureaucrats on the committee (including I. I. Ivanov who had loathed *The Wood Demon*) insulted the author and damned the play by demanding revisions: 'we recognise it as deserving of production on condition that minor cuts and revisions are carried out in accordance with the indications of the Committee's department and a second submission to the Committee.' Unfortunately, Nemirovich-Danchenko felt that as director of the Moscow Arts Theatre he could not allow a conflict of interests to arise by attending and swinging the committee's verdict by his single vote.

The committee sent Chekhov a more substantial, if obtuse, critique:

> Its staging has certain unevenness or gaps. Before Act 3 Uncle Vania and Astrov seem to merge into the type of failure, superfluous man which is fairly successfully sketched in Mr Chekhov's works. Nothing prepares us for that powerful burst of passion which occurs during his talk with Elena[13] [. . .] That Voinitsky might take a dislike to the professor as Elena's husband is understandable [. . .] but disillusion in Serebriakov's greatness as a scholar, especially as an art historian is somewhat strange [. . .] is no excuse for pursuing him firing a pistol, chasing him like a madman. If the spectator were to link this state with the drunken state in which the author for some reason too often portrays both Uncle Vania and Astrov, the unpleasant and unexpected introduction of these two shots into the play takes on a peculiar and undesirable nuance. The character of Elena might need somewhat more clarification [. . .] Perhaps the main female character on the stage, the cause of so many alarms and dramas, endowed with a 'tiresome' character, she arouses no interest in the spectator. The play has longueurs, from a literary point of view these drag out the action with no profit to it. One instance is the protracted praise of forests in Act 1, shared by Sonia and Astrov, and the explanation of Astrov's theory of afforestation, so is the explanation of the maps, so is even the finely conceived depiction of the peace that falls after Elena and her husband have left, in the end of the play, and Sonia's dreams. In this final scene which comes after the main dramatic interest is exhausted the contrast should have been reduced to brief, bare essentials.

In April Chekhov visited one committee member, Teliakovsky, after this letter for a 'conversation'. The latter recalls: 'Chekhov was absolute *sang-froid*. He asked me not to fuss about his play being blackballed, said that of course he would change nothing in the play [. . .] and to calm me promised to write a new play by autumn specially for the Maly.' Thus, thanks to the conservatism of the Imperial theatres,[14] Stanislavsky and Nemirovich-Danchenko were presented with the play they had hoped

Innokenty Smoktunovsky as Vanya and Irina Kupchenko as Sonia, in a 1970 Russian film adaptation of Uncle Vanya.

for to consolidate the success of their production of ***The Seagull.***

Meanwhile ***Uncle Vania*** was winning a shadowy provincial popularity. We know that it was performed in Kazan in October 1897 and with great success in Pavlovsk (the summer resort of many Petersburgers) in 1898. In autumn it played in Odessa and Kiev (a staging that Chekhov saw a few years later). Chekhov read the play to amateur actors who performed it in Serpukhov, a few miles from Melikhovo. In November it played in Chekhov's home town, Taganrog, where his cousin reported 'especially great success'. Nizhnii Novgorod, and Tiflis were other centres important enough to force Moscow and St Petersburg critics to take note of provincial reactions to what they had spurned. A critic who saw the Pavlovsk production already noted the Act 4 as 'a stage chef-d'œuvre' which made the play 'the most impressive work on the stage of recent years.' The Russian-language press in Tiflis (*Kavkaz,* 2 May 1899) showed the heartfelt empathy which provincial and colonial audiences in the Russian audience were to accord all the later Chekhovian drama, as if Chekhov were the first metropolitan writer to understand the dreary hopelessness of their lives on the fringe: 'in a truly Chekhovian way, that is with

fine observation and deep psychological analysis [. . .] we see clever, talented, educated people spending their whole lives on trivia and withering in unconscious quietism, busy with things that are beneath them, gradually sucked into base trivial lives, existing with no profit to others or themselves.'

One perceptive Chekhovian stood alone: A. I. Urusov stood by his fondness for ***The Wood Demon.*** 'I have carefully reread ***Uncle Vania*** and must with sadness tell you that in my opinion you have ruined ***The Wood Demon.*** You have crumpled it, reduced it to an outline and disfigured it. You had a splendid comic villain: he has vanished, and he was necessary to the internal symmetry, and rogues of that stature, with luxuriant and bright plumage, is what you are especially good at. It was precious to the play, bringing in a humorous note. The second sin, in my view, is still more heinous: changing the pace of the play. The suicide in Act 3 and the nocturnal scene by the river with the tea table in Act 4, the wife's return to the doctor—all that was newer, bolder, more interesting than the end you have now. When I was retelling ***The Wood Demon*** to the French, it was this that struck them: the hero is killed, but life goes on. The actors I spoke to were of the same opinion. Of course, ***Uncle Vania*** is good, better than anything being written now—but *The Wood Demon* was better' (letter to Chekhov, 27 i 99).

One might also take Tolstoy's play *A Living Corpse* of 1900 as expressing a marked preference for *The Wood Demon* over *Uncle Vania*: Tolstoy's wayward hero, after his fictitious death is exposed, shoots himself so that his wife may marry a man worthy of her love, a plot which seems to turn the suicide of Voinitsky and reconciliation of the Serebriakovs into a morally coherent sequence, however much it may seem to be at odds with the asceticism preached elsewhere by Tolstoy. The failure of *The Wood Demon* continued to haunt *Uncle Vania*: when in 1901 the Society of Russian Playwrights and Opera Composers was deciding what play to recommend as the outstanding play of the previous year for the Griboyedov prize, they refused to consider *Uncle Vania* on the grounds that it was 'an adaptation of the same author's *The Wood Demon* which had already been considered.'

In Spring 1899 Nemirovich-Danchenko was glad to accept *Uncle Vania* for the Moscow Arts Theatre with no changes: Nemirovich-Danchenko directed (Stanislavsky was too busy preparing A. K. Tolstoy's *The Death of Ivan the Terrible*). Nemirovich-Danchenko persuaded Stanislavsky to play Astrov, although the latter's first preference was the title role.[15] Chekhov was present at one rehearsal of two acts in May and intervened to supply maps of Serpukhov with Melikhovo at the centre for Act 3. Chekhov was laconic, even cryptic, to any actor who asked him for help in interpreting a role: 'It's all written there,' was his standard reply. Only questions of dress—especially Vania's splendid tie—were expanded on by the author. The remaining rehearsals went on in Chekhov's absence, but with Nemirovich-Danchenko, Meierkhold and Olga Knipper all giving the playwright slightly varying accounts of the play's progress. Except for Knipper, the final casting corresponded not at all with Chekhov's original preferences, particularly for Komissarzhevskaia as Sonia and Davydov (who acted in *The Wood Demon*) as Voinitsky. Stanislavsky's wife, Lilina, took Sonia, while Vishnevsky, who played Voinitsky, was probably the only actor whom Chekhov wholeheartedly trusted to interpret his part intelligently. As the theatre's co-director, and as Astrov on stage, Stanislavsky had more influence than Chekhov over Knipper's interpretation of Elena: 'For a greater difference from Arkadina, I'd give Elena—of course in the quiet places—more immobility, drawl, idleness, reserve and worldliness and, at the same time, I'd give more shadow to her temperament.' Their co-operation was close: Knipper confessed, 'When I felt [Astrov's] infatuated gaze, full of cunning, and heard his caressing irony, "You're cunning", I was always annoyed with that "intellectual" Elena for not going to visit him in his forest nursery.'

Meanwhile illness had forced Chekhov to retire to Yalta, from where he wrote to Vishnevsky (8 x 99): 'How upset and annoyed I am that I can't be with you all, that I am missing almost all rehearsals and the performances and know them only at second hand, whereas it would be

enough for me to be present at rehearsals to recharge myself, to get experience and get down to a new play.'

The production appears to have been an outstanding success. Nemirovich-Danchenko's and Stanislavsky's production copy[16] gives some hint of the care and ingenuity with which they realised Chekhov's directions and of their contribution to the play's success. . . . The greenery of the opening scene went far beyond Chekhov's specifications. For Act 1 Stanislavsky specified mosquitoes, real chickens for Marina to round up, and even a dog. In creating the mood he specified that Astrov should smoke with a long cigarette holder and roll his own *papirosy,* while Voinitsky was to appear in a dressing-gown, and Maria Vasilievna with both pince-nez and lorgnette with a handbag full of pencils. The prop list for Act 2 was likewise inventive: hot water bottles were added to Serebriakov's medicines. As with *The Cherry Orchard,* Stanislavsky came into his own in the more crowded choreography required for Act 3. He opens it with Elena and Sonia playing a piano duet (thus spoiling the symbolism of the silent piano), Voinitsky throwing his hat and overcoat on a chair and conducting the performance, correcting Sonia's wrong notes. When the clock strikes one, Voinitsky checks his watch. During Sonia and Elena's brief exchange Stanislavsky had Sonia on the verge of sobbing, chewing her fingernails, while Elena jerks her hand away from Sonia's lips. In the climax of the act Stanislavsky had all mention of numbers and figures heavily stressed. Voinitsky was to come to the front of the stage and, with his back to the audience, confront Serebriakov. Stanislavsky then crossed out Voinitsky's threatening words, 'You won't forget me' (*Budesh' menia pomnit'*) and after the bungled murder attempt had Voinitsky point the gun at his own forehead, with a ten-second silent freeze before the curtain fell. The same meticulous care and the same need to fiddle with the text is found in Act 4. The care is expressed in the orchestration of non-verbal elements at the end: the cricket chirping, the rain dripping from the roof, the banging of the night-watchman and the guitar climax with heavy rain. Much of Elena's and Astrov's farewell is rearranged, with a long pause inserted in which Elena leans with her elbows against the door frame, as if blocking any exit.

There is one touch that Stanislavsky puts on the last page after his own signature, 'Finished 27 May 1899, K. Alekseev: "And life anyway is stupid, boring," is Chekhov's own phrase.' It suggests how close Astrov is to Chekhov (at least in Stanislavsky's opinion), so that we may well interpret the progression from the Wood Demon to Astrov as representing a disillusion and coarsening in the author's own self.

Nemirovich-Danchenko and his colleagues kept sending telegrams to Yalta, rousing Chekhov from his sickbed, sending him barefoot in the dark to his newly installed telephone. Chekhov was irritated and embarrassed not to have seen the play even in rehearsal, even more by an item in a newspaper: 'A. P. Chekhov, very interested in the staging of his drama *Uncle Vania* by the Artistic-Popular Theatre troupe, has sent a writer-friend a letter asking for details of the staging of *Uncle Vania.*' But to judge by the telegrams Chekhov received, Stanislavsky's production met the same ecstatic audience response as his *Seagull.* Olga Knipper, however, like some of the cast, felt dissatisfied until several performances had taught the actors how to cope with the Chekhovian 'images'. Nemirovich-Danchenko felt that the text itself was still not perfect, that the motivation for Voinitsky's attack on the professor was so obscure that it inhibited audience response. (Later, in his articles, Nemirovich-Danchenko blamed his production for devoting more time to sound effects than the lyrical potential of the text.) Nevertheless, by the sixth performance (10 November 1899) Vishnevsky, who played Voinitsky, could write: 'We acted amazingly today!!! The theatre was crammed to overflowing. I have never known such a reception [. . .] Groans and shouts filled the theatre! We had fifteen curtain calls.'

Chekhov's rivals went to see it: Gorky, by no means a friend of Chekhovian drama, commented, 'I don't consider the play a pearl, but I see more content in it than others do; its content is enormous, symbolist, and in form it is a completely original, unique thing.' Shortly afterwards (24 January 1900), Tolstoy visited MKhaT. His dairy records, 'I went to see *Uncle Vania* and was indignant.' He is reported to have complained that 'despite brilliant passages there was no tragic situation, that it was pointless to hint at any meaning in the sound of the guitar or of the cricket, that Astrov and Voinitsky were rubbish, idlers, running from action, that they should have married peasant girls and stopped pestering Serebriakov.' The perversity of this response is outrageous when we consider Tolstoy's late drama, particularly *A Living Corpse,* where the best elements are very Chekhovian irrational touches and liberalism.

The success of *Uncle Vania,* performed by professionals and amateurs in the provinces, was unprecedented, so much so that the new director of the Imperial theatres overrode their previous decision and only MKhaT's intervention stopped the Aleksandrinsky theatre from performing it in Petersburg. Effectively, Stanislavsky was acquiring a monopoly of Chekhov in the metropolitan theatre, which Nemirovich-Danchenko defended as 'a defence of Chekhov's artistic interests'. (Nemirovich-Danchenko considered St Petersburg actors, especially in the Maly theatre, as unsuitable for Chekhovian characters because of their incorrigibly handsome voices and rhythms.)

In their letters to Chekhov it is remarkable how unanimously critics agreed that this play was closely linked with *The Seagull* as a basis for a new drama and a 'hammer to beat the public's head'. Likewise, attention focused on Act 4 and the tragic implication that Sonia and Voinitsky now had no future. Chekhov's cousin, Georgi Mitrofanovich, in his letter from Taganrog spoke for many: 'The tableau of the final act was extraordinarily sad and depressing, it left on all the spectators an impression that was heavier than any tragic scenes.' The reactions were often personal, even intrusive: one MKhaT actor wrote, 'I a man of 22 wept . . . not only for uncle

Vania, for Astrov, but mainly for you. God, how alone you are and how little personal happiness you have. Astrov's notes of universal grief are covered by a heavy chord of lack of love, happiness, personal happiness.' *Uncle Vania* may have been the first major Chekhov play to be performed abroad, for an amateur group of Russians played it in Paris in January 1902.[17] One spectator recorded in her diary, 'amid the merriment and noise of Paris I heard a sound penetrating right into my heart—a voice from the homeland, an echo of its life.' Many of these reactions, optimistic, pessimistic, puzzled or adoring, were addressed to Chekhov and his occasional, if taciturn responses are sometimes illuminating: for instance in one reply to an actress's letter he enlarged on his conception of Elena, 'Perhaps Elena Andreevna may seem incapable of thinking or even loving, but when I was writing *Uncle Vania* I had something quite different in mind.'

Faced with the play's success on stage, the literary critics began to run with the hare, not the hounds. The Moscow critics in particular drifted away from their usual assessments based on sociology and representativeness and began to appreciate novelty as a virtue: 'Mr Chekhov feels, thinks and perceives life in episodes, particulars, in its flotsam and jetsam and, if one may say so, infinite parallels that never intersect, at least, not on any visible plane,' wrote one of his most perceptive critics, Kugel (*Teatr i iskusstvo* [1900] 8, 168-9). In St Petersburg it was the symbolists who were readiest to welcome Chekhov for, as Filosofov put it, 'truly decadent refinement'. (Chekhov was less inclined to read, let alone respond to, professional criticism: 'I don't read such articles so as not to foul my mood' he wrote to Nemirovich-Danchenko [3 xii 99].) However, on 6 November 1899 Rakshanin in the Stock Exchange Gazette (*Birzhevaia gazeta*), usually the most aesthetically inclined of the Petersburg newspapers, took a broader view: 'Until recently playwrights of all countries and times wrote dramas, comedies and vaudevilles for the stage. For these writings there were definite forms, specific requirements, there was a tradition which seemed unshakeable. [. . .] We are now undoubtedly present at a battle of a new tendency in dramatic writing with the established forms, and Anton Chekhov is at the head of the movement. [. . .] *Uncle Vania* of course is not a comedy, even less a drama, undoubtedly it is not a vaudeville—it is in fact "a mood in four acts".'

It was not until 10 April 1900, when the MKhaT came to Sevastopol that Chekhov saw his play in production. Stanislavsky records: 'We were moved by the dark figure of the author hidden in the director's box behind the backs of Vl. Nemirovich-Danchenko and his wife. The first act had a chilly reception. By the end success had become a great ovation. The author was called for. He was in despair, but still came forth.' Chekhov went backstage with advice, especially on Astrov. Stanislavsky realised: 'Astrov is a cynic, he has become one from contempt for the vulgarity around him. He isn't sentimental and doesn't sulk . . . he cancels out the lyricism of Uncle Vania's and Sonia's finale.'

The influence of *Uncle Vania* grew with its reputation; in Germany it clearly affected Arthur Schnitzler, whose play *Der einsame Weg* (*The Lonely Way* [1903]),[18] with its dandy hero Stephan von Sala, stakes his claim to be called the 'German Chekhov'. 'Not much has made such an unforgettable impression on me as *Uncle Vania* in as staged by the Moscow Arts Theatre,' Schnitzler wrote.[19]

In Russia *Uncle Vania* became the least contentious of Chekhov's plays; its relative simplicity, its brevity and economy, the absence of complicated effects and sets made it accessible to provincial repertory and amateur theatre; its title role was easily identifiable with many a spectator's uncle and thus became a byword. Maiakovsky, an unlikely worshipper of Chekhov, argued in his *Two Chekhovs* (1914) that (like the futurists) Chekhov was an innovative artist of words, not ideas: 'Take his bloodless dramas. Behind the stained glass of words life is discernible only as much as is necessary. Where another writer would have needed to use a suicide to justify someone's parading round the stage, Chekhov gives the highest drama in the simple "grey" words: *Astrov:* "But the heat in that Africa there must be really terrific".'

After the revolution Chekhov became an official icon, and provoked reaction not so much against him as against the mummification of his work. Bulgakov satirises *Uncle Vania* in his play *The Days of the Turbins,* where the embattled heroes compete for the attention of an unhappily married Elena: no sooner does the poet-figure declare 'We shall rest' than nine gun-shots belie his hopes. Osip Mandelstam's sketch (1935) for a broadcast[20] on *Uncle Vania* is indignant. It opens with the cast list and then asks: 'Why are they together? [. . .] Try and define the qualities or kinship of Voinitsky, son of the widow of a privy councillor, of the mother of the professor's first wife, with Sofia Aleksandrovna, the professor's daughter by his first wife. I for one find it easier to understand the funnel-shaped outline of Dante's comedy with its circles, routes and spherical astronomy, than this petty-passport nonsense. A biologist would call the Chekhovian principle ecological. Cohabitation is the determining factor for Chekhov. There is no action in his plays, there is only contiguity and the unpleasantnesses that result. Chekhov takes a sample with a pipette from a non-existent human "mire". People live together and just cannot separate. That is all.'

In post-Soviet prose, Viacheslav P'etsukh showed the same touching irreverence in his sketch *Uncle Senia,*[21] where the actor of this name has to play Uncle Vania in a provincial performance: 'things were so bad that in the middle of Act 4 Voinitsky, thanks to a whim of the Vologda director, commits suicide.' Pretending to be dead, Uncle Senia snarls at the sufferings of Uncle Vania: 'No, what a life they screwed up, the dogs—it was a fairy tale, not life!'

The very success of *Uncle Vania* has prevented Russian directors from much experimentation—only the Soviet insistence on making Sonia's last speech a prophecy of post-revolutionary bliss temporarily blighted the Chekhovian

mood. With the fragmentation of Russia's theatres in the 1990s, however, some experimentation has taken place. Desnitsky's classically minimal production on the tiny stage of the theatre *U nikitskikh vorot* of 1993 contrasts with the Petersburg Maly theatre's attempt (directed by Sergei Soloviov) to prove Nemirovich-Danchenko wrong by assembling the maximum of detail and turning it into a compendium of Chekhoviana, giving Uncle Vania the cello that uncles traditionally play in Russian literature (e.g. in Turgenev's *Fathers and Sons* or Chekhov's *Ivanov*), making Sonia (however unlikely) a secret drinker of vodka like Masha in *The Seagull,* with Sonia's haymaking visible from the house (like the hay in Stanislavsky's production of *The Cherry Orchard*), emphasising the emotional weight behind every mention of the dead Vera Petrovna, amassing detail with an exactitude and fussiness that would amaze even Stanislavsky. *Uncle Vania* also acquired a second life in the Russian cinema. Notable is the 1975 version by Mikhail Konchalovsky in which Bondarchuk plays a rather middle-aged Astrov and Smoktunovsky plays an omni-present Vania, who, when not taking part in the action, is listening to it through the wall from his den of a room, in a house of almost Edgar Allen Poe atmosphere: the mood of brooding depression intensifying to the point of insanity is cinematically powerful, even though it is unfaithful to the callous comic strain of Chekhov's play.

Although Chekhov's second life can be said to be taking place in English, Chekhov's plays met the greatest resistance in England. The London production of *Uncle Vania* in 1914, however, roused *The Times* to commend it as 'a play utterly opposed to all our English notions of play making, a play of will-less people, futile people, drifters, just pottering on with their disappointed, frustrated lives[22] . . . not Vania, but little Sonia, is its central figure.' Other reviewers condemned it as 'a desolate, dreary, competent piece of work, no doubt good for us to see once . . .'. Directed by Komisarjevsky in 1921, the next English version of *Uncle Vania* was more successful: 'what Chekhov has done and what nobody else has ever attempted is to put on the stage that which in all other plays happens during the *entr'actes,'* commented Desmond McCarthy in *New Statesman,* while James Agate declared the play 'quite perfect,' a view which long remained challenged, however tragically or comically Chekhov's subtitle 'Scenes from country life' was interpreted. Howard Barker, a radical playwright turned producer, however, has now decided to resolve his 'quarrel with Chekhov a man [. . .] who has to some extent institutionalised failure' by staging a version of *Uncle Vania* in which Vania shoots straight at the professor, with catastrophic results.[23]

If in Germany *Uncle Vania* found a ready acceptance (until the coming of the Nazis), in France it had to overcome the prejudice of critics such as Schlumberger, who in 1921 declared that the play 'lacked gathering, sacrifice in establishing the plan, it scorns the underlining of action, without which our taste for architecture is unsatisfied.' When Georges Pitoëff (who had studied under Stanislavsky) staged *Uncle Vania* in 1922, however, the view was transformed: Lucien Descaves found it had 'an anguish and an undeniable beauty.' In Japan, after Maurice Baring's chapter on Chekhov's plays had been translated, *Uncle Vania* was singled out for attention, just as in China it became by the 1950s the favourite foreign play.

Not only readers, but theatre performers, have been swayed by the interpretations of literary critics. In the English-speaking world they tended to emphasise the elegiac, melancholy aspects of *Uncle Vania* and played down the farce. Some of the best (and most influential) critiques have come from scholars with no knowledge of Russian; few have equalled the insights of F. L. Lucas in his *The Drama of Chekhov, Synge, Yeats and Pirandello* (London: Cassell, 1963). Although Lucas dismisses *The Wood Demon* out of hand, [he identifies] *Uncle Vania* and its diatribe against Serebriakov with Chekhov's personal loathing of critics. In such critiques Chekhov's play was pulled out of its Russian context and placed in a wider and larger context of unhappy comedies of love, of sylvan settings destroyed, from Ronsard and Molière to Thomas Hardy and Flaubert, whose god-like Dr Rivière Lucas turns into a Titanic predecessor of the Chekhovian doctor. Such an approach, of course, is open to the accusation that it contradicts Chekhov's own insistence on the comic nature of his work and the critic, like critics of Molière, is forced to take refuge in the notorious phrase 'Then Chekhov [Molière] was wrong.'

Of the linguistically qualified critics in English, David Magarshack (in *Chekhov the Dramatist* [New York: Hill and Wang, 1960]) was the first to deal adequately with the relationship between *The Wood Demon* and *Uncle Vania.* He divides Chekhov's plays into conventional plays of direct action and innovative plays of indirect action; he called *The Wood Demon* a play of transition, and classified *Uncle Vania* as a play of indirect action, setting out in parallel columns at least one scene from Act 1 of each play to show how very similar texts have different impact in changed frameworks. Before Magarshack no critic had given *The Wood Demon* such a fair examination. Magarshack emphasises the complete opposition of Chekhov's intentions and achievement: 'teeming with coincidences and *deus ex machina* situations [. . .] the action of the play is in fact full of unlife-like melodramatic touches.'

Maurice Valency attracted attention to his study of Chekhov's drama by the serendipity of his title, *The Breaking String* (New York: Oxford University Press, 1966). He gave the first coherent account in English of the genesis of *The Wood Demon* and rightly points out that the play's contemporary critics never objected to the worst faults of the play: the use of 'found' letters and diaries to make the plot and hasten its dénouement. Valency is a loyal Chekhovian in insisting that *Uncle Vania*'s 'comedic aspects are quite incompatible with a tragic action' and sees the play as an ambiguous drama in which all the characters are mentally ill and 'have wrapped themselves up more or less comfortably against the elemental blasts'. The critical complacency becomes questionable only when Valency concludes that *Uncle Vania* shows 'Chekhov had achieved a certain proficiency in this exacting medium' (whereas 'the *Three Sisters* is not a well-made play. It

is a chronicle in which may be discerned only the vestiges of a plot.')

Other critics such as J. L. Styan (*Chekhov in Performance: A Commentary on the Major Plays* [Cambridge University Press, 1971]) have directed their efforts not so much towards a reader's interpretation but a director's staging. Styan is anxious that the director should appreciate the agrarian poverty of the world outside Chekhov's sets. Otherwise, too, this is an interpretation that centres on political issues: an interesting poll is produced to show how critics and directors of all nations split almost evenly on whether to interpret Sonia's last speech as a call for optimism or an illusion born of despair. The concern for consensus forces Styan to relegate his best insights to footnotes, notably a comment that the end of Act 2, in which Astrov and Sonia negotiate their future non-relationship foreshadows Act 4 of *The Cherry Orchard* and the even bleaker scene between Varia and Lopakhin.

The next generation of critics, such as Richard Peace (*Chekhov: A Study of the Four Major Plays* [Yale: Harvard University Press, 1983]) and Laurence Senelick (*Modern Dramatists: Anton Chekhov* [London: Macmillan, 1985]) have paid less attention to Chekhov's development as a whole and have treated *Uncle Vania* as a work in the modern canon. Peace pays special attention to the almost Japanese role of the tea-drinking around which Act 1 is constructed and investigates the symbolism of the names, Voinitsky representing the 'warring' principle (*voin-*) and Elena the principle of idleness (*len'-*). Senclick has been more concerned to integrate *Uncle Vania* with modern, especially French drama (Beckett). Senelick points out the Bergsonian nature of Chekhovian time, as a flow outside which the characters are unable to stand, imprisoned like Proust in subjective time. The play thus becomes more likc a novel, for time, it is implied in Chekhovian drama, must go on flowing after the curtain-fall. Senelick has fewer insights into the genesis of Chekhov's work than Russian critics, but his is one of the best attempts to fit it into the 20th-century European Zeitgeist, to see its link to the desolate symbolism of Strindberg. Perhaps the tendency to recruit Chekhov posthumously into the Theatre of the Absurd has gone too far; as the German critic Maria Deppermann has pointed out in a number of articles. *Uncle Vania* opens and closes with scenes of human affection which are completely uncharacteristic of the absurd and the alienated. However hopeless, Sonia's consolation of Vania and, however uncomprehending, Marina's concern for Astrov affirm some sort of sense and communion in human life.

NOTES

[13] Chekhov marked this part of the document in pencil with an irritated 'On whose part?' [*U kogo?*] As he was to insist to Olga Knipper, who not for the last time showed disappointing perversity in interpreting her roles, Astrov was not passionate towards Elena, but idly lecherous.

[14] In 1899, however, the Aleksandrinsky theatre in St Petersburg tried and failed to secure the play and override the Committee's ban.

[15] The power of Stanislavsky's acting may explain why some spectators felt that Astrov, not Voinitsky, should be the title role, that the centre of gravity had not really shifted from the doctor to Voinitsky in the conversion of *The Wood Demon* into *Uncle Vania.*

[16] I am very grateful to the curator and archivist of the Museum of MKhaT in Moscow for permission to study this copy. It is numbered 18890, and dated 27 May 1899, with additional notes for Acts 1 in Nemirovich-Danchenko's hand (in red and blue). As the copy awaits publication I have agreed to restrain from a comprehensive description of Stanislavsky's annotations and have limited myself to a few quotations and to a rough reproduction of Stanislavsky's sketches for the sets. Stanislavsky had unsewn a copy of Chekhov's *Plays* (1897) and for every page of Chekhov's text of *Uncle Vania* he interleaved a page of notes before rebinding the play. Most of Stanislavsky's many additional stage directions were not incorporated into Chekhov's next edition of the work (1901). It is clear, however, that the few changes in the final version of *Uncle Vania* in Chekhov's collected works stem mostly from Stanislavsky's alterations.

[17] There were, however, several performances in Czech in Prague and the Bohemian provinces in 1901.

[18] Schnitzler's play was performed in Russian in MKhaT on the same night in 1904 as *Uncle Vania* was first performed in the Künstlertheater in Vienna.

[19] See Maria Deppermann, *Tschechov und Arthur Schnizler,* in Kluge, op. cit., pp. 1161-85.

[20] The talk was never broadcast: see Osip Mandelstam, *Sobranie sochinenii IV* (Paris, 1981) 107-9.

[21] Viachelsav P'etsukh, *Tsikly* (Moscow, 1991) 155-61.

[22] A sentence repeated almost verbatim in another unsigned review of the play in *The Times* in 1945.

[23] *The Guardian* (9 April 1994) 29.

Three Sisters

Lionel Trilling (essay date 1967)

SOURCE: *"The Three Sisters,"* in *Prefaces to the Experience of Literature,* Harcourt Brace Jovanovich, 1967, pp. 28-36.

[*In the following essay, Trilling ruminates on Chekhov's insistence that* Three Sisters *is a comedy, speculating that when Chekhov maintained "that* Three Sisters *was a comedy, even a farce, he was not talking to critics or theorists of literature but to actors, and he was trying to suggest what should be brought to the text by those who put it on the stage, a complexity of meaning which the text might not at first reveal."*]

Three Sisters is surely one of the saddest works in all literature. It is also one of the most saddening. As it draws to a close, and for some time after Olga has uttered her hopeless desire to know whether life and its suffering have any meaning, we must make a conscious effort if we are not to be overcome by the depression that threatens our spirits. The frustration and hopelessness to which the persons of the drama fall prey seems to be not only their doom but ours as well. For between ourselves and those persons in *Three Sisters* with whom we sympathize there is remarkably little distance, certainly as compared, say, with the distance that separates us from Lear. Apart from the difference in nationality, nothing stands in the way of our saying that they are much like ourselves and our friends. They are decent, well-intentioned people, not extraordinary in their gifts but above the general run of mankind in intelligence and sensitivity, well enough educated to take pleasure in the arts and to aspire to freedom, the enjoyment of beauty, and the natural development of their personalities, all the benefits to which we give the name of "the good life."

And in fact, apart from their recognizability, these people are made especially easy for us to come close to because Chekhov, in representing them, takes full account of an element of human life that the tragic dramatists were not concerned with. Sophocles and Shakespeare represented life in terms of character and fate. Chekhov proposes the part that is played in our existence by environment. There is nothing that more readily fosters our intimacy with other people than an awareness of the actual and particular conditions in which they live their lives from day to day.

Character, in the sense in which we use it of the creations of the great tragic dramatists, means the way in which a person confronts the things that happen to him, a number of which may come about as a consequence of his characteristic behavior. Fate is the sum of the decisive things that happen to a person, whether as the result

The first edition of Three Sisters.

of his characteristic behavior, or fortuitously, or at the behest of some transcendent power. Environment signifies those material and social circumstances in which an individual leads his existence, in particular those that make for his well-being or lack of it and that seem to condition his character and fate.

Since all events take place under nameable conditions, environment is an integral element of all dramatic genres, including tragedy. In the story of Oedipus, for example, it is clearly of consequence that Oedipus is king of Thebes, not of Athens, and that he lives as befits a king and not, say, a merchant. But we are not asked to be aware of these circumstances except in a general way. Our imagination of Oedipus in his regal life does not include particularities such as the boring ceremonial a king must endure, the strain of being always in the public eye, his exasperated sense of the frivolity of the innumerable palace servants, whose gossip and petty intrigue are a perpetual nuisance . . . and so on.

The modern literary imagination almost always conceives environment as adverse, as comprising those material and social conditions of life which constrain and hamper the protagonist and thwart his ideal development and which, more than anything that might happen to him in a sudden dramatic way, make his destiny. The habit of thinking about a human life in relation to its environment is of relatively recent growth. It began, roughly speaking, in the eighteenth century. Since then it has achieved an importance that can scarcely be overestimated.

This sense of the influence of environment on character and fate has deeply changed the traditional way of thinking about morality and politics. It enables us to believe in an essential quality of humanity, about which predications can be made, usually to the effect that it is by nature good, and then to go on to judge whether a particular circumstance in which an individual is placed is appropriate or inappropriate to his essential humanity. It thus serves as a principle of explanation in the personal life, and as a ground of social action. Few people can hear the contemporary phrase "juvenile delinquent" without immediately thinking of the family and neighborhood circumstances—the environment—that fostered the undesirable behavior of the young person. And in our view of ourselves we have learned to give great significance to the conditions of our lives, those that made us what we are and those that keep us from being what we might wish to be.

The awareness of environment is, as I have said, salient in our response to *Three Sisters.* We are never permitted to forget that the people in Chekhov's play are required to live in a certain way—far from the metropolis, Moscow, in a dreary provincial city; possessing the tastes and desires of a certain social class yet lacking the money to fulfil their expectations of life; bored by and disaffected from their professions. Their desperate unhappiness is not the result of an event, of some catastrophic shock, but, rather, a condition of life itself, the slow relentless withdrawal of all that had once been promised of delight and satisfaction. To catastrophe we can sometimes respond by mustering up our energies of resistance or fortitude, but the unhappiness that Chekhov represents is that of people who, as the environment takes its toll of them, have fewer and fewer energies of resistance or endurance, let alone renovation. It is a state that few of us can fail in at least some degree to know from experience, and our knowledge of it makes us peculiarly responsive to the pathos of *Three Sisters.* We are not surprised to hear that when the manuscript of the play was read to the members of the Moscow Art Theatre who were to perform it, the company was so deeply moved that many wept as they listened.

Chekhov did not take their tears as a tribute. He told them that they had quite misconceived the nature of *Three Sisters,* which was, he said, a "gay comedy, almost a farce." This may well be the strangest comment on his own work that a writer ever made. And Chekhov did not make it casually or playfully, as a provocative paradox. He insisted on it. The famous head of the Moscow Theatre, Constantin Stanislavsky, who directed and championed Chekhov's plays, says in his memoirs that he can remember no opinion ever expressed by Chekhov that the author defended so passionately; he held it, Stanislavsky says, "until his dying day" and believed that his play had failed if it was understood otherwise. Yet he was never able to make clear what he meant by this strange idea. Another theatrical colleague, Vladimir Nemirovich Danchenko, who was even closer to Chekhov than Stanislavsky was, tells us that when the actors asked him for an explanation of such a view, he never could advance reasons to substantiate it. To his friends in the theatre it was plain that Chekhov was not being perverse, that he truly believed that this saddest of plays was a comedy. But why he believed this they did not know.

And perhaps we cannot know. At the end of Plato's *Symposium,* when all the other guests at the great party have fallen asleep, Socrates sits drinking with the comic poet Aristophanes and the tragic poet Agathon, compelling them "to acknowledge that the genius of comedy was the same with that of tragedy, and that the true artist in tragedy was an artist in comedy also. To this they were constrained to assent, being drowsy and not quite following the argument." How the argument ran was not reported and will never be known. And it may well be that Chekhov's reason for calling *Three Sisters* a comedy despite all its sadness will also never be known, even by inference.

But perhaps we today are in a better position to speculate about it than were the members of the Moscow Art Theatre. To the people of his own time, the new and striking thing about the plays of Chekhov was that they expressed so fully the pathos of personal aspiration frustrated by social and cultural circumstances. The latter part of the nineteenth century in Russia saw the rapid development of the class of intelligentsia, as it was called, people of sensibility and education, readily accessible to the influence of ideas and ideals, who could imagine and desire more in the way of fulness of life than they would ever achieve. This discrepancy is common to similar groups in all nations, but what made it especially marked in Russia was the repressiveness of the Czarist government and the backwardness of the economy. A young Russian who undertook to live the life of intellect and art, or simply the good life in which intellect and art have their place, had fewer opportunities to do so than a young person elsewhere in Europe. His will, checked and baffled, lost its impetus and turned back upon itself in bitterness and self-recrimination. All Chekhov's plays are concerned with the defeat of delicate and generous minds, and the warmth of feeling that the Russian intelligentsia directed to Chekhov in his lifetime was in gratitude for his having made its plight so fully explicit and for having treated its pathos with so affectionate a tenderness. It is not too much to say that the intelligentsia of Chekhov's time received the pathos of his plays as a precious gift and cherished it dearly.

But what was new at the turn of the century is now fairly old. Although the theme of the adverse social or cultural environment is still central to our thought, by the same token it is pretty much taken for granted. The personal frustration that Chekhov's characters suffered is now no longer assumed to be the inevitable fate of the members of the intelligentsia; today, at least in some countries, they can look forward to lives of considerable freedom and activity, even affluence and power. As a consequence, while we respond, and even deeply, to the pathos of Chekhov's plays, we are not likely to value it in the same degree that it was valued by the members of the Moscow Art Theatre.

This being so, it is easier for us than it was for his colleagues in the theatre to suppose that Chekhov himself did not want his audiences to feel only the sadness of *Three Sisters,* although it had of course been his purpose to evoke it and make it poignant and salient. He also had another and what might seem a contradictory intention: to lead his audience *away* from those very emotions in the play which they most cherished. When Chekhov said that *Three Sisters* was a comedy, even a farce, he was not talking to critics or theorists of literature but to actors, and he was trying to suggest what should be brought to the text by those who put it on the stage, a complexity of meaning which the text might not at first reveal. The meaning of a highly developed work of literature cannot ever be given in a formula, and Chekhov's plays resist formulation rather more than most. Chekhov did not undertake to solve life; he was averse to the propagation of ideas; his sole purpose, he said, was to represent life as it really is. But life cannot be seen without judgment of some kind, and throughout *Three Sisters,* as throughout his other great plays, Chekhov undertakes to influence our judgment in many ways, giving us ground for sympathy with one character, of antipathy to another, of contempt for yet another, of distaste for this or that circumstance of existence, controlling not only the direction of our feelings but their duration and intensity as well, so that contempt begins to give way suddenly to understanding, or admiration to irony. Much, then, of our sense of the meaning of *Three Sisters* when we see it performed depends upon the style of the performance—upon, that is, the ability of the actors to complicate its emotional communication.

Stanislavsky, we are told, had a tendency to produce all Chekhov's plays in a deliberate and dramatic style, which emphasized the moments of painful feeling and made the plays into what were called "heavy dramas." This method, which in effect invited the audience to self-pity before the hopelessness of life, was no doubt the loyal Stanislavsky's way of expressing his sense of Chekhov's seriousness and importance. But if *Three Sisters* is acted with the lightness and the rapid tempo of the comic style, or with some of the briskness of farce, the response of the audience is bound to be different. The play will not then offer an exactly cheerful view of things; it will still

be saying that life is, in all conscience, hard and bitterly disappointing. But this will not be its sole judgment. The seeming contradiction between the sadness of the text and the vivacity of the style will suggest an inconclusiveness of judgment, inviting the audience not to the indulgence of self-pity but to a thoughtful, perhaps even an ironic detachment.

Whether or not we accept the play as a comedy, we cannot fail to see that there is comedy in it, and a performance in the comic style will give full recognition to its abundant humor of character. All the male characters, in one degree or another, provoke our laughter or at least our smiles—Vershinin by his compulsion to make visionary speeches about mankind's future happiness, Andrey by his fatness, Chebutykin by his avowed total ignorance of medicine, Solyony by his absurd social behavior, especially his belief that he resembles the great romantic poet Lermontov, Kulygin by his pedantry and silliness, even poor good Tusenbach by his confidence that he can solve the problems of existence by going to work for a brick company. It is an aspect of his gift that Chekhov is able to make us laugh at these people without allowing us to despise them. Our laughter is a skeptical comment on the facile belief that nothing but the circumstances of environment accounts for people's destinies, for what we laugh at is the self-deception, or the pretension, or the infirmity of purpose that in some large part explains their pain and defeat—and our own.

The three sisters themselves, however, appear in a light very different from that in which the male characters are placed. We cannot say of them, as we do of the men, that they have helped contrive their defeat; the situation of women being what it was when Chekhov was writing, there was virtually no way by which they might have triumphed over circumstances to avoid the waste of their lives. Each of the three girls had, to be sure, overestimated the chances of happiness, but what they had imagined and desired was not beyond reason. Such deceptions as they practice on themselves do not warp their personalities into comic eccentricity, as happens with all the men. In the sisters, we feel, life appears in its normality, rather beautiful: they are finely developed human beings of delicate and generous mind. And the end of the play finds each of them doomed to unfulfilment, bitterly grieving over her fate, despite the resolution to live out her life in courageous affirmation. That this final scene is intensely sad goes without saying. But it is an open question for the reader or the stage director whether the exaltation of fortitude and faith that the sisters muster up in the face of defeat is to be taken ironically, as a delusion which makes the sadness yet more intense, or whether it is to be understood as sounding a true note of affirmation. The answer to the question should perhaps be conditioned by the knowledge that the scene was written by a dying man.

Chekhov suffered from tuberculosis, at that time a disease not easily cured. A physician of considerable skill, although he had given up the practice of medicine, he was not likely to be under any illusion about his chances of recovery; he died four years after the production of *Three Sisters,* at the age of forty-five. His illness did not deprive him of all gratification. He worked, although against odds. His work was honored, and he was much loved. But he had to live in exile from Moscow, even from Russia; he was often in pain; physical activity became ever less possible; he was often separated from his young wife for long periods. It could not have been without thought of himself that he wrote such despairing speeches as the one in which Irina says, "Where has it all gone? Where is it? . . . life's slipping by, and it will never, never return. . . ."

Yet as we read Chekhov's letters of the last years of his illness, we find no despair in them, no bitterness, not even the sorrow we might expect to find. They are full of the often trivial details of travel, business, and work, of expressions of concern and affection for others, they address themselves to ordinary, unexceptional life, without tragic reverberations, even without drama. Perhaps an unwillingness to burden others with his darker thoughts in some part explains why Chekhov wrote as he did, but as one reads the letters alongside the plays, one feels that Chekhov was living life as the speeches at the end of *Three Sisters* suggest it must be lived: without the expectation of joy, yet in full attachment, and cherishing what may be cherished, even if that is nothing more than the idea of life itself. A man of affectionate disposition upon whom death had laid its hand would probably not be concerned with making a rational or prudential judgment upon life: more likely he would be moved to wonder if a transcendent judgment might not be made. And when Chekhov wrote that "it will be winter soon, and everything will be covered with snow," he may well have wished to suggest that in the cycle of seasons the spring will follow and that, sad as we may be over what befalls ourselves and others, life itself is to be celebrated. Over the centuries the attributes and intentions of comedy have been numerous and various. But one of the oldest of them has been to say that, appearances to the contrary notwithstanding, all will be well, the life of the earth will renew itself.

Randall Jarrell   (essay date 1969)

SOURCE: "Chekhov and the Play," in *The Three Sisters,* by Anton Chekhov, translated by Randall Jarrell, The Macmillan Company, 1969, pp. 103-13.

[In the excerpt below, Jarrell discusses the themes of Three Sisters.]

In a sense **The Three Sisters** needs criticism less than almost any play I can think of. It is so marvelously organized, made, realized, that reading it or seeing it many times to be thoroughly acquainted with it is all one needs. In it Chekhov gives us a cluster of attitudes about values—happiness, marriage, work, duty, beauty, cultivation, the past, the present, the future—and shows us how these are meaningful or meaningless to people. Values

are presented to us through opposed opinions, opposed lives; at different ages in life with different emotions; and finally, on different levels.

Take the ways, for instance, that marriage is presented: so obviously, so tenuously, so alternatively. All the marriages we see are disasters; but Vershinin's goes wrong for different reasons than Andrei's, and Andrei's goes wrong for different reasons than Masha's. Still, Chekhov can lump them into one generalization that we accept when Vershinin says, "Why is a Russian always sick and tired of his wife . . . and his wife and children always sick and tired of him?" Then he uses a generalization from particular experience when he has Andrei tell us, "People shouldn't get married. They shouldn't because it's boring." These are bold truths. And yet, surrounded by bad models (and in Kulygin's case, involved in one), Olga remains convincingly dedicated to marriage as an ideal—woman's role, woman's duty. And Kulygin never loses his faith in its value as a value, or as an "institution" to belong to for its own sake, and continues to encourage the single ones to marry.

"Love and Marriage" is a little ballet for Irina and Tuzenbach of coming together and parting, of going separate ways yet looking over shoulders. First they are on the same side about love. Both of them idealize it and want it, but while his dream of love is Irina, hers is Moscow where she'll meet "the real one." Later, when she gives up her dream, they come together on the marriage level (long enough to be engaged) but not at the love level. Theirs is a poignant pas de deux when, first, Irina truthfully declares it is not in her power to love this homely man and, after that, Tuzenbach's own sensitive drawing back from marriage on those terms. Both of them achieve their maximum substance as human beings at this moment. When he says to her, "There isn't anything in my life terrible enough to frighten me, only that lost key . . ." (the key to Irina's love), and when he puts love ahead of the imminent duel, Tuzenbach is ennobled. The ambiguities here make it possible for us to wonder whether the marriage would really have gone ahead the next day if he had not been killed, whether the "dead tree" allusion of Tuzenbach's meant he *knew* (by willing it) that he was going to die.

Chekhov was nearly forty when he fell deeply in love with the actress Olga Knipper. He wrote Masha's part for her, and, significantly, love and marriage are examined in this play more than any other. The fact he had not married all this while is an indication of sorts, but of course, the stories tell us over and over in fiction what he often told his friends in letters. At age twenty-five he wrote, "I am above marriage." Ten years later he wrote, "Very well, I'll marry if you wish it. But here are my conditions: Everything must remain the same as before—that is she must live in Moscow and I in the country, and I'll make visits to her. The kind of happiness which continues day in and day out, from one morning to the next, I cannot endure. When people tell me the same thing in the same tone of voice every day, I become furious. . . . I promise to be a splendid husband, but give me a wife who, like the moon, will not appear in my sky every day." In a letter to his brother Misha, advising him on Misha's marriage, Chekhov wrote that the absolute essential was "love, sexual attraction, to be one flesh."

When the play was finished he and Olga Knipper were married, but in the months beforehand he delayed it by every possible tactic until she made it plain he could not hold her without it. Shortly after, he wrote his sister (five years later than the other letter about his "conditions" for marriage) and said, "That I'm married, you already know. I don't think the fact will in any way change my life or the conditions under which I have lived up to now . . . . everything will go on as before. At the end of July I'll be in Yalta, then in Moscow until December, and then back in Yalta. That is, my wife and I will live apart—a situation, by the way, to which I'm already accustomed." Partly accustomed, yes; and the marriage went ahead along the lines he'd laid down earlier, but not as easily as he'd assumed. He did get much writing done by himself in Yalta where he had to stay at times in the milder climate on account of his tuberculosis, but also he got bored and lonely. Among many letters to Olga (they wrote every day) he once said, "I keep waiting for you to order me to pack and travel to Moscow. To Moscow! To Moscow! that is not said by *three sisters* but by one husband." In *The Three Sisters* many voices tell us what he'd summarized in one sentence in 1898 in the story **"About Love"**: "The one incontestable truth about love is that it is a mystery and all that is written about it is not a solution but a series of questions that remain unanswered."

There is a real geometry to *The Three Sisters.* It has an ideological, character, and chain-of-events organization that develops with an inevitableness akin to Greek tragedy. After making his logical skeleton Chekhov invents and *invents* plausible disguises that keep the play from having the Ibsen-well-made surface and the symbols from having the Ibsen starkness. Indeed, having so many symbols and leitmotivs prevents the most important of any of them from sticking out or being too differentiated from the rest of the surface. While the underlying organization is extremely plain, parallel, and symmetrical, it is masked by a "spot-surface" or expressed in terms of these "spots" themselves.

A visual counterpart of this very method uncannily exists in the work of the painter Vuillard. In certain of his indoor and outdoor scenes of French domestic life, the foundation areas on the canvas are made less emphatic by the swarms of particles that mottle the walls with rose-printed paper, the rugs with swirls, the lawns with pools of sun and shade. From such variation and variegation comes his cohesion. Vuillard commingles plaids and dappled things as non sequitur as the jottings in Chebutykin's notebook. He alludes to a mysterious darkness by leaving a door ajar. He baffles the viewer by a woman's ear glowing red. What does she hear? In the same way, Masha's eccentric line "By the curved seastrand a green oak stands / A chain of gold upon it . . ." baffles us. What *does* it mean?

These Vuillard "spots" are found in bizarre, grotesque, homey touches in a speech, a mannerism, a trait, an incident that add up to several dozen possibly. Solyony, Chebutykin, Kulygin, Natasha, and Ferapont are covered with them; Olga and Irina and Vershinin scarcely have any; with Masha and Tuzenbach they are used sparingly but memorably. Chekhov made such imaginative and original use of the indeterminacy principle on the microscopic level (the opposite of Ibsen) while maintaining on the macroscopic level firm causality. The more his themes and characters were contradictory, inconsistent, and ambiguous, the more the play got a feeling of the randomness and personalness of real life. . . .

An essential part of the play is the meaning of life as opposed to the meaninglessness of life. Chekhov shows us what people say, believe, believe under their acts (unconsciously) until *The Three Sisters* becomes a poll of answers about his values and ultimates. How *many* answers there are and how paradoxical Chekhov thought they were can be seen immediately if they are listed as follows:

THEMES

MEANING	MEANINGLESSNESS
Specific meaning: Knowledge, the meaningful past, Moscow, father.	"What's the difference?" nonsense, stupidity, silliness, crudeness, provincial present.
Remembering this.	Forgetting, denying, departing.
Happiness: through love, dreams, work, progress, ("If only"-dreams).	Unhappiness: frustration, boredom, "work without poetry," loneliness, empty dutifulness.
Satisfactions: work, progress, duty.	Despair at lack of progress or slowness of it.
Fate or lot: accepting this, "We must live," "We shall live."	The life we reconcile ourselves to, nihilism, "What's the difference?" "It's all the same."
Dreams-wishes: dreams are necessary.	Tiredness, exhaustion, headaches due to weariness in waiting for dreams to come true, giving up on dreams.
Love.	Lack of love.
Youth.	Age and aging.

In a certain sense *The Three Sisters* is as well-made as an Ibsen play in that everything is related to everything else, except that Chekhov relates things in a musical way, or in a realistic-causal, rather than geometrical-rhetorical-causal, way. The repeated use of Wagnerian leitmotivs occurs not only for characters but for themes, ideology, and morality. Diffusing the themes required more concentration, he wrote in letters when he was working on *The Three Sisters,* than for any other play. He perfected it to relax the essential structural framework the play is built on. In the exchange of themes, overly defined edges of characterization and situation are blurred and, to him, more realistic. In particular, Chebutykin's "What's the difference?" is his own special leitmotiv that, however, is borrowed by nearly everyone at sometime or other, just as themes of fatigue, happiness, boredom, etc., are shared.

Loneliness (hardly a value or a philosophy) becomes a sort of ghost that haunts Andrei all the time, Irina until she gets older, and Solyony under cover of his Lermontov personality. Loneliness pervaded Chekhov's own life in similar ways. He wrote someone, "I positively cannot live without guests. When I am alone, for some reason I become terrified, just as though I were in a frail little boat on a great ocean." Though he kept people around him a lot of the time, there was an essential distance from, removal of everybody else from Chekhov in life. He joked and played jokes and behaved frivolously as a regular way of getting along with people. Even when he was so in love with Olga Knipper, it was hard for him to stay close, and he'd write her "silly" letters that she sometimes scolded him for. She wanted him to talk of the meaning of life once, and he wrote her (à la Tuzenbach's "See it's snowing" sentence), "You ask: What is life? That is just the same as asking: What is a carrot? A carrot is a carrot, and nothing more is known about it." For years he wore a seal ring with these words: "To the lonely man the world is a desert."

He keeps us conscious of the loneliness underneath the general animation. At the birthday party in Act I, there is Vershinin's line about the gloomy-looking bridge in Moscow where the water under it could be heard: "It makes a lonely man feel sad." Later on we hear again when Chebutykin tells Andrei about being unmarried, even if marriage is boring: "But the loneliness! You can philosophize as much as you please, but loneliness is a terrible thing, Andrei. . . ." With the "good-bye trees" and "good-bye echo" and the embraces, tears, *au revoir*'s and farewells, loneliness has built up like entropy as the good social group—that partly kept people from being lonely—has been broken into by the inferior outside world. The organized enclave of Act I, after being invaded by the relatively unorganized environment, loses its own organization like a physical system and runs down to almost nothing . . . Andrei.

The musical side of Russian life, and Chekhov, comes into the play in every act: Masha whistles, the carnival people play off-stage, Chebutykin sings nervously after the duel. Specifically, Act I opens with Olga remembering the band's funeral march after the father's death and Act IV ends with the band playing a march as the brigade leaves and Olga has her last, summarizing speech. The "yoo-hoos" beforehand have imparted a faintly mu-

sical nostalgia to the scene, too. In Acts I and II there are guitar and piano and singing. "My New Porch" is a song everyone knows like "Old MacDonald Had a Farm," so that when Tuzenbach starts it off, even lonely Andrei and old Chebutykin can carry it along. Masha and Vershinin's duet becomes a witty—but entirely different—parallel of this formula. The camaraderie at the bottom of the first is countered with the romantic insinuation of the second. "Unto love all ages bow, its pangs are blest . . ." leaves nothing in doubt, and when Masha sings a refrain of this and Vershinin adds another, they make a musical declaration of love. This is an excellent preparation for Act III when, after Masha's love confession, it would have been awkward for Vershinin and her to appear together on stage. Their intimacy is even strengthened, in our minds, by his off-stage song to Masha which she hears, comprehends, and answers in song before leaving the stage to join him.

There was always a piano in Chekhov's house, and having someone play helped him to write when he got stuck. Rhythms came naturally to him, and just as he has varied them in the lines of *The Three Sisters*—from the shortest (sounds, single words) to the arias and big set speeches—similarly there is a rhythmic pattern like that on a railway platform where all the people know each other and little groups leave, say good-bye, meet.

To me, Davchenko's comment on the lack of spontaneity of this play is really a tribute to its extraordinary solidity of construction. How frail, spontaneously lyric, and farcical *The Cherry Orchard* is in comparison. Chekhov said of it, "I call it a comedy." It was the work of a dying man who had strength to write only a few lines a day, whereas *The Three Sisters: A Drama in Four Acts* is his crowning work. It is the culmination of his whole writing life. *Uncle Vanya* is the nearest thing, but nothing equally long (none of the short novels) is as good as *The Three Sisters.*

Beverly Hahn (essay date 1977)

SOURCE: *"Three Sisters,"* in *Chekhov: A Study of the Major Stories and Plays,* Cambridge University Press, 1977, pp. 284-309.

[*In this essay, Hahn examines Chekhov's carefully constructed balance of opposing tensions in* Three Sisters.]

D. S. Mirsky defined something of the essential character of Chekhov's art when he said, in the course of an otherwise hostile account, 'Chekhov . . . must appeal to Classicist and Romanticist alike: the former will admire the balance and measure of his art and mind; the latter the naturalness of the balance, which in its very harmony remains true to self, and imposes no constraint on spontaneous experience.'[1] The satisfaction with which one reads the best Chekhov stories has undoubtedly to do with this peculiar quality of his art: the measure and clarity with which it balances one aspect of a situation against another, seeking a tentative result, and yet at the same time its unusual feeling for the spontaneous and unpredictable elements in people's behaviour. But it is in the late plays that we feel this quality of the art issuing into a distinctive tension, as the drama conveys both the provisional, chaotic and unpredictable nature of each moment of life and yet the peculiar consistency with which those moments add up to a given fate. And nowhere, perhaps, is this tension more evident or more fruitfully exploited than in the living and varied drama of *Three Sisters*. *Three Sisters* is, in my view, the consummate product of Chekhov's art—tactful, sensitive and deeply understanding in its representation of the Prozorov women; suggestive about the relationship between aspiration and suffering in people's lives; analytical about why it might be that even the best civilizations seem doomed to fail; and above all dramatically alive and challenging through all the shifting moods and changing situations of its fully imagined characters. It is Chekhov's true *'chef d'oeuvre'*; and in capturing the residue of humour, energy and purposiveness and, at the same time, the larger sadness, debilitation and suffering of the sisters' lives, he finally and triumphantly relates—within the quite specific social world of the play—the obvious ambivalences in his own more general response to life.

Considered as a whole, *Three Sisters* is a profoundly sad play (Lionel Trilling rightly calls it one of the saddest works in all literature). It knows what it is for people to yearn for self-realization and self-fulfilment, those two essentially Romantic ideals; and it knows the negative side of those ideals, where yearning produces only continuing frustration and pain. A century after the initial euphoria of the English Romantics about the possibilities open to the individual, Chekhov surrounds those possibilities with a pervasive sense of irony and even tragedy. Yet whatever the overall sadness of the sisters' situation, Chekhov will not allow it to subdue the moment-to-moment life of his characters, which has often an attractive, and even occasionally comic, buoyancy. Whether, as is often debated by both students and critics, that buoyancy is an effect of Russian manners in general or a particular Chekhovian heightening of the ordinary conventions (or, as is most likely, a combination of the two), there can be no doubt of the air of spontaneity and self-abandon pervading the characters' actions. The presence of such qualities in their behaviour ensures that we never lose sight of life's more exuberant and positive qualities:

> FEDOTIK. You may move, Irina Sergeyevna, you may move (*taking a photograph*). You look charming today (*taking a top out of his pocket*). Here is a top, by the way . . . It has a wonderful note . . .
>
> IRINA. How lovely!
>
> MASHA. By the sea-shore an oak-tree green . . . Upon that oak a chain of gold . . . (*Complainingly*) Why do I keep saying that? That phrase has been haunting me all day . . .
>
> KULIGIN. Thirteen at table!

> RODDEY (*loudly*). Surely you do not attach importance, to such superstitions? (*laughter*).
>
> KULIGIN. If there are thirteen at table, it means that someone present is in love. It's not you, Ivan Romanovitch, by any chance? (*laughter*).[2]

The intimacy and exuberance here are peculiar for so large a group and give the scene its unusual energy. There is no room for privacy or dejection. Each person responds to the situation in his or her way, but each responds with a sense of being part of a community. So, whatever the deficiencies in these characters' lives, there is something positive which they share. We are aware of feelings and impulses cutting across one another, and thus of the distances between people, but also of the unusual volatility and abundance of reaction in this scene. Moreover, the art itself, while 'impos[ing] no constraint on spontaneous experience', ensures that there is nothing random about these reactions or about the sequence in which they occur. The 'wonderful note' of Fedotik's top, for example, is not just an isolated effect designed to project a surface realism: at a deeper level it merges with Masha's fascination with the mysterious lines from Pushkin and with Kuligin's talk of love, so that together they suggest, beneath the laughing and the teasing, the romantic richness of Masha's personality, presaging her impending love affair with Vershinin.

Much of the effect of *Three Sisters* depends on this multiplicity of response. Manners in the play appear to be spontaneous and yet are subtly stylized; the overall sadness of the sisters' predicament does not preclude some memorably comic moments. Moreover, the characters' own senses of life, conditioned by their predicament as cultured people living in a period of social transition and geographically isolated in the provinces, hold in tension various social and philosophic possibilities. The sisters are frustrated with their lives, and their frustration is the source of their eloquent lyricism. Never finding true happiness, they create images to embody their sense of an ideal life—lovely clean images of birds and snow, blossoms and spring warmth. Their sensitivity to the passing things in nature is splendidly preserved:

> TUSENBACH. . . . Not only in two or three hundred years but in a million years life will be just the same; it does not change, it remains stationary, following its own laws which we have nothing to do with or which, anyway, we shall never find out. Migratory birds, cranes for instance, fly backwards and forwards . . . They fly and will continue to fly, however philosophic they may become; and it doesn't matter how philosophical they are so long as they go on flying . . .
>
> MASHA. But still there is a meaning?
>
> TUSENBACH. Meaning . . . Here it is snowing. What meaning is there in that? (*a pause*).
>
> MASHA. I think man ought to have faith or ought to seek a faith, or else his life is empty, empty . . . To

live and not to understand why cranes fly; why children are born; why there are stars in the sky . . . One must know what one is living for or else it is all nonsense and waste (*a pause*).[3]

But as this dialogue shows (and again it is not simply naturalistic, but poetically stylized to deepen the feeling of the scene), the sisters' aspirations and longings emerge always against a background of doubt. The waste of their lives as they go on living, themselves unfulfilled and unable properly to exercise their talents for the sake of others, prompts them to ask questions of life's meaning which deepen and diversify the dominantly social and cultural interests of the play. Thus Tusenbach, in answer to Masha's question, expresses his agnostic sense that life exists purely and simply for itself—'Here it is snowing. What meaning is there in that?'—words which capture something of our response to the sisters' own lives, dignified as they are and yet apparently without purpose. But it is Masha who takes up that other call which Chekhov seems equally to have felt—the call to *find* a purpose (socially, and in a sense metaphysically) if life itself lacks one—which lies behind the play's half-convinced idealism about work and about the happier future of man. This is another of the play's sources of tension. It is unlikely that the sisters will find any real fulfilment in their lives: the play dramatizes with great insight and subtlety the consistency with which even the most apparently random events work to disadvantage them, and suggests the complex factors involved in their defeat. But while *Three Sisters* suggests the bleakness of the future awaiting the sisters, it also contains a counterbalancing movement towards a peculiar variety of optimism about the general future of man. The 'Man must work . . .' speeches contain a certain amount of irony, especially when one sees what happens to Olga and Irina when they do work. But the faith in eventual human progress so often adumbrated by the characters, though placed in context by the near-tragic circumstances of the sisters, is just as essential to the play as Chekhov's other, more publicized, tendency towards scepticism.

As *The Cherry Orchard* shows, Chekhov is not a dramatist of the traditional kind. In *Three Sisters* the fire and the duel, which might seem the most likely dramatic climaxes, happen off-stage, and the characters seem to interact too obliquely for there to be any open conflict. But *Three Sisters* does have its own particular kind of tension, the tension of social change. It concerns a society—or, rather, an educated class—in a state of crisis, slowly disintegrating from within and without. That is, its social context is of that unstable kind which I have suggested as being particularly stimulating to Chekhov's dramatic imagination; and the conflict it dramatizes between two opposing ways of life is as fundamental as it is instinctive in the participants:

> IRINA. You say life is beautiful . . . Yes, but what if it only seems so! Life for us three sisters has not been beautiful yet, we have been stifled by it as plants are choked by weeds . . . I am shedding tears . . . I mustn't do that (*hurriedly wipes her eyes and smiles*).

I must work, I must work! The reason we are depressed and take such a gloomy view of life is that we know nothing of work. We come of people who despised work . . .

(*Enter* NATALYA IVANOVNA; *she is wearing a pink dress with a green sash.*)

NATASHA. They are sitting down to lunch already . . . I am late . . . (*Steals a glance at herself in the glass and sets herself to rights*) I think my hair is all right. (*Seeing* IRINA) Dear Irina Sergeyevna, I congratulate you! (*gives her a vigorous and prolonged kiss*) You have a lot of visitors, I really feel shy . . . Good day, Baron![4]

Natasha and her way of life are set against the sisters and theirs. Irina is sensitive and well-bred, and her way of expressing herself has a smooth and attractive lyricism. Natasha, obviously, is vulgar, affected and incorrigibly vain. Her staccato phrases and jerky movements, along with her pink dress and green sash, reveal by contrast with Irina a complete lack of taste. Yet, as most audiences realize, Natasha's gaudiness and clumsy energy also signify a rough vitality in her which contrasts with the lack of energy of the sisters. Irina is educated and refined but also exceptionally vulnerable, and behind her tears there is a dangerous passivity to life. Her lyricism gives her predicament real pathos: '. . . we have been stifled by [life] as plants are choked by weeds . . .'; but it is a lyricism which comes from an unusual quality of submission. Irina lacks real will, perhaps from the very nature of her upper-class education and what is hidden in it—what W. H. Bruford, in his 'sociological study' of Chekhov's Russia, calls 'a concealed fear of life'.[5] As Natasha enters, Irina makes the very important observation, 'We come of people who despised work'; and that is just where Natasha is different. Natasha feigns—she may actually feel—a sense of her social inferiority when she proclaims that she is shy; but in fact she has all the self-assertive energy of one who feels herself rising in the world. She does not seem actually to calculate her effects: she does not need to. With the steely, self-enclosed will of a person who, all her life, has had to 'know [something] of work', she is bound to triumph over the superior delicacy of the sisters.

Yet it is important that *Three Sisters* not be seen simply as a drama of class conflict, with Natasha the representative of the bourgeoisie. It appeals to us in terms quite different from those of *The Cherry Orchard,* with its more directly social emphases. For one thing, there is no simple choice to be made between one class and another, since Andrey, in actually marrying Natasha, creates something in between. Also, as I have suggested elsewhere, Natasha herself too often borders on caricature to occupy such an important role. Though she is frighteningly destructive as she gradually takes over the sisters' house, she remains an individual figure rather than a representative one, and she is less subtly and less interestingly developed than any other major character in the play. Her purpose in the drama is as the agent of the sisters'

The Moscow Art Theater cast of Three Sisters, *1901.*

defeat; but the way she defeats them—personal as it is—simply focuses more intently the vulnerability of the sisters' fineness and refined aspiration to the coarser and more primitively energetic elements of life.

Three Sisters, then, is less concerned with the outside threat to civilized standards represented by Natasha than with the paradoxical—and tragic—vulnerability of civilization to weaknesses within itself. The sisters, it is true, are caught in an environment peculiar to late-nineteenth-century Russia; but the social and psychological aspects of their predicament, as Chekhov portrays them, have the utmost relevance to other cultures as well. As civilized people surrounded by, and in some ways embodying, an almost defunct culture, the sisters make us aware of the dilemma which later preoccupied Yeats in 'Ancestral Houses', that of cultural refinement working unconsciously towards its own defeat. So although Natasha is necessary to the bolder dramatic outlines of the play, Chekhov I think puts proportionately much more stress on the *internal* nature of the sisters' world and its inbuilt momentum towards de-

struction. He is intensely sympathetic to the sisters, whose fineness and sensitivity is contrasted with Natasha's coarseness and bluntness; but he is likewise aware of their lack of energy and purpose (again by contrast with Natasha), which signals the decline of a previous phase of Russian civilization.

All three sisters are very attractive, I think, and from moment to moment they behave with a spontaneous—if rather brittle—gaiety:

> MASHA (*strikes her plate with her fork*). Ladies and gentlemen, I want to make a speech!
>
> KULIGIN. You deserve three bad marks for conduct.[6]

But beneath the liveliness and humour of these momentary outbursts there is in the sisters a deep-rooted and tragic inability to act. Beyond their openness—even spiritedness—in daily conversation there is an element of defeatism in their psychological make-up which makes them unusually vulnerable to the frustrating conditions of their lives. Masha exemplifies it least: in her manner—her whistling, her recitations from Pushkin and her occasional bluntness of speech—there is a sensuousness of a distinctly sexual kind. She does find fulfilment, with Vershinin, and her tragedy is that she has to forfeit it. But in Olga particularly, despite her dignity and gentleness, there is finally a damaging lack of flexibility—a deep inability to adapt and to make something positive of life. Olga is the most responsible of the sisters, the one with the most developed sense of duty. At times she acts towards Irina and Masha with the strength and stabilizing force which compensate for the loss of their mother. Yet her strength and stability at some points are matched by complete exhaustion at others, as we see in Act III on the night of the fire. Being the eldest, she has the longest memory, and the sheer strength of her memory of Moscow seems to leave her oddly disabled and unfitted for the present. She feels old, although she is only twenty-eight; and at twenty-eight her life does seem already in the past. Of her personal life she speaks with resignation, and in an implied past tense:

> It's all quite right, it's all from God, but it seems to me that if I were married and sitting at home all day, it would be better (*a pause*). I should be fond of my husband.[7]

Olga's gentleness and reserve give her an air of assurance, but she is in an intangible way prematurely aged. She cannot really conceive of a different future: her opportunities all seem to have been missed. She seems, on the surface, the very opposite of Irina; but while Irina, as the youngest, does have innocence and hope—her whole personality suspended towards that mythical future in Moscow—she too shares Olga's passivity. She waits for the happier future to happen to her, rather than taking initiatives of her own. In Act III, in fact, her passivity becomes almost a kind of living death:

> You are so pale and lovely and fascinating . . . It seems to me as though your paleness sheds a light through the dark air . . . You are melancholy; you are dissatisfied with life . . .[8]

So, attractive as Irina certainly is, her very refinement seems to shut out those more vigorous energies on which personal happiness often depends. Throughout *Three Sisters* her vitality remains conspicuously chaste, and her adolescence seems rather painfully extended. The fulfilment she awaits does not come. Like her sisters, she has not the psychological resources to seek it out. The sisters, as a group, have much to offer, but they are caught in circumstances that have very little to offer them. Worse, in this situation, where Olga and Irina find no real opportunity for fulfilment and Masha's is only fleeting, the sisters' very differentness from the provincial life around them seems to turn back on them to disable them. Their psychological disabilities, as they emerge to us, stem directly from their embodiment of certain standards of civilization in a world upon which such civilization has no hold. It is on this that the tragedy turns.

The sisters, of course, are as vulnerable as they are because they lack a sustaining environment. What is vulnerable within them has already been defeated in the world outside; or perhaps it never existed at all in the provinces. But it is clear that their predicament is not something they suffer alone, since there is a widespread *malaise* around them in their society. Very few of the characters who come in contact with the sisters show, for example, any sign of positive or virile energy, and they share a common propensity to philosophize as a way of passing time. Apart from the sisters themselves, only Tusenbach and Vershinin have anything like complete personalities—one attached to the future, the other to the past. But Tusenbach and his idealism cannot survive in the world of the play any more than Vershinin can persist in it. Vershinin, by a quiet calculation on Chekhov's part, comes from the world of the sisters' *father*—the former world of Moscow, in which Vershinin played the part of the 'lovesick major'. Vershinin has not had life all his own way, and he can be weak and ineffectual; yet he embodies some of the energy of an earlier age (presumably of the time when the civilization which the sisters reflect was stronger), and he brings that energy, positively, into the world of the play. It is with his entry that the two groups of characters finally come together in Act I, and it is as a result of his optimistic consolation that Masha takes heart and decides to stay for Irina's party. His whole presence—though he can occasionally seem sentimental and is sometimes a bit foolish—is pervaded by an energetic resilience to life which finds a contrast in nearly everyone else. At the end of *Three Sisters,* however, he departs and takes that energy with him. And his leaving with the battery (together with Tusenbach's death) marks the symbolic end of whatever energy has still remained in the sisters' refined society at the time when the play began.

The contrast between Vershinin and Kuligin, and between the roles they play in Masha's life, tells us much about the inability of the sisters' provincial environment to offer them fulfilment. For if Vershinin manifests something of an earlier and more energetic style of Moscow life, Masha's husband Kuligin is a relatively harmless but comically ineffectual, parochial and uninspired figure of the provincial present:

> Now I have always been successful, I am fortunate, I have even got the order of the Stanislav of the second degree and I am teaching others that *ut consecutivum.* Of course, I am clever, cleverer than very many people, but happiness does not lie in that . . . (*a pause*).[9]

Kuligin's stilted, comically pedagogical manner makes us feel at almost every point a truncated and limited personality. It is perhaps a fault of the play that he so often borders on mere caricature, a relation of the provincial types in Gogol (although there is, in fact, an undercurrent of sadness and self-doubt in this particular speech). He is a man of no stature; and to live with him involves living a life whose possibilities are painfully reduced. Masha's marriage with this provincial school-teacher thus suggests, in itself, the narrowness and limitation of the sisters' acquaintance. Yet it is important, in the context of the others who surround the sisters, that Kuligin is nevertheless a character with whom we can sympathize. For, along with the absurdity of his exaggerated gestures, his air of nervous confidence and his quoting and copying the school director, he does have a certain pathos. As Irina says, he is 'the kindest of men, but he is not the cleverest',[10] and there is something touching—as well as something irritating—about his refusal to know what has happened to his own domestic happiness. Chekhov's sympathies are too fully engaged by Masha for him not to feel a certain malice towards her limited husband; besides, Kuligin embodies some of the more tedious aspects of Russian bureaucracy. But Kuligin's presence around the sisters is no worse than limiting, and Olga in particular regards him with some sympathy. He lacks the capacity, so prevalent elsewhere in the sisters' society, to bring about actual destruction.

Few characters in the play can be described simply as victors or victims. As I have suggested earlier, there are factors operating both internally and externally to defeat its most civilized characters; and it is one of the play's saddest ironies that Andrey, himself weak and therefore Natasha's victim, should participate so actively in bringing about the downfall of his sisters. Through Andrey, Chekhov focuses the dissipation of the robust energies of an older generation of Prozorovs, while relating the social vulnerability of the present generation back to certain aspects of their family upbringing. We first hear Andrey in Act I playing his violin, deliberately secluded from company. When he appears, he seems somehow oppressed by the superior vitality of the sisters and by their large expectations of him. He is the only son of the Prozorov family and as such has an intolerable burden to bear. We note the bitterness with which Masha will later speak of him:

> Here is our Andrey . . . All our hopes are shattered. Thousands of people raised the bell, a lot of money and of labour was spent on it, and it suddenly fell and smashed. All at once, for no reason whatever. That's just how it is with Andrey . . .[11]

But Andrey's failure is not as unpredictable as the image would have us think, for to an even greater degree than his sisters he has been overshadowed psychologically by the imposing and austere figure of his father:

> Yes. Our father, the kingdom of heaven be his, oppressed us with education. It's absurd and silly, but it must be confessed I began to get fatter after his death, and I have grown too fat in one year, as though a weight had been taken off my body.[12]

After their father's death, Andrey and the sisters, while educated and refined, have been left without the stern direction he had given to their lives. They cannot find the energy and the discipline to continue on their own: Andrey's career, Masha's music and the sisters' knowledge of languages move backwards rather than forwards. The effort that has been made for them is one they can-

not make for themselves, and it is this that makes them all so vulnerable to Natasha's energy. Though the sisters disapprove of Natasha they take delight in the infectious proximity of Andrey's love for her, and by their teasing they directly, though inadvertently, forward their and Andrey's defeat. And Andrey himself, in proposing to Natasha, shows a weakness that has fundamentally to do with the psychological predicament of his family, and perhaps even of his class. Lacking any vitality of his own, he crucially mistakes Natasha's instinctive, yet half-calculated, flight from the table (her genuine, yet exploited, gaucherie) for a pure sign of innocence and youth: 'Oh youth, lovely, marvellous youth!'[13] It is a symptomatic mistake from which we feel the unhappiness and destruction to come. By his own defeat, expressed (as we come to feel) in the kiss that ends Act I, Andrey will subsequently co-operate with Natasha in bringing about the future defeat of his sisters. He will be unable to resist her as she assumes a day-to-day control over the house, and he will actually mortgage the house to Natasha's lover, Protopopov, when he takes to gambling as an escape from his unhappiness.

Yet the principal destroyers of life in *Three Sisters* who make us feel the destructive forces at work in society at large are the two extreme figures, Solyony and Tchebutykin. In one way they are opposites—Solyony with his psychopathic aggression, Tchebutykin indifferent and idle amid his self-absorbed nihilism: '"Tarara-boom-de-ay!" (*reads his paper*). It doesn't matter, it doesn't matter.'[14] But while Solyony cultivates the melodramatic postures of the European Romantic hero and Tchebutykin the postures of the fashionable nihilist, both are obsessively caught in the circular traces of riddles and recitations, and both represent principles totally hostile to civilization. By the fourth act, each is prototypically extreme—so much so that doubts arise as to the credibility of both characters. They contract from what they have been into something almost de-humanized—Solyony to a pair of scented hands from which nothing can remove the smell of a corpse, Tchebutykin to a set of disembodied jingles. But whatever their precise believability in the last act (and it is helped by the more rounded sense of them the play has given earlier), they provide a macabre and fatal combination. The sisters, intuiting the explosive violence of his temperament, are actually afraid of Solyony, but it is part of their predicament that they cannot keep him from the house:

> IRINA. No; please go, Vassily Vassilyitch, You can't stay here.
>
> SOLYONY. How is it the baron can be here and I can't?[15]

There is no answer they can give consistent with civilized manners. But with Tchebutykin the destruction is more insidious. He is tender towards Irina, and in Act IV he can still give Andrey a piece of honest advice. But his nihilism, his escape-route from responsibility, leaves him indifferent to any situation of moral consequence. Thus it is Tchebutykin who sets Andrey gambling in Act II; he who doesn't pay his rent when the sisters' house is mortgaged; he who breaks the treasured clock in Act III, having become drunk on the night of the fire; and he who attends—and so makes possible—the duel in the final scene.

From the evidence of the characters, then (even minor ones like Vershinin's bohemian wife, with her attempted suicide), the society in the play is a society in a state of crisis. In fact, the play itself is dominated by a prophecy of change:

> TUSENBACH. The yearning for work, oh dear, how well I understand it! I have never worked in my life. I was born in cold, idle Petersburg, in a family that had known nothing of work or cares of any kind. I remember, when I came home from the school of cadets, a footman used to pull off my boots . . . But I doubt if they have succeeded in guarding me completely, I doubt it! The time is at hand, an avalanche is moving down upon us, a mighty clearing storm which is coming, is already near and will soon blow the laziness, the indifference, the distaste for work, the rotten boredom out of our society.[16]

Tusenbach's image of the storm broods symbolically over the whole play: it is both his, and Chekhov's, way of articulating a sense of social crisis. Yet in context the image is not unequivocal: it is, precisely, a characteristic of Tusenbach's class that it reaches for large and unspecific images, rather than seeking specific social reforms. The storm certainly seems inevitable, and perhaps even necessary, but it may or may not take place. So the more relevant metaphor for the actual state of things in *Three Sisters* is, in fact, the one contained in the words of the old porter Ferapont, to whom Chekhov gives his classic image of cultural tension:

> And the same contractor says—maybe it's not true— that there's a rope stretched right across Moscow.[17]

This is not unlike the string that actually does snap at the end of *The Cherry Orchard,* releasing the old society into the new. But in *Three Sisters* the string does not snap, and the play remains taut to the very end. The tension is equally social and psychological, with a fastidious correspondence between outer and inner worlds.

Three Sisters has, at points, a strange, sometimes strained, exuberance; but its predominant mood is, I think, one of sadness—that peculiar lyrical sadness epitomized for many people by the emblem of the seagull on the curtains of the Moscow Art Theatre. The central image of the play is the sisters' Moscow, for which they yearn over a geographical and psychological distance they cannot cross. Indeed, as it is invoked from beyond the play's own horizon, the city of Moscow comes gradually to have a near-symbolic force. It is not just a city, nor completely a symbol, but something in between: a kind of metaphor for that unattainable condition of life to which the sisters aspire without success. Along with so many other images from Chekhov's drama, it has for too long been wrongly described as a symbol. In the first place, the reference of

the image is not metaphysical, expressing a sense of all life as crucially unfulfilled, but psychological with respect to the sisters and their past. Most important of all, Moscow—unlike the actual symbols in Ibsen's work (one thinks of the famous white horses of *Rosmersholm*)—is poetically defined, qualified and criticized by the varying perspectives of the play in such a way as to limit its resonance. I do not mean simply that *Three Sisters* contains images of Moscow very different from the one held by the sisters. It does do that, of course; and a number of critics have pointed to Vershinin's speech in Act I about the 'gloomy bridge' and to Ferapont's snatches of information that two thousand people have frozen to death or that a businessman died eating forty pancakes in a vulgar competition. But beyond this fairly obvious kind of checking and placing of the sisters' view of Moscow, the sisters' speeches themselves reveal the true intricacy of the psychological affinity they feel with that city. The image of Moscow is not left to stand vaguely, sentimentally, as an expression of unfulfilled aspiration in one of those 'lyrical gestures' of which Raymond Williams complains. Rather, the image is quite specific—and implicitly critical—in the emotions it conveys:

> (BARON TUSENBACH, TCHEBUTYKIN *and* SOLYONY *appear near the table in the dining-room, beyond the columns.*)

> OLGA. It is warm to-day, we can have the windows open, but the birches are not in leaf yet. Father was given his brigade and came here with us from Moscow eleven years ago and I remember distinctly that in Moscow at this time, at the beginning of May, everything was already in flower; it was warm, and everything was bathed in sunshine. It's eleven years ago, and yet I remember it all as though we had left it yesterday. Oh, dear! I woke up this morning, I saw a blaze of sunshine. I saw the spring, and joy stirred in my heart. I had a passionate longing to be back at home again!

> TCHEBUTYKIN. The devil it is!

> TUSENBACH. Of course, it's nonsense.[18]

Since the sisters' refinement is essentially urban in origin, their longing for the city has a well-founded psychological basis, and their expression of it is moving and lyrical. The images of blossoms, sunlight and warmth are finely evocative, touching on our sense of the peculiar freshness and warmth of early spring sunshine. But the effect is more than simply aesthetic: it captures a longing for security, a sudden rush of nostalgia, caught up in the phrase 'to be back *at home* again!' (my italics). With its longing and its nostalgia projected through the same speech rhythms, the whole feeling of Olga's speech suggests a deep-rooted longing for the past, for the irrecoverable (and now idealized) world of her childhood. And while this gives it its pathos, it also highlights the unreal and escapist nature of her dream of the city. The very way in which Olga conceives of Moscow represents Chekhov's sympathetic but critical appraisal of her failure to confront the present.

Tchebutykin's and Tusenbach's voices, intruding bluntly across the stage at the end of Olga's speech, provide of course another kind of critical check. The background stage suddenly and unnaturalistically asserts its action and its sounds over those of the foreground, to interrupt Olga's reverie at a carefully judged point. She has just so much space in which to amplify her feeling before the passive and past quality of it is placed by Tchebutykin's outburst—'The devil it is!'—which is not, of course, literally a response to Olga's speech but certainly feels as if it were. In fact the checking process at this point is fairly crude, cruder than at any later moment in the play; but it does show Chekhov combining certain effects of poetry with the methods of drama to define and place the image of Moscow, right from the beginning, in terms of a clearly formed psychological perception. As Olga goes on, we feel the superior intensity of her feelings, the pathos of her youth ebbing away drop by drop as the sunlight floods through the window. But we feel, too, the complexities which surround the image of Moscow she projects, complexities incompatible with the simple functions of what we recognize as symbol. Moscow epitomizes, poetically, a disabling backward-looking tendency in the sisters' psychology which affects their present lives. The provinces, certainly, give only limited opportunities to personalities with as much potential as theirs; but, then (as Tchebutykin announces in Act III, although the point of his remark is not immediately apparent, even to himself), even Balzac found happiness in the provinces—at Berdichev. As for Moscow, Chekhov subtly suggests the disillusionment that awaits the sisters there: the journey which they plan, beginning in the autumn, would bring them to Moscow for the winter freeze, and not for those delicate, balmy days of blossoms, sunlight and warmth.

The whole play, then, works in a much more complex way than is ordinarily suggested by the term 'symbolism'. It has no symbols as such. But it is, on the other hand, a highly stylized work which never quite asks to be accepted as a piece of naturalism. As my colleague Mr Robin Grove pointed out some years ago,[19] its meaning has a great deal to do with the way the action is paced and with the way Chekhov organizes the space on the stage. Verbal and visual details in *Three Sisters* are co-ordinated to an unusual degree, where even the conflict between Natasha and the sisters seems indirect and partly stylized. There is little in the way of overt climax: more, rather, of the subtle drama of finely wrought composition. The details are arranged visually and metaphorically to externalize the hidden tensions of the sisters' predicament and to create drama from that. So the opening scene, for example, while it is in a much lower key than the high-spirited dinner conversation towards the end of Act I, generates a peculiar visual and poetic drama of its own:

In the house of the PROZOROVS. *A drawing-room with columns beyond which a large room is visible. Midday; [outside] it is bright and sunny. The table in the further room is being laid for lunch.*

Chekhov on the writing of *Three Sisters*:

To His Sister

Yalta. Sept. 9, 1900.

The Three Sisters is very difficult to write, more difficult than my other plays. Oh well, it doesn't matter; perhaps something will come of it, next season if not this. It's very hard to write in Yalta, by the way: I am interrupted, and I feel as though I had no object in writing; what I wrote yesterday I don't like to-day. . . .

Letters of Anton Chekhov, in *Letters on the Short Story, Drama and Other Literary Topics,* by Anton Chekhov, edited by Louis S. Friedland, Minton, Balch, 1924, pp. 115-63.

OLGA *in the dark blue uniform of a high-school teacher, is correcting exercise books, at times standing still and then walking up and down;* MASHA, *in a black dress, with her hat on her knee, is reading a book;* IRINA, *in a white dress, is standing plunged in thought.*

OLGA. Father died just a year ago, on this very day— the fifth of May, your name-day, Irina. It was very cold, snow was falling. I felt as though I should not live through it; you lay fainting as though you were dead. But now a year has passed and we can think of it calmly; you are already in a white dress, your face is radiant. (*The clock strikes twelves*). The clock was striking then too (*a pause*). I remember the band playing and the firing at the cemetery as they carried the coffin. Though he was a general in command of a brigade, yet there weren't many people there. It was raining, though. Heavy rain and snow.[20]

For the beginning of a drama, the pacing of this is unusually slow, with very little sense of urgency. In fact, it is positively retarded by the chiming of the clock and the stage direction 'a pause', as if Chekhov were consciously slowing the action and at the same time giving his audience time to reflect on the stage-image before them. For the visual details here are as important to the overall effect as is the measured cadencing of Olga's speech. Outside it is 'mid-day', and 'it is bright and sunny'; but the action is set indoors where the light is less intense. The house itself, with its drawing-room and ballroom, is aristocratically proportioned, though homely enough with Olga correcting her pupils' work and the table being laid for lunch; and we find the sisters in postures which are relaxed but significantly different—Olga walking up and down, Masha reading and Irina 'plunged in thought'. These different postures immediately suggest both the sisters' separateness and their unself-conscious intimacy. But most important of all, the sisters, in the relative gloom of indoors, are in navy blue, black and white—colours which, while they suggest well-bred gentility and reserve, nonetheless also suggest a certain suppression of sexuality. Natasha, when she enters, is vulgar but sensuous in her flamboyant combinations of yellow and red, pink and green. So that visually, through the subdued light and the sisters' ascetic dress, Chekhov begins to convey an element of disquiet in his sense of their world. It is a sense of a peculiar pastness in their lives which the elegiac rhythms of Olga's speech confirm. Although the spring sunlight is streaming in through the window, Olga's mind is somehow fixed back in the cold, the rain and the snow of her father's funeral. Things *seem* to her to have changed, but Irina's name-day party, particularly at the beginning, adheres more to the past than to the present. Indeed, the painful weight of the past is felt with a peculiar tangibility in those twelve chimes of the clock which break across the first note of hope in Olga's speech. With a psychological delicacy we could expect only at this late stage in the development of his understanding of women, Chekhov is both sympathetic and implicitly critical. The sisters' lives go on, but there is something static in Olga's psychology, something that will not allow her to act freely in the present. Some part of her spirit is left behind, just as some part of Irina's remains unreleased. The sisters, that is, share a propensity (though in Masha it is more complicated) to project intense feeling backwards to the past or forwards to the future—rarely to release it, fully and spontaneously, in the present. Their consciousness, as sensitive and civilized people, of time-schemes outside the present and of all that life once contained or might contain—while it remains one of the most attractive things about them—has become sadly debilitating. Whether that over-consciousness, particularly of the past, is a result of the inadequacies of the sisters' present context or is itself a symptom of decadence, it makes the disintegration of their way of life—confronted with something less reflective and more energetic in the person of Natasha—virtually inevitable.

Throughout **Three Sisters** the past and its presences echo throughout the present in this peculiar way, and life seems, in the end, simply to retrace the tragic patterns of the past. Natasha, of course, moves forward all the time; and things do happen to the sisters—Masha falls in love, and Irina decides to marry. But the deepest poetic points in the play are pervaded by a strong and tragic feeling of recurrence, as in the remarkable exchange between Masha and Vershinin in Act II:

> VERSHININ . . . Strange, it's only to you I complain (*kisses her hand*). Don't be angry with me . . . Except for you I have no-one—no-one . . . (*a pause*).
>
> MASHA. What a noise in the stove! Before father died there was howling in the chimney. There, just like that.
>
> VERSHININ. Are you superstitious?
>
> MASHA. Yes.

> VERSHININ. That's strange (*kisses her hand*). You are a splendid, wonderful woman. Splendid! Wonderful! It's dark, but I see the light in your eyes.[21]

As a moment of love, the atmosphere of this is both intense and strangely other-worldly; and the wind in the stove, evoking the past, has also the force of an omen. Vershinin's presence, like so much else in the play, is surrounded by a peculiar fatality. He will have to leave the sisters at the end, and he will do so—as their father did—to the strains of a military band. Even the fire in Act III will prompt a memory from the old Ferapont:

> In 1812 Moscow was burnt too . . . Mercy on us! The French marvelled.[22]

Everything, it seems, has its counterpart in the past—everything, that is, except Natasha. In fact, it will be her exploitation of the present, along with the weight of the past which inhibits the sisters, that will cause them not only to remain unfulfilled and unhappy but also to lose the small consolations they do have.

Act I sets in motion the limited *action* of the play. We learn of Tusenbach's love for Irina, a love that is unreturned—and this provides one area of dramatic tension. Masha is unhappily married to Kuligin (while Kuligin's speeches reassuring everyone how happy *he* is show us, less directly, that he is unhappy too); and Act I introduces Masha to Vershinin, whose will to live reassures her and slowly becomes the basis of her dawning love for him. On the more obviously negative side, there is the disturbing fact of Solyony, with his strangely indrawn personality and his explosive aggression; and there is Andrey's 'love' for Natasha, the attraction which her energy has for a man consumed by inertia—an attraction fatal for the play's civilized world. All these things emerge in Act I in an oddly unstable mixture: no single element in the sisters' situation is allowed to predominate. In the first few moments we find Olga tearful, Irina joyful, Masha irritated: the sisters share the same life, the same fate, but each feels it somewhat differently, and they react to those differences in one another. Furthermore, after Vershinin's entry and during the actual evening of the party their spirits seem to mount towards real gaiety. We feel very strongly that the house we are in is the sisters' house and that, whatever the shortcomings in their lives, they have space in which to move with a certain amount of freedom.

Act II, however, is set in the same house twelve months later, and it takes only the contrast of the scene on which the curtain now rises to make us feel what kind of twelve months they have been. For although the setting of Act II is the same as that for Act I, the imaginative effect is deliberately reversed: it is inverted to provide, visually, an image of the sisters' worsened situation. From the effect of space and the outside sunshine of Act I, the stage in Act II has darkened and contracted: it is unlit, with the larger perspective of the ballroom lost. It is eight o'clock at night, and there is no sign of life: only the sounds of a concertina come in, significantly, from the street. So, with the light, noise, colour and high spirits of the party in Act I still lingering in our minds, we understand that the darkness and silence now reigning in the sisters' house signals a darkening in the whole mood of the play. When someone does enter, it is Natasha—alone. She carries a candle, which makes her seem symbolically in control of the situation and implicitly in possession of the sisters' house. That again is a deliberate contrast to the situation in Act I. Act I began with the sisters grouped together, and they were central to every conversation and every scene. Natasha, however noticeable she was by virtue of her abrupt manners and colourful dress, was on the periphery of the action, at least until the very end. But Act II begins with Natasha, and now it is the sisters who are pushed aside. They enter only belatedly, and then one after another; they are never all three grouped together as they were before. Faced with Natasha's absorbed domesticity, Andrey is beaten; and even the sense of community which has sustained the sisters is on the brink of collapse. They are dispersed from their quite intimate grouping in Act I into new and separate relationships. Masha is with Vershinin, Irina with Tusenbach, and Olga comes back with Kuligin from the school. The cause of the dispersal is clear. Natasha, now rapidly taking the reins of power, is instinctively afraid of upper-class social life. During the party in Act I, she was bewildered and confused; by the time of Act II, she is in a position to have such parties stopped. Nor is that all: in cancelling the carnival party, Natasha determines the sisters' fate in a single stroke. Andrey and Tchebutykin go off to gamble, and it is Andrey's gambling losses that will cause him to mortgage the house; Irina is left alone for that confrontation with Solyony which will precipitate the death of Tusenbach; and Natasha, to complete her triumph, goes off—she says—for a 'drive' with Protopopov.

One notices in Act II, even more than in the other acts, how the destructive characters in *Three Sisters* unconsciously but infallibly reinforce one another's destructiveness. At the end of that act, after Irina has just been through the psychic assault of first a proposal and then a threat from the sinister Solyony, Natasha takes advantage of Irina's momentary weakness to propose that she yield her room to Bobik. So although there may be little overt conflict between Natasha and the sisters, there is nevertheless a taut dramatic logic operating through events, always to the sisters' disadvantage. Their gradual loss of power in their own house is externalized in the visual details of Chekhov's stage settings, while the sisters themselves are grouped in finely managed postures and attitudes to manifest their psychological relationship to that loss. Thus throughout the first three acts, as the situation becomes more and more desperate, the scenes are set further into the night and the visual impressions become much more sombre. The climax, quite clearly, is Act III, where the night drags on into the early hours of the morning and the background is filled with the glow of fire and the ringing of alarms. It is also the point at which the sisters' longing for Moscow—produced by, and yet counterpointing, the general sense of loss—is at its most intense.

Stanislavsky as Vershinin in the Moscow Art Theater production of Three Sisters, *1901.*

At the beginning of Act III, then, the setting is a bedroom shared by Olga and Irina, and the space on the stage seems almost cramped. It is past two o'clock in the morning, but instead of darkness and sleep there is the ominous glow of fire and an atmosphere of combined tension and exhaustion, panic and fatigue. When the action begins, Olga moves between feverish activity and complete collapse; and in the course of the act the waning of energy through the night hours is felt as a progressive draining-away of the sources of the sisters' vitality. Around them, Tchebutykin has broken his oath of two years and has become hopelessly drunk, while the old Nanny, Anfisa, intuiting some crisis in the air, suddenly pleads not to be sent away. Emotionally, Act III is the play's real turning-point. That, in a way, is the significance of the fire: raging off-stage in the distance, it gives imaginative definition to the explosive domestic situation inside. It is, as I have said, not exactly symbolism, but that subtle extension of literal situations of which Chekhov was capable at his best. For amid the incipient hysteria of Olga's confrontation with Natasha over Anfisa and the many other direct conflicts unleashed in this act, there is an extremely sure timing of effect to give each moment a wider and decisive resonance:

OLGA. Well, let her sit still.

NATASHA (*surprised*). How, sit still? Why, she is a servant. (*Through tears*) I don't understand you, Olya.

I have a nurse to look after the children as well as a wet nurse for baby, and we have a housemaid and a cook, what do we want that old woman for? What's the use of her?

(The alarm bell rings behind the scenes.)

OLGA. This night has made me ten years older.[23]

It is not only that the alarm signals a crisis in Natasha's mounting fury and Olga's sad defeat: it penetrates deeper to the sisters' fate generally, giving something like a premonition of their future. As long as Natasha values people according to their utility—'What's the use of her?'—it is not only Anfisa, but the sisters too, who must eventually go. It is the same kind of thing that happens with Tchebutykin's famous breaking of the clock. His dropping it is, of course, a drunken accident, but it happens at exactly the point when the news that the battery is to be transferred shatters the growing tensions of the scene. Furthermore, Irina has just announced that the sisters will go away too: in that sense the breaking of the clock seems like the shattering of their dream. And the fact that it was the sisters' mother's clock and so has a sentimental value makes the accident upsetting in its own right. One loss—the anticipated departure of the brigade which gives the town its only social life—generates another which both externalizes the first and adds its own upset to it. Such incidents are not isolated, nor part of a loose chain of crises, but moments in which the major drama reaches a special kind of symbolic epiphany.

It is this kind of thing, which we have seen throughout Chekhov's work, which makes the charge of looseness or lack of control so difficult to accept. If anything, Chekhov's meaning in *Three Sisters* can be disconcertingly contrived, as with the reference to Balzac finding happiness at Berdichev, or the development of the association between Solyony and Lermontov. But for the most part Chekhov's effects are both highly dramatic and unobtrusive, with subtle but clear consistency. Under the crisis conditions of Act III, for example, there is a further change in the way the sisters are brought together on the stage. Emotionally and psychologically, the sisters are fatigued; they need one another's protection. In the face of this, they reaffirm their indissoluble relationship as sisters in meeting one another's needs. Masha can now confess her love for Vershinin, though Olga (who already knows about it) refuses to hear it spoken of. On Olga's advice, Irina decides to marry Tusenbach; and Olga herself confronts Andrey over his having mortgaged the house. Psychologically they are close to one another again. As if to emphasize this, and gently stylizing their physical behaviour, Chekhov groups and re-groups the sisters physically around one another more obviously than ever before. They move continuously closer until, at the end of Act IV, they are, as the play directs, literally 'huddled' together to face their future.

I do not myself consider the ending of *Three Sisters* a very hopeful one. Up to a point, Act IV gives a feeling of relief: it is midday again, and the outdoor setting gives a sense of space after the rather claustrophobic setting of Act III. But the brightness and crispness of the scene—it is autumn, and not (as in the first act) spring—and the receding perspectives of the long avenue of firs, the river and the forest give more the feeling of a crisis being over than of anything being solved. Natasha now has all of the house: she and her children appear at the windows, and the house is filled (Chekhov's irony against her is relentless) with the sounds of her 'Maiden's Prayer'. Moreover, any brightness suggested by the sunlight is overhung with shadow. The departure of the battery, in the play's own discreet symbolism, will leave the town 'extinguished' like a candle, and there is still something to be settled between Solyony and Tusenbach. The most moving moment of Act IV, certainly the one to which it gives most attention, is the farewell between Masha and Vershinin. Yet while that farewell is sad, and even tragic, there is something that is both more neglected by the other characters and, finally, more disturbing: the death of Tusenbach and its reception (or lack of reception) among those he loves.

Tusenbach is an idealist, his idealism coloured by his love. But he is also, unlike most of the other characters in the play, a man capable of action. He does leave the militia in order to work; and it is telling that none of the other characters is much interested when he does. But he does it, and—what is more—he is generous-hearted and able to respond deeply to the things around him. One of the finest speeches in the play belongs to him, and it is spoken immediately before his death:

> I feel as though I were seeing these pines, these maples, these birch-trees for the first time in my life, and they all seem to be looking at me with curiosity and waiting. What beautiful trees, and, really, how beautiful life ought to be under them! . . . See, that tree is dead, but it waves in the wind with the others. And so it seems to me that if I die I shall still have a part in life, one way or another. Good-bye, my darling . . .[24]

This speech reveals, with almost unbearable sadness, the real depth of Tusenbach's character. It manifests the special pressure of awareness and deliberation of response of a person seeing the world for the last time, and therefore in a sense for the first; but it also expands from that into an almost religious worship of life for its own sake, for its simple beauty and for sensations as simple as swaying in the wind. So when Tusenbach does die—killed by Solyony in a duel—his death is the death of a crucial possibility from the world of the play. It is the death of the possibility of life being lived for both work and love, or of life being felt as enough of a value in itself.

Of course, like all Chekhov's characters, Tusenbach does not simply embody a 'possibility': he is a complete character, and one with obvious social limitations. His mannerisms in company are frequently stiff (even bordering on the comic in his mild paranoia about his German name), and he shows a mixture of naivety and literal-mindedness both in his speeches about happiness and in his decision to fulfil his ideal of work and social usefulness by taking employment in a brickworks. Irina does seem to be compromising her life when, at that moment of despair in Act III, she agrees to marry him. But it is still a symptom of the state of provincial (and, by implication, of Russian) society, as it is represented in the play, that a man as purposive and sensitive as Tusenbach should fit into no one's world. Tusenbach has the loyalty of Irina, and yet in a way he dies that her innocence might be preserved. For, when we remember Irina's earlier speeches—

> IRINA. Tell me, why is it I am so happy to-day? As though I were sailing with the great blue sky above me and big white birds flying over it. Why is it? Why?

> TCHEBUTYKIN *(kissing both her hands, tenderly)*. My white bird . . .[25]

—it seems impossible that such expansiveness and such lovely cleanness, much less such chastity and fragility, should ever be immured in Tusenbach's brickworks. The standard of feminine refinement embodied in the sisters could not survive the robust masculinity of Tusenbach's 'new life'. But the tragedy is that the passivity to certain kinds of situations associated with that refinement unintentionally co-operates with Solyony's aggressive destructiveness in killing Tusenbach. Tusenbach tries to understand Solyony and be kind to him, and he dies for it. Yet Solyony's success depends on the fact that everyone—even, in a sense, Irina—unconsciously acquiesces in the possibility of his death. Even after a reference as obvious as the one to the 'dead tree', Irina cannot bring herself to intervene, and she cannot say those words of love which might mysteriously have rescued Tusenbach (as Laevsky was rescued in **'The Duel'**) by giving him new purpose.

Tusenbach's death amounts, from one point of view, to a defeat of the play's own values; but it is the way in which his death is received by the other characters which really consolidates the defeat. In Act IV the play's time-scale is relatively contracted: moments become precious in such a way as to give urgency to Vershinin's departure in particular. Tusenbach, however, attracts none of this sense of urgency. He makes his final plea to Irina in a calm, significantly measured tone. Then he goes off to the duel, to be virtually forgotten amid the more immediately pressing drama of Masha's and Vershinin's farewell. The news of his death hardly ruffles the surface of the play. It may of course be a fault, from the critic's point of view, that the shot which kills him goes almost unnoticed, at least by the characters on stage; but it is more likely that Chekhov meant it to indicate something sinister and disturbing. Tusenbach—able, youthful and idealistic, for all his minor faults—dies virtually unlamented by the sisters, and even before his death has been announced Natasha is busily destroying his last claim on life by planning to cut down the firs and maples, his

'beautiful trees', to replace them with the colourful and highly scented flowers which answer to her own spirit. Tusenbach's death is accepted with a sinister lack of protest by everyone in the play: that lack of protest is ominous in what it suggests not only about Natasha's values but about what has happened to the sisters' own, more civilized, world.

The ending of **Three Sisters,** then, looks very bleak indeed, with Tusenbach dead, Vershinin gone and the sisters grouped together in postures of mutual protection. Yet at that very point, when practically everything that has sustained their lives seems lost, the sisters visibly draw strength from their attempt to identify their condition. They find the courage to go on:

> MASHA. Oh, listen to that band! They are going away from us; one has gone altogether, gone forever. We are left alone to begin our life over again . . . We've got to live . . . we've got to live . . .

> IRINA *(lays her head on* OLGA *'s bosom)*. A time will come when everyone will know what all this is for, why there is this misery; there will be no mysteries and, meanwhile, we have got to live . . . we have got to work, only to work! Tomorrow I shall go alone; I shall teach in the school, and I will give all my life to those to whom it may be of use. Now it's autumn; soon winter will come and cover us with snow, and I will work, I will work.

> OLGA *(embraces both her sisters)*. The music is so gay, so confident, and one longs for life! O my God! Time will pass, and we shall go away for ever, and we shall be forgotten, our voices, and how many there were of us; but our sufferings will pass into joy for those who live after us, happiness and peace will be established upon earth, and they will remember kindly and bless those who have lived before. Oh, dear sisters, our life is not ended yet. We shall live! The music is so gay, so joyful, and it seems as though a little more and we shall know what we are living for, why we are suffering . . . If only we knew—if only we knew![26]

This is one of the few points in **Three Sisters** when the sisters' verbalizing of feeling and their introspection about their own states of mind have the effect of strengthening, rather than debilitating, them. As their voices take over from one another they assume, and build upon, one another's feelings, consolidating and forwarding them—from Masha's suffering assertion 'we've got to *live*' to Irina's 'we've got to *work*' to Olga's more positive '*longing*' for life. Masha, true to her usual character, takes the most difficult and energetic initiative; Irina takes up Tusenbach's call for a life made meaningful through work; and Olga looks into the distance for comfort and justification in the joys of others. Then, with Tchebutykin softly humming his nihilistic chant—'"Tarara-boom-dee-ay!" . . . It doesn't matter, it doesn't matter'—and Olga calling across the stage 'If only we knew, if only we knew!', the range of the drama itself may seem to have been extended into the metaphysical, as if Chekhov were embodying something of his own general reaction to life (quite independently of the sisters) in the finale of the play. But it is important to recognize that these are sentiments uttered in a particular context by characters who have been carefully individualized and to some extent (albeit sympathetically) criticized. The persuasiveness of the sisters' final speeches is almost entirely emotional, their content dictated by the sheer intensity of the sisters' needs; for if those speeches affirm the sisters' continuing and heroic aspiration to make something of their lives, and to do so on new terms, they are also a way of softening, or warding off, final defeat. To Chekhov, no fate is complete this side of death: the very fact that the sisters' lives are now so reduced that their last reserves of strength are needed merely to survive makes a new beginning conceivable. But, watching this scene, and even while one is drawn into the intensity of the sisters' feelings, it is impossible not to recognize how much has been lost both personally and socially in the world of the play, and to see the sisters' hopes for a new future in relation to the wider facts which the rest of the play has revealed. The sisters do go on living, but living has become virtually synonymous with suffering. They cannot, in fact, 'begin their lives over again', because the whole play has shown their past to be inescapable. And if they seem to draw strength from one another in this final scene, we cannot forget that they are about to go their separate ways, alone. They have abandoned their dream of Moscow which, according to at least one understanding of the play, ought to release them to live more realistically and fully in the present; but the opportunities which were embodied in their present—in Vershinin and Tusenbach—have already gone. There are, of course, those notes of hope of which I have already spoken. The sisters assert their will to go on living, and Olga in particular is roused by the strains of the military band:

> 'Oh, dear sisters, our life is not ended yet. We shall live! The music is so gay, so joyful . . .'

But even as she says it the band grows fainter and fainter in the distance. Winter is coming and the snow will cover everything: that much is certain. Irina, though, may or may not go on working. The stoical determination to live, to survive, and the optimistic determination to work are the two poles between which the feeling runs. Only life itself will decide. But it is characteristic of Chekhov's genius and the subtle tensions it holds in balance—the tensions, essentially, of a temperament both agnostic and humanist—that the doubt and the hope, in his greatest single work, are there as one.

NOTES

[1] 'Chekhov and the English', in Donald Davie (ed.), *Russian Literature and Modern English Fiction* (Chicago, 1965), p. 206.
[2] *Three Sisters and Other Plays* (Garnett), p. 27.
[3] Ibid. p. 40.
[4] Ibid. p. 25.
[5] *Chekhov and His Russia: A Sociological Study* (London, 1948), p. 36.
[6] *Three Sisters and Other Plays* (Garnett), p. 26.
[7] Ibid. p. 5. The tense-structure of the original is actually ambiguous: it might be translated in the present, as here, or cast more strongly in the past.
[8] Ibid. p. 65.
[9] Ibid. p. 79.
[10] Ibid. p. 24.
[11] Ibid. p. 80.
[12] Ibid. pp. 18-19.
[13] Ibid. p. 28.
[14] Ibid. p. 95.
[15] Ibid. p. 64.
[16] Ibid. p. 8.
[17] Ibid. p. 33.
[18] Ibid. p. 4.
[19] Unpublished lectures on Chekhov, delivered at the University of Melbourne, 1970.
[20] *Three Sisters and Other Plays* (Garnett), p. 3. I have inserted the word 'outside' into the Garnett translation of the stage directions here, as this detail seems to me important for a proper understanding of the scene and is clearly indicated in the original text. . . . Incidentally, the Fen translation of this particular work does seem to me on the whole rather more careful and exact than the Garnett; but I have kept to the Garnett for this quotation, for the sake of consistency.
[21] Ibid. p. 35.
[22] Ibid. p. 55.
[23] Ibid. p. 58.
[24] Ibid. pp. 85-6.
[25] Ibid. p. 7.
[26] Ibid. pp. 94-5.

Howard Moss   (essay date 1977-78)

SOURCE: "Three Sisters," in *The Hudson Review* XXX, No. 4, Winter 1977-78, pp. 525-43.

[*In the following essay, Moss focuses on the motivations, values, and interrelations of the characters in* Three Sisters, *maintaining that "the webs of characters obscure—and enrich—the scaffold of action" in the drama.*]

"Loneliness is a terrible thing, Andrei."

In *Three Sisters,* the inability to act becomes the action of the play. How to make stasis dramatic is its problem and Chekhov solves it by a gradual deepening of insight rather than by the play of event. The grandeur of great gestures and magnificent speeches remains a Shakespearian possibility—a diminishing one. Most often, we get to know people through the accretion of small details—minute responses, tiny actions, little gauze screens being lifted in the day-to-day pressure of relationships. In most plays, action builds toward a major crisis. In *Three Sisters,* it might be compared to the drip of a faucet in a water basin; a continuous process wears away the enamel of facade.

Many stories are being told simultaneously: the stories of the four Prozorov orphans—three girls, one boy, grown up in varying degrees—living in one of those Chekhovian provincial towns that have the literal detail of a newspaper story but keep drifting off into song. There is the old drunken doctor, Chebutykin, once in love with the Prozorovs' mother, there is a slew of battery officers stationed in the town—one of them, Vershinin, a married man, falls in love with the already married middle-sister, Masha; another proposes to the youngest, Irena; and still a third, Soliony, also declares his love for her. There is Olga, the oldest sister, and Kulighin, Masha's awkward school-teacher husband, and there is Natasha, the small town girl who sets her heart on Andrei, the brother. It is Natasha's and Andrei's marriage that provides the catalyst of change. Each of these characters might be conceived as a voice entering the score at intervals to announce or to develop its subject, to join and part in various combinations: duets, trios, and so on. *Three Sisters* is the most musical of all of Chekhov's plays in construction, the one that depends most heavily on the repetition of motifs. And it uses music throughout: marching bands, hummed tunes, "the faint sound of an accordion coming from the street," a guitar, a piano, the human voice raised in song.

Yet too much can be made of the "music" of the play at the expense of its command of narrative style. Private confrontation and social conflict are handled with equal authority, and a symbolism still amateur in *The Seagull* written five years earlier, has matured and gone underground to permeate the texture of the work. No dead bird is brought onstage weighted with meaning. No ideas are embalmed in objects. What we have instead is a kind of geometric structure, one angle of each story fitting into the triangular figure of another, and, overlaying that, a subtle web of connected images and words. Seemingly artless, it is made of steel. In a letter to his sister, Chekhov complained, "I find it very difficult to write *Three Sisters,* much more difficult than any of my other plays." One can well believe it.

Because immobility is the subject—no other play catches hold of the notion so definitively with the exception of *Hamlet*—secondary characters carry the burden of narration forward. Natasha and Andrei establish the main line of construction; their marriage is the network to which everything else attaches. Yet Andrei never spins the wheels of action. That task is left to Natasha, a character originally outside the immediate family, and to another stranger to the domestic circle, Soliony. One a provincial social climber, the other a neurotic captain, each takes on, in time, an ultimate coloration: Natasha, the devouring wife, Soliony, the lethal friend.

Natasha's motives are obvious enough to be disarming—disarming in its literal sense: to deprive one of weapons. No one need *suspect* her of the worst; her lies are so transparent that every civilized resource is called upon to deal with the transparency rather than the lie.

Soliony lacks accessible motivation but is easily recognizable as a true creature from life. Panicky and literal, he is repellent—one of the few repellent characters Chekhov ever created. If Soliony is shy, shyness is dangerous. Instinct, not insight leads him to the weak spot in other people. A deeply wounded man who has turned into a weapon, he is a member of a species: the seducer-duelist, a 19th century stock character Chekhov manages to twist into a perverse original.

When Irena rejects him, he says he will kill anyone who wins her; and in the name of affection, he makes good his threat. Ironically, Irena's half-hearted relationship to Tuzenbach becomes the fatal rivalry of the play; Tuzen-

bach has won Irena's hand but not her heart Moreover, Soliony is introduced into the Prozorov circle by Tuzenbach, who therefore begins the chain of events leading to his own death.

Nothing redeems Soliony except the barbarity of his manner, a symptom of an alienation deep enough, perhaps, to evoke pity. A person who cannot feel pleasure and destroys everyone else's, his touchy uneasiness is irrational, the punishment it exacts inexhaustible. Unwilling to be mollified by life's niceties or won over by its distractions, he is a definite negative force in a play in which a lack of energy is crucial. Natasha turned inside-out, a killer without her affectations and pieties, he is, if never likeable, at least not a liar. He tells us several times that, even to him, the scent he uses fails to disguise the smell of a dead man. That stench rises from a whole gallery of literary soldiers. No matter how heroic a military man may be, he is, functionally, a murderer. Soliony reminds us of that easily forgotten fact: He is the gunman of the play.

And the gunshot in *Three Sisters* is fired offstage—a shot heard before in *Ivanov, The Seagull,* and *The Wood Demon.* In *Uncle Vanya,* the shots occur *on*stage; half-farcical, they are not without psychological danger. Vanya shoots out of humiliation; his failure to hit anything only deepens it. The offstage gunshot in *Three Sisters* does more than end Tuzenbach's life and destroy Irena's marriage. A final fact, it leaves in its wake a slowly emerging revelation, the dark edge of an outline: the black side of Irena.

In the scene just preceding the shot, Tuzenbach makes a crucial request. Irena has described herself earlier as a locked piano to which she has lost the key.

> TUZENBACH: I was awake all night. Not that there's anything to be afraid of in my life, nothing's threatening . . . Only the thought of that lost key torments me and keeps me awake. Say something to me . . . (*A pause*) Say something!
>
> IRENA: What? What am I to say? What?
>
> TUZENBACH: Anything.

Tuzenbach, about to fight a duel with Soliony, needs Irena's reassurance. Forced to obscure a fact while trying to express an emotion, he says, ". . . nothing's threatening . . ." He is telling a lie, and unaware of his true situation, Irena can hardly be blamed for not understanding its desperateness. And there is something odd about Tuzenbach's request in the first place: he already knows Irena doesn't love him and is hoping against hope for a last reprieve. The inability to bare or face emotional realities—a favorite Chekhovian notion—is only partly in question here; here there is something worse: to feel the demand but not the attraction. For even if Irena understood Tuzenbach's request, her response, if honest, would have to be equivocal. They are both guilty; he for demanding love where he knows it doesn't exist; she for not loving. He is asking too much; she is offering too little.

Tuzenbach's request echoes almost exactly the one Katya makes to the Professor at the end of **"A Dreary Story,"** where it is met with the same failure:

> "Help me, help me!" she begs. "I can't stand any more." ****
> "There's nothing I can say, Katya." ****
> I am at a loss, embarrassed, moved by her sobbing, and I can hardly stand.
>
> "Let's have lunch, Katya," I say with a forced smile. "And stop that crying." "I shall soon be dead, Katya," I at once add in a low voice.
>
> "Just say one word, just one word!" she cries, holding out her hands.

Katya seems as impervious to the Professor's death sentence as he is to her despair. Each is too full of his own suffering. The characters in **Three Sisters,** like Katya and the Professor, do not hear each other's pleas, partly out of selfishness—other people's troubles are boring— partly out of self-protection. If they *did* hear them, what could they do?

Needs, revealed but never satisfied, drive Chekhov's characters toward two kinds of action: the deranged— Vanya's hysterical outbursts, Treplev's suicide—or flight. They desert each other—as Katya deserts the Professor half a page after the dialogue above, and as Trigorin abandons Nina in **The Seagull.** Nothing could be more Chekhovian than the last sentence of **"A Dreary Story."** The Professor, watching Katya go, wonders if she'll turn around and look back at him for the last time. She doesn't. Then he says to himself, "Goodbye, my treasure."—end of story. But those three words are endlessly and ambiguously illuminating. Does he love Katya? Is she his treasure because this is the last feeling he will ever have? Is this final desertion the one symptom of his being human? Is there a tiny sarcastic twinge to "treasure"? In regard to people, every credible truth is only partial.

The inability to respond evokes responses: coldness, hatred, contempt. Loneliness can be viewed as humiliation and misfortune as insult. What cannot be given is interpreted as being withheld. The wrong people always love each other—bad luck or the telltale sign of a fundamental incapacity to love. The typical Chekhovian character longs for what he can neither express nor have, and each unrequited wish is one more dream in a universal nightmare. If the great treachery lies in the disparity between what we feel and what we say, between what we want and what we get, do we have—through an unconscious perversity—a vested interest in disparity itself? Proust, the ultimate dissecter of jealousy, thought so, and it is odd to think that Chekhov, working with such different material and in such a different way, may have come to a similar conclusion. The truth is that what is interesting about love is how it doesn't work out, and

Proust and Chekhov saw that truth and that interest from different angles. Surprisingly, like Proust in *Remembrance of Things Past,* who provides us with not one example of a happy marriage in over 4,000 pages, Chekhov offers us none either.

And both Proust and Chekhov concern themselves with a social class that is about to be overwhelmed by forces rising from below. In Proust, the class distinctions are clear; we know exactly who is noble, and who is middle-class. We have to, because the impingement of one upon the other is one of the themes of the novel. That certainly eludes us in Chekhov's case. Olga, Masha, and Irena belong to a social class that has no counterpart in America. We see them as a kind of provincial nobility (partly because we have got to them so often through English accents) whereas they represent the lowest rung of a rural aristocracy, a sort of down-at-the-heels upper middle-class living in the country; squires going to seed, a gentry saddled with land that no longer interests them, fitful leftovers unable to cope with the unfamiliar and the new. Chekhov's plays suffer from classlessness in translation, and more than classlessness in certain productions: maids become heroines and stable boys stars. The main difficulty is: One can hardly imagine Irena in Kansas, say, stretching her hands toward an imaginary New York. She would have already been there, traveling by jet. And, in **The Seagull,** would anyone have the faintest notion of just what *kind* of bank Madame Arkadina kept her much-discussed securities in?

But power, as a source, is general no matter the specific version, and both Natasha and Soliony are interested in it. Each is allowed to inherit a particular world: domestic tyranny in Natasha's case, the completed fantasy of the romantic egoist in Soliony's: the destruction of the rival lover. The passivity of the others gives them permission, it invites them in.

An embittered fact-monger, Soliony is unable to respond to any shade of irony. And though Irena is too young to know it, to be literal and humorless—qualities equally at home in the romantic and the dullard—can be as poisonous as deception or ingrained meanness. Worldliness is never an issue in **Three Sisters** though it might well be. Vershinin brings a breath of it in the door with him with his arrival, but it is the weary urbanity of a disappointed middle-aged man. A lack of worldliness in people forced to live in the world is always a potential source of suffering. Those people doomed to love late and to be ultimately denied it, like Masha and Vershinin, arrive at it by way of lost opportunities and through a web of feeling. In **Three Sisters,** we get two warped version of it: Natasha's grasping selfishness and the doctor's cynicism. They are the merest echoes of the real thing. What we have in its place is innocence on the one hand and frustration on the other. There is no wise man in the play for the others to turn to; there is no mother and father for children who remain children, though they walk about as if they were adults, to run to for comfort and advice. In Chekhov's view, even worldliness, we suspect, would be another inadequate means of dealing with life, as powerless as innocence to fend off its evils, and, because it comes in the guise of wisdom, perhaps the most deceptive of all.

It is not always clear in various editions of the play that these revelations occur over a period of five years. We watch Irena, in fact, change from a young girl into a woman. The time scheme is relatively long, the roles are enigmatically written and need to be played with the finest gradations in order to develop their true flavors and poisons. If Natasha is immediately recognizable as evil, or Soliony as the threat of the play, a great deal is lost in characterization and suspense. Irena's cry of "Moscow! . . . Moscow!" at the end of the second act should be a note in a scale, not a final sounding. She has not realized, she is *beginning* to realize that what she hopes for will remain a dream.

Compared to *The Seagull* and *Uncle Vanya,* a technical advance occurs in *Three Sisters* that may account for a greater sounding of the depths. Chekhov's mastery of the techniques of playwriting may be measured by his use of the gun; it is farther offstage here than before—not in the next room but at the edge of town, which suggests that it might, finally, be dispensed with, as it is in *The Cherry Orchard,* where the only sound we hear, ultimately, is an axe cutting down trees. As he went on, Chekhov let go of the trigger, his one concession to the merciless demands of the stage. The gunshot in *Three Sisters,* unlike the shot in *Vanya,* is terminal. But Tuzenbach's death has further implications; it is partly the result of, and the price paid for, Irena's lack of love. Something suicidal colors Tuzenbach's death, and we pick it up in his last big speech:

> TUZENBACH: . . . Really, I feel quite elated. I feel as if I were seeing those fir trees and maples and birches for the first time in my life. They all seem to be looking at me with a sort of inquisitive look and waiting for something. What beautiful trees—and how beautiful, when you think of it, life ought to be with trees like these!
>
> (*Shouts of 'Ah-oo! Heigh-ho' are heard.*)
>
> I must go, it's time. . . . Look at that dead tree, it's all dried up, but it's still swaying in the wind along with the others. And in the same way, it seems to me that, if I die, I shall still have a share in life somehow or other. Goodbye, my dear . . . (*Kisses her hands.*) Your papers, the ones you gave me, are on my desk, under the calendar.

Tuzenbach never had much of "a share in life"; he has always been a "dried-up (tree) . . . swaying in the wind . . ." If Irena had been able to love him, would he have tried to talk to Soliony or to Dr. Chebutykin, in some way mediated the pointlessness of this ending? A pointlessness equally vivid, one suspects, whether he had married Irena or not.

The key to Irena's heart, that locked piano, is lost. Neither Tuzenbach nor Soliony ever had it. So their duel,

though in deadly earnest, turns out to be an ironic, even a ludicrous footnote. Who holds the key to Irena's heart? Someone offstage—like the gun—whom she hopes to meet in Moscow. "The right one" is how she describes him, the unmeetable ideal who dominates the fantasies of school-girls. The doctor may comfort himself with bogus philosophy and claim that nothing matters but the others tend to confirm not his thesis but its perverse corollary. By the indecisiveness of their actions, by their inability to deal head-on with what is central to their lives, they make, in the end, what matters futile. They unwittingly prove Dr. Chebutykin's false notion: what *does* Tuzenbach's death matter? Would Irena be any more lonely with him than without him? Would he have been content living with someone who doesn't love him, he who needs love to make himself feel loveable? Would Irena have joined him in "work"—her idealized version of it—and not be working alone? At what? Reality intrudes upon a pipedream, but even the reality is dreamlike. The Baron's sacrifice does little for the cause of either work or love.

* * *

Of the three sisters, Olga is the least interesting: nothing romantic attaches to her. She is neither unhappily married or unhappily *un*married. A person of feeling who has suppressed or never felt the pull of the irrational, she is the substitute mother or the spinster-mother—a recognizable type for whom the traditional role is the aunt, boringly earnest but secretly admirable. She represents a standard of behavior unwillingly, almost painfully, for her nerves are not equal to the moral battles in which she must take part, yet those very nerves are the barometric instruments that register ethical weather. Two sets of values are in conflict in *Three Sisters,* as well as two social classes, and nothing makes those values clearer than Olga's and Natasha's confrontation over Anfisa, the 80-year-old nurse. To Olga, Anfisa deserves the respect accorded the old and the faithful. Natasha uses Anfisa as another means of enforcing a pecking order whose main function is to make her status visible. She demands that Anfisa stand up in her presence like a soldier at attention. In this clash of feelings and wills, Olga doesn't defend Anfisa as she should: in true opposition, in attack. She is too stunned, too hurt. She says, ". . . everything went black." Natasha, out to win, wins in spite of what would ordinarily be a great drawback—her affair with Poptopopov. Even her open-faced adultery, commented upon by the doctor in the third act, doesn't undercut her position. People prefer to ignore her rather than precipitate a series of crises whose logical end could only be an attack on Andrei. And Andrei cannot be attacked. Affection, pity, and, most of all, necessity are his three shields. Natasha has found the perfect nest to despoil. Andrei was always too weak, too self-centered, in spite of his shyness, to guard his sisters' interests. Now he is not only weak; he is torn.

But Olga is too morally good to let Natasha's rudeness to Anfisa pass without protest—as so many other instances have passed: Natasha's request for Irena's room, made both to Irena and Andrei, for instance, which is

Act IV of the Moscow Art Theater production of Three Sisters, *1901.*

met with a kind of cowed acquiescence. It is a demand so basically impossible that no immediate way of dealing with it comes to hand. Natasha apologizes to Olga but it is an apology without understanding, without heart. Actually, it is motivated by Natasha's fear that she has revealed too much, gone too far. Finally, Olga removes Anfisa from the household. There is a tiny suite for her at the school where Olga becomes headmistress, a place where Anfisa may stay for the rest of her life. It is easier—and wiser, too—to get out than to go on fighting a battle already lost. But whether the existence of that suite sways Olga in her decision to *become* a headmistress is left hanging.

Though Natasha and Soliony are the movers and the shakers of the play, another neurotic character, invisible throughout, is a spur to its conflicts: Vershinin's suicidal fishwife of a mate, whom he fears, comes to detest, and yet who controls his life. He is weak, too, unable to make a clean break with his own misery. Chekhov points up one of the strangest true facts of emotional life: nothing binds people closer together than mutual unhappiness. And that is why Chekhov is sometimes so funny. The very horrors of people's lives—short of poverty and disease—are also the most ludicrous things about them. Vanya with a gun! How sad! Yet everyone laughs. The

absurd and the tragic are uncomfortably close. Like the figure of the clown, and the wit in black humor, Chekhov teeters on a seesaw. Even a suggestion of the excessive would be ruinous. One gunshot too many, one sob prolonged a second longer than necessary and we have crossed over to the other side. Chekhov, to be played properly, has to be played on a hairline.

Vershinin's mirror-image is Masha, the most interesting of the three sisters, an interest dramatically mysterious because we know so little about her. But we know she is a woman of temperament, a woman capable of passion—and that in itself distinguishes her from Olga, to whom something of the old maid clings, just as something of the ingenue mars Irena. Masha wears black throughout the play, reminding us of her namesake, Masha Shamrayev, in *The Seagull,* who also always wears black because she is "in mourning for my life." (It may be of some interest to note that, in the same play, Madame Arkadina's first name is Irena.)

Masha is the onlooker who comments or withholds comment, often to devastating effect. She is the one free-speaker of the play. She tells us the truth about Natasha from the beginning, if only by implication; as a matter of fact, she tells us the truth about everything, even herself, blurting out the facts to her unwilling listeners, Olga and Irena, who don't want to hear of her love for Vershinin, don't want to be involved in a family betrayal. If adultery is a black mark against the detested Natasha, what must one make of it with the beloved Masha? The categories begin to blur, the certainties become uncertain. Like a lot of truth tellers, Masha is morally impeccable in regard to honesty but something of a menace; she puts people in impossible positions. She is the romantic heart of the play just as Irena is the romantic lead. Unlike Irena, Masha is a lover disillusioned by life, not deluded by it. She married her schoolmaster when she was a young student and bitterly learns that the man who struck her as superior is at heart a fool. The reigning intelligence of the play is Masha's. It might have been the doctor's if intelligence were not so dangerous a gift for a man who has taught himself to be disingenuous.

Masha is still something of an impulsive child, a far different thing from being an adolescent like Irena, or living a self-imposed second childhood like the doctor, whose drunken dream is to make second childhood permanent. Masha isn't interested in intelligence per se and the doctor can't afford to be. If he ever let himself know what he knows, it would destroy him. And so he protects himself by a kind of slow-motion destruction, infinitely easier to handle. He keeps telling us how impossible it is to bear reality in a play in which everyone else keeps saying how impossible it is to know what reality is.

In spite of a loveless marriage (from *her* point of view), Masha has Kulighin, who, for all his absurdity, has something everyone else lacks: a true position. Too emasculated to oppose Masha's affair with Vershinin, he nevertheless loves her, sticks by her, and would be desperate without her. A stuffed shirt, a mollycoddle, a bower and a scraper, his ridiculousness masks the genuine feelings of a boy—he loves out of dependency but who else is able to love in *Three Sisters*? Masha, yes, but her love is romantic; Irena, no, *because* her love is romantic. Kulighin ends up with something: he may wander about the stage calling for Masha who never seems to be there, but he has the *right* to call her, and knows she will go home with him in the end. She has nowhere else to go.

The three marriages in the play—Masha-Kulighin, Vershinin and his offstage wife and Natasha-Andrei—are all unhappy. Strangely, Masha and Kulighin do not have children, and no mention is ever made of their childlessness. A matter of no significance, it seems, yet it becomes important in regard to Natasha for it is through the cardinal bourgeois virtue of motherhood that she manipulates the household. Masha provides no counterweight. A subterranean notion percolates at the lowest level of *Three Sisters*—moral righteousness as the chief disguise of self-interest. Power is consolidated under the smokescreen of moral urgency. The Dreyfus Affair, the Reichstag fire, and Watergate are extensions of the same basic principle. Natasha's emotions are as false as her values. Under the camouflage of maternal love, she gains possession of Irena's room and has the maskers dismissed. Whatever *she* may think, it is clear to us that what

motivates her action is not her love for her children but her love for herself.

And something similar may be said of Soliony. The duel, though illegal, was a process by which men of Soliony's day still settled matters of honor too refined or too personal for the courts. But it was also a vehicle for machismo pride hidden in the trappings of a gentleman's code. Emotional illness has never found a better front than ethical smugness.

In contrast to the Prozorovs as we first see them, and in spite of her malevolence, Natasha is creating a true family, one with a real mother, father, and children, where only a semblance of family life had existed before. The ghosts of family attachments haunt the wanderers crossing the thresholds of rooms, as if they were searching for a phrase impossible to recall, or had fixed their eyes on an invisible figure. The word "orphan" rings its bell. And Natasha, carrying the energetic serum of the new, has only one goal: to possess a material world. Starting out as a girl who doesn't even know how to dress, she ends up as an unwitting domestic servant of change, dusting a corner here, tearing down a cobweb there. Not one of these acts has a generous motive. She is only a force for progress by being lower-class and on the move. She thinks of herself as the mistress of a house that had for too long been in disorder without her. And in a certain sense, that view is not irrational. Two questions that can never be answered are asked *sotto voce* in the play: What would have happened to everyone if Andrei hadn't married Natasha? And: What will Andrei's and Natasha's children be like?

But even Natasha is up against something too subtle to control. Conquerors have their opposites—losers. But Natasha is working not in a house of losers but of survivors. Something too lively makes Chekhov's characters, even the desperate ones, convincing candidates for yet another day of hopes and dreams. One feels their mortality less than their indestructibility. Everyone casts the shadow of age ahead; it is hard to think of anyone dying in a Chekhov play who isn't actually killed during the action. Some predisposition to live, some strain of the *type* transfixes the individual into permanent amber, so that, unheroic as they may be, we think of them somewhat in the way we think of Shakespearian heroes. They may languish in life but they refuse to die in art, and with a peculiar insistence—an irony only good plays manage to achieve because it is only on the stage that the human figure is always wholly represented and representative. When we speak of "Masha" or "Vanya," we are already talking about the future. One of the side-effects of masterpieces is to make their characters as immortal as the works in which they appear. And so Natasha is stuck among her gallery-mates forever, always *about* to take over the house.

And she is about to do so by exploiting bourgeois morality for ugly ends—an old story. But the subject is the key to Chekhov's method here: the business of unmasking. The soldiers' uniforms hide the same boring civilians underneath. It is important for Tuzenbach literally to take off his clothes and become a civilian "so plain" that Olga cries when she first sees him. Natasha's sash is a tiny repetition of this motif when she reverses roles and comments on Irena's belt in the last act, a bit of signalling uncharacteristic of Chekhov, who rarely stoops to a device so crude. It is already clear that the outsider of Act I has become the dominating power of the household.

Unfulfilled wishes allow for seemingly random duets that enrich the texture of the play by showing us major characters in minor relationships—psychological side pockets of a sort that cast desperate or ironic lights. Olga and Kulighin, for instance, in their discussion of marriage defend it as an institution and as a source of happiness. Yet Olga is a spinster and Kulighin a cuckold. Both schoolteachers, they are drawn together by their profession and by a kind of innocent idealism that overrides fact and disappointment. Theirs might have been the only happy marriage in the play, and Kulighin says he often thinks if he hadn't married Masha, he would have married Olga. In the face of adultery, alcoholism, compulsive gambling, irrational rage, and attempted suicide, Olga still believes in the "finer things," in the vision of human goodness.

Similarly, Irena and Dr. Chebutykin are connected by a thread of sympathy and habit—the oldest and the youngest in one another's arms, each equally deluded, alcohol fuzzing the facts for the doctor, and the determined unawareness of youth providing Irena with a temporary protective barrier. These uneasy alliances are touching because they rise out of needs that bear little relation to their satisfactions. It is precisely Kulighin's marriage to Masha that makes Olga more deeply aware she is a spinster; it is Chebutykin's drinking and his smashing of her mother's clock that will finally curdle Irena's affection for him. And this kind of delicate interplay between the loving and the hateful aspects of relationships is re-enforced often by the action of the play itself. It is Chebutykin, for example, who is the Baron's second at the duel in which Irena is deprived of her husband-to-be, her one chance of making a bid for another life. Trusted by the Baron, Chebutykin has some reason for hoping the Baron is killed—namely, to protect the continuation of his relationship to Irena. If that is true, there is a further irony: the doctor doesn't realize that he has already put that relationship in serious jeopardy. And then there are relationships by omission: Andrei's outpourings to the deaf servant Ferapont, Masha's never addressing a single word to Natasha throughout the entire course of the play. Masha—like her creator—makes the inarticulate eloquent.

The random duets are complemented by a series of trios: two are obvious: Masha-Kulighin-Vershinin and Irena-Tuzenbach-Soliony. But a third is not: Chebutykin's ambiguous relationship to Irena provides her with an underground suitor; his is one of those fatherly-grandfatherly roles whose sexual, affectionate, and narcissistic aspects are impossible to unravel, and he places himself in position as a member of a male trio: Tuzenbach-Soliony-Chebutykin. The doctor has a claim on Irena; he was her protector in the past; she is his lifeline now. It is through the subtle shifts of Irena's relationship to Chebutykin that we watch Irena grow from an unknowing girl into a woman who is beginning to see the truth. Chebutykin is onstage, but by being a kind of subliminal lover, he brings to mind, or to the back of the mind, three *off*-stage characters essential to the conflicts of the play: Vershinin's wife; Natasha's lover, Protopopov; and the sisters' mother, each an invisible figure in a triangle. If Chebutykin was once in love with the Prozorovs' mother, he was part of an unacknowledged trio: the mother of the sisters, their father, and himself. The mother's image is kept alive in Irena, who resembles her. These offstage-onstage love affairs—one of which we see, one of which we watch being covered up, and one of which we merely hear about—complicate the action and re-enforce the play's design of interlocking triangles.

Irena is part of two other triangles, one onstage, one off. Our study in ingenuousness, an ingenuousness that will become educated before our eyes, she is joined to Second Lieutenant Fedotik and Rode by the enthusiasms and innocence of youth. If the play were a ballet, at some point they would have a divertissement to themselves. They isolate Chebutykin in a particular way: the contrast between their trio and the doctor makes time physically visible. And then Irena might be considered part of yet another triangle; her dreamed-of "someone" whom she hopes to meet in Moscow is as much of a threat to her happiness with Tuzenbach as Soliony is. It is he, in her mind, who holds the key to the locked piano. Overall, we have our fixed image of a trio, our superimposed stereotype: the three sisters themselves.

The themes of *Three Sisters,* the gulf between dream and action, between hope and disappointment, have finer variations. Even accepting the "real" is thwarted. Irena's compromise in marrying the Baron proves to be impossible. Having given up Moscow, Irena is not even allowed, so to speak, its drearier suburbs. She has met the fate that awaited her all along. Her cry of "work, work," echoed by Tuzenbach, is a hopeless cry. The issue is real, the solution false: what could a dreamy schoolgirl and a philosophical Baron contribute to a brickworks?

But something more than simple evasiveness frustrates the actors in *Three Sisters.* There is a grand plan working out its design, moving the players beyond their ability to act. And the military here perform a special function. When the battery is moved to Poland—its rumored destination was Siberia—the soldiers and officers reverse positions with the sisters who can never get to Moscow, the dreamland of easy solutions. The sisters are psychologically "stationed" in the house by a force as ineluctable as that which sends the soldiers on their way. The dispatchment of soldiers is an event inevitable in time. And illusion gathers strength in ratio to time: the longer an idea is believed the more powerful it becomes. "If we only knew," the sisters say at the end. "If we could only know . . ." Know what? Something already known—time moves people without their moving: the soldiers are forced to go, the sisters to stay. The object the doctor breaks in his drunkenness is a clock, and for good reason. Time's pervasiveness—its importance—is stressed many times in the play: the announcement of what time the maskers are to arrive; the hour set for the duel (at one point, the doctor takes out his hunting watch to verify it); the fifteen minutes Natasha allows herself on the sleigh ride with her lover; the no longer available date on which Andrei's papers have to be signed; the very first scene, in fact, which is both an anniversary and a name day. As the minutes tick themselves off, action is always being performed, even by omission. Deluded into thinking time is eternal, events infinitely postponable, the sisters keep hoping problems will solve themselves, somehow, in time. They do, but not as a requital to hope. Birth and death, introduced in the anniversary-name day occasion of the first scene, are more sharply contrasted and connected in the last. Natasha's newest baby is wheeled back and forth in a carriage, a bit of counterpoint to Tuzenbach's death. In between, we have, simply, age—the eighty years of Anfisa's life.

Time sounds a recurrent note in *Three Sisters*; place is more subtly emphasized. The idea of a journey hovers in the air and charges the atmosphere—the journey never taken, the journey never to *be* taken. The repeated sounding of "Moscow!" is more than the never-to-be-reached Eldorado of the work or its lost Eden; it is a symbol of distance itself, that past or future in space from which the characters are forever barred. On this score, the play peculiarly divides itself on sexual grounds: the men want to stay, the women to go. Memory lures them, in opposite directions, and Masha's halting bit of verse clues us in. What cannot be remembered takes on importance; it begins to have the force of a prediction in the same way that the unconscious, unable to bring significant material to the surface, determines future behavior. What does her verse mean? Where has she heard it? She says nothing for the first fifteen minutes of the play, she hums a little tune, remembers a line of verse she can't quite place. She has given up the piano. Enraged beyond speech, she feels—when we first see her—that any communication would be a betrayal. What Masha remembers most vividly, and whose betrayal she cannot forgive, is herself. Even music and poetry, because they evoke memory, are forms of conspiracy: they reveal the sensibility she has forfeited for the stupidity of the world she lives in.

The women want to go; more than that, they want to go *back*. Back to a life they once lived (they think), certainly not the one they are living. As for a brave new world, there are no explorers in *Three Sisters,* no wanderers ready to set forth for the unknown. The word "Siberia" runs its little chill through the kitchen. The play is nostalgic, for one set of people would do anything *not* to be removed from where they are (a form of self-miring in the present as if it *were* the past), and one set would do anything, short of what is necessary, to *be* removed. The setting is . . . where? A country town. But it is the least realistic of Chekhov's plays, or at least what is realistic about it always suggests the allusive, one image connecting with or piling up on a similar one. Masha gives up the piano; Irena is a locked piano; Andrei plays the violin. Vershinin receives letters; Kulighin has his note-

books; Andrei is translating an English novel. A whistled phrase is a signal from Vershinin to Masha or vice versa; the doctor bangs on the floor—his little Morse code. Irena gives her room up for a baby; Olga gives it up for an old woman, Anfisa. These networks are fine meshes thrown over the realistic surface of the play. The webs of character obscure—and enrich—the scaffold of action. And what is allusive about the play suggests the thematically symbolic. Where do people move? From room to room. (Is that why the first thing we see is a room within a room?) But two crucial moves, Irena and Olga doubling up in one bedroom, and Anfisa moving out, are overshadowed by the movement, the literal displacement, of the soldiers going to two possible destinations: Poland (where we are still within the limits of the civilized and the credible) and Siberia (where we move into the realm of fear and fantasy).

The sense of danger, a hairsbreadth away from the cozy, becomes actual in the fire of Act 3. People can really be forced out of their houses, they can be *made to move* by events beyond their power to predict or to control. The fire presents us with a true Apocalypse, its victims huddled downstairs, lost souls wandering about, crying, the rescuers, inside and out, trying to keep the contagion from spreading. Blankets, beds, food are commandeered. Still the shadow of the flames races up the walls. We are in a disaster area, a battlefield. We are also in Olga's and Irena's bedroom. The disaster outside is the general counterpart of the specific horrors within. They have one thing in common: dislocation. For the burning houses are no longer truly houses, any more than the room is now either Olga's *or* Irena's. Natasha has invaded the place of privacy, the source of identity, and we get to know that because it is *after* this scene that Olga moves out to become headmistress and *during* it that Irena decides to marry the Baron and Masha to sleep with Vershinin. And these three decisions prepare us for a fourth: the removal of Anfisa from the household. That is not as simple a decision as it first appears, for Anfisa is the basic—and the last—link with whatever living tradition ties the sisters to their childhoods. The issue of Anfisa is the scale that balances the strengths and weaknesses of Olga and Natasha, the turning point of the act and the breaking point of the play. In a psychological terror scene the fate of the Prozorovs is decided. Natasha's taking over of the house is played against the bigger landscape of the fire destroying the adjacent houses. But the small wreck and the large are equally devastating.

Each sister is given an opportunity for moral or emotional expansion and is finally enclosed in the limited world of the possible. Each outlasts a wish and is forced to go on living a life without any particular pleasure or savor. The sway of compulsion is important to the play because compulsion suggests what must be limited: to be compelled is the opposite of being able to make a free choice. And there are enough examples of the irrational in the air to make the fearful and the uncontrollable real: Vershinin's wife's suicide attempts, Andrei's gambling, the doctor's alcoholism, Natasha's temper. And Soliony, our capital case, because he brings about what we are most

Chekhov on the "dullness" of *Three Sisters*:

To V. F. Kommissarzhevskaya

Moscow. Nov. 13, 1900.

The Three Sisters is completed, but its future, at least its immediate future, is obscure to me. The play turned out dull, verbose, and awkward. I say awkward because it has only four female rôles, and its mood is duller than dull. Your artists would not take to it if I sent it to them at the Alexandra Theatre. Nevertheless, I shall send it to you. Read it and let me know if it would be a good idea to take it on tour for the summer.

Letters of Anton Chekhov, in *Letters on the Short Story, Drama and Other Literary Topics,* by Anton Chekhov, edited by Louis S. Friedland, Minton, Balch, 1924, pp. 115-63.

afraid of: death. The departed, the unloved, the disappointed—all these are pale imitations of true oblivion. Soliony is the darkest cloud of all.

Three Sisters is enigmatic—it would be hard to say just how the last speeches should be played—sadly, bitterly?—as a kind of cosmic, ridiculous joke? Realistically?—as if in the face of hopelessness it were possible to conceive a Utopia? Only *Hamlet* offers so many unresolved possibilities. Could the doctor have saved Tuzenbach in the last act? Does he let him die to ensure his own continuing relationship to Irena? Is there a homosexual undercurrent in the relationship between Soliony and Tuzenbach? It was suggested in the Olivier-Bates version of the play. Is the trio of Irena's suitors—the doctor, Soliony, and Tuzenbach—an ironic, or merely an instrumental little mirror-play of the sisters themselves, trio for trio? Is Vershinin's vision of the world to come just another more cosmic version of the never-to-be-attained Moscow of Irena's dreams? There are overtones and undertows. More clearly than in any of Chekhov's other plays, fantasy imbues consciousness with a strength similar to the power of dreams in the unconscious. The play teeters on an ambiguity: if coming to terms with reality is a sign of psychological maturity, philosophy offers a contrary alternative: in letting go of an ideal, the sisters may be depriving themselves—or are being deprived—of the one thing that makes life worth living.

These positive-negative aspects of the play are not easily resolved. Ambivalence enriches the action but fogs the ending. The problems *Three Sisters* raises have been presented to us with a complexity that allows for no easy solutions. Yet the curtain has to come down, the audience depart. And Chekhov, almost up to the last moment, keeps adding complications. In spite of its faultless construction, or because of it, the play is full of

surprises. Andrei's moving and unexpected speech about Natasha's vulgarity, for instance. He knows how awful she is, and yet he loves her, and can't understand why—an unusual, and far from simpleminded, admission.

The sisters long to accomplish the opposite of what they achieve, to become the contrary of what they are. Masha is most honest about this and most hopeless; she cannot console herself with the optimistic platitudes of Irena or shore herself up with the resigned Puritanism of Olga. Irena is about to rush off to her brick factory and Olga to her schoolroom. Masha lives with and within herself—a black person in a black dress, beautiful, loving, without joy. *Three Sisters,* in spite of its ambiguously worded life-may-be-better-in-the-future ending, might properly be subtitled, "Three Ways of Learning to Live without Hope." It is a drama of induced stupors and wounds and its tagged-on hopefulness is the one thing about it that doesn't ring true. People use each other in the play sentimentally, desperately, and, finally, fatally, and there is no reason to assume that, given the choice, they will ever do anything else.

What we hear in *Three Sisters* are the twin peals of longing and departure. They are amplified by human ineptitude, human error, human weakness. And behind them we hear the clangings of the extreme: the childish, the monstrous, the insane. The Brahmsian overcast of sadness that darkens the action—little outbursts of joy and gaiety always too soon stifled or abandoned—helps to make what is essentially a terrible indictment of life bearable. Sadness is at least not hopelessness. A play of girlhood, it is a play of loss, but not only feminine loss, though that strikes the deepest note. The drums and fifes offstage, the batteries that occasionally go off, the gambling house and the office—male institutions and trimmings—are shadowy and have nothing of the power and the immediacy of preparations for a meal, the giving of gifts, the temperature of a nursery—the force of the domestic, whether frustrated and virginal, or fulfilled and turning sour. A play about women—men are strangely absent even in the moment of their presence—its author clearly saw what lay at its most profound level: helplessness, a real, social, or contrived trait associated with, and sometimes promulgated by, women. Social class and the accident of sex work hand in hand to defeat desire and ambition. Watchers watching life go by, a stately frieze longing for the activity of movement, that is the central image of *Three Sisters.* Not so much "If we had only known . . ." as "If we could only *move* . . ." Temperament, breeding, upbringing fix the sisters to separate stakes. They go on, hoping for the best, getting the worst, which is, in their case, to stay exactly as they were.

Karl D. Kramer   (essay date 1981)

SOURCE: "*Three Sisters,* Or Taking a Chance on Love," in *Chekhov's Great Plays: A Critical Anthology,* edited by Jean-Pierre Barricelli, New York University Press, 1981, pp. 61-75.

[*In the essay below, Kramer traces "the variety of responses to love" among the main characters of* Three Sisters.]

For all the talk about **Three Sisters,** it is still extraordinarily difficult to determine exactly what the play is about. One prominent school places the emphasis on the sisters as inevitably ruined creatures. Beverly Hahn, for instance, speaks of the "inbuilt momentum towards destruction" in the sisters' world.[1] Another commentator claims that we cannot avoid contrasting the success of Natasha and Protopopov with the failures of the sisters.[2] We might do well to examine just what the first two do achieve: a house, an affair, and a businesslike manipulation of the professional positions of the others. It would, of course, be absurd to suggest that the sisters have in some way failed because they do not aspire to such heights of crass avarice as Natasha and Protopopov. But there is still the claim that the sisters continually yearn for a quality of life that they do not possess, and yet do very little, if anything, to make their dreams come true. Chekhov invited this response by initiating the to Moscow line. That goal remains unattained, while the desires of Natasha and Protopopov are richly fulfilled. This seems to present an opposition between those who get what they want and those who don't, as if the goals were equivalent, but abilities not. Natasha wants the big house on the hill and a union with the man who runs things in town—the boss. These may be attainable prizes, and certainly Natasha does wrestle their house away from the sisters, but the sisters never really enter into combat with her over such issues. If they did, they would themselves be transformed into first-class Natashas, an extremely dubious achievement at best. Natasha sees living in the big house at the top of the hill as an end in itself. The sisters' aspirations go considerably beyond this. Moscow as destination is equally illusory. Natasha, incidentally, isn't even up to that aspiration on the fanciful scale; she's quite content with a good view in a city much like Perm. The questions the sisters seek answers to are considerably more basic: how to seize and properly evaluate one's own experience, how to cope with experience, and when all one's delusions have been cast aside how to go on somehow from there. The particular area of experience around which the majority of the action in the play revolves is the question of love. The stance of nearly every character is determined by his ability to establish a close relationship with another. Love gone awry is in most instances the pattern. Ol'ga seems to have the least chance of finding a mate—a situation to which she has become largely reconciled, though in Act I she chides Masha for failing to value the man she does have. Kulygin himself—aware of the failure of his own marriage—pathetically suggests to Ol'ga in the third act that if he hadn't married Masha, he would have married her. Irina ultimately admits that her desire to reach Moscow is directly connected with her desire to find her true love. Masha is the only one of the sisters who does at least temporarily find real love, and in this sense her experience is the standard against which the experience of nearly all the other characters is to be measured. Chebutykin once loved their mother but has long since lost that love, and with

it his involvement in actual experience. Solenyy, on the other hand, capitalizes on his inability to inspire love by deliberately creating hostile relationships. But to determine the structure of the play as a whole and the way in which the experience depicted adds up to a statement about human capabilities, we must look in considerably more detail at the variety of responses to love among the main characters.

It is Andrey's fate to make the most ghastly miscalculation of them all in believing he loves Natasha. How could he, an educated man, brought up in the same environment as his sisters, believe he has fallen in love with her? Masha in the first act discounts the possibility that he could be serious about her. The answer seems to lie in a recognition that he has been constantly living under pressures he can't bear. "Father . . . oppressed us with education. . . . I grew fat in one year after he died, as if my body were liberated from his oppression," he tells Vershinin.[3] He has been preparing for a university career, bowing to his father's wishes—a course he abandons immediately after his marriage. Since the father's death, Andrey has been under constant pressure from his sisters to deliver them from this provincial town. His love for Natasha is simply a means of escaping these various responsibilities, which have been thrust upon him. But a relationship based on such motivation becomes a trap from which Andrey desperately wishes to escape. In some dialogue that Chekhov eventually deleted from the play, Andrey dreams of losing all his money, being deserted by his wife, running back to his sisters, crying, "I'm saved! I'm saved!"[4] In the finished play, Andrey and Chebutykin argue about the efficacy of marriage, Andrey maintaining it is to be avoided, Chebutykin asserting loneliness is worse. But by the end of the play, even Chebutykin admits that the best course for Andrey is to leave, "leave and keep going, don't ever look back" (XI, 295). This is, indeed, the course Chebutykin himself adopts at the end of the play. Andrey's escape from responsibility through love thus seems to lead only to an entrapment from which he would be only too happy to flee by the end of the play. His predicament stems not so much from Natasha's nature as from his own desire to avoid experience by hiding behind a very illusory kind of love.

Chebutykin's problems turn equally on love. He had at one time known a real love for the sisters' mother. That has long been in the past, but the only vaguely positive way he can deal with immediate experience is by the illusion that this love can be sustained through his relationship with the sisters, particularly Irina. His other protective screen is his growing insistence that nothing and nobody really exists and that therefore nothing matters. In his first appearance at stage center, he is talking sheer nonsense about a remedy for baldness and duly noting down this trivia. Shortly thereafter in Act I he displays his tender—almost sentimental—affection for Irina by presenting her with a silver samovar on her name day. The fact that the silver samovar is the traditional gift on the twenty-fifth wedding anniversary surely suggests that he is honoring the memory of the woman he loved and is exploiting the occasion of Irina's name day

Olga Knipper as Masha in Three Sisters.

for this purpose. During the first two acts he alternates between these two poles—the attempt to sustain a lost love and an abiding interest in trivia. The chief sign of the latter is his constant reading of old newspapers, a device for distracting himself from the actuality of the present moment.

In Act III his failure to handle his experience reaches a crisis when, drunk, realizing he is responsible for the death of a woman who was under his care, he retreats into a pretense that nothing and nobody exists. It may be a measure of his feeling that he so retreats, but I would suggest that he associates this recent death with that death in the past of the woman he loved. Death has denied him his love, and the recent event vividly reminds him of his own earlier loss. Within moments of this breakdown he smashes the clock which had belonged to the sisters' mother. This may of course suggest that he is trying to destroy time itself, which separates him from his love, but he is also deliberately destroying a material object that belonged to her; it may also be a gesture of denial—a denial that his love ever existed. He tries to

cover this by suggesting that perhaps there was no clock to break, and he accuses the others of refusing to see that Natasha and Protopopov are having an affair. The assumption is that if others don't see what's right before their eyes, why shouldn't Chebutykin refuse to recognize anything in the world that may hurt him? In any case, what comes out of this episode is our discovery that Chebutykin cannot deal with a death that takes away his love. His final stance in the play—"The baron is a fine fellow, but one baron more or less, what difference does it make?" (XI, 294)—is a pathetic indication of the lengths he is driven to in trying to cope with a love long since lost.

Solenyy is the only character in the play who turns away from love—turns away so completely that he commits himself to murder instead. He has an uncanny knack for turning a situation that is initially friendly into one of enmity. In Act II Tuzenbakh attempts to bury the hatchet with Solenyy, who immediately denies that there is any animus between them, thus provoking an argument and indirectly testifying to the correctness of Tuzenbakh's view of their relationship. Their discussion ends with

Solenyy's "Do not be angry, Aleko" (XI, 271), which distorts Tuzenbakh's friendly overtures into a rivalry, presumably over Irina. Dissatisfied in his exchange with Tuzenbakh, Solenyy seizes upon the first opportunity for further quarrel. Chebutykin enters, regaling Irina with an account of a dinner given in his honor. He is particularly pleased with the *chekhartma* (lamb). Solenyy insists that *cheremsha* (an onion) is totally disagreeable. This pointless argument ends with a victory on Chebutykin's side when he says: "You've never been to the Caucasus and have never eaten *chekhartma*" (XI, 271). Chebutykin is the clear victor here, because Solenyy prides himself on being a reincarnation of Lermontov, the nineteenth-century Russian romantic poet whose setting is regularly the Caucasus Mountains. To suggest that Solenyy has never been there totally undercuts his stance as a hero in the Lermontov mold. Having lost the argument with Chebutykin, Solenyy immediately proceeds to avenge himself in the best Lermontov tradition by picking a quarrel with Andrey over the number of universities in Moscow.

It is true that he declares his love for Irina toward the close of Act II, but one senses that he had expected a cool reception from her. In any case, the scene ends with what seems to be Solenyy's real message—that he will brook no rivals. To put it another way, Solenyy employs his declaration of love to establish a hostile relation with Tuzenbakh. We might also view the episode as a parody of the opening scene in Act II, where Vershinin declares his very real love to Masha. The initial exchange between Masha and Solenyy in the first act suggests that we are to view them as polar extremes in some sense. Solenyy's first speech implies a $1 + 1 = 3$ equation: "With one hand I can lift only fifty-five pounds, but with two hands I can lift a hundred and eighty—two hundred, even. From that I deduce that two men aren't twice as strong, they're three times as strong as one man . . . or even stronger . . ." (XI, 244). Masha's opening speech implies a retort to Solenyy: "In the old days, when Father was alive, there'd be thirty or forty officers here on our name days, there was lots of noise, but today there's a man and a half . . ." (XI, 247). In view of the fact that the only officers present are Solenyy, Tuzenbakh, and Chebutykin, Masha's equation is apparently $3 = 1.5$. Solenyy immediately picks up on this banter, if that's what it is, and compares one man philosophizing with two women trying to philosophize, the latter being equal to sucking one's thumb. Masha thereupon cuts him off: "And what is that supposed to mean, you terribly dreadful man?" (XI, 247). This exchange between Masha and Solenyy in the opening moments of *Three Sisters* is a vitally important one because, on the question of love, they represent polar extremes within the play: Masha is willing to take a chance on love; Solenyy can only capitalize on love as a pretense for a duel.

The wooing scenes between Vershinin and Masha are masterpieces in Chekhov's whimsical art. The process is initiated in the first act as Ol'ga and Irina laugh together over recollections of Moscow. It is Masha who suddenly pins down a real moment of connection in their lives when she recalls that they used to tease Vershinin as the lovesick major. In the first of his rather protracted philosophical speeches, Vershinin offers a justification for existence in response to Masha's statement that the sisters' lives will go unnoticed. She immediately responds to his attention by announcing she'll stay to lunch after all. This exchange initiates that special relationship between them. Shortly after this, Vershinin offers Masha another view with which she must be wholly in sympathy: ". . . if I were to begin life over again, I wouldn't get married. . . . No! No!" (XI, 254). This is the precise moment Chekhov chooses for Kulygin's entrance.

In Act II, Vershinin's speech on what life will be like in two or three hundred years is clearly directed toward Masha; indeed, his philosophical ramblings are primarily a way of wooing her. She understands this and laughs softly during his speech. Tuzenbakh is clearly not privy to this particular form of lovemaking. He believes he is engaged in a serious discussion with Vershinin and cannot understand why Masha is laughing. Vershinin, of course, has no reason to ask. It is interesting to note, incidentally, that in his musings about the future Vershinin almost never responds to Tuzenbakh's attempts to join in the discussion. Indeed, Chekhov revised the text of *Three Sisters* at a number of points to eliminate Vershinin's responses to Tuzenbakh's remarks.[5] In the first act Tuzenbakh announces Vershinin's arrival to the assembled company; Vershinin ignores the introduction and proceeds to identify himself by name. In his first monologue on the future, Vershinin dismisses Tuzenbakh's attempt to enter the discussion with a curt "Yes, yes, of course" (XI, 251). In the musings about life in two or three hundred years in Act II, Vershinin suggests the theme and Tuzenbakh offers his opinion about the future. Vershinin is apparently ruminating on his own views as Tuzenbakh speaks—the stage direction reads: *After a moment's thought* (XI, 266). His subsequent remarks bear no relation to Tuzenbakh's; we get the distinct impression the Vershinin has not the slightest interest in a debate, thus emphasizing the real motive for his musings, to converse indirectly with Masha. The ostensible discussion continues with Masha's observations on the necessity for meaning in life:

> It seems to me a man must believe, or search for some belief, or else his life is empty, empty. . . . To live and not know why the cranes fly, why children are born, why there are stars in the sky. . . . Either you know what you're living for, or else it's all nonsense, hocus-pocus.
>
> (XI, 267)

In effect, her words confirm her need for the kind of reassurance Vershinin has been offering her, that what man is presently doing is creating the possibility for future happiness and understanding. Vershinin's next line— "Still it's a pity our youth has passed" (XI, 267)—is almost a reproach to Masha: since youth has passed and each of them is set in his respective relationship, their mutual happiness is impossible for any protracted period of time. Masha greets his reproval with the famous line from Gogol': "It's dull in this world, gentlemen." Tuzenbakh, not comprehending the private dialogue, answers with a paraphrase of Masha's reference to Gogol', expressing his frustration over a conversation he was never meant to follow. Chebutykin does apparently follow at least the drift of the conversation—love—as he notes that Balzac was married in Berdichev. Irina, either consciously or unconsciously, picks up on this drift as she repeats Chebutykin's observation. Tuzenbakh, now attentive to one strand in the discussion—what can we do with our lives?—announces he's leaving the service. Having argued that life will always be pretty much the same, he now asserts that he will change the direction of his own. This is an important aspect of that contradiction of position so characteristic of Tuzenbakh and Vershinin. It is highly ironic that Vershinin consistently denies there is any happiness for us now, while achieving at least a momentary happiness with Masha. Tuzenbakh, on the other hand, argues that he is happy right now, in his love for Irina, while he is denied any return of that love. Masha, characteristically, disapproves of his determination to change, feeling herself denied any such opportunity.

In the third act, Vershinin's musings on life in the future are a direct response to Masha's arrival on the scene. After Chebutykin's rather shocking references to Natasha having an affair, perhaps partly to distract everyone's attention from the assumption that he and Masha are, too, Vershinin launches into a peroration on what his daughters have yet to go through in their lives. When Masha enters, he almost immediately shifts theme from daughters to life in the future, as though the topic has already become a secret code between them. His musings are intermixed with his laughter and expressions of happiness. Everybody has fallen asleep except Masha and Vershinin, making clear that his philosophizing *is* a way of talking about love. The episode ends with their strange love duet from Chaykovskiy's *Yevgeniy Onegin*.

Near the end of the third act Masha has her frank talk with her sisters. Ol'ga refuses to listen; Irina listens most attentively, as she presumably longs for a love of her own. Despite Ol'ga's disclaimers, Masha's confession of love brings the sisters closer together than they have been at any point in the play thus far and prepares the way for their final scene of coming together in the finale.

In the fourth act Masha speaks to Chebutykin of her love, implicitly comparing her own position with his at an earlier time:

MASHA: . . . Did you love my mother?

CHEBUTYKIN: Very much.

MASHA: Did she love you?

CHEBUTYKIN *after a pause*: That I don't remember anymore.

MASHA: Is mine here? That's the way our cook Marfa used to speak of her policeman: mine. Is mine here?

CHEBUTYKIN: Not yet.

MASHA: When you take happiness in snatches, in little pieces, and then lose it as I am, little by little you get coarse, you become furious. . . .

(XI, 293)

The ambiguity in Chebutykin's reply to Masha's question about her mother is remarkable. Is he trying to protect the honor of the woman he loved? Did she perhaps not return his love? Or is his reply part of his attempt to deny the past experience itself? We have no way of knowing. Masha's use of "mine" must refer to Vershinin, and Chebutykin so understands it. If he thought she were speaking of her husband, he could not reply "Not yet," for he has just seen Kulygin go in the house. Masha's remarks on happiness contain little joy, and yet she is admitting she has now known love, and the indications are that it will not turn her away from experience as it has Chebutykin. We shall see more of this in the finale.

As far as love is concerned, Irina would seem to be in the best position of the three sisters. She is unattached; two suitors pursue her; and yet she is unhappy because there is an imaginary third lover, whom she associates with Moscow. It is the dream of going to Moscow that animates her in the first act, and, although it is not clear why Moscow is so important to her at this point, it does become clear by the end of Act III. Still, there are hints, even in the opening scene, that it is love Irina seeks. When Tuzenbakh reports the arrival of the new battery commander, it is Irina who pricks up her ears, inquiring, "Is he old? . . . Is he interesting?" (XI, 244). Her desire to work looks like a second choice, and Tuzenbakh is at his most pathetic as he tries to ingratiate himself with her by sharing her desire for work: "That longing for work, Oh Lord, how well I understand it!" (XI, 245). Tuzenbakh seems to use the work theme to promote his standing with Irina in very much the way Vershinin talks of the future to woo Masha. Irina's cry at the end of Act II—"To Moscow! To Moscow! To Moscow!"—suggests that it is an appeal to love, if we look at the context out of which it arises. Solenyy has just made his rather ridiculous and thoroughly repulsive declaration of love to her; Vershinin has just returned bearing the news that his wife didn't poison herself after all; Kulygin is unable to find his wife; Natasha has just left with Protopopov; Ol'ga makes her first appearance in the act, complaining of professional responsibilities and of Andrey's gambling losses. Each situation suggests an abortive love relationship, including the absence of a love for Ol'ga. If all this is what provokes Irina's cry, it may well mean she is looking to Moscow for the kind of love that is simply unavailable to her here.

Her association of Moscow with love becomes explicit in the third act when she says: "I always expected we would move to Moscow, and there I would meet my real one, I've dreamed of him, I've loved him. . . . But it seems it was all nonsense, all nonsense . . ." (XI, 285). In the final lines of Act II she agrees to marry the baron, but still wants to go to Moscow: ". . . only let's go to Moscow! I beg you, let's go! There's nothing on earth better than Moscow! Let's go, Olya! Let's go!" (XI, 288). These words come after Masha's declaration that she loves Vershinin and would seem to suggest that though Irina has agreed to marry Tuzenbakh, she looks forward to finding her real love elsewhere, as Masha has.

Ol'ga has had the least opportunity to find happiness through love, and yet Ol'ga seems to cope with her situation better than the other two. She has very nearly reconciled herself to a single life even at the opening of the play, and during the course of it she expresses her love in an entirely different fashion. We see her love in her readiness to help with both clothing and lodging for those who have been left homeless by the fire; we see it in her comforting Irina in the third act and in the way she silently acquiesces to Masha's love for Vershinin, as she steps aside to allow them their last moment alone together.

Finally, we must compare the situations at the opening of the play and at its end to gather some measure of just what the intervening experience has meant for the sisters, how it has altered their conceptions of human possibility. Harvey Pitcher has observed that the fourth act is very nearly an "inversion" of the first.[6] He lists any number of actions and situations that occur in Act I and again in altered form in the fourth. He makes a convincing argument for seeing the finale as a negation of most of the positive elements that appeared in the opening, but I think that in addition to such negations, we see a number of positive elements in the finale that invert the hopeless and desperate attitudes of the opening. In one sense, the play moves from both naïve faith and despair to a heightened awareness of possibilities in life and a more solidly rooted ability to endure. At the opening, the sisters are both physically and temporally separated; Ol'ga is primarily oriented to the past as she recollects the death of their father a year ago and comments on how the last four years at the high school have aged her. Irina disclaims any interest in this past, as she remarks to Ol'ga: "Why talk about it?" (XI, 243). She also shares some of Irina's naïve faith in a future in Moscow, but even Moscow is in part a past orientation; certainly for Ol'ga it must be, since she is the eldest and would have the clearest memory of what their life had been like there. Irina's Moscow, on the other hand, is the land of the future; she can look only forward to Moscow and to going to work. Masha restricts her observations to an occasional whistle, is not particularly interested in either Ol'ga's sense of the past or Irina's hopes for the future; she is, as she sees it, buried in a present without hope. When Ol'ga suggests that Masha can come up to Moscow every summer to visit them, Masha's only comment is to whistle, as if, knowing her own present, she recognizes Ol'ga's wishful thinking as a mere whistling in the wind. Perhaps Masha's only departure from a present orientation is her remark about her mother: "Just imagine, I've already begun to forget her face. Just as they won't remember us. They'll forget" (XI, 250). But even here she seems to exploit both past and future to affirm the worthlessness of present existence. Thus, at the opening the sisters are totally at odds, as they contemplate three different perceptions of reality. Perhaps the only common strain here is their shared dissatisfaction with the present.[7] Spatially, there is some sense of their occupying a restricted area, particularly with Ol'ga, who either sits at her desk correcting papers or walks to and fro about the room. Even Masha seems initially restricted to her couch. Temperamentally, they are also separated from one another here, each involved in her own activity—Ol'ga correcting, Masha reading, Irina lost in thought, their dresses dark blue, black, and white.

Ol'ga's opening speech is full of strands connecting past, present, and future:

> Father died exactly a year ago on this very day, the fifth of May, your name day, Irina. It was very cold then, snow was falling. I thought I couldn't bear it, you lay in a dead faint. But a year has passed and we remember it easily; you're wearing a white dress now, your face is radiant. *The clock strikes twelve.* And the clock was striking then. *Pause.* I remember, when they were carrying Father, there was music playing and they fired a volley at the cemetery.

(XI, 242-43)

The play opens with the recollection of a death, just as it will end with the news of a death at the present moment. At the same time, Ol'ga's recollection of death is associated with birth; it is also Irina's name day. Ol'ga's reflections next focus the difficulty of facing the loss of a father whom both Ol'ga and Irina presumably loved, but, as if in anticipation of their stance at the end of the play, Ol'ga notes that they did survive the calamity. In short, Ol'ga's speech is a kind of summary of their reactions to calamitous experience: it is both unendurable and endurable, and calamity itself is mixed with elements of joy. The contrast between the weather a year ago and the weather today ("sunny and bright") underscores a recurrent cycle of anguish and joy. The funeral music of the military band of a year ago will be transformed at the end of the play into music that is played "so gaily, so eagerly, and one so wants to live" (X, 303).

The process of redressing natural relationships which were at the very least strained in Act I gets under way near the end of Act III. First, there is Masha, who refused to join in the sisters' conversation at the opening. In Act III she draws the sisters together, although against Ol'ga's better judgment, in her frank discussion of her love for Vershinin. This is followed shortly by Andrey's confession to at least two of his sisters that he is desperately unhappy, which constitutes a considerably more honest response to the family than his rapid departure from the scene as early as possible in Act I. The setting in Act IV is the garden attached to the house. On the one hand, it is true that Natasha dominates the house, but at the same time, if we recall that sense of the sisters' confinement in the living room of Act I, there is a compensatory feeling of openness in Act IV. The garden is unquestionably preferable to the living room now, and one is uncertain whether the sisters have been evicted or liberated—perhaps a combination of the two. The final tableau certainly contrasts the separation the sisters felt in the opening scene with their physical closeness at the end—*"The three sisters stand nestled up to one another"* (XI, 302). But the physical closeness reflects a far more basic sense of unity. Harvey Pitcher has quite justly commented on this scene: "The sisters feel perhaps closer to one another now than they have ever done before."[8] In the departure of the regiment and the death of Tuzenbakh, they give themselves to one another as they have not done earlier. They give themselves to their love for one another and discover a strength in this to endure.

Masha has the first of the sisters' final speeches, and I would like to look at her words, not as they are printed in texts today, but as they appear in Chekhov's original version of the speech, which, unfortunately in my view, has never been restored to the play. The speech was cut at the request of Ol'ga Knipper, who found the lines difficult to speak.[9] It would appear that Chekhov silently acquiesced. I've indicated the deleted lines by brackets:

> Oh, how the music is playing! They are leaving us, one has really gone, really and forever; and we'll stay here alone to begin our lives anew. I shall live, sisters! We must live. . . . [*Looks upward.* There are migratory birds above us; they have flown every spring and autumn for thousands of years now, and they don't know why, but they fly and will fly for a long, long time yet, for many thousands of years—until at last God reveals to them his mystery. . . .][10]

The reference to migratory birds connects a series of images that run through the play and that have two reference points for their meaning. The first is the rather familiar metaphor of birds' flight as man's passage through life. Irina is the first to use the image in Act I: "It's as if I were sailing with the wide blue sky over me and great white birds floating along" (XI, 245). Chebutykin picks up on this metaphor in Act IV when he tells Irina: "You have gone on far ahead, I'll never catch up with you. I'm left behind like a migratory bird which has grown old and can't fly. Fly on, my dears, fly on and God be with you" (XI, 291). Chebutykin makes the metaphorical meaning clear here: he may be too old a bird to continue the flight himself, but Irina must of necessity be engaged in her passage through life. Shortly after this Masha refers to the birds, apparently with reference to Vershinin: "When Vershinin comes, let me know. . . . *Walks away.* Migratory birds are leaving already. . . . *Looks upward.* Swans, or geese. . . . My dear ones, my happy ones . . ." (XI, 294). Like Chebutykin, Masha here refers to others whose lives go on, but in her final speech her "we must live" is connected with the bird imagery so that it becomes a positive image for her as well; her life—the life of all the sisters—will go on.

There is a second reference point for her speech, however, and that occurs in Act II when Tuzenbakh, as well, invokes the image. It comes in the midst of that scene in which Vershinin muses about the future, as a way of

wooing Masha—a scene in which Tuzenbakh is largely left out of the proceedings. He says: "Migratory birds, cranes, for instance, fly and fly and whatever great thoughts or small may wander through their heads, they'll go on flying, knowing neither where nor why. They fly and will fly whatever philosophers may appear among them; and let them philosophize as much as they like, so long as they go on flying . . ." (XI, 267). Masha's last speech is equally a tribute to Tuzenbakh. In paraphrasing his lines she both acknowledges his conception of experience and reconciles it with her own point of view, that eventually we must have some understanding of why we do what we do. Irina's betrothed—whatever the degree of affection she may have had for him—has just died. Masha has just parted with the man she loves, but she transforms their shared sorrow into a virtual panegyric to Tuzenbakh and finds in it a reason why the sisters must go on living.[11] In any case, the sisters have clearly come a long way from that point a year before the play began when death seemed unendurable.

In Ol'ga's final speech she answers that remark of Masha's in Act I—"they'll forget us too"—when she says: ". . . They'll forget us, forget our faces, our voices, and how many of us there were, but our sufferings will be transformed into joy for those who live after us, happiness and peace will reign on the earth and they will remember with a kind word and bless those who are living now" (XI, 303). Essentially, she is reiterating Masha's appeal that we must go on living because the experience is worth the effort, and reaffirming that the purpose will be revealed in the future. But whether it is or not, the continuation of living is essential.

The sisters' final speeches are interspersed with Chebutykin's nihilistic observations on the total indifference of the universe to anything that happens. The interchange may be read as an ultimately ambivalent attitude toward the nature of experience, or it may be read as a final tribute to the sisters' faith. They have not retreated to Chebutykin's fatalism, though their experience of love has been no more encouraging. The final interchange between Chebutykin and the sisters may suggest not an either/or response to life, but a measure of their capacity for endurance. After all, love is largely a matter of faith.[12]

NOTES

[1] *Chekhov: A Study of the Major Stories and Plays* (New York: Cambridge Univ. Press, 1977), p. 289. Hahn also offers a representative discussion of Natasha's role in ruining the sisters (p. 301).
[2] Harvey Pitcher, *The Chekhov Play: A New Interpretation* (New York: Harper and Row, 1973), p. 123.
[3] A. P. Chekhov, *Polnoye sobraniye sochineniy i pisem* (Moscow: Ogiz, 1944-51), XI, 253. Further references to the play will be cited by volume and page number in the text.
[4] *Literaturnoye nasledstvo: Chekhov,* ed. V. V. Vinogradov et al. (Moscow: Akademiya Nauk, 1960), LXVIII, 69.
[5] In *Literaturnoye nasledstvo* two earlier redactions of the play are included (pp. 1-87; see esp. pp. 27, 30, and 41.)
[6] *The Chekhov Play,* pp. 119-20.
[7] See J. L. Styan, *Chekhov in Performance: A Commentary on the Major Plays* (Cambridge: Cambridge Univ. Press, 1971), p. 162, for some further comments on the sisters' temporal orientation.

[8] *The Chekhov Play,* p. 151.
[9] See A. R. Vladimirskaya's introduction to the two earlier redactions of *Three Sisters* in *Literaturnoye nasledstvo,* pp. 13-14.
[10] *Literaturnoye nasledstvo,* p. 86.
[11] To delete the majority of Masha's final remarks may be a tribute to Chekhov's admiration, even love, for Ol'ga Knipper, but I see no reason why modern directors need bow to the actress' difficulties. They might well consider restoring this crowning link in the play's bird imagery.
[12] Many of the views expressed in this essay have emerged from interchanges between director, actors, and myself during work on a production of *Three Sisters* in Seattle in the summer of 1978 by the Intiman Theatre Company, Margaret Booker, artistic director.

Marina Majdalany (essay date 1983)

SOURCE: "Natasha Ivanovna, the Lonely *Bourgeoise,*" in *Modern Drama,* Vol. XXVI, No. 3, September 1983, pp. 305-09.

[*In this essay, Majdalany mounts a defense of Natasha Ivanovna in* Three Sisters, *in an effort to arrive at a more balanced interpretation of the character than the merely selfish and predatory figure she is commonly considered.*]

Whilst all commentators of Chekhov's play dwell at length upon the aesthetic longings of the three sisters, and tenderly evoke their sensitivity bruised by frustration, no comparable sympathy is extended to Natasha, their brother's young wife.[1] She is indeed as vain, selfish and even ruthless as she has been categorized; but what all these attributions have crowded out is the fact that first and foremost she is a disoriented *petite bourgeoise,* socially insecure and lonely in an alien and hostile environment.

To maintain objectivity, the critic must resist the temptation to redress the balance by tilting it in Natasha's favour. She is no more a flawless heroine than any of her sisters-in-law, but she deserves a fair appraisal. Natasha should be examined as an individual with feelings and attitudes which, although they may lack subtlety and charm, still have a right to our understanding and a claim on our compassion. Yet, what invariably seems to happen is that she is criticized as the sisters' antagonist, who she is in a sense, and it is not taken into account that the source of the conflict resides in a personal and social incompatibility for which all four women must share equal responsibility.

Harvey Pitcher comes close to explaining the reason for the general indictment of Natasha when he writes: "Everyone has always agreed that Natasha is an odious character and that to dislike her thoroughly is only right and proper. But there is such an impatient desire to find someone to blame in the *Three Sisters,* such a gleeful rush to castigate Natasha for her most obvious failings, that comment on her has often been superficial."[2] Yet, even after this caveat, he goes on to say: "When the gauche and tastelessly dressed Natasha makes her belated appearance, the audience is inclined to share the sisters' scepticism."[3]

By whose standards is Natasha's attire tasteless? Further, is Masha's venomous outburst which introduces the girl to the audience a mere expression of scepticism? This indirect presentation sets the tone and indicates the nature of the antagonism between the parties, as we see the balance of power shifting to the final effective dominance of Natasha. Her raw physicality explodes through Masha's outburst: she is garish, loves brightly coloured clothes, those yellows and reds which have no status amid the sober monochromes adopted by the sisters. Her shiny cheeks, which "look as though they've been scrubbed" (p. 261), reinforce the image of red-blooded sexuality, that earthy vitality which stirs the pallid emotions of Andrey: "Oh, how young you are, Natasha, how wonderfully, beautifully young!" (p. 271).

Natasha makes her first entrance *"wearing a pink dress with a green belt."* Awkward among a social élite, upset at being late, eager to please, her reactions are perfectly natural: she looks at the mirror, tidies her dress, and goes in to kiss Irena. Feeling shy, she admits as much to Olga, who takes one look at her and responds: "(*Alarmed, dropping her voice.*) You've got a green belt on! My dear, that's surely a mistake!" The bewildered young woman is guileless enough to believe that Olga's dismay is due to some esoteric knowledge of the occult: "Why, is it a bad omen, or what?" (p. 268).

Far from sharing the sisters' scepticism, an unbiased audience gasps at what J. L. Styan accurately describes as "Olga's feline cruelty."[4] But even as he credits Olga with the unpleasantness she richly deserves, he hints that Natasha's behaviour is already indicative of vanity, deceit and hypocrisy. As for David Magarshack, this exchange provides him with the Chekhov-sent opportunity of proving Natasha's vindictiveness[5] when, at the end of Act IV, she tells Irena: "My dear, that belt you're wearing doesn't suit you at all" (p. 328). If this is vindictiveness, it is amply justified by the family's behaviour towards her in the intervening years. When she has not been ignored, she has been either slighted (by Masha, Toozenbach, Soliony) or reminded of her lowly background (by Olga, e.g., in Act III, patronizingly: "Please try to understand me, dear. . . . It may be that we've been brought up in a peculiar way, but . . ." [p. 297]).

The cumulative effect of this disregard would be sufficient to account for the change in Natasha's character and attitude "from the timid fiancée" to the "mistress of the household."[6] In observing this evolution, the audience should recognize that Natasha's "sins of commission" are balanced by the Prozorovs' "sins of omission." The asperities of her selfishness collide with the granite of their egotism: she is vulgar and strives to become genteel; they are refined and never even attempt to groom her understanding or her manners. She grasps, they withdraw; she pushes, they recoil. Maurice Valency, no admirer of Natasha, nevertheless concedes: "She becomes a despot . . . [b]ut . . . she also demonstrates such strength of character as the well-bred sisters are incapable of developing."[7]

Once married to Andrey, quite understandably Natasha would like to feel that her new status lends her some measure of authority, and therefore she resents being overlooked: "[T]hey tell me that some carnival party's supposed to be coming here soon after nine" (Act II, pp. 272-273). Clearly no one had bothered to consult her, and no woman, now or then, in England or in Russia, would not be vexed at such evidence of neglect. It is her wounded vanity, not (as Magarshack assumes) her Satanic nature, that makes her countermand the party. Nor must we see her wish to secure Irena's room for her son as the stealthy move of a "ruthless predator"[8]; rather, it instances another collision between pusher and push-over which indicts both, albeit for contrasting reasons.

Furthermore, when Natasha tells her husband of her plans for the room, does he try to safeguard his sister's rights? As Natasha pauses for an answer, Andrey remains silent; when she shakes him into replying, his reaction is as limp as his violin-playing: "I was just day-dreaming. . . . There's nothing to say, anyway . . ." (p. 273). A more incisive husband, a more resolute sister-in-law, could have scotched Natasha's rise to power; but thwarted though she is in her desire to belong, Natasha never faces opposition in her wilfulness to possess.

Despised by her sisters-in-law, bound to a man cocooned in meditation on his wasted life, not surprisingly Natasha embarks on an affair with the gallant Protopopov, a man of her own social class and, like her, brash and determined to succeed. Here again, critics' prejudice supersedes fairness: whilst Natasha's dalliance is censured, not a word condemns Masha's passion for Vershinin. For all Masha's extolled sensitivity, the callousness she displays towards the long-suffering Koolyghin is breath-taking, even by modern standards. When in Act III the poor cuckold exclaims: ". . . I'm so happy, happy, happy!", his listless wife humiliates him publicly by retorting: "And I'm so bored, bored, bored!" (p. 304). Yet, it is Masha's volatile sister-in-law who is stigmatized for betraying a man who refers to her chillingly as "a sort of mean, blind, thick-skinned animal—anyway, not a human being" (p. 318).

Natasha's sense of inferiority and her wish to overcome it are both sharpened by the contempt in which she is held, so overt that even Andrey notices it. Like many *petites bourgeoises* who have jumped ranks, Natasha smarts at any mode of behaviour suggestive of disrespect. Petty by nature, vulgar by upbringing, and strident in response to the hostility of her surroundings, the girl who in Act I did not retort to Olga's criticism of her belt, by Act III has deteriorated spiritually without having improved socially.

Natasha's treatment of Anfisa, whilst not defensible, highlights the negativism that pervades the entire family and makes the relationship between Natasha and the sisters one of confrontation. As Natasha enters the room, she addresses Olga in her usual garrulous manner and ends her prattle on a note of motherly apprehension.

Chekhov's significant stage direction follows: "OLGA (*without listening to her*) . . ." (p. 296). Ignored again, Natasha's pent-up exasperation needs an outlet, and the hapless Anfisa becomes the object of her resentment. Natasha's words are cheap and cruel—but what are we to make of Masha's silence? Instead of going out *"in a huff"* (p. 296), filled with loathing for the vulgar intruder, Masha would have served Anfisa better had she stood her ground and given Natasha a piece of her mind. It is left to Olga to reprimand the young woman, as much for having distressed the old servant as for having troubled her own nerves: "Any cruel or tactless remark, even the slightest discourtesy, upsets me . . ." (p. 297). Natasha's behaviour is indeed condemnable, but she is not used to dealing with servants in the benevolent, paternalistic manner natural to the upper classes. Styan points out that she belongs to "the new ruling class who will adjust the old order of master and serf to the new order of rich and poor. . . ."[9]

It is well known how Chekhov observed the social change that was taking place in Russia, of which the dominant feature was the emergence of the new commercial middle class, and dramatized it through Natasha and later, in **The Cherry Orchard,** through Lopakhin. Perhaps from an aesthetic point of view the playwright regretted the passing of an upper class whose leisure admitted of dreams and wistful hopes, whose life unfurled with the gracefulness of a slow-motion picture. The three sisters stand for potential that could no longer be fulfilled in a new Russia where the need for work was becoming imperative for survival, and the doom to which their aspirations are condemned elicits our sympathy. In contrast to their effete longings, the concrete demands advanced by Natasha lead Magarshack, for example, to see her as a "convincing figure of evil."[10] But she should be appraised rather as a young woman whose upbringing in a provincial town, among people with few claims to culture and refinement, has not equipped her to understand that material acquisitiveness need not be the sole aim in life. The contrast with her sisters-in-law heightens the opposition between those who fail to achieve and the woman who overachieves. Pitcher writes discerningly that "we can be quite sure that had Natasha suddenly taken it into her head to move to Moscow, she would have allowed nothing and no one to stand in her way."[11]

To the very end, Natasha's impatient vitality challenges the moribund ethos of her surroundings: "I'll tell them to put flowers all round here, lots of flowers . . ." (p. 328). Her decision to have the trees felled is cited as yet another sign of her destructive nature and insensitivity to the past (whereas no similar criticism is levelled against Lopakhin's parallel resolution). How could she be awed by the sanctity of tradition when nothing in her background nurtured such sentiments? She has been educated, it seems, because Chekhov wrote that his play had "four responsible female parts, four educated young women."[12] But she belonged originally to a class with no heirlooms, arboreal or otherwise, and is concerned more with forging a congenial new environment than with preserving old relics sapped of the life force. (Toozenbach observes in Act IV: "Look at that dead tree, it's all dried-up, but it's still swaying in the wind along with the others" [p. 321].)

Beverly Hahn writes that Natasha "seems to have no ideals at all"[13], a statement with which even the most impartial of commentators cannot quarrel. However, we must beware of confusing ideals, which demand a modicum of active participation, with dreams, which leave us free to do nothing whatever by way of commitment. Since dreams, not ideals, dominate the lives of the Prozorovs throughout the play, it is harsh to single out Natasha for her lack of vision.

Innocent of ideals, the *petite bourgeoise* to whom only Koolyghin has ever shown any courtesy is not short on determination: if she cannot be accepted, Natasha makes sure at least that no one will ever again laugh at her. The last we hear of her is her shout at the maid, an explosion of bad temper that precedes the slowly unwinding finale of the play, with the sisters grouped together in contemplation of their future. Natasha is so petty that she elevates the most trivial domestic shortcoming into a major catastrophe; the sisters are so oblivious to reality that even the death of Toozenbach, a friend and Irena's fiancé, is subsumed by their hazy longings. There is little to choose between these antithetical attitudes. It is inequitable to scorn the rages of Natasha whilst indulging the egotism of her sisters-in-law, which even a tragedy cannot dent. If we are moved by Masha's frustrations, Irena's yearnings, and Olga's lassitude, we should also spare a thought for the young girl who came to lunch in her best frock, stayed on as Andrey's wife, and was never shown anything but contempt and aversion by her new family and their friends.

NOTES

[1] All quotations from *Three Sisters* are taken from Anton Chekhov, *Plays*, trans. Elisaveta Fen (Harmondsworth, 1959).
[2] Harvey Pitcher, *The Chekhov Play: A New Interpretation* (London, 1973), p. 127.
[3] Ibid., p. 135.
[4] J. L. Styan, *Chekhov in Performance* (Cambridge, Eng., 1971), p. 178.
[5] David Magarshack, *The Real Chekhov* (London, 1972), pp. 138-139.
[6] William Gerhardi, *Anton Chekhov: A Critical Study* (London, 1923), p. 27.
[7] Maurice Valency, *The Breaking String* (New York, 1966), p. 219.
[8] Magarshack, pp. 140, 138.
[9] Styan, p. 201.
[10] Magarshack, p. 140.
[11] Pitcher, p. 125.
[12] Anton Chekhov, Letter to Olga Knipper, 15 September 1900.
[13] Beverly Hahn, *Chekhov: A Study of the Major Stories and Plays* (Cambridge, Eng., 1977), p. 278.

Nils Åke Nilsson (essay date 1988)

SOURCE: "*Three Sisters:* The Battle between Carnival and Lent," in *Canadian American Slavic Studies,* Vol. 22, Nos. 1-4, Spring-Summer-Fall-Winter 1988, pp. 369-75.

[*In the following essay, Nilsson examines images of festivity and celebration counterpoised by images of abstinence and deprivation in* Three Sisters.]

One of the rooms devoted to modern pre-revolutionary art in the Leningrad Russian Museum is dominated by a large painting by Boris Kustodiev called *Maslenitsa*. It was first shown at the *Mir iskusstva* Exhibition in January 1916 where it attracted general attention. Although painted in the midst of the war and at a time when the artist was suffering from an illness which was to keep him handicapped for the rest of his life, it presented the light and timeless world of Russian provincial towns and national holidays, a theme which was a speciality of his art.

Using pure and bright colors and different perspectival planes, the picture shows the *maslenitsa* celebrations in a small provincial town. In the foreground, on the hills surrounding the town, some couples are taking a sleigh ride while children play with snowballs. Below the hills, a crowd of people gathers around a merry-go-round and some *balaganchiki* at a marketplace. In the background the little town with its roofs and church cupolas is glittering in a frosty sunset.

Even though the sleighs are placed in the foreground, their passengers do not play any significant role. The center of the entire canvas is instead occupied by the colorfully painted back of one of the sleighs, an organization of the space which stresses the decorative impression of the whole picture.

Maslenitsa was purchased by the acquisition commission of the Academy of Art but there were objections to the decision. This, one member maintained, was not art, but *lubok*.[1] This was meant as criticism but *lubok* had, in fact, a positive ring in other art circles at this time. These peasant woodcuts and other types of folk art had already been used for some time by young painters as models for a Russian avant-garde art and by designers of ballet décor. The ornamental-decorative style of Kustodiev's painting is clearly connected with both genres.

In another section of the Russian Museum a painting is exhibited which, except for the same big size, at first glance seems to have little in common with Kustodiev's *Maslenitsa*. It is entitled *Monastyrskaia trapeza* (Monastery Refectory) and was painted in the years 1865-76 by V. G. Perov, a member of the *Peredvizhniki* (The Wanderers), known for his paintings of social criticism. Some monks are sitting at the dinner table covered with an elegant, white tablecloth. The middle of the painting is dominated by the contented face of a very fat monk, probably the abbot, with his hands folded across the belly. At the right side a pair of wealthy patrons are welcomed at the door. A beggar woman sitting on the floor stretches out her hand asking for alms.

The dinner is in progress, but the dishes are mostly hidden behind the monks' backs. Wine is served, however. One of the monks is leaning back, emptying his glass. On the left side a waiter is busy uncorking bottles, while one of the monks is urging him to hurry up with an impatient gesture. It is clearly a dinner of a special kind and it could very well be a celebration during the *maslenitsa*.

We have here two very different ways of illustrating such a festive moment. Kustodiev lavishly spends his colors, choosing pure, cheerful, harmonious ones. Perov's picture, on the other hand, is all in dark, sombre colors. In *Maslenitsa* there is action and movement over the whole canvas. Here are sleigh rides, playing children, a merry-go-round, people enjoying themselves in a marketplace, a flock of (probably) jackdaws descending in the air. In Perov's picture the center is static, dominated by the contented monk. His folded hands contrast with the gestures on the right side (the beggar's outstretched hand) and on the left (the monk's impatient gesture, the waiter's hands busy with the uncorking of the wine bottles).

Maslenitsa clearly has no realistic ambitions. A Russian provincial town usually made—judging from the evidence of, for instance Chekhov's stories—a gray and gloomy impression. Kustodiev has changed it into a fairytale fantasy. Perov follows the patterns of the *Peredvizniki*: painstaking realism, some psychological portraits, social satire. The satire does not lapse into the grotesque but it is heavily underlined by numerous small details: the fat abbot at the table, the pair arriving at the door (she an elegantly dressed portly lady, he a meagre old man, half a head smaller than his wife; a comical pair, in other words), the beggar woman, a supplicant who has thrown himself at the feet of the abbot, the monk emptying his glass, the pantomimic scene on the left between the waiter and one of the monks. These details have a narrative character and could be used as elements in a story. They threaten to break up the whole picture into small scenes. Yet it is kept together by the dominating dark colors which clearly have a symbolic function, suggesting a "realm of darkness" as a part of tsarist Russia.[2]

These two paintings seem to be perfect illustrations of what Bakhtin has to say about banquet images and the traditional opposition of Carnival and Lent in medieval literature. By presenting the provincial town as a kind of fairytale land, Kustodiev's picture changes everyday norms in a carnivalesque way. There is something of Brueghel's villages in the organization of the painting and in Kustodiev's ability to evoke the joy and activity of a popular holiday, although the grotesque elements are missing. But, as in Brueghel's scenes, this is also a festivity "for all the world": the sleighs are for the wealthy (one of the passengers is a military officer), the merry-go-round and the *balaganchiki* are for the common people and the snow for all children.

Perov's painting is first of all connected with popular medieval stories of gluttonous monks. In his book on Rabelais, Bakhtin quotes several examples of this tradition which lived on and, of course, spread to Russia as well. But the painting is also an illustration of how medieval and renaissance banquet images changed in the nineteenth century literature of realism; "It is no longer 'the banquet for all the world,' in which all take part, but an intimate feast with hungry beggars at the door."[3] While in the medieval popular-festive tradition eating and drinking were seen as something positive, it was now considered as typical of an egoistic bourgeois life.

Perov's monastery scene has, as we see, all the proper components: the closed doors, the alliance of the Church and the wealthy class, the beggars at the door, the contrast between the servile welcoming of the guests on one side of the picture and the treatment of the waiter on the other side.

In a general sense these two pictures represent two different approaches to the world, one positive, stressing that the essence of life is joy and an openness of all senses to the world, while the other is moralistic and dogmatic, reminding of the futility of human life and endeavor (as, above all, in medieval literature) or of the injustice of modern society (as in realist literature and art). The contrasting of such different views was earlier manifested in mock battles between Carnival and Lent. A French poem, quoted by Bakhtin, describes such a "dispute du Gras et Maigre"[4] and it is the theme of the well-known painting by Peter Brueghel the Elder (from 1559), *The Battle between Carnival and Lent*.

This picture is divided into two parts. On the left side, dominated by an inn, people in masks and funny clothes dance, eat and drink. On the right side people in dark robes gather at the gate of a church and distribute alms to beggars who in turn are totally ignored on the other side of the painting. In the foreground a fat man on a beer barrel, representing Carnival, performs the traditional mock battle with Lent, a pale and scrawny man seated on a prayer stool. In Kustodiev's *Maslenitsa* a carnivalesque spirit prevails but the sunset and the descending black jackdaws give a presentiment of what is coming. The satire of Perov's painting rests, of course, on the contrast between a traditional conception of the "lenten" régime of monasteries and the wine and daintily spread table.

* * *

In modern literature this old, traditional opposition takes on new and modern forms. Russian literature has one interesting example in which the mock battle turns into a very real one: Chekhov's ***Three Sisters***.

A well-known structural line of Chekhov's plays is the appearance of someone coming from the outside who upsets an established static order and changes the lives of the main protagonists in a tragic (Konstantin, Tuzenbakh), resigned (Uncle Vania, the three sisters) or still uncertain (Nina, Ania) direction. In ***The Seagull,*** it is the writer Trigorin, in ***Uncle Vania*** it it is professor Serebriakov, in ***The Cherry Orchard*** Lopakhin. ***Three Sisters*** has two lines of catastrophe, one leading to the death of Tuzenbakh, the other one to the triumph of *byt*; of petty bourgeois life.

Scene from the 1901 Moscow Art Theater production of Three Sisters. *Stanislavsky as Vershinin and Olga Knipper as Masha.*

In two plays this line is accompanied by the theme of eating and drinking. Upon arriving at the estate, Professor Serebriabov changes the usual routine of tea drinking and Russian national dishes and introduces a more "Western" order of cuisine. Uncle Vania's first reply describes this new order: "I sleep at odd hours, eat all sorts of spicy sauces for lunch and dinner, drink wine."[5] ***Three Sisters*** begins with a namesday party and the first act ends in the fun and merriment of the breakfast. The second act seems at first to continue this tonality of festivity. In her first replies Natasha mentions that "this is Shrovetide" (*teper' maslenitsa*).

It soon becomes clear, however, that she is not a herald of the carnival. On the contrary, *maslenitsa,* as she sees it, brings only trouble: "There is no sense of order about the servants, one must keep one's eyes open so nothing happens. Yesterday I passed the living room at midnight and there was a candle burning." She then turns to her husband and asks—in a rhetorical way—for his approbation of her idea not to let the Shrovetide mummers come to the house in the evening—they may disturb their child. A direct order follows: "I've ordered clabber for dinner. The doctor says you ought to have nothing but clabber, or you'll never get thin."[6]

These decisions deprive the sisters and their friends of the traditional merriments of the holiday. It is only Thursday, the *maslenitsa* week has only started and many days

are still ahead before Shrove Tuesday and Lent. But there will be no traditional food, nor any Shrovetide masks and songs, and Natasha will watch over what she thinks is the best order in the house. She appears as a "spirit of Lent." But this is not a mock battle in the sense of the medieval tradition but a real struggle for power and mastery of the house.

Who then is the other side, the defenders of a carnivalesque spirit? The sisters and the army officers gradually gather to have a pleasant evening, in celebration of the holiday. No excesses are planned for, however. In Brueghel's painting Lent's weapon in the battle is a baker's paddle with two herrings. Natasha has, as we have seen, made an attack with a similar weapon: the sour milk. Brueghel's Carnival in turn has a spit garnished with succulent pieces of meat. The sisters' answer, in true Russian tradition, should, in other words, be *bliny.*

The exuberance, typical of the holiday, is, however, alien to them (as it was to Chekhov himself; compare his satirical sketches on *bliny* eating).[7] This attitude of modesty and unpretentiousness is stressed from the very beginning. In the first act a silver samovar is offered to Irina as a namesday present by Chebutykin but it only makes the sisters embarrassed. The second act has another example. After Natasha's replies at the beginning of the act, introducing an atmosphere of Lent, Ferapont, bringing some papers from the city council to Andrei, tells a story about a Moscow merchant who died after eating *bliny* ("it was either forty or fifty, I do not remember"). Natasha's *prostokvasha* diet is contrasted to but also connected with Ferapont's *bliny*. Both are seen as examples of grotesque exaggeration.

The sisters and the officers have planned for a *vecher* together. There is tea and also chocolate and brandy. There will be music and dancing and the appearance of the Shrovetide mummers. But when Natasha makes her thrust under the pretext that her child is sick and may be disturbed, all surrender at once. Solenyi, who plays a carnivalesque jester, this evening more than before, is the only one who dares a counter-attack. When Natasha tries to convince him of the extraordinary abilities of her Bobik, he answers with a joke in true *maslenitsa* style: "If that child were mine, I would have fried him in a skillet and eaten him."[8]

But all leave the house and Natasha is encouraged to complete her triumph. She tells Irina that she must give up her room for Bobik. After this she goes for a sleigh ride with her husband's principal. She feels that she is already master of the house and that she now freely can show her true egoistic face behind the lenten mask. There is a further point here. Sleighing was a very typical pleasure of *maslenitsa* and, as Kustodiev's painting shows, a pleasure reserved for the rich people. Her partner is the head of the city council and she feels flattered. This Protopopov is one of those characters in Chekhov's play who do not appear on stage but have an important role in the background. He has been introduced right at the beginning when he sends a cake for Irina's namesday party. She dismisses it with a short comment which makes it very clear what she and the sisters think of him: "Thank you. Tell him I said thank you" (*Spasibo. Poblagodari.*). He is—the reader or spectator immediately understands—a perfect match for Natasha.

The two first acts abound, as we have seen, in food images, reaching their climax in the *maslenitsa* of the second act. But the act ends with the victory of Lent, pointing to coming months of abstinence and privation. The third act has no food images at all, not even tea-drinking is mentioned. But the central image here is fire, a fire which consumes, literally and symbolically: homes, property, lives and hopes. There is one exception to this general picture of losses: Natasha has now a second child.

The last act shows, as it were, a landscape devastated by fire. Two food images, small but not insignificant, accompany the general picture of desolation and resignation. The stage directions mention a table on the terrace on which glasses and empty bottles of champagne stand. Usually a sign of festivity and celebration, they here have a different and more ominous meaning. They are connected with a small scene at the very end of the act, the last appearance of Natasha. On a bench she suddenly discovers a fork and in a last demonstration of power before the sisters she attacks the housemaid: "Why is this fork laying here, I'd like to know?" (*"Zachem zdes' valiaetsia vilka, ia sprashivaiu?"*).[9]

Empty glasses and bottles, a fork left behind—memories, signs of a happy time spent together, now lost for ever.

NOTES

[1] M. Etkind, *Boris Kustodijew. Malerei. Zeichnung. Buchgraphik. Bühnenbild-Gestaltung* (Leningrad: Aurora-Kunstverlag, 1983), p. 263.
[2] The Leningrad Russian Museum also possesses a small sketch on the same subject, made the same year as the large one, 1876. Most of the realistic details (for instance, the beggar woman, the supplicant, the drinking monk) are absent here. From an artistic point of view, this version is superior, while retaining the message of social criticism, in a more subdued, yet still effective manner.
[3] Mikhail Bakhtin, *Rabelais and his World* (Bloomington: Indiana Univ. Press, 1984), p. 302.
[4] *Ibid.*, p. 298.
[5] Anton Chekhov, *Uncle Vanya,* in *Chekhov: The Major Plays,* trans. Ann Dunnigan (New York: Signet, 1964), p. 175.
[6] Anton Chekhov, *Three Sisters, ibid.,* p. 258.
[7] Nils Åke Nilsson, "Food Images in Chekhov: A Bakhtinian Approach," *Scando-Slavica,* 32 (1986), 29f.
[8] *Three Sisters,* p. 268.
[9] *Ibid.,* p. 241.

Gordon McVay   (essay date 1995)

SOURCE: "Introduction," in *Chekhov's Three Sisters,* Bristol Classical Press, 1995, pp. v-xxviii.

[*In the essay below, McVay draws on comments by Chekhov in his correspondence regarding art in general and* Three Sisters *specifically in order to illuminate the play.*]

Chekhov's richest and greatest play has inspired a bewildering variety of interpretations since its premiére at the Moscow Arts Theatre on 31 January 1901. ***Three Sisters*** (***Tri sestry***) has been viewed both as tragedy and as comedy, as a poignant testimony to the eternal yearning for love, happiness, beauty, and meaning, or as a devastating indictment of the folly of inert gentility and vacuous daydreaming. Its characters have been deemed worthy embodiments of the universal 'human condition', keenly experiencing hope, disappointment, frustration, loneliness, and the passage of time—or passive products of pre-revolutionary Russian privilege, remnants fit only for the scrap-heap of history.

That the play has proved puzzling is hardly surprising, since Chekhov constantly shunned overt subjectivity and didacticism in his writings, just as he avoided ostentatious self-revelation in his personal life. Both as author and as man he appreciated the virtue of modesty and restraint. Like other plays of Chekhov's maturity, ***Three Sisters*** is multi-faceted and open-ended, rich in psychological and atmospheric nuance. To discern the dramatist's intentions requires—from reader and audience, director and cast—a corresponding delicacy of perception.

Detailed analysis of the text itself is of paramount importance. . . . Yet, since the play was not created by an automaton in a vacuum, it will be instructive first to consider briefly the author and his literary practice.

I

The outer facts of Chekhov's life are well established, thanks to his voluminous correspondence, the memoirs of relatives and acquaintances, and the efforts of scholars. Evidence suggests that, besides being a brilliantly innovative and subtle writer, he was also an unusually admirable person. Whereas other 'great' Russian authors incline to excess, with elements of neurosis and *folie des grandeurs* (Lermontov, Gogol, Dostoevsky, Tolstoy), Chekhov presents a remarkably unified and balanced personality, devoid of rhetoric and megalomania. In a land of preachers and partisans, he persistently refused to pontificate, with the result that he was often reviled for 'lack of principles' and absence of philosophical or political purpose. These charges worried him, although his life might serve as a model of positive practical endeavour. Despite his own ill-health,[1] he supported his family, treated peasants for their everyday ailments and at times of famine and cholera, planted trees, built schools, donated books to the Taganrog library, and performed innumerable undemonstrative acts of kindness.

There is an understandable temptation to regard Chekhov as a saintly figure, the gentle seer with tired, compassionate smile, pince-nez and blood-flecked beard. Yet, while not denying its attractiveness, virtually all biographers are struck by the 'elusiveness' of Chekhov's personality. His reticence may be interpreted as aloofness or detachment; his oft-repeated call for 'objectivity' as a writer may signify indifference; his playfully bantering tone in letters to enamoured females may betoken evasiveness and insensitivity; his gregariousness masks his loneliness; his concern may conceal an inner cold.

Some of these suspicions or accusations are not wholly without foundation. Chekhov devoted his limited energy to family, friends, creative work and charitable enterprise. It may well be that his equanimity and the early onset of his illness deprived him prematurely of youth's enviable elation. At the same time, however, his acute sense of proportion and his awareness of life's transience enabled him to see the folly of self-aggrandisement, and the vanity of rank, power and worldly success. 'Real talents always sit in the shadows', he wrote in March 1886.

His natural reserve was intensified by the application of will-power and self-control, as he endeavoured to protect his privacy and inner freedom. It has become almost commonplace to dub Chekhov an 'enigma', and a consequent legend has arisen of his total inscrutability. The fact remains, however, that the gregarious writer and doctor was usually surrounded by family and friends, and maintained a copious correspondence in addition to his output of stories and plays.

For a person supposedly 'isolated from others by a kind of inability to communicate, an impenetrability',[2] Chekhov proves an amazingly prolific correspondent. Between 1875 and 1904 he wrote more than 4,500 letters.[3] While it has been remarked that these missives are seldom, if ever, 'confessional' (what else was he meant to 'confess'?), perhaps few people would disagree with the general assertion: 'Certainly the best source of information about the mind and soul of Chekhov, the man and the writer, is his own correspondence.'[4] Conversance with these letters may assist the reader to understand (or, at least, not grossly misunderstand) the essence of *Three Sisters.*

It was in 1888, towards the start of a two-year period of intense self-scrutiny, that Chekhov made his most famous pronouncement on truth and freedom:

> I'm afraid of people who try to read between the lines to find my 'tendency' and who will insist on viewing me as a liberal or conservative. I'm not a liberal, or a conservative, or a gradualist, or a monk, or an indifferentist. I should like to be a free artist and that's all, and I regret that God has not given me the strength to be one. I hate lies and violence of all kinds . . . My holy of holies is the human body, health, intelligence, talent, inspiration, love and the most absolute freedom imaginable, freedom from violence and lies, no matter what form these may take. That is the programme I would adhere to if I were a great artist . . .
>
> (*To A. N. Pleshcheev,* 4 October 1888)[5]

As the son of a despotic, provincial grocer and grandson of a serf, Chekhov was acutely conscious of the gulf between slavery and freedom. On one occasion, with apparent reference to his own painful evolution, he suggested as the theme for a short story the depiction of how a young man 'squeezes the slave out of himself drop by drop and then wakes up one fine morning to discover that in his veins flows not the blood of a slave, but of a real human being' (letter of 7 January 1889).[6] As a writer, Chekhov consistently rejected any manifestation of coercion. He was appalled by coarse and spiteful literary critics, and by the perniciousness of State censorship. Sectarianism repelled him.

Chekhov's private letters indicate that his profound respect for personal freedom was matched by his love of truth. In his published writings, however, he carefully avoided grandiloquent declarations, preferring to pose questions rather than impose answers. As a result, towards the end of the 1880s a number of critics (mainly journalists of a utilitarian, socially committed hue) began to assail him for his apparent failure to propound aims, ideals, opinions and 'solutions' in his works.

In response to such attacks, between 1888 and 1890 Chekhov gradually formulated his own concept of the dispassionate, objective, non-judgemental author. As a point of principle, he not only disclaimed authorial omniscience and the right or duty to moralise, but actually professed the positive value of disclosing one's own ignorance:

> It seems to me that one shouldn't expect writers to solve such questions as God, pessimism, and so on. The writer's task is simply to record how and in what circumstances somebody spoke or thought about God

or pessimism. The artist should not be the judge of his characters and of what they say, but only an impartial witness. I heard a confused, totally inconclusive conversation of two Russians about pessimism and my duty is to convey this conversation exactly as I heard it, whereas the people to evaluate the conversation are the jury, that is, the readers. My only task is to be talented, that is, to know how to distinguish important evidence from the unimportant, to know how to illuminate characters and speak in their language . . . It's high time for writers, especially artists, to admit that in this world one can't understand anything; as Socrates once admitted, and Voltaire . . .

(*To A. S. Suvorin,* 30 May 1888)

You rebuke me for my objectivity, which you call indifference to good and evil, a lack of ideals and ideas, etc. When I depict horse-thieves, you want me to say: horse-stealing is wrong. But everyone knows that without me saying so! Let a jury judge them—my only task is to show them as they are . . . Whenever I write, I trust completely in my reader, and assume that he himself will add the subjective elements missing from my story . . .

(*To A. S. Suvorin,* 1 April 1890)

Although Chekhov's scientific training and habitual scepticism inclined him towards non-didactic objectivity, he nevertheless remained deeply aware of the value of 'aims' for an author, and of the aimlessness characteristic of himself and the writers of his own generation (the 1880s and 1890s).[7]

From these, and similar, statements it might be tempting to deduce that the modestly undogmatic Chekhov was totally self-effacing in his writings. Indeed, he once advised his elder brother, Alexander (letter of 8 May 1889):

Now—turning to your play . . . Above all, beware of the personal element. Your play will be no good whatsoever if all the characters resemble you . . . Who wants to know about my life and yours, my thoughts and your thoughts? Give people people—don't give them yourself . . .

If Chekhov's own personal sympathies were indeed entirely absent from his art, virtually all interpretations of his plays, including *Three Sisters,* might claim equal validity. Yet it should be realised that he cultivated 'indifference' and 'coldness' as a deliberate artistic method, to intensify the emotional effectiveness of his writing. He took pains to enlighten a fellow-author, Lidiya Avilova:

Here's my advice as a reader: when you're portraying unfortunate wretches and want to rouse the reader's pity, try to be colder—that gives a kind of backdrop to the characters' grief, and will make it stand out more sharply. As things are, your heroes weep, and you sigh. Yes, be cold . . .

(*Letter of 19 March 1892*)

I wrote to you once that one has to be indifferent when writing sad stories. You didn't understand what I meant. One can weep and groan as one writes, and suffer along with one's heroes, but I think one must do so without the reader noticing. It makes a more powerful impression the more objective one is. That's what I meant . . .

(*Letter of 29 April 1892*)

Despite his dispassionate air, Chekhov was never a totally neutral and impartial observer. As a writer, he had never pretended to be an unselecting lens, pointed at random to whatever passed before his eye. He assured Suvorin (letter of 27 October 1888):

An artist observes, selects, conjectures, arranges—and these very acts presuppose as their starting-point a question—for if from the start he's not set himself a question, there would be nothing to conjecture or select . . .

In demanding that an artist should have a conscious attitude towards his work you are right, but you are confusing two concepts: *solving a question* and *posing a question correctly.* Only the latter is obligatory for an artist. There's not a single question solved in either *Anna Karenina* or *Onegin,* and yet they remain fully satisfying, simply because the questions they raise are all posed correctly. The court is obliged to pose the questions correctly, but let the jury decide, each according to his own taste . . .

Chekhov's seemingly 'uncommitted' tone, in works such as *Three Sisters,* may thus disguise or conceal a considerable amount of 'commitment', albeit of a non-partisan, non-strident kind. He was never a proponent of 'amoral' art:

Literature is accepted as an art because it portrays life as it really is. Its aim is absolute and honest truth . . .[8]

(*To M. V. Kiseleva,* 14 January 1887)

II

Anton Chekhov was a reluctant dramatist. For many years he saw himself primarily as a doctor, reiterating the formula: 'Medicine is my lawful wife, and literature is my mistress . . .' (11 September 1888).[9] Furthermore, in the realm of literature he felt more at ease with the short story than with the drama, once colourfully remarking: 'The narrative form is a lawful wife, whereas the dramatic form is a gaudy, loud-mouthed, brazen and tiresome mistress . . .' (15 January 1889).

Throughout his life Chekhov had an ambivalent attitude towards the stage. In one letter he described the contemporary Russian theatre as a 'vile disease' which should be swept away (7 November 1888). When his first full-length play, *Ivanov,* received its memorably controversial première at Korsh's Theatre in Moscow on 19 November 1887, the dramatist was amazed by the actors' ad libbings and the director's 'blunders' (20 November 1887). Nine years later, at the first night of *The Seagull* (*Chaika*) he found the performers 'foul and foolish' (18 October 1896). He admired very few actors—Vera Komissarzhevskaya, Mariya Savina, to some extent Vladimir Davydov. Yet he loved the light-hearted vaudeville, and never fully lost his childhood enthusiasm, when he had frequented the Taganrog theatre and acted in amateur theatricals.

> You've become attached to the theatre, whereas I'm evidently drifting further and further away from it—and I regret that, for the theatre once afforded me much pleasure . . . Once upon a time I knew no greater delight than sitting in a theatre, but now I sit there with the sensation that someone up in the gods will call out at any moment: 'The building's on fire!' And I don't like actors. Being a playwright has spoilt me . . .
>
> (*To A. S. Suvorin,* 13 [25] March 1898)[10]

What particularly 'spoilt', and very nearly destroyed, his remaining benevolence towards the theatre was the disastrous Petersburg première of *The Seagull* on 17 October 1896. Chekhov never forgot his humiliation at the Alexandrinsky Theatre, after which he immediately vowed to abandon for ever the writing of plays. His letters indicate the extent of his hurt, and the vulnerability and wounded vanity of an essentially modest man.

> It's not the failure of my play which is to blame; after all, most of my earlier plays were failures too,[11] and that was always like water off a duck's back. On 17 October it wasn't my play which failed—it was my whole person . . . I'm calm now, and in my usual frame of mind, but I still can't forget what happened, just as I couldn't, for instance, forget a blow in the face . . .
>
> (*To A. S. Suvorin,* 14 December 1896)

That Chekhov's 'pride was hurt' (letter of 22 October 1896) is hardly surprising, since he was offering the public his first new full-length play since *The Wood Demon* seven years earlier. First-night reviews of *The Seagull* were mainly hostile, and, despite its relative success on subsequent nights, the play was taken off after only five performances. For some time thereafter, it seemed that Anton Chekhov might never again write for the theatre.[12]

III

Although 1898 was an extremely productive year for Chekhov as a short-story writer, in the annals of theatrical history it is notable for marking the opening of his association with the newly established Moscow Arts Theatre. The initiative of its co-founders, K. S. Stanislavsky and Vl. I. Nemirovich-Danchenko, was to stimulate a remarkable late flowering of Chekhov the dramatist. On 17 December 1898, in its inaugural season, the Moscow Arts Theatre staged a highly successful revival of *The Seagull,* thereby easing somewhat the pain of the

1896 fiasco. On a more personal level, on 9 September 1898, Chekhov had admired for the first time a woman who was to play a central role in his final years: the actress Olga Leonardovna Knipper.

Chekhov missed the Moscow Arts Theatre première of *The Seagull,* as tuberculosis 'confined' him to Yalta, 'like Dreyfus on Devil's Island' (telegram to Nemirovich-Danchenko, 18 December 1898). When he eventually saw the production, at a special private performance in Moscow on 1 May 1899, he disliked the acting of Mariya Roksanova (Nina) and Stanislavsky (Trigorin), but was otherwise impressed.

Chekhov had already promised *Uncle Vanya* to the Maly Theatre, but when the Theatrical and Literary Committee (a kind of censorship body for the 'Imperial' theatres) demanded various changes if the work were to be staged at the 'Imperial' Maly Theatre, he promptly transferred his play to the privately owned Moscow Arts Theatre. Chekhov was able to admire a rehearsal of *Uncle Vanya* in Moscow on 24 May, but again the Arts Theatre première (on 26 October 1899) found him languishing in his Yalta 'exile'.

Confined to the south by illness, the writer yearned for Moscow, where there was culture, and the Moscow Arts Theatre, and the actress Olga Knipper. His letters document his growing attachment to the new theatre, which was helping to bring about his rebirth as a dramatist.

Having successfully revived *The Seagull* and mounted a major production of *Uncle Vanya,*[13] Stanislavsky and Nemirovich-Danchenko were naturally eager to commission an original work from Chekhov, the first play to be written specially for the Moscow Arts Theatre company. Earlier in 1899 the dramatist had already hinted at his willingness to comply.[14]

In a letter to Nemirovich-Danchenko on 24 November 1899 he mentioned for the first time the title, *Three Sisters*:

> I'm not writing any play. I have a theme, *Three Sisters* (*Tri sestry*), but until I finish the stories which have been on my conscience for a long time, I shan't start on the play . . .

Chekhov spent most of 1900 as a 'prisoner' in the Crimea, plagued by illness and unwanted visitors. There were, however, several highlights to punctuate the gloom. In April he joyfully greeted the Moscow Arts Theatre company when it toured Sevastopol and Yalta, performing, among other plays, his *Seagull* and *Uncle Vanya.* In July 1900 Olga Knipper stayed with the Chekhov family in Yalta, and the intimacy of their subsequent letters indicates that during this time the author and the actress became lovers. In the closing months of the year he struggled to complete his new play *Three Sisters,* which the Arts Theatre eagerly awaited for its 1900-1 season.

His letters from Yalta in 1900 chronicle the evolution of the play:

Am I writing the new play? It's beginning to emerge, but I haven't started writing yet . . .

(*To Vl. I. Nemirovich-Danchenko,* 10 March 1900)

Yesterday Alekseev[15] visited me. We spoke of the play, I gave him my word, what's more I promised to finish the play no later than September . . .

(*To O. L. Knipper,* 9 August 1900)

My darling, I don't know when I'll be coming to Moscow—I don't know because, would you believe it, I'm now writing the play. Actually, it's not a play I'm writing, but more of a mess. There are lots of characters—perhaps I'll lose my way and abandon it . . .

(*To O. L. Knipper,* 14 August 1900)

I'm working in Yalta, not in Gurzuf, and people disturb me unmercifully, they disturb me vilely and abominably. The play's all in my head, it has already taken shape and levelled out, and is begging to be written down, but the moment I reach for my writing paper the door opens and some ugly mug crawls in . . .

(*To O. L. Knipper,* 18 August 1900)

I'm writing the play, but I'm afraid it will turn out boring . . .

(*To O. L. Knipper,* 23 August 1900)

Writing *Three Sisters* is very difficult, more difficult than my earlier plays . . . And writing's very difficult in Yalta; there are interruptions, and there seems no point in writing, and I don't like today what I wrote yesterday . . .

(*To his sister Masha,* 9 September 1900)

As for my play, it will be finished sooner or later, in September, or October, or even November, but I'm not sure whether to stage it this season . . . I'm not sure because, first, the play isn't quite ready—let it lie on my desk for a while, and, second, I must attend the rehearsals, I really must! I can't leave four important female roles, four educated young women, in Alekseev's hands, despite all my respect for his talent and insight. I must keep at least one eye on the rehearsals . . .

(*To O. L. Knipper,* 15 September 1900)

Oh, what a part I've got for you in *Three Sisters*! What a part![16] If you give me ten roubles you can have the part, otherwise I'll hand it over to another actress. I shan't offer *Three Sisters* this season. Let the play lie around for a bit and sweat, or—as merchants' wives say of a pie when they serve it up for dinner—let it breathe . . .

(*To O. L. Knipper,* 28 September 1900)

I'll probably make a fair copy of my new play when I'm in Moscow . . .

(*To O. L. Knipper,* 4 October 1900)

Would you believe it, I've written the play . . . It was terribly difficult to write *Three Sisters*. After all, it's got three heroines, each has to have her own shape and pattern, and all three are daughters of a general! The action takes place in a provincial town such as Perm, the milieu consists of soldiers, artillery . . .[17]

(*To M. Gorky,* 16 October 1900)

On 23 October 1900 Chekhov arrived in Moscow, bringing with him the first version or draft of *Three Sisters*.[18] According to the memoirs of Olga Knipper, on 29 October Chekhov read his play to the Moscow Arts Theatre company, who reacted by claiming that it was only a 'sketch' or 'outline', with no fully developed 'roles'.[19] In Moscow he continued to revise the play:

Three Sisters is finished . . . The play has turned out dull, protracted and awkward; I say—awkward, because, for instance, it has four heroines and a mood, as they say, gloomier than gloom itself . . .

My play is complex like a novel and its mood, people say, is murderous . . .

(*To V. F. Komissarzhevskaya,* 13 November 1900)

The ailing author left Moscow on 11 December 1900, arriving in Nice three days later. At the Pension Russe he continued his work on *Three Sisters*:

The windows in my room are wide open; and it seems as if my soul too is wide open. I'm copying out my play and feel amazed at how I could write this piece, and what for . . .

I'll go down to the sea now, I'll sit there and read the newspapers, and then, when I come home, I'll copy out the play—and tomorrow I'll be able to send Nemirovich Act III, and the day after tomorrow Act IV—or both of them together . . .[20]

(*To O. L. Knipper,* 15 [28] December 1900)

In Act III I've changed only a little, but in Act IV I've made drastic changes. I've added many words for you . . .

(*To O. L. Knipper,* 17 [30] December 1900)

The play is now finished and I've sent it off . . .

(*To O. L. Knipper,* 21 December 1900
[3 January 1901])

While the Moscow Arts Theatre company was rehearsing *Three Sisters*,[21] Chekhov sent further letters from Nice. Although willing to comment on specific details of the action and characterisation, he was reluctant to elaborate on the play's overall mood or 'message':

You write that in Act III, when Natasha is making her rounds of the house at night, she puts out the lights and looks for burglars under the furniture. But I think it would be better if she strode straight across the stage, *à la* Lady Macbeth, clutching a candle—that would be crisper and more horrifying . . .[22]

(*To K. S. Stanislavsky,* 2 [15] January 1901)

Indeed, Solyony thinks he looks like Lermontov; but of course he doesn't—the very idea is laughable . . .

He should be made up to look like Lermontov. The resemblance to Lermontov is enormous, but it exists only in Solyony's mind . . .[23]

(*To I. A. Tikhomirov,* 14 [27] January 1901)

Of course, you're absolutely right. Tuzenbakh's corpse shouldn't be shown at all. I felt this myself when I was writing, and spoke to you about it, if you remember.[24] As for the end being like **Uncle Vanya**—that's no great misfortune. After all, **Uncle Vanya** is my play, and not somebody else's, and when one echoes oneself in a work, people say that's how things should be . . .

(*To K. S. Stanislavsky,* 15 [28] January 1901)

With his typical love of understatement, Chekhov encouraged a subtle discernment in all aspects of the production:

Of course, Act III must be performed quietly, to convey the feeling that people are exhausted, and that they want to sleep . . . What noise are you talking about? I've indicated where bells should be ringing off-stage.[25]

(*To O. L. Knipper,* 17 [30] January 1901)

You write that in Act III there is noise and bustle . . . What do you mean? The noise and bustle are only in the distance, off-stage, a vague muffled noise, but here on stage everyone's exhausted, almost asleep . . . If you spoil Act III the play will be ruined and I'll be hissed off the stage in my old age . . .

(*To O. L. Knipper,* 20 January [2 February] 1901)

Masha's confession in Act III is not a real confession, but merely a candid conversation. Play it with agitation, but not despair, don't shout, do smile from time to time and, above all, play it in such a way that one can feel the exhaustion of night. And also so that one can feel you're cleverer than your sisters, or at least that you regard yourself as cleverer . . .

(*To O. L. Knipper,* 21 January [3 February] 1901)

You inform me that in Act III you lead Irina by the arm . . . What for? . . . Can't Irina cross the stage by herself? . . .

(*To O. L. Knipper,* 24 January [6 February] 1901)

I'm leaving for Italy at 12 midnight . . .

(*To O. R. Vasilieva,* 26 January [8 February] 1901)

Chekhov duly arrived in Pisa:

I'm writing this to you from Pisa, my darling. From here I'll be going to Florence, then Rome, and then Naples . . .

Was my play performed or not? I know nothing . . .

(*To O. L. Knipper,* 28 January [10 February] 1901)

On 31 January 1901, while Chekhov was in his beloved Italy, the première of **Three Sisters** took place in Moscow.

NOTES

[1] Chekhov first coughed blood in 1884, and tuberculosis was finally diagnosed in 1897 after he suffered a massive lung haemorrhage.

[2] Daniel Gillès, *Chekhov: Observer Without Illusion* (New York, 1968), p. 189.

[3] For the fullest edition, see A. P. Chekhov, *Polnoe sobranie sochinenii i pisem v tridtsati tomakh* (Moscow, 1974-83), where the twelve volumes of letters contain some 4,500 items. Many other letters have perished, been deliberately destroyed, or remain undiscovered.

[4] Carolina De Maegd-Soëp, *Chekhov and Women: Women in the Life and Work of Chekhov* (Ohio, 1987), p. 26.

[5] Most of the quotations from Chekhov's letters may be found in *Chekhov: A Life in Letters,* translated and edited by Gordon McVay (The Folio Society: London, 1994).

[6] It was perhaps his veneration of freedom which prompted him, in 1890, to undertake the unexpected and arduous journey across Siberia to Sakhalin, where he conducted a detailed census of some 10,000 convicts and settlers condemned to live out their lives in servitude.

[7] See his letter to A. S. Suvorin (25 November 1892).

[8] In a notebook, Chekhov observed: 'Man will become better when you show him what he is really like' (A. P. Chekhov, *Polnoe sobranie sochinenii i pisem v tridtsati tomakh: Sochineniia* XVII [Moscow, 1980], p. 90). Henceforth, references to the eighteen volumes of Chekhov's works will be cited from this edition thus: XVII, 90 (the Roman numeral denotes the volume, the Arabic indicates the page).

[9] A similar thought is expressed in letters of, for instance, 17 January 1887, 11 February 1893, and 15 March 1896.

[10] Chekhov was writing from Nice. The first date is according to the 'old style' Julian calendar used in Russia before the Revolution, and the second, according to the Gregorian calendar in use in Western Europe. In the nineteenth century, the Gregorian calendar was twelve days ahead of the Julian, and in the twentieth century, thirteen days ahead.

[11] Critics attending the first night of *Ivanov* (19 November 1887) were predominantly hostile. The Petersburg revival of a substantially revised *Ivanov* (31 January 1889) was better received, but the Moscow première of *The Wood Demon (Leshii)* (27 December 1889) attracted much adverse comment, and the play was taken off after only five or six performances. At some unknown point between 1890 and 1896, Chekhov transformed *The Wood Demon* into a new play, *Uncle Vanya (Diadia Vania).* To date, his most popular (and lucrative) plays had been the one-act vaudevilles or 'jests', such as *The Bear (Medved')* (1888) and *The Proposal (Predlozhenie)* (1888-9).

[12] In the spring of 1897 Suvorin published an edition of Chekhov's plays (including *Uncle Vanya*), but Chekhov's letters between October 1896 and January 1899 indicate his reluctance to write any further plays.

[13] *Uncle Vanya* had already been staged several times in the provinces in the second half of 1898.

[14] See his letters of 8 February, 19 February and 8 October 1899.

[15] The real name of K. S. Stanislavsky, who was born Konstantin Sergeevich Alekseev, son of a wealthy textile manufacturer. Stanislavsky was his stage name.

[16] The role of Masha in *Three Sisters* was written with Olga Knipper in mind.

[17] Chekhov's first-hand knowledge of military circles is said to date back to his acquaintance with the family of Colonel B. I. Maevsky (the local battery commander) and Lieutenant E. P. Egorov in Voskresensk in 1883-4. See, for instance, M. P. Chekhov, *Vokrug Chekhova: Vstrechi i vpechatleniia* (Moscow, 1964), pp. 132-3. The army milieu is also reflected in Chekhov's story *The Kiss (Potselui)* (1887).

[18] A comparison of this first, 'Yalta', version of *Three Sisters* and the 'final text' is most revealing. See the valuable publication by A. R. Vladimirskaya, 'Dve rannie redaktsii p'esy "Tri sestry"', in *Literaturnoe nasledstvo,* LXVIII: *Chekhov* (Moscow, 1960), pp. 1-86. For ease of reference, variants in Chekhov's text will be quoted from the notes to Volume XIII of his thirty-volume collected works (Moscow, 1978): XIII, 273-309.

[19] O. L. Knipper-Chekhova, in *Chekhov v vospominaniiakh sovremennikov* (Moscow, 1954), p. 606. Other sources (including Stanislavsky and Nemirovich-Danchenko) indicate that, although Chekhov attended this reading on 29 October, he himself did not recite the play. Chekhov's lifelong distaste for public declamation is well attested.

[20] Chekhov sent off Act III to Moscow on 16 December 1900, and Act IV on 20 December.

[21] Stanislavsky's meticulous work as director is recorded in his production score of *Three Sisters*—see *Rezhisserskie ekzempliary K. S. Stanislavskogo,* III: *1901-1904: P'esy A. P. Chekhova 'Tri sestry',*

'Vishnevyi sad' (Moscow, 1983), pp. 87-289. Henceforth, references to Stanislavsky's production score will cite the page only of this edition.

[22] In his reply later in January Stanislavsky explained: 'Natasha looks for burglars not in the third, but in the second act'. Natasha appears with a candle on two occasions in Act II (at the beginning and towards the end), and once in Act III (towards the end). The two men seem to be talking of different episodes—Stanislavsky evidently wanted Natasha to look for miscreants at the beginning of Act II, whereas Chekhov wished her to cross the stage '*à la* Lady Macbeth' late in Act III.

[23] On one level, Solyony may be regarded as a psychopathic murderous misfit, a tragi-comic parody of the Lermontovian hero. Lermontov (1814-41) was Russia's greatest Romantic poet.

[24] In the 'Yalta' version of the play, Chekhov's stage direction towards the end of Act IV included the words: 'there is a noise at the back of the stage; a crowd can be seen, looking on as the body of the Baron, who has been killed in the duel, is carried past' (XIII, 308). This stage direction led to a lively correspondence between Chekhov and Stanislavsky, both of whom seem determined to persuade the other to drop the idea (the Moscow Arts Theatre stage was too small, the spectacle of a corpse would distract from the mood of the sisters' closing speeches, etc.). See also Chekhov's letter to O. L. Knipper on 20 January (2 February) 1901. The episode was wisely excluded from the final version.

[25] In her letter to Chekhov on 11 January 1901 Olga Knipper had written that, when rehearsing Act III, Stanislavsky had emphasised 'a terrible commotion on stage, with everyone running about feverishly . . . '.

The Cherry Orchard

Francis Fergusson (essay date 1949)

SOURCE: "*Ghosts* and *The Cherry Orchard:* The Theater of Modern Realism," in *The Idea of a Theater: A Study of Ten Plays: The Art of Drama in Changing Perspective,* Princeton University Press, 1949, pp. 146-77.

[*In the excerpt below, Fergusson illuminates the carefully built structure underlying the seemingly plotless* Cherry Orchard.]

THE PLOT OF *THE CHERRY ORCHARD*

The Cherry Orchard is often accused of having no plot whatever, and it is true that the story gives little indication of the play's content or meaning; nothing happens, as the Broadway reviewers so often point out. Nor does it have a thesis, though many attempts have been made to attribute a thesis to it, to make it into a Marxian tract, or into a nostalgic defense of the old regime. The play does not have much of a plot in either of these accepted meanings of the word, for it is not addressed to the rationalizing mind but to the poetic and histrionic sensibility. It is an imitation of an action in the strictest sense, and it is plotted according to the first meaning of this word which I have distinguished in other contexts: the incidents are selected and arranged to define an action in a certain mode; a complete action, with a beginning, middle, and end in time. Its freedom from the mechanical order of the thesis or the intrigue is the sign of the perfection of Chekhov's realistic art. And its apparently casual incidents are actually composed with most elaborate and conscious skill to reveal the underlying life, and the natural, objective form of the play as a whole. . . .

[In Henrik Ibsen's *Ghosts*] the action is distorted by the stereotyped requirements of the thesis and the intrigue. That is partly a matter of the mode of action which Ibsen was trying to show; a quest "of ethical motivation" which requires some sort of intellectual framework, and yet can have no final meaning in the purely literal terms of Ibsen's theater. *The Cherry Orchard,* on the other hand, is a drama "of pathetic motivation," a theater-poem of the suffering of change; and this mode of action and awareness is much closer to the skeptical basis of modern realism, and to the histrionic basis of all realism. Direct perception before predication is always true, says Aristotle; and the extraordinary feat of Chekhov is to predicate nothing. This he achieves by means of his plot: he selects only those incidents, those moments in his characters' lives, between their rationalized efforts, when they sense their situation and destiny most directly. So he contrives to show the action of the play as a whole—the unsuccessful attempt to cling to the Cherry Orchard—in

Olga Knipper as Ranevskaya, in The Cherry Orchard.

many diverse reflectors and without propounding any thesis about it.

The slight narrative thread which ties these incidents and characters together for the inquiring mind, is quickly recounted. The family that owns the old estate named after its famous orchard—Lyubov, her brother Gaev, and her daughters Varya and Anya—is all but bankrupt, and the question is how to prevent the bailiffs from selling the estate to pay their debts. Lopahin, whose family were formerly serfs on the estate, is now rapidly growing rich as a businessman, and he offers a very sensible plan: chop down the orchard, divide the property into small lots, and sell them off to make a residential suburb for the growing industrial town nearby. Thus the cash value of the estate could be not only preserved, but increased. But this would not save what Lyubov and her brother find valuable in the old estate; they cannot consent to the destruction of the orchard. But they cannot find, or earn, or borrow the money to pay their debts either; and in due course the estate is sold at auction to Lopahin himself, who will make a very good thing of it. His workmen are hacking at the old trees before the family is out of the house.

The play may be briefly described as a realistic ensemble pathos: the characters all suffer the passing of the estate in different ways, thus adumbrating this change at a deeper and more generally significant level than that of any individual's experience. The action which they all share by analogy, and which informs the suffering of the destined change of the Cherry Orchard, is "to save the Cherry Orchard": that is, each character sees some value in it—economic, sentimental, social, cultural—which he wishes to keep. By means of his plot, Chekhov always focuses attention on the general action: his crowded stage, full of the characters I have mentioned as well as half a dozen hangers-on, is like an implicit discussion of the fatality which concerns them all; but Chekhov does not believe in their ideas, and the interplay he shows among his *dramatis personae* is not so much the play of thought as the alternation of his characters' perceptions of their situation, as the moods shift and the time for decision comes and goes.

Though the action which Chekhov chooses to show on-stage is "pathetic," i.e., suffering and perception, it is complete: the Cherry Orchard is constituted before our eyes, and then dissolved. The first act is a prologue: it is the occasion of Lyubov's return from Paris to try to resume her old life. Through her eyes and those of her daughter Anya, as well as from the complementary perspectives of Lopahin and Trofimov, we see the estate as it were in the round, in its many possible meanings. The second act corresponds to the agon; it is in this act that we become aware of the conflicting values of all the characters, and of the efforts they make (off-stage) to save each one *his* Orchard. The third act corresponds to the pathos and peripety of the traditional tragic form. The occasion is a rather hysterical party which Lyubov gives while her estate is being sold at auction in the nearby town; it ends with Lopahin's announcement, in pride and the bitterness of guilt, that he was the purchaser. The last act is the epiphany: we see the action, now completed, in a new and ironic light. The occasion is the departure of the family: the windows are boarded up, the furniture piled in the corners, and the bags packed. All the characters feel, and the audience sees in a thousand ways, that the wish to save the Orchard has amounted in fact to destroying it; the gathering of its denizens to separation; the homecoming to departure. What this "means" we are not told. But the action is completed, and the poem of the suffering of change concludes in a new and final perception, and a rich chord of feeling.

The structure of each act is based upon a more or less ceremonious social occasion. In his use of the social ceremony—arrivals, departures, anniversaries, parties—Chekhov is akin to James. His purpose is the same: to focus attention on an action which all share by analogy, instead of upon the reasoned purpose of any individual, as Ibsen does in his drama of ethical motivation. Chekhov uses the social occasion also to reveal the individual at moments when he is least enclosed in his private rationalization and most open to disinterested insights. The Chekhovian ensembles may appear superficially to be mere pointless stalemates—too like family gatherings and arbitrary meetings which we know off-stage. So they are. But in his miraculous arrangement the very discomfort of many presences is made to reveal fundamental aspects of the human situation.

That Chekhov's art of plotting is extremely conscious and deliberate is clear the moment one considers the distinction between the stories of his characters as we learn about them, and the moments of their lives which he chose to show directly onstage. Lopahin, for example, is a man of action like one of the new capitalists in Gorki's plays. Chekhov knew all about him, and could have shown us an exciting episode from his career if he had not chosen to see him only when he was forced to pause and pathetically sense his own motives in a wider context which qualifies their importance. Lyubov has been dragged about Europe for years by her ne'er-do-well lover, and her life might have yielded several sure-fire erotic intrigues like those of the commercial theater. But Chekhov, like all the great artists of modern times, rejected these standard motivations as both stale and false. The actress Arkadina, in *The Seagull,* remarks, as she closes a novel of Maupassant's, "Well, among the French that may be, but here with us there's nothing of the kind, we've no set program." In the context the irony of her remark is deep: she is herself a purest product of the commercial theater, and at that very time she is engaged in a love affair of the kind she objects to in Maupassant. But Chekhov, with his subtle art of plotting, has caught her in a situation, and at a brief moment of clarity and pause, when the falsity of her career is clear to all, even herself.

Thus Chekhov, by his art of plot-making, defines an action in the opposite mode to that of *Ghosts.* Ibsen defines a desperate quest for reasons and for ultimate, intelligible moral values. This action falls naturally into the form of the agon, and at the end of the play Ibsen is at a loss to develop the final pathos, or bring it to an end with an accepted perception. But the pathetic is the very mode of action and awareness which seems to Chekhov closest to the reality of the human situation, and by means of his plot he shows, even in characters who are not in themselves unusually passive, the suffering and the perception of change. The "moment" of human experience which *The Cherry Orchard* presents thus corresponds to that of the Sophoclean chorus, and of the evenings in the *Purgatorio. Ghosts* is a fighting play, armed for its sharp encounter with the rationalizing mind, its poetry concealed by its reasons. Chekhov's poetry, like Ibsen's, is behind the naturalistic surfaces; but the form of the play as a whole is "nothing but" poetry in the widest sense: the coherence of the concrete elements of the composition. Hence the curious vulnerability of Chekhov on the contemporary stage: he does not argue, he merely presents; and though his audiences even on Broadway are touched by the time they reach the last act, they are at a loss to say what it is all about.

It is this reticent objectivity of Chekhov also which makes him so difficult to analyze in words: he appeals exclusively to the histrionic sensibility where the little poetry of modern realism is to be found. Nevertheless, the effort of analysis must be made if one is to understand this art at all; and if the reader will bear with me, he is asked to consider one element, that of the scene, in the composition of the second act.

ACT II: THE SCENE AS A BASIC ELEMENT IN THE COMPOSITION

M. Cocteau writes, in his preface to *Les Mariés de la Tour Eiffel*: "The action of my play is in images (*imagée*) while the text is not: I attempt to substitute a 'poetry of the theater' for 'poetry in the theater.' Poetry in the theater is a piece of lace which it is impossible to see at a distance. Poetry of the theater would be coarse lace; a lace of ropes, a ship at sea. *Les Mariés* should have the frightening look of a drop of poetry under the microscope. The *scenes* are integrated like the *words* of a poem."

This description applies very exactly to **The Cherry Orchard:** the larger elements of the composition—the scenes or episodes, the setting and the developing story—are composed in such a way as to make a poetry of the theater; but the "text" as we read it literally, is not. Chekhov's method, as Mr. Stark Young puts it in the preface to his translation of **The Seagull,** "is to take actual material such as we find in life and manage it in such a way that the inner meanings are made to appear. On the surface the life in his plays, is natural, possible, and at times in effect even casual."

Mr. Young's translations of Chekhov's plays, together with his beautifully accurate notes, explanations, and interpretations, have made the text of Chekhov at last available for the English-speaking stage, and for any reader who will bring to his reading a little patience and imagination. Mr. Young shows us what Chekhov means in detail: by the particular words his characters use; by their rhythms of speech; by their gestures, pauses, and bits of stage business. In short, he makes the text transparent, enabling us to see through it to the music of action, the underlying poetry of the composition as a whole—and this is as much as to say that any study of Chekhov (lacking as we do adequate and available productions) must be based upon Mr. Young's work. At this point I propose to take this work for granted; to assume the translucent text; and to consider the role of the setting in the poetic or musical order of Act II.

The second act, as I have said, corresponds to the agon of the traditional plot scheme: it is here that we see most clearly the divisive purposes of the characters, the contrasts between their views of the Cherry Orchard itself.

But the center of interest is not in these individual conflicts, nor in the contrasting visions for their own sake, but in the common fatality which they reveal: the passing of the old estate. The setting, as we come to know it behind the casual surfaces of the text, is one of the chief elements in this poem of change: if Act II were a lyric, instead of an act of a play, the setting would be a crucial word appearing in a succession of rich contexts which endow it with a developing meaning.

Chekhov describes the setting in the following realistic terms. "A field. An old chapel, long abandoned, with crooked walls, near it a well, big stones that apparently were once tombstones, and an old bench. A road to the estate of Gaev can be seen. On one side poplars rise, casting their shadows, the cherry orchard begins there. In the distance a row of telegraph poles; and far, far away, faintly traced on the horizon, is a large town, visible only in the clearest weather. The sun will soon be down."

To make this set out of a cyclorama, flats, cut-out silhouettes, and lighting-effects, would be difficult, without producing that unbelievable but literally intended—and in any case indigestible—scene which modern realism demands; and here Chekhov is uncomfortably bound by the convention of his time. The best strategy in production is that adopted by Robert Edmund Jones in his setting for **The Seagull**: to pay lip service only to the convention of photographic realism, and make the trees, the chapel and all the other elements as simple as possible. The less closely the setting is defined by the carpenter, the freer it is to play the role Chekhov wrote for it: a role which changes and develops in relation to the story. Shakespeare did not have this problem; he could present his setting in different ways at different moments in a few lines of verse:

> Alack! the night comes on, and the bleak winds
> Do sorely ruffle; for many miles about
> There's scarce a bush.

Chekhov, as we shall see, gives his setting life and flexibility in spite of the visible elements on-stage, not by means of the poetry of words but by means of his characters' changing sense of it.

When the curtain rises we see the setting simply as the country at the sentimental hour of sunset. Epihodov is playing his guitar and other hangers-on of the estate are loafing, as is their habit, before supper. The dialogue which starts after a brief pause focuses attention upon individuals in the group: Charlotta, the governess, boasting of her culture and complaining that no one understands her; the silly maid Dunyasha, who is infatuated with Yasha, Lyubov's valet. The scene, as reflected by these characters, is a satirical period-piece like the "Stag at Eve" or "The Maiden's Prayer"; and when the group falls silent and begins to drift away (having heard Lyubov, Gaev, and Lopahin approaching along the path) Chekhov expects us to smile at the sentimental clichés which the place and the hour have produced.

But Lyubov's party brings with it a very different atmosphere: of irritation, frustration, and fear. It is here we learn that Lopahin cannot persuade Lyubov and Gaev to put their affairs in order; that Gaev has been making futile gestures toward getting a job and borrowing money; that Lyubov is worried about the estate, about her daughters, and about her lover, who has now fallen ill in Paris. Lopahin, in a huff, offers to leave; but Lyubov will not let him go—"It's more cheerful with you here," she says; and this group in its turn falls silent. In the distance we hear the music of the Jewish orchestra—when Chekhov wishes us to raise our eyes from the people in the foreground to their wider setting, he often uses music as a signal and an inducement. This time the musical entrance of the setting into our consciousness is more urgent and sinister than it was before: we see not so much the peace of evening as the silhouette of the dynamic industrial town on the horizon, and the approach of darkness. After a little more desultory conversation, there is another pause, this time without music, and the foreboding aspect of the scene in silence is more intense.

In this silence Firs, the ancient servant, hurries on with Gaev's coat, to protect him from the evening chill, and we briefly see the scene through Firs's eyes. He remembers the estate before the emancipation of the serfs, when it was the scene of a way of life which made sense to him; and now we become aware of the frail relics of this life: the old gravestones and the chapel "fallen out of the perpendicular."

In sharpest contrast with this vision come the young voices of Anya, Varya, and Trofimov who are approaching along the path. The middle-aged and the old in the foreground are pathetically grateful for this note of youth, of strength, and of hope; and presently they are listening happily (though without agreement or belief) to Trofimov's aspirations, his creed of social progress, and his conviction that their generation is no longer important to the life of Russia. When the group falls silent again, they are all disposed to contentment with the moment; and when Epihodov's guitar is heard, and we look up, we feel the country and the evening under the aspect of hope—as offering freedom from the responsibilities and conflicts of the estate itself:

(Epihodov passes by at the back, playing his guitar.)

LYUBOV. (Lost in thought.) Epihodov is coming—

ANYA. (Lost in though.) Epihodov is coming.

GAEV. The sun has set, ladies and gentlemen.

TROFIMOV. Yes.

GAEV. (Not loud and as if he were declaiming.) Oh, Nature, wonderful, you gleam with eternal radiance, beautiful and indifferent, you, whom we call Mother, combine in yourself both life and death, you give life and take it away.

VARYA. (Beseechingly.) Uncle!

Gaev's false, rhetorical note ends the harmony, brings us back to the to the present and to the awareness of change on the horizon, and produces a sort of empty stalemate—a silent pause with worry and fear in it.

(All sit absorbed in their thoughts. There is only the silence. FIRS is heard muttering to himself softly. Suddenly a distant sound is heard, as if from the sky, like the sound of a snapped string, dying away, mournful.)

This mysterious sound is used like Epihodov's strumming to remind us of the wider scene, but (though distant) it is sharp, almost a warning signal, and all the characters listen and peer toward the dim edges of the horizon. In their attitudes and guesses Chekhov reflects, in rapid succession, the contradictory aspects of the scene which have been developed at more length before us:

LYUBOV. What's that?

LOPAHIN. I don't know. Somewhere far off in a mine shaft a bucket fell. But somewhere very far off.

GAEV. And it may be some bird—like a heron.

TROFIMOV. Or an owl—

LYUBOV. (Shivering.) It's unpleasant, somehow. (A pause.)

FIRS. Before the disaster it was like that. The owl hooted and the samovar hummed without stopping, both.

GAEV. Before what disaster?

FIRS. Before the emancipation.

(A pause.)

LYUBOV. You know, my friends, let's go. . . .

Lyubov feels the need to retreat, but the retreat is turned into flight when "the wayfarer" suddenly appears on the path asking for money. Lyubov in her bewilderment, her sympathy, and her bad conscience, gives him gold. The party breaks up, each in his own way thwarted and demoralized.

Anya and Trofimov are left on-stage; and, to conclude his theatrical poem of the suffering of change, Chekhov reflects the setting in them:

ANYA. (A pause.) It's wonderful here today!

TROFIMOV. Yes, the weather is marvelous.

ANYA. What have you done to me, Petya, why don't I love the cherry orchard any longer the way I used to? I loved it too tenderly; it seemed to me there was not a better place on earth than our orchard.

TROFIMOV. All Russia is our garden. The earth is immense and beautiful. . . .

The sun has set, the moon is rising with its chill and its ancient animal excitement, and the estate is dissolved in the darkness as Nineveh is dissolved in a pile of rubble with vegetation creeping over it. Chekhov wishes to show the Cherry Orchard as "gone"; but for this purpose he employs not only the literal time-scheme (sunset to moonrise) but, as reflectors, Anya and Trofimov, for whom the present in any form is already gone and only the bodiless future is real. Anya's young love for Trofimov's intellectual enthusiasm (like Juliet's "all as boundless as the sea") has freed her from her actual childhood home, made her feel "at home in the world" anywhere. Trofimov's abstract aspirations give him a chillier and more artificial, but equally complete, detachment not only from the estate itself (he disapproves of it on theoretical grounds) but from Anya (he thinks it would be vulgar to be in love with her). We hear the worried Varya calling for Anya in the distance; Anya and Trofimov run down to the river to discuss the socialistic *Paradiso Terrestre*; and with these complementary images of the human scene, and this subtle chord of feeling, Chekhov ends the act.

The "scene" is only one element in the composition of Act II, but it illustrates the nature of Chekhov's poetry of the theater. It is very clear, I think, that Chekhov is not trying to present us with a rationalization of social change *à la* Marx, or even with a subtler rationalization *à la* Shaw. On the other hand, he is not seeking, like Wagner, to seduce us into one passion. He shows us a moment of change in society, and he shows us a "pathos"; but the elements of his composition are always taken as objectively real. He offers us various rationalizations, various images and various feelings, which cannot be reduced either to one emotion or to one idea: they indicate an action and a scene which is "there" before the rational formulations, or the emotionally charged attitudes, of any of the characters.

The surrounding scene of *The Cherry Orchard* corresponds to the significant stage of human life which Sophocles' choruses reveal, and to the empty wilderness beyond Ibsen's little parlor. We miss, in Chekhov's scene, any fixed points of human significance, and that is why, compared with Sophocles, he seems limited and partial—a bit too pathetic even for our bewildered times. But, precisely because he subtly and elaborately develops the moments of pathos with their sad insights, he sees much more in the little scene of modern realism than Ibsen does. Ibsen's snowpeaks strike us as rather hysterical; but the "stage of Europe" which we divine behind the Cherry Orchard is confirmed by a thousand impressions derived from other sources. We may recognize its main elements in a cocktail party in Connecticut or Westchester: someone's lawn full of voluble people; a dry white clapboard church (instead of an Orthodox chapel) just visible across a field; time passing, and the muffled roar of a four-lane highway under the hill—or we may be reminded of it in the final section of *The Wasteland*,

with its twittering voices, its old gravestones and deserted chapel, and its dim crowd on the horizon foreboding change. It is because Chekhov says so little that he reveals so much, providing a concrete basis for many conflicting rationalizations of contemporary social change: by accepting the immediacy and unintelligibility of modern realism so completely, he in some ways transcends its limitations, and prepares the way for subsequent developments in the modern theater.

CHEKHOV'S HISTRIONIC ART: AN END AND A BEGINNING

Era già l'ora che volge il disio
    ai naviganti, e intenercisce il core
    lo dì ch'han detto ai dolci amici addio;
e che lo nuovo peregrin d'amore
    punge, se ode squilla di lontano,
    che paia il giorno pianger che si more.

It was now the hour that turns back the desire of those who sail the seas and melts their heart, that day when they have said to their sweet friends adieu, and that pierces the new pilgrim with love, if from afar he hears the chimes which seem to mourn for the dying day.

—*Purgatorio*, CANTO VIII

The poetry of modern realistic drama is to be found in those inarticulate moments when the human creature is shown responding directly to his immediate situation. Such are the many moments—composed, interrelated, echoing each other—when the waiting and loafing characters in Act II get a fresh sense (one after the other, and each in his own way) of their situation on the doomed estate. It is because of the exactitude with which Chekhov perceives and imitates these tiny responses, that he can make them echo each other, and convey, when taken together, a single action with the scope, the general significance or suggestiveness, of poetry. Chekhov, like other great dramatists, has what might be called an ear for action, comparable to the trained musician's ear for musical sound.

The action which Chekhov thus imitates in his second act (that of lending ear, in a moment of freedom from practical pressures, to impending change) echoes, in its turn, a number of other poets: Laforgue's "poetry of waiting-rooms" comes to mind, as well as other works stemming from the period of hush before the first World War. The poets are to some extent talking about the same thing, and their works, like voices in a continuing colloquy, help to explain each other: hence the justification and the purpose of seeking comparisons. The eighth canto of the *Purgatorio* is widely separated from *The Cherry Orchard* in space and time, but these two poems unmistakably echo and confirm each other. Thinking of them together, one can begin to place Chekhov's curiously non-verbal dramaturgy and understand the purpose and the value of his reduction of the art to histrionic terms, as well as the more obvious limitations which he thereby accepts. For Dante accepts similar limitations at this point but locates the mode of action he shows here at a certain point in his vast scheme.

The explicit co-ordinates whereby Dante places the action of Canto VIII might alone suffice to give one a clue to the comparison with **The Cherry Orchard**: we are in the Valley of Negligent Rulers who, lacking light, unwillingly suffer their irresponsibility, just as Lyubov and Gaev do. The ante-purgatorio is behind us, and purgatory proper, with its hoped-for work, thought, and moral effort, is somewhere ahead, beyond the night which is now approaching. It is the end of the day; and as we wait, watch, and listen, evening moves slowly over our heads, from sunset to darkness to moonrise. Looking more closely at this canto, one can see that Dante the Pilgrim, and the Negligent Rulers he meets, are listening and looking as Chekhov's characters are in Act II: the action is the same; in both a childish and uninstructed responsiveness, an unpremeditated obedience to what is actual, informs the suffering of change. Dante the author, for his elaborate and completely conscious reasons, works here with the primitive histrionic sensibility, he composes with elements sensuously or sympathetically, but not rationally or verbally, defined. The rhythms, the pauses, and the sound effects he employs are strikingly similar to Chekhov's. And so he shows himself—Dante "the new Pilgrim"—meeting this mode of awareness for the first time: as delicately and ignorantly as Gaev when he feels all of a sudden the extent of evening, and before he falsifies this perception with his embarrassing apostrophe to Nature.

If Dante allows himself as artist and as protagonist only the primitive sensibility of the child, the naïf, the natural saint, at this point in the ascent, it is because, like Chekhov, he is presenting a threshold or moment of change in human experience. He wants to show the unbounded potentialities of the psyche before or between the moments when it is morally and intellectually realized. In Canto VIII the pilgrim is both a child, and a child who is changing; later moments of transition are different. Here he is virtually (but for the Grace of God) lost; all the dangers are present. Yet he remains uncommitted and therefore open to finding himself again and more truly. In all of this the parallel to Chekhov is close. But because Dante sees this moment as a moment only in the ascent, Canto VIII is also composed in ways in which Act II of **The Cherry Orchard** is not—ways which the reader of the *Purgatorio* will not understand until he looks back from the top of the mountain. Then he will see the homesickness which informs Canto VIII in a new light, and all of the concrete elements, the snake in the grass, the winged figures that roost at the edge of the valley like night-hawks, will be intelligible to the mind and, without losing their concreteness, take their places in a more general frame. Dante's fiction is laid in the scene beyond the grave, where every human action has its relation to ultimate reality, even though that relation becomes explicit only gradually. But Chekhov's characters are seen in the flesh and in their very secular emotional entanglements: in the contemporary world as any-

one can see it—nothing visible beyond the earth's horizon, with its signs of social change. The fatality of the *Zeitgeist* is the ultimate reality in the theater of modern realism; the anagoge is lacking. And though Ibsen and Chekhov are aware of both history and moral effort, they do not know what to make of them—perhaps they reveal only illusory perspectives, "masquerades which time resumes." If Chekhov echoes Dante, it is not because of what he ultimately understood but because of the accuracy with which he saw and imitated that moment of action.

If one thinks of the generation to which Anya and Trofimov were supposed to belong, it is clear that the new motives and reasons which they were to find, after their inspired evening together, were not such as to turn all Russia, or all the world, into a garden. The potentialities which Chekhov presented at that movement of change were not to be realized in the wars and revolutions which followed: what actually followed was rather that separation and destruction, that scattering and destinationless trekking, which he also sensed as possible. But, in the cultivation of the dramatic art after Chekhov, renewals, the realization of hidden potentialities, did follow. In Chekhov's histrionic art, the "desire is turned back" to its very root, to the immediate response, to the movements of the psyche before they are limited, defined, and realized in reasoned purpose. Thus Chekhov revealed hidden potentialities, if not in the life of the time, at least in ways of seeing and showing human life; if not in society, at least in the dramatic art. The first and most generally recognized result of these labors was to bring modern realism to its final perfection in the productions of the Moscow Art Theater and in those who learned from it. But the end of modern realism was also a return to very ancient sources; and in our time the fertilizing effect of Chekhov's humble objectivity may be traced in a number of dramatic forms which cannot be called modern realism at all.

The acting technique of the Moscow Art Theater is so closely connected, in its final development, with Chekhov's dramaturgy, that it would be hard to say which gave the more important clues. Stanislavsky and Nemirovitch-Dantchenko from one point of view, and Chekhov from another, approached the same conception: both were searching for an attitude and a method that would be less hidebound, truer to experience, than the cliché-responses of the commercial theater. The Moscow Art Theater taught the performer to make that direct and total response which is the root of poetry in the widest sense: they cultivated the histrionic sensibility in order to free the actor to realize, in his art, the situations and actions which the playwright had imagined. Chekhov's plays demand this accuracy and imaginative freedom from the performer; and the Moscow Art Theater's productions of his works were a demonstration of the perfection, the reticent poetry, of modern realism. And modern realism of this kind is still alive in the work of many artists who have been more or less directly influenced either by Chekhov or by the Moscow Art Theater. In our country, for instance, there is Clifford Odets; in France, Vildrac and

Bernard, and the realistic cinema, of which *Symphonie Pastorale* is a recent example.

But this cultivation of the histrionic sensibility, bringing modern realism to its end and its perfection, also provided fresh access to many other dramatic forms. The Moscow technique, when properly developed and critically understood, enables the producer and performer to find the life in any theatrical form; and before the revolution the Moscow Art Theater had thus revivified *Hamlet, Carmen,* the interludes of Cervantes, Neoclassic comedies of several kinds, and many other works which were not realistic in the modern sense at all. A closely related acting technique underlay Reinhardt's virtuosity; and Copeau, in the Vieux Colombier, used it to renew not only the art of acting but, by that means, the art of play-writing also. . . .

After periods when great drama is written, great performers usually appear to carry on the life of the theater for a few more generations. Such were the Siddonses and Macreadys who kept the great Shakespearian roles alive after Shakespeare's theater was gone, and such, at a further stage of degeneration, were the mimes of the Commedia dell'Arte, improvising on the themes of Terence and Plautus when the theater had lost most of its meaning. The progress of modern realism from Ibsen to Chekhov looks in some respects like a withering and degeneration of this kind: Chekhov does not demand the intellectual scope, the ultimate meanings, which Ibsen demanded, and to some critics Chekhov does not look like a real dramatist but merely an overdeveloped mime, a stage virtuoso. But the theater of modern realism did not afford what Ibsen demanded, and Chekhov is much the more perfect master of its little scene. If Chekhov drastically reduced the dramatic art, he did so in full consciousness, and in obedience both to artistic scruples and to a strict sense of reality. He reduced the dramatic art to its ancient root, from which new growths are possible.

But the tradition of modern realism is not the only version of the theater in our time. The stage itself, belying the realistic pretense of artlessness and pseudo-scientific truth, is there. Most of the best contemporary play-writing accepts the stage "as stage," and by so doing tries to escape realistic limitations altogether.

Jacqueline E. M. Latham (essay date 1958)

SOURCE: "*The Cherry Orchard* as Comedy," in *Educational Theatre Journal*, Vol. X, No. 1, March 1958, pp. 21-9.

[*In the following essay, Latham assembles evidence for her contention that* The Cherry Orchard *is not a tragedy, as it was commonly viewed, but rather a comedy, as Chekhov insisted. Latham states: "In his revelation of the ludicrous in human nature Chekhov successfully achieves a very rare blend of sympathetic and judicial comedy" in the play.*]

Chekhov suffered during his lifetime from bad productions of his plays. Even Stanislavsky, the founder of the Moscow Art Theatre, misunderstood the nature of his comedies, **The Seagull** and **The Cherry Orchard,** and after the production of the latter Chekhov wrote to his wife: "How awful it is! An act that ought to take twelve minutes at most lasts forty minutes. There is only one thing I can say: Stanislavsky has ruined my play for me."[1] Stanislavsky and his fellow-director Nemirovich-Danchenko believed that Chekhov was wrong in thinking that he had written comedies; when Stanislavsky had read **The Cherry Orchard** he wrote to Chekhov informing him that it was, in fact, a tragedy. These Moscow productions, which were, of course, in many ways very fine, displeased Chekhov who was too ill to protest forcibly about them, and so they became the first of the line of melancholy productions which today we accept almost without question in England and the United States. Indeed, the pattern is so well established that it was brilliantly and easily parodied in Peter Ustinov's *The Love of Four Colonels.* Desmond MacCarthy (as did Shaw and many others) fully accepted Chekhov's plays as tragedies of frustration and in 1937, in *The New Statesman and Nation,* he reviewed a production of **Uncle Vanya** sharply criticizing the humor and comedy in the performance. However, his criticisms elicited a letter from Dorothy Sayers (whose first acquaintance with Chekhov this was) in defense of the production, saying "But the whole tragedy of futility is that it never succeeds in achieving tragedy. In its blackest moments it is inevitably doomed to the comic gesture."[2] This, the central point of Chekhov's comedy, is what so many critics have missed. In the United States, too, Edmund Wilson writing in *The New Yorker*[3] admits that in rereading Chekhov's plays he can find a broader humour than he remembers in stage productions. Indeed, the tradition is established and Chekhov has been accepted as a writer of gloomy tragedies of frustration; I doubt whether he can be reinstated as he would wish.

The Cherry Orchard,[4] Chekhov's last play, was written slowly and painfully in 1903. It was produced in January, 1904, by Stanislavsky at the Moscow Art Threatre only six months before the author's death. The subject of the play is the impoverishment of an aristocratic family who sell their house and orchard to one of their ex-serfs who wishes to build summer cottages. The passing of an era is a favourite subject for sentimentalists and it would have been easy for Chekhov to have shown aristocratic nobility and integrity at the mercy of an unscrupulous bourgeois. But he did not write that play, although many producers have wished that he had. He wrote instead a comedy. "The play has turned out not a drama, but a comedy, in parts even a farce."[5] He did not see the passing of the old order as tragic, and, in emphasizing the social uselessness of the aristocratic family, he treats the subject from a comic viewpoint. He sees in them no love, no sense of responsibility; their deepest emotion is only sentiment.

Chekhov's father was of peasant stock, for the grandfather had purchased their freedom, although he was, said

Chekhov, "a most rabid upholder of serfdom."[6] Chekhov's love for humanity was universal; he neither idealized the serfs from whom he sprang nor did he fawn upon the rich who were now his friends. Lydia Avilov, in her memoir, *Chekhov in my Life,* quotes Chekhov as saying, "I will describe life to you truthfully, that is artistically, and you will see in it what you have not seen before, what you never noticed before: its divergence from the norms, its contradictions."[7] It is exactly this that Chekhov achieves in **The Cherry Orchard** (although it was not, of course, of this play that he was speaking). All classes of men were for Chekhov possible subjects of comedy; his plays are about human nature and his sympathies did not lie exclusively with one class, nor did he wish to satirize the other. It is because he shows "divergence from the norms" that **The Cherry Orchard** is a comedy, and these anormalities he sees in the wealthy as well as in their servants. The play has, certainly, tragic overtones, as has Molière's *Le Misanthrope,* but the point of view of the author is definitely comic, and as if he wishes to emphasize this he introduces certain farcical incidents: squeaking boots, clumsiness, conjuring tricks, a governess dressed as a man jumping about in a ballroom, and an accidental blow with a stick struck by Varya on the man she loves.

Chekhov's purpose in writing **The Cherry Orchard** was to give a criticism of life by showing characters who deviate from the norm. The cherry orchard itself is not a constant symbol of beauty wantonly destroyed, but, as the centre of the play, it has a different significance for each character. There are twelve people who make up the *comèdie humaine,* all individuals, all more or less comic, some contributing to a central pattern of meaning, others merely performing peripherally their own comic dance and only occasionally impinging on the central pattern.

Although Chekhov considered the merchant Lopahin the central figure in the play,[8] it is best for us to consider first the brother and sister, Gayeff and Madame Ranevskaya. They are middle-aged children. For Gayeff life is a game, no more serious than the game of billiards which cheers him when his estate is sold and which he plays in imagination (though with words and gestures) whenever the problems of the material world seem too much for him. He leaves his estate for a life as a bank official saying "I am a financier now—yellow ball into the side pocket."[9] Even his tardily acquired career as a financier—for which his own financial failure has ill-prepared him—seems to be only a continuation of his life at the billiard table: trying to make a big break before he finally loses.

Gayeff's ridiculousness is accentuated by his continual eating of candies. "They say I've eaten my fortune up in hard candies" (II) he says laughing, but we know he doesn't believe it. This candy eating is a symbol of his childishness, of his unfitness for the adult world. Even old Fiers, the butler, treats him like a child, worrying whether he is dressed properly when he goes out and bringing him his coat when it is cold. His sister, too, has never matured. When her husband had died and her son

had been drowned shortly afterwards, she left Russia with her lover, leaving her two daughters behind. Her lover has been unfaithful and has spent all her money, yet at the end of the play she returns to him. She has spent her life avoiding real sorrow, for she has not the depth of character to accept it and to be purified by it. She is a creature of moods and in Act I appears like a child in her unconscious self-consciousness: "Is it really me sitting here? (*Laughing*) I'd like to jump around and wave my arms. (*Covering her face with her hands*) But I may be dreaming." Soon she is tearful, then kissing Fiers and the bookcase too.[10] For the brother and sister the orchard is a symbol of their youth, the youth they have never left. As Madame Ranevskaya looks out at it from their childhood nursery, she imagines that one of the trees in blossom is their mother, dressed in white, walking through the orchard. "I slept in this nursery," she exclaims, "and looked out on the orchard from here, every morning happiness awoke with me, it was just as it is now, then, nothing has changed" (I). This is, of course, Chekhov's point. The brother and sister have not changed, yet the world has. They are children in an adult world, and for the most part they are unaware of reality; even in their rare moments of self-knowledge they lack the power of coming to grips with reality.

Madame Ranevskaya's embrace of the bookcase is matched by her brother's even more ludicrous piece of self-dramatization, also in Act I, when he salutes the bookcase (tearfully) as "sustaining through the generations of our family our courage and our faith in a better future and nurturing in us ideals of goodness and of a social consciousness." This comic gesture not only helps us to see Gayeff's essential ridiculousness, but serves as an ironic commentary on his sister's character. The generosity shown when Madame Ranevskaya gives the drunken stranger a gold piece despite their extreme poverty is ludicrous, not admirable, for it is not based upon altruism or love but is an automatic gesture paralleled by her extravagance at restaurants where they cannot pay the bills. There is no longer any ideal of "goodness and of a social consciousness" in the family; had there been, the play might have been a tragedy. Rather, there is continual self-deception, punctuated by mawkish moments of self-awareness, as when at the end of Act I Gayeff says "And today I made a speech to the bookcase—so silly! And it was only when I finished it that I could see it was silly," only to add shortly after "On my honour I'll swear, by anything you like, that the estate shall not be sold! By my happiness, I swear! Here's my hand, call me a worthless, dishonourable man, if I allow it to come up for auction! With all my soul I swear it!" Chekhov's stage directions indicate that before he says this he puts a candy in his mouth.

This brings us to the central dramatic action—whether the estate should be sold to raise the necessary money or whether Gayeff and his sister should be prepared to raise money by letting part or all of it for building summer cottages. This is their dilemma and this is the issue they steadfastly refuse to face. When Lopahin suggests that they let the land, they refuse to. Gayeff promises that the estate will not be auctioned, deceiving himself into confidence in uninterested generals and a parsimonious rich aunt. The estate, of course, is auctioned and while Gayeff bids 15,000 roubles (provided by the rich aunt and eventually spent in Paris by Madame Ranevskaya with her lover), his sister is giving a ball to which the stationmaster and post-office clerk are invited. With magnificent understatement she says "We planned the ball at an unfortunate moment—well, it doesn't matter" (III). Their essential indifference to the fate of their estate is shown in the absence of practical measures to preserve it. They dramatize, pose, and make unreal gestures but they have protested too much; in the end they have forfeited their claim to our sympathy.

Lopahin, the ex-serf who has succeeded in life, is presented far more sympathetically by Chekhov. It is he who has the plan which will enable Gayeff and his sister to keep the estate, and even when eventually he buys it Chekhov is careful to point out that he bid for it only against an outsider and after Gayeff had withdrawn from the auction. In a letter to Stanislavsky, Chekhov writes:

> Lopahin is a merchant, but he is a decent man in every sense; he has to behave with perfect manners, like an educated man . . . Varya, a serious and religious girl, loved Lopahin; she would not have fallen in love with a money-grubber.[11]

and later:

> Dunya and Epihodoff stand in Lopahin's presence; they do not sit. Lopahin, in fact, maintains his position like a gentleman. He addresses the servants "thou" and they "you" him.[12]

Lopahin, then, is not a Dogberry, neither is he a Monsieur Jourdain. In his efforts to save their estate he is practical, though perhaps a little unfeeling, but Chekhov does not ask us to laugh at him for this. Indeed he embodies in many ways Chekhov's hopes for the future as expressed in Act II by the perennial student Trofimoff: the past can only be atoned for "through uncommon, incessant labor." Lopahin, though, is comic in another way; he who is successful in business matters is unsuccessful in his private life. Despite the fact that he is loved and respected by the family he is incapable of proposing marriage to Varya of whom he is fond and who loves him. As he has said in Act I to Dunyasha the maid, "You must know your place." He knows his too well, or rather, he is caught in his childhood sense of inferiority. He idealizes Madame Ranevskaya and is unable to marry her adopted daughter. She had said to him, when he had been hit by his father as a child, "Don't cry . . . little peasant" (I), and he still sees himself as a peasant and still worships Madame Ranevskaya. The stick, as David Magarshack noted,[13] is a symbol of his servitude ("father . . . just beat me in his drunken fits and always with a stick" [II]) and it is ironical that when in Act I he mocks Anya and Varya, who are perturbed about the debts incurred by the family, Varya threatens "I'd land him one like that *(shaking her fist)*." In fact she

does, accidentally, hit him with a stick when he returns from the auction to tell them that he has bought the estate; he may be master of the house, but he is not the master in his private life. For all his success as a businessman, for all his kindness and integrity, he yet remains the slave, unable to master his own happiness in his relationship with the family.

As if to emphasize this gulf between practical success and success in personal relationships. Chekhov has associated a second symbol with Lopahin: his watch. At the very beginning of the play Lopahin, who has come especially to meet Madame Ranevskaya at the station, wakes up to find that the train is in and that he has overslept. He never seems to overcome this initial setback; though he can be decisive about the remedy the family should take to save their estate, yet he cannot meet the people around him on equal terms. He seems to need the moral support of his watch—which is associated with the well-regulated business world of which he is master—when he is with Gayeff and his family. When he tries to tell them his idea for saving the estate and to take his departure, he four times refers to his watch as if for support. Finally, in Act IV, during his last talk with Varya, when he has already told Madame Ranevskaya that he will ask Varya to marry him, he is unable to broach the subject at all to her. When she enters, he is looking at his watch and the conversation ends when he calls to someone offstage "This minute." The stick and watch are symbols of Lopahin's divided personality. He is still in subjection spiritually and he is unable to conquer time and circumstances in his private life and to impose his will upon them. We know from Chekhov's letters that he wished us to admire Lopahin, for in many ways he is the embodiment of Chekhov's ideal for society, practical hard work. Yet in his inability to bring his personal desires and relationships into his control in the same way that he has dominated the commercial world, he is anormal. It is thus that he is a comic figure, though he is far more sympathetically portrayed than Gayeff and his sister.

The action of the play revolves around the debts incurred by the family and the way they can raise money on the estate. The solution that Gayeff and his sister are forced to accept—in spite of their illusory belief that they deserve to be saved from their predicament—is not an ideal one. Neither is Lopahin's suggestion of letting the orchard for commercial building wholly satisfactory to us. However, Chekhov does imply a different course of action, though it is now too late to implement it. It is Fiers, the deaf butler to whom no-one listens, who in Act I indicates a positive solution:

> FIERS: There was a time forty-fifty years ago when the cherries were dried, soaked, pickled, cooked into jam and it used to be—
>
> GAYEFF: Keep quiet, Fiers.
>
> FIERS: And it used to be that the dried cherries were shipped by the wagon-load to Moscow and to Kharkov. And the money there was! And the dried cherries

were soft then, juicy, sweet, fragrant—They had a way of treating them then—

MADAME RANEVSKAYA: And where is that way now?

FIERS: They have forgotten it. Nobody remembers now.

Chekhov's criticism of this aristocratic family, then, goes deeper: they have not only lived in an imaginary world, avoiding responsibility like children, but they have lost the means by which a life like this can be made possible; they have lost the secret and they do not even realize what they have done.

Only Fiers realizes what has been lost and only he of the servants knows what it is to serve, to work, and to maintain order. Significantly enough, like Chekhov's grandfather, he refers to the emancipation of serfs as "the disaster" and says that he did not take his freedom but stayed instead with his master. Although his aim in life is to serve, the irony of his situation lies in the fact that those whom he serves are unworthy of this dedication. Madame Ranevskaya's affection for Fiers is merely sentimental. He is part of the world that is slipping from her; he does not exist as a human being worthy of love or of gratitude. His life-long devotion is not even rewarded by a warm farewell when she thinks he is going to the hospital. Instead she relies upon another servant to make certain that he is taken and cared for. His end, left behind in the doomed house, is the one discordant note in the comedy. His rejection is, of course, symbolic. The days of which he is a legacy are over, the days when, as he says, "there were generals, barons, admirals dancing at our parties" (III), and a new era has begun. Gayeff and his sister cannot even command respect from their other servants, and when at the end they lock the house with Fiers inside, it is their final gesture of irresponsibility; it is symbolically very effective. However, on the literal level it introduces an alien note into the play, though as David Magarshack points out[14] there is no reason to suppose that Fiers dies, for Chekhov states clearly that Epihodoff, the clerk, is to remain behind. There is fine irony in Fiers' last speech in which he worries lest Gayeff may not have worn his topcoat and then, as if in final recognition, he applies to himself the epithet he has been applying to others, "good-for-nothing." He seems at this moment to realize that his life has passed in a cause which was not worthy of him. This, I believe, is Chekhov's only wholly tragic note. It becomes tragic because, although Fiers is self-deceived as the other characters are, we can admire him for his devotion and integrity.

Of Madame Ranevskaya's two daughters, Chekov told Nemirovich-Danchenko:

> Anya can be acted by anyone, even by a quite unknown actress, provided she is young and looks like a girl, and speaks in a young ringing voice. This is not one of the important parts . . . Varya's is a more serious part . . . she is a figure in a black dress, nun-like, a silly, a cry-baby etc. etc.[15]

Varya is a complementary character to Lopahin. She is unable to secure happiness because of her indecision yet in her management of the household she imposes a severe discipline. She loves Lopahin but "is quite incapable of disregarding the conventions which demand that the lady has to wait for the gentleman to propose to her."[16] Varya, as Chekhov wrote to his wife, is "a foolish creature"[17] and it is in her lack of purpose, her frequent weeping, and above all her inability to show any affection to the man she loves, that she is a comic character. Anya, too, is a feeble person but she resembles her mother, as Gayeff notices. She is as easily reassured as her mother is, and Gayeff's promises that the estate will be saved make her at once confident. Her joy in the cherry orchard is, like her mother's, a child's joy and she wishes to run out into the orchard in the early morning. For Varya, her proposed marriage is "like a dream" (I) and for Anya, too, reality hardly exists. When at the end of the play her mother leaves again for Paris and her lover, Anya promises her that she will work and pass examinations: "Then I'll work, I will help you. We'll read all sorts of books together. Mama isn't that so? We'll read in the autumn evenings, read lots of books and a new, wonderful world will open up before us."

In Anya's love affair with Trofimoff one can see another theme with which Chekhov is preoccupied. Trofimoff is a young intellectual—a student who has been sent down from his university for political reasons—and he becomes in some measure a spokesman for Chekhov and hence in this respect a normative character. He sees physical work as the key to social progress: "One must work and must help with all one's might those who see the truth. With us in Russia so far only a few work" (II).[18] But, ironically he is not one of these few. He is as ineffectual as Gayeff and his sister, but whereas they will not act because they cannot see reality, he does not act although he can see the future plainly. He perceives the truth but does not act on it and he is in this a comic figure. His appearance reinforces his ineffectualness and he says that a peasant woman called him "a mangy-looking gentleman" (I). But it is in his affection for Anya that he is really made to look ludicrous. He believes that they are "above love" (II). It is Madame Ranevskaya who points out the absurdity of this pose saying that he is a "ridiculous crank, a freak" (III). However, Madame Ranevskaya, who has abandoned herself to an unworthy lover and whose love for her daughters is so sentimental, is not the norm but another extreme. The norm we must see to lie between these paths, yet not in the timidity of Varya and Lopahin. Different attitudes to love, one of Chekhov's main comic themes, are handled here far more simply than in *The Seagull*.

Madame Ranevskaya, Gayeff, Lopahin, Varya, Anya, Trofimoff, and Fiers are the central characters in *The Cherry Orchard* and in their divergence from the norms they illustrate most seriously and effectively Chekhov's main comic themes. However, around them are grouped less important characters who are perhaps more obviously comic in themselves though they have less bearing on the main comic purpose. David Magarshack points out that Semyonoff-Pischtchik's name is itself comic. "The first half of it is impressively aristocratic and the second farcical (its English equivalent would be Squeaker)."[19] He is the lucky fool, the third son of the fairy tales, the man who deserves nothing—he even asks Gayeff for money—yet who wins everything. He misses jokes and laughs in the wrong place; he is so absent minded that he even forgets that the house has been sold and promises to drop in on Thursday when they are just departing. Finally, with a reversal which Chekhov so loved, he gives back to Gayeff and his sister the money he owes them, for, extraordinarily, white clay has been found on his land. He is magnificently vague and inconsequential, talking about his daughter Dashenka who is of interest to no one in the self-centered family.

Charlotta, the governess, is another broadly comic character. She says very little but enlivens the untimely ball by a conjuring and ventriloquist display. She is completely alone in the world; she does not even know how old she is. In her loneliness she gains for herself a group of admirers by her conjuring. She, unlike Madame Ranevskaya, Varya, and Anya who love although they are not able to achieve happiness in their love, loves no one. She seems to thirst for affection and pathetically in her ventriloquist act she converses with herself thus: "'You are so nice, you're my ideal.' The Voice: 'Madame, you too please me greatly'" (III). Charlotta might easily have been a tragic figure except that Chekhov has not explored her character deeply. In a letter to his wife he insists that the actress "must be funny in Charlotta, that's the chief thing,"[20] and later he adds that her dog "must be long-haired, small with no life in it, with sour eyes."[21] A well-cast Charlotta and a well-cast dog would make an amusing pair.

Finally, there are the younger servants. Epihodoff—or twenty-two misfortunes as he is called—is a man in squeky boots who drops flowers on the floor, falls over the chair, and puts a suitcase on top of a hat-box crushing it just as the family are about to leave with their luggage. He even welcomes misfortunes which help to justify the nickname which he thinks has been given to him in affection. He is pedantic and priggish, congratulating himself on his culture and yet uncertain whether to live or to shoot himself. His lack of control, which manifests itself in his clumsiness, is a reflection of his master's lack of self-discipline, and in his self-conscious (and stupid) pedantry we can see something of Gayeff's eloquent dramatization. He is a microcosm of the family, the most ludicrous traits of which are brought together in him. He loves the foolish maid Dunyasha and sings sad songs celebrating his happiness, yet he has no sense of his position in the house as a clerk. Dunyasha, in her indecision over whether to marry the pompous Epihodoff or the good-for-nothing Yasha, both of whom consider themselves superior to her, reveals her essential triviality. One of the most telling indictments of the family is their inability to handle their insolent servants or to appreciate the devotion of Fiers. In Act II Yasha insults Gayeff with impunity, and Gayeff even turns to his sister

saying "Either I or he—." Dunyasha, in her abandoned love for the pretentious Yasha, echoes Madame Ranevskaya's passion for her lover and this preserves the balance of morality between servants and masters.

The purpose of this article has been to show in what ways *The Cherry Orchard* is a comedy. It cannot be denied that there are occasional overtones of pathos and tragedy but these contribute to the depth and complexity of the comedy and provide the "contradictions" which, Chekhov said, "you never noticed before." As Dorothy Sayers says, the "tragedy of futility is that . . . it is inevitably doomed to the comic gesture," and if one wishes to see *The Cherry Orchard* as a tragedy of futility, one must grant that it is revealed in comedy. In his revelation of the ludicrous in human nature Chekhov successfully achieves a very rare blend of sympathetic and judicial comedy; although the audience are aware of the triviality and inadequacies of the comic characters yet they cannot completely dissociate themselves from them, to assume a superior position. The picture is complex: Chekhov criticizes his characters both in their relation to the material world and in their relation to each other; they are self-deceived, complacent, self-indulgent, ill-adjusted to the outside world, ill-adjusted to themselves, and often merely foolish. The pattern of this criticism is most easily discerned in the main characters, yet the minor characters perform small steps to the same tune, while retaining their sharp individuality. Chekhov wrote of a story "I have let the subject filter through my memory, so that only what is important or typical is left, as in a filter,"[22] this is his method, too, in his very complex plays.

NOTES

[1] March 29, 1904. *The Letters of Anton Pavlovitch Tchehov to Olga Leonardovna Knipper,* trans. Constance Garnett (New York, n.d.), p. 374. The last sentence is omitted here. It is given in full by David Magarshack, in *Chekhov a Life* (London, 1952), footnote on p. 383.
[2] Dorothy Sayers, *The New Statesman and Nation,* Feb. 27, 1937, p. 324.
[3] Edmund Wilson, "Seeing Chekhov Plain," *The New Yorker,* Nov. 22, 1952, p. 180-194.
[4] The text used is the translation by Stark Young in *Best Plays by Chekhov* (New York, 1956). All names will be given in his spelling.
[5] Letter to Madame Stanislavsky, Sept. 15, 1903. *The Life and Letters of Anton Tchekhov,* ed. and trans. S. S. Koteliansky & Philip Tomlinson (New York, n.d.), p. 290.
[6] Quoted in *Chekhov a Life,* p. 18.
[7] *Chekhov in my Life,* trans. David Magarshack (London, 1950), p. 32.
[8] Letter to Stanislavsky, Oct. 30, 1903. *Life and Letters,* p. 291.
[9] Act IV. Subsequent quotations will be identified by act numbers in parentheses.
[10] It is in character that the only books she mentions are fairy tales.
[11] Oct. 30, 1903. *Life and Letters.* p. 291.
[12] Nov. 10, 1903. *Life and Letters,* p. 293.
[13] *Chekhov the Dramatist* (London, 1952), p. 281.
[14] *Chekhov the Dramatist,* p. 285-6.
[15] Nov. 2, 1903. *Life and Letters,* p. 292.
[16] *Chekhov the Dramatist,* p. 278.
[17] Nov. 1, 1903. *Letters to Olga Knipper,* p. 336.
[18] The orchard is for Trofimoff a symbol of tyranny. He says in Act II "All Russia is our orchard."
[19] *Chekhov the Dramatist,* p. 284.
[20] Nov. 8, 1903. *Letters to Olga Knipper,* p. 341.
[21] Nov. 27, 1903. *Letters to Olga Knipper,* p. 349.
[22] Letter to F. D. Batyushkov, Dec. 15, 1897. *Life and Letters,* p. 252.

Ronald Gaskell (essay date 1972)

SOURCE: "Chekhov: *The Cherry Orchard*," in *Drama and Reality:* The European Theatre since Ibsen, Routledge & Kegan Paul, 1972, pp. 94-8.

[*In this essay, Gaskell examines Chekhov's "uniquely honest and sensitive vision of life" in* The Cherry Orchard.]

Chekhov finished **The Cherry Orchard** in October 1903 and sent it immediately to the Moscow Art Theatre. Three weeks later, writing again from Yalta, he asked Vishnevsky, one of the actors with the company, to keep him a scat for *Pillars of Society*: 'I want to have a look at this amazing Norwegian play and will even pay for the privilege. Ibsen is my favourite author, you know.' If this was meant seriously, which seems unlikely, one would guess that it caused some surprise. Stanislavsky records that when they were acting *Hedda Gabler* Chekhov told him bluntly that Ibsen was not a playwright. On another occasion, at a rehearsal of *The Wild Duck,* he broke out: 'Look here, Ibsen does not know life. In life it does not happen like that.' Ibsen would have agreed that the theatre should present life as it happens. Life did not mean to him, however, what it meant to Chekhov. For Ibsen to live is to choose: to affirm an integrity assailed at once by others and by the trolls within the self. For Chekhov to live is to grow old; to recognize that we live alone, and that if life has any meaning we are not likely to discover it.

This may explain why his search for a dramatic form—a form that would reveal life as Chekhov saw it—proved so difficult. Ibsen, from *Pillars of Society* onwards, could explore his themes through a vigorous rehandling of conventions already available in the well-made play (the intrigue plot, the discovered secret, the effective confrontation). For the well-made play, from Scribe to Sartre, involves us in the life of moral action: a life, no doubt, more exciting than our own, but like our own in its commitment to desires and projects thwarted by other people. Ibsen sees this world more clearly, and presents it far more truthfully, than Scribe; his morality is not that of the Paris boulevards. But for Ibsen too, in his prose plays, this is the world we have to contend with.

Chekhov sees life less in terms of action than in terms of feeling. More exactly, perhaps, in terms of sensibility. (So in the first act of **The Cherry Orchard** it is partly the fatigue of the travellers, heightening their delight in the freshness of the trees, that makes the orchard real to our imagination.) The difference from an Ibsen play can be felt at once:

MRS RANEVSKY: How does it go now? Let me remember. 'Put the red in the corner. Double into the middle.'

GAEV: Screw shot into the corner. At one time, dear sister, we both used to sleep in this room. And now I'm fifty-one, unlikely as it may sound.

LOPAKHIN: Yes, time marches on.

GAEV: What's that?

LOPAKHIN: Time. It marches on, I was saying.

GAEV: This place smells of cheap scent.

Why do we recognize this instantly as Chekhov? Not just because Gaev starts reminiscing, doesn't at first hear Lopakhin, and then goes off at a tangent, but because the immediate sense impression ('This place smells of cheap scent') cuts across the track of thought and feeling. Chekhov's objection to *The Wild Duck* was that 'in life it does not happen like that'. Our response to **The Cherry Orchard** is surely that in life it happens very much like that: for Chekhov's apparently inconsequential dialogues, and monologues, trace out very precisely the actual movements of the psyche. In his letters Chekhov speaks of the writer's need to be 'as objective as a chemist'. But if he sees his people objectively, as he does—finite, vulnerable, comic and therefore sad—he feels them intuitively: as we feel ourselves, not as we observe others.

Chekhov's sympathy with men and women goes deep. It is more than a delight in traits of personality, more even than a delicate responsiveness to the play of feeling. It is the kind of awareness that we meet in Shakespeare in those phrases where, as Eric Bentley puts it, we move beyond a character's personality to his humanity. Hence, perhaps, those moments in **The Cherry Orchard** which make visible the intersection of two lives. As Lopakhin enters towards the end of the third act, the guests crowd into the drawing room and the band falls silent:

MRS RANEVSKY: Was the cherry orchard sold?

LOPAKHIN: It was.

MRS RAVENSKY: Who bought it?

LOPAKHIN: I did.

Varya flings her housekeeping keys to the floor and runs out. Gaev has already gone to change. Mrs Ranevsky is alone, beside the guests who form an audience for Lopakhin. His speech, with its pride at having justified his life, is the most passionate in the play:

If my father and grandfather could only rise from their graves and see what happened, see how their Yermolay—Yermolay who was always being beaten, who could hardly write his name and ran round barefoot in winter—how this same Yermolay bought this estate, the most beautiful place in the world. I've bought the estate where my father and grandfather were slaves, where they weren't even allowed inside the kitchen.

Mrs Ranevsky, a few minutes before, had told Trofimov: 'I was born here, my father and mother lived here, and my grandfather too. I love this house. Without the cherry orchard life has no meaning for me and if it really must be sold then you'd better sell me with it.' The ironic light that Lopakhin's words shed back on these does more than qualify our sympathy for Mrs Ranevsky; it reminds us, as Chekhov often reminds us, of the separate and equal reality of human lives.

Chekhov, we said, gives us little in the way of action. And because his people, in general, are withdrawn from action, they have time not only to reflect but to appreciate the world in which they live. In his stories Chekhov had trained himself to economy: no landscape painting but a single brushstroke—the smell of meadowsweet after rain, the dark blue of a wood below a stormy sky. In his plays, too, a few words are enough to suggest the heat of summer or the chill of an autumn evening. But a play, as Chekhov knew, is made with more than words. At the beginning of *The Cherry Orchard* the stage is growing light (Dunyasha almost at once blows out her candle). Somewhere outside a dog is howling: 'The dogs have been awake all night, they can tell the family are coming.' In a few minutes carriages are heard. The air is cold, birds are singing in the garden. Lopakhin explains his plan for saving the estate and at last takes himself off. The shutters are opened, the room fills with sunshine, Gaev and his sister look out at the branches whose shadows play against the wall.

Chekhov's feeling for sound, as for nuances of light, creates a sense of space, of the reality of the natural world, unusual in the theatre. At the same time he relates this world to human feeling. The setting for the second act is open country. As the sun drops Lopakhin is speaking of the plains and forests of Russia, of its vast horizons. Yepikhodov, romantic and absurd, crosses against the sky. We hear the plangent chords of his guitar, with a counterpoint of voices:

> There goes Yepikhodov.
>   —There goes Yepikhodov.
> The sun has set, my friends.
>   —Yes.

It is the climax of the play. Gaev, eloquent as ever, transposes into comedy the sentiment gathering in the air. Silence. The distant sound, as if from the sky, of a breaking string; then the intrusion of a passer-by to disrupt the group so that Anya and Trofimov are alone. (The moon rises, the guitar is heard again quietly.)

To be aware of nature in this way is to be aware of time, as the process of change. Chekhov's plays are saturated in time, so that the scene gradually expands and deepens till beyond each phrase and gesture we are conscious of the events that have brought these people together. Lopakhin and Mrs Ranevsky have known each other since she was a girl, and the play is crowded with recollections of the past. These are not, as they would be in Ibsen, references to a crucial moment that has shaped the present; they are casual, often nostalgic allusions to events of childhood, of the last few years, or of long ago. The bookcase which Gaev addresses in the first act, and which stands in a corner when they leave at the end, goes back,

to his delight, a hundred years. The first and last acts take place in the room where he and his sister slept as children—the room from which she would look out at the orchard and from which the boy Gaev saw his father setting off for church.

Chekhov's feeling for the reality of time gives his plays their typical curve of development. Each of his three finest plays starts with an arrival—with people recognizing each other, asking questions, recounting what has happened to them—and ends with the sadness of departure, with the breaking of relationships that have formed the emotional substance of the play. In *The Cherry Orchard* this design is strengthened by a second, taken from the natural world. The play begins in spring, moves through summer (the orchard is sold in August), and ends on a day—cold and sunny: an echo of the first act—in October. Characteristically, Chekhov looks ahead: to the return of spring, when the house will be pulled down. Meantime Gaev is taking a job at the bank, Varya going to keep house for the Ragulins, Lopakhin leaving for business affairs in Kharkov. Like a river seen through an open window, their lives have flowed through the play and flow beyond it.

The analogy is not exact, but it suggests the clarity and detachment of Chekhov's vision and the apparently casual movement of his plays. For most of us life has no more direction or unity than the paragraphs of a newspaper: a street burns down, a baron is killed in a duel, Balzac was married in Berdichev. No writer has caught this random quality of experience more exactly than Chekhov. Yet his characters do not just drift. Like the acrobats of Rilke's [fifth Duino Elegy], they travel from place to place, spending their skill and energy to group themselves in a pattern that holds for a moment and then collapses. The pattern has no significance, yet we feel it should have. For though this world may be all there is, we can never be content with it; beyond our migratory lives we look for something that would give them meaning 'if we could only know'.

There are writers, Eliot for example, who believe we can know. Chekhov records simply that we want to. Occasionally, as the light fails, we catch the sound of a breaking string, dying away sadly; an owl, perhaps, or a heron. Or we are reconciled for a moment to the world, seeing in the wind that sways the dead tree with the living an image of the life that we belong to.

Beyond the humour and humanity of *The Cherry Orchard* it is this that gives the play its depth. The selection and composition, the development of a theme through character, scene and speech, is the expression of a uniquely honest and sensitive vision of life. It is not a vision imposed on life, as one often feels that Eliot's or Ibsen's is, but an order discerned in life—an order that we glimpse ourselves faintly and imperfectly. In Chekhov we see, made coherent and intelligible, the interdependence of persons essentially solitary: changing in time, caring for each other, and at moments aware of the stillness at the centre of their lives.

Beverly Hahn (essay date 1973)

SOURCE: "Chekhov's *The Cherry Orchard*," in *The Critical Review*, No. 16, 1973, pp. 56-72.

[*In the essay below, Hahn interprets* The Cherry Orchard *as a comedy in the classical sense, with social and cultural significance. Hahn asserts: "The often comic characters in the play inhabit a world that is nonetheless felt to be humanly and historically serious."*]

The Cherry Orchard is the last of Chekhov's plays, one he always insisted was a comedy. **The Three Sisters,** he agreed, was a drama; but with his last play he had done something else:

> What has emerged from me is not a drama but a comedy, sometimes even a farce . . . the last act is gay, the whole play is gay, light . . . why on the posters and in the advertisements is my play so persistently called a *drama*? Nemirovich and Stanislavsky see in it a meaning different from what I intended. They never read it attentively, I am sure.
>
> (Quoted from Raymond Williams, "Anton Chekhov," *Drama from Ibsen to Eliot,* Peregrine, 1964, p. 149)

The dialogue between Chekhov and Stanislavsky on the subject is a famous one; but since it raises at least Chekhov's intention to make **The Cherry Orchard** a comedy, it provides a good point of departure for another look at the play itself. In recent years there has, of course, been a reaction against the older view that took Stanislavsky's side in the debate. David Magarshack (*Chekhov the Dramatist,* London, 1952) stresses to the last inch its elements of farce; Maurice Valency discovers the play to be, of all things, "cosmic *vaudeville*" (*The Breaking String,* New York 1966); and Logan Speirs finds it "astonishingly light and fresh" (*Tolstoy and Chekhov,* Cambridge 1971). Clearly, something along these lines, if not so extreme, needed to be said. But it is surely time to challenge the narrow definition of "comedy" that seems implicit in all these accounts, in the hope that applying the term in a more classical sense will help break through the debate.

There is a certain amount of common ground with which one can start. The cherry orchard itself is generally agreed to be Chekhov's means of imaging a quality of aristocratic life to which the central characters, Gaev and Lyubov, at the beginning of the play now only superficially belong. It forms the centre of a balanced composition that begins immediately Lopahin first suggests his plan to cut the orchard down:

> LYUBOV. Cut down? My dear fellow, forgive me, but you don't know what you are talking about. If there is one thing interesting—remarkable indeed—in the whole province, it's just our cherry orchard.
>
> LOPAHIN. The only thing remarkable about the orchard is that it's a very large one. There's a crop of cherries

every alternate year, and then there's nothing to be done with them, no one buys them.

> GAEV. This orchard is mentioned in the "Encyclopaedia".
>
> LOPAHIN (*glancing at his watch*). If we don't decide on something and don't take some steps, on the 22nd of August the cherry orchard and the whole estate too will be sold by auction. Make up your minds! There is no other way of saving it, I'll take my oath on that. No, no!
>
> FIRS. In old days, forty or fifty years ago, they used to dry the cherries, soak them, pickle them, make jam too, and they used—
>
> GAEV. Be quiet, Firs.
>
> FIRS. And they used to send the preserved cherries to Moscow and to Harkov by the waggon-load. That brought the money in! And the preserved cherries in those days were soft and juicy, sweet and fragrant . . . They knew the way to do them then . . .
>
> LYUBOV. And where is the recipe now?
>
> FIRS. It's forgotten. Nobody remembers it.
>
> [*The Cherry Orchard and Other Plays,* translated by Constance Garnett, London 1946, pp. 15-6]

The voices on the stage come from three directions in time. Firs's is from the past, when the orchard was abundant with life and work, beautiful but productive too. Lyubov and Gaev speak from the present of an orchard already more important for private reasons than for itself: it is a landmark mentioned in the "Encyclopaedia", a spectacle that is no longer useful but one intimately associated with their childhood. Finally, in Lopahin, we have the voice of the future, which assures us of the necessity of its sacrifice. The voices are intertwined to great effect, while being kept separate and distinct. And what they give us, as they emerge relative to each other, is a significantly deepening perspective on the centrally placed image of the cherry orchard. Like the gentry themselves, the orchard is a touching relic of the past: glorious in blossom, imaging a gracious and leisurely age, but essentially of no use. In its present state its vulnerability seems a cause for sadness, but its unproductiveness, compared with the juicy harvests of the past, partly qualifies the loss. Compared with it again, Lopahin's projected villas will be ugly and perhaps vulgar, but they will at least have their use as well as their vitality from a new and growing class.

This much is indicated very early in the first Act. But it is characteristic of Chekhov criticism generally that very few accounts of **The Cherry Orchard** get much beyond this sense of things (mixed up with discussions of character) and a definition of the "comic" or "tragic" or "tragi-comic" response Chekhov is supposed to have had to it. It is here that the disputes arise. For, on the one hand,

Chekhov creates a sense of social transition and of its cost, showing a serious interest in the nature and process of social evolution. The financial ruin of the old estates, the relation of that to the Emancipation of the serfs, and the growth of a new merchant class out of the ranks of the former serfs, all have some mention in the play and are in some ways the central psychic facts under whose impetus the characters act. But Firs's subservience, Lopahin's rather aggressive autonomy, and Gaev's failure to be realistic about his debts are not the deeply (even tragically) consequential states *The Three Sisters* might have made of them. They are presented, instead, with a finely achieved lightness of touch. Like *The Three Sisters,* the play is imbued with a sense of social and cultural tension, which the breaking string and the thud of the axe express at snapping-point. But even at the first ominous sound of that string a lighter note is not far away:

> (*All sit plunged in thought. Perfect stillness. The only thing audible is the muttering of* FIRS. *Suddenly there is a sound in the distance, as it were from the sky— the sound of a breaking harp-string, mournfully dying away.*)
>
> LYUBOV. What is that?
>
> LOPAHIN. I don't know. Somewhere far away a bucket fallen and broken in the pits. But somewhere very far away.
>
> GAEV. It might be a bird of some sort—such as a heron.
>
> TROFIMOV. Or an owl.
>
> LYUBOV. *(Shudders)* I don't know why, but it's horrid *(a pause).*
>
> FIRS. It was the same before the calamity—the owl hooted and the samovar hissed all the time.
>
> GAEV. Before what calamity?
>
> FIRS. Before the emancipation *(a pause).*
>
> (pp. 40-1)

The way the sound is placed, at an impasse in the conversation and immediately the sun has set, gives it clear symbolic force—which Maurice Valency's suggestively titled book, *The Breaking String,* somewhat disappointingly fails to specify. It is the sound of social transition, of the passing away of a particular class, as the wheels of a society begin to turn. As the string snaps over characters momentarily silent and stilled, the history that will absorb them feels sadly, and even horrifically, palpable. The play deepens suddenly into a premonition of the defeat awaiting its characters—with the exception, of course, of Lopahin. Yet the social significance of the snapping string is at once suggested and *lightened* by Firs's reference to similar omens before the Emancipation. The long perspective of time returns to the immediate comedy of Firs's remark.

This tension in the play's mood is even more obvious when it comes to Chekhov's balancing the old order against the new—a departure again from the tone and feeling of *The Three Sisters. The Cherry Orchard,* in fact, functions throughout in terms of symmetry. Realistically aware of what is gained, as well as what is lost, in the destruction of the orchard, it avoids naive or weak sentimentality. The old order had its bitterness, always present in Trofimov's mind, of which we are asked to be aware:

> Think only, Anya, your grandfather, and great-grandfather, and all your ancestors were slave-owners—the owners of living souls—and from every cherry in the orchard, from every leaf, from every trunk there are human creatures looking at you. Cannot you hear their voices? Oh, it is awful!
>
> (p. 43)

But, to balance this, the new one has its positive side:

> LOPAHIN. I sowed three thousand acres with poppies in the spring, and now I have cleared forty thousand profit. And when my poppies were in flower, wasn't it a picture! So here, as I say, I made forty thousand, and I'm offering you a loan because I can afford to. Why turn up your nose? I am a peasant—I speak bluntly.
>
> (p. 67)

Though Lopahin's practicality involves bluntness of manner and even downright destruction, he can be generous and he is not utterly impervious to beauty. His honesty and openness in the play can be as refreshing as a cool wind; and if his poppies are more flamboyant than the stately cherry-orchard and more transient in blossom, they are nevertheless what the cherry orchard no longer is. Though lacking the historical and in a sense cultural permanence of the orchard, they have a more colourful vitality; and, along with their beauty, they are—importantly—profitable. Their beauty *is* their "use", a beauty for which, unlike that of the orchard, people are prepared to pay.

The earliest plays that Chekhov wrote were vaudeville and farce, and indeed the comic sense of behaviour he exploited there was never far from his work. His sense of humour, while often expressed as irony, also involved a keen sense of the ridiculous in human gesture; and there *are* many individual effects in *The Cherry Orchard* that border on burlesque. The whole conception of Epihodov, "two and twenty misfortunes", for example, makes for a fairly primitive kind of comedy running through the whole play as he squashes, breaks and falls over everything. Trofimov, too, falls downstairs at the point of his indignant exit in Act III, and in the same Act Varya wields a stick that almost hits the wrong man. If there is a more sinister significance attaching to the distasteful Pishtchik and Yasha, the comic vein still continues. The characters of *The Cherry Orchard,* as Valency notices, are more formulaic than those of Chekhov's other major plays, though they are not caricatures; in fact, Mme Ranevsky

Act III of the Moscow Art Theater production of The Cherry Orchard, *1904.*

is the only figure who is even potentially tragic. But even Mme Ranevsky, if she is not herself comic, is set in a context where comedy is always likely to arise. When she pronounces herself so glad to find old Firs alive, he responds deafly "the day before yesterday", and her worldly, rather heavy-handed "wit" is made humorous, if it isn't already, by the solemnity with which it is received:

> PISHTCHIK (*to* LYUBOV ANDREYEVNA). What's it like in Paris? Did you eat frogs there?
>
> LYUBOV. Oh, I ate crocodiles.
>
> PISHTCHIK. Fancy that now!
>
> (p. 16)

Yet although the ridiculous is part of Chekhov's sense of *people,* it is not his ultimate response to life. The often comic characters in the play inhabit a world that is nonetheless felt to be humanly and historically serious. So that when Chekhov called **The Cherry Orchard** a "comedy" he may well have meant comedy in the classical sense: not something designed to provoke actual laughter, but a kind of art that, while being imbued with a strong sense of the destiny of its figures, refuses to see that destiny tragically. The sad and spasmodically anguished debate between Chekhov and Stanislavsky about the kind of play each deemed it to be does seem to have rested on a more literal-minded view, at least on Stanislavsky's part, of what the comic mode might involve. Looked at more broadly, however, **The Cherry Orchard** belongs to something like the category of *The Winter's Tale*: it contains a tragedy but does not allow it to be fulfilled. In Chekhov's case, this is not because the ending brings partial recovery: Lyubov and Gaev do finally lose their estate. But what is lost at the end of **The Cherry Orchard** has really already been lost at the beginning. Mme Ranevsky and her family have been away from the cherry-orchard and the play records their coming home; the pattern is primarily one of return—return to a way of life, idyllic and pure, but which there is really no hope of sustaining. So that, rather than a tragedy, **The Cherry**

Orchard might be seen, from one point of view, as a modern adaptation of Pastoral.

Pastoral, of course, has taken many forms over the centuries. Wordsworth's "nature" poetry, for example, or Corot's landscapes may not seem "pastoral" in the classical sense at all. But it does seem as if periods of very rapid social transition are often accompanied in the arts by a renewal of interest (on the part of both artists and their audiences) in images of rural content. At its simplest, the contrast between an ideal of rustic goodness and the sophisticated vanities of the world is the artist's most natural moral reaction to the competing energies of a society in rapid change. Yet even if the contrast takes more complicated artistic forms than this, the popular tendency at such times to equate the loss of an old way of life with the loss of cultural innocence may well supply the artist with a stock of potent psychological imagery. In **The Cherry Orchard** that imagery involves the orchard itself, identified by both Lyubov and Gaev with the purity of their childhood, to which, in coming back to the orchard, Lyubov is trying to return. And, together with that, Chekhov quite self-consciously adapts to his usual stage effects the pastoral shepherd's pipe and wayside shrine. In effect, just prior to the onset of one of the most momentous social transitions in modern history, Chekhov renovated stylized elements of an old pastoral mode for his own distinctly modern purposes: to define the yearning for lost innocence that is so central to Lyubov's individual psychology, and to indicate by ironic disjunctions from the pastoral ideal the state of a culture in which the loss of innocence (and energy) has long since happened.

Like **The Seagull, The Cherry Orchard** is constructed around a central image, not (as in **Uncle Vanya** and **The Three Sisters**) around a person or persons. On the whole, this has the disadvantaage of robbing the play of that interest in complex personalities that makes **The Three Sisters** so humanly rich. But the advantages for Chekhov of this quasi-symbolist way of conceiving his task are, firstly, the tightness it enables him to give to the shape of his work, and secondly, the opportunity it offers, by removing him from close psychological involvement with his characters, for a drama with an explicit cultural and historical dimension. Where the abundance of **The Three Sisters** may hinder an easy perception of its emergent pattern, **The Cherry Orchard** immediately feels to be a well-constructed play. And where our absorption by Olga's, Masha's and Irena's personalities in **The Three Sisters** may distract us from noticing the stage-composition, there is no such distraction from **The Cherry Orchard**'s changing visual tableaux. **The Cherry Orchard** begins and ends with a stage without people: in each case there is only the "nursery", cold and empty, with the cherry-orchard sparkling through its windows. The cherry-orchard itself is the *dramatis persona*. For, right from the beginning of Act I, it is from the static spectacle of the orchard, white with frost, that the play takes its psychological shape:

> *A room, which has always been called the nursery. One of the doors leads into* ANYA's *room. Dawn, sun rises during the scene. May, the cherry trees in flower, but it is cold in the garden with the frost of early morning. Windows closed. Enter* DUNYASHA *with a candle and* LOPAHIN *with a book in his hand.*

(p. 3)

The sunrise is just beginning as the Act begins, so that the light defines the cherry-orchard against the more shadowy inside foreground; and the whiteness of the blossoming trees and frosted earth gives the outside scene a static, timeless air. As the light gradually intensifies throughout the Act, the cherry-orchard pales back into the distance. But no account of the play can afford to disregard this immediate visual presentation of the orchard, impersonal and almost magically suspended in the morning frost. For its strangely timeless quality and mute purity become for a while, as in pastoral, the reference-points against which the ordinary human world seems burdened and exhausted by time. The room in which Act I takes place is a former nursery, a place full of memories. Lopahin and Dunyasha enter during those odd few minutes between night and day when time is most palpable:

> LOPAHIN. The train's in, thank God. What time is it?

> DUNYASHA. Nearly two o'clock *(puts out the candle)*. It's daylight already.

(p. 3)

And, when Lopahin begins his typically Chekhovian reverie, bringing a personal and social past simultaneously forward to sustain his anticipation of seeing Lyubov again, the complexity of human time is felt against the unvarying cycle of the cherry-blossoming, momentarily spellbound in three degrees of frost:

> Lyubov Andreyevna has been abroad five years; I don't know what she is like now . . . She's a splendid woman. A good-natured, kind-hearted woman. I remember when I was a lad of fifteen, my poor father—

he used to keep a little shop here in the village in those days—gave me a punch in the face with his fist and made my nose bleed. We were in the yard here, I forget what we'd come about—he had had a drop. Lyubov Andreyevna—I can see her now—she was a slim young girl then—took me to wash my face, and then brought me into this very room, into the nursery. "Don't cry, little peasant," says she, "it will be well in time for your wedding day" *(a pause)*.

(pp. 3-4)

Human time, as Chekhov envisages it, is both complicated by nostalgia and fraught with irony. This "little peasant" will later own Lyubov's estate, and her troubles will be increased by his failure to have that "wedding-day". But it is the *irrevocability* of time that occupies our attention in Act I as Lyubov and her entourage arrive back from the worldliness of Paris in the hope of a new life. When, towards the end of the Act, the windows are flung open to the orchard twittering with birds, the innocence of which it reminds Lyubov has an almost tragic past tense:

> VARYA *(softly)*. Anya's asleep. *(Softly opens the window)* Now the sun's risen, it's not a bit cold. Look, mamma, what exquisite trees! My goodness! And the air! The starlings are singing!

> GAEV *(opens another window)*. The orchard is all white. You've not forgotten it, Lyuba? That long avenue that runs straight, straight as an arrow, how it shines on a moonlight night. You remember? You've not forgotten?

> LYUBOV *(looking out of the window into the garden)*. Oh, my childhood, my innocence! It was in this nursery I used to sleep, from here I looked out into the orchard, happiness waked with me every morning and in those days the orchard was just the same, nothing has changed *(laughs with delight)*. All, all white! Oh, my orchard! After the dark gloomy autumn, and the cold winter, you are young again, and full of happiness, the heavenly angels have never left you . . . If I could cast off the burden that weighs on my heart, if I could forget the past!

(p. 20)

It is characteristic of Chekhov to avoid a surface nostalgia here (that emotion which is so attractive, yet so dangerous in unskilled hands), and instead to make Lyubov's, albeit somewhat theatrical, longing for childhood a longing for innocence and escape from time. The whiteness she prizes as purity in the orchard touches her because of the loss of that quality in her own life (just as Gaev, too, values the brilliance and symmetry that are missing from his). For although Mme Ranevsky is an attractive character, a woman of energy of whom Chekhov said "nothing but death could subdue a woman like that", there is a worldliness and incipient vulgarity about her that reveal her a long way, psychologically, from the cherry-orchard world of her youth. She feels the passing of time, not in terms of age, but in terms of guilt—guilt about her lover, about the death of her son, about all that

Paris has meant to her. And if, as the play goes on, she seems singularly inactive about any attempt to save the orchard that means so much to her, it is, first, because she feels morally that she does not *deserve* the orchard, and second, because in that world she does not actually *belong*. In her deepest self she regards the experience of losing the orchard, of letting it slip through her hands, as a form of penance—the loss of the *emblem* of that innocence whose reality has long since gone. In any case, the call of her life—and love—is to Paris. The telegrams that arrive at her estate even before she herself does are a persistent cause of tension, of self-division, which under the trying circumstances of Act III suddenly explodes into a defiant recognition of where her allegiances lie:

> LYUBOV. That's a telegram from Paris. I get one every day. One yesterday and one today. That savage creature is ill again, he's in trouble again. He begs forgiveness, beseeches me to go, and really I ought to go to Paris to see him. You look shocked, Petya. What am I to do, my dear boy, what am I to do? He is ill, he is alone and unhappy, and who'll look after him, who'll keep him from doing the wrong thing, who'll give him his medicine at the right time? And why hide it or be silent? I love him, that's clear. I love him! I love him! He's a millstone about my neck, I'm going to the bottom with him, but I love that stone and can't live without it *(presses* TROFIMOV'S *hand).* Don't think ill of me, Petya, don't tell me anything, don't tell me . . .
>
> (pp. 53-4)

After this speech, a few significantly placed lines from "The Magdalene" make it clear that, paradoxical as it may seem, the cherry-orchard, with all its metaphoric connotations of innocence for Lyubov, *has* to be lost for her to have peace of mind.

When the play begins, the only character to have anything like the purity the orchard represents is Anya, who bears so much likeness to Lyubov's younger self. In Act I all hope seems centred on her. Significantly, the shepherd's pipe plays as she retires to bed, and the last words of the Act are a spoken tribute to her (ordinary metaphors, perhaps, but meaningfully suggestive of natural radiance in this carefully established context):

> TROFIMOV *(tenderly).* My sunshine! My spring.

Later in the play, however, as Anya becomes more and more the victim of Trofimov's rhetoric, her value as embodying innocence is greatly qualified. In welcoming the "new dawn" with Trofimov, she subordinates her natural goodness to a shaky ideal; and at the end of Act III she comforts Lyubov with promises that are plainly empty. The pastoral shepherd's piping is not heard again after the end of Act I.

Chekhov, as I have said, is renovating certain elements of pastoral to define a process of cultural transition. The whole opening scene of Act II, as a pictorial composition, is pastoral in character—the initial illusion of purity about the pastoral setting becoming only gradually and subtly ironic as we discern the presence of the "great town" in the background. Then, more particularly, the ironic intention becomes manifest through the disintegration of the pure and exact visual impression (described in the elaborate stage-directions) into an incongruous awkwardness of movement and modernity of dialogue when the action actually begins. The "wider horizon" Chekhov wanted in the stage-setting provides an urban perspective to the pastoral image, foreshadowing the end of a country idyll. More importantly, however, the human groupings in the foreground (framed, in this case, by the wayside shrine and well, so clearly reminiscent of pastoral) recall Watteau's famous painting, *Les Charmes de la Vie,* bringing to mind the subtle melancholy of that picture. Epihodov is set apart with his guitar, while the others are clustered on the garden seat. The setting seems initially to invite delight and the pleasures of courtly love. But, while there is a love-triangle of a kind between Yasha, Dunyasha and Epihodov, it is not one to radiate innocence and joy. Like Yasha's and Epihodov's singing, something in the setting is vaguely off-key: there is a sense of disquiet, and each figure, "plunged in thought", seems oddly absorbed in himself.

Like Watteau's *Gilles,* Chekhov's composition shows his feeling for the fate of those secondary characters, like the artificer and the clown, who have been congenially parasitic on a high culture which is now entering a phase of decline. For, before the lifelessness of a culture is generally recognized, these people instinctively reflect the fact by a certain stiffness of posture and, in some cases, artlessness of gesture. Their demeanour reveals the emptiness of their art which, in no longer serving something vital, no longer serves them. So that it is no small calculation on Chekhov's part that Act II should begin with Charlotta—governess, conjurer and ventriloquist—captured at an artlessly confessional moment, speaking (unheard) to other subordinate people, all of whom seem, despite their stylized postures, lonely and bereft of resource:

> CHARLOTTA *(musingly).* I haven't a real passport of my own, and I don't know how old I am, and I always feel that I'm a young thing. When I was a little girl, my father and mother used to travel about to fairs and give performances—very good ones. And I used to dance *salto-mortale* and all sorts of things. And when papa and mamma died, a German lady took me and had me educated. And so I grew up and became a governess. But where I came from, and who I am, I don't know . . . who my parents were, very likely they weren't married . . . I don't know *(takes a cucumber out of her pocket and eats).* I know nothing at all *(a pause).* One wants to talk and has no one to talk to . . . I have nobody.
>
> EPIHODOV *(plays on the guitar and sings).* "What care I for the noisy world! What care I for friends and foes!" How agreeable it is to play on the mandoline!
>
> DUNYASHA. That's a guitar, not a mandoline *(looks in a hand-mirror and powders herself).*
>
> (pp. 28-9)

It is part of the comic convention that the sorrows of which Charlotta speaks are *recognized* rather than felt, partly balanced by, and partly deflected into, her cucumber-eating. The expressions of melancholy are stylized. But the fact that feelings are formalized in this arrangement does nothing to discount the fact that they are there. Though lacking the individualism, and indeed the cruelty, of tragedy, the scene gives classical expression to a state of cultural decay by which the characters are tangibly but unconsciously oppressed. With the setting sun, in deliberate contrast to the sunrise of Act I, Chekhov prepares imaginatively for the demise of the landed class in this play and for the loss of all that that has contributed positively to the culture.

Consistent with this stylized beginning, the Act in general assumes a processional character—three groups of figures in turn arriving to converse by the abandoned shrine before the sun finally sets and the string is heard snapping in the sky. The last of these groups includes Trofimov, the "perpetual student" whose opinions (were it not for their often ironic context in the play) are fairly close to what Chekhov's letters suggest were his own. Trofimov's speeches widen the specific social reference of the play:

> The vast majority of the intellectual people I know, seek nothing, do nothing, are not fit as yet for work of any kind. They call themselves intellectual, but they treat their servants as inferiors, behave to the peasants as though they were animals, learn little, read nothing seriously, do practically nothing, only talk about science and know very little about art.
>
> (p. 39)

It is characteristic of Chekhov's irony, however, that this character, who so often accords with his own attitudes, is a conspicuously inadequate person, embodying more than anyone the inactivity of which he speaks. What Trofimov advocates in his most rhetorical speeches is embodied before him in Lopahin; and though *he* cannot recognize it, Chekhov clearly does so in creating that symbolic stalemate between Lopahin and Lyubov on the subject of Russia's "giants":

> LOPAHIN. You know, I get up at five o'clock in the morning, and I work from morning to night; and I've money, my own and other people's, always passing through my hands, and I see what people are made of all round me. One has only to begin to do anything to see how few honest, decent people there are. Sometimes when I lie awake at night I think: "Oh! Lord, thou hast given us immense forests, boundless plains, the widest horizons, and living here we ourselves ought really to be giants."
>
> LYUBOV. You ask for giants! They are no good except in story-books; in real life they frighten us.
>
> (EPIHODOV *advances in the background, playing on the guitar*)
>
> LYUBOV (*dreamily*). There goes Epihodov.

ANYA (*dreamily*). There goes Epihodov.

GAEV. The sun has set, my friends.

(pp. 39-40)

Epihodov steps forth as if in answer to Lyubov's call: the most absurd representative of the old order, passing across the stage in the last rays of light. As the sun sets over him, the string in the sky snaps over all. Immediately, a change occurs. By its own inner momentum, the play works towards this as one of its crucial points of timing. The wayfarer enters, begging and then ridiculing Varya's money; Lopahin suddenly taunts her about their assumed marriage, which he has never done before; and Trofimov wins the loyalty of Anya. Although Lopahin's "giants" would at least be decent and incorruptible men, and although Trofimov the idealist prophesies happiness, there is nothing to endorse either hope in the play's structure. In fact, the rising moon, the poplars, Epihodov's melancholy tune, and the echo of Varya's voice—"Anya! Anya!"—say otherwise.

It is at this point, from the beginning of Act III, that the strong pastoral note fades away and Chekhov turns more directly to give an image of shifting power and social disintegration. From a beginning in which what is essentially a *family* is re-united in a setting of shared memories, the play accumulates people—only to loosen the bindings between them. The emphasis shifts from Lyubov's personal longing for lost innocence to the power-dynamics of social change. In Acts I and II Yasha and Dunyasha, coming only gradually into their own right as characters, are disruptive presences among the cherry-orchard people, breaking up any sense that Lyubov and Gaev are the unrivalled central persons in a stable community. Though officially subordinate in station, they dress and act like the class they serve; and Yasha's service to that class is often performed with irony. In Act III, however, beginning with the introduction of the post-office clerk and station-master as reluctant guests at Lyubov's party, Chekhov now brings directly into focus the stages of Lyubov's and Gaev's loss of power and the greater importance of a new factor in the determination of status—the factor of money. In no other of Chekhov's plays is money so important, so insidiously dominating the characters' lives. Pishtchik can think of nothing else, as he himself says. And the unusually nervous balance of relationships in Act III derives from the fact that, although the scales of power are presumed to have tipped with the sale of the orchard, no one knows exactly which way.

Like its counterparts in Chekhov's other major plays, Act III brings the drama to a climax by collecting its characters together in strained and untypical circumstances. Almost always, these occasions have the inbuilt irony of being gatherings that should not have been. Like Serebryakov's meeting to propose the sale of the estate in **Uncle Vanya,** and the fire that occurs by chance in **The Three Sisters** (so wholly inappropriate to the sisters' state of feeling at the time, that it seems as if it has been lit "on purpose" to spite them), Act III of **The Cherry Orchard** is "the wrong time to have the orchestra, and the wrong time to give a dance" (p. 48). The very presence of the post-office clerk and the station-master is a clear sign of change, a disappointment in terms of what has been prepared for by the double drawing-room, the arch and the burning chandelier. After the outdoor setting of Act II, this scene is burdened with the accessories of a past age, oppressing the non-aristocratic present with their disproportionate formality and weight. The dance, designed to promote high spirits, has only a forced gaiety, beneath which lie frustration and a flickering aggression. No one in the room (except perhaps the silly Dunyasha) is really happy, and only a convention of mock-abuse, freely indulged in, covers—or partly covers—the personal aggressions that are going on. The propensity for aggression infects nearly all the characters, but it is most obvious in Charlotta—that curiously disembodied and autonomous person, obscure as to class, mannish, and yet not without a feminine quota of loneliness. Charlotta works with artifice, is skilled in *illusion*; and it is by illusion that she distracts attention from the painful fate hanging over the cherry-orchard. In her check trousers and grey top hat, and springing into the air with shouts of "Bravo!", she is an unrealistic figure (belonging, one comes to see, to the stylized tradition of mime); and yet an intriguing and important one. For her tricks show more than a simple desire to entertain, being intensely self-assertive and in some ways frightening in their willed anarchy. Chekhov makes them, in fact, cleverly symbolic of just such cruel, almost predestined operations of "chance" and sudden overthrow of the old by which the world of the play works and which gives Lyubov's estate to Lopahin.

Significantly, the first definite news that the orchard has been sold provokes laughter from Yasha and irony from Firs: reactions in each case to Lyubov's loss of power, and coming with a quickness that betrays an aggression that has always been latent though masked. The process of loss culminates in the burlesque of Varya's taking a stick to Epihodov, perfectly timed to become her last frustrated gesture of authority. It is subverted by the entry of Lopahin, the new owner of the cherry-orchard. As Lopahin announces the fact that he owns the orchard, activity and dialogue stop to allow the shock to reverberate across the stage. Only after Varya has thrown down her keys do things resume their progress, but now at Lopahin's bidding, not Lyubov's. The final shift of power takes place, definitively, in that one moment, after which Lyubov is left only with the private hope of going to Paris and Anya's well-intentioned but empty promises.

So far as the characters are concerned, the drama at this point is effectively finished; and Act IV *is* in many ways thinner than the other Acts. What it does, however, is to shift the emphasis away from people and more towards social fact. The very setting of the scene is more impersonal, with the cold, hard reality of Mme Ranevsky's loss embodied in the new starkness of the former "nursery". The sense of space on the stage is a sense of "desolation", of emptiness—an emptiness in which Lopahin and Yasha with their glasses of champagne are somewhat at a loss. The house already has an abandoned and

hollow air. As in Act I, the weather is sunny and still, with three degrees of frost; but the significance of such weather now is simply that it is "just right for building". A pervasive shift has taken place in the culture represented in the play, from aristocratic to bourgeois values. Yet Chekhov's response is no more all sadness than it is all fun: he simply recognizes that, up to a point, life *is* change and that time usually brings at least some good:

> TROFIMOV. Your father was a peasant, mine was a chemist—and that proves absolutely nothing whatever. (LOPAHIN *takes out his pocket-book*). Stop that—stop that. If you were to offer me two hundred thousand I wouldn't take it. I am an independent man, and everything that all of you, rich and poor alike, prize so highly and hold so dear, hasn't the slightest power over me—it's like so much fluff fluttering in the air. I can get on without you. I can pass by you. I am strong and proud. Humanity is advancing towards the highest truth, the highest happiness, which is possible on earth, and I am in the front ranks.
>
> LOPAHIN. Will you get there?
>
> TROFIMOV. I shall get there *(a pause)*. I shall get there, or I shall show others the way to get there.
>
> *(In the distance is heard the stroke of an axe on a tree).*
>
> LOPAHIN. Good-bye, my dear fellow; it's time to be off. We turn up our noses at one another, but life is passing all the while. When I am working hard without resting, then my mind is more at ease, and it seems to me as though I too know what I exist for; but how many people there are in Russia, my dear boy, who exist, one doesn't know what for. Well, it doesn't matter. That's not what keeps things spinning.
>
> (pp. 67-8)

This dialogue between Lopahin and Trofimov is entirely without malice. It is the last salutation between men bent on opposite ways, and it rises to the occasion with an uneasy but touching reconciliation: "We turn up our noses at one another, but life is passing all the while". Trofimov has the vague idealism of the old class, Lopahin the quiet, instinctive pragmatism of the new. Lopahin has money and a confidence based on the utility of work; but the axe is also his that fells the cherry-trees. Trofimov has only a great dream; and, while it is in one way a democratic dream, it is in its self-aggrandizing pride and self-assurance unmistakably aristocratic in origin. It sounds, to say the least, a very precarious dream, placed up against the down-to-earth question—"Will you get there?"—and the distant sound of the axe.

It is significant, of course, that this balancing of gains and losses between the old order and the new is achieved through Lopahin and Trofimov. The ethical side of Chekhov's intelligence demands that he recognize Lopahin's basic decency and that he admire Lopahin's ability to get things done. To do so, he sets him beside one of the less sympathetic members of the old class, with whom our

Chekhov on performing the characters in
***The Cherry Orchard*:**

To Vl. I. Nemirovich-Danchenko

Yalta. Nov. 2, 1903.

And now about the play.

(1) Anya can be played by anybody convenient, even by an altogether unknown actress,—only she must be young and look young, and her voice must be youthful and ringing. This is not one of the important rôles.

(2) Varya is a more serious part, if Marya Petrovna [Stanislavsky's wife] takes it. Without Marya Petrovna it will be a little insipid and crude, and will have to be changed, softened. M. P. cannot repeat herself, first, because she is talented, and second, because Varya does not resemble Sonya and Natasha; she is a figure in a black dress, a bit nun-like, a bit stupid, somewhat tearful, etc., etc.

(3) Gaev and Lopakhin—let these rôles be left to Konst. Serg. [Stanislavsky] to try to make his choice. If he were to take Lopakhin and the rôle pleased him, then the play would be successful. But if Lopakhin is poorly played by a second-rate actor, both the rôle and the play will fail.

(4) Pishchik—Gribunin. God keep N. from this rôle.

(5) Charlotte—a question mark . . . of course, you must not give it away; Muratova will perhaps be good, but not comical. For this rôle Mme. Knipper.

(6) Epikhodov—if Moskvin wants it, let him have it. He will be an excellent Epikhodov. I supposed that Luzhsky was to play it.

(7) Firs—Artyom.

(8) Dunyasha—Khalutina.

(9) Yasha. If Alexandrov, of whom you write, is the one who is your assistant-manager, let him have Yasha. Moskvin would make a wonderful Yasha. And I should not object to Leonidov for the part.

(10) The Tramp—Gromov.

(11) The station-master, the one who reads "The Transgressor" in the third act,—an actor who has a bass voice.

Charlotte does not speak in a hybrid way, but uses the pure Russian tongue; but, on rare occasions, she pronounces the soft ending of a word, hard, and she confuses the masculine and feminine genders of adjectives. Pishchik is a Russian, an old man, worn out by the gout, age, and satiety; stout, dressed in a sleeveless undercoat (à la Simov), boots without heels. Lopakhin—a white waistcoat, yellow shoes; when walking, swings his arms, a broad stride, thinks deeply while walking, walks as if on a straight line. Hair not short, and therefore often throws back his head; while in thought he passes his hand through his beard, combing it from the back forward, i.e., from the neck toward the mouth. Trofimov, I think, is clear. Varya—black dress, wide belt.

Three years I spent writing **The Cherry Orchard,** and for three years I have been telling you that it is necessary to invite an actress for the rôle of Liubov Andreevna. And now you see you are trying to solve a puzzle that won't work out.

Letters of Anton Chekhov, in *Letters on the Short Story, Drama and Other Literary Topics,* by Anton Chekhov, edited by Louis S. Friedland, Minton, Balch, 1924, pp. 115-63.

sympathies are not so involved. In this way a fairly ready balance is achieved and Chekhov's *intellectual* grasp of the situation is left clear. For some time, in fact, the play counterpoints each response with another in order to prevent the feelings of any one character or group of characters from holding complete sway. Lyubov and Gaev are both saddened and relieved at the loss of the orchard, since their personal lives are somehow freed: freed perhaps too late, and certainly in an ambiguous way, but freed nonetheless. Lopahin, on the other hand, having triumphed in the purchase of the orchard, seems to have no *private* energy left. There is no doubt now that he will never marry Varya.

The emptiness of the house, left to stand during the winter to be knocked down in the spring, when "new life" theoretically begins, makes us feel this departure from the cherry-orchard to be the sad finale to a whole era of Russian life. Still the voices are set in dialogue:

ANYA. Good-bye, home! Good-bye to the old life!

TROFIMOV. Welcome to the new life!

There is not one response but many, deftly inter-twined:

LOPAHIN. Till the spring, then! Come, friends, till we meet! *(goes out).*

(LYUBOV ANDREYEVNA *and* GAEV *remain alone. As though they had been waiting for this, they throw themselves on each other's necks, and break into subdued smothered sobbing, afraid of being overheard)*

GAEV *(in despair).* Sister, my sister!

LYUBOV. Oh, my orchard!—my sweet, beautiful orchard! My life, my youth, my happiness, good-bye! good-bye!

VOICE OF ANYA *(calling gaily)*. Mamma!

VOICE OF TROFIMOV *(gaily, excitedly)*. Aa-oo!

(p. 77)

This counter-pointing of youth and age, hope and elegy, perfectly balances a sense of alternative social possibilities. It is a tribute to Chekhov's intelligence that that balance should persist to the very end. But as *all* the voices dissolve into silence and the dull thud of the axe, the moment has come for him to abandon the previous restraints on his own sympathies. The sounds retreating, then silence, and finally the axe and solitary footsteps, all echo life deserting the cherry-orchard and the destruction of the cherry-orchard itself. And with the appearance of Firs, old, sick and lying motionless on the stage as the curtain drops, a chapter of history seems to be coming to a close.

It is true, I think, that this image of Firs at the very end of the play softens and distorts our sense of the Russian past, evoking too simple a pathos. Since the cherry-orchard itself is, from one point of view, an intrinsically biased emblem of the past—its value, however finally ambiguous, being instantly established in its visual beauty, its glistening whiteness—the ending of the play with its historical implication needs to be firmer. Firs is a risky figure for Chekhov to give much importance to because he is so much a stock-creation, producing only a limited comedy and always tempting Chekhov to indulge over-simple effects. We might do well to compare the sense of the past as embodied in him with that of even the very recent past in *The Three Sisters,* where it takes such a complex form in Olga's, Masha's and Irena's characters, or with the late story **"A Woman's Kingdom",** where a past style of life is seen incongruously penetrating the one that has replaced it. Fortunately, Firs lying on the stage is not the only impression with which *The Cherry Orchard* leaves us. Above him is the sound of the string snapping in the sky, and behind him are the resounding strokes of the axe, conveying the eerie impression of the inevitability, pathos, and finally the chilling unalterability of a social transition taking place. Our sympathy for these people and this household is converted, I think, into a more abstract understanding of historical process. Certainly, after the simplification of feeling introduced by the figure of Firs, that is something that the end of the play needs.

Clayton A. Hubbs and Joanna T. Hubbs (essay date 1982)

SOURCE: "The Goddess of Love and the Tree of Knowledge: Some Elements of Myth and Folklore in Chekhov's *The Cherry Orchard,*" in *The South Carolina Review,* Vol. 14, No. 2, Spring 1982, pp. 66-77.

[In the following essay, the critics argue that "archetypes from myth and folklore" inform The Cherry Orchard *and exert significant influence on its plot.]*

In the climactic scene of *The Cherry Orchard,* Gayev recites the following hymn to the Great Mother Goddess:

> Oh, glorious Nature, shining with eternal light, so beautiful and yet so indifferent to our fate . . . you whom we call Mother, uniting in yourself both Life and Death, you live and you destroy. . . .[1]

Gayev's speech is followed by an embarrassed silence *"only broken by the subdued muttering of Feers. Suddenly a distant sound is heard, coming as if out of the sky, like the sound of a string snapping, slowly and sadly dying away."* In the stage directions for the scene, the trees of the cherry orchard are contrasted to man-made trees, telegraph poles:

> *A road leads to Gayev's estate. On one side and at some distance away there is a row of dark poplars, and it is there that the cherry orchard begins. Further away is seen a line of telegraph poles, and beyond them, on the horizon, the vague outlines of a large town, visible only in very good, clear weather.*

(354)

In the final scene of the play we hear the breaking string a second time, this time against the background of the cherry trees being cut down to make way for construction. Liubov, whose name means "love" and whose role in the play suggests her identification with the Mother Goddess, is cast out into the profane world as if she were Eve being cast out of Paradise: "Oh my darling, my precious, my beautiful orchard! My life, my youth, my happiness . . . good-bye! . . . Good-bye!"

Gayev's evocation of nature as an indifferent goddess juxtaposed with the sound of a breaking string produces a sense of sadness and dislocation, the prevailing tone of *The Cherry Orchard* and all of Chekhov's plays. "Out of the sky" suggests a break between man and the sustaining cosmos. The association of Liubov with the tree (the chopping down of the trees and the departure of the mother occur together against the sound of the breaking string) provides us with a clue to the complex symbolism and structure of the play: The role of the Great Goddess changes from that of the bringer of life to the agent of death, from an initial association with the Tree of Life to a final association with the Tree of Knowledge, from the central and totemic figure of the Goddess to the denigrated and sinful Eve.

The mother, in the double aspect that Gayev describes her, as the agent of life and of death, is clearly the central figure that informs *The Cherry Orchard.* The play's four acts follow the movement of the seasons, from spring and the promise of renewal of life with the return of the mother in act one to winter and the coming of death in act four. By isolating one aspect of the Great Mother Goddess, her totemic association with trees (in this case the cherry trees of the orchard) and noting the change that occurs as the nature of that association moves from one with the Tree of Life (the cherry as the fruit-bearing tree which feeds both peasant and gentry) to the Tree of Knowledge (tele-

graph poles, man-made trees which indicate the dislocation and human isolation of industrial society), we will
disclose the controlling symbolism of the play and outline
its movement from the promise of renewal of comedy and
to the suffering and death of tragedy.[2]

The historian of religion Fedotov argues that the cult of
nature as mother is deeply embedded in Russian life and
is the source of Russian religiosity. Christianization
merely transformed the caring Russian Demeter into the
all-encompassing *Bogoroditsa* (Mother of God).[3] At the
same time the evil aspects of the Mother Goddess—as
death dealer—were identified in part with the temptress
Eve, the sinful rebel, mother of mankind whose action
condemned her children to exile and death. Eve became
the prototype for the disobedient and hence evil wife
against whose snares the Orthodox church warned its
male members.[4] But the cult of the pagan all-powerful
Great Mother continued in Russia into the twentieth
century. As Gayev's speech reminds us, the two aspects
of the Great Goddess as bringer of life and death are
clearly united. What is involved here is a gradual displacement of her functions. To appreciate fully Chekhov's use of the complex symbolism of the double aspect
of the mother and of the feminine, we must consider the
disparity between her image in Russian folklore and in
Christian mythology.

Russian folklore is suffused with the worship of "Mother
Moist Earth" (*Mat' Syra Zemlia*) embodying the forces
of nature and the family bond. She appears to bear her
children parthenogenetically. Though she is without name,
she is akin to Demeter, goddess of fertility and motherly
love. The peasant is her child, tied to the earth umbili-
cally as though to the body of the nurturing mother.
Fedotov describes him as "the fatherless son of Mother
Earth" and though she taught him fidelity, he continues,
she did not instill in him the male virtues of freedom and
valor.[5] Since she represents the totality of being and
nature, she is the good, nurturing mother; but she is also
the evil *hetaera* and hag. Russian folklore presents us
with these two distinct aspects of her being in the figures
of the witch Baba Yaga and the nymphs called *rusalki*.
It is through them that the linkage of earth and tree, of
the Goddess with her Tree of Life, seems most apparent.

The cannibal witch Baba Yaga lives alone in the forest
but is frequently represented as the mother of many daughters and surrounded by all forms of animal life. Through
her fearsome hut on hen's feet youths must pass in their
rites of passage into manhood and womanhood. They
must escape her oven, her maw. But she is not merely a
dangerous obstacle in the quest; she can also provide the
key to success to the hero or heroine who knows how to
win her favor or outwit her.[6] This dual function, good
and evil, is also shared by the *rusalki*. Here the sexual
aspect suggested metaphorically in Baba Yaga's oven and
her "heraldry," the mortar and pestle, is more pronounced,
while the maternal aspects are diminished. The *rusalki*
or Russian sirens are thought to live in all three elements
of nature—water, earth, and sky—and their movement
from one to the other suggests their role in the process

of fertility as self-inseminatory. They are represented often
as half-birds, half-fish. From their perches in the trees to
which they migrate in the spring from their abodes in
lakes, rivers, or springs, they lure men to their death. At
the same time they bring fertility to the land.[7]

Both the Yaga and the *rusalki* are linked with trees—the
first as the mother living in the midst of her primeval
forest; the latter as *hetaera,* who lure the unwary. The
tree, which in the form of the birch is associated with the
Greek Goddess in Russian lore, is often represented as
her homologue. In folk art, particularly embroidery, one
often finds the motif of a goddess (perhaps "Mother Moist
Earth" herself) flanked by horsemen, animals, birds, and
many forms of vegetation. Frequently, the figure of a
woman is replaced by that of the universal symbol of the
Tree of Life, suggestive of the Mother Goddess encompassing her male child-consort.[8] In Russian folk tradition
the tree has an especially significant function. It is closely associated with the natural cycle of fertility for which
it is the totem. The "priestesses" of the Tree of Life are
peasant women—both young and mature.[9] In the rites of
the agrarian calendar which regulate all social and personal life of the peasantry, women are the midwives of
nature who help deliver her child in the form of the
harvest. Their homology with the fertile earth is suggested in the following Christianized proverb: "Your first
Mother is Mary, your second mother is the earth, and
your third is your own mother."[10] In the calenderic rites
that fertility is linked with trees. The festival of "bringing in the spring" which began the pagan year rites was
the most joyous of the Russian festivals. In some areas
before the Revolution, girls brought a doll figure or a
tree from the forest into the village and called it "our
Blessed Mother Spring"; and as though to suggest the
persistence of rites in Russia which recall those of Demeter and Kore, they sang: "My spring, where is your daughter?"[11] This ritual initiated a series of festivals in which
women appeared to transfer the power of the tree, its
rising sap—represented mythologically as the migration
of the *rusalki* from water to tree—into the village to
stimulate seeds planted in the fields and, analogously,
human fertility. Going into the forest during the spring
festival of Rusalia, girls and women decorated and
chopped down a tree called a "Rusalka." This tree was
used to augur future marrianges.[12]

While the tree is perceived as the symbol of the mother
as nature and has the significance of the Tree of Life in
the folkloric context, in Christian symbolism the Edenic
tree is no longer called the Tree of Life but the Tree of
Knowledge and is presided over by an angry male god
rather than a maternal goddess. The feminine, once anal-
ogous with the cosmos, is derogated to the function of
the helpmate of Adam, created rather than creating, born
through the masculine "womb"—Logos. (One might call
her "manufactured.") As Eve, she is the source of man's
fall, his willful seductress; and yet she is also the mother
of mankind—a disobedient and hence evil mother who
condemns her progeny to death. In her rebellion against
the just Jehovah, she sinned by reassociating herself with
the forbidden tree through the act of eating its fruit.

In *The Cherry Orchard* we see precisely the movement from the orchard presided over by the ancient form of the goddess as the Tree of Life, the fruit-producing tree, to the orchard which begins to lose its life-giving harvest, abandoned by its goddess and ceding to the Edenic Tree of Knowledge—of the bitter and divisive fruit. Chekhov's image of the orchard dissolving into the line of telegraph poles clearly suggests the displacement of one by the other: the domain of nature is to be dominated and subjected to man's design. Liubov, the mother, thus embodies both pagan and Christian mythologems: She is a mother goddess, giver of life and fertility, as her name implies; but she becomes increasingly impotent and thus evil, suggesting the unpredictable aspects of the *rusalki* and the Yaga who avenge themselves on those who disobey them. The once all-powerful goddess is displaced from her orchard—her own creation. As the fallen Eve, Liubov betrays the old Adam, her weak brother Gayev who is under her power, and abandons the orchard to the "New Adams," Trofimov and Lopahin. As the degraded Eve, her act is one of rebellion: She showers her last gold on the ground until she has none to give and leaves those who will no longer worship her former glory and her orchard. In so doing, she condemns the orchard to destruction and those who remain to the routine of meaningless work "by the sweat of their brow."

We now see the context for the complex symbolism of *The Cherry Orchard.* The Tree of Life which produces fruit is now, if not useless, not used. It stands as the "totem" of agrarian Russia, the place in which gentry and peasants communed in the cycle of nature. As old Feers says, "The peasant belonged to the gentry and the gentry belonged to the peasant; and now everything is separate and you can't understand a thing." All this has resulted from the orchard's falling into neglect after the initial departure of Liubov. The final break comes with her sale of the orchard and its abandonment. Liubov thus appears as a last representative of the sustaining power of the pagan nature myth; her "fall" brings to an end the old comic cycle of death and rebirth and suggests the "linear" finality of modern tragedy.

Having outlined the thematic and structural bases of the play in myth and folklore, we will examine its dramatic movement from the hope of renewed life to the fact of death. Despite our emphasis on chronology to show the mythic analogues, we wish to emphasize that Liubov's transformation from the goddess of love to the fallen Eve does not come as straightforward progression. Like the literal and historical levels of meaning, the mythic one remains richly ambiguous and cuts across the other two.

Liubov's springtime arrival as the sun comes up brings with it the promise of renewal. She is escorted by her worshipful entourage.[13] Her daughters, her former self, and her brother Gayev bring her, like the Goddess of Spring, into the nursery where she appears both as the resurrected child ("I feel as if I were little again") and the mother of her drowned son and two unmarried daughters. She is both a Russian Demeter and a Kore. However, the goddess has already forsaken her land; her beautiful Adonis-like child has died—as a result of what she calls "her sins," her sexual transgressions—and the peasants go hungry. It is the death of the child which has driven her away. To pay the debts for her sins, the orchard must be sold and her trees sacrificed.

But for the moment there is hope of a paradise regained, of the old order renewed. Only her adopted peasant daughter Varia, who "lives like a nun," suspects that "in fact there's nothing in it, it's all a kind of dream." But the old serf Feers, embodiment of the old order, says: "The Mistress is home again! Home at last! I don't mind if I die now . . . *(Weeps with joy)*" (340). Coming right after Ania's recapitulation of the past and announcement to the audience that little brother Grisha was drowned in the river, this reference to a "happy" death as though it were an old man's return to the maternal womb ironically unites the child-Adonis to the old man. Liubov leaves because of an unexpected death over which she appeared to have no control and returns not to life but to another death—that of the old man Feers, of the orchard, and of the "grandfather house" contained within it. Child, old man, house, and orchard—encompassing all in a maternal bond—will disappear at play's end as Liubov leaves. But for now she has returned, and she is happy: "God, how I love my own country! I love it so much, I could hardly see it from the train, I was crying all the time [*through tears*]. However, I must drink my coffee. Thank you, Feers, thank you, my dear old friend. I am so glad I found you still alive" (341-42).

In her tears she evokes the Orthodox version of the God-bearer Madonna whose image co-exists among the peasantry with that of Mother Earth. In her iconic as well as ritual and folkloric representation—as the embodiment of the orchard and the symbol of the Goddess of Love—she will be destroyed for money. But as we have seen, she is not only the grieving Madonna who weeps for the death of humanity, she is also the pagan goddess of sexual and profane love. She is a *rusalka,* a *siren,* in the guise of the Christianized temptress Eve. In Paris—the image of the West through which industrialization reaches Russia and through which the cycle of the seasons is superseded by the dictates of society and machine, in which woman rules as "coquette" rather than in her maternal role as goddess of bonding love—the consort of the former goddess is a sickly lover. Maternal love is replaced by a shady "liaison" in a society where pairings are determined by man, not nature, and not for the reproduction of life but for profane pleasures.

Meanwhile the orchard languishes. The "debate" over its fate is the apparent action of the play. Lopahin, who loves Liubov and still worships her, insists that the cherry orchard be cut down to pay the family debts. Although Lopahin's spiritual attachment to Liubov remains, his dependence on the natural cycle has been replaced by a compulsion to work and to accumulate capital. In the past the orchard provided nourishment to the entire county. In the old days, Feers says, "they had a recipe." But the "recipe," the contract or bond with the natural order made by both peasant and gentry, cemented by the nurturing mother, is now forgotten. Lopahin, the embodiment of one form of the new Adam, sums it up:

> Up to just recently there were only gentry and peasants living in the country, but now there are all these summer residents. All the towns, even quite small ones, are surrounded with villas. And probably in the course of the next twenty years or so, these people will multiply tremendously. At present they merely drink tea on the verandah, but they might start cultivating their plots of land, and then your cherry orchard would be gay with life and wealth and luxury. . . .

> (344)

Liubov's weak brother, Gayev, who remains more strongly under her spell, can only say, "What nonsense," anticipating the very words with which Liubov will chastise Lopahin for his sentimental belief in the future and work. Gayev—like the landowner Pishchik, Feers, and her children—are still in her sphere.

In act one it is Gayev who reminds Liubov of her identification with the orchard:

> GAYEV [*opens another window*]. The orchard is all white. You haven't forgotten, Liuba?. . . . Do you remember? You haven't forgotten?

> LIUBOV ANDRYEEVNA [*looks through the window at the orchard*]. Oh my childhood, my innocent childhood! I used to sleep in this nursery; I used to look on to the orchard from here, and I woke up happy every morning. In those days the orchard was just as it is now, nothing has changed. [*Laughs happily.*] All white! Oh, my orchard! After the dark, stormy autumn and the cold winter, you are young and joyous again. . . .

> (347)

She sees her mother "walking through the orchard . . . in a white dress! [*Laughs happily.*] It is her!" (348). The orchard is not only Liubov in youth, as Kore, it is also her Mother Demeter whose role she herself has now assumed in regard to her children. The cherry trees dressed in white appear as an embodiment of woman (348). Trofimov, who enters in his shabby clothes, links the orchard in its bloom with her drowned son Grisha: In a literal as well as symbolic sense he takes Grisha's place. While Lopahin will take the place of Liubov as the "owner" of the land which is organically attached to her, so Trofimov will take the place of the youth unattached to the mother and looking forward to history and man's actions outside the organic sphere of nature as mother. Trofimov, a prototype for the forward-looking intelligentsia which wishes to propel Russia into the industrialized and westernized future, replaces Grisha, the child-Adonis attached to the mother. Liubov at first fails to recognize him and then strongly dislikes him:

> LIUBOV ANDRYEEVNA [*quietly weeping*]. My little boy was lost . . . drowned . . . What for? What for, my friend? [*More quietly.*] How is it that you've lost your good looks? Why have you aged so?

> TROFIMOV. A peasant woman in the train called me "that motheaten gent."

> LIUBOV ANDRYEEVNA. In those days you were quite a boy, a nice young student, and now your hair is thin, you wear glasses. . . . Are you still a student? [*Walks to the door.*]

> TROFIMOV. I expect I shall be a student to the end of my days.

> (349)

The image of the mother and her drowned child suggests the interruption of the nurturance and continuance of life through the body of the mother. One can see in Trofimov, the petrified *puer eternus,* the symbol of that interrupted cycle. He is implicated in the child's death—most clearly in the sense that Grisha had been passed into his hands by Liubov to be "educated." Trofimov, the child substitute, exists only through his continued attachment to the Tree of Knowledge—the symbol of alienation, sin, and exile.

In the second act the focus shifts from the past to the present, from spring to summer, and the dream of regeneration of the first act is dramatically shattered. All the ancient folkloric motifs linking nature to mother and family are present in the background against which the servants, aping their betters, complain of loneliness and isolation. Here Gayev delivers his hymn to the Great Goddess. The shrine in the open fields is by a well, sacred in the folk tradition to the water nymphs, the *rusalki*; the discarded gravestones in the disused shrine evoke the image of the disintegration of the family clan with the dissolution of the worship of the mother-centered natural cycle. The action will still take place in the field, but the outline of a town looms on the horizon. The trees cede to telegraph poles threading their way out of the orchard and into the city. The servants' "dumb show" anticipates the one at play's end, the death of old Feers. Chekhov includes each character in the tragic action.

Lopahin attempts to persuade the lady to sell the estate for building plots. Liubov complains that her servants go hungry (the old servants get nothing but dried peas from her daughter Varia) while she spills coins on the open field. But she is not too distracted to admonish Lopahin, as she has Trofimov, for the drab and meaningless life he leads and to suggest, unsuccessfully, that he marry Varia. Liubov as matchmaker, as the goddess of the family who determines fates, finds herself unable to mate her own daughter to these "new men." Feers reminds them that in the old order "peasants belonged to the gentry and the gentry belonged to the peasants; but now everything is separate and you can't understand anything" (362). As a counterpoint, Trofimov pompously lectures Liubov and Gayev on the "progressive" opinions of a segment of the intelligentsia. Man is not a child of Mother Nature; he is a self-created being: "Where's the sense of being proud when you consider that Man, as a species, is not very well constructed physiologically and in the vast majority of cases is coarse, stupid, and profoundly

Stanislavsky as Gaev, in the 1904 Moscow Art Theater production of The Cherry Orchard.

Eve, whose sin makes mankind suffer. It is Liubov's regretable inattentiveness which results in the sale of the orchard and the necessity to "toil in the sweat of one's brow." It is through her that man is expelled from sacred to profane time, from the mythic realm of Eden to the stage of history where his sins must be expiated through labor and torment. She is the scapegoat and will be expelled in act four. As the orchard goes, so goes Mother Russia, Old Russia—subdivided into plots, industrialized to the rhythm of the machine and the clock. Liubov has lost all power:

> LIUBOV ANDRYEEVNA. What truth? *You* can see where the truth is and where it isn't, but I seem to have lost my power of vision. I don't see anything. . . . You look ahead so boldly—but isn't that because life is still hidden from your young eyes. . . . I can't conceive life without the cherry orchard and if it really has to be sold then sell me with it. . . . [*Embraces* TROFIMOV, *kisses him on the forehead.*] You know, my son was drowned here. . . . [*Weeps.*] Have pity on me.
>
> (375-76)

Trofimov has replaced Grisha, but he has not grown up; her daughter wishes to marry a "freak" who is "above love." When Lopahin enters to gloat over his purchase of the estate and order the trees cut, the sense of rape and despoliation of nature and her daemon Liubov is complete (384). Lopahin's "new life" will come at the expense of the destruction of an organic unity with nature. Chekhov's irony here is perhaps almost too apparent. The tyranny of nature—and of the old social order—is replaced by the tyranny of labor and of money:

> LOPAHIN. Everything must be just as *I* wish it now. [*Ironically.*] Here comes the new landowner, here comes the owner of the cherry orchard!
>
> (384)

Only Ania and Varia, the daughter "priestesses" of the Great Mother, each one linked with one aspect of the New Men, Trofimov and Lopahin, still attempt to worship Liubov's now empty powers (385).

Act four, winter, is marked by *"an oppressive sense of emptiness."* Liubov, the Great Goddess as Demeter, promising fertility and renewal in the spring of the first act, has now become Kore and Eve, reigning over the house of the dead. Lopahin and Trofimov combine as the patriarchal figures of Pluto and Jehovah who have captured her forever perhaps. When spring comes again, the house and its remaining inhabitants will no longer exist, ceding to the new industrial, patriarchal order.

Lopahin and Trofimov see salvation only in continuous planning for the future and in work. No longer attached to the regular cycle of the seasons, work becomes neurotic repetition with no cosmic pivot. Lopahin says, "When I work for long hours on end without taking any time off, I feel happier in my mind and *I even imagine I know why I exist*" (389, emphasis added). Man is not expendable in nature: he rejoins his family and ancestors and forms a

unhappy too? We ought to stop all this self-admiration. We ought to—just work" (363). Trofimov and Lopahin thus come together in opposition to Liubov and her weakling brother as the new men whose recipe for salvation is to oppose the natural order, "to work." Trofimov works for a new humanity, an "advanced" mankind; Lopahin, more practically, works to enhance his financial worth. One is absorbed in ideas, the other in amassing wealth. Neither has time for love.

As an ironic counterpoint to the progressive visions of these "new men," Gayev, the Old Adam, sings his hymn to the Great Goddess, and we hear the sound of the breaking string. The break with nature and the past is complete; but the men of the future, Lopahin and Trofimov, are false prophets. As it was for the three sisters, Chekhov shows us that all this knowledge is useless without a sustaining myth, a reason for existing.

In the autumn of act three the future already belongs to Trofimov and Lopahin. Liubov is now the patriarchalized version of the Great Mother of the ancient world,

collective unit with them in the natural cycle.[14] However, in society he is expendable, an often unnecessary cog—Trofimov's "coarse, stupid" humanity. With the departure of the mother goddess from whom the peasantry as well as their masters drew strength, meaningful life comes to an end.

> GAYEV [*with despair in his voice*]. Sister, my sister. . . .

> LIUBOV ANDRYEEVNA. Oh my darling, my precious, my beautiful orchard! My life, my youth, my happiness . . . good-bye! . . . Goodbye!

> (397-398)[15]

The world left in its new cycle of history and labor—the "new life" welcomed by Trofimov in his last line in the play—appears doomed to sterility and its children to a sense of orphanage, unable to communicate their sorrow or their love. The mother, as the totem holding the family together, leaves her children scattered. The extreme pathos of Chekhov's plays is thus focused in the breaking string—the break with nature as mother, the eternal ground of communion for humanity.

We must conclude that in Liubov's final relinquishment of the cherry orchard Chekhov presents us with the end of a myth, the displacement of the Tree of Life by the Tree of Knowledge and of the Great Mother Goddess by the sinful Eve. Man is driven from the paradise of comedy by a destiny which finally denies his cyclically based perceptions. In place of the reassuring continuum of the natural cycle, Chekhov's characters face discontinuity and death. In *Three Sisters,* Vershinin considers what it would be like to start life all over again: "If that happened, I think the thing you'd want most of all would be not to repeat yourself" (264). In *The Cherry Orchard* we see that hope fulfilled, with a suggestion of its consequences. It may be argued that Chekhov's plays represent the end of the evolution of drama from the fertility rites of traditional man who lives in myth to the empty repetitions of modern man who lives in a condition of constant material and spiritual dislocation. In Chekhov's earlier plays the mother's absence is the major source of pathos. In *The Cherry Orchard,* the reasons for the absence and the consequences are fully presented: Liubov, who first abandons and then is betrayed by her children, loses her power; with her departure the cord which had attached them to the land and its cyclic laws is broken.

In re-examining Chekhov's plays from the perspective of the archetypes from myth and folklore which inform them, we may better understand not only the structure of individual works but the nature and significance of all of Chekhov's dramatic works. We see that they are not limited to what Francis Fergusson has called "the little scene of modern realism" or to the absurd drama of arbitrary issue. Like the tragic drama of the ancient Greeks, Chekhov's plays dramatize man's relation to natural forces over which he attempts—and fails—to gain control. Attempts to subdue the forces of nature lead to psychic dissolution, alienation, and abandonment. The central

archetypes remain the same; the specific forms are drawn from the tradition of Russian folklore and Christian myth

NOTES

[1] Anton Chekhov, *Plays,* trans. Elisaveta Fen (Harmondsworth, Middlesex, 1959), p. 365. Subsequent references will appear in the text.
[2] For a full summary of critical responses to the sound of the breaking string, see Jean-Pierre Barricelli, "Counterpoint of the Snapping String: Chekhov's *The Cherry Orchard,*" *California Slavic Studies,* 10 (1977), 121-36. Barricelli persuasively argues that "Chekhov was too precise and self-conscious an artist to allow a gratuitous or solely mood-setting, isolated incident to enter his work," and—concurring with J. L. Styan, *Chekhov in Performance*—declares that "To interpret that sound is to interpret the play." We agree that the two soundings of the snapping string are central to our understanding of the play, that the play is a "drama of death," and that "the background of the snapping string must be sought in folklore." Barricelli's outline of the dialectic of life and death, symbolized most vividly by the heron and the owl that Gayev and Trofimov respectively suggest as the sources of the eerie sound when it first occurs in the second act, is an important reading. However, we do not agree with Barricelli's conclusion that the play's origin in folklore is a "distant" one.
The structural and thematic movement from comedy to tragedy encompasses a major theme in Russian literature and the experience of which it is a reflection—the movement from a woman-centered, cyclical agrarian society, dominated by the figure of the mother as avatar of nature to a society which is industrialized and intensely patriarchal. Like *The Cherry Orchard,* many of the major works of Russian literature are dominated by the figure of the woman. (See V. Dunham, "The Strong Woman Motif," in C. Black, ed., *The Transformation of Russian Society,* Cambridge, 1960.)
On the central role of the mother in Russian society and culture, see M. Matossian, "The Peasant Way of Life," in W. S. Vucinich, *The Peasant in Nineteenth-Century Russia* (Stanford, California, 1968), p. 18; and N. S. Arsen'ev, *Iz Russkoi kul' turnoi i tvorcheskoi traditsii* (Frankfort, 1959).
For a discussion of the allegorical structure of the play, see John Kelson, "Allegory and Myth in *The Cherry Orchard,*" *Western Humanities Review,* 13 (Summer 1959), 321-24: "Since, on the mythic level, the play is mimesis of the cycle of Nature, it is appropriate that one character (Liubov) should represent the continuing, sustaining, and life-giving power of Nature." Kelson concludes that the mother's departure is a ritual one: "Like Persephone, she will return to the world of the living, and when she does she will bring life back to the earth again." Kelson's reading is valuable; however, it ignores the deep and pervasive irony of the play. As usual—and here rather systematically—Chekhov "stands myth on its head." The movement is from life to death, from the comic to the tragic; and the promise of ritual return and renewal is pathetic and false.
In the life-to-death, spring-to-winter movement the four acts of the play follow rather closely the four phases of the seasonal cycle of the year and the organic cycle of human life upon which Northrop Frye bases his theory of genres: dawn, spring, and birth (romance); zenith, summer, and marriage (comedy, pastoral, and idyll); sunset, autumn and death (tragedy and elegy); darkness, winter, and dissolution (satire): *The Fables of Identity* (New York, 1963), p. 16, and *The Anatomy of Criticism* (Princeton, 1957). In our discussion of the play's mythic structure and folkloric symbolism, we pay little direct attention to its literal social implications. This may suggest an assumption that Chekhov takes the position of a political reactionary defending the old order, but this is not the case. Chekhov, as always, is ambivalent, and his satire cuts both ways. The old union of the peasant and gentry was cruel and despotic, assimilated as it was to the agrarian cycle (see Gayev's hymn to Nature), but it had represented a fixed and predictable structure (see Feers's speech in which he insists that the gentry belong to the peasants and the peasants to the gentry). The new order, with its capitalistic and individualistic concerns and its open-ended belief in progress freeing human life from the natural cycle, appears to deprive life of meaning. Thus Chekhov criticizes both the romantic vision of nature and of social progress.
[3] G. P. Fedotov, *The Russian Religious Mind* (New York, 1960), pp. 13 and 360-62. On the Christianization of the pagan Mother Goddess, see N. Matorin, *Zhenskoe bozhestvo v pravoslavnom kul'te* (Moscow, 1931).
[4] E. Elnett, *Historic Origins and Social Development of Family Life in Russia* (New York, 1926), pp. 22-23. On woman's resistance to Christianization in medieval Kiev, see S. Smirnov, "Baby bogomerzskiia," in *Sbornik statei posviashchennykh V. O. Kliuchevskomu* (Moscow, 1909), pp. 217-243.

[5] Fedotov, p. 19.

[6] For an extended discussion of the Baba Yaga, see A. A. Potebnia, "O mificheskom znachenii nekotorykh obriadov," *Chteniia v obshchestve istorii i drevnostei rossiiskikh*, numbers 2, 3, 4 (1865), 85-232; and on the initiatory function of the Yaga, see M. G. Wosien, *The Russian Folktale* (Munich, 1969), pp. 133-140.

[7] Archeological and ethnographic materials on the *rusalki* are gathered together by B. A. Rybakov, "Rusalii i bog Simargl-Pereplut," *Sovetskaia arkheologiia*, vol. 2 (1967), 102-125. For a full discussion of the importance of the *rusalka* image in Russian folk art, see V. M. Vasilenko, *Russkaia narodnaia rez'ba i rospis' po derevu v xviii-xx vv* (Moscow, 1960).

[8] On the universally found image of the tree of life, see E. O. James, *The Tree of Life* (Leiden, 1966) and G. d'Alviella, *The Migration of Symbols* (New York, 1956), pp. 122-174. The motif of the Mother Goddess represented both as woman and as tree of life in Russian folk art is discussed by B. A. Rybakov, "Drevnie elementy v russkom narodnom tvorchestve," *Sovetskaia etnografiia*, No. 1 (1948), 90-106 and A. Netting, "Images and Ideas in Russian Peasant Art," *Slavic Review* (March 1976), 65 ff.

[9] D. K. Zelenin, "Totemicheskii kul't derev'ev u russkikh i u belorussov," *Izvestiia akademii nauk SSR, otdelenie obshchestvennykh nauk*, No. 3 (Moscow, 1933), 591-629. See also B. A. Rybakov, "Drevnie elementy . . ." *op. cit.* Zelenin discusses the central role of women in fertility rites in Russia in "Istolkovanie perezhitochnykh religioznykh obriadov," *Sovetskaia etnografiia*, No. 5 (Moscow, 1934), 3-16.

[10] D. Strotmann, "Quelques apercus historiques sur le culte marial en Russie," *Irenikon* xxxii, p. 187 (translation ours).

[11] I. I. Zemtsovskii, ed., *Poezii krest'ianskikh prazdnikov* (Leningrad, 1970), p. 290 (translation ours).

[12] D. K. Zelenin, "Istolkovanie perezhitochnykh . . ." *op. cit.*, pp. 10-11; and V. Ya. Propp, *Russkie agrarnie prazdniki* (Leningrad, 1963), pp. 130-131, suggests that in this ceremony women assume the powers of fertility of the earth and bring it into the collectivity. On the calendrical cycle associated with women and incarnations of the feminine, see L. S. Nosova, *Iazychestvo v pravoslavii* (Moscow, 1975), p. 93. On the matristic sources of Russian pagan culture, see Z. R. Dittrich, "Zur Religiosen Urund Frühgeschichte der Slaven," *Jahrbuch für Geschichte Österuropas*, Band 9 (Wiesbaden, 1961), 481-510.

[13] Like the chthonian Mother Earth and her avatars in Russian folklore, Baba Yaga and the *rusalki*, Liubov lives without a husband. Like the representative of earth, the mother, she stands at the center of the family and the play's action. As a representative of the gentry class and like the maternal goddess, she stands above and yet among the peasantry—her estate enclosing them.

[14] Fedotov insists on the relationship of the pagan Russian cult of ancestors to the cult of earth as mother: "From the sperm of the parents man is brought forth into the everlasting *rod* [clan or extended family] for his short existence, just as the seed, buried in the earth's womb, gives a new life to the ear of corn which is procreated through the death of the seed itself. . . . Russian paganism (as well as the primitive Greek) considered the individual only as a transient moment in the eternal life of the *rod*. From the parents man comes and to the parents he returns, into the womb of the Mother Earth" (Fedotov, pp. 18-19).

[15] Chekhov could be echoing a refrain found in the popular religious verses called *Dukhovnye stikhy* in which Adam bewails his loss of Paradise with the following words: "Oh my Paradise, my beautiful orchard / I was happy, Paradise, to be in you / Eve was happy. . . ." But why is it Liubov who recites this lament while Gayev, the Old Adam, can only cry for his sister? Chekhov may be suggesting, obliquely again, the strength of the mother-centered pagan religion and the relative weakness of the Christian version of life in the old agrarian order. See P. Bezsonov, ed., *Kaleki perekhozhie*, Part VI (Moscow, 1861), pp. 242 ff.

G. J. Watson (essay date 1983)

SOURCE: "*Chekhov and the Drama of Social Change: The Cherry Orchard,*" in *Drama: An Introduction,* St. Martin's Press, 1983, pp. 132-46.

[*In this essay, Watson examines a number of factors contributing to the life-like quality of* The Cherry Orchard.]

The Russian dramatist Anton Chekhov, like Ibsen and Miller, is interested in man's relations with society—his last play, which might be regarded as his masterpiece, **The Cherry Orchard,** is a profound drama of social change. He is, however, a more 'open' dramatist than the other two. That is, Ibsen places a perhaps too insistent emphasis on the intractable nature of the opposition between individual aspiration and social constraints. His views are fixed: his protagonists *must* always, *will* always, be broken in their attempts at self-assertion. If there is a criticism of Ibsen's drama, it is that there is a hint of a predetermined thesis lying behind his plays. Miller's *Death of a Salesman* also suffers from its author's adoption of a rigid stance, in this case the desire to assert the possibility of the tragedy of the common man (Willy's very surname is Loman), which is juxtaposed uneasily with Miller's social insights.

CHEKHOV'S OBJECTIVITY

The most immediately apparent quality of Chekhov's art (he was a superb writer of short stories as well as of plays) is its dispassionateness or objectivity. This may be due in part to his direct experience and knowledge of a very wide social spectrum. He was a serf's son, but also a doctor, a landowner and an artist, and moved as easily in Russia's backward villages as in the artistic and intellectual circles of her major cities. Being a doctor brought Chekhov into contact with a wide range of life, but 'though it was important to Chekhov as a source of copy, medicine was still more important in a philosophical sense: it reinforced his pragmatical, down-to-earth view of life'.[1] He writes to a friend in a famous letter:

> You confuse two concepts: the solution of a problem and its correct presentation. Only the second is incumbent on the artist . . . In my view it's not the writer's job to solve such problems as God, pessimism and so on. The writer's job is only to show who, how, in what context, spoke or thought about God and pessimism. The artist must not be the judge of his character and of what they say: merely a dispassionate observer . . .[2]

This dispassionateness of outlook has a deep impact on the dramatic form of Chekhov's plays, giving them an 'open-ended' quality which makes considerable demands on the subtlety and responsiveness of actors and producers. Even more than in most authors is it damaging to separate Chekhov's 'form' from his 'content'. 'How he says it' is very much 'what he says'.

'REAL LIFE': CHEKHOV'S DISTASTE FOR THEATRICALITY

Chekhov is a master of dramatic anti-climax, going out of his way to avoid what he considered to be falsely 'theatrical' episodes or moments. He remarked with pride of **The Cherry Orchard** that there was not a single pistol-shot in it, but it is not only gross melodrama which he rejects. He cleverly subverts and confounds even more legitimate dramatic expectations raised by the pattern of his action. Thus the climactic action, Lopakhin's announcement that he has bought the orchard, is made almost apologetically, and in the disarmingly digressive context of Gayev's longing for anchovies, Black Sea herrings and a game of billiards, which affects him every bit as much as the loss of his ancestral lands. Again, a persistent motif in the play is the possibility of a marriage between Varya, Mrs Ranevsky's adopted daughter, and Lopakhin. This would unite two single characters, suggest the virtue of work as an antidote to social disintegration (Varya and Lopakhin are the play's hard workers), perhaps even symbolise a stage in the evolution of the Russian class system which would fit in with the play's major thematic interests—in short, a 'loose end' would be very neatly tied. What happens in the last Act, however, is that Lopakhin has more or less to be driven to a *tête-à-tête* with Varya. Chekhov dramatises it thus, in a way that perfectly illustrates his art of anti-climax and his mastery of apparently inconsequential dialogue. Lopakhin has been left on his own:

LOPAKHIN [*with a glance at his watch*]: Yes. [*Pause.*] [*Suppressed laughter and whispering are heard from behind the door. After some time Varya comes in.*]

VARYA [*spends a long time examining the luggage*]: That's funny, I can't find it anywhere.

LOPAKHIN: What are you looking for?

VARYA: I packed it myself and I still can't remember. [*Pause.*]

LOPAKHIN: Where are you going now, Varya?

VARYA: Me? To the Ragulins'. I've arranged to look after their place, a sort of housekeeper's job.

LOPAKHIN: That's in Yashnevo, isn't it? It must be fifty odd miles from here. [*Pause.*] So life has ended in this house.

VARYA [*examining the luggage*]: Oh, where can it be? Or could I have put it in the trunk? Yes, life has gone out of this house. And it will never come back.

LOPAKHIN: Well, I'm just off to Kharkov. By the next train. I have plenty to do there. And I'm leaving Yepikhodov in charge here, I've taken him on.

VARYA: Oh, have you?

LOPAKHIN: This time last year we already had snow, remember? But now it's calm and sunny. It's a bit cold though. Three degrees of frost, I should say.

VARYA: I haven't looked. [*Pause.*] Besides, our thermometer's broken. [*Pause.*]

[*A voice at the outer door:* 'Mr Lopakhin!']

LOPAKHIN: [*as if he had been expecting this summons*]: I'm just coming. [*Goes out quickly.*]

[*Varya sits on the floor with her head on a bundle of clothes, quietly sobbing.*]

It is necessary to quote at length to convey something of the fluidity of Chekhov's dramatic art, especially his handling of dialogue, which makes Ibsen (and indeed many other dramatists) seem stiff and wooden in comparison. Chekhov marries perfectly the naturalistic surface level of speech (with its hesitations, pauses and massive non-sequiturs) to a perception of the real emotional currents flowing in any act of human communication. So here, empty chat about a bit of luggage, train-journeys and the weather simultaneously masks and obliquely reveals the truth of the situation—Varya's inability to drop into tenderness from her usual bossy, managing kind of manner, her fear of being thought to be 'on offer', her hope that he will say something; Lopakhin's fear of his own adequacy, the absence of any genuine commitment to her, his overwhelming embarrassment. It is dramatically absorbing but never seems 'theatrical' in the pejorative sense of the word. Chekhov was very clear about this, writing in a letter which sums up his anti-theatrical stance:

> The demand is made that the hero and heroine should be dramatically effective. But in life people do not shoot themselves, or hang themselves, or fall in love, or deliver themselves of clever sayings every minute. They spend most of their time eating, drinking, running after women or men, talking nonsense. It is therefore necessary that this should be shown on the stage. A play ought to be written in which the people should come and go, dine, talk of the weather, or play cards, not because the author wants it, but because that is what happens in real life. Life on the stage should be as it really is, and the people, too, should be as they are, and not on stilts.[3]

CHEKHOV'S SENSE OF PLOT

Another way in which Chekhov gives *The Cherry Orchard* the texture of 'life as it really is' is by his careful construction of a plot which does not give the appearance of being a plot. There is no character in the play who is in any way manipulating events towards any sort of end—Mrs Ranevsky and her brother, indeed, seem incapable of action, simply standing aside helplessly doing nothing to prevent the sale of their estate. Lopakhin, whom it would have been very easy to cast in the role of the villain-despoiler, not only does nothing to get the estate into his power, but, far from employing schemes and stratagems from self-interest, tries hard to ensure that it stays in the hands of its hereditary owners. He only buys it at the last moment, on the spur of that moment, and is rather dazed at what he has done. A large part of any audience's sense of a dramatic plot comes from the presence of dynamic characters who manipulate the action—Edmund in *King Lear*, Volpone and Mosca, even Hedda Gabler. In suppressing this type of character in *The Cherry Orchard,* Chekhov contrives to give the action of the play the 'open', random feel of life—things seem to happen, rather than be made to happen.

GROUP SCENES

Chekhov characteristically employs a large group of characters, often on the stage at the one time, in such normal group contexts as arrivals, parties and departures, and other social ceremonies. This may be explained as deriving from his attempt to suggest the large social representativeness of his action (whereas Ibsen, concerned with the fate of single individuals, characteristically focuses on one or two characters in intense dialogue). These group scenes provide even more opportunities for Chekhov's mastery of random, inconsequential dialogue, as the characters speak not so much to each other as past each other, in contexts which permit of juxtapositions and non-sequiturs which are sometimes hilarious, sometimes poignant, and where the polyphony of voices does indeed create at times a musical effect. No one character dominates, and this in turn enables Chekhov to achieve his brilliantly subtle modulations of mood, which more than anything else, perhaps, make his dramatic texture seem so fluid.

Group or 'crowd' scenes work very well in dramas that attempt social representativeness. The confused history of an Ireland in the midst of revolution and civil war is captured brilliantly in O'Casey's three 'Dublin' plays, *The Shadow of a Gunman* (1923), *Juno and the Paycock* (1924), and *The Plough and the Stars* (1926), where the tenement or slum settings enable O'Casey to depict many characters with differing political views and loyalties in communal dispute. The same sense of communal integration and fission is illustrated in works such as Soyinka's *A Dance of the Forests* and in Edward Dorall's *A Tiger is Loose in Our Community,* where the crowd scenes depicting antagonisms between the Chinese and Tamil populations are especially vibrant. (Dorall has completed a postgraduate thesis on O'Casey's plays.)

'THEATRE-POETRY'

Chekhov's ability to create mood, and to convey his meaning through the suggestiveness of mood rather than through the much more explicit psychological analysis to be found in Ibsen, can be seen most clearly in the opening of Act 2 of *The Cherry Orchard.* Here all the elements in Chekhov's sense of dramatic form coalesce, to create what has been called 'theatre-poetry'. No verse is actually spoken: the 'poetry' comes from the setting, from the grouping of characters, from the dramatic rhythm (or pace of the action), and from the musical counterpoint of Yepikhodov's guitar. It is open country; a tumbledown old chapel and what seem like old tombstones give intimations of mortality and a hint of the decay of old certainties. The cherry orchard can be seen only dimly, and beyond it a row of telegraph poles and the distant outlines of a big town—a clear visual suggestion of the incursion of a newer modern world on an older, possibly outmoded way of life. The four characters converse after a fashion, but each is absorbed in his own separate thoughts. The sense of separation, of individual loneliness, is strong—Yepikhodov is in love with Dunyasha, but she loves Yasha, who loves only himself. Charlotte the governess says that she doesn't know who she is, where she comes from, and that she is 'alone in the world'. But these four are also a group, a group of servants, which lends ironic point to the demonstration of their separateness. The implication might be that they are all servants of a way of life which is disintegrating. The sun is setting, and from this and the other visual details of the setting, it could be argued that Chekhov is creating a kind of tone-poem on the demise of the landed class, and on the loss of everything which that class had contributed, positively, to the culture. Later in this Act comes the first ominous and symbolic sound of a breaking string, a device taken up and used again in effective counterpoint to the sound of Lopakhin's axes biting into the cherry orchard, in the play's conclusion—if anything, an even more powerful example of 'theatre-poetry'.

TRAGEDY OR COMEDY?

Chekhov the elegiac writer is certainly popular; he is the dramatist of the melancholy mood, the poet of the gloom and soulfulness of a Russia about to pass away for ever and aware in its bones of the nature of its lingering disease. But Chekhov is not to be so easily pinned down or labelled. The opening of Act 2 could also be played—and seen—in a much more comic way. Here is one detail from Charlotte's opening speech:

> Who my parents were I don't know either, very likely they weren't even married. [*Takes a cucumber out of her pocket and starts eating it.*] I don't know anything.

The cucumber is robustly bizarre, in the manner of some of Dickens's greatly eccentric and greatly comic unnecessary details; and eating a good firm cucumber is not, especially in a theatre, a silent business. Charlotte herself and Yepikhodov can be seen as essentially farcical, and Yasha and Dunyasha as riddled with comic affectations; the whole scene can be regarded as a parody of the melancholy of the 'superfluous man' (or class), a Russian literary type.

Indeed, Chekhov's ability to modulate tone, or to hold opposing moods in a delicate balance means that *The Cherry Orchard* as a whole resists generic classification. Is it a tragedy or a comedy? Stanislavsky (1863-1938), the great director of the Moscow Arts Theatre closely associated with Chekhov, was in no doubt of its tragic qualities—but this intensely irritated Chekhov, who firmly insisted on calling the play a comedy. This might seem to be conclusive, but the play's final moments—the farewell to the home and the orchard, and the bitter-sweet vignette of the abandoned old servant, Firs—can only be described as comic with some considerable strain. Ronald Hingley's view of the problem seems eminently sensible:

> In firmly describing his plays, above all *The Cherry Orchard,* as comedies, Chekhov was perhaps confusing matters by dragging in a traditional theatrical term inapplicable to his new form of drama. What he was really appealing for, we suggest, was a lightness of touch, a throw-away casual style, an abandonment of the traditional over-theatricality of the Russian (and not only the Russian) theatre.[4]

Once again, we are back with the salient point: that Chekhov's stance is that of a dispassionate (though not cynical) observer, and that consequently his dramatic mode embraces great tonal fluidity, an alert anti-theatricality, a subtle obliquity of dialogue, and an ability to suggest through 'theatre-poetry' what another dramatist might hammer home explicitly. Chekhov's own dramatic mastery in these respects has influenced dramatists as different as Shaw, Pinter and Beckett.

This technique, and the attitude which informs it, enable Chekhov to present his drama of social change both fairly and comprehensively. *The Cherry Orchard,* like nearly all of his plays, is about 'the fate of the cultured classes in the modern world'.[5] In many British stage productions, Chekhov's vision is sentimentalised, and *The Cherry Orchard* becomes an elegy for the doomed gentry, attractive and whimsically eccentric, lovable in spite (or because) of their faults. On the other hand, it is also easy to throw a falsifying over-emphasis in the other direction. This has been especially true of Soviet criticism, which tends to see Chekhov as a breezy extrovert, portraying with comic vigour the inadequacies of the decaying upper class, and looking forward by implication and with confidence to the brave new world which was to be ushered in, only thirteen years after his death, by the Bolshevik revolution. Both approaches distort Chekhov's remarkable flexibility, his ability to make a full diagnosis (to use the medical terminology he himself was fond of). To see this clearly requires a brief discussion of Chekhov's portrayal of Lopakhin, however difficult it is to isolate one aspect of a very closely woven work of art.

LOPAKHIN

The Cherry Orchard describes the dispossession of a family of land-owning gentry by the son of one of its former serfs, Lopakhin, who has become a self-made man, a dynamic member of the new rising business class. The possibilities of slotting Lopakhin into a melodramatic stereotype are sufficiently obvious, but the portrait is much more subtle.

Lopakhin's great moment in the play, and indeed the climax of whatever action there is, comes near the end of Act 3, when he comes back to the pathetic little party which Mrs Ranevsky is throwing, and announces to a shocked room that *he* has bought the cherry orchard:

> And now the cherry orchard is mine. Mine! [*Gives a loud laugh.*] Great God in heaven, the cherry orchard's mine! Tell me I'm drunk or crazy, say it's all a dream. [*Stamps his feet.*] Don't laugh at me. If my father and grandfather could only rise from their graves and see what happened, see how their Yermolay—Yermolay who was always being beaten, who could hardly write his name and ran round barefoot in winter—how this same Yermolay bought this estate . . . where my father and grandfather were slaves, where they weren't even allowed inside the kitchen . . . Hey, you in the band, give us a tune, I want to hear you. Come here, all of you, and just watch Yermolay Lopakhin get his axe into that cherry orchard, watch the trees come crashing down. We'll fill the place with cottages. Our grandchildren and our great grandchildren will see a few changes round here.

The words exude the confidence of a once-repressed class coming into its own. It is the turning-point of the play, and implicitly the turning-point for Russia, the death of the old order. In a good production, the audience should almost be able to feel the ground shaking underneath the characters' feet, as if the steamroller of history was already rumbling up the driveway: 'just watch Yermolay Lopakhin get his axe into that cherry orchard, watch the trees come crashing down'.

THE DEATH OF THE OLD ORDER

Lopakhin's words refer to some of the exploitative aspects of the old order, and in doing so recall a speech of considerable power and social bite given to the student Trofimov in Act 2. He is trying to point out to Mrs Ranevsky's daughter, whom he loves, the realities of the system on which her traditional status rests:

> Owning living souls, that's what has changed you all so completely, those who went before and those alive today, so that your mother, you yourself, your uncle—you don't realise that you're actually living on credit. You're living on other people, the very people you won't even let inside your own front door.

This whole speech so alarmed the State censor that he insisted that Chekhov should rewrite it. It—and Lopakhin's speech in Act 3 which contains obvious verbal echoes of it—suggest that Chekhov might have approved of the demise of a system of feudal exploitation.

Such a supposition rests on the argument that Chekhov created Lopakhin as a representative of the new dynamic order which was to supplant a decadent gentry. The play certainly paints a strong contrast between the utilitarian, practical Lopakhin (and the doctor in Chekhov approved of the practical and the utilitarian) and the almost incredible lassitude and negligence of Mrs Ranevsky and her brother. Lopakhin also comes extremely well out of the comparison with the play's other 'man of the future', Trofimov. Trofimov is very specific about the Russian disease—too much talking and theorising, and not enough work. The irony is that Trofimov is a spectacular example of the type that he criticises, the eternal student, full of empty theorising. His often inflated rhetoric about his 'being in the vanguard' as 'mankind marches towards a higher truth' compares unfavourably with Lopakhin's plain speech, that of a man more interested in *doing* than in *philosophising*:

> I'm always up by five o'clock, you know. I work from morning till night, and then—well, I'm always handling money, my own and other people's, and I can see what sort of men and women I have around me. You only have to start a job of work to realise how few decent, honest folk there are about.

Lopakhin's role, then, is dynamic, differentiated sharply from the dithering gentry and from the windy theorising of the intellectual; and in him we may feel that Chekhov has embodied his approval of the direction taken by social change in Russia since the emancipation of the serfs.

Lopakhin and the Orchard

It is possible, however, to take a very different view of Lopakhin. This could originate in a sense of the beauty of the cherry orchard itself. The play begins with it, sparkling white with frost through the windows of the empty nursery, and ends with the sound of its destruction. In its mute purity it may be seen as emblematic of a beautiful lost world—not just the lost world of a more expansive feudal life-style, but the lost world of childhood innocence and purity, a world outside time and change, which is locked up somewhere, in different shapes and forms, in all our imaginations. Mrs Ranevsky and her brother do not see in the orchard (as Trofimov insensitively can only see) a symbol of political and social power, once wielded, now lost. It is rather a living memento of the innocence and happiness of childhood: for Mrs Ranevsky it contains a *personal* truth which cannot be measured by the application of moralistic or political standards, as she tries to explain to Trofimov in Act 3. And in Act 1, as the windows are thrown open to the orchard, she exclaims:

> Oh, my childhood, my innocent childhood! This is the nursery where I slept and I used to look out at the orchard from here. When I woke up every morning happiness awoke with me, and the orchard was just the same in those days. Nothing's changed. [*Laughs happily.*] White! All white! Oh, my orchard! After the damp, dismal autumn and the cold winter here you are, young again and full of happiness. The angels in heaven have not forsaken you. If I could only shake off the heavy burden that weighs me down, if only I could forget my past.

Lopakhin seems cursed by an absolute insensitivity to the personal meaning of the orchard for Mrs Ranevsky. He fails to respond to its beauty, and crassly begins to chop it down before Mrs Ranevsky is even out of the house, a crassness that is underlined by his inappropriate production of celebratory champagne. His axes thud not only into wood, but into people's deeply felt past and present

lives. Chekhov's dramatic fluidity and mastery of tonal modulation easily accommodate the playing up of the pathos of Mrs Ranevsky's position, and accordingly as this is done, so does Lopakhin's position take on the tinge and colouring of the utilitarian barbarian, not actively malicious but so insensitive as to be almost as bad; and the play becomes an elegy for the passing of a culture and a way of life symbolised in the orchard itself—beautiful, but unproductive, and since commercially useless, however graceful, to be destroyed by a harsh new type.

Both views of Lopakhin, one friendly, one hostile, are based on the idea that Chekhov must have had one definite attitude to social change. If that attitude could be 'worked out', the character could be 'explained'. But Chekhov's dramatic complexity—and a good deal of his moral significance for our categorising and polarised modern world—insists that a human being cannot be explained in terms of his class role or his social status, that human acts are never just the products of socio-economic factors, but result from a blend of such factors with other, more unpredictable, personal ones. Chekhov makes it very difficult to pigeon-hole Lopakhin as representative of the new dynamic bourgeoisie.

Lopakhin and Mrs Ranevsky

Lopakhin does not see Mrs Ranevsky as the class enemy. Quite the contrary. Many details in the text suggest that he is in love with her, however difficult it might be to define precisely the nature of that love. As he says to her in Act 1, after getting over his agitation at the prospect of her return:

> This brother of yours calls me a lout of a peasant out for what I can get, but that doesn't bother me a bit. Let him talk. You must believe in me as you used to, that's all I ask, and look at me in the old way, with those wonderful, irresistible eyes. Merciful heavens! My father was a serf, belonged to your father and your grandfather before him. But you—you've done so much for me in the past that I've forgotten all that and love you as a brother. Or even more.

Clearly, with his constant efforts to help Mrs Ranevsky out of her financial predicament, which stem from his love for the woman he is to displace, a major and multiple irony of the play is established. Lopakhin may be cast by history as the man of the future but he is as besotted by the past and by admiration for the gentry's way of life as they themselves are.

The inheritance of serfdom is still powerfully active within him, spiritually and emotionally. He tells Dunyasha very early in the play that he has 'plenty of money, but when you really get down to it I'm just another country bumpkin;' and he goes on to rebuke her for her claims to ladylike 'nerves': 'You're too sensitive altogether, my girl. You dress like a lady and do your hair like one too. We can't have that. Remember your place.' These terms could easily have come from old Firs, the play's most absolute believer in the values of the feudal past. Lopakhin cannot entirely rid himself of feelings of inferiority to the cultured milieu he now dominates financially, and his decisiveness as a business man is undercut by his dithering in the area of personal relationships, where he is just as ineffective as, say, Gayev is when dealing with the practical problems of life. There is, for instance, his curiously abortive relationship with Varya—into which Chekhov also works Lopakhin's emotional dependence on Mrs Ranevsky: 'I don't feel I'll ever propose to her without you here.'

CHEKHOV'S MORAL TOLERANCE

Lopakhin, like all the major characters of the play, is seen in a kind of double perspective, which liberates him from dramatic or political stereotyping. The obviousness of what Chekhov says should not blind us to its moral importance: what we do, how we act, should never be taken as a definition of, or confused with, what we are—and vice versa. Lopakhin is no more a simple representative of the new bourgeoisie than Mrs Ranevsky is a simple representative of an obsolete gentry. Sympathy is aroused for her by the intensity with which she associates the orchard with her childhood happiness and innocence. Yet Chekhov also shows, with his infinitely lively sense of the complexity of human beings, that Mrs Ranevsky does not make any real effort to save the orchard because she knows that she no longer belongs to its world, but to Paris and her lover. In a sense, she even wants to lose it. While she still owns it, its very beauty and its associations can only jab the more at her conscience, exacerbate a depressed consciousness of her now rootless, feckless life. When the orchard is lost, her outer and her inner life come more into harmony again. Thus her brother says near the end:

> It's quite true, everything's all right now. Before the cherry orchard was sold we were all worried and upset, but when things were settled once and for all and we'd burnt our boats, we all calmed down and actually cheered up a bit . . . And you can say what you like, Lyuba, you're looking a lot better, no doubt about it.

She replies:

> Yes, I'm not so much on edge, that's true. And I'm sleeping better . . . I'm going to Paris and I'll live on the money your great-aunt sent from Yaroslavl to buy the estate—good old Aunty! Not that it will last very long.

THE BALANCE OF THE CONCLUSION

The indifference and irresponsibility shown in the insouciant attitude to 'Aunty's money' reminds us again, at this crucial point towards the play's close, of the negligence and extravagance of Mrs Ranevsky's life, in the end the main cause of her loss of her family estate. The

ending of the play could have easily, in the hands of a lesser dramatist, turned into a sentimental orgy as the charming aristocrat bids farewell to her home. Indeed, Chekhov's depiction of the leave-taking of Mrs Ranevsky and her brother is deeply moving. But the balance is held: the play ends with a superb picture of the old servant Firs, alone, forgotten by the family, lying down to think over the futility of his devoted service to a family whom even he seems to sense is finished. His words, and their context, clearly do more than refer to his own personal situation:

> Life's slipped by just as if I'd never lived at all. I'll lie down a bit. You've got no strength left, got nothing left, nothing at all. You're just a nincompoop. [*Lies motionless. A distant sound is heard. It seems to come from the sky and is the sound of a breaking string. It dies away sadly. Silence follows, broken only by the thud of an axe striking a tree far away in the orchard.*]

This is wryly funny, but also intensely moving—the distinctive Chekhovian emotional balance is held brilliantly right to the end of the play, that kind of double vision which enables him to see the desperate absurdity of his characters and at the same time the human values in their lives, which tempers his irony with compassion. The 'openness' of Chekhov's dramatic mode is the formal expression of the wide tolerance of his vision of men in society.

NOTES

[1] R. Hingley, *A New Life of Anton Chekhov* (London: Oxford University Press, 1976), p. 52.
[2] M. H. Heim and S. Karlinsky (eds), *Letters of Anton Chekhov* (London: Bodley Head, 1973), p. 117.
[3] Cited by R. Brustein, *The Theatre of Revolt* (London: Methuen, 1970), p. 142.
[4] Hingley, op. cit., p. 302.
[5] Brustein, op. cit., p. 178.

Greta Anderson (essay date 1991)

SOURCE: "The Music of *The Cherry Orchard*: Repetitions in the Russian Text," in *Modern Drama*, Vol. XXXIV, No. 3, September 1991, pp. 340-50

[*In the following essay, Anderson detects "musical structures" in* The Cherry Orchard.]

Kay Unruh Des Roches has recently demonstrated how an analysis of the verbal repetitions in the original text of Ibsen's *The Lady from the Sea* contributes to a specific understanding of the play which a close study of its English translations would not be able to yield. Her essay suggests that all plays in translation "need a criticism based on a detailed description of untranslatable elements in the original text," a criticism which would be as relevant to the theater as to the classroom.[1] Chekhov's major plays certainly merit such an approach, not only because they are so popular in both settings, but because, even in translation, their verbal repetitions (and acoustic repetitions) are such a significant part of our experience of them. Here, a reading of the Russian text of *The Cherry Orchard* will reveal the original shape and sound of its repetitions and probe the meanings inhering in their arrangement. As in Ibsen's play, the repetitions in Chekhov create local patterns which telescope into the play's larger thematic structure. By understanding the play in terms of musical structures, we can appreciate in greater detail the measured grace and good humor with which the playwright has his characters conduct themselves together, in the face of an uncertain future. Attention to structural rhythms tends toward a reading of the play more in accord with Chekhov's designation of the play as a comedy[2] than do most interpretations, particularly those which focus on its closing moments. Of the final snapped string, one critic has written, "to interpret that sound is to interpret the play"[3]: this essay will explicate the rhythmic framework in which that note sounds.

Throughout this play in which "nothing happens," Chekhov creates a dramatic "action" based on community and place—ultimately, the severance of the two. Thus, the characters appear on stage just as they would appear on the family estate, engaged in casual conversation or hysteric outburst, as the case may be. What makes such a loose "ensemble" structure cohere is, at least in part, the interplay of different types of verbal and acoustic repetition, with intermittant repetitions establishing a base rhythm upon which are layered the lyrical swells and lulls of local repetition. Through the effects of these two techniques on the audience's experience of time and emotion, Chekhov creates the boundaries of scenes and acts, and structures the play's close. The most common form of intermittant repetition occurs in character-specific "motifs," from Gayev's "cue ball into the corner" to Yepikhodov's sad song on the guitar. Such repetitions function to counter the strange with the familiar, the tragic with the perpetually comic, and recurring from beginning to end as they do, mark the play's progress through time, evoking the pulse of particular lives through fateful vicissitudes. Local repetitions, as when a word is sounded twice—"doubling"—or when characters repeat their own words or others' within the space of a speech or exchange, often serve to amplify the tenor of the moment, but may also "round off" scenes within acts and close the acts themselves, returning heightened emotions to a baseline level, bringing silence to the stage.

The first line we hear Pishchik utter is the phrase "Think of that now!"[4] in response to Charlotta's out-of-the-blue assertion: "My dog even eats nuts." He repeats this phrase twelve times in the play. This repetition establishes him as a gaping, vacuous character, but his character type is less important here than Chekhov's use of his "Think of that now!"s. The second delivery occurs later in Act One, following an equally bizarre exchange:

> PISHCHIK How was it in Paris? What's it like there? Did you eat frogs?

> LYUBOV I ate crocodiles.

> PISHCHIK Think of that now!

>   (p. 327)

Moments later, Pishchik interrupts Gayev's verbal tribute to an antique bookcase with the exclamation: "A hundred years! . . . Think of that now!"

Pishchik's repetitive exclamations form a pattern of response to the more eccentric, potentially discordant elements in the play. The absolute predictability of his reaction domesticates the wild unpredictability of speeches like those cited above, balancing out the outrageousness in which Chekhov, and Chekhov's audience, delights. Both *Uncle Vanya* and *The Three Sisters* are much about the social carrying capacities of their communities, and the strain on equilibrium caused by certain combinations of personalities. In this sense, the community of *The Cherry Orchard* could not tolerate another Charlotta, nor could it do without Pishchik's normalizing responses, "Think of that now!" But Pishchik is not a "blank" background character. We take interest in him, not only because he swallows a boxful of pills, but because his speech is so consistently vacant. Pishchik's repetitive domestications of eccentricity are in fact just another genre of eccentricity.

Like Pishchik's expressions, Gayev's billiards speeches, though strange or obsessive by the standards of the outside world, form a normalizing subtext within the play. In almost every scene in which he appears, we witness the soon familiar "Cut shot into the corner" or one of its variants, accompanied by an appropriate pantomime. Other characters encourage this behavior. Lyubov is the first to articulate the standard line, responding to her brother's gestural "cue" with "How does it go? Let's see if I can remember . . . cue ball into the corner! Double the rail to center table" (I. p. 323), a speech which, being her first upon entering the stage, reveals her desire to resume the patterned discourse of the community she left and now returns to. In a later scene, Trofimov suggests that Gayev "cue ball into the center" (p. 347), his attempts at grandiloquence having been unanimously shut down. Gayev's billiards habit is endorsed by his family as more tolerable than his tendency to apostrophize the closest object at hand. Other characters rave, but Gayev is silenced as soon as he launches into his fustian extemporizations, and it is precisely because the others are allowed to rave that Gayev must be limited to his billiards motif. Trofimov, Lyubov, and to a lesser extent, Lopakhin all express deeply held and contrasting points of view—about tradition and change, love, the peasants; Gayev's idiosyncratic lyricism clutters the arena of situated conflict, and participates in communal discourse only to be silenced.

"Cue ball into the corner" and its variants not only provide Gayev's community an alternative to his excessive speechifying, they also provide him a viable response to personal crisis. According to Chekhov's stage directions, he announces his imaginary billiards shots *"in deep* thought," "forlornly," and finally, "afraid of bursting into tears." Gayev's habitual dislocation of emotion in the billiards game is most acutely demonstrated in Act Three, during the public disclosure of his financial ruin. Gayev enters the scene of the party weeping from the auction's outcome. When, from the adjacent room, the click of billiard balls is heard, his expression changes: he stops weeping, and returns to his everyday concerns, leaving with Firs to change out of his business clothes. The allusion to billiards in this scene is most poignant because the symbolic language of billiards and the emotion Gayev brings to it are so unequal in value. Billiards is just a game, but it is Gayev's stronghold against debilitating change.

The repeated instances of Gayev's verbal tic might be charted as "ticks" on the play's temporal axis. Since these utterances are distributed equally throughout the play and, as Lyubov's initial speech makes clear, existed before the play, they form a constant that we can imagine will continue into the next phase of Gayev's life. Pishchik's banal "Think of that now"s produce a similar rhythmic effect. But while these intermittent repetitions might be said to "keep time" in the play, its local repetitions serve to amplify the dimensions of individual moments, as characters use them to express their joy or grief—their passions. Likewise, while the pre-existence and continuation of certain verbal patterns suggest the sensation of unbounded or existential time, those rhythms are counterbalanced by the containing power of local repetitions at the ends of scenes and acts.

Of the play's characters, Lyubov, Anya and Varya most frequently use local repetition for emotional emphasis:

> LYUBOV Today my fate is decided . . . my fate.
>
> (3. p. 356*)

> ANYA I'm at peace now! I'm at peace!
>
> (1. p. 335*)

Local repetition is often syntactically enhanced, as in these cases of anaphora and epistrophe:

> LYUVOV You should be a man, at your age you should understand those who love. And you yourself should love . . . you should fall in love! [Angrily] Yes, yes!
>
> (3. p. 359*)

> CHARLOTTA But where I come from and who I am— I don't know. . . . Who my parents were—perhaps they weren't even married—I don't know. . . . I don't know anything.
>
> (2. p. 337*)

Doubling, or the immediate repetition of a word, occurs frequently in the play; the words most often repeated thus are those of silencing or coming and going:

> VARYA Don't talk about it, don't talk about it.
>
> (1. p. 320)

> GAYEV I'll be silent, silent.
>
> (2. p. 347)

> LOPAKHIN I'm going, I'm going.
>
> (1. p. 329)[5]

> GAYEV I'm coming, I'm coming.
>
> (1. p. 335)

In the following passage, Gayev and Trofimov attempt to silence Lyubov by doubled repetition. The scattered repetition in Lyubov's initial speech reflects her disrupted emotions: "son," the word best modified by "my," is separated from her two utterances of that pronoun. As Lyubov gains control, she uses repetition—"For what? For what, my friend?"—to intensify her expression of grief:

> GAYEV [embarrassed] Now, now, Lyuba.
>
> VARYA [crying] Didn't I tell you, Petya, to wait until tomorrow?
>
> LYUBOV ANDREYEVNA My Grisha . . . my little boy . . . Grisha . . . son . . .
>
> VARYA What can we do, Mama dear? It's God's will.
>
> TROFIMOV [gently, through tears] There, there . . .
>
> LYUBOV ANDREYEVNA [crying softly] My little boy is dead, drowned . . . For what? For what, my friend? . . . But Petya, why do you look so bad? Why have you grown so old?
>
> (1. p. 331*)

Lyubov's repeated question paradoxically purges her emotion as it contains it; it aestheticizes, through rhythm, an emotion too strong for ordinary syntax. This frees her to move on to another gesture better suited to the social setting; she teases Trofimov about his "mangy" appearance. In other words, her verbal repetition ends the "scene" which her weeping began.

Chekhov broke from contemporary dramatic convention when he chose not to subdivide into "french scenes" his later one-acts and the acts of his full-length dramas from *The Seagull* onward.[6] Still, though they are not demarcated, there are within the acts distinct units of action, usually initiated or closed off by characters' entrances and exits, or one of the forty-three pauses written into the stage directions.[7] For example, in Act One, Dunyasha's exit as she goes to prepare coffee leaves Anya and Varya alone in a distinct scene. Her reappearance ends the scene. Verbal repetitions often directly precede or follow such breaks in the action, emphasizing the boundaries of what we identify as scenes. In this case, Varya begins and ends the tête-à-tête with the phrase: "My darling has arrived! My pretty one has arrived!" (pp. 320*, 321*). Afterwards, the coffee serving begins: a new scene. This perpetual ending and beginning conditions the audience's response to the ends of acts, and to the end of the play. The audience comes to expect the continuation of action after closure and silence.

The scene immediately preceding the first snapping of the string is initiated by a dramatic entrance, concluded by a pause, and bounded also by verbal doubling. Like so many scenes in Chekhov's plays, it does not further the action, but holds the characters in a static suspension. The logic that effects its dramatic coherence is based on musical structures, rather than the signifying processes of the serial increment—the "what happens" of the plot unit:

[*Yepikhodov crosses at the rear of the stage, playing the guitar.*]

LYUBOV ANDREYEVNA [*pensively*] There goes Yepikhodov . . .

ANYA [*pensively*] There goes Yepikhodov . . .

GAYEV The sun has set, ladies and gentlemen.

TROFIMOV Yes.

GAYEV [*in a low voice, as though reciting*] Oh, Nature, wondrous Nature, you shine with eternal radiance, beautiful and indifferent, you whom we call mother, unite within yourself both life and death, you give life and take it away . . .

VARYA [*beseechingly*] Uncle dear!

ANYA Uncle, you're doing it again!

TROFIMOV You'd better cue ball into the center.

GAYEV I'll be quiet, I'll be quiet.

[*All sit, lost in thought. Silence. All that's heard is the quiet muttering of* FIRS. *Suddenly a distant sound is heard, as if from* the sky, like the sound of a snapped string mournfully dying away.]

(2. pp. 347-48*)

The snapping string is the structural close to a scene which opens with several musical elements. Yepikhodov enters playing a guitar. The repeated anapests of *Yepikhódov idyót, Yepikhódov idyót,* create a distinct rhythm, to which the trochees of the next line answer: *Sólntze syélo, gòspodá.* Finally, the last syllable of this line is repeated immediately in Trofimov's *"Da".* In fact, the repeated *-da* or the acoustic image *-oda,* seems, as much as the setting sun, to inspire Gayev's rhapsody addressed to Nature, or *priróda.* Gayev expands beyond the acoustic coincidence to deliver a lyric speech crammed full of literary language: nature is divine, indifferent; she lives and destroys. His phrase "whom we call mother" acknowledges this literariness, as does the stage direction: ". . . *as though reciting.*" Finally, the abstraction of phonic repetition which introduced or generated Gayev's bathetic verbalization is reinstated in

the silence urged upon him by his nieces, and by the sound which follows.

The reasons for this specific suppression of verbality may be found in a long speech by Trofimov immediately preceding the passage cited above. In it he proclaims the hypocrisy of the intelligentsia, and states his distrust of "fine talk" and "serious conversations." But by its length and its polemical sophistication, the speech of the "eternal student" itself might well qualify as "fine talk." The others ignore his conclusion—"Better to remain silent"—and continue their verbal seriousness until they are interrupted by the entrance of Yepikhodov. The music which Yepikhodov introduces to the stage provides a simple alternative to literary language and political debate, and the ensuing "conversation" utilizes musical principles. In it Gayev, like a player in an orchestral ensemble, is instructed to either play his part or be silent.

The above scene illustrates Chekhov's use of local repetition to create verbal borders for scenes within the larger dramatic framework. But the repetitive element which closes the action also connects the unified part to the continuous whole, and to a time line which extends beyond the drama's borders. The sisters' pleas for silence are a motif introduced in Act One when Gayev makes a stupid speech shortly after lamenting this tendency of his. Here, Anya's "Uncle, you're doing it again!" comes close to duplicating her earlier complaint, "You're doing it again, uncle!" (p. 335*). But Varya, in this second instance, and in a similar instance in Act Four (p. 377), does not restate the substantive imperative, "be quiet"; she simply cries out, "Uncle dear." The content of the sisters' verbal gesture is implicit because it is a repetition, yet part of that content has shifted to the very fact of its repetition: we smile at the "[not] again!" Formally, the expression begins to approach the enigmatic "Cue ball into the center" as a trope of rhythmic continuity in communal discourse, a seme that constitutes both a constant and a constraint in lives which are now changing course, dispersing.

Chekhov's use of local repetition to contain dramatic action is most evident in the endings of his acts. The first three acts of **The Cherry Orchard** conclude with the doubled utterance of the Russian verb *poidyóm* (variously rendered in translation as "let's go," "come," or "come along"). The repetition of this verb at the end of acts works like a refrain or chorus in a ballad, closing off each part, while linking those parts in a continuing series, simultaneously creating linguistic closure and prompting a renewal of linguistic activity. Interestingly, the element of narrative stasis in a ballad becomes the repeated action of the play. Something does happen: the characters come and go. Finally, they go. The doubled *poidyóms* which close the first three acts prepare us for the last enunciation of this verb in the final and decisive exit of the family from the estate; the patterns created in the first three instances help inform our experience of that exit, and of the play's final events as a whole.

Varya supplies the refrain to Act One as she ushers her sister to bed:

> VARYA Come to your little bed . . . Come along. [*Leading her*] My little darling fell asleep. Come along. . . . [*They go*]
>
> [*In the distance, beyond the orchard, a shepherd is playing on a reed pipe.*
>
> TROFIMOV *crosses the stage and, seeing* VARYA *and* ANYA, *stops.*]
>
> VARYA Sh! She's asleep . . . asleep . . . Come along, darling.
>
> ANYA [*softly, half-asleep*] I'm so tired . . . Those bells . . . Uncle . . . darling . . . Mama and Uncle . . .
>
> VARYA Come along, darling, come along. [*They go into* ANYA'S *room*]
>
> TROFIMOV [*deeply moved*] My sunshine! My spring!
>
> (p. 336*)

In Act Two, the refrain is rendered by a shared repetition, heard over the familiar strum of Yepikhodov's guitar:

> VARYA'S VOICE Anya! Where are you?
>
> TROFIMOV That Varya again! [*Angrily*] It's revolting!
>
> ANYA Well? Let's go down to the river. It's lovely there.
>
> TROFIMOV Let's go. [*They go*]
>
> VARYA'S VOICE Anya! Anya!
>
> (p. 351*)

Anya's speech comforting her mother concludes Act Three:

> ANYA Mama! . . . Mama, are you crying? My dear, kind, good mama, my pretty one, I love you . . . I bless you. The cherry orchard is sold, it's gone, that's true, true, but don't cry, Mama, you still have your life before you, you still have your good, pure soul . . . Let's go together, let's go, darling, away from here, let's go! . . . We'll plant a new orchard, more splendid than this one, you will see it and understand, and joy, deep, quiet joy will sink into your soul, like the evening sun, and you will smile, Mama! Come, let's go, darling! Let's go! . . .
>
> (p. 367*)

Established in the endings of the first three acts is a pattern of alternating harmony and discord, from Trofimov's effusive infatuation to Varya's peskiness back to the shared dreams of mother and daughter. This pattern prepares us for the discord of the ending, and mollifies that discord with promise of a rhythmic renewal of joy and harmony. The invocation of the sun in the two up-

Stanislavsky as Gaev and Maria Petrovna Lilina as Anya, in a Moscow Art Theater production of The Cherry Orchard, *1908.*

beat passages is significant, presenting an image of that which is ever repeating. Like other motifs, this natural one both divides time and stresses its infinite extension; it also comforts the community with its rhythm. Paired with spring, as in Trofimov's speech, the sun suggests bright renewal; imagined at sunset, as in Anya's speech, it evokes suffusing warmth. The relative timing of these two images—sunshine and spring in the first act; the colored dusk in the third—might imply a dramatic progression in synch with the natural temporal structures of days and years. In fact, the play begins in spring and ends with the onset of winter. But Chekhov would remind us that nature's changes are cyclical and continuous; Lopakhin refers to the next spring twice in the final act. Likewise, the opening of Act One subverts temporal closure even as it establishes a structural correspondence to the unit of "day." In the play's first exchange, Dunyasha, responding to Lopakhin's query "What time is it?" replies, "Nearly two," snuffs the candle that she carries, and continues, "It's already light." The enacted drama begins at day's beginning, but alludes to the ever-present past, to the dark of the previous night.

Act One opens with Lopakhin's awakening and closes with Anya's retreat to her bedroom for sleep. Act Three also closes with the suggestion of bedtime, rendered by the lullaby qualities of the repetitions in Anya's speech to her mother. In inflected languages like Russian, the possibilities for acoustic repetition, especially through suffixal assonance, are greatly increased. In Russian, assonance through inflection is particularly pronounced in feminine nominative and accusative adjective endings, where the vowel sound is doubled,—"-aya, -yaya / -ooyoo, -yooyoo"—and acoustically imitates the feminine noun endings—"-a, -ya / -oo, -yoo." Chekhov utilizes this feature of his language in Anya's speech ending; the string of adjectives—*Mílaya, dóbraya, khoróshaya, moyá . . . moyá, prekrásnaya*—modifying "mama," and also those modifying the feminine nouns "joy" and "soul," add to the verbal repetition and syntactic parallelism a distinct acoustic repetition. These repeated soft sounds effectively calm and silence Lyubov. And by silencing Lyubov, Anya silences the stage, bringing the act to a rounded close.

But while Act Three ends precisely with the by now familiar refrain, *Poidyóm . . . poidyóm!*, the previous acts end with a refrain and a coda, a focused conclusion followed by an expression from off-center, or even offstage. Act One ends, not with the repetitive final words of the two characters whose conversation is central to the drama, but with the exclamation of the observing Trofimov, "My sunshine! My spring!" Likewise, Varya's call, from offstage, tags behind the happy closure of the lovers' exit at the end of Act Two. The end of Act Four and of the play itself is structured on a similar model of closure and coda, amplified and expanded.

Toward the close of Act Four the audience hears the sequence—

> GAYEV My sister, my sister!
>
> ANYA'S VOICE Mama!
>
> TROFIMOV'S VOICE Aa-ooo!
>
> (p. 379)

—repeated twice, then completed by Lyubov's *"Poidyóm"* as she and Gayev exit. A silence then falls upon the empty stage. The audience which has been sensitive to the play's structures feels the resolution of this moment, yet nevertheless anticipates a further note. And indeed, the stillness is broken by the thud of an axe against a tree somewhere offstage. The ensuing apperance of Firs, presumably removed to a hospital, is as shocking as if he had risen from the dead—and we understand that he is to die. His ragged speech provides the coda to the closing departure of his previous masters:

> FIRS [*goes to the door and tries the handle*]: Locked. They have gone . . . [*Sits down on the sofa.*] They've forgotten me . . . It's nothing . . . I'll sit here awhile . . . I expect Leonid Andreich hasn't put on his fur coat and has gone off in his overcoat. [*Sighs anxiously.*] And I didn't see to it . . . The greenhorn! [*Mumbles something which can't be understood.*] That life is gone, as if it never were lived . . . [*Lies down.*] I'll

> lie down awhile . . . There's no strength left in you, nothing's left, nothing . . . Ugh, you . . . addlepate! [*Lies motionless*]
>
> (p. 380*)

Early in his speech, Firs acknowledges the fact that would tend to give the play's ending a pessimistic tone: "They've forgotten me." But Firs goes on, repeating the habitual concern for and affectionate criticism of Gayev he has voiced all along, asserting the endurance of their relationship beyond the dramatic, or material, relevance of that relationship: Leonid Andreich is gone for good. It is as if Firs says, "They've forgotten me; what's more, as usual, the greenhorn's forgotten his coat. He'll never change." Firs lives for his master and through his master; in expressing that fussbudgety love of the life that will go on without him, he, in a sense, transcends his own death. The moment is followed by a darker view of his fate, and of the play's action. The line, "That life is gone, as if it never were lived," might serve as a gloss on the play itself.[8] Soon the audience will leave the theater and leave these other lives behind. "Nothing's left, nothing . . ." seems to be a definitive ending to the play, a doubled repetition to arrest the propulsive "Let's go . . . let's go" of previous endings. But this end too has a coda. Firs's last utterance subverts the closure of his death with a gritty assertion of continuity. "Addlepate" may be Firs's last word and the play's last word, but it is not the last time his word will be used. Lyubov has already adopted this epithet in her put-down of Trofimov in the third act, acknowledging Firs as her source: "You! You're not above love. As our Firs would say, you're just an addlepate!" (p. 358*). Firs's cranky expression will continue to sound in the community of which he was once an integral part.

Non-verbal sound has the "last word" in the play. A distant sound is heard, that of a snapped string "mournfully dying away." While the same sound in Act Two invited the characters' interpretations, this time it invites the audience's interpretation. Finding no referent for that noise, the audience might interpret the sound based on what it knows about the play's ending, rather than the other way around. Firs is abandoned, left to die alone. Outside someone is chopping down the orchard. In this context, the distant sound might be heard as the end punctuation to a cruel tragedy.

Searching for Chekhov's "intentions" regarding the sound raises difficult questions about the difference between playgoing versus play-reading. It is crucial to keep in mind that the reading audience will experience this "sound" differently from an audience in the theater; it will note that the string has sounded *"(as if) from the sky"* (angels on high?), that it is *"(like) the sound of a snapped string"* (reminiscent of Atropos's snip), that it *"dies away"* (like Firs), and that it does so "mournfully." But it might well note that these figures do not constitute but describe the sound, and that they are, to the word, the same figures used to describe it in Act Two. Chekhov is thwarting the reader's expectation for variation in literary language; his linguistic repetition stresses the structural, phonic identity of the two sounds, the acoustic repetition that a live audience would hear.

"The sound of the snapped string," in other words, indicates more a recurring motif than the sound *of* a snapped string. Recall the description of the first issuance of the string's sound:

> *All sit, lost in thought, Silence, All that's heard is the quiet muttering of FIRS. Suddenly a distant sound is heard, as if from the sky, like the sound of a snapped string mournfully dying away.*

In Act Two, silence, and Firs's mumbling, preceded the sonic event. In the second issuance, the volume is turned up, as it were; we hear the fragments of Firs's disconnected speech. The significance of the ending note may likewise seem amplified, momentous, but the momentum generated by its repetition prepares us for another act, another sounding of the string. Because of the patterns established and developed throughout the play, we expect another coda.

So, finally, the snapped string is followed by the sound of an axe continuing its work on the orchard. This sound is rhythmic, repetitive, and does not cease. It epitomizes not so much the ending or beginning of an era, but the current of the ongoing present, the infinitely receding coda to joy and grief, day and night, arrivals and departures, life and death. It answers the play's opening speech not with an apocalyptic gong, but with the repeated ticking of tocks. And thus the action of the play merges with the "action" of our own lives—the changes we do not so much "suffer" as endure or experience, the music we make with others while we can. For the final coda, the members of the audience will say to their companions, "Let's go," and, as they emerge outside under a changed sky, they may check their watches and note, as Lopakhin does in Act One: "Time passes . . . Time passes, I say."

NOTES

[1] "A Problem of Translation: Structural Patterns in the Language of Ibsen's *The Lady from the Sea*," *Modern Drama*, 30 (1987), 325.
[2] This is a major concern of Chekhov's biographical critics, David Magarshak (*Chekhov the Dramatist* [New York, 1952]) and Ronald Hingley (*A New Life of Anton Chekhov* [New York, 1976]). From the play's planning stages to its performances, Chekhov's letters are adamant about this point: *The Cherry Orchard* is a comedy, if not a farce.
[3] J. L. Styan, *Chekhov in Performance* (Cambridge 1971), p. 337. See also Maurice Valency, *The Breaking String* (Oxford, 1966), esp. p. 287, and Harvey Pitcher, *The Chekhov Play: A New Interpretation* (London, 1973), p. 182. These and other interpretations are summarized by Jean-Pierre Baricelli, preliminary to his argument in "Counterpoint of the Snapping String: Chekhov's *The Cherry Orchard* in *California Slavic Studies*, 10 (1976): 121-36.
[4] *The Cherry Orchard* in *Chekhov: The Major Plays*, trans. Ann Dunnigan, Signet Classic, 1964, p. 318. Hereafter act and page numbers, when not stated in the text, appear in parenthesis. I have significantly modified a number of Dunnigan's translations; in these instances, the page number is asterisked. The Russian text I've used is edited by Donald R. Hitchcock, Library of Russian Classics (Hertfordshire, 1978).

For a discussion of the relative merits of the various translations of *The Cherry Orchard*, see Andrew Durkin, "*The Cherry Orchard* in English: An Overview," *Yearbook of Comparative and General Literature*, 33

(1984), 74-82. Durkin concludes that, on the basis of its transparency, "Dunnigan's translation would seem to be the closest approximation in English to Chekhov's text, while [Ronald] Hingley (The *Oxford Chekhov*) and [Eugene] Bristow (Norton Critical Edition) offer versions that are perhaps better suited to a close study of the play" (p. 81). These latter include commentary on variant translations and the sound of the original text.
[5] In informal usage, the Russian verb absorbs the pronoun in its conjugation; hence, single words may speak a sentence: "I'm going" = *"idóo"*; "I'll be silent" = *"molchóo."* Such compact expressions make for more immediate, more musical repetition.
[6] Turgenev, before him, was the first to abandon this tradition, in *A Month in the Country*. Most of Chekhov's contemporaries maintained the practice of numbering discrete scenes each time an entrance or exit was made. (See Vera Gottlieb, *Chekhov and the Vaudeville* [London, 1982].)
[7] S. D. Balukhaty discusses the distribution of these pauses in his article "*The Cherry Orchard*: A Formalist Approach," in Robert Louis Jackson, *Chekhov: A Collection of Critical Essays*, Englewood NJ, 1967, p. 143.
[8] This line is curiously absent from the Signet edition.

Donald Rayfield   (essay date 1994)

SOURCE: "Critical Reception," in *The Cherry Orchard: Catastrophe and Comedy*, Twayne Publishers, 1994, pp. 15-28.

[*In the essay below, Rayfield surveys European and American responses to, and interpretations of,* The Cherry Orchard *throughout the twentiety century.*]

The Cherry Orchard began to reverberate in Russian literature even before it was performed or published. The first reaction, in November 1903, was that of the state censor Vasili Vereshchagin, who found two passages of social criticism in Trofimov's speeches in act 2 too outspoken and forced Chekhov to substitute less biting passages. In December, when Chekhov came to Moscow to attend rehearsals, the great director of the Moscow Arts Theater Konstantin Stanislavsky, and many of his actors appeared to react to the play as though it were a tragedy or a straightforward political diatribe. Stanislavsky's telegram of congratulations ended, "We wept in the last act."[1] His wife, Maria Lilina, who was to play Ania, dared to contradict the author's subtitle "comedy": "It's a tragedy, whatever outlet to a better life you reveal in the last act. . . . I wept, as a woman."[2] A little later she intuited, "*The Cherry Orchard* is not a play, but a work of music, a symphony." Vladimir Nemirovich-Danchenko, Stanislavsky's second in command, had for 12 years enjoyed Chekhov's trust. He had achieved a reputation in Russia as a playwright and sacrificed this career to serve the Moscow Arts Theater: his plays, such as *Tsena zhizni* (The Price of Life) of 1889, developed the merchant dramas of Nikolai Ostrovsky with a French vaudeville lightness and, despite their lack of original spark or subtlety, were apparently genuinely admired by Chekhov. Nemirovich-Danchenko sensed (in an extravagant telegram to Chekhov) that they had "overdone the tears."[3] Chekhov stressed the play's vaudeville qualities: the tears of the Ranevskaia household were only metaphorical. At the same time he edited the text to bring out the sensitivity of his capitalist Lopakhin. Chekhov was prepared to incorporate an actor's improvisation only if it enhanced the ludicrous side of the play. Some actors realized how complex the play was: A. L. Vishnevsky called it "the most expensive lace . . . the most difficult of your plays to perform."[4]

The play was first performed on 17 January 1904 to celebrate the twenty-fifth anniversary of Chekhov's literary career, but the sight of the dying author, unable to stand, wanly acknowledging applause, was hardly festive. The interpretation of the play as a tragic swan song was linked with the spectable of the playwright's lugubrious last bow. Nemirovich-Danchenko had packed the theater with a claque of spectators (known as "angels") standing behind the legitimate seated audience; many of them were Chekhov's Crimean neighbors—emaciated tubercular young men from Yalta—and their sobs as the play ended to the sound of the last blows of the ax on the cherry trees cast an elegiac pall over the performance.[5] Chekhov's reported reaction was annoyance: "It's all wrong, the play and the performance. That's not what I saw, and they couldn't understand what I wanted."[6] Yet over the 1904 season the theater could not believe its production had betrayed the author: "Never in my theatrical career do I remember seeing an audience react like that to the slightest detail of drama, genre, psychology, as today," Nemirovich-Danchenko telegraphed to Chekhov. "The overall tone of the performance has splendid assurance, precision, talent. More than any other of your plays, the success is due to the author, regardless of the theater."[7]

Only after Chekhov's death did Nemirovich-Danchenko concede that they had misinterpreted the play: "We didn't fully understand his subtle writing. Chekhov was refining realism to the point of symbols, and the theater took a long time to find this delicate weft in Chekhov's work."[8] One perceptive reviewer, the dramatist Aleksandr Amfiteatrov, insisted, "For all its great success neither the public nor the critics had grasped all its charm; they will take a very long time discovering one depth after another, sinking deeper and deeper into it, loving it and becoming used to it."[9] Amfiteatrov's review was one of the most penetrating: he realized that Chekhov was not to be understood as a political partisan or a social arbiter, that Ranevskaia and Gaev were not the traditional bad landowners rightfully deprived of their property: "The Gaevs perish not in revolt against modern times, but because fate has come to pass: a race is dying out."

Throughout the season, until Chekhov's death in July, there were some 80 reviews of the Moscow Arts Theater's performances. On the whole, the wittiest were the most negative. The doyenne of symbolist salons and head of the anti-Chekhovian school of criticism, Zinaida Gippius (writing as "Anton the Extreme"), dismissed the play as unperformable.[10] A year before she had caricatured the Chekhovian play this way: "It's raining. Leaves are falling. People are drinking tea with jam. They set out a game of patience. They're very bored. They drink, and a drunk laughs quietly for a long time. They're bored again. Sometimes a man feels a sexual urge, makes a pass, and says, 'Voluptuous woman!' They then drink tea again, are bored, and finally die, sometimes of an illness, sometimes by shooting themselves."[11]

The majority of critics, however, agreed with the Moscow Arts Theater: this, said Vlas Doroshevich, "was a comedy in name, a drama in content."[12] It was, he said, a narrative poem: the landowner Ranevskaia and her family were *morituri* (doomed to die). Russia's symbolists, constantly feuding with realism, were, however, detecting in Chekhov not a boring student of reality but a fellow poet mourning the destruction of beauty and the hatefulness of life. The signal was given in the spring of 1904 by the poet, novelist, manifesto writer, and theoretician Andrei Bely. While other symbolists (e.g., the self-proclaimed maestro Valeri Briusov) felt that the play was artifice and that only act 3 had real dramatic impact, Bely in an influential article proclaimed that Chekhov had married realism and symbolism, making the play "a continuous link between the fathers and the children. . . . In act 3 . . . Chekhov's devices crystallize; a family drama takes place in the hall, while in the back room, lit by candles, masks of horror dance in frenzy. . . . [W]hat from a distance seem to be shadowy cracks turn out to be openings into eternity."[13] In 1907 Bely redefined the play: "realism made transparent, naturally fused with symbolism."

In a letter to Chekhov, Vsevolod Meierkhold—the "dark genius" of the Russian theater and once a protégé of Stanislavsky but now a Lucifer cast out into St. Petersburg by the Moscow Arts Theater—claimed *The Cherry Orchard* as authentic symbolist repertory: "I don't much like the Moscow performance of this play. . . . Your play is as abstract as a Tchaikovsky symphony. And a director should use his ear above all to grasp it. In act 3 to the sound of idiotic stamping—and that stamping should be audible—Horror enters, unnoticed by the people. The cherry orchard is sold. They dance. 'It's sold!' They dance. And so on to the end. . . . When one reads plays by foreign authors, you stand apart by your originality. In drama, too, the West will have to learn from you."[14] Meierkhold worshiped Chekhov; he had played Treplev in *The Seagull* and, before his break with Nemirovich-Danchenko and Stanislavsky, was apparently the actor for whom the part of Tuzenbakh in *Three Sisters* was written. It seems that Meierkhold was encouraged by Chekhov's response to his alternative views and felt them to be part of a dialogue. Meierkhold is reported to have told A. K. Gladkov, "Do you know who first sowed doubts in me that not all the paths of the Moscow Arts Theater were right? Anton Chekhov. He disagreed with a lot in the theater, much he criticized outright."

Meierkhold's views on the symbolist nature of *The Cherry Orchard* were spectacularly graphic but never realized in the theater. His own three performances of the play in the Black Sea port of Kherson in February 1904 apparently differed little from the Moscow Arts Theater style he had been trained in. Moving to St. Petersburg and joining forces with the great actress-director Vera Komissarzhevskaia, Meierkhold found himself forced to submit to her view that *The Cherry Orchard* was unplayable except in the Moscow Arts Theater tradition.

Nevertheless, in 1906 Meierkhold did sketch an alternative mise-en-scène for the play, which was never produced, despite the 30 years of his career still left to run. The ideas he set out in a 1908 article of are persuasive: Epikhodov, Iasha, and Duniasha he saw as the circus figures of Pierrot, Harlequin, and Colombine, who figure prominently in French and Russian symbolist poetry, in Pablo Picasso's blue period, and in Igor Stravinsky's *Petrushka*.[15] Meierkhold's vision of Ranevskaia identifies her as the life force.

The progressive, realist camp who saw in Maksim Gorky's *Lower Depths* the real future of drama and revolution tended to dismiss the play as did Gorky: "Nothing new. Everything—moods, ideas, if you can call them that, characters—are to be found in the earlier plays. Of course it's beautiful, and raw anguish on the stage hits the audience. But what the anguish is about, I don't know."[16] Others as subjective as the symbolists reinterpreted Chekhov's play to suit their views: typical in its breathtaking naïveté is a letter Chekhov received from Viktor Baranovsky, a radical student in the provinces: "I heard . . . a call to an active, energetic life of ferment, to bold, fearless struggle—and so to the end of the play I felt intense pleasure. Lopakhin and the student are friends going arm in arm towards that bright star."[17] Many reviewers assumed that if the Ranevskaia household lost its estate deservedly, then Lopakhin or Trofimov were rightful heirs and would create "a future on the wreck of the old."[18] The ambiguity and irony of Chekhov's stance escaped the radicals, as it had for the previous 18 years, ever since Chekhov's neurotic idealist and villain Ivanov (in the play of the same name) first taxed their judgment with his equivocations.

Powerful disparagement was also heard: the most consistent for 50 years to come was from Chekhov's disciple, the great writer Ivan Bunin. He acknowledged Chekhov's supremacy in the short story but, like Tolstoy, felt that the plays were embarrassingly ignorant and incompetent. In vain, Chekhov's defenders pointed out that you did not have to be a nobleman to write about the landed gentry, that strict social realism was not Chekhov's aim. Bunin was upset by Soviet ideology hijacking the Moscow Arts Theater and the "progressive" speeches of Chekhov's characters. Bunin's loathing of *The Cherry Orchard* is important because it formed an undercurrent of opinion that still flows in Russia today. Bunin wrote, "There were never any orchards in Russia that were entirely given over to cherry trees and there's nothing wonderful about cherry trees. . . . Ranevskaia is supposed to be a landowner and yet a Parisian, she either weeps hysterically or laughs. . . . It's also quite implausible that Lopakhin should have these profitable trees cut down with such stupid haste before the former owner has even left the house. . . . Firs is fairly plausible, but the rest is unbearable."[19]

The breakup of the symbolist movement on the eve of World War I and the Bolsheviks' use of the theater as ideological centers turned *The Cherry Orchard* first into an unquestionable classic and then into a vehicle for illustrating the inevitability of the old order's collapse. Russian criticism concentrated on textual and intertextual problems, demonstrating the kinship of Chekhov's drama to the "new drama" that arose on the fringes of Western Europe—in Norway, Sweden, and Russia—so that the trio of Henrik Ibsen, August Strindberg, and Anton Chekhov took on a misleading similarity, as dramatists who protested against not only the congealed conventions of the theater but also the hypocrisy and oppression of bourgeois societies. Survivors of the formalist school made only modest inroads into such a simplistic view: the Bulgarian scholar Petr Bitsilli pointed out how daringly Chekhov uses conventional devices such as eavesdropping and soliloquy in *The Cherry Orchard*; Sergei Balukhaty emphasized the lyrical structure and demotion of the exterior world. But Soviet criticism had to subordinate all insights to one task—to prove that great prerevolutionary dramatists were humanists heralding a new dawn, entry to a Promised Land.

For this reason the current of rejection never waned. St. Petersburg poets sensed Chekhov's indifference to their city. The poet Anna Akhmatova was notorious for her dismissal of Chekhov's "grayness": one might suspect that the dislike was self-defense, for many of Akhmatova's early poems are condensed versions of ironic Chekhovian narratives. But the poet Osip Mandelstam, in an unbroadcast radio talk he prepared in 1935 while in exile in Voronezh, articulated his dislike: "A biologist would call the Chekhovian principle ecological. Cohabitation is the decisive factor in Chekhov. In his dramas there is no action—just contiguity and the consequent unpleasantnesses. Recently I went to the Voronezh Town Theater in time for act 3 of *The Cherry Orchard.* The actors were putting on their makeup and resting in the dressing rooms. . . . On the whole, the ruins of the play, backstage, were not bad. After acting Chekhov the actors came offstage as if chilled and a little shifty. The correlation of theater and so-called life in Chekhov is that of a chill to good health."[20]

To those who suffered starvation, persecution, and execution, the predicaments of Chekhov's characters seemed trivial: even after the collapse of the Soviet Union, the satirist Viacheslav Pietsukh has a character exclaim, "Ditherers, bastards, they had a bad life, did they? I'll bet they wore excellent overcoats, knocked back the Worontsoff vodka with caviar, mixed with lovely women, those reptiles philosophized from morning to night for want of anything to do—and then they say they have a bad life, you see? You sons of bitches ought to be in the clutches of a planned economy, you should be brought to an Executive Committee's attention—they'd show you what a cherry orchard was!"[21]

Abroad, Chekhov's reputation depended on two elements: the theatrical climate and the quality, even availability, of translations. In Slavonic cultures the theatrical climate was favorable, and there were literati familiar with Russian. Not surprisingly, the first performances of *The Cherry Orchard* abroad were in Bulgaria (1904) and Bohemia and Moravia (1905). But the nationalistic theater could catch only the "Russianness" and little else; the self-confidence of translators such as the Czech Boleslav Prusík resulted in ludicrously poor translation. In 1911 England was the first major Western European country to stage *The Cherry Orchard,* at first in an imperfect translation by Constance Garnett. The actors solemnly misinterpreted the morality: the English Duniasha was shocked at Charlotta's supposed illegitimacy. Critics found the play "stationary," "queer, outlandish, and even silly." They cited its "fantastic trivialities" and, at their most charitable, assumed it was a display of Russian temperament that no English actor was ready for.[22] (They unwittingly agreed with Chekhov, who had always assumed his drama was of purely local interest.) Half the audience had left the theater by act 3. The few receptive spectators were Russian specialists like Maurice Baring or innovative dramatists like George Bernard Shaw. Baring followed the progressive Russian interpretation, compared the play with Molière's *Le Misanthrope (The Misanthropist)* in its lack of violent action, and insisted that the play had to be seen, not read, for the sake of the "hundred effects that make themselves felt on the boards."[23] Shaw was extravagant: "When I hear a play of Chekhov's I want to tear my own up." He called *The Cherry Orchard* the "most important production in England since that of *A Doll's House.*"[24] His *Heartbreak House* (1919) was to pay explicit tribute to Chekhov's comedy.

World War I and the Revolution presented Russia in a militant, heroic light and led critics to discard Chekhov as irrelevant to modern times and his Russia as an ephemeral and uninteresting setting. When *The Cherry Orchard* was again staged in England, in a slightly better version by George Calderon in 1920, it was still judged to be "a decadent ritual," at best "a philosophical essay." Only major innovators responded with enthusiasm. Virginia Woolf declared after watching *The Cherry Orchard* that she felt "like a piano played upon at last . . . all over the keyboard and with the lid left open."[25] The novelist Frank Swinnerton considered *The Cherry Orchard* to be the best of Chekhov's plays for its "most beautifully varied . . . snatches of idle, puzzled, irrelevant talk."[26] Irish writers, like Shaw, saw common ground between Ranevskaia's household and decaying Irish estates. Very few, notably the dramatist and director Granville Barker, who had seen Chekhov produced in Moscow, understood that Stanislavskian acting principles were inseparable from Chekhov's textual innovations: they welcomed the play as a means of carrying out a similar revolution in the English theater.

In the United States Chekhov's plays were read a decade before they were produced, and most critical opinion derided them. The critic Storm Jameson in 1914 concluded that Chekhov was no great dramatist but "by virtue of the complexity of life . . . and an unresting note of revolt . . . a great artist."[27] When a 1915 anthology of "modern masterpieces" included *The Cherry Orchard,* an anonymous reviewer complained, "Why this streak of abstract life is included in a collection . . . is hard to say. . . . [I]t is a lazy dream of idle aristocrats . . . mere portrayal of inept circumstances. . . . [T]o plod through

Chekhov's cerebral abullitions . . . the rankest American amateur would be suspected of softening of the cerebellum."[28] In 1923 New Yorkers saw *The Cherry Orchard,* produced in Russian by the Moscow Arts Theater, with Chekhov's widow, Olga Knipper, playing Ranevskaia and also assisting English-language productions of other Chekhov plays, notably *Three Sisters.* A few critics saw in the aging Knipper-Chekhova merely Junoesque posing, but makers of opinion, such as Edmund Wilson, became apostles of Chekhovian drama, declaring the comedy one of "ineptitude touched with the tragedy of all human failure."[29]

Only after the ponderous performances of the Moscow Arts Theater abroad (by both Stanislavsky's "Soviet" and Vasili Kachalov's "émigré" troupes) had given way to more confident English and American productions did critics and directors begin to see the comedy implicit in *The Cherry Orchard.* Brooks Atkinson in the *New York Times* in 1928 concluded that "despite the melancholy of the conclusion, this comedy . . . sealed an epoch . . . stream of consciousness. . . . [N]othing since *The Cherry Orchard* has woven the new method into such a luminous pattern of beguiling life."[30] By 1933 Tyrone Guthrie in his London production (yet another translation by Charles Butler) had declared Chekhov to be "a thoroughly amusing and flippant dramatist"[31] and based his comedienne's Ranevskaia on Knipper's performance. The influential Miss Le Gallienne productions in the 1940s compromised by making *The Cherry Orchard* a "tragicomedy in which the hero and villain were both aspects of progress and the victim was beauty."[32] In England, too, James Agate had swung opinion in 1925 by declaring it "one of the great plays of the world" and "a comedy of guesswork,"[33] thereby rescuing Chekhov from the contempt of populist critics (e.g., the *Daily Express:* "This silly, tiresome, boring comedy. . . . I know of no reason why this fatuous drivel should be translated at all. There is no plot. The cherry orchard is for sale, and certain dull people are upset because it must be sold").[34]

Germany was one of the first countries to appreciate Chekhov's drama. His play *Ivanov* has such striking echoes in Gerhart Hauptmann's *Einsame Menschen (Lonely People)* that it is tempting to see Chekhov imitated in it. Rainer Maria Rilke, spellbound after seeing *The Seagull* at the Moscow Arts Theater, wrote plays such as *Das tägliche Leben* (Daily Life), in which a Mascha, dressed in black, was enthralled by the artist hero. In February 1906 the Moscow Arts Theater (including Knipper) performed in Russian in Berlin: they brought with them the only two Chekhov plays—*Uncle Vania* and *Three Sisters*—then available in German. But their performance was shattering: the notoriously tight-lipped Hauptmann burst into tears in the hall and shrieked in the foyer that this was the greatest stage experience of his life; others, such as the poet Christian Morgenstern, were moved to tears. This created a climate that would be favorable to Chekhov's *The Cherry Orchard* as yet another example of *Stimmungstheater* (mood theater). Despite wartime Russophobia, *The Cherry Orchard* was first performed in German in Vienna in 1916 and again in Munich in 1917. The novelist and dramatist Lion Feuchtwanger had a hand in polishing the German version. He cryptically declared the play "a gloomy mirror of the human spirit which is measuring its limits against the limitless."[35] When the Moscow Arts Theater returned to Germany in 1922, however, it again omitted *The Cherry Orchard* (as it had *The Seagull*), but scorn for Russian inertia was so ingrained that Chekhov's mature plays were rarely performed until well after World War II, and Nazi hostility to all things Slav had prevented significant appreciation of *The Cherry Orchard* in Germany, even though Chekhov was not banned under Hitler. A divided Germany brought a divided view of *The Cherry Orchard*: the Tübingen production of 1947 was slapstick; the East Berlin version of 1950 was coarse, alienating, and Brechtian.

France had esteemed the Russian novel earlier than any other foreign culture, yet, despite the efforts of the translator Denis Roche, reaction to Chekhov had been muted. He was seen primarily as a disciple of Maupassant. The French lack of interest justifies Chekhov's protest to his wife against allowing a translation of *The Cherry Orchard*: "Why translate my play into French? It's crazy, the French won't understand anything about Ermolai [Lopakhin] or the sale of the estate and will only be bored." "I can't forbid it, let anyone who wants translate, it will still be pointless."[36] Not until 1921 was a major play of Chekhov's professionally staged in Paris, and despite the success of *The Seagull, Uncle Vania,* and *Three Sisters* in 1929, *The Cherry Orchard* had to wait until 1944 before it was staged at all. This neglect is all the more surprising when we consider that the French director Georges Pitoëff was of Russian origin and had studied under Stanislavsky and Meierkhold. He had been present at the first performance of *The Cherry Orchard* on 17 January 1904, and between 1915 and 1920, while in exile in Switzerland, he had translated the play into French. (The Roche version was rehearsed in Paris in 1914 but aborted when war broke out.) The absurdist dramatist Arthur Adamov translated several of Chekhov's plays, and his essays collected in the 1964 volume *Ici et maintenant* (Here and Now) show that he regarded *The Cherry Orchard* as the first progenitor of comedy where language fails its primary functions. "Chekhov's characters," he said, "don't say what they think at any given moment but what forms a sort of continual scheme of their thinking."[37] It is the falsity of Chekhov's characters' speeches that made for Adamov potential tragedy comic.

In 1954 Jean-Louis Barrault won acclaim for *The Cherry Orchard,* which he put forward as the greatest of Chekhov's plays: "The play's action actually unfolds through silence and, aside from the poem-tirades which are separate, the dialogues exist, as in music, only to make the silence resound."[38] The delay in presenting the play to the French was evidently justified, for Barrault had catapulted his spectators straight into a modern view of the play as a play around the unspoken, as a musical structure not primarily about the fate of human individuals. Barrault's explanatory remarks are the most illuminating of any made by an actor-director, even more profound than Stanislavsky's. "It is a play about time," Barrault wrote. "And therefore it doesn't matter whether the storyline is Russian or Japanese." Although Barrault paid tribute to the Russian spirit "on the boundaries of East and West" for revealing a way of "penetrating and perceiving the imperceptible passage of time," he insisted on its universality as a play about time: "The action never slackens; it is tense, solid, for, I repeat, every minute is full. Every minute has its own saturation, but not with dialogues, but silence, life itself passing."

By breaking down the framework of a social message, Chekhov's ideological impact, Barrault asserted, was like acupuncture: the impact was out of all proportion to the force exerted. The three male protagonists—Gaev, Lopakhin, and Trofimov—Barrault saw in terms of time as past, present, and future—a view subsequent directors and critics have adopted. In France, Barrault's view that Chekhov had shown maximum economy in representation—"Not a single thing can be crossed out"—accredited *The Cherry Orchard* as a play that met all the criteria of art set by Racine and Flaubert. Chekhov was naturalized. France could now accept a Russian writer so un-Dostoyevskian, and the perfection of the play led critics to doubt that it should be subjected to the inevitable imperfections of production. Only the visit of the Moscow Arts Theater in 1958 with *The Cherry Orchard* sobered susceptible audiences into a pedestrian, Soviet-oriented view of Chekhov and his theater as faithful reproducers of reality and a herald of a brighter future.

By the 1950s, all over the Western world and in Japan, where overtones of *Macbeth* and the symbolism of the cherry blossom were particularly appreciated, *The Cherry Orchard* was established as a classic. Criticism was now concerned with providing guidance for correct interpretation. As modern structuralist brains drained from Prague to Boston, Paris, and Oxford, attention was paid to the integrity of Chekhov's text, casting the mold in which this study is set. The significance of every detail in the play—from the breaking string to the Duniasha's saucer, from traditional farce such as the dialogue of the deaf to the new absurdities of extraneous imagery (e.g., fish and billiards)—challenges critics to resolve the overall equivocations, to "make the silences resound" as Barrault put it. Research in Russia has established how manifold Chekhov's sources were, so that the very texture of the play seems as much a collage of phrases read and overheard as a linearly composed narrative. The new release of material from archives will uncover more sources for the raw material of the play. Questions of genre also preoccupy critics in Russia and abroad: In what sense can a play about the loss of property, love, and death be termed a "comedy," and is the answer in the play's formal structure rather than in the audience's stock responses to these losses?

Today, as new and antagonistic schools of criticism—whether feminist or deconstructionist—proliferate rapidly, *The Cherry Orchard* has been spared the gutting that other modern "classics" have undergone. But some recent productions of the play amount to a deconstructionist critical reception. Russian directors, once the thaw permitted dissent from official practices, rebelled against leisurely productions by the Moscow Arts Theater (its performance of *The Cherry Orchard* in Poland allegedly lasted five hours). Anatoli Efros's production in 1975 at Moscow's Taganka Theater, then the nearest to a radical theater in the Soviet Union, stretched neurosis in the characterization and morbidity in the sets to give an expressionist hysteria to Lopakhin and Ranevskaia and to create an atmosphere of funeral gloom. Efros's follower, Leonid Trushkin, produced a "cooperative" *Cherry Orchard* in 1990, where the "much esteemed bookcase" of act 1 becomes the whole set, turning the actors into marionettelike automata: against this background Ranevskaia appears as an Edith Piaf-like amoral life force, undefeated by the loss of the estate, filling the finale with comic optimism. In the October 1992 Moscow Festival, foreign *Cherry Orchard*s returned to Moscow to bewilder the Russians with German expressionism (Peter Stain) or Czech hysteria (Otomar Krejčí).

Recent non-Russian productions have translated not just the text but the whole setting. There have been Irish and even confederate American *Cherry Orchard*s (one being *The Wisteria Trees,* with black Dunia and Yasha; another Michael Schultz's all-black cast), although few spectators found universality unlocked by such transformations. Trevor Griffiths in Britain rewrote the text in order to give the play a neo-Trotskyist political analysis, a transformation so radical that it implies Chekhov's original play to be irrelevant to modern audiences. Peter Brook's 1981 Paris production sought universality by using an international cast, so that Chekhov was performed in French with English, Danish, and other accents, and almost no props, ridding the play of its Russianness. Trying "to play the myth—the secret play" was a high price paid to make Everyman and Everywoman protagonists of the play. The flight from Chekhov's explicit settings and dynamics and from the Moscow Art Theater's heritage led to an unfortunately unforgettable American interpretation of 1985: Joel Gersmann reduced the play to "They buy the farm, they lose the farm," kept only the theory of time zones (future shock and derelict past) from critical tradition, and subjected what was left to transvestism, punk rock, and violence, with Ranevskaia wielding a chainsaw, Trofimov having sexual intercourse with Ania on a stage free from props. Gersmann's sole achievement in "playing the subtext" was to use song to bring out the significance for what happens onstage to Ranevskaia's drowned son, Grisha: "Grisha's dead, Grisha's dead / Drowned in the river, No-one heard his screams."

Just as in classical music, the critical pendulum, however, has swung back in favor of observing the composer's original dynamics and even using period instruments to reconstruct original performances. Thus, in performing Chekhov, where we have to hand a body of interpretative guidance from the author and his first directors, the most powerful contemporary Russian productions, such as Vladimir Pakhomov's in the Lipetsk Theater, have reverted to a modified Stanislavskian interpretation, trust-

ing the original text to bridge the increasing distance between us and Chekhov's times and using the archival and interpretative discoveries of Chekhov critics only where one might reasonably imagine the ghost of the author approving. In the West the publication of new translations, notably Michael Frayn's, where the language works onstage and is yet a professional rendering of Chekhov's Russian, has saved innovative directors coping with quaint, unintelligible, and unspeakable lines but at the same time deprived them of a pretext for radical misinterpretation.

NOTES

[1] Konstantin Stanislavsky, telegram to Chekhov, 21 October 1903.
[2] Maria Lilina, letter to Chekhov, 18 October 1903.
[3] Vladimir Nemirovich-Danchenko, telegram to Chekhov, 21 October 1903.
[4] A. L. Vishnevsky, letter to Chekhov, undated [November 1903].
[5] See Osip Dymov, "Pervoe predstavlenie Vishniovogo sada v Sankt-Peterburge," *Utro Rossii* 4 (1904): 1.
[6] See Vladimir Nemirovich-Danchenko, *Iz proshlogo,* vol. 1 (Moscow: Iskusstvo, 1952), 177.
[7] Vladimir Nemirovich-Danchenko, telegram to Chekhov, 2 April 1904.
[8] Nemirovich-Danchenko, *Iz proshlogo,* 1: 107.
[9] Aleksandr Amfiteatrov, *Rus'* [newspaper], no. 110, 31 March 1904; no. 111, 1 April 1904.
[10] See Zinaida Gippius, *Novy Put'* [St. Petersburg journal] 5 (1904): 251-67.
[11] See Zinaida Gippius, *Nova Put'* [St. Petersburg journal] 8 (1903): 184-87.
[12] Vlas Doroshevich, *Russkoe Slovo* [St. Petersburg newspaper], no. 19, 1904.
[13] Andrei Bely, *Arabeski* (Moscow: Skepion, 1911), 400.
[14] Vsevolod Meierkhold, letter to Chekhov, 8 May 1904; see *Literaturnoe Nasledstvo* [Moscow] 68 (1960): 448.
[15] Vsevolod Meierkhold, "Teatr. K istorii i tekhnike," in *Teatr. Kniga o novom teatre* (St. Petersburg: Shipovnik, 1908), 143.
[16] Maksim Gorky, *Sobranie sochineii v 30i tomax,* vol. 28 (Moscow: Nauka, 1954), 291.
[17] Viktor Baranovsky, letter to Chekhov, 20 March 1904, RGB Archives.
[18] M. Khosidov, letter to Chekhov, 13 June 1904, RGB Archives.
[19] Ivan Bunin, *O Chekhove* (New York: Chekhov Publishing House, 1955), 216.
[20] Osip Mandelstam, *Sobranie sochinenii,* vol. 4 (Paris: YMCA Press, 1981), 108-109.
[21] Viacheslav Pietsukh, *Ia i prochee* (Moscow, 1990), 42.
[22] For example, London *Daily Telegraph,* no. 21, 1911; see Victor Emeljanow, *Chekhov: The Critical Heritage* (London: Routledge & Kegan Paul, 1981), 10-11.
[23] Maurice Baring, "Russian Literature," *New Quarterly* [London] 1 (1907-1908): 405-29.
[24] George Bernard Shaw, quoted by H.M.W. in the *Nation* [London], 16 May 1914, 265-66.
[25] Virginia Woolf, in Emeljanow, *Critical Heritage,* 200.
[26] Frank Swinnerton, in Emeljanow, *Critical Heritage,* 192.
[27] Storm Jameson, "Modern Dramatists," *Egoist,* 16 March 1914, 116-17.
[28] Anonymous reviewer, *Dramatist* 4 (July 1915): 590-91.
[29] Edmund Wilson, "The Moscow Arts Theatre," *Dial* 74 (January 1923): 319.
[30] Brooks Atkinson, "The Cherry Orchard," *New York Times,* 11 March 1928, pt. 8, p. 1.
[31] Tyrone Guthrie, in Emeljanow, *Critical Heritage,* 380.
[32] Miss Le Gallienne, in Emeljanow, *Critical Heritage,* 441.
[33] James Agate, Sunday *Times* [London], 31 May 1925.
[34] *Daily Express,* quoted by Patrick Miles, *Chekhov on the British Stage, 1909-1987* (London: Sam and Sam, 1987), 26.
[35] Lion Feuchtwanger, "Der Kirschgarten," *Die Schaubühne* [Munich] 33 (1916): 175-182.
[36] Letter to Olga Knipper, in *Polnoe sobranie sochinenii i pisem v 30i tomakh* (Moscow: Nauka, 1974-83), letter nos. 4214 and 4238. Letters from these volumes are hereafter cited in text by number.
[37] Arthur Adamov, *Ici et maintenant* (Paris: NRF, 1969), 197.
[38] Jean-Louis Barrault, "Pourquois *La Cerisaie?*" in *Cahiers de la Compagnie Madeleine Renard-Jean-Louis Barrault* (Paris: Gallimard, 1954), 87-97.

Further Reading

Balukhaty, S. D., ed. *The Seagull Produced by Stanislavsky,* trans. David Magarshack. London: Dennis Dobson, Ltd., n.d., 292 p.

Detailed examination of the Moscow Art Theater production of Chekhov's play. Includes the full text of the drama with notations and comments by Stanislavsky.

Beckerman, Bernard. "Dramatic Analysis and Literary Interpretation: 'The Cherry Orchard' as Exemplum." *New Literary History* II, No. 3 (Spring 1971): 391-406.

Uses *The Cherry Orchard* as a case in point in his argument that most critics fail to distinguish between two different approaches to dramatic works.

Bill, Valentine Tschebotarioff. *Chekhov: The Silent Voice of Freedom.* New York: Philosophical Library, 1987, 277 p.

Argues that the primary goal of Chekhov's work is "to light the path of the human individual toward freedom."

Bitsilli, Peter M. "Dramatic Works." in *Chekhov's Art: A Stylistic Analysis,* trans. Toby W. Clyman and Edwina Jannie Cruise, pp. 115-23. Ann Arbor, Mich.: Ardis, 1983.

Dismisses Chekhov's plays, declaring that "Chekhov's creativity was on the wane when he began writing for the theater."

Bruford, W. H. "The Playwright." In *Anton Chekhov,* pp. 39-59. New Haven, Conn.: Yale University Press, 1957.

Traces the development of what the critic terms "psychological naturalism" throughout Chekhov's dramatic career.

Clayton, J. Douglas. " Čexov's *Djadja Vanja* and Traditional Comic Structure." *Russian Language Journal* XL, Nos. 136-137 (Spring-Fall 1986): 103-10.

Argues that *Uncle Vanya* acquires its subtlety from Chekhov's sophisticated manipulation of theatrical conventions rather than his rejection of them.

Corrigan, Robert W. "The Plays of Chekhov." In *The Theatre in Search of a Fix,* pp. 125-46. New York: Delacorte Press, 1973.

Discusses Chekhov's continuing relevance for modern audiences.

Cousin, Geraldine. "Revisiting the Prozorovs." *Modern Drama* XL, No. 3 (Fall 1997): 325-33.

Finds significant parallels between Timberlake Wertenbaker's *The Break of Day* and *Three Sisters.*

De Maegd-Soëp, Carolina. *Chekhov and Women: Women in the Life and Work of Chekhov.* Columbus, Ohio: Slavica Publishers, 1987, 373 p.

Surveys Chekhov's correspondence from a feminist perspective to gauge contemporary reaction to his works.

Emeljanow, Victor. *Chekhov: The Critical Heritage.* London: Routledge & Kegan Paul, 1981, 471 p.

Collection of English-language reviews of Chekhov's works from the time of their first appearance in England and America through 1945.

Fen, Elisaveta. Introduction to *Plays,* by Anton Chekhov, trans. Elisaveta Fen, pp. 7-34. Harmondsworth, Middlesex: Penguin Books, 1959.

Biographical and critical survey of the playwright.

Finke, Michael. "The Hero's Descent to the Underworld in Chekhov." *The Russian Review* 53, No. 1 (January 1994): 67-80.

Traces the archetypal motif of the descent to hell throughout Chekhov's works.

Gassner, John. "Chekhov and the Sublimation of Realism." In *Masters of the Drama,* third edition, pp. 508-20. New York: Dover Publications, 1951.

Surveys Chekhov's career, stressing his "sense of unity with mankind."

Gilman, Richard. "Chekhov." In *The Making of Modern Drama: A Study of Büchner, Ibsen, Strindberg, Chekhov, Pirandello, Brecht, Beckett, Handke,* pp. 116-56. New York: Farrar, Straus, and Giroux, 1975.

Analyzes the origins and impact of Chekhov's theatrical innovations.

————. "*Ivanov*: Prologue to a Revolution." *Theatre* XXII, No. 2 (Spring 1991): 14-27.

Declares that "*Ivanov* stands as something more than an apprentice work; it's a preliminary to Chekhov's mature manner, in some ways a rehearsal for it."

Hahn, Beverly. *Chekhov: A Study of the Major Stories and Plays.* Cambridge: Cambridge University Press, 1977, 350 p.

Regards Chekhov's work as highly psychological and claims the author is "a more positive writer than even his strongest supporters often contend."

Hingley, Ronald. *A New Life of Anton Chekhov.* New York: Alfred A. Knopf, 1976, 352 p.

Sequel to Hingley's 1950 volume, *Chekhov: A Biographical and Critical Study* (excerpted above), taking advantage of more recent scholarship and the uncovering of additional documentary evidence concerning Chekhov's life and career.

Hingley, Ronald. Introduction to *Chekhov: Five Major Plays,* trans. Ronald Hingley, pp. ix-xxxiv. New York: Bantam Books, 1982.
Biographical and critical survey of the playwright.

Karlinsky, Simon, ed. *Letters of Anton Chekhov,* trans. Michael Henry Heim and Simon Karlinsky. New York: Harper & Row, 1973, 494 p.
Correspondence in which Chekhov expresses his views on art, literature, and his own work.

Koteliansky, S. S., ed. *Anton Tchekhov: Literary and Theatrical Reminiscences.* 1927. Reprint. New York: Benjamin Blom, 1965, 249 p.
Collection of personal essays on the playwright and his works, including excerpts from his diary and several previously unpublished stories and dramas.

Lafitte, Sophie. *Chekhov, 1860-1904,* trans. Moura Budberg and Gordon Latta. New York: Charles Scribner's Sons, 1973, 246 p.
Literary biography with an introduction that outlines major themes in Chekhov scholarship.

Lantz, K. A. *Anton Chekhov: A Reference Guide to Literature.* Boston: G. K. Hall & Co., 1985, 287 p.
Annotated bibliography of sources of Chekhov criticism in English, Russian, German, and French.

Lewis, Allan. "The Comedy of Frustration—Chekhov: *The Cherry Orchard.*" In *The Contemporary Theatre: The Significant Playwrights of Our Time,* pp. 59-80. New York: Crown Publishers, 1962.
Explores the comic elements in the play.

Maurois, André. "The Art and Philosophy of Anton Tchekov." in *The Art of Writing,* trans. Gerard Hopkins, pp. 224-64. London: The Bodley Head, 1960.
Broad overview of Chekhov's works.

Meister, Charles W. *Chekhov Bibliography: Works in English by and about Anton Chekhov; American, British, and Canadian Performances.* Jefferson, N. C.: McFarland & Co., 1985, 184 p.
Lists English editions of Chekhov's works, critical and biographical sources, and information on stage performances of the plays.

———. *Chekhov Criticism, 1880 through 1986.* Jefferson, N. C.: McFarland & Co., 1988, 350 p.
Surveys commentary on Chekhov's works, from early reviews to modern critical evaluations.

Melchinger, Siegfried. *Anton Chekhov,* trans. Edith Tarcov. New York: Frederick Ungar Publishing Co., 1972, 184 p.
Detailed study of how Chekhov's plays should be produced in order to best convey the author's intentions.

Meyerhold, Vsévolod. "The Naturalistic Theatre and the Theatre of Mood." In *Meyerhold on Theatre,* trans. and ed. Edward Braun, pp. 23-34. New York: Hill and Wang, 1969.

Comments on the original Moscow Art Theater productions of Chekhov's plays, noting that *The Seagull* and *Uncle Vanya* were great successes because the actors captured the rhythm of the plays' language, which was "the secret of Chekhov's mood."

Miles, Patrick, ed. and trans. *Chekhov on the British Stage.* Cambridge: Cambridge University Press, 1993, 258 p.
Collection of essays by John Russell Brown, Vera Gottlieb, Richard Peace, and others, on a variety of topics, including the Moscow Art Theater's English productions of Chekhov's plays and Chekhov's impact on George Bernard Shaw.

Morson, Gary Saul. "Prosaic Chekhov: Metadrama, the Intelligentsia, and *Uncle Vanya.*" *TriQuarterly* 80 (Winter 1990-1991): 118-59.
Asserts that in *Uncle Vanya* and his other plays, "Chekhov gives us dramatic characters in an undramatic world in order to satirize all theatrical poses and all attempts to behave as if life were literary and theatrical."

Orr, John. "The Everyday and the Transient in Chekhov's Tragedy." In *Tragic Drama and Modern Society: A Sociology of Dramatic Form from 1880 to the Present,* second ed., pp. 57-83. Houndsmills, Basingstoke, Hampshire: Macmillan, 1989.
Finds Chekhov's plays have more in common with the great Russian novels of the nineteenth century than with the drama of that period.

Pitcher, Harvey. "The Chekhov Play: A New Interpretation." London: Chatto & Windus, 1973, 224 p.
Attempts to "define the essential nature and characteristics of the Chekhov play," and traces their evolution through the four major plays.

Pritchett, V. S. *Chekhov: A Spirit Set Free.* London: Hodder & Stoughton, 1988, 235 p.
Offers a critical examination of Chekhov's works.

Rayfield, Donald. *Chekhov: The Evolution of His Art.* New York: Barnes & Noble, 1975, 266 p.
Traces the development of Chekhov's literary career, treating the dominant themes in his works and attempting to reconcile seemingly contradictory facets of his art.

Saunders, Beatrice. *Tchehov, the Man.* Philadelphia: Dufour Editions, 1961, 195 p.
Hagiographic depiction of the writer.

Senelick, Laurence. *Anton Chekhov.* Macmillan Modern Dramatists. Houndsmills, Basingstoke, Hampshire: Macmillan, 1985, 173 p.
Biographical and critical introduction to the author. Includes discussions of the one-act and early works, as well as the major plays.

Silverstein, Norman. "Chekhov's Comic Spirit and *The Cherry Orchard.*" *Modern Drama* 1, No. 2 (September 1958); 91-100.

Views *The Cherry Orchard* as a comedy and provides biographical anecdotes about Chekhov in order to support this claim.

Simmons, Ernest J. *Chekhov: A Biography.* Boston: Little, Brown and Company, 1962, 669 p.
Seeks to present the "enigma of Chekhov's complex personality" by drawing on his correspondence, diaries and reminiscences of cohorts, and other materials.

Speirs, Logan. *Tolstoy and Chekhov.* Cambridge: At the University Press, 1971, 237 p.
Traces Tolstoy's influence on his younger contemporary. Includes three chapters on the major plays.

Stanislavsky, Constantin. *My Life in Art,* trans. J. J. Robbins. New York: Theatre Arts Books, 586 p.
Includes chapters on the Moscow Art Theater productions of each of Chekhov's major plays. In his discussion of *The Seagull,* Stanislavsky admits that he "did not understand the essence, the aroma, the beauty" of the play.

Styan, J. L. "Naturalistic Shading." In *The Dark Comedy: The Development of Modern Comic Tragedy,* pp. 59-126. Cambridge: Cambridge at the University Press, 1962.
Detailed explication of the fourth act of *The Cherry Orchard* that reveals the development toward the play's climax and denouement.

————. *Chekhov in Performance: A Commentary on the Major Plays.* Cambridge: Cambridge at the University Press, 1971, 341 p.
Well-respected and influential study of Chekhov's dramatic works.

Troyat, Henri. *Chekhov,* trans. Michael Henry Heim. New York: E. P. Dutton, 1986.
Popular biography of the writer.

Tufts, Carol Strongin. "Prisoners of Their Plots: Literary Allusion and the Satiric Drama of Self-Consciousness in

Chekhov's *Three Sisters.*" *Modern Drama* XXXII, No. 4 (December 1989): 485-501.
Contends that the characters in *Three Sisters* are "prisoners of self-created romantic dreams and self-imprisoning plots," a fact "apparent to an audience at once familiar enough with the literary allusions that permeate the play and careful enough as listeners to pick up the satiric counterpoint that Chekhov opposes to the characters' visions of themselves."

Tulloch, John. *Chekhov: A Structuralist Study.* New York: Barnes and Noble, 1980, 225 p.
Analysis of the thematic structures of Chekhov's works, with chapters devoted to *Three Sisters* and *The Cherry Orchard.*

Turkov, Andrei, ed. *Anton Chekhov and His Times,* trans. Cynthia Carlile and Sharon McKee. Fayetteville: University of Arkansas Press, 1995, 327 p.
Includes reminiscences of Chekhov by Stanislavsky, Olga Knipper, and others, as well as a selection of his correspondence.

Worrall, Nick, ed. *File on Chekhov.* London: Methuen, 1986, 96 p.
Provides background, critical, and production information on each of Chekhov's plays, including one-act pieces.

Worrall, Nick. "Stanislavsky's Production of Chekhov's *Three Sisters.*" In *Russian Theatre in the Age of Modernism,* ed. Robert Russell and Andrew Barratt, pp. 1-32. Houndsmills, Basingstoke, Hampshire: Macmillan, 1990.
Analyzes the Moscow Art Theater staging of Chekhov's play.

Yermilov, Vladimir. *Anton Pavlovich Chekhov, 1860-1904.* Moscow: Foreign Languages Publishing House, 1956, 415 p.
Biography with an emphasis on factors significant to Chekhov's development as a writer.

Additional coverage of Chekhov's life and career is contained in the following sources published by Gale Research: *Contemporary Authors,* **Vols. 104, 124;** *DISCovering Authors, DISCovering Authors: British Edition; DISCovering Authors: Canadian Edition; DISCovering Authors Modules*—**Dramatist Module and Most-Studied Authors Module;** *Short Story Criticism,* **Vols. 2, 28;** *Something about the Author,* **Vol. 90;** *Twentieth Century Literary Criticism,* **Vols, 3, 10, 31, 55;** *World Literature Criticism,* **Vol. 1.**

CUMULATIVE INDEXES

How to Use This Index

The main references

Calvino, Italo
1923–1985 .... CLC 5, 8, 11, 22, 33, 39,
73; SSC 3

list all author entries in the following Gale Literary Criticism series:

BLC = *Black Literature Criticism*
CLC = *Contemporary Literary Criticism*
CLR = *Children's Literature Review*
CMLC = *Classical and Medieval Literature Criticism*
DA = *DISCovering Authors*
DAB = *DISCovering Authors: British*
DAC = *DISCovering Authors: Canadian*
DAM = *DISCovering Authors: Modules*
    DRAM: *Dramatists Module;* *MST*: *Most-Studied Authors Module;*
    MULT: *Multicultural Authors Module;* *NOV*: *Novelists Module;*
    POET: *Poets Module;* *POP*: *Popular Fiction and Genre Authors Module*
DC = *Drama Criticism*
HLC = *Hispanic Literature Criticism*
LC = *Literature Criticism from 1400 to 1800*
NCLC = *Nineteenth-Century Literature Criticism*
PC = *Poetry Criticism*
SSC = *Short Story Criticism*
TCLC = *Twentieth-Century Literary Criticism*
WLC = *World Literature Criticism, 1500 to the Present*

The cross-references

See also CANR 23; CA 85-88;
obituary CA116

list all author entries in the following Gale biographical and literary sources:

AAYA = *Authors & Artists for Young Adults*
AITN = *Authors in the News*
BEST = *Bestsellers*
BW = *Black Writers*
CA = *Contemporary Authors*
CAAS = *Contemporary Authors Autobiography Series*
CABS = *Contemporary Authors Bibliographical Series*
CANR = *Contemporary Authors New Revision Series*
CAP = *Contemporary Authors Permanent Series*
CDALB = *Concise Dictionary of American Literary Biography*
CDBLB = *Concise Dictionary of British Literary Biography*
DLB = *Dictionary of Literary Biography*
DLBD = *Dictionary of Literary Biography Documentary Series*
DLBY = *Dictionary of Literary Biography Yearbook*
HW = *Hispanic Writers*
JRDA = *Junior DISCovering Authors*
MAICYA = *Major Authors and Illustrators for Children and Young Adults*
MTCW = *Major 20th-Century Writers*
NNAL = *Native North American Literature*
SAAS = *Something about the Author Autobiography Series*
SATA = *Something about the Author*
YABC = *Yesterday's Authors of Books for Children*

Literary Criticism Series
Cumulative Author Index

Anodos
See Coleridge, Mary E(lizabeth)

Anon, Charles Robert
See Pessoa, Fernando (Antonio Nogueira)

Anouilh, Jean (Marie Lucien Pierre) 1910-1987
CLC 1, 3, 8, 13, 40, 50; DAM DRAM; DC 8
See also CA 17-20R; 123; CANR 32; MTCW

Anthony, Florence
See Ai

Anthony, John
See Ciardi, John (Anthony)

Anthony, Peter
See Shaffer, Anthony (Joshua); Shaffer, Peter (Levin)

Anthony, Piers 1934- ...... **CLC 35; DAM POP**
See also AAYA 11; CA 21-24R; CANR 28, 56; DLB 8; MTCW; SAAS 22; SATA 84

Antoine, Marc
See Proust, (Valentin-Louis-George-Eugene-) Marcel

Antoninus, Brother
See Everson, William (Oliver)

Antonioni, Michelangelo 1912- .... **CLC 20**
See also CA 73-76; CANR 45

Antschel, Paul 1920-1970
See Celan, Paul
See also CA 85-88; CANR 33, 61; MTCW

Anwar, Chairil 1922-1949 .... **TCLC 22**
See also CA 121

Apollinaire, Guillaume 1880-1918...**TCLC 3, 8, 51; DAM POET; PC 7**
See also Kostrowitzki, Wilhelm Apollinaris de
See also CA 152

Appelfeld, Aharon 1932- .... **CLC 23, 47**
See also CA 112; 133

Apple, Max (Isaac) 1941- .... **CLC 9, 33**
See also CA 81-84; CANR 19, 54; DLB 130

Appleman, Philip (Dean) 1926- .... **CLC 51**
See also CA 13-16R; CAAS 18; CANR 6, 29, 56

Appleton, Lawrence
See Lovecraft, H(oward) P(hillips)

Apteryx
See Eliot, T(homas) S(tearns)

Apuleius, (Lucius Madaurensis) 125(?)-175(?)
CMLC 1

Aquin, Hubert 1929-1977 .... **CLC 15**
See also CA 105; DLB 53

Aragon, Louis 1897-1982 ... **CLC 3, 22; DAM NOV, POET**
See also CA 69-72; 108; CANR 28; DLB 72; MTCW

Arany, Janos 1817-1882 .... **NCLC 34**

Arbuthnot, John 1667-1735 .... **LC 1**
See also DLB 101

Archer, Herbert Winslow
See Mencken, H(enry) L(ouis)

Archer, Jeffrey (Howard) 1940- ...... **CLC 28; DAM POP**
See also AAYA 16; BEST 89:3; CA 77-80; CANR 22, 52; INT CANR-22

Archer, Jules 1915- .... **CLC 12**
See also CA 9-12R; CANR 6, 69; SAAS 5; SATA 4, 85

Archer, Lee
See Ellison, Harlan (Jay)

Arden, John 1930-...**CLC 6, 13, 15; DAM DRAM**
See also CA 13-16R; CAAS 4; CANR 31, 65, 67; DLB 13; MTCW

Arenas, Reinaldo 1943-1990 ... **CLC 41; DAM MULT; HLC**
See also CA 124; 128; 133; DLB 145; HW

Arendt, Hannah 1906-1975 .... **CLC 66, 98**
See also CA 17-20R; 61-64; CANR 26, 60; MTCW

Aretino, Pietro 1492-1556 .... **LC 12**

Arghezi, Tudor .... **CLC 80**
See also Theodorescu, Ion N.

Arguedas, Jose Maria 1911-1969...**CLC 10, 18**
See also CA 89-92; DLB 113; HW

Argueta, Manlio 1936- .... **CLC 31**
See also CA 131; DLB 145; HW

Ariosto, Ludovico 1474-1533 .... **LC 6**

Aristides
See Epstein, Joseph

Aristophanes 450B.C.-385B.C....**CMLC 4; DA; DAB; DAC; DAM DRAM, MST; DC 2; WLCS**
See also DLB 176

Arlt, Roberto (Godofredo Christophersen) 1900-1942 ... **TCLC 29; DAM MULT; HLC**
See also CA 123; 131; CANR 67; HW

Armah, Ayi Kwei 1939- .... **CLC 5, 33; BLC 1; DAM MULT, POET**
See also BW 1; CA 61-64; CANR 21, 64; DLB 117; MTCW

Armatrading, Joan 1950- .... **CLC 17**
See also CA 114

Arnette, Robert
See Silverberg, Robert

Arnim, Achim von (Ludwig Joachim von Arnim) 1781-1831 .... **NCLC 5; SSC 29**
See also DLB 90

Arnim, Bettina von 1785-1859 .... **NCLC 38**
See also DLB 90

Arnold, Matthew 1822-1888 .. **NCLC 6, 29; DA; DAB; DAC; DAM MST, POET; PC 5; WLC**
See also CDBLB 1832-1890; DLB 32, 57

Arnold, Thomas 1795-1842 .... **NCLC 18**
See also DLB 55

Arnow, Harriette (Louisa) Simpson 1908-1986
CLC 2, 7, 18
See also CA 9-12R; 118; CANR 14; DLB 6; MTCW; SATA 42; SATA-Obit 47

Arp, Hans
See Arp, Jean

Arp, Jean 1887-1966 .... **CLC 5**
See also CA 81-84; 25-28R; CANR 42

Arrabal
See Arrabal, Fernando

Arrabal, Fernando 1932- ...... **CLC 2, 9, 18, 58**
See also CA 9-12R; CANR 15

Arrick, Fran .... **CLC 30**
See also Gaberman, Judie Angell

Artaud, Antonin (Marie Joseph) 1896-1948
TCLC 3, 36; DAM DRAM
See also CA 104; 149

Arthur, Ruth M(abel) 1905-1979 .... **CLC 12**
See also CA 9-12R; 85-88; CANR 4; SATA 7, 26

Artsybashev, Mikhail (Petrovich) 1878-1927
TCLC 31

Arundel, Honor (Morfydd) 1919-1973...**CLC 17**
See also CA 21-22; 41-44R; CAP 2; CLR 35; SATA 4; SATA-Obit 24

Arzner, Dorothy 1897-1979 .... **CLC 98**

Asch, Sholem 1880-1957 .... **TCLC 3**
See also CA 105

Ash, Shalom
See Asch, Sholem

Ashbery, John (Lawrence) 1927-...**CLC 2, 3, 4, 6, 9, 13, 15, 25, 41, 77; DAM POET**
See also CA 5-8R; CANR 9, 37, 66; DLB 5, 165; DLBY 81; INT CANR-9; MTCW

Ashdown, Clifford
See Freeman, R(ichard) Austin

Ashe, Gordon
See Creasey, John

Ashton-Warner, Sylvia (Constance) 1908-1984
CLC 19
See also CA 69-72; 112; CANR 29; MTCW

Asimov, Isaac 1920-1992...**CLC 1, 3, 9, 19, 26, 76, 92; DAM POP**
See also AAYA 13; BEST 90:2; CA 1-4R; 137; CANR 2, 19, 36, 60; CLR 12; DLB 8; DLBY 92; INT CANR-19; JRDA; MAICYA; MTCW; SATA 1, 26, 74

Assis, Joaquim Maria Machado de
See Machado de Assis, Joaquim Maria

Astley, Thea (Beatrice May) 1925-...... **CLC 41**
See also CA 65-68; CANR 11, 43

Aston, James
See White, T(erence) H(anbury)

Asturias, Miguel Angel 1899-1974...**CLC 3, 8, 13; DAM MULT, NOV; HLC**
See also CA 25-28; 49-52; CANR 32; CAP 2; DLB 113; HW; MTCW

Atares, Carlos Saura
See Saura (Atares), Carlos

Atheling, William
See Pound, Ezra (Weston Loomis)

Atheling, William, Jr.
See Blish, James (Benjamin)

Atherton, Gertrude (Franklin Horn) 1857-1948
TCLC 2
See also CA 104; 155; DLB 9, 78, 186

Atherton, Lucius
See Masters, Edgar Lee

Atkins, Jack
See Harris, Mark

Atkinson, Kate .... **CLC 99**
See also CA 166

Attaway, William (Alexander) 1911-1986
CLC 92; BLC 1; DAM MULT
See also BW 2; CA 143; DLB 76

Atticus
See Fleming, Ian (Lancaster); Wilson, (Thomas) Woodrow

Atwood, Margaret (Eleanor) 1939-...**CLC 2, 3, 4, 8, 13, 15, 25, 44, 84; DA; DAB; DAC; DAM MST, NOV, POET; PC 8; SSC 2; WLC**
See also AAYA 12; BEST 89:2; CA 49-52; CANR 3, 24, 33, 59; DLB 53; INT CANR-24; MTCW; SATA 50

Aubigny, Pierre d'
See Mencken, H(enry) L(ouis)

Aubin, Penelope 1685-1731(?).................. **LC 9**
See also DLB 39

Auchincloss, Louis (Stanton) 1917-...**CLC 4, 6, 9, 18, 45; DAM NOV; SSC 22**
See also CA 1-4R; CANR 6, 29, 55; DLB 2; DLBY 80; INT CANR-29; MTCW

Auden, W(ystan) H(ugh) 1907-1973...**CLC 1, 2, 3, 4, 6, 9, 11, 14, 43; DA; DAB; DAC; DAM DRAM, MST, POET; PC 1; WLC**
See also AAYA 18; CA 9-12R; 45-48; CANR 5, 61; CDBLB 1914-1945; DLB 10, 20; MTCW

Audiberti, Jacques 1900-1965...**CLC 38; DAM DRAM**
See also CA 25-28R

Audubon, John James 1785-1851 ... **NCLC 47**

Auel, Jean M(arie) 1936-...**CLC 31, 107; DAM POP**
See also AAYA 7; BEST 90:4; CA 103; CANR 21, 64; INT CANR-21; SATA 91

Auerbach, Erich 1892-1957 .... **TCLC 43**
See also CA 118; 155

Augier, Emile 1820-1889 .... **NCLC 31**
See also DLB 192

Barnes, Julian (Patrick) 1946-...CLC 42; DAB
See also CA 102; CANR 19, 54; DLB 194;
DLBY 93
Barnes, Peter 1931- .... CLC 5, 56
See also CA 65-68; CAAS 12; CANR 33, 34,
64; DLB 13; MTCW
Baroja (y Nessi), Pio 1872-1956...TCLC 8; HLC
See also CA 104
Baron, David
See Pinter, Harold
Baron Corvo
See Rolfe, Frederick (William Serafino Austin
Lewis Mary)
Barondess, Sue K(aufman) 1926-1977...CLC 8
See also Kaufman, Sue
See also CA 1-4R; 69-72; CANR 1
Baron de Teive
See Pessoa, Fernando (Antonio Nogueira)
Barres, (Auguste-) Maurice 1862-1923
TCLC 47
See also CA 164; DLB 123
Barreto, Afonso Henrique de Lima
See Lima Barreto, Afonso Henrique de
Barrett, (Roger) Syd 1946- .... CLC 35
Barrett, William (Christopher) 1913-1992
CLC 27
See also CA 13-16R; 139; CANR 11, 67; INT
CANR-11
Barrie, J(ames) M(atthew) 1860-1937...TCLC
2; DAB; DAM DRAM
See also CA 104; 136; CDBLB 1890-1914; CLR
16; DLB 10, 141, 156; MAICYA; YABC 1
Barrington, Michael
See Moorcock, Michael (John)
Barrol, Grady
See Bograd, Larry
Barry, Mike
See Malzberg, Barry N(athaniel)
Barry, Philip 1896-1949 .... TCLC 11
See also CA 109; DLB 7
Bart, Andre Schwarz
See Schwarz-Bart, Andre
Barth, John (Simmons) 1930-...CLC 1, 2, 3, 5,
7, 9, 10, 14, 27, 51, 89; DAM NOV; SSC 10
See also AITN 1, 2; CA 1-4R; CABS 1; CANR
5, 23, 49, 64; DLB 2; MTCW
Barthelme, Donald 1931-1989...CLC 1, 2, 3,
5, 6, 8, 13, 23, 46, 59; DAM NOV; SSC 2
See also CA 21-24R; 129; CANR 20, 58; DLB 2;
DLBY 80,89; MTCW; SATA 7; SATA-Obit 62
Barthelme, Frederick 1943- .... CLC 36
See also CA 114; 122; DLBY 85; INT 122
Barthes, Roland (Gerard) 1915-1980 ..C L C
24, 83
See also CA 130; 97-100; CANR 66; MTCW
Barzun, Jacques (Martin) 1907- .... CLC 51
See also CA 61-64; CANR 22
Bashevis, Isaac
See Singer, Isaac Bashevis
Bashkirtseff, Marie 1859-1884 .... NCLC 27
Basho
See Matsuo Basho
Bass, Kingsley B., Jr.
See Bullins, Ed
Bass, Rick 1958- .... CLC 79
See also CA 126; CANR 53
Bassani, Giorgio 1916- .... CLC 9
See also CA 65-68; CANR 33; DLB 128, 177;
MTCW
Bastos, Augusto (Antonio) Roa
See Roa Bastos, Augusto (Antonio)
Bataille, Georges 1897-1962 .... CLC 29
See also CA 101; 89-92

Bates, H(erbert) E(rnest) 1905-1974...CLC 46;
DAB; DAM POP; SSC 10
See also CA 93-96; 45-48; CANR 34; DLB 162,
191; MTCW
Bauchart
See Camus, Albert
Baudelaire, Charles 1821-1867...NCLC 6, 29,
55; DA; DAB; DAC; DAM MST, POET; PC
1; SSC 18; WLC
Baudrillard, Jean 1929- .... CLC 60
Baum, L(yman) Frank 1856-1919 ..... TCLC 7
See also CA 108; 133; CLR 15; DLB 22; JRDA;
MAICYA; MTCW; SATA 18
Baum, Louis F.
See Baum, L(yman) Frank
Baumbach, Jonathan 1933- .... CLC 6, 23
See also CA 13-16R; CAAS 5; CANR 12, 66;
DLBY 80; INT CANR-12; MTCW
Bausch, Richard (Carl) 1945- .... CLC 51
See also CA 101; CAAS 14; CANR 43, 61; DLB
130
Baxter, Charles (Morley) 1947- . CLC 45, 78;
DAM POP
See also CA 57-60; CANR 40, 64; DLB 130
Baxter, George Owen
See Faust, Frederick (Schiller)
Baxter, James K(eir) 1926-1972 .... CLC 14
See also CA 77-80
Baxter, John
See Hunt, E(verette) Howard, (Jr.)
Bayer, Sylvia
See Glassco, John
Baynton, Barbara 1857-1929 .... TCLC 57
Beagle, Peter S(oyer) 1939- .... CLC 7, 104
See also CA 9-12R; CANR 4, 51; DLBY 80; INT
CANR-4; SATA 60
Bean, Normal
See Burroughs, Edgar Rice
Beard, Charles A(ustin) 1874-1948...TCLC 15
See also CA 115; DLB 17; SATA 18
Beardsley, Aubrey 1872-1898 .... NCLC 6
Beattie, Ann 1947- ....CLC 8, 13, 18, 40, 63;
DAM NOV, POP; SSC 11
See also BEST 90:2; CA 81-84; CANR 53;
DLBY 82; MTCW
Beattie, James 1735-1803 .... NCLC 25
See also DLB 109
Beauchamp, Kathleen Mansfield 1888-1923
See Mansfield, Katherine
See also CA 104; 134; DA; DAC; DAM MST
Beaumarchais, Pierre-Augustin Caron de 1732-
1799 .... DC 4
See also DAM DRAM
Beaumont, Francis 1584(?)-1616...LC 33; DC 6
See also CDBLB Before 1660; DLB 58, 121
Beauvoir, Simone (Lucie Ernestine Marie
Bertrand) de 1908-1986...CLC 1, 2, 4, 8,
14, 31, 44, 50, 71; DA; DAB; DAC; DAM
MST, NOV; WLC
See also CA 9-12R; 118; CANR 28, 61; DLB
72; DLBY 86; MTCW
Becker, Carl (Lotus) 1873-1945 ...... TCLC 63
See also CA 157; DLB 17
Becker, Jurek 1937-1997 .... CLC 7, 19
See also CA 85-88; 157; CANR 60; DLB 75
Becker, Walter 1950- .... CLC 26
Beckett, Samuel (Barclay) 1906-1989...C L C
1, 2, 3, 4, 6, 9, 10, 11, 14, 18, 29, 57, 59, 83;
DA; DAB; DAC; DAM DRAM, MST, NOV;
SSC 16; WLC
See also CA 5-8R; 130; CANR 33, 61; CDBLB
1945-1960; DLB 13, 15; DLBY 90;
MTCW

Beckford, William 1760-1844 .... NCLC 16
See also DLB 39
Beckman, Gunnel 1910- .... CLC 26
See also CA 33-36R; CANR 15; CLR 25;
MAICYA; SAAS 9; SATA 6
Becque, Henri 1837-1899 .... NCLC 3
See also DLB 192
Beddoes, Thomas Lovell 1803-1849 . NCLC 3
See also DLB 96
Bede c. 673-735 .... CMLC 20
See also DLB 146
Bedford, Donald F.
See Fearing, Kenneth (Flexner)
Beecher, Catharine Esther 1800-1878...N C L C
30
See also DLB 1
Beecher, John 1904-1980 .... CLC 6
See also AITN 1; CA 5-8R; 105; CANR 8
Beer, Johann 1655-1700 .... LC 5
See also DLB 168
Beer, Patricia 1924- .... CLC 58
See also CA 61-64; CANR 13, 46; DLB 40
Beerbohm, Max
See Beerbohm, (Henry) Max(imilian)
Beerbohm, (Henry) Max(imilian) 1872-1956
TCLC 1, 24
See also CA 104; 154; DLB 34, 100
Beer-Hofmann, Richard 1866-1945...TCLC 60
See also CA 160; DLB 81
Begiebing, Robert J(ohn) 1946- .... CLC 70
See also CA 122; CANR 40
Behan, Brendan 1923-1964CLC 1, 8, 11, 15, 79;
DAM DRAM
See also CA 73-76; CANR 33; CDBLB 1945-
1960; DLB 13; MTCW
Behn, Aphra 1640(?)-1689 .... LC 1, 30; DA;
DAB; DAC; DAM DRAM, MST, NOV,
POET; DC 4; PC 13; WLC
See also DLB 39, 80, 131
Behrman, S(amuel) N(athaniel) 1893-1973
CLC 40
See also CA 13-16; 45-48; CAP 1; DLB 7, 44
Belasco, David 1853-1931 .... TCLC 3
See also CA 104; DLB 7
Belcheva, Elisaveta 1893- .... CLC 10
See also Bagryana, Elisaveta
Beldone, Phil "Cheech"
See Ellison, Harlan (Jay)
Beleno
See Azuela, Mariano
Belinski, Vissarion Grigoryevich 1811-1848
NCLC 5
See also DLB 198
Belitt, Ben 1911- .... CLC 22
See also CA 13-16R; CAAS 4; CANR 7; DLB 5
Bell, Gertrude (Margaret Lowthian) 1868-1926
TCLC 67
See also DLB 174
Bell, James Madison 1826-1902 ... TCLC 43;
BLC 1; DAM MULT
See also BW 1; CA 122; 124; DLB 50
Bell, Madison Smartt 1957- .... CLC 41, 102
See also CA 111; CANR 28, 54
Bell, Marvin (Hartley) 1937- ..... CLC 8, 31;
DAM POET
See also CA 21-24R; CAAS 14; CANR 59; DLB
5; MTCW
Bell, W. L. D.
See Mencken, H(enry) L(ouis)
Bellamy, Atwood C.
See Mencken, H(enry) L(ouis)
Bellamy, Edward 1850-1898 .... NCLC 4
See also DLB 12

Cavallo, Evelyn
  See Spark, Muriel (Sarah)
Cavanna, Betty .... CLC 12
  See also Harrison, Elizabeth Cavanna
  See also JRDA; MAICYA; SAAS 4; SATA 1, 30
Cavendish, Margaret Lucas 1623-1673...LC 30
  See also DLB 131
Caxton, William 1421(?)-1491(?) .... LC 17
  See also DLB 170
Cayer, D. M.
  See Duffy, Maureen
Cayrol, Jean 1911- .... CLC 11
  See also CA 89-92; DLB 83
Cela, Camilo Jose 1916-.... CLC 4, 13, 59;
  DAM MULT; HLC
  See also BEST 90:2; CA 21-24R; CAAS 10;
  CANR 21, 32; DLBY 89; HW; MTCW
Celan, Paul .... CLC 10, 19, 53, 82; PC 10
  See also Antschel, Paul
  See also DLB 69
Celine, Louis-Ferdinand. .CLC 1, 3, 4, 7, 9, 15, 47
  See also Destouches, Louis-Ferdinand
  See also DLB 72
Cellini, Benvenuto 1500-1571 .... LC 7
Cendrars, Blaise 1887-1961 .... CLC 18, 106
  See also Sauser-Hall, Frederic
Cernuda (y Bidon), Luis 1902-1963 . CLC 54;
  DAM POET
  See also CA 131; 89-92; DLB 134; HW
Cervantes (Saavedra), Miguel de 1547-1616
  LC 6, 23; DA; DAB; DAC; DAM MST,
  NOV; SSC 12; WLC
Cesaire, Aime (Fernand) 1913- ...CLC 19, 32,
  112; BLC 1; DAM MULT, POET
  See also BW 2; CA 65-68; CANR 24, 43; MTCW
Chabon, Michael 1963- .... CLC 55
  See also CA 139; CANR 57
Chabrol, Claude 1930- .... CLC 16
  See also CA 110
Challans, Mary 1905-1983
  See Renault, Mary
  See also CA 81-84; 111; SATA 23; SATA-Obit 36
Challis, George
  See Faust, Frederick (Schiller)
Chambers, Aidan 1934- .... CLC 35
  See also CA 25-28R; CANR 12, 31, 58; JRDA;
  MAICYA; SAAS 12; SATA 1, 69
Chambers, James 1948-
  See Cliff, Jimmy
  See also CA 124
Chambers, Jessie
  See Lawrence, D(avid) H(erbert Richards)
Chambers, Robert W(illiam) 1865-1933
  TCLC 41
  See also CA 165
Chandler, Raymond (Thornton) 1888-1959
  TCLC 1, 7; SSC 23
  See also AAYA 25; CA 104; 129; CANR 60;
  CDALB 1929-1941; DLBD 6; MTCW
Chang, Eileen 1920-1995 .... SSC 28
  See also CA 166
Chang, Jung 1952- .... CLC 71
  See also CA 142
Chang Ai-Ling
  See Chang, Eileen
Channing, William Ellery 1780-1842..NCLC 17
  See also DLB 1, 59
Chaplin, Charles Spencer 1889-1977...CLC 16
  See also Chaplin, Charlie
  See also CA 81-84; 73-76
Chaplin, Charlie
  See Chaplin, Charles Spencer
  See also DLB 44

Chapman, George 1559(?)-1634 ......LC 22;
  DAM DRAM
  See also DLB 62, 121
Chapman, Graham 1941-1989 .... CLC 21
  See also Monty Python
  See also CA 116; 129; CANR 35
Chapman, John Jay 1862-1933 .... TCLC 7
  See also CA 104
Chapman, Lee
  See Bradley, Marion Zimmer
Chapman, Walker
  See Silverberg, Robert
Chappell, Fred (Davis) 1936- .... CLC 40, 78
  See also CA 5-8R; CAAS 4; CANR 8, 33, 67;
  DLB 6, 105
Char, Rene(-Emile) 1907-1988...CLC 9, 11, 14,
  55; DAM POET
  See also CA 13-16R; 124; CANR 32; MTCW
Charby, Jay
  See Ellison, Harlan (Jay)
Chardin, Pierre Teilhard de
  See Teilhard de Chardin, (Marie Joseph) Pierre
Charles I 1600-1649 .... LC 13
Charriere, Isabelle de 1740-1805 .... NCLC 66
Charyn, Jerome 1937- .... CLC 5, 8, 18
  See also CA 5-8R; CAAS 1; CANR 7, 61; DLBY
  83; MTCW
Chase, Mary (Coyle) 1907-1981 .... DC 1
  See also CA 77-80; 105; SATA 17; SATA-Obit 29
Chase, Mary Ellen 1887-1973 .... CLC 2
  See also CA 13-16; 41-44R; CAP 1; SATA 10
Chase, Nicholas
  See Hyde, Anthony
Chateaubriand, Francois Rene de 1768-1848
  NCLC 3
  See also DLB 119
Chatterje, Sarat Chandra 1876-1936(?)
  See Chatterji, Saratchandra
  See also CA 109
Chatterji, Bankim Chandra 1838-1894
  NCLC 19
Chatterji, Saratchandra .... TCLC 13
  See also Chatterje, Sarat Chandra
Chatterton, Thomas 1752-1770 .... LC 3; DAM
  POET
  See also DLB 109
Chatwin, (Charles) Bruce 1940-1989...CLC 28,
  57, 59; DAM POP
  See also AAYA 4; BEST 90:1; CA 85-88; 127;
  DLB 194
Chaucer, Daniel
  See Ford, Ford Madox
Chaucer, Geoffrey 1340(?)-1400...LC 17; DA;
  DAB; DAC; DAM MST, POET; PC 19;
  WLCS
  See also CDBLB Before 1660; DLB 146
Chaviaras, Strates 1935-
  See Haviaras, Stratis
  See also CA 105
Chayefsky, Paddy .... CLC 23
  See also Chayefsky, Sidney
  See also DLB 7, 44; DLBY 81
Chayefsky, Sidney 1923-1981
  See Chayefsky, Paddy
  See also CA 9-12R; 104; CANR 18; DAM DRAM
Chedid, Andree 1920- .... CLC 47
  See also CA 145
Cheever, John 1912-1982... CLC 3, 7, 8, 11,
  15, 25, 64; DA; DAB; DAC; DAM MST,
  NOV, POP; SSC 1; WLC
  See also CA 5-8R; 106; CABS 1; CANR 5, 27;
  CDALB 1941-1968; DLB 2, 102; DLBY 80,
  82; INT CANR-5; MTCW

Cheever, Susan 1943- .... CLC 18, 48
  See also CA 103; CANR 27, 51; DLBY 82; INT
  CANR-27
Chekhonte, Antosha
  See Chekhov, Anton (Pavlovich)
Chekhov, Anton (Pavlovich) 1860-1904
  TCLC 3, 10, 31, 55; DA; DAB; DAC;
  DAM DRAM, MST; DC 9; SSC 2, 28;
  WLC
  See also CA 104; 124; SATA 90
Chernyshevsky, Nikolay Gavrilovich 1828-1889
  NCLC 1
Cherry, Carolyn Janice 1942-
  See Cherryh, C. J.
  See also CA 65-68; CANR 10
Cherryh, C. J. .... CLC 35
  See also Cherry, Carolyn Janice
  See also AAYA 24; DLBY 80; SATA 93
Chesnutt, Charles W(addell) 1858-1932
  TCLC 5, 39; BLC 1; DAM MULT; SSC 7
  See also BW 1; CA 106; 125; DLB 12, 50, 78;
  MTCW
Chester, Alfred 1929(?)-1971 .... CLC 49
  See also CA 33-36R; DLB 130
Chesterton, G(ilbert) K(eith) 1874-1936
  TCLC 1, 6, 64; DAM NOV, POET; SSC 1
  See also CA 104; 132; CDBLB 1914-1945; DLB
  10, 19, 34, 70, 98, 149, 178; MTCW; SATA
  27
Chiang, Pin-chin 1904-1986
  See Ding Ling
  See also CA 118
Ch'ien Chung-shu 1910- .... CLC 22
  See also CA 130; MTCW
Child, L. Maria
  See Child, Lydia Maria
Child, Lydia Maria 1802-1880 .... NCLC 6
  See also DLB 1, 74; SATA 67
Child, Mrs.
  See Child, Lydia Maria
Child, Philip 1898-1978 .... CLC 19, 68
  See also CA 13-14; CAP 1; SATA 47
Childers, (Robert) Erskine 1870-1922
  TCLC 65
  See also CA 113; 153; DLB 70
Childress, Alice 1920-1994...CLC 12, 15, 86,
  96; BLC 1; DAM DRAM, MULT, NOV;
  DC 4
  See also AAYA 8; BW 2; CA 45-48; 146; CANR
  3, 27, 50; CLR 14; DLB 7, 38; JRDA;
  MAICYA; MTCW; SATA 7, 48, 81
Chin, Frank (Chew, Jr.) 1940- .... DC 7
  See also CA 33-36R; DAM MULT
Chislett, (Margaret) Anne 1943- .... CLC 34
  See also CA 151
Chitty, Thomas Willes 1926- .... CLC 11
  See also Hinde, Thomas
  See also CA 5-8R
Chivers, Thomas Holley 1809-1858...NCLC 49
  See also DLB 3
Chomette, Rene Lucien 1898-1981
  See Clair, Rene
  See also CA 103
Chopin, Kate .. TCLC 5, 14; DA; DAB; SSC 8;
  WLCS
  See also Chopin, Katherine
  See also CDALB 1865-1917; DLB 12, 78
Chopin, Katherine 1851-1904
  See Chopin, Kate
  See also CA 104; 122; DAC; DAM MST, NOV
Chretien de Troyes c. 12th cent. - .... CMLC 10
Christie
  See Ichikawa, Kon

Cowper, William 1731-1800 .. NCLC 8; DAM POET
See also DLB 104, 109
Cox, William Trevor 1928- .... CLC 9, 14, 71; DAM NOV
See also Trevor, William
See also CA 9-12R; CANR 4, 37, 55; DLB 14; INT CANR-37; MTCW
Coyne, P. J.
See Masters, Hilary
Cozzens, James Gould 1903-1978...CLC 1, 4, 11, 92
See also CA 9-12R; 81-84; CANR 19; CDALB 1941-1968; DLB 9; DLBD 2; DLBY 84, 97; MTCW
Crabbe, George 1754-1832 .... NCLC 26
See also DLB 93
Craddock, Charles Egbert
See Murfree, Mary Noailles
Craig, A. A.
See Anderson, Poul (William)
Craik, Dinah Maria (Mulock) 1826-1887 NCLC 38
See also DLB 35, 163; MAICYA; SATA 34
Cram, Ralph Adams 1863-1942 ...... TCLC 45
See also CA 160
Crane, (Harold) Hart 1899-1932...TCLC 2, 5, 80; DA; DAB; DAC; DAM MST, POET; PC 3; WLC
See also CA 104; 127; CDALB 1917-1929; DLB 4, 48; MTCW
Crane, R(onald) S(almon) 1886-1967...CLC 27
See also CA 85-88; DLB 63
Crane, Stephen (Townley) 1871-1900...TCLC 11, 17, 32; DA; DAB; DAC; DAM MST, NOV, POET; SSC 7; WLC
See also AAYA 21; CA 109; 140; CDALB 1865-1917; DLB 12, 54, 78; YABC 2
Crase, Douglas 1944- .... CLC 58
See also CA 106
Crashaw, Richard 1612(?)-1649 .... LC 24
See also DLB 126
Craven, Margaret 1901-1980 .. CLC 17; DAC
See also CA 103
Crawford, F(rancis) Marion 1854-1909 TCLC 10
See also CA 107; DLB 71
Crawford, Isabella Valancy 1850-1887 NCLC 12
See also DLB 92
Crayon, Geoffrey
See Irving, Washington
Creasey, John 1908-1973 .... CLC 11
See also CA 5-8R; 41-44R; CANR 8, 59; DLB 77; MTCW
Crebillon, Claude Prosper Jolyot de (fils) 1707-1777 .... LC 28
Credo
See Creasey, John
Credo, Alvaro J. de
See Prado (Calvo), Pedro
Creeley, Robert (White) 1926-...CLC 1, 2, 4, 8, 11, 15, 36, 78; DAM POET
See also CA 1-4R; CAAS 10; CANR 23, 43; DLB 5, 16, 169; MTCW
Crews, Harry (Eugene) 1935- .. CLC 6, 23, 49
See also AITN 1; CA 25-28R; CANR 20, 57; DLB 6, 143, 185; MTCW
Crichton, (John) Michael 1942-...CLC 2, 6, 54, 90; DAM NOV, POP
See also AAYA 10; AITN 2; CA 25-28R; CANR 13, 40, 54; DLBY 81; INT CANR-13; JRDA; MTCW; SATA 9, 88

Crispin, Edmund .... CLC 22
See also Montgomery, (Robert) Bruce
See also DLB 87
Cristofer, Michael 1945(?)- .... CLC 28; DAM DRAM
See also CA 110; 152; DLB 7
Croce, Benedetto 1866-1952 .... TCLC 37
See also CA 120; 155
Crockett, David 1786-1836 .... NCLC 8
See also DLB 3, 11
Crockett, Davy
See Crockett, David
Crofts, Freeman Wills 1879-1957 ... TCLC 55
See also CA 115; DLB 77
Croker, John Wilson 1780-1857 ...... NCLC 10
See also DLB 110
Crommelynck, Fernand 1885-1970 ... CLC 75
See also CA 89-92
Cromwell, Oliver 1599-1658 .... LC 43
Cronin, A(rchibald) J(oseph) 1896-1981...CLC 32
See also CA 1-4R; 102; CANR 5; DLB 191; SATA 47; SATA-Obit 25
Cross, Amanda
See Heilbrun, Carolyn G(old)
Crothers, Rachel 1878(?)-1958 .... TCLC 19
See also CA 113; DLB 7
Croves, Hal
See Traven, B.
Crow Dog, Mary (Ellen) (?)- .... CLC 93
See also Brave Bird, Mary
See also CA 154
Crowfield, Christopher
See Stowe, Harriet (Elizabeth) Beecher
Crowley, Aleister .... TCLC 7
See also Crowley, Edward Alexander
Crowley, Edward Alexander 1875-1947
See Crowley, Aleister
See also CA 104
Crowley, John 1942- .... CLC 57
See also CA 61-64; CANR 43; DLBY 82; SATA 65
Crud
See Crumb, R(obert)
Crumarums
See Crumb, R(obert)
Crumb, R(obert) 1943- .... CLC 17
See also CA 106
Crumbum
See Crumb, R(obert)
Crumski
See Crumb, R(obert)
Crum the Bum
See Crumb, R(obert)
Crunk
See Crumb, R(obert)
Crustt
See Crumb, R(obert)
Cryer, Gretchen (Kiger) 1935- .... CLC 21
See also CA 114; 123
Csath, Geza 1887-1919 .... TCLC 13
See also CA 111
Cudlip, David 1933- .... CLC 34
Cullen, Countee 1903-1946 ... TCLC 4, 37; BLC 1; DA; DAC; DAM MST, MULT, POET; PC 20; WLCS
See also BW 1; CA 108; 124; CDALB 1917-1929; DLB 4, 48, 51; MTCW; SATA 18
Cum, R.
See Crumb, R(obert)
Cummings, Bruce F(rederick) 1889-1919
See Barbellion, W. N. P.
See also CA 123

Cummings, E(dward) E(stlin) 1894-1962 CLC 1, 3, 8, 12, 15, 68; DA; DAB; DAC; DAM MST, POET; PC 5; WLC 2
See also CA 73-76; CANR 31; CDALB 1929-1941; DLB 4, 48; MTCW
Cunha, Euclides (Rodrigues Pimenta) da 1866-1909 .... TCLC 24
See also CA 123
Cunningham, E. V.
See Fast, Howard (Melvin)
Cunningham, J(ames) V(incent) 1911-1985 CLC 3, 31
See also CA 1-4R; 115; CANR 1; DLB 5
Cunningham, Julia (Woolfolk) 1916-...CLC 12
See also CA 9-12R; CANR 4, 19, 36; JRDA; MAICYA; SAAS 2; SATA 1, 26
Cunningham, Michael 1952- .... CLC 34
See also CA 136
Cunninghame Graham, R(obert) B(ontine) 1852-1936 .... TCLC 19
See also Graham, R(obert) B(ontine) Cunninghame
See also CA 119; DLB 98
Currie, Ellen 19(?)- .... CLC 44
Curtin, Philip
See Lowndes, Marie Adelaide (Belloc)
Curtis, Price
See Ellison, Harlan (Jay)
Cutrate, Joe
See Spiegelman, Art
Cynewulf c. 770-c. 840 .... CMLC 23
Czaczkes, Shmuel Yosef
See Agnon, S(hmuel) Y(osef Halevi)
Dabrowska, Maria (Szumska) 1889-1965 CLC 15
See also CA 106
Dabydeen, David 1955- .... CLC 34
See also BW 1; CA 125; CANR 56
Dacey, Philip 1939- .... CLC 51
See also CA 37-40R; CAAS 17; CANR 14, 32, 64; DLB 105
Dagerman, Stig (Halvard) 1923-1954 TCLC 17
See also CA 117; 155
Dahl, Roald 1916-1990 ..... CLC 1, 6, 18, 79; DAB; DAC; DAM MST, NOV, POP
See also AAYA 15; CA 1-4R; 133; CANR 6, 32, 37, 62; CLR 1, 7, 41; DLB 139; JRDA; MAICYA; MTCW; SATA 1, 26, 73; SATA-Obit 65
Dahlberg, Edward 1900-1977 .... CLC 1, 7, 14
See also CA 9-12R; 69-72; CANR 31, 62; DLB 48; MTCW
Daitch, Susan 1954- .... CLC 103
See also CA 161
Dale, Colin .... TCLC 18
See also Lawrence, T(homas) E(dward)
Dale, George E.
See Asimov, Isaac
Daly, Elizabeth 1878-1967 .... CLC 52
See also CA 23-24; 25-28R; CANR 60; CAP 2
Daly, Maureen 1921- .... CLC 17
See also AAYA 5; CANR 37; JRDA; MAICYA; SAAS 1; SATA 2
Damas, Leon-Gontran 1912-1978 ...... CLC 84
See also BW 1; CA 125; 73-76
Dana, Richard Henry Sr. 1787-1879 NCLC 53
Daniel, Samuel 1562(?)-1619 .... LC 24
See also DLB 62
Daniels, Brett
See Adler, Renata

French, Marilyn 1929-..... CLC 10, 18, 60; DAM DRAM, NOV, POP
See also CA 69-72; CANR 3, 31; INT CANR-31; MTCW

French, Paul
See Asimov, Isaac ·

Freneau, Philip Morin 1752-1832 ..... NCLC 1
See also DLB 37, 43

Freud, Sigmund 1856-1939 .... TCLC 52
See also CA 115; 133; CANR 69; MTCW

Friedan, Betty (Naomi) 1921-............. CLC 74
See also CA 65-68; CANR 18, 45; MTCW

Friedlander, Saul 1932-....................... CLC 90
See also CA 117; 130

Friedman, B(ernard) H(arper) 1926-.. CLC 7
See also CA 1-4R; CANR 3, 48

Friedman, Bruce Jay 1930- .... CLC 3, 5, 56
See also CA 9-12R; CANR 25, 52; DLB 2, 28; INT CANR-25

Friel, Brian 1929- .... CLC 5, 42, 59; DC 8
See also CA 21-24R; CANR 33, 69; DLB 13; MTCW

Friis-Baastad, Babbis Ellinor 1921-1970 CLC 12
See also CA 17-20R; 134; SATA 7

Frisch, Max (Rudolf) 1911-1991...CLC 3, 9, 14, 18, 32, 44; DAM DRAM, NOV
See also CA 85-88; 134; CANR 32; DLB 69, 124; MTCW

Fromentin, Eugene (Samuel Auguste) 1820-1876 NCLC 10
See also DLB 123

Frost, Frederick
See Faust, Frederick (Schiller)

Frost, Robert (Lee) 1874-1963...CLC 1, 3, 4, 9, 10, 13, 15, 26, 34, 44; DA; DAB; DAC; DAM MST, POET; PC 1; WLC
See also AAYA 21; CA 89-92; CANR 33; CDALB 1917-1929; DLB 54; DLBD 7; MTCW; SATA 14

Froude, James Anthony 1818-1894 NCLC 43
See also DLB 18, 57, 144

Froy, Herald
See Waterhouse, Keith (Spencer)

Fry, Christopher 1907- ... CLC 2, 10, 14; DAM DRAM
See also CA 17-20R; CAAS 23; CANR 9, 30; DLB 13; MTCW; SATA 66

Frye, (Herman) Northrop 1912-1991 ..C L C 24, 70
See also CA 5-8R; 133; CANR 8, 37; DLB 67, 68; MTCW

Fuchs, Daniel 1909-1993 .... CLC 8, 22
See also CA 81-84; 142; CAAS 5; CANR 40; DLB 9, 26, 28; DLBY 93

Fuchs, Daniel 1934-............................. CLC 34
See also CA 37-40R; CANR 14, 48

Fuentes, Carlos 1928-... CLC 3, 8, 10, 13, 22, 41, 60, 113; DA; DAB; DAC; DAM MST, MULT, NOV; HLC; SSC 24; WLC
See also AAYA 4; AITN 2; CA 69-72; CANR 10, 32, 68; DLB 113; HW; MTCW

Fuentes, Gregorio Lopez y
See Lopez y Fuentes, Gregorio

Fugard, (Harold) Athol 1932-...CLC 5, 9, 14, 25, 40, 80; DAM DRAM; DC 3
See also AAYA 17; CA 85-88; CANR 32, 54; MTCW

Fugard, Sheila 1932- .... CLC 48
See also CA 125

Fuller, Charles (H., Jr.) 1939- ... CLC 25; BLC 2; DAM DRAM, MULT; DC 1
See also BW 2; CA 108; 112; DLB 38; INT 112; MTCW

Fuller, John (Leopold) 1937-.............. CLC 62
See also CA 21-24R; CANR 9, 44; DLB 40

Fuller, Margaret .... NCLC 5, 50
See also Ossoli, Sarah Margaret (Fuller marchesa d')

Fuller, Roy (Broadbent) 1912-1991 CLC 4, 28
See also CA 5-8R; 135; CAAS 10; CANR 53; DLB 15, 20; SATA 87

Fulton, Alice 1952- .... CLC 52
See also CA 116; CANR 57; DLB 193

Furphy, Joseph 1843-1912 .... TCLC 25
See also CA 163

Fussell, Paul 1924-................................ CLC 74
See also BEST 90:1; CA 17-20R; CANR 8, 21, 35, 69; INT CANR-21; MTCW

Futabatei, Shimei 1864-1909 .... TCLC 44
See also CA 162; DLB 180

Futrelle, Jacques 1875-1912 .... TCLC 19
See also CA 113; 155

Gaboriau, Emile 1835-1873 .... NCLC 14

Gadda, Carlo Emilio 1893-1973 .... CLC 11
See also CA 89-92; DLB 177

Gaddis, William 1922-...CLC 1, 3, 6, 8, 10, 19, 43, 86
See also CA 17-20R; CANR 21, 48; DLB 2; MTCW

Gage, Walter
See Inge, William (Motter)

Gaines, Ernest J(ames) 1933-...CLC 3, 11, 18, 86; BLC 2; DAM MULT
See also AAYA 18; AITN 1; BW 2; CA 9-12R; CANR 6, 24, 42; CDALB 1968-1988; DLB 2, 33, 152; DLBY 80; MTCW; SATA 86

Gaitskill, Mary 1954- .... CLC 69
See also CA 128; CANR 61

Galdos, Benito Perez
See Perez Galdos, Benito

Gale, Zona 1874-1938 .... TCLC 7; DAM DRAM
See also CA 105; 153; DLB 9, 78

Galeano, Eduardo (Hughes) 1940-..... CLC 72
See also CA 29-32R; CANR 13, 32; HW

Galiano, Juan Valera y Alcala
See Valera y Alcala-Galiano, Juan

Galilei, Galileo 1546-1642 .... LC 45

Gallagher, Tess 1943- ...... CLC 18, 63; DAM POET; PC 9
See also CA 106; DLB 120

Gallant, Mavis 1922- ... CLC 7, 18, 38; DAC; DAM MST; SSC 5
See also CA 69-72; CANR 29, 69; DLB 53; MTCW

Gallant, Roy A(rthur) 1924- .... CLC 17
See also CA 5-8R; CANR 4, 29, 54; CLR 30; MAICYA; SATA 4, 68

Gallico, Paul (William) 1897-1976 .... CLC 2
See also AITN 1; CA 5-8R; 69-72; CANR 23; DLB 9, 171; MAICYA; SATA 13

Gallo, Max Louis 1932- .... CLC 95
See also CA 85-88

Gallois, Lucien
See Desnos, Robert

Gallup, Ralph
See Whitemore, Hugh (John)

Galsworthy, John 1867-1933 ... TCLC 1, 45; DA; DAB; DAC; DAM DRAM, MST, NOV; SSC 22; WLC 2
See also CA 104; 141; CDBLB 1890-1914; DLB 10, 34, 98, 162; DLBD 16

Galt, John 1779-1839 .... NCLC 1
See also DLB 99, 116, 159

Galvin, James 1951- .... CLC 38
See also CA 108; CANR 26

Gamboa, Federico 1864-1939 .... TCLC 36

Gandhi, M. K.
See Gandhi, Mohandas Karamchand

Gandhi, Mahatma
See Gandhi, Mohandas Karamchand

Gandhi, Mohandas Karamchand 1869-1948 TCLC 59; DAM MULT
See also CA 121; 132; MTCW

Gann, Ernest Kellogg 1910-1991 .... CLC 23
See also AITN 1; CA 1-4R; 136; CANR 1

Garcia, Cristina 1958- .... CLC 76
See also CA 141

Garcia Lorca, Federico 1898-1936...TCLC 1, 7, 49; DA; DAB; DAC; DAM DRAM, MST, MULT, POET; DC 2; HLC; PC 3; WLC
See also CA 104; 131; DLB 108; HW; MTCW

Garcia Marquez, Gabriel (Jose) 1928-...CLC 2, 3, 8, 10, 15, 27, 47, 55, 68; DA; DAB; DAC; DAM MST, MULT, NOV, POP; HLC; SSC 8; WLC
See also AAYA 3; BEST 89:1, 90:4; CA 33-36R; CANR 10, 28, 50; DLB 113; HW; MTCW

Gard, Janice
See Latham, Jean Lee

Gard, Roger Martin du
See Martin du Gard, Roger

Gardam, Jane 1928-............................. CLC 43
See also CA 49-52; CANR 2, 18, 33, 54; CLR 12; DLB 14, 161; MAICYA; MTCW; SAAS 9; SATA 39, 76; SATA-Brief 28

Gardner, Herb(ert) 1934- .... CLC 44
See also CA 149

Gardner, John (Champlin), Jr. 1933-1982 CLC 2, 3, 5, 7, 8, 10, 18, 28, 34; DAM NOV, POP; SSC 7
See also AITN 1; CA 65-68; 107; CANR 33; DLB 2; DLBY 82; MTCW; SATA 40; SATA-Obit 31

Gardner, John (Edmund) 1926- ..... CLC 30; DAM POP
See also CA 103; CANR 15, 69; MTCW

Gardner, Miriam
See Bradley, Marion Zimmer

Gardner, Noel
See Kuttner, Henry

Gardons, S. S.
See Snodgrass, W(illiam) D(e Witt)

Garfield, Leon 1921-1996 .... CLC 12
See also AAYA 8; CA 17-20R; 152; CANR 38, 41; CLR 21; DLB 161; JRDA; MAICYA; SATA 1, 32, 76; SATA-Obit 90

Garland, (Hannibal) Hamlin 1860-1940 TCLC 3; SSC 18
See also CA 104; DLB 12, 71, 78, 186

Garneau, (Hector de) Saint-Denys 1912-1943 TCLC 13
See also CA 111; DLB 88

Garner, Alan 1934-....CLC 17; DAB; DAM POP
See also AAYA 18; CA 73-76; CANR 15, 64; CLR 20; DLB 161; MAICYA; MTCW; SATA 18, 69

Garner, Hugh 1913-1979 .... CLC 13
See also CA 69-72; CANR 31; DLB 68

Garnett, David 1892-1981 .... CLC 3
See also CA 5-8R; 103; CANR 17; DLB 34

Garos, Stephanie
See Katz, Steve

Garrett, George (Palmer) 1929-...**CLC 3, 11, 51; SSC 30**
See also CA 1-4R; CAAS 5; CANR 1, 42, 67; DLB 2, 5, 130, 152; DLBY 83

Garrick, David 1717-1779 ...... **LC 15; DAM DRAM**
See also DLB 84

Garrigue, Jean 1914-1972 .... **CLC 2, 8**
See also CA 5-8R; 37-40R; CANR 20

Garrison, Frederick
See Sinclair, Upton (Beall)

Garth, Will
See Hamilton, Edmond; Kuttner, Henry

Garvey, Marcus (Moziah, Jr.) 1887-1940
TCLC 41; BLC 2; DAM MULT
See also BW 1; CA 120; 124

Gary, Romain .... **CLC 25**
See also Kacew, Romain
See also DLB 83

Gascar, Pierre .... **CLC 11**
See also Fournier, Pierre

Gascoyne, David (Emery) 1916- .... **CLC 45**
See also CA 65-68; CANR 10, 28, 54; DLB 20; MTCW

Gaskell, Elizabeth Cleghorn 1810-1865**NCLC 70; DAB; DAM MST; SSC 25**
See also CDBLB 1832-1890; DLB 21, 144, 159

Gass, William H(oward) 1924-...**CLC 1, 2, 8, 11, 15, 39; SSC 12**
See also CA 17-20R; CANR 30; DLB 2; MTCW

Gasset, Jose Ortega y
See Ortega y Gasset, Jose

Gates, Henry Louis, Jr. 1950- .... **CLC 65; BLCS; DAM MULT**
See also BW 2; CA 109; CANR 25, 53; DLB 67

Gautier, Theophile 1811-1872 ... **NCLC 1, 59; DAM POET; PC 18; SSC 20**
See also DLB 119

Gawsworth, John
See Bates, H(erbert) E(rnest)

Gay, Oliver
See Gogarty, Oliver St. John

Gaye, Marvin (Penze) 1939-1984 .... **CLC 26**
See also CA 112

Gebler, Carlo (Ernest) 1954- .... **CLC 39**
See also CA 119; 133

Gee, Maggie (Mary) 1948- .... **CLC 57**
See also CA 130

Gee, Maurice (Gough) 1931-............. **CLC 29**
See also CA 97-100; CANR 67; SATA 46

Gelbart, Larry (Simon) 1923- ...... **CLC 21, 61**
See also CA 73-76; CANR 45

Gelber, Jack 1932-................. **CLC 1, 6, 14, 79**
See also CA 1-4R; CANR 2; DLB 7

Gellhorn, Martha (Ellis) 1908-1998..**CLC 14, 60**
See also CA 77-80; 164; CANR 44; DLBY 82

Genet, Jean 1910-1986**CLC 1, 2, 5, 10, 14, 44, 46; DAM DRAM**
See also CA 13-16R; CANR 18; DLB 72; DLBY 86; MTCW

Gent, Peter 1942- .... **CLC 29**
See also AITN 1; CA 89-92; DLBY 82

Gentlewoman in New England, A
See Bradstreet, Anne

Gentlewoman in Those Parts, A
See Bradstreet, Anne

George, Jean Craighead 1919-........... **CLC 35**
See also AAYA 8; CA 5-8R; CANR 25; CLR 1; DLB 52; JRDA; MAICYA; SATA 2, 68

George, Stefan (Anton) 1868-1933..**TCLC 2, 14**
See also CA 104

Georges, Georges Martin
See Simenon, Georges (Jacques Christian)

Gerhardi, William Alexander
See Gerhardie, William Alexander

Gerhardie, William Alexander 1895-1977
CLC 5
See also CA 25-28R; 73-76; CANR 18; DLB 36

Gerstler, Amy 1956- .... **CLC 70**
See also CA 146

Gertler, T. .... **CLC 34**
See also CA 116; 121; INT 121

Ghalib .... **NCLC 39**
See also Ghalib, Hsadullah Khan

Ghalib, Hsadullah Khan 1797-1869
See Ghalib
See also DAM POET

Ghelderode, Michel de 1898-1962...**CLC 6, 11; DAM DRAM**
See also CA 85-88; CANR 40

Ghiselin, Brewster 1903-..................... **CLC 23**
See also CA 13-16R; CAAS 10; CANR 13

Ghose, Aurabinda 1872-1950 .... **TCLC 63**
See also CA 163

Ghose, Zulfikar 1935- .... **CLC 42**
See also CA 65-68; CANR 67

Ghosh, Amitav 1956-.......................... **CLC 44**
See also CA 147

Giacosa, Giuseppe 1847-1906............ **TCLC 7**
See also CA 104

Gibb, Lee
See Waterhouse, Keith (Spencer)

Gibbon, Lewis Grassic .... **TCLC 4**
See also Mitchell, James Leslie

Gibbons, Kaye 1960- ....**CLC 50, 88; DAM POP**
See also CA 151

Gibran, Kahlil 1883-1931 .. **TCLC 1, 9; DAM POET, POP; PC 9**
See also CA 104; 150

Gibran, Khalil
See Gibran, Kahlil

Gibson, William 1914-..... **CLC 23; DA; DAB; DAC; DAM DRAM, MST**
See also CA 9-12R; CANR 9, 42; DLB 7; SATA 66

Gibson, William (Ford) 1948-..... **CLC 39, 63; DAM POP**
See also AAYA 12; CA 126; 133; CANR 52

Gide, Andre (Paul Guillaume) 1869-1951
TCLC 5, 12, 36; DA; DAB; DAC; DAM MST, NOV; SSC 13; WLC
See also CA 104; 124; DLB 65; MTCW

Gifford, Barry (Colby) 1946- .... **CLC 34**
See also CA 65-68; CANR 9, 30, 40

Gilbert, Frank
See De Voto, Bernard (Augustine)

Gilbert, W(illiam) S(chwenck) 1836-1911
TCLC 3; DAM DRAM, POET
See also CA 104; SATA 36

Gilbreth, Frank B., Jr. 1911- .... **CLC 17**
See also CA 9-12R; SATA 2

Gilchrist, Ellen 1935-.... **CLC 34, 48; DAM POP; SSC 14**
See also CA 113; 116; CANR 41, 61; DLB 130; MTCW

Giles, Molly 1942- .... **CLC 39**
See also CA 126

Gill, Patrick
See Creasey, John

Gilliam, Terry (Vance) 1940- .... **CLC 21**
See also Monty Python
See also AAYA 19; CA 108; 113; CANR 35; INT 113

Gillian, Jerry
See Gilliam, Terry (Vance)

Gilliatt, Penelope (Ann Douglass) 1932-1993
CLC 2, 10, 13, 53
See also AITN 2; CA 13-16R; 141; CANR 49; DLB 14

Gilman, Charlotte (Anna) Perkins (Stetson) 1860-1935 .... **TCLC 9, 37; SSC 13**
See also CA 106; 150

Gilmour, David 1949- .... **CLC 35**
See also CA 138, 147

Gilpin, William 1724-1804 .... **NCLC 30**

Gilray, J. D.
See Mencken, H(enry) L(ouis)

Gilroy, Frank D(aniel) 1925- .... **CLC 2**
See also CA 81-84; CANR 32, 64; DLB 7

Gilstrap, John 1957(?)- .... **CLC 99**
See also CA 160

Ginsberg, Allen 1926-1997...**CLC 1, 2, 3, 4, 6, 13, 36, 69, 109; DA; DAB; DAC; DAM MST, POET; PC 4; WLC 3**
See also AITN 1; CA 1-4R; 157; CANR 2, 41, 63; CDALB 1941-1968; DLB 5, 16, 169; MTCW

Ginzburg, Natalia 1916-1991...**CLC 5, 11, 54, 70**
See also CA 85-88; 135; CANR 33; DLB 177; MTCW

Giono, Jean 1895-1970 .... **CLC 4, 11**
See also CA 45-48; 29-32R; CANR 2, 35; DLB 72; MTCW

Giovanni, Nikki 1943- ....**CLC 2, 4, 19, 64; BLC 2; DA; DAB; DAC; DAM MST, MULT, POET; PC 19; WLCS**
See also AAYA 22; AITN 1; BW 2; CA 29-32R; CAAS 6; CANR 18, 41, 60; CLR 6; DLB 5, 41; INT CANR-18; MAICYA; MTCW; SATA 24

Giovene, Andrea 1904- .... **CLC 7**
See also CA 85-88

Gippius, Zinaida (Nikolayevna) 1869-1945
See Hippius, Zinaida
See also CA 106

Giraudoux, (Hippolyte) Jean 1882-1944
TCLC 2, 7; DAM DRAM
See also CA 104; DLB 65

Gironella, Jose Maria 1917- .... **CLC 11**
See also CA 101

Gissing, George (Robert) 1857-1903...**TCLC 3, 24, 47**
See also CA 105; DLB 18, 135, 184

Giurlani, Aldo
See Palazzeschi, Aldo

Gladkov, Fyodor (Vasilyevich) 1883-1958
TCLC 27

Glanville, Brian (Lester) 1931- .... **CLC 6**
See also CA 5-8R; CAAS 9; CANR 3; DLB 15, 139; SATA 42

Glasgow, Ellen (Anderson Gholson) 1873-1945
TCLC 2, 7
See also CA 104; 164; DLB 9, 12

Glaspell, Susan 1882(?)-1948 .... **TCLC 55**
See also CA 110; 154; DLB 7, 9, 78; YABC 2

Glassco, John 1909-1981 .... **CLC 9**
See also CA 13-16R; 102; CANR 15; DLB 68

Glasscock, Amnesia
See Steinbeck, John (Ernst)

Glasser, Ronald J. 1940(?)- .... **CLC 37**

Glassman, Joyce
See Johnson, Joyce

Glendinning, Victoria 1937- .... **CLC 50**
See also CA 120; 127; CANR 59; DLB 155

Glissant, Edouard 1928- ... **CLC 10, 68; DAM MULT**
See also CA 153

Graves, Robert (von Ranke) 1895-1985
    **CLC 1, 2, 6, 11, 39, 44, 45; DAB; DAC;
    DAM MST, POET; PC 6**
    See also CA 5-8R; 117; CANR 5, 36; CDBLB
    1914-1945; DLB 20, 100, 191; DLBY 85;
    MTCW; SATA 45
Graves, Valerie
    See Bradley, Marion Zimmer
Gray, Alasdair (James) 1934- .... **CLC 41**
    See also CA 126; CANR 47, 69; DLB 194; INT
    126; MTCW
Gray, Amlin 1946- .... **CLC 29**
    See also CA 138
Gray, Francine du Plessix 1930- ..... **CLC 22;
    DAM NOV**
    See also BEST 90:3; CA 61-64; CAAS 2; CANR
    11, 33; INT CANR-11; MTCW
Gray, John (Henry) 1866-1934 .... **TCLC 19**
    See also CA 119; 162
Gray, Simon (James Holliday) 1936-...**C L C
    9, 14, 36**
    See also AITN 1; CA 21-24R; CAAS 3; CANR
    32, 69; DLB 13; MTCW
Gray, Spalding 1941-**CLC 49, 112; DAM POP;
    DC 7**
    See also CA 128
Gray, Thomas 1716-1771 ..... **LC 4, 40; DA;
    DAB; DAC; DAM MST; PC 2; WLC**
    See also CDBLB 1660-1789; DLB 109

Grayson, David
    See Baker, Ray Stannard

Grayson, Richard (A.) 1951- .... **CLC 38**
    See also CA 85-88; CANR 14, 31, 57
Greeley, Andrew M(oran) 1928- .... **CLC 28;
    DAM POP**
    See also CA 5-8R; CAAS 7; CANR 7, 43, 69;
    MTCW
Green, Anna Katharine 1846-1935...**TCLC 63**
    See also CA 112; 159
Green, Brian
    See Card, Orson Scott
Green, Hannah
    See Greenberg, Joanne (Goldenberg)
Green, Hannah 1927(?)-1996 .... **CLC 3**
    See also CA 73-76; CANR 59
Green, Henry 1905-1973 .... **CLC 2, 13, 97**
    See also Yorke, Henry Vincent
    See also DLB 15
Green, Julian (Hartridge) 1900-
    See Green, Julien
    See also CA 21-24R; CANR 33; DLB 4, 72;
    MTCW
Green, Julien .... **CLC 3, 11, 77**
    See also Green, Julian (Hartridge)
Green, Paul (Eliot) 1894-1981 ...... **CLC 25;
    DAM DRAM**
    See also AITN 1; CA 5-8R; 103; CANR 3; DLB
    7, 9; DLBY 81
Greenberg, Ivan 1908-1973
    See Rahv, Philip
    See also CA 85-88
Greenberg, Joanne (Goldenberg) 1932-..**CLC
    7, 30**
    See also AAYA 12; CA 5-8R; CANR 14, 32, 69;
    SATA 25
Greenberg, Richard 1959(?)- .... **CLC 57**
    See also CA 138
Greene, Bette 1934-.............................. **CLC 30**
    See also AAYA 7; CA 53-56; CANR 4; CLR 2;
    JRDA; MAICYA; SAAS 16; SATA 8
Greene, Gael .... **CLC 8**
    See also CA 13-16R; CANR 10

Greene, Graham (Henry) 1904-1991.. **CLC 1,
    3, 6, 9, 14, 18, 27, 37, 70, 72; DA; DAB;
    DAC; DAM MST, NOV; SSC 29; WLC**
    See also AITN 2; CA 13-16R; 133; CANR 35,
    61; CDBLB 1945-1960; DLB 13, 15, 77, 100,
    162; DLBY 91; MTCW; SATA 20
Greene, Robert 1558-1592 .... **LC 41**
    . See also DLB 62, 167
Greer, Richard
    See Silverberg, Robert
Gregor, Arthur 1923-............................. **CLC 9**
    See also CA 25-28R; CAAS 10; CANR 11; SATA 36
Gregor, Lee
    See Pohl, Frederik
Gregory, Isabella Augusta (Persse) 1852-1932
    TCLC 1
    See also CA 104; DLB 10
Gregory, J. Dennis
    See Williams, John A(lfred)
Grendon, Stephen
    See Derleth, August (William)
Grenville, Kate 1950- .... **CLC 61**
    See also CA 118; CANR 53
Grenville, Pelham
    See Wodehouse, P(elham) G(renville)
Greve, Felix Paul (Berthold Friedrich) 1879-
    1948
    See Grove, Frederick Philip
    See also CA 104; 141; DAC; DAM MST
Grey, Zane 1872-1939 ... **TCLC 6; DAM POP**
    See also CA 104; 132; DLB 9; MTCW
Grieg, (Johan) Nordahl (Brun) 1902-1943
    TCLC 10
    See also CA 107
Grieve, C(hristopher) M(urray) 1892-1978
    CLC 11, 19; DAM POET
    See also MacDiarmid, Hugh; Pteleon
    See also CA 5-8R; 85-88; CANR 33; MTCW
Griffin, Gerald 1803-1840 .... **NCLC 7**
    See also DLB 159
Griffin, John Howard 1920-1980 .... **CLC 68**
    See also AITN 1; CA 1-4R; 101; CANR 2
Griffin, Peter 1942- .... **CLC 39**
    See also CA 136
Griffith, D(avid Lewelyn) W(ark) 1875(?)-1948
    TCLC 68
    See also CA 119; 150
Griffith, Lawrence
    See Griffith, D(avid Lewelyn) W(ark)
Griffiths, Trevor 1935- .... **CLC 13, 52**
    See also CA 97-100; CANR 45; DLB 13
Griggs, Sutton Elbert 1872-1930(?)...**TCLC 77**
    See also CA 123; DLB 50
Grigson, Geoffrey (Edward Harvey) 1905-1985
    CLC 7, 39
    See also CA 25-28R; 118; CANR 20, 33; DLB
    27; MTCW
Grillparzer, Franz 1791-1872 .... **NCLC 1**
    See also DLB 133
Grimble, Reverend Charles James
    See Eliot, T(homas) S(tearns)
Grimke, Charlotte L(ottie) Forten 1837(?)-1914
    See Forten, Charlotte L.
    See also BW 1; CA 117; 124; DAM MULT,
    POET
Grimm, Jacob Ludwig Karl 1785-1863
    NCLC 3
    See also DLB 90; MAICYA; SATA 22
Grimm, Wilhelm Karl 1786-1859 ..... **NCLC 3**
    See also DLB 90; MAICYA; SATA 22
Grimmelshausen, Johann Jakob Christoffel von
    1621-1676 .... **LC 6**
    See also DLB 168

Grindel, Eugene 1895-1952
    See Eluard, Paul
    See also CA 104
Grisham, John 1955- ...... **CLC 84; DAM POP**
    See also AAYA 14; CA 138; CANR 47, 69
Grossman, David 1954-..................... **CLC 67**
    See also CA 138
Grossman, Vasily (Semenovich) 1905-1964
    CLC 41
    See also CA 124; 130; MTCW
Grove, Frederick Philip .... **TCLC 4**
    See also Greve, Felix Paul (Berthold Friedrich)
    See also DLB 92
Grubb
    See Crumb, R(obert)
Grumbach, Doris (Isaac) 1918-...**CLC 13, 22,
    64**
    See also CA 5-8R; CAAS 2; CANR 9, 42; INT
    CANR-9
Grundtvig, Nicolai Frederik Severin 1783-1872
    NCLC 1
Grunge
    See Crumb, R(obert)
Grunwald, Lisa 1959-.......................... **CLC 44**
    See also CA 120
Guare, John 1938-... **CLC 8, 14, 29, 67; DAM
    DRAM**
    See also CA 73-76; CANR 21, 69; DLB 7;
    MTCW
Gudjonsson, Halldor Kiljan 1902-1998
    See Laxness, Halldor
    See also CA 103; 164
Guenter, Erich
    See Eich, Guenter
Guest, Barbara 1920- .... **CLC 34**
    See also CA 25-28R; CANR 11, 44; DLB 5, 193
Guest, Judith (Ann) 1936- .. **CLC 8, 30; DAM
    NOV, POP**
    See also AAYA 7; CA 77-80; CANR 15; INT
    CANR-15; MTCW
Guevara, Che .... **CLC 87; HLC**
    See also Guevara (Serna), Ernesto
Guevara (Serna), Ernesto 1928-1967
    See Guevara, Che
    See also CA 127; 111; CANR 56; DAM MULT;
    HW
Guild, Nicholas M. 1944- .... **CLC 33**
    See also CA 93-96
Guillemin, Jacques
    See Sartre, Jean-Paul
Guillen, Jorge 1893-1984........ **CLC 11; DAM
    MULT, POET**
    See also CA 89-92; 112; DLB 108; HW
Guillen, Nicolas (Cristobal) 1902-1989...**C L C
    48, 79; BLC 2; DAM MST, MULT, POET;
    HLC; PC 23**
    See also BW 2; CA 116; 125; 129; HW
Guillevic, (Eugene) 1907- .... **CLC 33**
    See also CA 93-96
Guillois
    See Desnos, Robert
Guillois, Valentin
    See Desnos, Robert
Guiney, Louise Imogen 1861-1920... **TCLC 41**
    See also CA 160; DLB 54
Guiraldes, Ricardo (Guillermo) 1886-1927
    TCLC 39
    See also CA 131; HW; MTCW
Gumilev, Nikolai (Stepanovich) 1886-1921
    TCLC 60
    See also CA 165
Gunesekera, Romesh 1954- .... **CLC 91**
    See also CA 159

Hellenhofferu, Vojtech Kapristian z
See Hasek, Jaroslav (Matej Frantisek)
Heller, Joseph 1923-...CLC 1, 3, 5, 8, 11, 36, 63; DA; DAB; DAC; DAM MST, NOV, POP; WLC
See also AAYA 24; AITN 1; CA 5-8R; CABS 1; CANR 8, 42, 66; DLB 2, 28; DLBY 80; INT CANR-8; MTCW
Hellman, Lillian (Florence) 1906-1984...CLC 2, 4, 8, 14, 18, 34, 44, 52; DAM DRAM; DC 1
See also AITN 1, 2; CA 13-16R; 112; CANR 33; DLB 7; DLBY 84; MTCW
Helprin, Mark 1947- .... CLC 7, 10, 22, 32; DAM NOV, POP
See also CA 81-84; CANR 47, 64; DLBY 85; MTCW
Helvetius, Claude-Adrien 1715-1771 ... LC 26
Helyar, Jane Penelope Josephine 1933-
See Poole, Josephine
See also CA 21-24R; CANR 10, 26; SATA 82
Hemans, Felicia 1793-1835 .... NCLC 71
See also DLB 96
Hemingway, Ernest (Miller) 1899-1961...CLC 1, 3, 6, 8, 10, 13, 19, 30, 34, 39, 41, 44, 50, 61, 80; DA; DAB; DAC; DAM MST, NOV; SSC 25; WLC
See also AAYA 19; CA 77-80; CANR 34; CDALB 1917-1929; DLB 4, 9, 102; DLBD 1, 15, 16; DLBY 81, 87, 96; MTCW
Hempel, Amy 1951- .... CLC 39
See also CA 118; 137
Henderson, F. C.
See Mencken, H(enry) L(ouis)
Henderson, Sylvia
See Ashton-Warner, Sylvia (Constance)
Henderson, Zenna (Chlarson) 1917-1983... SSC 29
See also CA 1-4R; 133; CANR 1; DLB 8; SATA 5
Henley, Beth .... CLC 23; DC 6
See also Henley, Elizabeth Becker
See also CABS 3; DLBY 86
Henley, Elizabeth Becker 1952-
See Henley, Beth
See also CA 107; CANR 32; DAM DRAM, MST; MTCW
Henley, William Ernest 1849-1903 ... TCLC 8
See also CA 105; DLB 19
Hennissart, Martha
See Lathen, Emma
See also CA 85-88; CANR 64
Henry, O. .... TCLC 1, 19; SSC 5; WLC
See also Porter, William Sydney
Henry, Patrick 1736-1799 .... LC 25
Henryson, Robert 1430(?)-1506(?) ...... LC 20
See also DLB 146
Henry VIII 1491-1547 .... LC 10
Henschke, Alfred
See Klabund
Hentoff, Nat(han Irving) 1925- .... CLC 26
See also AAYA 4; CA 1-4R; CAAS 6; CANR 5, 25; CLR 1, 52; INT CANR-25; JRDA; MAICYA; SATA 42, 69; SATA-Brief 27
Heppenstall, (John) Rayner 1911-1981... CLC 10
See also CA 1-4R; 103; CANR 29
Heraclitus c. 540B.C.-c. 450B.C. .... CMLC 22
See also DLB 176
Herbert, Frank (Patrick) 1920-1986 CLC 12, 23, 35, 44, 85; DAM POP
See also AAYA 21; CA 53-56; 118; CANR 5, 43; DLB 8; INT CANR-5; MTCW; SATA 9, 37; SATA-Obit 47

Herbert, George 1593-1633 .... LC 24; DAB; DAM POET; PC 4
See also CDBLB Before 1660; DLB 126
Herbert, Zbigniew 1924- .... CLC 9, 43; DAM POET
See also CA 89-92; CANR 36; MTCW
Herbst, Josephine (Frey) 1897-1969...CLC 34
See also CA 5-8R; 25-28R; DLB 9
Hergesheimer, Joseph 1880-1954 ... TCLC 11
See also CA 109; DLB 102, 9
Herlihy, James Leo 1927-1993 .... CLC 6
See also CA 1-4R; 143; CANR 2
Hermogenes fl. c. 175- .... CMLC 6
Hernandez, Jose 1834-1886 .... NCLC 17
Herodotus c. 484B.C.-429B.C. .... CMLC 17
See also DLB 176
Herrick, Robert 1591-1674 ..... LC 13; DA; DAB; DAC; DAM MST, POP; PC 9
See also DLB 126
Herring, Guilles
See Somerville, Edith
Herriot, James 1916-1995 ... CLC 12; DAM POP
See also Wight, James Alfred
See also AAYA 1; CA 148; CANR 40; SATA 86
Herrmann, Dorothy 1941- .... CLC 44
See also CA 107
Herrmann, Taffy
See Herrmann, Dorothy
Hersey, John (Richard) 1914-1993...CLC 1, 2, 7, 9, 40, 81, 97; DAM POP
See also CA 17-20R; 140; CANR 33; DLB 6, 185; MTCW; SATA 25; SATA-Obit 76
Herzen, Aleksandr Ivanovich 1812-1870 NCLC 10, 61
Herzl, Theodor 1860-1904 .... TCLC 36
Herzog, Werner 1942- .... CLC 16
See also CA 89-92
Hesiod c. 8th cent. B.C.- .... CMLC 5
See also DLB 176
Hesse, Hermann 1877-1962...CLC 1, 2, 3, 6, 11, 17, 25, 69; DA; DAB; DAC; DAM MST, NOV; SSC 9; WLC
See also CA 17-18; CAP 2; DLB 66; MTCW; SATA 50
Hewes, Cady
See De Voto, Bernard (Augustine)
Heyen, William 1940- .... CLC 13, 18
See also CA 33-36R; CAAS 9; DLB 5
Heyerdahl, Thor 1914- .... CLC 26
See also CA 5-8R; CANR 5, 22, 66; MTCW; SATA 2, 52
Heym, Georg (Theodor Franz Arthur) 1887-1912 .... TCLC 9
See also CA 106
Heym, Stefan 1913- .... CLC 41
See also CA 9-12R; CANR 4; DLB 69
Heyse, Paul (Johann Ludwig von) 1830-1914 TCLC 8
See also CA 104; DLB 129
Heyward, (Edwin) DuBose 1885-1940 TCLC 59
See also CA 108; 157; DLB 7, 9, 45; SATA 21
Hibbert, Eleanor Alice Burford 1906-1993 CLC 7; DAM POP
See also BEST 90:4; CA 17-20R; 140; CANR 9, 28, 59; SATA 2; SATA-Obit 74
Hichens, Robert (Smythe) 1864-1950 ...TCLC 64
See also CA 162; DLB 153
Higgins, George V(incent) 1939-...CLC 4, 7, 10, 18
See also CA 77-80; CAAS 5; CANR 17, 51; DLB 2; DLBY 81; INT CANR-17; MTCW

Higginson, Thomas Wentworth 1823-1911 TCLC 36
See also CA 162; DLB 1, 64
Highet, Helen
See MacInnes, Helen (Clark)
Highsmith, (Mary) Patricia 1921-1995...CLC 2, 4, 14, 42, 102; DAM NOV, POP
See also CA 1-4R; 147; CANR 1, 20, 48, 62; MTCW
Highwater, Jamake (Mamake) 1942(?)-...CLC 12
See also AAYA 7; CA 65-68; CAAS 7; CANR 10, 34; CLR 17; DLB 52; DLBY 85; JRDA; MAICYA; SATA 32, 69; SATA-Brief 30
Highway, Tomson 1951-..... CLC 92; DAC; DAM MULT
See also CA 151; NNAL
Higuchi, Ichiyo 1872-1896 .... NCLC 49
Hijuelos, Oscar 1951- .... CLC 65; DAM MULT, POP; HLC
See also AAYA 25; BEST 90:1; CA 123; CANR 50; DLB 145; HW
Hikmet, Nazim 1902(?)-1963 .... CLC 40
See also CA 141; 93-96
Hildegard von Bingen 1098-1179 .. CMLC 20
See also DLB 148
Hildesheimer, Wolfgang 1916-1991 ... CLC 49
See also CA 101; 135; DLB 69, 124
Hill, Geoffrey (William) 1932-...CLC 5, 8, 18, 45; DAM POET
See also CA 81-84; CANR 21; CDBLB 1960 to Present; DLB 40; MTCW
Hill, George Roy 1921- .... CLC 26
See also CA 110; 122
Hill, John
See Koontz, Dean R(ay)
Hill, Susan (Elizabeth) 1942- ..... CLC 4, 113; DAB; DAM MST, NOV
See also CA 33-36R; CANR 29, 69; DLB 14, 139; MTCW
Hillerman, Tony 1925- ... CLC 62; DAM POP
See also AAYA 6; BEST 89:1; CA 29-32R; CANR 21, 42, 65; SATA 6
Hillesum, Etty 1914-1943 .... TCLC 49
See also CA 137
Hilliard, Noel (Harvey) 1929- .... CLC 15
See also CA 9-12R; CANR 7, 69
Hillis, Rick 1956- .... CLC 66
See also CA 134
Hilton, James 1900-1954 .... TCLC 21
See also CA 108; DLB 34, 77; SATA 34
Himes, Chester (Bomar) 1909-1984... CLC 2, 4, 7, 18, 58, 108; BLC 2; DAM MULT
See also BW 2; CA 25-28R; 114; CANR 22; DLB 2, 76, 143; MTCW
Hinde, Thomas .... CLC 6, 11
See also Chitty, Thomas Willes
Hindin, Nathan
See Bloch, Robert (Albert)
Hine, (William) Daryl 1936- .... CLC 15
See also CA 1-4R; CAAS 15; CANR 1, 20; DLB 60
Hinkson, Katharine Tynan
See Tynan, Katharine
Hinton, S(usan) E(loise) 1950- .. CLC 30, 111; DA; DAB; DAC; DAM MST, NOV
See also AAYA 2; CA 81-84; CANR 32, 62; CLR 3, 23; JRDA; MAICYA; MTCW; SATA 19, 58
Hippius, Zinaida .... TCLC 9
See also Gippius, Zinaida (Nikolayevna)
Hiraoka, Kimitake 1925-1970
See Mishima, Yukio
See also CA 97-100; 29-32R; DAM DRAM; MTCW

Hirsch, E(ric) D(onald), Jr. 1928- ...... **CLC 79**
See also CA 25-28R; CANR 27, 51; DLB 67;
INT CANR-27; MTCW
Hirsch, Edward 1950- .... **CLC 31, 50**
See also CA 104; CANR 20, 42; DLB 120
Hitchcock, Alfred (Joseph) 1899-1980...**CLC 16**
See also AAYA 22; CA 159; 97-100; SATA 27;
SATA-Obit 24
Hitler, Adolf 1889-1945 .... **TCLC 53**
See also CA 117; 147
Hoagland, Edward 1932- .... **CLC 28**
See also CA 1-4R; CANR 2, 31, 57; DLB 6;
SATA 51
Hoban, Russell (Conwell) 1925- ... **CLC 7, 25; DAM NOV**
See also CA 5-8R; CANR 23, 37, 66; CLR 3;
DLB 52; MAICYA; MTCW; SATA 1, 40, 78
Hobbes, Thomas 1588-1679 .... **LC 36**
See also DLB 151
Hobbs, Perry
See Blackmur, R(ichard) P(almer)
Hobson, Laura Z(ametkin) 1900-1986...**CLC 7, 25**
See also CA 17-20R; 118; CANR 55; DLB 28;
SATA 52
Hochhuth, Rolf 1931- .... **CLC 4, 11, 18; DAM DRAM**
See also CA 5-8R; CANR 33; DLB 124; MTCW
Hochman, Sandra 1936- .... **CLC 3, 8**
See also CA 5-8R; DLB 5
Hochwaelder, Fritz 1911-1986...**CLC 36; DAM DRAM**
See also CA 29-32R; 120; CANR 42; MTCW
Hochwalder, Fritz
See Hochwaelder, Fritz
Hocking, Mary (Eunice) 1921- .... **CLC 13**
See also CA 101; CANR 18, 40
Hodgins, Jack 1938- .... **CLC 23**
See also CA 93-96; DLB 60
Hodgson, William Hope 1877(?)-1918...**TCLC 13**
See also CA 111; 164; DLB 70, 153, 156, 178
Hoeg, Peter 1957- .... **CLC 95**
See also CA 151
Hoffman, Alice 1952- .... **CLC 51; DAM NOV**
See also CA 77-80; CANR 34, 66; MTCW
Hoffman, Daniel (Gerard) 1923-...**CLC 6, 13, 23**
See also CA 1-4R; CANR 4; DLB 5
Hoffman, Stanley 1944- .... **CLC 5**
See also CA 77-80
Hoffman, William M(oses) 1939- .... **CLC 40**
See also CA 57-60; CANR 11
Hoffmann, E(rnst) T(heodor) A(madeus) 1776-
1822 .... **NCLC 2; SSC 13**
See also DLB 90; SATA 27
Hofmann, Gert 1931- .... **CLC 54**
See also CA 128
Hofmannsthal, Hugo von 1874-1929 .. **T C L C 11; DAM DRAM; DC 4**
See also CA 106; 153; DLB 81, 118
Hogan, Linda 1947- .... **CLC 73; DAM MULT**
See also CA 120; CANR 45, 69; DLB 175;
NNAL
Hogarth, Charles
See Creasey, John
Hogarth, Emmett
See Polonsky, Abraham (Lincoln)
Hogg, James 1770-1835 .... **NCLC 4**
See also DLB 93, 116, 159
Holbach, Paul Henri Thiry Baron 1723-1789
LC 14

Holberg, Ludvig 1684-1754 .... **LC 6**
Holden, Ursula 1921- .... **CLC 18**
See also CA 101; CAAS 8; CANR 22
Holderlin, (Johann Christian) Friedrich 1770-
1843...**NCLC 16; PC 4**
Holdstock, Robert
See Holdstock, Robert P.
Holdstock, Robert P. 1948- .... **CLC 39**
See also CA 131
Holland, Isabelle 1920- .... **CLC 21**
See also AAYA 11; CA 21-24R; CANR 10, 25,
47; JRDA; MAICYA; SATA 8, 70
Holland, Marcus
See Caldwell, (Janet Miriam) Taylor (Holland)
Hollander, John 1929- .... **CLC 2, 5, 8, 14**
See also CA 1-4R; CANR 1, 52; DLB 5; SATA
13
Hollander, Paul
See Silverberg, Robert
Holleran, Andrew 1943(?)- .... **CLC 38**
See also CA 144
Hollinghurst, Alan 1954- .... **CLC 55, 91**
See also CA 114
Hollis, Jim
See Summers, Hollis (Spurgeon, Jr.)
Holly, Buddy 1936-1959 .... **TCLC 65**
Holmes, Gordon
See Shiel, M(atthew) P(hipps)
Holmes, John
See Souster, (Holmes) Raymond
Holmes, John Clellon 1926-1988 .... **CLC 56**
See also CA 9-12R; 125; CANR 4; DLB 16
Holmes, Oliver Wendell, Jr. 1841-1935
TCLC 77
See also CA 114
Holmes, Oliver Wendell 1809-1894...**NCLC 14**
See also CDALB 1640-1865; DLB 1, 189; SATA
34
Holmes, Raymond
See Souster, (Holmes) Raymond
Holt, Victoria
See Hibbert, Eleanor Alice Burford
Holub, Miroslav 1923- .... **CLC 4**
See also CA 21-24R; CANR 10
Homer c. 8th cent. B.C.- .... **CMLC 1, 16; DA; DAB; DAC; DAM MST, POET; PC 23; WLCS**
See also DLB 176
Hongo, Garrett Kaoru 1951- .... **PC 23**
See also CA 133; CAAS 22; DLB 120
Honig, Edwin 1919- .... **CLC 33**
See also CA 5-8R; CAAS 8; CANR 4, 45; DLB
5
Hood, Hugh (John Blagdon) 1928-...**CLC 15, 28**
See also CA 49-52; CAAS 17; CANR 1, 33; DLB
53
Hood, Thomas 1799-1845 .... **NCLC 16**
See also DLB 96
Hooker, (Peter) Jeremy 1941- .... **CLC 43**
See also CA 77-80; CANR 22; DLB 40
hooks, bell .... **CLC 94; BLCS**
See also Watkins, Gloria
Hope, A(lec) D(erwent) 1907-......... **CLC 3, 51**
See also CA 21-24R; CANR 33; MTCW
Hope, Anthony 1863-1933 .... **TCLC 83**
See also CA 157; DLB 153, 156
Hope, Brian
See Creasey, John
Hope, Christopher (David Tully) 1944-...**CLC 52**
See also CA 106; CANR 47; SATA 62

Hopkins, Gerard Manley 1844-1889 .. **N C L C 17; DA; DAB; DAC; DAM MST, POET; PC 15; WLC**
See also CDBLB 1890-1914; DLB 35, 57
Hopkins, John (Richard) 1931- .... **CLC 4**
See also CA 85-88
Hopkins, Pauline Elizabeth 1859-1930 **T C L C 28; BLC 2; DAM MULT**
See also BW 2; CA 141; DLB 50
Hopkinson, Francis 1737-1791 .... **LC 25**
See also DLB 31
Hopley-Woolrich, Cornell George 1903-1968
See Woolrich, Cornell
See also CA 13-14; CANR 58; CAP 1
Horatio
See Proust, (Valentin-Louis-George-Eugene-)
Marcel
Horgan, Paul (George Vincent O'Shaughnessy)
1903-1995 .... **CLC 9, 53; DAM NOV**
See also CA 13-16R; 147; CANR 9, 35; DLB
102; DLBY 85; INT CANR-9; MTCW; SATA
13; SATA-Obit 84
Horn, Peter
See Kuttner, Henry
Hornem, Horace Esq.
See Byron, George Gordon (Noel)
Horney, Karen (Clementine Theodore Danielsen)
1885-1952 .... **TCLC 71**
See also CA 114; 165
Hornung, E(rnest) W(illiam) 1866-1921
TCLC 59
See also CA 108; 160; DLB 70
Horovitz, Israel (Arthur) 1939- ..... **CLC 56; DAM DRAM**
See also CA 33-36R; CANR 46, 59; DLB 7
Horvath, Odon von
See Horvath, Oedoen von
See also DLB 85, 124
Horvath, Oedoen von 1901-1938 .... **TCLC 45**
See also Horvath, Odon von
See also CA 118
Horwitz, Julius 1920-1986 .... **CLC 14**
See also CA 9-12R; 119; CANR 12
Hospital, Janette Turner 1942- .... **CLC 42**
See also CA 108; CANR 48
Hostos, E. M. de
See Hostos (y Bonilla), Eugenio Maria de
Hostos, Eugenio M. de
See Hostos (y Bonilla), Eugenio Maria de
Hostos, Eugenio Maria
See Hostos (y Bonilla), Eugenio Maria de
Hostos (y Bonilla), Eugenio Maria de 1839-1903
TCLC 24
See also CA 123; 131; HW
Houdini
See Lovecraft, H(oward) P(hillips)
Hougan, Carolyn 1943-....................... **CLC 34**
See also CA 139
Household, Geoffrey (Edward West) 1900-1988
CLC 11
See also CA 77-80; 126; CANR 58; DLB 87;
SATA 14; SATA-Obit 59
Housman, A(lfred) E(dward) 1859-1936
TCLC 1, 10; DA; DAB; DAC; DAM MST, POET; PC 2; WLCS
See also CA 104; 125; DLB 19; MTCW
Housman, Laurence 1865-1959 .... **TCLC 7**
See also CA 106; 155; DLB 10; SATA 25
Howard, Elizabeth Jane 1923- .... **CLC 7, 29**
See also CA 5-8R; CANR 8, 62
Howard, Maureen 1930- ....**CLC 5, 14, 46**
See also CA 53-56; CANR 31; DLBY 83; INT
CANR-31; MTCW

John, Saint 7th cent. - .... **CMLC 27**

John of the Cross, St. 1542-1591 .... **LC 18**

Johnson, B(ryan) S(tanley William) 1933-1973
    CLC 6, 9
    See also CA 9-12R; 53-56; CANR 9; DLB 14, 40

Johnson, Benj. F. of Boo
    See Riley, James Whitcomb

Johnson, Benjamin F. of Boo
    See Riley, James Whitcomb

Johnson, Charles (Richard) 1948-...**CLC 7, 51,
    65; BLC 2; DAM MULT**
    See also BW 2; CA 116; CAAS 18; CANR 42,
    66; DLB 33

Johnson, Denis 1949- .... **CLC 52**
    See also CA 117; 121; DLB 120

Johnson, Diane 1934- .... **CLC 5, 13, 48**
    See also CA 41-44R; CANR 17, 40, 62; DLBY
    80; INT CANR-17; MTCW

Johnson, Eyvind (Olof Verner) 1900-1976
    CLC 14
    See also CA 73-76; 69-72; CANR 34

Johnson, J. R.
    See James, C(yril) L(ionel) R(obert)

Johnson, James Weldon 1871-1938...**TCLC 3,
    19; BLC 2; DAM MULT, POET**
    See also BW 1; CA 104; 125; CDALB 1917-
    1929; CLR 32; DLB 51; MTCW; SATA 31

Johnson, Joyce 1935- .... **CLC 58**
    See also CA 125; 129

Johnson, Lionel (Pigot) 1867-1902...**TCLC 19**
    See also CA 117; DLB 19

Johnson, Mel
    See Malzberg, Barry N(athaniel)

Johnson, Pamela Hansford 1912-1981...**CLC 1,
    7, 27**
    See also CA 1-4R; 104; CANR 2, 28; DLB 15;
    MTCW

Johnson, Robert 1911(?)-1938 .... **TCLC 69**

Johnson, Samuel 1709-1784 ......**LC 15; DA;
    DAB; DAC; DAM MST; WLC**
    See also CDBLB 1660-1789; DLB 39, 95, 104, 142

Johnson, Uwe 1934-1984 ....**CLC 5, 10, 15, 40**
    See also CA 1-4R; 112; CANR 1, 39; DLB 75;
    MTCW

Johnston, George (Benson) 1913- ......**CLC 51**
    See also CA 1-4R; CANR 5, 20; DLB 88

Johnston, Jennifer 1930- .... **CLC 7**
    See also CA 85-88; DLB 14

Jolley, (Monica) Elizabeth 1923- ...**CLC 46;
    SSC 19**
    See also CA 127; CAAS 13; CANR 59

Jones, Arthur Llewellyn 1863-1947
    See Machen, Arthur
    See also CA 104

Jones, D(ouglas) G(ordon) 1929- ....**CLC 10**
    See also CA 29-32R; CANR 13; DLB 53

Jones, David (Michael) 1895-1974...**CLC 2,
    4, 7, 13, 42**
    See also CA 9-12R; 53-56; CANR 28; CDBLB
    1945-1960; DLB 20, 100; MTCW

Jones, David Robert 1947-
    See Bowie, David
    See also CA 103

Jones, Diana Wynne 1934-...................... **CLC 26**
    See also AAYA 12; CA 49-52; CANR 4, 26, 56;
    CLR 23; DLB 161; JRDA; MAICYA; SAAS
    7; SATA 9, 70

Jones, Edward P. 1950- .... **CLC 76**
    See also BW 2; CA 142

Jones, Gayl 1949- .....**CLC 6, 9; BLC 2; DAM
    MULT**
    See also BW 2; CA 77-80; CANR 27, 66; DLB
    33; MTCW

Jones, James 1921-1977 ....**CLC 1, 3, 10, 39**
    See also AITN 1, 2; CA 1-4R; 69-72; CANR 6;
    DLB 2, 143; MTCW

Jones, John J.
    See Lovecraft, H(oward) P(hillips)

Jones, LeRoi .... **CLC 1, 2, 3, 5, 10, 14**
    See also Baraka, Amiri

Jones, Louis B. .... **CLC 65**
    See also CA 141

Jones, Madison (Percy, Jr.) 1925- .... **CLC 4**
    See also CA 13-16R; CAAS 11; CANR 7, 54;
    DLB 152

Jones, Mervyn 1922-...................... **CLC 10, 52**
    See also CA 45-48; CAAS 5; CANR 1; MTCW

Jones, Mick 1956(?)- .... **CLC 30**

Jones, Nettie (Pearl) 1941- .... **CLC 34**
    See also BW 2; CA 137; CAAS 20

Jones, Preston 1936-1979 .... **CLC 10**
    See also CA 73-76; 89-92; DLB 7

Jones, Robert F(rancis) 1934- .... **CLC 7**
    See also CA 49-52; CANR 2, 61

Jones, Rod 1953- .... **CLC 50**
    See also CA 128

Jones, Terence Graham Parry 1942-...**CLC 21**
    See also Jones, Terry; Monty Python
    See also CA 112; 116; CANR 35; INT 116

Jones, Terry
    See Jones, Terence Graham Parry
    See also SATA 67; SATA-Brief 51

Jones, Thom 1945(?)- .... **CLC 81**
    See also CA 157

Jong, Erica 1942- ..**CLC 4, 6, 8, 18, 83; DAM
    NOV, POP**
    See also AITN 1; BEST 90:2; CA 73-76; CANR
    26, 52; DLB 2, 5, 28, 152; INT CANR-26;
    MTCW

Jonson, Ben(jamin) 1572(?)-1637...**LC 6, 33;
    DA; DAB; DAC; DAM DRAM, MST,
    POET; DC 4; PC 17; WLC**
    See also CDBLB Before 1660; DLB 62, 121

Jordan, June 1936-....**CLC 5, 11, 23; BLCS;
    DAM MULT, POET**
    See also AAYA 2; BW 2; CA 33-36R; CANR
    25; CLR 10; DLB 38; MAICYA; MTCW;
    SATA 4

Jordan, Neil (Patrick) 1950- .... **CLC 110**
    See also CA 124; 130; CANR 54; INT 130

Jordan, Pat(rick M.) 1941- .... **CLC 37**
    See also CA 33-36R

Jorgensen, Ivar
    See Ellison, Harlan (Jay)

Jorgenson, Ivar
    See Silverberg, Robert

Josephus, Flavius c. 37-100 .... **CMLC 13**

Josipovici, Gabriel 1940- .... **CLC 6, 43**
    See also CA 37-40R; CAAS 8; CANR 47; DLB 14

Joubert, Joseph 1754-1824 .... **NCLC 9**

Jouve, Pierre Jean 1887-1976 .... **CLC 47**
    See also CA 65-68

Jovine, Francesco 1902-1950 .... **TCLC 79**

Joyce, James (Augustine Aloysius) 1882-1941
    **TCLC 3, 8, 16, 35, 52; DA; DAB; DAC;
    DAM MST, NOV, POET; PC 22; SSC 3, 26;
    WLC**
    See also CA 104; 126; CDBLB 1914-1945; DLB
    10, 19, 36, 162; MTCW

Jozsef, Attila 1905-1937 .... **TCLC 22**
    See also CA 116

Juana Ines de la Cruz 1651(?)-1695 ....**LC 5**

Judd, Cyril
    See Kornbluth, C(yril) M.; Pohl, Frederik

Julian of Norwich 1342(?)-1416(?) ....**LC 6**
    See also DLB 146

Junger, Sebastian 1962- .... **CLC 109**
    See also CA 165

Juniper, Alex
    See Hospital, Janette Turner

Junius
    See Luxemburg, Rosa

Just, Ward (Swift) 1935- .... **CLC 4, 27**
    See also CA 25-28R; CANR 32; INT CANR-32

Justice, Donald (Rodney) 1925- ..**CLC 6, 19,
    102; DAM POET**
    See also CA 5-8R; CANR 26, 54; DLBY 83; INT
    CANR-26

Juvenal c. 55-c. 127 .... **CMLC 8**

Juvenis
    See Bourne, Randolph S(illiman)

Kacew, Romain 1914-1980
    See Gary, Romain
    See also CA 108; 102

Kadare, Ismail 1936-......................... **CLC 52**
    See also CA 161

Kadohata, Cynthia .... **CLC 59**
    See also CA 140

Kafka, Franz 1883-1924....**TCLC 2, 6, 13,
    29, 47, 53; DA; DAB; DAC; DAM MST,
    NOV; SSC 5, 29; WLC**
    See also CA 105; 126; DLB 81; MTCW

Kahanovitsch, Pinkhes
    See Der Nister

Kahn, Roger 1927-............................. **CLC 30**
    See also CA 25-28R; CANR 44, 69; DLB 171;
    SATA 37

Kain, Saul
    See Sassoon, Siegfried (Lorraine)

Kaiser, Georg 1878-1945 .... **TCLC 9**
    See also CA 106; DLB 124

Kaletski, Alexander 1946- .... **CLC 39**
    See also CA 118; 143

Kalidasa fl. c. 400- .... **CMLC 9; PC 22**

Kallman, Chester (Simon) 1921-1975 .**CLC 2**
    See also CA 45-48; 53-56; CANR 3

Kaminsky, Melvin 1926-
    See Brooks, Mel
    See also CA 65-68; CANR 16

Kaminsky, Stuart M(elvin) 1934-........**CLC 59**
    See also CA 73-76; CANR 29, 53

Kane, Francis
    See Robbins, Harold

Kane, Paul
    See Simon, Paul (Frederick)

Kane, Wilson
    See Bloch, Robert (Albert)

Kanin, Garson 1912-............................ **CLC 22**
    See also AITN 1; CA 5-8R; CANR 7; DLB 7

Kaniuk, Yoram 1930-......................... **CLC 19**
    See also CA 134

Kant, Immanuel 1724-1804 .... **NCLC 27, 67**
    See also DLB 94

Kantor, MacKinlay 1904-1977 .... **CLC 7**
    See also CA 61-64; 73-76; CANR 60, 63; DLB
    9, 102

Kaplan, David Michael 1946- .... **CLC 50**

Kaplan, James 1951- .... **CLC 59**
    See also CA 135

Karageorge, Michael
    See Anderson, Poul (William)

Karamzin, Nikolai Mikhailovich 1766-1826
    NCLC 3
    See also DLB 150

Karapanou, Margarita 1946- .... **CLC 13**
    See also CA 101

Karinthy, Frigyes 1887-1938 .... **TCLC 47**

Karl, Frederick R(obert) 1927-.......... **CLC 34**
    See also CA 5-8R; CANR 3, 44

Livesay, Dorothy (Kathleen) 1909-...CLC 4, 15, 79; DAC; DAM MST, POET
See also AITN 2; CA 25-28R; CAAS 8; CANR 36, 67; DLB 68; MTCW

Livy c. 59B.C.-c. 17 .... CMLC 11

Lizardi, Jose Joaquin Fernandez de 1776-1827 NCLC 30

Llewellyn, Richard
See Llewellyn Lloyd, Richard Dafydd Vivian
See also DLB 15

Llewellyn Lloyd, Richard Dafydd Vivian 1906-1983 .... CLC 7, 80
See also Llewellyn, Richard
See also CA 53-56; 111; CANR 7; SATA 11; SATA-Obit 37

Llosa, (Jorge) Mario (Pedro) Vargas
See Vargas Llosa, (Jorge) Mario (Pedro)

Lloyd, Manda
See Mander, (Mary) Jane

Lloyd Webber, Andrew 1948-
See Webber, Andrew Lloyd
See also AAYA 1; CA 116; 149; DAM DRAM; SATA 56

Llull, Ramon c. 1235-c. 1316 .... CMLC 12

Locke, Alain (Le Roy) 1886-1954 .. TCLC 43; BLCS
See also BW 1; CA 106; 124; DLB 51

Locke, John 1632-1704 .... LC 7, 35
See also DLB 101

Locke-Elliott, Sumner
See Elliott, Sumner Locke

Lockhart, John Gibson 1794-1854 .... NCLC 6
See also DLB 110, 116, 144

Lodge, David (John) 1935- .... CLC 36; DAM POP
See also BEST 90:1; CA 17-20R; CANR 19, 53; DLB 14, 194; INT CANR-19; MTCW

Lodge, Thomas 1558-1625 .... LC 41
See also DLB 172

Lodge, Thomas 1558-1625 .... LC 41

Loennbohm, Armas Eino Leopold 1878-1926
See Leino, Eino
See also CA 123

Loewinsohn, Ron(ald William) 1937-...CLC 52
See also CA 25-28R

Logan, Jake
See Smith, Martin Cruz

Logan, John (Burton) 1923-1987 .... CLC 5
See also CA 77-80; 124; CANR 45; DLB 5

Lo Kuan-chung 1330(?)-1400(?) .... LC 12

Lombard, Nap
See Johnson, Pamela Hansford

London, Jack 1876-1916 .. TCLC 9, 15, 39; SSC 4; WLC
See also London, John Griffith
See also AAYA 13; AITN 2; CDALB 1865-1917; DLB 8, 12, 78; SATA 18

London, John Griffith 1876-1916
See London, Jack
See also CA 110; 119; DA; DAB; DAC; DAM MST, NOV; JRDA; MAICYA; MTCW

Long, Emmett
See Leonard, Elmore (John, Jr.)

Longbaugh, Harry
See Goldman, William (W.)

Longfellow, Henry Wadsworth 1807-1882 NCLC 2, 45; DA; DAB; DAC; DAM MST, POET; WLCS
See also CDALB 1640-1865; DLB 1, 59; SATA 19

Longinus c. 1st cent. - .... CMLC 27
See also DLB 176

Longley, Michael 1939-...................... CLC 29
See also CA 102; DLB 40

Longus fl. c. 2nd cent. - .... CMLC 7

Longway, A. Hugh
See Lang, Andrew

Lonnrot, Elias 1802-1884 .... NCLC 53

Lopate, Phillip 1943- .... CLC 29
See also CA 97-100; DLBY 80; INT 97-100

Lopez Portillo (y Pacheco), Jose 1920- . C L C 46
See also CA 129; HW

Lopez y Fuentes, Gregorio 1897(?)-1966 CLC 32
See also CA 131; HW

Lorca, Federico Garcia
See Garcia Lorca, Federico

Lord, Bette Bao 1938-........................CLC 23
See also BEST 90:3; CA 107; CANR 41; INT 107; SATA 58

Lord Auch
See Bataille, Georges

Lord Byron
See Byron, George Gordon (Noel)

Lorde, Audre (Geraldine) 1934-1992...C L C 18, 71; BLC 2; DAM MULT, POET; PC 12
See also BW 1; CA 25-28R; 142; CANR 16, 26, 46; DLB 41; MTCW

Lord Houghton
See Milnes, Richard Monckton

Lord Jeffrey
See Jeffrey, Francis

Lorenzini, Carlo 1826-1890
See Collodi, Carlo
See also MAICYA; SATA 29

Lorenzo, Heberto Padilla
See Padilla (Lorenzo), Heberto

Loris
See Hofmannsthal, Hugo von

Loti, Pierre .... TCLC 11
See also Viaud, (Louis Marie) Julien
See also DLB 123

Louie, David Wong 1954- .... CLC 70
See also CA 139

Louis, Father M.
See Merton, Thomas

Lovecraft, H(oward) P(hillips) 1890-1937 TCLC 4, 22; DAM POP; SSC 3
See also AAYA 14; CA 104; 133; MTCW

Lovelace, Earl 1935- .... CLC 51
See also BW 2; CA 77-80; CANR 41; DLB 125; MTCW

Lovelace, Richard 1618-1657 .... LC 24
See also DLB 131

Lowell, Amy 1874-1925 ..... TCLC 1, 8; DAM POET; PC 13
See also CA 104; 151; DLB 54, 140

Lowell, James Russell 1819-1891 ...... NCLC 2
See also CDALB 1640-1865; DLB 1, 11, 64, 79, 189

Lowell, Robert (Traill Spence, Jr.) 1917-1977 CLC 1, 2, 3, 4, 5, 8, 9, 11, 15, 37; DA; DAB; DAC; DAM MST, NOV; PC 3; WLC
See also CA 9-12R; 73-76; CABS 2; CANR 26, 60; DLB 5, 169; MTCW

Lowndes, Marie Adelaide (Belloc) 1868-1947 TCLC 12
See also CA 107; DLB 70

Lowry, (Clarence) Malcolm 1909-1957 TCLC 6, 40; SSC 31
See also CA 105; 131; CANR 62; CDBLB 1945-1960; DLB 15; MTCW

Lowry, Mina Gertrude 1882-1966
See Loy, Mina
See also CA 113

Loxsmith, John
See Brunner, John (Kilian Houston)

Loy, Mina .... CLC 28; DAM POET; PC 16
See also Lowry, Mina Gertrude
See also DLB 4, 54

Loyson-Bridet
See Schwob, (Mayer Andre) Marcel

Lucas, Craig 1951- .... CLC 64
See also CA 137

Lucas, E(dward) V(errall) 1868-1938...T C L C 73
See also DLB 98, 149, 153; SATA 20

Lucas, George 1944- .... CLC 16
See also AAYA 1, 23; CA 77-80; CANR 30; SATA 56

Lucas, Hans
See Godard, Jean-Luc

Lucas, Victoria
See Plath, Sylvia

Ludlam, Charles 1943-1987 .... CLC 46, 50
See also CA 85-88; 122

Ludlum, Robert 1927-.... CLC 22, 43; DAM NOV, POP
See also AAYA 10; BEST 89:1, 90:3; CA 33-36R; CANR 25, 41, 68; DLBY 82; MTCW

Ludwig, Ken .... CLC 60

Ludwig, Otto 1813-1865 .... NCLC 4
See also DLB 129

Lugones, Leopoldo 1874-1938 .... TCLC 15
See also CA 116; 131; HW

Lu Hsun 1881-1936 .... TCLC 3; SSC 20
See also Shu-Jen, Chou

Lukacs, George .... CLC 24
See also Lukacs, Gyorgy (Szegeny von)

Lukacs, Gyorgy (Szegeny von) 1885-1971
See Lukacs, George
See also CA 101; 29-32R; CANR 62

Luke, Peter (Ambrose Cyprian) 1919-1995 CLC 38
See also CA 81-84; 147; DLB 13

Lunar, Dennis
See Mungo, Raymond

Lurie, Alison 1926-................. CLC 4, 5, 18, 39
See also CA 1-4R; CANR 2, 17, 50; DLB 2; MTCW; SATA 46

Lustig, Arnost 1926- .... CLC 56
See also AAYA 3; CA 69-72; CANR 47; SATA 56

Luther, Martin 1483-1546 .... LC 9, 37
See also DLB 179

Luxemburg, Rosa 1870(?)-1919 ...... TCLC 63
See also CA 118

Luzi, Mario 1914-............................... CLC 13
See also CA 61-64; CANR 9; DLB 128

Lyly, John 1554(?)-1606 .... LC 41; DAM DRAM; DC 7
See also DLB 62, 167

L'Ymagier
See Gourmont, Remy (-Marie-Charles) de

Lynch, B. Suarez
See Bioy Casares, Adolfo; Borges, Jorge Luis

Lynch, David (K.) 1946-..................... CLC 66
See also CA 124; 129

Lynch, James
See Andreyev, Leonid (Nikolaevich)

Lynch Davis, B.
See Bioy Casares, Adolfo; Borges, Jorge Luis

Lyndsay, Sir David 1490-1555 .... LC 20

Lynn, Kenneth S(chuyler) 1923- .... CLC 50
See also CA 1-4R; CANR 3, 27, 65

Lynx
See West, Rebecca

Lyons, Marcus
See Blish, James (Benjamin)

McLoughlin, R. B.
See Mencken, H(enry) L(ouis)
McLuhan, (Herbert) Marshall 1911-1980**CLC 37, 83**
See also CA 9-12R; 102; CANR 12, 34, 61; DLB 88; INT CANR-12; MTCW
McMillan, Terry (L.) 1951- **CLC 50, 61, 112; BLCS; DAM MULT, NOV, POP**
See also AAYA 21; BW 2; CA 140; CANR 60
McMurtry, Larry (Jeff) 1936-**CLC 2, 3, 7, 11, 27, 44; DAM NOV, POP**
See also AAYA 15; AITN 2; BEST 89:2; CA 5-8R; CANR 19, 43, 64; CDALB 1968-1988; DLB 2, 143; DLBY 80, 87; MTCW
McNally, T. M. 1961- .... **CLC 82**
McNally, Terrence 1939-**CLC 4, 7, 41, 91; DAM DRAM**
See also CA 45-48; CANR 2, 56; DLB 7
McNamer, Deirdre 1950- .... **CLC 70**
McNeile, Herman Cyril 1888-1937
See Sapper
See also DLB 77
McNickle, (William) D'Arcy 1904-1977 . **C L C 89; DAM MULT**
See also CA 9-12R; 85-88; CANR 5, 45; DLB 175; NNAL; SATA-Obit 22
McPhee, John (Angus) 1931- .... **CLC 36**
See also BEST 90:1; CA 65-68; CANR 20, 46, 64, 69; DLB 185; MTCW
McPherson, James Alan 1943- ... **CLC 19, 77; BLCS**
See also BW 1; CA 25-28R; CAAS 17; CANR 24; DLB 38; MTCW
McPherson, William (Alexander) 1933- . **C L C 34**
See also CA 69-72; CANR 28; INT CANR-28
Mead, Margaret 1901-1978 .... **CLC 37**
See also AITN 1; CA 1-4R; 81-84; CANR 4; MTCW; SATA-Obit 20
Meaker, Marijane (Agnes) 1927-
See Kerr, M. E.
See also CA 107; CANR 37, 63; INT 107; JRDA; MAICYA; MTCW; SATA 20, 61
Medoff, Mark (Howard) 1940- .... **CLC 6, 23; DAM DRAM**
See also AITN 1; CA 53-56; CANR 5; DLB 7; INT CANR-5
Medvedev, P. N.
See Bakhtin, Mikhail Mikhailovich
Meged, Aharon
See Megged, Aharon
Meged, Aron
See Megged, Aharon
Megged, Aharon 1920- .... **CLC 9**
See also CA 49-52; CAAS 13; CANR 1
Mehta, Ved (Parkash) 1934- .... **CLC 37**
See also CA 1-4R; CANR 2, 23, 69; MTCW
Melanter
See Blackmore, R(ichard) D(oddridge)
Melies, Georges 1861-1938 .... **TCLC 81**
Melikow, Loris
See Hofmannsthal, Hugo von
Melmoth, Sebastian
See Wilde, Oscar (Fingal O'Flahertie Wills)
Meltzer, Milton 1915- .... **CLC 26**
See also AAYA 8; CA 13-16R; CANR 38; CLR 13; DLB 61; JRDA; MAICYA; SAAS 1; SATA 1, 50, 80
Melville, Herman 1819-1891 **NCLC 3, 12, 29, 45, 49; DA; DAB; DAC; DAM MST, NOV; SSC 1, 17; WLC**
See also AAYA 25; CDALB 1640-1865; DLB 3, 74; SATA 59

Menander c. 342B.C.-c. 292B.C. .....**CMLC 9; DAM DRAM; DC 3**
See also DLB 176
Mencken, H(enry) L(ouis) 1880-1956...**TCLC 13**
See also CA 105; 125; CDALB 1917-1929; DLB 11, 29, 63, 137; MTCW
Mendelsohn, Jane 1965(?)- .... **CLC 99**
See also CA 154
Mercer, David 1928-1980 .... **CLC 5; DAM DRAM**
See also CA 9-12R; 102; CANR 23; DLB 13; MTCW
Merchant, Paul
See Ellison, Harlan (Jay)
Meredith, George 1828-1909 ... **TCLC 17, 43; DAM POET**
See also CA 117; 153; CDBLB 1832-1890; DLB 18, 35, 57, 159
Meredith, William (Morris) 1919-...**CLC 4, 13, 22, 55; DAM POET**
See also CA 9-12R; CAAS 14; CANR 6, 40; DLB 5
Merezhkovsky, Dmitry Sergeyevich 1865-1941 **TCLC 29**
Merimee, Prosper 1803-1870 ... **NCLC 6, 65; SSC 7**
See also DLB 119, 192
Merkin, Daphne 1954- .... **CLC 44**
See also CA 123
Merlin, Arthur
See Blish, James (Benjamin)
Merrill, James (Ingram) 1926-1995...**CLC 2, 3, 6, 8, 13, 18, 34, 91; DAM POET**
See also CA 13-16R; 147; CANR 10, 49, 63; DLB 5, 165; DLBY 85; INT CANR-10; MTCW
Merriman, Alex
See Silverberg, Robert
Merriman, Brian 1747-1805 .... **NCLC 70**
Merritt, E. B.
See Waddington, Miriam
Merton, Thomas 1915-1968...**CLC 1, 3, 11, 34, 83; PC 10**
See also CA 5-8R; 25-28R; CANR 22, 53; DLB 48; DLBY 81; MTCW
Merwin, W(illiam) S(tanley) 1927-...**CLC 1, 2, 3, 5, 8, 13, 18, 45, 88; DAM POET**
See also CA 13-16R; CANR 15, 51; DLB 5, 169; INT CANR-15; MTCW
Metcalf, John 1938- .... **CLC 37**
See also CA 113; DLB 60
Metcalf, Suzanne
See Baum, L(yman) Frank
Mew, Charlotte (Mary) 1870-1928 ... **TCLC 8**
See also CA 105; DLB 19, 135
Mewshaw, Michael 1943- .... **CLC 9**
See also CA 53-56; CANR 7, 47; DLBY 80
Meyer, June
See Jordan, June
Meyer, Lynn
See Slavitt, David R(ytman)
Meyer-Meyrink, Gustav 1868-1932
See Meyrink, Gustav
See also CA 117
Meyers, Jeffrey 1939- .... **CLC 39**
See also CA 73-76; CANR 54; DLB 111
Meynell, Alice (Christina Gertrude Thompson) 1847-1922 .... **TCLC 6**
See also CA 104; DLB 19, 98
Meyrink, Gustav .... **TCLC 21**
See also Meyer-Meyrink, Gustav
See also DLB 81

Michaels, Leonard 1933-...**CLC 6, 25; SSC 16**
See also CA 61-64; CANR 21, 62; DLB 130; MTCW
Michaux, Henri 1899-1984 .... **CLC 8, 19**
See also CA 85-88; 114
Micheaux, Oscar 1884-1951 .... **TCLC 76**
See also DLB 50
Michelangelo 1475-1564 .... **LC 12**
Michelet, Jules 1798-1874 .... **NCLC 31**
Michener, James A(lbert) 1907(?)-1997 **CLC 1, 5, 11, 29, 60, 109; DAM NOV, POP**
See also AITN 1; BEST 90:1; CA 5-8R; 161; CANR 21, 45, 68; DLB 6; MTCW
Mickiewicz, Adam 1798-1855 .... **NCLC 3**
Middleton, Christopher 1926- .... **CLC 13**
See also CA 13-16R; CANR 29, 54; DLB 40
Middleton, Richard (Barham) 1882-1911 **TCLC 56**
See also DLB 156
Middleton, Stanley 1919- .... **CLC 7, 38**
See also CA 25-28R; CAAS 23; CANR 21, 46; DLB 14
Middleton, Thomas 1580-1627 . **LC 33; DAM DRAM, MST; DC 5**
See also DLB 58
Migueis, Jose Rodrigues 1901- .... **CLC 10**
Mikszath, Kalman 1847-1910 .... **TCLC 31**
Miles, Jack ....**CLC 100**
Miles, Josephine (Louise) 1911-1985...**CLC 1, 2, 14, 34, 39; DAM POET**
See also CA 1-4R; 116; CANR 2, 55; DLB 48
Militant
See Sandburg, Carl (August)
Mill, John Stuart 1806-1873 ..... **NCLC 11, 58**
See also CDBLB 1832-1890; DLB 55, 190
Millar, Kenneth 1915-1983 ....**CLC 14; DAM POP**
See also Macdonald, Ross
See also CA 9-12R; 110; CANR 16, 63; DLB 2; DLBD 6; DLBY 83; MTCW
Millay, E. Vincent
See Millay, Edna St. Vincent
Millay, Edna St. Vincent 1892-1950...**TCLC 4, 49; DA; DAB; DAC; DAM MST, POET; PC 6; WLCS**
See also CA 104; 130; CDALB 1917-1929; DLB 45; MTCW
Miller, Arthur 1915-...**CLC 1, 2, 6, 10, 15, 26, 47, 78; DA; DAB; DAC; DAM DRAM, MST; DC 1; WLC**
See also AAYA 15; AITN 1; CA 1-4R; CABS 3; CANR 2, 30, 54; CDALB 1941-1968; DLB 7; MTCW
Miller, Henry (Valentine) 1891-1980...**CLC 1, 2, 4, 9, 14, 43, 84; DA; DAB; DAC; DAM MST, NOV; WLC**
See also CA 9-12R; 97-100; CANR 33, 64; CDALB 1929-1941; DLB 4, 9; DLBY 80; MTCW
Miller, Jason 1939(?)- .... **CLC 2**
See also AITN 1; CA 73-76; DLB 7
Miller, Sue 1943- .... **CLC 44; DAM POP**
See also BEST 90:3; CA 139; CANR 59; DLB 143
Miller, Walter M(ichael, Jr.) 1923-...**CLC 4, 30**
See also CA 85-88; DLB 8
Millett, Kate 1934- .... **CLC 67**
See also AITN 1; CA 73-76; CANR 32, 53; MTCW
Millhauser, Steven (Lewis) 1943-...**CLC 21, 54, 109**
See also CA 110; 111; CANR 63; DLB 2; INT 111

Morgan, Robin (Evonne) 1941- .... **CLC 2**
See also CA 69-72; CANR 29, 68; MTCW; SATA 80

Morgan, Scott
See Kuttner, Henry

Morgan, Seth 1949(?)-1990 .... **CLC 65**
See also CA 132

Morgenstern, Christian 1871-1914 .. **TCLC 8**
See also CA 105

Morgenstern, S.
See Goldman, William (W.)

Moricz, Zsigmond 1879-1942 .... **TCLC 33**
See also CA 165

Morike, Eduard (Friedrich) 1804-1875
NCLC 10
See also DLB 133

Moritz, Karl Philipp 1756-1793 .... **LC 2**
See also DLB 94

Morland, Peter Henry
See Faust, Frederick (Schiller)

Morren, Theophil
See Hofmannsthal, Hugo von

Morris, Bill 1952- .... **CLC 76**

Morris, Julian
See West, Morris L(anglo)

Morris, Steveland Judkins 1950(?)-
See Wonder, Stevie
See also CA 111

Morris, William 1834-1896 .... **NCLC 4**
See also CDBLB 1832-1890; DLB 18, 35, 57, 156, 178, 184

Morris, Wright 1910- .... **CLC 1, 3, 7, 18, 37**
See also CA 9-12R; CANR 21; DLB 2; DLBY 81; MTCW

Morrison, Arthur 1863-1945 .... **TCLC 72**
See also CA 120; 157; DLB 70, 135, 197

Morrison, Chloe Anthony Wofford
See Morrison, Toni

Morrison, James Douglas 1943-1971
See Morrison, Jim
See also CA 73-76; CANR 40

Morrison, Jim .... **CLC 17**
See also Morrison, James Douglas

Morrison, Toni 1931-...**CLC 4, 10, 22, 55, 81, 87; BLC 3; DA; DAB; DAC; DAM MST, MULT, NOV, POP**
See also AAYA 1, 22; BW 2; CA 29-32R; CANR 27, 42, 67; CDALB 1968-1988; DLB 6, 33, 143; DLBY 81; MTCW; SATA 57

Morrison, Van 1945- .... **CLC 21**
See also CA 116

Morrissy, Mary 1958- .... **CLC 99**

Mortimer, John (Clifford) 1923-...**CLC 28, 43; DAM DRAM, POP**
See also CA 13-16R; CANR 21, 69; CDBLB 1960 to Present; DLB 13; INT CANR-21; MTCW

Mortimer, Penelope (Ruth) 1918- .... **CLC 5**
See also CA 57-60; CANR 45

Morton, Anthony
See Creasey, John

Mosca, Gaetano 1858-1941 .... **TCLC 75**

Mosher, Howard Frank 1943- .... **CLC 62**
See also CA 139; CANR 65

Mosley, Nicholas 1923- .... **CLC 43, 70**
See also CA 69-72; CANR 41, 60; DLB 14

Mosley, Walter 1952- . **CLC 97; BLCS; DAM MULT, POP**
See also AAYA 17; BW 2; CA 142; CANR 57

Moss, Howard 1922-1987...**CLC 7, 14, 45, 50; DAM POET**
See also CA 1-4R; 123; CANR 1, 44; DLB 5

Mossgiel, Rab
See Burns, Robert

Motion, Andrew (Peter) 1952- .... **CLC 47**
See also CA 146; DLB 40

Motley, Willard (Francis) 1909-1965...**CLC 18**
See also BW 1; CA 117; 106; DLB 76, 143

Motoori, Norinaga 1730-1801 .... **NCLC 45**

Mott, Michael (Charles Alston) 1930-...**CLC 15, 34**
See also CA 5-8R; CAAS 7; CANR 7, 29

Mountain Wolf Woman 1884-1960 .... **CLC 92**
See also CA 144; NNAL

Moure, Erin 1955- .... **CLC 88**
See also CA 113; DLB 60

Mowat, Farley (McGill) 1921-...**CLC 26; DAC; DAM MST**
See also AAYA 1; CA 1-4R; CANR 4, 24, 42, 68; CLR 20; DLB 68; INT CANR-24; JRDA; MAICYA; MTCW; SATA 3, 55

Moyers, Bill 1934- .... **CLC 74**
See also AITN 2; CA 61-64; CANR 31, 52

Mphahlele, Es'kia
See Mphahlele, Ezekiel
See also DLB 125

Mphahlele, Ezekiel 1919-1983 .... **CLC 25; BLC 3; DAM MULT**
See also Mphahlele, Es'kia
See also BW 2; CA 81-84; CANR 26

Mqhayi, S(amuel) E(dward) K(rune Loliwe) 1875-1945 ...... **TCLC 25; BLC 3; DAM MULT**
See also CA 153

Mrozek, Slawomir 1930- .... **CLC 3, 13**
See also CA 13-16R; CAAS 10; CANR 29; MTCW

Mrs. Belloc-Lowndes
See Lowndes, Marie Adelaide (Belloc)

Mtwa, Percy (?)- .... **CLC 47**

Mueller, Lisel 1924- .... **CLC 13, 51**
See also CA 93-96; DLB 105

Muir, Edwin 1887-1959 .... **TCLC 2**
See also CA 104; DLB 20, 100, 191

Muir, John 1838-1914 .... **TCLC 28**
See also CA 165; DLB 186

Mujica Lainez, Manuel 1910-1984 .... **CLC 31**
See also Lainez, Manuel Mujica
See also CA 81-84; 112; CANR 32; HW

Mukherjee, Bharati 1940- ... **CLC 53; DAM NOV**
See also BEST 89:2; CA 107; CANR 45; DLB 60; MTCW

Muldoon, Paul 1951- ...... **CLC 32, 72; DAM POET**
See also CA 113; 129; CANR 52; DLB 40; INT 129

Mulisch, Harry 1927- .... **CLC 42**
See also CA 9-12R; CANR 6, 26, 56

Mull, Martin 1943- .... **CLC 17**
See also CA 105

Mulock, Dinah Maria
See Craik, Dinah Maria (Mulock)

Munford, Robert 1737(?)-1783 .... **LC 5**
See also DLB 31

Mungo, Raymond 1946- .... **CLC 72**
See also CA 49-52; CANR 2

Munro, Alice 1931-.... **CLC 6, 10, 19, 50, 95; DAC; DAM MST, NOV; SSC 3; WLCS**
See also AITN 2; CA 33-36R; CANR 33, 53; DLB 53; MTCW; SATA 29

Munro, H(ector) H(ugh) 1870-1916
See Saki
See also CA 104; 130; CDBLB 1890-1914; DA; DAB; DAC; DAM MST, NOV; DLB 34, 162; MTCW; WLC

Murasaki, Lady .... **CMLC 1**

Murdoch, (Jean) Iris 1919-...**CLC 1, 2, 3, 4, 6, 8, 11, 15, 22, 31, 51; DAB; DAC; DAM MST, NOV**
See also CA 13-16R; CANR 8, 43, 68; CDBLB 1960 to Present; DLB 14, 194; INT CANR-8; MTCW

Murfree, Mary Noailles 1850-1922 .... **SSC 22**
See also CA 122; DLB 12, 74

Murnau, Friedrich Wilhelm
See Plumpe, Friedrich Wilhelm

Murphy, Richard 1927- .... **CLC 41**
See also CA 29-32R; DLB 40

Murphy, Sylvia 1937- .... **CLC 34**
See also CA 121

Murphy, Thomas (Bernard) 1935-...... **CLC 51**
See also CA 101

Murray, Albert L. 1916- .... **CLC 73**
See also BW 2; CA 49-52; CANR 26, 52; DLB 38

Murray, Judith Sargent 1751-1820...**NCLC 63**
See also DLB 37, 200

Murray, Les(lie) A(llan) 1938- .... **CLC 40; DAM POET**
See also CA 21-24R; CANR 11, 27, 56

Murry, J. Middleton
See Murry, John Middleton

Murry, John Middleton 1889-1957...**TCLC 16**
See also CA 118; DLB 149

Musgrave, Susan 1951- .... **CLC 13, 54**
See also CA 69-72; CANR 45

Musil, Robert (Edler von) 1880-1942 .. **TCLC 12, 68; SSC 18**
See also CA 109; CANR 55; DLB 81, 124

Muske, Carol 1945- .... **CLC 90**
See also Muske-Dukes, Carol (Anne)

Muske-Dukes, Carol (Anne) 1945-
See Muske, Carol
See also CA 65-68; CANR 32

Musset, (Louis Charles) Alfred de 1810-1857
NCLC 7
See also DLB 192

My Brother's Brother
See Chekhov, Anton (Pavlovich)

Myers, L(eopold) H(amilton) 1881-1944
TCLC 59
See also CA 157; DLB 15

Myers, Walter Dean 1937-... **CLC 35; BLC 3; DAM MULT, NOV**
See also AAYA 4, 23; BW 2; CA 33-36R; CANR 20, 42, 67; CLR 4, 16, 35; DLB 33; INT CANR-20; JRDA; MAICYA; SAAS 2; SATA 41, 71; SATA-Brief 27

Myers, Walter M.
See Myers, Walter Dean

Myles, Symon
See Follett, Ken(neth Martin)

Nabokov, Vladimir (Vladimirovich) 1899-1977
CLC 1, 2, 3, 6, 8, 11, 15, 23, 44, 46, 64; DA; DAB; DAC; DAM MST, NOV; SSC 11; WLC
See also CA 5-8R; 69-72; CANR 20; CDALB 1941-1968; DLB 2; DLBD 3; DLBY 80, 91; MTCW

Nagai Kafu 1879-1959 .... **TCLC 51**
See also Nagai Sokichi
See also DLB 180

Nagai Sokichi 1879-1959
See Nagai Kafu
See also CA 117

Nagy, Laszlo 1925-1978 .... **CLC 7**
See also CA 129; 112

Naidu, Sarojini 1879-1943 .... **TCLC 80**

Osborne, John (James) 1929-1994... **CLC 1, 2, 5, 11, 45; DA; DAB; DAC; DAM DRAM, MST; WLC**
See also CA 13-16R; 147; CANR 21, 56; CDBLB 1945-1960; DLB 13; MTCW

Osborne, Lawrence 1958- .... **CLC 50**

Oshima, Nagisa 1932- .... **CLC 20**
See also CA 116; 121

Oskison, John Milton 1874-1947 ... **TCLC 35; DAM MULT**
See also CA 144; DLB 175; NNAL

Ossian c. 3rd cent. - .... **CMLC 28**
See also Macpherson, James

Ossoli, Sarah Margaret (Fuller marchesa d') 1810-1850
See Fuller, Margaret
See also SATA 25

Ostrovsky, Alexander 1823-1886... **NCLC 30, 57**

Otero, Blas de 1916-1979 .... **CLC 11**
Scc also CA 89-92; DLB 134

Otto, Whitney 1955- .... **CLC 70**
See also CA 140

Ouida .... **TCLC 43**
See also De La Ramee, (Marie) Louise
See also DLB 18, 156

Ousmane, Sembene 1923- ..... **CLC 66; BLC 3**
See also BW 1; CA 117; 125; MTCW

Ovid 43B.C.-18(?)...**CMLC 7; DAM POET; PC 2**

Owen, Hugh
See Faust, Frederick (Schiller)

Owen, Wilfred (Edward Salter) 1893-1918 **TCLC 5, 27; DA; DAB; DAC; DAM MST, POET; PC 19; WLC**
See also CA 104; 141; CDBLB 1914-1945; DLB 20

Owens, Rochelle 1936- .... **CLC 8**
See also CA 17-20R; CAAS 2; CANR 39

Oz, Amos 1939- .... **CLC 5, 8, 11, 27, 33, 54; DAM NOV**
See also CA 53-56; CANR 27, 47, 65; MTCW

Ozick, Cynthia 1928-...**CLC 3, 7, 28, 62; DAM NOV, POP; SSC 15**
See also BEST 90:1; CA 17-20R; CANR 23, 58; DLB 28, 152; DLBY 82; INT CANR-23; MTCW

Ozu, Yasujiro 1903-1963 .... **CLC 16**
See also CA 112

Pacheco, C.
See Pessoa, Fernando (Antonio Nogueira)

Pa Chin .... **CLC 18**
See also Li Fei-kan

Pack, Robert 1929- .... **CLC 13**
See also CA 1-4R; CANR 3, 44; DLB 5

Padgett, Lewis
See Kuttner, Henry

Padilla (Lorenzo), Heberto 1932- ...... **CLC 38**
See also AITN 1; CA 123; 131; HW

Page, Jimmy 1944- .... **CLC 12**

Page, Louise 1955- .... **CLC 40**
See also CA 140

Page, P(atricia) K(athleen) 1916-...**CLC 7, 18; DAC; DAM MST; PC 12**
See also CA 53-56; CANR 4, 22, 65; DLB 68; MTCW

Page, Thomas Nelson 1853-1922 .... **SSC 23**
See also CA 118; DLB 12, 78; DLBD 13

Pagels, Elaine Hiesey 1943- ....**CLC 104**
See also CA 45-48; CANR 2, 24, 51

Paget, Violet 1856-1935
See Lee, Vernon
See also CA 104; 166

Paget-Lowe, Henry
See Lovecraft, H(oward) P(hillips)

Paglia, Camille (Anna) 1947- .... **CLC 68**
See also CA 140

Paige, Richard
See Koontz, Dean R(ay)

Paine, Thomas 1737-1809 .... **NCLC 62**
See also CDALB 1640-1865; DLB 31, 43, 73, 158

Pakenham, Antonia
See Fraser, (Lady) Antonia (Pakenham)

Palamas, Kostes 1859-1943 .... **TCLC 5**
See also CA 105

Palazzeschi, Aldo 1885-1974 .... **CLC 11**
See also CA 89-92; 53-56; DLB 114

Paley, Grace 1922-...**CLC 4, 6, 37; DAM POP; SSC 8**
See also CA 25-28R; CANR 13, 46; DLB 28; INT CANR-13; MTCW

Palin, Michael (Edward) 1943- .... **CLC 21**
See also Monty Python
See also CA 107; CANR 35; SATA 67

Palliser, Charles 1947- .... **CLC 65**
See also CA 136

Palma, Ricardo 1833-1919 .... **TCLC 29**

Pancake, Breece Dexter 1952-1979
See Pancake, Breece D'J
See also CA 123; 109

Pancake, Breece D'J .... **CLC 29**
See also Pancake, Breece Dexter
See also DLB 130

Panko, Rudy
See Gogol, Nikolai (Vasilyevich)

Papadiamantis, Alexandros 1851-1911...**TCLC 29**

Papadiamantopoulos, Johannes 1856-1910
See Moreas, Jean
See also CA 117

Papini, Giovanni 1881-1956 .... **TCLC 22**
See also CA 121

Paracelsus 1493-1541 .... **LC 14**
See also DLB 179

Parasol, Peter
See Stevens, Wallace

Pardo Bazán, Emilia 1851-1921 .... **SSC 30**

Pareto, Vilfredo 1848-1923 .... **TCLC 69**

Parfenie, Maria
See Codrescu, Andrei

Parini, Jay (Lee) 1948-........................ **CLC 54**
See also CA 97-100; CAAS 16; CANR 32

Park, Jordan
See Kornbluth, C(yril) M.; Pohl, Frederik

Park, Robert E(zra) 1864-1944 .... **TCLC 73**
See also CA 122; 165

Parker, Bert
See Ellison, Harlan (Jay)

Parker, Dorothy (Rothschild) 1893-1967 **CLC 15, 68; DAM POET; SSC 2**
See also CA 19-20; 25-28R; CAP 2; DLB 11, 45, 86; MTCW

Parker, Robert B(rown) 1932-...**CLC 27; DAM NOV, POP**
See also BEST 89:4; CA 49-52; CANR 1, 26, 52; INT CANR-26; MTCW

Parkin, Frank 1940- .... **CLC 43**
See also CA 147

Parkman, Francis, Jr. 1823-1893 .... **NCLC 12**
See also DLB 1, 30, 186

Parks, Gordon (Alexander Buchanan) 1912- **CLC 1, 16; BLC 3; DAM MULT**
See also AITN 2; BW 2; CA 41-44R; CANR 26, 66; DLB 33; SATA 8

Parmenides c. 515B.C.-c. 450B.C. .. **CMLC 22**
See also DLB 176

Parnell, Thomas 1679-1718 .... **LC 3**
See also DLB 94

Parra, Nicanor 1914- ...... **CLC 2, 102; DAM MULT; HLC**
See also CA 85-88; CANR 32; HW; MTCW

Parrish, Mary Frances
See Fisher, M(ary) F(rances) K(ennedy)

Parson
See Coleridge, Samuel Taylor

Parson Lot
See Kingsley, Charles

Partridge, Anthony
See Oppenheim, E(dward) Phillips

Pascal, Blaise 1623-1662 .... **LC 35**

Pascoli, Giovanni 1855-1912 .... **TCLC 45**

Pasolini, Pier Paolo 1922-1975 .. **CLC 20, 37, 106; PC 17**
See also CA 93-96; 61-64; CANR 63; DLB 128, 177; MTCW

Pasquini
See Silone, Ignazio

Pastan, Linda (Olenik) 1932-.. **CLC 27; DAM POET**
See also CA 61-64; CANR 18, 40, 61; DLB 5

Pasternak, Boris (Leonidovich) 1890-1960 **CLC 7, 10, 18, 63; DA; DAB; DAC; DAM MST, NOV, POET; PC 6; SSC 31; WLC**
See also CA 127; 116; MTCW

Patchen, Kenneth 1911-1972 .... **CLC 1, 2, 18; DAM POET**
See also CA 1-4R; 33-36R; CANR 3, 35; DLB 16, 48; MTCW

Pater, Walter (Horatio) 1839-1894 ... **NCLC 7**
See also CDBLB 1832-1890; DLB 57, 156

Paterson, A(ndrew) B(arton) 1864-1941 **TCLC 32**
See also CA 155; SATA 97

Paterson, Katherine (Womeldorf) 1932-...**CLC 12, 30**
See also AAYA 1; CA 21-24R; CANR 28, 59; CLR 7, 50; DLB 52; JRDA; MAICYA; MTCW; SATA 13, 53, 92

Patmore, Coventry Kersey Dighton 1823-1896 **NCLC 9**
See also DLB 35, 98

Paton, Alan (Stewart) 1903-1988...**CLC 4, 10, 25, 55, 106; DA; DAB; DAC; DAM MST, NOV; WLC**
See also CA 13-16; 125; CANR 22; CAP 1; MTCW; SATA 11; SATA-Obit 56

Paton Walsh, Gillian 1937-
See Walsh, Jill Paton
See also CANR 38; JRDA; MAICYA; SAAS 3; SATA 4, 72

Patton, George S. 1885-1945 .... **TCLC 79**

Paulding, James Kirke 1778-1860 .... **NCLC 2**
See also DLB 3, 59, 74

Paulin, Thomas Neilson 1949-
See Paulin, Tom
See also CA 123; 128

Paulin, Tom .... **CLC 37**
See also Paulin, Thomas Neilson
See also DLB 40

Paustovsky, Konstantin (Georgievich) 1892-1968 .... **CLC 40**
See also CA 93-96; 25-28R

Pavese, Cesare 1908-1950 ..**TCLC 3; PC 13; SSC 19**
See also CA 104; DLB 128, 177

Pavic, Milorad 1929-........................... **CLC 60**
See also CA 136; DLB 181

Payne, Alan
See Jakes, John (William)

Private 19022
See Manning, Frederic
Probst, Mark 1925- .... **CLC 59**
See also CA 130
Prokosch, Frederic 1908-1989 .... **CLC 4, 48**
See also CA 73-76; 128; DLB 48
Prophet, The
See Dreiser, Theodore (Herman Albert)
Prose, Francine 1947- .... **CLC 45**
See also CA 109; 112; CANR 46
Proudhon
See Cunha, Euclides (Rodrigues Pimenta) da
Proulx, Annie
See Proulx, E(dna) Annie
Proulx, E(dna) Annie 1935- ...**CLC 81; DAM
POP**
See also CA 145; CANR 65
**Proust, (Valentin-Louis-George-Eugene-)
Marcel** 1871-1922...**TCLC 7, 13, 33; DA;
DAB; DAC; DAM MST, NOV; WLC**
See also CA 104; 120; DLB 65; MTCW
Prowler, Harley
See Masters, Edgar Lee
Prus, Boleslaw 1845-1912 .... **TCLC 48**
Pryor, Richard (Franklin Lenox Thomas) 1940-
CLC 26
See also CA 122
Przybyszewski, Stanislaw 1868-1927...**T C L C
36**
See also CA 160; DLB 66
Pteleon
See Grieve, C(hristopher) M(urray)
See also DAM POET
Puckett, Lute
See Masters, Edgar Lee
Puig, Manuel 1932-1990...**CLC 3, 5, 10, 28, 65;
DAM MULT; HLC**
See also CA 45-48; CANR 2, 32, 63; DLB 113;
HW; MTCW
Pulitzer, Joseph 1847-1911 .... **TCLC 76**
See also CA 114; DLB 23
Purdy, A(lfred) W(ellington) 1918-...**CLC 3, 6,
14, 50; DAC; DAM MST, POET**
See also CA 81-84; CAAS 17; CANR 42, 66;
DLB 88
Purdy, James (Amos) 1923-...**CLC 2, 4, 10, 28,
52**
See also CA 33-36R; CAAS 1; CANR 19, 51;
DLB 2; INT CANR-19; MTCW
Pure, Simon
See Swinnerton, Frank Arthur
Pushkin, Alexander (Sergeyevich) 1799-1837
**NCLC 3, 27; DA; DAB; DAC; DAM
DRAM, MST, POET; PC 10; SSC 27; WLC**
See also SATA 61
P'u Sung-ling 1640-1715 .... **LC 3; SSC 31**
Putnam, Arthur Lee
See Alger, Horatio, Jr.
Puzo, Mario 1920-...... **CLC 1, 2, 6, 36, 107;
DAM NOV, POP**
See also CA 65-68; CANR 4, 42, 65; DLB 6;
MTCW
Pygge, Edward
See Barnes, Julian (Patrick)
Pyle, Ernest Taylor 1900-1945
See Pyle, Ernie
See also CA 115; 160
Pyle, Ernie 1900-1945 .... **TCLC 75**
See also Pyle, Ernest Taylor
See also DLB 29
Pyle, Howard 1853-1911 .... **TCLC 81**
See also CA 109; 137; CLR 22; DLB 42, 188;
DLBD 13; MAICYA; SATA 16

Pym, Barbara (Mary Crampton) 1913-1980
CLC 13, 19, 37, 111
See also CA 13-14; 97-100; CANR 13, 34; CAP
1; DLB 14; DLBY 87; MTCW
Pynchon, Thomas (Ruggles, Jr.) 1937-...**CLC 2,
3, 6, 9, 11, 18, 33, 62, 72; DA; DAB; DAC;
DAM MST, NOV, POP; SSC 14; WLC**
See also BEST 90:2; CA 17-20R; CANR 22, 46;
DLB 2, 173; MTCW
Pythagoras c. 570B.C.-c. 500B.C. ... **CMLC 22**
See also DLB 176
Q
See Quiller-Couch, SirArthur (Thomas)
Qian Zhongshu
See Ch'ien Chung-shu
Qroll
See Dagerman, Stig (Halvard)
Quarrington, Paul (Lewis) 1953- .... **CLC 65**
See also CA 129; CANR 62
Quasimodo, Salvatore 1901-1968 ...... **CLC 10**
See also CA 13-16; 25-28R; CAP 1; DLB 114;
MTCW
Quay, Stephen 1947- .... **CLC 95**
Quay, Timothy 1947- .... **CLC 95**
Queen, Ellery .... **CLC 3, 11**
See also Dannay, Frederic; Davidson, Avram; Lee,
Manfred B(ennington); Marlowe, Stephen;
Sturgeon, Theodore (Hamilton); Vance, John
Holbrook
Queen, Ellery, Jr.
See Dannay, Frederic; Lee, Manfred B(ennington)
Queneau, Raymond 1903-1976...**CLC 2, 5, 10, 42**
See also CA 77-80; 69-72; CANR 32; DLB 72;
MTCW
Quevedo, Francisco de 1580-1645 .... **LC 23**
Quiller-Couch, SirArthur (Thomas) 1863-1944
TCLC 53
See also CA 118; 166; DLB 135, 153, 190
Quin, Ann (Marie) 1936-1973 .... **CLC 6**
See also CA 9-12R; 45-48; DLB 14
Quinn, Martin
See Smith, Martin Cruz
Quinn, Peter 1947- .... **CLC 91**
Quinn, Simon
See Smith, Martin Cruz
Quiroga, Horacio (Sylvestre) 1878-1937
TCLC 20; DAM MULT; HLC
See also CA 117; 131; HW; MTCW
Quoirez, Francoise 1935- .... **CLC 9**
See also Sagan, Francoise
See also CA 49-52; CANR 6, 39; MTCW
Raabe, Wilhelm 1831-1910 .... **TCLC 45**
See also DLB 129
Rabe, David (William) 1940- .... **CLC 4, 8, 33;
DAM DRAM**
See also CA 85-88; CABS 3; CANR 59; DLB 7
Rabelais, Francois 1483-1553 ..... **LC 5; DA;
DAB; DAC; DAM MST; WLC**
Rabinovitch, Sholem 1859-1916
See Aleichem, Sholom
See also CA 104
Rachilde 1860-1953 .... **TCLC 67**
See also DLB 123, 192
Racine, Jean 1639-1699 .. **LC 28; DAB; DAM
MST**
Radcliffe, Ann (Ward) 1764-1823...**NCLC 6, 55**
See also DLB 39, 178
Radiguet, Raymond 1903-1923 .... **TCLC 29**
See also CA 162; DLB 65
Radnoti, Miklos 1909-1944 .... **TCLC 16**
See also CA 118
Rado, James 1939- ....**CLC 17**
See also CA 105

Radvanyi, Netty 1900-1983
See Seghers, Anna
See also CA 85-88; 110
Rae, Ben
See Griffiths, Trevor
Raeburn, John (Hay) 1941- .... **CLC 34**
See also CA 57-60
Ragni, Gerome 1942-1991 .... **CLC 17**
See also CA 105; 134
Rahv, Philip 1908-1973 .... **CLC 24**
See also Greenberg, Ivan
See also DLB 137
Raimund, Ferdinand Jakob 1790-1836
NCLC 69
See also DLB 90
Raine, Craig 1944- .... **CLC 32, 103**
See also CA 108; CANR 29, 51; DLB 40
Raine, Kathleen (Jessie) 1908- .... **CLC 7, 45**
See also CA 85-88; CANR 46; DLB 20; MTCW
Rainis, Janis 1865-1929 .... **TCLC 29**
Rakosi, Carl 1903-............................. **CLC 47**
See also Rawley, Callman
See also CAAS 5; DLB 193
Raleigh, Richard
See Lovecraft, H(oward) P(hillips)
Raleigh, Sir Walter 1554(?)-1618... **LC 31, 39**
See also CDBLB Before 1660; DLB 172
Rallentando, H. P.
See Sayers, Dorothy L(eigh)
Ramal, Walter
See de la Mare, Walter (John)
Ramon, Juan
See Jimenez (Mantecon), Juan Ramon
Ramos, Graciliano 1892-1953 .... **TCLC 32**
Rampersad, Arnold 1941- .... **CLC 44**
See also BW 2; CA 127; 133; DLB 111; INT
133
Rampling, Anne
See Rice, Anne
Ramsay, Allan 1684(?)-1758 .... **LC 29**
See also DLB 95
Ramuz, Charles-Ferdinand 1878-1947...**TCLC
33**
See also CA 165
Rand, Ayn 1905-1982...**CLC 3, 30, 44, 79; DA;
DAC; DAM MST, NOV, POP; WLC**
See also AAYA 10; CA 13-16R; 105; CANR 27;
MTCW
Randall, Dudley (Felker) 1914- .....**CLC 1;
BLC 3; DAM MULT**
See also BW 1; CA 25-28R; CANR 23; DLB 41
Randall, Robert
See Silverberg, Robert
Ranger, Ken
See Creasey, John
Ransom, John Crowe 1888-1974...**CLC 2, 4, 5,
11, 24; DAM POET**
See also CA 5-8R; 49-52; CANR 6, 34; DLB 45,
63; MTCW
Rao, Raja 1909- .... **CLC 25, 56; DAM NOV**
See also CA 73-76; CANR 51; MTCW
Raphael, Frederic (Michael) 1931-...**CLC 2, 14**
See also CA 1-4R; CANR 1; DLB 14
Ratcliffe, James P.
See Mencken, H(enry) L(ouis)
Rathbone, Julian 1935- .... **CLC 41**
See also CA 101; CANR 34
Rattigan, Terence (Mervyn) 1911-1977...**CLC
7; DAM DRAM**
See also CA 85-88; 73-76; CDBLB 1945-1960;
DLB 13; MTCW
Ratushinskaya, Irina 1954-................ **CLC 54**
See also CA 129; CANR 68

Roth, Philip (Milton) 1933-...CLC 1, 2, 3, 4, 6, 9, 15, 22, 31, 47, 66, 86; DA; DAB; DAC; DAM MST, NOV, POP; SSC 26; WLC
See also BEST 90:3; CA 1-4R; CANR 1, 22, 36, 55; CDALB 1968-1988; DLB 2, 28, 173; DLBY 82; MTCW
Rothenberg, Jerome 1931- .... CLC 6, 57
See also CA 45-48; CANR 1; DLB 5, 193
Roumain, Jacques (Jean Baptiste) 1907-1944 TCLC 19; BLC 3; DAM MULT
See also BW 1; CA 117; 125
Rourke, Constance (Mayfield) 1885-1941 TCLC 12
See also CA 107; YABC 1
Rousseau, Jean-Baptiste 1671-1741 ....LC 9
Rousseau, Jean-Jacques 1712-1778...LC 14, 36; DA; DAB; DAC; DAM MST; WLC
Roussel, Raymond 1877-1933 .... TCLC 20
See also CA 117
Rovit, Earl (Herbert) 1927- .... CLC 7
See also CA 5-8R; CANR 12
Rowe, Elizabeth Singer 1674-1737 ...... LC 44
See also DLB 39, 95
Rowe, Nicholas 1674-1718 .... LC 8
See also DLB 84
Rowley, Ames Dorrance
See Lovecraft, H(oward) P(hillips)
Rowson, Susanna Haswell 1762(?)-1824 NCLC 5, 69
See also DLB 37, 200
Roy, Arundhati 1960(?)- .... CLC 109
See also CA 163; DLBY 97
Roy, Gabrielle 1909-1983 .CLC 10, 14; DAB; DAC; DAM MST
See also CA 53-56; 110; CANR 5, 61; DLB 68; MTCW
Royko, Mike 1932-1997 .... CLC 109
See also CA 89-92; 157; CANR 26
Rozewicz, Tadeusz 1921- ..... CLC 9, 23; DAM POET
See also CA 108; CANR 36, 66; MTCW
Ruark, Gibbons 1941- .... CLC 3
See also CA 33-36R; CAAS 23; CANR 14, 31, 57; DLB 120
Rubens, Bernice (Ruth) 1923- ...... CLC 19, 31
See also CA 25-28R; CANR 33, 65; DLB 14; MTCW
Rubin, Harold
See Robbins, Harold
Rudkin, (James) David 1936- .... CLC 14
See also CA 89-92; DLB 13
Rudnik, Raphael 1933- .... CLC 7
See also CA 29-32R
Ruffian, M.
See Hasek, Jaroslav (Matej Frantisek)
Ruiz, Jose Martinez .... CLC 11
See also Martinez Ruiz, Jose
Rukeyser, Muriel 1913-1980...CLC 6, 10, 15, 27; DAM POET; PC 12
See also CA 5-8R; 93-96; CANR 26, 60; DLB 48; MTCW; SATA-Obit 22
Rule, Jane (Vance) 1931- .... CLC 27
See also CA 25-28R; CAAS 18; CANR 12; DLB 60
Rulfo, Juan 1918-1986 .... CLC 8, 80; DAM MULT; HLC; SSC 25
See also CA 85-88; 118; CANR 26; DLB 113; HW; MTCW
Rumi, Jalal al-Din 1297-1373 .... CMLC 20
Runeberg, Johan 1804-1877 .... NCLC 41
Runyon, (Alfred) Damon 1884(?)-1946...TCLC 10
See also CA 107; 165; DLB 11, 86, 171

Rush, Norman 1933- .... CLC 44
See also CA 121; 126; INT 126
Rushdie, (Ahmed) Salman 1947-...CLC 23, 31, 55, 100; DAB; DAC; DAM MST, NOV, POP; WLCS
See also BEST 89:3; CA 108; 111; CANR 33, 56; DLB 194; INT 111; MTCW
Rushforth, Peter (Scott) 1945- .... CLC 19
See also CA 101
Ruskin, John 1819-1900 .... TCLC 63
See also CA 114; 129; CDBLB 1832-1890; DLB 55, 163, 190; SATA 24
Russ, Joanna 1937- .... CLC 15
See also CANR 11, 31, 65; DLB 8; MTCW
Russell, George William 1867-1935
See Baker, Jean H.
See also CA 104; 153; CDBLB 1890-1914, DAM POET
Russell, (Henry) Ken(neth Alfred) 1927-CLC 16
See also CA 105
Russell, William Martin 1947- .... CLC 60
See also CA 164
Rutherford, Mark .... TCLC 25
See also White, William Hale
See also DLB 18
Ruyslinck, Ward 1929- .... CLC 14
See also Belser, Reimond Karel Maria de
Ryan, Cornelius (John) 1920-1974 ...... CLC 7
See also CA 69-72; 53-56; CANR 38
Ryan, Michael 1946- .... CLC 65
See also CA 49-52; DLBY 82
Ryan, Tim
See Dent, Lester
Rybakov, Anatoli (Naumovich) 1911- .. C L C 23, 53
See also CA 126; 135; SATA 79
Ryder, Jonathan
See Ludlum, Robert
Ryga, George 1932-1987 .... CLC 14; DAC; DAM MST
See also CA 101; 124; CANR 43; DLB 60
S. H.
See Hartmann, Sadakichi
S. S.
See Sassoon, Siegfried (Lorraine)
Saba, Umberto 1883-1957 .... TCLC 33
See also CA 144; DLB 114
Sabatini, Rafael 1875-1950 .... TCLC 47
See also CA 162
Sabato, Ernesto (R.) 1911-...CLC 10, 23; DAM MULT; HLC
See also CA 97-100; CANR 32, 65; DLB 145; HW; MTCW
Sa-Carniero, Mario de 1890-1916 .. TCLC 83
Sacastru, Martin
See Bioy Casares, Adolfo
Sacher-Masoch, Leopold von 1836(?)-1895 NCLC 31
Sachs, Marilyn (Stickle) 1927- .... CLC 35
See also AAYA 2; CA 17-20R; CANR 13, 47; CLR 2; JRDA; MAICYA; SAAS 2; SATA 3, 68
Sachs, Nelly 1891-1970 .... CLC 14, 98
See also CA 17-18; 25-28R; CAP 2
Sackler, Howard (Oliver) 1929-1982...CLC 14
See also CA 61-64; 108; CANR 30; DLB 7
Sacks, Oliver (Wolf) 1933- .... CLC 67
See also CA 53-56; CANR 28, 50; INT CANR-28; MTCW
Sadakichi
See Hartmann, Sadakichi
Sade, Donatien Alphonse Francois, Comte de 1740-1814 .... NCLC 47

Sadoff, Ira 1945- .... CLC 9
See also CA 53-56; CANR 5, 21; DLB 120
Saetone
See Camus, Albert
Safire, William 1929- .... CLC 10
See also CA 17-20R; CANR 31, 54
Sagan, Carl (Edward) 1934-1996...CLC 30, 112
See also AAYA 2; CA 25-28R; 155; CANR 11, 36; MTCW; SATA 58; SATA-Obit 94
Sagan, Francoise .... CLC 3, 6, 9, 17, 36
See also Quoirez, Francoise
See also DLB 83
Sahgal, Nayantara (Pandit) 1927- ...... CLC 41
See also CA 9-12R; CANR 11
Saint, H(arry) F. 1941- .... CLC 50
See also CA 127

St. Aubin de Teran, Lisa 1953-
See Teran, Lisa St. Aubin de
See also CA 118; 126; INT 126

Saint Birgitta of Sweden c. 1303-1373...CMLC 24
Sainte-Beuve, Charles Augustin 1804-1869 NCLC 5
Saint-Exupery, Antoine (Jean Baptiste Marie Roger) de 1900-1944 ..... TCLC 2, 56; DAM NOV; WLC
See also CA 108; 132; CLR 10; DLB 72; MAICYA; MTCW; SATA 20
St. John, David
See Hunt, E(verette) Howard, (Jr.)
Saint-John Perse
See Leger, (Marie-Rene Auguste) Alexis Saint-Leger
Saintsbury, George (Edward Bateman) 1845-1933 .... TCLC 31
See also CA 160; DLB 57, 149
Sait Faik .... TCLC 23
See also Abasiyanik, Sait Faik
Saki .... TCLC 3; SSC 12
See also Munro, H(ector) H(ugh)
Sala, George Augustus .... NCLC 46
Salama, Hannu 1936- .... CLC 18
Salamanca, J(ack) R(ichard) 1922-...CLC 4, 15
See also CA 25-28R
Sale, J. Kirkpatrick
See Sale, Kirkpatrick
Sale, Kirkpatrick 1937- .... CLC 68
See also CA 13-16R; CANR 10
Salinas, Luis Omar 1937- .... CLC 90; DAM MULT; HLC
See also CA 131; DLB 82; HW
Salinas (y Serrano), Pedro 1891(?)-1951 TCLC 17
See also CA 117; DLB 134
Salinger, J(erome) D(avid) 1919-...CLC 1, 3, 8, 12, 55, 56; DA; DAB; DAC; DAM MST, NOV, POP; SSC 2, 28; WLC
See also AAYA 2; CA 5-8R; CANR 39; CDALB 1941-1968; CLR 18; DLB 2, 102, 173; MAICYA; MTCW; SATA 67
Salisbury, John
See Caute, (John) David
Salter, James 1925- .... CLC 7, 52, 59
See also CA 73-76; DLB 130
Saltus, Edgar (Everton) 1855-1921 .. TCLC 8
See also CA 105
Saltykov, Mikhail Evgrafovich 1826-1889 NCLC 16
Samarakis, Antonis 1919- .... CLC 5
See also CA 25-28R; CAAS 16; CANR 36
Sanchez, Florencio 1875-1910 .... TCLC 37
See also CA 153; HW

Sanchez, Luis Rafael 1936- .... CLC 23
See also CA 128; DLB 145; HW

Sanchez, Sonia 1934- ... CLC 5; BLC 3; DAM
MULT; PC 9
See also BW 2; CA 33-36R; CANR 24, 49; CLR
18; DLB 41; DLBD 8; MAICYA; MTCW;
SATA 22

Sand, George 1804-1876 .. NCLC 2, 42, 57;
DA; DAB; DAC; DAM MST, NOV; WLC
See also DLB 119, 192

Sandburg, Carl (August) 1878-1967...CLC 1, 4,
10, 15, 35; DA; DAB; DAC; DAM MST,
POET; PC 2; WLC
See also AAYA 24; CA 5-8R; 25-28R; CANR
35; CDALB 1865-1917; DLB 17, 54;
MAICYA; MTCW; SATA 8

Sandburg, Charles
See Sandburg, Carl (August)

Sandburg, Charles A.
See Sandburg, Carl (August)

Sanders, (James) Ed(ward) 1939- ...... CLC 53
See also CA 13-16R; CAAS 21; CANR 13, 44;
DLB 16

Sanders, Lawrence 1920-1998...CLC 41; DAM
POP
See also BEST 89:4; CA 81-84; 165; CANR 33,
62; MTCW

Sanders, Noah
See Blount, Roy (Alton), Jr.

Sanders, Winston P.
See Anderson, Poul (William)

Sandoz, Mari(e Susette) 1896-1966 ... CLC 28
See also CA 1-4R; 25-28R; CANR 17, 64; DLB
9; MTCW; SATA 5

Saner, Reg(inald Anthony) 1931- .... CLC 9
See also CA 65-68

Sannazaro, Jacopo 1456(?)-1530 .... LC 8

Sansom, William 1912-1976...CLC 2, 6; DAM
NOV; SSC 21
See also CA 5-8R; 65-68; CANR 42; DLB 139;
MTCW

Santayana, George 1863-1952 .... TCLC 40
See also CA 115; DLB 54, 71; DLBD 13

Santiago, Danny .... CLC 33
See also James, Daniel (Lewis)
See also DLB 122

Santmyer, Helen Hoover 1895-1986 .. CLC 33
See also CA 1-4R; 118; CANR 15, 33; DLBY
84; MTCW

Santoka, Taneda 1882-1940 .... TCLC 72

Santos, Bienvenido N(uqui) 1911-1996...C L C
22; DAM MULT
See also CA 101; 151; CANR 19, 46

Sapper .... TCLC 44
See also McNeile, Herman Cyril

Sapphire 1950- .... CLC 99

Sappho fl. 6th cent. B.C.- .... CMLC 3; DAM
POET; PC 5
See also DLB 176

Sarduy, Severo 1937-1993 .... CLC 6, 97
See also CA 89-92; 142; CANR 58; DLB 113; HW

Sargeson, Frank 1903-1982 .... CLC 31
See also CA 25-28R; 106; CANR 38

Sarmiento, Felix Ruben Garcia
See Dario, Ruben

Saroyan, William 1908-1981...CLC 1, 8, 10, 29,
34, 56; DA; DAB; DAC; DAM DRAM,
MST, NOV; SSC 21; WLC
See also CA 5-8R; 103; CANR 30; DLB 7, 9, 86;
DLBY 81; MTCW; SATA 23; SATA-Obit 24

Sarraute, Nathalie 1900-...CLC 1, 2, 4, 8, 10, 31,
80
See also CA 9-12R; CANR 23, 66; DLB 83; MTCW

Sarton, (Eleanor) May 1912-1995...CLC 4, 14,
49, 91; DAM POET
See also CA 1-4R; 149; CANR 1, 34, 55; DLB
48; DLBY 81; INT CANR-34; MTCW; SATA
36; SATA-Obit 86

Sartre, Jean-Paul 1905-1980...CLC 1, 4, 7, 9,
13, 18, 24, 44, 50, 52; DA; DAB; DAC;
DAM DRAM, MST, NOV; DC 3; WLC
See also CA 9-12R; 97-100; CANR 21; DLB 72;
MTCW

Sassoon, Siegfried (Lorraine) 1886-1967
CLC 36; DAB; DAM MST, NOV, POET;
PC 12
See also CA 104; 25-28R; CANR 36; DLB 20,
191; MTCW

Satterfield, Charles
See Pohl, Frederik

Saul, John (W. III) 1942- .... CLC 46; DAM
NOV, POP
See also AAYA 10; BEST 90:4; CA 81-84;
CANR 16, 40; SATA 98

Saunders, Caleb
See Heinlein, Robert A(nson)

Saura (Atares), Carlos 1932- .... CLC 20
See also CA 114; 131; HW

Sauser-Hall, Frederic 1887-1961 .... CLC 18
See also Cendrars, Blaise
See also CA 102; 93-96; CANR 36, 62; MTCW

Saussure, Ferdinand de 1857-1913 . TCLC 49

Savage, Catharine
See Brosman, Catharine Savage

Savage, Thomas 1915- .... CLC 40
See also CA 126; 132; CAAS 15; INT 132

Savan, Glenn 19(?)- .... CLC 50

Sayers, Dorothy L(eigh) 1893-1957 . TCLC 2,
15; DAM POP
See also CA 104; 119; CANR 60; CDBLB 1914-
1945; DLB 10, 36, 77, 100; MTCW

Sayers, Valerie 1952- .... CLC 50
See also CA 134; CANR 61

Sayles, John (Thomas) 1950- .... CLC 7, 10, 14
See also CA 57-60; CANR 41; DLB 44

Scammell, Michael 1935- .... CLC 34
See also CA 156

Scannell, Vernon 1922- .... CLC 49
See also CA 5-8R; CANR 8, 24, 57; DLB 27;
SATA 59

Scarlett, Susan
See Streatfeild, (Mary) Noel

Schaeffer, Susan Fromberg 1941-..CLC 6, 11, 22
See also CA 49-52; CANR 18, 65; DLB 28;
MTCW; SATA 22

Schary, Jill
See Robinson, Jill

Schell, Jonathan 1943- .... CLC 35
See also CA 73-76; CANR 12

Schelling, Friedrich Wilhelm Joseph von 1775-
1854 .... NCLC 30
See also DLB 90

Schendel, Arthur van 1874-1946 .... TCLC 56

Scherer, Jean-Marie Maurice 1920-
See Rohmer, Eric
See also CA 110

Schevill, James (Erwin) 1920- .... CLC 7
See also CA 5-8R; CAAS 12

Schiller, Friedrich 1759-1805 .. NCLC 39, 69;
DAM DRAM
See also DLB 94

Schisgal, Murray (Joseph) 1926- .... CLC 6
See also CA 21-24R; CANR 48

Schlee, Ann 1934- .... CLC 35
See also CA 101; CANR 29; SATA 44; SATA-
Brief 36

Schlegel, August Wilhelm von 1767-1845
NCLC 15
See also DLB 94

Schlegel, Friedrich 1772-1829 .... NCLC 45
See also DLB 90

Schlegel, Johann Elias (von) 1719(?)-1749
LC 5

Schlesinger, Arthur M(eier), Jr. 1917-
CLC 84
See also AITN 1; CA 1-4R; CANR 1, 28, 58;
DLB 17; INT CANR-28; MTCW; SATA 61

Schmidt, Arno (Otto) 1914-1979 .... CLC 56
See also CA 128; 109; DLB 69

Schmitz, Aron Hector 1861-1928
See Svevo, Italo
See also CA 104; 122; MTCW

Schnackenberg, Gjertrud 1953- .... CLC 40
See also CA 116; DLB 120

Schneider, Leonard Alfred 1925-1966
See Bruce, Lenny
See also CA 89-92

Schnitzler, Arthur 1862-1931 ....TCLC 4;
SSC 15
See also CA 104; DLB 81, 118

Schoenberg, Arnold 1874-1951 .... TCLC 75
See also CA 109

Schonberg, Arnold
See Schoenberg, Arnold

Schopenhauer, Arthur 1788-1860 ... NCLC 51
See also DLB 90

Schor, Sandra (M.) 1932(?)-1990 .... CLC 65
See also CA 132

Schorer, Mark 1908-1977 .... CLC 9
See also CA 5-8R; 73-76; CANR 7; DLB 103

Schrader, Paul (Joseph) 1946- .... CLC 26
See also CA 37-40R; CANR 41; DLB 44

Schreiner, Olive (Emilie Albertina) 1855-1920
TCLC 9
See also CA 105; 154; DLB 18, 156, 190

Schulberg, Budd (Wilson) 1914- .... CLC 7, 48
See also CA 25-28R; CANR 19; DLB 6, 26, 28;
DLBY 81

Schulz, Bruno 1892-1942...TCLC 5, 51; SSC
13
See also CA 115; 123

Schulz, Charles M(onroe) 1922- .... CLC 12
See also CA 9-12R; CANR 6; INT CANR-6;
SATA 10

Schumacher, E(rnst) F(riedrich) 1911-1977
CLC 80
See also CA 81-84; 73-76; CANR 34

Schuyler, James Marcus 1923-1991....CLC 5,
23; DAM POET
See also CA 101; 134; DLB 5, 169; INT 101

Schwartz, Delmore (David) 1913-1966... C L C
2, 4, 10, 45, 87; PC 8
See also CA 17-18; 25-28R; CANR 35; CAP 2;
DLB 28, 48; MTCW

Schwartz, Ernst
See Ozu, Yasujiro

Schwartz, John Burnham 1965- .... CLC 59
See also CA 132

Schwartz, Lynne Sharon 1939- .... CLC 31
See also CA 103; CANR 44

Schwartz, Muriel A.
See Eliot, T(homas) S(tearns)

Schwarz-Bart, Andre 1928- .... CLC 2, 4
See also CA 89-92

Schwarz-Bart, Simone 1938- ... CLC 7; BLCS
See also BW 2; CA 97-100

Schwob, (Mayer Andre) Marcel 1867-1905
TCLC 20
See also CA 117; DLB 123

Spacks, Barry (Bernard) 1931- .... **CLC 14**
See also CA 154; CANR 33; DLB 105
Spanidou, Irini 1946- .... **CLC 44**
Spark, Muriel (Sarah) 1918-...**CLC 2, 3, 5, 8,
13, 18, 40, 94; DAB; DAC; DAM MST,
NOV; SSC 10**
See also CA 5-8R; CANR 12, 36; CDBLB 1945-
1960; DLB 15, 139; INT CANR-12; MTCW
Spaulding, Douglas
See Bradbury, Ray (Douglas)
Spaulding, Leonard
See Bradbury, Ray (Douglas)
Spence, J. A. D.
See Eliot, T(homas) S(tearns)
Spencer, Elizabeth 1921- .... **CLC 22**
See also CA 13-16R; CANR 32, 65; DLB 6;
MTCW; SATA 14
Spencer, Leonard G.
See Silverberg, Robert
Spencer, Scott 1945- .... **CLC 30**
See also CA 113; CANR 51; DLBY 86
Spender, Stephen (Harold) 1909-1995...**C L C
1, 2, 5, 10, 41, 91; DAM POET**
See also CA 9-12R; 149; CANR 31, 54; CDBLB
1945-1960; DLB 20; MTCW
Spengler, Oswald (Arnold Gottfried) 1880-1936
TCLC 25
See also CA 118
Spenser, Edmund 1552(?)-1599...**LC 5, 39; DA;
DAB; DAC; DAM MST, POET; PC 8;
WLC**
See also CDBLB Before 1660; DLB 167
Spicer, Jack 1925-1965...**CLC 8, 18, 72; DAM
POET**
See also CA 85-88; DLB 5, 16, 193
Spiegelman, Art 1948- .... **CLC 76**
See also AAYA 10; CA 125; CANR 41, 55
Spielberg, Peter 1929-.......................... **CLC 6**
See also CA 5-8R; CANR 4, 48; DLBY 81
Spielberg, Steven 1947- .... **CLC 20**
See also AAYA 8, 24; CA 77-80; CANR 32;
SATA 32
Spillane, Frank Morrison 1918-
See Spillane, Mickey
See also CA 25-28R; CANR 28, 63; MTCW;
SATA 66
Spillane, Mickey .... **CLC 3, 13**
See also Spillane, Frank Morrison
Spinoza, Benedictus de 1632-1677 .... **LC 9**
Spinrad, Norman (Richard) 1940- ..... **CLC 46**
See also CA 37-40R; CAAS 19; CANR 20; DLB
8; INT CANR-20
Spitteler, Carl (Friedrich Georg) 1845-1924
TCLC 12
See also CA 109; DLB 129
Spivack, Kathleen (Romola Drucker) 1938-
CLC 6
See also CA 49-52
Spoto, Donald 1941- .... **CLC 39**
See also CA 65-68; CANR 11, 57
Springsteen, Bruce (F.) 1949- .... **CLC 17**
See also CA 111
Spurling, Hilary 1940- .... **CLC 34**
See also CA 104; CANR 25, 52
Spyker, John Howland
See Elman, Richard (Martin)
Squires, (James) Radcliffe 1917-1993...**CLC 51**
See also CA 1-4R; 140; CANR 6, 21
Srivastava, Dhanpat Rai 1880(?)-1936
See Premchand
See also CA 118
Stacy, Donald
See Pohl, Frederik

Stael, Germaine de 1766-1817
See Stael-Holstein, Anne Louise Germaine
Necker Baronn
See also DLB 119
Stael-Holstein, Anne Louise Germaine Necker
Baronn 1766-1817 .... **NCLC 3**
See also Stael, Germaine de
See also DLB 192
Stafford, Jean 1915-1979...**CLC 4, 7, 19, 68;
SSC 26**
See also CA 1-4R; 85-88; CANR 3, 65; DLB 2,
173; MTCW; SATA-Obit 22
Stafford, William (Edgar) 1914-1993...**CLC 4,
7, 29; DAM POET**
See also CA 5-8R; 142; CAAS 3; CANR 5, 22;
DLB 5; INT CANR-22
Stagnelius, Eric Johan 1793-1823 ... **NCLC 61**
Staines, Trevor
See Brunner, John (Kilian Houston)
Stairs, Gordon
See Austin, Mary (Hunter)
Stannard, Martin 1947- .... **CLC 44**
See also CA 142; DLB 155
Stanton, Elizabeth Cady 1815-1902...**TCLC 73**
See also DLB 79
Stanton, Maura 1946- .... **CLC 9**
See also CA 89-92; CANR 15; DLB 120
Stanton, Schuyler
See Baum, L(yman) Frank
Stapledon, (William) Olaf 1886-1950
TCLC 22
See also CA 111; 162; DLB 15
Starbuck, George (Edwin) 1931-1996...**C L C
53; DAM POET**
See also CA 21-24R; 153; CANR 23
Stark, Richard
See Westlake, Donald E(dwin)
Staunton, Schuyler
See Baum, L(yman) Frank
Stead, Christina (Ellen) 1902-1983... **C L C
2, 5, 8, 32, 80**
See also CA 13-16R; 109; CANR 33, 40; MTCW
Stead, William Thomas 1849-1912 . **TCLC 48**
Steele, Richard 1672-1729 .... **LC 18**
See also CDBLB 1660-1789; DLB 84, 101
Steele, Timothy (Reid) 1948- .... **CLC 45**
See also CA 93-96; CANR 16, 50; DLB 120
Steffens, (Joseph) Lincoln 1866-1936
TCLC 20
See also CA 117
Stegner, Wallace (Earle) 1909-1993...**CLC 9,
49, 81; DAM NOV; SSC 27**
See also AITN 1; BEST 90:3; CA 1-4R; 141;
CAAS 9; CANR 1, 21, 46; DLB 9; DLBY 93;
MTCW
Stein, Gertrude 1874-1946...**TCLC 1, 6, 28,
48; DA; DAB; DAC; DAM MST, NOV,
POET; PC 18; WLC**
See also CA 104; 132; CDALB 1917-1929; DLB
4, 54, 86; DLBD 15; MTCW
Steinbeck, John (Ernst) 1902-1968...**CLC 1, 5,
9, 13, 21, 34, 45, 75; DA; DAB; DAC; DAM
DRAM, MST, NOV; SSC 11; WLC**
See also AAYA 12; CA 1-4R; 25-28R; CANR 1,
35; CDALB 1929-1941; DLB 7, 9; DLBD 2;
MTCW; SATA 9
Steinem, Gloria 1934- .... **CLC 63**
See also CA 53-56; CANR 28, 51; MTCW
Steiner, George 1929-.... **CLC 24; DAM NOV**
See also CA 73-76; CANR 31, 67; DLB 67;
MTCW; SATA 62
Steiner, K. Leslie
See Delany, Samuel R(ay, Jr.)

Steiner, Rudolf 1861-1925 .... **TCLC 13**
See also CA 107
Stendhal 1783-1842...**NCLC 23, 46; DA; DAB;
DAC; DAM MST, NOV; SSC 27; WLC**
See also DLB 119
Stephen, Adeline Virginia
See Woolf, (Adeline) Virginia
Stephen, SirLeslie 1832-1904 .... **TCLC 23**
See also CA 123; DLB 57, 144, 190
Stephen, Sir Leslie
See Stephen, SirLeslie
Stephen, Virginia
See Woolf, (Adeline) Virginia
Stephens, James 1882(?)-1950 .... **TCLC 4**
See also CA 104; DLB 19, 153, 162
Stephens, Reed
See Donaldson, Stephen R.
Steptoe, Lydia
See Barnes, Djuna
Sterchi, Beat 1949- .... **CLC 65**
Sterling, Brett
See Bradbury, Ray (Douglas); Hamilton, Edmond
Sterling, Bruce 1954- .... **CLC 72**
See also CA 119; CANR 44
Sterling, George 1869-1926 .... **TCLC 20**
See also CA 117; 165; DLB 54
Stern, Gerald 1925- .... **CLC 40, 100**
See also CA 81-84; CANR 28; DLB 105
Stern, Richard (Gustave) 1928- ..... **CLC 4, 39**
See also CA 1-4R; CANR 1, 25, 52; DLBY 87;
INT CANR-25
Sternberg, Josef von 1894-1969......... **CLC 20**
See also CA 81-84
Sterne, Laurence 1713-1768 ...... **LC 2; DA;
DAB; DAC; DAM MST, NOV; WLC**
See also CDBLB 1660-1789; DLB 39
Sternheim, (William Adolf) Carl 1878-1942
TCLC 8
See also CA 105; DLB 56, 118
Stevens, Mark 1951- .... **CLC 34**
See also CA 122
Stevens, Wallace 1879-1955...**TCLC 3, 12, 45;
DA; DAB; DAC; DAM MST, POET; PC 6;
WLC**
See also CA 104; 124; CDALB 1929-1941; DLB
54; MTCW
Stevenson, Anne (Katharine) 1933-...**CLC 7, 33**
See also CA 17-20R; CAAS 9; CANR 9, 33; DLB
40; MTCW
Stevenson, Robert Louis (Balfour) 1850-1894
**NCLC 5, 14, 63; DA; DAB; DAC; DAM
MST, NOV; SSC 11; WLC**
See also AAYA 24; CDBLB 1890-1914; CLR 10,
11; DLB 18, 57, 141, 156, 174; DLBD 13;
JRDA; MAICYA; YABC 2
Stewart, J(ohn) I(nnes) M(ackintosh) 1906-1994
CLC 7, 14, 32
See also CA 85-88; 147; CAAS 3; CANR 47;
MTCW
Stewart, Mary (Florence Elinor) 1916-..**CLC
7, 35; DAB**
See also CA 1-4R; CANR 1, 59; SATA 12
Stewart, Mary Rainbow
See Stewart, Mary (Florence Elinor)
Stifle, June
See Campbell, Maria
Stifter, Adalbert 1805-1868...**NCLC 41; SSC 28**
See also DLB 133
Still, James 1906- .... **CLC 49**
See also CA 65-68; CAAS 17; CANR 10, 26;
DLB 9; SATA 29
Sting
See Sumner, Gordon Matthew

Stirling, Arthur
See Sinclair, Upton (Beall)
Stitt, Milan 1941- .... **CLC 29**
See also CA 69-72
Stockton, Francis Richard 1834-1902
See Stockton, Frank R.
See also CA 108; 137; MAICYA; SATA 44
Stockton, Frank R. .... **TCLC 47**
See also Stockton, Francis Richard
See also DLB 42, 74; DLBD 13; SATA-Brief 32
Stoddard, Charles
See Kuttner, Henry
Stoker, Abraham 1847-1912
See Stoker, Bram
See also CA 105; 150; DA; DAC; DAM MST,
NOV; SATA 29
Stoker, Bram 1847-1912...**TCLC 8; DAB; WLC**
See also Stoker, Abraham
See also AAYA 23; CDBLB 1890-1914; DLB
36, 70, 178
Stolz, Mary (Slattery) 1920- .... **CLC 12**
See also AAYA 8; AITN 1; CA 5-8R; CANR 13,
41; JRDA; MAICYA; SAAS 3; SATA 10, 71
Stone, Irving 1903-1989 .. **CLC 7; DAM POP**
See also AITN 1; CA 1-4R; 129; CAAS 3; CANR
1, 23; INT CANR-23; MTCW; SATA 3;
SATA-Obit 64
Stone, Oliver (William) 1946- .... **CLC 73**
See also AAYA 15; CA 110; CANR 55
Stone, Robert (Anthony) 1937-...**CLC 5, 23, 42**
See also CA 85-88; CANR 23, 66; DLB 152; INT
CANR-23; MTCW
Stone, Zachary
See Follett, Ken(neth Martin)
Stoppard, Tom 1937-...**CLC 1, 3, 4, 5, 8, 15, 29,
34, 63, 91; DA; DAB; DAC; DAM DRAM,
MST; DC 6; WLC**
See also CA 81-84; CANR 39, 67; CDBLB 1960
to Present; DLB 13; DLBY 85; MTCW
Storey, David (Malcolm) 1933-...**CLC 2, 4, 5, 8;
DAM DRAM**
See also CA 81-84; CANR 36; DLB 13, 14;
MTCW
Storm, Hyemeyohsts 1935- .... **CLC 3; DAM
MULT**
See also CA 81-84; CANR 45; NNAL
Storm, (Hans) Theodor (Woldsen) 1817-1888
NCLC 1; SSC 27
See also DLB 129
Storni, Alfonsina 1892-1938 .. **TCLC 5; DAM
MULT; HLC**
See also CA 104; 131; HW
Stoughton, William 1631-1701 .... **LC 38**
See also DLB 24
Stout, Rex (Todhunter) 1886-1975....... **CLC 3**
See also AITN 2; CA 61-64
Stow, (Julian) Randolph 1935- ..... **CLC 23, 48**
See also CA 13-16R; CANR 33; MTCW
Stowe, Harriet (Elizabeth) Beecher 1811-1896
**NCLC 3, 50; DA; DAB; DAC; DAM MST,
NOV; WLC**
See also CDALB 1865-1917; DLB 1, 12, 42, 74,
189; JRDA; MAICYA; YABC 1
Strachey, (Giles) Lytton 1880-1932...**TCLC 12**
See also CA 110; DLB 149; DLBD 10
Strand, Mark 1934- . **CLC 6, 18, 41, 71; DAM
POET**
See also CA 21-24R; CANR 40, 65; DLB 5;
SATA 41
Straub, Peter (Francis) 1943- ... **CLC 28, 107;
DAM POP**
See also BEST 89:1; CA 85-88; CANR 28, 65;
DLBY 84; MTCW

Strauss, Botho 1944- .... **CLC 22**
See also CA 157; DLB 124
Streatfeild, (Mary) Noel 1895(?)-1986..**CLC 21**
See also CA 81-84; 120; CANR 31; CLR 17;
DLB 160; MAICYA; SATA 20; SATA-Obit 48
Stribling, T(homas) S(igismund) 1881-1965
CLC 23
See also CA 107; DLB 9
Strindberg, (Johan) August 1849-1912...**TCLC
1, 8, 21, 47; DA; DAB; DAC; DAM DRAM,
MST; WLC**
See also CA 104; 135
Stringer, Arthur 1874-1950 .... **TCLC 37**
See also CA 161; DLB 92
Stringer, David
See Roberts, Keith (John Kingston)
Stroheim, Erich von 1885-1957 ...... **TCLC 71**
Strugatskii, Arkadii (Natanovich) 1925-1991
CLC 27
See also CA 106; 135
Strugatskii, Boris (Natanovich) 1933-...**CLC 27**
See also CA 106
Strummer, Joe 1953(?)- .... **CLC 30**
Stuart, Don A.
See Campbell, John W(ood, Jr.)
Stuart, Ian
See MacLean, Alistair (Stuart)
Stuart, Jesse (Hilton) 1906-1984...**CLC 1, 8, 11,
14, 34; SSC 31**
See also CA 5-8R; 112; CANR 31; DLB 9, 48,
102; DLBY 84; SATA 2; SATA-Obit 36
Sturgeon, Theodore (Hamilton) 1918-1985
CLC 22, 39
See also Queen, Ellery
See also CA 81-84; 116; CANR 32; DLB 8;
DLBY 85; MTCW
Sturges, Preston 1898-1959 .... **TCLC 48**
See also CA 114; 149; DLB 26
Styron, William 1925-...**CLC 1, 3, 5, 11, 15, 60;
DAM NOV, POP; SSC 25**
See also BEST 90:4; CA 5-8R; CANR 6, 33;
CDALB 1968-1988; DLB 2, 143; DLBY 80;
INT CANR-6; MTCW
Su, Chien 1884-1918
See Su Man-shu
See also CA 123
Suarez Lynch, B.
See Bioy Casares, Adolfo; Borges, Jorge Luis
Suckow, Ruth 1892-1960 .... **SSC 18**
See also CA 113; DLB 9, 102
Sudermann, Hermann 1857-1928 ... **TCLC 15**
See also CA 107; DLB 118
Sue, Eugene 1804-1857 .... **NCLC 1**
See also DLB 119
Sueskind, Patrick 1949- .... **CLC 44**
See also Suskind, Patrick
Sukenick, Ronald 1932- .... **CLC 3, 4, 6, 48**
See also CA 25-28R; CAAS 8; CANR 32; DLB
173; DLBY 81
Suknaski, Andrew 1942- .... **CLC 19**
See also CA 101; DLB 53
Sullivan, Vernon
See Vian, Boris
Sully Prudhomme 1839-1907 .... **TCLC 31**
Su Man-shu .... **TCLC 24**
See also Su, Chien
Summerforest, Ivy B.
See Kirkup, James
Summers, Andrew James 1942- .... **CLC 26**
Summers, Andy
See Summers, Andrew James
Summers, Hollis (Spurgeon, Jr.) 1916-...**CLC 10**
See also CA 5-8R; CANR 3; DLB 6

**Summers, (Alphonsus Joseph-Mary Augustus)
Montague** 1880-1948 .... **TCLC 16**
See also CA 118; 163
Sumner, Gordon Matthew 1951- .... **CLC 26**
Surtees, Robert Smith 1803-1864 ... **NCLC 14**
See also DLB 21
Susann, Jacqueline 1921-1974............. **CLC 3**
See also AITN 1; CA 65-68; 53-56; MTCW
Su Shih 1036-1101 .... **CMLC 15**
Suskind, Patrick
See Sueskind, Patrick
See also CA 145
Sutcliff, Rosemary 1920-1992...**CLC 26; DAB;
DAC; DAM MST, POP**
See also AAYA 10; CA 5-8R; 139; CANR 37;
CLR 1, 37; JRDA; MAICYA; SATA 6, 44, 78;
SATA-Obit 73
Sutro, Alfred 1863-1933 .... **TCLC 6**
See also CA 105; DLB 10
Sutton, Henry
See Slavitt, David R(ytman)
Svevo, Italo 1861-1928 .. **TCLC 2, 35; SSC 25**
See also Schmitz, Aron Hector
Swados, Elizabeth (A.) 1951- .... **CLC 12**
See also CA 97-100; CANR 49; INT 97-100
Swados, Harvey 1920-1972 .... **CLC 5**
See also CA 5-8R; 37-40R; CANR 6; DLB 2
Swan, Gladys 1934- .... **CLC 69**
See also CA 101; CANR 17, 39
Swarthout, Glendon (Fred) 1918-1992...**CLC 35**
See also CA 1-4R; 139; CANR 1, 47; SATA 26
Sweet, Sarah C.
See Jewett, (Theodora) Sarah Orne
Swenson, May 1919-1989 ...**CLC 4, 14, 61,
106; DA; DAB; DAC; DAM MST,
POET; PC 14**
See also CA 5-8R; 130; CANR 36, 61; DLB 5;
MTCW; SATA 15
Swift, Augustus
See Lovecraft, H(oward) P(hillips)
Swift, Graham (Colin) 1949- .... **CLC 41, 88**
See also CA 117; 122; CANR 46; DLB 194
Swift, Jonathan 1667-1745 .. **LC 1; DA; DAB;
DAC; DAM MST, NOV, POET; PC 9; WLC**
See also CDBLB 1660-1789; DLB 39, 95, 101;
SATA 19
Swinburne, Algernon Charles 1837-1909
**TCLC 8, 36; DA; DAB; DAC; DAM MST,
POET; WLC**
See also CA 105; 140; CDBLB 1832-1890; DLB
35, 57
Swinfen, Ann .... **CLC 34**
Swinnerton, Frank Arthur 1884-1982...**CLC 31**
See also CA 108; DLB 34
Swithen, John
See King, Stephen (Edwin)
Sylvia
See Ashton-Warner, Sylvia (Constance)
Symmes, Robert Edward
See Duncan, Robert (Edward)
Symonds, John Addington 1840-1893...**NCLC
34**
See also DLB 57, 144
Symons, Arthur 1865-1945 .... **TCLC 11**
See also CA 107; DLB 19, 57, 149
Symons, Julian (Gustave) 1912-1994...**CLC 2,
14, 32**
See also CA 49-52; 147; CAAS 3; CANR 3, 33,
59; DLB 87, 155; DLBY 92; MTCW
Synge, (Edmund) J(ohn) M(illington) 1871-1909
TCLC 6, 37; DAM DRAM; DC 2
See also CA 104; 141; CDBLB 1890-1914; DLB
10, 19

Syruc, J.
See Milosz, Czeslaw

Szirtes, George 1948- .... **CLC 46**
See also CA 109; CANR 27, 61

Szymborska, Wislawa 1923- .... **CLC 99**
See also CA 154; DLBY 96

T. O., Nik
See Annensky, Innokenty (Fyodorovich)

Tabori, George 1914- .... **CLC 19**
See also CA 49-52; CANR 4, 69

Tagore, Rabindranath 1861-1941 .. **TCLC 3, 53; DAM DRAM, POET; PC 8**
See also CA 104; 120; MTCW

Taine, Hippolyte Adolphe 1828-1893..**NCLC 15**

Talese, Gay 1932- .... **CLC 37**
See also AITN 1; CA 1-4R; CANR 9, 58; DLB 185; INT CANR-9; MTCW

Tallent, Elizabeth (Ann) 1954- .... **CLC 45**
See also CA 117; DLB 130

Tally, Ted 1952- .... **CLC 42**
See also CA 120; 124; INT 124

Tamayo y Baus, Manuel 1829-1898 .. **NCLC 1**

Tammsaare, A(nton) H(ansen) 1878-1940
TCLC 27
See also CA 164

Tam'si, Tchicaya U
See Tchicaya, Gerald Felix

Tan, Amy (Ruth) 1952- .... **CLC 59; DAM MULT, NOV, POP**
See also AAYA 9; BEST 89:3; CA 136; CANR 54; DLB 173; SATA 75

Tandem, Felix
See Spitteler, Carl (Friedrich Georg)

Tanizaki, Jun'ichiro 1886-1965 . **CLC 8, 14, 28; SSC 21**
See also CA 93-96; 25-28R; DLB 180

Tanner, William
See Amis, Kingsley (William)

Tao Lao
See Storni, Alfonsina

Tarassoff, Lev
See Troyat, Henri

Tarbell, Ida M(inerva) 1857-1944 ... **TCLC 40**
See also CA 122; DLB 47

Tarkington, (Newton) Booth 1869-1946
TCLC 9
See also CA 110; 143; DLB 9, 102; SATA 17

Tarkovsky, Andrei (Arsenyevich) 1932-1986
CLC 75
See also CA 127

Tartt, Donna 1964(?)- .... **CLC 76**
See also CA 142

Tasso, Torquato 1544-1595 .... **LC 5**

Tate, (John Orley) Allen 1899-1979...**CLC 2, 4, 6, 9, 11, 14, 24**
See also CA 5-8R; 85-88; CANR 32; DLB 4, 45, 63; MTCW

Tate, Ellalice
See Hibbert, Eleanor Alice Burford

Tate, James (Vincent) 1943- .... **CLC 2, 6, 25**
See also CA 21-24R; CANR 29, 57; DLB 5, 169

Tavel, Ronald 1940- .... **CLC 6**
See also CA 21-24R; CANR 33

Taylor, C(ecil) P(hilip) 1929-1981 ...... **CLC 27**
See also CA 25-28R; 105; CANR 47

Taylor, Edward 1642(?)-1729 ..... **LC 11; DA; DAB; DAC; DAM MST, POET**
See also DLB 24

Taylor, Eleanor Ross 1920- .... **CLC 5**
See also CA 81-84

Taylor, Elizabeth 1912-1975 .... **CLC 2, 4, 29**
See also CA 13-16R; CANR 9; DLB 139; MTCW; SATA 13

Taylor, Frederick Winslow 1856-1915...**T C L C 76**

Taylor, Henry (Splawn) 1942- .... **CLC 44**
See also CA 33-36R; CAAS 7; CANR 31; DLB 5

Taylor, Kamala (Purnaiya) 1924-
See Markandaya, Kamala
See also CA 77-80

Taylor, Mildred D. ....CLC 21
See also AAYA 10; BW 1; CA 85-88; CANR 25; CLR 9; DLB 52; JRDA; MAICYA; SAAS 5; SATA 15, 70

Taylor, Peter (Hillsman) 1917-1994...**CLC 1, 4, 18, 37, 44, 50, 71; SSC 10**
See also CA 13-16R; 147; CANR 9, 50; DLBY 81, 94; INT CANR-9; MTCW

Taylor, Robert Lewis 1912- .... **CLC 14**
See also CA 1-4R; CANR 3, 64; SATA 10

Tchekhov, Anton
See Chekhov, Anton (Pavlovich)

Tchicaya, Gerald Felix 1931-1988 .... **CLC 101**
See also CA 129; 125

Tchicaya U Tam'si
See Tchicaya, Gerald Felix

Teasdale, Sara 1884-1933 .... **TCLC 4**
See also CA 104; 163; DLB 45; SATA 32

Tegner, Esaias 1782-1846 .... **NCLC 2**

Teilhard de Chardin, (Marie Joseph) Pierre 1881-1955 .... **TCLC 9**
See also CA 105

Temple, Ann
See Mortimer, Penelope (Ruth)

Tennant, Emma (Christina) 1937-...**CLC 13, 52**
See also CA 65-68; CAAS 9; CANR 10, 38, 59; DLB 14

Tenneshaw, S. M.
See Silverberg, Robert

Tennyson, Alfred 1809-1892 ... **NCLC 30, 65; DA; DAB; DAC; DAM MST, POET; PC 6; WLC**
See also CDBLB 1832-1890; DLB 32

Teran, Lisa St. Aubin de .... **CLC 36**
See also St. Aubin de Teran, Lisa

Terence 195(?)B.C.-159B.C....**CMLC 14; DC 7**

Teresa de Jesus, St. 1515-1582 .... **LC 18**

Terkel, Louis 1912-
See Terkel, Studs
See also CA 57-60; CANR 18, 45, 67; MTCW

Terkel, Studs .... **CLC 38**
See also Terkel, Louis
See also AITN 1

Terry, C. V.
See Slaughter, Frank G(ill)

Terry, Megan 1932- .... **CLC 19**
See also CA 77-80; CABS 3; CANR 43; DLB 7

Tertullian c. 155-c. 245 .... **CMLC 29**

Tertz, Abram
See Sinyavsky, Andrei (Donatevich)

Tesich, Steve 1943(?)-1996 .... **CLC 40, 69**
See also CA 105; 152; DLBY 83

Teternikov, Fyodor Kuzmich 1863-1927
See Sologub, Fyodor
See also CA 104

Tevis, Walter 1928-1984 .... **CLC 42**
See also CA 113

Tey, Josephine .... **TCLC 14**
See also Mackintosh, Elizabeth
See also DLB 77

Thackeray, William Makepeace 1811-1863
NCLC 5, 14, 22, 43; DA; DAB; DAC; DAM MST, NOV; WLC
See also CDBLB 1832-1890; DLB 21, 55, 159, 163; SATA 23

Thakura, Ravindranatha
See Tagore, Rabindranath

Tharoor, Shashi 1956- .... **CLC 70**
See also CA 141

Thelwell, Michael Miles 1939- .... **CLC 22**
See also BW 2; CA 101

Theobald, Lewis, Jr.
See Lovecraft, H(oward) P(hillips)

Theodorescu, Ion N. 1880-1967
See Arghezi, Tudor
See also CA 116

Theriault, Yves 1915-1983 .... **CLC 79; DAC; DAM MST**
See also CA 102; DLB 88

Theroux, Alexander (Louis) 1939-...**CLC 2, 25**
See also CA 85-88; CANR 20, 63

Theroux, Paul (Edward) 1941-...**CLC 5, 8, 11, 15, 28, 46; DAM POP**
See also BEST 89:4; CA 33-36R; CANR 20, 45; DLB 2; MTCW; SATA 44

Thesen, Sharon 1946- .... **CLC 56**
See also CA 163

Thevenin, Denis
See Duhamel, Georges

Thibault, Jacques Anatole Francois 1844-1924
See France, Anatole
See also CA 106; 127; DAM NOV; MTCW

Thiele, Colin (Milton) 1920- .... **CLC 17**
See also CA 29-32R; CANR 12, 28, 53; CLR 27; MAICYA; SAAS 2; SATA 14, 72

Thomas, Audrey (Callahan) 1935-...**CLC 7, 13, 37, 107; SSC 20**
See also AITN 2; CA 21-24R; CAAS 19; CANR 36, 58; DLB 60; MTCW

Thomas, D(onald) M(ichael) 1935- . **CLC 13, 22, 31**
See also CA 61-64; CAAS 11; CANR 17, 45; CDBLB 1960 to Present; DLB 40; INT CANR-17; MTCW

Thomas, Dylan (Marlais) 1914-1953... **T C L C 1, 8, 45; DA; DAB; DAC; DAM DRAM, MST, POET; PC 2; SSC 3; WLC**
See also CA 104; 120; CANR 65; CDBLB 1945-1960; DLB 13, 20, 139; MTCW; SATA 60

Thomas, (Philip) Edward 1878-1917 .. **T C L C 10; DAM POET**
See also CA 106; 153; DLB 19

Thomas, Joyce Carol 1938- .... **CLC 35**
See also AAYA 12; BW 2; CA 113; 116; CANR 48; CLR 19; DLB 33; INT 116; JRDA; MAICYA; MTCW; SAAS 7; SATA 40, 78

Thomas, Lewis 1913-1993 .... **CLC 35**
See also CA 85-88; 143; CANR 38, 60; MTCW

Thomas, Paul
See Mann, (Paul) Thomas

Thomas, Piri 1928- .... **CLC 17**
See also CA 73-76; HW

Thomas, R(onald) S(tuart) 1913-...**CLC 6, 13, 48; DAB; DAM POET**
See also CA 89-92; CAAS 4; CANR 30; CDBLB 1960 to Present; DLB 27; MTCW

Thomas, Ross (Elmore) 1926-1995 .... **CLC 39**
See also CA 33-36R; 150; CANR 22, 63

Thompson, Francis Clegg
See Mencken, H(enry) L(ouis)

Thompson, Francis Joseph 1859-1907
TCLC 4
See also CA 104; CDBLB 1890-1914; DLB 19

Thompson, Hunter S(tockton) 1939-...**CLC 9, 17, 40, 104; DAM POP**
See also BEST 89:1; CA 17-20R; CANR 23, 46; DLB 185; MTCW

Wallace, (Richard Horatio) Edgar 1875-1932
   TCLC 57
   See also CA 115; DLB 70
Wallace, Irving 1916-1990 .. CLC 7, 13; DAM
   NOV, POP
   See also AITN 1; CA 1-4R; 132; CAAS 1; CANR
   1, 27; INT CANR-27; MTCW
Wallant, Edward Lewis 1926-1962...CLC 5, 10
   See also CA 1-4R; CANR 22; DLB 2, 28, 143;
   MTCW
Walley, Byron
   See Card, Orson Scott
Walpole, Horace 1717-1797 .... LC 2
   See also DLB 39, 104
Walpole, Hugh (Seymour) 1884-1941...TCLC 5
   See also CA 104; 165; DLB 34
Walser, Martin 1927- .... CLC 27
   See also CA 57-60; CANR 8, 46; DLB 75, 124
Walser, Robert 1878-1956...TCLC 18; SSC 20
   See also CA 118; 165; DLB 66
Walsh, Jill Paton .... CLC 35
   See also Paton Walsh, Gillian
   See also AAYA 11; CLR 2; DLB 161; SAAS 3
Walter, William Christian
   See Andersen, Hans Christian
Wambaugh, Joseph (Aloysius, Jr.) 1937-...CLC
   3, 18; DAM NOV, POP
   See also AITN 1; BEST 89:3; CA 33-36R;
   CANR 42, 65; DLB 6; DLBY 83; MTCW
Wang Wei 699(?)-761(?) .... PC 18
Ward, Arthur Henry Sarsfield 1883-1959
   See Rohmer, Sax
   See also CA 108
Ward, Douglas Turner 1930- .... CLC 19
   See also BW 1; CA 81-84; CANR 27; DLB 7, 38
Ward, Mary Augusta
   See Ward, Mrs. Humphry
Ward, Mrs. Humphry 1851-1920 .... TCLC 55
   See also DLB 18
Ward, Peter
   See Faust, Frederick (Schiller)
Warhol, Andy 1928(?)-1987 .... CLC 20
   See also AAYA 12; BEST 89:4; CA 89-92; 121;
   CANR 34
Warner, Francis (Robert le Plastrier) 1937-
   CLC 14
   See also CA 53-56; CANR 11
Warner, Marina 1946- .... CLC 59
   See also CA 65-68; CANR 21, 55; DLB 194
Warner, Rex (Ernest) 1905-1986 .... CLC 45
   See also CA 89-92; 119; DLB 15
Warner, Susan (Bogert) 1819-1885...NCLC 31
   See also DLB 3, 42
Warner, Sylvia (Constance) Ashton
   See Ashton-Warner, Sylvia (Constance)
Warner, Sylvia Townsend 1893-1978 .. CLC 7,
   19; SSC 23
   See also CA 61-64; 77-80; CANR 16, 60; DLB
   34, 139; MTCW
Warren, Mercy Otis 1728-1814 ...... NCLC 13
   See also DLB 31, 200
Warren, Robert Penn 1905-1989...CLC 1, 4, 6,
   8, 10, 13, 18, 39, 53, 59; DA; DAB; DAC;
   DAM MST, NOV, POET; SSC 4; WLC
   See also AITN 1; CA 13-16R; 129; CANR 10,
   47; CDALB 1968-1988; DLB 2, 48, 152;
   DLBY 80, 89; INT CANR-10; MTCW; SATA
   46; SATA-Obit 63
Warshofsky, Isaac
   See Singer, Isaac Bashevis
Warton, Thomas 1728-1790 ...... LC 15; DAM
   POET
   See also DLB 104, 109

Waruk, Kona
   See Harris, (Theodore) Wilson
Warung, Price 1855-1911 .... TCLC 45
Warwick, Jarvis
   See Garner, Hugh
Washington, Alex
   See Harris, Mark
Washington, Booker T(aliaferro) 1856-1915
   TCLC 10; BLC 3; DAM MULT
   See also BW 1; CA 114; 125; SATA 28
Washington, George 1732-1799 .... LC 25
   See also DLB 31
Wassermann, (Karl) Jakob 1873-1934
   TCLC 6
   See also CA 104; DLB 66
Wasserstein, Wendy 1950- .... CLC 32, 59, 90;
   DAM DRAM; DC 4
   See also CA 121; 129; CABS 3; CANR 53; INT
   129; SATA 94
Waterhouse, Keith (Spencer) 1929- ...CLC 47
   See also CA 5-8R; CANR 38, 67; DLB 13, 15;
   MTCW
Waters, Frank (Joseph) 1902-1995 ....CLC 88
   See also CA 5-8R; 149; CAAS 13; CANR 3, 18,
   63; DLBY 86
Waters, Roger 1944- .... CLC 35
Watkins, Frances Ellen
   See Harper, Frances Ellen Watkins
Watkins, Gerrold
   See Malzberg, Barry N(athaniel)
Watkins, Gloria 1955(?)-
   See hooks, bell
   See also BW 2; CA 143
Watkins, Paul 1964-........................... CLC 55
   See also CA 132; CANR 62
Watkins, Vernon Phillips 1906-1967 ...CLC 43
   See also CA 9-10; 25-28R; CAP 1; DLB 20
Watson, Irving S.
   See Mencken, H(enry) L(ouis)
Watson, John H.
   See Farmer, Philip Jose
Watson, Richard F.
   See Silverberg, Robert
Waugh, Auberon (Alexander) 1939- .... CLC 7
   See also CA 45-48; CANR 6, 22; DLB 14, 194
Waugh, Evelyn (Arthur St. John) 1903-1966
   CLC 1, 3, 8, 13, 19, 27, 44, 107; DA; DAB;
   DAC; DAM MST, NOV, POP; WLC
   See also CA 85-88; 25-28R; CANR 22; CDBLB
   1914-1945; DLB 15, 162, 195; MTCW
Waugh, Harriet 1944- .... CLC 6
   See also CA 85-88; CANR 22
Ways, C. R.
   See Blount, Roy (Alton), Jr.
Waystaff, Simon
   See Swift, Jonathan
Webb, (Martha) Beatrice (Potter) 1858-1943
   TCLC 22
   See also Potter, (Helen) Beatrix
   See also CA 117
Webb, Charles (Richard) 1939- .... CLC 7
   See also CA 25-28R
Webb, James H(enry), Jr. 1946-......... CLC 22
   See also CA 81-84
Webb, Mary (Gladys Meredith) 1881-1927
   TCLC 24
   See also CA 123; DLB 34
Webb, Mrs. Sidney
   See Webb, (Martha) Beatrice (Potter)
Webb, Phyllis 1927-........................... CLC 18
   See also CA 104; CANR 23; DLB 53
Webb, Sidney (James) 1859-1947 ... TCLC 22
   See also CA 117; 163; DLB 190

Webber, Andrew Lloyd .... CLC 21
   See also Lloyd Webber, Andrew
Weber, Lenora Mattingly 1895-1971...CLC 12
   See also CA 19-20; 29-32R; CAP 1; SATA 2;
   SATA-Obit 26
Weber, Max 1864-1920 .... TCLC 69
   See also CA 109
Webster, John 1579(?)-1634(?).... LC 33; DA;
   DAB; DAC; DAM DRAM, MST; DC 2;
   WLC
   See also CDBLB Before 1660; DLB 58
Webster, Noah 1758-1843 .... NCLC 30
Wedekind, (Benjamin) Frank(lin) 1864-1918
   TCLC 7; DAM DRAM
   See also CA 104; 153; DLB 118
Weidman, Jerome 1913- .... CLC 7
   See also AITN 2; CA 1-4R; CANR 1; DLB 28
Weil, Simone (Adolphine) 1909-1943
   TCLC 23
   See also CA 117; 159
Weinstein, Nathan
   See West, Nathanael
Weinstein, Nathan von Wallenstein
   See West, Nathanael
Weir, Peter (Lindsay) 1944- .... CLC 20
   See also CA 113; 123
Weiss, Peter (Ulrich) 1916-1982 .. CLC 3,
   15, 51; DAM DRAM
   See also CA 45-48; 106; CANR 3; DLB 69, 124
Weiss, Theodore (Russell) 1916-...CLC 3, 8, 14
   See also CA 9-12R; CAAS 2; CANR 46; DLB 5
Welch, (Maurice) Denton 1915-1948..TCLC 22
   See also CA 121; 148
Welch, James 1940- .... CLC 6, 14, 52; DAM
   MULT, POP
   See also CA 85-88; CANR 42, 66; DLB 175;
   NNAL
Weldon, Fay 1931-... CLC 6, 9, 11, 19, 36, 59;
   DAM POP
   See also CA 21-24R; CANR 16, 46, 63; CDBLB
   1960 to Present; DLB 14, 194; INT CANR-
   16; MTCW
Wellek, Rene 1903-1995 .... CLC 28
   See also CA 5-8R; 150; CAAS 7; CANR 8; DLB
   63; INT CANR-8
Weller, Michael 1942- .... CLC 10, 53
   See also CA 85-88
Weller, Paul 1958- .... CLC 26
Wellershoff, Dieter 1925- .... CLC 46
   See also CA 89-92; CANR 16, 37
Welles, (George) Orson 1915-1985...CLC 20,
   80
   See also CA 93-96; 117
Wellman, John McDowell 1945-
   See Wellman, Mac
   See also CA 166
Wellman, Mac 1945- .... CLC 65
   See also Wellman, John McDowell; Wellman,
   John McDowell
Wellman, Manly Wade 1903-1986 ..... CLC 49
   See also CA 1-4R; 118; CANR 6, 16, 44; SATA
   6; SATA-Obit 47
Wells, Carolyn 1869(?)-1942 .... TCLC 35
   See also CA 113; DLB 11
Wells, H(erbert) G(eorge) 1866-1946
   TCLC 6, 12, 19; DA; DAB; DAC; DAM
   MST, NOV; SSC 6; WLC
   See also AAYA 18; CA 110; 121; CDBLB 1914-
   1945; DLB 34, 70, 156, 178; MTCW; SATA
   20
Wells, Rosemary 1943- .... CLC 12
   See also AAYA 13; CA 85-88; CANR 48; CLR
   16; MAICYA; SAAS 1; SATA 18, 69

Welty, Eudora 1909-...CLC 1, 2, 5, 14, 22, 33, 105; DA; DAB; DAC; DAM MST, NOV; SSC 1, 27; WLC
  See also CA 9-12R; CABS 1; CANR 32, 65; CDALB 1941-1968; DLB 2, 102, 143; DLBD 12; DLBY 87; MTCW

Wen I-to 1899-1946 .... TCLC 28

Wentworth, Robert
  See Hamilton, Edmond

Werfel, Franz (Viktor) 1890-1945 ..... TCLC 8
  See also CA 104; 161; DLB 81, 124

Wergeland, Henrik Arnold 1808-1845 NCLC 5

Wersba, Barbara 1932- .... CLC 30
  See also AAYA 2; CA 29-32R; CANR 16, 38; CLR 3; DLB 52; JRDA; MAICYA; SAAS 2; SATA 1, 58

Wertmueller, Lina 1928- .... CLC 16
  See also CA 97-100; CANR 39

Wescott, Glenway 1901-1987 .... CLC 13
  See also CA 13-16R; 121; CANR 23; DLB 4, 9, 102

Wesker, Arnold 1932- .... CLC 3, 5, 42; DAB; DAM DRAM
  See also CA 1-4R; CAAS 7; CANR 1, 33; CDBLB 1960 to Present; DLB 13; MTCW

Wesley, Richard (Errol) 1945- .... CLC 7
  See also BW 1; CA 57-60; CANR 27; DLB 38

Wessel, Johan Herman 1742-1785 .... LC 7

West, Anthony (Panther) 1914-1987 .. CLC 50
  See also CA 45-48; 124; CANR 3, 19; DLB 15

West, C. P.
  See Wodehouse, P(elham) G(renville)

West, (Mary) Jessamyn 1902-1984...CLC 7, 17
  See also CA 9-12R; 112; CANR 27; DLB 6; DLBY 84; MTCW; SATA-Obit 37

West, Morris L(anglo) 1916- .... CLC 6, 33
  See also CA 5-8R; CANR 24, 49, 64; MTCW

West, Nathanael 1903-1940 .. TCLC 1, 14, 44; SSC 16
  See also CA 104; 125; CDALB 1929-1941; DLB 4, 9, 28; MTCW

West, Owen
  See Koontz, Dean R(ay)

West, Paul 1930- .... CLC 7, 14, 96
  See also CA 13-16R; CAAS 7; CANR 22, 53; DLB 14; INT CANR-22

West, Rebecca 1892-1983 ..... CLC 7, 9, 31, 50
  See also CA 5-8R; 109; CANR 19; DLB 36; DLBY 83; MTCW

Westall, Robert (Atkinson) 1929-1993 CLC 17
  See also AAYA 12; CA 69-72; 141; CANR 18, 68; CLR 13; JRDA; MAICYA; SAAS 2; SATA 23, 69; SATA-Obit 75

Westlake, Donald E(dwin) 1933- .. CLC 7, 33; DAM POP
  See also CA 17-20R; CAAS 13; CANR 16, 44, 65; INT CANR-16

Westmacott, Mary
  See Christie, Agatha (Mary Clarissa)

Weston, Allen
  See Norton, Andre

Wetcheek, J. L.
  See Feuchtwanger, Lion

Wetering, Janwillem van de
  See van de Wetering, Janwillem

Wetherald, Agnes Ethelwyn 1857-1940 TCLC 81
  See also DLB 99

Wetherell, Elizabeth
  See Warner, Susan (Bogert)

Whale, James 1889-1957 .... TCLC 63

Whalen, Philip 1923- .... CLC 6, 29
  See also CA 9-12R; CANR 5, 39; DLB 16

Wharton, Edith (Newbold Jones) 1862-1937 TCLC 3, 9, 27, 53; DA; DAB; DAC; DAM MST, NOV; SSC 6; WLC
  See also AAYA 25; CA 104; 132; CDALB 1865-1917; DLB 4, 9, 12, 78, 189; DLBD 13; MTCW

Wharton, James
  See Mencken, H(enry) L(ouis)

Wharton, William (a pseudonym) ..CLC 18, 37
  See also CA 93-96; DLBY 80; INT 93-96

Wheatley (Peters), Phillis 1754(?)-1784...LC 3; BLC 3; DA; DAC; DAM MST, MULT, POET; PC 3; WLC
  See also CDALB 1640-1865; DLB 31, 50

Wheelock, John Hall 1886-1978 .... CLC 14
  See also CA 13-16R; 77-80; CANR 14; DLB 45

White, E(lwyn) B(rooks) 1899-1985...CLC 10, 34, 39; DAM POP
  See also AITN 2; CA 13-16R; 116; CANR 16, 37; CLR 1, 21; DLB 11, 22; MAICYA; MTCW; SATA 2, 29; SATA-Obit 44

White, Edmund (Valentine III) 1940-...CLC 27, 110; DAM POP
  See also AAYA 7; CA 45-48; CANR 3, 19, 36, 62; MTCW

White, Patrick (Victor Martindale) 1912-1990 CLC 3, 4, 5, 7, 9, 18, 65, 69
  See also CA 81-84; 132; CANR 43; MTCW

White, Phyllis Dorothy James 1920-
  See James, P. D.
  See also CA 21-24R; CANR 17, 43, 65; DAM POP; MTCW

White, T(erence) H(anbury) 1906-1964 CLC 30
  See also AAYA 22; CA 73-76; CANR 37; DLB 160; JRDA; MAICYA; SATA 12

White, Terence de Vere 1912-1994 .... CLC 49
  See also CA 49-52; 145; CANR 3

White, Walter F(rancis) 1893-1955...TCLC 15
  See also White, Walter
  See also BW 1; CA 115; 124; DLB 51

White, William Hale 1831-1913
  See Rutherford, Mark
  See also CA 121

Whitehead, E(dward) A(nthony) 1933-...CLC 5
  See also CA 65-68; CANR 58

Whitemore, Hugh (John) 1936- .... CLC 37
  See also CA 132; INT 132

Whitman, Sarah Helen (Power) 1803-1878 NCLC 19
  See also DLB 1

Whitman, Walt(er) 1819-1892 .. NCLC 4, 31; DA; DAB; DAC; DAM MST, POET; PC 3; WLC
  See also CDALB 1640-1865; DLB 3, 64; SATA 20

Whitney, Phyllis A(yame) 1903- ..... CLC 42; DAM POP
  See also AITN 2; BEST 90:3; CA 1-4R; CANR 3, 25, 38, 60; JRDA; MAICYA; SATA 1, 30

Whittemore, (Edward) Reed (Jr.) 1919- CLC 4
  See also CA 9-12R; CAAS 8; CANR 4; DLB 5

Whittier, John Greenleaf 1807-1892...NCLC 8, 59
  See also DLB 1

Whittlebot, Hernia
  See Coward, Noel (Peirce)

Wicker, Thomas Grey 1926-
  See Wicker, Tom
  See also CA 65-68; CANR 21, 46

Wicker, Tom .... CLC 7
  See also Wicker, Thomas Grey

Wideman, John Edgar 1941-...CLC 5, 34, 36, 67; BLC 3; DAM MULT
  See also BW 2; CA 85-88; CANR 14, 42, 67; DLB 33, 143

Wiebe, Rudy (Henry) 1934- .... CLC 6, 11, 14; DAC; DAM MST
  See also CA 37-40R; CANR 42, 67; DLB 60

Wieland, Christoph Martin 1733-1813 NCLC 17
  See also DLB 97

Wiene, Robert 1881-1938 .... TCLC 56

Wieners, John 1934- .... CLC 7
  See also CA 13-16R; DLB 16

Wiesel, Elie(zer) 1928-...CLC 3, 5, 11, 37; DA; DAB; DAC; DAM MST, NOV; WLCS 2
  See also AAYA 7; AITN 1; CA 5-8R; CAAS 4; CANR 8, 40, 65; DLB 83; DLBY 87; INT CANR-8; MTCW; SATA 56

Wiggins, Marianne 1947- .... CLC 57
  See also BEST 89:3; CA 130; CANR 60

Wight, James Alfred 1916-1995
  See Herriot, James
  See also CA 77-80; SATA 55; SATA-Brief 44

Wilbur, Richard (Purdy) 1921-...CLC 3, 6, 9, 14, 53, 110; DA; DAB; DAC; DAM MST, POET
  See also CA 1-4R; CABS 2; CANR 2, 29; DLB 5, 169; INT CANR-29; MTCW; SATA 9

Wild, Peter 1940- .... CLC 14
  See also CA 37-40R; DLB 5

Wilde, Oscar (Fingal O'Flahertie Wills) 1854(?)-1900 ... TCLC 1, 8, 23, 41; DA; DAB; DAC; DAM DRAM, MST, NOV; SSC 11; WLC
  See also CA 104; 119; CDBLB 1890-1914; DLB 10, 19, 34, 57, 141, 156, 190; SATA 24

Wilder, Billy .... CLC 20
  See also Wilder, Samuel
  See also DLB 26

Wilder, Samuel 1906-
  See Wilder, Billy
  See also CA 89-92

Wilder, Thornton (Niven) 1897-1975... C L C 1, 5, 6, 10, 15, 35, 82; DA; DAB; DAC; DAM DRAM, MST, NOV; DC 1; WLC
  See also AITN 2; CA 13-16R; 61-64; CANR 40; DLB 4, 7, 9; DLBY 97; MTCW

Wilding, Michael 1942- .... CLC 73
  See also CA 104; CANR 24, 49

Wiley, Richard 1944- .... CLC 44
  See also CA 121; 129

Wilhelm, Kate .... CLC 7
  See also Wilhelm, Katie Gertrude
  See also AAYA 20; CAAS 5; DLB 8; INT CANR-17

Wilhelm, Katie Gertrude 1928-
  See Wilhelm, Kate
  See also CA 37-40R; CANR 17, 36, 60; MTCW

Wilkins, Mary
  See Freeman, Mary Eleanor Wilkins

Willard, Nancy 1936- .... CLC 7, 37
  See also CA 89-92; CANR 10, 39, 68; CLR 5; DLB 5, 52; MAICYA; MTCW; SATA 37, 71; SATA-Brief 30

Williams, C(harles) K(enneth) 1936-...CLC 33, 56; DAM POET
  See also CA 37-40R; CAAS 26; CANR 57; DLB 5

Williams, Charles
  See Collier, James L(incoln)

Williams, Charles (Walter Stansby) 1886-1945 TCLC 1, 11
  See also CA 104; 163; DLB 100, 153

Woollcott, Alexander (Humphreys) 1887-1943
TCLC 5
See also CA 105; 161; DLB 29
Woolrich, Cornell 1903-1968 .... **CLC 77**
See also Hopley-Woolrich, Cornell George
Wordsworth, Dorothy 1771-1855 ... **NCLC 25**
See also DLB 107
Wordsworth, William 1770-1850 ..**NCLC 12, 38; DA; DAB; DAC; DAM MST, POET; PC 4; WLC**
See also CDBLB 1789-1832; DLB 93, 107
Wouk, Herman 1915-....**CLC 1, 9, 38; DAM NOV, POP**
See also CA 5-8R; CANR 6, 33, 67; DLBY 82; INT CANR-6; MTCW
Wright, Charles (Penzel, Jr.) 1935-...**CLC 6, 13, 28**
See also CA 29-32R; CAAS 7; CANR 23, 36, 62; DLB 165; DLBY 82; MTCW
Wright, Charles Stevenson 1932- ... **CLC 49; BLC 3; DAM MULT, POET**
See also BW 1; CA 9-12R; CANR 26; DLB 33
Wright, Jack R.
See Harris, Mark
Wright, James (Arlington) 1927-1980... **C L C 3, 5, 10, 28; DAM POET**
See also AITN 2; CA 49-52; 97-100; CANR 4, 34, 64; DLB 5, 169; MTCW
Wright, Judith (Arandell) 1915-...**CLC 11, 53; PC 14**
See also CA 13-16R; CANR 31; MTCW; SATA 14
Wright, L(aurali) R. 1939-.................. **CLC 44**
See also CA 138
Wright, Richard (Nathaniel) 1908-1960
CLC 1, 3, 4, 9, 14, 21, 48, 74; BLC 3; DA; DAB; DAC; DAM MST, MULT, NOV; SSC 2; WLC
See also AAYA 5; BW 1; CA 108; CANR 64; CDALB 1929-1941; DLB 76, 102; DLBD 2; MTCW
Wright, Richard B(ruce) 1937- .... **CLC 6**
See also CA 85-88; DLB 53
Wright, Rick 1945-............................... **CLC 35**
Wright, Rowland
See Wells, Carolyn
Wright, Stephen 1946- .... **CLC 33**
Wright, Willard Huntington 1888-1939
See Van Dine, S. S.
See also CA 115; DLBD 16
Wright, William 1930- .... **CLC 44**
See also CA 53-56; CANR 7, 23
Wroth, LadyMary 1587-1653(?) .... **LC 30**
See also DLB 121
Wu Ch'eng-en 1500(?)-1582(?) .... **LC 7**
Wu Ching-tzu 1701-1754 .... **LC 2**
Wurlitzer, Rudolph 1938(?)- ....**CLC 2, 4, 15**
See also CA 85-88; DLB 173
Wycherley, William 1641-1715 .....**LC 8, 21; DAM DRAM**
See also CDBLB 1660-1789; DLB 80
Wylie, Elinor (Morton Hoyt) 1885-1928
TCLC 8; PC 23
See also CA 105; 162; DLB 9, 45
Wylie, Philip (Gordon) 1902-1971 .....**CLC 43**
See also CA 21-22; 33-36R; CAP 2; DLB 9
Wyndham, John ....**CLC 19**
See also Harris, John (Wyndham Parkes Lucas) Beynon
Wyss, Johann David Von 1743-1818...**NCLC 10**
See also JRDA; MAICYA; SATA 29; SATA-Brief 27
Xenophon c. 430B.C.-c. 354B.C. ..... **CMLC 17**
See also DLB 176

Yakumo Koizumi
See Hearn, (Patricio) Lafcadio (Tessima Carlos)
Yanez, Jose Donoso
See Donoso (Yanez), Jose
Yanovsky, Basile S.
See Yanovsky, V(assily) S(emenovich)
Yanovsky, V(assily) S(emenovich) 1906-1989
CLC 2, 18
See also CA 97-100; 129
Yates, Richard 1926-1992 .... **CLC 7, 8, 23**
See also CA 5-8R; 139; CANR 10, 43; DLB 2; DLBY 81, 92; INT CANR-10
Yeats, W. B.
See Yeats, William Butler
Yeats, William Butler 1865-1939...**TCLC 1, 11, 18, 31; DA; DAB; DAC; DAM DRAM, MST, POET; PC 20; WLC**
See also CA 104; 127; CANR 45; CDBLB 1890-1914; DLB 10, 19, 98, 156; MTCW
Yehoshua, A(braham) B. 1936- .... **CLC 13, 31**
See also CA 33-36R; CANR 43
Yep, Laurence Michael 1948- .... **CLC 35**
See also AAYA 5; CA 49-52; CANR 1, 46; CLR 3, 17; DLB 52; JRDA; MAICYA; SATA 7, 69
Yerby, Frank G(arvin) 1916-1991...**CLC 1, 7, 22; BLC 3; DAM MULT**
See also BW 1; CA 9-12R; 136; CANR 16, 52; DLB 76; INT CANR-16; MTCW
Yesenin, Sergei Alexandrovich
See Esenin, Sergei (Alexandrovich)
Yevtushenko, Yevgeny (Alexandrovich) 1933-
CLC 1, 3, 13, 26, 51; DAM POET
See also CA 81-84; CANR 33, 54; MTCW
Yezierska, Anzia 1885(?)-1970 .... **CLC 46**
See also CA 126; 89-92; DLB 28; MTCW
Yglesias, Helen 1915- .... **CLC 7, 22**
See also CA 37-40R; CAAS 20; CANR 15, 65; INT CANR-15; MTCW
Yokomitsu Riichi 1898-1947 .... **TCLC 47**
Yonge, Charlotte (Mary) 1823-1901 **TCLC 48**
See also CA 109; 163; DLB 18, 163; SATA 17
York, Jeremy
See Creasey, John
York, Simon
See Heinlein, Robert A(nson)
Yorke, Henry Vincent 1905-1974 .... **CLC 13**
See also Green, Henry
See also CA 85-88; 49-52
Yosano Akiko 1878-1942 ..... **TCLC 59; PC 11**
See also CA 161
Yoshimoto, Banana .... **CLC 84**
See also Yoshimoto, Mahoko
Yoshimoto, Mahoko 1964-
See Yoshimoto, Banana
See also CA 144
Young, Al(bert James) 1939-...**CLC 19; BLC 3; DAM MULT**
See also BW 2; CA 29-32R; CANR 26, 65; DLB 33
Young, Andrew (John) 1885-1971 .... **CLC 5**
See also CA 5-8R; CANR 7, 29
Young, Collier
See Bloch, Robert (Albert)
Young, Edward 1683-1765 .... **LC 3, 40**
See also DLB 95
Young, Marguerite (Vivian) 1909-1995...**CLC 82**
See also CA 13-16; 150; CAP 1
Young, Neil 1945- .... **CLC 17**
See also CA 110
Young Bear, Ray A. 1950- .... **CLC 94; DAM MULT**
See also CA 146; DLB 175; NNAL

Yourcenar, Marguerite 1903-1987...**CLC 19, 38, 50, 87; DAM NOV**
See also CA 69-72; CANR 23, 60; DLB 72; DLBY 88; MTCW
Yurick, Sol 1925- .... **CLC 6**
See also CA 13-16R; CANR 25
Zabolotsky, Nikolai Alekseevich 1903-1958
TCLC 52
See also CA 116; 164
Zamiatin, Yevgenii
See Zamyatin, Evgeny Ivanovich
Zamora, Bernice (B. Ortiz) 1938-.... **CLC 89; DAM MULT; HLC**
See also CA 151; DLB 82; HW
Zamyatin, Evgeny Ivanovich 1884-1937
TCLC 8, 37
See also CA 105; 166
Zangwill, Israel 1864-1926 .... **TCLC 16**
See also CA 109; DLB 10, 135, 197
Zappa, Francis Vincent, Jr. 1940-1993
See Zappa, Frank
See also CA 108; 143; CANR 57
Zappa, Frank ....**CLC 17**
See also Zappa, Francis Vincent, Jr.
Zaturenska, Marya 1902-1982 .... **CLC 6, 11**
See also CA 13-16R; 105; CANR 22
Zeami 1363-1443 .... **DC 7**
Zelazny, Roger (Joseph) 1937-1995...**CLC 21**
See also AAYA 7; CA 21-24R; 148; CANR 26, 60; DLB 8; MTCW; SATA 57; SATA-Brief 39
Zhdanov, Andrei A(lexandrovich) 1896-1948
TCLC 18
See also CA 117
Zhukovsky, Vasily 1783-1852 .... **NCLC 35**
Ziegenhagen, Eric .... **CLC 55**
Zimmer, Jill Schary
See Robinson, Jill
Zimmerman, Robert
See Dylan, Bob
Zindel, Paul 1936-.... **CLC 6, 26; DA; DAB; DAC; DAM DRAM, MST, NOV; DC 5**
See also AAYA 2; CA 73-76; CANR 31, 65; CLR 3, 45; DLB 7, 52; JRDA; MAICYA; MTCW; SATA 16, 58
Zinov'Ev, A. A.
See Zinoviev, Alexander (Aleksandrovich)
Zinoviev, Alexander (Aleksandrovich) 1922-
CLC 19
See also CA 116; 133; CAAS 10
Zoilus
See Lovecraft, H(oward) P(hillips)
Zola, Emile (Edouard Charles Antoine) 1840-1902 ... **TCLC 1, 6, 21, 41; DA; DAB; DAC; DAM MST, NOV; WLC**
See also CA 104; 138; DLB 123
Zoline, Pamela 1941- .... **CLC 62**
See also CA 161
Zorrilla y Moral, Jose 1817-1893 ..... **NCLC 6**
Zoshchenko, Mikhail (Mikhailovich) 1895-1958
TCLC 15; SSC 15
See also CA 115; 160
Zuckmayer, Carl 1896-1977 .... **CLC 18**
See also CA 69-72; DLB 56, 124
Zuk, Georges
See Skelton, Robin
Zukofsky, Louis 1904-1978...**CLC 1, 2, 4, 7, 11, 18; DAM POET; PC 11**
See also CA 9-12R; 77-80; CANR 39; DLB 5, 165; MTCW
Zweig, Paul 1935-1984 .... **CLC 34, 42**
See also CA 85-88; 113
Zweig, Stefan 1881-1942 .... **TCLC 17**
See also CA 112; DLB 81, 118

Author Index

Drama Criticism
Cumulative Nationality Index

ALGERIAN
Camus, Albert **2**

AMERICAN
Baldwin, James (Arthur) **1**
Baraka, Amiri **6**
Brown, William Wells **1**
Bullins, Ed **6**
Chase, Mary (Coyle) **1**
Childress, Alice **4**
Chin, Frank (Chew Jr.) **7**
Elder, Lonne III **8**
Fuller, Charles (H. Jr.) **1**
Gordone, Charles **8**
Gray, Spalding **7**
Hansberry, Lorraine (Vivian) **2**
Hellman, Lillian (Florence) **1**
Henley, Beth **6**
Hughes, (James) Langston **3**
Hwang, David Henry **4**
Kennedy, Adrienne (Lita) **5**
Kramer, Larry **8**
Mamet, David (Alan) **4**
Mann, Emily **7**
Miller, Arthur **1**
Norman, Marsha **8**
Odets, Clifford **6**
Shange, Ntozake **3**
Shepard, Sam **5**
Sheridan, Richard Brinsley **1**
Wasserstein, Wendy **4**
Wilder, Thornton (Niven) **1**
Williams, Tennessee **4**
Wilson, August **2**
Zindel, Paul **5**

AUSTRIAN
Hofmannsthal, Hugo von **4**

BARBADIAN
Kennedy, Adrienne (Lita) **5**

CZECH
Capek, Karel **1**
Havel, Vaclav **6**

ENGLISH
Beaumont, Francis **6**
Behn, Aphra **4**
Churchill, Caryl **5**
Congreve, William **2**
Dryden, John **3**
Fletcher, John **6**
Ford, John **8**
Jonson, Ben(jamin) **4**
Kyd, Thomas **3**
Lyly, John **7**
Marlowe, Christopher **1**
Middleton, Thomas **5**
Orton, Joe **3**
Shaffer, Peter (Levin) **7**
Stoppard, Tom **6**
Webster, John **2**

FRENCH
Anouilh, Jean (Marie Lucien Pierre) **8**
Beaumarchais, Pierre-Augustin
  Caron de **4**
Camus, Albert **2**
Dumas, Alexandre **1**
Marivaux, Pierre Carlet de Chamblain de **7**
Sartre, Jean-Paul **3**
Scribe, (Augustin) Eugene **5**

GERMAN
Brecht, (Eugen) Bertolt (Friedrich) **3**

GREEK
Aeschylus **8**
Aristophanes **2**
Euripides **4**
Menander **3**
Sophocles **1**

IRISH
Friel, Brian **8**
Goldsmith, Oliver **8**
Synge, (Edmund) J(ohn) M(illington) **2**

ITALIAN
Pirandello, Luigi **5**

JAPANESE
Mishima, Yukio **1**
Zeami **7**

NIGERIAN
Clark, John Pepper **5**
Soyinka, Wole **2**

NORWEGIAN
Ibsen, Henrik (Johan) **2**

ROMAN
Seneca, Lucius Annaeus **5**
Terence **7**

RUSSIAN
Chekhov, Anton Pavlovich **9**
Gogol, Nikolai Vasilyevich **1**
Turgenev, Ivan **7**

SOUTH AFRICAN
Fugard, (Harold) Athol **3**

SPANISH
Calderon de la Barca, Pedro **3**
Garcia Lorca, Federico **2**

ST. LUCIAN
Walcott, Derek (Alton) **7**

Drama Criticism
Cumulative Title Index

Arlequin poli par l'amour (Marivaux) **7**:124, 126, 129-30, 132, 147, 149,-50, 155, 163-65

"Arm Yourself or Harm Yourself: A One-Act Play: A Message of Self-Defense to Black Men" (Baraka) **6**:8, 15

Artist Descending a Staircase (Stoppard) **6**:294, 308-09, 312, 314-15, 347

As Well as Before, Better than Before (Pirandello)
 See *Come prima, meglio di prima*

As You Desire Me (Pirandello)
 See *Come tu mi vuoi*

Ashikari (Zeami) **7**:348, 350

Asi que pasen cinco anos (Garcia Lorca) **2**:199-200, 202, 204, 206, 213

Asinaria (Plautus) **6**:242, 275-78, 286, 290

Aspis (Menander) **3**:362, 364, 366, 368-70

The Assassins (Camus)
 See *Les justes*

Assembly of Women (Aristophanes)
 See *Ekklesiazousai*

The Assignation (Dryden) **3**:167-68, 188

Asya (Turgenev) **7**:

"At a Spritualist Seance" (Chekhov) **9**:33

"At Christmas-Time" (Chekhov) **9**:36

"At Sea" (Chekhov) **9**:32-4

At the Exit (Pirandello)
 See *All'uscita*

At the Gate (Pirandello)
 See *All'uscita*

"An Attack of Nerves" (Chekhov) **9**:122

"Audience" (Havel) **6**:150-51, 156-57, 163, 166, 170-73, 175

The Audience (Garcia Lorca)
 See *El publico*

Aufstieg und Fall der Stadt Mahagonny (Brecht) **3**:19-20, 27

"The Augsburg Chalk Circle" (Brecht)
 See "Der Augsburger Kreidekreis"

"Der Augsburger Kreidekreis" (Brecht) **3**:81

Aulularia (Plautus) **6**:241-42, 244-46, 249, 269, 278-79, 281-83

"Aunt Maggie, the Strong One" (Friel) **8**:213

Aureng-Zebe (Dryden) **3**:154, 158, 160-62, 168-69, 177, 179, 184, 188, 190-91, 193-96, 198, 212, 216-17

l'autre Tartuffe; ou La mere coupable (Beaumarchais) **4**:2-6, 10-12, 14, 18, 20, 25

The Autumn Garden (Hellman) **1**:188, 190-91, 208

Awake and Sing! (Odets) **6**:205-07, 209, 211, 214-16, 223-32, 234

Aya no tsuzumi (Mishima) **1**:361-62, 363-66, 368-70, 372

L'azione parlata (Pirandello) **5**:215, 217, 233

Baal (Brecht) **3**:15-16, 25-6, 34, 78

Baby Doll (Williams) **4**:371-72

The Babylonians (Aristophanes) **2**:9, 18, 35-6, 41

Bacchae (Aeschylus) **8**:16

Bacchae (Euripides) **4**:96, 98-9, 101-5, 107-9, 121-2, 142-4, 152-3, 156-7

The Bacchae of Euripides: A Communion Rite (Soyinka) **2**:366, 368

Bacchanals (Euripides)
 See *Bacchae*

The Bacchants (Euripides)
 See *Bacchae*

Bacchides (Plautus) **6**:242, 246, 250-51, 255, 262-64, 290

The Bacchis Sisters (Plautus)
 See *Bacchides*

The Bachelor (Turgenev)
 See *Kholostiak*

Bachelor Girls (Wasserstein) **4**:366

Back Bog Beast Bait (Shepard) **5**:359-60

Bad Temper (Menander)
 See *Orge*

Le bal des voleurs (Anouilh) **8**:71, 75

Balance of Terror (Shaffer) **7**:183

La banda y la flor (Calderon de la Barca) **3**:104

The Banqueters (Aristophanes) **2**:8, 18, 42

"The Baptism" (Baraka) **6**:10-12, 15-17, 25, 30, 32

Ba-Ra-Ka (Baraka) **6**:15

The Barber of Seville (Beaumarchais)
 See *Le barbier de Séville; ou, La précaution inutile*

Le barbier de Séville; ou, La précaution inutile (Beaumarchais) **4**:2-9, 11-2, 14-18, 21-5, 30-1

Bartholomew Fair (Jonson) **4**:227, 229, 232, 235, 240, 242, 248, 256-59, 263, 276

Bataille de dames; ou, Un duel en amour (Scribe) **5**:247-49, 253

Batrakhoi (Aristophanes) **2**:4, 6, 13-14, 16-17, 40, 45, 47-51, 68

The Battle at Yashima (Zeami)
 See *Yashima*

Battle of Angels (Williams) **4**:371, 383, 391

The Battle of Shrivings (Shaffer) **7**:183-84, 189-90, 197, 202, 205

"The Bear" (Chekhov)
 See "Medvéd"

A Beast Story (Kennedy) **5**:76, 89, 91-2

Beautie (Jonson)
 See *Masque of Beauty*

"The Beauties" (Chekhov) **9**:153

"Because of the King of France" (Kennedy) **5**:90

Becket; or, The Honor of God (Anouilh)
 See *Becket; ou, L'honneur de Dieu*

Becket; ou, L'honneur de Dieu (Anouilh) **8**:85, 88, 91, 95, 104-10

The Bee (Goldsmith) **8**:281

Beef, No Chicken (Walcott) **7**:320, 323-25

Before the Marriage (Menander) **3**:346

Beggar's Bush (Beaumont) **6**:84

Beggar's Bush (Fletcher) **6**:84

The Beggar's Opera (Havel) **6**:151, 163

The Begging Priest (Menander) **3**:346

A Begonia for Miss Applebaum (Zindel) **5**:425

Die beiden Gotter (Hofmannsthal) **4**:169

Being and Nothingness: An Essay on Phenomenological Ontology (Sartre)
 See *L'etre et le néant: Essai d'ontologie phénoménologique*

Bellerophon (Euripides) **4**:104

Ben Jonson: Selected Works (Jonson) **4**:277

Bernarda Alba's Family (Garcia Lorca)
 See *La casa de Bernarda Alba*

Bernardine (Chase) **1**:84

Il berretto a sonagli (Pirandello) **5**:206

Bertrand et Raton; ou, L'art de conspirer (Scribe) **5**:251, 261

"The Betrothed" (Chekhov) **9**:127-29

Betsey Brown (Shange) **3**:473

Beware of Smooth Water (Calderon de la Barca)
 See *Guardate del agua mensa*

"Bezdenezh'e" (Turgenev) **7**:281, 285, 288-289, 297

The Bible (Brecht) **3**:37

The Big Knife (Odets) **6**:208-10, 216, 218-20, 222

The Big Sea: An Autobiography (Hughes) **3**:279, 282

Bila nemoc (Capek) **1**:66, 73

The Birds (Aristophanes)
 See *Ornithes*

Bitter Oleander (Garcia Lorca)
 See *Bodas de sangre*

Black Children's Day (Kennedy) **5**:78, 95, 97

"Black Comedy" (Shaffer) **7**:184, 193, 203

The Black Domino (Scribe)
 See *Le domino noir*

A Black Mass (Baraka) **6**:7, 9, 16, 18

"The Black Monk" (Chekhov) **9**:36, 42

Black Nativity (Hughes) **3**:275, 277, 287-90

Black Power Chant (Baraka) **6**:15

Blacknesse (Jonson)
 See *Masque of Blacknesse*

Les blancs (Hansberry) **2**:247, 250

The Bleeding Nun (Scribe)
 See *La Nonne Saglante*

The Blind Mice (Friel) **8**:209-10, 233, 259

The Blood Knot (Fugard) **3**:222-24, 227-30, 232, 236-45, 248-49, 252

Blood Wedding (Garcia Lorca)
 See *Bodas de sangre*

Bloodrites (Baraka) **6**:15

The Blood-stained Nun (Scribe)
 See *La Nonne Saglante*

The Bloody Brother, or Rollo Duke of Normandy (Fletcher) **6**:65

Blue Bitch (Shepard) **5**:360

Blues for Mister Charlie (Baldwin) **1**:2, 5-9, 14-24, 26

The Boarder (Turgenev)
 See *Nakhlebnik*

Boats (Kennedy) **5**:89, 94

Bodas de sangre (Garcia Lorca) 200-11, 213-22, 229-32

Boesman and Lena (Fugard) **3**:226-27, 229, 232-33, 235, 237, 248-49, 251

Bohemia the Beautiful Bohemia Mine (Havel) **6**:151

Boogie Woogie Landscapes (Shange) **3**:474, 478, 487-90

Book of Friends (Hofmannsthal)
 See *Buch der Freunde*

Book of Gypsy Ballads (Garcia Lorca)
 See *Primer romancero gitano*

Book of Songs (Garcia Lorca)
 See *Canciones*

Book of Transmission of the Flower (Zeami)
 See *Kadensho*

"A Boring Story" (Chekhov) **9**:23, 36, 69, 218, 238-39, 248, 304

Both Were Young (Menander) **3**:346

The Bow at Hachiman Shrine (Zeami)
 See *Yumi Yawata*

Braggart Warrior (Plautus)
 See *Miles Glorious*

A Branch of the Blue Nile (Walcott) **7**:320, 324-25

Brand (Ibsen) **2**:278, 291, 299-300, 314, 319-20

"Breakfast at a Nobleman's Home" (Turgenev)
 See "Zavtrak u predvoritelya"

The Bride of Gomez Arias (Calderon de la Barca)
 See *La nina de Gomez Arias*

The Brocade Tree (Zeami)
 See *Nishikigi*

The Broken Heart (Ford) **8**:131-37, 139, 143, 145, 148, 150-55, 158, 174, 180-93

The Brothers (Terence)
 See *Adelphoe*

The Brownsville Raid (Fuller) **1**:135-36, 139

Title Index